STATE PROFILES

STATE PROFILES

THE POPULATION AND ECONOMY OF EACH U.S. STATE

Eighth Edition
2016

Edited by Hannah M. Anderson

Bernan Press

Lanham, Maryland

Published in the United States of America
by Bernan Press, a wholly owned subsidiary of
The Rowman & Littlefield Publishing Group, Inc.
4501 Forbes Boulevard, Suite 200
Lanham, Maryland 20706

Bernan Press
800-462-6420
www.rowman.com

ISBN 13: 978-1-59888-871-3
E-ISBN: 978-1-59888-872-0

∞™ The paper used in this publication meets the minimum requirements of
American National Standard for Information Sciences—Permanence of
Paper for Printed Library Materials, ANSI/NISO Z39.48-1992.
Manufactured in the United States of America.

CONTENTS

The following tables are included for each state and the District of Columbia:

Bernan Press is pleased to present the eighth edition of *State Profiles*, a publication that provides a state-by-state view of the United States. Topics covered include population composition by age, sex, race, and ethnicity; marital status; migration, origin, and language; households and housing; income and poverty; health insurance; employment; educational indicators; voting; crime; and other important aspects of the economy.

The publication's primary focus is on the 50 states and the District of Columbia, each of which possesses considerable differences in economic structure and demographics and has experienced various changes over time. Changes at the national level, including the diminished importance of agriculture and manufacturing and the growing influence of global trade, have resulted in today's information-based, service-providing economy. While national trends have laid the broad framework for change, each state has been affected differently. Cyclical fluctuations have also affected states in various ways during the nationwide recessions and the subsequent recovery periods. Recessions and recoveries spread unevenly among regions and states. Migration patterns have also reflected these changes, as states have experienced different influxes of workers from within the country and new residents from abroad.

Beyond the market forces, local and national government policies and expenditures on items such as education, health care, energy production and conservation, national defense, and homeland security have influenced economic circumstances.

The information provided in *State Profiles* aims to illuminate these trends. As such, the analysis and statistics are of interest not only to researchers and policy analysts but also to businesses seeking a broad basis for investments and expansion or relocation plans. The volume also profiles recent voting patterns, which will be of interest to political scientists.

DATA SELECTION

This edition of *State Profiles* generally continues the broad selection of information from previous editions. Most, but not all, of the data items have been updated through 2013, 2014, and even 2015, as demographic estimates from the U.S. Census Bureau became available.

As in the past, space constraints have influenced the amount of data presented for each state. The most meaningful and relevant data have thus been selected, analyzed, and highlighted. This edition expands upon the available information to include more detailed data on the demographics of each state, especially in regard to diversity of spoken languages and the foreign-born population. For most of the subjects addressed in this edition, further data are generally available from the source government agencies. Locations of sources of information are listed in notes and definitions at the end of the volume.

Although the editor has taken care to present accurate data, all statistical data are subject to a degree of error, resulting from sampling variability, erroneous reporting, and other causes. Many of the data are subject to subsequent revision.

The data in this book meet the publication standards of the federal agencies from which they were obtained. The responsibilities of the editor and publisher of this volume are limited to reasonable care in the reproduction and presentation of the data from the established sources.

Hannah M. Anderson has edited the past two editions of *State Profiles*. She previously worked as an assistant editor for Bernan Press and is now a freelance writer and editor for several reference titles. She has a B.A. in journalism at the University of Maryland.

USING THIS BOOK: ORGANIZATION AND CONTENTS

STATE PROFILES 2016 PROVIDES:

- Rankings of states for key demographic and economic indicators
- A chapter for each state, complete with tables and figures that summarize and illustrate demographic and economic characteristics
- Notes and definitions to assist with interpreting the information contained in this volume

THE U.S. OVERVIEW. This short introduction to the demographics of the United States provides commentary on overall trends within the country.

THE STATE RANKINGS. The ranking tables that follow the national overview give state rankings by more than 30 characteristics, including population, demographic and age composition, income, per capita gross domestic product, homeownership, poverty, health indicators, education, and federal aid. These rankings provide the user with a quick analysis of the performance of each state in relation to the other states.

THE STATE CHAPTERS. The state chapters are the focus of this book. Each chapter follows a standard format and contains text highlighting the key features shown in the tables and figures. Some of these tables and figures contain references to the U.S. averages for the same characteristics.

Each of the state chapters is organized as follows:

Population: This table provides data on the state's total population and average annual population growth in comparison with the national average. It also shows the major population groups by sex, age, race, and ethnicity.

Marital status: The table shows the marital status for all men and women age 15 years and over.

Housing: This table showcases data pertaining to housing, such as number of households, types of households, housing characteristics, and median gross rent, mortgage, and monthly owner cost amounts.

Origin, migration, and language: This table provides statistics on residence one year ago, year of entry, place of origin, language spoken at home, and the native-born and foreign-born populations.

Income and poverty: Median household and family income and poverty rates by sex and age are contained in this table.

Health insurance coverage: This table provides information on health insurance, by type and coverage.

Employment: These tables illustrate each state's particular economic configuration. Employment status by detailed demographic group, labor force, participation rates, employment, unemployment, average wages and salaries by industry, and employment by family type.

Education: This section provides the user with details on educational attainment, elementary and secondary school enrollment, student/teacher ratios, per student expenditures, and higher education enrollments.

Voter participation: Information is given on voter registration and voter participation in the 2014 election, categorized by sex and race and ethnicity.

Crime: This table includes the number and rates of violent and property crime.

Government finance: These tables provide data on revenues and expenditures by source. In addition, tax information is included.

NOTES AND DEFINITIONS. Each chapter relies on the same standard set of federal data sources. Since the basic data sources are common to all chapters, the main body of the volume contains few footnotes. Basic data and corresponding definitions and sources are identified in the notes and definition section at the end of the volume. It provides brief descriptions, methodologies, data availability, information on calculations made by the editors, and references to additional sources of information.

Introduction

During the early 2000s, the United States experienced several economic fluctuations that had a great impact on the strength, size, and performance of its economy. The recession that began in March 2001 was concluded in a few months; however, the longer-lasting recession that began in December 2007 has had a more serious impact on the country. This edition of *State Profiles: The Population and Economy of Each U.S. State* creates a snapshot of the people and economy in each state and the District of Columbia. Each chapter (one per state/district) includes information on topics such as population, health, marital status, crime, government finance, housing, education, and language.

Summary

The U.S. population grew 3.9 percent between 2010 and 2015. North Dakota experienced the largest population growth in the nation at 12.2 percent. The states and areas with the largest population growth included the District of Columbia (11.1 percent), Texas (8.8 percent), Colorado (8.1 percent), Utah (7.9 percent), Florida (7.5 percent), Nevada (6.9 percent), Arizona (6.6 percent), Washington (6.3 percent), South Carolina (5.6 percent), Idaho (5.3 percent), South Dakota (5.2 percent), and Georgia (5.2 percent). States that grew in population by 0.5 percent or less included Michigan, Connecticut, Rhode Island, Illinois, Maine, and Vermont. The population of West Virginia fell by 0.5 percent.

Maine had the highest percentage of White alone residents in 2015, at 94.9 percent, followed by Vermont at 94.8 percent. Hawaii had the lowest number of White alone residents, at 26.7 percent. The District of Columbia had the highest percentage of Black or African American alone residents at 48.3 percent, followed by Mississippi at 37.6 percent. At 0.6 percent, Montana had the lowest percentage of Black or African American alone residents.

New Mexico had the highest percent of Hispanic or Latino residents (48.0 percent), and West Virginia had the lowest percentage at 1.5 percent. Those classified as Hispanic or Latino may be of any race.

In 2014, the median household income in the United States was $53,657. Maryland had the highest median household income at $73,971, followed by New Jersey ($71,919), the District of Columbia ($71,648), Alaska ($71,583), and Connecticut ($70,048). The states with the lowest median household incomes were Mississippi ($39,680), West Virginia ($41,059), Arkansas ($42,262), Alabama ($42,830), and Kentucky ($42,958). Some correlation to the percentage of residents with a bachelor's degree or more can be inferred, as Maryland, and the District of Columbia rank in the top five states in this category. Mississippi, West Virginia, and Arkansas rank as the bottom three states in this category, with Alabama ranking 45th and Kentucky ranking 48th. The unemployment rate for the United States was 5.3 percent in 2015, which is down from 6.2 percent in 2014. The District of Columbia had the highest percentage of unemployed residents in 2015 (6.9 percent), followed by West Virginia and Nevada (6.7 percent each). North Dakota (2.7 percent) had the lowest percentage of unemployed residents.

In the United States in 2014, 15.5 percent of the population lived below the poverty level. Mississippi, which had the lowest median household income, also had the highest poverty rate, with 21.5 percent of its residents below the poverty level. New Hampshire had the lowest poverty rate, at 9.2 percent. New Mexico had the highest rate of persons under 18 years of age below the poverty level (29.5 percent), followed by Mississippi (29.4 percent), Louisiana (27.9 percent), Alabama (27.7 percent), and South Carolina (27.1 percent). The states with the fewest residents under 18 years of age below the poverty level included Wyoming (12.8 percent), New Hampshire (13.0 percent), Maryland (13.0 percent), Utah (13.3 percent), and Hawaii (14.7 percent).

UNITED STATES RANKINGS

Population, 2015		
Rank	State	Population
	United States......................	321,418,820
1	California............................	39,144,818
2	Texas.................................	27,469,114
3	Florida...............................	20,271,272
4	New York............................	19,795,791
5	Illinois...............................	12,859,995
6	Pennsylvania......................	12,802,503
7	Ohio..................................	11,613,423
8	Georgia..............................	10,214,860
9	North Carolina.....................	10,042,802
10	Michigan............................	9,922,576
11	New Jersey.........................	8,958,013
12	Virginia..............................	8,382,993
13	Washington.........................	7,170,351
14	Arizona..............................	6,828,065
15	Massachusetts.....................	6,794,422
16	Indiana..............................	6,619,680
17	Tennessee..........................	6,600,299
18	Missouri.............................	6,083,672
19	Maryland............................	6,006,401
20	Wisconsin...........................	5,771,337
21	Minnesota...........................	5,489,594
22	Colorado............................	5,456,574
23	South Carolina.....................	4,896,146
24	Alabama.............................	4,858,979
25	Louisiana............................	4,670,724
26	Kentucky............................	4,425,092
27	Oregon..............................	4,028,977
28	Oklahoma...........................	3,911,338
29	Connecticut.........................	3,590,886
30	Iowa..................................	3,123,899
31	Utah..................................	2,995,919
32	Mississippi..........................	2,992,333
33	Arkansas............................	2,978,204
34	Kansas...............................	2,911,641
35	Nevada..............................	2,890,845
36	New Mexico.........................	2,085,109
37	Nebraska............................	1,896,190
38	West Virginia.......................	1,844,128
39	Idaho.................................	1,654,930
40	Hawaii...............................	1,431,603
41	New Hampshire....................	1,330,608
42	Maine................................	1,329,328
43	Rhode Island.......................	1,056,298
44	Montana.............................	1,032,949
45	Delaware............................	945,934
46	South Dakota.......................	858,469
47	North Dakota.......................	756,927
48	Alaska...............................	738,432
49	District of Columbia...............	672,228
50	Vermont.............................	626,042
51	Wyoming............................	586,107

Population, Percent Change, 2010–2015		
Rank	State	Percent
	United States......................	3.9
1	North Dakota.......................	12.2
2	District of Columbia...............	11.1
3	Texas.................................	8.8
4	Colorado............................	8.1
5	Utah..................................	7.9
6	Florida...............................	7.5
7	Nevada..............................	6.9
8	Arizona..............................	6.6
9	Washington.........................	6.3
10	South Carolina.....................	5.6
11	Idaho.................................	5.3
12	South Dakota.......................	5.2
12	Georgia..............................	5.2
14	Delaware............................	5.1
14	North Carolina.....................	5.1
16	Oregon..............................	5.0
16	Hawaii...............................	5.0
18	California............................	4.9
19	Virginia..............................	4.5
20	Montana.............................	4.3
21	Oklahoma...........................	4.0
22	Tennessee..........................	3.8
22	Wyoming............................	3.8
22	Maryland............................	3.8
25	Nebraska............................	3.6
26	Massachusetts.....................	3.5
27	Alaska...............................	3.4
27	Minnesota...........................	3.4
29	Louisiana............................	2.8
30	Iowa..................................	2.4
31	New York............................	2.0
31	Indiana..............................	2.0
33	Arkansas............................	1.9
34	Kansas...............................	1.8
34	Kentucky............................	1.8
34	New Jersey.........................	1.8
37	Alabama.............................	1.5
37	Missouri.............................	1.5
39	Wisconsin...........................	1.4
40	New Hampshire....................	1.1
41	New Mexico.........................	1.0
42	Mississippi..........................	0.7
42	Pennsylvania......................	0.7
44	Ohio..................................	0.6
45	Michigan............................	0.5
46	Connecticut.........................	0.3
46	Rhode Island.......................	0.3
48	Illinois...............................	0.1
48	Maine................................	0.1
50	Vermont.............................	Z
51	West Virginia.......................	-0.5

Z = An amount greater than zero but less than half of the unit shown.

Population Under 18 Years Old, 2015		
Rank	State	Percent
	United States......................	22.9
1	Utah..................................	30.5
2	Texas.................................	26.3
3	Idaho.................................	26.2
4	Alaska...............................	25.2
5	Nebraska............................	24.8
6	Kansas...............................	24.7
7	South Dakota.......................	24.6
7	Oklahoma...........................	24.6
9	Georgia..............................	24.5
10	Mississippi..........................	24.3
11	Louisiana............................	23.9
11	Indiana..............................	23.9
13	New Mexico.........................	23.8
13	Arizona..............................	23.8
15	Wyoming............................	23.7
15	Arkansas............................	23.7
17	Minnesota...........................	23.4
18	Iowa..................................	23.3
18	California............................	23.3
20	Nevada..............................	23.1
21	Colorado............................	23.0
21	Illinois...............................	23.0
21	North Dakota.......................	23.0
24	Missouri.............................	22.9
24	Kentucky............................	22.9
26	North Carolina.....................	22.8
27	Alabama.............................	22.7
27	Tennessee..........................	22.7
29	Ohio..................................	22.6
30	Washington.........................	22.5
31	Maryland............................	22.4
31	Wisconsin...........................	22.4
33	New Jersey.........................	22.3
33	Virginia..............................	22.3
33	South Carolina.....................	22.3
36	Michigan............................	22.2
37	Montana.............................	21.9
38	Hawaii...............................	21.7
39	Delaware............................	21.6
40	Oregon..............................	21.4
41	Connecticut.........................	21.3
41	New York............................	21.3
43	Pennsylvania......................	21.0
44	West Virginia.......................	20.6
45	Massachusetts.....................	20.4
46	Florida...............................	20.3
47	Rhode Island.......................	20.0
48	New Hampshire....................	19.8
49	Maine................................	19.3
50	Vermont.............................	19.2
51	District of Columbia...............	17.6

Population 65 Years and Over, 2015

Rank	State	Percent
	United States	14.9
1	Florida	19.4
2	Maine	18.8
3	West Virginia	18.2
4	Vermont	17.6
5	Montana	17.2
6	Pennsylvania	17.0
6	Delaware	17.0
8	Hawaii	16.5
8	New Hampshire	16.5
10	Arizona	16.4
10	Oregon	16.4
12	South Carolina	16.2
13	Iowa	16.1
13	Rhode Island	16.1
15	Arkansas	16.0
16	Ohio	15.9
17	New Mexico	15.8
17	Michigan	15.8
17	Connecticut	15.8
20	Alabama	15.7
20	Missouri	15.7
20	South Dakota	15.7
23	Wisconsin	15.6
24	Tennessee	15.4
24	Massachusetts	15.4
26	Kentucky	15.2
27	North Carolina	15.1
28	New Jersey	15.0
28	New York	15.0
30	Oklahoma	14.7
30	Idaho	14.7
30	Nebraska	14.7
30	Mississippi	14.7
30	Minnesota	14.7
35	Kansas	14.6
35	Nevada	14.6
35	Indiana	14.6
38	Wyoming	14.5
39	Washington	14.4
40	Illinois	14.2
40	Virginia	14.2
40	North Dakota	14.2
43	Maryland	14.1
44	Louisiana	14.0
45	California	13.3
46	Colorado	13.0
47	Georgia	12.8
48	Texas	11.7
49	District of Columbia	11.5
50	Utah	10.3
51	Alaska	9.9

Percent White Alone, 2015

Rank	State	Percent
	United States	77.1
1	Maine	94.9
2	Vermont	94.8
3	New Hampshire	93.9
4	West Virginia	93.6
5	Idaho	93.4
6	Wyoming	92.7
7	Iowa	91.8
8	Utah	91.2
9	Montana	89.2
10	Nebraska	89.1
11	North Dakota	88.6
12	Kentucky	88.1
13	Wisconsin	87.6
13	Oregon	87.6
15	Colorado	87.5
16	Kansas	86.7
17	Indiana	85.8
18	South Dakota	85.5
19	Minnesota	85.4
20	Rhode Island	84.8
21	Arizona	83.5
22	Missouri	83.3
23	Ohio	82.7
24	Pennsylvania	82.6
25	New Mexico	82.5
26	Massachusetts	82.1
27	Connecticut	80.8
28	Washington	80.3
29	Michigan	79.7
29	Texas	79.7
31	Arkansas	79.5
32	Tennessee	78.8
33	Florida	77.7
34	Illinois	77.3
35	Nevada	75.7
36	Oklahoma	74.8
37	California	72.9
38	New Jersey	72.6
39	North Carolina	71.2
40	Delaware	70.4
41	Virginia	70.2
42	New York	70.1
43	Alabama	69.5
44	South Carolina	68.4
45	Alaska	66.5
46	Louisiana	63.2
47	Georgia	61.6
48	Maryland	59.6
49	Mississippi	59.5
50	District of Columbia	44.1
51	Hawaii	26.7

Percent Black or African American Alone, 2015

Rank	State	Percent
	United States	13.3
1	District of Columbia	48.3
2	Mississippi	37.6
3	Louisiana	32.5
4	Georgia	31.7
5	Maryland	30.5
6	South Carolina	27.6
7	Alabama	26.8
8	Delaware	22.4
9	North Carolina	22.1
10	Virginia	19.7
11	New York	17.6
12	Tennessee	17.1
13	Florida	16.8
14	Arkansas	15.7
15	New Jersey	14.8
16	Illinois	14.7
17	Michigan	14.2
18	Ohio	12.7
19	Texas	12.5
20	Missouri	11.8
21	Pennsylvania	11.7
22	Connecticut	11.6
23	Indiana	9.6
24	Nevada	9.3
25	Massachusetts	8.4
26	Kentucky	8.3
27	Rhode Island	7.9
28	Oklahoma	7.8
29	Wisconsin	6.6
30	California	6.5
31	Kansas	6.3
32	Minnesota	6.0
33	Nebraska	5.0
34	Arizona	4.8
35	Colorado	4.5
36	Washington	4.1
37	Alaska	3.9
38	West Virginia	3.6
39	Iowa	3.5
40	Hawaii	2.6
40	New Mexico	2.6
42	North Dakota	2.4
43	Oregon	2.1
44	South Dakota	1.8
45	New Hampshire	1.5
46	Maine	1.4
46	Wyoming	1.4
48	Utah	1.3
48	Vermont	1.3
50	Idaho	0.8
51	Montana	0.6

Percent American Indian and Alaska Native Alone, 2015

Rank	State	Percent
	United States......................	1.2
1	Alaska	14.8
2	New Mexico	10.5
3	Oklahoma............................	9.1
4	South Dakota	8.9
5	Montana..............................	6.6
6	North Dakota.......................	5.5
7	Arizona...............................	5.3
8	Wyoming	2.7
9	Washington.........................	1.9
10	Oregon	1.8
11	Idaho..................................	1.7
11	California............................	1.7
13	Nevada	1.6
13	Colorado	1.6
13	North Carolina.....................	1.6
16	Utah	1.5
17	Nebraska.............................	1.4
18	Minnesota...........................	1.3
19	Kansas	1.2
20	Wisconsin	1.1
21	Texas..................................	1.0
21	Arkansas	1.0
21	Rhode Island.......................	1.0
21	New York............................	1.0
25	Louisiana	0.8
26	Michigan	0.7
26	Alabama	0.7
26	Maine	0.7
26	Delaware	0.7
30	New Jersey	0.6
30	Mississippi..........................	0.6
30	Illinois................................	0.6
30	Maryland.............................	0.6
30	District of Columbia	0.6
30	Missouri..............................	0.6
36	Virginia...............................	0.5
36	South Carolina	0.5
36	Connecticut.........................	0.5
36	Georgia	0.5
36	Iowa	0.5
36	Florida................................	0.5
36	Massachusetts	0.5
36	Hawaii	0.5
44	Tennessee	0.4
44	Indiana	0.4
44	Vermont	0.4
44	Pennsylvania.......................	0.4
48	Kentucky	0.3
48	New Hampshire....................	0.3
48	Ohio	0.3
51	West Virginia.......................	0.2

Percent Asian Alone, 2015

Rank	State	Percent
	United States......................	5.6
1	Hawaii	37.3
2	California............................	14.7
3	New Jersey	9.7
4	New York............................	8.8
5	Nevada	8.5
6	Washington.........................	8.4
7	Massachusetts	6.6
8	Maryland.............................	6.5
8	Virginia...............................	6.5
10	Alaska	6.3
11	Illinois................................	5.5
12	Minnesota...........................	4.9
13	Texas..................................	4.7
14	Connecticut.........................	4.6
15	Oregon	4.4
16	District of Columbia	4.2
17	Georgia	4.0
18	Delaware	3.9
19	Rhode Island.......................	3.6
20	Pennsylvania.......................	3.4
20	Arizona...............................	3.4
22	Colorado	3.2
23	Michigan	3.0
24	Kansas	2.9
25	Florida................................	2.8
25	North Carolina.....................	2.8
25	Wisconsin	2.8
28	New Hampshire....................	2.6
29	Utah	2.5
30	Iowa	2.4
31	Nebraska.............................	2.3
32	Oklahoma............................	2.2
33	Indiana	2.1
33	Ohio	2.1
35	Missouri..............................	2.0
36	Louisiana	1.8
36	Tennessee	1.8
38	New Mexico	1.7
39	Vermont	1.6
39	South Carolina	1.6
39	Arkansas	1.6
42	Idaho..................................	1.5
43	Kentucky	1.4
43	North Dakota.......................	1.4
43	Alabama	1.4
43	South Dakota	1.4
47	Maine	1.2
48	Mississippi..........................	1.1
49	Wyoming	1.0
50	West Virginia.......................	0.8
50	Montana..............................	0.8

Percent Native Hawaiian and Other Pacific Islander Alone, 2015

Rank	State	Percent
	United States......................	0.2
1	Hawaii	9.9
2	Alaska	1.3
3	Utah	1.0
4	Nevada	0.8
5	Washington.........................	0.7
6	California............................	0.5
7	Oregon	0.4
8	Arkansas	0.3
8	Arizona...............................	0.3
10	Idaho..................................	0.2
10	Colorado	0.2
10	Rhode Island.......................	0.2
10	Oklahoma............................	0.2
10	New Mexico	0.2
10	District of Columbia	0.2
16	Missouri..............................	0.1
16	Texas..................................	0.1
16	New York............................	0.1
16	North Carolina.....................	0.1
16	Nebraska.............................	0.1
16	Georgia	0.1
16	Virginia...............................	0.1
16	Wyoming	0.1
16	Kansas	0.1
16	Florida................................	0.1
16	Connecticut.........................	0.1
16	Maryland.............................	0.1
16	Alabama	0.1
16	Iowa	0.1
16	New Jersey	0.1
16	Massachusetts	0.1
16	Tennessee	0.1
16	South Carolina	0.1
16	Delaware	0.1
16	Montana..............................	0.1
16	Kentucky	0.1
16	North Dakota.......................	0.1
16	South Dakota	0.1
16	Pennsylvania.......................	0.1
16	Louisiana	0.1
16	Minnesota...........................	0.1
16	Illinois................................	0.1
16	Indiana	0.1
16	Mississippi..........................	0.1
16	Ohio	0.1
16	Wisconsin	0.1
47	New Hampshire....................	Z
47	Michigan	Z
47	Vermont	Z
47	Maine	Z
47	West Virginia.......................	Z

Z = Value greater than zero but less than half of the unit shown.

Percent Two or More Races, 2015		
Rank	State	Percent
	United States......................	2.6
1	Hawaii.............................	23.0
2	Alaska.............................	7.2
3	Oklahoma.........................	6.0
4	Washington.......................	4.6
5	Nevada............................	4.1
6	California.........................	3.8
7	Oregon............................	3.7
8	Colorado..........................	2.9
9	Virginia...........................	2.9
10	Kansas............................	2.9
11	Arizona............................	2.7
12	Maryland..........................	2.7
13	District of Columbia	2.7
14	Montana...........................	2.7
15	Rhode Island.....................	2.6
16	Delaware..........................	2.5
17	New Mexico	2.5
18	New York..........................	2.4
19	Utah...............................	2.4
20	Minnesota.........................	2.4
21	Idaho..............................	2.3
22	Michigan..........................	2.3
23	Massachusetts...................	2.3
24	Connecticut.......................	2.2
25	South Dakota	2.2
26	Missouri...........................	2.2
27	Ohio...............................	2.1
28	New Jersey	2.1
29	North Carolina....................	2.1
30	Nebraska..........................	2.1
31	North Dakota......................	2.1
32	Wyoming..........................	2.1
33	Florida............................	2.0
34	Georgia	2.0
35	Arkansas..........................	2.0
36	Indiana............................	1.9
37	Pennsylvania.....................	1.9
38	Texas..............................	1.9
39	Illinois............................	1.9
40	Vermont...........................	1.9
41	Wisconsin.........................	1.8
42	Kentucky..........................	1.8
43	Tennessee	1.8
44	South Carolina	1.8
45	Iowa...............................	1.8
46	Maine..............................	1.7
47	New Hampshire...................	1.6
48	West Virginia.....................	1.6
49	Alabama...........................	1.6
50	Louisiana	1.6
51	Mississippi........................	1.2

Percent Hispanic or Latino,[1] 2015		
Rank	State	Percent
	United States......................	17.6
1	New Mexico	48.0
2	Texas..............................	38.8
2	California.........................	38.8
4	Arizona............................	30.7
5	Nevada............................	28.1
6	Florida............................	24.5
7	Colorado	21.3
8	New Jersey	19.7
9	New York..........................	18.8
10	Illinois............................	16.9
11	Connecticut.......................	15.4
12	Rhode Island.....................	14.4
13	Utah...............................	13.7
14	Oregon............................	12.7
15	Washington.......................	12.4
16	Idaho..............................	12.2
17	Kansas............................	11.6
18	Massachusetts...................	11.2
19	District of Columbia	10.6
20	Nebraska..........................	10.4
20	Hawaii.............................	10.4
22	Oklahoma.........................	10.1
23	Wyoming..........................	9.9
24	Maryland..........................	9.5
25	Georgia	9.4
26	North Carolina....................	9.1
27	Delaware..........................	9.0
27	Virginia...........................	9.0
29	Arkansas..........................	7.2
30	Alaska.............................	7.0
31	Pennsylvania.....................	6.8
32	Indiana............................	6.7
33	Wisconsin.........................	6.6
34	Iowa...............................	5.7
35	South Carolina	5.5
36	Minnesota.........................	5.2
36	Tennessee	5.2
38	Louisiana	5.0
39	Michigan..........................	4.9
40	Alabama...........................	4.2
41	Missouri...........................	4.1
42	South Dakota	3.6
42	Montana...........................	3.6
42	Ohio...............................	3.6
45	North Dakota......................	3.5
46	Kentucky..........................	3.4
46	New Hampshire...................	3.4
48	Mississippi........................	3.1
49	Vermont...........................	1.8
50	Maine..............................	1.6
51	West Virginia.....................	1.5

[1]May be of any race.

Percent White Alone, Not Hispanic or Latino, 2015		
Rank	State	Percent
	United States......................	61.6
1	Maine..............................	93.6
2	Vermont...........................	93.3
3	West Virginia.....................	92.3
4	New Hampshire...................	91.0
5	Iowa...............................	86.7
6	Montana...........................	86.5
7	North Dakota......................	85.8
8	Kentucky..........................	85.1
9	Wyoming..........................	84.0
10	South Dakota	82.9
11	Idaho..............................	82.5
12	Wisconsin.........................	81.9
13	Minnesota.........................	81.0
14	Nebraska..........................	80.0
14	Indiana............................	80.0
16	Missouri...........................	79.8
16	Ohio...............................	79.8
18	Utah...............................	79.0
19	Pennsylvania.....................	77.4
20	Oregon............................	76.6
21	Kansas............................	76.4
22	Michigan..........................	75.6
23	Tennessee	74.4
24	Rhode Island.....................	73.9
25	Massachusetts...................	73.5
26	Arkansas..........................	73.1
27	Washington.......................	69.8
28	Colorado	68.7
29	Connecticut.......................	68.2
30	Oklahoma.........................	66.5
31	Alabama...........................	66.0
32	South Carolina	63.8
32	North Carolina....................	63.8
34	Delaware..........................	63.2
35	Virginia...........................	62.7
36	Illinois............................	61.9
37	Alaska.............................	61.5
38	Louisiana	59.1
39	Mississippi........................	57.0
40	New Jersey	56.2
41	New York..........................	56.0
42	Arizona............................	55.8
43	Florida............................	55.3
44	Georgia	53.9
45	Maryland..........................	52.0
46	Nevada............................	50.7
47	Texas..............................	43.0
48	New Mexico	38.4
49	California.........................	38.0
50	District of Columbia	36.1
51	Hawaii.............................	22.9

Infant Mortality Rate, 2014

Rank	State	Rate per 1,000 live births (infants under 1 year old)
	United States	5.82
1	Alabama	8.68
2	Mississippi	8.24
3	Oklahoma	8.14
4	Arkansas	7.53
5	Louisiana	7.49
6	Georgia	7.45
7	District of Columbia	7.26
8	Kentucky	7.09
9	Indiana	7.08
9	North Carolina	7.08
11	West Virginia	7.04
12	Tennessee	6.91
13	Ohio	6.85
14	Delaware	6.74
15	Maine	6.69
16	Illinois	6.59
17	Alaska	6.58
18	Michigan	6.51
19	Maryland	6.47
20	South Carolina	6.46
21	Wyoming	6.37
22	Kansas	6.30
23	Arizona	6.15
24	Florida	6.06
24	Missouri	6.06
26	Pennsylvania	5.89
27	South Dakota	5.86
28	Texas	5.85
29	Virginia	5.76
30	Wisconsin	5.67
31	Montana	5.47
31	Nevada	5.47
33	Idaho	5.46
34	New Mexico	5.41
35	Oregon	5.14
36	Nebraska	5.08
37	Minnestoa	5.04
38	North Dakota	5.02
39	Utah	4.91
40	Connecticut	4.85
41	Iowa	4.81
42	Colorado	4.79
43	New York	4.65
44	Vermont	4.57
45	Washington	4.54
46	Hawaii	4.47
47	Rhode Island	4.43
48	New Jersey	4.39
49	Massachusetts	4.38
50	New Hampshire	4.31
51	California	4.30

Birth Rate, 2014

Rank	State	Rate per 1,000 population
	United States	12.5
1	Utah	17.4
2	Alaska	15.5
3	North Dakota	15.4
4	Texas	14.8
5	District of Columbia	14.4
5	South Dakota	14.4
7	Nebraska	14.2
8	Idaho	14.0
9	Louisiana	13.9
10	Oklahoma	13.8
11	Kansas	13.5
12	Wyoming	13.2
13	Hawaii	13.1
14	Arkansas	13.0
14	California	13.0
14	Georgia	13.0
17	Arizona	12.9
17	Mississippi	12.9
19	Iowa	12.8
19	Minnesota	12.8
21	Indiana	12.7
21	Kentucky	12.7
23	Nevada	12.6
24	New Mexico	12.5
24	Tennessee	12.5
24	Washington	12.5
27	Maryland	12.4
27	Missouri	12.4
27	Virginia	12.4
30	Alabama	12.3
30	Colorado	12.3
30	Illinois	12.3
33	North Carolina	12.2
34	Montana	12.1
34	New York	12.1
36	Ohio	12.0
37	South Carolina	11.9
38	Delaware	11.7
39	Wisconsin	11.7
40	New Jersey	11.6
41	Michigan	11.5
41	Oregon	11.5
43	Florida	11.1
43	Pennsylvania	11.1
45	West Virginia	11.0
46	Massachusetts	10.7
47	Rhode Island	10.3
48	Connecticut	10.1
49	Vermont	9.8
50	Maine	9.5
51	New Hampshire	9.3

Voting Population, 2014

Rank	State	Percent voted, total population
	United States	38.5
1	Maine	60.5
2	Colorado	55.2
3	Wisconsin	53.8
4	Oregon	51.8
5	Iowa	51.5
6	Minnesota	49.9
7	Montana	49.7
8	North Dakota	49.2
9	Alaska	49.0
10	Louisiana	48.6
10	New Hampshire	48.6
12	Kentucky	45.9
13	District of Columbia	45.8
14	Kansas	45.3
15	Michigan	45.1
16	Washington	44.8
17	Maryland	44.7
18	South Dakota	43.7
19	Connecticut	43.0
20	Massachusetts	42.8
20	North Carolina	42.8
22	New Mexico	42.1
23	Delaware	42.0
24	Mississippi	41.6
24	Vermont	41.6
26	Nebraska	41.4
27	South Carolina	41.3
28	Alabama	40.9
29	Florida	40.4
29	Rhode Island	40.4
31	Georgia	40.0
32	Virginia	39.4
33	Idaho	39.1
33	Wyoming	39.1
35	Hawaii	38.6
36	Ohio	38.5
37	Illinois	38.3
37	Pennsylvania	38.3
39	Missouri	38.0
40	Arkansas	36.5
41	Arizona	35.7
42	Tennessee	35.4
43	Utah	34.7
44	Indiana	33.5
45	West Virginia	33.4
46	Nevada	32.6
47	Oklahoma	32.3
48	New Jersey	31.5
49	California	30.8
50	New York	30.6
51	Texas	30.2

Percent of Persons 25 Years and Over with a Bachelor's Degree or More, 2014

Rank	State	Percent
	United States....................	30.1
1	District of Columbia	55.0
2	Massachusetts....................	41.2
3	Colorado	38.3
4	Maryland	38.2
5	Connecticut........................	38.0
6	New Jersey	37.4
7	Virginia..............................	36.7
8	New Hampshire..................	35.0
9	Vermont.............................	34.9
10	New York...........................	34.5
11	Minnesota..........................	34.3
12	Washington........................	33.1
13	Illinois...............................	32.8
14	California............................	31.7
15	Kansas	31.5
16	Utah	31.1
17	Hawaii	31.0
18	Oregon..............................	30.8
19	Delaware............................	30.6
20	Rhode Island......................	30.4
21	Nebraska...........................	29.5
22	Maine................................	29.4
23	Montana............................	29.3
24	Georgia.............................	29.1
25	Pennsylvania......................	29.0
26	North Carolina....................	28.7
27	Wisconsin..........................	28.4
28	Alaska...............................	28.0
29	South Dakota	27.8
29	Texas................................	27.8
31	Iowa.................................	27.7
32	Arizona..............................	27.6
33	Missouri.............................	27.5
34	Michigan............................	27.4
34	North Dakota......................	27.4
36	Florida...............................	27.3
37	Ohio..................................	26.6
37	Wyoming	26.6
39	New Mexico	26.4
40	South Carolina	26.3
41	Tennessee.........................	25.3
42	Idaho................................	25.0
43	Indiana..............................	24.7
44	Oklahoma..........................	24.2
45	Alabama............................	23.5
46	Nevada..............................	23.1
47	Louisiana...........................	22.9
48	Kentucky............................	22.2
49	Arkansas	21.4
50	Mississippi.........................	21.1
51	West Virginia......................	19.2

Violent Crime, 2014

Rank	State	Rate per 100,000 population
	United States......................	365.5
1	District of Columbia	1,244.4
2	Alaska	635.8
3	Nevada..............................	635.6
4	Tennessee.........................	608.4
5	New Mexico	597.4
6	Florida...............................	540.5
7	Louisiana	514.7
8	South Carolina	497.7
9	Delaware............................	489.1
10	Arkansas	480.1
11	Maryland	446.1
12	Missouri.............................	442.9
13	Alabama............................	427.4
14	Michigan............................	427.3
15	Oklahoma..........................	406.0
16	Texas................................	405.9
17	Arizona..............................	399.9
18	California............................	396.1
19	Massachusetts....................	391.4
20	New York...........................	381.8
21	Georgia.............................	377.3
22	Illinois...............................	370.0
23	Indiana..............................	365.3
24	Kansas	348.6
25	North Carolina....................	329.5
26	South Dakota	326.5
27	Montana............................	323.7
28	Pennsylvania......................	314.1
29	Colorado	309.1
30	West Virginia......................	302.0
31	Wisconsin..........................	290.3
32	Washington........................	285.2
33	Ohio..................................	284.9
34	Nebraska...........................	280.4
35	Mississippi.........................	278.5
36	Iowa.................................	273.5
37	North Dakota......................	265.1
38	New Jersey	261.2
39	Hawaii	259.2
40	Connecticut........................	236.9
41	Oregon..............................	232.3
42	Minnesota..........................	229.1
43	Rhode Island......................	219.2
44	Utah	215.6
45	Idaho................................	212.2
46	Kentucky............................	211.6
47	Virginia..............................	196.2
48	New Hampshire..................	196.1
49	Wyoming	195.5
50	Maine................................	127.8
51	Vermont.............................	99.3

Property Crime, 2014

Rank	State	Rate per 100,000 population
	United States......................	2,596.1
1	District of Columbia[1]	5,182.5
2	Washington........................	3,706.1
3	New Mexico	3,542.3
4	South Carolina	3,460.3
5	Louisiana	3,458.8
6	Florida...............................	3,415.5
7	Arkansas	3,338.0
8	Georgia.............................	3,281.2
9	Arizona..............................	3,197.5
10	Alabama............................	3,177.6
11	Tennessee.........................	3,060.6
12	Hawaii	3,050.0
13	Texas................................	3,019.4
14	Oklahoma..........................	2,990.7
15	Delaware............................	2,982.0
16	Mississippi.........................	2,921.2
17	Missouri.............................	2,906.5
18	Oregon..............................	2,879.0
19	Utah	2,878.5
20	North Carolina....................	2,873.1
21	Ohio..................................	2,799.1
22	Alaska...............................	2,760.0
23	Kansas	2,735.2
24	Indiana..............................	2,649.4
25	Nevada..............................	2,625.4
26	Colorado	2,530.1
27	Nebraska...........................	2,523.5
28	Maryland	2,507.5
29	Montana............................	2,472.9
30	California............................	2,441.1
31	Minnesota..........................	2,297.5
32	Kentucky............................	2,246.9
33	Rhode Island......................	2,173.6
34	North Dakota......................	2,110.3
35	Iowa.................................	2,093.8
36	Wisconsin..........................	2,088.3
37	Illinois...............................	2,075.9
38	Michigan............................	2,043.9
39	West Virginia......................	2,034.7
40	Maine................................	1,986.4
41	Wyoming	1,964.7
42	New Hampshire..................	1,962.7
43	Pennsylvania......................	1,931.7
44	Virginia..............................	1,930.3
45	Connecticut........................	1,920.4
46	South Dakota	1,863.9
47	Massachusetts....................	1,857.1
48	Idaho................................	1,854.8
49	New Jersey	1,734.1
50	New York...........................	1,718.2
51	Vermont.............................	1,524.4

[1]Includes offenses reported by the Zoological Police and the Metro Transit Police.

State Government Employment, 2014
(Full-time equivalent employees)

Rank	State	State employees per 1,000 residents
	United States......................	13.5
1	Hawaii......................	40.8
2	Alaska......................	36.6
3	Delaware......................	27.6
4	North Dakota......................	24.8
5	Vermont......................	23.1
6	Wyoming......................	23.0
7	New Mexico......................	22.1
8	West Virginia......................	21.8
9	Arkansas......................	20.8
10	Montana......................	20.1
11	Mississippi......................	19.0
12	Kentucky......................	18.8
13	Alabama......................	18.3
14	Utah......................	18.0
15	Rhode Island......................	17.7
16	Connecticut......................	17.5
17	Oklahoma......................	17.1
18	South Dakota......................	17.0
18	Kansas......................	17.0
20	Nebraska......................	16.9
21	Washington......................	16.7
22	Oregon......................	16.6
23	Louisiana......................	16.3
24	South Carolina......................	16.1
25	New Jersey......................	16.0
25	Iowa......................	16.0
27	Maine......................	15.8
28	Virginia......................	15.2
29	Minnesota......................	15.0
30	Colorado......................	14.6
30	Massachusetts......................	14.6
32	Missouri......................	14.5
32	North Carolina......................	14.5
34	Maryland......................	14.4
34	Idaho......................	14.4
36	Michigan......................	14.3
37	New Hampshire......................	14.1
38	Indiana......................	13.2
39	Georgia......................	12.9
40	Wisconsin......................	12.6
40	Pennsylvania......................	12.6
42	New York......................	12.2
43	Tennessee......................	12.0
44	Ohio......................	11.8
45	Arizona......................	11.5
46	Texas......................	11.4
47	California......................	10.4
48	Illinois......................	9.6
49	Nevada......................	9.4
50	Florida......................	8.7
	District of Columbia......................	X

X = Not applicable.

Unemployment Rate, 2015

Rank	State	Unemployment rate
	United States......................	5.3
1	District of Columbia......................	6.9
2	Nevada......................	6.7
2	West Virginia......................	6.7
4	New Mexico......................	6.6
5	Alaska......................	6.5
5	Mississippi......................	6.5
7	Louisiana......................	6.3
8	California......................	6.2
9	Alabama......................	6.1
9	Arizona......................	6.1
11	Rhode Island......................	6.0
11	South Carolina......................	6.0
13	Georgia......................	5.9
13	Illinois......................	5.9
15	Tennessee......................	5.8
16	North Carolina......................	5.7
16	Oregon......................	5.7
16	Washington......................	5.7
19	Connecticut......................	5.6
19	New Jersey......................	5.6
21	Florida......................	5.4
21	Kentucky......................	5.4
21	Michigan......................	5.4
24	New York......................	5.3
25	Arkansas......................	5.2
25	Maryland......................	5.2
27	Pennsylvania......................	5.1
28	Massachusetts......................	5.0
28	Missouri......................	5.0
30	Delaware......................	4.9
30	Ohio......................	4.9
32	Indiana......................	4.8
33	Wisconsin......................	4.6
34	Texas......................	4.5
35	Maine......................	4.4
35	Virginia......................	4.4
37	Kansas......................	4.2
37	Oklahoma......................	4.2
37	Wyoming......................	4.2
40	Idaho......................	4.1
40	Montana......................	4.1
42	Colorado......................	3.9
43	Iowa......................	3.7
43	Minnesota......................	3.7
43	Vermont......................	3.7
46	Hawaii......................	3.6
47	Utah......................	3.5
48	New Hampshire......................	3.4
49	South Dakota......................	3.1
50	Nebraska......................	3.0
51	North Dakota......................	2.7

Employees on Nonfarm Payrolls, Percent Change, 2014–2015

Rank	State	Percent
	United States......................	2.1
1	Utah......................	3.8
2	Florida......................	3.4
3	Nevada......................	3.3
3	Oregon......................	3.3
5	Colorado......................	3.1
6	California......................	3.0
6	Idaho......................	3.0
8	Georgia......................	2.9
8	Washington......................	2.9
10	South Carolina......................	2.7
11	Arizona......................	2.6
12	Tennessee......................	2.5
13	North Carolina......................	2.4
13	Texas......................	2.4
15	Delaware......................	2.3
16	Indiana......................	1.8
16	Virginia......................	1.8
16	Arkansas......................	1.8
19	Massachusetts......................	1.7
19	District of Columbia......................	1.7
19	Montana......................	1.7
19	New York......................	1.7
19	Missouri......................	1.7
24	Hawaii......................	1.5
24	Minnesota......................	1.5
24	New Hampshire......................	1.5
24	Michigan......................	1.5
24	Maryland......................	1.5
24	Kentucky......................	1.5
30	Ohio......................	1.4
30	New Jersey......................	1.4
30	Illinois......................	1.4
33	Nebraska......................	1.3
33	Alabama......................	1.3
33	Wisconsin......................	1.3
36	Rhode Island......................	1.2
36	Mississippi......................	1.2
38	South Dakota......................	1.0
38	Iowa......................	1.0
40	Vermont......................	0.9
41	Pennsylvania......................	0.8
41	New Mexico......................	0.8
41	Maine......................	0.8
41	Connecticut......................	0.8
45	Oklahoma......................	0.7
46	Kansas......................	0.6
47	Alaska......................	0.5
48	Louisiana......................	0.2
49	West Virginia......................	-0.7
50	Wyoming......................	-0.9
51	North Dakota......................	-1.6

Per Capita Personal Income, 2014 (2014 Dollars)		
Rank	State	Dollars
	United States	46,049
1	District of Columbia	69,838
2	Connecticut	64,864
3	Massachusetts	58,737
4	New Jersey	57,620
5	North Dakota	55,802
6	New York	55,611
7	Wyoming	54,584
8	Maryland	54,176
9	Alaska	54,012
10	New Hampshire	52,773
11	Virginia	50,345
12	California	49,985
13	Washington	49,610
14	Minnesota	48,998
15	Colorado	48,869
16	Rhode Island	48,359
17	Pennsylvania	47,679
18	Illinois	47,643
19	Nebraska	47,557
20	Vermont	46,428
21	Delaware	46,378
22	Hawaii	46,034
23	Texas	45,669
24	South Dakota	45,279
25	Iowa	44,937
26	Kansas	44,891
27	Wisconsin	44,186
28	Oklahoma	43,637
29	Florida	42,737
30	Ohio	42,236
31	Louisiana	42,030
32	Missouri	41,639
33	Oregon	41,220
34	Maine	40,745
35	Nevada	40,742
36	Michigan	40,740
37	Tennessee	40,457
38	Montana	39,903
39	Indiana	39,578
40	North Carolina	39,171
41	Georgia	38,980
42	Arizona	37,895
43	Arkansas	37,782
44	Utah	37,664
45	Alabama	37,512
46	Kentucky	37,396
47	New Mexico	37,091
48	Idaho	36,734
49	South Carolina	36,677
50	West Virginia	36,132
51	Mississippi	34,431

Real Gross Domestic Product in Chained (2009) Dollars, 2014		
Rank	State	Dollars (billions)
	United States	15,653
1	California	2,119
2	Texas	1,422
3	New York	1,248
4	Florida	766
5	Illinois	674
6	Pennsylvania	616
7	Ohio	535
8	New Jersey	499
9	Georgia	431
9	North Carolina	431
11	Virginia	425
12	Massachusetts	419
13	Michigan	413
14	Washington	386
15	Maryland	322
16	Indiana	294
17	Minnesota	292
18	Colorado	279
19	Tennessee	275
20	Wisconsin	269
21	Arizona	259
22	Missouri	258
23	Connecticut	229
24	Louisiana	210
25	Oregon	192
26	Alabama	180
27	South Carolina	174
28	Kentucky	172
29	Oklahoma	169
30	Iowa	153
31	Kansas	132
32	Utah	127
33	Nevada	123
34	Arkansas	111
35	District of Columbia	105
36	Nebraska	98
37	Mississippi	95
38	New Mexico	85
39	Hawaii	70
40	West Virginia	67
41	New Hampshire	65
42	Delaware	59
43	Idaho	57
44	North Dakota	51
45	Rhode Island	50
45	Maine	50
45	Alaska	50
48	South Dakota	40
48	Montana	40
50	Wyoming	35
51	Vermont	27

Real Gross Domestic Product in Chained (2009) Dollars, Percent Change, 2013–2014		
Rank	State	Percent
	United States	2.2
1	North Dakota	6.0
2	Delaware	4.3
3	Colorado	4.1
4	Texas	3.8
5	Nevada	3.4
6	Ohio	3.3
6	Oklahoma	3.3
8	California	3.1
9	Washington	3.0
10	Iowa	2.8
11	Florida	2.6
11	Minnesota	2.6
11	New Mexico	2.6
14	Georgia	2.5
14	South Carolina	2.5
16	New Hampshire	2.4
17	Pennsylvania	2.3
18	Indiana	2.2
18	Rhode Island	2.2
18	Utah	2.2
21	Arkansas	2.1
21	Idaho	2.1
21	North Carolina	2.1
21	Wisconsin	2.1
25	Montana	2.0
26	Louisiana	1.9
26	Nebraska	1.9
28	Arizona	1.8
28	District of Columbia	1.8
28	Massachusetts	1.8
31	Maryland	1.6
31	Tennessee	1.6
33	Michigan	1.5
33	Vermont	1.5
35	Connecticut	1.2
35	Kansas	1.2
35	New York	1.2
38	Kentucky	1.1
38	Maine	1.1
38	Missouri	1.1
41	Illinois	1.0
42	Alabama	0.9
42	Oregon	0.9
44	Hawaii	0.8
44	New Jersey	0.8
46	West Virginia	0.7
47	Wyoming	0.5
48	South Dakota	0.4
49	Virginia	0.2
50	Mississippi	-0.3
51	Alaska	-3.5

Median Household Income, 2014		
Rank	State	Dollars
	United States	53,657
1	Maryland	73,971
2	New Jersey	71,919
3	District of Columbia	71,648
4	Alaska	71,583
5	Connecticut	70,048
6	Hawaii	69,592
7	Massachusetts	69,160
8	New Hampshire	66,532
9	Virginia	64,902
10	California	61,933
11	Minnesota	61,481
12	Washington	61,366
13	Colorado	61,303
14	Utah	60,922
15	Delaware	59,716
16	North Dakota	59,029
17	New York	58,878
18	Illinois	57,444
19	Wyoming	57,055
20	Rhode Island	54,891
21	Vermont	54,166
22	Iowa	53,712
23	Pennsylvania	53,234
24	Texas	53,035
25	Nebraska	52,686
26	Wisconsin	52,622
27	Kansas	52,504
28	Nevada	51,450
29	Oregon	51,075
30	South Dakota	50,979
31	Arizona	50,068
32	Michigan	49,847
33	Maine	49,462
34	Indiana	49,446
35	Georgia	49,321
36	Ohio	49,308
37	Missouri	48,363
38	Idaho	47,861
39	Oklahoma	47,529
40	Florida	47,463
41	North Carolina	46,556
42	Montana	46,328
43	South Carolina	45,238
44	New Mexico	44,803
45	Louisiana	44,555
46	Tennessee	44,361
47	Kentucky	42,958
48	Alabama	42,830
49	Arkansas	41,262
50	West Virginia	41,059
51	Mississippi	39,680

Median Family Income, 2014		
Rank	State	Dollars
	United States	65,910
1	Maryland	89,678
2	Connecticut	88,819
3	New Jersey	88,419
4	Massachusetts	87,951
5	District of Columbia	84,094
6	Alaska	82,307
7	New Hampshire	80,581
8	Hawaii	79,187
9	Virginia	78,290
10	Minnesota	77,941
11	Colorado	75,405
12	North Dakota	75,221
13	Washington	74,193
14	Delaware	72,594
15	Wyoming	72,460
16	Illinois	71,796
17	Rhode Island	71,212
18	New York	71,115
19	California	71,015
20	Utah	69,535
21	Pennsylvania	67,876
22	Iowa	67,771
23	Wisconsin	67,187
24	Vermont	67,154
25	South Dakota	66,936
26	Kansas	66,425
27	Nebraska	66,120
28	Texas	62,830
29	Oregon	62,670
30	Ohio	62,300
31	Michigan	62,143
32	Maine	62,078
33	Missouri	61,299
34	Nevada	60,824
35	Indiana	60,780
36	Montana	60,643
37	Arizona	59,700
38	Georgia	58,885
39	Oklahoma	58,710
40	Idaho	58,101
41	North Carolina	57,380
42	Florida	57,212
43	Louisiana	56,573
44	South Carolina	56,491
45	Tennessee	55,557
46	Kentucky	54,776
47	New Mexico	54,705
48	Alabama	53,764
49	West Virginia	52,413
50	Arkansas	51,528
51	Mississippi	50,178

Persons Below Poverty Level, 2014		
Rank	State	Percent
	United States	15.5
1	Mississippi	21.5
2	New Mexico	21.3
3	Louisiana	19.8
4	Alabama	19.3
5	Kentucky	19.1
6	Arkansas	18.9
7	Georgia	18.3
7	Tennessee	18.3
7	West Virginia	18.3
10	Arizona	18.2
11	South Carolina	18.0
12	District of Columbia	17.7
13	North Carolina	17.2
13	Texas	17.2
15	Oklahoma	16.6
15	Oregon	16.6
17	Florida	16.5
18	California	16.4
19	Michigan	16.2
20	New York	15.9
21	Ohio	15.8
22	Missouri	15.5
23	Montana	15.4
24	Indiana	15.2
24	Nevada	15.2
26	Idaho	14.8
27	Illinois	14.4
28	Rhode Island	14.3
29	South Dakota	14.2
30	Maine	14.1
31	Kansas	13.6
31	Pennsylvania	13.6
33	Washington	13.2
33	Wisconsin	13.2
35	Delaware	12.5
36	Nebraska	12.4
37	Iowa	12.2
37	Vermont	12.2
39	Colorado	12.0
40	Virginia	11.8
41	Utah	11.7
42	Massachusetts	11.6
43	Minnesota	11.5
43	North Dakota	11.5
45	Hawaii	11.4
46	Alaska	11.2
46	Wyoming	11.2
48	New Jersey	11.1
49	Connecticut	10.8
50	Maryland	10.1
51	New Hampshire	9.2

Persons Under 18 Years Old Below Poverty Level, 2014

Rank	State	Percent
	United States......................	21.7
1	New Mexico	29.5
2	Mississippi......................	29.4
3	Louisiana	27.9
4	Alabama......................	27.7
5	South Carolina	27.1
6	Arkansas......................	26.4
7	Georgia......................	26.3
8	Kentucky......................	26.2
8	Tennessee......................	26.2
10	District of Columbia	26.0
11	Arizona......................	25.6
12	West Virginia......................	24.7
13	Texas......................	24.6
14	North Carolina......................	24.3
15	Florida......................	23.8
16	Ohio......................	22.9
17	California......................	22.7
18	Michigan......................	22.6
18	New York......................	22.6
20	Oklahoma......................	22.4
21	Nevada......................	22.0
22	Oregon......................	21.6
23	Indiana......................	21.5
24	Missouri......................	21.1
25	Illinois......................	20.2
26	Rhode Island......................	19.8
27	Pennsylvania......................	19.4
28	Maine......................	19.1
29	Idaho......................	18.8
30	Montana......................	18.5
31	Wisconsin......................	18.4
32	South Dakota	18.0
33	Delaware......................	17.7
33	Kansas......................	17.7
35	Washington......................	17.5
36	Nebraska......................	16.2
37	New Jersey	15.9
38	Alaska......................	15.8
38	Vermont......................	15.8
38	Virginia......................	15.8
41	Colorado	15.4
42	Iowa......................	15.3
43	Massachusetts......................	15.2
44	Connecticut......................	14.9
44	Minnesota......................	14.9
46	North Dakota......................	14.8
47	Hawaii......................	14.7
48	Utah......................	13.3
49	Maryland......................	13.0
49	New Hampshire......................	13.0
51	Wyoming......................	12.8

Energy Consumption Per Capita, 2014

Rank	State	Million Btu
	United States......................	308.5
1	Louisiana	920.5
2	Wyoming	916.7
3	North Dakota......................	864.9
4	Alaska......................	818.3
5	Iowa......................	495.9
6	Texas......................	478.1
7	South Dakota......................	459.2
8	Nebraska......................	459.0
9	Indiana......................	444.3
10	Oklahoma......................	433.0
11	West Virginia......................	407.3
12	Alabama......................	404.1
13	Kentucky......................	401.3
14	Montana......................	394.3
15	Kansas......................	390.1
16	Mississippi......................	386.0
17	Arkansas......................	375.6
18	Minnesota......................	350.4
19	South Carolina	338.0
20	Tennessee......................	335.2
21	Ohio......................	328.5
22	New Mexico	325.6
23	Wisconsin......................	324.5
24	Idaho......................	318.0
25	Missouri......................	314.0
26	Illinois......................	313.8
27	Maine......................	308.6
28	Pennsylvania......................	305.0
29	Delaware......................	292.8
30	Virginia......................	291.8
31	Michigan......................	290.6
32	Washington......................	284.8
33	Georgia......................	282.4
34	Colorado	275.8
35	District of Columbia	271.2
36	Utah......................	271.0
37	New Jersey	261.8
38	North Carolina......................	257.0
39	Oregon......................	248.6
40	Maryland......................	234.4
41	New Hampshire......................	233.5
42	Nevada......................	232.6
43	Vermont......................	223.2
44	Massachusetts......................	212.8
45	Arizona......................	211.4
46	Connecticut......................	208.6
47	Florida......................	207.1
48	Hawaii......................	198.0
49	California......................	196.4
50	Rhode Island......................	193.8
51	New York......................	189.5

Homeownership Rate, 2015

Rank	State	Percent
	United States......................	63.7
1	West Virginia......................	74.9
2	Michigan......................	74.6
3	Delaware......................	73.3
4	Vermont......................	71.8
5	New Hampshire......................	71.6
6	Mississippi......................	70.7
7	Minnesota......................	70.1
8	South Dakota	70.1
9	Alabama......................	70.0
10	Idaho......................	70.0
11	Maine......................	69.9
12	Utah......................	69.9
13	Wyoming	69.9
14	Pennsylvania......................	69.6
15	Indiana......................	69.4
16	Iowa......................	68.8
17	Missouri......................	68.5
18	Nebraska......................	68.1
19	Kentucky......................	67.9
20	Oklahoma......................	67.4
21	Arkansas......................	67.1
22	Maryland......................	67.1
23	South Carolina	67.1
24	Virginia......................	67.1
25	Wisconsin......................	66.6
26	Connecticut......................	66.5
27	New Mexico	66.5
28	Tennessee......................	66.5
29	Montana......................	66.4
30	Ohio......................	66.4
31	Illinois......................	65.4
32	North Carolina......................	65.2
33	Kansas......................	64.9
34	Florida......................	64.8
35	New Jersey	64.0
36	Colorado	63.6
37	Louisiana	63.3
38	Georgia......................	62.9
39	Washington......................	62.6
40	Alaska......................	62.3
41	Texas......................	61.9
42	North Dakota......................	61.8
43	Arizona......................	61.7
44	Oregon......................	61.1
45	Massachusetts......................	60.5
46	Hawaii......................	59.3
47	Rhode Island......................	58.9
48	Nevada......................	54.8
49	California......................	54.3
50	New York......................	51.5
51	District of Columbia	40.4

One-Unit Detached or Attached Housing Units, Percent of Total Housing Units, 2014

Rank	State	Percent
	United States	67.3
1	Iowa	77.8
2	Kansas	77.5
3	Michigan	76.6
4	Indiana	76.2
5	Nebraska	76.0
6	Idaho	75.5
6	Pennsylvania	75.5
8	Minnesota	74.8
9	Utah	74.6
10	Oklahoma	74.6
10	Missouri	73.7
12	Delaware	73.1
13	Ohio	72.8
14	South Dakota	72.6
14	Virginia	72.6
16	Maryland	72.5
17	West Virginia	72.3
18	Montana	71.9
19	Maine	71.7
20	Arkansas	71.5
20	Tennessee	71.5
22	Wisconsin	70.8
23	Mississippi	70.5
24	Georgia	70.1
25	Alabama	69.9
26	Vermont	69.8
26	Wyoming	69.8
28	Alaska	69.6
28	Colorado	69.6
30	Kentucky	69.2
31	North Carolina	69.0
32	New Mexico	68.8
33	Arizona	68.3
34	New Hampshire	67.8
34	Oregon	67.8
36	Louisiana	67.7
37	Texas	67.5
38	Washington	67.0
39	South Carolina	65.5
40	California	64.9
41	Illinois	64.4
41	North Dakota	64.4
43	Connecticut	64.0
44	Nevada	63.6
45	New Jersey	62.6
46	Hawaii	61.6
47	Florida	60.0
48	Rhode Island	57.7
49	Massachusetts	57.5
50	New York	46.5
51	District of Columbia	37.0

Percent of Population Not Covered by Private or Public Insurance, 2014

Rank	State	Percent
	United States	11.7
1	Texas	19.1
2	Alaska	17.2
3	Florida	16.6
4	Georgia	15.8
5	Oklahoma	15.4
6	Nevada	15.2
7	Louisiana	14.8
8	Mississippi	14.5
8	New Mexico	14.5
10	Montana	14.2
11	Arizona	13.6
11	Idaho	13.6
11	South Carolina	13.6
14	North Carolina	13.1
15	Utah	12.5
16	California	12.4
17	Alabama	12.1
18	Tennessee	12.0
18	Wyoming	12.0
20	Indiana	11.9
21	Arkansas	11.8
22	Missouri	11.7
23	New Jersey	10.9
23	Virginia	10.9
25	Colorado	10.3
26	Kansas	10.2
27	Maine	10.1
28	South Dakota	9.8
29	Illinois	9.7
29	Nebraska	9.7
29	Oregon	9.7
32	New Hampshire	9.2
32	Washington	9.2
34	New York	8.7
35	West Virginia	8.6
36	Kentucky	8.5
36	Michigan	8.5
36	Pennsylvania	8.5
39	Ohio	8.4
40	Maryland	7.9
40	North Dakota	7.9
42	Delaware	7.8
43	Rhode Island	7.4
44	Wisconsin	7.3
45	Connecticut	6.9
46	Iowa	6.2
47	Minnesota	5.9
48	District of Columbia	5.3
48	Hawaii	5.3
50	Vermont	5.0
51	Massachusetts	3.3

Traffic Fatalities Per 100 Million Vehicle Miles, 2014

Rank	State	Rate
	United States	1.08
1	South Carolina	1.65
2	Wyoming	1.59
3	Montana	1.58
4	Mississippi	1.54
5	Louisiana	1.53
6	New Mexico	1.51
7	Alaska	1.50
8	South Dakota	1.47
9	Texas	1.46
10	West Virginia	1.42
11	Kentucky	1.40
11	Oklahoma	1.40
13	Arkansas	1.37
14	Tennessee	1.33
15	North Dakota	1.28
16	Delaware	1.26
17	Alabama	1.25
17	Kansas	1.25
19	Florida	1.24
20	Arizona	1.23
21	Pennsylvania	1.20
22	North Carolina	1.19
23	Idaho	1.15
23	Nebraska	1.15
23	Nevada	1.15
26	Missouri	1.08
27	Georgia	1.04
28	Oregon	1.03
29	Iowa	1.02
30	Colorado	1.00
31	Indiana	0.94
32	Hawaii	0.93
32	Michigan	0.93
32	Utah	0.93
35	California	0.92
35	Maine	0.92
37	Ohio	0.89
38	Illinois	0.88
39	Virginia	0.87
40	Wisconsin	0.84
41	Connecticut	0.80
41	New York	0.80
41	Washington	0.80
44	Maryland	0.78
45	New Jersey	0.74
46	New Hampshire	0.73
47	Rhode Island	0.68
48	District of Columbia	0.65
49	Minnesota	0.63
50	Vermont	0.62
51	Massachusetts	0.57

ALABAMA

Facts and Figures

Location: Southeastern United States; bordered on the N by Tennessee, on the E by Georgia, on the S by Florida and the Gulf of Mexico, and on the W by Mississippi

Area: 52,420 sq. mi. (135,765 sq. km.); rank—30th

Population: 4,858,979 (2015 est.); rank—24th

Principal Cities: capital—Montgomery; largest—Birmingham

Statehood: December 14, 1819; 22nd state

U.S. Congress: 2 senators, 7 representatives

State Motto: *Audemus jura nostra defendere* ("We dare defend our rights")

State Song: "Alabama"

State Nicknames: The Yellowhammer State; The Heart of Dixie; The Cotton State

Abbreviations: AL; Ala.

State Symbols: flower—camellia; tree—Southern longleaf pine; bird—yellowhammer

At a Glance

- With an increase in population of 1.5 percent, Alabama ranked 37th among the states in growth from 2010 to 2015.

- Alabama's per capita personal income in 2014 was $37,512, ranking 45th in the nation.

- With 8.68 deaths per 1,000 live births, Alabama's infant mortality rate was the highest in the nation in 2014.

- In 2014, 19.3 percent of Alabama residents lived below the poverty level, a percentage that ranked 4th in the nation.

- Alabama's violent crime rate in 2014 was 427.3 per 100,000 residents, compared to 365.5 for the entire nation.

- Alabama's median household income of $42,830 ranked 48th in the nation.

Table AL-1. Population by Age, Sex, Race, and Hispanic Origin

(Number, percent, except where noted.)

Sex, age, race, and Hispanic origin	2000	2010	2015[1]	Average annual percent change, 2010–2015
Total Population..	4,447,100	4,779,736	4,858,979	0.1
Percent of total U.S. population	1.6	1.5	1.5	X
Sex				
Male..	2,146,504	2,320,188	2,353,184	0.1
Female	2,300,596	2,459,548	2,505,795	0.1
Age				
Under 5 years...	295,992	304,957	292,973	-0.3
5 to 19 years..	960,177	971,355	935,562	-0.3
20 to 64 years..	2,611,133	2,845,632	2,866,282	0.1
65 years and over..	579,798	657,792	764,162	1.1
Median age (years)..	35.8	37.9	38.7	0.1
Race and Hispanic Origin				
One race				
White	3,162,808	3,362,877	3,374,569	-
Black..	1,155,930	1,259,224	1,300,596	0.2
American Indian and Alaska Native	22,430	32,903	33,980	0.2
Asian..	31,346	55,240	67,196	1.4
Native Hawaiian or Other Pacific Islander	1,409	5,208	5,067	-0.2
Two or more races..	44,179	64,284	77,571	1.4
Hispanic (of any race)...	75,830	192,498	203,325	0.4

X = Not applicable.
[1]Population figures for 2015 are July 1 estimates. The 2010 estimates are taken from the 2010 Census.
- = Zero or rounds to zero.

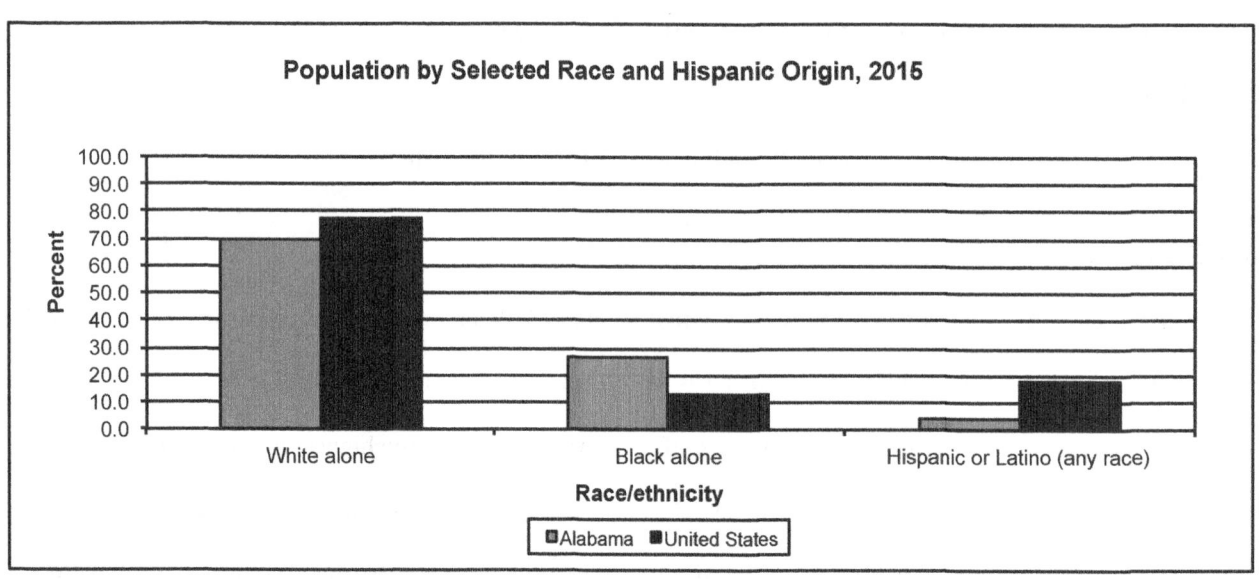

Table AL-2. Marital Status

(Number, percent distribution.)

Sex, age, and marital status	2000	2010	2014
Males, 15 Years and Over	1,666,798	1,844,661	1,863,744
Never married	26.7	32.5	32.4
Now married, except separated..	59.0	50.6	51.0
Separated..	1.8	2.5	2.1
Widowed...	2.8	3.0	3.0
Divorced...	9.8	11.4	11.5
Females, 15 Years and Over	1,847,401	2,004,450	2,028,847
Never married	21.4	26.1	26.7
Now married, except separated..	52.5	45.9	46.0
Separated..	2.5	3.1	3.0
Widowed...	12.4	11.2	10.9
Divorced...	11.2	13.6	13.5

Table AL-3. Households and Housing Characteristics

(Number, percent, dollars.)

Item	2000	2010	2014	Average annual percent change, 2000–2014
Total Households..................................	1,737,080	1,815,152	1,841,217	0.4
Family households........................	1,215,968	1,227,884	1,232,515	0.1
Married-couple family..............	906,916	868,946	870,026	-0.3
Other family........................	309,052	358,938	362,489	1.2
Male householder, no wife present....	62,586	79,308	77,605	1.7
Female householder, no husband present.....	246,466	279,630	284,884	1.1
Nonfamily households.....................	521,112	587,268	608,702	1.2
Householder living alone..............	453,898	511,708	530,916	1.2
Householder not living alone...........	67,214	75,560	77,786	1.1
Housing Characteristics				
Total housing units.....................	1,963,711	2,174,428	2,208,030	0.9
Occupied housing units	1,737,080	1,815,152	1,841,217	0.4
Owner occupied........................	1,258,705	1,272,846	1,246,080	-0.1
Renter occupied.......................	478,375	542,306	595,137	1.7
Average household size................	2.49	2.57	2.57	0.2
Financial Characteristics				
Median gross rent of renter-occupied housing	447	667	717	4.3
Median monthly owner costs for housing units with a mortgage	816	1,130	1,119	2.7
Median value of owner-occupied housing units.............	85,100	123,900	125,600	3.4

Table AL-4. Migration, Origin, and Language

(Number, percent.)

Characteristic	State			U.S.		
	2013	2014	Percent change	2013	2014	Percent change
Residence 1 Year Ago						
Population 1 year and over	4,781,296	4,791,931	0.2	312,432,820	315,095,393	0.9
Same house...............................	85.1	85.2	X	85.0	85.1	X
Different house in the U.S.	14.6	14.5	X	14.4	14.3	X
Same county...........................	9.1	9.0	X	8.9	8.7	X
Different county	5.5	5.5	X	5.5	5.6	X
Same state	3.3	3.2	X	3.2	3.3	X
Different state	2.2	2.3	X	2.3	2.3	X
Abroad...............................	0.3	0.3	X	0.6	0.6	X
Place of Birth						
Native born	4,671,496	4,692,021	0.4	274,780,773	276,465,262	0.6
Male................................	48.3	48.4	X	49.3	49.3	X
Female..............................	51.7	51.6	X	50.7	50.7	X
Foreign born	162,226	157,356	-3.0	41,348,066	42,391,794	2.5
Male................................	51.8	50	X	48.8	48.7	X
Female..............................	48.2	50	X	51.2	51.3	X
Foreign born; naturalized U.S. citizen......	59,782	54,716	X	19,294,710	19,984,738	3.6
Male................................	48.9	42.6	X	45.9	45.9	X
Female..............................	51.1	57.4	X	54.1	54.1	X
Foreign born; not a U.S. citizen...........	102,444	102,640	0.2	22,053,356	22,407,056	1.6
Male................................	53.5	54	X	51.3	51.2	X
Female..............................	46.5	46	X	48.7	48.8	X
Entered 2010 or later....................	11.9	14.3	X	9.7	12.3	X
Entered 2000 to 2009...................	42.4	38.6	X	29.4	28.6	X
Entered before 2000....................	45.7	47.2	X	61.0	59.1	X
World Region of Birth, Foreign						
Foreign-born population, excluding population born at sea	162,226	157,356	-3.0	41,347,945	42,390,705	2.5
Europe	10.7	11.0	X	11.6	11.2	X
Asia...............................	30.9	30.7	X	29.5	30.1	X
Africa.............................	4.6	4.5	X	4.4	4.6	X
Oceania...........................	0.6	0.5	X	0.5	0.6	X
Latin America......................	51.1	50.7	X	51.9	51.6	X
North America.....................	2.1	2.6	X	2.0	1.9	X
Language Spoken at Home and Ability to Speak English						
Population 5 years and over........................	4,541,368	4,558,217	0.4	296,358,760	299,084,046	0.9
English only	94.9	95.1	X	79.2	78.9	X
Language other than English...........	5.1	4.9	X	20.8	21.1	X
Speaks English less than "very well".........	2.2	2.0	X	8.5	8.6	X

X = Not applicable.
- = Zero or rounds to zero.

Table AL-5. Median Income and Poverty Status, 2014

(Number, percent, except as noted.)

Characteristic	State		U.S.	
	Number	Percent	Number	Percent
Median Income				
Households (dollars)...	42,830	X	53,657	X
Families (dollars)	53,764	X	65,910	X
Below Poverty Level (All People)	910,175	19.3	48,208,387	15.5
Sex				
Male..	396,012	17.4	21,590,918	14.2
Female	514,163	21.0	26,617,469	16.8
Age				
Under 18 years..	302,736	27.7	15,686,012	21.7
Related children under 18 years...........................	299,717	27.5	15,372,705	21.3
18 to 64 years...	526,246	18.1	28,267,482	14.6
65 years and over	81,193	11.2	4,254,893	9.5

X = Not applicable.

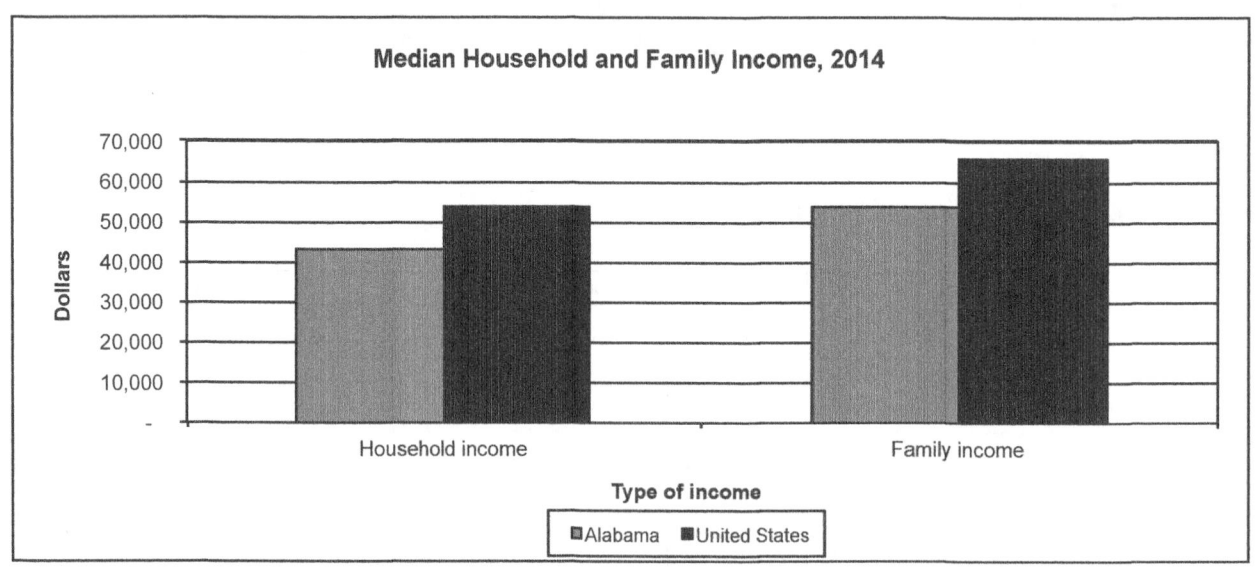

Table AL-6. Health Insurance Coverage Status for the Civilian Noninstitutionalized Population and Children Under 18 Years of Age

(Numbers in thousands, percent.)

Item	2006	2007	2008	2009	2010	2011	2012	2013	2014
Civilian Noninstitutionalized Population	4,532	4,570	4,574	4,616	4,703	4,720	4,742	4,755	4,767
Covered by Private or Public Insurance									
Number..	3,843	4,021	4,023	3,979	4,016	4,046	4,109	4,110	4,118
Percent..	84.8	88.0	88.0	86.2	85.4	85.7	86.7	86.4	87.9
Not Covered									
Number..	689	549	551	637	687	674	632	645	579
Percent..	15.2	12.0	12.0	13.8	14.6	14.3	13.3	13.6	12.1
Percent in the U.S. not covered.............................	15.8	15.3	15.1	15.1	15.5	15.1	14.8	14.5	11.7
Children Under 18 Years of Age	1,114	1,083	1,120	1,124	1,134	1,122	1,123	1,108	1,107
Covered by Private or Public Insurance									
Number..	1,032	1,041	1,030	1,057	1,067	1,063	1,077	1,060	1,064
Percent..	92.6	92.7	92.0	94.1	94.1	94.7	95.9	95.7	96.2
Not Covered									
Number..	82	82	90	67	67	59	46	48	42
Percent..	7.4	7.3	8.0	5.9	5.9	5.3	4.1	4.3	3.8
Percent in the U.S. not covered.............................	11.7	11.0	9.7	8.6	8.0	7.5	7.2	7.1	6.0

Table AL-7. Employment Status by Demographic Group, 2015

(Numbers in thousands, percent.)

Characteristic	Civilian noninstitutional population	Civilian labor force		Employed		Unemployed	
		Number	Percent of population	Number	Percent of population	Number	Percent of population
Total....................	3,807	2,158	56.7	2,026	53.2	132	6.1
Sex							
Male....................	1,800	1,134	63.0	1,065	59.2	69	6.1
Female	2,008	1,023	51.0	960	47.8	63	6.2
Race, Sex, and Hispanic Origin							
White...................	2,706	1,523	56.3	1,457	53.8	66	4.3
Male...................	1,306	849	65.0	811	62.1	38	4.4
Female	1,400	674	48.2	646	46.1	29	4.2
Black or African American..................	977	567	58.0	506	51.8	60	10.6
Male...................	433	249	57.5	220	50.8	29	11.7
Female	544	318	58.4	286	52.6	31	9.8
Hispanic or Latino ethnicity[1]	124	82	66.1	77	61.8	5	6.5
Male...................	68	55	81.1	51	75.5	4	7.0
Female	NA	NA	NA	NA	NA	NA	NA
Age							
16 to 19 years...........	275	82	30.0	70	25.3	13	15.6
20 to 24 years...........	347	238	68.5	208	59.9	30	12.5
25 to 34 years...........	576	451	78.3	409	71.0	42	9.3
35 to 44 years...........	586	468	80.0	449	76.7	19	4.1
45 to 54 years...........	620	454	73.3	441	71.1	14	3.0
55 to 64 years...........	665	361	54.3	350	52.6	11	3.0
65 years and over..........	739	103	14.0	100	13.5	3	3.3

NOTE: Data in Table 7 are from the Current Population Survey (CPS) and do not match the estimates in Table 8. See notes and definitions for further information.
[1]May be of any race.
NA = Not available.

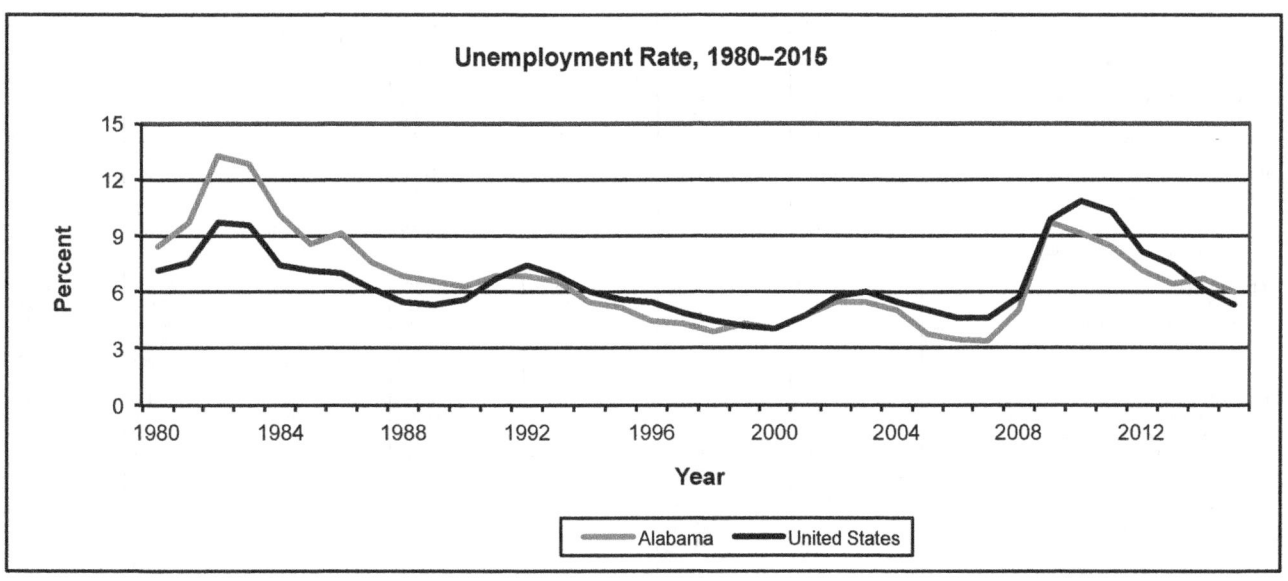

Unemployment Rate, 1980–2015

Table AL-8. Employment Status of the Civilian Noninstitutional Population Age 16 Years and Over

(Number, percent.)

Year	Civilian labor force	Civilian participation rate	Employed	Unemployed	Unemployment rate
2007....................	2,175,612	61.1	2,089,127	86,485	4.0
2008....................	2,176,489	60.6	2,053,477	123,012	5.7
2009....................	2,162,999	59.7	1,924,747	238,252	11.0
2010....................	2,196,042	59.5	1,964,559	231,483	10.5
2011....................	2,202,670	59.1	1,990,413	212,257	9.6
2012....................	2,174,972	58.1	2,001,849	173,123	8.0
2013....................	2,167,238	57.6	2,010,431	156,807	7.2
2014....................	2,161,313	57.1	2,014,284	147,029	6.8
2015....................	2,146,157	56.4	2,015,189	130,968	6.1

Table AL-9. Employment and Average Wages by Industry

(Estimates through 2010 are based on the 2007 North American Industry Classification System [NAICS]. Estimates from 2011 onward are based on the 2012 NAICS.)

Industry	2008	2009	2010	2011	2012	2013	2014
	Number of Jobs						
Wage and Salary Employment by Industry..............	2,082,617	1,978,414	1,960,904	1,962,049	1,967,479	1,983,624	2,000,031
Farm Wage and Salary Employment......................	7,750	9,482	7,957	8,074	8,015	8,597	5,311
Nonfarm Wage and Salary Employment....................	2,074,867	1,968,932	1,952,947	1,953,975	1,959,464	1,975,027	1,994,720
Private wage and salary employment.....................	1,664,029	1,557,480	1,539,991	1,545,888	1,556,449	1,574,326	1,594,919
Forestry, fishing, and related activities..................	8,708	8,503	8,727	8,857	8,482	8,713	8,919
Mining..	8,267	7,723	7,771	8,289	8,595	7,990	7,548
Utilities..	13,971	13,865	14,093	14,262	14,248	14,377	14,295
Construction	112,693	95,983	91,361	85,262	82,318	82,463	82,409
Manufacturing..	282,951	246,592	236,733	237,815	243,884	249,574	253,188
Durable goods manufacturing............................	178,501	152,566	146,428	148,023	154,486	159,866	165,126
Nondurable goods manufacturing.......................	104,450	94,026	90,305	89,792	89,398	89,708	88,062
Wholesale trade	81,737	75,203	72,336	72,563	72,930	73,476	73,402
Retail trade...	240,716	228,378	226,793	228,106	226,180	226,637	229,529
Transportation and warehousing...........................	58,524	53,443	53,269	54,180	55,668	57,083	58,992
Information..	27,380	25,325	24,016	23,098	22,709	22,607	21,938
Finance and insurance	73,664	71,718	70,355	71,988	72,218	73,265	74,347
Real estate and rental and leasing.......................	25,659	24,041	22,753	21,878	21,800	22,415	22,255
Professional, scientific, and technical services	100,795	97,910	95,809	95,059	95,095	95,402	95,435
Management of companies and enterprises...............	14,439	15,190	15,496	15,982	16,878	15,952	15,134
Administrative and waste services........................	108,209	94,485	100,596	104,600	108,133	109,279	113,931
Educational services	25,905	27,042	28,053	28,817	29,491	29,078	29,879
Health care and social assistance........................	196,005	195,152	197,749	199,466	201,226	204,075	206,070
Arts, entertainment, and recreation......................	17,787	18,082	16,616	16,278	15,796	16,077	16,328
Accommodation and food services........................	158,467	153,918	153,104	155,098	159,136	163,951	168,682
Other services, except public administration..............	108,152	104,927	104,361	104,290	101,662	101,912	102,638
Government and government enterprises..................	410,838	411,452	412,956	408,087	403,015	400,701	399,801
	Dollars						
Average Wages and Salaries by Industry	38,085	38,701	39,607	40,461	41,288	41,579	42,594
Average Farm Wages and Salaries	23,102	18,923	22,692	20,050	22,475	21,643	25,427
Average Nonfarm Wages and Salaries	38,141	38,796	39,676	40,546	41,365	41,665	42,639
Average private wages and salaries.......................	37,345	37,841	38,802	39,653	40,673	41,037	41,996
Forestry, fishing, and related activities..................	30,634	29,997	32,117	32,801	33,685	34,373	35,435
Mining..	67,255	68,446	74,346	77,705	76,342	77,961	80,884
Utilities..	81,835	80,520	78,785	85,859	88,189	88,407	88,422
Construction	40,970	41,761	43,398	43,496	45,255	45,524	47,788
Manufacturing..	45,149	45,770	48,313	49,094	50,348	50,900	52,870
Durable goods manufacturing............................	47,563	48,039	51,079	51,728	52,901	53,251	55,082
Nondurable goods manufacturing.......................	41,026	42,088	43,827	44,752	45,934	46,710	48,724
Wholesale trade	53,580	53,268	54,900	56,108	56,903	57,896	59,920
Retail trade...	23,821	24,139	24,523	24,734	25,295	25,622	25,872
Transportation and warehousing...........................	40,641	40,471	41,919	43,059	43,938	44,568	45,891
Information..	48,804	47,929	48,328	50,897	51,274	51,562	54,120
Finance and insurance	58,570	58,364	58,243	62,143	64,393	65,097	67,919
Real estate and rental and leasing.......................	33,444	32,982	35,275	36,598	38,746	38,450	40,052
Professional, scientific, and technical services	62,245	65,076	65,906	68,022	69,673	70,590	71,459
Management of companies and enterprises...............	70,406	69,189	74,595	78,602	80,746	83,380	85,332
Administrative and waste services........................	24,258	25,148	26,251	26,113	26,713	26,697	27,107
Educational services	23,660	24,069	24,045	24,536	24,627	25,296	25,538
Health care and social assistance........................	39,966	41,221	41,615	42,230	43,263	43,395	44,122
Arts, entertainment, and recreation......................	19,310	18,934	18,935	18,915	19,903	20,174	20,410
Accommodation and food services........................	14,346	14,700	15,353	15,715	15,964	15,952	16,419
Other services, except public administration..............	25,935	26,389	27,569	28,092	29,150	29,834	30,545
Government and government enterprises..................	41,366	42,412	42,937	43,929	44,035	44,133	45,208

Table AL-10. Employment Characteristics by Family Type

(Number, percent.)

Family type and labor force status	2012 Total	2012 Families with own children under 18 years	2013 Total	2013 Families with own children under 18 years	2014 Total	2014 Families with own children under 18 years
All Families...	1,233,937	502,537	1,222,568	492,554	1,229,579	485,990
FAMILY TYPE AND LABOR FORCE STATUS						
Married-Couple Families............................	883,291	323,513	857,865	305,444	867,090	305,881
Both husband and wife in labor force.......................	47.2	63.7	46.7	63.6	46.3	63.6
Husband in labor force, wife not in labor force	24.1	30.0	23.4	28.8	23.7	29.0
Wife in labor force, husband not in labor force	8.2	4.2	8.7	5.1	8.5	4.8
Both husband and wife not in labor force..................	20.4	2.1	20.9	2.3	21.5	2.5
Other Families	350,646	179,024	364,703	187,110	362,489	180,109
Female householder, no husband present.....................	79.2	83.2	77.9	81.4	78.6	82.7
In labor force	52.0	67.2	49.5	64.4	48.8	64.5
Not in labor force	27.2	16.0	28.5	16.9	29.8	18.2
Male householder, no wife present.........................	20.8	16.8	22.1	18.6	21.4	17.3
In labor force......................................	14.3	14.2	16.1	16.7	14.4	14.7
Not in labor force	6.5	2.6	6	2.0	7.0	2.6

Table AL-11. School Enrollment and Educational Attainment, 2014

(Number, percent.)

Item	State	U.S.
Enrollment		
Total population 3 years and over, enrolled in school..............	1,190,580	82,063,714
Enrolled in nursery school or preschool (percent).................	5.0	6.0
Enrolled in kindergarten (percent)...............................	5.2	5.1
Enrolled in elementary school, grades 1-8 (percent)...............	42.4	40.2
Enrolled in high school, grades 9-12 (percent)...................	21.4	20.7
Enrolled in college or graduate school (percent).................	26.0	28.0
Attainment		
Total population 25 years and over	3,256,766	213,725,624
Less than ninth grade (percent)	5.1	5.6
9th to 12th grade, no diploma (percent).........................	10.2	7.5
High school graduate, including equivalency (percent)............	31.6	27.7
Some college, no degree (percent)	21.8	21.0
Associate's degree (percent)	7.9	8.2
Bachelor's degree (percent)	14.7	18.7
Graduate or professional degree (percent).......................	8.8	11.4
High school graduate or higher (percent)	84.7	86.9
Bachelor's degree or higher (percent)...........................	23.5	30.1

Table AL-12. Public School Characteristics and Educational Indicators

(Number, percent; data derived from National Center of Education Statistics.)

Item	State	U.S.
Public Schools, 2013–2014 (except where noted)		
Number of school districts......................................	177	18,194
Number of schools...	1,637	98,271
Number of students (in thousands)	746	50,045
Number of teachers (in thousands)	47	3,114
Student-teacher ratio	15.8	16.1
Expenditures per student (dollars), FY 2013	8,773	107,637
Four-year adjusted cohort graduation rate (ACGR)[1,2]	86.3	82.3
Students eligible for free or reduced-price lunch (in thousands)	434	25,596
English language learners (in thousands)	17	4,461
Students age 3 to 21 served under IDEA, part B (in thousands) ...	81	6,464

Public Schools by Type	Number	Percent of state public schools
Total number of schools...	1,637	100.0
Regular	1,402	85.6
Special education...	44	2.7
Vocational education..	72	4.4
Alternative education...	119	7.3

NOTE: Every school is assigned only one school type based on its instructional emphasis.
[1] ACGR data represents a new method of calculating high-school completion rates and may not be comparable to previous years' data for Averaged Freshmen Graduation Rates (AFGR).
[2] The United States 4-year ACGRs were estimated using both the reported 4-year ACGR data from 49 states and the District of Columbia and using imputed data for Idaho. The estimate for American Indian/Alaska Native students also includes imputed data for Virginia.

Table AL-13. Reported Voting and Registration of the Voting-Age Population, November 2014

(Numbers in thousands, percent.)

Item	Total population	Total citizen population	Registered			Voted		
			Total registered	Percent registered (total population)	Percent registered (total citizen population)	Total voted	Percent voted (total population)	Percent voted (total citizen population)
U.S. Total	239,874	219,941	142,166	59.3	64.6	92,251	38.5	41.9
State Total.............................	3,656	3,519	2,366	64.7	67.2	1,497	40.9	42.5
Sex								
Male...	1,734	1,642	1,063	61.3	64.7	677	39.0	41.2
Female	1,922	1,877	1,303	67.8	69.4	820	42.6	43.7
Race								
White alone..............................	2,586	2,503	1,700	65.8	67.9	1,045	40.4	41.8
White, non-Hispanic alone	2,478	2,473	1,686	68.0	68.2	1,045	42.2	42.3
Black alone................................	922	910	596	64.6	65.4	414	44.9	45.5
Asian alone...............................	51	23	17	(B)	(B)	9	(B)	(B)
Hispanic (of any race)	136	41	17	(B)	(B)	3	(B)	(B)
White alone or in combination	2,660	2,572	1,746	65.6	67.9	1,071	40.2	41.6
Black alone or in combination.........	937	925	604	64.5	65.3	414	44.2	44.8
Asian alone or in combination..........	51	23	17	(B)	(B)	9	(B)	(B)
Age								
18 to 24 years...........................	482	449	181	37.4	40.2	77	16.1	17.2
25 to 34 years...........................	555	519	330	59.4	63.6	155	27.9	29.9
35 to 44 years...........................	610	566	373	61.1	65.9	244	40.0	43.2
45 to 64 years...........................	1,298	1,277	951	73.3	74.5	630	48.5	49.3
65 years and over	710	708	532	74.9	75.1	390	54.9	55.1

- = Zero or rounds to zero.
B = Base is less than 75,000 and therefore too small to show the derived measure.

Table AL-14. Crime

(Number, rate per 100,000. Data are derived from the FBI Uniform Crime Reports.)

Item	State[1]			U.S.[1,2,3,4]		
	2013	2014	Percent change	2013	2014	Percent change
TOTAL POPULATION[5]..	4,833,722	4,849,377	0.3	316,128,839	318,857,056	0.9
VIOLENT CRIME						
Number..................................	20,210	20,727	2.6	1,163,146	1,165,383	0.2
Rate	418.1	427.4	2.2	367.9	365.5	-0.7
Murder and Nonnegligent Manslaughter						
Number..................................	347	276	-20.5	14,196	14,249	0.4
Rate	7.2	5.7	-20.8	4.5	4.5	-
Rape[6]						
Number..................................	2,044	2,005	X	108,612	116,645	X
Rate	42.3	41.3	X	34.4	36.6	X
Robbery						
Number..................................	4,648	4,701	1.1	345,031	325,802	-5.6
Rate	96.2	96.9	0.7	109.1	102.2	-6.3
Aggravated Assault						
Number..................................	13,787	13,745	-0.3	724,149	741,291	2.4
Rate	285.2	283.4	-0.6	229.1	232.5	1.5
PROPERTY CRIME						
Number..................................	161,993	154,094	-4.9	8,632,512	8,277,829	-4.1
Rate	3,351.3	3,177.6	-5.2	2,730.7	2,596.1	-4.9
Burglary						
Number..................................	42,429	39,715	-6.4	1,928,465	1,729,806	-10.3
Rate	877.8	819.0	-6.7	610.0	542.5	-11.1
Larceny-Theft						
Number..................................	108,993	104,238	-4.4	6,004,453	5,858,496	-2.4
Rate	2,254.8	2,149.5	-4.7	1,899.4	1,837.3	-3.3
Motor Vehicle Theft						
Number..................................	10,571	10,141	-4.1	699,594	689,527	-1.4
Rate	218.7	209.1	-4.4	221.3	216.2	-2.3

NOTE: Although arson data are included in the trend and clearance tables, sufficient data are not available to estimate totals for this offense. Therefore, no arson data are published in this table.
X = Not applicable.
- = Zero or rounds to zero.
[1]Because of changes in the state's reporting practices, figures are not comparable to previous years' data.
[2]The crime figures have been adjusted.
[3]The data collection methodology for the offense of forcible rape used by the Minnesota state Uniform Crime Reporting (UCR) Program (with the exception of Minneapolis and St. Paul, Minnesota) does not comply with national UCR Program guidelines. Consequently, its figures for forcible rape and violent crime (of which forcible rape is a part) are not published in this table.
[4]Includes offenses reported by the Zoological Police and the Metro Transit Police.
[5]Populations are U.S. Census Bureau provisional estimates as of July 1 of each year.
[6]The figures shown for the 2013 offense of rape were estimated using the revised Uniform Crime Reporting (UCR) definition of rape. Figures are not comparable to data from previous years.

Table AL-15. State Government Finances, 2014

(Dollar amounts in thousands, percent distribution.)

Item	Dollars	Percent distribution
Total Revenue	28,280,058	100.0
General revenue	22,948,381	81.1
Intergovernmental revenue	8,135,043	28.8
Taxes	9,293,754	32.9
General sales	2,393,192	8.5
Selective sales	2,419,482	8.6
License taxes	386,378	1.4
Individual income tax	3,206,583	11.3
Corporate income tax	406,408	1.4
Other taxes	481,711	1.7
Current charges	4,255,483	15.0
Miscellaneous general revenue	1,264,101	4.5
Utility revenue	0	-
Liquor stores revenue	288,982	1.0
Insurance trust revenue[1]	5,042,695	17.8
Total Expenditure	28,127,696	100.0
Intergovernmental expenditure	6,474,302	23.0
Direct expenditure	21,653,394	77.0
Current operation	15,550,184	55.3
Capital outlay	1,636,827	5.8
Insurance benefits and repayments	3,358,956	11.9
Assistance and subsidies	653,499	2.3
Interest on debt	453,928	1.6
Exhibit: Salaries and wages	4,658,023	16.6
Total Expenditure	28,127,696	100.0
General expenditure	24,501,856	87.1
Intergovernmental expenditure	6,474,302	23.0
Direct expenditure	21,653,394	77.0
General expenditure, by function:		
Education	10,367,010	36.9
Public welfare	6,619,150	23.5
Hospitals	2,184,917	7.8
Health	520,967	1.9
Highways	1,684,932	6.0
Police protection	164,276	0.6
Correction	541,554	1.9
Natural resources	262,297	0.9
Parks and recreation	19,829	0.1
Governmental administration	583,739	2.1
Interest on general debt	453,928	1.6
Other and unallocable	1,099,257	3.9
Utility expenditure	0	-
Liquor stores expenditure	266,884	0.9
Insurance trust expenditure	3,358,956	11.9
Debt at End of Fiscal Year	8,907,686	X
Cash and Security Holdings	43,515,389	X

X = Not applicable.

- = Zero or rounds to zero.

[1]Within insurance trust revenue, net earnings of state retirement systems is a calculated statistic (the item code in the data file is X08), and thus can be positive or negative. Net earnings is the sum of earnings on investments plus gains on investments minus losses on investments. The change made in 2002 for asset valuation from book to market value in accordance with Statement 34 of the Governmental Accounting Standards Board is reflected in the calculated statistics.

Table AL-16. State Government Tax Collections, 2014

(Dollars in thousands, percent.)

Item	Dollars	Percent distribution
Total Taxes	9,293,754	100.0
Property taxes	329,598	3.5
Sales and gross receipts	4,812,674	51.8
General sales and gross receipts	2,393,192	25.8
Selective sales and gross receipts	2,419,482	26.0
Alcoholic beverages	181,427	2.0
Amusements	70	-
Insurance premiums	304,441	3.3
Motor fuels	534,396	5.8
Pari-mutuels	1,547	0.0
Public utilities	734,105	7.9
Tobacco products	117,112	1.3
Other selective sales	546,384	5.9
Licenses	386,378	4.2
Alcoholic beverages	4,225	-
Amusements	0	-
Corporations in general	78,166	0.8
Hunting and fishing	21,311	0.2
Motor vehicle	189,345	2.0
Motor vehicle operators	20,920	0.2
Public utilities	14,233	0.2
Occupation and business, NEC	58,178	0.6
Other licenses	0	-
Income taxes	3,612,991	38.9
Individual income	3,206,583	34.5
Corporation net income	406,408	4.4
Other taxes	152,113	1.6
Death and gift	8	-
Documentary and stock transfer	36,668	0.4
Severance	115,437	1.2
Taxes, NEC	0	-

- = Zero or rounds to zero.

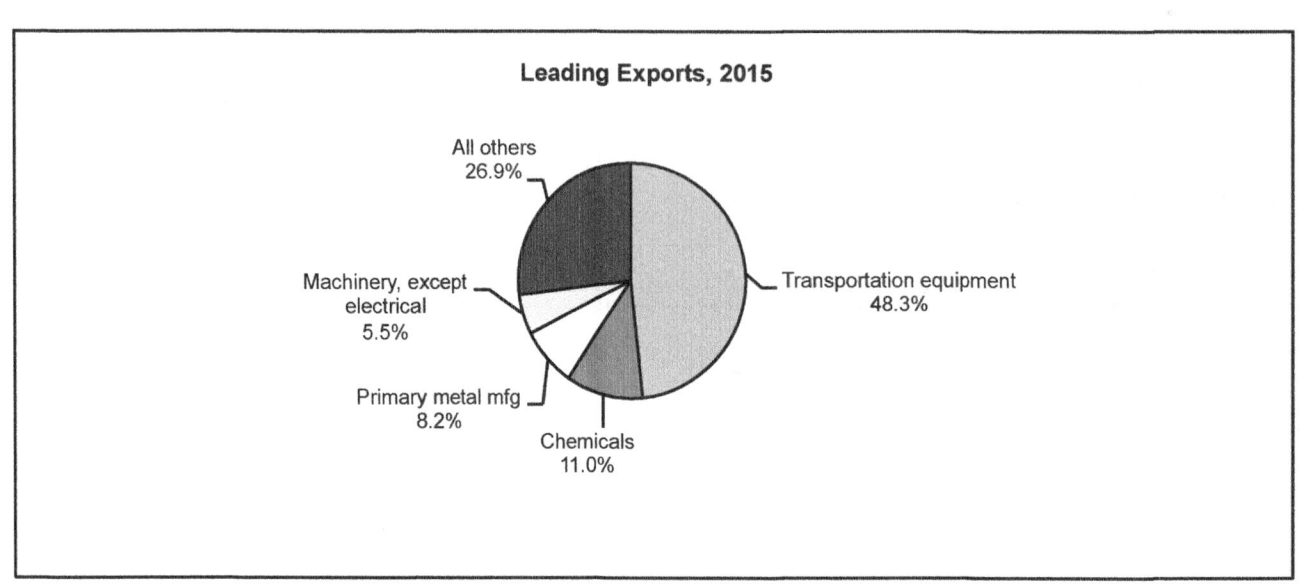

Leading Exports, 2015

All others 26.9%

Machinery, except electrical 5.5%

Primary metal mfg 8.2%

Chemicals 11.0%

Transportation equipment 48.3%

ALASKA

Facts and Figures

Location: Northwestern North America; bordered on the N by the Arctic Ocean, on the E by Canada, on the S by the Pacific Ocean and the Gulf of Alaska, and on the W by the Bering Sea

Area: 665,384 sq. mi. (1,717,854 sq. sq. km.); rank—1st

Population: 738,432 (2015 est.); rank—48th

Principal Cities: capital—Juneau; largest—Anchorage

Statehood: January 3, 1959; 49th state

U.S. Congress: 2 senators, 1 representative

State Motto: North to the Future

State Song: "Alaska's Flag"

State Nicknames: The Last Frontier; The Land of the Midnight Sun

Abbreviations: AK

State Symbols: flower—forget-me-not; tree—Sitka spruce; bird—willow ptarmigan

At a Glance

- With an increase in population of 3.4 percent, Alaska ranked 27th among the states for growth from 2010 to 2015.

- Alaska's 2014 violent crime rate ranked 2nd in the nation at 635.8 per 100,000 population, and the property crime rate (2,760.0 per 100,000 population) ranked 22nd.

- Alaska was the state with the second highest birth rate in 2014, at 15.5 births per 1,000 population.

- In 2014, 11.2 percent of Alaskans lived below the poverty level, a percentage that ranked 46th in the nation.

- Of all the states, Alaska had the 4th highest percentage of residents under 18 years old (25.2 percent) and the lowest percentage of residents age 65 and over (9.9 percent) in 2015.

Table AK-1. Population by Age, Sex, Race, and Hispanic Origin

(Number, percent, except where noted.)

Sex, age, race, and Hispanic origin	2000	2010	2015[1]	Average annual percent change, 2010–2015
Total Population..	626,932	710,231	738,432	0.3
Percent of total U.S. population	0.2	0.2	0.2	X
Sex				
Male..	324,112	369,628	389,025	0.4
Female	302,820	340,603	349,407	0.2
Age				
Under 5 years..	47,591	53,996	55,449	0.2
5 to 19 years...	160,526	153,844	149,121	-0.2
20 to 64 years...	383,116	447,453	461,025	0.2
65 years and over...	35,699	54,938	72,837	2.0
Median age (years)...	32.4	33.8	33.3	-0.1
Race and Hispanic Origin				
One race				
White	434,534	483,873	491,362	0.1
Black..	21,787	24,441	28,825	1.2
American Indian and Alaska Native	98,043	106,268	109,515	0.2
Asian..	25,116	38,882	46,191	1.2
Native Hawaiian or Other Pacific Islander	3,309	7,622	9,612	1.7
Two or more races..	34,146	49,105	52,927	0.5
Hispanic (of any race)...	25,852	44,490	51,826	1.1

X = Not applicable.
[1]Population figures for 2015 are July 1 estimates. The 2010 estimates are taken from the 2010 Census.

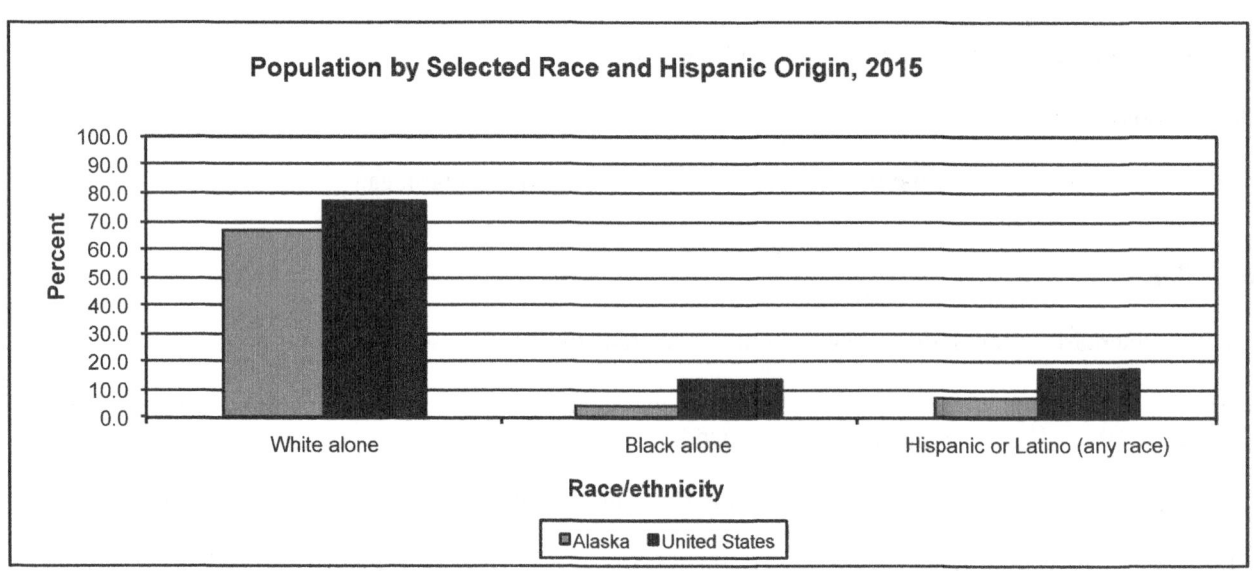

Table AK-2. Marital Status

(Number, percent distribution.)

Sex, age, and marital status	2000	2010	2014
Males, 15 Years and Over	243,024	290,598	299,493
Never married	32.5	35.5	37.5
Now married, except separated..............................	53.6	49.7	48.0
Separated...	1.7	1.7	1.6
Widowed..	1.4	1.8	1.8
Divorced..	10.8	11.4	11.1
Females, 15 Years and Over	225,837	267,563	271,697
Never married	24.1	27.3	29.0
Now married, except separated..............................	55.6	50.2	49.7
Separated...	2.3	2.6	2.2
Widowed..	5.6	6.1	6.0
Divorced..	12.5	13.7	13.1

Table AK-3. Households and Housing Characteristics

(Number, percent, dollars.)

Item	2000	2010	2014	Average annual percent change, 2000–2014
Total Households..	221,600	254,610	249,659	0.9
Family households..	152,337	170,859	165,015	0.6
Married-couple family..	116,318	127,969	124,028	0.5
Other family..	36,019	42,890	40,987	1.0
Male householder, no wife present....................	12,082	14,211	14,666	1.5
Female householder, no husband present..........................	23,937	28,679	26,321	0.7
Nonfamily households	69,263	83,751	84,644	1.6
Householder living alone..	52,060	63,698	63,973	1.6
Householder not living alone..	17,203	20,053	20,671	1.4
Housing Characteristics				
Total housing units...	260,978	307,065	308,571	1.3
Occupied housing units	221,600	254,610	249,659	0.9
Owner occupied..	138,509	162,785	156,006	0.9
Renter occupied..	83,091	91,825	93,653	0.9
Average household size..	2.74	2.70	2.84	0.3
Financial Characteristics				
Median gross rent of renter-occupied housing	720	981	1,183	4.6
Median monthly owner costs for housing units with a mortgage	1,315	1,772	1,797	2.6
Median value of owner-occupied housing units	144,200	241,400	254,500	5.5

Table AK-4. Migration, Origin, and Language

(Number, percent.)

Characteristic	State			U.S.		
	2013	2014	Percent change	2013	2014	Percent change
Residence 1 Year Ago						
Population 1 year and over	725,193	725,206	–	312,432,820	315,095,393	0.9
Same house	80.5	80.8	X	85.0	85.1	X
Different house in the U.S.	18.5	18.6	X	14.4	14.3	X
Same county	11.2	10.9	X	8.9	8.7	X
Different county	7.4	7.7	X	5.5	5.6	X
Same state	2.6	2.5	X	3.2	3.3	X
Different state	4.7	5.2	X	2.3	2.3	X
Abroad...	1.0	0.6	X	0.6	0.6	X
Place of Birth						
Native born	684,372	682,060	-0.3	274,780,773	276,465,262	0.6
Male...	53.0	52.5	X	49.3	49.3	X
Female...	47.0	47.5	X	50.7	50.7	X
Foreign born	50,760	54,672	7.7	41,348,066	42,391,794	2.5
Male...	47.2	49.9	X	48.8	48.7	X
Female...	52.8	50.1	X	51.2	51.3	X
Foreign born; naturalized U.S. citizen...	28,509	30,598	7.3	19,294,710	19,984,738	3.6
Male...	46.9	49	X	45.9	45.9	X
Female...	53.1	51	X	54.1	54.1	X
Foreign born; not a U.S. citizen..	22,251	24,074	8.2	22,053,356	22,407,056	1.6
Male...	47.6	51	X	51.3	51.2	X
Female...	52.4	49	X	48.7	48.8	X
Entered 2010 or later	10.7	10.7	X	9.7	12.3	X
Entered 2000 to 2009	27.7	32.5	X	29.4	28.6	X
Entered before 2000..	61.6	56.8	X	61.0	59.1	X
World Region of Birth, Foreign						
Foreign-born population, excluding population born at sea	50,760	54,672	7.7	41,347,945	42,390,705	2.5
Europe...	14.2	17.1	X	11.6	11.2	X
Asia..	56.4	53.7	X	29.5	30.1	X
Africa...	3.1	4	X	4.4	4.6	X
Oceania..	3.3	2.2	X	0.5	0.6	X
Latin America...	17.2	17.6	X	51.9	51.6	X
North America...	5.7	5.4	X	2.0	1.9	X
Language Spoken at Home and Ability to Speak English						
Population 5 years and over..	680,427	683,324	0.4	296,358,760	299,084,046	0.9
English only..	84.5	83.4	X	79.2	78.9	X
Language other than English..	15.5	16.6	X	20.8	21.1	X
Speaks English less than "very well"..	4.8	5.1	X	8.5	8.6	X

X = Not applicable.
- = Zero or rounds to zero.

Table AK-5. Median Income and Poverty Status, 2014

(Number, percent, except as noted.)

Characteristic	State		U.S.	
	Number	Percent	Number	Percent
Median Income				
Households (dollars)...	71,583	X	53,657	X
Families (dollars)	82,307	X	65,910	X
Below Poverty Level (All People)	80,627	11.2	48,208,387	15.5
Sex				
Male...	37,392	10.1	21,590,918	14.2
Female	43,235	12.5	26,617,469	16.8
Age				
Under 18 years..	28,851	15.8	15,686,012	21.7
Related children under 18 years.....................	27,741	15.3	15,372,705	21.3
18 to 64 years	48,793	10.5	28,267,482	14.6
65 years and over	2,983	4.3	4,254,893	9.5

X = Not applicable.

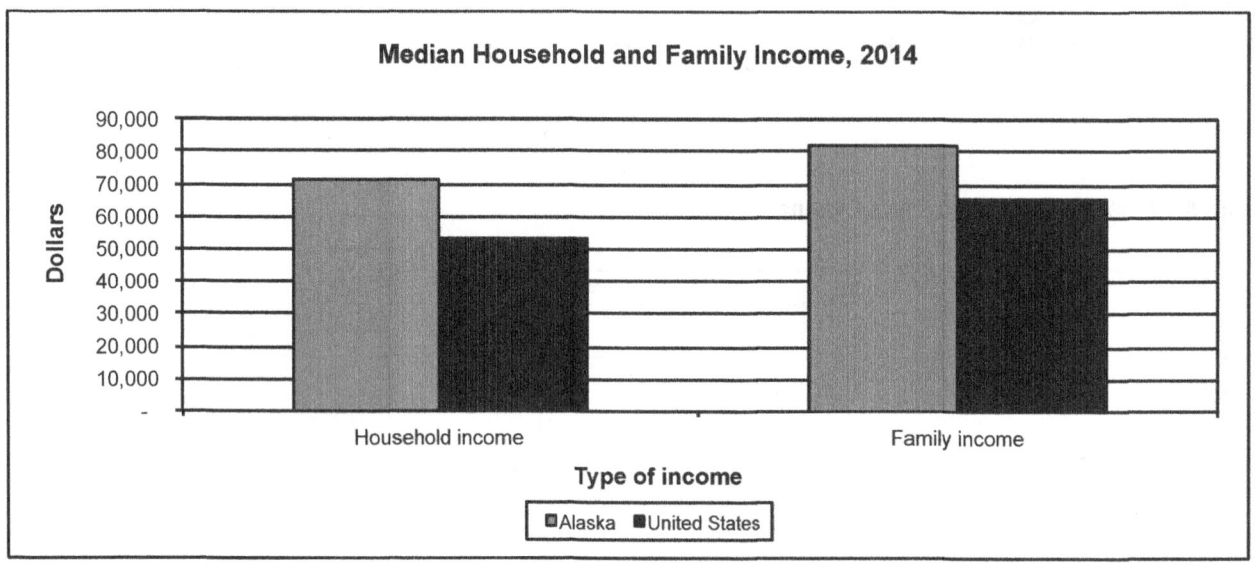

Table AK-6. Health Insurance Coverage Status for the Civilian Noninstitutionalized Population and Children Under 18 Years of Age

(Numbers in thousands, percent.)

Item	2006	2007	2008	2009	2010	2011	2012	2013	2014
Civilian Noninstitutionalized Population	659	675	659	678	689	699	709	712	712
Covered by Private or Public Insurance									
Number..	550	552	635	535	552	559	564	580	589
Percent..	83.5	81.8	96.4	78.9	80.1	79.9	79.5	81.5	82.8
Not Covered									
Number..	109	123	24	143	137	141	145	132	122
Percent..	16.5	18.2	3.6	21.1	19.9	20.1	20.5	18.5	17.2
Percent in the U.S. not covered..	15.8	15.3	15.1	15.1	15.5	15.1	14.8	14.5	11.7
Children Under 18 Years of Age	181	185	180	183	188	188	187	188	186
Covered by Private or Public Insurance									
Number..	163	164	156	158	165	166	161	166	165
Percent..	89.7	88.6	86.7	86.4	87.8	88.2	86.1	88.4	88.6
Not Covered									
Number..	19	21	24	25	23	22	26	22	21
Percent..	10.3	11.4	13.3	13.6	12.2	11.8	13.9	11.6	11.4
Percent in the U.S. not covered..	11.7	11.0	9.7	8.6	8.0	7.5	7.2	7.1	6.0

Table AK-7. Employment Status by Demographic Group, 2015

(Numbers in thousands, percent.)

Characteristic	Civilian noninstitutional population	Civilian labor force		Employed		Unemployed	
		Number	Percent of population	Number	Percent of population	Number	Percent of population
Total..	540	362	67.0	338	62.5	24	6.7
Sex							
Male	277	198	71.4	182	65.9	15	7.7
Female	264	164	62.3	155	58.9	9	5.6
Race, Sex, and Hispanic Origin							
White	359	243	67.6	230	64.1	13	5.2
Male	188	136	72.3	128	67.9	8	6.1
Female	171	107	62.5	102	60.0	4	4.0
Black or African American..............	19	14	72.9	13	69.5	1	4.6
Male	NA	NA	NA	NA	NA	NA	NA
Female	NA	NA	NA	NA	NA	NA	NA
Hispanic or Latino ethnicity[1]	36	28	77.0	27	73.1	1	5.1
Male	19	16	84.0	15	81.2	1	3.4
Female	18	12	69.6	12	64.6	1	7.3
Age							
16 to 19 years...........................	38	15	39.4	13	33.2	2	15.4
20 to 24 years...........................	52	39	75.0	35	66.9	4	11.1
25 to 34 years...........................	110	88	79.3	82	73.9	6	6.7
35 to 44 years...........................	84	69	81.5	65	76.7	4	5.8
45 to 54 years...........................	92	73	79.5	70	75.8	3	4.6
55 to 64 years...........................	93	62	66.4	59	63.0	3	5.2
65 years and over	71	17	23.7	16	22.0	1	7.2

NOTE: Data in Table 7 are from the Current Population Survey (CPS) and do not match the estimates in Table 8. See notes and definitions for further information.
[1]May be of any race.
NA = Not available.

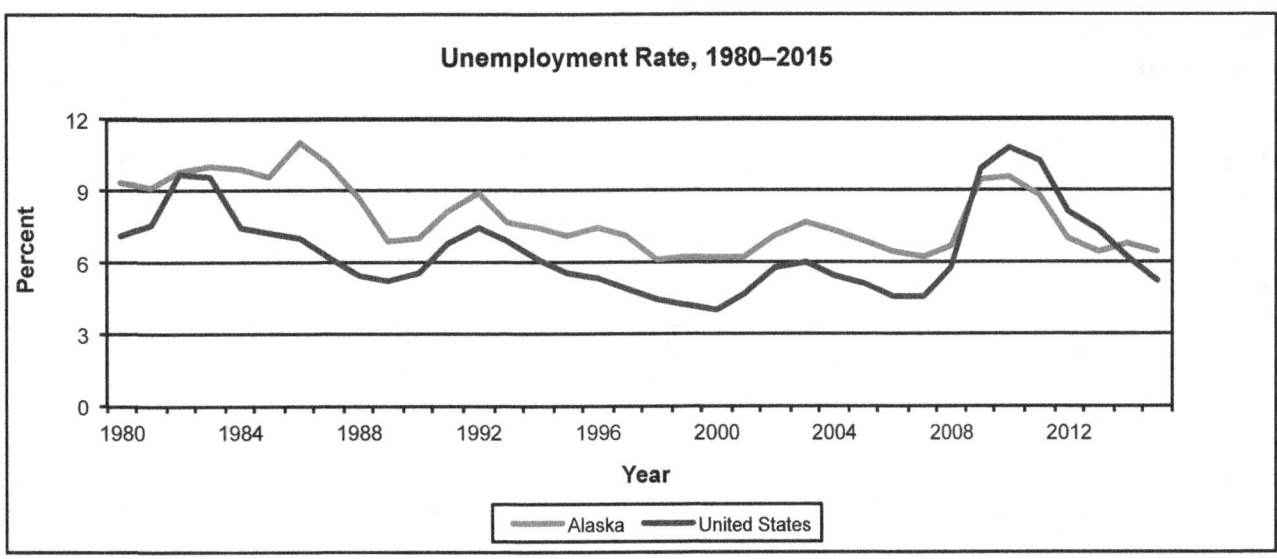

Table AK-8. Employment Status of the Civilian Noninstitutional Population Age 16 Years and Over

(Number, percent.)

Year	Civilian labor force	Civilian participation rate	Employed	Unemployed	Unemployment rate
2007.............................	350,785	70.7	328,579	22,206	6.3
2008.............................	356,109	71.0	332,285	23,824	6.7
2009.............................	359,647	70.3	331,792	27,855	7.7
2010.............................	361,913	69.8	333,416	28,497	7.9
2011.............................	365,913	69.2	338,161	27,752	7.6
2012.............................	365,674	68.3	339,608	26,066	7.1
2013.............................	365,216	67.8	339,957	25,259	6.9
2014.............................	365,890	67.7	340,804	25,086	6.9
2015.............................	363,822	67.1	340,227	23,595	6.5

Table AK-9. Employment and Average Wages by Industry

(Estimates through 2010 are based on the 2007 North American Industry Classification System [NAICS]. Estimates from 2011 onward are based on the 2012 NAICS.)

Industry	2008	2009	2010	2011	2012	2013	2014
	Number of Jobs						
Wage and Salary Employment by Industry..................	351,532	351,192	353,467	359,669	365,031	366,027	367,291
Farm Wage and Salary Employment..........................	179	175	187	210	188	244	509
Nonfarm Wage and Salary Employment.....................	351,353	351,017	353,280	359,459	364,843	365,783	366,782
Private wage and salary employment..........................	245,649	243,126	245,102	250,423	255,968	258,749	261,044
Forestry, fishing, and related activities......................	485	508	677	941	708	673	693
Mining...	15,206	14,877	15,040	15,591	16,600	16,999	17,609
Utilities..	1,895	1,982	2,142	2,107	2,120	2,136	2,113
Construction..	17,945	17,050	16,812	16,673	16,997	17,189	17,660
Manufacturing..	13,015	12,879	12,771	13,708	13,910	14,278	14,438
Durable goods manufacturing............................	2,186	2,042	1,891	1,865	2,015	2,079	2,076
Nondurable goods manufacturing.......................	10,829	10,837	10,880	11,843	11,895	12,199	12,362
Wholesale trade...	6,596	6,376	6,333	6,360	6,287	6,650	6,540
Retail trade...	36,724	36,150	36,033	36,275	36,146	36,262	37,117
Transportation and warehousing............................	20,264	19,575	19,141	19,416	19,927	19,633	19,592
Information...	7,000	6,607	6,458	6,316	6,205	6,161	6,248
Finance and insurance	9,145	8,955	9,085	9,047	8,730	7,416	7,322
Real estate and rental and leasing..........................	4,801	4,899	5,073	5,013	4,891	4,992	4,969
Professional, scientific, and technical services	13,379	13,825	14,055	14,641	14,962	15,140	14,932
Management of companies and enterprises...................	1,206	1,247	1,156	1,240	1,822	3,056	3,003
Administrative and waste services	11,979	11,571	11,474	11,636	12,138	12,191	12,303
Educational services	3,048	3,023	3,128	3,236	3,277	3,300	3,330
Health care and social assistance..........................	37,103	38,701	40,627	42,054	43,959	44,655	44,293
Arts, entertainment, and recreation.........................	4,638	4,573	4,463	4,860	4,910	4,929	4,873
Accommodation and food services..........................	27,979	26,908	27,379	28,039	28,607	29,038	29,579
Other services, except public administration.................	13,241	13,420	13,255	13,270	13,772	14,051	14,430
Government and government enterprises..........................	105,704	107,891	108,178	109,036	108,875	107,034	105,738
	Dollars						
Average Wages and Salaries by Industry	47,088	48,401	49,543	50,806	53,579	54,523	56,313
Average Farm Wages and Salaries	28,430	28,320	28,487	29,324	19,867	33,156	35,658
Average Nonfarm Wages and Salaries	47,098	48,411	49,554	50,819	53,597	54,538	56,342
Average private wages and salaries..........................	46,001	47,125	48,041	49,206	52,250	53,392	55,547
Forestry, fishing, and related activities......................	45,831	44,037	47,266	51,692	54,523	62,468	61,475
Mining...	110,499	114,364	116,055	118,956	128,178	130,818	137,491
Utilities..	70,620	74,032	73,526	78,613	85,671	88,125	88,539
Construction..	66,902	69,498	71,000	70,793	74,703	77,367	81,786
Manufacturing..	38,163	37,869	39,476	39,535	41,334	44,516	45,432
Durable goods manufacturing............................	47,471	49,774	49,620	49,568	53,282	55,315	59,758
Nondurable goods manufacturing.......................	36,285	35,625	37,713	37,955	41,052	42,675	43,027
Wholesale trade...	51,329	52,283	52,303	53,477	56,129	56,038	57,730
Retail trade...	28,441	28,536	28,997	29,478	31,370	31,587	32,505
Transportation and warehousing............................	55,641	58,086	59,113	60,778	63,057	64,124	66,028
Information...	55,511	56,738	56,105	59,742	62,106	63,397	65,857
Finance and insurance	56,815	57,805	59,910	61,358	66,115	63,502	65,911
Real estate and rental and leasing..........................	35,354	37,045	38,255	38,912	41,665	42,450	44,042
Professional, scientific, and technical services	63,161	64,443	65,970	68,859	72,021	73,796	77,095
Management of companies and enterprises...................	77,402	77,772	81,629	79,747	78,980	81,459	87,644
Administrative and waste services	39,836	41,766	42,586	42,389	44,550	44,360	46,441
Educational services	28,340	28,229	28,092	27,795	28,567	29,553	28,916
Health care and social assistance..........................	41,597	43,000	43,588	45,279	47,473	48,876	50,470
Arts, entertainment, and recreation.........................	19,874	19,137	20,478	21,405	22,372	23,304	24,269
Accommodation and food services..........................	22,199	21,907	22,619	23,430	24,579	24,901	26,518
Other services, except public administration.................	31,682	32,817	34,283	34,569	35,987	37,013	37,314
Government and government enterprises..........................	49,647	51,309	52,980	54,522	56,762	57,308	58,305

Table AK-10. Employment Characteristics by Family Type

(Number, percent.)

Family type and labor force status	2012		2013		2014	
	Total	Families with own children under 18 years	Total	Families with own children under 18 years	Total	Families with own children under 18 years
All Families..	166,400	82,259	165,431	76,918	164,518	81,338
FAMILY TYPE AND LABOR FORCE STATUS						
Married-Couple Families...............................	123,248	54,673	126,502	54,850	123,531	56,246
Both husband and wife in labor force..................	56.7	62.6	58.1	64.2	55.9	61.4
Husband in labor force, wife not in labor force	22.2	29.3	22	28.5	23.2	30.0
Wife in labor force, husband not in labor force	9.5	5.9	8.8	5.2	8.2	5.3
Both husband and wife not in labor force..............	11.6	2.2	10.9	2	12.8	3.3
Other Families	43,152	27,586	38,929	22,068	40,987	25,092
Female householder, no husband present............	68.6	73.4	63.8	64.4	64.2	65.7
In labor force..	49.7	57.6	47.6	54.6	47.6	54.1
Not in labor force	19.0	15.8	16.2	9.8	16.6	11.5
Male householder, no wife present....................	31.4	26.6	36.2	35.6	35.8	34.3
In labor force..	26.2	23.7	30.5	32.4	28.5	30.5
Not in labor force	5.1	2.8	5.7	3.2	7.3	3.9

Table AK-11. School Enrollment and Educational Attainment, 2014

(Number, percent.)

Item	State	U.S.
Enrollment		
Total population 3 years and over, enrolled in school...............	195,830	82,063,714
Enrolled in nursery school or preschool (percent).....................	5.0	6.0
Enrolled in kindergarten (percent).......................................	5.8	5.1
Enrolled in elementary school, grades 1-8 (percent).................	41.6	40.2
Enrolled in high school, grades 9-12 (percent).......................	22.1	20.7
Enrolled in college or graduate school (percent)......................	25.6	28.0
Attainment		
Total population 25 years and over	465,149	213,725,624
Less than ninth grade (percent)	2.7	5.6
9th to 12th grade, no diploma (percent)	4.4	7.5
High school graduate, including equivalency (percent)...............	28.4	27.7
Some college, no degree (percent)	28.3	21.0
Associate's degree (percent)	8.2	8.2
Bachelor's degree (percent)	18.4	18.7
Graduate or professional degree (percent)............................	9.6	11.4
High school graduate or higher (percent)	92.9	86.9
Bachelor's degree or higher (percent)	28.0	30.1

Table AK-12. Public School Characteristics and Educational Indicators

(Number, percent; data derived from National Center of Education Statistics.)

Item	State	U.S.
Public Schools, 2013–2014 (except where noted)		
Number of school districts..	54	18,194
Number of schools...	507	98,271
Number of students (in thousands)	131	50,045
Number of teachers (in thousands)	8	3,114
Student-teacher ratio	16.6	16.1
Expenditures per student (dollars), FY 2013...........................	18,217	107,637
Four-year adjusted cohort graduation rate (ACGR)[1,2]	71.1	82.3
Students eligible for free or reduced-price lunch (in thousands) ...	56	25,596
English language learners (in thousands)	15	4,461
Students age 3 to 21 served under IDEA, part B (in thousands)	18	6,464

Public Schools by Type	Number	Percent of state public schools
Total number of schools..	507	100.0
Regular..	440	86.8
Special education..	3	0.6
Vocational education..	3	0.6
Alternative education..	61	12.0

NOTE: Every school is assigned only one school type based on its instructional emphasis.
[1] ACGR data represents a new method of calculating high-school completion rates and may not be comparable to previous years' data for Averaged Freshmen Graduation Rates (AFGR).
[2] The United States 4-year ACGRs were estimated using both the reported 4-year ACGR data from 49 states and the District of Columbia and using imputed data for Idaho. The estimate for American Indian/Alaska Native students also includes imputed data for Virginia.

Table AK-13. Reported Voting and Registration of the Voting-Age Population, November 2014

(Numbers in thousands, percent.)

Item	Total population	Total citizen population	Registered			Voted		
			Total registered	Percent registered (total population)	Percent registered (total citizen population)	Total voted	Percent voted (total population)	Percent voted (total citizen population)
U.S. Total	239,874	219,941	142,166	59.3	64.6	92,251	38.5	41.9
State Total...............................	521	503	336	64.6	66.8	255	49.0	50.7
Sex								
Male..	264	256	168	63.8	65.7	128	48.4	49.9
Female	257	247	168	65.4	68.0	127	49.6	51.5
Race								
White alone.............................	340	331	234	68.9	70.7	188	55.5	56.9
White, non-Hispanic alone...........	318	312	223	70.1	71.4	181	56.8	57.8
Black alone..............................	18	18	9	(B)	(B)	6	(B)	(B)
Asian alone..............................	28	21	8	(B)	(B)	7	(B)	(B)
Hispanic (of any race).................	28	24	12	(B)	(B)	8	(B)	(B)
White alone or in combination	360	350	245	68.2	70.0	196	54.6	56.1
Black alone or in combination...........	21	20	11	(B)	(B)	8	(B)	(B)
Asian alone or in combination..........	32	25	11	(B)	(B)	9	(B)	(B)
Age								
18 to 24 years...........................	76	74	34	(B)	(B)	19	(B)	(B)
25 to 34 years...........................	111	107	70	62.7	65.2	46	41.3	42.9
35 to 44 years...........................	78	75	47	(B)	(B)	34	(B)	(B)
45 to 64 years...........................	189	184	136	71.8	74.0	113	59.8	61.6
65 years and over	66	64	49	(B)	(B)	43	(B)	(B)

B = Base is less than 75,000 and therefore too small to show the derived measure.

Table AK-14. Crime

(Number, rate per 100,000. Data are derived from the FBI Uniform Crime Reports.)

Item	State			U.S. [1,2,3,4]		
	2013	2014	Percent change	2013	2014	Percent change
TOTAL POPULATION[5]...........................	735,132	736,732	0.7	316,128,839	318,857,056	0.9
VIOLENT CRIME						
Number..	4,430	4,684	0.4	1,163,146	1,165,383	0.2
Rate	602.6	635.8	-0.3	367.9	365.5	-0.7
Murder and Nonnegligent Manslaughter						
Number..	34	41	13.3	14,196	14,249	0.4
Rate	4.6	5.6	12.6	4.5	4.5	-
Forcible Rape						
Number..	922	771	X	108,612	116,645	X
Rate	125.4	104.7	X	34.4	36.6	X
Robbery						
Number..	624	629		345,031	325,802	-5.6
Rate	84.9	85.4	-1.6	109.1	102.2	-6.3
Aggravated Assault						
Number..	3,128	3,243	-1.3	724,149	741,291	2.4
Rate	425.5	440.2	-1.9	229.1	232.5	1.5
PROPERTY CRIME						
Number..	21,210	20,334	5.9	8,632,512	8,277,829	-4.1
Rate	2,885.2	2,760.0	5.2	2,730.7	2,596.1	-4.9
Burglary						
Number..	2,916	3,150	-1.2	1,928,465	1,729,806	-10.3
Rate	396.7	427.6	-1.8	610.0	542.5	-11.1
Larceny-Theft						
Number..	16,599	15,445	6.6	6,004,453	5,858,496	-2.4
Rate	2,258.0	2,096.4	5.9	1,899.4	1,837.3	-3.3
Motor Vehicle Theft						
Number..	1,695	1,739	11.4	699,594	689,527	-1.4
Rate	230.6	236.0	10.6	221.3	216.2	-2.3

NOTE: Although arson data are included in the trend and clearance tables, sufficient data are not available to estimate totals for this offense. Therefore, no arson data are published in this table.
X = Not applicable.
- = Zero or rounds to zero.
[1]Because of changes in the state's reporting practices, figures are not comparable to previous years' data.
[2]The crime figures have been adjusted.
[3]The data collection methodology for the offense of forcible rape used by the Minnesota state Uniform Crime Reporting (UCR) Program (with the exception of Minneapolis and St. Paul, Minnesota) does not comply with national UCR Program guidelines. Consequently, its figures for forcible rape and violent crime (of which forcible rape is a part) are not published in this table.
[4]Includes offenses reported by the Zoological Police and the Metro Transit Police.
[5]Populations are U.S. Census Bureau provisional estimates as of July 1 of each year.
[6]The figures shown for the offense of rape were estimated using the revised Uniform Crime Reporting (UCR) definition of rape.

Table AK-15. State Government Finances, 2014

(Dollar amounts in thousands, percent distribution.)

Item	Dollars	Percent distribution
Total Revenue	12,871,274	100.0
General revenue	10,436,362	81.1
Intergovernmental revenue	2,810,194	21.8
Taxes	3,392,869	26.4
General sales	0	0.0
Selective sales	257,696	2.0
License taxes	141,947	1.1
Individual income tax	0	0.0
Corporate income tax	408,938	3.2
Other taxes	2,584,288	20.1
Current charges	627,605	4.9
Miscellaneous general revenue	3,605,694	28.0
Utility revenue	17,542	0.1
Liquor stores revenue	0	-
Insurance trust revenue[1]	2,417,370	18.8
Total Expenditure	12,920,065	100.0
Intergovernmental expenditure	2,059,333	15.9
Direct expenditure	10,860,732	84.1
Current operation	7,836,410	60.7
Capital outlay	1,309,067	10.1
Insurance benefits and repayments	1,266,607	9.8
Assistance and subsidies	194,111	1.5
Interest on debt	254,537	2.0
Exhibit: Salaries and wages	1,909,523	14.8
Total Expenditure	12,920,065	100.0
General expenditure	11,427,172	88.4
Intergovernmental expenditure	2,059,333	15.9
Direct expenditure	9,367,839	72.5
General expenditure, by function:		
Education	2,768,833	21.4
Public welfare	2,168,639	16.8
Hospitals	70,127	0.5
Health	323,760	2.5
Highways	1,243,655	9.6
Police protection	157,803	1.2
Correction	335,504	2.6
Natural resources	353,554	2.7
Parks and recreation	23,989	0.2
Governmental administration	664,797	5.1
Interest on general debt	250,410	1.9
Other and unallocable	3,066,101	23.7
Utility expenditure	226,286	1.8
Liquor stores expenditure	0	-
Insurance trust expenditure	1,266,607	9.8
Debt at End of Fiscal Year	6,048,619	X
Cash and Security Holdings	84,380,171	X

X = Not applicable.
- = Zero or rounds to zero.
[1]Within insurance trust revenue, net earnings of state retirement systems is a calculated statistic (the item code in the data file is X08), and thus can be positive or negative. Net earnings is the sum of earnings on investments plus gains on investments minus losses on investments. The change made in 2002 for asset valuation from book to market value in accordance with Statement 34 of the Governmental Accounting Standards Board is reflected in the calculated statistics.

Table AK-16. State Government Tax Collections, 2014

(Dollars in thousands, percent.)

Item	Dollars	Percent distribution
Total Taxes	3,392,869	100.0
Property taxes	128,076	3.8
Sales and gross receipts	257,696	7.6
General sales and gross receipts	X	X
Selective sales and gross receipts	257,696	7.6
Alcoholic beverages	39,078	1.2
Amusements	9,205	0.3
Insurance premiums	62,292	1.8
Motor fuels	42,467	1.3
Pari-mutuels	X	X
Public utilities	4,230	0.1
Tobacco products	72,004	2.1
Other selective sales	28,420	0.8
Licenses	141,947	4.2
Alcoholic beverages	1,905	0.1
Amusements	0	-
Corporations in general	0	-
Hunting and fishing	27,833	0.8
Motor vehicle	59,497	1.8
Motor vehicle operators	0	-
Public utilities	840	-
Occupation and business, NEC	43,060	1.3
Other licenses	8,812	0.3
Income taxes	408,938	12.1
Individual income	X	X
Corporation net income	408,938	12.1
Other taxes	2,456,212	72.4
Death and gift	0	-
Documentary and stock transfer	X	X
Severance	2,456,212	72.4
Taxes, NEC	0	-

X = Not applicable.
- = Zero or rounds to zero.

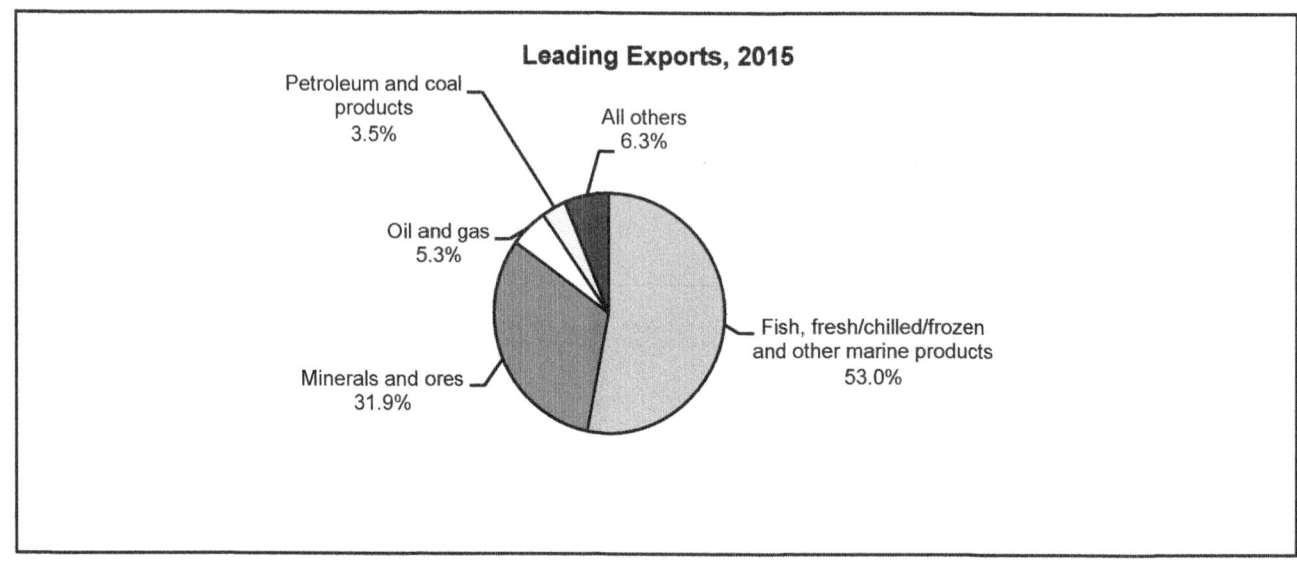

Leading Exports, 2015

Petroleum and coal products 3.5%

All others 6.3%

Oil and gas 5.3%

Fish, fresh/chilled/frozen and other marine products 53.0%

Minerals and ores 31.9%

ARIZONA

Facts and Figures

Location: Southwestern United States; bordered on the North by Utah, on the East by New Mexico, on the South by Mexico, and on the West by Nevada and California; Arizona is one of the Four Corner states—at its NE corner it touches Colorado, New Mexico, and Utah

Area: 113,990 sq, mi. (295,254 sq. km.); rank—6th

Population: 6,828,065 (2015 est.); rank—14th

Principal Cities: capital—Phoenix; largest—Phoenix

Statehood: February 14, 1912; 48th state

U.S. Congress: 2 senators, 9 representatives

State Motto: *Ditat Deus* ("God enriches")

State Song: "Arizona"

State Nickname: The Grand Canyon State

Abbreviations: AZ; Ariz.

State Symbols: flower—saguaro cactus blossom; tree—paloverde; bird—cactus wren

At a Glance

- With an increase in population of 6.6 percent, Arizona ranked 8th among the states in growth from 2010 to 2015.

- In 2015, 16.4 percent of Arizonans were age 65 and older, the 10th highest percent in the nation.

- Arizona's median household income in 2014 was $50,068, compared to the national median household income of $53,657.

- In 2014, 18.2 percent of Arizonans lived below the poverty level, a percentage that ranked 10th in the country.

- Arizona's violent crime rate in 2014 was 399.9 per 100,000 population, ranking 17th in the nation.

Table AZ-1. Population by Age, Sex, Race, and Hispanic Origin

(Number, percent, except where noted.)

Sex, age, race, and Hispanic origin	2000	2010	2015[1]	Average annual percent change, 2010–2015
Total Population...	5,130,632	6,392,017	6,828,065	0.5
Percent of total U.S. population	1.8	2.1	2.1	X
Sex				
Male...	2,561,057	3,175,823	3,391,490	0.5
Female	2,569,575	3,216,814	3,436,575	0.5
Age				
Under 5 years...	382,386	455,715	429,244	-0.4
5 to 19 years...	1,135,802	1,363,926	1,378,779	0.1
20 to 64 years...	2,944,605	3,690,545	3,899,988	0.4
65 years and over...	667,839	881,831	1,120,054	1.7
Median age (years)...	34.2	35.9	37.3	0.3
Race and Hispanic Origin				
One race				
White	3,873,611	5,418,483	5,698,416	0.4
Black...	158,873	280,905	330,467	1.2
American Indian and Alaska Native	255,879	335,278	362,968	0.6
Asian...	92,236	188,456	231,462	1.5
Native Hawaiian or Other Pacific Islander	6,733	16,112	18,166	0.9
Two or more races	146,526	152,783	186,586	1.4
Hispanic (of any race)...	1,295,617	1,943,466	2,098,410	0.5

X = Not applicable.
[1]Population figures for 2015 are July 1 estimates. The 2010 estimates are taken from the 2010 Census.

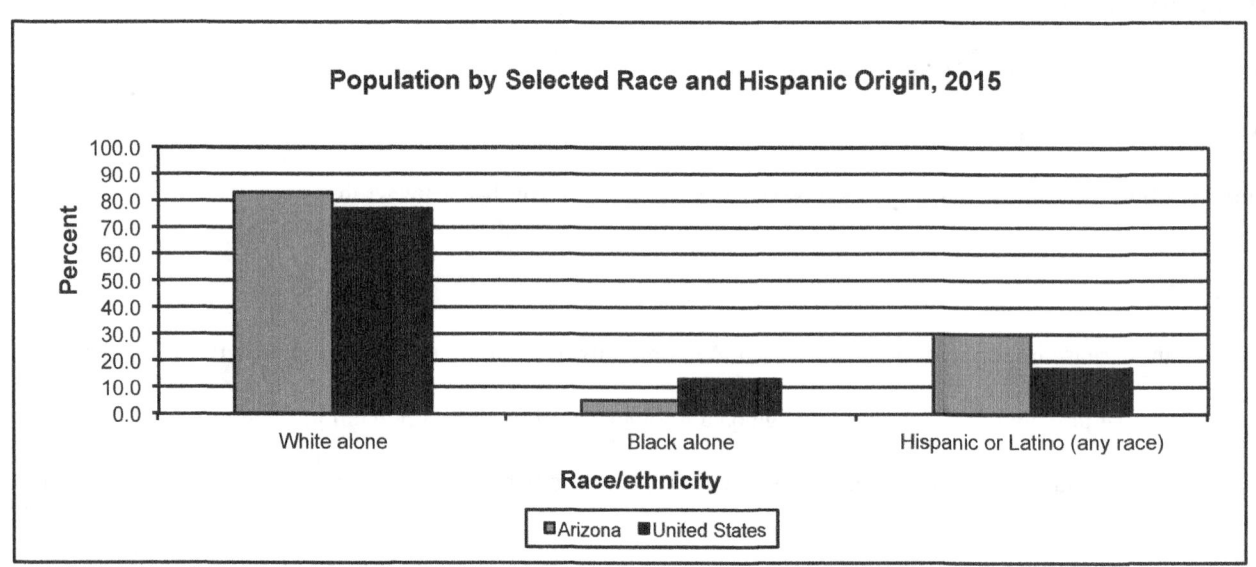

Population by Selected Race and Hispanic Origin, 2015

Table AZ-2. Marital Status

(Number, percent distribution.)

Sex, age, race, and Hispanic origin	2000	2010	2014
Males, 15 Years and Over	1,966,032	2,492,590	2,570,191
Never married	29.6	35.3	36.0
Now married, except separated...	56.4	50.1	49.0
Separated...	1.6	1.4	1.6
Widowed...	2.6	2.5	2.6
Divorced...	9.8	10.7	10.8
Females, 15 Years and Over	2,013,304	2,559,409	2,640,886
Never married	22.5	28.0	28.8
Now married, except separated...	53.6	48.0	46.6
Separated...	2.1	2.2	2.2
Widowed...	9.4	8.3	8.5
Divorced...	12.3	13.5	13.9

Table AZ-3. Households and Housing Characteristics

(Number, percent, dollars.)

Item	2000	2010	2014	Average annual percent change, 2000–2014
Total Households..	1,901,327	2,334,050	2,428,743	2.0
Family households	1,287,367	1,548,428	1,579,481	1.6
Married-couple family	986,303	1,134,229	1,141,295	1.1
Other family	310,064	414,199	438,186	3.0
Male householder, no wife present............	90,283	123,772	134,120	3.5
Female householder, no husband present...	210,781	290,427	304,066	3.2
Nonfamily households	613,960	785,622	849,262	2.7
Householder living alone.........................	472,006	621,291	669,627	3.0
Householder not living alone...................	141,954	164,331	179,635	1.9
Housing Characteristics				
Total housing units.....................................	2,189,189	2,846,738	2,909,336	2.3
Occupied housing units	1,901,327	2,334,050	2,428,743	2.0
Owner occupied	1,293,556	1,522,938	1,484,857	1.1
Renter occupied	607,771	811,112	943,886	4.0
Average household size................................	2.64	2.69	2.71	0.2
Financial Characteristics				
Median gross rent of renter-occupied housing	619	844	916	3.4
Median monthly owner costs for housing units with a mortgage	1,039	1,442	1,273	1.6
Median value of owner-occupied housing units	121,300	168,800	176,700	3.3

Table AZ-4. Migration, Origin, and Language

(Number, percent.)

Characteristic	State 2013	State 2014	State Percent change	U.S. 2013	U.S. 2014	U.S. Percent change
Residence 1 Year Ago						
Population 1 year and over	6,543,362	6,651,964	1.7	312,432,820	315,095,393	0.9
Same house	81.3	81.6	X	85.0	85.1	X
Different house in the U.S.	18.0	17.6	X	14.4	14.3	X
Same county	12.5	12.1	X	8.9	8.7	X
Different county	5.5	5.5	X	5.5	5.6	X
Same state	1.9	1.8	X	3.2	3.3	X
Different state	3.6	3.8	X	2.3	2.3	X
Abroad	0.7	0.7	X	0.6	0.6	X
Place of Birth						
Native born	5,730,314	5,811,925	1.4	274,780,773	276,465,262	0.6
Male	50.0	49.9	X	49.3	49.3	X
Female	50.0	50.1	X	50.7	50.7	X
Foreign born	896,310	919,559	2.6	41,348,066	42,391,794	2.5
Male	48.5	48.4	X	48.8	48.7	X
Female	51.5	51.6	X	51.2	51.3	X
Foreign born; naturalized U.S. citizen...........	342,265	358,978	4.9	19,294,710	19,984,738	3.6
Male	45.5	45.3	X	45.9	45.9	X
Female	54.5	54.7	X	54.1	54.1	X
Foreign born; not a U.S. citizen	554,045	560,581	1.2	22,053,356	22,407,056	1.6
Male	50.3	50.4	X	51.3	51.2	X
Female	49.7	49.6	X	48.7	48.8	X
Entered 2010 or later	9.4	11.7	X	9.7	12.3	X
Entered 2000 to 2009	26.9	27.1	X	29.4	28.6	X
Entered before 2000.....................................	63.7	61.2	X	61.0	59.1	X
World Region of Birth, Foreign						
Foreign-born population, excluding population born at sea	896,310	919,559	2.6	41,347,945	42,390,705	2.5
Europe	9.0	8.9	X	11.6	11.2	X
Asia..	18.0	19.5	X	29.5	30.1	X
Africa	3.2	2.6	X	4.4	4.6	X
Oceania	0.5	0.6	X	0.5	0.6	X
Latin America..	64.3	63.5	X	51.9	51.6	X
North America...	5.0	4.8	X	2.0	1.9	X
Language Spoken at Home and Ability to Speak English						
Population 5 years and over...........................	6,196,543	6,298,821	1.7	296,358,760	299,084,046	0.9
English only	73.2	73	X	79.2	78.9	X
Language other than English......................	26.8	27	X	20.8	21.1	X
Speaks English less than "very well"...........	9.1	9.3	X	8.5	8.6	X

X = Not applicable.
- = Zero or rounds to zero.

Table AZ-5. Median Income and Poverty Status, 2014

(Number, percent, except as noted.)

Characteristic	State		U.S.	
	Number	Percent	Number	Percent
Median Income				
Households (dollars)...........................	50,068	X	53,657	X
Families (dollars)	59,700	X	65,910	X
Below Poverty Level (All People)	1,199,061	18.2	48,208,387	15.5
Sex				
Male..............	558,163	17.3	21,590,918	14.2
Female	640,898	19.2	26,617,469	16.8
Age				
Under 18 years................	407,695	25.6	15,686,012	21.7
Related children under 18 years................	398,754	25.2	15,372,705	21.3
18 to 64 years..................	691,417	17.6	28,267,482	14.6
65 years and over	99,949	9.4	4,254,893	9.5

X = Not applicable.

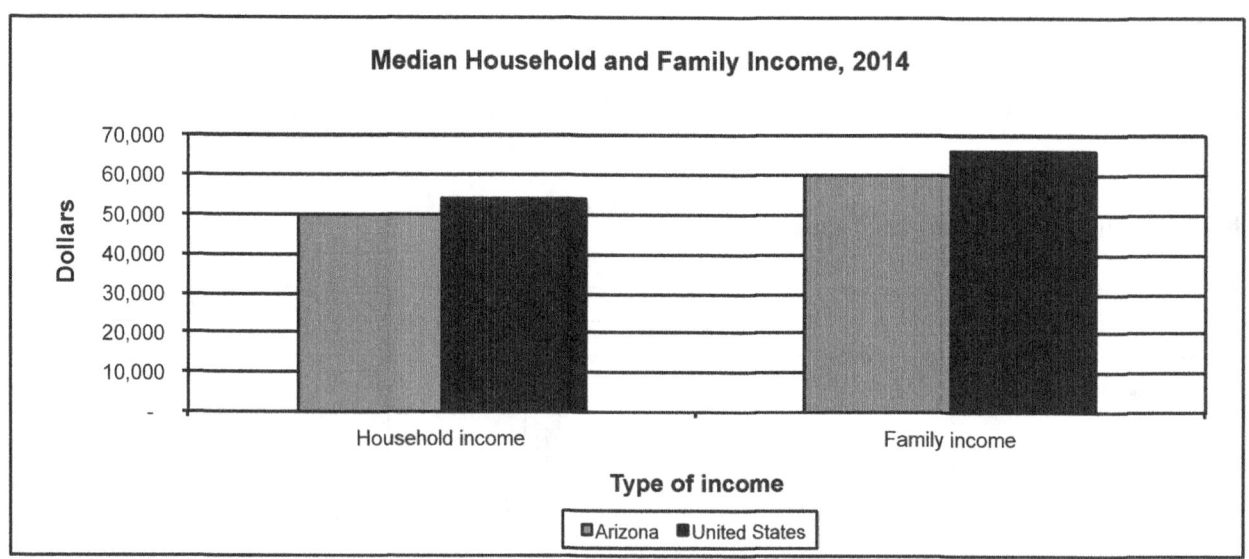

Table AZ-6. Health Insurance Coverage Status for the Civilian Noninstitutionalized Population and Children Under 18 Years of Age

(Numbers in thousands, percent.)

Item	2006	2007	2008	2009	2010	2011	2012	2013	2014
Civilian Noninstitutionalized Population	6,269	6,368	6,403	6,502	6,310	6,378	6,444	6,521	6,623
Covered by Private or Public Insurance									
Number............................	4,958	5,204	5,207	5,375	5,245	5,283	5,313	5,403	5,720
Percent...........................	79.1	81.7	81.3	82.7	83.1	82.8	82.4	82.9	86.4
Not Covered									
Number............................	1,311	1,164	1,196	1,127	1,065	1,095	1,131	1,118	903
Percent...........................	20.9	18.3	18.7	17.3	16.9	17.2	17.6	17.1	13.6
Percent in the U.S. not covered...........................	15.8	15.3	15.1	15.1	15.5	15.1	14.8	14.5	11.7
Children Under 18 Years of Age	1,662	1,697	1,706	1,730	1,630	1,622	1,617	1,614	1,621
Covered by Private or Public Insurance									
Number............................	1,379	1,463	1,430	1,522	1,422	1,622	1,403	1,422	1,459
Percent...........................	83.0	86.2	83.8	88.0	87.2	87.1	86.8	88.1	90.0
Not Covered									
Number............................	283	234	276	208	208	208	214	192	162
Percent...........................	17.0	13.8	16.2	12.0	12.8	12.9	13.2	11.9	10.0
Percent in the U.S. not covered...........................	11.7	11.0	9.7	8.6	8.0	7.5	7.2	7.1	6.0

Table AZ-7. Employment Status by Demographic Group, 2015

(Numbers in thousands, percent.)

Characteristic	Civilian noninstitutional population	Civilian labor force		Employed		Unemployed	
		Number	Percent of population	Number	Percent of population	Number	Percent of population
Total.............................	5,256	3,155	60.0	2,964	56.4	191	6.0
Sex							
Male..............................	2,558	1,701	66.5	1,593	62.3	108	6.3
Female	2,699	1,454	53.9	1,371	50.8	83	5.7
Race, Sex, and Hispanic Origin							
White............................	4,513	2,684	59.5	2,530	56.1	154	5.7
Male..........................	2,189	1,448	66.1	1,362	62.2	86	5.9
Female	2,324	1,236	53.2	1,168	50.3	68	5.5
Black or African American.................	227	157	69.2	143	62.9	14	9.1
Male..........................	122	88	72.6	80	65.5	9	9.8
Female	106	69	65.3	63	60.0	6	8.2
Hispanic or Latino ethnicity[1]	1,861	1,193	64.1	1,094	58.8	99	8.3
Male..........................	908	665	73.3	610	67.1	56	8.4
Female	953	528	55.3	485	50.8	43	8.2
Age							
16 to 19 years......................	362	132	36.4	108	29.9	24	17.9
20 to 24 years......................	442	316	71.5	284	64.3	32	10.0
25 to 34 years......................	883	689	78.0	645	73.0	44	6.4
35 to 44 years......................	839	646	76.9	617	73.6	28	4.4
45 to 54 years......................	899	704	78.3	674	74.9	30	4.3
55 to 64 years......................	839	523	62.3	499	59.4	24	4.7
65 years and over	993	146	14.7	137	13.8	9	5.9

NOTE: Data in Table 7 are from the Current Population Survey (CPS) and do not match the estimates in Table 8. See notes and definitions for further information.
[1]May be of any race.

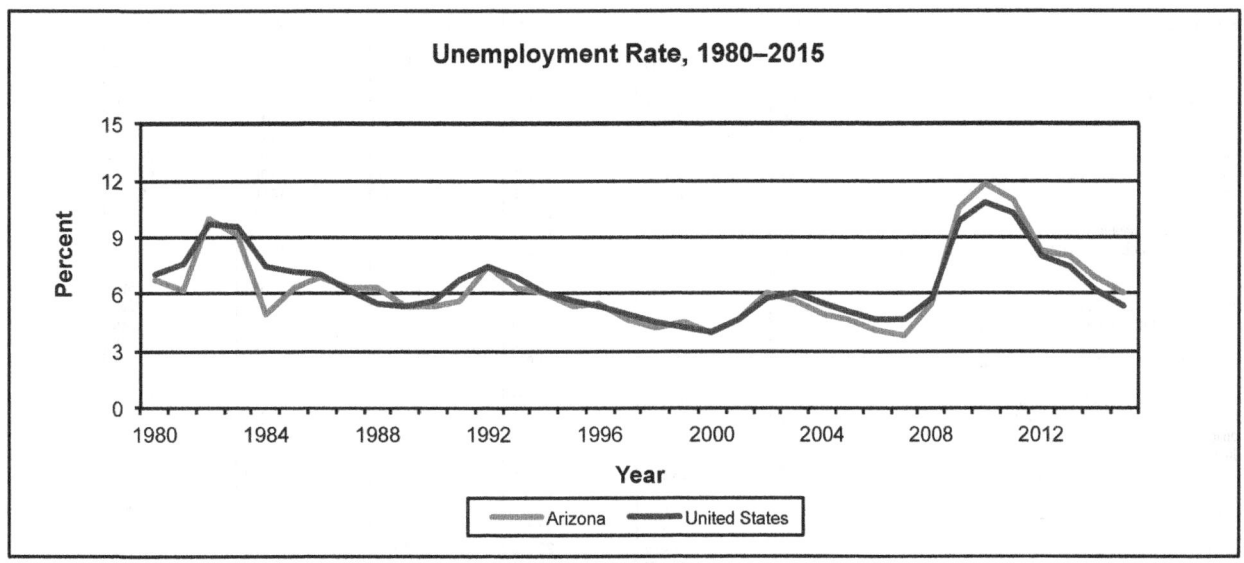

Unemployment Rate, 1980–2015

Table AZ-8. Employment Status of the Civilian Noninstitutional Population Age 16 Years and Over

(Number, percent.)

Year	Civilian labor force	Civilian participation rate	Employed	Unemployed	Unemployment rate
2007....................	3,034,016	63.7	2,917,117	116,899	3.9
2008....................	3,104,863	63.8	2,913,903	190,960	6.2
2009....................	3,128,110	63.2	2,817,577	310,533	9.9
2010....................	3,089,705	63.1	2,769,454	320,251	10.4
2011....................	3,037,017	61.7	2,748,470	288,547	9.5
2012....................	3,031,199	60.6	2,778,425	252,774	8.3
2013....................	3,039,865	59.8	2,804,338	235,527	7.7
2014....................	3,097,112	59.8	2,886,412	210,700	6.8
2015....................	3,152,708	59.8	2,959,518	193,190	6.1

Table AZ-9. Employment and Average Wages by Industry

(Estimates through 2010 are based on the 2007 North American Industry Classification System [NAICS]. Estimates from 2011 onward are based on the 2012 NAICS.)

Industry	2008	2009	2010	2011	2012	2013	2014
				Number of Jobs			
Wage and Salary Employment by Industry................	2,713,899	2,524,521	2,483,674	2,510,358	2,558,795	2,619,055	2,672,673
Farm Wage and Salary Employment.........................	11,632	12,134	11,583	11,342	12,000	13,751	12,345
Nonfarm Wage and Salary Employment....................	2,702,267	2,512,387	2,472,091	2,499,016	2,546,795	2,605,304	2,660,328
Private wage and salary employment.........................	2,243,239	2,059,730	2,024,116	2,058,758	2,104,563	2,163,547	2,215,519
Forestry, fishing, and related activities....................	13,180	11,880	12,431	12,954	12,157	12,081	12,142
Mining..	12,976	10,559	10,285	10,925	11,931	12,616	12,302
Utilities...	12,738	12,435	12,079	11,975	12,290	11,932	11,954
Construction	193,649	134,757	116,705	117,015	120,118	128,145	128,984
Manufacturing..	172,214	151,959	146,695	148,251	153,645	154,018	155,082
Durable goods manufacturing............................	139,141	121,379	116,492	117,601	121,694	121,388	121,590
Nondurable goods manufacturing......................	33,073	30,580	30,203	30,650	31,951	32,630	33,492
Wholesale trade	110,611	102,513	98,769	98,543	98,903	99,361	95,712
Retail trade..	326,188	302,597	297,827	299,718	300,584	302,633	315,716
Transportation and warehousing...........................	74,922	70,120	67,604	70,860	73,011	73,342	75,834
Information	40,878	38,185	36,733	36,683	38,284	41,847	43,382
Finance and insurance	127,573	123,284	121,948	125,932	129,752	135,954	140,650
Real estate and rental and leasing.........................	53,938	49,042	47,092	46,332	46,947	48,424	48,911
Professional, scientific, and technical services	135,400	125,170	123,415	125,862	124,752	128,710	131,852
Management of companies and enterprises..............	27,646	26,577	25,422	25,216	26,735	28,748	29,702
Administrative and waste services.........................	229,569	199,382	197,672	200,946	208,545	221,058	226,455
Educational services	45,006	47,281	51,291	53,767	56,000	56,587	56,750
Health care and social assistance..........................	279,644	285,598	296,275	304,151	312,598	319,598	326,363
Arts, entertainment, and recreation.......................	36,226	33,492	33,467	33,781	34,976	35,853	38,302
Accommodation and food services.........................	236,949	225,280	223,334	228,368	233,536	241,850	249,759
Other services, except public administration..........	113,932	109,619	105,072	107,479	109,799	110,790	115,667
Government and government enterprises..........................	459,028	452,657	447,975	440,258	442,232	441,757	444,809
				Dollars			
Average Wages and Salaries by Industry	43,309	43,580	44,145	45,396	46,417	46,797	47,823
Average Farm Wages and Salaries	35,735	38,035	34,616	36,679	29,631	38,734	41,808
Average Nonfarm Wages and Salaries	43,341	43,607	44,190	45,435	46,496	46,840	47,851
Average private wages and salaries.........................	42,994	43,149	43,948	45,258	46,471	46,763	47,887
Forestry, fishing, and related activities....................	20,414	22,363	22,730	23,549	23,869	24,027	26,005
Mining...	70,644	68,479	71,447	78,827	80,923	78,939	79,312
Utilities...	87,512	91,045	92,192	95,114	95,384	97,378	102,326
Construction	45,101	44,867	45,018	45,931	47,964	48,426	49,512
Manufacturing..	62,020	63,447	66,902	70,052	70,645	70,743	72,547
Durable goods manufacturing............................	67,051	69,137	73,482	77,173	77,819	78,007	80,114
Nondurable goods manufacturing......................	40,856	40,862	41,523	42,728	43,322	43,721	45,076
Wholesale trade	62,201	62,405	64,391	66,939	71,333	68,506	72,196
Retail trade..	28,964	28,679	29,366	30,909	30,859	30,259	31,150
Transportation and warehousing...........................	46,428	46,747	48,814	49,744	50,046	50,749	50,882
Information	55,738	57,476	57,915	59,814	61,620	62,888	66,530
Finance and insurance	60,329	58,925	61,003	63,500	67,007	69,577	71,031
Real estate and rental and leasing.........................	43,606	42,085	42,624	44,623	46,810	46,491	48,547
Professional, scientific, and technical services	65,255	66,152	67,406	69,857	73,607	74,254	74,768
Management of companies and enterprises..............	76,555	75,094	74,940	77,325	82,548	85,637	92,388
Administrative and waste services.........................	32,804	33,206	33,325	33,607	34,078	34,733	35,951
Educational services	37,183	39,065	39,625	40,119	40,700	40,585	40,733
Health care and social assistance..........................	47,546	48,233	48,018	48,532	48,962	49,422	50,243
Arts, entertainment, and recreation.......................	34,719	36,293	37,062	37,101	38,100	38,267	39,453
Accommodation and food services.........................	19,778	19,475	20,005	20,467	20,873	20,892	21,733
Other services, except public administration..........	28,105	27,993	28,541	29,086	29,445	30,523	31,957
Government and government enterprises..........................	45,037	45,691	45,281	46,265	46,616	47,217	47,671

Table AZ-10. Employment Characteristics by Family Type

(Number, percent.)

Family type and labor force status	2012 Total	2012 Families with own children under 18 years	2013 Total	2013 Families with own children under 18 years	2014 Total	2014 Families with own children under 18 years
All Families..	1,560,687	674,358	1,572,310	671,500	1,573,546	657,330
FAMILY TYPE AND LABOR FORCE STATUS						
Married-Couple Families............................	1,122,884	429,016	1,136,593	429,785	1,135,360	428,399
Both husband and wife in labor force...............	45.6	60.3	43.3	57.6	43.9	58.9
Husband in labor force, wife not in labor force.........	23	33.7	23.8	35.3	23.9	34.4
Wife in labor force, husband not in labor force...........	7.5	4.0	7.8	4.4	7.7	3.9
Both husband and wife not in labor force.............	23.9	2.0	24.7	2.5	24.5	2.7
Other Families	437,803	245,342	435,717	241,715	438,186	228,931
Female householder, no husband present................	70.5	71.5	70.3	73.2	69.4	71.8
In labor force................................	50.7	58.4	49.9	59.6	48.3	58.0
Not in labor force	19.8	13.1	20.3	13.6	21.1	13.8
Male householder, no wife present..................	29.5	28.5	29.7	26.8	30.6	28.2
In labor force..............................	23.1	25.7	23.1	24.0	24.3	25.6
Not in labor force	6.5	2.8	6.6	2.7	6.3	2.6

Table AZ-11. School Enrollment and Educational Attainment, 2014

(Number, percent.)

Item	State	U.S.
Enrollment		
Total population 3 years and over, enrolled in school...............	1,757,664	82,063,714
Enrolled in nursery school or preschool (percent)...........	4.9	6.0
Enrolled in kindergarten (percent)...............	5.1	5.1
Enrolled in elementary school, grades 1-8 (percent)...............	41.3	40.2
Enrolled in high school, grades 9-12 (percent)...............	21.3	20.7
Enrolled in college or graduate school (percent)...............	27.4	28.0
Attainment		
Total population 25 years and over	4,436,226	213,725,624
Less than ninth grade (percent)...............	6.4	5.6
9th to 12th grade, no diploma (percent)	7.5	7.5
High school graduate, including equivalency (percent)...............	24.3	27.7
Some college, no degree (percent)	25.7	21.0
Associate's degree (percent)...............	8.5	8.2
Bachelor's degree (percent)...............	17.3	18.7
Graduate or professional degree (percent)...............	10.3	11.4
High school graduate or higher (percent)	86.1	86.9
Bachelor's degree or higher (percent)	27.6	30.1

Table AZ-12. Public School Characteristics and Educational Indicators

(Number, percent; data derived from National Center of Education Statistics.)

Item	State	U.S.
Public Schools, 2013–2014 (except where noted)		
Number of school districts................	684	18,194
Number of schools................	2,252	98,271
Number of students (in thousands)................	1,102	50,045
Number of teachers (in thousands)	48	3,114
Student-teacher ratio................	22.8	16.1
Expenditures per student (dollars), FY 2013................	74,957	107,637
Four-year adjusted cohort graduation rate (ACGR)[1,2]	75.7	82.3
Students eligible for free or reduced-price lunch (in thousands)	544	25,596
English language learners (in thousands)................	63	4,461
Students age 3 to 21 served under IDEA, part B (in thousands)................	130	6,464

Public Schools by Type	Number	Percent of state public schools
Total number of schools................	2,252	100.0
Regular................	1,943	86.3
Special education................	21	0.9
Vocational education................	227	10.1
Alternative education................	61	2.7

NOTE: Every school is assigned only one school type based on its instructional emphasis.

[1]ACGR data represents a new method of calculating high-school completion rates and may not be comparable to previous years' data for Averaged Freshmen Graduation Rates (AFGR).

[2]The United States 4-year ACGRs were estimated using both the reported 4-year ACGR data from 49 states and the District of Columbia and using imputed data for Idaho. The estimate for American Indian/Alaska Native students also includes imputed data for Virginia.

Table AZ-13. Reported Voting and Registration of the Voting-Age Population, November 2014

(Numbers in thousands, percent.)

Item	Total population	Total citizen population	Registered			Voted		
			Total registered	Percent registered (total population)	Percent registered (total citizen population)	Total voted	Percent voted (total population)	Percent voted (total citizen population)
U.S. Total	239,874	219,941	142,166	59.3	64.6	92,251	38.5	41.9
State Total.............................	4,994	4,397	2,738	54.8	62.3	1,785	35.7	40.6
Sex								
Male.......................................	2,423	2,133	1,309	54.0	61.4	823	34.0	38.6
Female	2,571	2,264	1,430	55.6	63.1	961	37.4	42.5
Race								
White alone..............................	4,226	3,742	2,386	56.5	63.8	1,583	37.5	42.3
White, non-Hispanic alone	2,743	2,694	1,757	64.1	65.2	1,250	45.6	46.4
Black alone..............................	215	199	120	55.9	60.3	66	30.8	33.1
Asian alone	189	98	39	20.4	39.3	20	10.6	20.3
Hispanic (of any race)	1,580	1,145	687	43.5	60.0	364	23.1	31.8
White alone or in combination	4,315	3,827	2,425	56.2	63.4	1,614	37.4	42.2
Black alone or in combination..........	248	229	120	48.5	52.4	66	26.7	28.8
Asian alone or in combination..........	205	115	48	23.3	41.7	25	12.0	21.5
Age								
18 to 24 years	514	491	181	35.1	36.8	74	14.4	15.1
25 to 34 years	859	735	411	47.9	56.0	170	19.8	23.1
35 to 44 years.............................	948	760	458	48.3	60.3	245	25.8	32.2
45 to 64 years.............................	1,725	1,526	1,012	58.7	66.3	710	41.1	46.5
65 years and over	947	885	676	71.4	76.3	587	61.9	66.3

Table AZ-14. Crime

(Number, rate per 100,000. Data are derived from the FBI Uniform Crime Reports.)

Item	State			U.S.[1,2,3,4]		
	2013	2014	Percent change	2013	2014	Percent change
TOTAL POPULATION[5]...............................	6,626,624	6,731,484	1.6	316,128,839	318,857,056	0.9
VIOLENT CRIME						
Number...................................	26,892	26,916	0.1	1,163,146	1,165,383	0.2
Rate	405.8	399.9	-1.5	367.9	365.5	-0.7
Murder and Nonnegligent Manslaughter						
Number...................................	357	319	-10.6	14,196	14,249	0.4
Rate	5.4	4.7	-13.0	4.5	4.5	-
Rape[6]						
Number...................................	3,050	3,378	X	108,612	116,645	X
Rate	46.0	50.2	X	34.4	36.6	X
Robbery						
Number...................................	6,702	6,249	-6.8	345,031	325,802	-5.6
Rate	101.1	92.8	-8.2	109.1	102.2	-6.3
Aggravated Assault						
Number...................................	17,490	16,970	-3.0	724,149	741,291	2.4
Rate	263.9	252.1	-4.5	229.1	232.5	1.5
PROPERTY CRIME						
Number...................................	225,243	215,240	-4.4	8,632,512	8,277,829	-4.1
Rate	3,399.1	3,197.5	-5.9	2,730.7	2,596.1	-4.9
Burglary						
Number...................................	48,533	43,562	-10.2	1,928,465	1,729,806	-10.3
Rate	732.4	647.1	-11.6	610.0	542.5	-11.1
Larceny-Theft						
Number...................................	159,272	154,091	-3.3	6,004,453	5,858,496	-2.4
Rate	2,403.5	2,289.1	-4.8	1,899.4	1,837.3	-3.3
Motor Vehicle Theft						
Number...................................	17,438	17,587	0.9	699,594	689,527	-1.4
Rate	263.2	261.3	-0.7	221.3	216.2	-2.3

NOTE: Although arson data are included in the trend and clearance tables, sufficient data are not available to estimate totals for this offense. Therefore, no arson data are published in this table.
X = Not applicable.
- = Zero or rounds to zero.
[1]Because of changes in the state's reporting practices, figures are not comparable to previous years' data.
[2]The data collection methodology for the offense of forcible rape used by the Minnesota state Uniform Crime Reporting (UCR) Program (with the exception of Minneapolis and St. Paul, Minnesota) does not comply with national UCR Program guidelines. Consequently, its figures for forcible rape and violent crime (of which forcible rape is a part) are not published in this table.
[3]Includes offenses reported by the Zoological Police and the Metro Transit Police.
[4]The crime figures have been adjusted.
[5]Populations are U.S. Census Bureau provisional estimates as of July 1 of each year.
[6]The figures shown for the offense of rape were estimated using the revised Uniform Crime Reporting (UCR) definition of rape.

Table AZ-15. State Government Finances, 2014

(Dollar amounts in thousands, percent distribution.)

Item	Dollars	Percent distribution
Total Revenue	39,053,409	100.0
General revenue	29,349,780	75.2
Intergovernmental revenue	10,951,041	28.0
Taxes	13,084,043	33.5
General sales	5,994,048	15.3
Selective sales	1,765,577	4.5
License taxes	437,127	1.1
Individual income tax	3,462,413	8.9
Corporate income tax	575,180	1.5
Other taxes	849,698	2.2
Current charges	3,682,132	9.4
Miscellaneous general revenue	1,632,564	4.2
Utility revenue	28,763	0.1
Liquor stores revenue	0	-
Insurance trust revenue [1]	9,674,866	24.8
Total Expenditure	33,231,219	100.0
Intergovernmental expenditure	7,448,459	22.4
Direct expenditure	25,782,760	77.6
Current operation	18,131,047	54.6
Capital outlay	1,168,587	3.5
Insurance benefits and repayments	4,107,480	12.4
Assistance and subsidies	1,855,005	5.6
Interest on debt	520,641	1.6
Exhibit: Salaries and wages	3,465,853	10.4
Total Expenditure	33,231,219	100.0
General expenditure	29,093,708	87.5
Intergovernmental expenditure	7,448,459	22.4
Direct expenditure	21,645,249	65.1
General expenditure, by function:		
Education	9,714,410	29.2
Public welfare	9,080,843	27.3
Hospitals	854,563	2.6
Health	2,041,887	6.1
Highways	1,758,371	5.3
Police protection	221,187	0.7
Correction	1,059,088	3.2
Natural resources	263,324	0.8
Parks and recreation	78,676	0.2
Governmental administration	695,711	2.1
Interest on general debt	519,164	1.6
Other and unallocable	2,806,484	8.4
Utility expenditure	30,031	0.1
Liquor stores expenditure	0	-
Insurance trust expenditure	4,107,480	12.4
Debt at End of Fiscal Year	14,315,828	X
Cash and Security Holdings	57,816,282	X

X = Not applicable.
- = Zero or rounds to zero.
[1]Within insurance trust revenue, net earnings of state retirement systems is a calculated statistic (the item code in the data file is X08), and thus can be positive or negative. Net earnings is the sum of earnings on investments plus gains on investments minus losses on investments. The change made in 2002 for asset valuation from book to market value in accordance with Statement 34 of the Governmental Accounting Standards Board is reflected in the calculated statistics.

Table AZ-16. State Government Tax Collections, 2014

(Dollars in thousands, percent.)

Item	Dollars	Percent distribution
Total Taxes	13,084,043	100.0
Property taxes	823,508	6.3
Sales and gross receipts	7,759,625	59.3
General sales and gross receipts	5,994,048	45.8
Selective sales and gross receipts	1,765,577	13.5
Alcoholic beverages	71,136	0.5
Amusements	533	-
Insurance premiums	448,115	3.4
Motor fuels	779,970	6.0
Pari-mutuels	216	-
Public utilities	21,760	0.2
Tobacco products	311,811	2.4
Other selective sales	132,036	1.0
Licenses	437,127	3.3
Alcoholic beverages	5,246	-
Amusements	0	-
Corporations in general	10,368	0.1
Hunting and fishing	32,787	0.3
Motor vehicle	198,227	1.5
Motor vehicle operators	30,215	0.2
Public utilities	25,986	0.2
Occupation and business, NEC	131,360	1.0
Other licenses	2,938	-
		-
Income taxes	4,037,593	30.9
Individual income	3,462,413	26.5
Corporation net income	575,180	4.4
Other taxes	26,190	0.2
Death and gift	0	-
Documentary and stock transfer	0	-
Severance	26,190	0.2
Taxes, NEC	0	-

- = Zero or rounds to zero.

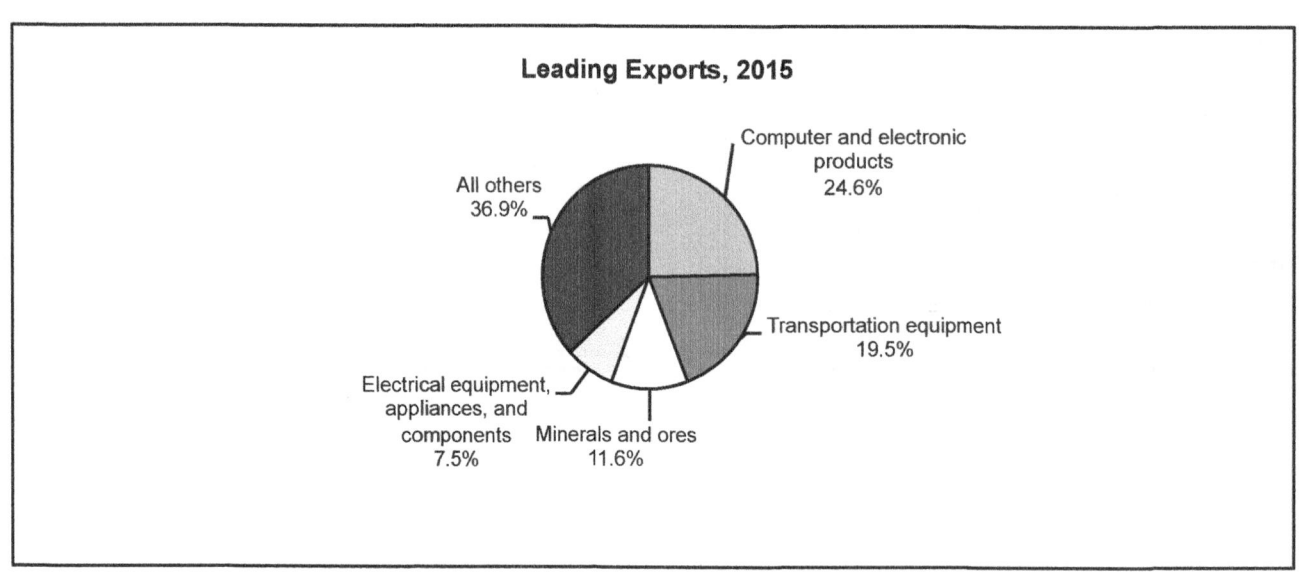

Leading Exports, 2015

Computer and electronic products 24.6%

All others 36.9%

Transportation equipment 19.5%

Electrical equipment, appliances, and components 7.5%

Minerals and ores 11.6%

Facts and Figures

Location: South central United States; bordered on the N by Missouri, on the E by Tennessee and Mississippi, on the S by Louisiana, and on the W by Oklahoma and Texas

Area: 53,178 sq. mi. (137,733 sq. km.); rank—29th

Population: 2,978,204 (2015 est.); rank—33rd

Principal Cities: capital—Little Rock; largest—Little Rock

Statehood: June 15, 1836; 25th state

U.S. Congress: 2 senators, 4 representatives

State Motto: *Regnat populus* ("The people rule")

State Song: "Arkansas"

State Nicknames: The Natural State; The Land of Opportunity

Abbreviations: AR; Ark.

State Symbols: flower—apple blossom; tree—pine; bird—mockingbird

At a Glance

- With an increase in population of 1.9 percent, Arkansas ranked 33rd among the states in growth from 2010 to 2015.

- The infant mortality rate in Arkansas in 2014 was 7.53 per 1,000 live births, which ranked 4th in the nation.

- Arkansas's median household income in 2014 was $41,262, and 18.9 percent of its population lived below the poverty level.

- In 2015, 11.8 percent of Arkansans did not have health insurance, which was down from 16.0 percent the previous year.

- Arkansas's property crime rate in 2014 was 3,338.0 per 100,000 population, which ranked 7th in the nation.

Table AR-1. Population by Age, Sex, Race, and Hispanic Origin

(Number, percent, except where noted.)

Sex, age, race, and Hispanic origin	2000	2010	2015[1]	Average annual percent change, 2010–2015
Total Population...........................	2,673,400	2,915,918	2,978,204	0.2
Percent of total U.S. population	0.9	0.9	0.9	X
Sex				
Male...........................	1,304,693	1,431,637	1,462,856	0.2
Female	1,368,707	1,484,281	1,515,348	0.1
Age				
Under 5 years...........................	181,585	197,689	190,858	-0.3
5 to 19 years...........................	578,924	598,241	592,246	-0.1
20 to 64 years...........................	1,538,872	1,700,007	1,717,951	0.1
65 years and over...........................	374,019	419,981	477,149	0.9
Median age (years)	36.0	37.4	37.9	0.1
Race and Hispanic Origin				
One race				
White...........................	2,138,598	2,342,403	2,367,701	0.1
Black...........................	418,950	454,021	466,112	0.2
American Indian and Alaska Native	17,808	26,134	29,268	0.8
Asian...........................	20,220	37,537	46,911	1.6
Native Hawaiian or				
Other Pacific Islander...........................	1,668	6,685	8,757	1.9
Two or more races...........................	35,744	49,138	59,455	1.4
Hispanic (of any race)...........................	86,866	191,535	213,957	0.8

X = Not applicable.
[1]Population figures for 2015 are July 1 estimates. The 2010 estimates are taken from the 2010 Census.

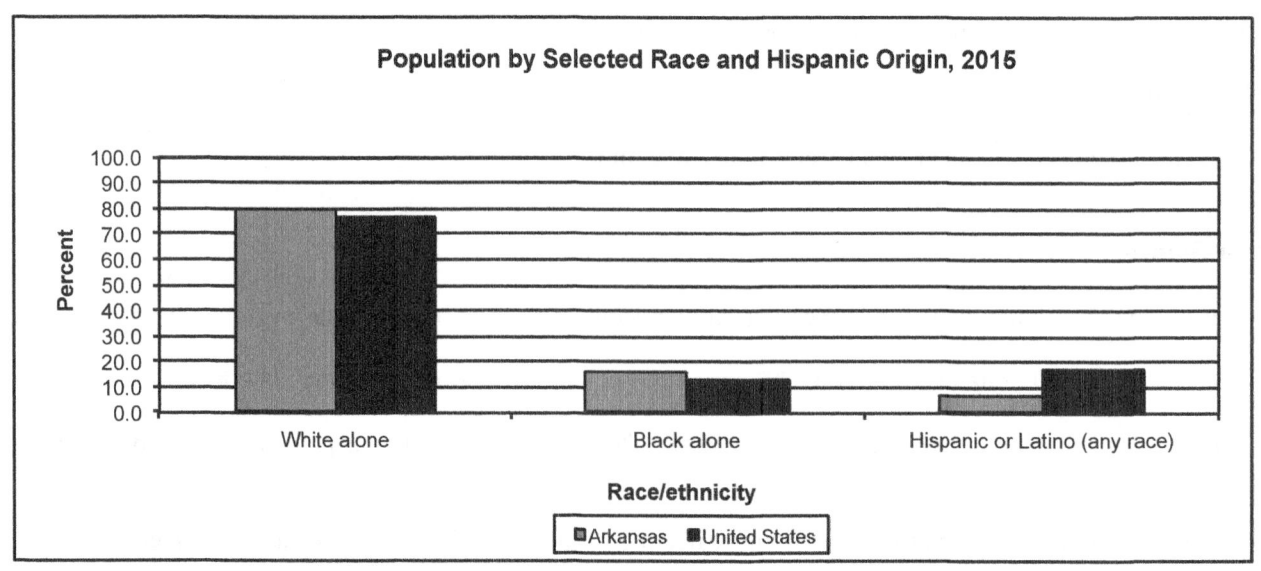

Table AR-2. Marital Status

(Number, percent distribution.)

Sex, age, race, and Hispanic origin	2000	2010	2014
Males, 15 Years and Over	1,015,594	1,128,804	1,144,409
Never married	24.2	29.5	30.2
Now married, except separated...........................	61.0	53.3	52.8
Separated...........................	1.6	2.2	2.0
Widowed...........................	2.7	3.1	2.8
Divorced...........................	10.4	12.0	12.1
Females, 15 Years and Over	1,096,069	1,200,974	1,211,598
Never married	18.4	23.5	23.8
Now married, except separated...........................	55.7	48.8	48.9
Separated...........................	2.2	2.9	2.7
Widowed...........................	12.2	11.2	10.7
Divorced...........................	11.6	13.6	13.9

Table AR-3. Households and Housing Characteristics

(Number, percent, dollars.)

Item	2000	2010	2014	Average annual percent change, 2000–2014
Total Households................................	1,042,696	1,114,902	1,131,288	0.6
Family households	732,261	761,361	752,212	0.2
Married-couple family	566,401	554,946	546,528	-0.3
Other family	165,860	206,415	205,684	1.7
Male householder, no wife present................................	39,299	51,620	53,552	2.6
Female householder, no husband present................................	126,561	154,795	152,132	1.4
Nonfamily households	310,435	353,541	379,076	1.6
Householder living alone................................	266,585	302,127	323,420	1.5
Householder not living alone................................	43,850	51,414	55,656	1.9
Housing Characteristics				
Total housing units................................	1,173,043	1,317,818	1,341,081	1.0
Occupied housing units	1,042,696	1,114,902	1,131,288	0.6
Owner occupied	723,535	751,568	744,318	0.2
Renter occupied	319,161	363,334	386,970	1.5
Average household size................................	2.49	2.55	2.55	0.2
Financial Characteristics				
Median gross rent of renter-occupied housing	453	638	683	3.6
Median monthly owner costs for housing units with a mortgage	737	987	995	2.5
Median value of owner-occupied housing units................................	72,800	106,300	112,500	3.9

Table AR-4. Migration, Origin, and Language

(Number, percent.)

Characteristic	State 2013	State 2014	State Percent change	U.S. 2013	U.S. 2014	U.S. Percent change
Residence 1 Year Ago						
Population 1 year and over	2,923,642	2,931,123	0.3	312,432,820	315,095,393	0.9
Same house................................	84.7	84.1	X	85.0	85.1	X
Different house in the U.S.	15.0	15.6	X	14.4	14.3	X
Same county	9.1	9.5	X	8.9	8.7	X
Different county	5.9	6.2	X	5.5	5.6	X
Same state	3.5	3.6	X	3.2	3.3	X
Different state	2.4	2.5	X	2.3	2.3	X
Abroad	0.3	0.3	X	0.6	0.6	X
Place of Birth						
Native born	2,825,485	2,826,372	-	274,780,773	276,465,262	0.6
Male................................	49.3	49	X	49.3	49.3	X
Female................................	50.7	51	X	50.7	50.7	X
Foreign born	133,888	139,997	4.6	41,348,066	42,391,794	2.5
Male................................	50.4	50.9	X	48.8	48.7	X
Female................................	49.6	49.1	X	51.2	51.3	X
Foreign born; naturalized U.S. citizen................................	43,677	42,221	-3.3	19,294,710	19,984,738	3.6
Male................................	46.4	43.9	X	45.9	45.9	X
Female................................	53.6	56.1	X	54.1	54.1	X
Foreign born; not a U.S. citizen	90,211	97,776	8.4	22,053,356	22,407,056	1.6
Male................................	52.3	53.9	X	51.3	51.2	X
Female................................	47.7	46.1	X	48.7	48.8	X
Entered 2010 or later	13.6	13.6	X	9.7	12.3	X
Entered 2000 to 2009	34.4	36	X	29.4	28.6	X
Entered before 2000................................	52.0	50.5	X	61.0	59.1	X
World Region of Birth, Foreign						
Foreign-born population, excluding population born at sea	133,888	139,997	4.6	41,347,945	42,390,705	2.5
Europe	7.2	7.6	X	11.6	11.2	X
Asia................................	24.6	21	X	29.5	30.1	X
Africa	2.2	1.2	X	4.4	4.6	X
Oceania	0.7	3.1	X	0.5	0.6	X
Latin America................................	63.4	65.7	X	51.9	51.6	X
North America................................	2.0	1.4	X	2.0	1.9	X
Language Spoken at Home and Ability to Speak English						
Population 5 years and over................................	2,769,171	2,775,973	0.2	296,358,760	299,084,046	0.9
English only	93.1	93.1	X	79.2	78.9	X
Language other than English................................	6.9	6.9	X	20.8	21.1	X
Speaks English less than "very well"................................	3.1	3.3	X	8.5	8.6	X

X = Not applicable.
- = Zero or rounds to zero.

Table AR-5. Median Income and Poverty Status, 2014

(Number, percent, except as noted.)

Characteristic	State		U.S.	
	Number	Percent	Number	Percent
Median Income				
Households (dollars)...	41,262	X	53,657	X
Families (dollars)	51,528	X	65,910	X
Below Poverty Level (All People)	543,882	18.9	48,208,387	15.5
Sex				
Male..	240,527	17.1	21,590,918	14.2
Female	303,355	20.6	26,617,469	16.8
Age				
Under 18 years..	183,830	26.4	15,686,012	21.7
Related children under 18 years............................	179,355	26.0	15,372,705	21.3
18 to 64 years...	312,639	18.0	28,267,482	14.6
65 years and over	47,413	10.6	4,254,893	9.5

X = Not applicable.

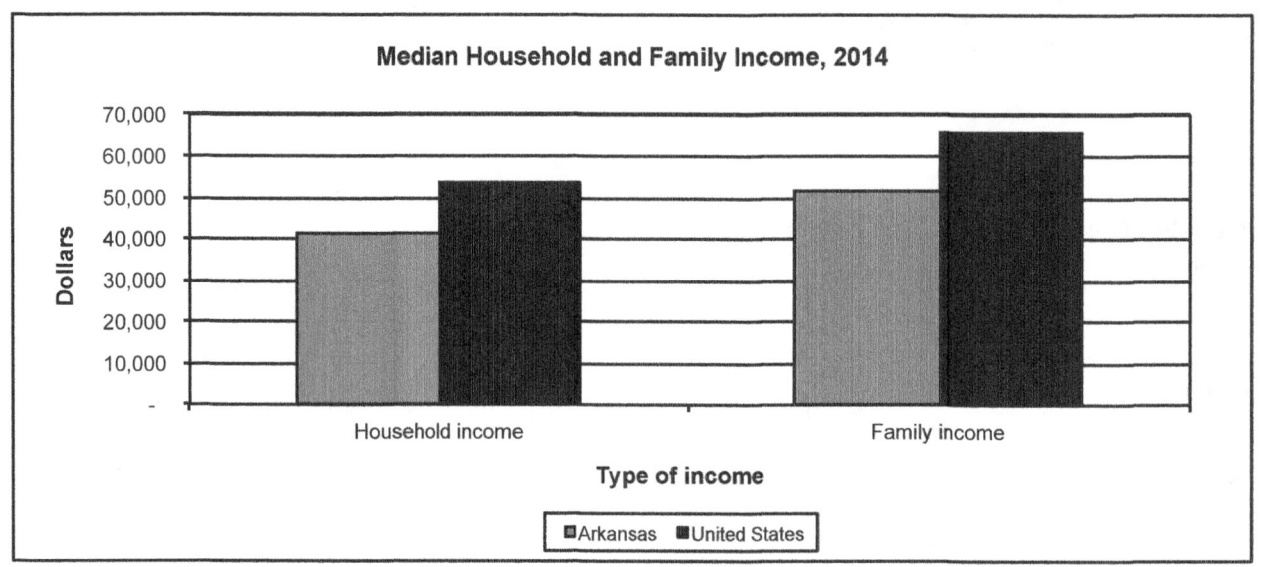

Table AR-6. Health Insurance Coverage Status for the Civilian Noninstitutionalized Population and Children Under 18 Years of Age

(Numbers in thousands, percent.)

Item	2006	2007	2008	2009	2010	2011	2012	2013	2014
Civilian Noninstitutionalized Population	2,758	2,805	2,802	2,833	2,868	2,885	2,896	2,907	2,914
Covered by Private or Public Insurance									
Number...	2,237	2,354	2,296	2,351	2,367	2,393	2,420	2,442	2,571
Percent...	81.1	83.9	81.9	83.0	82.5	82.9	83.6	84.0	88.2
Not Covered									
Number...	521	451	506	483	501	492	476	465	343
Percent...	18.9	16.1	18.1	17.0	17.5	17.1	16.4	16.0	11.8
Percent in the U.S. not covered..	15.8	15.3	15.1	15.1	15.5	15.1	14.8	14.5	11.7
Children Under 18 Years of Age	699	720	701	707	709	709	709	709	704
Covered by Private or Public Insurance									
Number...	634	679	640	663	663	669	667	670	670
Percent...	90.7	93.8	91.3	93.8	93.4	94.4	94.1	94.5	95.2
Not Covered									
Number...	65	44	61	44	46	40	42	39	34
Percent...	9.3	6.2	8.7	6.2	6.6	5.6	5.9	5.5	4.8
Percent in the U.S. not covered..	11.7	11.0	9.7	8.6	8.0	7.5	7.2	7.1	6.0

Table AR-7. Employment Status by Demographic Group, 2015

(Numbers in thousands, percent.)

Characteristic	Civilian noninstitutional population	Civilian labor force		Employed		Unemployed	
		Number	Percent of population	Number	Percent of population	Number	Percent of population
Total..............................	2,299	1,337	58.1	1,266	55.1	70	5.2
Sex							
Male.............................	1,105	704	63.7	664	60.1	40	5.7
Female	1,193	632	53.0	602	50.5	30	4.7
Race, Sex, and Hispanic Origin							
White.............................	1,889	1,107	58.6	1,059	56.0	48	4.3
Male..........................	920	597	64.9	570	61.9	27	4.6
Female	969	510	52.6	490	50.5	21	4.0
Black or African American................	333	184	55.1	165	49.4	19	10.3
Male..........................	149	84	56.3	73	48.9	11	13.2
Female	184	99	54.0	92	49.8	8	7.9
Hispanic or Latino ethnicity[1]............	149	99	66.2	92	61.8	7	6.7
Male..........................	81	61	75.6	57	70.3	4	7.0
Female	69	38	55.1	36	51.7	2	6.2
Age							
16 to 19 years.....................	155	48	31.3	41	26.4	8	15.9
20 to 24 years.....................	182	127	69.9	116	63.4	12	9.3
25 to 34 years.....................	394	311	79.0	291	73.8	20	6.5
35 to 44 years.....................	356	282	79.3	269	75.5	14	4.8
45 to 54 years.....................	396	293	74.1	284	71.7	10	3.3
55 to 64 years.....................	378	209	55.4	203	53.8	6	2.7
65 years and over..................	439	65	14.9	64	14.6	1	2.1

NOTE: Data in Table 7 are from the Current Population Survey (CPS) and do not match the estimates in Table 8. See notes and definitions for further information.
[1] May be of any race.

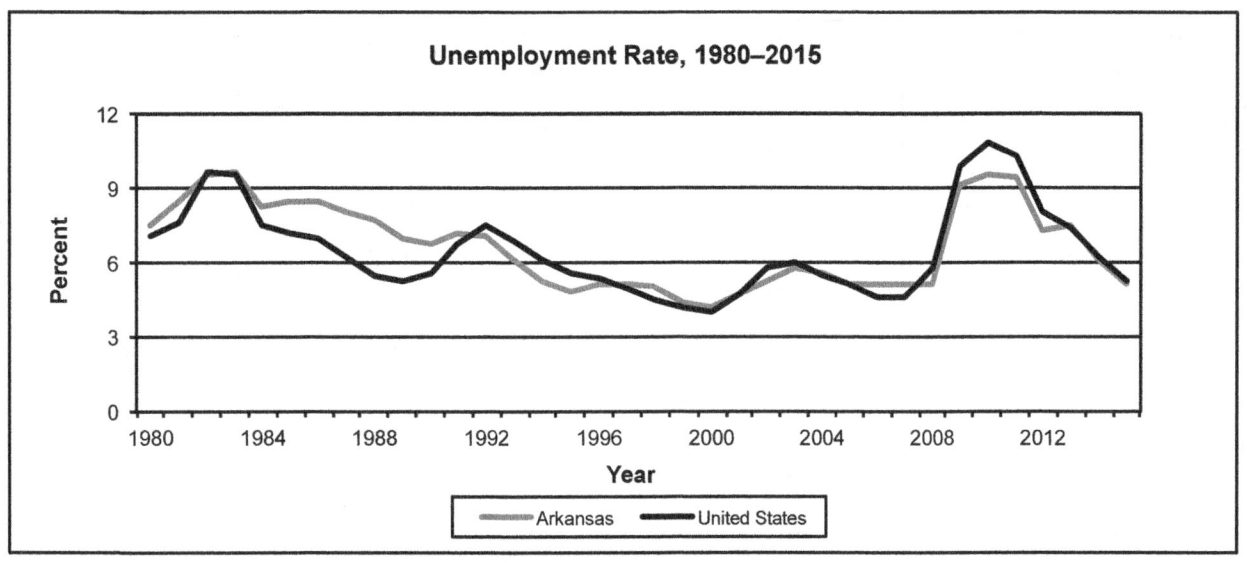

Table AR-8. Employment Status of the Civilian Noninstitutional Population Age 16 Years and Over

(Number, percent.)

Year	Civilian labor force	Civilian participation rate	Employed	Unemployed	Unemployment rate
2007..............................	1,369,284	63.2	1,296,572	72,712	5.3
2008..............................	1,375,257	62.9	1,300,017	75,240	5.5
2009..............................	1,358,911	61.7	1,252,399	106,512	7.8
2010..............................	1,353,338	60.6	1,242,496	110,842	8.2
2011..............................	1,362,682	60.5	1,249,514	113,168	8.3
2012..............................	1,342,327	59.3	1,240,646	101,681	7.6
2013..............................	1,307,986	57.5	1,212,009	95,977	7.3
2014..............................	1,304,141	57.0	1,224,398	79,743	6.1
2015..............................	1,330,099	57.9	1,260,615	69,484	5.2

Table AR-9. Employment and Average Wages by Industry

(Estimates through 2010 are based on the 2007 North American Industry Classification System [NAICS]. Estimates from 2011 onward are based on the 2012 NAICS.)

Industry	2008	2009	2010	2011	2012	2013	2014
	Number of Jobs						
Wage and Salary Employment by Industry..................	1,263,298	1,227,077	1,226,354	1,229,913	1,231,172	1,234,941	1,245,380
Farm Wage and Salary Employment..........................	12,453	12,493	13,208	11,972	8,820	11,397	11,305
Nonfarm Wage and Salary Employment....................	1,250,845	1,214,584	1,213,146	1,217,941	1,222,352	1,223,544	1,234,075
Private wage and salary employment..........................	1,018,122	978,490	976,519	983,731	987,787	988,208	1,002,084
Forestry, fishing, and related activities.....................	8,061	7,774	8,163	8,244	7,963	7,979	8,174
Mining..	8,322	8,432	8,574	9,014	8,662	7,540	6,728
Utilities..	6,971	7,028	7,315	7,170	7,700	8,088	7,904
Construction..	58,642	54,361	51,129	49,824	49,041	47,155	47,569
Manufacturing..	181,870	162,703	159,290	158,294	154,704	152,141	153,262
Durable goods manufacturing...........................	94,796	80,067	77,864	78,484	76,862	75,449	76,265
Nondurable goods manufacturing......................	87,074	82,636	81,426	79,810	77,842	76,692	76,997
Wholesale trade	49,087	47,341	46,792	46,968	47,488	46,443	46,728
Retail trade..	135,130	131,360	131,391	133,167	133,703	134,327	137,346
Transportation and warehousing..........................	59,287	53,350	52,891	54,211	54,772	53,984	55,163
Information..	18,518	17,437	16,545	16,077	15,594	15,362	14,842
Finance and insurance	37,616	36,472	36,135	36,797	36,850	37,091	37,075
Real estate and rental and leasing........................	14,754	14,334	14,074	13,719	13,543	13,534	13,245
Professional, scientific, and technical services	39,391	38,313	39,141	39,756	39,150	40,547	41,002
Management of companies and enterprises..................	26,130	26,357	25,904	26,048	30,901	31,442	32,432
Administrative and waste services	53,823	50,018	53,783	56,173	54,657	57,821	61,210
Educational services	14,170	14,454	14,841	15,224	15,855	15,756	16,665
Health care and social assistance.........................	149,162	153,207	156,158	157,082	160,170	160,028	160,793
Arts, entertainment, and recreation.......................	10,026	9,954	9,881	9,875	9,809	10,187	10,594
Accommodation and food services.........................	91,945	90,991	90,288	91,548	93,708	95,552	97,820
Other services, except public administration................	55,217	54,604	54,224	54,540	53,517	53,231	53,532
Government and government enterprises...........................	232,723	236,094	236,627	234,210	234,565	235,336	231,991
	Dollars						
Average Wages and Salaries by Industry	35,321	36,032	36,686	37,787	38,897	39,532	40,560
Average Farm Wages and Salaries	22,276	18,839	19,023	19,145	24,550	27,352	23,551
Average Nonfarm Wages and Salaries	35,451	36,209	36,878	37,970	39,000	39,645	40,716
Average private wages and salaries..........................	35,251	35,914	36,667	37,771	39,017	39,784	40,884
Forestry, fishing, and related activities.....................	29,126	29,499	30,403	31,440	32,308	33,455	34,656
Mining..	61,034	62,564	64,277	67,647	67,915	69,169	71,763
Utilities..	72,220	72,644	71,533	74,513	76,612	79,103	82,637
Construction..	39,321	40,284	40,169	40,709	42,307	41,704	43,247
Manufacturing..	38,563	38,731	40,788	42,050	43,568	44,332	45,865
Durable goods manufacturing...........................	40,064	40,397	42,621	44,068	45,640	46,665	48,221
Nondurable goods manufacturing......................	36,928	37,116	39,036	40,066	41,522	42,037	43,531
Wholesale trade	54,190	54,294	56,314	57,927	59,765	62,222	63,926
Retail trade..	23,004	23,340	23,904	24,286	24,941	25,254	25,887
Transportation and warehousing..........................	40,824	40,433	41,564	44,092	44,900	46,592	47,677
Information..	50,957	65,601	48,243	50,025	49,713	50,659	53,427
Finance and insurance	50,838	51,213	52,920	55,027	57,740	57,983	60,021
Real estate and rental and leasing........................	30,007	30,480	31,376	32,788	34,354	34,651	35,909
Professional, scientific, and technical services	50,492	51,509	53,072	56,330	55,126	56,813	58,268
Management of companies and enterprises..................	77,734	81,263	90,405	91,222	96,145	103,349	105,412
Administrative and waste services	24,195	25,240	25,843	26,898	27,278	26,905	27,673
Educational services	24,105	25,937	26,232	26,894	26,441	27,263	27,260
Health care and social assistance.........................	35,599	36,104	36,284	37,279	38,303	39,151	40,330
Arts, entertainment, and recreation.......................	19,771	19,644	19,311	20,360	20,664	20,882	21,364
Accommodation and food services.........................	13,826	14,097	14,688	15,144	15,511	15,501	16,102
Other services, except public administration................	25,237	25,244	26,277	26,864	27,276	27,854	29,044
Government and government enterprises...........................	36,323	37,431	37,749	38,808	38,927	39,064	39,991

Table AR-10. Employment Characteristics by Family Type

(Number, percent.)

Family type and labor force status	2012 Total	2012 Families with own children under 18 years	2013 Total	2013 Families with own children under 18 years	2014 Total	2014 Families with own children under 18 years
All Families..	758,601	315,273	751,124	313,438	749,751	310,218
FAMILY TYPE AND LABOR FORCE STATUS						
Married-Couple Families................................	557,982	206,752	548,537	204,825	544,067	197,290
Both husband and wife in labor force............................	48.0	63.4	46.4	63.5	46.9	64.9
Husband in labor force, wife not in labor force	22.6	28.8	22.9	28.7	22.5	27.5
Wife in labor force, husband not in labor force	9.5	5.2	9.3	5.2	9.1	5.0
Both husband and wife not in labor force.........................	20.0	2.6	21.2	2.6	21.5	2.6
Other Families	200,619	108,521	202,587	108,613	205,684	112,928
Female householder, no husband present	74.9	77.0	74.1	75.7	74.0	75.6
In labor force	50.7	60.2	48.5	59.8	48.3	59.8
Not in labor force	24.2	16.7	25.6	15.8	25.6	15.8
Male householder, no wife present...........................	25.1	23.0	25.9	24.3	26.0	24.4
In labor force...	18.9	20.2	18.3	19.9	19.5	21.5
Not in labor force	6.2	2.9	7.6	4.4	6.6	3.0

Table AR-11. School Enrollment and Educational Attainment, 2014

(Number, percent.)

Item	State	U.S.
Enrollment		
Total population 3 years and over, enrolled in school................	746,254	82,063,714
Enrolled in nursery school or preschool (percent)	7.0	6.0
Enrolled in kindergarten (percent)...................................	5.3	5.1
Enrolled in elementary school, grades 1-8 (percent).................	41.4	40.2
Enrolled in high school, grades 9-12 (percent)......................	21.7	20.7
Enrolled in college or graduate school (percent)....................	24.7	28.0
Attainment		
Total population 25 years and over	1,968,414	213,725,624
Less than ninth grade (percent)	5.6	5.6
9th to 12th grade, no diploma (percent)	9.0	7.5
High school graduate, including equivalency (percent)...............	34.9	27.7
Some college, no degree (percent)	22.8	21.0
Associate's degree (percent)..	6.3	8.2
Bachelor's degree (percent)...	13.8	18.7
Graduate or professional degree (percent)..........................	7.5	11.4
High school graduate or higher (percent)	85.3	86.9
Bachelor's degree or higher (percent)	21.4	30.1

Table AR-12. Public School Characteristics and Educational Indicators

(Number, percent; data derived from National Center of Education Statistics.)

Item	State	U.S.
Public Schools, 2013–2014 (except where noted)		
Number of school districts...................................	288	18,194
Number of schools...	1,112	98,271
Number of students (in thousands)	490	50,045
Number of teachers (in thousands)	35	3,114
Student-teacher ratio	14.0	16.1
Expenditures per student (dollars), FY 2013.................	95,387	107,637
Four-year adjusted cohort graduation rate (ACGR)[1,2]	86.9	82.3
Students eligible for free or reduced-price lunch (in thousands)	300	25,596
English language learners (in thousands)	36	4,461
Students age 3 to 21 served under IDEA, part B (in thousands)	65	6,464

Public Schools by Type	Number	Percent of state public schools
Total number of schools..................................	1,112	100.0
Regular	1,073	96.5
Special education..	4	0.4
Vocational education.....................................	26	2.3
Alternative education....................................	9	0.8

NOTE: Every school is assigned only one school type based on its instructional emphasis.
[1]ACGR data represents a new method of calculating high-school completion rates and may not be comparable to previous years' data for Averaged Freshmen Graduation Rates (AFGR).
[2]The United States 4-year ACGRs were estimated using both the reported 4-year ACGR data from 49 states and the District of Columbia and using imputed data for Idaho. The estimate for American Indian/Alaska Native students also includes imputed data for Virginia.

Table AR-13. Reported Voting and Registration of the Voting-Age Population, November 2014

(Numbers in thousands, percent.)

Item	Total population	Total citizen population	Registered			Voted		
			Total registered	Percent registered (total population)	Percent registered (total citizen population)	Total voted	Percent voted (total population)	Percent voted (total citizen population)
U.S. Total	239,874	219,941	142,166	59.3	64.6	92,251	38.5	41.9
State Total............................	2,189	2,057	1,292	59.0	62.8	798	36.5	38.8
Sex								
Male.................................	1,058	993	592	55.9	59.6	364	34.4	36.7
Female	1,131	1,064	700	61.9	65.8	434	38.3	40.8
Race								
White alone.....................................	1,763	1,680	1,076	61.0	64.0	661	37.5	39.3
White, non-Hispanic alone	1,645	1,633	1,058	64.3	64.8	647	39.3	39.6
Black alone..........................	307	303	184	60.0	60.7	116	37.7	38.2
Asian alone	54	28	8	(B)	(B)	2	(B)	(B)
Hispanic (of any race)......................	136	55	20	(B)	(B)	14	(B)	(B)
White alone or in combination	1,795	1,712	1,087	60.6	63.5	670	37.3	39.1
Black alone or in combination..........	311	307	184	59.3	60.0	116	37.3	37.7
Asian alone or in combination..........	57	31	8	(B)	(B)	2	(B)	(B)
Age								
18 to 24 years..........................	242	230	116	48.2	50.7	36	14.7	15.5
25 to 34 years..........................	388	347	194	49.9	55.8	76	19.6	21.9
35 to 44 years..........................	352	313	202	57.4	64.5	127	36.2	40.8
45 to 64 years..........................	797	767	484	60.7	63.1	341	42.8	44.5
65 years and over	410	401	296	72.2	73.9	218	53.1	54.4

B = Base is less than 75,000 and therefore too small to show the derived measure.

Table AR-14. Crime

(Number, rate per 100,000. Data are derived from the FBI Uniform Crime Reports.)

Item	State			U.S.[1,2,3,4]		
	2013	2014	Percent change	2013	2014	Percent change
TOTAL POPULATION[5]..	2,959,373	2,966,369	0.2	316,128,839	318,857,056	0.9
VIOLENT CRIME						
Number........	13,191	14,243	8.0	1,163,146	1,165,383	0.2
Rate	445.7	480.1	7.7	367.9	365.5	-0.7
Murder and Nonnegligent Manslaughter						
Number........	159	165	3.8	14,196	14,249	0.4
Rate	5.4	5.6	3.7	4.5	4.5	-
Rape[6]						
Number........	1,423	1,763	X	108,612	116,645	X
Rate	48.1	59.4	X	34.4	36.6	X
Robbery						
Number........	2,258	2,050	-9.2	345,031	325,802	-5.6
Rate	76.3	69.1	-9.4	109.1	102.2	-6.3
Aggravated Assault						
Number........	9,781	10,265	4.9	724,149	741,291	2.4
Rate	330.5	346.0	4.7	229.1	232.5	1.5
PROPERTY CRIME						
Number........	106,613	99,018	-7.1	8,632,512	8,277,829	-4.1
Rate	3,602.6	3,338.0	-7.3	2,730.7	2,596.1	-4.9
Burglary						
Number........	30,485	24,790	-18.7	1,928,465	1,729,806	-10.3
Rate	1,030.1	835.7	-18.9	610.0	542.5	-11.1
Larceny-Theft						
Number........	70,450	68,627	-2.6	6,004,453	5,858,496	-2.4
Rate	2,380.6	2,313.5	-2.8	1,899.4	1,837.3	-3.3
Motor Vehicle Theft						
Number........	5,678	5,601	-1.4	699,594	689,527	-1.4
Rate	191.9	188.8	-1.6	221.3	216.2	-2.3

NOTE: Although arson data are included in the trend and clearance tables, sufficient data are not available to estimate totals for this offense. Therefore, no arson data are published in this table.
X = Not applicable.
- = Zero or rounds to zero.
[1]The crime figures have been adjusted.
[2]The data collection methodology for the offense of forcible rape used by the Minnesota state Uniform Crime Reporting (UCR) Program (with the exception of Minneapolis and St. Paul, Minnesota) does not comply with national UCR Program guidelines. Consequently, its figures for forcible rape and violent crime (of which forcible rape is a part) are not published in this table.
[3]Includes offenses reported by the Zoological Police and the Metro Transit Police.
[4]Because of changes in the state's reporting practices, figures are not comparable to previous years' data.
[5]Populations are U.S. Census Bureau provisional estimates as of July 1 of each year.
[6]The figures shown for the offense of rape were estimated using the revised Uniform Crime Reporting (UCR) definition of rape.

Table AR-15. State Government Finances, 2014

(Dollar amounts in thousands, percent distribution.)

Item	Dollars	Percent distribution
Total Revenue	23,417,228	100.0
General revenue	18,058,204	77.1
Intergovernmental revenue	6,096,896	26.0
Taxes	8,936,781	38.2
General sales	3,130,274	13.4
Selective sales	1,193,883	5.1
License taxes	368,622	1.6
Individual income tax	2,602,160	11.1
Corporate income tax	398,493	1.7
Other taxes	1,243,349	5.3
Current charges	2,200,450	9.4
Miscellaneous general revenue	824,077	3.5
Utility revenue	0	-
Liquor stores revenue	0	-
Insurance trust revenue[1]	5,359,024	22.9
Total Expenditure	20,410,423	100.0
Intergovernmental expenditure	5,199,089	25.5
Direct expenditure	15,211,334	74.5
Current operation	11,638,914	57.0
Capital outlay	1,088,469	5.3
Insurance benefits and repayments	1,852,440	9.1
Assistance and subsidies	491,271	2.4
Interest on debt	140,240	0.7
Exhibit: Salaries and wages	3,148,070	15.4
Total Expenditure	20,410,423	100.0
General expenditure	18,557,983	90.9
Intergovernmental expenditure	5,199,089	25.5
Direct expenditure	13,358,894	65.5
General expenditure, by function:		
Education	7,610,604	37.3
Public welfare	5,713,188	28.0
Hospitals	942,018	4.6
Health	305,095	1.5
Highways	1,372,565	6.7
Police protection	119,311	0.6
Correction	392,988	1.9
Natural resources	256,092	1.3
Parks and recreation	64,052	0.3
Governmental administration	631,150	3.1
Interest on general debt	140,240	0.7
Other and unallocable	1,010,680	5.0
Utility expenditure	0	-
Liquor stores expenditure	0	-
Insurance trust expenditure	1,852,440	9.1
Debt at End of Fiscal Year	4,533,255	X
Cash and Security Holdings	34,233,660	X

X = Not applicable.
- = Zero or rounds to zero.
[1]Within insurance trust revenue, net earnings of state retirement systems is a calculated statistic (the item code in the data file is X08), and thus can be positive or negative. Net earnings is the sum of earnings on investments plus gains on investments minus losses on investments. The change made in 2002 for asset valuation from book to market value in accordance with Statement 34 of the Governmental Accounting Standards Board is reflected in the calculated statistics.

Table AR-16. State Government Tax Collections, 2014

(Dollars in thousands, percent.)

Item	Dollars	Percent distribution
Total Taxes	8,936,781	100.0
Property taxes	1,077,377	12.1
Sales and gross receipts	4,324,157	48.4
General sales and gross receipts	3,130,274	35.0
Selective sales and gross receipts	1,193,883	13.4
Alcoholic beverages	51,618	0.6
Amusements	39,660	0.4
Insurance premiums	182,092	2.0
Motor fuels	454,909	5.1
Pari-mutuels	3,090	0.0
Public utilities	0	-
Tobacco products	225,809	2.5
Other selective sales	236,705	2.6
Licenses	368,622	4.1
Alcoholic beverages	4,187	-
Amusements	426	-
Corporations in general	27,999	0.3
Hunting and fishing	23,533	0.3
Motor vehicle	153,445	1.7
Motor vehicle operators	17,657	0.2
Public utilities	9,985	0.1
Occupation and business, NEC	129,711	1.5
Other licenses	1,679	-
Income taxes	3,000,653	33.6
Individual income	2,602,160	29.1
Corporation net income	398,493	4.5
Other taxes	165,972	1.9
Death and gift	3	-
Documentary and stock transfer	32,715	0.4
Severance	108,511	1.2
Taxes, NEC	24,743	0.3

- = Zero or rounds to zero.

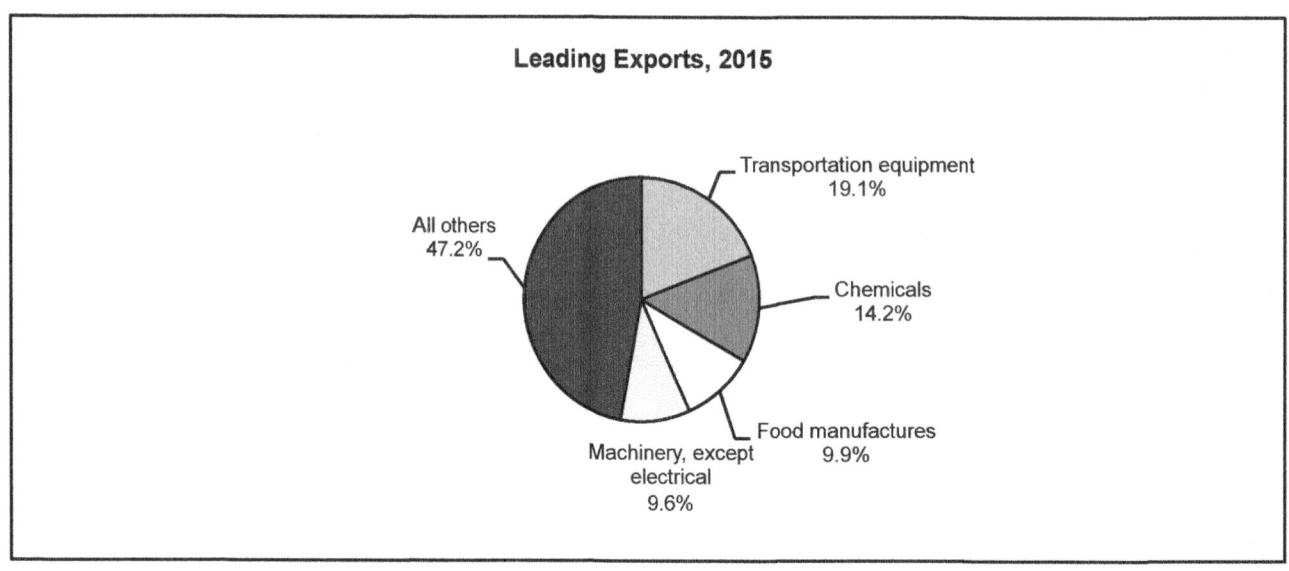

Leading Exports, 2015

Transportation equipment 19.1%

Chemicals 14.2%

Food manufactures 9.9%

Machinery, except electrical 9.6%

All others 47.2%

Facts and Figures

Location: Western United States; bordered on the N by Oregon, on the E by Nevada and Arizona, on the S by Mexico, and on the W by the Pacific Ocean

Area: 163,694 sq. mi. (423,970 sq. km.); rank—3rd

Population: 39,144,818 (2015 est.); rank—1st

Principal Cities: capital—Sacramento; largest—Los Angeles

Statehood: September 9, 1850; 31st state

U.S. Congress: 2 senators, 53 representatives

State Motto: *Eureka* ("I have found it")

State Song: "I Love You, California"

State Nickname: The Golden State

Abbreviations: CA; Calif.

State Symbols: flower—California poppy; tree—redwood; bird—California valley quail

At a Glance

- With an increase in population of 4.9 percent, California ranked 18th among the states in growth from 2010 to 2015.

- In 2014, California's median household income was $61,933, and 16.4 percent of the population lived below the poverty level.

- California's violent crime rate in 2014 was 396.1 per 100,000 population, compared to 365.5 for the entire nation.

- In 2015, California's unemployment rate of 6.2 percent ranked 8th in the nation.

- Approximately 14.7 percent of Californians self-identified their race as "Asian Alone" in 2015, which was the second highest in the country.

Table CA-1. Population by Age, Sex, Race, and Hispanic Origin

(Number, percent, except where noted.)

Sex, age, race, and Hispanic origin	2000	2010	2015[1]	Average annual percent change, 2010–2015
Total population	33,871,648	37,253,956	39,144,818	0.4
Percent of total U.S. population	12.0	12.1	12.2	X
Sex				
Male	16,874,892	18,517,830	19,443,068	0.3
Female	16,996,756	18,736,126	19,701,750	0.4
Age				
Under 5 years	2,486,981	2,531,333	2,508,752	-0.1
5 to 19 years	7,747,590	7,920,709	7,664,160	-0.2
20 to 64 years	20,041,419	22,555,400	23,783,152	0.4
65 years and over	3,595,658	4,246,514	5,188,754	1.4
Median age (years)	33.3	35.2	36.2	0.2
Race and Hispanic origin				
One race				
White	20,170,059	27,636,403	28,535,273	0.2
Black	2,263,882	2,486,549	2,552,858	0.2
American Indian and Alaska Native	333,346	622,107	648,172	0.3
Asian	3,697,513	5,038,123	5,736,988	0.9
Native Hawaiian or Other Pacific Islander	116,961	181,431	196,652	0.6
Two or more races	1,607,646	1,289,343	1,474,875	1.0
Hispanic (of any race)	10,966,556	14,440,187	15,184,548	0.4

X = Not applicable.
[1]Population figures for 2015 are July 1 estimates. The 2010 estimates are taken from the 2010 Census.

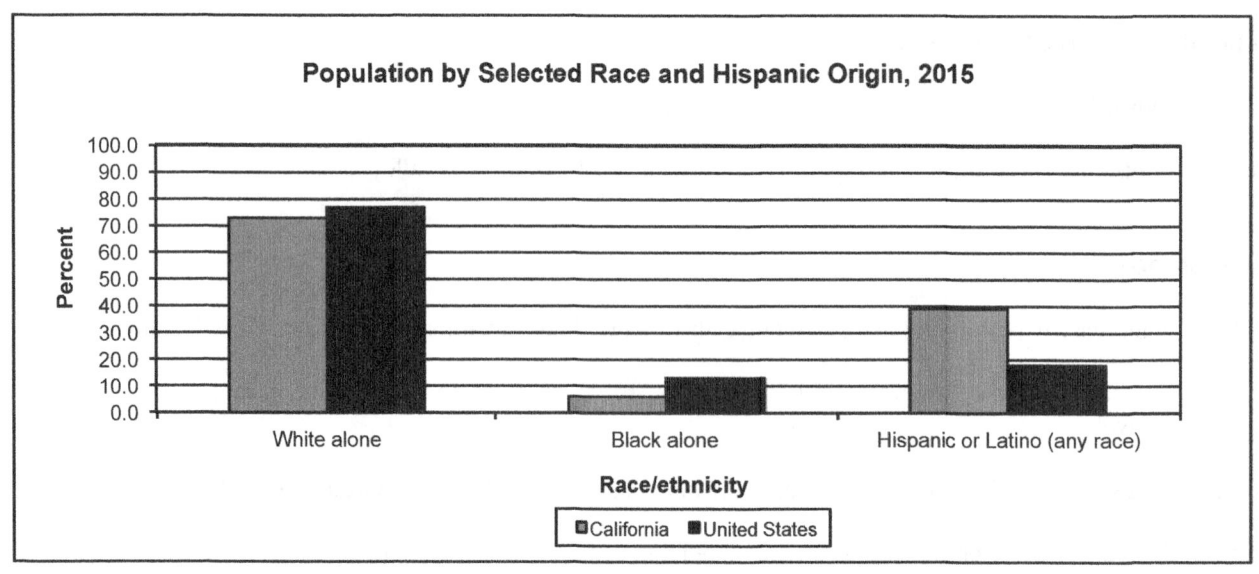

Population by Selected Race and Hispanic Origin, 2015

Table CA-2. Marital Status

(Number, percent distribution.)

Sex, age, race, and Hispanic origin	2000	2010	2014
Males, 15 Years and Over	12,844,669	14,662,335	15,026,838
Never married	33.8	39.8	40.0
Now married, except separated	54.1	48.2	48.0
SeparatedW	2.0	1.9	1.9
Widowed	2.2	2.1	2.1
Divorced	7.9	8.0	8.1
Females, 15 Years and Over	13,231,494	15,043,190	15,435,415
Never married	26.5	32.3	32.8
Now married, except separated	50.7	45.7	45.4
Separated	2.9	2.7	2.7
Widowed	8.9	8.1	8.0
Divorced	11.0	11.2	11.2

Table CA-3. Households and Housing Characteristics

(Number, percent, dollars.)

Item	2000	2010	2014	Average annual percent change, 2000–2014
Total Households...........	11,502,870	12,406,475	12,758,648	0.8
Family households	7,920,049	8,507,856	8,762,059	0.8
Married-couple family	5,877,084	6,082,566	6,239,143	0.4
Other family	2,042,965	2,425,290	2,522,916	1.7
Male householder, no wife present...........	594,455	736,626	772,276	2.1
Female householder, no husband present...........	1,448,510	1,688,664	1,750,640	1.5
Nonfamily households	3,582,821	3,898,619	3,996,589	0.8
Householder living alone...........	2,708,308	3,001,307	3,062,500	0.9
Householder not living alone...........	874,513	897,312	934,089	0.5
Housing Characteristics				
Total housing units...........	12,214,549	13,682,976	13,901,594	1.0
Occupied housing units	11,502,870	12,406,475	12,758,648	0.8
Owner occupied	6,546,334	6,903,175	6,855,688	0.3
Renter occupied	4,956,536	5,503,300	5,902,960	1.4
Average household size...........	2.87	2.94	2.98	0.3
Financial Characteristics				
Median gross rent of renter-occupied housing	747	1,163	1,268	5.0
Median monthly owner costs for housing units with a mortgage	1,478	2,242	2,068	2.9
Median value of owner-occupied housing units...........	211,500	370,900	412,700	6.8

Table CA-4. Migration, Origin, and Language

(Number, percent.)

Characteristic	State			U.S.		
	2013	2014	Percent change	2013	2014	Percent change
Residence 1 Year Ago						
Population 1 year and over	37,873,189	38,340,324	1.2	312,432,820	315,095,393	0.9
Same house...........	85.0	85.7	X	85.0	85.1	X
Different house in the U.S.	14.2	13.5	X	14.4	14.3	X
Same county...........	10.1	9.3	X	8.9	8.7	X
Different county	4.1	4.2	X	5.5	5.6	X
Same state	2.8	2.8	X	3.2	3.3	X
Different state	1.3	1.3	X	2.3	2.3	X
Abroad...........	0.8	0.8	X	0.6	0.6	X
Place of Birth						
Native born	28,021,321	28,290,101	1.0	274,780,773	276,465,262	0.6
Male	50.2	50.1	X	49.3	49.3	X
Female	49.8	49.9	X	50.7	50.7	X
Foreign born	10,311,200	10,512,399	2.0	41,348,066	42,391,794	2.5
Male	48.5	48.5	X	48.8	48.7	X
Female	51.5	51.5	X	51.2	51.3	X
Foreign born; naturalized U.S. citizen...........	5,006,979	5,154,783	3.0	19,294,710	19,984,738	3.6
Male	46.1	46.2	X	45.9	45.9	X
Female	53.9	53.8	X	54.1	54.1	X
Foreign born; not a U.S. citizen...........	5,304,221	5,357,616	1.0	22,053,356	22,407,056	1.6
Male	50.7	50.7	X	51.3	51.2	X
Female	49.3	49.3	X	48.7	48.8	X
Entered 2010 or later	6.6	8.6	X	9.7	12.3	X
Entered 2000 to 2009	24.6	24.3	X	29.4	28.6	X
Entered before 2000...........	68.8	67.1	X	61.0	59.1	X
World Region of Birth, Foreign						
Foreign-born population, excluding population born at sea	10,311,079	10,512,292	2.0	41,347,945	42,390,705	2.5
Europe	6.5	6.4	X	11.6	11.2	X
Asia...........	37.2	37.8	X	29.5	30.1	X
Africa...........	1.7	1.6	X	4.4	4.6	X
Oceania	0.7	0.7	X	0.5	0.6	X
Latin America...........	52.6	52.1	X	51.9	51.6	X
North America	1.3	1.3	X	2.0	1.9	X
Language Spoken at Home and Ability to Speak English						
Population 5 years and over...........	35,831,956	36,290,808	1.3	296,358,760	299,084,046	0.9
English only	56.2	56.1	X	79.2	78.9	X
Language other than English...........	43.8	43.9	X	20.8	21.1	X
Speaks English less than "very well"	18.9	18.5	X	8.5	8.6	X

X = Not applicable.
- = Zero or rounds to zero.

Table CA-5. Median Income and Poverty Status, 2014

(Number, percent, except as noted.)

Characteristic	State		U.S.	
	Number	Percent	Number	Percent
Median Income				
Households (dollars)...	61,933	X	53,657	X
Families (dollars)	71,015	X	65,910	X
Below Poverty Level (All People)	6,259,098	16.4	48,208,387	15.5
Sex				
Male.............................	2,883,050	15.3	21,590,918	14.2
Female	3,376,048	17.5	26,617,469	16.8
Age				
Under 18 years.............................	2,047,259	22.7	15,686,012	21.7
Related children under 18 years........................	2,007,029	22.4	15,372,705	21.3
18 to 64 years	3,692,707	15.3	28,267,482	14.6
65 years and over	519,132	10.6	4,254,893	9.5

X = Not applicable.

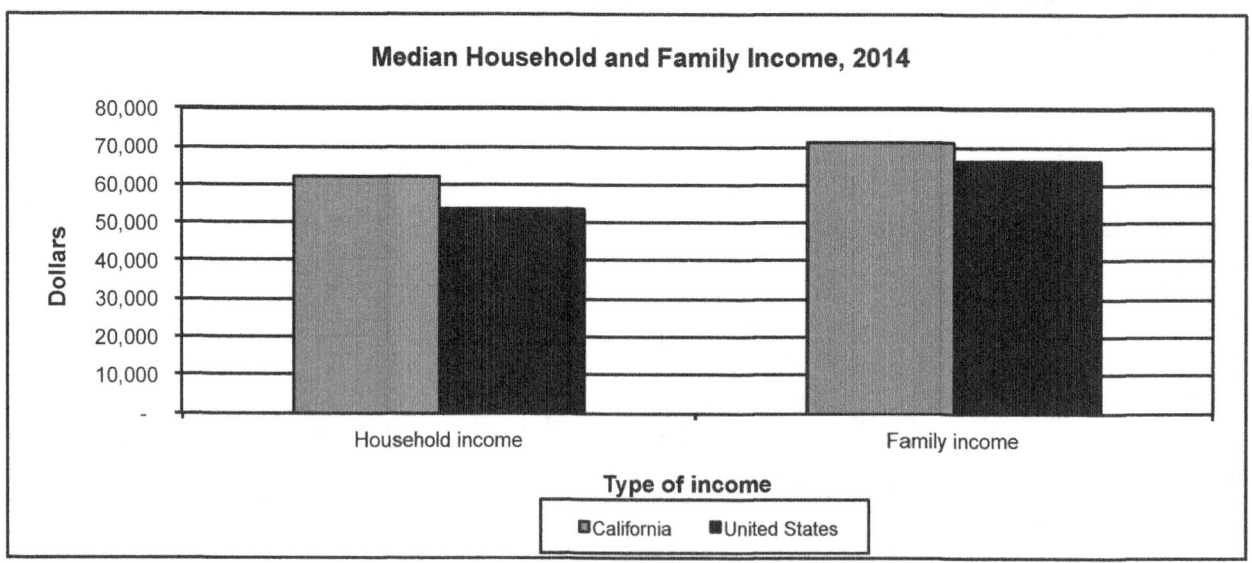

Median Household and Family Income, 2014

Table CA-6. Health Insurance Coverage Status for the Civilian Noninstitutionalized Population and Children Under 18 Years of Age

(Numbers in thousands, percent.)

Item	2006	2007	2008	2009	2010	2011	2012	2013	2014
Civilian Noninstitutionalized Population	36,208	36,295	36,161	36,377	36,816	37,162	37,524	37,832	38,297
Covered by Private or Public Insurance									
Number............................	29,417	29,682	29,730	29,818	29,990	30,436	30,815	31,331	33,531
Percent............................	81.2	81.8	82.2	82.0	81.5	81.9	82.1	82.8	87.6
Not Covered									
Number............................	6,791	6,613	6,431	6,559	6,835	6,726	6,709	6,500	4,767
Percent............................	18.8	18.2	17.8	18.0	18.5	18.1	17.9	17.2	12.4
Percent in the U.S. not covered..........................	15.8	15.3	15.1	15.1	15.5	15.1	14.8	14.5	11.7
Children Under 18 Years of Age	9,571	9,423	9,348	9,423	9,289	9,252	9,223	9,158	9,135
Covered by Private or Public Insurance									
Number............................	8,346	8,410	8,337	8,532	8,456	8,507	8,503	8,485	8,638
Percent............................	87.2	89.3	89.2	90.5	91.0	92.0	92.1	92.6	94.6
Not Covered									
Number............................	1,225	1,013	1,011	891	833	745	720	673	497
Percent............................	12.8	10.7	10.8	9.5	9.0	8.0	7.9	7.4	5.4
Percent in the U.S. not covered..........................	11.7	11.0	9.7	8.6	8.0	7.5	7.2	7.1	6.0

Table CA-7. Employment Status by Demographic Group, 2015

(Numbers in thousands, percent.)

Characteristic	Civilian noninstitutional population	Civilian labor force		Employed		Unemployed	
		Number	Percent of population	Number	Percent of population	Number	Percent of population
Total..............................	30,493	18,966	62.2	17,798	58.4	1,168	6.2
Sex							
Male..........................	14,886	10,379	69.7	9,751	65.5	628	6.1
Female	15,607	8,586	55.0	8,047	51.6	540	6.3
Race, Sex, and Hispanic Origin							
White	22,292	13,974	62.7	13,136	58.9	837	6.0
Male	10,997	7,810	71.0	7,360	66.9	450	5.8
Female	11,295	6,164	54.6	5,777	51.1	387	6.3
Black or African American..................	1,932	1,168	60.5	1,039	53.8	129	11.0
Male	916	582	63.5	520	56.8	62	10.6
Female	1,016	586	57.7	519	51.1	67	11.4
Hispanic or Latino ethnicity[1]	10,628	6,878	64.7	6,353	59.8	525	7.6
Male	5,297	3,956	74.7	3,675	69.4	282	7.1
Female	5,331	2,922	54.8	2,678	50.2	243	8.3
Age							
16 to 19 years.............	2,100	590	28.1	466	22.2	124	21.1
20 to 24 years.............	2,972	1,944	65.4	1,730	58.2	214	11.0
25 to 34 years.............	5,405	4,259	78.8	3,992	73.9	268	6.3
35 to 44 years.............	5,161	4,114	79.7	3,916	75.9	198	4.8
45 to 54 years.............	5,223	4,103	78.6	3,920	75.0	183	4.5
55 to 64 years.............	4,578	2,947	64.4	2,812	61.4	135	4.6
65 years and over	5,054	1,009	20.0	962	19.0	47	4.6

NOTE: Data in Table 7 are from the Current Population Survey (CPS) and do not match the estimates in Table 8. See notes and definitions for further information.
[1]May be of any race.

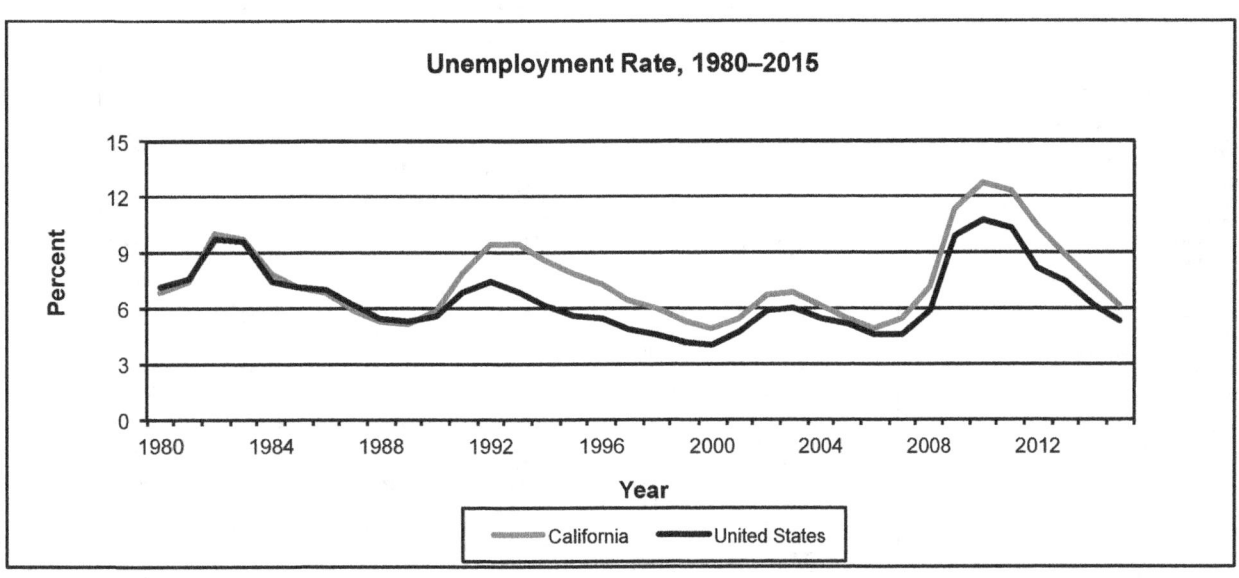

Table CA-8. Employment Status of the Civilian Noninstitutional Population Age 16 Years and Over

(Number, percent.)

Year	Civilian labor force	Civilian participation rate	Employed	Unemployed	Unemployment rate
2007..................	17,893,080	65.6	16,931,590	961,490	5.4
2008..................	18,178,123	65.8	16,854,482	1,323,641	7.3
2009..................	18,215,140	65.2	16,182,572	2,032,568	11.2
2010..................	18,336,271	64.2	16,091,945	2,244,326	12.2
2011..................	18,415,100	63.5	16,258,133	2,156,967	11.7
2012..................	18,551,413	63.1	16,627,835	1,923,578	10.4
2013..................	18,670,058	62.7	17,001,033	1,669,025	8.9
2014..................	18,827,925	62.4	17,418,042	1,409,883	7.5
2015..................	18,981,770	62.2	17,798,614	1,183,156	6.2

Table CA-9. Employment and Average Wages by Industry

(Estimates through 2010 are based on the 2007 North American Industry Classification System [NAICS]. Estimates from 2011 onward are based on the 2012 NAICS.)

Industry	2008	2009	2010	2011	2012	2013	2014
	Number of Jobs						
Wage and Salary Employment by Industry..................	16,110,889	15,233,396	15,047,583	15,204,435	15,443,410	16,225,103	16,688,639
Farm Wage and Salary Employment..........................	156,022	161,058	169,614	160,906	152,310	165,882	179,996
Nonfarm Wage and Salary Employment....................	15,954,867	15,072,338	14,877,969	15,043,529	15,291,100	16,059,221	16,508,643
Private wage and salary employment.......................	13,198,099	12,342,534	12,195,802	12,422,179	12,700,623	13,470,529	13,892,015
Forestry, fishing, and related activities........................	191,649	181,927	192,710	201,708	203,469	214,225	217,278
Mining..	26,281	23,952	24,427	26,341	28,033	27,873	28,586
Utilities..	58,774	60,033	57,126	58,304	59,382	58,937	57,874
Construction	818,256	650,724	585,150	590,831	609,226	659,968	693,580
Manufacturing..	1,422,847	1,284,607	1,241,475	1,246,809	1,252,809	1,253,079	1,271,636
Durable goods manufacturing..........................	898,963	800,113	770,103	777,998	781,436	780,445	793,732
Nondurable goods manufacturing.....................	523,884	484,494	471,372	468,811	471,373	472,634	477,904
Wholesale trade..	714,862	655,084	650,177	663,909	679,074	701,750	715,303
Retail trade..	1,666,081	1,546,001	1,538,490	1,559,965	1,584,601	1,617,740	1,647,037
Transportation and warehousing...........................	453,409	420,712	414,620	420,114	429,625	445,135	466,206
Information..	464,230	435,783	427,352	429,627	434,780	448,765	461,361
Finance and insurance	591,900	558,634	536,180	544,545	555,424	552,710	550,590
Real estate and rental and leasing...........................	286,684	267,267	261,542	258,009	258,077	267,333	271,909
Professional, scientific, and technical services	1,107,746	1,040,459	1,037,800	1,074,788	1,116,929	1,153,603	1,185,512
Management of companies and enterprises..................	206,764	198,742	192,985	199,149	203,448	218,846	227,011
Administrative and waste services............................	959,603	854,098	868,144	890,638	942,434	990,012	1,036,072
Educational services	326,221	335,608	338,629	349,487	358,825	367,262	372,932
Health care and social assistance...........................	1,443,788	1,470,049	1,502,221	1,527,790	1,559,226	1,982,552	2,049,056
Arts, entertainment, and recreation.........................	258,853	249,738	250,178	255,015	260,723	272,611	282,318
Accommodation and food services...........................	1,329,333	1,270,556	1,272,004	1,301,337	1,347,228	1,414,682	1,486,721
Other services, except public administration.................	870,818	838,560	804,592	823,813	817,310	823,446	871,033
Government and government enterprises........................	2,756,768	2,729,804	2,682,167	2,621,350	2,590,477	2,588,692	2,616,628
	Dollars						
Average Wages and Salaries by Industry	52,474	52,641	54,355	56,097	58,259	57,608	59,391
Average Farm Wages and Salaries	32,196	33,633	31,788	29,768	25,973	38,119	30,913
Average Nonfarm Wages and Salaries	52,672	52,844	54,613	56,379	58,581	57,810	59,702
Average private wages and salaries...........................	52,262	52,307	54,298	56,170	58,635	57,596	59,461
Forestry, fishing, and related activities........................	22,278	22,579	23,173	24,053	25,019	25,774	26,580
Mining..	118,023	114,505	130,923	129,702	135,591	136,062	139,017
Utilities..	96,972	100,935	103,261	108,002	111,080	117,409	118,061
Construction	55,127	55,846	55,814	57,238	59,070	59,152	60,245
Manufacturing..	67,279	69,765	74,165	76,527	79,122	79,474	82,931
Durable goods manufacturing..........................	75,953	77,579	85,553	88,777	90,699	90,291	94,948
Nondurable goods manufacturing.....................	52,396	56,860	55,560	56,199	59,930	61,612	62,972
Wholesale trade..	64,144	63,855	65,842	68,418	70,078	70,414	73,378
Retail trade..	31,597	31,114	31,923	32,639	33,708	33,499	34,241
Transportation and warehousing...........................	47,251	47,191	48,557	49,951	51,131	51,944	52,695
Information..	92,922	92,646	101,563	107,712	114,823	133,886	137,799
Finance and insurance	93,323	89,206	93,938	97,258	103,042	103,372	109,350
Real estate and rental and leasing...........................	50,237	48,526	49,852	52,639	55,728	57,039	60,311
Professional, scientific, and technical services	86,900	87,010	91,051	94,848	103,795	98,978	105,145
Management of companies and enterprises..................	92,037	90,436	97,434	103,817	108,749	112,989	121,734
Administrative and waste services............................	36,602	36,916	38,007	39,229	40,831	40,067	40,718
Educational services	37,941	39,081	41,151	42,187	42,778	43,653	44,626
Health care and social assistance...........................	50,943	52,548	53,445	54,684	55,752	47,382	47,855
Arts, entertainment, and recreation.........................	52,827	52,078	53,203	55,439	56,522	55,494	57,462
Accommodation and food services...........................	21,205	20,815	21,455	22,154	22,558	22,455	23,449
Other services, except public administration.................	28,655	28,515	29,752	30,353	31,378	32,001	32,509
Government and government enterprises........................	54,632	55,274	56,041	57,366	58,318	58,922	60,983

Table CA-10. Employment Characteristics by Family Type

(Number, percent.)

Family type and labor force status	2012 Total	2012 Families with own children under 18 years	2013 Total	2013 Families with own children under 18 years	2014 Total	2014 Families with own children under 18 years
All Families..	8,585,787	4,046,765	8,645,970	3,984,574	8,708,774	3,976,389
FAMILY TYPE AND LABOR FORCE STATUS						
Married-Couple Families..............................	6,104,099	2,787,943	6,160,314	2,753,934	6,185,858	2,754,933
Both husband and wife in labor force................	51.3	60.7	50.5	60.2	50.0	59.9
Husband in labor force, wife not in labor force.....	25.9	33.3	25.8	33.8	26.5	34.0
Wife in labor force, husband not in labor force.....	7.3	4.0	7.4	3.8	7.6	4.1
Both husband and wife not in labor force...........	15.5	2.0	15.7	2.0	15.9	2.0
Other Families	2,481,688	1,258,822	2,485,656	1,230,640	2,522,916	1,221,456
Female householder, no husband present............	69.4	72.2	69.5	72.4	69.4	71.9
In labor force	48.9	57.6	48.2	56.8	48.0	56.9
Not in labor force	20.5	14.6	21.3	15.6	21.4	15.0
Male householder, no wife present...................	30.6	27.8	30.5	27.6	30.6	28.1
In labor force..	24.9	25.5	24.5	25.1	24.8	25.6
Not in labor force	5.7	2.3	6.0	2.5	5.8	2.5

Table CA-11. School Enrollment and Educational Attainment, 2014

(Number, percent.)

Item	State	U.S.
Enrollment		
Total population 3 years and over, enrolled in school.............	10,531,321	82,063,714
Enrolled in nursery school or preschool (percent).................	5.5	6.0
Enrolled in kindergarten (percent)................................	4.8	5.1
Enrolled in elementary school, grades 1-8 (percent)...............	38.3	40.2
Enrolled in high school, grades 9-12 (percent)...................	21.0	20.7
Enrolled in college or graduate school (percent).................	30.3	28.0
Attainment		
Total population 25 years and over	25,654,292	213,725,624
Less than ninth grade (percent)..................................	10.0	5.6
9th to 12th grade, no diploma (percent)	7.9	7.5
High school graduate, including equivalency (percent)............	20.9	27.7
Some college, no degree (percent)	21.7	21.0
Associate's degree (percent).....................................	7.8	8.2
Bachelor's degree (percent)......................................	20.0	18.7
Graduate or professional degree (percent)........................	11.8	11.4
High school graduate or higher (percent)	82.1	86.9
Bachelor's degree or higher (percent)............................	31.7	30.1

Table CA-12. Public School Characteristics and Educational Indicators

(Number, percent; data derived from National Center of Education Statistics.)

Item	State	U.S.
Public Schools, 2013–2014 (except where noted)		
Number of school districts.......................................	1,172	18,194
Number of schools..	10,276	98,271
Number of students (in thousands)	6,313	50,045
Number of teachers (in thousands)	260	3,114
Student-teacher ratio	24.3	16.1
Expenditures per student (dollars), FY 2013......................	92,587	107,637
Four-year adjusted cohort graduation rate (ACGR)[1,2]	81.0	82.3
Students eligible for free or reduced-price lunch (in thousands) ...	3610	25,596
English language learners (in thousands)	1393	4,461
Students age 3 to 21 served under IDEA, part B (in thousands)	699	6,464

Public Schools by Type	Number	Percent of state public schools
Total number of schools..	10,276	100.0
Regular	8,811	85.7
Special education..	151	1.5
Vocational education...	76	0.7
Alternative education..	1,238	12.0

NOTE: Every school is assigned only one school type based on its instructional emphasis.
[1]ACGR data represents a new method of calculating high-school completion rates and may not be comparable to previous years' data for Averaged Freshmen Graduation Rates (AFGR).
[2]The United States 4-year ACGRs were estimated using both the reported 4-year ACGR data from 49 states and the District of Columbia and using imputed data for Idaho. The estimate for American Indian/Alaska Native students also includes imputed data for Virginia.

Table CA-13. Reported Voting and Registration of the Voting-Age Population, November 2014

(Numbers in thousands, percent.)

Item	Total population	Total citizen population	Registered			Voted		
			Total registered	Percent registered (total population)	Percent registered (total citizen population)	Total voted	Percent voted (total population)	Percent voted (total citizen population)
U.S. Total	239,874	219,941	142,166	59.3	64.6	92,251	38.5	41.9
State Total.............................	29,030	24,455	14,113	48.6	57.7	8,949	30.8	36.6
Sex								
Male..........	14,156	11,811	6,622	46.8	56.1	4,240	30.0	35.9
Female	14,874	12,645	7,491	50.4	59.2	4,708	31.7	37.2
Race								
White alone..........	21,429	18,060	10,753	50.2	59.5	7,093	33.1	39.3
White, non-Hispanic alone	12,326	11,907	7,830	63.5	65.8	5,551	45.0	46.6
Black alone..........	1,846	1,787	1,043	56.5	58.4	535	29.0	29.9
Asian alone	4,409	3,486	1,628	36.9	46.7	933	21.2	26.8
Hispanic (of any race).........	10,023	6,859	3,294	32.9	48.0	1,707	17.0	24.9
White alone or in combination	21,993	18,565	11,107	50.5	59.8	7,252	33.0	39.1
Black alone or in combination..........	1,997	1,913	1,134	56.8	59.3	570	28.5	29.8
Asian alone or in combination..........	4,598	3,660	1,742	37.9	47.6	986	21.5	27.0
Age								
18 to 24 years.........	4,129	3,708	1,438	34.8	38.8	591	14.3	15.9
25 to 34 years.........	5,288	4,242	2,082	39.4	49.1	917	17.3	21.6
35 to 44 years.........	5,025	3,845	2,117	42.1	55.1	1,172	23.3	30.5
45 to 64 years.........	9,672	8,163	5,377	55.6	65.9	3,712	38.4	45.5
65 years and over	4,916	4,498	3,099	63.0	68.9	2,558	52.0	56.9

Table CA-14. Crime

(Number, rate per 100,000. Data are derived from the FBI Uniform Crime Reports.)

Item	State			U.S. [1,2,3,4]		
	2014	2014	Percent change	2013	2014	Percent change
TOTAL POPULATION[5]..........	38,332,521	38,802,500	1.2	316,128,839	318,857,056	0.9
VIOLENT CRIME						
Number..........	151,879	153,709	1.2	1,163,146	1,165,383	0.2
Rate	396.2	396.1	-	367.9	365.5	-0.7
Murder and Nonnegligent Manslaughter						
Number..........	1,746	1,699	-2.7	14,196	14,249	0.4
Rate	4.6	4.4	-4.3	4.5	4.5	-
Rape[6]						
Number..........	9,714	11,527	X	108,612	116,645	X
Rate	25.3	29.7	X	34.4	36.6	X
Robbery						
Number..........	53,640	48,680	-9.2	345,031	325,802	-5.6
Rate	139.9	125.5	-10.3	109.1	102.2	-6.3
Aggravated Assault						
Number..........	89,029	91,803	3.1	724,149	741,291	2.4
Rate	232.3	236.6	1.9	229.1	232.5	1.5
PROPERTY CRIME						
Number..........	1,018,907	947,192	-7.0	8,632,512	8,277,829	-4.1
Rate	2,658.1	2,441.1	-8.2	2,730.7	2,596.1	-4.9
Burglary						
Number..........	232,058	202,670	-12.7	1,928,465	1,729,806	-10.3
Rate	605.4	522.3	-13.7	610.0	542.5	-11.1
Larceny-Theft						
Number..........	621,557	592,670	-4.6	6,004,453	5,858,496	-2.4
Rate	1,621.5	1,527.4	-5.8	1,899.4	1,837.3	-3.3
Motor Vehicle Theft						
Number..........	165,292	151,852	-8.1	699,594	689,527	-1.4
Rate	431.2	391.3	-9.3	221.3	216.2	-2.3

NOTE: Although arson data are included in the trend and clearance tables, sufficient data are not available to estimate totals for this offense. Therefore, no arson data are published in this table.
X = Not applicable.
- = Zero or rounds to zero.
[1]The crime figures have been adjusted.
[2]The data collection methodology for the offense of forcible rape used by the Minnesota state Uniform Crime Reporting (UCR) Program (with the exception of Minneapolis and St. Paul, Minnesota) does not comply with national UCR Program guidelines. Consequently, its figures for forcible rape and violent crime (of which forcible rape is a part) are not published in this table.
[3]Includes offenses reported by the Zoological Police and the Metro Transit Police.
[4]Because of changes in the state's reporting practices, figures are not comparable to previous years' data.
[5]Populations are U.S. Census Bureau provisional estimates as of July 1 of each year.
[6]The figures shown for the offense of rape were estimated using the revised Uniform Crime Reporting (UCR) definition of rape.

Table CA-15. State Government Finances, 2014

(Dollar amounts in thousands, percent distribution.)

Item	Dollars	Percent distribution
Total Revenue	353,368,448	100.0
General revenue	230,741,509	65.3
Intergovernmental revenue	63,516,604	18.0
Taxes	138,069,870	39.1
General sales	37,224,077	10.5
Selective sales	12,777,976	3.6
License taxes	8,922,534	2.5
Individual income tax	67,995,659	19.2
Corporate income tax	8,858,498	2.5
Other taxes	2,291,126	0.6
Current charges	19,371,442	5.5
Miscellaneous general revenue	9,783,593	2.8
Utility revenue	993,952	0.3
Liquor stores revenue	0	-
Insurance trust revenue[1]	121,632,987	34.4
Total Expenditure	284,555,886	100.0
Intergovernmental expenditure	91,869,167	32.3
Direct expenditure	192,686,719	67.7
Current operation	123,718,282	43.5
Capital outlay	9,199,016	3.2
Insurance benefits and repayments	47,787,558	16.8
Assistance and subsidies	4,532,899	1.6
Interest on debt	7,448,964	2.6
Exhibit: Salaries and wages	30,734,262	10.8
Total Expenditure	284,555,886	100.0
General expenditure	234,831,197	82.5
Intergovernmental expenditure	91,869,167	32.3
Direct expenditure	142,962,030	50.2
General expenditure, by function:		
Education	79,812,818	28.0
Public welfare	83,486,422	29.3
Hospitals	9,822,407	3.5
Health	8,842,113	3.1
Highways	12,631,699	4.4
Police protection	1,671,332	0.6
Correction	8,949,885	3.1
Natural resources	3,719,571	1.3
Parks and recreation	548,053	0.2
Governmental administration	7,973,800	2.8
Interest on general debt	7,205,964	2.5
Other and unallocable	10,167,133	3.6
Utility expenditure	1,937,131	0.7
Liquor stores expenditure	0	-
Insurance trust expenditure	47,787,558	16.8
Debt at End of Fiscal Year	156,807,868	X
Cash and Security Holdings	639,185,874	X

X = Not applicable.
- = Zero or rounds to zero.
[1]Within insurance trust revenue, net earnings of state retirement systems is a calculated statistic (the item code in the data file is X08), and thus can be positive or negative. Net earnings is the sum of earnings on investments plus gains on investments minus losses on investments. The change made in 2002 for asset valuation from book to market value in accordance with Statement 34 of the Governmental Accounting Standards Board is reflected in the calculated statistics.

Table CA-16. State Government Tax Collections, 2014

(Dollars in thousands, percent.)

Item	Dollars	Percent distribution
Total Taxes	138,069,870	100.0
Property taxes	2,176,236	1.6
Sales and gross receipts	50,002,053	36.2
General sales and gross receipts	37,224,077	27.0
Selective sales and gross receipts	12,777,976	9.3
Alcoholic beverages	354,297	0.3
Amusements	0	-
Insurance premiums	2,362,738	1.7
Motor fuels	6,063,356	4.4
Pari-mutuels	13,899	-
Public utilities	663,448	0.5
Tobacco products	833,126	0.6
Other selective sales	2,487,112	1.8
Licenses	8,922,534	6.5
Alcoholic beverages	55,550	-
Amusements	15,457	-
Corporations in general	59,777	-
Hunting and fishing	101,237	0.1
Motor vehicle	3,745,377	2.7
Motor vehicle operators	280,038	0.2
Public utilities	388,443	0.3
Occupation and business, NEC	4,269,033	3.1
Other licenses	7,622	-
Income taxes	76,854,157	55.7
Individual income	67,995,659	49.2
Corporation net income	8,858,498	6.4
Other taxes	114,890	0.1
Death and gift	0	-
Documentary and stock transfer	0	-
Severance	38,686	-
Taxes, NEC	76,204	0.1

- = Zero or rounds to zero.

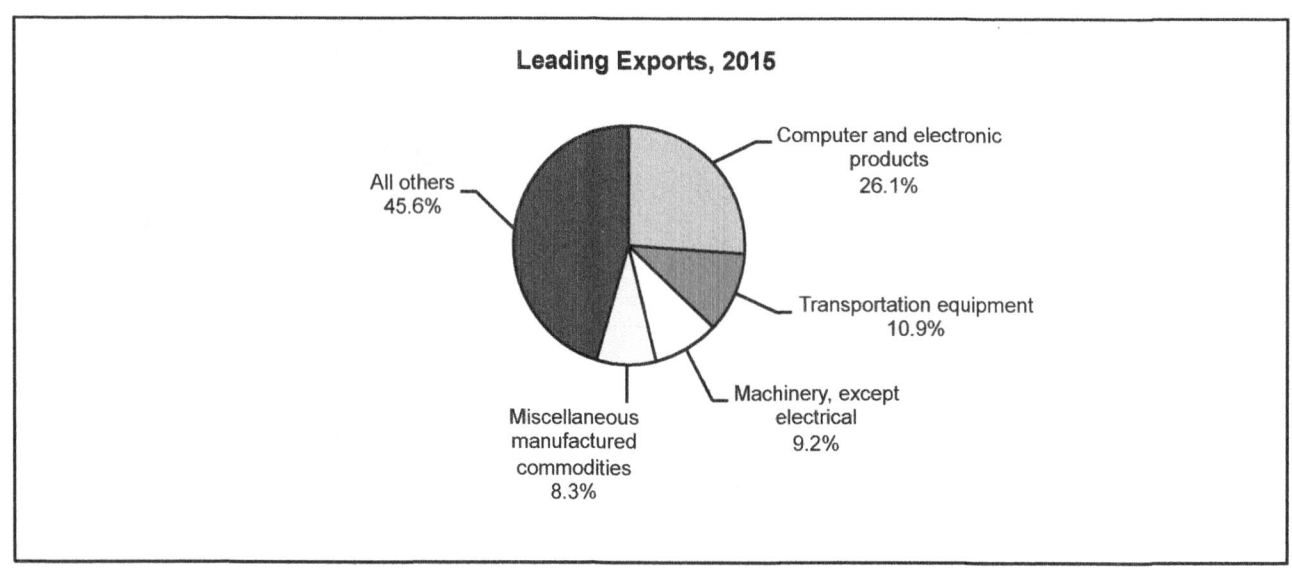

Leading Exports, 2015

Computer and electronic products 26.1%

Transportation equipment 10.9%

Machinery, except electrical 9.2%

Miscellaneous manufactured commodities 8.3%

All others 45.6%

COLORADO

Facts and Figures

Location: Western United States; bordered on the N by Wyoming and Nebraska, on the E by Nebraska and Kansas, on the S by Oklahoma and New Mexico, and on the W by Utah; Colorado is one of the Four Corner states—at its SW corner it touches Arizona, New Mexico, and Utah

Area: 104,093 sq. mi. (269,601 sq. km.); rank—8th

Population: 5,456,574 (2015 est.); rank—22nd

Principal Cities: capital—Denver; largest—Denver

Statehood: August 1, 1876; 38th state

U.S. Congress: 2 senators, 7 representatives

State Motto: *Nil sine numine* ("Nothing without providence")

State Songs: "Where the Columbines Grow"; "Rocky Mountain High"

State Nicknames: The Centennial State; Colorful Colorado

Abbreviations: CO; Colo.

State Symbols: flower—Rocky Mountain columbine; tree—Colorado blue spruce; bird—lark bunting

At a Glance

- With an increase in population of 8.1 percent, Colorado ranked 4th among the states in growth from 2010 to 2015.

- In 2014, 10.3 percent of Coloradans did not have health insurance, compared to 11.7 percent of the total U.S. population.

- The birth rate in Colorado in 2015 was 12.3 per 1,000 population, slightly less than the U.S. average of 12.5 births.

- In Colorado, 12.0 percent of the total population and 15.4 percent of persons under 18 years old lived below the poverty level in 2014, compared to nationwide poverty levels of 15.5 percent and 21.7 percent, respectively.

Table CO-1. Population by Age, Sex, Race, and Hispanic Origin

(Number, percent, except where noted.)

Sex, age, race, and Hispanic origin	2000	2010	2015[1]	Average annual percent change, 2010–2015
Total Population..	4,301,261	5,029,196	5,456,574	0.6
Percent of total U.S. population	1.5	1.6	1.7	X
Sex				
Male...	2,165,983	2,520,662	2,743,763	0.6
Female...	2,135,278	2,508,534	2,712,811	0.6
Age				
Under 5 years...	297,505	343,960	335,607	-0.2
5 to 19 years..	927,163	1,020,732	1,062,473	0.3
20 to 64 years...	2,660,520	3,114,879	3,346,869	0.5
65 years and over	416,073	549,625	711,625	1.9
Median age (years)...	34.3	36.1	36.5	0.1
Race and Hispanic Origin				
One race				
White	3,560,005	4,450,623	4,776,848	0.5
Black..	165,063	214,919	245,197	0.9
American Indian and Alaska Native	44,241	78,144	86,567	0.7
Asian...	95,213	144,819	176,793	1.4
Native Hawaiian or				
Other Pacific Islander.................................	4,621	8,420	10,525	1.6
Two or more races	122,187	132,271	160,644	1.4
Hispanic (of any race).......................................	735,601	1,078,225	1,164,274	0.5

X = Not applicable.
[1]Population figures for 2015 are July 1 estimates. The 2010 estimates are taken from the 2010 Census.

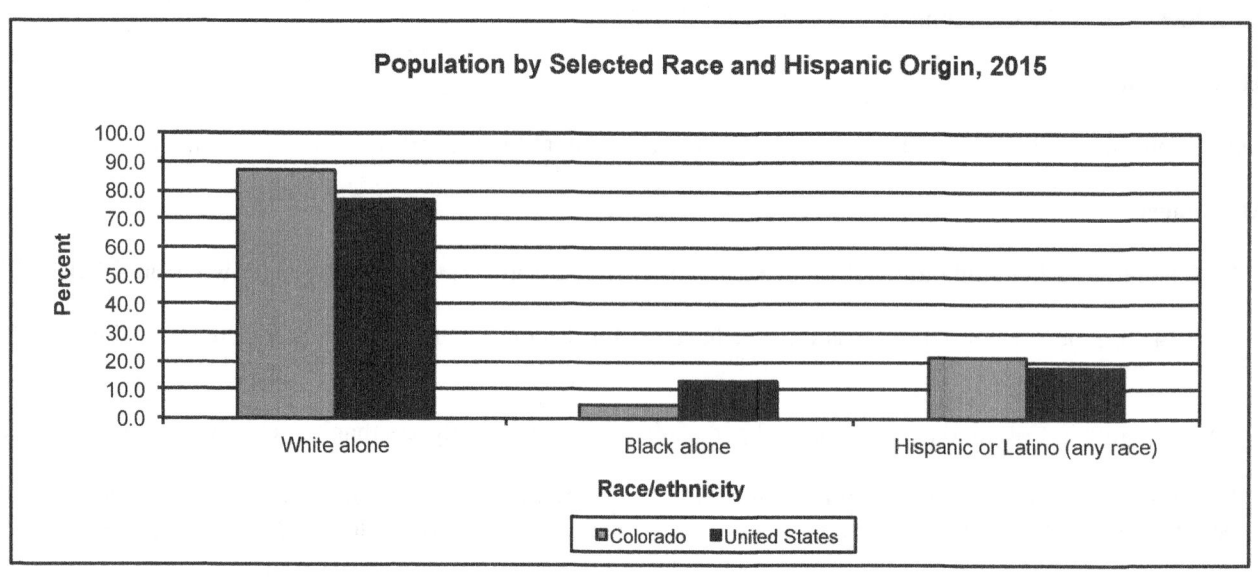

Table CO-2. Marital Status

(Number, percent distribution.)

Sex, age, race, and Hispanic origin	2000	2010	2014
Males, 15 Years and Over	1,694,635	2,004,303	2,078,151
Never married	30.5	34.4	34.7
Now married, except separated............................	56.6	51.7	51.5
Separated..	1.4	1.6	1.4
Widowed..	1.9	2.0	2.1
Divorced..	9.6	10.3	10.3
Females, 15 Years and Over	1,690,734	2,017,425	2,084,638
Never married	23.4	26.9	27.3
Now married, except separated............................	54.7	50.8	50.4
Separated..	1.8	2.0	1.9
Widowed..	7.6	7.0	6.9
Divorced..	12.5	13.3	13.6

Table CO-3. Households and Housing Characteristics

(Number, percent, dollars.)

Item	2000	2010	2014	Average annual percent change, 2000–2014
Total Households...	1,658,238	1,960,585	2,039,592	1.6
Family households	1,084,461	1,258,885	1,315,283	1.5
Married-couple family	858,671	959,624	1,005,726	1.2
Other family	225,790	299,261	309,557	2.6
Male householder, no wife present.............................	66,811	90,518	99,135	3.5
Female householder, no husband present......................	158,979	208,743	210,422	2.3
Nonfamily households	573,777	701,700	724,309	1.9
Householder living alone...	435,778	555,080	559,912	2.0
Householder not living alone......................................	137,999	146,620	164,397	1.4
Housing Characteristics				
Total housing units...	1,808,037	2,214,262	2,276,280	1.8
Occupied housing units	1,658,238	1,960,585	2,039,592	1.6
Owner occupied	1,116,173	1,292,792	1,302,533	1.2
Renter occupied	542,101	667,793	737,059	2.6
Average household size...	2.53	2.52	2.57	0.1
Financial Characteristics				
Median gross rent of renter-occupied housing	671	863	1,020	3.7
Median monthly owner costs for housing units with a mortgage	1,197	1,590	1,536	2.0
Median value of owner-occupied housing units................	166,600	236,600	255,200	3.8

Table CO-4. Migration, Origin, and Language

(Number, percent.)

Characteristic	State 2013	State 2014	State Percent change	U.S. 2013	U.S. 2014	U.S. Percent change
Residence 1 Year Ago						
Population 1 year and over	5,206,012	5,293,943	1.7	312,432,820	315,095,393	0.9
Same house	80.4	80.5	X	85.0	85.1	X
Different house in the U.S.	18.9	18.8	X	14.4	14.3	X
Same county	10.1	9.5	X	8.9	8.7	X
Different county	8.9	9.3	X	5.5	5.6	X
Same state	4.9	5.2	X	3.2	3.3	X
Different state	4.0	4.1	X	2.3	2.3	X
Abroad	0.7	0.6	X	0.6	0.6	X
Place of Birth						
Native born	4,767,733	4,817,622	1.0	274,780,773	276,465,262	0.6
Male..	50.4	50.4	X	49.3	49.3	X
Female..	49.6	49.6	X	50.7	50.7	X
Foreign born	500,634	538,244	7.5	41,348,066	42,391,794	2.5
Male..	48.7	49.6	X	48.8	48.7	X
Female..	51.3	50.4	X	51.2	51.3	X
Foreign born; naturalized U.S. citizen..	197,600	214,373	8.5	19,294,710	19,984,738	3.6
Male..	45.7	45.5	X	45.9	45.9	X
Female..	54.3	54.5	X	54.1	54.1	X
Foreign born; not a U.S. citizen...	303,034	323,871	6.9	22,053,356	22,407,056	1.6
Male..	50.6	52.3	X	51.3	51.2	X
Female..	49.4	47.7	X	48.7	48.8	X
Entered 2010 or later	9.4	12.0	X	9.7	12.3	X
Entered 2000 to 2009	32.1	31.3	X	29.4	28.6	X
Entered before 2000...	58.5	56.7	X	61.0	59.1	X
World Region of Birth, Foreign						
Foreign-born population, excluding population born at sea	500,634	538,244	7.5	41,347,945	42,390,705	2.5
Europe	14.2	14.6	X	11.6	11.2	X
Asia...	22.7	22.7	X	29.5	30.1	X
Africa	5.8	6.5	X	4.4	4.6	X
Oceania	0.6	0.7	X	0.5	0.6	X
Latin America...	53.4	52.8	X	51.9	51.6	X
North America..	3.3	2.6	X	2.0	1.9	X
Language Spoken at Home and Ability to Speak English						
Population 5 years and over..	4,934,794	5,023,808	1.8	296,358,760	299,084,046	0.9
English only	83.3	82.8	X	79.2	78.9	X
Language other than English..	16.7	17.2	X	20.8	21.1	X
Speaks English less than "very well"	6.2	6.2	X	8.5	8.6	X

X = Not applicable.
- = Zero or rounds to zero.

Table CO-5. Median Income and Poverty Status, 2014

(Number, percent, except as noted.)

Characteristic	State		U.S.	
	Number	Percent	Number	Percent
Median Income				
Households (dollars)...	61,303	X	53,657	X
Families (dollars)	75,405	X	65,910	X
Below Poverty Level (All People)	630,786	16.4	48,208,387	15.5
Sex				
Male..	293,198	15.3	21,590,918	14.2
Female	337,588	17.5	26,617,469	16.8
Age				
Under 18 years..	190,045	22.7	15,686,012	21.7
Related children under 18 years...	185,393	22.4	15,372,705	21.3
18 to 64 years...	393,728	15.3	28,267,482	14.6
65 years and over	47,013	10.6	4,254,893	9.5

X = Not applicable.

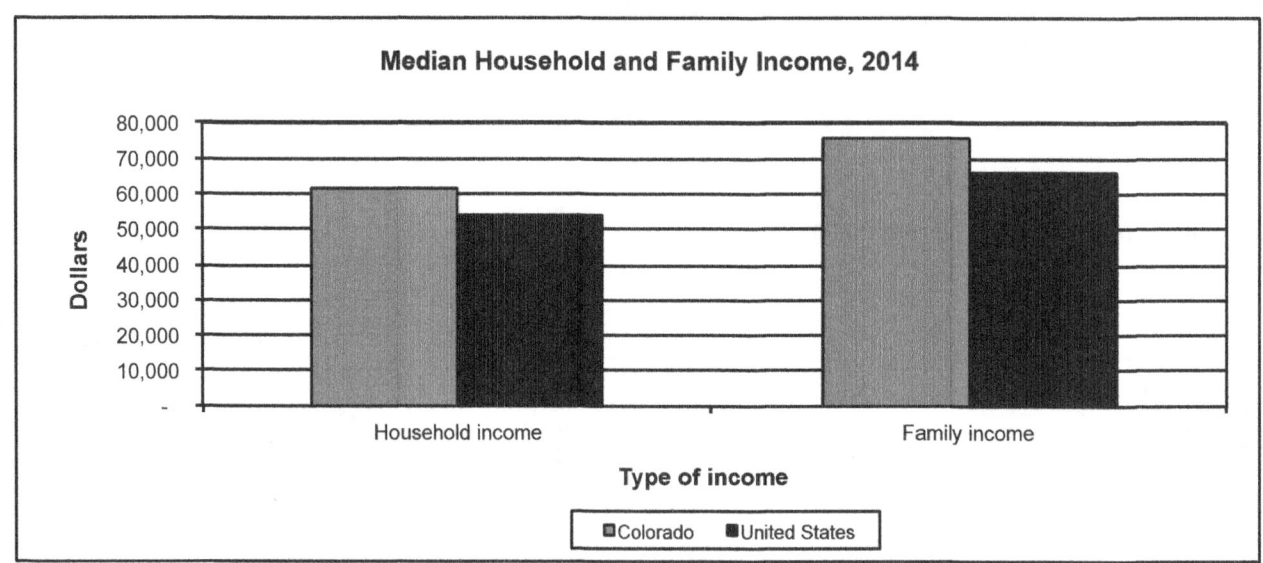

Median Household and Family Income, 2014

Table CO-6. Health Insurance Coverage Status for the Civilian Noninstitutionalized Population and Children Under 18 Years of Age

(Numbers in thousands, percent.)

Item	2006	2007	2008	2009	2010	2011	2012	2013	2014
Civilian Noninstitutionalized Population	4,803	4,877	4,853	4,930	4,957	5,025	5,095	5,173	5,266
Covered by Private or Public Insurance									
Number..	3,977	4,077	4,020	4,152	4,168	4,265	4,344	4,444	4,723
Percent..	82.8	83.6	82.8	84.2	84.1	84.9	85.3	85.9	89.7
Not Covered									
Number..	826	801	833	778	789	760	751	729	543
Percent..	17.2	16.4	17.2	15.8	15.9	15.1	14.7	14.1	10.3
Percent in the U.S. not covered..	15.8	15.3	15.1	15.1	15.5	15.1	14.8	14.5	11.7
Children Under 18 Years of Age	1,209	1,208	1,204	1,225	1,226	1,227	1,229	1,239	1,245
Covered by Private or Public Insurance									
Number..	1,033	1,051	1,031	1,101	1,102	1,111	1,120	1,137	1,175
Percent..	85.4	87.0	85.6	89.8	89.9	90.6	91.2	91.8	94.4
Not Covered									
Number..	176	157	173	124	124	116	109	102	70
Percent..	14.6	13.0	14.4	10.2	10.1	9.4	8.8	8.2	5.6
Percent in the U.S. not covered..	11.7	11.0	9.7	8.6	8.0	7.5	7.2	7.1	6.0

Table CO-7. Employment Status by Demographic Group, 2015

(Numbers in thousands, percent.)

Characteristic	Civilian noninstitutional population	Civilian labor force		Employed		Unemployed	
		Number	Percent of population	Number	Percent of population	Number	Percent of population
Total	4,213	2,800	66.5	2,692	63.9	109	3.9
Sex							
Male	2,083	1,524	73.2	1,464	70.3	60	3.9
Female	2,130	1,276	59.9	1,228	57.6	49	3.8
Race, Sex, and Hispanic Origin							
White	3,765	2,516	66.8	2,422	64.3	95	3.8
Male	1,868	1,376	73.6	1,322	70.8	53	3.9
Female	1,897	1,141	60.1	1,099	57.9	42	3.7
Black or African American	164	106	64.4	100	60.6	6	5.9
Male	80	53	65.5	50	61.7	3	5.8
Female	84	53	63.4	50	59.5	3	6.0
Hispanic or Latino ethnicity[1]	692	478	69.1	452	65.3	26	5.5
Male	348	275	79.0	263	75.5	12	4.4
Female	345	204	59.1	190	55.0	14	6.9
Age							
16 to 19 years	252	85	33.8	73	28.8	13	14.9
20 to 24 years	332	254	76.6	239	72.0	15	6.1
25 to 34 years	800	667	83.3	645	80.6	22	3.3
35 to 44 years	757	651	86.0	630	83.3	21	3.1
45 to 54 years	667	532	79.8	511	76.7	21	3.9
55 to 64 years	692	477	69.0	462	66.8	15	3.1
65 years and over	713	134	18.8	132	18.5	2	1.6

NOTE: Data in Table 7 are from the Current Population Survey (CPS) and do not match the estimates in Table 8. See notes and definitions for further information.
[1]May be of any race.

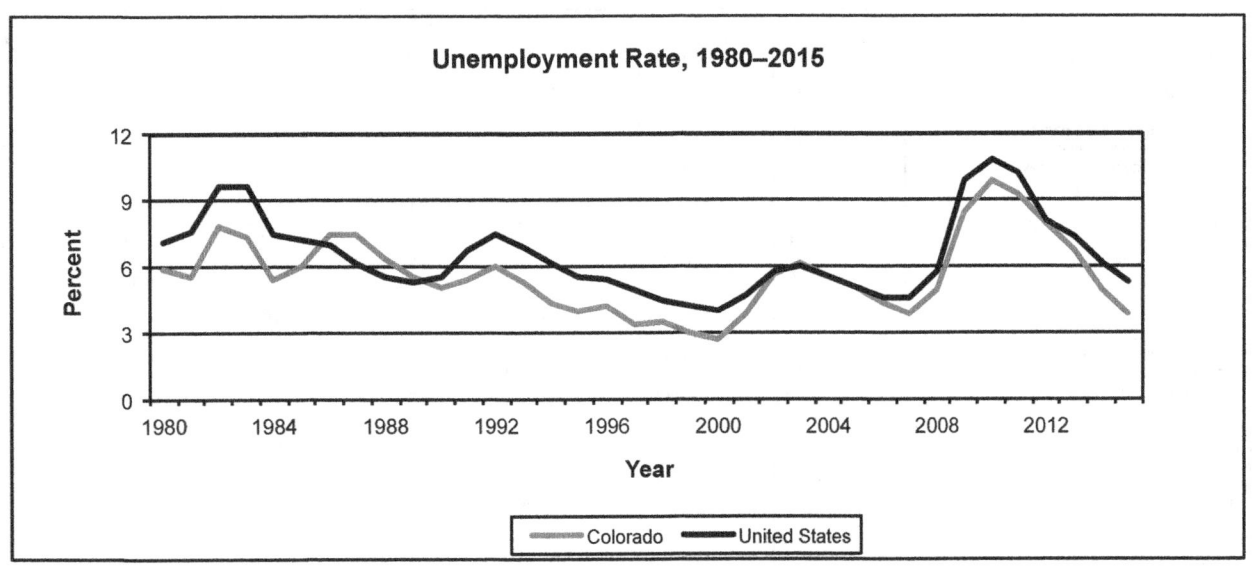

Unemployment Rate, 1980–2015

Table CO-8. Employment Status of the Civilian Noninstitutional Population Age 16 Years and Over

(Number, percent.)

Year	Civilian labor force	Civilian participation rate	Employed	Unemployed	Unemployment rate
2007	2,664,677	72.2	2,565,218	99,459	3.7
2008	2,716,625	72.1	2,585,243	131,382	4.8
2009	2,722,982	70.9	2,524,443	198,539	7.3
2010	2,724,417	70.4	2,486,404	238,013	8.7
2011	2,736,079	69.7	2,507,265	228,814	8.4
2012	2,759,437	69.1	2,542,267	217,170	7.9
2013	2,780,536	68.3	2,590,651	189,885	6.8
2014	2,815,200	67.9	2,674,635	140,565	5.0
2015	2,828,529	66.7	2,718,698	109,831	3.9

Table CO-9. Employment and Average Wages by Industry

(Estimates through 2010 are based on the 2007 North American Industry Classification System [NAICS]. Estimates from 2011 onward are based on the 2012 NAICS.)

Industry	2008	2009	2010	2011	2012	2013	2014
	Number of Jobs						
Wage and Salary Employment by Industry..................	2,478,747	2,373,917	2,355,555	2,393,084	2,441,958	2,514,654	2,596,484
Farm Wage and Salary Employment.........................	12,505	12,051	12,775	11,691	11,605	12,833	11,960
Nonfarm Wage and Salary Employment....................	2,466,242	2,361,866	2,342,780	2,381,393	2,430,353	2,501,821	2,584,524
Private wage and salary employment..........................	2,028,998	1,914,438	1,888,408	1,926,691	1,974,494	2,036,039	2,113,151
Forestry, fishing, and related activities.....................	4,967	5,035	5,304	5,598	5,568	6,180	6,451
Mining...	28,423	23,956	24,096	27,633	30,046	30,270	33,702
Utilities..	8,142	8,313	8,181	8,140	8,045	7,839	8,150
Construction	168,329	137,237	120,670	118,361	119,775	132,446	146,812
Manufacturing..	144,043	129,909	125,705	129,345	132,185	132,930	136,541
Durable goods manufacturing.................................	95,828	84,535	81,247	84,053	86,451	86,113	88,189
Nondurable goods manufacturing..........................	48,215	45,374	44,458	45,292	45,734	46,817	48,352
Wholesale trade	100,941	94,114	91,575	92,873	94,628	97,181	100,456
Retail trade...	256,017	242,207	240,644	243,733	246,114	251,893	257,543
Transportation and warehousing................................	67,863	63,291	61,351	62,042	64,090	66,362	69,565
Information	77,101	74,824	71,864	72,033	69,990	70,008	70,154
Finance and insurance	107,554	103,408	101,846	102,542	104,620	107,681	108,879
Real estate and rental and leasing.............................	48,596	44,742	43,415	42,920	42,997	44,251	45,608
Professional, scientific, and technical services	178,999	172,348	170,403	174,799	180,040	190,847	198,555
Management of companies and enterprises..................	29,026	28,556	28,823	29,921	31,802	34,648	35,474
Administrative and waste services..............................	148,263	133,816	135,539	139,134	147,146	150,285	155,584
Educational services	39,631	39,930	40,984	42,344	43,819	44,570	46,386
Health care and social assistance.............................	224,710	230,712	237,152	244,151	250,833	254,275	265,448
Arts, entertainment, and recreation...........................	46,337	45,357	45,435	46,757	47,481	48,137	49,813
Accommodation and food services.............................	229,772	220,157	220,787	228,234	234,287	243,670	252,797
Other services, except public administration..............	120,284	116,526	114,634	116,131	121,028	122,566	125,233
Government and government enterprises	437,244	447,428	454,372	454,702	455,859	465,782	471,373
	Dollars						
Average Wages and Salaries by Industry	47,201	47,427	48,477	49,788	51,211	51,537	53,401
Average Farm Wages and Salaries	34,126	39,317	32,222	36,532	31,456	42,611	44,261
Average Nonfarm Wages and Salaries	47,267	47,469	48,566	49,853	51,305	51,583	53,443
Average private wages and salaries...........................	47,647	47,684	48,872	50,279	51,980	52,169	54,183
Forestry, fishing, and related activities......................	22,560	23,827	24,186	25,041	25,771	26,396	27,534
Mining...	97,885	91,239	100,062	106,045	105,197	110,037	113,806
Utilities..	82,256	82,187	87,106	91,672	100,640	90,921	93,372
Construction	48,488	48,650	48,775	49,866	51,226	52,030	54,532
Manufacturing..	59,136	59,687	61,692	63,392	64,097	64,142	66,928
Durable goods manufacturing.................................	63,279	64,868	67,783	69,996	70,928	71,036	73,629
Nondurable goods manufacturing..........................	50,903	50,033	50,561	51,137	51,186	51,462	54,706
Wholesale trade	68,909	66,832	69,618	73,015	75,070	75,500	78,901
Retail trade...	27,695	27,633	27,840	28,170	28,961	29,265	30,238
Transportation and warehousing................................	45,394	45,346	46,404	47,767	49,341	52,354	54,326
Information	78,235	79,114	83,528	85,778	90,319	91,880	97,697
Finance and insurance	72,428	70,751	73,396	76,280	79,786	81,450	84,914
Real estate and rental and leasing.............................	42,676	41,997	43,100	45,260	48,429	50,438	51,897
Professional, scientific, and technical services	78,227	78,876	81,054	82,808	85,715	86,274	88,555
Management of companies and enterprises..................	112,467	119,266	127,683	133,814	155,824	126,899	137,094
Administrative and waste services..............................	34,214	34,764	35,342	36,183	37,019	35,838	37,160
Educational services	32,160	32,943	34,003	34,312	35,006	35,118	35,284
Health care and social assistance.............................	44,061	45,218	45,370	46,052	46,953	47,352	48,200
Arts, entertainment, and recreation...........................	34,056	33,864	33,778	34,527	34,652	35,601	36,950
Accommodation and food services.............................	19,501	19,261	19,882	20,598	21,018	21,250	22,247
Other services, except public administration..................	31,887	31,959	32,860	33,368	33,483	34,510	35,892
Government and government enterprises	45,504	46,549	47,295	48,050	48,380	49,021	50,128

Table CO-10. Employment Characteristics by Family Type

(Number, percent.)

Family type and labor force status	2012		2013		2014	
	Total	Families with own children under 18 years	Total	Families with own children under 18 years	Total	Families with own children under 18 years
All Families............................	1,278,264	589,021	1,279,941	584,086	1,309,702	599,088
FAMILY TYPE AND LABOR FORCE STATUS						
Married-Couple Families...........................	975,070	411,938	982,202	411,595	1,000,145	421,101
Both husband and wife in labor force...................	55.7	65.0	54.1	64.9	54.0	64.4
Husband in labor force, wife not in labor force...........	23.2	30.0	23.6	30.4	23.3	30.5
Wife in labor force, husband not in labor force..........	6.6	3.5	7.0	3.3	6.8	3.6
Both husband and wife not in labor force................	14.5	1.5	15.0	1.2	15.8	1.5
Other Families	303,194	177,083	297,739	172,491	309,557	177,987
Female householder, no husband present................	69.6	72.4	70.3	72.9	68.0	69.1
In labor force................	53.2	60.9	52.8	61.5	51.2	58.6
Not in labor force............	16.3	11.5	17.5	11.4	16.8	10.5
Male householder, no wife present....................	30.4	27.6	29.7	27.1	32.0	30.9
In labor force....................	26.1	25.7	24.5	25.2	26.9	29.0
Not in labor force	4.4	1.9	5.2	1.9	5.1	1.9

Table CO-11. School Enrollment and Educational Attainment, 2014

(Number, percent.)

Item	State	U.S.
Enrollment		
Total population 3 years and over, enrolled in school................	1,404,518	82,063,714
Enrolled in nursery school or preschool (percent)	6.4	6.0
Enrolled in kindergarten (percent)................	5.4	5.1
Enrolled in elementary school, grades 1-8 (percent)................	40.4	40.2
Enrolled in high school, grades 9-12 (percent)................	19.4	20.7
Enrolled in college or graduate school (percent)................	28.3	28.0
Attainment		
Total population 25 years and over	3,584,463	213,725,624
Less than ninth grade (percent)................	4.1	5.6
9th to 12th grade, no diploma (percent)	5.3	7.5
High school graduate, including equivalency (percent)................	21.9	27.7
Some college, no degree (percent)	22.1	21.0
Associate's degree (percent)	8.2	8.2
Bachelor's degree (percent)	24.1	18.7
Graduate or professional degree (percent)................	14.3	11.4
High school graduate or higher (percent)	90.5	86.9
Bachelor's degree or higher (percent)................	38.3	30.1

Table CO-12. Public School Characteristics and Educational Indicators

(Number, percent; data derived from National Center of Education Statistics.)

Item	State	U.S.
Public Schools, 2013–2014 (except where noted)		
Number of school districts................	261	18,194
Number of schools................	1,832	98,271
Number of students (in thousands)................	877	50,045
Number of teachers (in thousands)	50	3,114
Student-teacher ratio	17.5	16.1
Expenditures per student (dollars), FY 2013	8,693	107,637
Four-year adjusted cohort graduation rate (ACGR)[1,2]	77.3	82.3
Students eligible for free or reduced-price lunch (in thousands)	368	25,596
English language learners (in thousands)	106	4,461
Students age 3 to 21 served under IDEA, part B (in thousands)	91	6,464

Public Schools by Type	Number	Percent of state public schools
Total number of schools................	1,832	100.0
Regular................	1,728	94.3
Special education................	6	0.3
Vocational education................	6	0.3
Alternative education................	92	5.0

NOTE: Every school is assigned only one school type based on its instructional emphasis.
[1]ACGR data represents a new method of calculating high-school completion rates and may not be comparable to previous years' data for Averaged Freshmen Graduation Rates (AFGR).
[2]The United States 4-year ACGRs were estimated using both the reported 4-year ACGR data from 49 states and the District of Columbia and using imputed data for Idaho. The estimate for American Indian/Alaska Native students also includes imputed data for Virginia.

Table CO-13. Reported Voting and Registration of the Voting-Age Population, November 2014

(Numbers in thousands, percent.)

Item	Total population	Total citizen population	Registered Total registered	Registered Percent registered (total population)	Registered Percent registered (total citizen population)	Voted Total voted	Voted Percent voted (total population)	Voted Percent voted (total citizen population)
U.S. Total	239,874	219,941	142,166	59.3	64.6	92,251	38.5	41.9
State Total...............................	239,874	219,941	142,166	59.3	64.6	92,251	38.5	41.9
Sex								
Male................................	1,979	1,849	1,288	65.1	69.7	1,059	53.5	57.3
Female...............................	2,030	1,883	1,366	67.3	72.5	1,152	56.8	61.2
Race								
White alone	3,637	3,427	2,453	67.4	71.6	2,085	57.3	60.8
White, non-Hispanic alone	3,010	2,965	2,192	72.8	73.9	1,888	62.7	63.7
Black alone............................	147	132	75	51.2	57.0	56	38.0	42.3
Asian alone	112	63	48	(B)	(B)	40	(B)	(B)
Hispanic (of any race)....................	701	534	321	45.8	60.1	218	31.1	40.9
White alone or in combination	3,688	3,478	2,498	67.7	71.8	2,105	57.1	60.5
Black alone or in combination..........	157	142	78	49.9	55.1	57	36.5	40.4
Asian alone or in combination..........	138	88	74	53.3	83.1	48	35.0	54.6
Age								
18 to 24 years..........................	374	347	131	35.0	37.7	64	17.1	18.4
25 to 34 years..........................	853	795	506	59.3	63.7	368	43.1	46.3
35 to 44 years..........................	743	658	477	64.3	72.5	386	51.9	58.6
45 to 64 years..........................	1,317	1,217	939	71.3	77.1	833	63.3	68.4
65 years and over	722	715	601	83.2	84.2	561	77.6	78.5

B = Base is less than 75,000 and therefore too small to show the derived measure.

Table CO-14. Crime

(Number, rate per 100,000. Data are derived from the FBI Uniform Crime Reports.)

Item	State 2013	State 2014	State Percent change	U.S.[1,2,3,4] 2013	U.S.[1,2,3,4] 2014	U.S.[1,2,3,4] Percent change
TOTAL POPULATION[5]	5,268,367	5,355,866	1.7	316,128,839	318,857,056	0.9
VIOLENT CRIME						
Number....................................	15,342	16,554	7.9	1,163,146	1,165,383	0.2
Rate	291.2	309.1	6.1	367.9	365.5	-0.7
Murder and Nonnegligent Manslaughter						
Number....................................	178	151	-15.2	14,196	14,249	0.4
Rate	3.4	2.8	-17.6	4.5	4.5	-
Rape[6]						
Number....................................	2,934	3,039	X	108,612	116,645	X
Rate	55.7	56.7	X	34.4	36.6	X
Robbery						
Number....................................	3,151	3,039	-3.6	345,031	325,802	-5.6
Rate	59.8	56.7	-5.2	109.1	102.2	-6.3
Aggravated Assault						
Number....................................	9,963	10,325	3.6	724,149	741,291	2.4
Rate	189.1	192.8	2.0	229.1	232.5	1.5
PROPERTY CRIME						
Number....................................	140,057	135,510	-3.2	8,632,512	8,277,829	-4.1
Rate	2,658.5	2,530.1	-4.8	2,730.7	2,596.1	-4.9
Burglary						
Number....................................	25,081	23,472	-6.4	1,928,465	1,729,806	-10.3
Rate	476.1	438.2	-8.0	610.0	542.5	-11.1
Larceny-Theft						
Number....................................	102,443	99,464	-2.9	6,004,453	5,858,496	-2.4
Rate	1,944.5	1,857.1	-4.5	1,899.4	1,837.3	-3.3
Motor Vehicle Theft						
Number....................................	12,533	12,574	0.3	699,594	689,527	-1.4
Rate	237.9	234.8	-1.3	221.3	216.2	-2.3

NOTE: Although arson data are included in the trend and clearance tables, sufficient data are not available to estimate totals for this offense. Therefore, no arson data are published in this table.
X = Not applicable.
- = Zero or rounds to zero.
[1]The crime figures have been adjusted.
[2]The data collection methodology for the offense of forcible rape used by the Minnesota state Uniform Crime Reporting (UCR) Program (with the exception of Minneapolis and St. Paul, Minnesota) does not comply with national UCR Program guidelines. Consequently, its figures for forcible rape and violent crime (of which forcible rape is a part) are not published in this table.
[3]Includes offenses reported by the Zoological Police and the Metro Transit Police.
[4]Because of changes in the state's reporting practices, figures are not comparable to previous years' data.
[5]Populations are U.S. Census Bureau provisional estimates as of July 1 of each year.
[6]The figures shown for the offense of rape were estimated using the revised Uniform Crime Reporting (UCR) definition of rape.

Table CO-15. State Government Finances, 2014

(Dollar amounts in thousands, percent distribution.)

Item	Dollars	Percent distribution
Total Revenue	34,387,619	100.0
General revenue	24,739,273	71.9
Intergovernmental revenue	7,277,716	21.2
Taxes	11,755,394	34.2
General sales	2,615,601	7.6
Selective sales	1,858,693	5.4
License taxes	659,616	1.9
Individual income tax	5,658,457	16.5
Corporate income tax	717,506	2.1
Other taxes	245,521	0.7
Current charges	3,416,228	9.9
Miscellaneous general revenue	2,289,935	6.7
Utility revenue	0	-
Liquor stores revenue	0	-
Insurance trust revenue[1]	9,648,346	28.1
Total Expenditure	30,648,903	100.0
Intergovernmental expenditure	6,749,839	22.0
Direct expenditure	23,899,064	78.0
Current operation	15,842,492	51.7
Capital outlay	1,398,048	4.6
Insurance benefits and repayments	5,430,094	17.7
Assistance and subsidies	381,541	1.2
Interest on debt	846,889	2.8
Exhibit: Salaries and wages	4,226,503	13.8
Total Expenditure	30,648,903	100.0
General expenditure	25,202,339	82.2
Intergovernmental expenditure	6,749,839	22.0
Direct expenditure	18,452,500	60.2
General expenditure, by function:		
Education	10,078,562	32.9
Public welfare	6,714,964	21.9
Hospitals	808,437	2.6
Health	1,074,785	3.5
Highways	1,644,687	5.4
Police protection	186,457	0.6
Correction	965,306	3.1
Natural resources	342,944	1.1
Parks and recreation	96,853	0.3
Governmental administration	845,055	2.8
Interest on general debt	833,187	2.7
Other and unallocable	1,611,102	5.3
Utility expenditure	16,470	0.1
Liquor stores expenditure	0	-
Insurance trust expenditure	5,430,094	17.7
Debt at End of Fiscal Year	16,929,327	X
Cash and Security Holdings	74,146,731	X

X = Not applicable.
- = Zero or rounds to zero.
[1]Within insurance trust revenue, net earnings of state retirement systems is a calculated statistic (the item code in the data file is X08), and thus can be positive or negative. Net earnings is the sum of earnings on investments plus gains on investments minus losses on investments. The change made in 2002 for asset valuation from book to market value in accordance with Statement 34 of the Governmental Accounting Standards Board is reflected in the calculated statistics.

Table CO-16. State Government Tax Collections, 2014

(Dollars in thousands, percent.)

Item	Dollars	Percent distribution
Total Taxes	11,755,394	100.0
Property taxes	X	X
Sales and gross receipts	4,474,294	38.1
General sales and gross receipts	2,615,601	22.3
Selective sales and gross receipts	1,858,693	15.8
Alcoholic beverages	40,886	0.3
Amusements	105,420	0.9
Insurance premiums	239,431	2.0
Motor fuels	647,104	5.5
Pari-mutuels	609	-
Public utilities	10,819	0.1
Tobacco products	194,192	1.7
Other selective sales	620,232	5.3
Licenses	659,616	5.6
Alcoholic beverages	7,212	0.1
Amusements	791	-
Corporations in general	17,569	0.1
Hunting and fishing	71,142	0.6
Motor vehicle	474,534	4.0
Motor vehicle operators	28,660	0.2
Public utilities	14,156	0.1
Occupation and business, NEC	44,577	0.4
Other licenses	975	-
Income taxes	6,375,963	54.2
Individual income	5,658,457	48.1
Corporation net income	717,506	6.1
Other taxes	245,521	2.1
Death and gift	434	-
Documentary and stock transfer	0	-
Severance	245,087	2.1
Taxes, NEC	0	-

X = Not applicable.
- = Zero or rounds to zero.

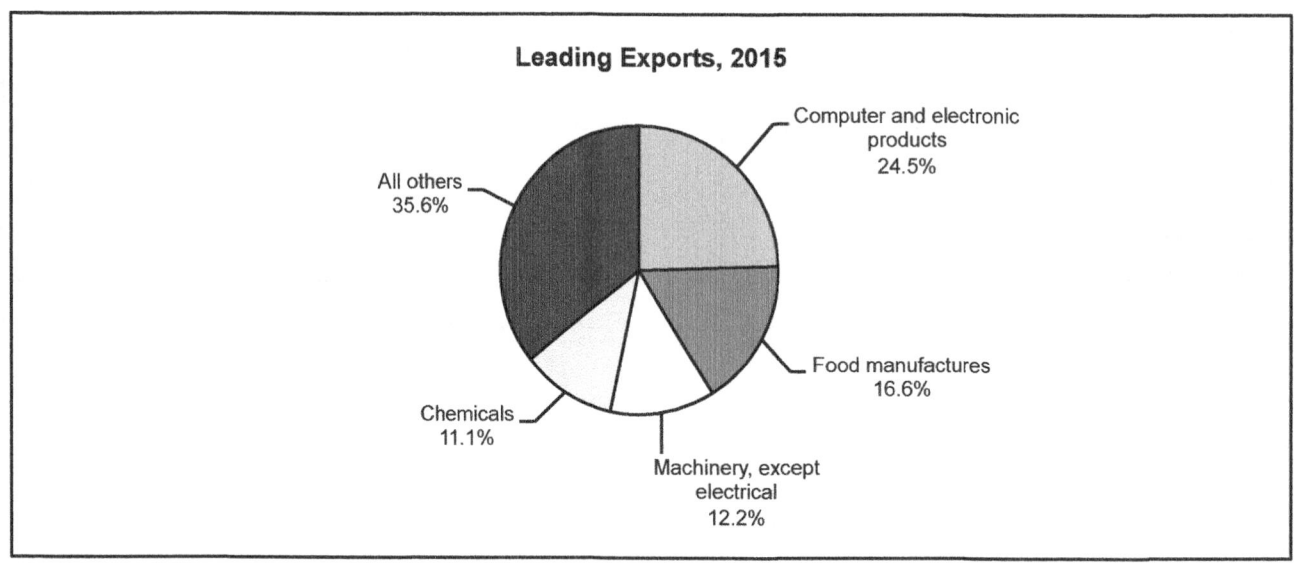

Leading Exports, 2015

- Computer and electronic products 24.5%
- All others 35.6%
- Chemicals 11.1%
- Machinery, except electrical 12.2%
- Food manufactures 16.6%

CONNECTICUT

Facts and Figures

Location: Northeastern United States; bordered on the N by Massachusetts, on the E by Rhode Island, on the S by Long Island Sound, and on the W by New York

Area: 5,543 sq. mi. (14,357); rank—48th

Population: 3,590,886 (2015 est.); rank—29th

Principal Cities: capital—Hartford; largest—Bridgeport

Statehood: January 9, 1788; 5th state

U.S. Congress: 2 senators, 5 representatives

State Motto: *Qui transtulit sustinet* ("He who transplanted still sustains")

State Song: "Yankee Doodle"

State Nicknames: The Constitution State; The Nutmeg State

Abbreviations: CT; Conn.

State Symbols: flower—mountain laurel; tree—white oak; bird—American robin

At a Glance

- With an increase in population of 0.3 percent, Connecticut ranked 46th among the states in growth from 2010 to 2015.

- Connecticut's median household income in 2014 was $70,048, and 10.8 percent of its population lived below the poverty level.

- In 2014, Connecticut's unemployment rate was 5.6 percent, down from 6.6 percent in 2013.

- Connecticut's violent crime rate in 2014 was 236.9 per 100,000 population, compared to 365.5 for the entire nation.

- The property crime rate in Connecticut in 2014 ranked 45th in the nation, with 1920.4 incidents per 100,000 population.

Table CT-1. Population by Age, Sex, Race, and Hispanic Origin

(Number, percent, except where noted.)

Sex, age, race, and Hispanic origin	2000	2010	2015[1]	Average annual percent change, 2010–2015
Total Population...	3,405,565	3,574,097	3,590,886	-
Percent of total U.S. population	1.2	1.2	1.1	X
Sex				
Male...	1,649,319	1,739,614	1,751,747	-
Female	1,756,246	1,834,483	1,839,139	-
Age				
Under 5 years...	233,344	202,106	187,620	-0.5
5 to 19 years...	702,358	713,670	681,854	-0.3
20 to 64 years...	2,009,680	2,151,762	2,154,606	-
65 years and over...	470,183	506,559	566,806	0.8
Median age (years)...	37.4	40.0	40.6	0.1
Race and Hispanic Origin				
One race				
White...	2,780,355	2,950,820	2,902,834	-0.1
Black...	309,843	392,131	418,185	0.5
American Indian and Alaska Native	9,639	16,734	19,132	1.0
Asian...	82,313	140,516	166,341	1.2
Native Hawaiian or				
Other Pacific Islander...	1,366	3,491	3,942	0.9
Two or more races...	74,848	70,405	80,452	1.0
Hispanic (of any race)...	320,323	498,638	553,781	0.8

X = Not applicable.
[1]Population figures for 2015 are July 1 estimates. The 2010 estimates are taken from the 2010 Census.
- = Zero or rounds to zero.

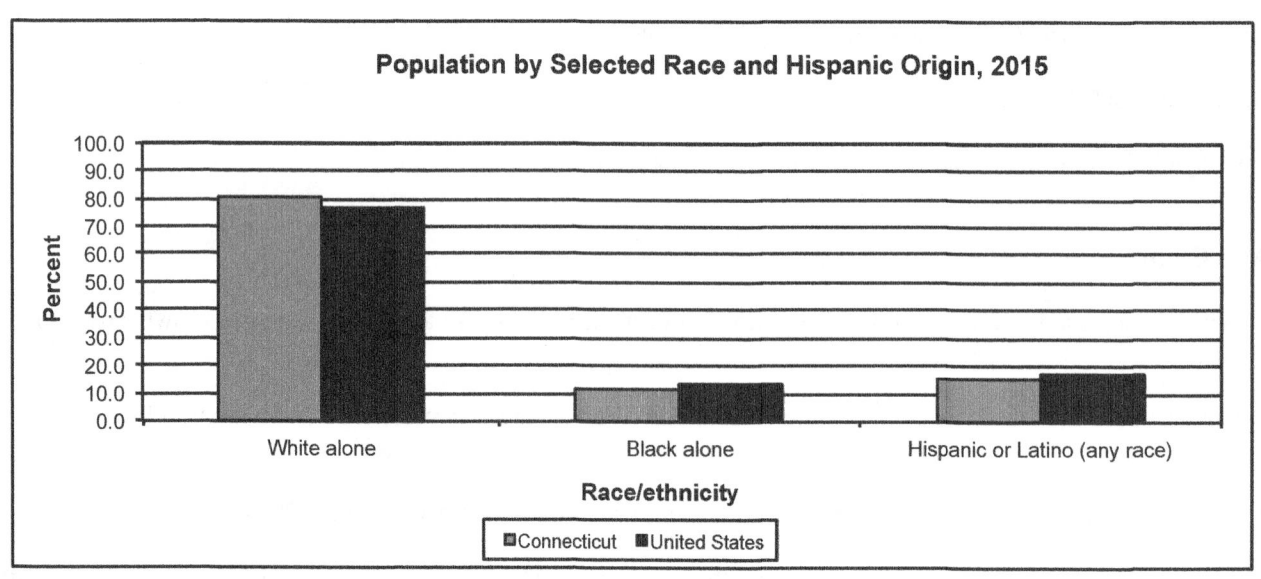

Table CT-2. Marital Status

(Number, percent distribution.)

Sex, age, race, and Hispanic origin	2000	2010	2014
Males, 15 Years and Over	1,284,881	1,399,329	1,420,207
Never married...	30.0	36.3	36.8
Now married, except separated.................................	58.0	50.6	50.5
Separated...	1.3	1.1	1.1
Widowed...	2.7	2.7	2.6
Divorced...	7.9	9.3	9.0
Females, 15 Years and Over	1,411,369	1,512,492	1,525,351
Never married...	24.5	29.9	30.5
Now married, except separated.................................	52.3	46.5	46.4
Separated...	1.8	1.8	1.6
Widowed...	10.8	9.3	9.1
Divorced...	10.5	12.5	12.3

Table CT-3. Households and Housing Characteristics

(Number, percent, dollars.)

Item	2000	2010	2014	Average annual percent change, 2000–2014
Total Households........................	1,301,670	1,358,809	1,355,817	0.3
Family households	881,170	890,770	887,263	-
Married-couple family	676,467	656,629	650,673	-0.3
Other family	204,703	234,141	236,590	1.1
Male householder, no wife present........................	47,292	58,325	64,771	2.6
Female householder, no husband present........................	157,411	175,816	171,819	0.7
Nonfamily households	420,500	468,039	468,554	0.8
Householder living alone........................	334,224	384,382	392,309	1.2
Householder not living alone........................	76,276	83,657	76,245	-
Housing Characteristics				
Total housing units........................	1,385,975	1,488,215	1,493,632	0.6
Occupied housing units	1,301,670	1,358,809	1,355,817	0.3
Owner occupied	869,729	923,617	900,039	0.2
Renter occupied	431,941	435,192	455,778	0.4
Average household size........................	2.53	2.55	2.57	0.1
Financial Characteristics				
Median gross rent of renter-occupied housing	681	992	1,076	4.1
Median monthly owner costs for housing units with a mortgage	1,426	2,068	1,994	2.8
Median value of owner-occupied housing units........................	166,900	288,800	267,200	4.3

- = Zero or rounds to zero

Table CT-4. Migration, Origin, and Language

(Number, percent.)

Characteristic	State			U.S.		
	2013	2014	Percent change	2013	2014	Percent change
Residence 1 Year Ago						
Population 1 year and over	3,562,959	3,558,915	-0.1	312,432,820	315,095,393	0.9
Same house........................	87.8	87.4	X	85.0	85.1	X
Different house in the U.S.	11.6	11.7	X	14.4	14.3	X
Same county	7.2	7.7	X	8.9	8.7	X
Different county	4.4	4	X	5.5	5.6	X
Same state	2.0	1.7	X	3.2	3.3	X
Different state	2.5	2.3	X	2.3	2.3	X
Abroad........................	0.6	0.8	X	0.6	0.6	X
Place of Birth						
Native born	3,096,437	3,104,758	0.3	274,780,773	276,465,262	0.6
Male........................	48.8	48.7	X	49.3	49.3	X
Female........................	51.2	51.3	X	50.7	50.7	X
Foreign born	499,643	491,919	-1.5	41,348,066	42,391,794	2.5
Male........................	48.3	49.5	X	48.8	48.7	X
Female........................	51.7	50.5	X	51.2	51.3	X
Foreign born; naturalized U.S. citizen........................	244,730	235,905	-3.6	19,294,710	19,984,738	3.6
Male........................	44.3	44.8	X	45.9	45.9	X
Female........................	55.7	55.2	X	54.1	54.1	X
Foreign born; not a U.S. citizen........................	254,913	256,014	0.4	22,053,356	22,407,056	1.6
Male........................	52.0	53.9	X	51.3	51.2	X
Female........................	48.0	46.1	X	48.7	48.8	X
Entered 2010 or later	10.3	14.3	X	9.7	12.3	X
Entered 2000 to 2009	29.9	29.6	X	29.4	28.6	X
Entered before 2000........................	59.7	56.1	X	61.0	59.1	X
World Region of Birth, Foreign						
Foreign-born population, excluding population born at sea	499,643	491,839	-1.6	41,347,945	42,390,705	2.5
Europe	25.9	25.1	X	11.6	11.2	X
Asia........................	23.3	25.2	X	29.5	30.1	X
Africa........................	2.8	4.6	X	4.4	4.6	X
Oceania........................	0.2	0.3	X	0.5	0.6	X
Latin America........................	45.0	41.8	X	51.9	51.6	X
North America........................	2.7	3.0	X	2.0	1.9	X
Language Spoken at Home and Ability to Speak English						
Population 5 years and over........................	3,405,334	3,407,815	0.1	296,358,760	299,084,046	0.9
English only........................	78.5	78.2	X	79.2	78.9	X
Language other than English........................	21.5	21.8	X	20.8	21.1	X
Speaks English less than "very well"........................	8.2	8.1	X	8.5	8.6	X

X = Not applicable.
- = Zero or rounds to zero.

Table CT-5. Median Income and Poverty Status, 2014

(Number, percent, except as noted.)

Characteristic	State		U.S.	
	Number	Percent	Number	Percent
Median Income				
Households (dollars)..	70,048	X	53,657	X
Families (dollars)	88,819	X	65,910	X
Below Poverty Level (All People)	374,772	10.8	48,208,387	15.5
Sex				
Male..	164,880	9.7	21,590,918	14.2
Female	209,892	11.7	26,617,469	16.8
Age				
Under 18 years................................	113,712	14.9	15,686,012	21.7
Related children under 18 years...........	109,751	14.4	15,372,705	21.3
18 to 64 years................................	219,686	10.0	28,267,482	14.6
65 years and over	41,374	7.8	4,254,893	9.5

X = Not applicable.

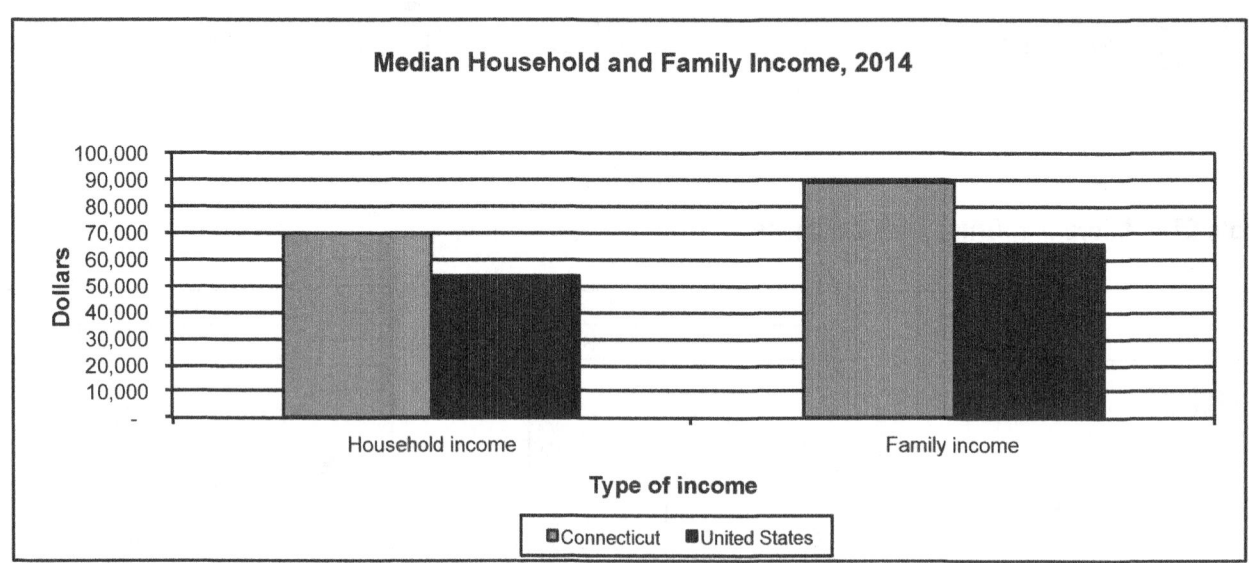

Table CT-6. Health Insurance Coverage Status for the Civilian Noninstitutionalized Population and Children Under 18 Years of Age

(Numbers in thousands, percent.)

Item	2006	2007	2008	2009	2010	2011	2012	2013	2014
Civilian Noninstitutionalized Population	3,462	3,476	3,441	3,457	3,520	3,523	3,535	3,541	3,541
Covered by Private or Public Insurance									
Number..........................	3,137	3,150	3,130	3,152	3,200	3,214	3,213	3,209	3,296
Percent..........................	90.6	90.6	91.0	91.2	90.9	91.2	90.9	90.6	93.1
Not Covered									
Number..........................	325	326	311	305	320	309	322	333	245
Percent..........................	9.4	9.4	9.0	8.8	9.1	8.8	9.1	9.4	6.9
Percent in the U.S. not covered........................	15.8	15.3	15.1	15.1	15.5	15.1	14.8	14.5	11.7
Children Under 18 Years of Age	820	819	810	807	815	803	791	784	774
Covered by Private or Public Insurance									
Number..........................	771	776	770	777	791	780	761	751	745
Percent..........................	94.0	94.8	95.1	96.2	97.0	97.1	96.2	95.7	96.3
Not Covered									
Number..........................	49	43	40	30	24	23	30	34	29
Percent..........................	6.0	5.2	4.9	3.8	3.0	2.9	3.8	4.3	3.7
Percent in the U.S. not covered........................	11.7	11.0	9.7	8.6	8.0	7.5	7.2	7.1	6.0

Table CT-7. Employment Status by Demographic Group, 2015

(Numbers in thousands, percent.)

Characteristic	Civilian noninstitutional population	Civilian labor force		Employed		Unemployed	
		Number	Percent of population	Number	Percent of population	Number	Percent of population
Total..	2,880	1,896	65.8	1,790	62.1	106	5.6
Sex							
Male..	1,383	977	70.6	921	66.6	56	5.7
Female...	1,497	920	61.4	869	58.1	51	5.5
Race, Sex, and Hispanic Origin							
White..	2,375	1,564	65.9	1,494	62.9	70	4.5
Male..	1,152	810	70.3	774	67.2	37	4.5
Female...	1,223	754	61.6	720	58.9	34	4.5
Black or African American..................	309	197	63.9	171	55.4	26	13.2
Male..	141	98	69.4	84	59.9	13	13.7
Female...	168	100	59.2	87	51.6	13	12.7
Hispanic or Latino ethnicity[1]............	337	225	66.8	199	59.2	26	11.3
Male..	153	112	73.4	100	65.3	12	11.0
Female...	184	112	61.2	99	54.1	13	11.7
Age							
16 to 19 years...................................	214	57	26.4	46	21.5	11	18.6
20 to 24 years...................................	233	165	70.9	154	65.9	12	7.0
25 to 34 years...................................	433	372	85.9	343	79.3	29	7.8
35 to 44 years...................................	419	354	84.5	335	79.8	19	5.5
45 to 54 years...................................	574	480	83.5	459	80.0	20	4.2
55 to 64 years...................................	476	351	73.8	340	71.3	12	3.4
65 years and over..............................	530	117	22.1	114	21.4	4	3.1

NOTE: Data in Table 7 are from the Current Population Survey (CPS) and do not match the estimates in Table 8. See notes and definitions for further information.
[1]May be of any race.

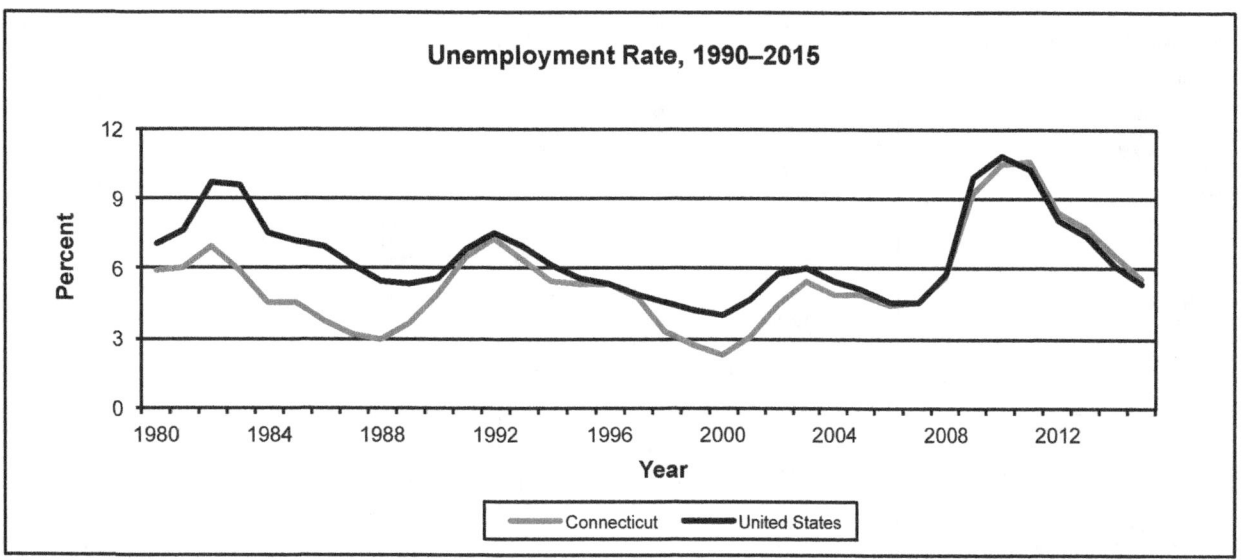

Unemployment Rate, 1990–2015

Table CT-8. Employment Status of the Civilian Noninstitutional Population Age 16 Years and Over

(Number, percent.)

Year	Civilian labor force	Civilian participation rate	Employed	Unemployed	Unemployment rate
2007..................	1,856,209	68.5	1,773,159	83,050	4.5
2008..................	1,881,454	69.0	1,774,681	106,773	5.7
2009..................	1,891,077	68.8	1,740,971	150,106	7.9
2010..................	1,911,712	68.3	1,737,449	174,263	9.1
2011..................	1,914,775	67.7	1,745,967	168,808	8.8
2012..................	1,888,336	66.4	1,730,695	157,641	8.3
2013..................	1,872,031	65.5	1,726,875	145,156	7.8
2014..................	1,886,398	65.8	1,761,610	124,788	6.6
2015..................	1,888,001	65.7	1,781,517	106,484	5.6

Table CT-9. Employment and Average Wages by Industry

(Estimates through 2010 are based on the 2007 North American Industry Classification System [NAICS]. Estimates from 2011 onward are based on the 2012 NAICS.)

Industry	2008	2009	2010	2011	2012	2013	2014
	Number of Jobs						
Wage and Salary Employment by Industry.................	1,768,627	1,697,796	1,678,439	1,695,049	1,705,660	1,718,531	1,734,286
Farm Wage and Salary Employment........................	4,612	4,449	4,460	4,730	4,789	5,675	5,471
Nonfarm Wage and Salary Employment....................	1,764,015	1,693,347	1,673,979	1,690,319	1,700,871	1,712,856	1,728,815
Private wage and salary employment...........................	1,491,508	1,424,167	1,407,694	1,428,832	1,441,703	1,452,960	1,467,004
Forestry, fishing, and related activities.........................	815	800	830	906	921	656	709
Mining...	737	629	571	542	554	543	547
Utilities..	6,759	6,644	6,310	6,173	5,934	6,038	5,943
Construction...	67,888	57,044	52,304	54,272	53,351	55,612	57,629
Manufacturing...	187,230	171,479	165,835	166,442	165,431	164,043	159,833
Durable goods manufacturing............................	143,485	132,078	127,377	128,576	128,779	127,652	124,436
Nondurable goods manufacturing.......................	43,745	39,401	38,458	37,866	36,652	36,391	35,397
Wholesale trade	69,891	65,526	63,209	63,914	63,527	63,465	63,454
Retail trade...	191,035	181,585	181,490	183,247	184,098	185,592	186,734
Transportation and warehousing..............................	43,337	40,829	40,274	41,375	41,920	42,519	43,765
Information	37,521	34,261	31,827	31,446	31,368	32,152	32,046
Finance and insurance	125,204	120,584	118,635	118,257	115,692	114,325	111,638
Real estate and rental and leasing...........................	21,279	19,820	19,780	19,485	19,237	19,632	19,758
Professional, scientific, and technical services	93,970	88,629	87,408	89,298	90,365	91,273	96,148
Management of companies and enterprises....................	28,516	27,779	27,826	28,622	31,618	30,694	31,898
Administrative and waste services............................	87,546	77,461	78,853	81,765	84,818	85,852	86,495
Educational services	61,087	63,159	64,153	66,405	67,317	67,834	68,851
Health care and social assistance............................	243,264	248,409	251,509	255,468	258,687	261,472	264,511
Arts, entertainment, and recreation..........................	24,211	23,964	23,873	24,538	3,886	26,299	26,739
Accommodation and food services............................	114,430	111,349	111,542	114,648	118,492	122,249	124,820
Other services, except public administration..................	86,788	84,216	81,465	82,029	83,159	82,710	85,486
Government and government enterprises...........................	272,507	269,180	266,285	261,487	259,168	259,896	261,811
	Dollars						
Average Wages and Salaries by Industry	57,517	56,809	58,501	60,138	61,221	61,312	62,871
Average Farm Wages and Salaries	28,805	28,367	26,728	22,547	24,961	28,700	31,258
Average Nonfarm Wages and Salaries	57,592	56,884	58,585	60,243	61,323	61,420	62,971
Average private wages and salaries............................	58,670	57,627	59,713	61,357	62,602	62,585	64,223
Forestry, fishing, and related activities........................	22,004	23,028	22,981	23,056	23,811	25,942	26,388
Mining..	64,171	64,526	67,965	68,950	64,549	64,164	70,324
Utilities..	109,587	106,692	103,576	111,584	109,758	111,008	111,317
Construction	57,966	57,799	58,614	58,336	59,246	59,373	61,069
Manufacturing..	70,484	70,207	73,403	76,894	78,934	81,100	81,376
Durable goods manufacturing.............................	69,674	69,702	73,005	76,332	78,597	81,022	82,082
Nondurable goods manufacturing.........................	73,142	71,900	74,724	78,801	80,117	81,374	78,893
Wholesale trade	79,758	79,147	81,467	83,383	85,392	85,925	87,683
Retail trade..	30,356	30,636	30,909	31,211	31,496	31,572	32,102
Transportation and warehousing...............................	47,040	46,145	46,410	47,499	47,870	46,867	47,773
Information	70,196	71,374	77,158	78,945	86,820	89,035	92,972
Finance and insurance	141,147	130,078	143,395	152,330	153,964	150,126	158,939
Real estate and rental and leasing............................	52,902	51,556	54,133	58,140	61,971	63,970	65,793
Professional, scientific, and technical services	85,411	85,225	88,164	89,592	91,723	92,541	95,818
Management of companies and enterprises....................	136,632	135,450	135,150	139,171	154,553	160,079	162,914
Administrative and waste services............................	38,188	38,583	40,063	40,837	41,257	40,800	42,998
Educational services	44,406	45,609	46,391	47,415	48,569	50,582	52,399
Health care and social assistance............................	45,815	46,433	46,972	47,523	48,405	48,594	49,795
Arts, entertainment, and recreation..........................	29,742	29,230	29,054	29,259	189,738	29,010	30,066
Accommodation and food services............................	19,788	19,804	20,491	20,779	21,125	20,918	21,844
Other services, except public administration..................	30,166	30,344	31,253	31,708	32,015	32,623	33,470
Government and government enterprises........................	51,688	52,951	52,625	54,157	54,206	54,907	55,951

Table CT-10. Employment Characteristics by Family Type

(Number, percent.)

Family type and labor force status	2012		2013		2014	
	Total	Families with own children under 18 years	Total	Families with own children under 18 years	Total	Families with own children under 18 years
All Families.............................	902,369	401,316	890,293	384,072	881,355	378,078
FAMILY TYPE AND LABOR FORCE STATUS						
Married-Couple Families...................	660,876	272,625	657,885	262,395	644,765	256,409
Both husband and wife in labor force............	58.8	70.9	58.1	70.4	57.2	70.7
Husband in labor force, wife not in labor force...........	19.6	25.0	19.9	24.3	20.1	25.0
Wife in labor force, husband not in labor force............	7.3	3.1	7.3	3.8	7.8	3.1
Both husband and wife not in labor force............	14.4	1.0	14.0	1.1	14.9	1.2
Other Families	241,493	128,691	232,408	121,677	236,590	121,669
Female householder, no husband present............	73.8	78.1	75.4	80.5	72.6	76.5
In labor force............	56.2	68.3	55.7	67.8	55.5	65.7
Not in labor force............	17.6	9.8	19.6	12.7	17.1	10.8
Male householder, no wife present.....................	26.2	21.9	24.6	19.5	27.4	23.5
In labor force............	21.2	20.1	19.6	17.9	22.6	21.7
Not in labor force............	5.0	1.9	5.1	1.6	4.8	1.8

Table CT-11. School Enrollment and Educational Attainment, 2014

(Number, percent.)

Item	State	U.S.
Enrollment		
Total population 3 years and over, enrolled in school................	928,526	82,063,714
Enrolled in nursery school or preschool (percent)	6.3	6.0
Enrolled in kindergarten (percent)	4.2	5.1
Enrolled in elementary school, grades 1-8 (percent)................	38.7	40.2
Enrolled in high school, grades 9-12 (percent)................	21.7	20.7
Enrolled in college or graduate school (percent)	29.1	28.0
Attainment		
Total population 25 years and over	2,471,818	213,725,624
Less than ninth grade (percent)	4.2	5.6
9th to 12th grade, no diploma (percent)	5.8	7.5
High school graduate, including equivalency (percent)	27.5	27.7
Some college, no degree (percent)	17.1	21.0
Associate's degree (percent)	7.5	8.2
Bachelor's degree (percent)	21.3	18.7
Graduate or professional degree (percent)................	16.7	11.4
High school graduate or higher (percent)	90.1	86.9
Bachelor's degree or higher (percent)................	38.0	30.1

Table CT-12. Public School Characteristics and Educational Indicators

(Number, percent; data derived from National Center of Education Statistics.)

Item	State	U.S.
Public Schools, 2013–2014 (except where noted)		
Number of school districts................	201	18,194
Number of schools................	1,152	98,271
Number of students (in thousands)	546	50,045
Number of teachers (in thousands)	43	3,114
Student-teacher ratio	12.6	16.1
Expenditures per student (dollars), FY 2013	173,217	107,637
Four-year adjusted cohort graduation rate (ACGR)[1,2]	87.0	82.3
Students eligible for free or reduced-price lunch (in thousands)	203	25,596
English language learners (in thousands)	30	4,461
Students age 3 to 21 served under IDEA, part B (in thousands)	71	6,464

Public Schools by Type	Number	Percent of state public schools
Total number of schools................	1,152	100.0
Regular	1,042	90.5
Special education................	44	3.8
Vocational education................	16	1.4
Alternative education................	50	4.3

NOTE: Every school is assigned only one school type based on its instructional emphasis.
[1]ACGR data represents a new method of calculating high-school completion rates and may not be comparable to previous years' data for Averaged Freshmen Graduation Rates (AFGR).
[2]The United States 4-year ACGRs were estimated using both the reported 4-year ACGR data from 49 states and the District of Columbia and using imputed data for Idaho. The estimate for American Indian/Alaska Native students also includes imputed data for Virginia.

Table CT-13. Reported Voting and Registration of the Voting-Age Population, November 2014

(Numbers in thousands, percent.)

Item	Total population	Total citizen population	Registered			Voted		
			Total registered	Percent registered (total population)	Percent registered (total citizen population)	Total voted	Percent voted (total population)	Percent voted (total citizen population)
U.S. Total	239,874	219,941	142,166	59.3	64.6	92,251	38.5	41.9
State Total............................	2,783	2,560	1,668	59.9	65.1	1,195	43.0	46.7
Sex								
Male....................................	1,333	1,217	765	57.4	62.9	588	44.1	48.3
Female	1,450	1,343	903	62.3	67.2	607	41.9	45.2
Race								
White alone..........................	2,344	2,198	1,475	62.9	67.1	1,065	45.4	48.4
White, non-Hispanic alone	2,076	2,014	1,374	66.2	68.2	1,009	48.6	50.1
Black alone...........................	291	246	121	41.7	49.2	83	28.4	33.5
Asian alone	101	72	40	(B)	(B)	28	(B)	(B)
Hispanic (of any race)	319	220	116	36.3	52.6	68	21.3	30.8
White alone or in combination	2,376	2,231	1,502	63.2	67.4	1,083	45.6	48.5
Black alone or in combination...........	305	261	131	42.8	50.1	86	28.1	32.9
Asian alone or in combination..........	101	72	40	(B)	(B)	28	(B)	(B)
Age								
18 to 24 years.......................	319	280	112	35.2	40.1	56	17.7	20.1
25 to 34 years.......................	434	387	202	46.5	52.2	118	27.2	30.5
35 to 44 years.......................	451	391	246	54.5	62.8	150	33.2	38.3
45 to 64 years.......................	1,047	991	719	68.6	72.5	556	53.1	56.1
65 years and over	531	511	389	73.2	76.1	315	59.4	61.7

B = Base is less than 75,000 and therefore too small to show the derived measure.

Table CT-14. Crime

(Number, rate per 100,000. Data are derived from the FBI Uniform Crime Reports.)

Item	State			U.S.[1,2,3,4]		
	2013	2014	Percent change	2013	2014	Percent change
TOTAL POPULATION[5]....................................	3,596,080	3,596,677	-	316,128,839	318,857,056	0.9
VIOLENT CRIME						
Number..................	9,153	8,522	-6.9	1,163,146	1,165,383	0.2
Rate	254.5	236.9	-6.9	367.9	365.5	-0.7
Murder and Nonnegligent Manslaughter						
Number..................	86	86	-	14,196	14,249	0.4
Rate	2.4	2.4	-	4.5	4.5	-
Rape[6]						
Number..................	955	782	X	108,612	116,645	X
Rate	26.6	21.7	X	34.4	36.6	X
Robbery						
Number..................	3,530	3,159	-10.5	345,031	325,802	-5.6
Rate	98.2	87.8	-10.6	109.1	102.2	-6.3
Aggravated Assault						
Number..................	4,869	4,495	-7.7	724,149	741,291	2.4
Rate	135.4	125.0	-7.7	229.1	232.5	1.5
PROPERTY CRIME						
Number..................	70,990	69,070	-2.7	8,632,512	8,277,829	-4.1
Rate	1,974.1	1,920.4	-2.7	2,730.7	2,596.1	-4.9
Burglary						
Number..................	12,892	11,955	-7.3	1,928,465	1,729,806	-10.3
Rate	358.5	332.4	-7.3	610.0	542.5	-11.1
Larceny-Theft						
Number..................	51,876	51,005	-1.7	6,004,453	5,858,496	-2.4
Rate	1,442.6	1,418.1	-1.7	1,899.4	1,837.3	-3.3
Motor Vehicle Theft						
Number..................	6,222	6,110	-1.8	699,594	689,527	-1.4
Rate	173.0	169.9	-1.8	221.3	216.2	-2.3

NOTE: Although arson data are included in the trend and clearance tables, sufficient data are not available to estimate totals for this offense. Therefore, no arson data are published in this table.
X = Not applicable.
- = Zero or rounds to zero.
[1]The crime figures have been adjusted.
[2]The data collection methodology for the offense of forcible rape used by the Minnesota state Uniform Crime Reporting (UCR) Program (with the exception of Minneapolis and St. Paul, Minnesota) does not comply with national UCR Program guidelines. Consequently, its figures for forcible rape and violent crime (of which forcible rape is a part) are not published in this table.
[3]Includes offenses reported by the Zoological Police and the Metro Transit Police.
[4]Because of changes in the state's reporting practices, figures are not comparable to previous years' data.
[5]Populations are U.S. Census Bureau provisional estimates as of July 1 of each year.
[6]The figures shown for the offense of rape were estimated using the revised Uniform Crime Reporting (UCR) definition of rape.

Table CT-15. State Government Finances, 2014

(Dollar amounts in thousands, percent distribution.)

Item	Dollars	Percent distribution
Total Revenue	31,291,641	100.0
General revenue	25,845,190	82.6
Intergovernmental revenue	6,364,610	20.3
Taxes	15,937,742	50.9
General sales	3,981,362	12.7
Selective sales	2,801,042	9.0
License taxes	433,024	1.4
Individual income tax	7,772,602	24.8
Corporate income tax	627,358	2.0
Other taxes	322,354	1.0
Current charges	1,898,869	6.1
Miscellaneous general revenue	1,643,969	5.3
Utility revenue	36,417	0.1
Liquor stores revenue	0	-
Insurance trust revenue[1]	5,410,034	17.3
Total Expenditure	29,308,254	100.0
Intergovernmental expenditure	4,899,005	16.7
Direct expenditure	24,409,249	83.3
Current operation	16,335,038	55.7
Capital outlay	1,609,133	5.5
Insurance benefits and repayments	4,517,037	15.4
Assistance and subsidies	525,692	1.8
Interest on debt	1,422,349	4.9
Exhibit: Salaries and wages	4,468,395	15.2
Total Expenditure	29,308,254	100.0
General expenditure	24,176,398	82.5
Intergovernmental expenditure	4,899,005	16.7
Direct expenditure	19,277,393	65.8
General expenditure, by function:		
Education	7,226,247	24.7
Public welfare	7,232,636	24.7
Hospitals	1,327,430	4.5
Health	992,468	3.4
Highways	1,063,513	3.6
Police protection	233,572	0.8
Correction	699,060	2.4
Natural resources	159,594	0.5
Parks and recreation	47,940	0.2
Governmental administration	1,299,721	4.4
Interest on general debt	1,422,349	4.9
Other and unallocable	2,471,868	8.4
Utility expenditure	614,819	2.1
Liquor stores expenditure	0	-
Insurance trust expenditure	4,517,037	15.4
Debt at End of Fiscal Year	33,229,567	X
Cash and Security Holdings	46,444,170	X

X = Not applicable.
- = Zero or rounds to zero.
[1]Within insurance trust revenue, net earnings of state retirement systems is a calculated statistic (the item code in the data file is X08), and thus can be positive or negative. Net earnings is the sum of earnings on investments plus gains on investments minus losses on investments. The change made in 2002 for asset valuation from book to market value in accordance with Statement 34 of the Governmental Accounting Standards Board is reflected in the calculated statistics.

Table CT-16. State Government Tax Collections, 2014

(Dollars in thousands, percent.)

Item	Dollars	Percent distribution
Total Taxes	15,937,742	100.0
Property taxes	X	X
Sales and gross receipts	6,782,404	42.6
General sales and gross receipts	3,981,362	25.0
Selective sales and gross receipts	2,801,042	17.6
Alcoholic beverages	60,686	0.4
Amusements	348,353	2.2
Insurance premiums	205,690	1.3
Motor fuels	503,252	3.2
Pari-mutuels	6,085	-
Public utilities	315,287	2.0
Tobacco products	376,489	2.4
Other selective sales	985,200	6.2
Licenses	433,024	2.7
Alcoholic beverages	9,265	0.1
Amusements	232	-
Corporations in general	27,828	0.2
Hunting and fishing	5,269	-
Motor vehicle	211,091	1.3
Motor vehicle operators	43,717	0.3
Public utilities	676	-
Occupation and business, NEC	132,703	0.8
Other licenses	2,243	-
Income taxes	8,399,960	52.7
Individual income	7,772,602	48.8
Corporation net income	627,358	3.9
Other taxes	322,354	2.0
Death and gift	147,737	0.9
Documentary and stock transfer	173,839	1.1
Severance	0	-
Taxes, NEC	778	-

- = Zero or rounds to zero.
X = Not applicable.

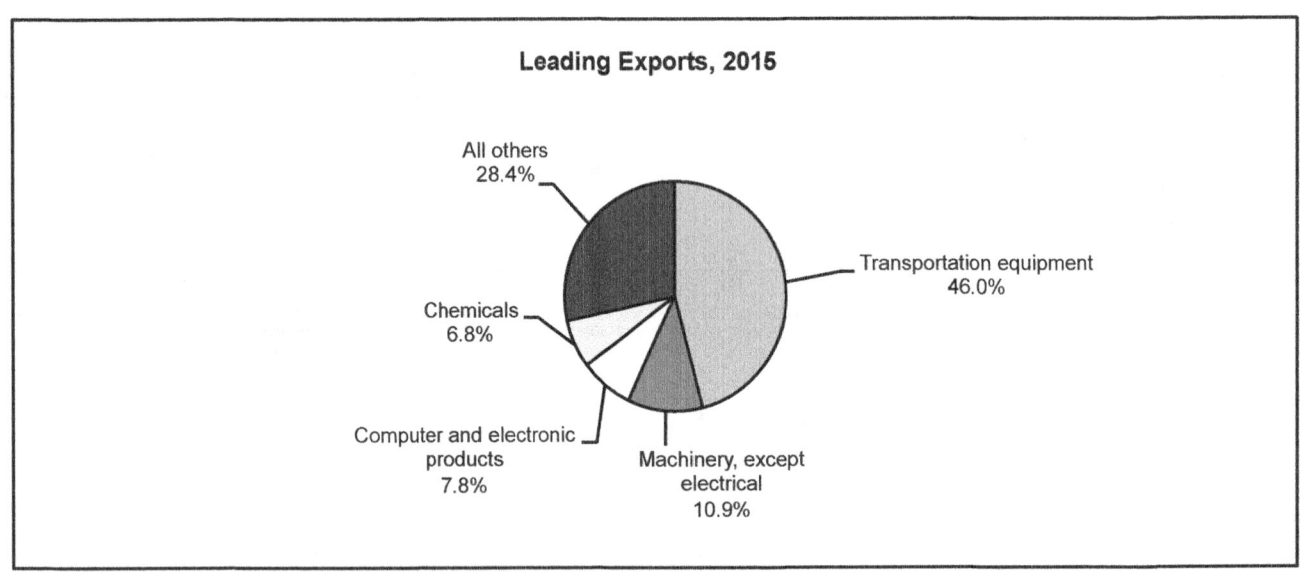

Leading Exports, 2015

All others 28.4%

Transportation equipment 46.0%

Chemicals 6.8%

Computer and electronic products 7.8%

Machinery, except electrical 10.9%

DELAWARE

Facts and Figures

Location: Northeastern United States; bordered on the N by Pennsylvania, on the E by New Jersey, and on the S and W by Maryland

Area: 2,488 sq. mi. (6,447 sq. km.); rank—49th

Population: 945,934 (2015 est.); rank—45th

Principal Cities: capital—Dover; largest—Wilmington

Statehood: December 7, 1787; 1st state

U.S. Congress: 2 senators, 1 representative

State Motto: Liberty and Independence

State Song: "Our Delaware"

State Nickname: The First State

Abbreviations: DE; Del.

State Symbols: flower—peach blossom; tree—American holly; bird—blue hen chicken

At a Glance

- With an increase in population of 5.1 percent, Delaware ranked 14th among the states in growth from 2010 to 2015.

- In 2014, 7.8 percent of Delawareans did not have health insurance, compared to 11.7 percent of the total U.S. population.

- Delaware's violent crime rate in 2014 was 489.1 per 100,000 population, compared to 365.5 for the entire nation.

- Delaware's median household income was $59,716 in 2014, ranking 15th in the nation.

- In 2014, 12.5 percent of Delawareans lived below the poverty level, compared to 15.5 percent of the total U.S. population.

Table DE-1. Population by Age, Sex, Race, and Hispanic Origin

(Number, percent, except where noted.)

Sex, age, race, and Hispanic origin	2000	2010	2015[1]	Average annual percent change, 2010–2015
Total Population...	783,600	897,934	945,934	0.4
Percent of total U.S. population	0.3	0.3	0.3	X
Sex				
Male..	380,541	434,939	457,809	0.4
Female	403,059	462,995	488,125	0.4
Age				
Under 5 years...	51,531	55,886	55,838	-
5 to 19 years..	166,719	177,917	173,626	-0.2
20 to 64 years..	463,624	648,387	555,955	-1.1
65 years and over	101,726	129,277	160,515	1.6
Median age (years)	36.0	38.8	40.0	0.2
Race and Hispanic Origin				
One race				
White..	584,773	645,770	666,187	0.2
Black...	150,666	196,281	211,859	0.5
American Indian and Alaska Native	2,731	5,929	6,189	0.3
Asian...	16,259	29,342	36,972	1.7
Native Hawaiian or				
Other Pacific Islander...	283	690	866	1.6
Two or more races	13,033	19,922	23,861	1.3
Hispanic (of any race)...	37,277	76,137	85,305	0.8

X = Not applicable.
[1]Population figures for 2015 are July 1 estimates. The 2010 estimates are taken from the 2010 Census.
- = Zero or rounds to zero.

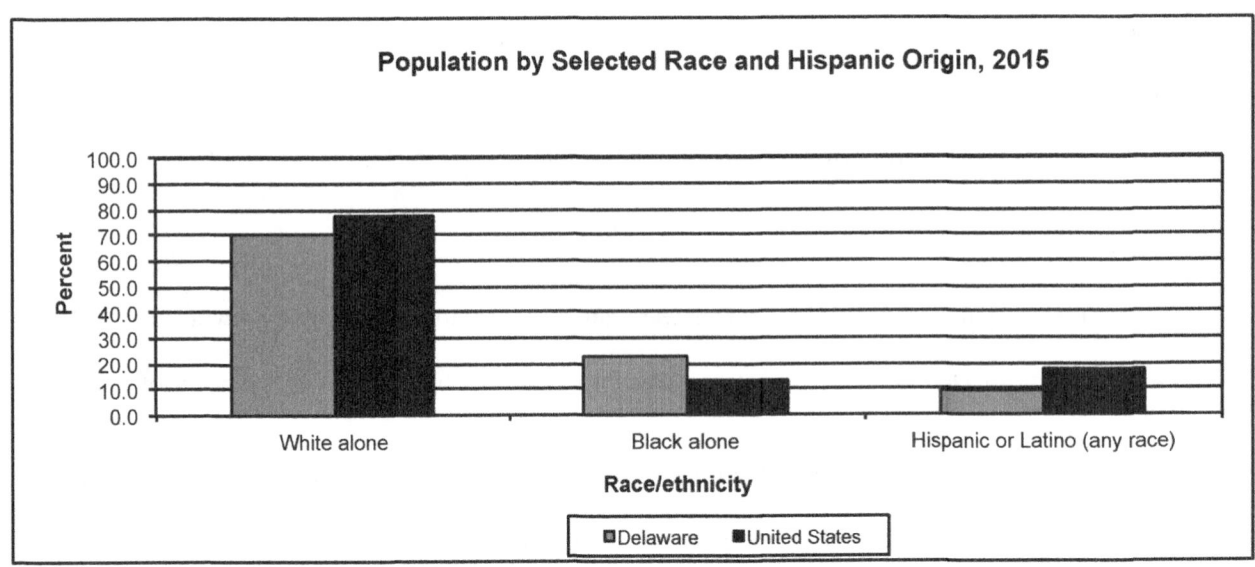

Table DE-2. Marital Status

(Number, percent distribution.)

Sex, age, race, and Hispanic origin	2000	2010	2014
Males, 15 Years and Over	296,619	350,025	357,646
Never married	29.4	35.3	35.6
Now married, except separated......................................	57.4	50.4	49.7
Separated..	1.8	1.9	1.7
Widowed..	2.8	2.9	2.9
Divorced..	8.7	9.4	10.0
Females, 15 Years and Over	324,042	380,618	389,580
Never married	25.3	30.8	30.7
Now married, except separated......................................	50.9	45.3	45.4
Separated..	2.2	2.0	2.0
Widowed..	10.7	9.8	9.1
Divorced..	10.9	12.1	12.8

Table DE-3. Households and Housing Characteristics

(Number, percent, dollars.)

Item	2000	2010	2014	Average annual percent change, 2000–2014
Total Households	298,736	328,765	349,743	1.2
Family households	204,590	221,233	233,000	1.0
Married-couple family	153,136	161,575	165,362	0.6
Other family	51,454	59,658	67,638	2.2
Male householder, no wife present	12,468	14,124	18,157	3.3
Female householder, no husband present	38,986	45,534	49,481	1.9
Nonfamily households	94,146	107,532	116,743	1.7
Householder living alone	74,639	86,990	96,302	2.1
Householder not living alone	19,507	20,542	20,441	0.3
Housing Characteristics				
Total housing units	343,072	406,489	417,413	1.5
Occupied housing units	298,736	328,765	349,743	1.2
Owner occupied	216,038	239,884	245,808	1.0
Renter occupied	86,698	88,881	103,935	1.4
Average household size	2.54	2.66	2.6	0.2
Financial Characteristics				
Median gross rent of renter-occupied housing	639	952	1,024	4.3
Median monthly owner costs for housing units with a mortgage	1,101	1,569	1,460	2.3
Median value of owner-occupied housing units	130,400	243,600	230,500	5.5

Table DE-4. Migration, Origin, and Language

(Number, percent.)

Characteristic	State 2013	State 2014	State Percent change	U.S. 2013	U.S. 2014	U.S. Percent change
Residence 1 Year Ago						
Population 1 year and over	914,025	924,770	1.2	312,432,820	315,095,393	0.9
Same house	86.6	87.7	X	85.0	85.1	X
Different house in the U.S.	12.9	11.8	X	14.4	14.3	X
Same county	7.9	7.3	X	8.9	8.7	X
Different county	5.0	4.5	X	5.5	5.6	X
Same state	1.0	1.0	X	3.2	3.3	X
Different state	4.0	3.5	X	2.3	2.3	X
Abroad	0.5	0.5	X	0.6	0.6	X
Place of Birth						
Native born	848,981	855,314	0.7	274,780,773	276,465,262	0.6
Male	48.2	48.5	X	49.3	49.3	X
Female	51.8	51.5	X	50.7	50.7	X
Foreign born	76,768	80,300	4.6	41,348,066	42,391,794	2.5
Male	50.7	49.1	X	48.8	48.7	X
Female	49.3	50.9	X	51.2	51.3	X
Foreign born; naturalized U.S. citizen	34,625	39,169	13.1	19,294,710	19,984,738	3.6
Male	47.1	49.2	X	45.9	45.9	X
Female	52.9	50.8	X	54.1	54.1	X
Foreign born; not a U.S. citizen	42,143	41,131	-2.4	22,053,356	22,407,056	1.6
Male	53.6	49.1	X	51.3	51.2	X
Female	46.4	50.9	X	48.7	48.8	X
Entered 2010 or later	13.0	15.1	X	9.7	12.3	X
Entered 2000 to 2009	33.7	35.2	X	29.4	28.6	X
Entered before 2000	53.3	49.7	X	61.0	59.1	X
World Region of Birth, Foreign						
Foreign-born population, excluding population born at sea	76,768	80,300	4.6	41,347,945	42,390,705	2.5
Europe	15	13	X	11.6	11.2	X
Asia	32.2	38.4	X	29.5	30.1	X
Africa	11.1	8.9	X	4.4	4.6	X
Oceania	-	0.0	X	0.5	0.6	X
Latin America	40.0	38.2	X	51.9	51.6	X
North America	1.8	1.4	X	2.0	1.9	X
Language Spoken at Home and Ability to Speak English						
Population 5 years and over	869,514	879,604	1.2	296,358,760	299,084,046	0.9
English only	87.9	87.0	X	79.2	78.9	X
Language other than English	12.1	13.0	X	20.8	21.1	X
Speaks English less than "very well"	4.5	4.4	X	8.5	8.6	X

X = Not applicable.
- = Zero or rounds to zero.

Table DE-5. Median Income and Poverty Status, 2014

(Number, percent, except as noted.)

Characteristic	State		U.S.	
	Number	Percent	Number	Percent
Median Income				
Households (dollars)...	59,716	X	53,657	X
Families (dollars)	72,594	X	65,910	X
Below Poverty Level (All People)	113,508	12.5	48,208,387	15.5
Sex				
Male..	49,496	11.3	21,590,918	14.2
Female	64,012	13.6	26,617,469	16.8
Age				
Under 18 years..	35,491	17.7	15,686,012	21.7
Related children under 18 years...........................	34,966	17.5	15,372,705	21.3
18 to 64 years..	66,834	11.9	28,267,482	14.6
65 years and over	11,183	7.5	4,254,893	9.5

X = Not applicable.

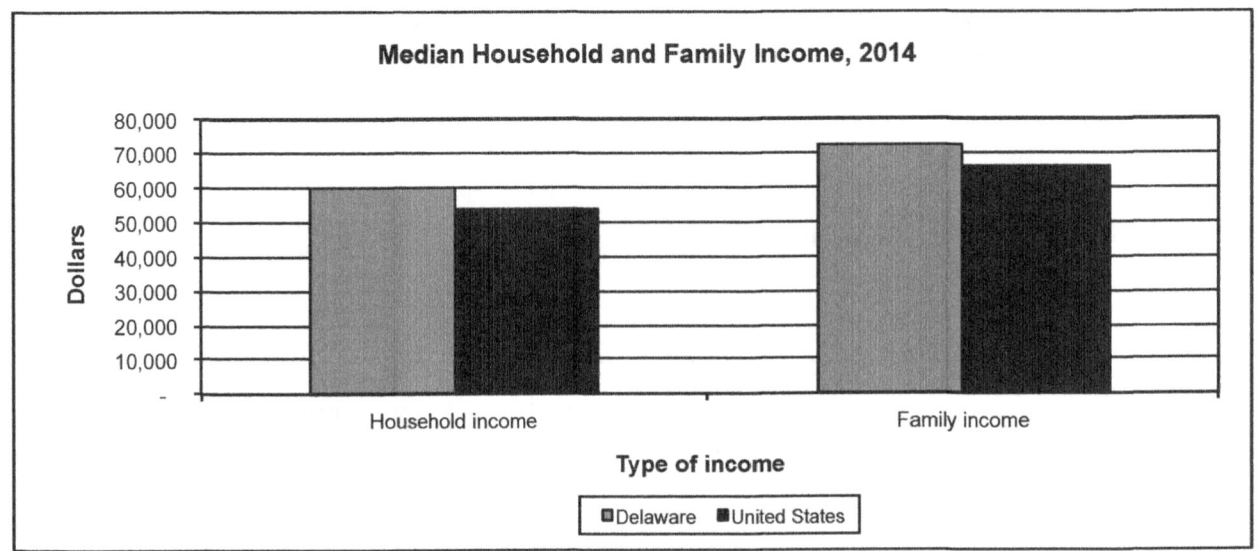

Table DE-6. Health Insurance Coverage Status for the Civilian Noninstitutionalized Population and Children Under 18 Years of Age

(Numbers in thousands, percent.)

Item	2006	2007	2008	2009	2010	2011	2012	2013	2014
Civilian Noninstitutionalized Population	862	863	856	869	885	892	903	912	921
Covered by Private or Public Insurance									
Number..	757	766	768	780	799	808	823	828	849
Percent..	87.9	88.8	89.7	89.8	90.3	90.6	91.2	90.9	92.2
Not Covered									
Number..	105	96	88	89	86	84	80	83	72
Percent..	12.1	11.2	10.3	10.2	9.7	9.4	8.8	9.1	7.8
Percent in the U.S. not covered............................	15.8	15.3	15.1	15.1	15.5	15.1	14.8	14.5	11.7
Children Under 18 Years of Age	206	209	206	207	206	204	204	203	203
Covered by Private or Public Insurance									
Number..	182	194	190	196	195	110	197	194	192
Percent..	88.3	92.5	92.2	94.5	94.7	95.4	96.5	95.5	94.3
Not Covered									
Number..	24	16	16	11	11	9	7	9	12
Percent..	11.7	7.5	7.8	5.5	5.3	4.6	3.5	4.5	5.7
Percent in the U.S. not covered............................	11.7	11.0	9.7	8.6	8.0	7.5	7.2	7.1	6.0

Table DE-7. Employment Status by Demographic Group, 2015

(Numbers in thousands, percent.)

Characteristic	Civilian noninstitutional population	Civilian labor force		Employed		Unemployed	
		Number	Percent of population	Number	Percent of population	Number	Percent of population
Total...	747	468	62.6	444	59.5	23	5.0
Sex							
Male..........	353	235	66.6	224	63.5	11	4.7
Female	394	233	59.1	220	55.9	12	5.3
Race, Sex, and Hispanic Origin							
White...........	549	338	61.4	323	58.8	15	4.3
Male..........	262	172	65.4	165	62.7	7	4.1
Female	287	166	57.8	158	55.2	7	4.5
Black or African American.........	157	103	65.7	95	60.5	8	8.0
Male..........	70	48	68.0	44	63.0	4	7.3
Female	87	55	63.9	51	58.4	5	8.6
Hispanic or Latino ethnicity[1]	55	41	73.8	39	69.5	2	6.0
Male..........	28	23	83.0	22	79.2	1	4.5
Female	28	18	64.5	16	59.4	1	7.9
Age							
16 to 19 years.........	41	15	35.9	13	30.7	2	14.7
20 to 24 years.........	54	39	71.2	34	63.6	4	10.9
25 to 34 years.........	120	101	83.7	95	78.7	6	6.1
35 to 44 years.........	122	104	85.3	99	81.7	4	4.2
45 to 54 years.........	122	101	82.8	97	79.3	4	4.2
55 to 64 years.........	124	78	62.8	76	61.4	2	2.2
65 years and over.........	164	31	19.1	31	18.6	1	2.2

NOTE: Data in Table 7 are from the Current Population Survey (CPS) and do not match the estimates in Table 8. See notes and definitions for further information.
[1]May be of any race.

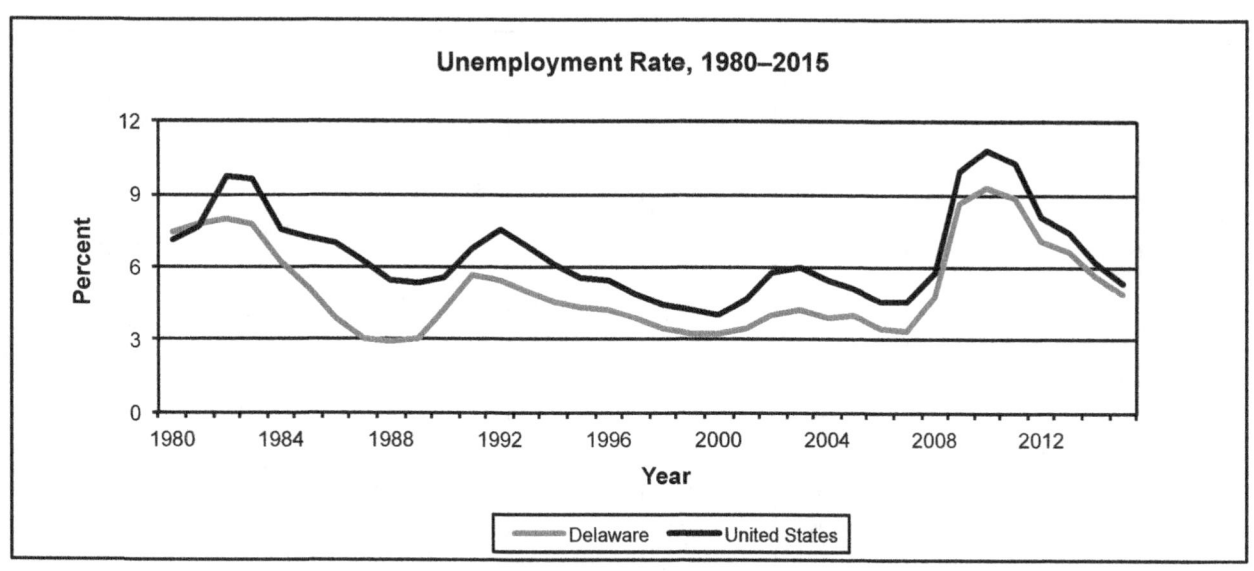

Table DE-8. Employment Status of the Civilian Noninstitutional Population Age 16 Years and Over

(Number, percent.)

Year	Civilian labor force	Civilian participation rate	Employed	Unemployed	Unemployment rate
2007.........	443,573	66.4	428,312	15,261	3.4
2008.........	447,041	65.9	424,914	22,127	4.9
2009.........	437,500	63.8	401,312	36,188	8.3
2010.........	434,419	62.0	397,869	36,550	8.4
2011.........	443,346	62.3	410,086	33,260	7.5
2012.........	445,708	61.9	413,589	32,119	7.2
2013.........	442,518	60.7	412,766	29,752	6.7
2014.........	453,631	61.4	427,708	25,923	5.7
2015.........	467,472	62.4	444,578	22,894	4.9

Table DE-9. Employment and Average Wages by Industry

(Estimates through 2010 are based on the 2007 North American Industry Classification System [NAICS]. Estimates from 2011 onward are based on the 2012 NAICS.)

Industry	2008	2009	2010	2011	2012	2013	2014
				Number of Jobs			
Wage and Salary Employment by Industry...................	451,791	430,104	428,089	432,161	433,304	442,726	452,023
Farm Wage and Salary Employment..........................	1,069	1,036	1,161	1,126	1,459	1,396	1,794
Nonfarm Wage and Salary Employment.....................	450,722	429,068	426,928	431,035	431,845	441,330	450,229
Private wage and salary employment........................	379,042	357,441	354,081	358,212	358,813	367,068	375,593
Forestry, fishing, and related activities...........................	D	D	D	D	D	D	D
Mining...	D	D	D	D	D	D	D
Utilities..	2,204	2,129	2,090	1,961	2,014	2,086	2,148
Construction...	25,636	20,959	20,265	20,318	19,158	20,291	21,025
Manufacturing...	31,813	27,987	26,181	25,698	25,787	25,361	25,708
Durable goods manufacturing................................	12,968	10,211	9,737	9,691	9,649	9,424	9,197
Nondurable goods manufacturing............................	18,845	17,776	16,444	16,007	16,138	15,937	16,511
Wholesale trade	14,667	13,355	12,599	12,592	12,533	12,253	12,038
Retail trade..	53,635	50,475	50,723	51,364	51,150	51,968	52,882
Transportation and warehousing..............................	11,196	10,215	10,092	10,261	10,553	11,719	12,993
Information...	7,072	6,502	5,985	5,661	5,461	5,257	4,894
Finance and insurance...	39,591	38,507	37,764	37,845	38,056	39,263	40,645
Real estate and rental and leasing..........................	6,708	6,164	5,894	5,732	5,568	5,667	5,414
Professional, scientific, and technical services	26,132	24,563	24,166	26,292	27,448	28,751	29,156
Management of companies and enterprises.................	10,745	9,933	9,409	8,048	7,490	5,966	5,497
Administrative and waste services...........................	23,737	21,527	21,440	22,068	21,795	23,530	25,508
Educational services	6,981	6,865	6,974	7,179	6,991	6,745	6,961
Health care and social assistance...........................	55,114	56,354	57,290	58,699	59,871	61,925	64,197
Arts, entertainment, and recreation..........................	8,439	8,223	8,817	9,224	8,898	8,784	10,250
Accommodation and food services............................	33,497	33,233	34,064	34,748	35,308	36,391	37,316
Other services, except public administration.................	21,532	20,085	19,925	19,978	20,214	20,464	18,291
Government and government enterprises.............................	71,680	71,627	72,847	72,823	73,032	74,262	74,636
				Dollars			
Average Wages and Salaries by Industry	46,831	47,075	47,961	49,661	50,860	51,093	52,281
Average Farm Wages and Salaries	32,054	31,419	26,482	24,429	21,132	30,092	27,086
Average Nonfarm Wages and Salaries	46,866	47,113	48,020	49,727	50,961	51,160	52,381
Average private wages and salaries.........................	47,097	47,132	48,446	50,316	51,546	51,757	53,127
Forestry, fishing, and related activities.........................	D	D	D	D	D	D	D
Mining...	D	D	D	D	D	D	D
Utilities..	88,640	94,420	94,430	96,294	95,593	98,759	104,333
Construction	49,628	48,641	49,049	52,483	50,990	53,079	53,835
Manufacturing...	56,464	57,897	56,995	56,148	57,087	57,900	59,591
Durable goods manufacturing................................	64,317	69,954	65,811	67,990	67,241	68,246	70,865
Nondurable goods manufacturing............................	51,059	50,971	51,776	48,979	51,016	51,782	53,311
Wholesale trade	69,948	72,291	76,872	82,623	82,041	79,192	83,247
Retail trade..	25,504	25,714	25,809	26,002	26,184	26,471	27,187
Transportation and warehousing..............................	40,885	43,197	43,126	44,551	46,121	46,002	45,997
Information...	55,013	55,492	56,439	57,380	59,118	61,039	62,346
Finance and insurance...	76,765	74,028	79,068	84,043	86,353	89,511	90,975
Real estate and rental and leasing..........................	40,138	39,671	40,745	41,443	41,997	42,630	44,527
Professional, scientific, and technical services	79,826	80,985	85,311	89,362	97,492	94,542	100,137
Management of companies and enterprises.................	90,221	88,304	105,373	127,272	130,107	143,164	143,808
Administrative and waste services...........................	31,245	31,075	32,443	32,770	33,877	34,332	35,341
Educational services	34,012	35,465	35,617	36,172	36,858	38,458	40,235
Health care and social assistance...........................	45,687	46,857	47,294	48,700	49,738	49,883	50,950
Arts, entertainment, and recreation..........................	26,862	27,626	28,568	30,865	30,148	29,015	26,582
Accommodation and food services............................	18,840	18,364	18,853	18,637	18,635	18,507	19,286
Other services, except public administration.................	28,818	28,893	29,255	29,443	29,284	29,801	33,363
Government and government enterprises.............................	45,687	47,015	45,948	46,827	48,086	48,207	48,628

D = Not shown to avoid disclosure of confidential information, but the estimates for this item are included in the total.

Table DE-10. Employment Characteristics by Family Type

(Number, percent.)

Family type and labor force status	2012		2013		2014	
	Total	Families with own children under 18 years	Total	Families with own children under 18 years	Total	Families with own children under 18 years
All Families...	225,593	92,860	228,364	88,214	230,988	89,297
FAMILY TYPE AND LABOR FORCE STATUS						
Married-Couple Families.....................	163,460	59,809	164,733	55,941	163,350	55,964
Both husband and wife in labor force...........	53.3	70.7	49.9	72.5	51.8	73.2
Husband in labor force, wife not in labor force........	19.3	24.1	20.4	22.6	16.9	21.3
Wife in labor force, husband not in labor force........	8.3	3.7	8.2	3.2	8.9	3.2
Both husband and wife not in labor force............	19.1	1.5	21.0	1.7	22.4	2.3
Other Families	62,133	33,051	63,631	32,273	67,638	33,333
Female householder, no husband present................	73.8	74.1	77.0	77.2	73.2	77.5
In labor force	55.7	65.2	55.6	63.7	53.6	64.5
Not in labor force	18.1	8.8	21.4	13.5	19.6	13.0
Male householder, no wife present....................	26.2	25.9	23.0	22.8	26.8	22.5
In labor force..	21.4	24.4	18.0	20.9	20.9	21.6
Not in labor force	4.8	1.5	5.1	2.0	5.9	0.9

Table DE-11. School Enrollment and Educational Attainment, 2014

(Number, percent.)

Item	State	U.S.
Enrollment		
Total population 3 years and over, enrolled in school...............	235,650	82,063,714
Enrolled in nursery school or preschool (percent)	6.9	6.0
Enrolled in kindergarten (percent)............................	5.3	5.1
Enrolled in elementary school, grades 1-8 (percent)............	37.4	40.2
Enrolled in high school, grades 9-12 (percent)................	19.7	20.7
Enrolled in college or graduate school (percent)...............	30.6	28.0
Attainment		
Total population 25 years and over	640,343	213,725,624
Less than ninth grade (percent)	3.4	5.6
9th to 12th grade, no diploma (percent)	7.7	7.5
High school graduate, including equivalency (percent)...........	31.2	27.7
Some college, no degree (percent)	19.2	21.0
Associate's degree (percent)	7.9	8.2
Bachelor's degree (percent)	18.3	18.7
Graduate or professional degree (percent).....................	12.3	11.4
High school graduate or higher (percent)	89.0	86.9
Bachelor's degree or higher (percent).........................	30.6	30.1

Table DE-12. Public School Characteristics and Educational Indicators

(Number, percent; data derived from National Center of Education Statistics.)

Item	State	U.S.
Public Schools, 2013–2014 (except where noted)		
Number of school districts...........................	43	18,194
Number of schools..................................	219	98,271
Number of students (in thousands)	132	50,045
Number of teachers (in thousands)	9	3,114
Student-teacher ratio	14.0	16.1
Expenditures per student (dollars), FY 2013	13,653	107,637
Four-year adjusted cohort graduation rate (ACGR)[1][2]	87.0	82.3
Students eligible for free or reduced-price lunch (in thousands)	52	25,596
English language learners (in thousands)	8	4,461
Students age 3 to 21 served under IDEA, part B (in thousands)	19	6,464

Public Schools by Type	Number	Percent of state public schools
Total number of schools.......................................	219	100.0
Regular	187	85.4
Special education..	19	8.7
Vocational education...	6	2.7
Alternative education..	7	3.2

NOTE: Every school is assigned only one school type based on its instructional emphasis.
[1]ACGR data represents a new method of calculating high-school completion rates and may not be comparable to previous years' data for Averaged Freshmen Graduation Rates (AFGR).
[2]The United States 4-year ACGRs were estimated using both the reported 4-year ACGR data from 49 states and the District of Columbia and using imputed data for Idaho. The estimate for American Indian/Alaska Native students also includes imputed data for Virginia.

Table DE-13. Reported Voting and Registration of the Voting-Age Population, November 2014

(Numbers in thousands, percent.)

Item	Total population	Total citizen population	Registered			Voted		
			Total registered	Percent registered (total population)	Percent registered (total citizen population)	Total voted	Percent voted (total population)	Percent voted (total citizen population)
U.S. Total	239,874	219,941	142,166	59.3	64.6	92,251	38.5	41.9
State Total............................	712	661	442	62.0	66.8	299	42.0	45.2
Sex								
Male...............................	337	311	206	61.2	66.2	139	41.2	44.6
Female	375	350	236	62.8	67.3	160	42.7	45.7
Race								
White alone..........................	510	484	336	65.9	69.4	229	44.9	47.2
White, non-Hispanic alone	471	465	326	69.3	70.2	224	47.7	48.3
Black alone..........................	147	138	91	61.9	66.1	59	40.3	43.0
Asian alone	32	20	4	(B)	(B)	3	(B)	(B)
Hispanic (of any race)	56	31	14	(B)	(B)	5	(B)	(B)
White alone or in combination	523	496	344	65.7	69.2	234	44.7	47.2
Black alone or in combination..........	157	146	98	62.4	67.0	64	40.7	43.7
Asian alone or in combination..........	33	20	5	(B)	(B)	3	(B)	(B)
Age								
18 to 24 years......................	78	72	36	(B)	(B)	12	(B)	(B)
25 to 34 years......................	120	103	58	48.4	56.6	31	25.9	30.3
35 to 44 years......................	111	97	62	55.8	63.7	36	32.1	36.6
45 to 64 years......................	246	237	171	69.6	72.3	123	50.1	52.1
65 years and over	157	152	115	73.2	75.3	97	62.0	63.7

B = Base is less than 75,000 and therefore too small to show the derived measure.

Table DE-14. Crime

(Number, rate per 100,000. Data are derived from the FBI Uniform Crime Reports.)

Item	State			U.S.[1,2,3,4]		
	2013	2014	Percent change	2013	2014	Percent change
TOTAL POPULATION[5]..	925,749	935,614	1.1	316,128,839	318,857,056	0.9
VIOLENT CRIME						
Number..............................	4,435	4,576	3.2	1,163,146	1,165,383	0.2
Rate................................	479.1	489.1	2.1	367.9	365.5	-0.7
Murder and Nonnegligent Manslaughter						
Number..............................	39	54	38.5	14,196	14,249	0.4
Rate	4.2	5.8	38.1	4.5	4.5	-
Rape[6]						
Number..............................	380	386	X	108,612	116,645	X
Rate................................	41.0	41.3	X	34.4	36.6	X
Robbery						
Number..............................	1,226	1,269	3.5	345,031	325,802	-5.6
Rate................................	132.4	135.6	2.4	109.1	102.2	-6.3
Aggravated Assault						
Number..............................	2,904	2,867	-1.3	724,149	741,291	2.4
Rate	313.7	306.4	-2.3	229.1	232.5	1.5
PROPERTY CRIME						
Number..............................	28,379	27,900	-1.7	8,632,512	8,277,829	-4.1
Rate................................	3,065.5	2,982.0	-2.7	2,730.7	2,596.1	-4.9
Burglary						
Number..............................	6,131	5,768	-5.9	1,928,465	1,729,806	-10.3
Rate................................	662.3	616.5	-6.9	610.0	542.5	-11.1
Larceny-Theft						
Number..............................	20,916	20,865	-0.2	6,004,453	5,858,496	-2.4
Rate................................	2,259.4	2,230.1	-1.3	1,899.4	1,837.3	-3.3
Motor Vehicle Theft						
Number..............................	1,332	1,267	-4.9	699,594	689,527	-1.4
Rate................................	143.9	135.4	-5.9	221.3	216.2	-2.3

NOTE: Although arson data are included in the trend and clearance tables, sufficient data are not available to estimate totals for this offense. Therefore, no arson data are published in this table.
X = Not applicable.
- = Zero or rounds to zero.
[1]The crime figures have been adjusted.
[2]The data collection methodology for the offense of forcible rape used by the Minnesota state Uniform Crime Reporting (UCR) Program (with the exception of Minneapolis and St. Paul, Minnesota) does not comply with national UCR Program guidelines. Consequently, its figures for forcible rape and violent crime (of which forcible rape is a part) are not published in this table.
[3]Includes offenses reported by the Zoological Police and the Metro Transit Police.
[4]Because of changes in the state's reporting practices, figures are not comparable to previous years' data.
[5]Populations are U.S. Census Bureau provisional estimates as of July 1 of each year.
[6]The figures shown for the offense of rape were estimated using the revised Uniform Crime Reporting (UCR) definition of rape.

Table DE-15. State Government Finances, 2014

(Dollar amounts in thousands, percent distribution.)

Item	Dollars	Percent distribution
Total Revenue	9,298,130	100.0
General revenue	7,605,276	81.8
Intergovernmental revenue	2,101,677	22.6
Taxes	3,176,169	34.2
General sales	0	-
Selective sales	480,352	5.2
License taxes	1,301,737	14.0
Individual income tax	1,040,341	11.2
Corporate income tax	278,872	3.0
Other taxes	74,867	0.8
Current charges	1,141,170	12.3
Miscellaneous general revenue	1,186,260	12.8
Utility revenue	18,666	0.2
Liquor stores revenue	0	-
Insurance trust revenue[1]	1,674,188	18.0
Total Expenditure	8,786,763	100.0
Intergovernmental expenditure	1,390,686	15.8
Direct expenditure	7,396,077	84.2
Current operation	5,481,855	62.4
Capital outlay	601,095	6.8
Insurance benefits and repayments	679,828	7.7
Assistance and subsidies	277,165	3.2
Interest on debt	356,134	4.1
Exhibit: Salaries and wages	2,483,946	28.3
Total Expenditure	8,786,763	100.0
General expenditure	7,978,002	90.8
Intergovernmental expenditure	1,390,686	15.8
Direct expenditure	6,587,316	75.0
General expenditure, by function:		
Education	2,841,666	32.3
Public welfare	2,142,011	24.4
Hospitals	44,786	0.5
Health	443,210	5.0
Highways	530,890	6.0
Police protection	121,044	1.4
Correction	291,531	3.3
Natural resources	87,912	1.0
Parks and recreation	42,102	0.5
Governmental administration	496,483	5.7
Interest on general debt	356,134	4.1
Other and unallocable	580,233	6.6
Utility expenditure	128,933	1.5
Liquor stores expenditure	0	-
Insurance trust expenditure	679,828	7.7
Debt at End of Fiscal Year	5,354,253	X
Cash and Security Holdings	15,881,262	X

X = Not applicable.
- = Zero or rounds to zero.
[1]Within insurance trust revenue, net earnings of state retirement systems is a calculated statistic (the item code in the data file is X08), and thus can be positive or negative. Net earnings is the sum of earnings on investments plus gains on investments minus losses on investments. The change made in 2002 for asset valuation from book to market value in accordance with Statement 34 of the Governmental Accounting Standards Board is reflected in the calculated statistics.

Table DE-16. State Government Tax Collections, 2014

(Dollars in thousands, percent.)

Item	Dollars	Percent distribution
Total Taxes	3,176,169	100.0
Property taxes	X	X
Sales and gross receipts	480,352	15.1
General sales and gross receipts	X	X
Selective sales and gross receipts	480,352	15.1
Alcoholic beverages	19,616	0.6
Amusements	0	-
Insurance premiums	85,735	2.7
Motor fuels	113,326	3.6
Pari-mutuels	82	-
Public utilities	59,128	1.9
Tobacco products	114,659	3.6
Other selective sales	87,806	2.8
Licenses	1,301,737	41.0
Alcoholic beverages	1,547	-
Amusements	328	-
Corporations in general	1,002,576	31.6
Hunting and fishing	2,916	0.1
Motor vehicle	51,790	1.6
Motor vehicle operators	5,712	0.2
Public utilities	0	-
Occupation and business, NEC	231,407	7.3
Other licenses	5,461	0.2
Income taxes	1,319,213	41.5
Individual income	1,040,341	32.8
Corporation net income	278,872	8.8
Other taxes	74,867	2.4
Death and gift	1,434	-
Documentary and stock transfer	72,347	2.3
Severance	X	X
Taxes, NEC	1,086	

X = Not applicable.
- = Zero or rounds to zero.

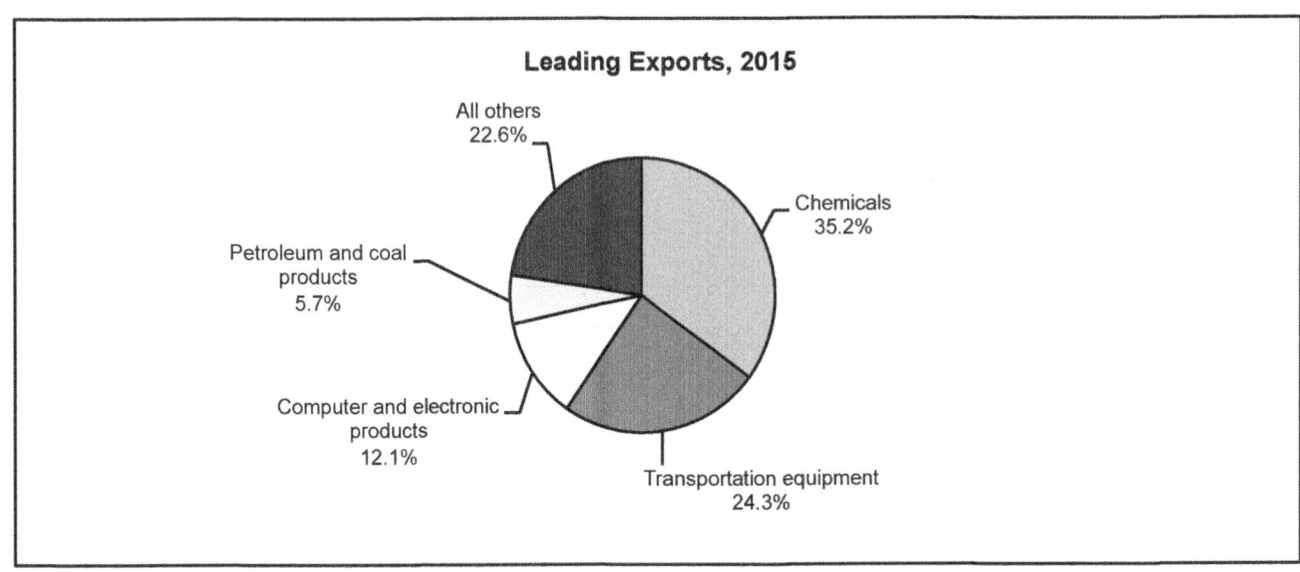

Leading Exports, 2015

- All others 22.6%
- Chemicals 35.2%
- Petroleum and coal products 5.7%
- Computer and electronic products 12.1%
- Transportation equipment 24.3%

Facts and Figures

Location: South Atlantic United States; bordered on the SE, NE, and NW by Maryland and on the SW by Virginia

Area: 68 sq. mi.

Population: 672,228 (2015 est.); rank—49th

Official Motto: Justitia omnibus ("Justice for All")

U.S. Congress: 1 delegate

Abbreviation: D.C.

Symbols: flower—American Beauty rose; tree—scarlet oak; bird—wood thrush

At a Glance

- From 2010 to 2015, the population of the District of Columbia increased by 11.1 percent, the second highest increase in the country.

- The violent crime rate in the District of Columbia was 1,244.4 per 100,000 population in 2014, more than triple the national rate of 367.9 per 100,000.

- In 2014, The District of Columbia's property crime rate was 5,182.5 per 100,000 population, compared to 2,596.1 for the U.S. as a whole.

- Compared to the 50 states, the District of Columbia had the lowest percentage of people under 18 years of age (17.6 percent), and the third lowest percentage of people over age 65 (11.5 percent) in 2015.

- In 2014, 17.7 percent of all District of Columbia residents lived in poverty and 26.0 percent of children under 18 years of age lived in poverty.

Table DC-1. Population by Age, Sex, Race, and Hispanic Origin

(Number, percent, except where noted.)

Sex, age, race, and Hispanic origin	2000	2010	2015[1]	Average annual percent change, 2010–2015
Total Population..................................	572,059	601,723	672,228	0.8
Percent of total U.S. population	0.2	0.2	0.2	X
Sex				
Male..................................	269,366	284,222	318,601	0.8
Female	302,693	317,501	353,627	0.8
Age				
Under 5 years..................................	32,536	32,613	43,352	2.1
5 to 19 years..................................	103,270	91,107	96,409	0.4
20 to 64 years..................................	366,355	409,194	455,463	0.8
65 years and over	69,898	68,809	77,004	0.8
Median age (years)	34.8	33.8	33.8	-
Race and Hispanic Origin				
One race				
White	176,101	251,265	296,292	1.2
Black..................................	343,312	310,379	324,694	0.3
American Indian and Alaska Native	1,713	3,264	3,750	1.0
Asian..................................	15,189	21,705	28,298	1.9
Native Hawaiian or Other Pacific Islander	348	770	1063	2.3
Two or more races	13,446	14,340	18,131	1.7
Hispanic (of any race)..................................	44,953	57,833	71,128	1.5

X = Not applicable.
- = Zero or rounds to zero.
[1]Population figures for 2015 are July 1 estimates. The 2010 estimates are taken from the 2010 Census.

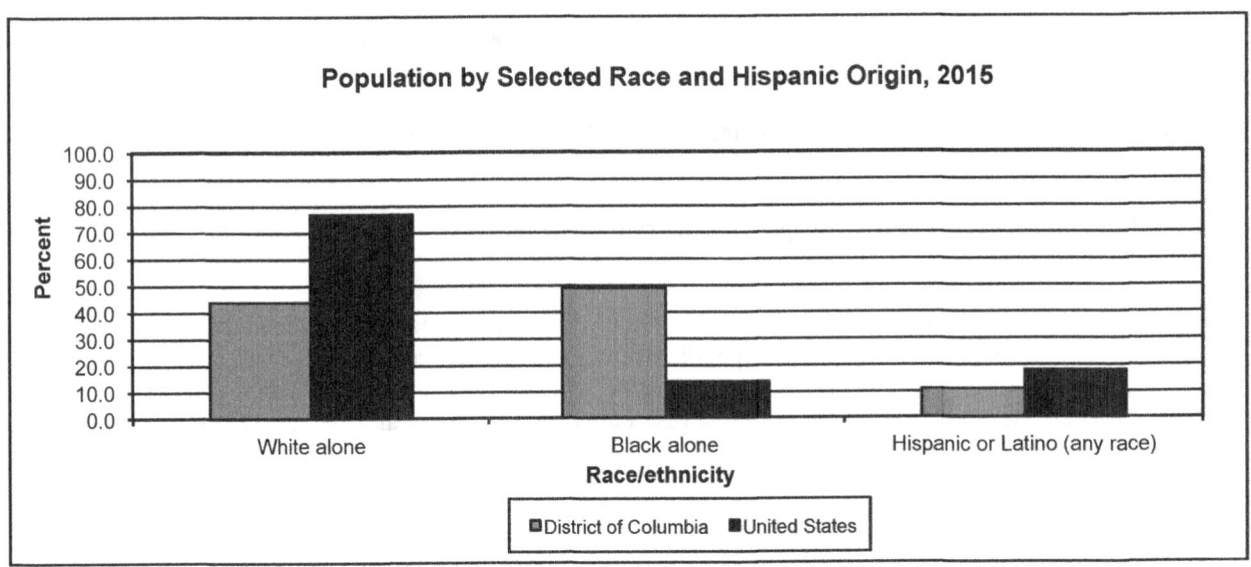

Table DC-2. Marital Status

(Number, percent distribution.)

Sex, age, race, and Hispanic origin	2000	2010	2014
Males, 15 Years and Over	219,706	243,152	253,450
Never married	51.2	58.9	58.3
Now married, except separated..................................	32.8	28.2	28.9
Separated..................................	3.9	2.4	2.3
Widowed..................................	3.4	2.1	1.9
Divorced..................................	8.7	8.4	8.6
Females, 15 Years and Over	254,711	277,203	288,250
Never married	46.0	55.8	55.9
Now married, except separated..................................	27.5	22.8	24.3
Separated..................................	4.4	3.1	2.5
Widowed..................................	11.6	7.5	7.1
Divorced..................................	10.6	10.8	10.2

Table DC-3. Households and Housing Characteristics

(Number, percent, dollars.)

Item	2000	2010	2014	Average annual percent change, 2000–2014
Total Households...	248,338	252,388	277,378	0.8
Family households	114,166	101,519	117,864	0.2
Married-couple family	56,631	57,275	66,244	1.2
Other family	57,535	44,244	51,620	-0.7
Male householder, no wife present...................	10,503	8,740	9,496	-0.7
Female householder, no husband present..........	47,032	35,504	42,124	-0.7
Nonfamily households	134,172	150,869	159,514	1.3
Householder living alone...	108,744	121,036	123,743	1.0
Householder not living alone...................................	25,428	29,833	35,771	2.9
Housing Characteristics				
Total housing units...	274,845	296,836	306,184	0.8
Occupied housing units	248,338	252,388	277,378	0.8
Owner occupied	101,214	107,193	112,492	0.8
Renter occupied	147,124	145,195	164,886	0.9
Average household size..	2.16	2.24	2.23	0.2
Financial Characteristics				
Median gross rent of renter-occupied housing	618	1,198	1,360	8.6
Median monthly owner costs for housing units with a mortgage	1,291	2,297	2,194	5.0
Median value of owner-occupied housing units.............	157,200	426,900	486,900	15.0

Table DC-4. Migration, Origin, and Language

(Number, percent.)

Characteristic	State			U.S.		
	2013	2014	Percent change	2013	2014	Percent change
Residence 1 Year Ago						
Population 1 year and over	636,535	648,586	1.9	312,432,820	315,095,393	0.9
Same house...	80.1	79.2	X	85.0	85.1	X
Different house in the U.S..	18.1	19	X	14.4	14.3	X
Same county	10.8	10.4	X	8.9	8.7	X
Different county	7.3	8.7	X	5.5	5.6	X
Same state	0.0	0	X	3.2	3.3	X
Different state	7.3	8.7	X	2.3	2.3	X
Abroad	1.7	1.8	X	0.6	0.6	X
Place of Birth						
Native born	553,630	566,944	2.4	274,780,773	276,465,262	0.6
Male..	47.1	47.4	X	49.3	49.3	X
Female	52.9	52.6	X	50.7	50.7	X
Foreign born	92,819	91,949	-0.9	41,348,066	42,391,794	2.5
Male..	48.9	47.6	X	48.8	48.7	X
Female	51.1	52.4	X	51.2	51.3	X
Foreign born; naturalized U.S. citizen........................	38,038	35,515	-6.6	19,294,710	19,984,738	3.6
Male..	48.0	42	X	45.9	45.9	X
Female	52.0	58	X	54.1	54.1	X
Foreign born; not a U.S. citizen	54,781	56,434	3.0	22,053,356	22,407,056	1.6
Male..	49.5	51.1	X	51.3	51.2	X
Female	50.5	48.9	X	48.7	48.8	X
Entered 2010 or later	17.3	21.7	X	9.7	12.3	X
Entered 2000 to 2009	35.8	35.5	X	29.4	28.6	X
Entered before 2000..	46.9	42.8	X	61.0	59.1	X
World Region of Birth, Foreign						
Foreign-born population, excluding population born at sea	92,819	91,949	-0.9	41,347,945	42,390,705	2.5
Europe	19.1	20	X	11.6	11.2	X
Asia..	17.5	18.3	X	29.5	30.1	X
Africa...	17.1	15.9	X	4.4	4.6	X
Oceania	1.0	0.9	X	0.5	0.6	X
Latin America..	43.1	43.1	X	51.9	51.6	X
North America...	2.1	2.0	X	2.0	1.9	X
Language Spoken at Home and Ability to Speak English						
Population 5 years and over..	605,388	616,130	1.8	296,358,760	299,084,046	0.9
English only	82.1	82.2	X	79.2	78.9	X
Language other than English.....................................	17.9	17.8	X	20.8	21.1	X
Speaks English less than "very well".....................	5.5	5.9	X	8.5	8.6	X

X = Not applicable.
- = Zero or rounds to zero.

Table DC-5. Median Income and Poverty Status, 2014

(Number, percent, except as noted.)

Characteristic	State		U.S.	
	Number	Percent	Number	Percent
Median Income				
Households (dollars)...	71,648	X	53,657	X
Families (dollars)	84,094	X	65,910	X
Below Poverty Level (All People)	110,666	17.7	48,208,387	15.5
Sex				
Male..	47,584	16.1	21,590,918	14.2
Female	63,082	19.2	26,617,469	16.8
Age				
Under 18 years..	29,404	26.0	15,686,012	21.7
Related children under 18 years.............................	29,202	25.9	15,372,705	21.3
18 to 64 years..	70,792	16.1	28,267,482	14.6
65 years and over	10,470	14.5	4,254,893	9.5

X = Not applicable.

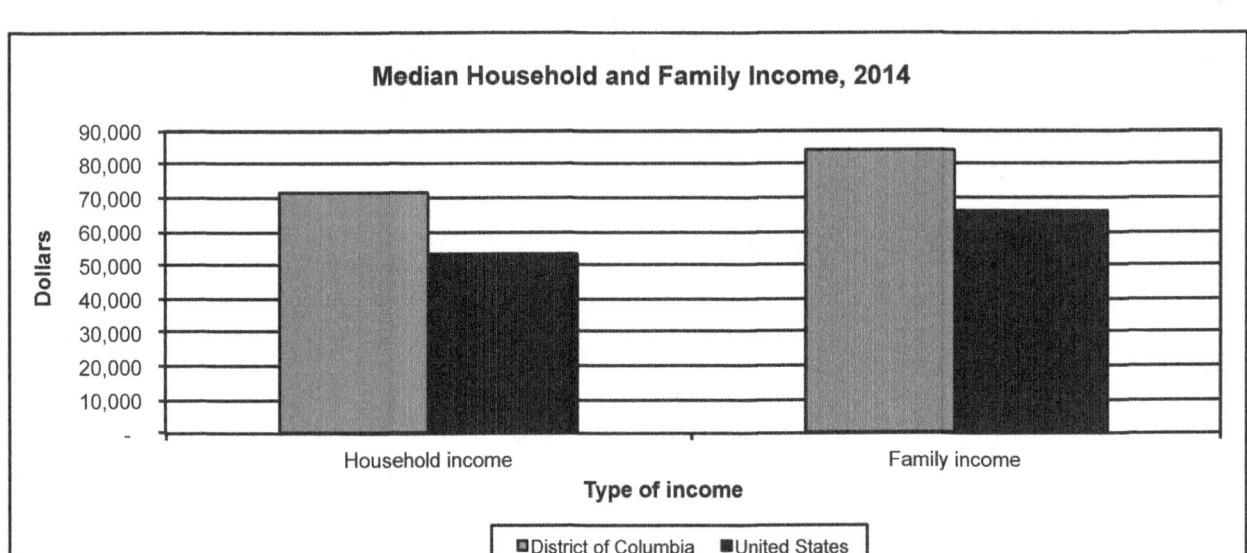

Table DC-6. Health Insurance Coverage Status for the Civilian Noninstitutionalized Population and Children Under 18 Years of Age

(Numbers in thousands, percent.)

Item	2006	2007	2008	2009	2010	2011	2012	2013	2014
Civilian Noninstitutionalized Population	569	582	580	589	594	608	621	636	648
Covered by Private or Public Insurance									
Number...	503	526	534	548	549	566	585	594	614
Percent...	88.5	90.5	92.1	93.0	92.4	93.1	94.1	93.3	94.7
Not Covered									
Number...	66	55	46	41	45	42	36	42	34
Percent...	11.6	9.5	7.9	7.0	7.6	6.9	5.9	6.7	5.3
Percent in the U.S. not covered...............................	15.8	15.3	15.1	15.1	15.5	15.1	14.8	14.5	11.7
Children Under 18 Years of Age	115	112	111	114	101	105	109	111	115
Covered by Private or Public Insurance									
Number...	105	105	106	111	99	101	107	109	112
Percent...	91.3	93.8	95.5	97.2	97.7	96.1	98.3	97.6	97.9
Not Covered									
Number...	10	7	5	3	2	4	2	3	2
Percent...	8.7	6.2	4.5	2.8	2.3	3.9	1.7	2.4	2.1
Percent in the U.S. not covered...............................	11.7	11.0	9.7	8.6	8.0	7.5	7.2	7.1	6.0

Table DC-7. Employment Status by Demographic Group, 2015

(Numbers in thousands, percent.)

Characteristic	Civilian noninstitutional population	Civilian labor force		Employed		Unemployed	
		Number	Percent of population	Number	Percent of population	Number	Percent of population
Total	551	386	70.1	359	65.3	27	6.9
Sex							
Male	256	189	74.0	177	69.3	12	6.3
Female	295	197	66.8	182	61.8	15	7.5
Race, Sex, and Hispanic Origin							
White	251	206	82.1	200	79.7	6	2.9
Male	125	107	84.9	104	82.5	3	2.9
Female	125	99	79.2	96	76.9	3	2.9
Black or African American	258	148	57.3	128	49.7	20	13.3
Male	113	69	60.4	60	53.0	8	12.3
Female	145	80	54.9	68	47.1	11	14.1
Hispanic or Latino ethnicity[1]	55	42	76.9	41	73.8	2	4.0
Male	25	21	81.7	20	78.7	1	3.5
Female	30	22	72.7	21	69.5	1	4.6
Age							
16 to 19 years	24	5	19.7	3	13.6	1	30.1
20 to 24 years	57	39	68.5	34	59.8	5	12.8
25 to 34 years	157	138	87.6	130	82.8	8	5.5
35 to 44 years	93	81	86.4	77	82.0	4	5.0
45 to 54 years	77	62	80.7	57	74.8	5	7.4
55 to 64 years	63	41	65.1	38	59.9	3	8.0
65 years and over	79	21	26.7	20	25.3	1	4.7

NOTE: Data in Table 7 are from the Current Population Survey (CPS) and do not match the estimates in Table 8. See notes and definitions for further information.
[1] May be of any race.

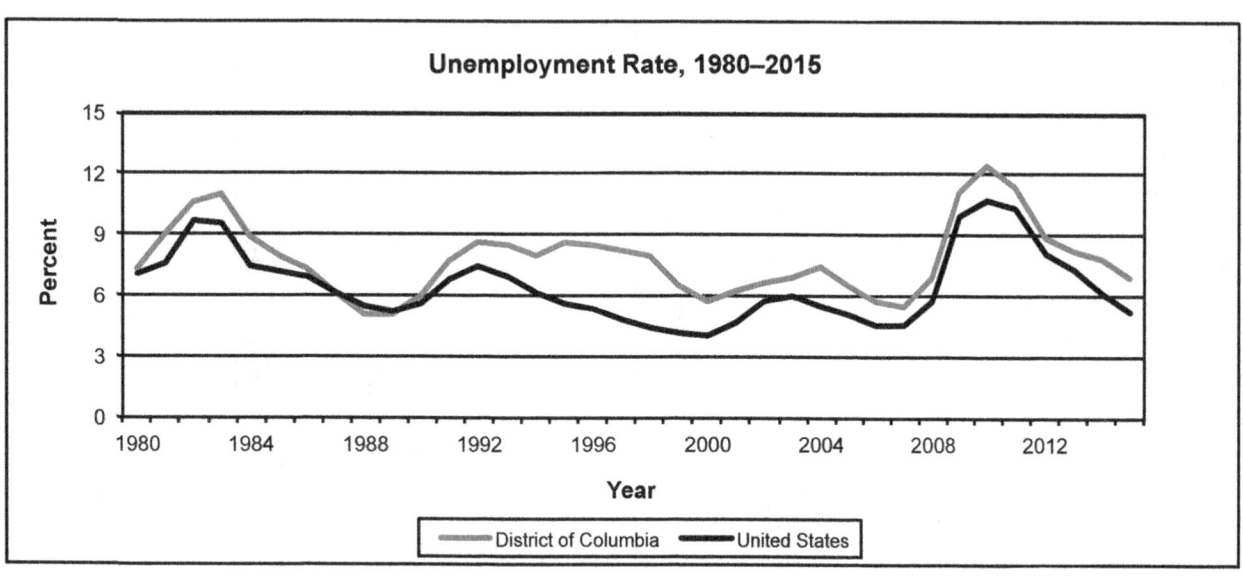

Table DC-8. Employment Status of the Civilian Noninstitutional Population Age 16 Years and Over

(Number, percent.)

Year	Civilian labor force	Civilian participation rate	Employed	Unemployed	Unemployment rate
2007	322,237	68.1	304,426	17,811	5.5
2008	330,544	69.2	309,192	21,352	6.5
2009	335,672	69.1	304,500	31,172	9.3
2010	346,065	68.8	313,508	32,557	9.4
2011	350,778	67.9	315,171	35,607	10.2
2012	365,055	69.2	332,068	32,987	9.0
2013	373,835	69.6	342,061	31,774	8.5
2014	378,082	69.4	348,729	29,353	7.8
2015	388,388	70.1	361,544	26,844	6.9

Table DC-9. Employment and Average Wages by Industry

(Estimates through 2010 are based on the 2007 North American Industry Classification System [NAICS]. Estimates from 2011 onward are based on the 2012 NAICS.)

Industry	2008	2009	2010	2011	2012	2013	2014
	Number of Jobs						
Wage and Salary Employment by Industry..................	733,517	733,350	744,878	757,818	748,009	757,897	768,122
Farm Wage and Salary Employment.........................	D	D	D	D	D	D	D
Nonfarm Wage and Salary Employment....................	733,517	733,350	744,878	757,818	748,009	757,897	768,122
Private wage and salary employment......................	481,877	474,925	476,224	489,895	493,348	506,757	516,516
Forestry, fishing, and related activities..........................	D	D	D	D	D	D	D
Mining..	D	D	D	D	D	D	D
Utilities..	2,346	2,459	1,833	1,830	1,850	1,891	1,920
Construction...	13,598	12,281	11,251	12,828	14,121	14,535	14,751
Manufacturing...	1,623	1,431	1,280	1,043	971	1,007	1,032
Durable goods manufacturing.....................	579	528	476	424	423	441	418
Nondurable goods manufacturing............................	1,044	903	804	619	548	566	614
Wholesale trade	4,852	4,673	4,819	4,651	4,980	4,899	4,940
Retail trade...	18,906	18,309	18,993	18,983	19,157	20,079	21,529
Transportation and warehousing........................	4,132	4,102	4,165	4,080	4,102	4,045	4,125
Information...	20,900	19,379	18,759	18,690	17,588	17,092	17,224
Finance and insurance	15,746	14,746	15,029	14,956	14,998	14,824	15,142
Real estate and rental and leasing......................	10,481	10,563	10,456	10,641	10,940	11,057	12,142
Professional, scientific, and technical services	105,097	102,924	102,220	104,222	107,473	108,794	109,665
Management of companies and enterprises..................	1,422	1,294	2,020	2,018	2,011	2,045	2,157
Administrative and waste services	44,695	42,286	42,712	45,578	45,879	46,454	47,053
Educational services	48,206	49,770	49,090	50,908	49,853	55,298	56,624
Health care and social assistance.....................	56,702	58,017	59,950	61,752	62,890	64,570	65,282
Arts, entertainment, and recreation..................	7,296	7,338	7,207	7,164	7,129	7,050	7,318
Accommodation and food services....................	51,596	51,897	53,781	56,053	58,700	61,313	63,053
Other services, except public administration..................	74,279	73,456	72,659	74,498	70,706	71,804	72,559
Government and government enterprises..........................	251,640	258,425	268,654	267,923	254,661	251,140	251,606
	Dollars						
Average Wages and Salaries by Industry	74,759	75,910	78,560	79,851	81,663	81,902	84,190
Average Farm Wages and Salaries	D	D	D	D	D	D	D
Average Nonfarm Wages and Salaries	74,759	75,910	78,560	79,851	81,663	81,902	84,190
Average private wages and salaries........................	70,075	69,872	72,019	73,536	75,551	76,028	78,182
Forestry, fishing, and related activities........................	D	D	D	D	D	D	D
Mining..	D	D	D	D	D	D	D
Utilities..	134,725	130,292	125,669	138,570	126,814	98,345	98,391
Construction	55,750	56,397	61,048	63,382	63,503	63,068	64,749
Manufacturing...	77,417	80,783	84,192	104,606	106,494	109,981	94,337
Durable goods manufacturing.....................	79,097	78,275	78,029	83,026	83,135	83,803	80,115
Nondurable goods manufacturing............................	76,486	82,250	87,841	119,388	124,526	130,378	104,020
Wholesale trade	95,595	97,341	100,782	107,748	113,590	116,136	120,259
Retail trade...	29,003	29,420	30,688	31,739	33,848	33,396	33,211
Transportation and warehousing........................	67,129	65,654	66,085	69,395	71,749	75,390	72,541
Information...	103,994	102,813	103,198	106,842	112,165	122,414	120,739
Finance and insurance	133,784	120,567	128,361	137,434	143,100	148,721	156,373
Real estate and rental and leasing......................	69,104	64,471	70,628	74,778	75,884	79,454	94,170
Professional, scientific, and technical services	113,138	113,173	117,448	120,221	122,662	122,534	126,544
Management of companies and enterprises..................	237,873	273,999	218,147	201,919	235,191	218,814	232,694
Administrative and waste services	42,388	42,808	43,764	45,846	47,076	48,278	48,983
Educational services	43,550	44,413	45,190	45,369	47,327	46,513	47,327
Health care and social assistance...................................	54,254	55,691	56,786	57,529	58,054	58,121	60,537
Arts, entertainment, and recreation...........................	60,157	61,914	63,999	55,361	50,225	54,597	58,024
Accommodation and food services..........................	30,918	30,575	31,751	32,479	32,417	32,934	34,087
Other services, except public administration..................	67,754	69,914	72,831	75,100	78,616	81,388	83,405
Government and government enterprises..........................	83,727	87,005	90,156	91,399	93,505	93,756	96,524

D = Not shown to avoid disclosure of confidential information, but the estimates for this item are included in the total.

Table DC-10. Employment Characteristics by Family Type

(Number, percent.)

Family type and labor force status	2012 Total	2012 Families with own children under 18 years	2013 Total	2013 Families with own children under 18 years	2014 Total	2014 Families with own children under 18 years
All Families	112,493	46,568	120,467	51,277	115,477	48,881
FAMILY TYPE AND LABOR FORCE STATUS						
Married-Couple Families	62,149	23,187	65,805	25,218	63,857	24,341
Both husband and wife in labor force	62.2	76.1	58.9	71.3	62.0	71.6
Husband in labor force, wife not in labor force	16.9	19.6	18.5	22.3	17.2	22.8
Wife in labor force, husband not in labor force	8.3	3.2	6.9	3.5	7.5	4.3
Both husband and wife not in labor force	12.6	1.2	13.2	1.3	13.2	1.3
Other Families	50,344	23,381	54,662	26,059	51,620	24,540
Female householder, no husband present	81.4	85.8	78.5	79.1	81.6	85.3
In labor force	54.8	68.5	52.3	61.6	55.8	69.3
Not in labor force	26.5	17.3	26.1	17.5	25.8	16.0
Male householder, no wife present	18.6	14.2	21.5	20.9	18.4	14.7
In labor force	13.9	11.4	16.0	17.0	13.6	13.7
Not in labor force	4.7	2.9	5.5	4.0	4.8	1.0

Table DC-11. School Enrollment and Educational Attainment, 2014

(Number, percent.)

Item	District	U.S.
Enrollment		
Total population 3 years and over, enrolled in school	164,598	82,063,714
Enrolled in nursery school or preschool (percent)	9.9	6.0
Enrolled in kindergarten (percent)	3.8	5.1
Enrolled in elementary school, grades 1-8 (percent)	27.4	40.2
Enrolled in high school, grades 9-12 (percent)	14.6	20.7
Enrolled in college or graduate school (percent)	44.3	28.0
Attainment		
Total population 25 years and over	463,211	213,725,624
Less than ninth grade (percent)	4.1	5.6
9th to 12th grade, no diploma (percent)	5.7	7.5
High school graduate, including equivalency (percent)	18.2	27.7
Some college, no degree (percent)	13.6	21.0
Associate's degree (percent)	3.4	8.2
Bachelor's degree (percent)	24.3	18.7
Graduate or professional degree (percent)	30.6	11.4
High school graduate or higher (percent)	90.2	86.9
Bachelor's degree or higher (percent)	55.0	30.1

Table DC-12. Public School Characteristics and Educational Indicators

(Number, percent; data derived from National Center of Education Statistics.)

Item	District	U.S.
Public Schools, 2013–2014 (except where noted)		
Number of school districts	62	18,194
Number of schools	225	98,271
Number of students (in thousands)	78	50,045
Number of teachers (in thousands)	6	3,114
Student-teacher ratio	13.0	16.1
Expenditures per student (dollars), FY 2013	20,530	107,637
Four-year adjusted cohort graduation rate (ACGR)[1,2]	61.4	82.3
Students eligible for free or reduced-price lunch (in thousands)	78	25,596
English language learners (in thousands)	5	4,461
Students age 3 to 21 served under IDEA, part B (in thousands)	12	6,464

Public Schools by Type	Number	Percent of D.C. public schools
Total number of schools	225	100.0
Regular	207	92.0
Special education	5	2.2
Vocational education	2	0.9
Alternative education	11.0	4.9

NOTE: Every school is assigned only one school type based on its instructional emphasis.
[1]ACGR data represents a new method of calculating high-school completion rates and may not be comparable to previous years' data for Averaged Freshmen Graduation Rates (AFGR).
[2]The United States 4-year ACGRs were estimated using both the reported 4-year ACGR data from 49 states and the District of Columbia and using imputed data for Idaho. The estimate for American Indian/Alaska Native students also includes imputed data for Virginia.

Table DC-13. Reported Voting and Registration of the Voting-Age Population, November 2014

(Numbers in thousands, percent.)

Item	Total population	Total citizen population	Registered			Voted		
			Total registered	Percent registered (total population)	Percent registered (total citizen population)	Total voted	Percent voted (total population)	Percent voted (total citizen population)
U.S. Total	239,874	219,941	142,166	59.3	64.6	92,251	38.5	41.9
State Total.............................	538	480	353	65.6	73.5	247	45.8	51.4
Sex								
Male..................................	249	219	165	66.2	75.3	118	47.1	53.6
Female...............................	289	261	188	65.1	71.9	129	44.8	49.5
Race								
White alone................................	251	220	176	70.1	79.7	123	49.1	55.8
White, non-Hispanic alone	213	202	162	76.3	80.6	113	53.3	56.2
Black alone................................	248	235	164	66.1	69.7	114	46.1	48.6
Asian alone	21	10	5	(B)	(B)	2	(B)	(B)
Hispanic (of any race)	53	28	19	(B)	(B)	13	(B)	(B)
White alone or in combination	262	231	182	69.7	79.0	128	48.9	55.4
Black alone or in combination..........	259	244	169	65.3	69.3	119	45.9	48.8
Asian alone or in combination..........	25	13	7	(B)	(B)	3	(B)	(B)
Age								
18 to 24 years.............................	69	62	35	(B)	(B)	17	(B)	(B)
25 to 34 years.............................	168	142	101	60.0	70.7	62	36.8	43.4
35 to 44 years.............................	82	67	51	(B)	(B)	35	(B)	(B)
45 to 64 years.............................	139	130	101	72.3	77.3	81	58.0	62.0
65 years and over	80	78	66	81.6	83.7	52	64.9	66.6

B = Base is less than 75,000 and therefore too small to show the derived measure.

Table DC-14. Crime

(Number, rate per 100,000. Data are derived from the FBI Uniform Crime Reports.)

Item	State[1]			U.S.[1,2,3,4]		
	2013	2014	Percent change	2013	2014	Percent change
TOTAL POPULATION[5]...	646,449	658,893	1.9	316,128,839	318,857,056	0.9
VIOLENT CRIME						
Number...............................	8,287	8,199	-1.1	1,163,146	1,165,383	0.2
Rate	1,281.9	1,244.4	-2.9	367.9	365.5	-0.7
Murder and Nonnegligent Manslaughter						
Number...............................	103	105	1.9	14,196	14,249	0.4
Rate	15.9	15.9	-	4.5	4.5	-
Rape[6]						
Number...............................	395	472	X	108,612	116,645	X
Rate	61.1	71.6	X	34.4	36.6	X
Robbery						
Number...............................	4,078	3,497	-14.2	345,031	325,802	-5.6
Rate	630.8	530.7	-15.9	109.1	102.2	-6.3
Aggravated Assault						
Number...............................	3,830	4,125	7.7	724,149	741,291	2.4
Rate	592.5	626.1	5.7	229.1	232.5	1.5
PROPERTY CRIME						
Number...............................	31,083	34,147	9.9	8,632,512	8,277,829	-4.1
Rate	4,808.3	5,182.5	7.8	2,730.7	2,596.1	-4.9
Burglary						
Number...............................	3,316	3,466	4.5	1,928,465	1,729,806	-10.3
Rate	513.0	526.0	2.5	610.0	542.5	-11.1
Larceny-Theft						
Number...............................	24,533	26,898	9.6	6,004,453	5,858,496	-2.4
Rate	3,795.0	4,082.3	7.6	1,899.4	1,837.3	-3.3
Motor Vehicle Theft						
Number...............................	3,234	3,783	17.0	699,594	689,527	-1.4
Rate	500.3	574.1	14.8	221.3	216.2	-2.3

NOTE: Although arson data are included in the trend and clearance tables, sufficient data are not available to estimate totals for this offense. Therefore, no arson data are published in this table.
X = Not applicable.
- = Zero or rounds to zero.
[1]Includes offenses reported by the Zoological Police and the Metro Transit Police.
[2]The crime figures have been adjusted.
[3]The data collection methodology for the offense of forcible rape used by the Minnesota state Uniform Crime Reporting (UCR) Program (with the exception of Minneapolis and St. Paul, Minnesota) does not comply with national UCR Program guidelines. Consequently, its figures for forcible rape and violent crime (of which forcible rape is a part) are not published in this table.
[4]Because of changes in the state's reporting practices, figures are not comparable to previous years' data.
[5]Populations are U.S. Census Bureau provisional estimates as of July 1 of each year.
[6]The figures shown for the offense of rape were estimated using the revised Uniform Crime Reporting (UCR) definition of rape.

Table DC-15. Local Government Finances, 2013[1]

(Dollar amounts in thousands, percent distribution.)

Item	Dollars	Percent distribution
Total Revenue	14,093,322	100.0
General revenue	11,949,370	84.8
Intergovernmental revenue	3,982,425	28.3
Taxes	6,179,767	43.8
General sales	1,085,547	7.7
Selective sales	425,531	3.0
License taxes	36,219	0.3
Individual income tax	1,640,899	11.6
Corporate income tax	453,280	3.2
Other taxes	568,573	4.0
Current charges	656,709	4.7
Miscellaneous general revenue	1,130,469	8.0
Utility revenue	951,210	6.7
Liquor stores revenue	0	-
Insurance trust revenue[2]	1,192,742	8.5
Total Expenditure	14,948,803	100.0
Intergovernmental expenditure	0	-
Direct expenditure	14,948,803	100.0
Current operation	10,845,567	72.6
Capital outlay	2,813,646	18.8
Insurance benefits and repayments	596,172	4.0
Assistance and subsidies	148,892	1.0
Interest on debt	544,526	3.6
Exhibit: Salaries and wages	3,365,733	22.5
Direct Expenditure	14,948,803	100.0
Direct expenditure by function:		
Direct general expenditure	11,556,724	77.3
Education services	2,586,000	17.3
Public welfare	3,192,152	21.4
Hospitals	233,868	1.6
Health	447,400	3.0
Highways	637,671	4.3
Police protection	559,765	3.7
Correction	250,999	1.7
Natural resources	46,074	0.3
Parks and recreation	207,666	1.4
Governmental administration	461,301	3.1
Interest on general debt	528,739	3.5
Other and unallocable	788,924	5.3
Utility expenditure	2,795,907	18.7
Liquor stores expenditure	0	-
Insurance trust expenditure	596,172	4.0
Debt at End of Fiscal Year	12,408,748	X
Cash and Security Holdings	13,016,210	X

X = Not applicable.
- = Zero or rounds to zero.
[1]Note: At the time of publication, the Census Bureau had not yet released 2014 finance data for the District of Columbia.
[2]Within insurance trust revenue, net earnings of state retirement systems is a calculated statistic (the item code in the data file is X08), and thus can be positive or negative. Net earnings is the sum of earnings on investments plus gains on investments minus losses on investments. The change made in 2002 for asset valuation from book to market value in accordance with Statement 34 of the Governmental Accounting Standards Board is reflected in the calculated statistics.

NOTE: Since the Census Bureau does not provide detailed data for the District of Columbia, there is no Table 16 for D.C.

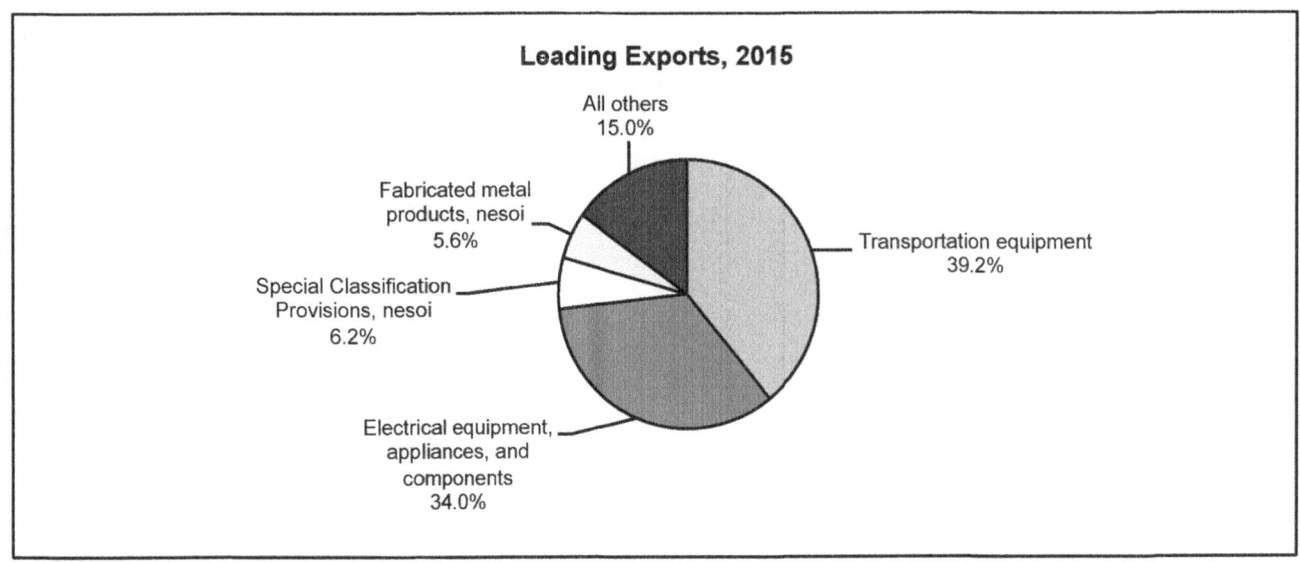

FLORIDA

Facts and Figures

Location: Southeastern United States; bordered on the N by Georgia and Alabama, on the E by the Atlantic Ocean, on the S by the Straits of Florida, and on the W by Alabama and the Gulf of Mexico

Area: 65,757 sq. mi. (170,304 sq. km.); rank—22nd

Population: 20,271,272 (2015 est.); rank—3rd

Principal Cities: capital—Tallahassee; largest—Jacksonville

Statehood: March 3, 1845; 27th state

U.S. Congress: 2 senators, 27 representatives

State Motto: In God We Trust

State Song: "The Swanee River (Old Folks at Home)"

State Nickname: The Sunshine State

Abbreviations: FL; Fla.

State Symbols: flower—orange blossom; tree—Sabal palm (cabbage palm); bird—mockingbird

At a Glance

- With an increase in population of 7.5 percent, Florida ranked 6th among the states in growth from 2010 to 2015.

- Florida's violent crime rate in 2014 was 540.5 incidents per 100,000 population, compared to 365.5 for the entire nation.

- In 2015, Florida was the state with the largest percentage of its population in the 65 and older age group (19.4 percent).

- Florida ranked 6th among the states for the highest percent of Hispanic or Latino residents (24.5 percent). Hispanic or Latino residents may be of any race.

- In 2014, 16.6 percent of all Florida residents and 9.3 percent of children under 18 years of age were uninsured, compared to the national levels of 11.7 percent and 6.0 percent respectively.

Table FL-1. Population by Age, Sex, Race, and Hispanic Origin

(Number, percent, except where noted.)

Sex, age, race, and Hispanic origin	2000	2010	2015[1]	Average annual percent change, 2010–2015
Total Population............	15,982,378	18,801,310	20,271,272	0.5
Percent of total U.S. population	5.7	6.1	6.3	X
Sex				
Male.........	7,797,715	9,189,355	9,902,539	0.5
Female	8,184,663	9,611,955	10,368,733	0.5
Age				
Under 5 years.........	945,823	1,073,506	1,101,071	0.2
5 to 19 years.........	3,102,809	3,439,484	3,466,436	0.1
20 to 64 years.........	9,126,149	11,034,718	11,761,297	0.5
65 years and over.........	2,807,597	3,259,602	3,942,468	1.4
Median age (years)	38.7	40.7	41.9	0.2
Race and Hispanic Origin				
One race				
White	12,465,029	14,808,867	15,748,458	0.4
Black	2,335,505	3,078,067	3,408,632	0.7
American Indian and Alaska Native	53,541	89,119	101,060	0.9
Asian.........	266,256	474,199	576,690	1.4
Native Hawaiian or Other Pacific Islander	8,625	18,790	22,857	1.4
Two or more races	376,315	332,268	413,575	1.6
Hispanic (of any race).........	2,682,715	4,301,853	4,964,077	1.0

X = Not applicable.
[1] Population figures for 2015 are July 1 estimates. The 2010 estimates are taken from the 2010 Census.

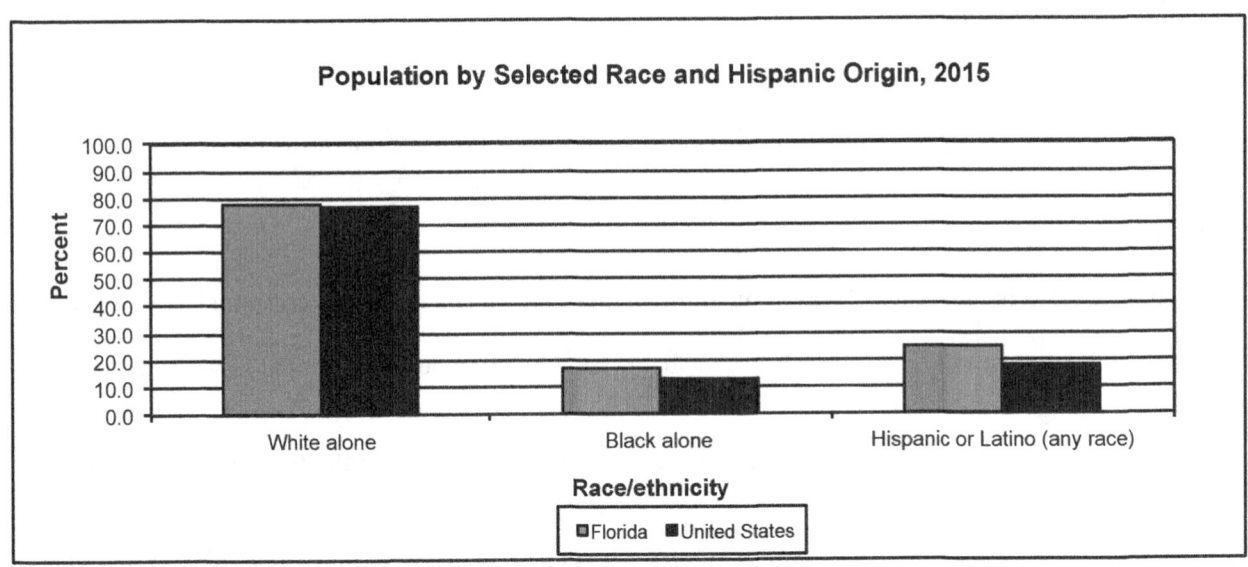

Population by Selected Race and Hispanic Origin, 2015

Florida   United States

Table FL-2. Marital Status

(Number, percent distribution.)

Sex, age, race, and Hispanic origin	2000	2010	2014
Males, 15 Years and Over	6,232,987	7,534,535	7,772,434
Never married	27.3	33.9	34.6
Now married, except separated.........	56.9	49.3	48.7
Separated.........	2.1	2.2	2.1
Widowed.........	3.2	3.2	3.2
Divorced.........	10.5	11.5	11.4
Females, 15 Years and Over	6,714,003	8,021,290	8,276,331
Never married	20.5	26.6	27.4
Now married, except separated.........	51.9	45.1	44.5
Separated.........	2.7	3.0	2.9
Widowed.........	12.3	10.8	10.8
Divorced.........	12.7	14.5	14.4

Table FL-3. Households and Housing Characteristics

(Number, percent, dollars.)

Item	2000	2010	2014	Average annual percent change, 2000–2014
Total Households..	6,337,929	7,035,068	7,328,046	1.1
Family households	4,210,760	4,556,930	4,693,411	0.8
Married-couple family	3,192,266	3,307,884	3,380,103	0.4
Other family	1,018,494	1,249,046	1,313,308	2.1
Male householder, no wife present.........................	259,924	313,305	353,537	2.6
Female householder, no husband present................	759,000	935,741	959,771	1.9
Nonfamily households	2,127,169	2,478,138	2,634,635	1.7
Householder living alone......................................	1,687,303	2,013,028	2,135,355	1.9
Householder not living alone................................	439,886	465,110	499,280	1.0
Housing Characteristics				
Total housing units..	7,302,947	8,994,091	9,144,650	1.8
Occupied housing units	6,337,929	7,035,068	7,328,046	1.1
Owner occupied	4,441,799	4,794,130	4,693,821	0.4
Renter occupied..	1,896,130	2,240,938	2,634,225	2.8
Average household size..	2.46	2.62	2.66	0.6
Financial Characteristics				
Median gross rent of renter-occupied housing	641	947	1,003	4.0
Median monthly owner costs for housing units with a mortgage	1,004	1,505	1,364	2.6
Median value of owner-occupied housing units...........	105,500	164,200	162,700	3.9

Table FL-4. Migration, Origin, and Language

(Number, percent.)

Characteristic	State 2013	State 2014	State Percent change	U.S. 2013	U.S. 2014	U.S. Percent change
Residence 1 Year Ago						
Population 1 year and over	19,345,059	19,683,763	1.8	312,432,820	315,095,393	0.9
Same house	83.7	83.9	X	85.0	85.1	X
Different house in the U.S.	15.4	15.2	X	14.4	14.3	X
Same county	9.5	9.3	X	8.9	8.7	X
Different county	5.8	5.9	X	5.5	5.6	X
Same state	3.1	3.1	X	3.2	3.3	X
Different state	2.7	2.8	X	2.3	2.3	X
Abroad...	0.9	1.0	X	0.6	0.6	X
Place of Birth						
Native born	15,754,798	15,919,782	1.0	274,780,773	276,465,262	0.6
Male...	49.4	49.3	X	49.3	49.3	X
Female..	50.6	50.7	X	50.7	50.7	X
Foreign born	3,798,062	3,973,515	4.6	41,348,066	42,391,794	2.5
Male...	47.1	47.2	X	48.8	48.7	X
Female..	52.9	52.8	X	51.2	51.3	X
Foreign born; naturalized U.S. citizen.................	2,028,738	2,136,462	5.3	19,294,710	19,984,738	3.6
Male...	44.5	44.1	X	45.9	45.9	X
Female..	55.5	55.9	X	54.1	54.1	X
Foreign born; not a U.S. citizen........................	1,769,324	1,837,053	3.8	22,053,356	22,407,056	1.6
Male...	50.1	50.8	X	51.3	51.2	X
Female..	49.9	49.2	X	48.7	48.8	X
Entered 2010 or later	10.1	12.9	X	9.7	12.3	X
Entered 2000 to 2009	30.0	28.4	X	29.4	28.6	X
Entered before 2000.......................................	59.8	58.7	X	61.0	59.1	X
World Region of Birth, Foreign						
Foreign-born population, excluding population born at sea	3,798,062	3,972,753	4.6	41,347,945	42,390,705	2.5
Europe	9.8	9.8	X	11.6	11.2	X
Asia..	10.7	10.6	X	29.5	30.1	X
Africa	1.5	1.6	X	4.4	4.6	X
Oceania..	0.2	0.2	X	0.5	0.6	X
Latin America..	74.8	75.1	X	51.9	51.6	X
North America..	3.1	2.7	X	2.0	1.9	X
Language Spoken at Home and Ability to Speak English						
Population 5 years and over...............................	18,478,811	18,815,725	1.8	296,358,760	299,084,046	0.9
English only	72.6	71.7	X	79.2	78.9	X
Language other than English............................	27.4	28.3	X	20.8	21.1	X
Speaks English less than "very well"..................	11.5	11.7	X	8.5	8.6	X

X = Not applicable.
- = Zero or rounds to zero.

Table FL-5. Median Income and Poverty Status, 2014

(Number, percent, except as noted.)

Characteristic	State		U.S.	
	Number	Percent	Number	Percent
Median Income				
Households (dollars)..	47,463	X	53,657	X
Families (dollars)	57,212	X	65,910	X
Below Poverty Level (All People)	3,211,615	16.5	48,208,387	15.5
Sex				
Male..	1,451,114	15.4	21,590,918	14.2
Female	1,760,501	17.6	26,617,469	16.8
Age				
Under 18 years...	948,465	23.8	15,686,012	21.7
Related children under 18 years...........................	933,030	23.5	15,372,705	21.3
18 to 64 years..	1,873,344	15.9	28,267,482	14.6
65 years and over	389,806	10.5	4,254,893	9.5

X = Not applicable.

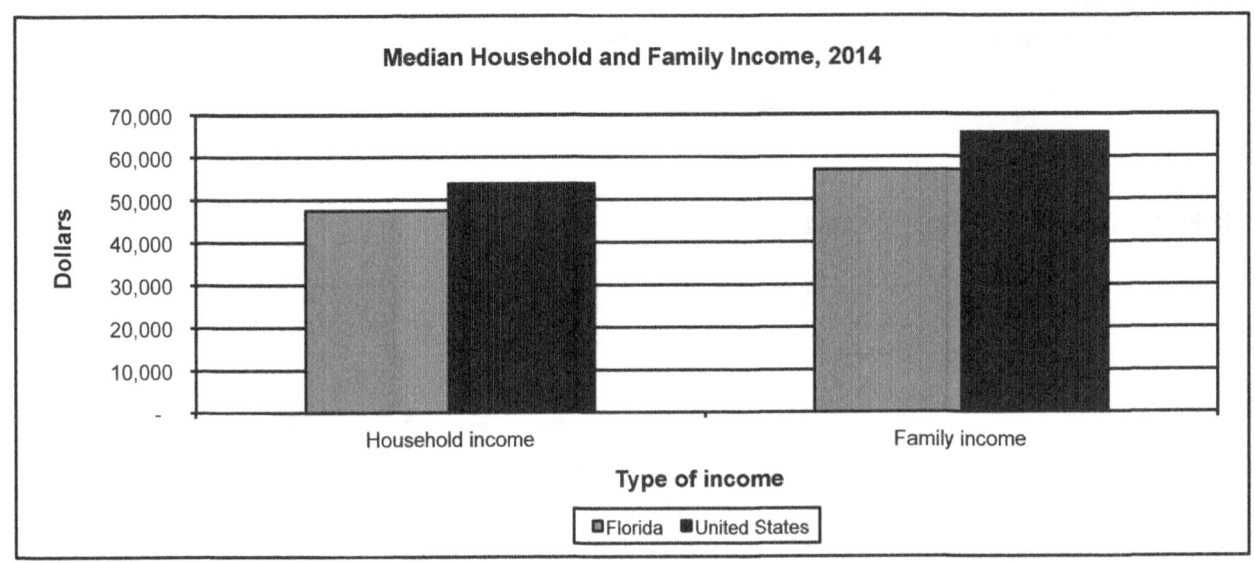

Table FL-6. Health Insurance Coverage Status for the Civilian Noninstitutionalized Population and Children Under 18 Years of Age

(Numbers in thousands, percent.)

Item	2006	2007	2008	2009	2010	2011	2012	2013	2014
Civilian Noninstitutionalized Population	18,062	18,074	17,996	18,193	18,534	18,752	19,011	19,245	19,583
Covered by Private or Public Insurance									
Number..	14,233	14,426	14,247	14,397	14,593	14,841	15,195	15,392	16,338
Percent..	78.8	79.8	79.2	79.1	78.7	79.1	79.9	80.0	83.4
Not Covered									
Number..	3,828	3,648	3,749	3,795	3,941	3,911	3,816	3,853	3,245
Percent..	21.2	20.2	20.8	20.9	21.3	20.9	20.1	20.0	16.6
Percent in the U.S. not covered............................	15.8	15.3	15.1	15.1	15.5	15.1	14.8	14.5	11.7
Children Under 18 Years of Age	4,076	4,084	3,996	4,051	3,990	3,987	3,991	4,020	4,046
Covered by Private or Public Insurance									
Number..	3,305	3,298	3,295	3,450	3,483	3,512	3,555	3,575	3,668
Percent..	81.1	80.8	82.5	85.2	87.3	88.1	89.1	88.9	90.7
Not Covered									
Number..	771	785	701	601	507	475	436	445	378
Percent..	18.9	19.2	17.5	14.8	12.7	11.9	10.9	11.1	9.3
Percent in the U.S. not covered............................	11.7	11.0	9.7	8.6	8.0	7.5	7.2	7.1	6.0

Table FL-7. Employment Status by Demographic Group, 2015

(Numbers in thousands, percent.)

Characteristic	Civilian noninstitutional population	Civilian labor force		Employed		Unemployed	
		Number	Percent of population	Number	Percent of population	Number	Percent of population
Total..	16,243	9,540	58.7	9,023	55.6	517	5.4
Sex							
Male..	7,774	5,042	64.9	4,767	61.3	276	5.5
Female	8,469	4,498	53.1	4,257	50.3	241	5.4
Race, Sex, and Hispanic Origin							
White...	13,060	7,572	58.0	7,221	55.3	350	4.6
Male..	6,320	4,089	64.7	3,904	61.8	185	4.5
Female	6,740	3,483	51.7	3,318	49.2	165	4.7
Black or African American..............	2,492	1,547	62.1	1,407	56.5	139	9.0
Male..	1,139	731	64.2	658	57.8	72	9.9
Female	1,353	816	60.3	749	55.4	67	8.2
Hispanic or Latino ethnicity[1]	3,901	2,476	63.5	2,333	59.8	143	5.8
Male..	1,915	1,389	72.6	1,307	68.2	83	5.9
Female	1,986	1,087	54.7	1,026	51.7	60	5.6
Age							
16 to 19 years	987	282	28.6	239	24.2	43	15.2
20 to 24 years	1,166	797	68.4	720	61.8	77	9.6
25 to 34 years	2,545	2,066	81.2	1,948	76.5	118	5.7
35 to 44 years	2,360	1,935	82.0	1,839	77.9	97	5.0
45 to 54 years	2,845	2,209	77.6	2,124	74.6	85	3.8
55 to 64 years	2,694	1,639	60.8	1,561	58.0	78	4.7
65 years and over	3,646	612	16.8	592	16.2	20	3.2

NOTE: Data in Table 7 are from the Current Population Survey (CPS) and do not match the estimates in Table 8. See notes and definitions for further information.
[1]May be of any race.

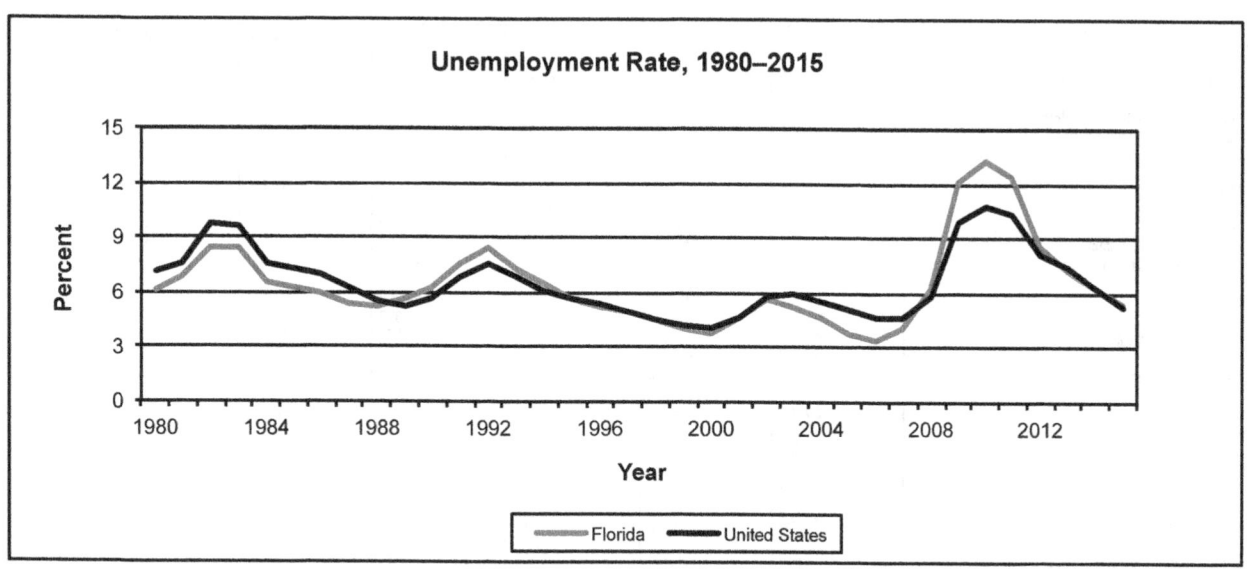

Table FL-8. Employment Status of the Civilian Noninstitutional Population Age 16 Years and Over

(Number, percent.)

Year	Civilian labor force	Civilian participation rate	Employed	Unemployed	Unemployment rate
2007................................	9,157,124	63.9	8,789,770	367,354	4.0
2008................................	9,215,524	63.7	8,637,164	578,360	6.3
2009................................	9,094,825	62.3	8,148,123	946,702	10.4
2010................................	9,212,066	61.6	8,193,659	1,018,407	11.1
2011................................	9,300,542	61.0	8,371,638	928,904	10.0
2012................................	9,391,203	60.7	8,592,418	798,785	8.5
2013................................	9,460,552	60.2	8,771,158	689,394	7.3
2014................................	9,606,715	60.1	8,999,446	607,269	6.3
2015................................	9,675,328	59.3	9,153,264	522,064	5.4

Table FL-9. Employment and Average Wages by Industry

(Estimates through 2010 are based on the 2007 North American Industry Classification System [NAICS]. Estimates from 2011 onward are based on the 2012 NAICS.)

Industry	2008	2009	2010	2011	2012	2013	2014
	Number of Jobs						
Wage and Salary Employment by Industry	8,125,945	7,630,376	7,563,323	7,649,469	7,779,074	7,948,084	8,200,167
Farm Wage and Salary Employment	45,006	40,631	43,823	43,610	46,283	44,696	48,712
Nonfarm Wage and Salary Employment	8,080,939	7,589,745	7,519,500	7,605,859	7,732,791	7,903,388	8,151,455
Private wage and salary employment	6,861,100	6,385,235	6,317,449	6,425,016	6,564,678	6,740,663	6,993,567
Forestry, fishing, and related activities	46,733	45,698	47,225	48,809	49,100	42,333	45,427
Mining	4,491	3,716	3,621	3,867	3,950	3,957	4,099
Utilities	23,899	23,635	22,536	22,449	22,654	22,296	22,009
Construction	533,034	411,498	363,731	352,460	353,977	379,181	409,471
Manufacturing	371,848	324,409	307,997	311,760	317,251	322,442	331,752
Durable goods manufacturing	250,147	214,229	202,824	205,712	209,521	215,080	222,873
Nondurable goods manufacturing	121,701	110,180	105,173	106,048	107,730	107,362	108,879
Wholesale trade	349,063	321,204	310,983	310,640	318,664	323,478	329,594
Retail trade	1,002,198	938,837	943,845	970,895	990,048	1,015,278	1,052,058
Transportation and warehousing	224,977	209,413	206,261	213,907	220,954	227,298	236,184
Information	156,989	143,058	136,033	134,453	134,280	134,400	136,957
Finance and insurance	360,662	334,599	331,483	340,393	351,288	356,304	363,515
Real estate and rental and leasing	177,961	161,689	158,406	157,696	164,977	171,122	175,476
Professional, scientific, and technical services	465,317	440,476	441,971	452,113	454,959	473,401	491,264
Management of companies and enterprises	82,146	79,963	78,138	81,001	83,737	91,048	94,192
Administrative and waste services	603,182	541,284	540,834	534,702	546,791	564,121	590,327
Educational services	135,985	139,499	146,429	151,325	149,307	148,992	153,562
Health care and social assistance	915,482	922,747	936,552	954,874	973,443	989,348	1,014,424
Arts, entertainment, and recreation	188,382	186,789	186,468	194,114	198,123	200,730	211,013
Accommodation and food services	770,528	735,030	745,657	773,615	807,546	844,460	881,618
Other services, except public administration	448,223	421,691	409,279	415,943	423,629	430,474	450,625
Government and government enterprises	1,219,839	1,204,510	1,202,051	1,180,843	1,168,113	1,162,725	1,157,888
	Dollars						
Average Wages and Salaries by Industry	41,818	42,146	42,871	43,660	44,556	45,064	46,228
Average Farm Wages and Salaries	28,713	30,381	28,183	25,536	17,416	30,306	25,122
Average Nonfarm Wages and Salaries	41,891	42,209	42,956	43,764	44,719	45,148	46,354
Average private wages and salaries	41,051	41,209	42,029	42,933	44,075	44,534	45,749
Forestry, fishing, and related activities	21,531	21,449	22,205	23,045	24,134	24,848	25,054
Mining	57,534	56,325	59,818	61,206	68,273	64,288	66,491
Utilities	76,318	80,133	80,142	84,153	86,106	88,031	93,236
Construction	42,914	42,484	42,173	42,044	42,774	43,242	44,733
Manufacturing	50,491	52,102	53,838	54,449	55,480	56,154	57,694
Durable goods manufacturing	52,660	54,854	56,778	57,454	58,657	59,262	60,826
Nondurable goods manufacturing	46,034	46,751	48,168	48,621	49,301	49,927	51,283
Wholesale trade	60,133	60,012	62,426	64,969	67,149	68,166	70,265
Retail trade	27,581	27,740	28,095	28,326	28,839	29,104	29,845
Transportation and warehousing	45,062	45,607	47,072	48,077	48,970	50,761	52,011
Information	60,097	60,896	63,321	66,495	68,969	70,525	72,961
Finance and insurance	66,651	65,488	68,184	70,986	73,616	75,621	79,245
Real estate and rental and leasing	39,866	39,360	40,310	41,834	43,164	44,195	46,645
Professional, scientific, and technical services	64,195	64,394	65,418	66,954	69,756	69,581	71,509
Management of companies and enterprises	86,320	85,668	91,656	95,799	106,503	101,676	104,438
Administrative and waste services	32,267	33,037	33,431	34,123	34,908	34,584	35,457
Educational services	35,264	35,821	36,176	37,532	37,304	37,887	38,310
Health care and social assistance	44,290	45,327	45,926	46,711	47,591	48,220	49,285
Arts, entertainment, and recreation	37,133	36,096	36,864	37,366	38,256	37,903	38,950
Accommodation and food services	20,810	20,434	21,174	21,844	22,285	22,559	23,369
Other services, except public administration	28,520	28,746	29,697	29,872	30,607	31,542	32,416
Government and government enterprises	46,613	47,508	47,829	48,285	48,333	48,706	50,008

Table FL-10. Employment Characteristics by Family Type

(Number, percent.)

Family type and labor force status	2012 Total	2012 Families with own children under 18 years	2013 Total	2013 Families with own children under 18 years	2014 Total	2014 Families with own children under 18 years
All Families..................................	4,598,222	1,781,769	4,626,388	1,753,872	4,675,046	1,744,542
FAMILY TYPE AND LABOR FORCE STATUS						
Married-Couple Families........................	3,319,620	1,121,347	3,334,383	1,109,448	3,361,738	1,094,773
Both husband and wife in labor force.....................	46.3	66.1	45.3	65.3	44.7	64.3
Husband in labor force, wife not in labor force.........	20.3	27.6	20.5	28.4	20.9	28.9
Wife in labor force, husband not in labor force.........	8.2	4.3	8.3	4.3	8.4	4.7
Both husband and wife not in labor force.............	25.2	2.0	25.5	1.7	26.0	2.2
Other Families	1,278,602	660,422	1,292,005	644,424	1,313,308	649,769
Female householder, no husband present..................	74.7	77.3	74.0	77.4	73.1	76.1
In labor force....................................	53.9	64.9	52.2	63.9	51.7	63.4
Not in labor force..............................	20.8	12.5	21.8	13.4	21.4	12.7
Male householder, no wife present........................	25.3	22.7	26.0	22.6	26.9	23.9
In labor force....................................	19.7	20.5	19.8	20.5	20.8	21.9
Not in labor force..............................	5.7	2.2	6.2	2.1	6.1	2.1

Table FL-11. School Enrollment and Educational Attainment, 2014

(Number, percent.)

Item	State	U.S.
Enrollment		
Total population 3 years and over, enrolled in school....................	4,674,255	82,063,714
Enrolled in nursery school or preschool (percent).........................	6.0	6.0
Enrolled in kindergarten (percent).........................	4.8	5.1
Enrolled in elementary school, grades 1-8 (percent)......................	39.2	40.2
Enrolled in high school, grades 9-12 (percent)...........................	20.9	20.7
Enrolled in college or graduate school (percent).........................	29.1	28.0
Attainment		
Total population 25 years and over	14,041,196	213,725,624
Less than ninth grade (percent).........................	5.2	5.6
9th to 12th grade, no diploma (percent).........................	7.6	7.5
High school graduate, including equivalency (percent).....................	29.6	27.7
Some college, no degree (percent).........................	20.7	21.0
Associate's degree (percent)..........................	9.7	8.2
Bachelor's degree (percent)...........................	17.4	18.7
Graduate or professional degree (percent).........................	9.8	11.4
High school graduate or higher (percent)	87.2	86.9
Bachelor's degree or higher (percent).........................	27.3	30.1

Table FL-12. Public School Characteristics and Educational Indicators

(Number, percent; data derived from National Center of Education Statistics.)

Item	State	U.S.
Public Schools, 2013–2014 (except where noted)		
Number of school districts....................	76	18,194
Number of schools....................	4,295	98,271
Number of students (in thousands)	2,721	50,045
Number of teachers (in thousands)	178	3,114
Student-teacher ratio	15.3	16.1
Expenditures per student (dollars), FY 2013....................	86,237	107,637
Four-year adjusted cohort graduation rate (ACGR)[1,2]	76.1	82.3
Students eligible for free or reduced-price lunch (in thousands)	1590	25,596
English language learners (in thousands)	250	4,461
Students age 3 to 21 served under IDEA, part B (in thousands)	356	6,464

Public Schools by Type	Number	Percent of state public schools
Total number of schools....................	4,295	100.0
Regular	3,660	85.2
Special education....................	186	4.3
Vocational education....................	51	1.2
Alternative education....................	398	9.3

NOTE: Every school is assigned only one school type based on its instructional emphasis.
[1]ACGR data represents a new method of calculating high-school completion rates and may not be comparable to previous years' data for Averaged Freshmen Graduation Rates (AFGR).
[2]The United States 4-year ACGRs were estimated using both the reported 4-year ACGR data from 49 states and the District of Columbia and using imputed data for Idaho. The estimate for American Indian/Alaska Native students also includes imputed data for Virginia.

Table FL-13. Reported Voting and Registration of the Voting-Age Population, November 2014

(Numbers in thousands, percent.)

Item	Total population	Total citizen population	Registered			Voted		
			Total registered	Percent registered (total population)	Percent registered (total citizen population)	Total voted	Percent voted (total population)	Percent voted (total citizen population)
U.S. Total	239,874	219,941	142,166	59.3	64.6	92,251	38.5	41.9
State Total..............................	15,414	13,879	8,691	56.4	62.6	6,220	40.4	44.8
Sex								
Male..........................	7,335	6,551	4,008	54.6	61.2	2,840	38.7	43.4
Female	8,079	7,327	4,683	58.0	63.9	3,380	41.8	46.1
Race								
White alone..........................	12,507	11,266	7,010	56.1	62.2	5,071	40.6	45.0
White, non-Hispanic alone	9,134	8,922	5,596	61.3	62.7	4,237	46.4	47.5
Black alone..........................	2,331	2,112	1,358	58.2	64.3	929	39.8	44.0
Asian alone	374	299	184	49.0	61.5	128	34.3	43.0
Hispanic (of any race)	3,530	2,480	1,493	42.3	60.2	892	25.3	36.0
White alone or in combination	12,646	11,406	7,101	56.2	62.3	5,127	40.5	45.0
Black alone or in combination..........	2,401	2,182	1,386	57.7	63.5	948	39.5	43.5
Asian alone or in combination..........	407	331	206	50.5	62.1	143	35.2	43.2
Age								
18 to 24 years..........................	1,406	1,301	486	34.5	37.3	229	16.3	17.6
25 to 34 years..........................	2,372	2,047	1,113	46.9	54.4	613	25.8	30.0
35 to 44 years..........................	2,634	2,269	1,335	50.7	58.8	812	30.8	35.8
45 to 64 years..........................	5,221	4,640	3,142	60.2	67.7	2,395	45.9	51.6
65 years and over	3,781	3,621	2,615	69.2	72.2	2,171	57.4	60.0

Table FL-14. Crime

(Number, rate per 100,000. Data are derived from the FBI Uniform Crime Reports.)

Item	State			U.S. [1,2,3,4]		
	2013	2014	Percent change	2013	2014	Percent change
TOTAL POPULATION[5]............................	19,552,860	19,893,297	1.7	316,128,839	318,857,056	0.9
VIOLENT CRIME						
Number..........................	89,948	107,521	19.5	1,163,146	1,165,383	0.2
Rate	460.0	540.5	17.5	367.9	365.5	-0.7
Murder and Nonnegligent Manslaughter						
Number..........................	972	1,149	18.2	14,196	14,249	0.4
Rate	5.0	5.8	16.0	4.5	4.5	-
Rape[6]						
Number..........................	6,760	8,563	X	108,612	116,645	X
Rate	34.6	43.0	X	34.4	36.6	X
Robbery						
Number..........................	23,200	24,914	7.4	345,031	325,802	-5.6
Rate	118.7	125.2	5.5	109.1	102.2	-6.3
Aggravated Assault						
Number..........................	61,054	72,895	19.4	724,149	741,291	2.4
Rate	312.3	366.4	17.3	229.1	232.5	1.5
PROPERTY CRIME						
Number..........................	607,172	679,446	11.9	8,632,512	8,277,829	-4.1
Rate	3,105.3	3,415.5	10.0	2,730.7	2,596.1	-4.9
Burglary						
Number..........................	138,916	143,220	3.1	1,928,465	1,729,806	-10.3
Rate	710.5	719.9	1.3	610.0	542.5	-11.1
Larceny-Theft						
Number..........................	433,344	493,647	13.9	6,004,453	5,858,496	-2.4
Rate	2,216.3	2,481.5	12.0	1,899.4	1,837.3	-3.3
Motor Vehicle Theft						
Number..........................	34,912	42,579	22.0	699,594	689,527	-1.4
Rate	178.6	214.0	19.8	221.3	216.2	-2.3

NOTE Although arson data are included in the trend and clearance tables, sufficient data are not available to estimate totals for this offense. Therefore, no arson data are published in this table.
X = Not applicable.
- = Zero or rounds to zero.
[1]The crime figures have been adjusted.
[2]The data collection methodology for the offense of forcible rape used by the Minnesota state Uniform Crime Reporting (UCR) Program (with the exception of Minneapolis and St. Paul, Minnesota) does not comply with national UCR Program guidelines. Consequently, its figures for forcible rape and violent crime (of which forcible rape is a part) are not published in this table.
[3]Includes offenses reported by the Zoological Police and the Metro Transit Police.
[4]Because of changes in the state's reporting practices, figures are not comparable to previous years' data.
[5]Populations are U.S. Census Bureau provisional estimates as of July 1 of each year.
[6]The figures shown for the offense of rape were estimated using the revised Uniform Crime Reporting (UCR) definition of rape.

Table FL-15. State Government Finances, 2014

(Dollar amounts in thousands, percent distribution.)

Item	Dollars	Percent distribution
Total Revenue	104,127,723	100.0
General revenue	76,827,084	73.8
Intergovernmental revenue	25,801,529	24.8
Taxes	35,384,350	34.0
General sales	21,480,910	20.6
Selective sales	7,566,020	7.3
License taxes	2,133,240	2.0
Individual income tax	0	-
Corporate income tax	2,043,750	2.0
Other taxes	2,160,430	2.1
Current charges	9,345,243	9.0
Miscellaneous general revenue	6,295,962	6.0
Utility revenue	24,196	-
Liquor stores revenue	0	-
Insurance trust revenue[1]	27,276,443	26.2
Total Expenditure	83,274,449	100.0
Intergovernmental expenditure	18,707,624	22.5
Direct expenditure	64,566,825	77.5
Current operation	47,031,141	56.5
Capital outlay	5,750,166	6.9
Insurance benefits and repayments	8,615,075	10.3
Assistance and subsidies	1,985,221	2.4
Interest on debt	1,185,222	1.4
Exhibit: Salaries and wages	9,231,552	11.1
Total Expenditure	83,274,449	100.0
General expenditure	74,476,907	89.4
Intergovernmental expenditure	18,707,624	22.5
Direct expenditure	55,769,283	67.0
General expenditure, by function:		
Education	25,075,684	30.1
Public welfare	24,368,280	29.3
Hospitals	890,293	1.1
Health	3,848,555	4.6
Highways	6,595,817	7.9
Police protection	512,060	0.6
Correction	2,191,117	2.6
Natural resources	1,115,770	1.3
Parks and recreation	114,024	0.1
Governmental administration	2,261,100	2.7
Interest on general debt	1,185,222	1.4
Other and unallocable	6,318,985	7.6
Utility expenditure	182,467	0.2
Liquor stores expenditure	0	-
Insurance trust expenditure	8,615,075	10.3
Debt at End of Fiscal Year	36,348,245	X
Cash and Security Holdings	223,236,115	X

X = Not applicable.
- = Zero or rounds to zero.
[1]Within insurance trust revenue, net earnings of state retirement systems is a calculated statistic (the item code in the data file is X08), and thus can be positive or negative. Net earnings is the sum of earnings on investments plus gains on investments minus losses on investments. The change made in 2002 for asset valuation from book to market value in accordance with Statement 34 of the Governmental Accounting Standards Board is reflected in the calculated statistics.

Table FL-16. State Government Tax Collections, 2014

(Dollars in thousands, percent.)

Item	Dollars	Percent distribution
Total Taxes	35,384,350	100.0
Property taxes	250	-
Sales and gross receipts	29,046,930	82.1
General sales and gross receipts	21,480,910	60.7
Selective sales and gross receipts	7,566,020	21.4
Alcoholic beverages	452,370	1.3
Amusements	187,639	0.5
Insurance premiums	702,340	2.0
Motor fuels	2,422,718	6.8
Pari-mutuels	10,412	-
Public utilities	2,719,350	7.7
Tobacco products	370,993	1.0
Other selective sales	700,198	2.0
Licenses	2,133,240	6.0
Alcoholic beverages	8,663	-
Amusements	14,000	-
Corporations in general	298,604	0.8
Hunting and fishing	16,275	-
Motor vehicle	1,380,910	3.9
Motor vehicle operators	187,182	0.5
Public utilities	24,569	0.1
Occupation and business, NEC	198,483	0.6
Other licenses	4,554	-
Income taxes	2,043,750	5.8
Individual income	X	X
Corporation net income	2,043,750	5.8
Other taxes	2,160,180	6.1
Death and gift	1,710	-
Documentary and stock transfer	2,109,370	6.0
Severance	49,100	0.1
Taxes, NEC	0	

X = Not applicable.
- = Zero or rounds to zero.

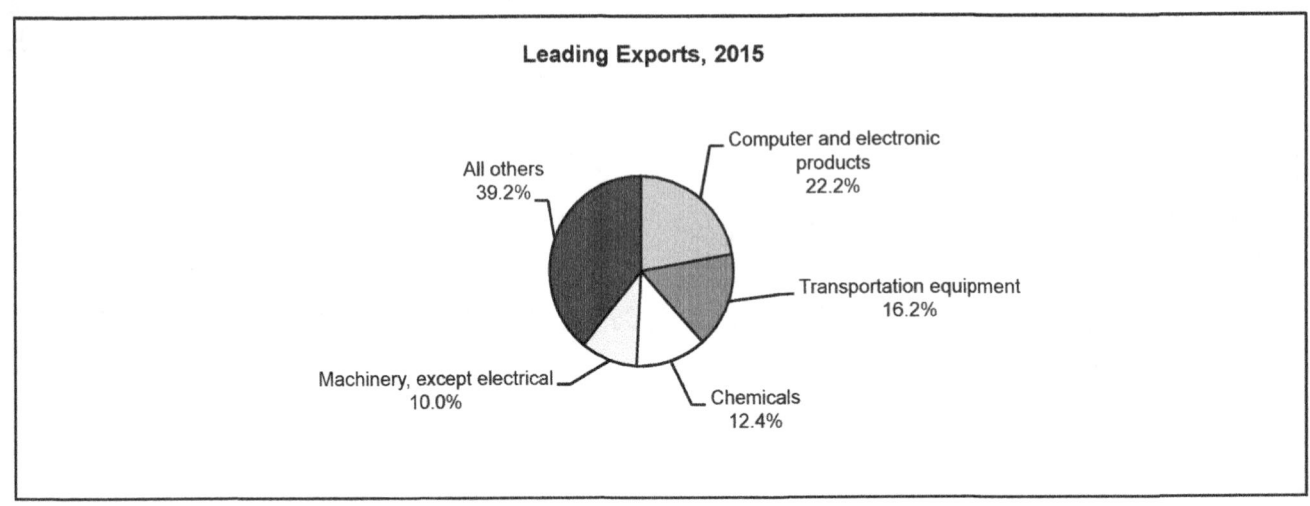

Leading Exports, 2015

All others 39.2%
Computer and electronic products 22.2%
Transportation equipment 16.2%
Chemicals 12.4%
Machinery, except electrical 10.0%

Facts and Figures

Location: Southeastern United States; bordered on the N by Tennessee and North Carolina, on the E by South Carolina and the Atlantic Ocean, on the S by Florida, and on the W by Florida and Alabama

Area: 59,425 sq. mi. (153,909 sq. km.); rank—21st

Population: 10,214,860 (2015 est.); rank—8th

Principal Cities: capital—Atlanta; largest—Atlanta

Statehood: January 2, 1788; 4th state

U.S. Congress: 2 senators, 14 representatives

State Motto: Wisdom, Justice, and Moderation

State Song: "Georgia on My Mind"

State Nicknames: The Empire State of the South; The Peach State

Abbreviations: GA; Ga.

State Symbols: flower—Cherokee rose; tree—live oak; bird—brown thrasher

At a Glance

- With an increase in population of 5.2 percent, Georgia ranked 12th among the states in growth from 2010 to 2015.

- Georgia's median household income in 2014 was $49,321, and 18.3 percent of the population lived below the poverty level.

- In 2014, 15.8 percent of Georgians did not have health insurance, compared to 11.7 percent of the total U.S. population.

- Georgia's violent crime rate was 377.3 per 100,000 population, compared to 365.5 for the U.S. as a whole in 2014.

- The property crime rate in Georgia in 2014 was 3,281.2 per 100,000 population, a rate that ranked 8th among the states.

Table GA-1. Population by Age, Sex, Race, and Hispanic Origin

(Number, percent, except where noted.)

Sex, age, race, and Hispanic origin	2000	2010	2015[1]	Average annual percent change, 2010–2015
Total Population.....................................	8,186,453	9,687,653	10,214,860	0.4
Percent of total U.S. population	2.9	3.1	3.2	X
Sex				
Male................................	4,027,113	4,729,171	4,979,882	0.4
Female	4,159,340	4,958,482	5,234,978	0.4
Age				
Under 5 years............................	595,150	686,785	660,045	-0.3
5 to 19 years...........................	1,819,620	2,094,844	2,123,861	0.1
20 to 64 years.........................	4,986,408	5,873,989	6,126,030	0.3
65 years and over.......................	785,275	1,032,035	1,304,924	1.7
Median age (years)	33.4	35.3	36.3	0.2
Race and Hispanic Origin				
One race				
White..................................	5,327,281	6,144,931	6,295,964	0.2
Black..................................	2,349,542	2,993,927	3,240,294	0.6
American Indian and Alaska Native	21,737	48,599	51,405	0.4
Asian..................................	173,170	323,459	409,119	1.7
Native Hawaiian or Other Pacific Islander............	4,246	10,454	12,229	1.1
Two or more races........................	114,188	166,283	205,849	1.5
Hispanic (of any race).....................	435,227	911,863	955,434	0.3

X = Not applicable.
[1]Population figures for 2015 are July 1 estimates. The 2010 estimates are taken from the 2010 Census.

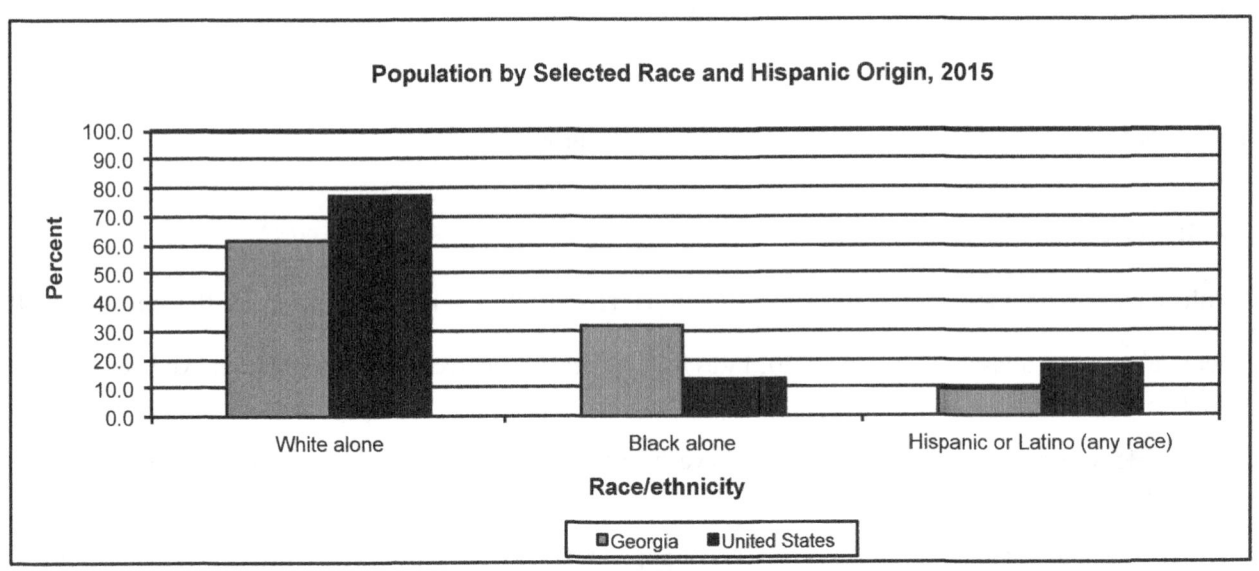

Population by Selected Race and Hispanic Origin, 2015

Table GA-2. Marital Status

(Number, percent distribution.)

Sex, age, race, and Hispanic origin	2000	2010	2014
Males, 15 Years and Over	3,092,736	3,683,258	3,779,687
Never married	30.4	35.4	36.2
Now married, except separated..................	56.5	50.5	49.5
Separated..................................	2.0	2.1	2.1
Widowed...................................	2.1	2.2	2.3
Divorced..................................	9.0	9.9	9.8
Females, 15 Years and Over	3,273,889	3,954,542	4,052,928
Never married	24.4	29.7	30.5
Now married, except separated..................	51.5	46.1	45.1
Separated..................................	2.7	2.9	2.9
Widowed...................................	9.8	8.6	8.6
Divorced..................................	11.6	12.7	12.9

Table GA-3. Households and Housing Characteristics

(Number, percent, dollars.)

Item	2000	2010	2014	Average annual percent change, 2000–2014
Total Households	3,006,369	3,482,420	3,587,521	1.4
Family households	2,111,647	2,385,969	2,426,392	1.1
Married-couple family	1,548,800	1,688,896	1,692,033	0.7
Other family	562,847	697,073	734,359	2.2
Male householder, no wife present	127,437	161,001	172,404	2.5
Female householder, no husband present	435,410	536,072	561,955	2.1
Nonfamily households	894,722	1,096,451	1,161,129	2.1
Householder living alone	710,523	921,005	964,072	2.5
Householder not living alone	184,199	175,446	197,057	0.5
Housing Characteristics				
Total housing units	3,281,737	4,091,482	4,151,387	1.9
Occupied housing units	3,006,369	3,482,420	3,587,521	1.4
Owner occupied	2,029,154	2,304,165	2,232,553	0.7
Renter occupied	977,215	1,178,255	1,354,968	2.8
Average household size	2.65	2.72	2.74	0.2
Financial Characteristics				
Median gross rent of renter-occupied housing	613	819	882	3.1
Median monthly owner costs for housing units with a mortgage	1,039	1,390	1,285	1.7
Median value of owner-occupied housing units	111,200	156,200	147,900	2.4

Table GA-4. Migration, Origin, and Language

(Number, percent.)

Characteristic	State			U.S.		
	2013	2014	Percent change	2013	2014	Percent change
Residence 1 Year Ago						
Population 1 year and over	9,870,319	9,970,167	1.0	312,432,820	315,095,393	0.9
Same house	83.6	84.3	X	85.0	85.1	X
Different house in the U.S.	15.8	15.2	X	14.4	14.3	X
Same county	8.7	7.7	X	8.9	8.7	X
Different county	7.1	7.5	X	5.5	5.6	X
Same state	4.2	4.7	X	3.2	3.3	X
Different state	2.8	2.7	X	2.3	2.3	X
Abroad	0.6	0.5	X	0.6	0.6	X
Place of Birth						
Native born	9,021,188	9,102,692	0.9	274,780,773	276,465,262	0.6
Male	48.6	48.6	X	49.3	49.3	X
Female	51.4	51.4	X	50.7	50.7	X
Foreign born	970,979	994,651	2.4	41,348,066	42,391,794	2.5
Male	51.2	50.2	X	48.8	48.7	X
Female	48.8	49.8	X	51.2	51.3	X
Foreign born; naturalized U.S. citizen	375,460	410,445	9.3	19,294,710	19,984,738	3.6
Male	47.0	47.6	X	45.9	45.9	X
Female	53.0	52.4	X	54.1	54.1	X
Foreign born; not a U.S. citizen	595,519	584,206	-1.9	22,053,356	22,407,056	1.6
Male	53.8	52.1	X	51.3	51.2	X
Female	46.2	47.9	X	48.7	48.8	X
Entered 2010 or later	10.5	12.1	X	9.7	12.3	X
Entered 2000 to 2009	35.9	34.7	X	29.4	28.6	X
Entered before 2000	53.6	53.2	X	61.0	59.1	X
World Region of Birth, Foreign						
Foreign-born population, excluding population born at sea	970,979	994,651	2.4	41,347,945	42,390,705	2.5
Europe	9.3	9	X	11.6	11.2	X
Asia	28.2	28.1	X	29.5	30.1	X
Africa	8.7	9	X	4.4	4.6	X
Oceania	0.2	0.4	X	0.5	0.6	X
Latin America	51.8	51.4	X	51.9	51.6	X
North America	1.8	2	X	2.0	1.9	X
Language Spoken at Home and Ability to Speak English						
Population 5 years and over	9,335,151	9,442,904	1.2	296,358,760	299,084,046	0.9
English only	86.4	86.4	X	79.2	78.9	X
Language other than English	13.6	13.6	X	20.8	21.1	X
Speaks English less than "very well"	5.7	5.5	X	8.5	8.6	X

X = Not applicable.
- = Zero or rounds to zero.

Table GA-5. Median Income and Poverty Status, 2014

(Number, percent, except as noted.)

Characteristic	State		U.S.	
	Number	Percent	Number	Percent
Median Income				
Households (dollars).........................	49,321	X	53,657	X
Families (dollars)	58,885	X	65,910	X
Below Poverty Level (All People)	1,797,969	18.3	48,208,387	15.5
Sex				
Male..........................	795,388	16.8	21,590,918	14.2
Female	1,002,581	19.7	26,617,469	16.8
Age				
Under 18 years..........................	645,855	26.3	15,686,012	21.7
Related children under 18 years....................	638,868	26.1	15,372,705	21.3
18 to 64 years..........................	1,025,404	16.7	28,267,482	14.6
65 years and over	126,710	10.4	4,254,893	9.5

X = Not applicable.

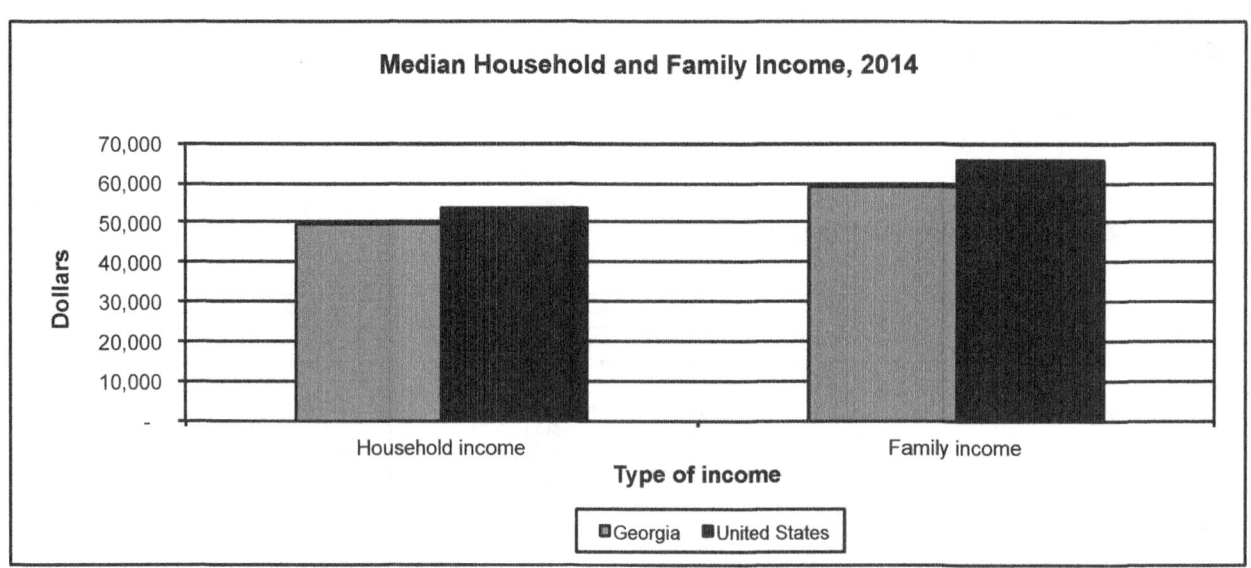

Table GA-6. Health Insurance Coverage Status for the Civilian Noninstitutionalized Population and Children Under 18 Years of Age

(Numbers in thousands, percent.)

Item	2006	2007	2008	2009	2010	2011	2012	2013	2014
Civilian Noninstitutionalized Population	9,347	9,493	9,473	9,594	9,520	9,620	9,719	9,801	9,907
Covered by Private or Public Insurance									
Number..	7,688	7,831	7,694	7,758	7,644	7,737	7,927	7,955	8,338
Percent..	82.3	82.5	81.2	80.9	80.3	80.4	81.6	81.2	84.2
Not Covered									
Number..	1,659	1,662	1,779	1,836	1,876	1,883	1,792	1,846	1,568
Percent..	17.7	17.5	18.8	19.1	19.7	19.6	18.4	18.8	15.8
Percent in the U.S. not covered................................	15.8	15.3	15.1	15.1	15.5	15.1	14.8	14.5	11.7
Children Under 18 Years of Age	2,455	2,517	2,536	2,576	2,492	2,485	2,492	2,487	2,488
Covered by Private or Public Insurance									
Number..	2,141	2,228	2,245	2,295	2,248	2,248	2,272	2,249	2,299
Percent..	87.2	88.5	88.5	89.1	90.2	90.5	91.2	90.4	92.4
Not Covered									
Number..	314	289	291	281	244	237	220	238	189
Percent..	12.8	11.5	11.5	10.9	9.8	9.5	8.8	9.6	7.6
Percent in the U.S. not covered................................	11.7	11.0	9.7	8.6	8.0	7.5	7.2	7.1	6.0

Table GA-7. Employment Status by Demographic Group, 2015

(Numbers in thousands, percent.)

Characteristic	Civilian noninstitutional population	Civilian labor force		Employed		Unemployed	
		Number	Percent of population	Number	Percent of population	Number	Percent of population
Total...	7,755	4,746	61.2	4,471	57.7	275	5.8
Sex							
Male..	3,669	2,481	67.6	2,348	64.0	133	5.4
Female..	4,086	2,265	55.4	2,123	52.0	142	6.3
Race, Sex, and Hispanic Origin							
White..	4,913	2,964	60.3	2,844	57.9	120	4.0
Male...	2,401	1,654	68.9	1,594	66.4	60	3.6
Female...	2,511	1,310	52.1	1,250	49.8	60	4.6
Black or African American....................	2,370	1,475	62.2	1,337	56.4	138	9.3
Male...	1,052	673	64.0	609	57.9	64	9.5
Female...	1,318	802	60.8	728	55.2	74	9.3
Hispanic or Latino ethnicity[1]	630	428	67.9	406	64.4	22	5.1
Male...	330	265	80.1	256	77.3	9	3.4
Female...	300	163	54.4	150	50.1	13	7.9
Age							
16 to 19 years....................................	506	138	27.2	109	21.5	29	21.1
20 to 24 years....................................	677	459	67.8	401	59.2	58	12.7
25 to 34 years....................................	1,381	1,066	77.2	1,002	72.5	64	6.0
35 to 44 years....................................	1,345	1,112	82.6	1,072	79.7	39	3.5
45 to 54 years....................................	1,353	1,040	76.9	999	73.8	42	4.0
55 to 64 years....................................	1,209	707	58.4	673	55.7	34	4.8
65 years and over...............................	1,283	225	17.5	216	16.9	9	3.8

NOTE: Data in Table 7 are from the Current Population Survey (CPS) and do not match the estimates in Table 8. See notes and definitions for further information.
[1] May be of any race.

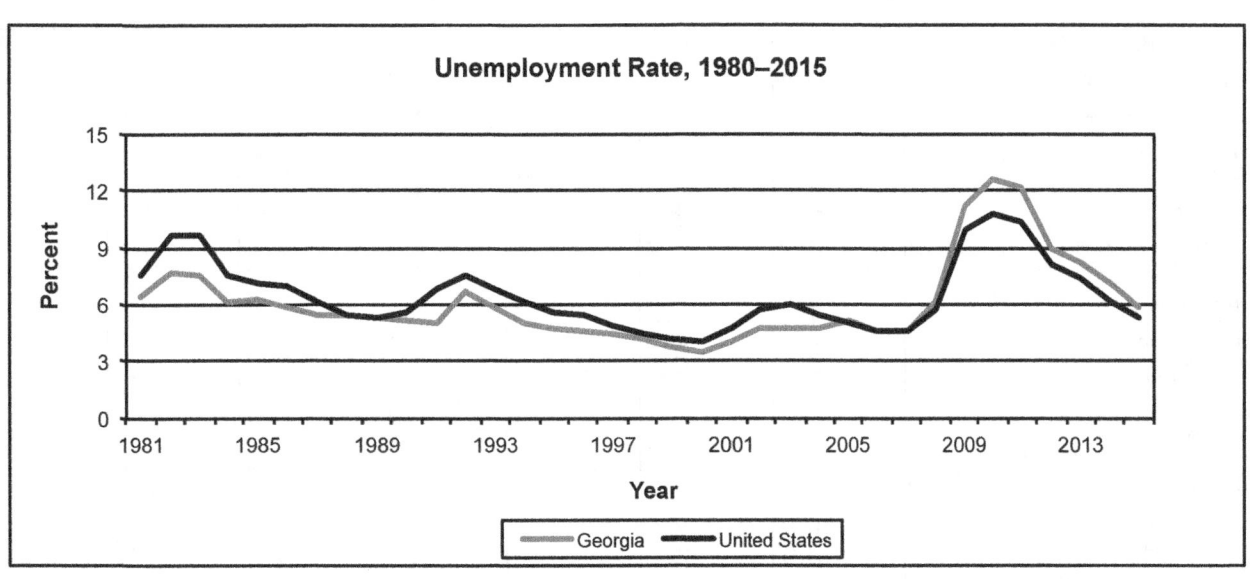

Table GA-8. Employment Status of the Civilian Noninstitutional Population Age 16 Years and Over

(Number, percent.)

Year	Civilian labor force	Civilian participation rate	Employed	Unemployed	Unemployment rate
2007...	4,815,818	68.1	4,597,640	218,178	4.5
2008...	4,879,253	67.8	4,575,010	304,243	6.2
2009...	4,787,749	65.6	4,311,854	475,895	9.9
2010...	4,696,676	64.1	4,202,052	494,624	10.5
2011...	4,748,754	64.3	4,263,305	485,449	10.2
2012...	4,788,068	63.9	4,349,796	438,272	9.2
2013...	4,759,506	62.8	4,369,349	390,157	8.2
2014...	4,753,765	62.0	4,416,715	337,050	7.1
2015...	4,770,873	61.3	4,490,931	279,942	5.9

Table GA-9. Employment and Average Wages by Industry

(Estimates through 2010 are based on the 2007 North American Industry Classification System [NAICS]. Estimates from 2011 onward are based on the 2012 NAICS.)

Industry	2008	2009	2010	2011	2012	2013	2014
				Number of Jobs			
Wage and Salary Employment by Industry..................	4,326,738	4,092,799	4,050,847	4,089,152	4,125,128	4,200,830	4,326,887
Farm Wage and Salary Employment........................	17,301	16,401	13,804	14,578	14,650	15,025	16,174
Nonfarm Wage and Salary Employment....................	4,309,437	4,076,398	4,037,043	4,074,574	4,110,478	4,185,805	4,310,713
Private wage and salary employment.......................	3,500,784	3,275,382	3,240,704	3,292,162	3,333,977	3,420,001	3,546,443
Forestry, fishing, and related activities....................	14,169	13,756	14,477	14,895	14,198	14,856	15,416
Mining..	5,943	5,013	4,942	4,792	4,671	4,708	4,855
Utilities...	20,625	20,437	19,738	20,011	19,850	19,858	19,787
Construction...	213,709	174,419	157,079	154,046	146,376	151,500	161,754
Manufacturing...	411,541	359,528	346,160	351,084	354,694	357,649	367,341
Durable goods manufacturing...........................	190,194	161,496	155,681	161,698	166,741	171,342	176,746
Nondurable goods manufacturing.......................	221,347	198,032	190,479	189,386	187,953	186,307	190,595
Wholesale trade...	219,879	201,601	198,258	199,538	202,769	206,413	211,777
Retail trade..	472,635	444,911	441,958	448,738	449,418	458,336	471,712
Transportation and warehousing..........................	173,231	162,834	162,081	165,995	169,234	169,670	177,607
Information..	110,244	101,744	97,935	98,631	100,074	102,835	107,264
Finance and insurance	164,341	160,226	156,825	159,145	163,398	166,470	171,968
Real estate and rental and leasing........................	64,997	59,978	58,451	58,078	57,531	58,908	60,920
Professional, scientific, and technical services	231,527	221,601	221,109	227,474	234,165	241,039	254,119
Management of companies and enterprises..................	54,251	52,583	52,879	54,026	57,410	60,052	62,923
Administrative and waste services........................	278,869	247,546	259,493	269,090	275,817	291,467	307,152
Educational services	75,806	77,301	79,567	81,954	81,601	81,492	82,992
Health care and social assistance........................	387,896	394,137	402,734	408,783	418,197	430,152	438,592
Arts, entertainment, and recreation.......................	42,415	41,471	39,828	41,138	41,724	43,262	44,544
Accommodation and food services........................	357,622	342,524	339,751	345,699	355,174	371,494	387,634
Other services, except public administration..............	201,084	193,772	187,439	189,045	187,676	189,840	198,086
Government and government enterprises	808,653	801,016	796,339	782,412	776,501	765,804	764,270
				Dollars			
Average Wages and Salaries by Industry	43,568	43,873	44,924	46,170	47,419	47,823	49,149
Average Farm Wages and Salaries	23,731	18,790	23,004	20,178	22,255	22,925	25,634
Average Nonfarm Wages and Salaries	43,648	43,974	44,999	46,263	47,509	47,912	49,237
Average private wages and salaries........................	43,988	44,160	45,335	46,678	48,281	48,727	50,068
Forestry, fishing, and related activities....................	29,761	30,078	31,128	31,585	32,668	33,752	34,273
Mining..	54,253	53,581	55,430	57,491	59,454	61,222	63,374
Utilities...	78,570	81,539	76,775	84,511	84,932	85,496	87,064
Construction...	45,449	45,940	46,524	47,134	48,898	49,873	51,788
Manufacturing...	47,931	48,957	51,805	53,702	54,980	55,840	56,969
Durable goods manufacturing...........................	50,599	52,057	54,755	56,989	57,182	58,298	59,818
Nondurable goods manufacturing.......................	45,639	46,429	49,394	50,895	53,026	53,580	54,328
Wholesale trade	65,646	65,394	67,527	69,803	71,440	72,326	74,110
Retail trade..	26,557	26,631	27,112	27,388	27,889	28,224	28,883
Transportation and warehousing..........................	49,645	48,753	51,081	52,918	54,063	56,739	58,834
Information..	74,449	73,878	76,733	79,875	85,779	85,858	88,943
Finance and insurance	72,191	70,080	72,883	76,669	80,087	81,890	84,271
Real estate and rental and leasing........................	46,902	45,213	45,955	48,695	50,958	51,857	53,734
Professional, scientific, and technical services	70,645	70,734	72,372	74,401	78,155	77,367	79,537
Management of companies and enterprises..................	83,871	85,454	89,287	94,652	100,560	98,874	106,000
Administrative and waste services........................	33,546	34,251	34,517	35,021	35,802	35,681	36,441
Educational services	39,002	39,754	40,262	41,022	42,047	43,012	43,831
Health care and social assistance........................	43,174	44,342	44,681	45,588	46,887	47,601	48,483
Arts, entertainment, and recreation.......................	33,577	33,892	35,321	35,834	34,889	35,449	36,695
Accommodation and food services........................	17,731	17,778	18,519	19,027	19,413	19,253	19,982
Other services, except public administration..................	28,617	28,691	29,763	30,144	30,760	31,455	31,655
Government and government enterprises	42,174	43,213	43,633	44,514	44,193	44,273	45,379

Table GA-10. Employment Characteristics by Family Type

(Number, percent.)

Family type and labor force status	2012		2013		2014	
	Total	Families with own children under 18 years	Total	Families with own children under 18 years	Total	Families with own children under 18 years
All Families..	2,406,226	1,103,278	2,389,803	1,087,559	2,419,167	1,103,236
FAMILY TYPE AND LABOR FORCE STATUS						
Married-Couple Families...........................	1,693,386	715,266	1,672,704	692,412	1,684,808	702,051
Both husband and wife in labor force...............	51.8	64.0	51.6	65.2	50.7	63.8
Husband in labor force, wife not in labor force	24.4	30.4	23.2	29.0	24.3	30.0
Wife in labor force, husband not in labor force	7.6	3.9	7.7	3.8	8.2	4.3
Both husband and wife not in labor force..............	16.2	1.7	17.0	1.8	16.8	1.9
Other Families	712,840	388,012	717,099	395,147	734,359	401,185
Female householder, no husband present..............	76.7	80.1	75.5	78.1	76.5	78.5
In labor force...............	54.3	66.0	53.8	64.7	54.1	65.2
Not in labor force	22.3	14.1	21.7	13.4	22.4	13.3
Male householder, no wife present....................	23.3	19.9	24.5	21.9	23.5	21.5
In labor force..............	17.8	17.9	19.3	19.9	18.2	19.4
Not in labor force	5.5	2.1	5.2	2.0	5.2	2.0

Table GA-11. School Enrollment and Educational Attainment, 2014

(Number, percent.)

Item	State	U.S.
Enrollment		
Total population 3 years and over, enrolled in school..............................	2,780,545	82,063,714
Enrolled in nursery school or preschool (percent)	6.2	6.0
Enrolled in kindergarten (percent)	5.3	5.1
Enrolled in elementary school, grades 1-8 (percent)............................	41.1	40.2
Enrolled in high school, grades 9-12 (percent)	20.9	20.7
Enrolled in college or graduate school (percent)...........................	26.4	28.0
Attainment		
Total population 25 years and over	6,576,408	213,725,624
Less than ninth grade (percent)	5.4	5.6
9th to 12th grade, no diploma (percent)	9.0	7.5
High school graduate, including equivalency (percent)............................	28.4	27.7
Some college, no degree (percent)	21.1	21.0
Associate's degree (percent)	7.0	8.2
Bachelor's degree (percent)	18.2	18.7
Graduate or professional degree (percent)............................	10.8	11.4
High school graduate or higher (percent)	85.6	86.9
Bachelor's degree or higher (percent)	29.1	30.1

Table GA-12. Public School Characteristics and Educational Indicators

(Number, percent; data derived from National Center of Education Statistics.)

Item	State	U.S.
Public Schools, 2013–2014 (except where noted)		
Number of school districts..............................	218	18,194
Number of schools..............................	2,379	98,271
Number of students (in thousands)	1,724	50,045
Number of teachers (in thousands)	109	3,114
Student-teacher ratio	15.8	16.1
Expenditures per student (dollars), FY 2013..............................	91,217	107,637
Four-year adjusted cohort graduation rate (ACGR)[1,2]	72.5	82.3
Students eligible for free or reduced-price lunch (in thousands)	1071	25,596
English language learners (in thousands)	90	4,461
Students age 3 to 21 served under IDEA, part B (in thousands)	191	6,464

Public Schools by Type	Number	Percent of state public schools
Total number of schools..	2,379	100.0
Regular	2,246	94.4
Special education..............................	60	2.5
Vocational education..............................	1	0.0
Alternative education..............................	72	3.0

NOTE: Every school is assigned only one school type based on its instructional emphasis.

[1]ACGR data represents a new method of calculating high-school completion rates and may not be comparable to previous years' data for Averaged Freshmen Graduation Rates (AFGR).

[2]The United States 4-year ACGRs were estimated using both the reported 4-year ACGR data from 49 states and the District of Columbia and using imputed data for Idaho. The estimate for American Indian/Alaska Native students also includes imputed data for Virginia.

Table GA-13. Reported Voting and Registration of the Voting-Age Population, November 2014

(Numbers in thousands, percent.)

Item	Total population	Total citizen population	Registered			Voted		
			Total registered	Percent registered (total population)	Percent registered (total citizen population)	Total voted	Percent voted (total population)	Percent voted (total citizen population)
U.S. Total	239,874	219,941	142,166	59.3	64.6	92,251	38.5	41.9
State Total..........................	7,306	6,759	4,306	58.9	63.7	2,919	40.0	43.2
Sex								
Male..................................	3,458	3,143	1,959	56.7	62.3	1,297	37.5	41.3
Female	3,848	3,616	2,347	61.0	64.9	1,622	42.2	44.9
Race								
White alone..........................	4,569	4,236	2,764	60.5	65.3	1,866	40.8	44.0
White, non-Hispanic alone...........	4,142	4,097	2,708	65.4	66.1	1,835	44.3	44.8
Black alone..........................	2,199	2,150	1,339	60.9	62.3	925	42.1	43.0
Asian alone	388	242	108	27.7	44.5	62	16.0	25.7
Hispanic (of any race)..............	508	207	99	19.6	48.1	62	12.1	29.8
White alone or in combination	4,655	4,317	2,826	60.7	65.4	1,901	40.8	44.0
Black alone or in combination..........	2,272	2,224	1,385	61.0	62.3	968	42.6	43.5
Asian alone or in combination..........	413	267	133	32.1	49.7	71	17.1	26.5
Age								
18 to 24 years......................	975	895	376	38.6	42.0	201	20.6	22.4
25 to 34 years......................	1,204	1,039	622	51.7	59.9	334	27.7	32.2
35 to 44 years......................	1,353	1,230	801	59.2	65.1	541	40.0	44.0
45 to 64 years......................	2,624	2,469	1,625	61.9	65.8	1,160	44.2	47.0
65 years and over	1,151	1,126	882	76.6	78.3	684	59.4	60.7

Table GA-14. Crime

(Number, rate per 100,000. Data are derived from the FBI Uniform Crime Reports.)

Item	State			U.S.[1,2,3,4]		
	2013	2014	Percent change	2013	2014	Percent change
TOTAL POPULATION[5]..........................	9,992,167	10,097,343	1.1	316,128,839	318,857,056	0.9
VIOLENT CRIME						
Number..............................	35,943	38,097	6.0	1,163,146	1,165,383	0.2
Rate	359.7	377.3	4.9	367.9	365.5	-0.7
Murder and Nonnegligent Manslaughter						
Number..............................	556	580	4.3	14,196	14,249	0.4
Rate	5.6	5.7	1.8	4.5	4.5	-
Rape[6]						
Number..............................	2,582	3,048	X	108,612	116,645	X
Rate	25.8	30.2	X	34.4	36.6	X
Robbery						
Number..............................	12,488	12,417	-0.6	345,031	325,802	-5.6
Rate	125.0	123.0	-1.6	109.1	102.2	-6.3
Aggravated Assault						
Number..............................	20,915	22,052	5.4	724,149	741,291	2.4
Rate	209.3	218.4	4.3	229.1	232.5	1.5
PROPERTY CRIME						
Number..............................	334,399	331,316	-0.9	8,632,512	8,277,829	-4.1
Rate	3,346.6	3,281.2	-2.0	2,730.7	2,596.1	-4.9
Burglary						
Number..............................	82,258	76,428	-7.1	1,928,465	1,729,806	-10.3
Rate	823.2	756.9	-8.1	610.0	542.5	-11.1
Larceny-Theft						
Number..............................	225,315	228,034	1.2	6,004,453	5,858,496	-2.4
Rate	2,254.9	2,258.4	0.2	1,899.4	1,837.3	-3.3
Motor Vehicle Theft						
Number..............................	26,826	26,854	0.1	699,594	689,527	-1.4
Rate	268.5	266.0	-0.9	221.3	216.2	-2.3

NOTE: Although arson data are included in the trend and clearance tables, sufficient data are not available to estimate totals for this offense. Therefore, no arson data are published in this table.
X = Not applicable.
- = Zero or rounds to zero.
[1]The crime figures have been adjusted.
[2]The data collection methodology for the offense of forcible rape used by the Minnesota state Uniform Crime Reporting (UCR) Program (with the exception of Minneapolis and St. Paul, Minnesota) does not comply with national UCR Program guidelines. Consequently, its figures for forcible rape and violent crime (of which forcible rape is a part) are not published in this table.
[3]Includes offenses reported by the Zoological Police and the Metro Transit Police.
[4]Because of changes in the state's reporting practices, figures are not comparable to previous years' data.
[5]Populations are U.S. Census Bureau provisional estimates as of July 1 of each year.
[6]The figures shown for the offense of rape were estimated using the revised Uniform Crime Reporting (UCR) definition of rape.

Table GA-15. State Government Finances, 2014

(Dollar amounts in thousands, percent distribution.)

Item	Dollars	Percent distribution
Total Revenue	54,206,860	100.0
General revenue	39,007,185	72.0
Intergovernmental revenue	14,611,862	27.0
Taxes	18,628,502	34.4
General sales	5,125,502	9.5
Selective sales	2,184,630	4.0
License taxes	609,944	1.1
Individual income tax	8,965,572	16.5
Corporate income tax	943,806	1.7
Other taxes	799,048	1.5
Current charges	3,589,728	6.6
Miscellaneous general revenue	2,177,093	4.0
Utility revenue	6,418	-
Liquor stores revenue	0	-
Insurance trust revenue[1]	15,193,257	28.0
Total Expenditure	45,452,071	100.0
Intergovernmental expenditure	10,557,747	23.2
Direct expenditure	34,894,324	76.8
Current operation	24,296,987	53.5
Capital outlay	2,560,000	5.6
Insurance benefits and repayments	6,370,406	14.0
Assistance and subsidies	1,006,855	2.2
Interest on debt	660,076	1.5
Exhibit: Salaries and wages	5,931,608	13.1
Total Expenditure	45,452,071	100.0
General expenditure	39,048,586	85.9
Intergovernmental expenditure	10,557,747	23.2
Direct expenditure	28,490,839	62.7
General expenditure, by function:		
Education	17,402,185	38.3
Public welfare	11,741,940	25.8
Hospitals	1,150,727	2.5
Health	1,179,452	2.6
Highways	2,300,070	5.1
Police protection	309,129	0.7
Correction	1,461,927	3.2
Natural resources	452,303	1.0
Parks and recreation	187,124	0.4
Governmental administration	847,860	1.9
Interest on general debt	660,076	1.5
Other and unallocable	1,355,793	3.0
Utility expenditure	33,079	0.1
Liquor stores expenditure	0	-
Insurance trust expenditure	6,370,406	14.0
Debt at End of Fiscal Year	13,380,184	X
Cash and Security Holdings	95,876,600	X

X = Not applicable.
- = Zero or rounds to zero.
[1]Within insurance trust revenue, net earnings of state retirement systems is a calculated statistic (the item code in the data file is X08), and thus can be positive or negative. Net earnings is the sum of earnings on investments plus gains on investments minus losses on investments. The change made in 2002 for asset valuation from book to market value in accordance with Statement 34 of the Governmental Accounting Standards Board is reflected in the calculated statistics.

Table GA-16. State Government Tax Collections, 2014

(Dollars in thousands, percent.)

Item	Dollars	Percent distribution
Total Taxes	18,628,502	100.0
Property taxes	788,350	4.2
Sales and gross receipts	7,310,132	39.2
General sales and gross receipts	5,125,502	27.5
Selective sales and gross receipts	2,184,630	11.7
Alcoholic beverages	181,875	1.0
Amusements	0	-
Insurance premiums	372,122	2.0
Motor fuels	1,006,494	5.4
Pari-mutuels	0	-
Public utilities	0	-
Tobacco products	216,640	1.2
Other selective sales	407,499	2.2
Licenses	609,944	3.3
Alcoholic beverages	3,829	-
Amusements	148	-
Corporations in general	48,078	0.3
Hunting and fishing	24,899	0.1
Motor vehicle	337,456	1.8
Motor vehicle operators	91,117	0.5
Public utilities	0	-
Occupation and business, NEC	83,662	0.4
Other licenses	20,755	0.1
Income taxes	9,909,378	53.2
Individual income	8,965,572	48.1
Corporation net income	943,806	5.1
Other taxes	10,698	0.1
Death and gift	0	-
Documentary and stock transfer	10,698	0.1
Severance	X	X
Taxes, NEC	0	-

X = Not applicable.
- = Zero or rounds to zero.

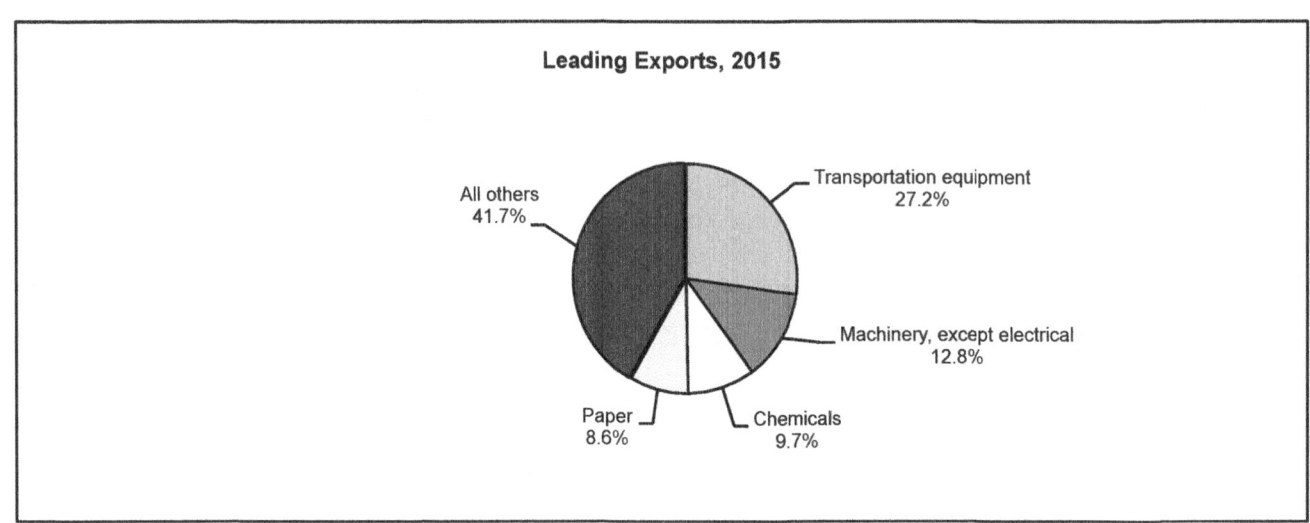

Leading Exports, 2015

Transportation equipment 27.2%
Machinery, except electrical 12.8%
Chemicals 9.7%
Paper 8.6%
All others 41.7%

HAWAII

Facts and Figures

Location: North Pacific Ocean

Area: 10,931 sq. mi. (28,311 sq. km.); rank—43rd

Population: 1,431,603 (2015 est.); rank—40th

Principal Cities: capital—Honolulu; largest—Honolulu

Statehood: August 21, 1959; 50th state

U.S. Congress: 2 senators, 2 representatives

State Motto: *Ua mau ke ea o ka'ina i ka pono* ("The life of the land is perpetuated in righteousness")

State Song: "Hawai'i Pono' (Hawaii's Own)"

State Nickname: The Aloha State

Abbreviations: HI

State Symbols: flower—native yellow hibiscus; tree—kukui (candlenut tree); bird—nene (Hawaiian goose)

At a Glance

- With an increase in population of 5.0 percent, Hawaii ranked 16th among the states in growth from 2010 to 2015.

- In 2014, 5.3 percent of Hawaiians did not have health insurance, compared to 11.7 percent of the total U.S. population.

- Hawaii's violent crime rate in 2014 was 259.2 per 100,000 population, compared to 365.5 for the entire nation.

- Hawaii had the highest proportion of state government employees to total residents in 2014, with 40.8 state employees per 1,000 residents, compared to the national average of 13.5 employees per 1,000 residents.

- Hawaii had the largest percent of Asian Alone residents in 2015, with 37.3 percent of its residents in this category.

Table HI-1. Population by Age, Sex, Race, and Hispanic Origin

(Number, percent, except where noted.)

Sex, age, race, and Hispanic origin	2000	2010	2015[1]	Average annual percent change, 2010–2015
Total Population..	1,211,537	1,360,301	1,431,603	0.4
Percent of total U.S. population	0.4	0.4	0.4	X
Sex				
Male..	563,891	681,243	725,372	0.4
Female	544,338	679,058	706,231	0.3
Age				
Under 5 years...	78,163	87,407	92,412	0.4
5 to 19 years...	249,088	250,894	249,930	-
20 to 64 years...	723,685	826,868	852,347	0.2
65 years and over	160,601	195,138	236,914	1.4
Median age (years)	36.2	38.6	37.8	-0.1
Race and Hispanic Origin				
One race				
White	294,102	349,051	382,852	0.7
Black..	22,003	22,473	37,413	3.7
American Indian and Alaska Native	3,535	4,960	6,475	1.9
Asian..	503,868	531,633	533,402	-
Native Hawaiian or				
Other Pacific Islander...................................	113,539	138,292	142,260	0.2
Two or more races	259,343	313,892	329,201	0.3
Hispanic (of any race)	87,699	133,342	148,705	0.8

X = Not applicable.
- = Zero or rounds to zero.
[1]Population figures for 2015 are July 1 estimates. The 2010 estimates are taken from the 2010 Census.

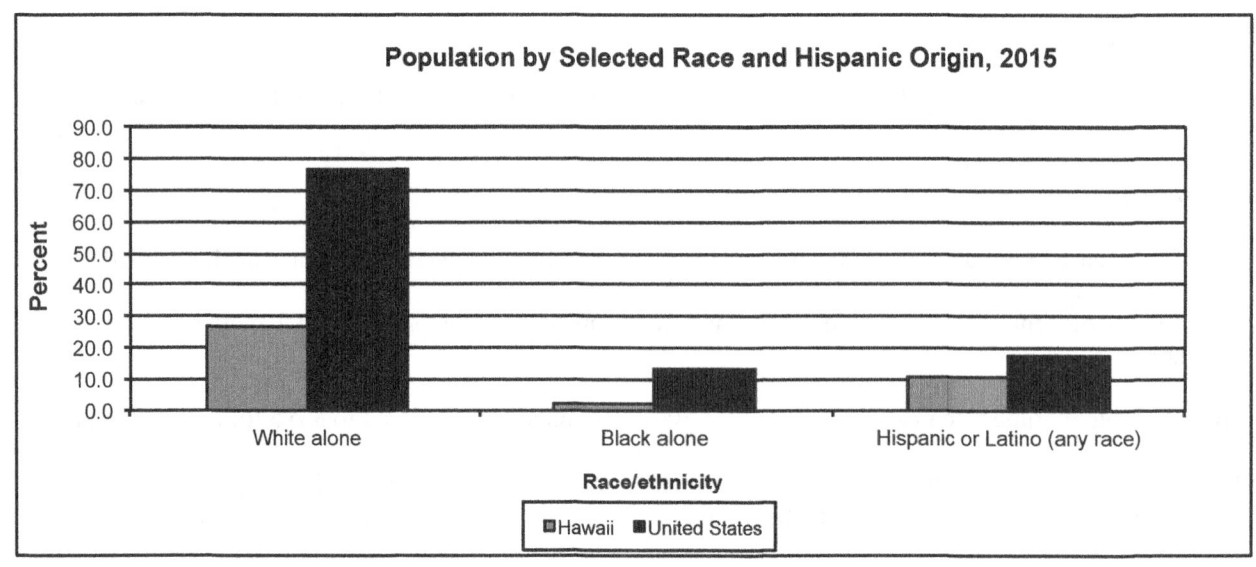

Table HI-2. Marital Status

(Number, percent distribution.)

Sex, age, race, and Hispanic origin	2000	2010	2014
Males, 15 Years and Over	481,768	554,154	569,152
Never married	34.6	37.8	37.5
Now married, except separated......................................	53.7	49.1	50.3
Separated..	1.4	1.2	1.2
Widowed..	2.2	2.7	2.5
Divorced..	8.1	9.2	8.5
Females, 15 Years and Over	484,107	556,915	566,217
Never married	25.9	28.7	28.8
Now married, except separated......................................	52.5	48.5	49.3
Separated..	1.7	1.8	1.5
Widowed..	9.8	10.1	10.0
Divorced..	10.0	11.0	10.5

Table HI-3. Households and Housing Characteristics

(Number, percent, dollars.)

Item	2000	2010	2014	Average annual percent change, 2000–2014
Total Households...	403,240	445,812	450,769	0.8
Family households	287,068	303,075	314,151	0.7
Married-couple family	216,077	224,402	232,049	0.5
Other family	70,991	78,673	82,102	1.1
Male householder, no wife present........................	21,068	24,247	26,199	1.7
Female householder, no husband present...............	49,923	54,426	55,903	0.9
Nonfamily households	116,172	142,737	136,618	1.3
Householder living alone....................................	88,153	108,872	106,271	1.5
Householder not living alone..............................	28,019	33,865	30,347	0.6
Housing Characteristics				
Total housing units..	460,542	519,992	530,118	1.1
Occupied housing units	403,240	445,812	450,769	0.8
Owner occupied	227,888	258,533	255,375	0.9
Renter occupied	175,352	187,279	195,394	0.8
Average household size..	2.92	2.96	3.05	0.3
Financial Characteristics				
Median gross rent of renter-occupied housing	779	1,291	1,448	6.1
Median monthly owner costs for housing units with a mortgage	1,636	2,240	2,173	2.3
Median value of owner-occupied housing units...........	272,700	525,400	528,000	6.7

Table HI-4. Migration, Origin, and Language

(Number, percent.)

Characteristic	State 2013	State 2014	State Percent change	U.S. 2013	U.S. 2014	U.S. Percent change
Residence 1 Year Ago						
Population 1 year and over	1,387,361	1,401,004	1.0	312,432,820	315,095,393	0.9
Same house	84.9	85.6	X	85.0	85.1	X
Different house in the U.S.	14.0	13.6	X	14.4	14.3	X
Same county	9.3	8.9	X	8.9	8.7	X
Different county	4.7	4.7	X	5.5	5.6	X
Same state	0.5	0.5	X	3.2	3.3	X
Different state	4.2	4.2	X	2.3	2.3	X
Abroad	1.1	0.9	X	0.6	0.6	X
Place of Birth						
Native born	1,157,590	1,169,289	1.0	274,780,773	276,465,262	0.6
Male	52.1	52.3	X	49.3	49.3	X
Female	47.9	47.7	X	50.7	50.7	X
Foreign born	246,464	250,272	1.5	41,348,066	42,391,794	2.5
Male	43.6	42.4	X	48.8	48.7	X
Female	56.4	57.6	X	51.2	51.3	X
Foreign born; naturalized U.S. citizen....................	139,732	142,503	2.0	19,294,710	19,984,738	3.6
Male	42.3	41	X	45.9	45.9	X
Female	57.7	59	X	54.1	54.1	X
Foreign born; not a U.S. citizen...........................	106,732	107,769	1.0	22,053,356	22,407,056	1.6
Male	45.3	44.2	X	51.3	51.2	X
Female	54.7	55.8	X	48.7	48.8	X
Entered 2010 or later	9.4	11.3	X	9.7	12.3	X
Entered 2000 to 2009	27.5	27.8	X	29.4	28.6	X
Entered before 2000..	63.1	61	X	61.0	59.1	X
World Region of Birth, Foreign						
Foreign-born population, excluding population born at sea	246,464	250,272	1.5	41,347,945	42,390,705	2.5
Europe..	4.5	4.2	X	11.6	11.2	X
Asia..	79.2	78.4	X	29.5	30.1	X
Africa..	0.8	0.9	X	4.4	4.6	X
Oceania...	9.3	10.8	X	0.5	0.6	X
Latin America...	4.1	4.1	X	51.9	51.6	X
North America..	2.1	1.7	X	2.0	1.9	X
Language Spoken at Home and Ability to Speak English						
Population 5 years and over..................................	1,313,348	1,328,554	1.2	296,358,760	299,084,046	0.9
English only	74.9	74.8	X	79.2	78.9	X
Language other than English...............................	25.1	25.2	X	20.8	21.1	X
Speaks English less than "very well"....................	13.1	12.8	X	8.5	8.6	X

X = Not applicable.
- = Zero or rounds to zero.

Table HI-5. Median Income and Poverty Status, 2014

(Number, percent, except as noted.)

Characteristic	State		U.S.	
	Number	Percent	Number	Percent
Median Income				
Households (dollars)..	69,592	X	53,657	X
Families (dollars)	79,187	X	65,910	X
Below Poverty Level (All People)	156,729	11.4	48,208,387	15.5
Sex				
Male...	71,319	10.3	21,590,918	14.2
Female	85,410	12.4	26,617,469	16.8
Age				
Under 18 years..	44,363	14.7	15,686,012	21.7
Related children under 18 years......................	43,019	14.4	15,372,705	21.3
18 to 64 years...	94,026	11	28,267,482	14.6
65 years and over	18,340	8.2	4,254,893	9.5

X = Not applicable.

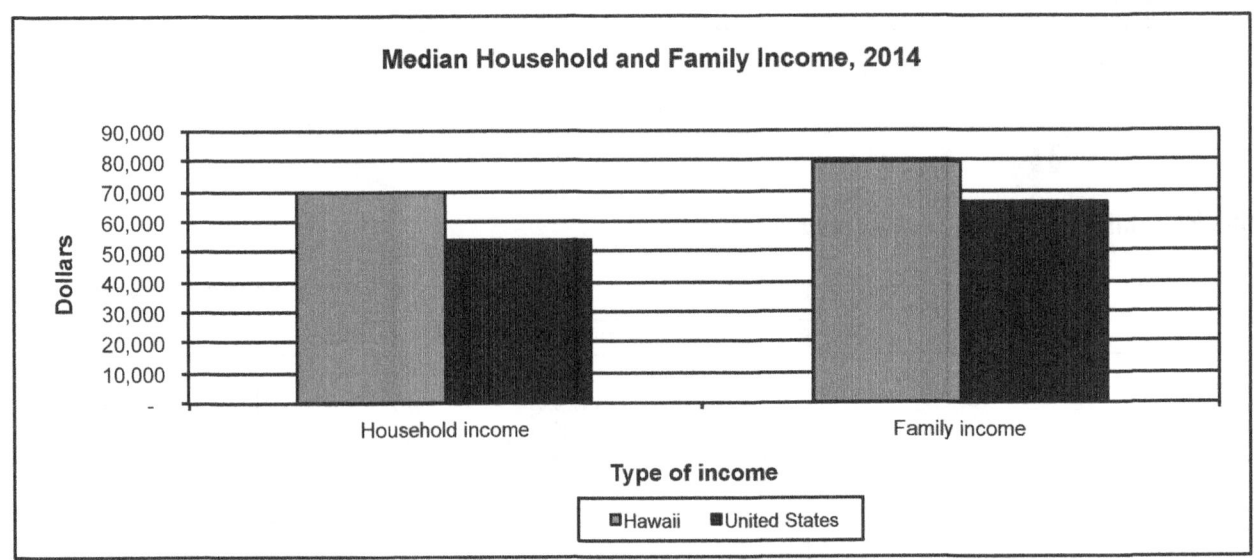

Table HI-6. Health Insurance Coverage Status for the Civilian Noninstitutionalized Population and Children Under 18 Years of Age

(Numbers in thousands, percent.)

Item	2006	2007	2008	2009	2010	2011	2012	2013	2014
Civilian Noninstitutionalized Population	1,255	1,267	1,237	1,232	1,316	1,326	1,342	1,345	1,368
Covered by Private or Public Insurance									
Number..	1,144	1,172	1,154	1,146	1,212	1,232	1,249	1,254	1,296
Percent...	91.2	92.5	93.3	93.0	92.1	92.9	93.1	93.3	94.7
Not Covered									
Number..	110	96	83	86	104	94	93	91	72
Percent...	8.8	7.5	6.7	7.0	7.9	7.1	6.9	6.7	5.3
Percent in the U.S. not covered...........................	15.8	15.3	15.1	15.1	15.5	15.1	14.8	14.5	11.7
Children Under 18 Years of Age	298	291	284	288	304	304	303	307	308
Covered by Private or Public Insurance									
Number..	279	277	274	281	293	293	293	298	298
Percent...	93.7	47.5	96.5	97.5	96.3	96.4	96.5	97.0	96.9
Not Covered									
Number..	19	14	10	7	11	11	10	9	10
Percent...	6.3	4.8	3.5	2.5	3.7	3.6	3.5	3.0	3.1
Percent in the U.S. not covered...........................	11.7	11.0	9.7	8.6	8.0	7.5	7.2	7.1	6.0

Table HI-7. Employment Status by Demographic Group, 2015

(Numbers in thousands, percent.)

Characteristic	Civilian noninstitutional population	Civilian labor force		Employed		Unemployed	
		Number	Percent of population	Number	Percent of population	Number	Percent of population
Total...	1,092	678	62.1	652	59.7	25	3.7
Sex							
Male...	533	356	66.7	341	63.9	15	4.3
Female..	559	322	57.6	312	55.8	10	3.2
Race, Sex, and Hispanic Origin							
White...	236	143	60.8	137	58.0	6	4.5
Male..	125	82	66.0	79	63.0	4	4.5
Female...	111	61	54.9	58	52.5	3	4.4
Black or African American................	22	12	54.1	11	51.8	1	4.1
Male..	NA	NA	NA	NA	NA	NA	NA
Female...	NA	NA	NA	NA	NA	NA	NA
Hispanic or Latino ethnicity[1]	95	60	63.1	57	60.5	3	4.1
Male..	45	29	64.0	27	61.3	1	4.2
Female...	50	31	62.3	30	59.8	1	4.1
Age							
16 to 19 years...............................	77	24	31.3	21	27.3	3	13.0
20 to 24 years...............................	97	64	66.0	60	61.4	5	7.0
25 to 34 years...............................	173	140	80.9	133	77.2	7	4.6
35 to 44 years...............................	160	136	84.7	132	82.5	4	2.6
45 to 54 years...............................	178	144	80.7	140	78.7	4	2.4
55 to 64 years...............................	181	121	67.0	119	65.6	3	2.1
65 years and over...........................	226	49	21.6	47	20.8	2	3.3

NOTE: Data in Table 7 are from the Current Population Survey (CPS) and do not match the estimates in Table 8. See notes and definitions for further information.
[1]May be of any race.
NA = Not available.

Unemployment Rate, 1980–2015

Table HI-8. Employment Status of the Civilian Noninstitutional Population Age 16 Years and Over

(Number, percent.)

Year	Civilian labor force	Civilian participation rate	Employed	Unemployed	Unemployment rate
2007.............................	638,395	65.9	620,535	17,860	2.8
2008.............................	639,691	65.6	612,120	27,571	4.3
2009.............................	631,690	64.3	586,522	45,168	7.2
2010.............................	647,249	62.8	602,282	44,967	6.9
2011.............................	660,253	62.6	615,319	44,934	6.8
2012.............................	647,625	60.9	608,722	38,903	6.0
2013.............................	650,708	60.6	619,088	31,620	4.9
2014.............................	668,346	61.7	639,148	29,198	4.4
2015.............................	677,439	62.0	652,939	24,500	3.6

Table HI-9. Employment and Average Wages by Industry

(Estimates through 2010 are based on the 2007 North American Industry Classification System [NAICS]. Estimates from 2011 onward are based on the 2012 NAICS.)

Industry	2008	2009	2010	2011	2012	2013	2014
	Number of Jobs						
Wage and Salary Employment by Industry..................	695,721	668,418	665,430	674,452	681,963	695,044	704,326
Farm Wage and Salary Employment.........................	5,822	5,699	6,087	6,808	6,106	6,359	7,366
Nonfarm Wage and Salary Employment.....................	689,899	662,719	659,343	667,644	675,857	688,685	696,960
Private wage and salary employment..........................	509,528	481,507	477,378	484,522	493,164	506,104	513,460
Forestry, fishing, and related activities..........................	1,193	1,151	1,171	1,285	1,309	1,444	1,546
Mining...	330	340	338	332	298	255	252
Utilities...	3,086	3,193	3,215	3,329	3,568	3,769	3,808
Construction..	39,066	32,516	29,925	29,882	30,114	31,832	32,751
Manufacturing..	14,906	13,716	12,954	13,179	13,349	13,575	13,914
Durable goods manufacturing............................	4,607	4,154	3,793	3,881	3,619	3,633	3,591
Nondurable goods manufacturing............................	10,299	9,562	9,161	9,298	9,730	9,942	10,323
Wholesale trade	18,937	17,992	17,849	17,596	17,736	17,828	17,794
Retail trade...	70,876	67,641	67,119	68,182	69,509	70,371	70,499
Transportation and warehousing................................	26,686	23,862	23,478	23,997	25,140	25,981	26,648
Information	10,083	9,095	9,931	8,510	8,470	8,811	8,490
Finance and insurance	17,206	16,725	16,154	16,016	16,046	15,771	15,675
Real estate and rental and leasing.............................	13,126	11,864	11,888	11,775	11,811	12,121	12,279
Professional, scientific, and technical services	25,447	25,039	24,553	24,675	24,577	24,625	24,562
Management of companies and enterprises....................	7,442	7,001	6,649	6,926	7,508	8,252	8,379
Administrative and waste services	43,516	40,458	41,345	44,446	45,578	47,695	49,909
Educational services	15,664	15,778	15,790	16,072	16,502	16,125	15,996
Health care and social assistance...............................	60,819	61,416	62,098	62,401	62,942	64,936	65,845
Arts, entertainment, and recreation.............................	11,767	10,877	10,548	10,836	11,454	12,167	12,195
Accommodation and food services..............................	96,394	90,989	90,918	93,410	96,476	99,698	101,762
Other services, except public administration.................	32,984	31,854	31,455	31,673	30,777	30,848	31,156
Government and government enterprises...........................	180,371	181,212	181,965	183,122	182,693	182,581	183,500
	Dollars						
Average Wages and Salaries by Industry	42,012	42,708	43,202	44,085	44,885	45,302	46,649
Average Farm Wages and Salaries	28,365	28,219	28,395	29,353	19,847	31,649	35,665
Average Nonfarm Wages and Salaries	42,127	42,833	43,338	44,236	45,111	45,428	46,765
Average private wages and salaries..........................	39,090	39,306	39,925	40,572	41,622	42,253	43,430
Forestry, fishing, and related activities..........................	22,105	21,284	21,976	22,674	23,346	24,458	24,530
Mining...	81,870	77,894	73,485	77,443	82,839	88,251	93,825
Utilities...	78,450	80,427	83,879	88,489	90,370	92,368	94,514
Construction..	62,052	62,750	62,573	63,604	64,809	65,104	66,574
Manufacturing..	38,773	38,818	39,245	40,354	40,050	40,699	41,315
Durable goods manufacturing............................	47,183	47,850	48,272	50,996	49,964	50,807	53,343
Nondurable goods manufacturing............................	35,012	34,894	35,508	35,912	36,363	37,006	37,131
Wholesale trade	47,975	48,169	48,175	49,747	51,363	52,586	54,265
Retail trade...	27,064	27,419	28,193	28,183	28,363	28,814	29,682
Transportation and warehousing................................	41,197	41,024	42,112	43,535	44,716	46,158	48,112
Information	54,887	55,815	55,593	57,663	58,627	58,561	61,924
Finance and insurance	56,764	56,897	58,145	60,284	63,148	64,483	65,697
Real estate and rental and leasing.............................	40,717	40,386	41,368	42,542	44,025	46,202	47,067
Professional, scientific, and technical services	61,791	62,342	63,054	63,420	65,877	66,729	68,324
Management of companies and enterprises....................	71,675	71,200	76,806	79,812	83,741	82,599	84,360
Administrative and waste services	29,299	30,283	30,312	29,710	30,840	31,051	31,585
Educational services	31,430	32,337	33,386	34,416	33,477	34,514	34,329
Health care and social assistance...............................	43,364	45,348	45,549	46,630	47,886	48,317	49,728
Arts, entertainment, and recreation.............................	29,078	29,151	28,107	27,292	27,524	28,388	29,752
Accommodation and food services..............................	28,777	27,819	29,329	30,557	31,771	32,209	33,571
Other services, except public administration.................	30,402	30,727	31,896	32,405	33,326	33,705	34,827
Government and government enterprises...........................	50,707	52,204	52,294	53,929	54,531	54,229	56,099

Table HI-10. Employment Characteristics by Family Type

(Number, percent.)

Family type and labor force status	2012		2013		2014	
	Total	Families with own children under 18 years	Total	Families with own children under 18 years	Total	Families with own children under 18 years
All Families...	309,165	121,971	311,203	120,365	312,380	122,610
FAMILY TYPE AND LABOR FORCE STATUS						
Married-Couple Families...	229,027	89,864	235,190	91,038	230,278	89,744
Both husband and wife in labor force........................	54.0	69.1	53.8	66.8	51.1	64.3
Husband in labor force, wife not in labor force	20.0	25.0	21.0	28.8	21.9	28.9
Wife in labor force, husband not in labor force	8.7	4.4	7.8	3.1	9.7	4.5
Both husband and wife not in labor force....................	17.4	1.5	17.1	1.1	17.3	2.3
Other Families	80,138	32,107	76,013	29,327	82,102	32,866
Female householder, no husband present....................	70.6	76.0	69.7	70.0	68.1	70.9
In labor force...	42.4	59.0	44.3	57.1	44.4	58.4
Not in labor force...	28.1	17.0	25.4	12.9	23.7	12.5
Male householder, no wife present...........................	29.4	24.0	30.3	30.0	31.9	29.1
In labor force...	22.5	22.5	21.7	26.3	22.1	25.9
Not in labor force	6.9	1.5	8.6	3.7	9.8	3.2

Table HI-11. School Enrollment and Educational Attainment, 2014

(Number, percent.)

Item	State	U.S.
Enrollment		
Total population 3 years and over, enrolled in school........................	335,539	82,063,714
Enrolled in nursery school or preschool (percent)	5.9	6.0
Enrolled in kindergarten (percent)	4.8	5.1
Enrolled in elementary school, grades 1-8 (percent)........................	40.1	40.2
Enrolled in high school, grades 9-12 (percent)	19.3	20.7
Enrolled in college or graduate school (percent)........................	29.9	28.0
Attainment		
Total population 25 years and over	974,586	213,725,624
Less than ninth grade (percent)	4.0	5.6
9th to 12th grade, no diploma (percent)	4.3	7.5
High school graduate, including equivalency (percent)........................	28.5	27.7
Some college, no degree (percent)	21.7	21.0
Associate's degree (percent)	10.5	8.2
Bachelor's degree (percent)	20.6	18.7
Graduate or professional degree (percent)........................	10.5	11.4
High school graduate or higher (percent)	91.7	86.9
Bachelor's degree or higher (percent)........................	31.0	30.1

Table HI-12. Public School Characteristics and Educational Indicators

(Number, percent; data derived from National Center of Education Statistics.)

Item	State	U.S.
Public Schools, 2013–2014 (except where noted)		
Number of school districts........................	1	18,194
Number of schools........................	288	98,271
Number of students (in thousands)	187	50,045
Number of teachers (in thousands)	12	3,114
Student-teacher ratio	15.9	16.1
Expenditures per student (dollars), FY 2013........................	11,743	107,637
Four-year adjusted cohort graduation rate (ACGR)[1,2]	81.8	82.3
Students eligible for free or reduced-price lunch (in thousands)	94	25,596
English language learners (in thousands)	16	4,461
Students age 3 to 21 served under IDEA, part B (in thousands)	19	6,464

Public Schools by Type	Number	Percent of state public schools
Total number of schools........................	288	100.0
Regular	286	99.3
Special education........................	1	0.3
Vocational education........................	0	0.0
Alternative education........................	1	0.3

NOTE: Every school is assigned only one school type based on its instructional emphasis.
[1]ACGR data represents a new method of calculating high-school completion rates and may not be comparable to previous years' data for Averaged Freshmen Graduation Rates (AFGR).
[2]The United States 4-year ACGRs were estimated using both the reported 4-year ACGR data from 49 states and the District of Columbia and using imputed data for Idaho. The estimate for American Indian/Alaska Native students also includes imputed data for Virginia.

Table HI-13. Reported Voting and Registration of the Voting-Age Population, November 2014

(Numbers in thousands, percent.)

Item	Total population	Total citizen population	Registered			Voted		
			Total registered	Percent registered (total population)	Percent registered (total citizen population)	Total voted	Percent voted (total population)	Percent voted (total citizen population)
U.S. Total	239,874	219,941	142,166	59.3	64.6	92,251	38.5	41.9
State Total............................	1,035	956	490	47.4	51.3	399	38.6	41.8
Sex								
Male.................................	502	475	243	48.4	51.2	197	39.2	41.4
Female	533	481	247	46.4	51.4	202	38.0	42.1
Race								
White alone..........................	228	217	117	51.6	54.2	95	41.8	44.0
White, non-Hispanic alone	211	201	110	52.1	54.6	91	43.0	45.1
Black alone...........................	19	18	8	(B)	(B)	7	(B)	(B)
Asian alone	482	428	228	47.2	53.2	196	40.6	45.8
Hispanic (of any race)................	64	62	31	(B)	(B)	21	(B)	(B)
White alone or in combination	352	340	189	53.7	55.5	146	41.3	42.8
Black alone or in combination.........	26	25	10	(B)	(B)	7	(B)	(B)
Asian alone or in combination.........	605	550	297	49.1	54.1	243	40.1	44.2
Age								
18 to 24 years......................	133	125	31	23.4	24.8	11	8.2	8.7
25 to 34 years......................	143	131	55	38.6	42.2	39	27.0	29.4
35 to 44 years......................	181	157	72	39.8	46.0	56	31.0	35.8
45 to 64 years......................	353	328	195	55.4	59.6	170	48.0	51.7
65 years and over	225	215	136	60.6	63.5	124	55.1	57.7

B = Base is less than 75,000 and therefore too small to show the derived measure.

Table HI-14. Crime

(Number, rate per 100,000. Data are derived from the FBI Uniform Crime Reports.)

Item	State			U.S.[1,2,3,4]		
	2013	2014	Percent change	2013	2014	Percent change
TOTAL POPULATION[5]........................	1,404,054	1,419,561	1.1	316,128,839	318,857,056	0.9
VIOLENT CRIME						
Number..............................	3,444	3,680	6.9	1,163,146	1,165,383	0.2
Rate	245.3	259.2	5.7	367.9	365.5	-0.7
Murder and Nonnegligent Manslaughter						
Number..............................	21	26	23.8	14,196	14,249	0.4
Rate	1.5	1.8	20.0	4.5	4.5	-
Rape[6]						
Number..............................	385	445	X	108,612	116,645	X
Rate	27.4	31.3	X	34.4	36.6	X
Robbery						
Number..............................	1,131	1,107	-2.1	345,031	325,802	-5.6
Rate	80.6	78.0	-3.2	109.1	102.2	-6.3
Aggravated Assault						
Number..............................	1,996	2,102	5.3	724,149	741,291	2.4
Rate	142.2	148.1	4.1	229.1	232.5	1.5
PROPERTY CRIME						
Number..............................	42,875	43,297	1.0	8,632,512	8,277,829	-4.1
Rate	3,053.7	3,050.0	-0.1	2,730.7	2,596.1	-4.9
Burglary						
Number..............................	7,533	7,778	3.3	1,928,465	1,729,806	-10.3
Rate	536.5	547.9	2.1	610.0	542.5	-11.1
Larceny-Theft						
Number..............................	31,658	31,640	-0.1	6,004,453	5,858,496	-2.4
Rate	2,254.8	2,228.9	-1.1	1,899.4	1,837.3	-3.3
Motor Vehicle Theft						
Number..............................	3,684	3,879	5.3	699,594	689,527	-1.4
Rate	262.4	273.3	4.2	221.3	216.2	-2.3

NOTE: Although arson data are included in the trend and clearance tables, sufficient data are not available to estimate totals for this offense. Therefore, no arson data are published in this table.
X = Not applicable.
- = Zero or rounds to zero.
[1]The crime figures have been adjusted.
[2]The data collection methodology for the offense of forcible rape used by the Minnesota state Uniform Crime Reporting (UCR) Program (with the exception of Minneapolis and St. Paul, Minnesota) does not comply with national UCR Program guidelines. Consequently, its figures for forcible rape and violent crime (of which forcible rape is a part) are not published in this table.
[3]Includes offenses reported by the Zoological Police and the Metro Transit Police.
[4]Because of changes in the state's reporting practices, figures are not comparable to previous years' data.
[5]Populations are U.S. Census Bureau provisional estimates as of July 1 of each year.
[6]The figures shown for the offense of rape were estimated using the revised Uniform Crime Reporting (UCR) definition of rape.

Table HI-15. State Government Finances, 2014

(Dollar amounts in thousands, percent distribution.)

Item	Dollars	Percent distribution
Total Revenue	15,055,561	100.0
General revenue	11,304,424	75.1
Intergovernmental revenue	2,810,537	18.7
Taxes	6,033,331	40.1
General sales	2,825,041	18.8
Selective sales	1,022,621	6.8
License taxes	223,543	1.5
Individual income tax	1,745,461	11.6
Corporate income tax	126,045	0.8
Other taxes	90,620	0.6
Current charges	1,664,748	11.1
Miscellaneous general revenue	795,808	5.3
Utility revenue	0	-
Liquor stores revenue	0	-
Insurance trust revenue[1]	3,751,137	24.9
Total Expenditure	12,378,789	100.0
Intergovernmental expenditure	255,885	2.1
Direct expenditure	12,122,904	97.9
Current operation	9,576,856	77.4
Capital outlay	682,348	5.5
Insurance benefits and repayments	1,328,588	10.7
Assistance and subsidies	151,888	1.2
Interest on debt	383,224	3.1
Exhibit: Salaries and wages	2,567,750	20.7
Total Expenditure	12,378,789	100.0
General expenditure	11,045,050	89.2
Intergovernmental expenditure	255,885	2.1
Direct expenditure	10,789,165	87.2
General expenditure, by function:		
Education	3,275,517	26.5
Public welfare	2,582,963	20.9
Hospitals	818,591	6.6
Health	528,294	4.3
Highways	414,444	3.3
Police protection	36,352	0.3
Correction	215,302	1.7
Natural resources	112,112	0.9
Parks and recreation	91,742	0.7
Governmental administration	488,872	3.9
Interest on general debt	383,224	3.1
Other and unallocable	2,097,637	16.9
Utility expenditure	5,151	-
Liquor stores expenditure	0	-
Insurance trust expenditure	1,328,588	10.7
Debt at End of Fiscal Year	8,426,573	X
Cash and Security Holdings	19,176,589	X

X = Not applicable.
- = Zero or rounds to zero.
[1]Within insurance trust revenue, net earnings of state retirement systems is a calculated statistic (the item code in the data file is X08), and thus can be positive or negative. Net earnings is the sum of earnings on investments plus gains on investments minus losses on investments. The change made in 2002 for asset valuation from book to market value in accordance with Statement 34 of the Governmental Accounting Standards Board is reflected in the calculated statistics.

Table HI-16. State Government Tax Collections, 2014

(Dollars in thousands, percent.)

Item	Dollars	Percent distribution
Total Taxes	6,033,331	100.0
Property taxes	X	X
Sales and gross receipts	3,847,662	63.8
General sales and gross receipts	2,825,041	46.8
Selective sales and gross receipts	1,022,621	16.9
Alcoholic beverages	48,305	0.8
Amusements	0	-
Insurance premiums	142,051	2.4
Motor fuels	93,598	1.6
Pari-mutuels	0	-
Public utilities	166,179	2.8
Tobacco products	107,685	1.8
Other selective sales	464,803	7.7
Licenses	223,543	3.7
Alcoholic beverages	0	-
Amusements	0	-
Corporations in general	1,691	-
Hunting and fishing	536	-
Motor vehicle	168,980	2.8
Motor vehicle operators	360	-
Public utilities	21,183	0.4
Occupation and business, NEC	29,480	0.5
Other licenses	1,313	-
Income taxes	1,871,506	31.0
Individual income	1,745,461	28.9
Corporation net income	126,045	2.1
Other taxes	90,620	1.5
Death and gift	14,789	0.2
Documentary and stock transfer	75,831	1.3
Severance	X	X
Taxes, NEC	0	-

X = Not applicable.
- = Zero or rounds to zero.

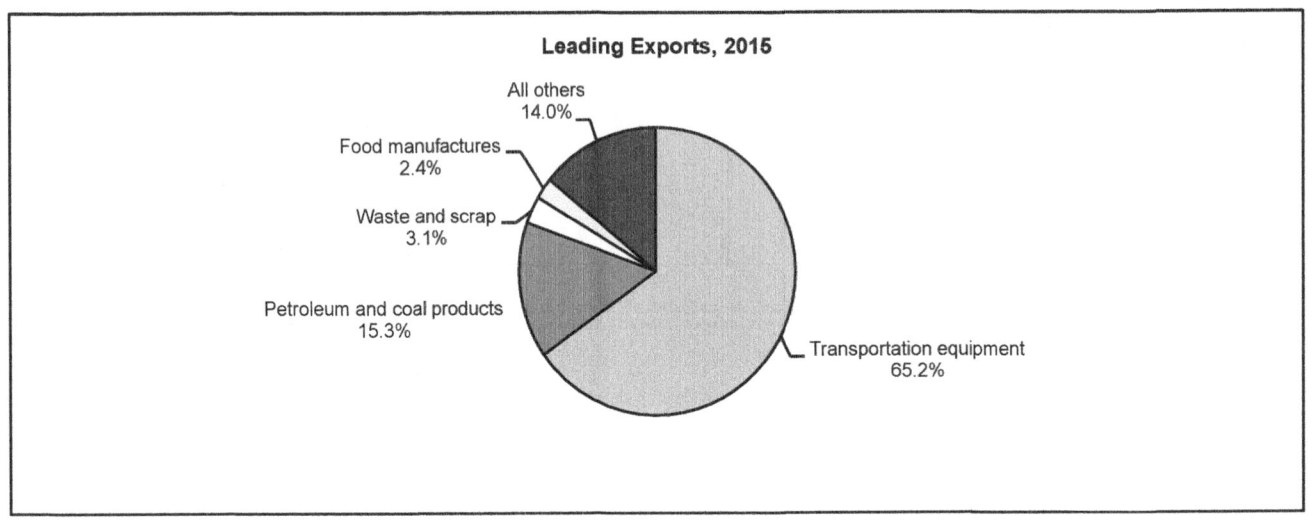

Leading Exports, 2015

All others 14.0%
Food manufactures 2.4%
Waste and scrap 3.1%
Petroleum and coal products 15.3%
Transportation equipment 65.2%

IDAHO

Facts and Figures

Location: Northwestern United States; bordered on the N by Canada, on the E by Montana and Wyoming, on the S by Nevada and Utah, and on the W by Washington and Oregon

Area: 83,568 sq. mi. (216,446 sq. km.); rank—14th

Population: 1,654,930 (2015 est.); rank—39th

Principal Cities: capital—Boise; largest—Boise

Statehood: July 3, 1890; 43rd state

U.S. Congress: 2 senators, 2 representatives

State Motto: *Esto perpetua* ("Let it be perpetual")

State Song: "Here We Have Idaho"

State Nickname: The Gem State

Abbreviations: ID

State Symbols: flower—syringa (mock orange); tree—Western white pine; bird—mountain bluebird

At a Glance

- With an increase in population of 5.3 percent, Idaho ranked 11th among the states in growth from 2010 to 2015.

- With 1,854.8 incidents per 100,000 population, Idaho had the 4th lowest property crime rate in the country in 2014.

- Idaho's violent crime rate in 2014 was 212.2 per 100,000 population, compared to 365.5 for the entire nation.

- With 26.2 percent of its population under age 18, Idaho ranked 3rd among the states for the highest percent children in 2015.

- Idaho's birth rate of 14.0 births per 1,000 population ranked 8th in the nation in 2014.

Table ID-1. Population by Age, Sex, Race, and Hispanic Origin

(Number, percent, except where noted.)

Sex, age, race, and Hispanic origin	2000	2010	2015[1]	Average annual percent change, 2010–2015
Total Population..	1,293,953	1,567,582	1,654,930	0.4
Percent of total U.S. population	0.5	0.5	0.5	X
Sex				
Male..	648,660	785,324	828,747	0.4
Female	645,293	782,258	826,183	0.4
Age				
Under 5 years..	97,643	121,772	112,923	-0.5
5 to 19 years...	316,222	353,509	364,485	0.2
20 to 64 years..	734,172	897,633	934,028	0.3
65 years and over	145,916	194,668	243,494	1.6
Median age (years)	33.2	34.6	35.9	0.3
Race and Hispanic Origin				
One race				
White..	1,177,304	1,476,097	1,545,478	0.3
Black..	5,456	10,950	13,932	1.7
American Indian and Alaska Native	17,645	25,782	28,833	0.8
Asian..	11,889	20,034	24,609	1.5
Native Hawaiian or Other Pacific Islander	1,308	2,786	3,383	1.4
Two or more races	25,609	31,933	38,695	1.4
Hispanic (of any race)..	101,690	182,424	202,430	0.7

X = Not applicable.
[1]Population figures for 2015 are July 1 estimates. The 2010 estimates are taken from the 2010 Census.

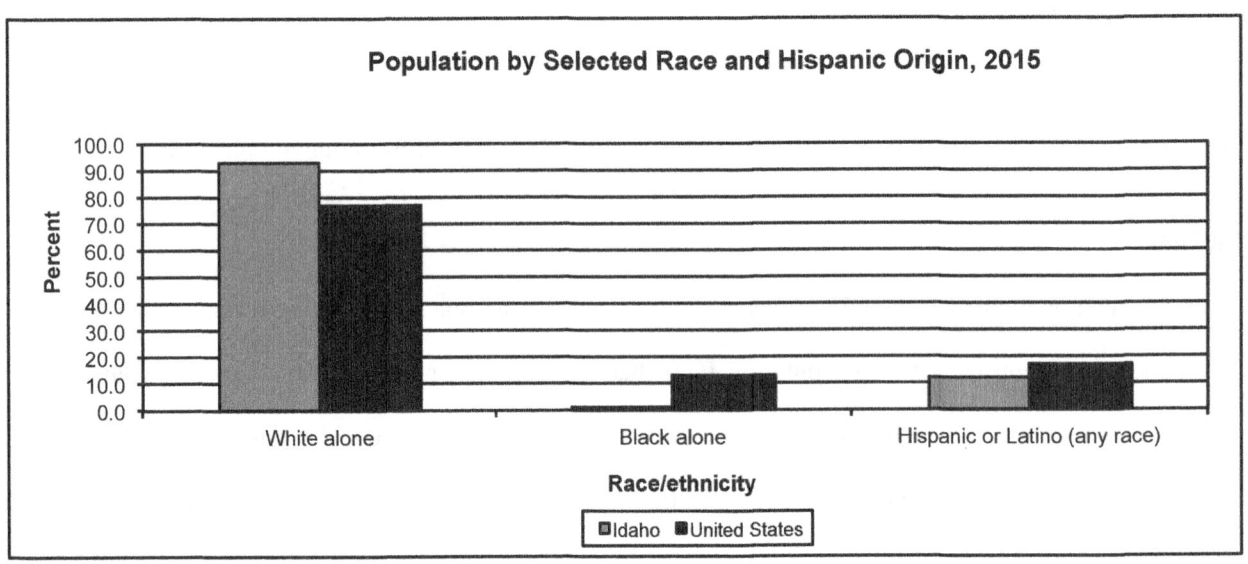

Table ID-2. Marital Status

(Number, percent distribution.)

Sex, age, race, and Hispanic origin	2000	2010	2014
Males, 15 Years and Over	493,045	602,308	617,796
Never married	26.1	28.3	29.1
Now married, except separated..	61.0	57.0	56.3
Separated...	1.0	1.4	1.1
Widowed...	2.1	2.4	2.4
Divorced...	9.9	10.9	11.0
Females, 15 Years and Over	498,579	608,900	622,771
Never married	19.6	22.4	22.7
Now married, except separated..	59.0	55.3	54.8
Separated...	1.3	1.6	1.6
Widowed...	8.6	7.6	7.9
Divorced...	11.4	13.1	13.2

Table ID-3. Households and Housing Characteristics

(Number, percent, dollars.)

Item	2000	2010	2014	Average annual percent change, 2000–2014
Total Households...	469,645	576,709	591,587	1.9
Family households..	333,588	401,806	407,499	1.6
Married-couple family..	276,511	322,129	324,619	1.2
Other family..	59,077	79,677	82,880	2.9
Male householder, no wife present........................	18,228	23,583	27,575	3.7
Female householder, no husband present...............	40,849	56,094	55,305	2.5
Nonfamily households	134,057	174,903	184,088	2.7
Householder living alone...	105,175	139,909	151,201	3.1
Householder not living alone......................................	28,882	34,994	32,887	1.0
Housing Characteristics				
Total housing units...	527,824	668,634	685,098	2.1
Occupied housing units	469,645	576,709	591,587	1.9
Owner occupied..	339,960	401,532	402,394	1.3
Renter occupied..	129,685	175,177	189,193	3.3
Average household size..	2.69	2.67	2.71	0.1
Financial Characteristics				
Median gross rent of renter-occupied housing	515	683	755	3.3
Median monthly owner costs for housing units with a mortgage	887	1,187	1,138	2.0
Median value of owner-occupied housing units.............	106,300	165,100	165,300	4.0

- = Zero or rounds to zero.

Table ID-4. Migration, Origin, and Language

(Number, percent.)

Characteristic	State			U.S.		
	2013	2014	Percent change	2013	2014	Percent change
Residence 1 Year Ago						
Population 1 year and over	1,592,596	1613068	1.3	312,432,820	315,095,393	0.9
Same house	82.7	82.8	X	85.0	85.1	X
Different house in the U.S.	16.8	16.8	X	14.4	14.3	X
Same county	9.4	9.2	X	8.9	8.7	X
Different county	7.4	7.6	X	5.5	5.6	X
Same state	3.5	3.6	X	3.2	3.3	X
Different state	3.9	4.0	X	2.3	2.3	X
Abroad	0.5	0.4	X	0.6	0.6	X
Place of Birth						
Native born	1,516,611	1,537,111	1.4	274,780,773	276,465,262	0.6
Male	50.3	50.0	X	49.3	49.3	X
Female	49.7	50.0	X	50.7	50.7	X
Foreign born	95,525	97,353	1.9	41,348,066	42,391,794	2.5
Male	51.1	50.3	X	48.8	48.7	X
Female	48.9	49.7	X	51.2	51.3	X
Foreign born; naturalized U.S. citizen.................	35,903	35,239	-1.8	19,294,710	19,984,738	3.6
Male	44.5	46	X	45.9	45.9	X
Female	55.5	54	X	54.1	54.1	X
Foreign born; not a U.S. citizen........................	59,622	62,114	4.2	22,053,356	22,407,056	1.6
Male	55.0	52.7	X	51.3	51.2	X
Female	45.0	47.3	X	48.7	48.8	X
Entered 2010 or later	14.6	11.3	X	9.7	12.3	X
Entered 2000 to 2009	28.6	29.6	X	29.4	28.6	X
Entered before 2000.......................................	56.8	59.0	X	61.0	59.1	X
World Region of Birth, Foreign						
Foreign-born population, excluding population born at sea	95,525	97,353	1.9	41,347,945	42,390,705	2.5
Europe	13.7	9.8	X	11.6	11.2	X
Asia	20.2	20.3	X	29.5	30.1	X
Africa	3.0	2.6	X	4.4	4.6	X
Oceania	1.2	0.6	X	0.5	0.6	X
Latin America...	57.2	60.8	X	51.9	51.6	X
North America..	4.7	6.0	X	2.0	1.9	X
Language Spoken at Home and Ability to Speak English						
Population 5 years and over...............................	1,500,897	1,522,757	1.5	296,358,760	299,084,046	0.9
English only	89.1	89.7	X	79.2	78.9	X
Language other than English.............................	10.9	10.3	X	20.8	21.1	X
Speaks English less than "very well"..................	4.1	4.1	X	8.5	8.6	X

X = Not applicable.
- = Zero or rounds to zero.

Table ID-5. Median Income and Poverty Status, 2014

(Number, percent, except as noted.)

Characteristic	State		U.S.	
	Number	Percent	Number	Percent
Median Income				
Households (dollars)...	47,861	X	53,657	X
Families (dollars)	58,101	X	65,910	X
Below Poverty Level (All People)	237,981	14.8	48,208,387	15.5
Sex				
Male..	107,009	13.4	21,590,918	14.2
Female	130,972	16.2	26,617,469	16.8
Age				
Under 18 years..	80,025	18.8	15,686,012	21.7
Related children under 18 years............................	78,394	18.5	15,372,705	21.3
18 to 64 years...	136,054	14.4	28,267,482	14.6
65 years and over	21,902	9.5	4,254,893	9.5

X = Not applicable.

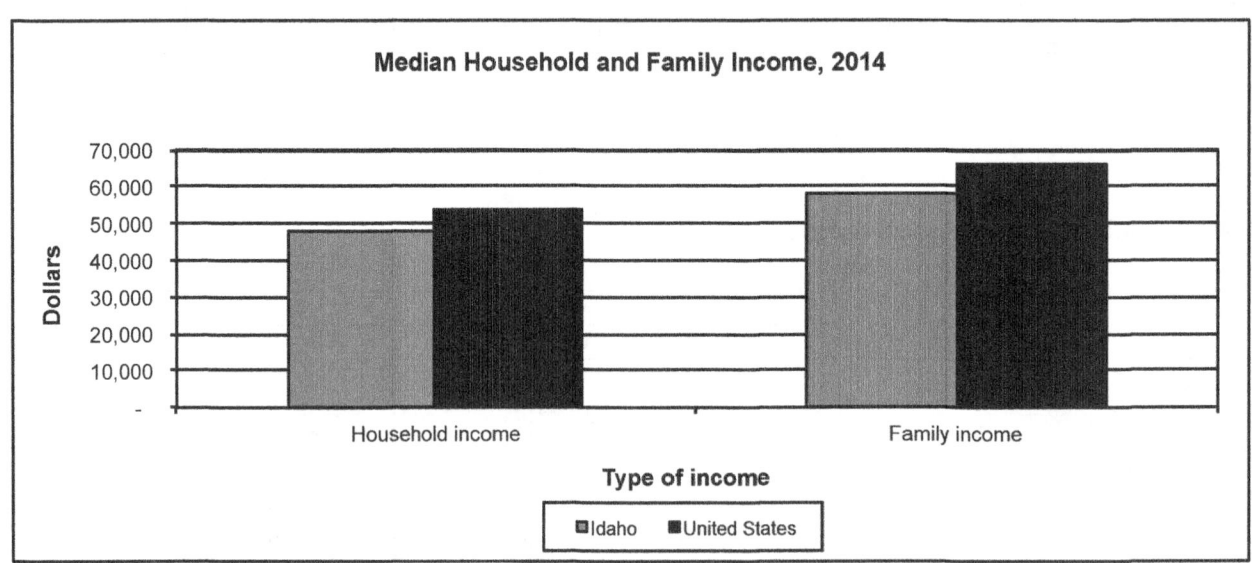

Table ID-6. Health Insurance Coverage Status for the Civilian Noninstitutionalized Population and Children Under 18 Years of Age

(Numbers in thousands, percent.)

Item	2006	2007	2008	2009	2010	2011	2012	2013	2014
Civilian Noninstitutionalized Population	1,475	1,501	1,499	1,521	1,552	1,566	1,576	1,592	1,613
Covered by Private or Public Insurance									
Number..	1,248	1,292	1,232	1,256	1,276	1,307	1,321	1,335	1,394
Percent...	84.6	86.1	82.2	82.6	82.3	83.5	83.8	83.8	86.4
Not Covered									
Number..	227	209	267	264	275	259	255	257	219
Percent...	15.4	13.9	17.8	17.4	17.7	16.5	16.2	16.2	13.6
Percent in the U.S. not covered................................	15.8	15.3	15.1	15.1	15.5	15.1	14.8	14.5	11.7
Children Under 18 Years of Age	420	415	413	418	428	427	424	426	431
Covered by Private or Public Insurance									
Number..	350	369	357	371	383	388	388	388	397
Percent...	87.0	89.0	86.4	88.8	89.5	90.9	91.5	91.1	92.2
Not Covered									
Number..	52	46	56	47	45	39	36	38	34
Percent...	13.0	11.0	13.6	11.2	10.5	9.1	8.5	8.9	7.8
Percent in the U.S. not covered................................	11.7	11.0	9.7	8.6	8.0	7.5	7.2	7.1	6.0

Table ID-7. Employment Status by Demographic Group, 2015

(Numbers in thousands, percent.)

Characteristic	Civilian noninstitutional population	Civilian labor force		Employed		Unemployed	
		Number	Percent of population	Number	Percent of population	Number	Percent of population
Total..	1,246	801	64.3	767	61.6	34	4.3
Sex							
Male..	615	437	71.2	417	67.8	21	4.7
Female.....................................	631	364	57.6	350	55.5	14	3.7
Race, Sex, and Hispanic Origin							
White.......................................	1,183	760	64.2	728	61.6	32	4.2
Male....................................	579	413	71.4	394	68.1	19	4.6
Female.................................	604	347	57.4	334	55.3	13	3.7
Black or African American...............	NA	NA	NA	NA	NA	NA	NA
Male....................................	NA	NA	NA	NA	NA	NA	NA
Female.................................	NA	NA	NA	NA	NA	NA	NA
Hispanic or Latino ethnicity[1]..........	140	102	73.2	96	68.8	6	5.9
Male....................................	75	63	83.9	60	79.7	3	5.0
Female.................................	65	39	60.7	36	56.3	3	7.2
Age							
16 to 19 years............................	90	41	45.2	36	39.7	5	12.2
20 to 24 years............................	112	82	73.0	77	68.6	5	6.1
25 to 34 years............................	208	170	81.7	162	78.2	7	4.3
35 to 44 years............................	200	168	83.8	162	80.8	6	3.6
45 to 54 years............................	213	173	81.1	167	78.5	5	3.1
55 to 64 years............................	201	130	64.7	126	62.7	4	3.1
65 years and over........................	222	39	17.3	37	16.8	1	3.4

NOTE: Data in Table 7 are from the Current Population Survey (CPS) and do not match the estimates in Table 8. See notes and definitions for further information.
[1]May be of any race.
NA = Not available.

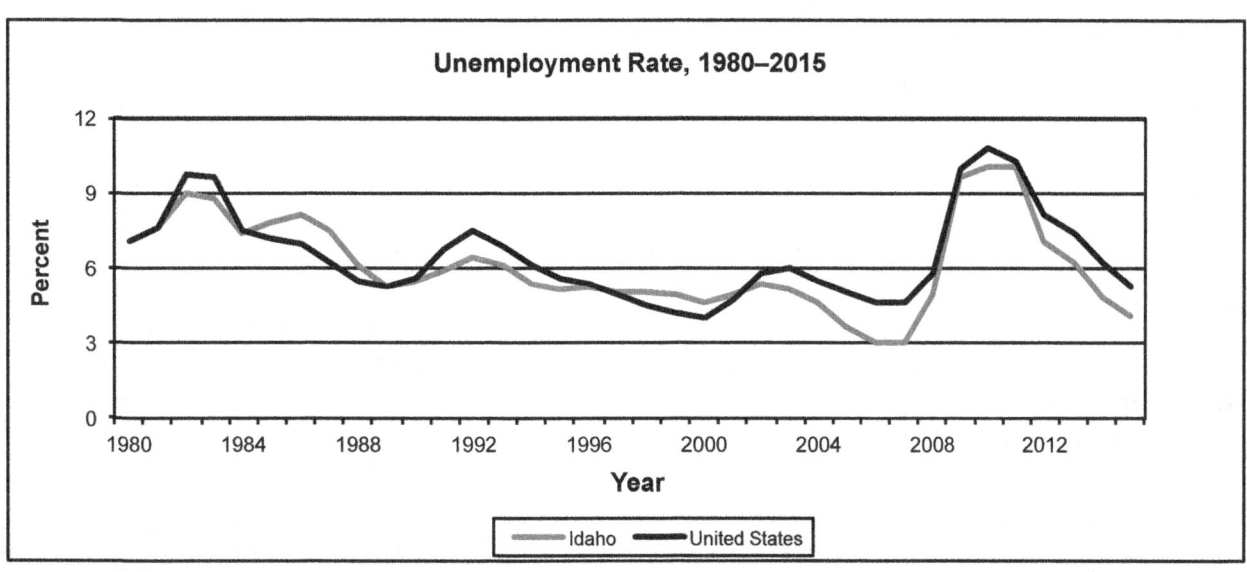

Unemployment Rate, 1980–2015

Table ID-8. Employment Status of the Civilian Noninstitutional Population Age 16 Years and Over

(Number, percent.)

Year	Civilian labor force	Civilian participation rate	Employed	Unemployed	Unemployment rate
2007....................................	754,438	67.8	731,235	23,203	3.1
2008....................................	755,153	66.6	716,653	38,500	5.1
2009....................................	757,131	65.8	690,722	66,409	8.8
2010....................................	761,056	65.3	692,826	68,230	9.0
2011....................................	765,178	64.9	701,466	63,712	8.3
2012....................................	769,617	64.5	713,981	55,636	7.2
2013....................................	772,513	63.9	724,955	47,558	6.2
2014....................................	781,390	63.6	743,574	37,816	4.8
2015....................................	797,475	63.9	764,463	33,012	4.1

Table ID-9. Employment and Average Wages by Industry

(Estimates through 2010 are based on the 2007 North American Industry Classification System [NAICS]. Estimates from 2011 onward are based on the 2012 NAICS.)

Industry	2008	2009	2010	2011	2012	2013	2014
	Number of Jobs						
Wage and Salary Employment by Industry..................	694,229	653,408	646,725	649,999	654,214	670,896	686,595
Farm Wage and Salary Employment.........................	15,287	14,323	14,700	16,442	17,023	17,526	17,602
Nonfarm Wage and Salary Employment....................	678,942	639,085	632,025	633,557	637,191	653,370	668,993
Private wage and salary employment.............................	550,215	510,255	503,538	507,403	510,169	526,463	541,678
Forestry, fishing, and related activities.....................	7,502	7,128	7,316	7,485	7,094	7,975	8,446
Mining..	2,780	2,167	2,273	2,568	2,674	2,547	2,419
Utilities..	2,161	2,098	2,729	2,798	2,826	2,805	2,914
Construction...	47,063	36,067	32,693	31,140	30,563	32,942	35,024
Manufacturing...	63,059	55,052	53,383	54,598	56,599	59,248	59,948
Durable goods manufacturing............................	38,378	31,182	29,954	31,309	32,653	34,072	34,489
Nondurable goods manufacturing.......................	24,681	23,870	23,429	23,289	23,946	25,176	25,459
Wholesale trade..	27,922	26,315	25,950	26,413	27,007	28,285	28,804
Retail trade..	83,774	77,551	76,232	76,151	77,178	78,698	80,489
Transportation and warehousing...........................	19,358	18,402	18,377	18,504	18,693	18,673	19,520
Information...	11,075	10,077	9,702	9,424	9,312	9,256	9,229
Finance and insurance	21,997	21,063	20,980	21,343	21,359	21,768	22,244
Real estate and rental and leasing.........................	8,615	7,515	7,168	6,924	6,726	6,889	7,003
Professional, scientific, and technical services	34,494	33,003	32,795	32,794	31,686	31,339	32,806
Management of companies and enterprises.................	7,250	6,719	5,863	5,874	5,916	5,435	5,479
Administrative and waste services...........................	40,620	36,959	36,571	37,024	37,393	39,922	40,422
Educational services	9,890	10,043	10,295	10,585	11,009	11,176	11,370
Health care and social assistance.........................	70,562	73,380	76,111	77,474	77,998	80,852	83,775
Arts, entertainment, and recreation.........................	9,038	8,704	8,621	8,663	9,077	9,394	9,840
Accommodation and food services..........................	54,748	50,606	50,047	51,144	52,081	53,763	56,224
Other services, except public administration..............	28,307	27,406	26,432	26,497	24,978	25,496	25,722
Government and government enterprises........................	128,727	128,830	128,487	126,154	127,022	126,907	127,315
	Dollars						
Average Wages and Salaries by Industry	34,651	35,066	35,781	36,452	36,911	37,800	38,893
Average Farm Wages and Salaries	35,696	42,301	35,808	33,216	27,421	39,897	40,141
Average Nonfarm Wages and Salaries	34,628	34,904	35,781	36,536	37,165	37,744	38,861
Average private wages and salaries..........................	34,467	34,647	35,729	36,595	37,241	37,963	39,141
Forestry, fishing, and related activities......................	27,349	26,300	27,268	28,854	28,618	29,434	30,483
Mining..	59,909	57,883	67,925	69,470	71,675	76,081	76,561
Utilities..	62,911	65,184	73,834	75,159	77,161	79,131	80,860
Construction...	38,167	37,942	39,040	39,436	40,207	39,915	39,963
Manufacturing...	48,028	48,132	50,941	51,881	52,287	54,819	59,922
Durable goods manufacturing............................	54,184	54,423	58,795	58,355	58,267	62,185	69,744
Nondurable goods manufacturing.......................	38,455	39,913	40,900	43,177	44,134	44,849	46,615
Wholesale trade	45,887	45,910	47,440	48,927	49,857	51,222	53,184
Retail trade..	25,270	25,330	25,847	26,308	27,024	27,684	28,712
Transportation and warehousing...........................	37,119	37,036	37,745	39,150	40,133	41,463	41,822
Information...	41,268	41,888	42,599	44,478	47,257	46,788	48,052
Finance and insurance	47,440	47,444	48,734	49,575	52,832	54,124	55,645
Real estate and rental and leasing.........................	28,616	28,478	28,465	28,854	30,455	32,061	33,900
Professional, scientific, and technical services	52,533	54,833	56,536	58,158	57,439	59,088	59,229
Management of companies and enterprises.................	77,648	78,219	81,421	87,177	90,193	87,420	79,101
Administrative and waste services...........................	25,777	26,126	26,740	27,217	27,362	27,112	27,813
Educational services	24,594	25,495	26,243	26,993	27,204	27,177	27,393
Health care and social assistance.........................	35,224	35,982	36,401	37,454	37,600	38,706	39,590
Arts, entertainment, and recreation.........................	19,585	18,399	19,522	18,973	18,802	19,335	19,889
Accommodation and food services..........................	14,306	14,482	15,110	15,442	15,835	15,730	16,412
Other services, except public administration..............	23,208	23,040	23,855	24,065	25,553	26,252	27,459
Government and government enterprises........................	35,315	35,921	35,983	36,296	36,859	36,835	37,669

Table ID-10. Employment Characteristics by Family Type

(Number, percent.)

Family type and labor force status	2012 Total	2012 Families with own children under 18 years	2013 Total	2013 Families with own children under 18 years	2014 Total	2014 Families with own children under 18 years
All Families	405,908	184,148	410,061	190,524	406,767	180,018
FAMILY TYPE AND LABOR FORCE STATUS						
Married-Couple Families	322,225	133,177	324,922	137,775	323,887	131,393
Both husband and wife in labor force	49.7	62.6	48.9	60.1	48.7	61.0
Husband in labor force, wife not in labor force	24.1	31.9	25.1	34.6	23.9	33.6
Wife in labor force, husband not in labor force	7.6	3.8	7.5	3.2	6.8	3.0
Both husband and wife not in labor force	18.6	1.7	18.3	2.0	20.6	2.5
Other Families	83,683	50,971	85,139	52,749	82,880	48,625
Female householder, no husband present	70.9	70.8	67.6	67.1	66.7	67.9
In labor force	50.8	57.7	46.1	53.4	47.8	53.1
Not in labor force	20.1	13.1	21.4	13.7	18.9	14.8
Male householder, no wife present	29.1	29.2	32.4	32.9	33.3	32.1
In labor force	23.6	26.7	26.1	29.5	26.3	29.2
Not in labor force	5.5	2.4	6.4	3.3	7.0	2.9

Table ID-11. School Enrollment and Educational Attainment, 2014

(Number, percent.)

Item	State	U.S.
Enrollment		
Total population 3 years and over, enrolled in school	445,627	82,063,714
Enrolled in nursery school or preschool (percent)	4.6	6.0
Enrolled in kindergarten (percent)	5.7	5.1
Enrolled in elementary school, grades 1-8 (percent)	43.3	40.2
Enrolled in high school, grades 9-12 (percent)	22.1	20.7
Enrolled in college or graduate school (percent)	24.3	28.0
Attainment		
Total population 25 years and over	1,045,193	213,725,624
Less than ninth grade (percent)	3.9	5.6
9th to 12th grade, no diploma (percent)	6.0	7.5
High school graduate, including equivalency (percent)	28.2	27.7
Some college, no degree (percent)	27.6	21.0
Associate's degree (percent)	9.3	8.2
Bachelor's degree (percent)	16.8	18.7
Graduate or professional degree (percent)	8.3	11.4
High school graduate or higher (percent)	90.1	86.9
Bachelor's degree or higher (percent)	25.0	30.1

Table ID-12. Public School Characteristics and Educational Indicators

(Number, percent; data derived from National Center of Education Statistics.)

Item	State	U.S.
Public Schools, 2013–2014 (except where noted)		
Number of school districts	152	18,194
Number of schools	706	98,271
Number of students (in thousands)	296	50,045
Number of teachers (in thousands)	15	3,114
Student-teacher ratio	19.8	16.1
Expenditures per student (dollars), FY 2013	67,617	107,637
Four-year adjusted cohort graduation rate (ACGR)[1,2]	77.3	82.3
Students eligible for free or reduced-price lunch (in thousands)	139	25,596
English language learners (in thousands)	13	4,461
Students age 3 to 21 served under IDEA, part B (in thousands)	28	6,464

Public Schools by Type	Number	Percent of state public schools
Total number of schools	706	100.0
Regular	633	89.7
Special education	13	1.8
Vocational education	9	1.3
Alternative education	51	7.2

NOTE: Every school is assigned only one school type based on its instructional emphasis.
[1]ACGR data represents a new method of calculating high-school completion rates and may not be comparable to previous years' data for Averaged Freshmen Graduation Rates (AFGR).
[2]The United States 4-year ACGRs were estimated using both the reported 4-year ACGR data from 49 states and the District of Columbia and using imputed data for Idaho. The estimate for American Indian/Alaska Native students also includes imputed data for Virginia.

Table ID-13. Reported Voting and Registration of the Voting-Age Population, November 2014

(Numbers in thousands, percent.)

Item	Total population	Total citizen population	Registered			Voted		
			Total registered	Percent registered (total population)	Percent registered (total citizen population)	Total voted	Percent voted (total population)	Percent voted (total citizen population)
U.S. Total	239,874	219,941	142,166	59.3	64.6	92,251	38.5	41.9
State Total.............................	1,182	1,105	671	56.8	60.7	462	39.1	41.8
Sex								
Male.................................	585	535	312	53.3	58.2	213	36.5	39.9
Female	597	569	359	60.1	63.1	248	41.6	43.6
Race								
White alone........................	1,110	1,044	648	58.4	62.1	452	40.7	43.3
White, non-Hispanic alone	963	951	625	64.9	65.8	435	45.2	45.8
Black alone........................	10	10	1	(B)	(B)	-	(B)	(B)
Asian alone	20	12	4	(B)	(B)	2	(B)	(B)
Hispanic (of any race)	153	96	23	15.1	24.0	17	11.1	17.6
White alone or in combination	1,127	1,060	658	58.4	62.1	458	40.7	43.2
Black alone or in combination	15	15	3	(B)	(B)	-	(B)	(B)
Asian alone or in combination..........	22	14	7	(B)	(B)	2	(B)	(B)
Age								
18 to 24 years.....................	181	171	53	29.4	31.1	21	11.8	12.5
25 to 34 years.....................	181	167	94	52.0	56.2	52	28.9	31.2
35 to 44 years.....................	194	169	96	49.5	56.9	51	26.0	30.0
45 to 64 years.....................	419	395	271	64.6	68.4	207	49.3	52.2
65 years and over	206	202	157	75.9	77.6	131	63.5	64.9

- = Zero or rounds to zero.
B = Base is less than 75,000 and therefore too small to show the derived measure.

Table ID-14. Crime

(Number, rate per 100,000. Data are derived from the FBI Uniform Crime Reports.)

Item	State			U.S.[1,2,3,4]		
	2013	2014	Percent change	2013	2014	Percent change
TOTAL POPULATION[5]..	1,612,136	1,634,464	1.4	316,128,839	318,857,056	0.9
VIOLENT CRIME						
Number........................	3,300	3,468	5.1	1,163,146	1,165,383	0.2
Rate..........................	204.7	212.2	3.7	367.9	365.5	-0.7
Murder and Nonnegligent Manslaughter						
Number........................	27	32	18.5	14,196	14,249	0.4
Rate..........................	1.7	2.0	17.6	4.5	4.5	-
Rape[6]						
Number........................	655	609	X	108,612	116,645	X
Rate..........................	40.6	37.3	X	34.4	36.6	X
Robbery						
Number........................	220	204	-7.3	345,031	325,802	-5.6
Rate..........................	13.6	12.5	-8.1	109.1	102.2	-6.3
Aggravated Assault						
Number........................	2,596	2,623	1.0	724,149	741,291	2.4
Rate..........................	161.0	160.5	-0.3	229.1	232.5	1.5
PROPERTY CRIME						
Number........................	30,055	30,316	0.9	8,632,512	8,277,829	-4.1
Rate	1,864.3	1,854.8	-0.5	2,730.7	2,596.1	-4.9
Burglary						
Number........................	6,640	6,428	-3.2	1,928,465	1,729,806	-10.3
Rate..........................	411.9	393.3	-4.5	610.0	542.5	-11.1
Larceny-Theft						
Number........................	21,879	22,227	1.6	6,004,453	5,858,496	-2.4
Rate..........................	1,357.1	1,359.9	0.2	1,899.4	1,837.3	-3.3
Motor Vehicle Theft						
Number........................	1,536	1,661	8.1	699,594	689,527	-1.4
Rate..........................	95.3	101.6	6.6	221.3	216.2	-2.3

NOTE: Although arson data are included in the trend and clearance tables, sufficient data are not available to estimate totals for this offense. Therefore, no arson data are published in this table.
X = Not applicable.
- = Zero or rounds to zero.
[1]The crime figures have been adjusted.
[2]The data collection methodology for the offense of forcible rape used by the Minnesota state Uniform Crime Reporting (UCR) Program (with the exception of Minneapolis and St. Paul, Minnesota) does not comply with national UCR Program guidelines. Consequently, its figures for forcible rape and violent crime (of which forcible rape is a part) are not published in this table.
[3]Includes offenses reported by the Zoological Police and the Metro Transit Police.
[4]Because of changes in the state's reporting practices, figures are not comparable to previous years' data.
[5]Populations are U.S. Census Bureau provisional estimates as of July 1 of each year.
[6]The figures shown for the offense of rape were estimated using the revised Uniform Crime Reporting (UCR) definition of rape.

Table ID-15. State Government Finances, 2014

(Dollar amounts in thousands, percent distribution.)

Item	Dollars	Percent distribution
Total Revenue	10,511,073	100.0
General revenue	7,435,715	70.7
Intergovernmental revenue	2,531,469	24.1
Taxes	3,671,715	34.9
General sales	1,373,666	13.1
Selective sales	447,637	4.3
License taxes	316,331	3.0
Individual income tax	1,338,075	12.7
Corporate income tax	190,002	1.8
Other taxes	6,004	0.1
Current charges	756,657	7.2
Miscellaneous general revenue	475,874	4.5
Utility revenue	0	-
Liquor stores revenue	136,343	1.3
Insurance trust revenue[1]	2,939,015	28.0
Total Expenditure	8,449,255	100.0
Intergovernmental expenditure	2,015,071	23.8
Direct expenditure	6,434,184	76.2
Current operation	4,724,383	55.9
Capital outlay	411,306	4.9
Insurance benefits and repayments	1,013,767	12.0
Assistance and subsidies	132,899	1.6
Interest on debt	151,829	1.8
Exhibit: Salaries and wages	1,099,510	13.0
Total Expenditure	8,449,255	100.0
General expenditure	7,328,860	86.7
Intergovernmental expenditure	2,015,071	23.8
Direct expenditure	5,313,789	62.9
General expenditure, by function:		
Education	2,646,641	31.3
Public welfare	2,225,688	26.3
Hospitals	52,849	0.6
Health	178,972	2.1
Highways	667,410	7.9
Police protection	50,518	0.6
Correction	255,955	3.0
Natural resources	207,169	2.5
Parks and recreation	32,685	0.4
Governmental administration	305,189	3.6
Interest on general debt	151,829	1.8
Other and unallocable	553,955	6.6
Utility expenditure	0	-
Liquor stores expenditure	106,628	1.3
Insurance trust expenditure	1,013,767	12.0
Debt at End of Fiscal Year	3,606,305	X
Cash and Security Holdings	22,070,702	X

X = Not applicable.
- = Zero or rounds to zero.
[1]Within insurance trust revenue, net earnings of state retirement systems is a calculated statistic (the item code in the data file is X08), and thus can be positive or negative. Net earnings is the sum of earnings on investments plus gains on investments minus losses on investments. The change made in 2002 for asset valuation from book to market value in accordance with Statement 34 of the Governmental Accounting Standards Board is reflected in the calculated statistics.

Table ID-16. State Government Tax Collections, 2014

(Dollars in thousands, percent.)

Item	Dollars	Percent distribution
Total Taxes	3,671,715	100.0
Property taxes	X	X
Sales and gross receipts	1,821,303	49.6
General sales and gross receipts	1,373,666	37.4
Selective sales and gross receipts	447,637	12.2
Alcoholic beverages	8,780	0.2
Amusements	0	
Insurance premiums	75,205	2.0
Motor fuels	248,454	6.8
Pari-mutuels	1,209	-
Public utilities	1,840	0.1
Tobacco products	47,816	1.3
Other selective sales	64,333	1.8
Licenses	316,331	8.6
Alcoholic beverages	1,617	-
Amusements	754	-
Corporations in general	2,203	0.1
Hunting and fishing	34,436	0.9
Motor vehicle	135,169	3.7
Motor vehicle operators	9,943	0.3
Public utilities	53,613	1.5
Occupation and business, NEC	74,790	2.0
Other licenses	3,806	0.1
Income taxes	1,528,077	41.6
Individual income	1,338,075	36.4
Corporation net income	190,002	5.2
Other taxes	6,004	0.2
Death and gift	0	-
Documentary and stock transfer	0	-
Severance	6,004	0.2
Taxes, NEC	0	-

X = Not applicable.
- = Zero or rounds to zero.

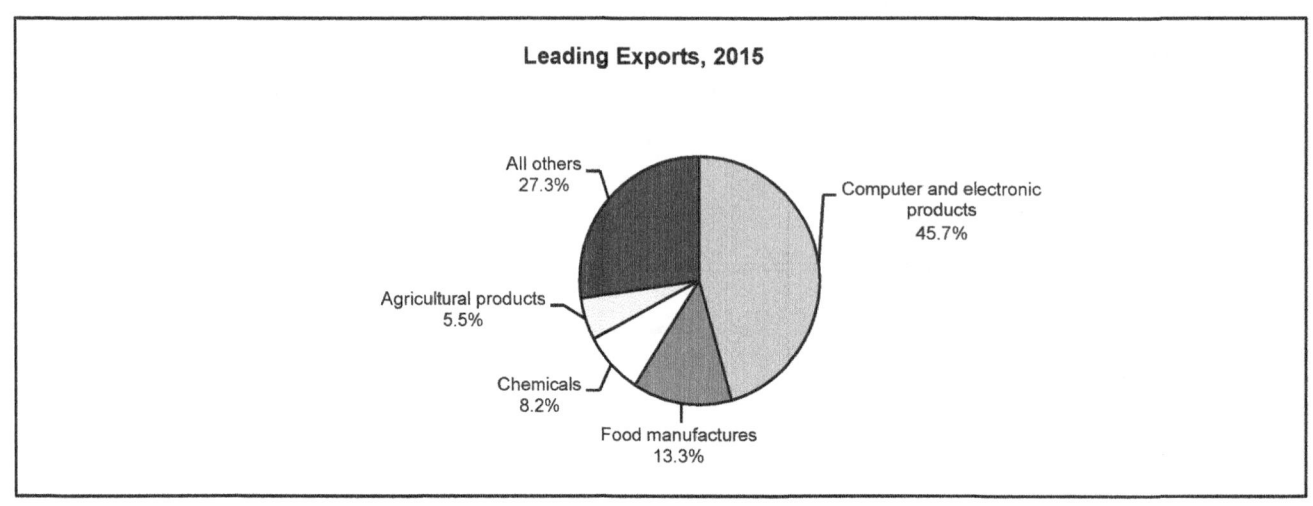

Leading Exports, 2015

All others 27.3%

Computer and electronic products 45.7%

Agricultural products 5.5%

Chemicals 8.2%

Food manufactures 13.3%

Facts and Figures

Location: North central United States; bordered on the N by Wisconsin, on the E by Lake Michigan and Indiana, on the S by Kentucky, and on the W by Iowa and Missouri

Area: 57,913 sq. mi. (149,998 sq. km.); rank—25th

Population: 12,859,995 (2015 est.); rank—5th

Principal Cities: capital—Springfield; largest—Chicago

Statehood: December 3, 1818; 21st state

U.S. Congress: 2 senators, 18 representatives

State Motto: State Sovereignty, National Union

State Song: "Illinois"

State Nicknames: The Prairie State; The Land of Lincoln

Abbreviations: IL; Ill.

State Symbols: flower—native violet; tree—white oak; bird—cardinal

At a Glance

- With an increase in population of 0.1 percent, Illinois ranked 48th among the states in growth from 2010 to 2015.

- Illinois's birth rate in 2014 was 12.3 per 1,000 population, slightly below the U.S. rate of 12.5 per 1,000 population.

- The violent crime rate in Illinois in 2014 was 370.0 per 100,000 population, compared to the U.S. rate of 365.5 per 100,000 population.

- Illinois ranked 18th for median household income in 2014, with an income of $57,444.

- In 2014, 9.7 percent of Illinois residents did not have health insurance, compared to 11.7 percent of the entire U.S. population.

Table IL-1. Population by Age, Sex, Race, and Hispanic Origin

(Number, percent, except where noted.)

Sex, age, race, and Hispanic origin	2000	2010	2015[1]	Average annual percent change, 2010–2015
Total Population...	12,419,293	12,830,632	12,859,995	-
Percent of total U.S. population	4.4	4.2	4.0	X
Sex				
Male..	6,080,336	6,292,276	6,314,495	-
Female	6,338,957	6,538,356	6,545,500	-
Age				
Under 5 years...	876,549	835,557	783,662	-0.5
5 to 19 years..	2,728,957	2,660,945	2,511,065	-0.4
20 to 64 years...	7,313,762	7,724,917	7,734,991	-
65 years and over...	1,500,025	1,609,213	1,830,277	0.9
Median age (years)	34.7	36.6	37.7	0.2
Race and Hispanic Origin				
One race				
White..	9,125,471	10,030,587	9,939,733	-0.1
Black..	1,878,875	1,903,458	1,888,404	-0.1
American Indian and Alaska Native	31,006	73,486	75,460	0.2
Asian..	423,603	604,399	707,192	1.1
Native Hawaiian or Other Pacific Islander	4,610	7,436	8,317	0.8
Two or more races...	235,016	210,906	240,889	1.0
Hispanic (of any race)..	1,530,262	2,073,054	2,175,116	0.3

X = Not applicable.
[1]Population figures for 2015 are July 1 estimates. The 2010 estimates are taken from the 2010 Census.
- = Zero or rounds to zero.

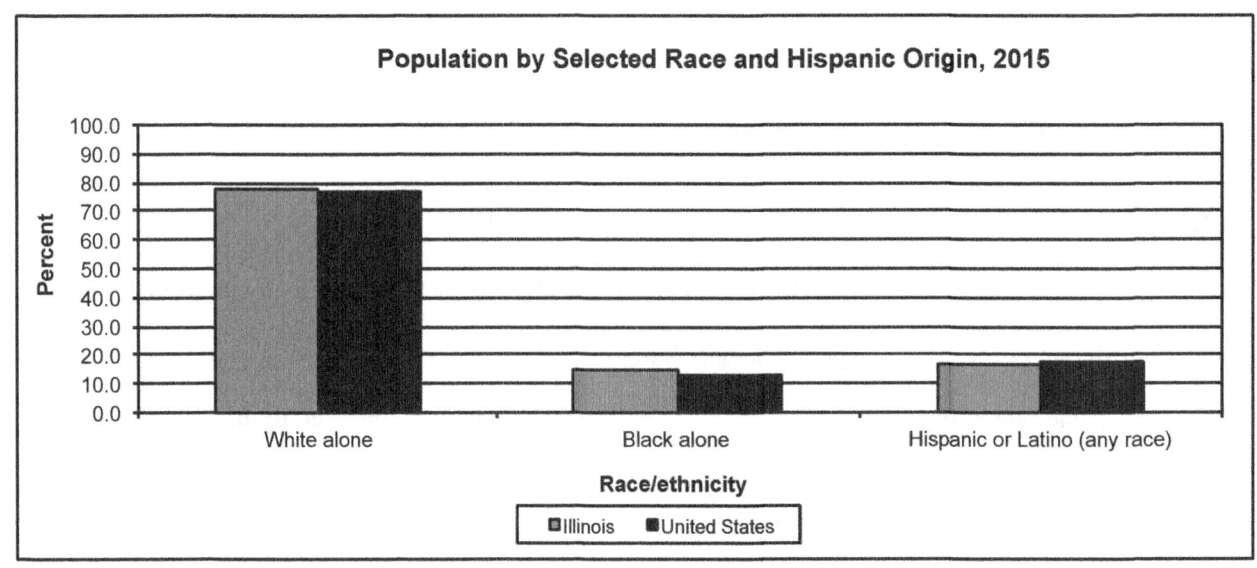

Table IL-2. Marital Status

(Number, percent distribution.)

Sex, age, race, and Hispanic origin	2000	2010	2014
Males, 15 Years and Over	4,685,982	4,977,964	5,027,649
Never married	31.9	37.2	37.5
Now married, except separated.................................	56.1	50.0	49.9
Separated..	1.6	1.4	1.5
Widowed..	2.5	2.6	2.5
Divorced...	7.9	8.8	8.6
Females, 15 Years and Over	5,021,855	5,289,803	5,319,835
Never married	26.1	31.1	31.5
Now married, except separated.................................	51.3	46.3	46.2
Separated..	2.0	2.1	2.0
Widowed..	10.7	9.5	9.3
Divorced...	9.9	11.0	11.0

Table IL-3. Households and Housing Characteristics

(Number, percent, dollars.)

Item	2000	2010	2014	Average annual percent change, 2000–2014
Total Households..	4,591,779	4,752,857	4,772,421	0.3
Family households	3,105,513	3,133,813	3,099,184	-
Married-couple family	2,353,892	2,301,009	2,269,298	-0.3
Other family	751,621	832,804	829,886	0.7
Male householder, no wife present................................	187,903	220,197	227,528	1.5
Female householder, no husband present......................	563,718	612,607	602,358	0.5
Nonfamily households	1,486,266	1,619,044	1,673,237	0.9
Householder living alone	1,229,807	1,340,394	1,379,600	0.9
Householder not living alone	256,459	278,650	293,637	1.0
Housing Characteristics				
Total housing units..	4,885,615	5,297,077	5,307,508	0.6
Occupied housing units	4,591,779	4,752,857	4,772,421	0.3
Owner occupied	3,088,884	3,219,338	3,125,655	0.1
Renter occupied	1,502,895	1,533,519	1,646,766	0.7
Average household size...	2.63	2.64	2.64	-
Financial Characteristics				
Median gross rent of renter-occupied housing	605	848	905	3.5
Median monthly owner costs for housing units with a mortgage	1,198	1,655	1,584	2.3
Median value of owner-occupied housing units.....................	130,800	191,800	171,900	2.2

- = Zero or rounds to zero.

Table IL-4. Migration, Origin, and Language

(Number, percent.)

	State			U.S.		
Characteristic	2013	2014	Percent change	2013	2014	Percent change
Residence 1 Year Ago						
Population 1 year and over	12,740,816	12,730,206	-0.1	312,432,820	315,095,393	0.9
Same house	86.6	86.6	X	85.0	85.1	X
Different house in the U.S.	12.8	12.9	X	14.4	14.3	X
Same county	8.6	8.6	X	8.9	8.7	X
Different county	4.2	4.3	X	5.5	5.6	X
Same state	2.5	2.7	X	3.2	3.3	X
Different state	1.8	1.6	X	2.3	2.3	X
Abroad	0.5	0.5	X	0.6	0.6	X
Place of Birth						
Native born	11,074,667	11,096,177	0.2	274,780,773	276,465,262	0.6
Male..	48.9	48.9	X	49.3	49.3	X
Female...	51.1	51.1	X	50.7	50.7	X
Foreign born	1,807,468	1,784,403	-1.3	41,348,066	42,391,794	2.5
Male..	50.2	50.1	X	48.8	48.7	X
Female...	49.8	49.9	X	51.2	51.3	X
Foreign born; naturalized U.S. citizen.............................	852,962	882,032	3.4	19,294,710	19,984,738	3.6
Male...	47.6	47.4	X	45.9	45.9	X
Female..	52.4	52.6	X	54.1	54.1	X
Foreign born; not a U.S. citizen	954,506	902,371	-5.5	22,053,356	22,407,056	1.6
Male...	52.4	52.7	X	51.3	51.2	X
Female..	47.6	47.3	X	48.7	48.8	X
Entered 2010 or later	8.2	10.0	X	9.7	12.3	X
Entered 2000 to 2009	28.4	26.2	X	29.4	28.6	X
Entered before 2000..	63.4	63.8	X	61.0	59.1	X
World Region of Birth, Foreign						
Foreign-born population, excluding population born at sea	1,807,468	1,784,403	-1.3	41,347,945	42,390,705	2.5
Europe	21.4	20.7	X	11.6	11.2	X
Asia	28.3	29.7	X	29.5	30.1	X
Africa	3.6	3.1	X	4.4	4.6	X
Oceania	0.2	0.2	X	0.5	0.6	X
Latin America...	45.3	45.3	X	51.9	51.6	X
North America...	1.2	1.0	X	2.0	1.9	X
Language Spoken at Home and Ability to Speak English						
Population 5 years and over..	12,085,046	12,091,454	0.1	296,358,760	299,084,046	0.9
English only	77.3	77.4	X	79.2	78.9	X
Language other than English..	22.7	22.6	X	20.8	21.1	X
Speaks English less than "very well"................................	9.2	8.9	X	8.5	8.6	X

X = Not applicable.
- = Zero or rounds to zero.

Table IL-5. Median Income and Poverty Status, 2014

(Number, percent, except as noted.)

Characteristic	State		U.S.	
	Number	Percent	Number	Percent
Median Income				
Households (dollars)..	57,444	X	53,657	X
Families (dollars)	71,796	X	65,910	X
Below Poverty Level (All People)	1,804,535	14.4	48,208,387	15.5
Sex				
Male..	792,846	12.9	21,590,918	14.2
Female	1,011,689	15.7	26,617,469	16.8
Age				
Under 18 years...	593,186	20.2	15,686,012	21.7
Related children under 18 years...........................	582,212	19.9	15,372,705	21.3
18 to 64 years..	1,059,126	13.4	28,267,482	14.6
65 years and over	152,223	8.8	4,254,893	9.5

X = Not applicable.

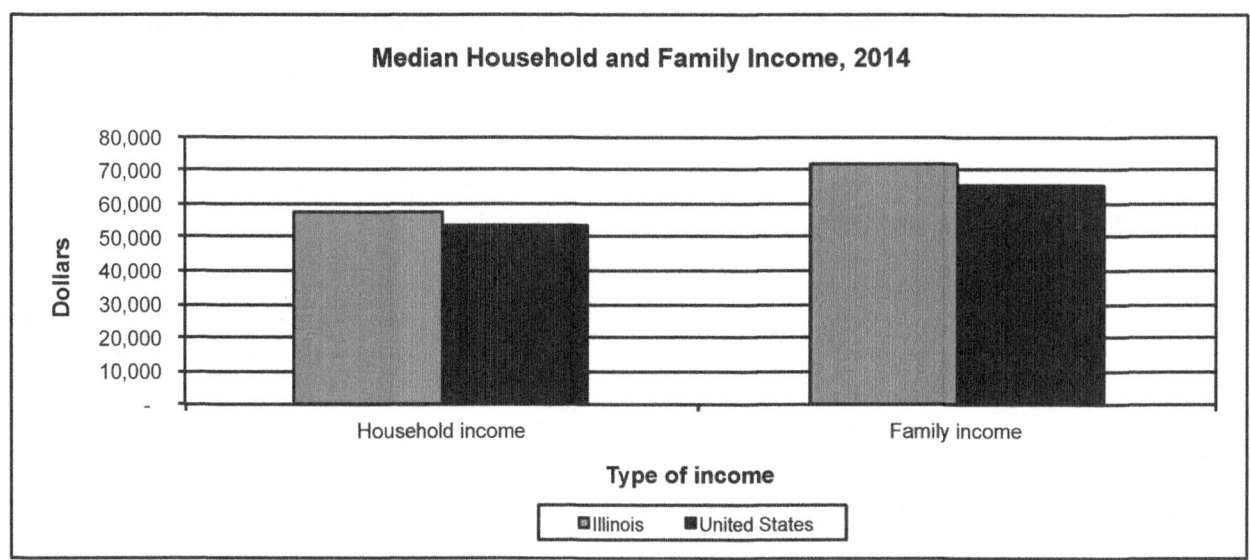

Table IL-6. Health Insurance Coverage Status for the Civilian Noninstitutionalized Population and Children Under 18 Years of Age

(Numbers in thousands, percent.)

Item	2006	2007	2008	2009	2010	2011	2012	2013	2014
Civilian Noninstitutionalized Population	12,644	12,688	12,709	12,720	12,673	12,689	12,698	12,705	12,702
Covered by Private or Public Insurance									
Number...	10,867	10,988	11,086	11,025	10,928	11,029	11,076	11,086	11,464
Percent...	86.0	86.6	87.2	86.7	86.2	86.9	87.2	87.3	90.3
Not Covered									
Number...	1,776	1,700	1,623	1,694	1,746	1,659	1,622	1,618	1,238
Percent...	14.0	13.4	12.8	13.3	13.8	13.1	12.8	12.7	9.7
Percent in the U.S. not covered................................	15.8	15.3	15.1	15.1	15.5	15.1	14.8	14.5	11.7
Children Under 18 Years of Age	3,188	3,180	3,176	3,168	3,122	3,092	3,059	3,018	2,981
Covered by Private or Public Insurance									
Number...	2,886	2,970	2,997	3,026	2,982	2,979	2,958	2,893	2,881
Percent...	90.5	93.4	94.4	95.5	95.5	96.3	96.7	95.8	96.7
Not Covered									
Number...	302	210	179	142	140	113	101	125	100
Percent...	9.5	6.6	5.6	4.5	4.5	3.7	3.3	4.2	3.3
Percent in the U.S. not covered................................	11.7	11.0	9.7	8.6	8.0	7.5	7.2	7.1	6.0

Table IL-7. Employment Status by Demographic Group, 2015

(Numbers in thousands, percent.)

Characteristic	Civilian noninstitutional population	Civilian labor force		Employed		Unemployed	
		Number	Percent of population	Number	Percent of population	Number	Percent of population
Total..	10,082	6,519	64.7	6,133	60.8	386	5.9
Sex							
Male...	4,868	3,454	70.9	3,228	66.3	225	6.5
Female..	5,214	3,066	58.8	2,905	55.7	161	5.2
Race, Sex, and Hispanic Origin							
White	7,940	5,195	65.4	4,936	62.2	258	5.0
Male...	3,881	2,792	71.9	2,642	68.1	150	5.4
Female..	4,059	2,403	59.2	2,294	56.5	108	4.5
Black or African American.................................	1,408	847	60.2	744	52.8	103	12.2
Male...	626	388	62.0	329	52.6	58	15.1
Female..	782	459	58.7	415	53.0	45	9.7
Hispanic or Latino ethnicity[1]	1,424	983	69.0	912	64.1	71	7.2
Male...	727	585	80.4	544	74.8	41	6.9
Female..	697	398	57.2	368	52.9	30	7.5
Age							
16 to 19 years..	685	262	38.2	213	31.1	49	18.7
20 to 24 years..	897	640	71.3	570	63.6	70	10.9
25 to 34 years..	1,816	1,516	83.4	1,434	78.9	82	5.4
35 to 44 years..	1,535	1,255	81.8	1,197	78.0	58	4.6
45 to 54 years..	1,696	1,393	82.1	1,332	78.5	62	4.4
55 to 64 years..	1,632	1,092	66.9	1,041	63.8	51	4.6
65 years and over	1,823	362	19.9	346	19.0	16	4.4

NOTE: Data in Table 7 are from the Current Population Survey (CPS) and do not match the estimates in Table 8. See notes and definitions for further information.
[1]May be of any race.

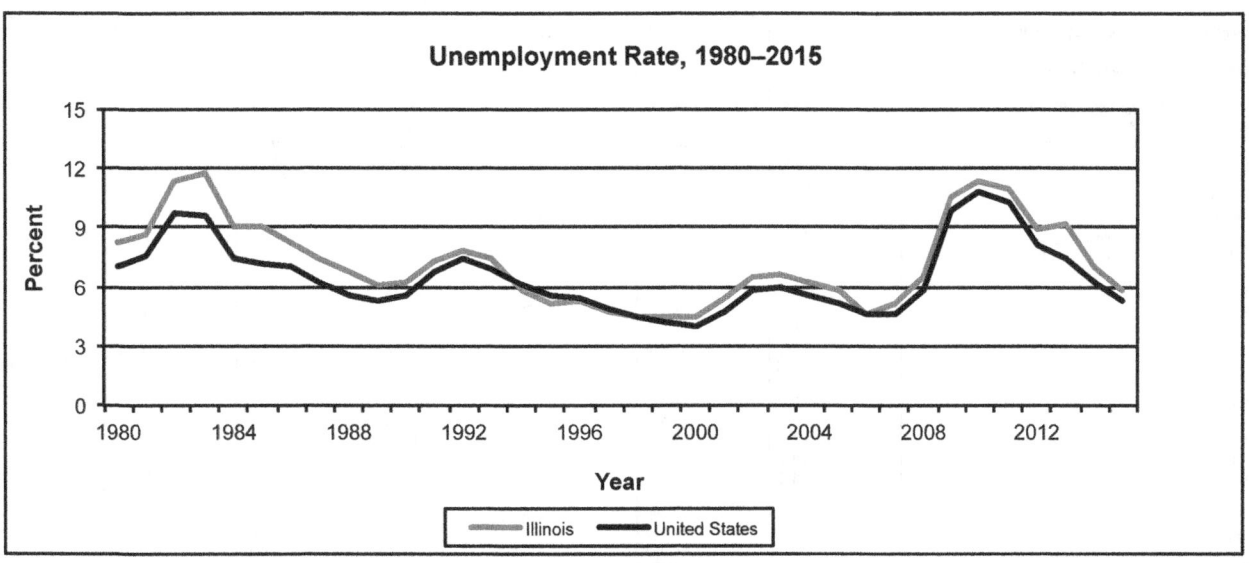

Table IL-8. Employment Status of the Civilian Noninstitutional Population Age 16 Years and Over

(Number, percent.)

Year	Civilian labor force	Civilian participation rate	Employed	Unemployed	Unemployment rate
2007..	6,665,601	68.4	6,334,010	331,591	5.0
2008..	6,657,227	67.8	6,238,611	418,616	6.3
2009..	6,618,658	67.0	5,943,229	675,429	10.2
2010..	6,625,321	66.9	5,937,047	688,274	10.4
2011..	6,586,893	66.2	5,948,366	638,527	9.7
2012..	6,584,691	65.9	5,993,148	591,543	9.0
2013..	6,561,142	65.5	5,964,580	596,562	9.1
2014..	6,515,198	64.8	6,053,884	461,314	7.1
2015..	6,512,386	64.7	6,126,307	386,079	5.9

Table IL-9. Employment and Average Wages by Industry

(Estimates through 2010 are based on the 2007 North American Industry Classification System [NAICS]. Estimates from 2011 onward are based on the 2012 NAICS.)

Industry	2008	2009	2010	2011	2012	2013	2014
	Number of Jobs						
Wage and Salary Employment by Industry..................	6,153,026	5,869,095	5,821,234	5,882,915	5,932,144	5,974,045	6,048,181
Farm Wage and Salary Employment.........................	16,207	15,271	18,237	17,069	16,174	12,222	11,695
Nonfarm Wage and Salary Employment....................	6,136,819	5,853,824	5,802,997	5,865,846	5,915,970	5,961,823	6,036,486
Private wage and salary employment........................	5,228,543	4,939,399	4,896,135	4,976,577	5,033,129	5,083,782	5,165,948
Forestry, fishing, and related activities.........................	4,362	4,261	3,820	4,068	4,078	4,725	5,982
Mining...	9,672	9,303	9,052	9,507	10,084	9,649	9,844
Utilities..	23,520	23,716	23,189	23,528	23,857	23,788	23,984
Construction...	269,100	229,839	208,243	206,472	195,541	198,343	208,107
Manufacturing..	659,693	579,317	561,722	574,540	584,275	580,152	580,204
Durable goods manufacturing................................	403,843	340,047	329,461	343,356	354,586	350,932	349,883
Nondurable goods manufacturing............................	255,850	239,270	232,261	231,184	229,689	229,220	230,321
Wholesale trade	312,742	295,062	288,749	291,888	295,640	300,325	301,556
Retail trade...	637,807	606,122	598,108	605,006	602,901	605,101	610,708
Transportation and warehousing.................................	244,327	230,887	231,795	238,612	244,352	244,358	250,897
Information...	115,305	106,957	101,883	100,183	100,561	99,051	99,401
Finance and insurance	313,174	298,307	293,720	291,833	294,661	293,926	292,624
Real estate and rental and leasing..............................	83,548	77,976	75,984	74,436	73,855	76,024	76,990
Professional, scientific, and technical services	374,287	353,699	351,122	360,573	367,226	381,107	391,488
Management of companies and enterprises.................	97,693	95,264	96,365	98,340	102,697	103,652	103,309
Administrative and waste services..............................	398,574	348,271	366,269	383,498	400,229	413,125	428,426
Educational services	148,711	155,293	160,381	165,620	166,775	166,810	168,583
Health care and social assistance...............................	678,901	690,647	700,048	711,121	721,617	730,326	740,589
Arts, entertainment, and recreation.............................	81,602	78,617	77,391	78,617	80,110	81,273	83,139
Accommodation and food services.............................	458,044	445,269	444,352	450,849	459,981	469,209	478,341
Other services, except public administration..................	317,481	310,592	303,942	307,886	304,689	302,838	311,776
Government and government enterprises...........................	908,276	914,425	906,862	889,269	882,841	878,041	870,538
	Dollars						
Average Wages and Salaries by Industry	49,415	49,012	50,271	51,711	53,078	53,541	55,136
Average Farm Wages and Salaries	32,632	31,157	24,440	34,006	24,929	35,420	38,804
Average Nonfarm Wages and Salaries	49,459	49,059	50,353	51,762	53,155	53,578	55,167
Average private wages and salaries...........................	49,988	49,335	50,673	52,169	53,636	53,909	55,623
Forestry, fishing, and related activities.........................	29,039	30,025	28,236	28,973	29,102	27,539	30,220
Mining...	61,714	61,591	68,078	66,616	68,108	70,817	74,301
Utilities..	102,320	98,866	98,417	104,422	107,901	106,768	112,986
Construction...	61,204	60,378	59,921	60,768	61,376	62,921	65,688
Manufacturing..	57,654	57,560	61,015	63,001	64,899	65,196	67,804
Durable goods manufacturing................................	58,749	58,578	61,613	64,517	65,803	65,489	67,090
Nondurable goods manufacturing............................	55,925	56,113	60,167	60,748	63,504	64,746	68,888
Wholesale trade	67,928	66,951	69,366	73,149	75,593	75,383	77,966
Retail trade...	26,771	26,537	27,260	27,824	28,548	28,747	29,237
Transportation and warehousing.................................	48,425	47,509	48,979	50,597	51,744	53,019	54,273
Information...	68,607	67,216	68,704	72,819	74,964	77,244	79,676
Finance and insurance	94,533	89,628	91,361	97,120	101,123	99,750	105,532
Real estate and rental and leasing..............................	51,702	49,771	51,723	53,603	56,535	58,298	60,949
Professional, scientific, and technical services	81,811	81,516	84,215	86,166	89,131	88,821	91,858
Management of companies and enterprises.................	108,889	107,457	114,816	117,501	121,268	123,360	124,785
Administrative and waste services..............................	33,970	33,908	34,811	35,004	35,908	35,138	36,719
Educational services	39,346	40,063	40,989	42,103	42,655	43,945	45,114
Health care and social assistance...............................	43,195	44,120	44,654	45,209	45,794	46,354	47,329
Arts, entertainment, and recreation.............................	33,922	33,922	34,953	35,783	36,949	36,753	36,340
Accommodation and food services.............................	18,906	18,807	19,510	20,189	20,693	20,710	21,382
Other services, except public administration..................	32,578	32,808	33,887	34,749	35,270	36,222	37,681
Government and government enterprises...........................	46,412	47,565	48,623	49,487	50,413	51,664	52,461

Table IL-10. Employment Characteristics by Family Type

(Number, percent.)

Family type and labor force status	2012		2013		2014	
	Total	Families with own children under 18 years	Total	Families with own children under 18 years	Total	Families with own children under 18 years
All Families...	3,121,020	1,398,372	3,128,369	1,383,676	3,086,335	1,350,738
FAMILY TYPE AND LABOR FORCE STATUS						
Married-Couple Families...	2,289,429	958,861	2,299,644	950,188	2,256,449	926,959
Both husband and wife in labor force................................	55.8	68.1	55.1	67.4	54.3	67.1
Husband in labor force, wife not in labor force...................	21.3	27.7	21.2	27.2	22.1	28.1
Wife in labor force, husband not in labor force....................	7.6	3.1	7.8	3.8	7.7	3.6
Both husband and wife not in labor force...........................	15.3	1.2	15.5	1.4	15.9	1.3
Other Families	831,591	439,511	828,725	433,488	829,886	423,779
Female householder, no husband present...........................	73.5	77.0	73.2	76.4	72.6	76.4
In labor force...	54.3	66.2	53.1	65.2	51.9	64.0
Not in labor force..	19.2	10.8	20.1	11.1	20.6	12.5
Male householder, no wife present...................................	26.5	23.0	26.8	23.6	27.4	23.6
In labor force...	21.2	21.2	21.5	21.9	21.6	21.7
Not in labor force..	5.3	1.8	5.3	1.7	5.9	1.9

Table IL-11. School Enrollment and Educational Attainment, 2014

(Number, percent.)

Item	State	U.S.
Enrollment		
Total population 3 years and over, enrolled in school..............................	3,379,651	82,063,714
Enrolled in nursery school or preschool (percent)................................	6.8	6.0
Enrolled in kindergarten (percent)..	5.0	5.1
Enrolled in elementary school, grades 1-8 (percent).............................	39.7	40.2
Enrolled in high school, grades 9-12 (percent)..................................	20.7	20.7
Enrolled in college or graduate school (percent)................................	27.9	28.0
Attainment		
Total population 25 years and over	8,639,076	213,725,624
Less than ninth grade (percent)...	5.2	5.6
9th to 12th grade, no diploma (percent)	6.6	7.5
High school graduate, including equivalency (percent)...........................	26.7	27.7
Some college, no degree (percent)..	20.9	21.0
Associate's degree (percent)	7.8	8.2
Bachelor's degree (percent)	20.1	18.7
Graduate or professional degree (percent)..	12.7	11.4
High school graduate or higher (percent)...	88.2	86.9
Bachelor's degree or higher (percent)..	32.8	30.1

Table IL-12. Public School Characteristics and Educational Indicators

(Number, percent; data derived from National Center of Education Statistics.)

Item	State	U.S.
Public Schools, 2013–2014 (except where noted)		
Number of school districts..	1,068	18,194
Number of schools...	4,204	98,271
Number of students (in thousands)	2,067	50,045
Number of teachers (in thousands)	136	3,114
Student-teacher ratio	15.2	16.1
Expenditures per student (dollars), FY 2013......................................	124,437	107,637
Four-year adjusted cohort graduation rate (ACGR)[1,2]	86.0	82.3
Students eligible for free or reduced-price lunch (in thousands)	1,045	25,596
English language learners (in thousands)	191	4,461
Students age 3 to 21 served under IDEA, part B (in thousands)	294	6,464

Public Schools by Type	Number	Percent of state public schools
Total number of schools...	4,204	100.0
Regular	3,923	93.3
Special education..	137	3.3
Vocational education...	0	0.0
Alternative education..	144	3.4

NOTE: Every school is assigned only one school type based on its instructional emphasis.
[1]ACGR data represents a new method of calculating high-school completion rates and may not be comparable to previous years' data for Averaged Freshmen Graduation Rates (AFGR).
[2]The United States 4-year ACGRs were estimated using both the reported 4-year ACGR data from 49 states and the District of Columbia and using imputed data for Idaho. The estimate for American Indian/Alaska Native students also includes imputed data for Virginia.

Table IL-13. Reported Voting and Registration of the Voting-Age Population, November 2014

(Numbers in thousands, percent.)

Item	Total population	Total citizen population	Registered			Voted		
			Total registered	Percent registered (total population)	Percent registered (total citizen population)	Total voted	Percent voted (total population)	Percent voted (total citizen population)
U.S. Total	239,874	219,941	142,166	59.3	64.6	92,251	38.5	41.9
State Total...........................	9,757	8,951	5,716	58.6	63.9	3,734	38.3	41.7
Sex								
Male..........	4,714	4,239	2,574	54.6	60.7	1,730	36.7	40.8
Female	5,042	4,712	3,142	62.3	66.7	2,004	39.7	42.5
Race								
White alone.......................	7,648	7,097	4,673	61.1	65.9	3,070	40.1	43.3
White, non-Hispanic alone	6,382	6,237	4,269	66.9	68.4	2,857	44.8	45.8
Black alone	1,348	1,329	768	57.0	57.8	535	39.7	40.2
Asian alone	616	396	167	27.1	42.2	73	11.9	18.5
Hispanic (of any race)......................	1,316	892	410	31.1	45.9	218	16.6	24.4
White alone or in combination	7,739	7,176	4,743	61.3	66.1	3,102	40.1	43.2
Black alone or in combination..........	1,387	1,368	801	57.7	58.6	558	40.2	40.8
Asian alone or in combination..........	659	427	192	29.2	45.0	78	11.8	18.2
Age								
18 to 24 years..........	1,385	1,273	519	37.5	40.7	191	13.8	15.0
25 to 34 years.................	1,713	1,458	831	48.5	57.0	406	23.7	27.8
35 to 44 years..........	1,534	1,351	794	51.8	58.8	456	29.7	33.7
45 to 64 years..........	3,402	3,208	2,347	69.0	73.2	1,727	50.8	53.8
65 years and over	1,722	1,661	1,225	71.1	73.8	955	55.4	57.5

Table IL-14. Crime

(Number, rate per 100,000. Data are derived from the FBI Uniform Crime Reports.)

Item	State			U.S.[1,2,3,4]		
	2013	2014	Percent change	2013	2014	Percent change
TOTAL POPULATION[5]..	12,882,135	12,880,580	-	316,128,839	318,857,056	0.9
VIOLENT CRIME						
Number..........	47,987	47,663	-0.7	1,163,146	1,165,383	0.2
Rate..........	372.5	370.0	-0.7	367.9	365.5	-0.7
Murder and Nonnegligent Manslaughter						
Number..........	706	685	-3.0	14,196	14,249	0.4
Rate..........	5.5	5.3	-3.6	4.5	4.5	-
Rape[6]						
Number..........	4,263	4,159	X	108,612	116,645	X
Rate..........	33.1	32.3	X	34.4	36.6	X
Robbery						
Number..........	17,722	15,299	-13.7	345,031	325,802	-5.6
Rate..........	137.6	118.8	-13.7	109.1	102.2	-6.3
Aggravated Assault						
Number..........	26,283	27,520	4.7	724,149	741,291	2.4
Rate..........	204.0	213.7	4.8	229.1	232.5	1.5
PROPERTY CRIME						
Number..........	292,983	267,385	-8.7	8,632,512	8,277,829	-4.1
Rate..........	2,274.3	2,075.9	-8.7	2,730.7	2,596.1	-4.9
Burglary						
Number..........	58,237	50,008	-14.1	1,928,465	1,729,806	-10.3
Rate..........	452.1	388.2	-14.1	610.0	542.5	-11.1
Larceny-Theft						
Number..........	213,813	199,926	-6.5	6,004,453	5,858,496	-2.4
Rate..........	1,659.8	1,552.2	-6.5	1,899.4	1,837.3	-3.3
Motor Vehicle Theft						
Number..........	20,933	17,451	-16.6	699,594	689,527	-1.4
Rate..........	162.5	135.5	-16.6	221.3	216.2	-2.3

NOTE: Although arson data are included in the trend and clearance tables, sufficient data are not available to estimate totals for this offense. Therefore, no arson data are published in this table.
X = Not applicable.
- = Zero or rounds to zero.
[1]The crime figures have been adjusted.
[2]The data collection methodology for the offense of forcible rape used by the Minnesota state Uniform Crime Reporting (UCR) Program (with the exception of Minneapolis and St. Paul, Minnesota) does not comply with national UCR Program guidelines. Consequently, its figures for forcible rape and violent crime (of which forcible rape is a part) are not published in this table.
[3]Includes offenses reported by the Zoological Police and the Metro Transit Police.
[4]Because of changes in the state's reporting practices, figures are not comparable to previous years' data.
[5]Populations are U.S. Census Bureau provisional estimates as of July 1 of each year.
[6]The figures shown for the offense of rape were estimated using the revised Uniform Crime Reporting (UCR) definition of rape.

Table IL-15. State Government Finances, 2014

(Dollar amounts in thousands, percent distribution.)

Item	Dollars	Percent distribution
Total Revenue	90,167,626	100.0
General revenue	66,636,637	73.9
Intergovernmental revenue	18,227,252	20.2
Taxes	39,182,894	43.5
General sales	8,515,410	9.4
Selective sales	7,243,099	8.0
License taxes	2,675,943	3.0
Individual income tax	16,058,396	17.8
Corporate income tax	4,284,646	4.8
Other taxes	405,400	0.4
Current charges	4,805,005	5.3
Miscellaneous general revenue	4,421,486	4.9
Utility revenue	0	-
Liquor stores revenue	0	-
Insurance trust revenue[1]	23,530,989	26.1
Total Expenditure	77,319,107	100.0
Intergovernmental expenditure	16,924,035	21.9
Direct expenditure	60,395,072	78.1
Current operation	37,820,634	48.9
Capital outlay	3,879,103	5.0
Insurance benefits and repayments	13,939,457	18.0
Assistance and subsidies	1,365,789	1.8
Interest on debt	3,390,089	4.4
Exhibit: Salaries and wages	9,195,758	11.9
Total Expenditure	77,319,107	100.0
General expenditure	63,379,650	82.0
Intergovernmental expenditure	16,924,035	21.9
Direct expenditure	46,455,615	60.1
General expenditure, by function:		
Education	17,695,676	22.9
Public welfare	21,227,555	27.5
Hospitals	1,182,564	1.5
Health	2,232,510	2.9
Highways	5,258,682	6.8
Police protection	477,567	0.6
Correction	1,408,780	1.8
Natural resources	281,133	0.4
Parks and recreation	249,875	0.3
Governmental administration	1,401,554	1.8
Interest on general debt	3,390,089	4.4
Other and unallocable	8,573,665	11.1
Utility expenditure	0	-
Liquor stores expenditure	0	-
Insurance trust expenditure	13,939,457	18.0
Debt at End of Fiscal Year	65,831,516	X
Cash and Security Holdings	155,146,804	X

X = Not applicable.
- = Zero or rounds to zero.
[1]Within insurance trust revenue, net earnings of state retirement systems is a calculated statistic (the item code in the data file is X08), and thus can be positive or negative. Net earnings is the sum of earnings on investments plus gains on investments minus losses on investments. The change made in 2002 for asset valuation from book to market value in accordance with Statement 34 of the Governmental Accounting Standards Board is reflected in the calculated statistics.

Table IL-16. State Government Tax Collections, 2014

(Dollars in thousands, percent.)

Item	Dollars	Percent distribution
Total Taxes	39,182,894	100.0
Property taxes	54,710	0.1
Sales and gross receipts	15,758,509	40.2
General sales and gross receipts	8,515,410	21.7
Selective sales and gross receipts	7,243,099	18.5
Alcoholic beverages	279,587	0.7
Amusements	662,592	1.7
Insurance premiums	359,240	0.9
Motor fuels	1,293,967	3.3
Pari-mutuels	6,534	-
Public utilities	1,651,211	4.2
Tobacco products	859,865	2.2
Other selective sales	2,130,103	5.4
Licenses	2,675,943	6.8
Alcoholic beverages	12,626	-
Amusements	14,972	-
Corporations in general	345,889	0.9
Hunting and fishing	42,936	0.1
Motor vehicle	1,623,571	4.1
Motor vehicle operators	116,206	0.3
Public utilities	16,217	-
Occupation and business, NEC	469,458	1.2
Other licenses	34,068	0.1
Income taxes	20,343,042	51.9
Individual income	16,058,396	41.0
Corporation net income	4,284,646	10.9
Other taxes	350,690	0.9
Death and gift	294,138	0.8
Documentary and stock transfer	56,552	0.1
Severance	X	X
Taxes, NEC	0	-

X = Not applicable.
- = Zero or rounds to zero.

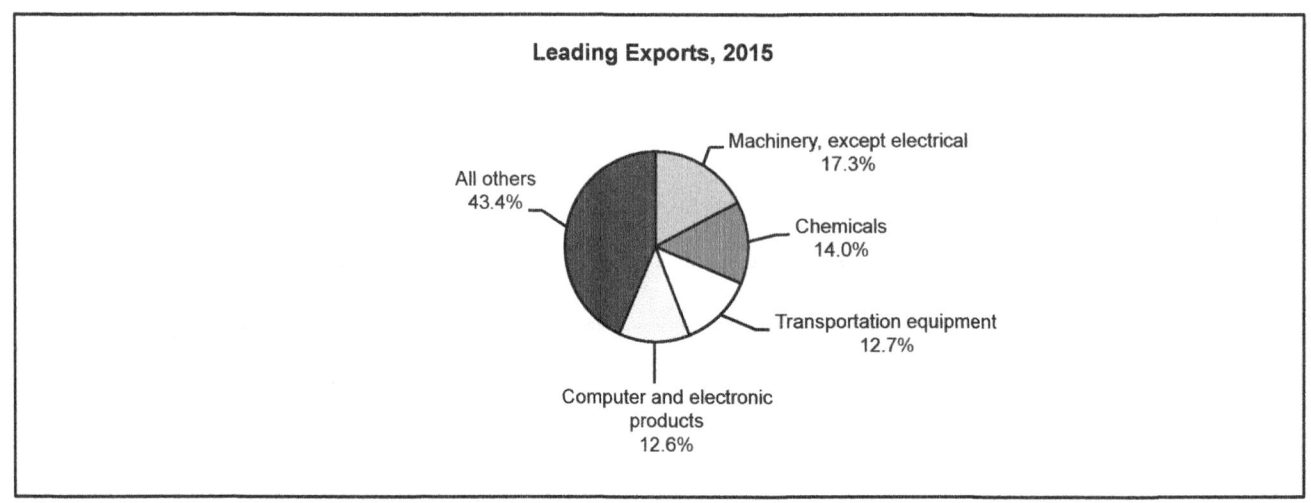

Leading Exports, 2015

Machinery, except electrical 17.3%
Chemicals 14.0%
Transportation equipment 12.7%
Computer and electronic products 12.6%
All others 43.4%

Facts and Figures

Location: East north central United States; bordered on the N by Michigan and Lake Michigan, on the E by Ohio, on the S by Kentucky, and on the W by Illinois

Area: 36,418 sq. mi. (94,321 sq. km.); rank—38th

Population: 6,619,680 (2015 est.); rank—16th

Principal Cities: capital—Indianapolis; largest—Indianapolis

Statehood: December 11, 1816; 19th state

U.S. Congress: 2 senators, 9 representatives

State Motto: The Crossroads of America

State Song: "On the Banks of the Wabash, Far Away"

State Nickname: The Hoosier State

Abbreviations: IN; Ind.

State Symbols: flower—peony; tree—tulip tree; bird—cardinal

At a Glance

- With an increase in population of 2.0 percent, Indiana ranked 31st among the states in growth from 2010 to 2015.

- Indiana's violent crime rate in 2014 was 365.3 per 100,000 population, compared to 365.5 for the entire nation.

- The property crime rate in Indiana in 2014 was 2,649.4 per 100,000 population, ranking 24th in the nation.

- The median household income in Indiana in 2014 was $49,446, compared to the nationwide median of $53,657.

- Approximately 15.2 percent of all Indianans and 21.5 percent of children under 18 years of age lived in poverty in 2014.

Table IN-1. Population by Age, Sex, Race, and Hispanic Origin

(Number, percent, except where noted.)

Sex, age, race, and Hispanic origin	2000	2010	2015[1]	Average annual percent change, 2010–2015
Total Population...	6,080,485	6,483,802	6,619,680	0.1
Percent of total U.S. population	2.2	2.1	2.1	X
Sex				
Male..	2,982,474	3,189,737	3,261,865	0.2
Female	3,098,011	3,294,065	3,357,815	0.1
Age				
Under 5 years..	423,215	434,075	419,490	-0.2
5 to 19 years...	1,340,171	1,372,507	1,341,984	-0.2
20 to 64 years..	3,564,268	3,836,112	3,892,079	0.1
65 years and over	752,831	841,108	966,127	1.0
Median age (years)	35.2	37.0	37.5	0.1
Race and Hispanic Origin				
One race				
White...	5,320,022	5,638,833	5,681,607	0.1
Black...	510,034	603,797	636,646	0.4
American Indian and Alaska Native	15,815	24,487	26,656	0.6
Asian...	59,126	105,535	141,740	2.1
Native Hawaiian or Other Pacific Islander	2,005	3,532	4,149	1.2
Two or more races	75,672	107,618	128,882	1.3
Hispanic (of any race)......................................	214,536	403,234	441,909	0.7

X = Not applicable.
[1]Population figures for 2015 are July 1 estimates. The 2010 estimates are taken from the 2010 Census.

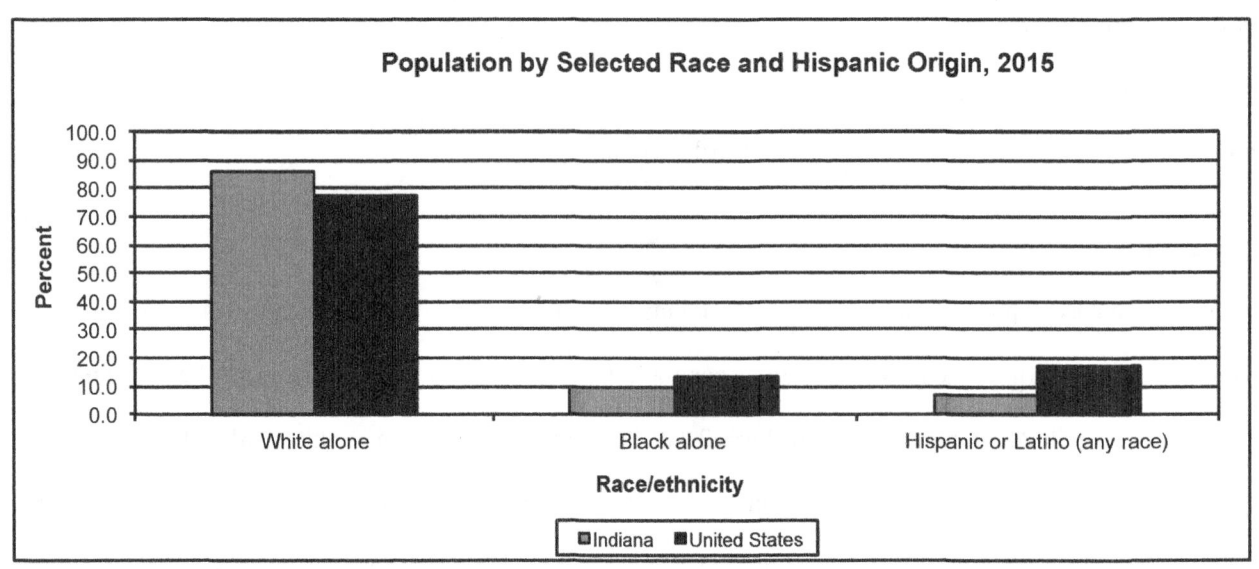

Population by Selected Race and Hispanic Origin, 2015

Table IN-2. Marital Status

(Number, percent distribution.)

Sex, age, race, and Hispanic origin	2000	2010	2014
Males, 15 Years and Over	2,308,917	2,513,953	2,545,970
Never married	27.9	32.6	33.1
Now married, except separated.............................	58.5	52.3	51.6
Separated..	1.3	1.1	1.2
Widowed..	2.4	2.5	2.6
Divorced..	10.0	11.4	11.5
Females, 15 Years and Over	2,462,123	2,644,068	2,677,102
Never married	22.0	26.7	27.1
Now married, except separated.............................	54.3	49.1	48.3
Separated..	1.5	1.8	1.8
Widowed..	10.6	9.2	9.2
Divorced..	11.6	13.2	13.5

Table IN-3. Households and Housing Characteristics

(Number, percent, dollars.)

Item	2000	2010	2014	Average annual percent change, 2000–2014
Total Households..	2,336,306	2,470,905	2,502,739	0.5
Family households	1,602,501	1,656,386	1,657,223	0.2
Married-couple family	1,251,458	1,236,518	1,219,395	-0.2
Other family	351,043	419,868	437,828	1.8
Male householder, no wife present........................	91,671	110,663	120,564	2.3
Female householder, no husband present.............	259,372	309,205	317,264	1.6
Nonfamily households	733,805	814,519	845,516	1.1
Householder living alone......................................	605,428	678,460	693,396	1.0
Householder not living alone.................................	128,377	136,059	152,120	1.3
Housing Characteristics				
Total housing units...	2,532,319	2,797,172	2,829,630	0.8
Occupied housing units	2,336,306	2,470,905	2,502,739	0.5
Owner occupied..	1,669,192	1,736,751	1,716,341	0.2
Renter occupied..	667,144	734,154	786,398	1.3
Average household size...	2.53	2.55	2.56	0.1
Financial Characteristics				
Median gross rent of renter-occupied housing	521	683	753	3.2
Median monthly owner costs for housing units with a mortgage	869	1,090	1,082	1.8
Median value of owner-occupied housing units..........................	94,300	123,300	124,300	2.3

Table IN-4. Migration, Origin, and Language

(Number, percent.)

Characteristic	State			U.S.		
	2013	2014	Percent change	2013	2014	Percent change
Residence 1 Year Ago						
Population 1 year and over	6,492,306	6,516,181	0.4	312,432,820	315,095,393	0.9
Same house	84.7	85.0	X	85.0	85.1	X
Different house in the U.S.	14.9	14.6	X	14.4	14.3	X
Same county	9.2	8.9	X	8.9	8.7	X
Different county	5.7	5.7	X	5.5	5.6	X
Same state	3.6	3.6	X	3.2	3.3	X
Different state	2.1	2.1	X	2.3	2.3	X
Abroad	0.4	0.4	X	0.6	0.6	X
Place of Birth						
Native born	6,256,401	6,277,275	0.3	274,780,773	276,465,262	0.6
Male	49.1	49.1	X	49.3	49.3	X
Female	50.9	50.9	X	50.7	50.7	X
Foreign born	314,501	319,580	1.6	41,348,066	42,391,794	2.5
Male	50.6	50.3	X	48.8	48.7	X
Female	49.4	49.7	X	51.2	51.3	X
Foreign born; naturalized U.S. citizen........................	110,657	123,697	11.8	19,294,710	19,984,738	3.6
Male	46.1	47.8	X	45.9	45.9	X
Female	53.9	52.2	X	54.1	54.1	X
Foreign born; not a U.S. citizen..................................	203,844	195,883	-3.9	22,053,356	22,407,056	1.6
Male	53.0	51.9	X	51.3	51.2	X
Female	47.0	48.1	X	48.7	48.8	X
Entered 2010 or later	15.5	17.3	X	9.7	12.3	X
Entered 2000 to 2009	39.0	36.4	X	29.4	28.6	X
Entered before 2000..	45.5	46.3	X	61.0	59.1	X
World Region of Birth, Foreign						
Foreign-born population, excluding population born at sea	314,501	319,580	1.6	41,347,945	42,390,705	2.5
Europe	13.5	12.9	X	11.6	11.2	X
Asia	32.2	34.7	X	29.5	30.1	X
Africa	6.9	5.3	X	4.4	4.6	X
Oceania	0.6	0.4	X	0.5	0.6	X
Latin America	44.8	44.5	X	51.9	51.6	X
North America	2.0	2.2	X	2.0	1.9	X
Language Spoken at Home and Ability to Speak English						
Population 5 years and over......................................	6,146,838	6,178,831	0.5	296,358,760	299,084,046	0.9
English only	91.8	92.1	X	79.2	78.9	X
Language other than English.....................................	8.2	7.9	X	20.8	21.1	X
Speaks English less than "very well"....................	3.2	3.1	X	8.5	8.6	X

X = Not applicable.
- = Zero or rounds to zero.

Table IN-5. Median Income and Poverty Status, 2014

(Number, percent, except as noted.)

Characteristic	State		U.S.	
	Number	Percent	Number	Percent
Median Income				
Households (dollars)...	49,446	X	53,657	X
Families (dollars)...	60,780	X	65,910	X
Below Poverty Level (All People)	974,218	15.2	48,208,387	15.5
Sex				
Male...	427,710	13.7	21,590,918	14.2
Female...	546,508	16.8	26,617,469	16.8
Age				
Under 18 years..	333,348	21.5	15,686,012	21.7
Related children under 18 years.............................	326,069	21.2	15,372,705	21.3
18 to 64 years...	577,701	14.7	28,267,482	14.6
65 years and over	63,169	7.0	4,254,893	9.5

X = Not applicable.

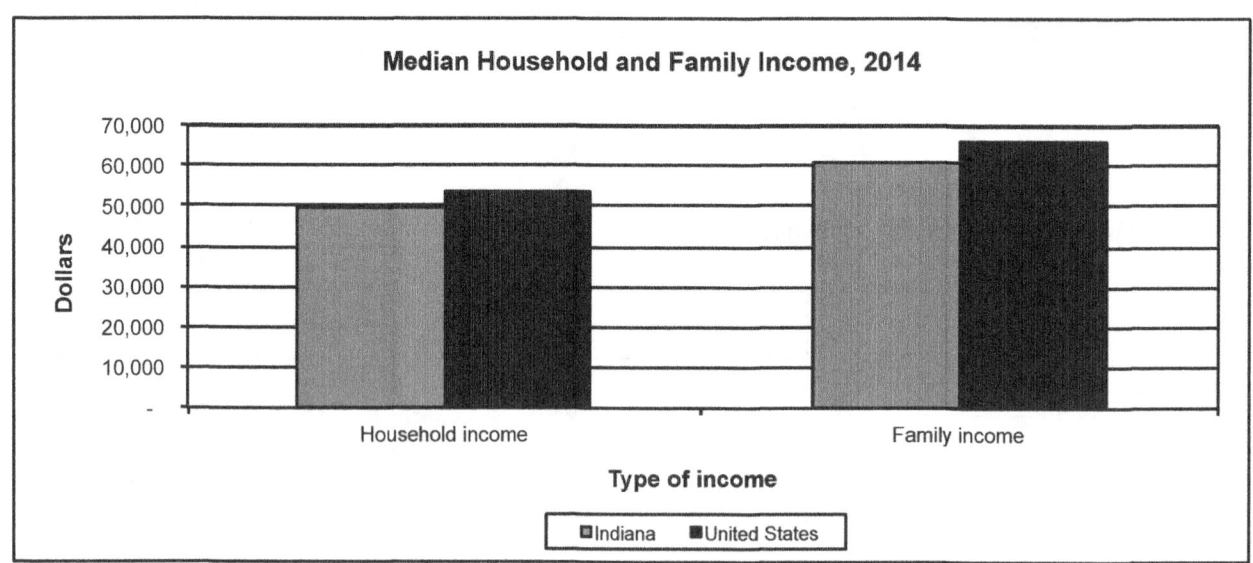

Table IN-6. Health Insurance Coverage Status for the Civilian Noninstitutionalized Population and Children Under 18 Years of Age

(Numbers in thousands, percent.)

Item	2006	2007	2008	2009	2010	2011	2012	2013	2014
Civilian Noninstitutionalized Population	6,337	6,263	6,271	6,316	6,391	6,418	6,437	6,472	6,498
Covered by Private or Public Insurance									
Number...	5,590	5,546	5,400	5,415	5,444	5,487	5,517	5,569	5,722
Percent..	88.2	88.6	86.1	85.7	85.2	85.5	85.7	86.0	88.1
Not Covered									
Number...	748	717	871	901	948	931	920	903	776
Percent..	11.8	11.4	13.9	14.3	14.8	14.5	14.3	14.0	11.9
Percent in the U.S. not covered.................................	15.8	15.3	15.1	15.1	15.5	15.1	14.8	14.5	11.7
Children Under 18 Years of Age	1,582	1,593	1,580	1,583	1,602	1,594	1,585	1,584	1,580
Covered by Private or Public Insurance									
Number...	1,459	1,511	1,420	1,443	1,459	1,465	1,451	1,454	1,466
Percent..	92.2	94.8	89.9	91.2	91.1	91.9	91.5	91.8	92.8
Not Covered									
Number...	123	83	160	140	143	129	134	130	113
Percent..	7.8	5.2	10.1	8.8	8.9	8.1	8.5	8.2	7.2
Percent in the U.S. not covered.................................	11.7	11.0	9.7	8.6	8.0	7.5	7.2	7.1	6.0

Table IN-7. Employment Status by Demographic Group, 2015

(Numbers in thousands, percent.)

Characteristic	Civilian noninstitutional population	Civilian labor force		Employed		Unemployed	
		Number	Percent of population	Number	Percent of population	Number	Percent of population
Total...	5,132	3,273	63.8	3,116	60.7	156	4.8
Sex							
Male..	2,485	1,723	69.4	1,641	66.0	82	4.8
Female..	2,648	1,550	58.5	1,476	55.7	74	4.8
Race, Sex, and Hispanic Origin							
White...	4,487	2,879	64.2	2,750	61.3	129	4.5
Male..	2,174	1,524	70.1	1,453	66.8	71	4.7
Female.....................................	2,313	1,355	58.6	1,297	56.1	57	4.2
Black or African American...............	454	283	62.2	263	57.8	20	7.0
Male..	205	130	63.5	121	59.2	9	6.8
Female.....................................	250	153	61.1	142	56.7	11	7.2
Hispanic or Latino ethnicity[1]...........	355	260	73.2	245	69.1	15	5.6
Male..	191	164	85.8	157	82.2	7	4.2
Female.....................................	164	96	58.7	89	53.9	8	8.0
Age							
16 to 19 years...............................	353	140	39.6	113	32.1	27	19.2
20 to 24 years...............................	428	309	72.1	284	66.4	25	8.0
25 to 34 years...............................	883	725	82.1	689	78.0	36	5.0
35 to 44 years...............................	804	676	84.0	652	81.0	24	3.5
45 to 54 years...............................	837	677	80.8	652	77.9	25	3.7
55 to 64 years...............................	854	565	66.2	551	64.6	14	2.5
65 years and over..........................	974	182	18.7	176	18.1	6	3.2

NOTE: Data in Table 7 are from the Current Population Survey (CPS) and do not match the estimates in Table 8. See notes and definitions for further information.
[1]May be of any race.

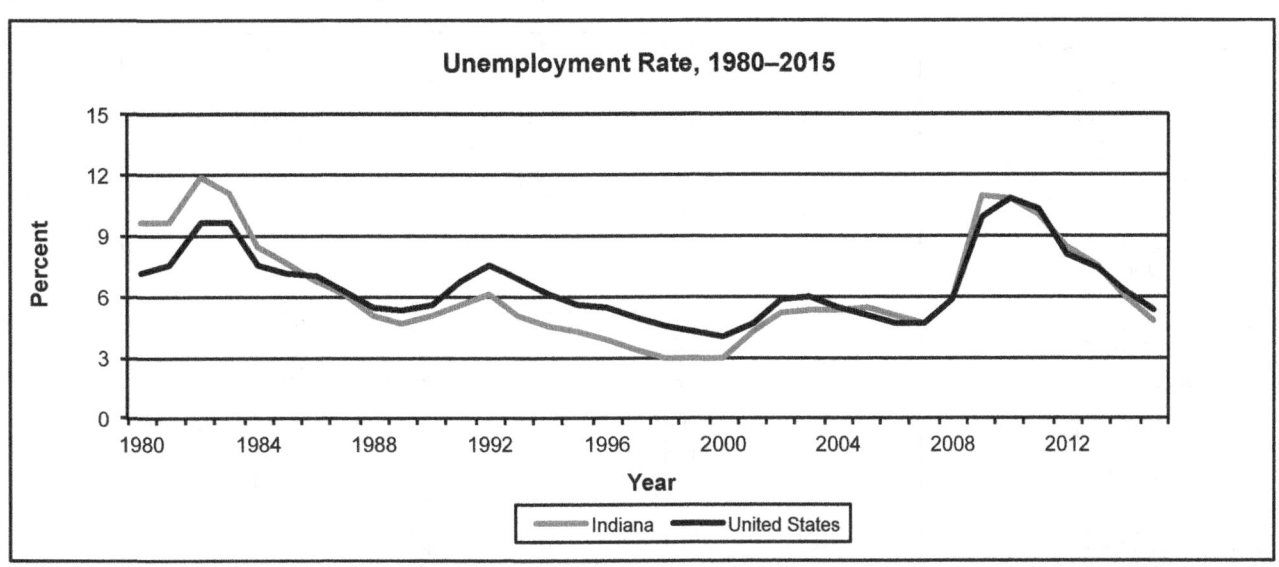

Table IN-8. Employment Status of the Civilian Noninstitutional Population Age 16 Years and Over

(Number, percent.)

Year	Civilian labor force	Civilian participation rate	Employed	Unemployed	Unemployment rate
2007..	3,207,687	66.3	3,061,042	146,645	4.6
2008..	3,232,097	66.3	3,041,828	190,269	5.9
2009..	3,193,989	65.1	2,864,985	329,004	10.3
2010..	3,175,192	64.0	2,845,608	329,584	10.4
2011..	3,181,991	63.6	2,891,945	290,046	9.1
2012..	3,171,569	63.0	2,907,130	264,439	8.3
2013..	3,193,427	63.0	2,948,941	244,486	7.7
2014..	3,227,970	63.3	3,035,984	191,986	5.9
2015..	3,265,761	63.7	3,109,217	156,544	4.8

Table IN-9. Employment and Average Wages by Industry

(Estimates through 2010 are based on the 2007 North American Industry Classification System [NAICS]. Estimates from 2011 onward are based on the 2012 NAICS.)

Industry	2008	2009	2010	2011	2012	2013	2014
	Number of jobs						
Wage and Salary Employment by Industry..................	3,042,659	2,877,302	2,886,635	2,930,409	2,982,649	3,016,449	3,057,584
Farm Wage and Salary Employment.........................	9,368	10,488	13,576	10,314	13,535	12,721	11,519
Nonfarm Wage and Salary Employment....................	3,033,291	2,866,814	2,873,059	2,920,095	2,969,114	3,003,728	3,046,065
Private wage and salary employment.........................	2,572,832	2,405,042	2,415,138	2,470,191	2,521,092	2,559,886	2,603,447
Forestry, fishing, and related activities.........................	3,152	2,985	3,158	3,183	3,243	3,313	4,137
Mining...	6,455	6,296	6,268	6,580	6,738	6,684	6,857
Utilities..	14,996	15,291	14,952	14,729	14,349	14,172	14,129
Construction...	150,313	126,089	121,231	126,627	129,260	127,819	126,843
Manufacturing.......................................	521,405	442,761	448,527	464,552	482,919	492,560	507,834
Durable goods manufacturing..........................	377,451	309,284	314,026	330,610	346,630	352,396	363,527
Nondurable goods manufacturing...................	143,954	133,477	134,501	133,942	136,289	140,164	144,307
Wholesale trade	126,047	116,318	114,851	115,978	116,691	117,517	118,351
Retail trade..	326,542	312,887	309,475	312,756	315,285	319,332	321,808
Transportation and warehousing......................	118,012	110,784	111,987	115,179	117,925	120,755	124,448
Information	39,759	37,772	35,811	34,274	35,829	35,826	35,589
Finance and insurance	101,823	98,256	97,609	98,073	98,138	97,815	99,300
Real estate and rental and leasing...................	35,920	34,329	33,286	33,249	33,162	33,488	33,628
Professional, scientific, and technical services ...	100,029	97,236	97,668	99,962	100,883	102,977	106,163
Management of companies and enterprises.........	29,218	27,518	26,995	28,043	29,106	31,082	32,178
Administrative and waste services...................	157,324	139,298	153,626	164,333	171,745	176,403	185,357
Educational services	61,830	61,146	62,728	64,520	65,737	66,620	66,799
Health care and social assistance...................	341,927	349,939	355,805	360,872	367,403	374,617	375,601
Arts, entertainment, and recreation.................	44,269	43,782	42,417	41,966	41,521	41,886	41,276
Accommodation and food services..................	243,915	236,425	234,685	239,687	245,647	250,846	254,693
Other services, except public administration........	149,896	145,930	144,059	145,628	145,511	146,174	148,456
Government and government enterprises...........................	460,459	461,772	457,921	449,904	448,022	443,842	442,618
	Dollars						
Average Wages and Salaries by Industry	38,950	38,869	39,885	40,970	41,830	42,328	43,296
Average Farm Wages and Salaries	33,586	32,706	25,400	33,141	24,449	34,539	38,387
Average Nonfarm Wages and Salaries	38,966	38,891	39,954	40,998	41,910	42,361	43,315
Average private wages and salaries.........................	39,396	39,153	40,335	41,461	42,488	42,913	43,908
Forestry, fishing, and related activities................	21,266	21,845	22,565	23,165	24,164	24,686	29,120
Mining...	59,481	59,059	62,666	65,326	65,302	68,335	70,656
Utilities..	75,360	76,469	79,645	82,447	84,740	88,413	90,462
Construction...	47,883	47,845	50,401	52,444	55,052	54,484	53,378
Manufacturing.......................................	53,793	54,025	56,098	57,108	58,046	58,013	59,453
Durable goods manufacturing..........................	53,426	53,484	55,455	56,727	57,978	57,340	58,768
Nondurable goods manufacturing...................	54,757	55,279	57,600	58,047	58,220	59,702	61,177
Wholesale trade	53,909	53,345	55,051	57,000	58,516	59,463	61,981
Retail trade..	23,642	23,809	24,497	24,866	25,324	25,465	26,194
Transportation and warehousing......................	41,521	41,056	41,857	43,020	43,509	44,243	45,270
Information	49,087	49,371	50,488	52,277	54,146	55,344	56,497
Finance and insurance	54,888	54,304	56,496	59,275	62,108	63,277	65,699
Real estate and rental and leasing...................	34,066	34,024	35,267	36,779	38,082	38,979	41,450
Professional, scientific, and technical services ...	55,068	54,734	56,197	58,657	60,311	62,930	62,578
Management of companies and enterprises.........	75,634	74,953	79,612	84,796	86,569	88,180	90,681
Administrative and waste services...................	27,130	27,832	28,019	28,591	28,892	29,133	29,616
Educational services	27,890	29,731	30,030	30,984	30,997	31,182	32,005
Health care and social assistance...................	39,857	40,532	40,982	41,982	43,246	43,909	44,899
Arts, entertainment, and recreation.................	32,893	31,624	32,922	32,971	32,938	33,145	33,683
Accommodation and food services..................	14,374	14,553	15,157	15,576	15,881	15,839	16,341
Other services, except public administration........	27,037	27,043	28,031	28,512	29,032	29,643	30,541
Government and government enterprises...........................	36,564	37,526	37,946	38,455	38,654	39,182	39,825

Table IN-10. Employment Characteristics by Family Type

(Number, percent.)

Family type and labor force status	2012 Total	2012 Families with own children under 18 years	2013 Total	2013 Families with own children under 18 years	2014 Total	2014 Families with own children under 18 years
All Families..........	1,648,172	719,823	1,647,941	720,081	1,651,536	707,467
FAMILY TYPE AND LABOR FORCE STATUS						
Married-Couple Families............................	1,229,106	477,058	1,226,204	476,033	1,213,708	459,653
Both husband and wife in labor force...........	53.5	67.8	52.8	67.8	53.6	69.8
Husband in labor force, wife not in labor force........	21.3	26.9	21.8	27.1	21.0	25.1
Wife in labor force, husband not in labor force..........	7.8	4.0	8.1	3.4	7.8	3.3
Both husband and wife not in labor force..........	17.4	1.4	17.1	1.5	17.6	1.8
Other Families	419,066	242,765	421,737	244,048	437,828	247,814
Female householder, no husband present..........	72.6	74.4	72.9	74.5	72.5	74.3
In labor force.................	52.5	62.4	51.4	61.0	52.3	62.3
Not in labor force	20.1	12.0	21.5	13.5	20.1	12.1
Male householder, no wife present..........	27.4	25.6	27.1	25.5	27.5	25.7
In labor force........	22.3	23.3	21.3	22.6	21.8	23.7
Not in labor force	5.1	2.3	5.8	2.9	5.8	2.0

Table IN-11. School Enrollment and Educational Attainment, 2014

(Number, percent.)

Item	State	U.S.
Enrollment		
Total population 3 years and over, enrolled in school..........	1,727,143	82,063,714
Enrolled in nursery school or preschool (percent)........	5.8	6.0
Enrolled in kindergarten (percent)........	5.0	5.1
Enrolled in elementary school, grades 1-8 (percent)........	41.6	40.2
Enrolled in high school, grades 9-12 (percent)........	21.1	20.7
Enrolled in college or graduate school (percent)........	26.5	28.0
Attainment		
Total population 25 years and over	4,342,916	213,725,624
Less than ninth grade (percent)........	3.9	5.6
9th to 12th grade, no diploma (percent)........	7.7	7.5
High school graduate, including equivalency (percent)........	34.3	27.7
Some college, no degree (percent)	21.1	21.0
Associate's degree (percent)........	8.5	8.2
Bachelor's degree (percent)........	15.7	18.7
Graduate or professional degree (percent)........	8.9	11.4
High school graduate or higher (percent)	88.4	86.9
Bachelor's degree or higher (percent)	24.7	30.1

Table IN-12. Public School Characteristics and Educational Indicators

(Number, percent; data derived from National Center of Education Statistics.)

Item	State	U.S.
Public Schools, 2013–2014 (except where noted)		
Number of school districts..........	408	18,194
Number of schools..........	1,928	98,271
Number of students (in thousands)	1,047	50,045
Number of teachers (in thousands)	60	3,114
Student-teacher ratio	17.5	16.1
Expenditures per student (dollars), FY 2013..........	94,217	107,637
Four-year adjusted cohort graduation rate (ACGR)[1,2]	87.9	82.3
Students eligible for free or reduced-price lunch (in thousands)	515	25,596
English language learners (in thousands)	54	4,461
Students age 3 to 21 served under IDEA, part B (in thousands)	170	6,464

Public Schools by Type	Number	Percent of state public schools
Total number of schools..........	1,928	100.0
Regular	1,865	96.7
Special education..........	27	1.4
Vocational education..........	27	1.4
Alternative education..........	9	0.5

NOTE: Every school is assigned only one school type based on its instructional emphasis.
[1]ACGR data represents a new method of calculating high-school completion rates and may not be comparable to previous years' data for Averaged Freshmen Graduation Rates (AFGR).
[2]The United States 4-year ACGRs were estimated using both the reported 4-year ACGR data from 49 states and the District of Columbia and using imputed data for Idaho. The estimate for American Indian/Alaska Native students also includes imputed data for Virginia.

Table IN-13. Reported Voting and Registration of the Voting-Age Population, November 2014

(Numbers in thousands, percent.)

Item	Total population	Total citizen population	Registered			Voted		
			Total registered	Percent registered (total population)	Percent registered (total citizen population)	Total voted	Percent voted (total population)	Percent voted (total citizen population)
U.S. Total	239,874	219,941	142,166	59.3	64.6	92,251	38.5	41.9
State Total............................	4,913	4,693	3,048	62.0	64.9	1,646	33.5	35.1
Sex								
Male..................................	2,357	2,244	1,426	60.5	63.5	795	33.7	35.4
Female	2,556	2,449	1,622	63.5	66.2	850	33.3	34.7
Race								
White alone..........................	4,365	4,212	2,788	63.9	66.2	1,498	34.3	35.6
White, non-Hispanic alone..........	4,062	4,042	2,715	66.8	67.2	1,463	36.0	36.2
Black alone..........................	395	385	226	57.4	58.8	143	36.4	37.3
Asian alone	95	38	4	(B)	(B)	-	(B)	(B)
Hispanic (of any race)...............	314	180	78	24.8	43.1	35	11.2	19.4
White alone or in combination	4,395	4,242	2,801	63.7	66.0	1,502	34.2	35.4
Black alone or in combination..........	420	410	240	57.1	58.4	147	35.1	35.9
Asian alone or in combination..........	99	42	4	(B)	(B)	-	(B)	(B)
Age								
18 to 24 years......................	559	505	268	48.0	53.1	91	16.3	18.0
25 to 34 years......................	879	831	487	55.4	58.6	168	19.1	20.2
35 to 44 years......................	830	749	464	55.9	61.9	208	25.1	27.8
45 to 64 years......................	1,759	1,725	1,142	64.9	66.2	701	39.8	40.6
65 years and over	886	883	688	77.6	77.9	478	53.9	54.1

B = Base is less than 75,000 and therefore too small to show the derived measure.

Table IN-14. Crime

(Number, rate per 100,000. Data are derived from the FBI Uniform Crime Reports.)

Item	State			U.S.[1,2,3,4]		
	2013	2014	Percent change	2013	2014	Percent change
TOTAL POPULATION[5]............................	6,570,902	6,596,855	0.4	316,128,839	318,857,056	0.9
VIOLENT CRIME						
Number...........................	22,991	24,099	4.8	1,163,146	1,165,383	0.2
Rate	349.9	365.3	4.4	367.9	365.5	-0.7
Murder and Nonnegligent Manslaughter						
Number............................	355	330	-7.0	14,196	14,249	0.4
Rate	5.4	5.0	-7.4	4.5	4.5	-
Rape[6]						
Number............................	2,142	2,186	X	108,612	116,645	X
Rate	32.6	33.1	X	34.4	36.6	X
Robbery						
Number............................	7,108	6,897	-3.0	345,031	325,802	-5.6
Rate	108.2	104.5	-3.4	109.1	102.2	-6.3
Aggravated Assault						
Number............................	13,882	14,686	5.8	724,149	741,291	2.4
Rate	211.3	222.6	5.3	229.1	232.5	1.5
PROPERTY CRIME						
Number............................	187,536	174,776	-6.8	8,632,512	8,277,829	-4.1
Rate	2,854.0	2,649.4	-7.2	2,730.7	2,596.1	-4.9
Burglary						
Number............................	42,909	36,893	-14.0	1,928,465	1,729,806	-10.3
Rate	653.0	559.3	-14.3	610.0	542.5	-11.1
Larceny-Theft						
Number............................	130,423	124,022	-4.9	6,004,453	5,858,496	-2.4
Rate	1,984.9	1,880.0	-5.3	1,899.4	1,837.3	-3.3
Motor Vehicle Theft						
Number............................	14,204	13,861	-2.4	699,594	689,527	-1.4
Rate	216.2	210.1	-2.8	221.3	216.2	-2.3

NOTE: Although arson data are included in the trend and clearance tables, sufficient data are not available to estimate totals for this offense. Therefore, no arson data are published in this table.
X = Not applicable.
- = Zero or rounds to zero.
[1]The crime figures have been adjusted.
[2]The data collection methodology for the offense of forcible rape used by the Minnesota state Uniform Crime Reporting (UCR) Program (with the exception of Minneapolis and St. Paul, Minnesota) does not comply with national UCR Program guidelines. Consequently, its figures for forcible rape and violent crime (of which forcible rape is a part) are not published in this table.
[3]Includes offenses reported by the Zoological Police and the Metro Transit Police.
[4]Because of changes in the state's reporting practices, figures are not comparable to previous years' data.
[5]Populations are U.S. Census Bureau provisional estimates as of July 1 of each year.
[6]The figures shown for the offense of rape were estimated using the revised Uniform Crime Reporting (UCR) definition of rape.

Table IN-15. State Government Finances, 2014

(Dollar amounts in thousands, percent distribution.)

Item	Dollars	Percent distribution
Total Revenue	39,528,798	100.0
General revenue	33,259,949	84.1
Intergovernmental revenue	11,055,684	28.0
Taxes	16,846,961	42.6
General sales	7,003,426	17.7
Selective sales	3,391,724	8.6
License taxes	590,483	1.5
Individual income tax	4,896,317	12.4
Corporate income tax	866,747	2.2
Other taxes	98,264	0.2
Current charges	3,480,034	8.8
Miscellaneous general revenue	1,877,270	4.7
Utility revenue	0	-
Liquor stores revenue	0	-
Insurance trust revenue[1]	6,268,849	15.9
Total Expenditure	35,990,274	100.0
Intergovernmental expenditure	9,314,957	25.9
Direct expenditure	26,675,317	74.1
Current operation	19,835,693	55.1
Capital outlay	1,860,061	5.2
Insurance benefits and repayments	2,972,075	8.3
Assistance and subsidies	1,036,749	2.9
Interest on debt	970,739	2.7
Exhibit: Salaries and wages	4,389,808	12.2
Total Expenditure	35,990,274	100.0
General expenditure	33,018,199	91.7
Intergovernmental expenditure	9,314,957	25.9
Direct expenditure	23,703,242	65.9
General expenditure, by function:		
Education	14,602,891	40.6
Public welfare	10,592,684	29.4
Hospitals	166,968	0.5
Health	495,609	1.4
Highways	2,417,655	6.7
Police protection	215,907	0.6
Correction	673,575	1.9
Natural resources	335,365	0.9
Parks and recreation	81,112	0.2
Governmental administration	598,153	1.7
Interest on general debt	970,739	2.7
Other and unallocable	1,867,541	5.2
Utility expenditure	0	-
Liquor stores expenditure	0	-
Insurance trust expenditure	2,972,075	8.3
Debt at End of Fiscal Year	21,120,303	X
Cash and Security Holdings	60,138,509	X

X = Not applicable.
- = Zero or rounds to zero.
[1]Within insurance trust revenue, net earnings of state retirement systems is a calculated statistic (the item code in the data file is X08), and thus can be positive or negative. Net earnings is the sum of earnings on investments plus gains on investments minus losses on investments. The change made in 2002 for asset valuation from book to market value in accordance with Statement 34 of the Governmental Accounting Standards Board is reflected in the calculated statistics.

Table IN-16. State Government Tax Collections, 2014

(Dollars in thousands, percent.)

Item	Dollars	Percent distribution
Total Taxes	16,846,961	100.0
Property taxes	8,052	-
Sales and gross receipts	10,395,150	61.7
General sales and gross receipts	7,003,426	41.6
Selective sales and gross receipts	3,391,724	20.1
Alcoholic beverages	45,955	0.3
Amusements	655,894	3.9
Insurance premiums	223,072	1.3
Motor fuels	814,549	4.8
Pari-mutuels	2,273	-
Public utilities	252,652	1.5
Tobacco products	447,561	2.7
Other selective sales	949,768	5.6
Licenses	590,483	3.5
Alcoholic beverages	13,073	0.1
Amusements	5,722	-
Corporations in general	7,045	-
Hunting and fishing	20,011	0.1
Motor vehicle	208,572	1.2
Motor vehicle operators	207,097	1.2
Public utilities	0	-
Occupation and business, NEC	46,157	0.3
Other licenses	82,806	0.5
Income taxes	5,763,064	34.2
Individual income	4,896,317	29.1
Corporation net income	866,747	5.1
Other taxes	90,212	0.5
Death and gift	87,712	0.5
Documentary and stock transfer	0	-
Severance	2,500	-
Taxes, NEC	0	-

- = Zero or rounds to zero.

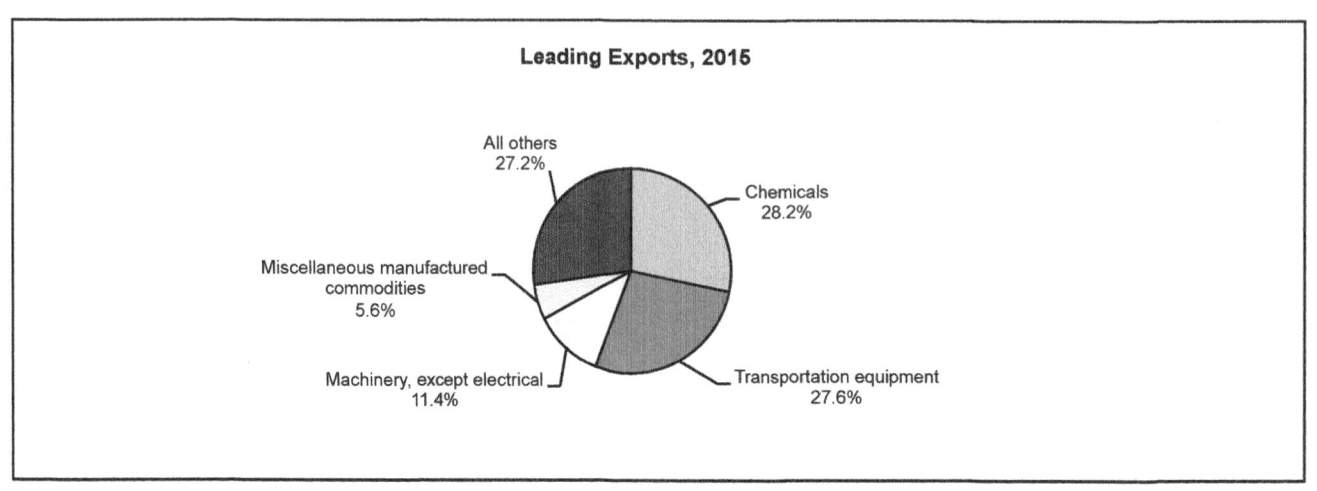

Leading Exports, 2015

All others 27.2%

Chemicals 28.2%

Miscellaneous manufactured commodities 5.6%

Machinery, except electrical 11.4%

Transportation equipment 27.6%

Facts and Figures

Location: North central United States; bordered on the N by Minnesota, on the E by Wisconsin and Illinois, on the S by Missouri, and on the W by Nebraska and South Dakota

Area: 56,272 sq. mi. (145,743 sq. km.); rank—26th

Population: 3,123,899 (2015 est.); rank—30th

Principal Cities: capital—Des Moines; largest—Des Moines

Statehood: December 28, 1846; 29th state

U.S. Congress: 2 senators, 4 representatives

State Motto: Our Liberties We Prize and Our Rights We Will Maintain

State Song: "The Song of Iowa"

State Nickname: The Hawkeye State

Abbreviations: IA; Ia.

State Symbols: flower—wild prairie rose; tree—oak; bird—Eastern goldfinch

At a Glance

- With an increase in population of 2.4 percent, Iowa ranked 30th among the states in growth from 2010 to 2015.

- Iowa's median household income in 2014 was $53,712, and 12.2 percent of the population lived below the poverty level.

- In 2014, 6.2 percent of Iowans did not have health insurance, compared to 11.7 percent of the total U.S. population.

- Iowa's violent crime rate in 2014 was 273.5 per 100,000 population, compared to the rate of 365.5 for the United States as a whole.

- In 2014, Iowa ranked 41st among the states for its infant mortality rate of 4.81 deaths per 1,000 live births.

Table IA-1. Population by Age, Sex, Race, and Hispanic Origin

(Number, percent, except where noted.)

Sex, age, race, and Hispanic origin	2000	2010	2015[1]	Average annual percent change, 2010–2015
Total Population...	2,926,324	3,046,355	3,123,899	0.2
Percent of total U.S. population	1.0	1.0	1.0	X
Sex				
Male..	1,435,515	1,508,319	1,552,026	0.2
Female	1,490,809	1,538,036	1,571,873	0.2
Age				
Under 5 years...	188,413	202,123	196,781	-0.2
5 to 19 years..	639,570	618,387	623,102	0.1
20 to 64 years..	1,662,128	1,772,957	1,801,139	0.1
65 years and over	436,213	452,888	502,877	0.8
Median age (years)	36.6	38.1	38.1	-
Race and Hispanic Origin				
One race				
White	2,748,640	2,839,615	2,866,320	0.1
Black	61,853	91,695	110,050	1.3
American Indian and Alaska Native	8,989	13,563	15,662	1.0
Asian...	36,635	54,232	73,564	2.2
Native Hawaiian or Other Pacific Islander	1,009	2,419	3,209	2.0
Two or more races..	31,778	44,831	55,094	1.5
Hispanic (of any race)...	82,473	156,932	178,620	0.9

X = Not applicable.
- = Zero or rounds to zero.
[1]Population figures for 2015 are July 1 estimates. The 2010 estimates are taken from the 2010 Census.

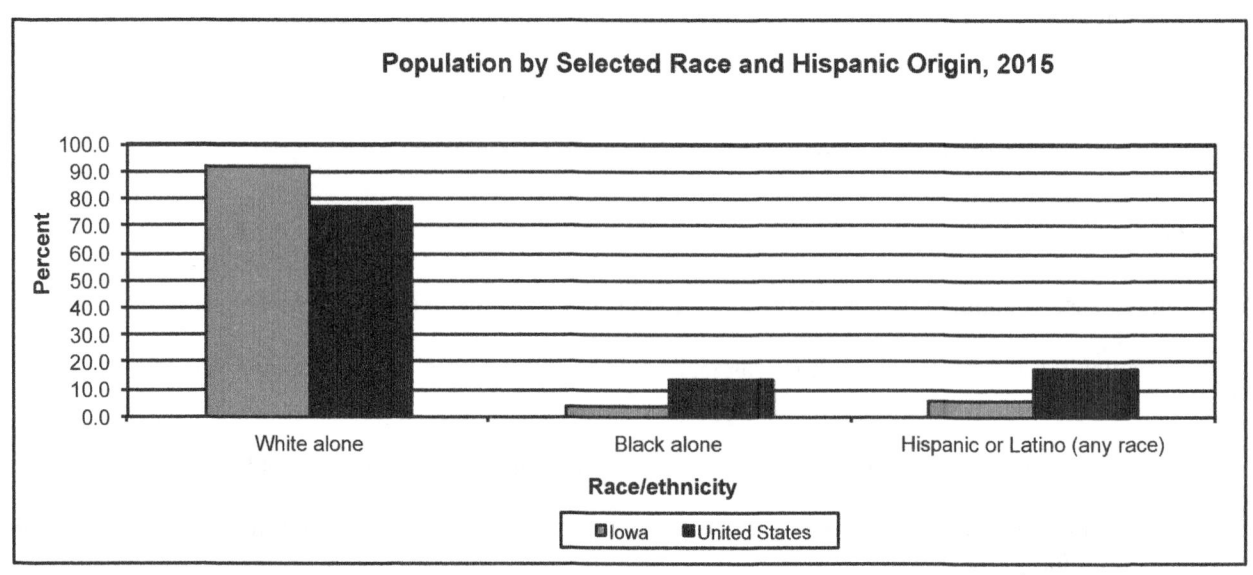

Table IA-2. Marital Status

(Number, percent distribution.)

Sex, age, race, and Hispanic origin	2000	2010	2014
Males, 15 Years and Over	1,126,566	1,199,509	1,217,529
Never married	28.2	31.3	31.9
Now married, except separated...	59.8	55.2	54.4
Separated...	0.9	1.1	1.1
Widowed..	2.5	2.6	2.6
Divorced..	8.5	9.7	10.0
Females, 15 Years and Over	1,198,297	1,250,612	1,257,647
Never married	21.8	24.7	25.2
Now married, except separated...	55.8	52.4	52.1
Separated...	1.1	1.5	1.5
Widowed..	11.6	10.2	9.9
Divorced..	9.6	11.2	11.3

Table IA-3. Households and Housing Characteristics

(Number, percent, dollars.)

Item	2000	2010	2014	Average annual percent change, 2000–2014
Total Households..	1,149,276	1,223,439	1,241,471	0.6
Family households	769,684	793,768	801,562	0.3
Married-couple family	633,254	633,602	636,747	-
Other family	136,430	160,166	164,815	1.5
Male householder, no wife present...............	38,160	46,829	54,441	3.0
Female householder, no husband present	98,270	113,337	110,374	0.9
Nonfamily households..	379,592	429,671	439,909	1.1
Householder living alone..................................	313,083	349,736	356,774	1.0
Householder not living alone...........................	66,509	79,935	83,135	1.8
Housing Characteristics				
Total housing units..	1,232,511	1,337,563	1,362,034	0.8
Occupied housing units	1,149,276	1,223,439	1,241,471	0.6
Owner occupied	831,419	885,284	879,878	0.4
Renter occupied	317,857	338,155	361,593	1.0
Average household size...	2.46	2.41	2.42	-0.1
Financial Characteristics				
Median gross rent of renter-occupied housing	470	629	711	3.7
Median monthly owner costs for housing units with a mortgage	829	1,140	1,173	3.0
Median value of owner-occupied housing units.............................	82,500	123,400	133,100	4.4

- = Zero or rounds to zero.

Table IA-4. Migration, Origin, and Language

(Number, percent.)

Characteristic	State			U.S.		
	2013	2014	Percent change	2013	2014	Percent change
Residence 1 Year Ago						
Population 1 year and over	3,053,635	3,067,872	0.5	312,432,820	315,095,393	0.9
Same house	84.7	84.6	X	85.0	85.1	X
Different house in the U.S.	14.9	15	X	14.4	14.3	X
Same county	8.8	8.7	X	8.9	8.7	X
Different county	6.1	6.2	X	5.5	5.6	X
Same state	3.7	3.7	X	3.2	3.3	X
Different state	2.5	2.6	X	2.3	2.3	X
Abroad	0.4	0.5	X	0.6	0.6	X
Place of Birth						
Native born	2,941,294	2,953,805	0.4	274,780,773	276,465,262	0.6
Male	49.4	49.6	X	49.3	49.3	X
Female	50.6	50.4	X	50.7	50.7	X
Foreign born	149,122	153,321	2.8	41,348,066	42,391,794	2.5
Male	50.8	52.5	X	48.8	48.7	X
Female	49.2	47.5	X	51.2	51.3	X
Foreign born; naturalized U.S. citizen...........................	55,195	54,750	-0.8	19,294,710	19,984,738	3.6
Male	48.9	48.3	X	45.9	45.9	X
Female	51.1	51.7	X	54.1	54.1	X
Foreign born; not a U.S. citizen...................................	93,927	98,571	4.9	22,053,356	22,407,056	1.6
Male	51.9	54.9	X	51.3	51.2	X
Female	48.1	45.1	X	48.7	48.8	X
Entered 2010 or later	17.6	26.7	X	9.7	12.3	X
Entered 2000 to 2009	36.1	27.4	X	29.4	28.6	X
Entered before 2000..	46.2	45.9	X	61.0	59.1	X
World Region of Birth, Foreign						
Foreign-born population, excluding population born at sea	149,122	153,321	2.8	41,347,945	42,390,705	2.5
Europe	15.5	12.8	X	11.6	11.2	X
Asia..	35.0	38.4	X	29.5	30.1	X
Africa..	8.0	9.1	X	4.4	4.6	X
Oceania	0.3	1.0	X	0.5	0.6	X
Latin America..	38.4	37	X	51.9	51.6	X
North America...	2.7	1.6	X	2.0	1.9	X
Language Spoken at Home and Ability to Speak English						
Population 5 years and over..	2,897,339	2,913,555	0.6	296,358,760	299,084,046	0.9
English only	92.8	92.8	X	79.2	78.9	X
Language other than English..	7.2	7.2	X	20.8	21.1	X
Speaks English less than "very well"........................	3.1	3.0	X	8.5	8.6	X

X = Not applicable.
- = Zero or rounds to zero.

Table IA-5. Median Income and Poverty Status, 2014

(Number, percent, except as noted.)

Characteristic	State		U.S.	
	Number	Percent	Number	Percent
Median Income				
Households (dollars)...	53,712	X	53,657	X
Families (dollars)	67,771	X	65,910	X
Below Poverty Level (All People)	367,816	12.2	48,208,387	15.5
Sex				
Male...	163,465	10.9	21,590,918	14.2
Female	204,351	13.5	26,617,469	16.8
Age				
Under 18 years..	108,888	15.3	15,686,012	21.7
Related children under 18 years...........................	105,497	14.9	15,372,705	21.3
18 to 64 years...	224,483	12.3	28,267,482	14.6
65 years and over	34,445	7.4	4,254,893	9.5

X = Not applicable.

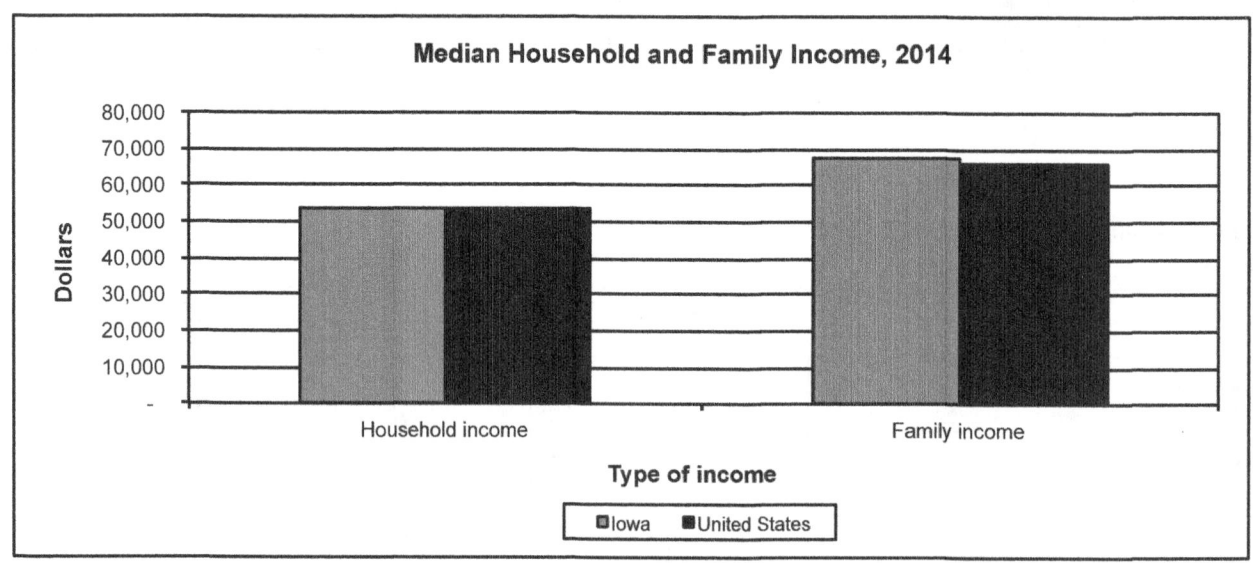

Table IA-6. Health Insurance Coverage Status for the Civilian Noninstitutionalized Population and Children Under 18 Years of Age

(Numbers in thousands, percent.)

Item	2006	2007	2008	2009	2010	2011	2012	2013	2014
Civilian Noninstitutionalized Population	2,919	2,970	2,951	2,957	3,005	3,017	3,029	3,045	3,063
Covered by Private or Public Insurance									
Number...	2,612	2,695	2,683	2,702	2,725	2,748	2,775	2,798	2,874
Percent...	89.5	90.7	90.9	91.4	90.7	91.1	91.6	91.9	93.8
Not Covered									
Number...	307	275	268	255	280	269	254	248	189
Percent...	10.5	9.3	9.1	8.6	9.3	8.9	8.4	8.1	6.2
Percent in the U.S. not covered..................................	15.8	15.3	15.1	15.1	15.5	15.1	14.8	14.5	11.7
Children Under 18 Years of Age	708	709	708	707	722	722	720	721	723
Covered by Private or Public Insurance									
Number...	664	675	668	675	693	690	691	692	700
Percent...	93.7	95.2	94.4	95.4	96.0	95.6	96.0	95.9	96.8
Not Covered									
Number...	44	34	40	32	29	32	29	30	23
Percent...	6.3	4.8	5.6	4.6	4.0	4.4	4.0	4.1	3.2
Percent in the U.S. not covered..................................	11.7	11.0	9.7	8.6	8.0	7.5	7.2	7.1	6.0

Table IA-7. Employment Status by Demographic Group, 2015

(Numbers in thousands, percent.)

Characteristic	Civilian noninstitutional population	Civilian labor force		Employed		Unemployed	
		Number	Percent of population	Number	Percent of population	Number	Percent of population
Total...	2,439	1,700	69.7	1,639	67.2	61	3.6
Sex							
Male...	1,202	888	73.8	855	71.1	33	3.7
Female...	1,237	812	65.7	785	63.5	28	3.4
Race, Sex, and Hispanic Origin							
White...	2,263	1,575	69.6	1,525	67.4	50	3.2
Male...	1,118	825	73.8	798	71.4	27	3.3
Female...	1,145	750	65.5	727	63.5	23	3.1
Black or African American................	72	47	64.9	40	55.4	7	14.8
Male...	38	24	62.4	20	53.8	3	13.6
Female...	34	23	67.7	19	56.9	4	15.9
Hispanic or Latino ethnicity[1]...........	102	81	78.7	77	75.2	4	4.5
Male...	52	42	80.7	40	76.5	2	5.2
Female...	50	38	76.6	37	73.7	1	3.8
Age							
16 to 19 years.................................	153	86	56.3	77	50.6	9	10.1
20 to 24 years.................................	212	170	80.3	157	74.1	13	7.6
25 to 34 years.................................	445	401	90.1	385	86.6	16	3.9
35 to 44 years.................................	337	304	90.1	296	87.7	8	2.7
45 to 54 years.................................	390	346	88.7	340	87.1	7	1.9
55 to 64 years.................................	422	304	72.0	296	70.2	8	2.5
65 years and over............................	480	89	18.6	88	18.4	1	1.3

NOTE: Data in Table 7 are from the Current Population Survey (CPS) and do not match the estimates in Table 8. See notes and definitions for further information.
[1]May be of any race.

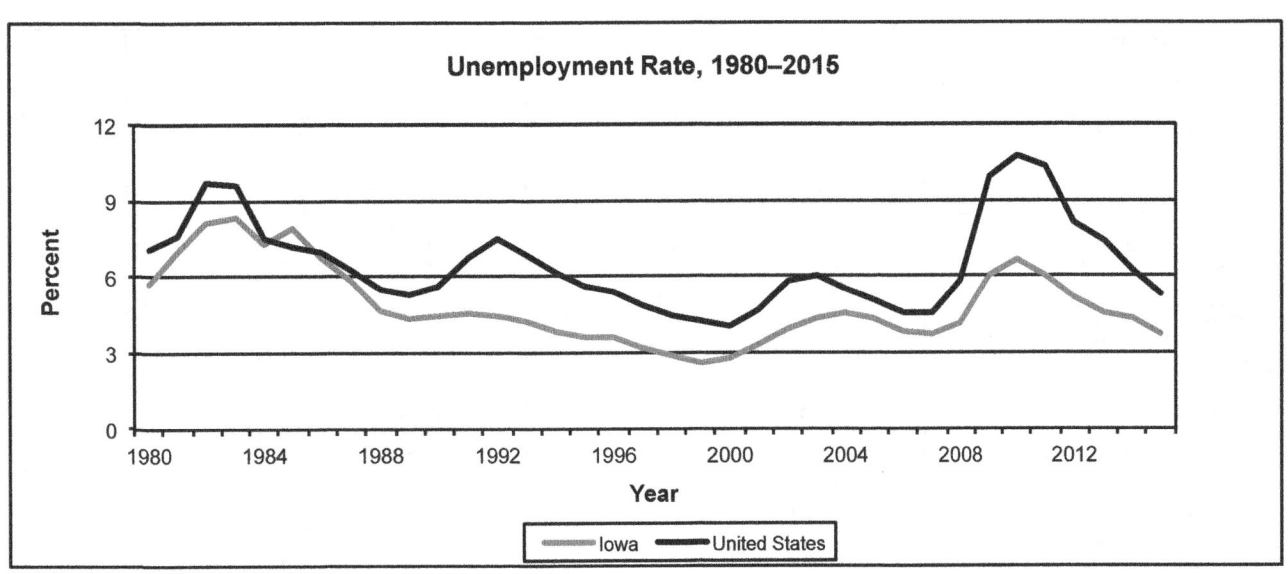

Unemployment Rate, 1980–2015

Table IA-8. Employment Status of the Civilian Noninstitutional Population Age 16 Years and Over

(Number, percent.)

Year	Civilian labor force	Civilian participation rate	Employed	Unemployed	Unemployment rate
2007..	1,660,677	72.0	1,599,332	61,345	3.7
2008..	1,679,293	72.4	1,608,695	70,598	4.2
2009..	1,687,411	72.3	1,579,248	108,163	6.4
2010..	1,678,281	71.2	1,577,447	100,834	6.0
2011..	1,662,376	70.0	1,570,177	92,199	5.5
2012..	1,649,169	69.0	1,565,874	83,295	5.1
2013..	1,672,399	69.5	1,593,027	79,372	4.7
2014..	1,697,712	70.1	1,626,270	71,442	4.2
2015..	1,701,329	69.9	1,638,868	62,461	3.7

Table IA-9. Employment and Average Wages by Industry

(Estimates through 2010 are based on the 2007 North American Industry Classification System [NAICS]. Estimates from 2011 onward are based on the 2012 NAICS.)

Industry	2008	2009	2010	2011	2012	2013	2014
	Number of jobs						
Wage and Salary Employment by Industry..................	1,590,045	1,546,421	1,541,196	1,556,200	1,574,044	1,595,727	1,609,473
Farm Wage and Salary Employment.........................	18,140	16,360	18,966	18,011	15,276	19,266	14,815
Nonfarm Wage and Salary Employment.....................	1,571,905	1,530,061	1,522,230	1,538,189	1,558,768	1,576,461	1,594,658
Private wage and salary employment............................	1,305,760	1,260,011	1,253,690	1,270,493	1,289,105	1,308,804	1,327,181
Forestry, fishing, and related activities.............................	5,606	5,754	6,550	6,776	7,115	8,331	7,673
Mining...	2,148	2,181	2,132	2,175	2,199	2,228	2,180
Utilities...	7,103	7,007	6,785	6,605	6,499	6,451	6,483
Construction	75,946	67,998	64,513	65,729	66,772	70,333	76,604
Manufacturing...	227,885	203,661	201,315	206,393	211,078	214,829	217,263
Durable goods manufacturing...............................	139,276	117,787	116,664	122,271	126,667	129,046	130,975
Nondurable goods manufacturing............................	88,609	85,874	84,651	84,122	84,411	85,783	86,288
Wholesale trade	69,641	67,350	66,581	67,390	68,961	69,638	69,363
Retail trade...	180,283	177,577	175,618	176,933	177,470	179,632	180,422
Transportation and warehousing..............................	57,393	55,432	55,371	56,908	57,595	57,651	58,217
Information..	31,944	30,269	28,786	28,192	27,047	26,164	25,711
Finance and insurance	92,084	91,221	92,004	92,320	92,991	94,108	94,496
Real estate and rental and leasing.............................	14,278	14,489	14,089	13,531	13,372	13,854	14,311
Professional, scientific, and technical services	43,946	42,881	43,288	43,841	45,101	47,081	48,698
Management of companies and enterprises.................	12,934	13,152	13,208	14,902	16,083	16,532	18,177
Administrative and waste services	67,482	62,500	66,552	68,103	69,826	69,673	70,550
Educational services	36,887	37,938	38,091	38,752	40,686	40,568	40,716
Health care and social assistance.............................	173,569	177,162	179,031	180,609	182,955	185,911	187,924
Arts, entertainment, and recreation...........................	20,988	20,764	19,931	20,701	19,776	18,788	18,829
Accommodation and food services............................	115,983	113,441	111,486	112,472	115,113	118,585	119,822
Other services, except public administration.................	69,660	69,234	68,359	68,161	68,466	68,447	69,742
Government and government enterprises.........................	266,145	270,050	268,540	267,696	269,663	267,657	267,477
	Dollars						
Average Wages and Salaries by Industry	36,259	36,413	37,323	38,386	39,468	40,213	41,750
Average Farm Wages and Salaries	30,211	33,470	29,462	30,892	38,063	33,629	50,307
Average Nonfarm Wages and Salaries	36,328	36,445	37,421	38,473	39,482	40,293	41,671
Average private wages and salaries............................	36,106	36,023	37,179	38,333	39,463	40,210	41,666
Forestry, fishing, and related activities.......................	24,169	24,953	25,161	26,320	27,769	27,158	29,610
Mining...	44,226	42,644	43,546	45,485	45,558	46,906	51,523
Utilities...	75,231	75,802	76,433	80,037	82,985	80,974	86,374
Construction	44,009	43,507	43,749	45,122	47,068	48,502	51,936
Manufacturing...	47,181	47,287	49,765	51,117	52,103	52,885	54,397
Durable goods manufacturing...............................	49,249	49,696	52,516	54,519	55,169	55,972	57,391
Nondurable goods manufacturing............................	43,930	43,982	45,972	46,171	47,503	48,241	49,852
Wholesale trade	49,557	49,730	51,514	53,943	55,839	57,041	58,754
Retail trade...	22,018	22,307	22,646	23,212	23,785	23,975	24,690
Transportation and warehousing..............................	39,718	39,061	40,388	41,255	41,973	42,960	44,585
Information..	43,267	43,600	45,192	46,745	47,014	48,938	50,746
Finance and insurance	56,584	55,622	59,010	61,219	63,398	65,911	68,256
Real estate and rental and leasing.............................	33,576	36,264	37,415	39,330	41,057	41,065	42,798
Professional, scientific, and technical services	49,175	50,327	51,550	53,774	57,569	58,845	60,372
Management of companies and enterprises.................	71,217	69,756	70,069	71,396	76,921	75,678	77,951
Administrative and waste services	25,038	25,716	26,379	26,248	27,244	27,733	28,554
Educational services	23,429	23,553	24,048	24,540	24,016	24,623	24,623
Health care and social assistance.............................	35,418	35,900	36,388	37,364	38,134	38,407	39,401
Arts, entertainment, and recreation...........................	20,534	20,120	20,702	20,698	20,222	18,773	19,633
Accommodation and food services............................	13,533	13,444	13,875	14,426	15,061	15,336	16,029
Other services, except public administration.................	24,852	25,407	26,192	26,827	27,255	28,183	29,250
Government and government enterprises.........................	37,418	38,409	38,553	39,141	39,572	40,701	41,696

Table IA-10. Employment Characteristics by Family Type

(Number, percent.)

Family type and labor force status	2012 Total	2012 Families with own children under 18 years	2013 Total	2013 Families with own children under 18 years	2014 Total	2014 Families with own children under 18 years
All Families..	796,744	347,214	793,749	345,493	796,909	348,223
FAMILY TYPE AND LABOR FORCE STATUS						
Married-Couple Families...........................	625,952	239,520	625,107	238,739	632,094	245,038
Both husband and wife in labor force.............	59.5	77.5	59.2	78.5	59.6	78.2
Husband in labor force, wife not in labor force	16.2	18.5	16.1	17.5	16.6	17.9
Wife in labor force, husband not in labor force	7.4	3.2	7.3	2.9	7.2	2.8
Both husband and wife not in labor force................	16.8	0.8	16.9	0.9	16.6	1.2
Other Families	170,792	107,694	168,642	106,754	164,815	103,185
Female householder, no husband present............	70.9	71.8	68.6	70.3	67.0	67.5
In labor force.............................	54.3	62.1	51.5	60.4	51.4	58.6
Not in labor force.........................	16.6	9.7	17.1	9.8	15.6	8.9
Male householder, no wife present.................	29.1	28.2	31.4	29.7	33.0	32.5
In labor force................................	24.1	25.4	25.7	26.2	27.1	30.2
Not in labor force	5.1	2.7	5.7	3.5	5.9	2.3

Table IA-11. School Enrollment and Educational Attainment, 2014

(Number, percent.)

Item	State	U.S.
Enrollment		
Total population 3 years and over, enrolled in school..........................	804,095	82,063,714
Enrolled in nursery school or preschool (percent)	7.0	6.0
Enrolled in kindergarten (percent)................................	5.5	5.1
Enrolled in elementary school, grades 1-8 (percent).................	40.0	40.2
Enrolled in high school, grades 9-12 (percent)	19.9	20.7
Enrolled in college or graduate school (percent)........................	27.5	28.0
Attainment		
Total population 25 years and over	2,062,734	213,725,624
Less than ninth grade (percent)	3.1	5.6
9th to 12th grade, no diploma (percent)	4.8	7.5
High school graduate, including equivalency (percent)..............	31.7	27.7
Some college, no degree (percent).............................	21.4	21.0
Associate's degree (percent)	11.3	8.2
Bachelor's degree (percent)	18.6	18.7
Graduate or professional degree (percent)..........................	9.0	11.4
High school graduate or higher (percent)	92.1	86.9
Bachelor's degree or higher (percent).............................	27.7	30.1

Table IA-12. Public School Characteristics and Educational Indicators

(Number, percent; data derived from National Center of Education Statistics.)

Item	State	U.S.
Public Schools, 2013–2014 (except where noted)		
Number of school districts.........................	355	18,194
Number of schools.............................	1,382	98,271
Number of students (in thousands)	503	50,045
Number of teachers (in thousands)	35	3,114
Student-teacher ratio	14.2	16.1
Expenditures per student (dollars), FY 2013	10,291	107,637
Four-year adjusted cohort graduation rate (ACGR)[1,2]	90.5	82.3
Students eligible for free or reduced-price lunch (in thousands)	202	25,596
English language learners (in thousands)	23	4,461
Students age 3 to 21 served under IDEA, part B (in thousands)	65	6,464

Public Schools by Type	Number	Percent of state public schools
Total number of schools..........................	1,382	100.0
Regular	1,349	97.6
Special education	7	0.5
Vocational education	0	0.0
Alternative education..............................	26	1.9

NOTE: Every school is assigned only one school type based on its instructional emphasis.
[1]ACGR data represents a new method of calculating high-school completion rates and may not be comparable to previous years' data for Averaged Freshmen Graduation Rates (AFGR).
[2]The United States 4-year ACGRs were estimated using both the reported 4-year ACGR data from 49 states and the District of Columbia and using imputed data for Idaho. The estimate for American Indian/Alaska Native students also includes imputed data for Virginia.

Table IA-13. Reported Voting and Registration of the Voting-Age Population, November 2014

(Numbers in thousands, percent.)

Item	Total population	Total citizen population	Registered			Voted		
			Total registered	Percent registered (total population)	Percent registered (total citizen population)	Total voted	Percent voted (total population)	Percent voted (total citizen population)
U.S. Total	239,874	219,941	142,166	59.3	64.6	92,251	38.5	41.9
State Total.............................	2,336	2,275	1,584	67.8	69.6	1,203	51.5	52.9
Sex								
Male...........................	1,154	1,120	755	65.4	67.4	569	49.3	50.8
Female	1,182	1,155	829	70.2	71.8	634	53.7	54.9
Race								
White alone....................	2,171	2,146	1,515	69.8	70.6	1,154	53.1	53.7
White, non-Hispanic alone	2,099	2,096	1,496	71.3	71.4	1,143	54.5	54.5
Black alone...................	69	61	31	(B)	(B)	20	(B)	(B)
Asian alone	54	33	17	(B)	(B)	12	(B)	(B)
Hispanic (of any race)......................	81	52	21	(B)	(B)	11	(B)	(B)
White alone or in combination	2,197	2,169	1,532	69.7	70.6	1,167	53.1	53.8
Black alone or in combination..........	84	75	38	45.0	50.1	22	26.9	29.9
Asian alone or in combination..........	60	39	21	(B)	(B)	16	(B)	(B)
Age								
18 to 24 years.....................	256	250	110	43.0	44.0	51	19.7	20.2
25 to 34 years.....................	445	414	247	55.6	59.7	141	31.6	33.9
35 to 44 years.....................	344	329	238	69.1	72.2	179	52.1	54.5
45 to 64 years.....................	819	810	598	73.0	73.8	488	59.5	60.2
65 years and over	471	471	390	82.9	82.9	345	73.3	73.3

B = Base is less than 75,000 and therefore too small to show the derived measure.

Table IA-14. Crime

(Number, rate per 100,000. Data are derived from the FBI Uniform Crime Reports.)

Item	State			U.S.[1,2,3,4]		
	2013	2014	Percent change	2013	2014	Percent change
TOTAL POPULATION[5]......................................	3,090,416	3,107,126	0.5	316,128,839	318,857,056	0.9
VIOLENT CRIME						
Number....................................	8,062	8,497	5.4	1,163,146	1,165,383	0.2
Rate	260.9	273.5	4.8	367.9	365.5	-0.7
Murder and Nonnegligent Manslaughter						
Number....................................	43	60	39.5	14,196	14,249	0.4
Rate	1.4	1.9	35.7	4.5	4.5	-
Rape[6]						
Number....................................	1,083	1,128	X	108,612	116,645	X
Rate	35.0	36.3	X	34.4	36.6	X
Robbery						
Number....................................	939	1,045	11.3	345,031	325,802	-5.6
Rate	30.4	33.6	10.5	109.1	102.2	-6.3
Aggravated Assault						
Number....................................	6,323	6,264	-0.9	724,149	741,291	2.4
Rate	204.6	201.6	-1.5	229.1	232.5	1.5
PROPERTY CRIME						
Number....................................	67,800	65,056	-4.0	8,632,512	8,277,829	-4.1
Rate	2,193.9	2,093.8	-4.6	2,730.7	2,596.1	-4.9
Burglary						
Number....................................	15,868	14,428	-9.1	1,928,465	1,729,806	-10.3
Rate	513.5	464.4	-9.6	610.0	542.5	-11.1
Larceny-Theft						
Number....................................	47,686	46,477	-2.5	6,004,453	5,858,496	-2.4
Rate	1,543.0	1,495.8	-3.1	1,899.4	1,837.3	-3.3
Motor Vehicle Theft						
Number....................................	4,246	4,151	-2.2	699,594	689,527	-1.4
Rate	137.4	133.6	-2.8	221.3	216.2	-2.3

NOTE: Although arson data are included in the trend and clearance tables, sufficient data are not available to estimate totals for this offense. Therefore, no arson data are published in this table.
- = Zero or rounds to zero.
X = Not applicable.
[1]The crime figures have been adjusted.
[2]The data collection methodology for the offense of forcible rape used by the Minnesota state Uniform Crime Reporting (UCR) Program (with the exception of Minneapolis and St. Paul, Minnesota) does not comply with national UCR Program guidelines. Consequently, its figures for forcible rape and violent crime (of which forcible rape is a part) are not published in this table.
[3]Includes offenses reported by the Zoological Police and the Metro Transit Police.
[4]Because of changes in the state's reporting practices, figures are not comparable to previous years' data.
[5]Populations are U.S. Census Bureau provisional estimates as of July 1 of each year.
[6]The figures shown for the offense of rape were estimated using the revised Uniform Crime Reporting (UCR) definition of rape.

Table IA-15. State Government Finances, 2014

(Dollar amounts in thousands, percent distribution.)

Item	Dollars	Percent distribution
Total Revenue	25,196,625	100.0
General revenue	18,889,101	75.0
Intergovernmental revenue	6,218,631	24.7
Taxes	8,271,839	32.8
General sales	2,659,231	10.6
Selective sales	1,112,707	4.4
License taxes	808,047	3.2
Individual income tax	3,197,578	12.7
Corporate income tax	388,699	1.5
Other taxes	105,577	0.4
Current charges	3,096,274	12.3
Miscellaneous general revenue	1,302,357	5.2
Utility revenue	0	-
Liquor stores revenue	265,900	1.1
Insurance trust revenue[1]	6,041,624	24.0
Total Expenditure	21,214,460	100.0
Intergovernmental expenditure	4,963,899	23.4
Direct expenditure	16,250,561	76.6
Current operation	11,405,834	53.8
Capital outlay	1,602,042	7.6
Insurance benefits and repayments	2,434,288	11.5
Assistance and subsidies	573,661	2.7
Interest on debt	234,736	1.1
Exhibit: Salaries and wages	2,736,971	12.9
Total Expenditure	21,214,460	100.0
General expenditure	18,597,927	87.7
Intergovernmental expenditure	4,963,899	23.4
Direct expenditure	13,634,028	64.3
General expenditure, by function:		
Education	6,729,017	31.7
Public welfare	5,538,117	26.1
Hospitals	1,584,419	7.5
Health	257,591	1.2
Highways	1,807,014	8.5
Police protection	95,383	0.4
Correction	291,549	1.4
Natural resources	301,160	1.4
Parks and recreation	31,391	0.1
Governmental administration	573,662	2.7
Interest on general debt	234,736	1.1
Other and unallocable	1,153,888	5.4
Utility expenditure	0	-
Liquor stores expenditure	182,245	-
Insurance trust expenditure	2,434,288	11.5
Debt at End of Fiscal Year	6,343,482	X
Cash and Security Holdings	43,410,552	X

X = Not applicable.
- = Zero or rounds to zero.
[1]Within insurance trust revenue, net earnings of state retirement systems is a calculated statistic (the item code in the data file is X08), and thus can be positive or negative. Net earnings is the sum of earnings on investments plus gains on investments minus losses on investments. The change made in 2002 for asset valuation from book to market value in accordance with Statement 34 of the Governmental Accounting Standards Board is reflected in the calculated statistics.

Table IA-16. State Government Tax Collections, 2014

(Dollars in thousands, percent.)

Item	Dollars	Percent distribution
Total Taxes	8,271,839	100.0
Property taxes	X	X
Sales and gross receipts	3,771,938	45.6
General sales and gross receipts	2,659,231	32.1
Selective sales and gross receipts	1,112,707	13.5
Alcoholic beverages	14,187	0.2
Amusements	282,713	3.4
Insurance premiums	105,532	1.3
Motor fuels	452,596	5.5
Pari-mutuels	3,962	-
Public utilities	0	-
Tobacco products	225,375	2.7
Other selective sales	28,342	0.3
Licenses	808,047	9.8
Alcoholic beverages	14,879	0.2
Amusements	22,703	0.3
Corporations in general	35,438	0.4
Hunting and fishing	28,262	0.3
Motor vehicle	548,670	6.6
Motor vehicle operators	21,867	0.3
Public utilities	17,590	0.2
Occupation and business, NEC	115,632	1.4
Other licenses	3,006	-
Income taxes	3,586,277	43.4
Individual income	3,197,578	38.7
Corporation net income	388,699	4.7
Other taxes	105,577	1.3
Death and gift	90,791	1.1
Documentary and stock transfer	14,786	0.2
Severance	X	X
Taxes, NEC	0	-

X = Not applicable.
- = Zero or rounds to zero.

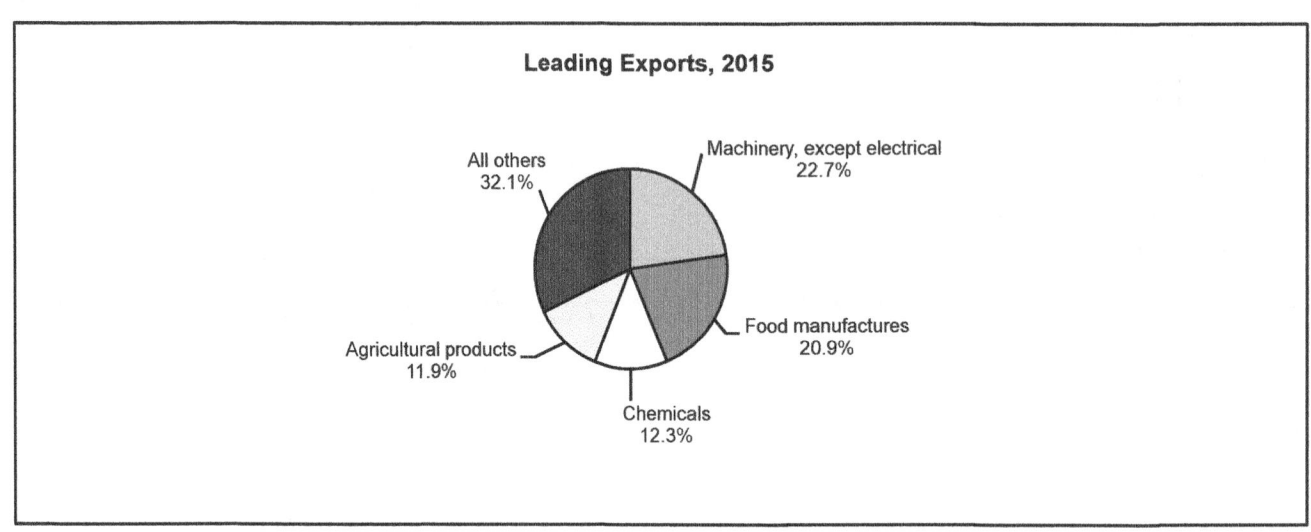

Leading Exports, 2015

All others 32.1%

Machinery, except electrical 22.7%

Agricultural products 11.9%

Chemicals 12.3%

Food manufactures 20.9%

Facts and Figures

Location: Central United States; bordered on the N by Nebraska, on the E by Missouri, on the S by Oklahoma, and on the W by Colorado

Area: 82,277 sq. mi. (213,096 sq. km.); rank—15th

Population: 2,911,641 (2015 est.); rank—34th

Principal Cities: capital—Topeka; largest—Wichita

Statehood: January 29, 1861; 34th state

U.S. Congress: 2 senators, 4 representatives

State Motto: *Ad astra per aspera* ("To the stars through difficulties")

State Song: "Home on the Range"

State Nicknames: The Sunflower State; The Jayhawk State

Abbreviations: KS; Kan.; Kans.

State Symbols: flower—wild native sunflower; tree—cottonwood; bird—Western meadowlark

At a Glance

- With an increase in population of 1.8 percent, Kansas ranked 34th among the states in growth from 2010 to 2015.

- In 2014, 10.2 percent of Kansans did not have health insurance, compared to 11.7 percent of the total U.S. population.

- Approximately 24.7 percent of Kansans were under 18 years old in 2015, the 6th highest percentage in the United States.

- Kansas had an unemployment rate of 4.2 percent in 2015, compared to the national rate of 5.3 percent.

- In Kansas, 13.6 percent of the total population and 17.7 percent of children under age 18 lived in poverty in 2014, compared to that national averages of 15.5 percent and 21.7 percent respectively.

Table KS-1. Population by Age, Sex, Race, and Hispanic Origin

(Number, percent, except where noted.)

Sex, age, race, and Hispanic origin	2000	2010	2015[1]	Average annual percent change, 2010–2015
Total Population..	2,688,418	2,853,118	2,911,641	0.1
Percent of total U.S. population	1.0	0.9	0.9	X
Sex				
Male..	1,328,474	1,415,408	1,453,633	0.2
Female...	1,359,944	1,437,710	1,458,008	0.1
Age				
Under 5 years...	188,708	205,492	197,480	-0.3
5 to 19 years..	609,710	605,152	603,130	-
20 to 64 years..	1,533,771	1,666,358	1,684,621	0.1
65 years and over..	356,229	376,116	426,410	0.9
Median age (years)	35.2	36.0	36.1	-
Race and Hispanic Origin				
One race				
White...	2,313,944	2,501,057	2,523,011	0.1
Black...	154,198	173,298	182,881	0.4
American Indian and Alaska Native	24,936	33,044	34,810	0.4
Asian...	46,806	69,628	84,577	1.4
Native Hawaiian or Other Pacific Islander	1,313	2,864	3,300	1.0
Two or more races..	56,496	73,227	83,062	0.9
Hispanic (of any race)...	188,252	311,460	336,594	0.6

X = Not applicable.
- = Zero or rounds to zero.
[1]Population figures for 2015 are July 1 estimates. The 2010 estimates are taken from the 2010 Census.

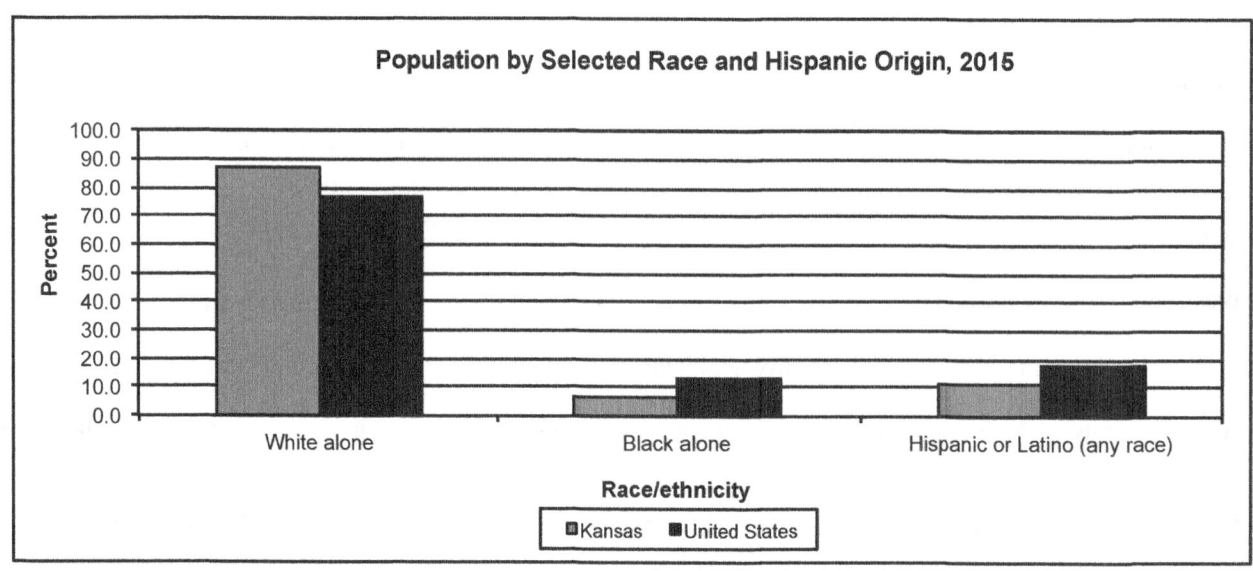

Table KS-2. Marital Status

(Number, percent distribution.)

Sex, age, race, and Hispanic origin	2000	2010	2014
Males, 15 Years and Over	1,025,114	1,106,102	1,123,431
Never married	27.4	31.6	31.7
Now married, except separated.................................	59.9	53.9	53.9
Separated...	1.1	1.4	1.2
Widowed...	2.3	2.6	2.7
Divorced...	9.2	10.5	10.4
Females, 15 Years and Over	1,075,542	1,145,453	1,152,985
Never married	20.8	25.1	25.2
Now married, except separated.................................	56.4	51.4	51.5
Separated...	1.3	1.7	1.6
Widowed...	10.6	9.2	9.1
Divorced...	10.9	12.6	12.6

Table KS-3. Households and Housing Characteristics

(Number, percent, dollars.)

Item	2000	2010	2014	Average annual percent change, 2000–2014
Total Households	1,037,891	1,101,658	1,109,280	0.5
Family households	701,547	721,592	728,602	0.3
Married-couple family	567,924	559,199	564,871	-
Other family	133,623	162,393	163,731	1.6
Male householder, no wife present	36,962	46,692	51,140	2.7
Female householder, no husband present	96,661	115,701	112,591	1.2
Nonfamily households	336,344	380,066	380,678	0.9
Householder living alone	280,387	313,390	320,616	1.0
Householder not living alone	55,957	66,676	60,062	0.5
Housing Characteristics				
Total housing units	1,131,200	1,234,037	1,248,861	0.7
Occupied housing units	1,037,891	1,101,658	1,109,280	0.5
Owner occupied	718,703	749,907	739,168	0.2
Renter occupied	319,188	351,751	370,112	1.1
Average household size	2.51	2.52	2.55	0.1
Financial Characteristics				
Median gross rent of renter-occupied housing	498	682	773	3.9
Median monthly owner costs for housing units with a mortgage	888	1,239	1,256	3.0
Median value of owner-occupied housing units	83,500	127,300	132,100	4.2

- = Zero or rounds to zero.

Table KS-4. Migration, Origin, and Language

(Number, percent.)

Characteristic	State			U.S.		
	2013	2014	Percent change	2013	2014	Percent change
Residence 1 Year Ago						
Population 1 year and over	2,854,869	2,866,584	0.4	312,432,820	315,095,393	0.9
Same house	2,386,028	83	X	85.0	85.1	X
Different house in the U.S.	453641.0	16.5	X	14.4	14.3	X
Same county	272,447	9.7	X	8.9	8.7	X
Different county	181194.0	6.8	X	5.5	5.6	X
Same state	91,459	3.5	X	3.2	3.3	X
Different state	89,735	3.4	X	2.3	2.3	X
Abroad	15,200	0.5	X	0.6	0.6	X
Place of Birth						
Native born	2,695,784	2,699,601	0.1	274,780,773	276,465,262	0.6
Male	49.6	49.6	X	49.3	49.3	X
Female	50.4	50.4	X	50.7	50.7	X
Foreign born	198,173	204,420	3.2	41,348,066	42,391,794	2.5
Male	51.6	51.3	X	48.8	48.7	X
Female	48.4	48.7	X	51.2	51.3	X
Foreign born; naturalized U.S. citizen	66,850	77,384	15.8	19,294,710	19,984,738	3.6
Male	49.0	49.1	X	45.9	45.9	X
Female	51.0	50.9	X	54.1	54.1	X
Foreign born; not a U.S. citizen	131,323	127,036	-3.3	22,053,356	22,407,056	1.6
Male	52.9	52.6	X	51.3	51.2	X
Female	47.1	47.4	X	48.7	48.8	X
Entered 2010 or later	14.2	16.1	X	9.7	12.3	X
Entered 2000 to 2009	34.5	33.3	X	29.4	28.6	X
Entered before 2000	51.3	50.6	X	61.0	59.1	X
World Region of Birth, Foreign						
Foreign-born population, excluding population born at sea	198,173	204,420	3.2	41,347,945	42,390,705	2.5
Europe	7.2	7.2	X	11.6	11.2	X
Asia	29.1	29.9	X	29.5	30.1	X
Africa	5.8	6.5	X	4.4	4.6	X
Oceania	0.6	0.7	X	0.5	0.6	X
Latin America	56.0	54.3	X	51.9	51.6	X
North America	1.3	1.4	X	2.0	1.9	X
Language Spoken at Home and Ability to Speak English						
Population 5 years and over	2,694,653	2,704,673	0.4	296,358,760	299,084,046	0.9
English only	89.1	88.7	X	79.2	78.9	X
Language other than English	10.9	11.3	X	20.8	21.1	X
Speaks English less than "very well"	4.3	4.4	X	8.5	8.6	X

X = Not applicable.
- = Zero or rounds to zero.

Table KS-5. Median Income and Poverty Status, 2014

(Number, percent, except as noted.)

Characteristic	State		U.S.	
	Number	Percent	Number	Percent
Median Income				
Households (dollars)..	52,504	X	53,657	X
Families (dollars)	66,425	X	65,910	X
Below Poverty Level (All People)	382,712	13.6	48,208,387	15.5
Sex				
Male..	175,534	12.6	21,590,918	14.2
Female	207,178	14.5	26,617,469	16.8
Age				
Under 18 years..	126,063	17.7	15,686,012	21.7
Related children under 18 years...............................	122,934	17.4	15,372,705	21.3
18 to 64 years..	225,078	13.2	28,267,482	14.6
65 years and over	31,571	7.9	4,254,893	9.5

X = Not applicable.

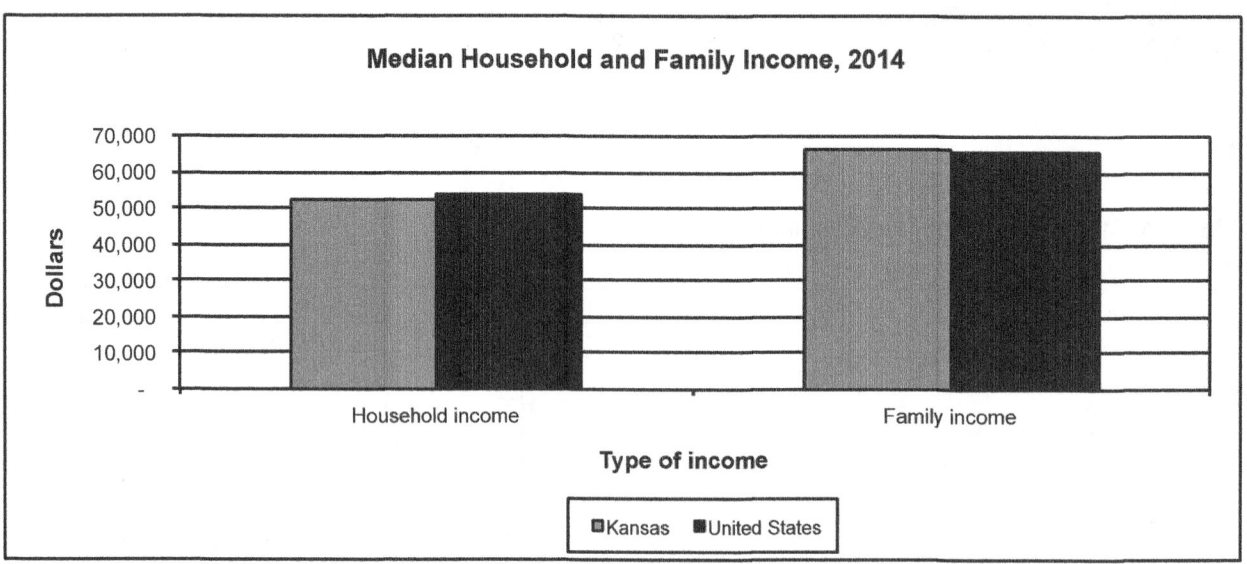

Table KS-6. Health Insurance Coverage Status for the Civilian Noninstitutionalized Population and Children Under 18 Years of Age

(Numbers in thousands, percent.)

Item	2006	2007	2008	2009	2010	2011	2012	2013	2014
Civilian Noninstitutionalized Population	2,723	2,722	2,739	2,757	2,804	2,814	2,825	2,837	2,845
Covered by Private or Public Insurance									
Number..	2,387	2,376	2,405	2,394	2,415	2,459	2,470	2,489	2,554
Percent..	87.7	87.3	87.8	86.8	86.1	87.4	87.4	87.7	89.8
Not Covered									
Number..	335	345	334	363	389	355	355	348	291
Percent..	12.3	12.7	12.2	13.2	13.9	12.6	12.6	12.3	10.2
Percent in the U.S. not covered..	15.8	15.3	15.1	15.1	15.5	15.1	14.8	14.5	11.7
Children Under 18 Years of Age	697	710	698	701	725	721	720	719	721
Covered by Private or Public Insurance									
Number..	646	655	640	643	665	675	672	675	681
Percent..	92.7	92.3	91.7	91.8	91.8	93.6	93.4	93.9	94.5
Not Covered									
Number..	51	54	58	58	60	46	48	44	39
Percent..	7.3	7.7	8.3	8.2	8.2	6.4	6.6	6.1	5.5
Percent in the U.S. not covered..	11.7	11.0	9.7	8.6	8.0	7.5	7.2	7.1	6.0

Table KS-7. Employment Status by Demographic Group, 2015

(Numbers in thousands, percent.)

Characteristic	Civilian noninstitutional population	Civilian labor force		Employed		Unemployed	
		Number	Percent of population	Number	Percent of population	Number	Percent of population
Total..	2,210	1,495	67.6	1,430	64.7	65	4.3
Sex							
Male..	1,080	798	73.9	762	70.6	36	4.5
Female	1,130	696	61.6	668	59.1	29	4.1
Race, Sex, and Hispanic Origin							
White	1,921	1,303	67.8	1,250	65.1	54	4.1
Male......................................	941	705	74.9	675	71.7	30	4.3
Female...................................	980	598	61.0	575	58.6	23	3.9
Black or African American................	133	89	66.9	83	62.5	6	6.6
Male......................................	65	41	63.7	38	58.9	3	7.5
Female...................................	68	47	70.0	45	65.8	3	5.9
Hispanic or Latino ethnicity[1]	219	166	75.8	159	72.3	8	4.5
Male......................................	117	98	84.0	93	79.8	5	5.0
Female...................................	102	68	66.3	65	63.8	3	3.9
Age							
16 to 19 years...............................	151	71	46.9	64	42.1	7	10.2
20 to 24 years...............................	191	148	77.5	139	72.6	9	6.3
25 to 34 years...............................	384	329	85.5	317	82.5	12	3.6
35 to 44 years...............................	348	303	87.3	292	84.1	11	3.6
45 to 54 years...............................	354	299	84.5	286	80.8	13	4.4
55 to 64 years...............................	369	249	67.4	240	65.0	9	3.6
65 years and over	413	96	23.3	93	22.5	3	3.3

NOTE: Data in Table 7 are from the Current Population Survey (CPS) and do not match the estimates in Table 8. See notes and definitions for further information.
[1] May be of any race.

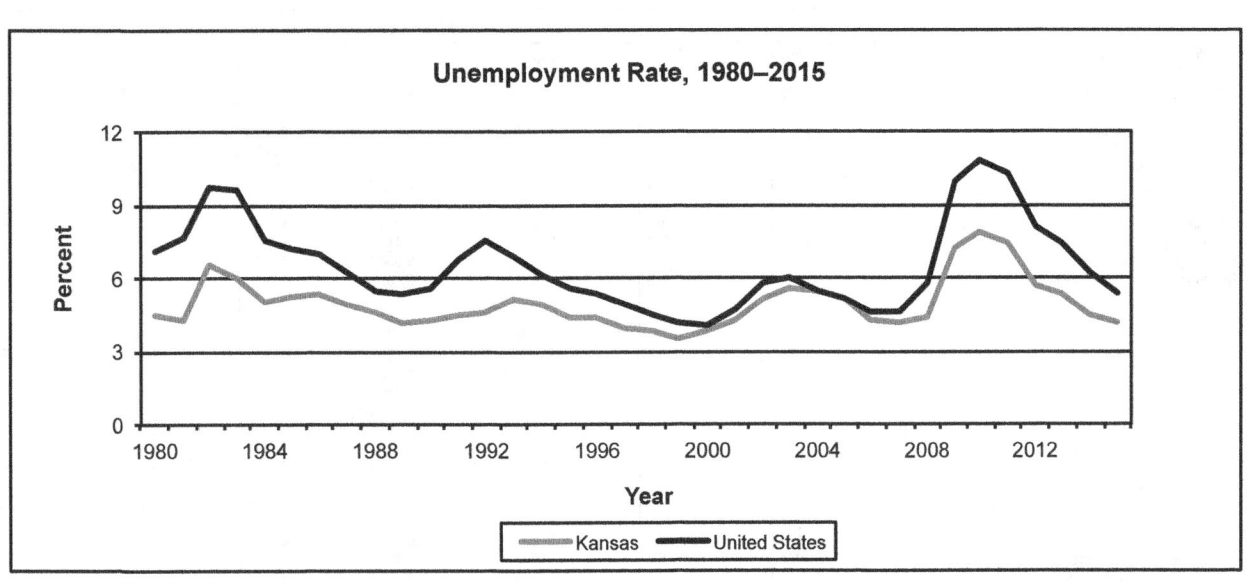

Table KS-8. Employment Status of the Civilian Noninstitutional Population Age 16 Years and Over

(Number, percent.)

Year	Civilian labor force	Civilian participation rate	Employed	Unemployed	Unemployment rate
2007..	1,483,458	70.8	1,420,449	63,009	4.2
2008..	1,499,676	71.0	1,430,628	69,048	4.6
2009..	1,518,207	71.3	1,413,873	104,334	6.9
2010..	1,500,764	69.8	1,394,958	105,806	7.1
2011..	1,491,087	69.0	1,394,082	97,005	6.5
2012..	1,483,574	68.2	1,398,474	85,100	5.7
2013..	1,485,405	68.0	1,406,374	79,031	5.3
2014..	1,494,188	68.0	1,425,970	68,218	4.6
2015..	1,499,009	67.9	1,435,884	63,125	4.2

Table KS-9. Employment and Average Wages by Industry

(Estimates through 2010 are based on the 2007 North American Industry Classification System [NAICS]. Estimates from 2011 onward are based on the 2012 NAICS.)

Industry	2008	2009	2010	2011	2012	2013	2014
	Number of jobs						
Wage and Salary Employment by Industry.................	1,478,020	1,428,586	1,414,533	1,425,056	1,434,672	1,449,149	1,471,776
Farm Wage and Salary Employment........................	9,499	8,833	10,270	11,830	10,207	9,475	11,892
Nonfarm Wage and Salary Employment....................	1,468,521	1,419,753	1,404,263	1,413,226	1,424,465	1,439,674	1,459,884
Private wage and salary employment..........................	1,170,143	1,119,434	1,100,661	1,113,281	1,125,846	1,143,243	1,164,401
Forestry, fishing, and related activities.........................	3,621	3,489	3,646	3,799	3,915	4,514	4,900
Mining......................................	10,010	8,353	8,521	9,047	9,907	10,384	10,401
Utilities..	7,565	7,726	7,808	8,049	7,978	7,750	7,780
Construction....................................	67,786	60,872	56,968	55,810	56,895	59,000	61,676
Manufacturing....................................	187,572	167,633	160,506	161,350	163,067	163,238	162,477
Durable goods manufacturing........................	121,515	104,021	97,481	98,111	100,029	100,607	98,720
Nondurable goods manufacturing......................	66,057	63,612	63,025	63,239	63,038	62,631	63,757
Wholesale trade	63,280	61,439	59,981	59,911	59,265	60,138	61,764
Retail trade...	148,774	144,390	143,075	143,980	144,065	145,703	147,780
Transportation and warehousing.......................	48,206	45,379	44,651	46,482	48,140	48,319	49,538
Information..	38,908	34,741	29,403	27,945	27,847	27,579	27,813
Finance and insurance	59,734	58,356	58,366	60,274	61,033	61,437	62,500
Real estate and rental and leasing....................	15,576	15,078	15,029	15,242	14,127	14,365	14,856
Professional, scientific, and technical services	63,482	61,957	61,452	61,464	63,263	66,893	68,005
Management of companies and enterprises................	13,739	13,452	15,182	13,984	13,636	15,193	18,627
Administrative and waste services......................	75,664	69,727	71,027	75,368	78,067	81,540	84,142
Educational services	18,904	18,879	19,343	19,929	20,082	20,546	20,948
Health care and social assistance......................	161,946	165,136	164,929	168,169	169,857	170,896	172,669
Arts, entertainment, and recreation.....................	13,572	13,403	13,336	14,033	15,660	16,117	16,346
Accommodation and food services......................	103,860	102,165	101,445	102,518	104,878	106,165	107,357
Other services, except public administration..............	67,944	67,259	65,993	66,027	64,164	63,466	64,822
Government and government enterprises.....................	298,378	300,319	303,602	299,945	298,619	296,431	295,483
	Dollars						
Average Wages and Salaries by Industry	39,091	39,046	39,824	40,958	42,215	42,713	43,801
Average Farm Wages and Salaries	50,280	44,140	35,828	39,315	41,878	43,442	44,083
Average Nonfarm Wages and Salaries	39,018	39,014	39,853	40,972	42,218	42,708	43,798
Average private wages and salaries.......................	39,594	39,330	40,320	41,464	43,007	43,549	44,708
Forestry, fishing, and related activities.....................	22,236	23,230	24,442	24,710	25,671	25,431	25,875
Mining..	52,426	49,114	50,987	54,896	57,680	56,495	59,947
Utilities..	75,535	78,281	79,209	87,794	84,981	88,282	89,319
Construction..	44,119	43,977	45,580	45,925	48,251	48,817	50,535
Manufacturing..	49,673	50,051	52,052	53,411	53,840	54,566	55,282
Durable goods manufacturing........................	52,920	53,844	56,405	58,084	58,510	58,674	59,408
Nondurable goods manufacturing......................	43,701	43,849	45,319	46,163	46,430	47,968	48,894
Wholesale trade	56,712	56,822	59,143	59,887	63,410	62,988	65,327
Retail trade...	23,895	23,839	24,134	24,788	25,573	25,651	26,090
Transportation and warehousing.......................	43,448	42,853	43,871	45,997	47,035	48,805	49,333
Information..	65,252	62,395	64,040	64,533	67,241	69,621	73,185
Finance and insurance	56,062	55,670	57,718	61,059	66,263	66,905	69,719
Real estate and rental and leasing....................	33,176	32,981	33,767	35,296	36,280	36,989	38,425
Professional, scientific, and technical services	55,782	56,122	57,269	59,584	62,416	63,636	65,804
Management of companies and enterprises................	85,476	79,859	81,323	87,707	95,254	93,145	94,893
Administrative and waste services......................	32,468	32,645	33,615	35,543	36,862	37,313	36,805
Educational services	26,876	27,528	27,481	28,249	29,003	28,897	29,506
Health care and social assistance......................	37,175	38,033	38,688	39,262	40,738	40,891	41,557
Arts, entertainment, and recreation.....................	17,247	17,222	17,872	18,328	20,431	20,816	20,847
Accommodation and food services......................	14,175	14,277	14,779	15,186	15,588	15,738	16,510
Other services, except public administration..............	26,447	26,097	26,898	27,605	28,467	29,442	30,391
Government and government enterprises.....................	36,759	37,836	38,162	39,147	39,243	39,466	40,212

Table KS-10. Employment Characteristics by Family Type

(Number, percent.)

Family type and labor force status	2012		2013		2014	
	Total	Families with own children under 18 years	Total	Families with own children under 18 years	Total	Families with own children under 18 years
All Families.........................	727,171	332,812	735,596	335,294	726,061	325,507
FAMILY TYPE AND LABOR FORCE STATUS						
Married-Couple Families...........................	563,407	232,015	568,165	236,490	562,330	226,937
Both husband and wife in labor force................	56.6	69.6	56.5	70.1	55.7	69.0
Husband in labor force, wife not in labor force	21.9	26.6	21.2	25.4	21.3	26.5
Wife in labor force, husband not in labor force	6.6	3.0	7.4	3.5	7.2	3.0
Both husband and wife not in labor force................	14.9	0.9	14.6	0.9	15.9	1.4
Other Families	163,764	100,797	167,431	98,804	163,731	98,570
Female householder, no husband present................	69.3	71.1	71.1	72.8	68.8	70.1
In labor force................	52.7	61.1	51.7	60.6	50.4	59.2
Not in labor force	16.6	9.9	19.4	12.2	18.4	10.9
Male householder, no wife present................	30.7	28.9	28.9	27.2	31.2	29.9
In labor force................	25.6	26.6	24.3	25.8	26.5	28.1
Not in labor force	5.1	2.4	4.6	1.5	4.7	1.8

Table KS-11. School Enrollment and Educational Attainment, 2014

(Number, percent.)

Item	State	U.S.
Enrollment		
Total population 3 years and over, enrolled in school................	785,489	82,063,714
Enrolled in nursery school or preschool (percent)	6.4	6.0
Enrolled in kindergarten (percent)................	5.3	5.1
Enrolled in elementary school, grades 1-8 (percent)................	40.7	40.2
Enrolled in high school, grades 9-12 (percent)	20.5	20.7
Enrolled in college or graduate school (percent)................	27.0	28.0
Attainment		
Total population 25 years and over	1,881,521	213,725,624
Less than ninth grade (percent)	3.9	5.6
9th to 12th grade, no diploma (percent)	5.8	7.5
High school graduate, including equivalency (percent)................	26.5	27.7
Some college, no degree (percent)	24.1	21.0
Associate's degree (percent)	8.1	8.2
Bachelor's degree (percent)	20.3	18.7
Graduate or professional degree (percent)................	11.3	11.4
High school graduate or higher (percent)	90.3	86.9
Bachelor's degree or higher (percent)................	31.5	30.1

Table KS-12. Public School Characteristics and Educational Indicators

(Number, percent; data derived from National Center of Education Statistics.)

Item	State	U.S.
Public Schools, 2013–2014 (except where noted)		
Number of school districts................	321	18,194
Number of schools................	1,346	98,271
Number of students (in thousands)	496	50,045
Number of teachers (in thousands)	38	3,114
Student-teacher ratio	13.0	16.1
Expenditures per student (dollars), FY 2013................	10,011	107,637
Four-year adjusted cohort graduation rate (ACGR)[1,2]	85.7	82.3
Students eligible for free or reduced-price lunch (in thousands)	246	25,596
English language learners (in thousands)	46	4,461
Students age 3 to 21 served under IDEA, part B (in thousands)	69	6,464

Public Schools by Type	Number	Percent of state public schools
Total number of schools................	1,346	100.0
Regular	1,333	99.0
Special education	10	0.7
Vocational education................	1	0.1
Alternative education................	2	0.1

NOTE: Every school is assigned only one school type based on its instructional emphasis.
[1]ACGR data represents a new method of calculating high-school completion rates and may not be comparable to previous years' data for Averaged Freshmen Graduation Rates (AFGR).
[2]The United States 4-year ACGRs were estimated using both the reported 4-year ACGR data from 49 states and the District of Columbia and using imputed data for Idaho. The estimate for American Indian/Alaska Native students also includes imputed data for Virginia.

Table KS-13. Reported Voting and Registration of the Voting-Age Population, November 2014

(Numbers in thousands, percent.)

Item	Total population	Total citizen population	Registered			Voted		
			Total registered	Percent registered (total population)	Percent registered (total citizen population)	Total voted	Percent voted (total population)	Percent voted (total citizen population)
U.S. Total	239,874	219,941	142,166	59.3	64.6	92,251	38.5	41.9
State Total..............................	2,125	1,993	1,353	63.7	67.9	962	45.3	48.3
Sex								
Male....................................	1,037	956	635	61.2	66.4	453	43.7	47.4
Female..................................	1,088	1,037	718	66.0	69.2	509	46.8	49.1
Race								
White alone..............................	1,853	1,770	1,220	65.8	68.9	873	47.1	49.3
White, non-Hispanic alone	1,673	1,671	1,170	69.9	70.0	838	50.1	50.1
Black alone..............................	129	122	73	56.3	59.8	53	40.8	43.3
Asian alone	76	45	30	(B)	(B)	22	(B)	(B)
Hispanic (of any race)	216	125	70	32.4	55.8	44	20.5	35.3
White alone or in combination	1,892	1,799	1,234	65.3	68.6	879	46.5	48.9
Black alone or in combination	139	131	75	53.7	56.8	54	39.2	41.5
Asian alone or in combination..........	84	53	34	(B)	(B)	25	(B)	(B)
Age								
18 to 24 years..........................	258	240	87	33.7	36.1	34	13.3	14.3
25 to 34 years..........................	414	370	217	52.5	58.8	108	26.0	29.2
35 to 44 years..........................	324	290	190	58.6	65.6	129	39.8	44.6
45 to 64 years..........................	714	678	524	73.4	77.2	417	58.4	61.4
65 years and over	415	415	335	80.7	80.7	274	66.0	66.0

B = Base is less than 75,000 and therefore too small to show the derived measure.

Table KS-14. Crime

(Number, rate per 100,000. Data are derived from the FBI Uniform Crime Reports.)

Item	State			U.S.[1,2,3,4]		
	2013	2014	Percent change	2013	2014	Percent change
TOTAL POPULATION[5].............................	2,893,957	2,904,021	0.3	316,128,839	318,857,056	0.9
VIOLENT CRIME						
Number.................................	9,478	10,123	6.8	1,163,146	1,165,383	0.2
Rate	327.5	348.6	6.4	367.9	365.5	-0.7
Murder and Nonnegligent Manslaughter						
Number.................................	112	91	-18.8	14,196	14,249	0.4
Rate	3.9	3.1	-20.5	4.5	4.5	-
Rape[6]						
Number.................................	1,195	1,411	X	108,612	116,645	X
Rate	41.3	48.6	X	34.4	36.6	X
Robbery						
Number.................................	1,350	1,362	0.9	345,031	325,802	-5.6
Rate	46.6	46.9	0.6	109.1	102.2	-6.3
Aggravated Assault						
Number.................................	7,181	7,259	1.1	724,149	741,291	2.4
Rate	248.1	250.0	0.8	229.1	232.5	1.5
PROPERTY CRIME						
Number.................................	85,280	79,431	-6.9	8,632,512	8,277,829	-4.1
Rate	2,946.8	2,735.2	-7.2	2,730.7	2,596.1	-4.9
Burglary						
Number.................................	17,375	15,828	-8.9	1,928,465	1,729,806	-10.3
Rate	600.4	545.0	-9.2	610.0	542.5	-11.1
Larceny-Theft						
Number.................................	61,264	56,697	-7.5	6,004,453	5,858,496	-2.4
Rate	2,117.0	1,952.4	-7.8	1,899.4	1,837.3	-3.3
Motor Vehicle Theft						
Number.................................	6,641	6,906	4.0	699,594	689,527	-1.4
Rate	229.5	237.8	3.6	221.3	216.2	-2.3

NOTE: Although arson data are included in the trend and clearance tables, sufficient data are not available to estimate totals for this offense. Therefore, no arson data are published in this table.
X = Not applicable.
- = Zero or rounds to zero.
[1]The crime figures have been adjusted.
[2]The data collection methodology for the offense of forcible rape used by the Minnesota state Uniform Crime Reporting (UCR) Program (with the exception of Minneapolis and St. Paul, Minnesota) does not comply with national UCR Program guidelines. Consequently, its figures for forcible rape and violent crime (of which forcible rape is a part) are not published in this table.
[3]Includes offenses reported by the Zoological Police and the Metro Transit Police.
[4]Because of changes in the state's reporting practices, figures are not comparable to previous years' data.
[5]Populations are U.S. Census Bureau provisional estimates as of July 1 of each year.
[6]The figures shown for the offense of rape were estimated using the revised Uniform Crime Reporting (UCR) definition of rape.

Table KS-15. State Government Finances, 2014

(Dollar amounts in thousands, percent distribution.)

Item	Dollars	Percent distribution
Total Revenue	19,012,887	100.0
General revenue	15,391,445	81.0
Intergovernmental revenue	3,975,772	20.9
Taxes	7,334,481	38.6
General sales	2,983,664	15.7
Selective sales	907,236	4.8
License taxes	395,454	2.1
Individual income tax	2,511,660	13.2
Corporate income tax	330,181	1.7
Other taxes	206,286	1.1
Current charges	3,041,825	16.0
Miscellaneous general revenue	1,039,367	5.5
Utility revenue	0	-
Liquor stores revenue	0	-
Insurance trust revenue[1]	3,621,442	19.0
Total Expenditure	16,920,498	100.0
Intergovernmental expenditure	4,108,481	24.3
Direct expenditure	12,812,017	75.7
Current operation	9,726,565	57.5
Capital outlay	855,300	5.1
Insurance benefits and repayments	1,844,928	10.9
Assistance and subsidies	159,324	0.9
Interest on debt	225,900	1.3
Exhibit: Salaries and wages	3,689,102	21.8
Total Expenditure	16,920,498	100.0
General expenditure	15,075,570	89.1
Intergovernmental expenditure	4,108,481	24.3
Direct expenditure	10,967,089	64.8
General expenditure, by function:		
Education	6,094,686	36.0
Public welfare	3,789,145	22.4
Hospitals	1,586,252	9.4
Health	443,059	2.6
Highways	1,189,214	7.0
Police protection	90,463	0.5
Correction	351,420	2.1
Natural resources	223,527	1.3
Parks and recreation	37,607	0.2
Governmental administration	412,379	2.4
Interest on general debt	225,900	1.3
Other and unallocable	631,918	3.7
Utility expenditure	0	-
Liquor stores expenditure	0	-
Insurance trust expenditure	1,844,928	10.9
Debt at End of Fiscal Year	6,742,696	X
Cash and Security Holdings	22,578,556	X

X = Not applicable.
- = Zero or rounds to zero.
[1]Within insurance trust revenue, net earnings of state retirement systems is a calculated statistic (the item code in the data file is X08), and thus can be positive or negative. Net earnings is the sum of earnings on investments plus gains on investments minus losses on investments. The change made in 2002 for asset valuation from book to market value in accordance with Statement 34 of the Governmental Accounting Standards Board is reflected in the calculated statistics.

Table KS-16. State Government Tax Collections, 2014

(Dollars in thousands, percent.)

Item	Dollars	Percent distribution
Total Taxes	7,334,481	100.0
Property taxes	81,267	1.1
Sales and gross receipts	3,890,900	53.0
General sales and gross receipts	2,983,664	40.7
Selective sales and gross receipts	907,236	12.4
Alcoholic beverages	126,861	1.7
Amusements	343	-
Insurance premiums	198,355	2.7
Motor fuels	441,843	6.0
Pari-mutuels	0	-
Public utilities	353	-
Tobacco products	97,813	1.3
Other selective sales	41,668	0.6
Licenses	395,454	5.4
Alcoholic beverages	3,575	-
Amusements	15	-
Corporations in general	63,582	0.9
Hunting and fishing	23,522	0.3
Motor vehicle	212,064	2.9
Motor vehicle operators	19,622	0.3
Public utilities	5,340	0.1
Occupation and business, NEC	65,516	0.9
Other licenses	2,218	-
Income taxes	2,841,841	38.7
Individual income	2,511,660	34.2
Corporation net income	330,181	4.5
Other taxes	125,019	1.7
Death and gift	136	-
Documentary and stock transfer	0	-
Severance	124,883	1.7
Taxes, NEC	0	-

- = Zero or rounds to zero.

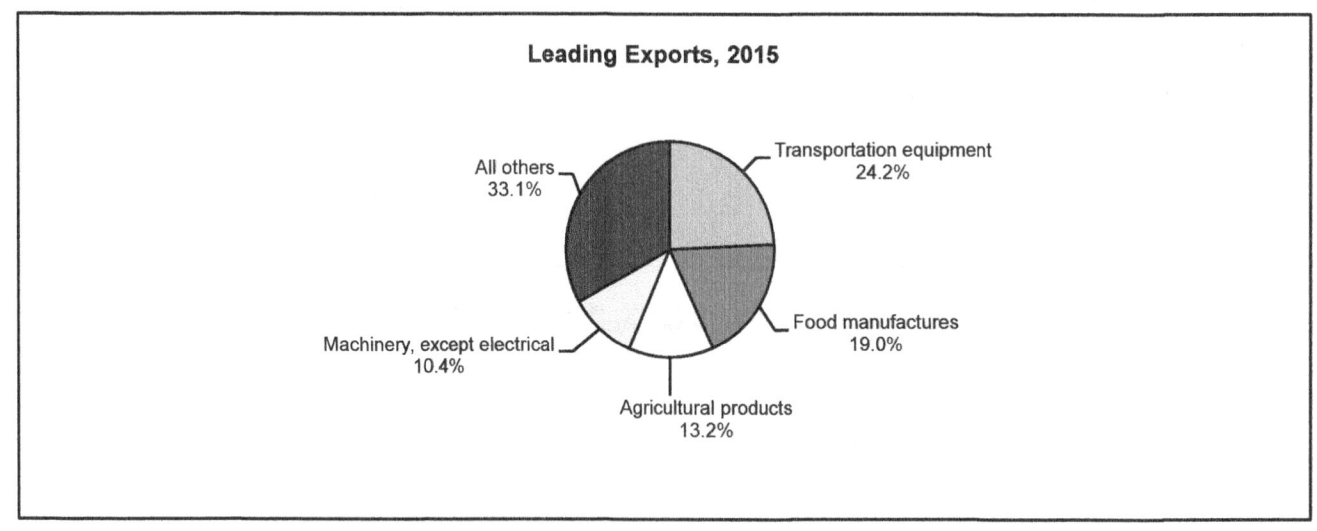

Leading Exports, 2015

- Transportation equipment 24.2%
- Food manufactures 19.0%
- Agricultural products 13.2%
- Machinery, except electrical 10.4%
- All others 33.1%

KENTUCKY

Facts and Figures

Location: East central United States; bordered on the N by Illinois, Indiana, and Ohio, on the E by West Virginia and Virginia, on the S by Tennessee, and on the W by Missouri and Illinois

Area: 40,409 sq. mi. (104,659 sq. km.); rank—37th

Population: 4,425,092 (2015 est.); rank—26th

Principal Cities: capital—Frankfort; largest—Lexington

Statehood: June 1, 1792; 15th state

U.S. Congress: 2 senators, 6 representatives

State Motto: United We Stand, Divided We Fall

State Song: "My Old Kentucky Home"

State Nickname: The Bluegrass State

Abbreviations: KY; Ky.

State Symbols: flower—goldenrod; tree—tulip poplar; bird—cardinal

At a Glance

- With an increase in population of 1.8 percent, Kentucky ranked 34th among the states in growth from 2010 to 2015.

- In Kentucky, 22.9 percent of the population was under age 18 in 2015, which was the same as the national average.

- In 2014, Kentucky's median household income was $42,958, the fifth lowest in the country, and 19.1 percent of the population lived below the poverty level.

- The property crime rate in Kentucky in 2014 was 2,246.9 per 100,000 population, compared to the U.S. rate of 2,596.1 per 100,000 population.

- In 2014, 8.5 percent of Kentucky residents did not have health insurance, down from 14.3 percent in 2013.

Table KY-1. Population by Age, Sex, Race, and Hispanic Origin

(Number, percent, except where noted.)

Sex, age, race, and Hispanic origin	2000	2010	2015[1]	Average annual percent change, 2010–2015
Total Population...	4,041,769	4,339,367	4,425,092	0.1
Percent of total U.S. population	1.4	1.4	1.4	X
Sex				
Male...	1,975,368	2,134,952	2,179,094	0.1
Female	2,066,401	2,204,425	2,245,998	0.1
Age				
Under 5 years..	265,901	282,367	277,389	-0.1
5 to 19 years...	847,743	863,837	846,841	-0.1
20 to 64 years...	2,423,332	2,614,936	2,628,097	-
65 years and over	504,793	578,227	672,765	1.1
Median age (years)	35.9	38.1	38.7	0.1
Race and Hispanic Origin				
One race				
White...	3,640,889	3,864,193	3,897,987	0.1
Black...	295,994	342,804	366,396	0.5
American Indian and Alaska Native	8,616	12,105	13,012	0.5
Asian...	29,744	50,177	63,953	1.7
Native Hawaiian or Other Pacific Islander	1,460	3,199	3,701	1.0
Two or more races	42,443	66,889	80,043	1.3
Hispanic (of any race)...	59,939	138,618	152,224	0.7

X = Not applicable.
- = Zero or rounds to zero.
[1]Population figures for 2015 are July 1 estimates. The 2010 estimates are taken from the 2010 Census.

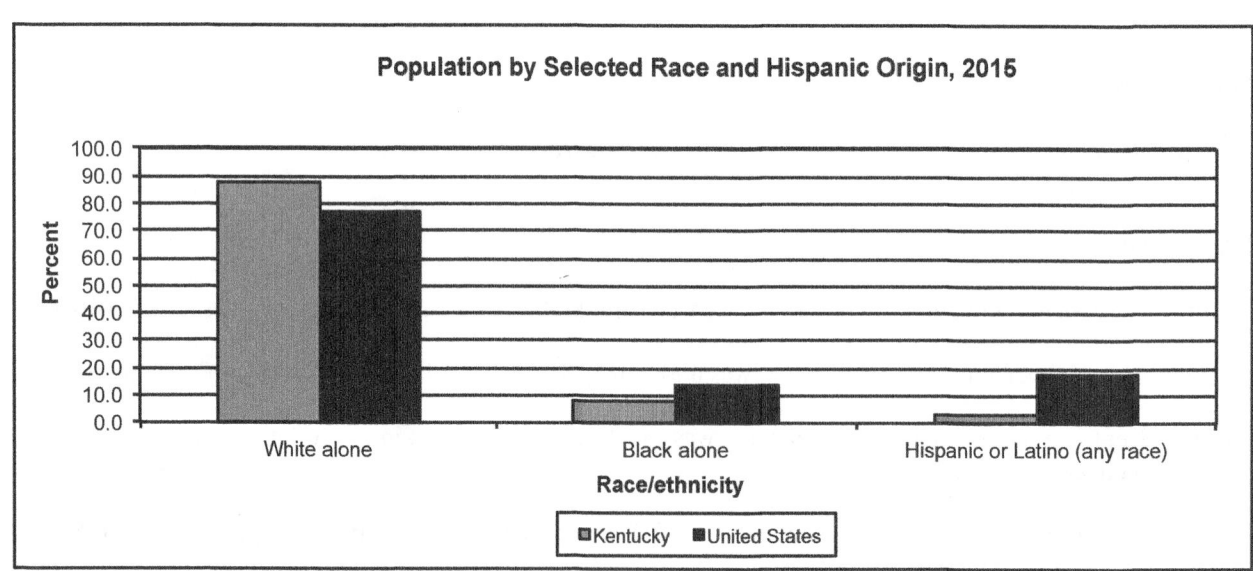

Population by Selected Race and Hispanic Origin, 2015

Table KY-2. Marital Status

(Number, percent distribution.)

Sex, age, race, and Hispanic origin	2000	2010	2014
Males, 15 Years and Over	1,551,174	1,702,020	1,722,001
Never married	25.9	30.8	31.0
Now married, except separated.....................................	59.9	52.0	51.9
Separated...	1.5	2.1	2.0
Widowed...	2.6	2.8	2.9
Divorced...	10.2	12.3	12.1
Females, 15 Years and Over	1,665,993	1,794,164	1,813,618
Never married	19.7	24.2	24.5
Now married, except separated.....................................	55.0	48.9	48.7
Separated...	2.1	2.6	2.5
Widowed...	11.5	10.6	10.2
Divorced...	11.8	13.7	14.1

Table KY-3. Households and Housing Characteristics

(Number, percent, dollars.)

Item	2000	2010	2014	Average annual percent change, 2000–2014
Total Households..	1,590,647	1,684,348	1,712,094	0.5
Family households	1,104,398	1,126,685	1,124,586	0.1
Married-couple family..	857,944	833,872	828,926	-0.2
Other family	246,454	292,813	295,660	1.4
Male householder, no wife present..................	58,497	76,832	79,241	2.5
Female householder, no husband present	187,957	215,981	216,419	1.1
Nonfamily households	486,249	557,663	587,508	1.5
Householder living alone.....................................	414,095	470,103	487,576	1.3
Householder not living alone	72,154	87,560	99,932	2.7
Housing Characteristics				
Total housing units..	1,750,927	1,928,617	1,950,504	0.8
Occupied housing units	1,590,647	1,684,348	1,712,094	0.5
Owner occupied...	1,125,397	1,156,292	1,131,197	-
Renter occupied..	465,250	528,056	580,897	1.8
Average household size..	2.47	2.51	2.5	0.1
Financial Characteristics				
Median gross rent of renter-occupied housing	445	613	678	3.7
Median monthly owner costs for housing units with a mortgage	816	1,072	1,100	2.5
Median value of owner-occupied housing units............	86,700	121,600	123,800	3.1

- = Zero or rounds to zero.

Table KY-4. Migration, Origin, and Language

(Number, percent.)

Characteristic	State 2013	State 2014	State Percent change	U.S. 2013	U.S. 2014	U.S. Percent change
Residence 1 Year Ago						
Population 1 year and over	4,345,186	4,357,819	0.3	312,432,820	315,095,393	0.9
Same house	84.4	84.1	X	85.0	85.1	X
Different house in the U.S.	15.2	15.6	X	14.4	14.3	X
Same county	8.9	9.1	X	8.9	8.7	X
Different county	6.3	6.5	X	5.5	5.6	X
Same state..	4.0	4.1	X	3.2	3.3	X
Different state...	2.4	2.4	X	2.3	2.3	X
Abroad	0.4	0.3	X	0.6	0.6	X
Place of Birth						
Native born	4,246,279	4,251,417	0.1	274,780,773	276,465,262	0.6
Male..	49.1	49.1	X	49.3	49.3	X
Female...	50.9	50.9	X	50.7	50.7	X
Foreign born	149,016	162,040	8.7	41,348,066	42,391,794	2.5
Male..	51.8	53.1	X	48.8	48.7	X
Female...	48.2	46.9	X	51.2	51.3	X
Foreign born; naturalized U.S. citizen.....................	56,085	58,742	4.7	19,294,710	19,984,738	3.6
Male..	44.2	48.0	X	45.9	45.9	X
Female...	55.8	52.0	X	54.1	54.1	X
Foreign born; not a U.S. citizen.............................	92,931	103,298	11.2	22,053,356	22,407,056	1.6
Male..	56.4	56.0	X	51.3	51.2	X
Female...	43.6	44.0	X	48.7	48.8	X
Entered 2010 or later	17.7	19.6	X	9.7	12.3	X
Entered 2000 to 2009	41.7	41.7	X	29.4	28.6	X
Entered before 2000...	40.5	38.7	X	61.0	59.1	X
World Region of Birth, Foreign						
Foreign-born population, excluding population born at sea	149,016	162,040	8.7	41,347,945	42,390,705	2.5
Europe	15.1	14.0	X	11.6	11.2	X
Asia..	32.4	31.6	X	29.5	30.1	X
Africa	8.5	12.3	X	4.4	4.6	X
Oceania...	0.1	0.7	X	0.5	0.6	X
Latin America...	42.0	39.1	X	51.9	51.6	X
North America..	1.9	2.3	X	2.0	1.9	X
Language Spoken at Home and Ability to Speak English						
Population 5 years and over.......................................	4,123,458	4,138,825	0.4	296,358,760	299,084,046	0.9
English only	95.0	94.8	X	79.2	78.9	X
Language other than English.................................	5.0	5.2	X	20.8	21.1	X
Speaks English less than "very well"..................	2.0	2.3	X	8.5	8.6	X

X = Not applicable.
- = Zero or rounds to zero.

Table KY-5. Median Income and Poverty Status, 2014

(Number, percent, except as noted.)

Characteristic	State		U.S.	
	Number	Percent	Number	Percent
Median Income				
Households (dollars)................................	42,958	X	53,657	X
Families (dollars)	54,776	X	65,910	X
Below Poverty Level (All People)	817,542	19.1	48,208,387	15.5
Sex				
Male................................	370,766	17.7	21,590,918	14.2
Female	446,776	20.5	26,617,469	16.8
Age				
Under 18 years................................	259,751	26.2	15,686,012	21.7
Related children under 18 years................	253,973	25.8	15,372,705	21.3
18 to 64 years................................	486,720	18.3	28,267,482	14.6
65 years and over................................	71,071	11.3	4,254,893	9.5

X = Not applicable.

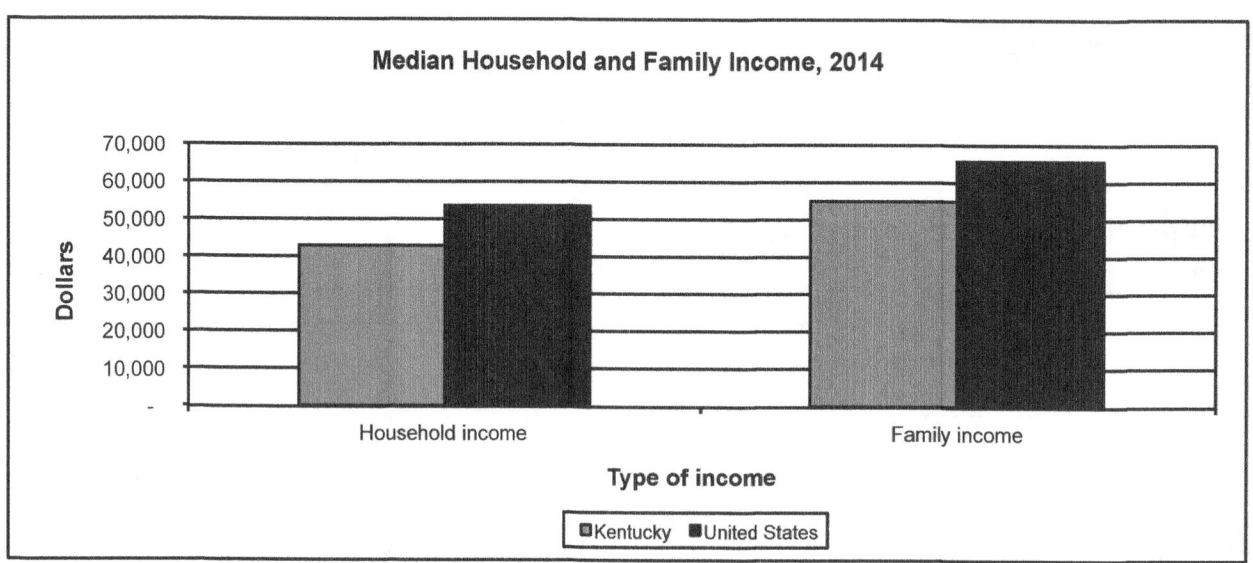

Table KY-6. Health Insurance Coverage Status for the Civilian Noninstitutionalized Population and Children Under 18 Years of Age

(Numbers in thousands, percent.)

Item	2006	2007	2008	2009	2010	2011	2012	2013	2014
Civilian Noninstitutionalized Population	4,106	4,207	4,188	4,225	4,243	4,284	4,293	4,312	4,329
Covered by Private or Public Insurance									
Number................................	3,467	3,637	3,598	3,612	3,596	3,666	3,697	3,696	3,962
Percent................................	84.4	86.4	85.9	85.5	84.7	85.6	86.1	85.7	91.5
Not Covered									
Number................................	639	570	590	613	647	618	596	616	366
Percent................................	15.6	13.6	14.1	14.5	15.3	14.4	13.9	14.3	8.5
Percent in the U.S. not covered................	15.8	15.3	15.1	15.1	15.5	15.1	14.8	14.5	11.7
Children Under 18 Years of Age	1,006	1,026	1,004	1,015	1,018	1,023	1,016	1,012	1,013
Covered by Private or Public Insurance									
Number................................	908	944	934	951	957	961	960	953	969
Percent................................	90.3	92.0	93.0	93.7	94.0	93.9	94.5	94.1	95.7
Not Covered									
Number................................	98	82	70	64	61	62	56	60	43
Percent................................	9.7	8.0	7.0	6.3	6.0	6.1	5.5	5.9	4.3
Percent in the U.S. not covered................	11.7	11.0	9.7	8.6	8.0	7.5	7.2	7.1	6.0

Table KY-7. Employment Status by Demographic Group, 2015

(Numbers in thousands, percent.)

Characteristic	Civilian noninstitutional population	Civilian labor force		Employed		Unemployed	
		Number	Percent of population	Number	Percent of population	Number	Percent of population
Total..	3,444	1,946	56.5	1,841	53.4	106	5.4
Sex							
Male..	1,659	1,024	61.7	962	58.0	62	6.1
Female.......................................	1,785	922	51.7	879	49.2	44	4.7
Race, Sex, and Hispanic Origin							
White	3,093	1,742	56.3	1,658	53.6	85	4.9
Male..	1,501	927	61.7	874	58.3	52	5.7
Female.......................................	1,592	816	51.2	783	49.2	33	4.0
Black or African American..................	253	149	58.7	132	52.1	17	11.2
Male..	113	68	59.6	59	51.9	9	12.9
Female.......................................	140	81	58.0	73	52.3	8	9.8
Hispanic or Latino ethnicity[1]	97	72	74.6	65	67.4	7	9.7
Male..	59	52	87.3	47	79.9	4	8.4
Female.......................................	NA	NA	NA	NA	NA	NA	NA
Age							
16 to 19 years...............................	211	72	34.3	58	27.6	14	19.7
20 to 24 years...............................	296	208	70.3	185	62.5	23	11.2
25 to 34 years...............................	555	435	78.3	411	74.0	24	5.4
35 to 44 years...............................	551	410	74.4	394	71.4	16	4.0
45 to 54 years...............................	615	438	71.3	423	68.8	15	3.5
55 to 64 years...............................	554	281	50.8	271	49.0	10	3.5
65 years and over	663	102	15.4	99	14.9	3	3.3

NOTE: Data in Table 7 are from the Current Population Survey (CPS) and do not match the estimates in Table 8. See notes and definitions for further information.
[1]May be of any race.
NA = Not available.

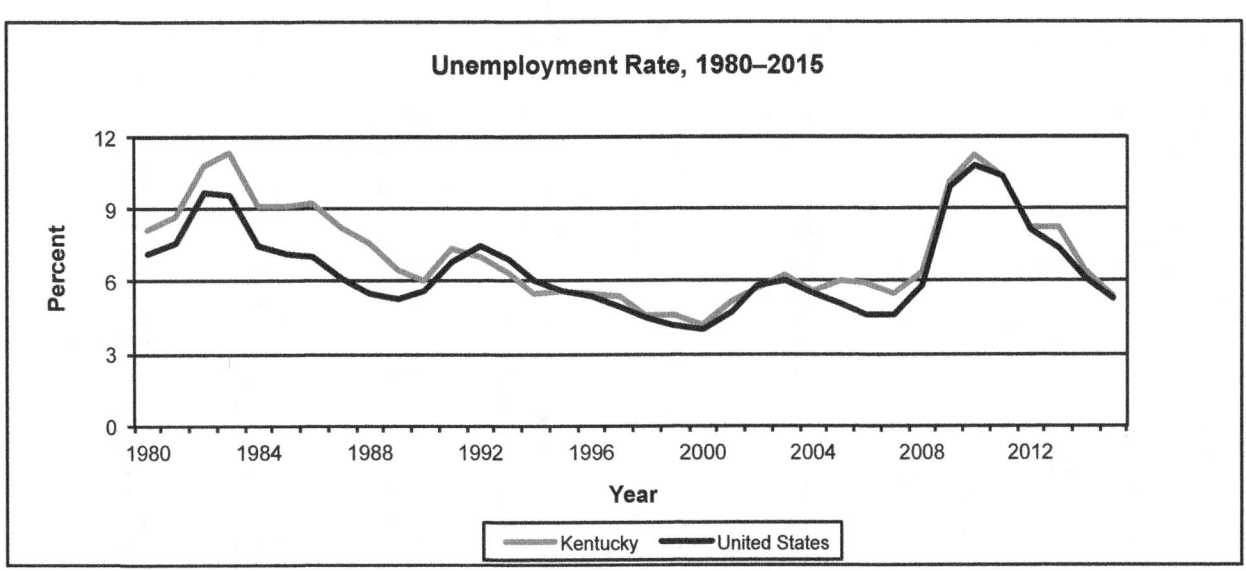

Table KY-8. Employment Status of the Civilian Noninstitutional Population Age 16 Years and Over

(Number, percent.)

Year	Civilian labor force	Civilian participation rate	Employed	Unemployed	Unemployment rate
2007..	2,032,082	62.1	1,922,220	109,862	5.4
2008..	2,030,738	61.4	1,900,683	130,055	6.4
2009..	2,060,162	61.9	1,847,126	213,036	10.3
2010..	2,054,375	61.3	1,844,650	209,725	10.2
2011..	2,056,410	61.0	1,862,928	193,482	9.4
2012..	2,058,982	60.8	1,891,038	167,944	8.2
2013..	2,058,186	60.4	1,892,027	166,159	8.1
2014..	2,005,603	58.6	1,875,932	129,671	6.5
2015..	1,953,393	56.8	1,847,938	105,455	5.4

Table KY-9. Employment and Average Wages by Industry

(Estimates through 2010 are based on the 2007 North American Industry Classification System [NAICS]. Estimates from 2011 onward are based on the 2012 NAICS.)

Industry	2008	2009	2010	2011	2012	2013	2014
	Number of jobs						
Wage and Salary Employment by Industry..................	1,950,323	1,871,120	1,876,202	1,900,942	1,913,171	1,928,456	1,952,624
Farm Wage and Salary Employment.........................	14,146	12,629	12,847	13,783	14,407	13,793	14,597
Nonfarm Wage and Salary Employment....................	1,936,177	1,858,491	1,863,355	1,887,159	1,898,764	1,914,663	1,938,027
Private wage and salary employment..............................	1,565,902	1,483,765	1,478,322	1,501,396	1,522,720	1,540,783	1,574,760
Forestry, fishing, and related activities........................	7,594	7,351	7,362	7,437	7,091	7,183	7,538
Mining..........	23,671	23,299	21,807	22,654	20,310	17,207	16,227
Utilities..........	6,453	6,501	6,424	6,522	6,566	6,509	6,625
Construction..........	88,033	77,487	71,126	71,270	69,642	70,565	75,089
Manufacturing..........	245,322	213,078	209,208	213,009	224,210	228,785	234,983
Durable goods manufacturing..........	153,729	127,339	124,800	128,920	139,540	143,023	149,095
Nondurable goods manufacturing..........	91,593	85,739	84,408	84,089	84,670	85,762	85,888
Wholesale trade..........	77,519	73,268	72,395	72,816	73,086	74,360	74,787
Retail trade..........	213,372	204,735	203,527	204,083	204,740	205,081	206,801
Transportation and warehousing..........	88,992	83,173	83,287	86,108	87,487	86,828	91,068
Information..........	29,192	27,206	26,277	26,849	26,617	26,314	26,353
Finance and insurance..........	73,261	71,045	69,826	70,243	72,232	73,931	75,003
Real estate and rental and leasing..........	20,166	19,164	18,978	18,465	18,284	18,752	18,635
Professional, scientific, and technical services..........	70,664	71,154	70,580	70,323	68,276	70,328	72,473
Management of companies and enterprises..........	19,582	19,700	19,454	19,563	20,081	20,513	20,661
Administrative and waste services..........	95,691	83,516	92,469	99,465	105,822	111,002	119,152
Educational services..........	29,125	29,794	30,613	31,673	32,396	32,281	33,023
Health care and social assistance..........	216,916	219,644	222,834	226,556	229,700	230,107	231,818
Arts, entertainment, and recreation..........	19,967	19,779	18,950	18,845	19,895	20,414	20,340
Accommodation and food services..........	154,499	150,416	150,872	152,893	156,429	160,411	163,375
Other services, except public administration..........	85,883	83,455	82,333	82,622	79,856	80,212	80,809
Government and government enterprises..........	370,275	374,726	385,033	385,763	376,044	373,880	363,267
	Dollars						
Average Wages and Salaries by Industry	37,207	37,783	38,532	39,538	40,279	40,674	41,778
Average Farm Wages and Salaries	21,403	22,775	20,748	17,634	18,910	26,912	24,142
Average Nonfarm Wages and Salaries	37,323	37,885	38,655	39,698	40,441	40,773	41,911
Average private wages and salaries..........	36,732	37,264	38,090	39,080	40,003	40,431	41,648
Forestry, fishing, and related activities..........	25,728	26,215	26,453	26,682	27,162	28,099	28,280
Mining..........	61,405	63,143	67,281	69,509	66,765	68,318	68,671
Utilities..........	67,238	70,540	70,655	72,214	74,125	76,467	79,768
Construction..........	42,062	43,479	43,597	44,021	45,908	47,396	49,891
Manufacturing..........	47,555	47,944	49,665	51,294	52,427	53,503	55,089
Durable goods manufacturing..........	48,853	49,507	51,125	53,250	54,012	55,177	56,405
Nondurable goods manufacturing..........	45,376	45,622	47,506	48,295	49,816	50,712	52,804
Wholesale trade..........	51,269	51,022	51,741	53,665	54,853	55,060	57,409
Retail trade..........	22,719	23,356	23,743	24,117	24,674	24,797	25,145
Transportation and warehousing..........	45,791	46,490	47,938	47,876	48,748	49,674	50,430
Information..........	41,598	42,749	43,463	44,510	45,906	46,321	49,010
Finance and insurance..........	53,410	53,825	56,627	58,941	60,342	60,921	63,880
Real estate and rental and leasing..........	32,268	32,233	33,474	35,370	36,413	35,396	37,201
Professional, scientific, and technical services..........	49,993	49,913	50,984	52,753	55,131	56,199	57,803
Management of companies and enterprises..........	82,602	81,553	86,292	92,016	95,382	91,305	92,905
Administrative and waste services..........	24,093	25,148	25,445	25,779	26,837	26,863	27,207
Educational services..........	22,346	23,467	24,318	24,649	24,362	24,580	24,298
Health care and social assistance..........	38,881	40,139	40,801	41,958	42,790	43,328	44,544
Arts, entertainment, and recreation..........	21,450	20,804	21,594	21,953	22,089	22,337	23,849
Accommodation and food services..........	14,358	14,775	15,294	15,635	15,974	15,842	16,664
Other services, except public administration..........	25,670	26,183	26,923	27,379	28,535	29,763	30,805
Government and government enterprises..........	39,821	40,344	40,825	42,105	42,215	42,183	43,050

Table KY-10. Employment Characteristics by Family Type

(Number, percent.)

Family type and labor force status	2012		2013		2014	
	Total	Families with own children under 18 years	Total	Families with own children under 18 years	Total	Families with own children under 18 years
All Families..	1,140,771	475,764	1,139,596	469,000	1,121,747	464,494
FAMILY TYPE AND LABOR FORCE STATUS						
Married-Couple Families............................	834,642	308,124	833,340	305,408	826,087	307,360
Both husband and wife in labor force........................	50.2	66.5	48.4	66.3	48.5	65.6
Husband in labor force, wife not in labor force................	20.0	24.7	21.0	25.8	20.8	25.9
Wife in labor force, husband not in labor force................	9.1	5.3	8.9	4.3	9.0	4.5
Both husband and wife not in labor force....................	20.8	3.5	21.3	3.3	21.7	4.0
Other Families	306,129	167,640	306,256	163,592	295,660	157,134
Female householder, no husband present....................	73.5	75.9	71.6	75.5	73.2	74.9
In labor force....................................	46.1	57.6	44.7	57.5	45.2	57.4
Not in labor force................................	27.4	18.3	27.0	18.0	28.0	17.4
Male householder, no wife present........................	26.5	24.1	28.4	24.5	26.8	25.1
In labor force....................................	18.9	20.5	19.7	21.2	18.1	20.3
Not in labor force................................	7.6	3.6	8.7	3.3	8.7	4.8

Table KY-11. School Enrollment and Educational Attainment, 2014

(Number, percent.)

Item	State	U.S.
Enrollment		
Total population 3 years and over, enrolled in school.........................	1,078,943	82,063,714
Enrolled in nursery school or preschool (percent).........................	5.3	6.0
Enrolled in kindergarten (percent).........................	5.4	5.1
Enrolled in elementary school, grades 1-8 (percent).........................	42.5	40.2
Enrolled in high school, grades 9-12 (percent).........................	21.1	20.7
Enrolled in college or graduate school (percent).........................	25.6	28.0
Attainment		
Total population 25 years and over	2,967,181	213,725,624
Less than ninth grade (percent)..........................	6.6	5.6
9th to 12th grade, no diploma (percent)..........................	8.9	7.5
High school graduate, including equivalency (percent)..........................	33.8	27.7
Some college, no degree (percent)	20.7	21.0
Associate's degree (percent)..........................	7.7	8.2
Bachelor's degree (percent)..........................	13.0	18.7
Graduate or professional degree (percent)..........................	9.2	11.4
High school graduate or higher (percent)..........................	84.5	86.9
Bachelor's degree or higher (percent)..........................	22.2	30.1

Table KY-12. Public School Characteristics and Educational Indicators

(Number, percent; data derived from National Center of Education Statistics.)

Item	State	U.S.
Public Schools, 2013–2014 (except where noted)		
Number of school districts..........................	194	18,194
Number of schools..........................	1,565	98,271
Number of students (in thousands)	677	50,045
Number of teachers (in thousands)	42	3,114
Student-teacher ratio	16.2	16.1
Expenditures per student (dollars), FY 2013	9,274	107,637
Four-year adjusted cohort graduation rate (ACGR)[1,2]	87.5	82.3
Students eligible for free or reduced-price lunch (in thousands)	368	25,596
English language learners (in thousands)	20	4,461
Students age 3 to 21 served under IDEA, part B (in thousands)	97	6,464

Public Schools by Type	Number	Percent of state public schools
Total number of schools..........................	1,565	100.0
Regular	1,286	82.2
Special education..........................	5	0.3
Vocational education..........................	122	7.8
Alternative education..........................	152	9.7

NOTE: Every school is assigned only one school type based on its instructional emphasis.
[1]ACGR data represents a new method of calculating high-school completion rates and may not be comparable to previous years' data for Averaged Freshmen Graduation Rates (AFGR).
[2]The United States 4-year ACGRs were estimated using both the reported 4-year ACGR data from 49 states and the District of Columbia and using imputed data for Idaho. The estimate for American Indian/Alaska Native students also includes imputed data for Virginia.

Table KY-13. Reported Voting and Registration of the Voting-Age Population, November 2014

(Numbers in thousands, percent.)

Item	Total population	Total citizen population	Registered			Voted		
			Total registered	Percent registered (total population)	Percent registered (total citizen population)	Total voted	Percent voted (total population)	Percent voted (total citizen population)
U.S. Total	239,874	219,941	142,166	59.3	64.6	92,251	38.5	41.9
State Total.............................	3,323	3,207	2,298	69.2	71.6	1,525	45.9	47.5
Sex								
Male...............................	1,597	1,532	1,091	68.3	71.2	754	47.2	49.2
Female	1,725	1,675	1,207	70.0	72.1	770	44.6	46.0
Race								
White alone...................................	2,943	2,870	2,059	70.0	71.8	1,367	46.4	47.6
White, non-Hispanic alone	2,842	2,821	2,031	71.5	72.0	1,349	47.5	47.8
Black alone...................	271	263	184	67.7	70.0	117	43.2	44.7
Asian alone	53	26	23	(B)	(B)	23	(B)	(B)
Hispanic (of any race)	113	55	34	(B)	(B)	23	(B)	(B)
White alone or in combination	2,985	2,912	2,089	70.0	71.7	1,382	46.3	47.5
Black alone or in combination..........	295	286	198	66.9	69.0	123	41.6	42.9
Asian alone or in combination..........	53	26	23	(B)	(B)	23	(B)	(B)
Age								
18 to 24 years....................	433	406	226	52.3	55.7	101	23.4	24.9
25 to 34 years....................	559	518	349	62.5	67.4	202	36.1	38.9
35 to 44 years....................	512	490	382	74.5	77.9	236	46.0	48.1
45 to 64 years....................	1,196	1,172	866	72.4	73.9	619	51.8	52.8
65 years and over	623	621	475	76.2	76.5	367	59.0	59.2

B = Base is less than 75,000 and therefore too small to show the derived measure.

Table KY-14. Crime

(Number, rate per 100,000. Data are derived from the FBI Uniform Crime Reports.)

Item	State			U.S.[1,2,3,4]		
	2013	2014	Percent change	2013	2014	Percent change
TOTAL POPULATION[5]......................................	4,395,295	4,413,457	0.4	316,128,839	318,857,056	0.9
VIOLENT CRIME						
Number..	8,737	9,340	6.9	1,163,146	1,165,383	0.2
Rate	198.8	211.6	6.4	367.9	365.5	-0.7
Murder and Nonnegligent Manslaughter						
Number..	167	160	-4.2	14,196	14,249	0.4
Rate	3.8	3.6	-5.3	4.5	4.5	-
Rape[6]						
Number..	1,611	1,440	X	108,612	116,645	X
Rate	36.7	32.6	X	34.4	36.6	X
Robbery						
Number..	3,246	3,336	2.8	345,031	325,802	-5.6
Rate	73.9	75.6	2.3	109.1	102.2	-6.3
Aggravated Assault						
Number..	4,198	4,404	4.9	724,149	741,291	2.4
Rate	95.5	99.8	4.5	229.1	232.5	1.5
PROPERTY CRIME						
Number..	103,857	99,166	-4.5	8,632,512	8,277,829	-4.1
Rate	2,362.9	2,246.9	-4.9	2,730.7	2,596.1	-4.9
Burglary						
Number..	26,213	23,244	-11.3	1,928,465	1,729,806	-10.3
Rate	596.4	526.7	-11.7	610.0	542.5	-11.1
Larceny-Theft						
Number..	71,612	69,604	-2.8	6,004,453	5,858,496	-2.4
Rate	1,629.3	1,577.1	-3.2	1,899.4	1,837.3	-3.3
Motor Vehicle Theft						
Number..	6,032	6,318	4.7	699,594	689,527	-1.4
Rate	137.2	143.2	4.4	221.3	216.2	-2.3

NOTE: Although arson data are included in the trend and clearance tables, sufficient data are not available to estimate totals for this offense. Therefore, no arson data are published in this table.
X = Not applicable.
- = Zero or rounds to zero.
[1]The crime figures have been adjusted.
[2]The data collection methodology for the offense of forcible rape used by the Minnesota state Uniform Crime Reporting (UCR) Program (with the exception of Minneapolis and St. Paul, Minnesota) does not comply with national UCR Program guidelines. Consequently, its figures for forcible rape and violent crime (of which forcible rape is a part) are not published in this table.
[3]Includes offenses reported by the Zoological Police and the Metro Transit Police.
[4]Because of changes in the state's reporting practices, figures are not comparable to previous years' data.
[5]Populations are U.S. Census Bureau provisional estimates as of July 1 of each year.
[6]The figures shown for the offense of rape were estimated using the revised Uniform Crime Reporting (UCR) definition of rape.

Table KY-15. State Government Finances, 2014

(Dollar amounts in thousands, percent distribution.)

Item	Dollars	Percent distribution
Total Revenue	31,507,525	100.0
General revenue	25,268,291	80.2
Intergovernmental revenue	9,768,931	31.0
Taxes	11,103,545	35.2
General sales	3,131,157	9.9
Selective sales	2,222,967	7.1
License taxes	472,225	1.5
Individual income tax	3,749,258	11.9
Corporate income tax	674,464	2.1
Other taxes	853,474	2.7
Current charges	3,127,988	9.9
Miscellaneous general revenue	1,267,827	4.0
Utility revenue	0	-
Liquor stores revenue	0	-
Insurance trust revenue[1]	6,239,234	19.8
Total Expenditure	29,938,181	100.0
Intergovernmental expenditure	4,649,395	15.5
Direct expenditure	25,288,786	84.5
Current operation	17,534,553	58.6
Capital outlay	1,955,992	6.5
Insurance benefits and repayments	4,199,381	14.0
Assistance and subsidies	925,106	3.1
Interest on debt	673,754	2.3
Exhibit: Salaries and wages	4,034,285	13.5
Total Expenditure	29,938,181	100.0
General expenditure	25,711,108	85.9
Intergovernmental expenditure	4,649,395	15.5
Direct expenditure	21,061,713	70.4
General expenditure, by function:		
Education	9,252,839	30.9
Public welfare	8,348,927	27.9
Hospitals	1,256,865	4.2
Health	712,375	2.4
Highways	2,500,595	8.4
Police protection	181,811	0.6
Correction	521,445	1.7
Natural resources	316,719	1.1
Parks and recreation	94,202	0.3
Governmental administration	892,585	3.0
Interest on general debt	673,754	2.3
Other and unallocable	958,991	3.2
Utility expenditure	27,692	0.1
Liquor stores expenditure	0	-
Insurance trust expenditure	4,199,381	14.0
Debt at End of Fiscal Year	14,829,986	X
Cash and Security Holdings	40,861,806	X

X = Not applicable.
- = Zero or rounds to zero.
[1]Within insurance trust revenue, net earnings of state retirement systems is a calculated statistic (the item code in the data file is X08), and thus can be positive or negative. Net earnings is the sum of earnings on investments plus gains on investments minus losses on investments. The change made in 2002 for asset valuation from book to market value in accordance with Statement 34 of the Governmental Accounting Standards Board is reflected in the calculated statistics.

Table KY-16. State Government Tax Collections, 2014

(Dollars in thousands, percent.)

Item	Dollars	Percent distribution
Total Taxes	11,103,545	100.0
Property taxes	562,370	5.1
Sales and gross receipts	5,354,124	48.2
General sales and gross receipts	3,131,157	28.2
Selective sales and gross receipts	2,222,967	20.0
Alcoholic beverages	128,534	1.2
Amusements	214	-
Insurance premiums	141,639	1.3
Motor fuels	886,161	8.0
Pari-mutuels	2,421	-
Public utilities	63,898	0.6
Tobacco products	248,979	2.2
Other selective sales	751,121	6.8
Licenses	472,225	4.3
Alcoholic beverages	6,374	0.1
Amusements	291	-
Corporations in general	100,843	0.9
Hunting and fishing	26,536	0.2
Motor vehicle	190,370	1.7
Motor vehicle operators	16,600	0.1
Public utilities	0	-
Occupation and business, NEC	126,113	1.1
Other licenses	5,098	-
Income taxes	4,423,722	39.8
Individual income	3,749,258	33.8
Corporation net income	674,464	6.1
Other taxes	291,104	2.6
Death and gift	45,844	0.4
Documentary and stock transfer	3,271	-
Severance	241,989	2.2
Taxes, NEC	0	-

- = Zero or rounds to zero.

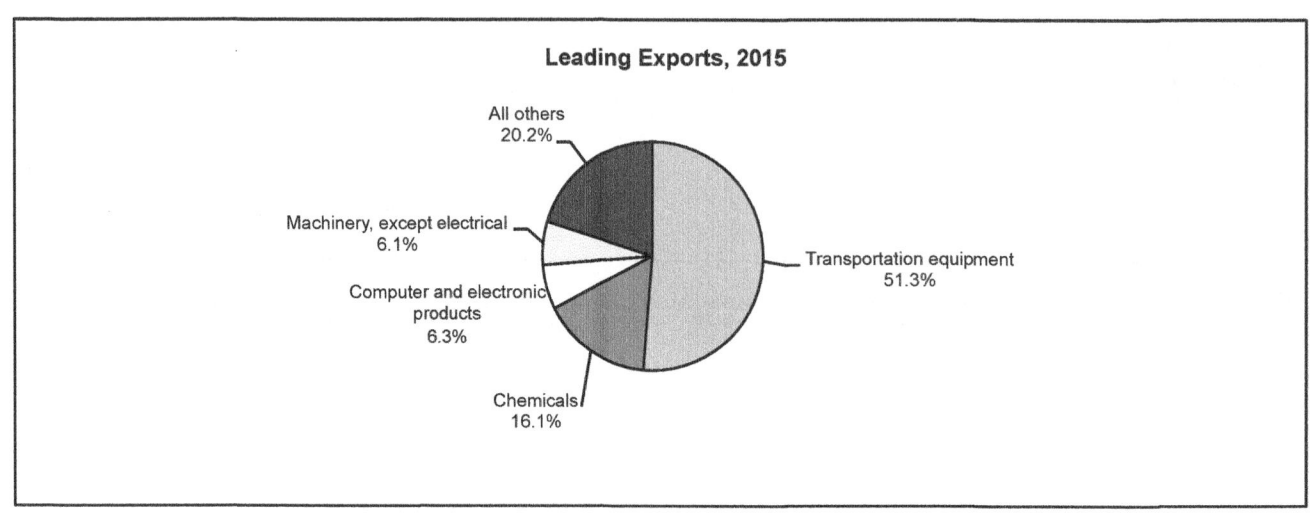

Leading Exports, 2015

- All others 20.2%
- Machinery, except electrical 6.1%
- Computer and electronic products 6.3%
- Chemicals 16.1%
- Transportation equipment 51.3%

LOUISIANA

Facts and Figures

Location: South central United States; bordered on the N by Arkansas, on the E by Mississippi, on the S by the Gulf of Mexico, and on the W by Texas

Area: 51,840 sq. mi. (134,264 sq. km.); rank—31st

Population: 4,670,724 (2015 est.); rank—25th

Principal Cities: capital—Baton Rouge; largest—New Orleans

Statehood: April 30, 1812; 18th state

U.S. Congress: 2 senators, 6 representatives

State Motto: Union, Justice, Confidence

State Song: "Give Me Louisiana"

State Nicknames: The Pelican State; The Bayou State

Abbreviations: LA; La.

State Symbols: flower—magnolia; tree—bald cypress; bird—Eastern brown pelican

At a Glance

- With an increase in population of 2.8 percent, Louisiana ranked 29th in population growth from 2010 to 2015.

- Louisiana's median household income in 2014 was $44,555, and 19.8 percent of the population lived below the poverty level.

- Louisiana's violent crime rate in 2014 was 514.7 per 100,000 population, compared to 365.5 for the entire nation.

- In 2014, 14.8 percent of Louisiana's population did not have health insurance, compared to 11.7 percent of the entire U.S. population.

- With an infant mortality rate of 7.49 deaths per 1,000 live births, Louisiana ranked 5th in the nation in 2014.

Table LA-1. Population by Age, Sex, Race, and Hispanic Origin

(Number, percent, except where noted.)

Sex, age, race, and Hispanic origin	2000	2010	2015[1]	Average annual percent change, 2010–2015
Total Population..	4,468,976	4,533,372	4,670,724	0.2
Percent of total U.S. population	1.6	1.5	1.5	X
Sex				
Male..	2,162,903	2,219,292	2,283,809	0.2
Female	2,306,073	2,314,080	2,386,915	0.2
Age				
Under 5 years..	317,392	314,260	310,817	-0.1
5 to 19 years...	1,050,637	939,977	919,390	-0.2
20 to 64 years...	2,584,018	2,721,278	2,787,423	0.2
65 years and over...	516,929	557,857	653,094	1.1
Median age (years)	34.0	35.8	36.4	0.1
Race and Hispanic Origin				
One race				
White	2,856,161	2,902,875	2,954,189	0.1
Black	1,451,944	1,462,969	1,517,482	0.3
American Indian and Alaska Native	25,477	33,037	35,648	0.5
Asian	54,758	71,829	85,870	1.3
Native Hawaiian or Other Pacific Islander	1,240	2,588	3,131	1.4
Two or more races	48,265	60,074	74,404	1.5
Hispanic (of any race)..	107,738	200,653	232,532	1.1

X = Not applicable.
[1]Population figures for 2015 are July 1 estimates. The 2010 estimates are taken from the 2010 Census.

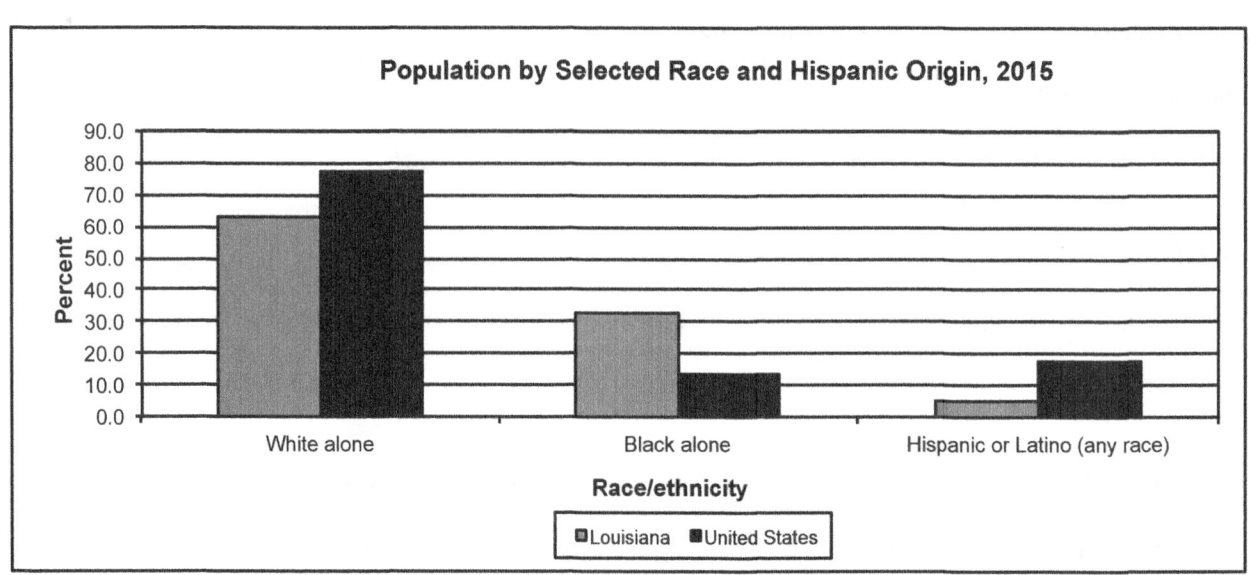

Population by Selected Race and Hispanic Origin, 2015

Table LA-2. Marital Status

(Number, percent distribution.)

Sex, age, race, and Hispanic origin	2000	2010	2014
Males, 15 Years and Over	1,648,133	1,751,556	1,775,744
Never married	31.2	37.0	37.4
Now married, except separated..................................	54.5	47.2	46.6
Separated...	2.2	2.2	2.3
Widowed...	2.8	2.8	2.9
Divorced...	9.2	10.8	10.8
Females, 15 Years and Over	1,828,247	1,861,490	1,894,309
Never married	26.3	30.8	31.5
Now married, except separated..................................	48.2	42.6	42.1
Separated...	2.9	3.2	3.2
Widowed...	11.5	10.1	10.2
Divorced...	11.1	13.3	13.1

Table LA-3. Households and Housing Characteristics

(Number, percent, dollars.)

Item	2000	2010	2014	Average annual percent change, 2000–2014
Total Households..	1,656,053	1,689,822	1,718,194	0.3
Family households...	1,156,438	1,129,117	1,112,659	-0.3
Married-couple family..	809,498	753,423	741,899	-0.6
Other family...	346,940	375,694	370,760	0.5
Male householder, no wife present............................	71,865	79,560	92,643	2.1
Female householder, no husband present...................	275,075	296,134	278,117	0.1
Nonfamily households...	499,615	560,705	605,535	1.5
Householder living alone...	419,200	468,853	511,005	1.6
Householder not living alone....................................	80,415	91,852	94,530	1.3
Housing Characteristics				
Total housing units..	1,847,181	1,967,947	2,011,037	0.6
Occupied housing units	1,656,053	1,689,822	1,718,194	0.3
Owner occupied...	1,125,135	1,141,504	1,106,785	-0.1
Renter occupied..	530,918	548,318	611,409	1.1
Average household size..	2.62	2.61	2.63	-
Financial Characteristics				
Median gross rent of renter-occupied housing	466	736	801	5.1
Median monthly owner costs for housing units with a mortgage	816	1,163	1,178	3.2
Median value of owner-occupied housing units............	85,000	137,500	143,600	4.9

- = Zero or rounds to zero

Table LA-4. Migration, Origin, and Language

(Number, percent.)

Characteristic	State			U.S.		
	2013	2014	Percent change	2013	2014	Percent change
Residence 1 Year Ago						
Population 1 year and over	4,568,320	4,593,505	0.6	312,432,820	315,095,393	0.9
Same house	86.3	86.4	X	85.0	85.1	X
Different house in the U.S.	13.4	13.3	X	14.4	14.3	X
Same county..	7.8	7.9	X	8.9	8.7	X
Different county	5.5	5.4	X	5.5	5.6	X
Same state..	3.5	3.3	X	3.2	3.3	X
Different state..	2.0	2.1	X	2.3	2.3	X
Abroad...	0.4	0.3	X	0.6	0.6	X
Place of Birth						
Native born	4,442,911	4,455,399	0.3	274,780,773	276,465,262	0.6
Male...	48.5	48.7	X	49.3	49.3	X
Female...	51.5	51.3	X	50.7	50.7	X
Foreign born	182,559	194,277	6.4	41,348,066	42,391,794	2.5
Male...	54.6	52.9	X	48.8	48.7	X
Female...	45.4	47.1	X	51.2	51.3	X
Foreign born; naturalized U.S. citizen........................	76,033	77,978	2.6	19,294,710	19,984,738	3.6
Male...	46.8	49.5	X	45.9	45.9	X
Female...	53.2	50.5	X	54.1	54.1	X
Foreign born; not a U.S. citizen...............................	106,526	116,299	9.2	22,053,356	22,407,056	1.6
Male...	60.2	55.1	X	51.3	51.2	X
Female...	39.8	44.9	X	48.7	48.8	X
Entered 2010 or later	18.0	20.2	X	9.7	12.3	X
Entered 2000 to 2009..	33.1	33.6	X	29.4	28.6	X
Entered before 2000...	48.9	46.3	X	61.0	59.1	X
World Region of Birth, Foreign						
Foreign-born population, excluding population born at sea	182,559	194,277	6.4	41,347,945	42,390,705	2.5
Europe..	9.4	7.8	X	11.6	11.2	X
Asia..	32.8	32.6	X	29.5	30.1	X
Africa	3.2	4.2	X	4.4	4.6	X
Oceania..	0.1	0.5	X	0.5	0.6	X
Latin America..	52.8	53.4	X	51.9	51.6	X
North America..	1.7	1.4	X	2.0	1.9	X
Language Spoken at Home and Ability to Speak English						
Population 5 years and over......................................	4,320,472	4,344,222	0.5	296,358,760	299,084,046	0.9
English only	91.7	91.6	X	79.2	78.9	X
Language other than English...................................	8.3	8.4	X	20.8	21.1	X
Speaks English less than "very well"........................	2.8	3.0	X	8.5	8.6	X

X = Not applicable.
- = Zero or rounds to zero.

Table LA-5. Median Income and Poverty Status, 2014

(Number, percent, except as noted.)

Characteristic	State		U.S.	
	Number	Percent	Number	Percent
Median Income				
Households (dollars)...	44,555	X	53,657	X
Families (dollars)	56,573	X	65,910	X
Below Poverty Level (All People)	896,524	19.8	48,208,387	15.5
Sex				
Male..	388,006	17.8	21,590,918	14.2
Female..	508,518	21.8	26,617,469	16.8
Age				
Under 18 years..	306,198	27.9	15,686,012	21.7
Related children under 18 years.................................	302,101	27.6	15,372,705	21.3
18 to 64 years...	511,918	18.2	28,267,482	14.6
65 years and over	78,408	12.8	4,254,893	9.5

X = Not applicable.

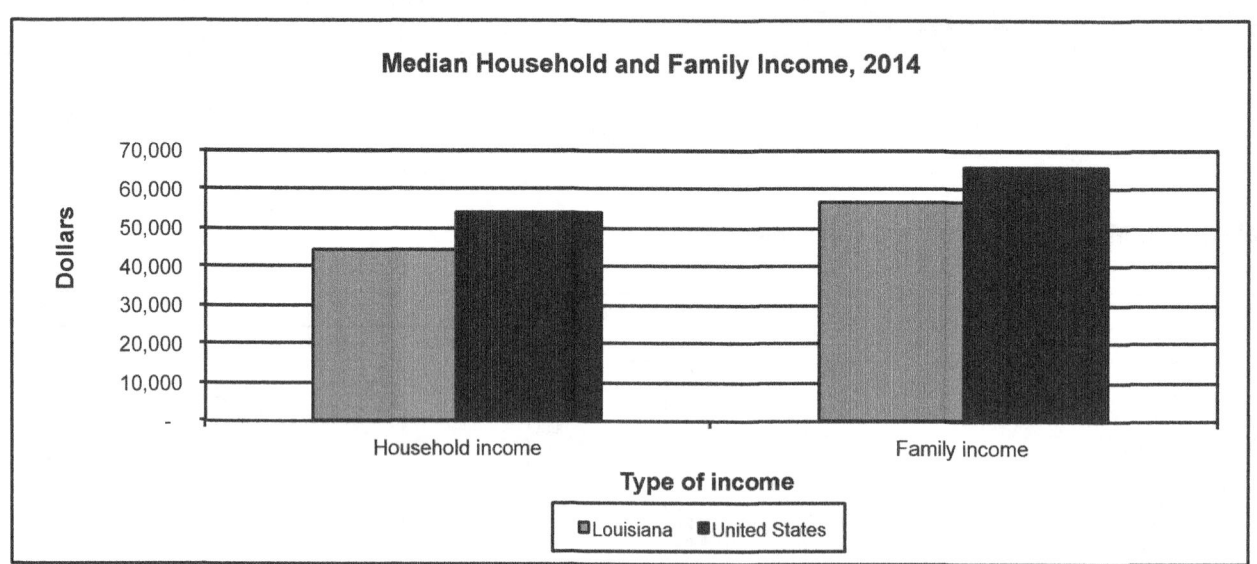

Table LA-6. Health Insurance Coverage Status for the Civilian Noninstitutionalized Population and Children Under 18 Years of Age

(Numbers in thousands, percent.)

Item	2006	2007	2008	2009	2010	2011	2012	2013	2014
Civilian Noninstitutionalized Population	4,212	4,197	4,313	4,392	4,440	4,473	4,499	4,523	4,548
Covered by Private or Public Insurance									
Number..	3,291	3,421	3,546	3,629	3,649	3,689	3,739	3,772	3,876
Percent..	78.1	81.5	82.2	82.6	82.2	82.5	83.1	83.4	85.2
Not Covered									
Number..	921	776	767	762	791	784	760	751	672
Percent..	21.9	18.5	17.8	17.4	17.8	17.5	16.9	16.6	14.8
Percent in the U.S. not covered...	15.8	15.3	15.1	15.1	15.5	15.1	14.8	14.5	11.7
Children Under 18 Years of Age	1,067	1,097	1,106	1,120	1,113	1,117	1,117	1,111	1,113
Covered by Private or Public Insurance									
Number..	897	960	1,020	1,047	1,051	1,052	1,058	1,048	1,055
Percent..	84.1	87.5	92.2	93.5	94.5	94.2	94.7	94.3	94.8
Not Covered									
Number..	170	137	86	73	62	65	59	63	58
Percent..	15.9	12.5	7.8	6.5	5.5	5.8	5.3	5.7	5.2
Percent in the U.S. not covered...	11.7	11.0	9.7	8.6	8.0	7.5	7.2	7.1	6.0

Table LA-7. Employment Status by Demographic Group, 2015

(Numbers in thousands, percent.)

Characteristic	Civilian noninstitutional population	Civilian labor force		Employed		Unemployed	
		Number	Percent of population	Number	Percent of population	Number	Percent of population
Total....................................	3,574	2,166	60.6	2,032	56.9	134	6.2
Sex							
Male....................	1,695	1,125	66.3	1,052	62.1	72	6.4
Female................	1,879	1,042	55.4	980	52.1	62	5.9
Race, Sex, and Hispanic Origin							
White..........................	2,336	1,438	61.6	1,369	58.6	69	4.8
Male....................	1,137	789	69.3	751	66.1	37	4.7
Female................	1,199	650	54.2	618	51.5	32	4.9
Black or African American..............	1,096	633	57.8	571	52.2	61	9.7
Male....................	490	285	58.2	252	51.4	33	11.5
Female................	606	348	57.5	320	52.7	29	8.2
Hispanic or Latino ethnicity[1]	173	117	67.5	108	62.4	9	7.6
Male....................	92	76	81.8	72	77.5	4	5.2
Female................	81	41	51.2	36	45.1	5	11.9
Age							
16 to 19 years..............	239	81	34.1	66	27.7	15	18.7
20 to 24 years..............	340	231	67.8	203	59.8	27	11.8
25 to 34 years..............	654	524	80.2	493	75.4	32	6.0
35 to 44 years..............	528	416	78.7	393	74.4	23	5.4
45 to 54 years..............	640	476	74.3	455	71.1	21	4.4
55 to 64 years..............	586	333	56.8	320	54.5	14	4.2
65 years and over	587	105	17.9	102	17.4	3	2.9

NOTE: Data in Table 7 are from the Current Population Survey (CPS) and do not match the estimates in Table 8. See notes and definitions for further information.
[1]May be of any race.

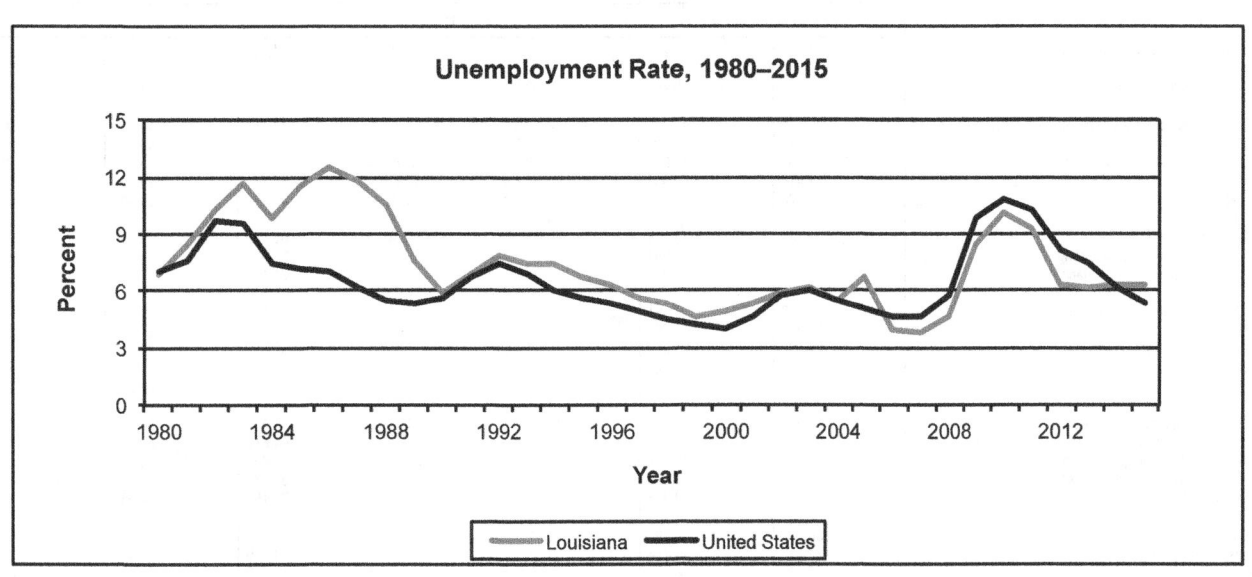

Unemployment Rate, 1980–2015

Table LA-8. Employment Status of the Civilian Noninstitutional Population Age 16 Years and Over

(Number, percent.)

Year	Civilian labor force	Civilian participation rate	Employed	Unemployed	Unemployment rate
2007..	2,030,434	61.7	1,944,038	86,396	4.3
2008..	2,084,835	62.2	1,982,381	102,454	4.9
2009..	2,064,768	60.9	1,923,884	140,884	6.8
2010..	2,086,076	60.7	1,919,852	166,224	8.0
2011..	2,073,217	59.6	1,911,021	162,196	7.8
2012..	2,080,664	59.4	1,932,880	147,784	7.1
2013..	2,106,424	59.7	1,964,634	141,790	6.7
2014..	2,156,737	60.8	2,018,593	138,144	6.4
2015..	2,160,195	60.5	2,025,102	135,093	6.3

Table LA-9. Employment and Average Wages by Industry

(Estimates through 2010 are based on the 2007 North American Industry Classification System [NAICS]. Estimates from 2011 onward are based on the 2012 NAICS.)

Industry	2008	2009	2010	2011	2012	2013	2014
	Number of jobs						
Wage and Salary Employment by Industry..................	2,040,323	2,003,169	1,990,201	2,005,804	2,022,998	2,042,221	2,069,930
Farm Wage and Salary Employment.........................	7,734	8,817	8,969	8,089	6,958	6,285	6,178
Nonfarm Wage and Salary Employment....................	2,032,589	1,994,352	1,981,232	1,997,715	2,016,040	2,035,936	2,063,752
Private wage and salary employment.......................	1,631,605	1,587,934	1,572,459	1,600,373	1,626,782	1,657,896	1,696,507
Forestry, fishing, and related activities.........................	7,311	7,062	7,230	7,227	7,023	7,119	7,382
Mining...	51,888	48,039	48,652	49,902	51,591	51,143	50,949
Utilities..	9,328	9,523	9,482	9,348	9,158	9,151	8,837
Construction...	140,889	136,972	126,709	127,925	130,758	136,086	143,736
Manufacturing..	152,927	142,703	137,621	139,983	141,987	144,079	147,226
Durable goods manufacturing..................................	82,805	74,529	69,661	71,156	73,079	74,662	77,089
Nondurable goods manufacturing............................	70,122	68,174	67,960	68,827	68,908	69,417	70,137
Wholesale trade	76,499	72,598	71,035	72,873	72,836	73,690	73,822
Retail trade..	228,562	224,211	221,236	224,125	224,650	226,296	229,156
Transportation and warehousing..................................	75,311	70,438	69,810	72,335	74,727	76,954	80,426
Information..	28,606	24,778	24,628	23,709	24,810	26,537	26,051
Finance and insurance..	60,294	58,857	60,615	62,178	61,045	60,602	61,182
Real estate and rental and leasing...........................	33,580	31,397	31,349	32,022	32,314	33,565	32,740
Professional, scientific, and technical services	83,757	80,848	80,830	82,403	85,490	87,378	89,233
Management of companies and enterprises..................	23,512	24,189	23,860	24,368	25,126	25,274	25,234
Administrative and waste services...............................	99,858	91,546	91,510	92,439	94,822	97,073	100,210
Educational services	36,063	36,795	37,716	39,051	40,988	41,905	43,512
Health care and social assistance.............................	224,622	232,150	236,656	240,782	244,026	248,311	256,601
Arts, entertainment, and recreation............................	33,506	28,899	28,522	28,412	28,879	30,019	30,667
Accommodation and food services.............................	165,158	168,102	168,568	174,942	179,632	184,927	191,839
Other services, except public administration..................	99,934	98,827	96,430	96,349	151,160	97,787	97,704
Government and government enterprises........................	400,984	406,418	408,773	397,342	389,258	378,040	367,245
	Dollars						
Average Wages and Salaries by Industry	41,097	41,216	42,181	43,154	44,047	44,828	46,856
Average Farm Wages and Salaries	21,339	18,758	18,557	18,447	23,864	27,288	23,376
Average Nonfarm Wages and Salaries	41,172	41,315	42,288	43,254	44,117	44,882	46,206
Average private wages and salaries............................	41,181	41,190	42,276	43,353	44,364	45,183	46,708
Forestry, fishing, and related activities.........................	31,593	30,515	32,382	33,109	34,190	35,621	36,038
Mining...	82,414	79,934	82,129	85,218	88,738	90,800	95,725
Utilities..	73,578	73,572	72,406	76,596	78,489	80,446	84,436
Construction...	50,192	51,721	51,220	51,894	52,501	53,554	56,564
Manufacturing..	58,606	58,888	61,563	64,047	65,769	66,486	69,265
Durable goods manufacturing..................................	51,827	51,561	54,313	56,764	57,912	58,443	60,813
Nondurable goods manufacturing............................	66,611	66,898	68,994	71,578	74,102	75,137	78,554
Wholesale trade	54,488	54,591	55,825	57,293	59,829	60,985	63,157
Retail trade..	25,043	25,087	25,536	25,983	26,734	27,057	27,355
Transportation and warehousing..................................	54,998	54,755	57,247	57,858	59,858	62,258	64,663
Information..	45,494	48,121	49,770	51,482	52,217	50,038	52,471
Finance and insurance..	53,342	52,520	55,110	58,855	60,207	62,225	65,786
Real estate and rental and leasing...........................	43,294	42,759	45,710	48,216	48,411	49,040	49,915
Professional, scientific, and technical services	58,536	59,248	61,153	63,001	64,670	66,802	68,152
Management of companies and enterprises..................	67,830	65,151	67,592	71,194	73,448	79,506	78,456
Administrative and waste services...............................	33,186	33,480	34,920	34,460	35,234	35,392	36,813
Educational services	30,973	32,485	33,256	33,857	34,167	34,055	34,221
Health care and social assistance.............................	36,633	37,597	38,116	38,808	39,288	39,929	41,149
Arts, entertainment, and recreation............................	34,339	33,016	35,217	35,272	34,389	34,524	34,600
Accommodation and food services.............................	17,572	18,089	18,898	19,152	19,433	19,482	20,179
Other services, except public administration..................	27,492	27,758	28,751	29,368	18,996	30,603	32,092
Government and government enterprises........................	41,139	41,803	42,333	42,855	43,087	43,559	43,888

Table LA-10. Employment Characteristics by Family Type

(Number, percent.)

Family type and labor force status	2012 Total	2012 Families with own children under 18 years	2013 Total	2013 Families with own children under 18 years	2014 Total	2014 Families with own children under 18 years
All Families..........................	1,125,659	491,081	1,129,437	484,007	1,109,475	468,474
FAMILY TYPE AND LABOR FORCE STATUS						
Married-Couple Families............................	744,806	280,552	745,632	282,943	738,715	270,836
Both husband and wife in labor force...........	49.8	67.7	49.3	66.0	47.4	63.4
Husband in labor force, wife not in labor force........	23.5	25.9	25.3	28.8	24.9	30.0
Wife in labor force, husband not in labor force...........	8.6	4.4	7.8	3.4	8.8	4.4
Both husband and wife not in labor force..........	18.1	2.0	17.3	1.7	18.9	2.2
Other Families........................	380,853	210,529	383,805	201,064	370,760	197,638
Female householder, no husband present........................	76.3	78.4	76.3	80.4	75.0	78.8
In labor force........................	53.3	64.3	51.0	64.2	49.1	62.1
Not in labor force........................	23.0	14.1	25.3	16.2	26.0	16.6
Male householder, no wife present........................	23.7	21.6	23.7	19.6	25.0	21.2
In labor force........................	17.3	19.1	17.2	17.1	18.6	18.7
Not in labor force........................	6.4	2.5	6.5	2.5	6.4	2.6

Table LA-11. School Enrollment and Educational Attainment, 2014

(Number, percent.)

Item	State	U.S.
Enrollment		
Total population 3 years and over, enrolled in school........................	1,179,507	82,063,714
Enrolled in nursery school or preschool (percent)........................	7.0	6.0
Enrolled in kindergarten (percent)........................	5.5	5.1
Enrolled in elementary school, grades 1-8 (percent)........................	43.4	40.2
Enrolled in high school, grades 9-12 (percent)........................	19.8	20.7
Enrolled in college or graduate school (percent)........................	24.4	28.0
Attainment		
Total population 25 years and over........................	3,060,688	213,725,624
Less than ninth grade (percent)........................	5.7	5.6
9th to 12th grade, no diploma (percent)........................	10.7	7.5
High school graduate, including equivalency (percent)........................	33.8	27.7
Some college, no degree (percent)........................	21.5	21.0
Associate's degree (percent)........................	5.4	8.2
Bachelor's degree (percent)........................	15.2	18.7
Graduate or professional degree (percent)........................	7.8	11.4
High school graduate or higher (percent)........................	83.6	86.9
Bachelor's degree or higher (percent)........................	22.9	30.1

Table LA-12. Public School Characteristics and Educational Indicators

(Number, percent; data derived from National Center of Education Statistics.)

Item	State	U.S.
Public Schools, 2013–2014 (except where noted)		
Number of school districts........................	133	18,194
Number of schools........................	1,412	98,271
Number of students (in thousands)........................	711	50,045
Number of teachers (in thousands)........................	46	3,114
Student-teacher ratio........................	15.3	16.1
Expenditures per student (dollars), FY 2012........................	105,397	107,637
Four-year adjusted cohort graduation rate (ACGR)[1,2]........................	74.6	82.3
Students eligible for free or reduced-price lunch (in thousands)........................	464	25,596
English language learners (in thousands)........................	14	4,461
Students age 3 to 21 served under IDEA, part B (in thousands)........................	79	6,464

Public Schools by Type	Number	Percent of state public schools
Total number of schools........................	1,412	100.0
Regular........................	1,277	90.4
Special education........................	30	2.1
Vocational education........................	8	0.6
Alternative education........................	97	6.9

NOTE: Every school is assigned only one school type based on its instructional emphasis.
[1]ACGR data represents a new method of calculating high-school completion rates and may not be comparable to previous years' data for Averaged Freshmen Graduation Rates (AFGR).
[2]The United States 4-year ACGRs were estimated using both the reported 4-year ACGR data from 49 states and the District of Columbia and using imputed data for Idaho. The estimate for American Indian/Alaska Native students also includes imputed data for Virginia.

Table LA-13. Reported Voting and Registration of the Voting-Age Population, November 2014

(Numbers in thousands, percent.)

Item	Total population	Total citizen population	Registered			Voted		
			Total registered	Percent registered (total population)	Percent registered (total citizen population)	Total voted	Percent voted (total population)	Percent voted (total citizen population)
U.S. Total	239,874	219,941	142,166	59.3	64.6	92,251	38.5	41.9
State Total.............................	3,450	3,342	2,398	69.5	71.7	1,677	48.6	50.2
Sex								
Male..	1,645	1,583	1,108	67.3	70.0	768	46.7	48.5
Female	1,805	1,759	1,290	71.5	73.4	908	50.3	51.7
Race								
White alone.............................	2,250	2,170	1,596	70.9	73.5	1,094	48.6	50.4
White, non-Hispanic alone	2,094	2,080	1,543	73.7	74.2	1,065	50.8	51.2
Black alone..............................	1,042	1,034	729	70.0	70.5	533	51.2	51.6
Asian alone	82	62	24	(B)	(B)	13	(B)	(B)
Hispanic (of any race)......................	165	100	57	34.4	56.7	31	19.0	31.3
White alone or in combination	2,280	2,200	1,616	70.9	73.4	1,109	48.7	50.4
Black alone or in combination..........	1,072	1,063	752	70.2	70.7	552	51.5	51.9
Asian alone or in combination..........	85	64	24	(B)	(B)	13	(B)	(B)
Age								
18 to 24 years..............................	501	484	258	51.6	53.4	132	26.2	27.2
25 to 34 years..............................	643	610	410	63.8	67.2	232	36.2	38.1
35 to 44 years..............................	502	463	306	60.9	66.0	183	36.5	39.6
45 to 64 years..............................	1,179	1,162	913	77.5	78.6	703	59.7	60.5
65 years and over	625	623	510	81.6	81.9	426	68.2	68.5

B = Base is less than 75,000 and therefore too small to show the derived measure.

Table LA-14. Crime

(Number, rate per 100,000. Data are derived from the FBI Uniform Crime Reports.)

Item	State			U.S.[1,2,3,4]		
	2013	2014	Percent change	2013	2014	Percent change
TOTAL POPULATION[5]............................	4,625,470	4,649,676	0.5	316,128,839	318,857,056	0.9
VIOLENT CRIME						
Number...	23,609	23,934	1.4	1,163,146	1,165,383	0.2
Rate	510.4	514.7	0.8	367.9	365.5	-0.7
Murder and Nonnegligent Manslaughter						
Number...	498	477	-4.2	14,196	14,249	0.4
Rate	10.8	10.3	-4.6	4.5	4.5	-
Rape[6]						
Number...	1,619	1,375	X	108,612	116,645	X
Rate	35.0	29.6	X	34.4	36.6	X
Robbery						
Number...	5,548	5,695	2.6	345,031	325,802	-5.6
Rate	119.9	122.5	2.2	109.1	102.2	-6.3
Aggravated Assault						
Number...	16,319	16,387	0.4	724,149	741,291	2.4
Rate	352.8	352.4	-0.1	229.1	232.5	1.5
PROPERTY CRIME						
Number...	165,686	160,824	-2.9	8,632,512	8,277,829	-4.1
Rate	3,582.0	3,458.8	-3.4	2,730.7	2,596.1	-4.9
Burglary						
Number...	41,184	38,337	-6.9	1,928,465	1,729,806	-10.3
Rate	890.4	824.5	-7.4	610.0	542.5	-11.1
Larceny-Theft						
Number...	115,342	112,596	-2.4	6,004,453	5,858,496	-2.4
Rate	2,493.6	2,421.6	-2.9	1,899.4	1,837.3	-3.3
Motor Vehicle Theft						
Number...	9,160	9,891	8.0	699,594	689,527	-1.4
Rate	198.0	212.7	7.4	221.3	216.2	-2.3

NOTE: Although arson data are included in the trend and clearance tables, sufficient data are not available to estimate totals for this offense. Therefore, no arson data are published in this table.
X = Not applicable.
- = Zero or rounds to zero.
[1]The crime figures have been adjusted.
[2]The data collection methodology for the offense of forcible rape used by the Minnesota state Uniform Crime Reporting (UCR) Program (with the exception of Minneapolis and St. Paul, Minnesota) does not comply with national UCR Program guidelines. Consequently, its figures for forcible rape and violent crime (of which forcible rape is a part) are not published in this table.
[3]Includes offenses reported by the Zoological Police and the Metro Transit Police.
[4]Because of changes in the state's reporting practices, figures are not comparable to previous years' data.
[5]Populations are U.S. Census Bureau provisional estimates as of July 1 of each year.
[6]The figures shown for the offense of rape were estimated using the revised Uniform Crime Reporting (UCR) definition of rape.

Table LA-15. State Government Finances, 2014

(Dollar amounts in thousands, percent distribution.)

Item	Dollars	Percent distribution
Total Revenue	33,275,548	100.0
General revenue	25,351,939	76.2
Intergovernmental revenue	10,214,940	30.7
Taxes	9,695,281	29.1
General sales	2,923,336	8.8
Selective sales	2,192,300	6.6
License taxes	427,090	1.3
Individual income tax	2,753,680	8.3
Corporate income tax	481,212	1.4
Other taxes	917,663	2.8
Current charges	3,031,797	9.1
Miscellaneous general revenue	2,409,921	7.2
Utility revenue	8,658	-
Liquor stores revenue	0	-
Insurance trust revenue[1]	7,914,951	23.8
Total Expenditure	31,803,632	100.0
Intergovernmental expenditure	6,053,019	19.0
Direct expenditure	25,750,613	81.0
Current operation	18,387,545	57.8
Capital outlay	1,508,021	4.7
Insurance benefits and repayments	4,310,455	13.6
Assistance and subsidies	743,671	2.3
Interest on debt	800,921	2.5
Exhibit: Salaries and wages	3,885,153	12.2
Total Expenditure	31,803,632	100.0
General expenditure	27,487,861	86.4
Intergovernmental expenditure	6,053,019	19.0
Direct expenditure	21,434,842	67.4
General expenditure, by function:		
Education	8,592,518	27.0
Public welfare	8,081,372	25.4
Hospitals	1,845,153	5.8
Health	500,686	1.6
Highways	1,522,816	4.8
Police protection	349,895	1.1
Correction	698,086	2.2
Natural resources	719,794	2.3
Parks and recreation	348,698	1.1
Governmental administration	972,613	3.1
Interest on general debt	800,921	2.5
Other and unallocable	3,055,309	9.6
Utility expenditure	5,316	-
Liquor stores expenditure	0	-
Insurance trust expenditure	4,310,455	13.6
Debt at End of Fiscal Year	18,996,129	X
Cash and Security Holdings	63,886,163	X

X = Not applicable.
- = Zero or rounds to zero.
[1]Within insurance trust revenue, net earnings of state retirement systems is a calculated statistic (the item code in the data file is X08), and thus can be positive or negative. Net earnings is the sum of earnings on investments plus gains on investments minus losses on investments. The change made in 2002 for asset valuation from book to market value in accordance with Statement 34 of the Governmental Accounting Standards Board is reflected in the calculated statistics.

Table LA-16. State Government Tax Collections, 2014

(Dollars in thousands, percent.)

Item	Dollars	Percent distribution
Total Taxes	9,695,281	100.0
Property taxes	55,363	0.6
Sales and gross receipts	5,115,636	52.8
General sales and gross receipts	2,923,336	30.2
Selective sales and gross receipts	2,192,300	22.6
Alcoholic beverages	56,967	0.6
Amusements	675,386	7.0
Insurance premiums	429,146	4.4
Motor fuels	588,860	6.1
Pari-mutuels	4,385	-
Public utilities	9,158	0.1
Tobacco products	130,045	1.3
Other selective sales	298,353	3.1
Licenses	427,090	4.4
Alcoholic beverages	0	-
Amusements	0	-
Corporations in general	188,197	1.9
Hunting and fishing	29,665	0.3
Motor vehicle	75,628	0.8
Motor vehicle operators	11,581	0.1
Public utilities	7,622	0.1
Occupation and business, NEC	110,176	1.1
Other licenses	4,221	-
Income taxes	3,234,892	33.4
Individual income	2,753,680	28.4
Corporation net income	481,212	5.0
Other taxes	862,300	8.9
Death and gift	150	-
Documentary and stock transfer	0	-
Severance	862,150	8.9
Taxes, NEC	0	0.0

- = Zero or rounds to zero.

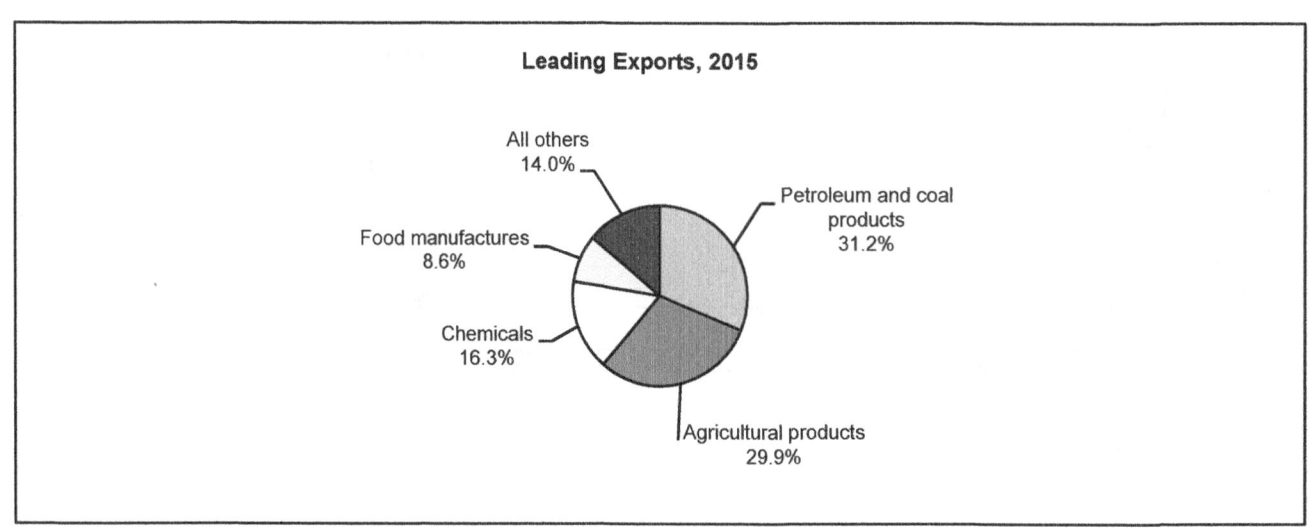

Leading Exports, 2015

All others 14.0%

Petroleum and coal products 31.2%

Food manufactures 8.6%

Chemicals 16.3%

Agricultural products 29.9%

MAINE

Facts and Figures

Location: Northeast corner of the United States; bordered on the N and E by New Brunswick, Canada; on the S by the Atlantic Ocean; on the W by New Hampshire; and on the NW by Quebec, Canada

Area: 35,385 sq. mi. (91,646 sq. km.); rank—39th

Population: 1,329,328 (2015 est.); rank—42nd

Principal Cities: capital—Augusta; largest—Portland

Statehood: March 15, 1820; 23rd state

U.S. Congress: 2 senators, 2 representatives

State Motto: *Dirigo* ("I lead")

State Song: "State of Maine Song"

State Nickname: The Pine Tree State

Abbreviations: ME; Me.

State Symbols: flower—white pinecone and tassel; tree—Eastern white pine; bird—chickadee

At a Glance

- With a population that grew 0.1 percent, Maine ranked 48th among the states in growth from 2010 to 2015.

- In 2014, 10.1 percent of Mainers did not have health insurance, compared to 11.7 percent of the total U.S. population.

- Maine's violent crime rate was 127.8 per 100,000 population, the second lowest in the country in 2014.

- With 18.8 percent of its population in the 65 and older age group, Maine ranked 2nd in this category in 2015.

- Maine's birth rate of 9.5 per 1,000 population was the second lowest in the country in 2014.

Table ME-1. Population by Age, Sex, Race, and Hispanic Origin

(Number, percent, except where noted.)

Sex, age, race, and Hispanic origin	2000	2010	2015[1]	Average annual percent change, 2010–2015
Total Population...	1,274,923	1,328,361	1,329,328	-
Percent of total U.S. population	0.5	0.4	0.4	X
Sex				
Male..	620,309	650,056	651,257	-
Female	654,614	678,305	678,071	-
Age				
Under 5 years..	70,726	69,520	64,687	-0.5
5 to 19 years...	264,729	241,439	224,934	-0.5
20 to 64 years...	756,036	806,322	789,171	-0.2
65 years and over...	183,402	211,080	250,536	1.2
Median age (years)	38.6	42.7	44.5	0.3
Race and Hispanic Origin				
One race				
White	1,236,014	1,269,764	1,261,773	-
Black	6,760	16,269	19,272	1.2
American Indian and Alaska Native	7,098	8,771	9,194	0.3
Asian..	9,111	13,783	16,378	1.2
Native Hawaiian or Other Pacific Islander	382	377	478	1.7
Two or more races	12,647	19,397	22,233	1.0
Hispanic (of any race)...	9,360	18,261	20,924	1.0

X = Not applicable.
- = Zero or rounds to zero.
[1]Population figures for 2015 are July 1 estimates. The 2010 estimates are taken from the 2010 Census.

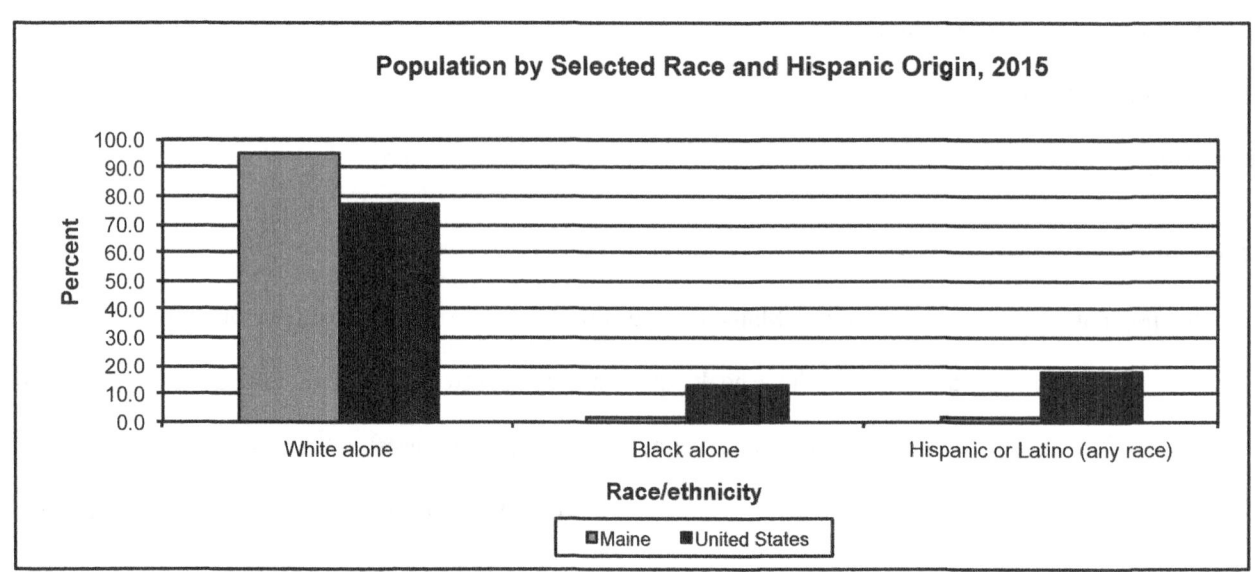

Table ME-2. Marital Status

(Number, percent distribution.)

Sex, age, race, and Hispanic origin	2000	2010	2014
Males, 15 Years and Over	494,217	534,474	538,760
Never married	26.8	31.0	30.6
Now married, except separated.......................................	58.8	52.5	52.7
Separated...	1.1	1.2	0.9
Widowed...	2.8	2.9	3.0
Divorced...	10.5	12.5	12.8
Females, 15 Years and Over	534,606	570,281	573,514
Never married	21.2	24.2	24.7
Now married, except separated.......................................	54.1	49.3	49.4
Separated...	1.3	1.6	1.3
Widowed...	11.0	9.9	9.5
Divorced...	12.4	15.0	15.0

Table ME-3. Households and Housing Characteristics

(Number, percent, dollars.)

Item	2000	2010	2014	Average annual percent change, 2000–2014
Total Households..	518,200	545,417	549,841	0.4
Family households	340,685	345,328	344,585	0.1
Married-couple family	272,152	266,670	263,704	-0.2
Other family	68,533	78,658	80,881	1.3
Male householder, no wife present................................	19,511	23,620	25,981	2.4
Female householder, no husband present	49,022	55,038	54,900	0.9
Nonfamily households	177,515	200,089	205,256	1.1
Householder living alone	139,969	155,623	161,859	1.1
Householder not living alone.....................................	37,546	44,466	43,397	1.1
Housing Characteristics				
Total housing units..	651,901	722,217	727,693	0.8
Occupied housing units	518,200	545,417	549,841	0.4
Owner occupied	370,905	396,395	392,139	0.4
Renter occupied	147,295	149,022	157,702	0.5
Average household size..	2.39	2.37	2.35	-0.1
Financial Characteristics				
Median gross rent of renter-occupied housing	497	707	776	4.0
Median monthly owner costs for housing units with a mortgage	923	1,289	1,322	3.1
Median value of owner-occupied housing units	98,700	179,100	174,800	5.5

- = Zero or rounds to zero.

Table ME-4. Migration, Origin, and Language

(Number, percent.)

Characteristic	State			U.S.		
	2013	2014	Percent change	2013	2014	Percent change
Residence 1 Year Ago						
Population 1 year and over	1,315,753	1,317,638	0.1	312,432,820	315,095,393	0.9
Same house	85.8	86.4	X	85.0	85.1	X
Different house in the U.S.	13.9	13.2	X	14.4	14.3	X
Same county	8.5	7.3	X	8.9	8.7	X
Different county	5.5	5.9	X	5.5	5.6	X
Same state	2.7	2.9	X	3.2	3.3	X
Different state	2.8	3.0	X	2.3	2.3	X
Abroad	0.3	0.4	X	0.6	0.6	X
Place of Birth						
Native born	1,283,615	1,280,403	0.1	274,780,773	276,465,262	0.6
Male	49.2	48.9	X	49.3	49.3	X
Female	50.8	51.1	X	50.7	50.7	X
Foreign born	44,687	49,686	0.1	41,348,066	42,391,794	2.5
Male	41.6	43.4	X	48.8	48.7	X
Female	58.4	56.6	X	51.2	51.3	X
Foreign born; naturalized U.S. citizen...........................	25,351	26,457	0.1	19,294,710	19,984,738	3.6
Male	41.3	44.8	X	45.9	45.9	X
Female	58.7	55.2	X	54.1	54.1	X
Foreign born; not a U.S. citizen	19,336	23,229	0.1	22,053,356	22,407,056	1.6
Male	41.9	41.8	X	51.3	51.2	X
Female	58.1	58.2	X	48.7	48.8	X
Entered 2010 or later	13.6	22.1	X	9.7	12.3	X
Entered 2000 to 2009	25.8	22.9	X	29.4	28.6	X
Entered before 2000..	60.6	55.0	X	61.0	59.1	X
World Region of Birth, Foreign						
Foreign-born population, excluding population born at sea	44,687	49,686	0.1	41,347,945	42,390,705	2.5
Europe	23.1	24.0	X	11.6	11.2	X
Asia	28.9	28.4	X	29.5	30.1	X
Africa	12.2	16.0	X	4.4	4.6	X
Oceania	1.3	0.8	X	0.5	0.6	X
Latin America..	9.8	10.7	X	51.9	51.6	X
North America...	24.8	20.2	X	2.0	1.9	X
Language Spoken at Home and Ability to Speak English						
Population 5 years and over..	1,264,125	1,267,172	0.1	296,358,760	299,084,046	0.9
English only	93.7	93.2	X	79.2	78.9	X
Language other than English.......................................	6.3	6.8	X	20.8	21.1	X
Speaks English less than "very well"...........................	1.5	1.8	X	8.5	8.6	X

X = Not applicable.
- = Zero or rounds to zero.

Table ME-5. Median Income and Poverty Status, 2014

(Number, percent, except as noted.)

Characteristic	State		U.S.	
	Number	Percent	Number	Percent
Median Income				
Households (dollars)...	49,462	X	53,657	X
Families (dollars)	62,078	X	65,910	X
Below Poverty Level (All People)	182,791	14.1	48,208,387	15.5
Sex				
Male..	79,771	12.7	21,590,918	14.2
Female..	103,020	15.5	26,617,469	16.8
Age				
Under 18 years...	48,007	19.1	15,686,012	21.7
Related children under 18 years...........................	46,689	18.7	15,372,705	21.3
18 to 64 years..	113,870	14.1	28,267,482	14.6
65 years and over	20,914	8.9	4,254,893	9.5

X = Not applicable.

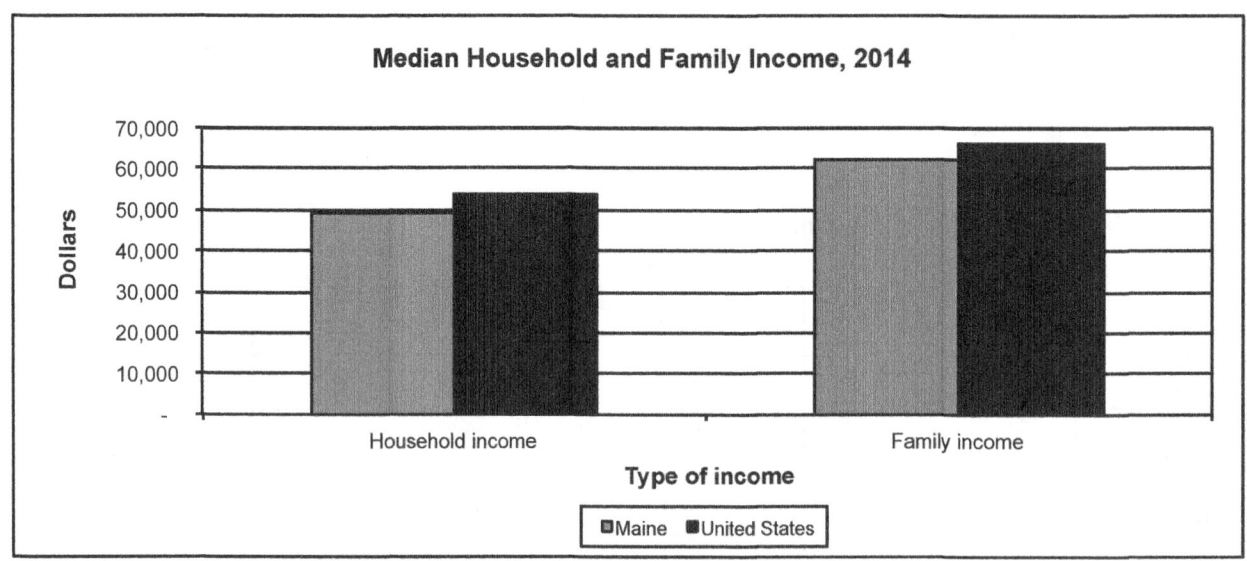

Table ME-6. Health Insurance Coverage Status for the Civilian Noninstitutionalized Population and Children Under 18 Years of Age

(Numbers in thousands, percent.)

Item	2006	2007	2008	2009	2010	2011	2012	2013	2014
Civilian Noninstitutionalized Population	1,315	1,313	1,299	1,301	1,313	1,314	1,316	1,314	1,316
Covered by Private or Public Insurance									
Number..	1,192	1,197	1,157	1,164	1,180	1,174	1,181	1,167	1,182
Percent..	90.7	91.2	89.1	89.5	89.8	89.3	89.8	88.8	89.9
Not Covered									
Number..	122	115	142	137	133	140	135	147	134
Percent..	9.3	8.8	10.9	10.5	10.1	10.7	10.2	11.2	10.1
Percent in the U.S. not covered............................	15.8	15.3	15.1	15.1	15.5	15.1	14.8	14.5	11.7
Children Under 18 Years of Age	286	281	275	270	273	270	265	260	257
Covered by Private or Public Insurance									
Number..	258	268	255	255	262	256	253	244	241
Percent..	93.6	94.9	92.7	94.4	96.0	94.8	95.4	94.1	93.7
Not Covered									
Number..	18	14	20	15	11	14	12	15	16
Percent..	6.4	5.1	7.3	5.6	4.0	5.2	4.6	5.9	6.3
Percent in the U.S. not covered............................	11.7	11.0	9.7	8.6	8.0	7.5	7.2	7.1	6.0

Table ME-7. Employment Status by Demographic Group, 2015

(Numbers in thousands, percent.)

Characteristic	Civilian noninstitutional population	Civilian labor force		Employed		Unemployed	
		Number	Percent of population	Number	Percent of population	Number	Percent of population
Total..	1,093	678	62.0	649	59.3	30	4.4
Sex							
Male...	530	354	66.8	338	63.8	16	4.6
Female..	563	324	57.5	311	55.1	14	4.2
Race, Sex, and Hispanic Origin							
White	1,033	640	62.0	613	59.4	27	4.2
Male...	502	334	66.6	319	63.6	15	4.4
Female..	531	306	57.7	294	55.3	12	4.0
Black or African American....................	11	9	82.8	8	74.3	1	10.1
Male...	NA	NA	NA	NA	NA	NA	NA
Female..	NA	NA	NA	NA	NA	NA	NA
Hispanic or Latino ethnicity[1]	14	8	59	7	53	1	12
Male...	NA	NA	NA	NA	NA	NA	NA
Female..	NA	NA	NA	NA	NA	NA	NA
Age							
16 to 19 years................................	60	26	43.3	22	36.8	4	15.1
20 to 24 years................................	73	54	73.0	49	66.8	5	8.4
25 to 34 years................................	140	111	79.0	105	74.9	6	5.1
35 to 44 years................................	172	138	80.5	134	77.9	5	3.3
45 to 54 years................................	180	149	82.8	144	80.3	5	3.0
55 to 64 years................................	218	148	67.8	143	65.6	5	3.2
65 years and over	250	53	21.3	52	20.6	2	3.6

NOTE. Data in Table 7 are from the Current Population Survey (CPS) and do not match the estimates in Table 8. See notes and definitions for further information.
[1] May be of any race.
NA = Not available.

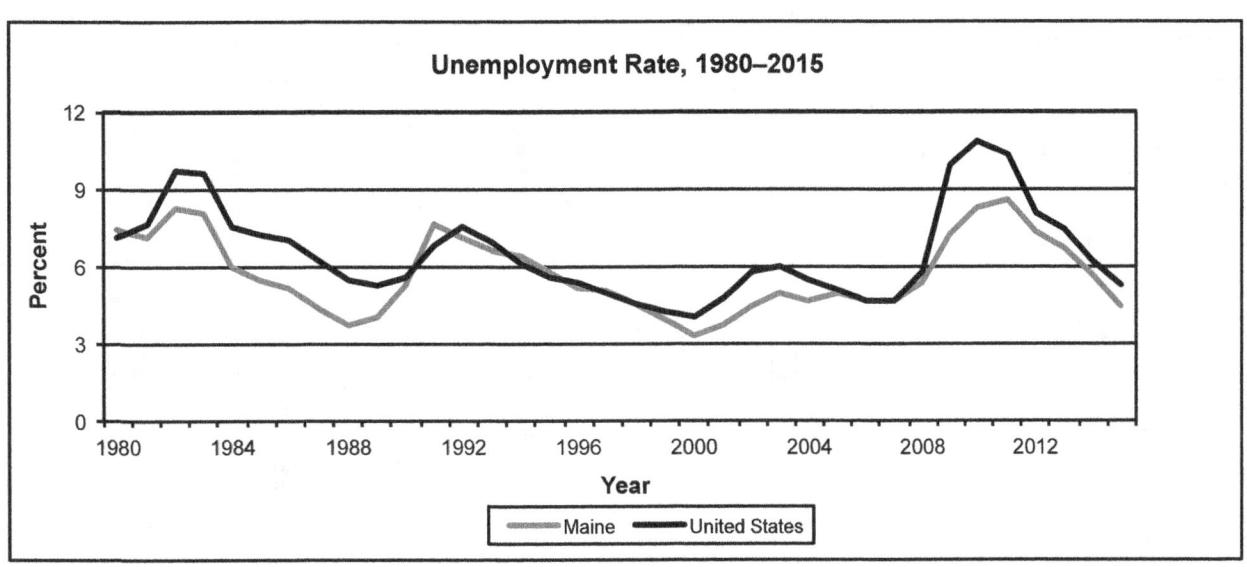

Table ME-8. Employment Status of the Civilian Noninstitutional Population Age 16 Years and Over

(Number, percent.)

Year	Civilian labor force	Civilian participation rate	Employed	Unemployed	Unemployment rate
2007...	700,468	66.3	667,781	32,687	4.7
2008...	701,646	66.0	663,158	38,488	5.5
2009...	696,219	65.4	639,954	56,265	8.1
2010...	695,182	64.8	638,630	56,552	8.1
2011...	699,281	64.8	644,085	55,196	7.9
2012...	702,799	64.9	650,249	52,550	7.5
2013...	707,623	65.2	660,662	46,961	6.6
2014...	696,578	63.9	657,302	39,276	5.6
2015...	679,756	62.3	649,855	29,901	4.4

Table ME-9. Employment and Average Wages by Industry

(Estimates through 2010 are based on the 2007 North American Industry Classification System [NAICS]. Estimates from 2011 onward are based on the 2012 NAICS.)

Industry	2008	2009	2010	2011	2012	2013	2014
	Number of jobs						
Wage and Salary Employment by Industry..................	637,589	616,379	611,786	613,325	613,326	616,647	620,233
Farm Wage and Salary Employment.........................	2,946	2,843	2,849	3,023	3,060	3,626	4,162
Nonfarm Wage and Salary Employment....................	634,643	613,536	608,937	610,302	610,266	613,021	616,071
Private wage and salary employment........................	521,727	501,937	498,170	501,526	502,293	506,080	509,476
Forestry, fishing, and related activities........................	D	D	4,071	4,094	D	4,081	4,201
Mining..	D	D	179	203	D	187	190
Utilities...	1,895	1,862	1,817	1,609	1,630	1,619	1,551
Construction...	30,502	26,371	25,484	26,588	26,443	26,446	26,770
Manufacturing...	58,801	52,436	50,716	50,855	50,832	50,407	50,277
Durable goods manufacturing............................	31,337	27,643	26,974	27,219	27,101	27,266	27,768
Nondurable goods manufacturing.........................	27,464	24,793	23,742	23,636	23,731	23,141	22,509
Wholesale trade..	20,968	19,746	19,170	19,190	19,516	19,679	19,828
Retail trade..	86,720	83,496	82,742	82,565	82,086	82,172	82,451
Transportation and warehousing.............................	16,929	15,944	15,696	15,875	15,743	16,064	16,578
Information...	10,146	9,239	9,159	8,289	7,920	7,651	7,443
Finance and insurance	25,369	24,841	24,775	25,288	24,965	25,014	23,704
Real estate and rental and leasing...........................	7,260	6,931	6,749	6,510	6,497	6,654	6,605
Professional, scientific, and technical services	24,812	24,128	23,830	23,854	23,968	24,853	25,015
Management of companies and enterprises..................	7,025	6,899	6,990	7,113	7,565	7,425	9,090
Administrative and waste services	26,028	25,314	25,808	27,120	27,169	28,340	29,726
Educational services	13,613	13,536	14,228	14,480	14,853	14,990	15,370
Health care and social assistance...........................	100,355	101,479	101,138	101,362	102,149	102,226	102,488
Arts, entertainment, and recreation.........................	8,399	8,170	8,182	8,251	8,852	8,925	8,445
Accommodation and food services...........................	52,345	51,679	52,319	52,713	53,236	54,253	55,100
Other services, except public administration.................	26,365	25,743	25,117	25,567	24,632	25,094	24,644
Government and government enterprises.........................	112,916	111,599	110,767	108,776	107,973	106,941	106,595
	Dollars						
Average Wages and Salaries by Industry	37,374	37,539	38,329	39,055	39,716	40,295	41,587
Average Farm Wages and Salaries	28,813	28,365	26,735	22,542	24,961	28,700	31,255
Average Nonfarm Wages and Salaries	37,413	37,582	38,384	39,137	39,790	40,363	41,657
Average private wages and salaries.........................	36,904	36,846	37,766	38,691	39,482	40,047	41,406
Forestry, fishing, and related activities.........................	D	D	38,248	40,511	D	40,580	41,937
Mining...	D	D	53,469	53,493	D	55,770	58,953
Utilities...	67,348	66,236	71,138	75,606	77,785	79,755	87,606
Construction...	41,160	41,016	41,257	42,576	43,605	44,616	45,855
Manufacturing...	48,074	48,119	51,576	52,263	52,484	53,201	54,464
Durable goods manufacturing............................	48,695	48,590	51,619	52,725	52,480	53,197	54,460
Nondurable goods manufacturing.........................	47,365	47,594	51,526	51,730	52,489	53,206	54,469
Wholesale trade	51,944	52,209	52,979	54,738	55,929	56,719	59,578
Retail trade	24,459	24,763	25,083	25,349	25,631	25,790	26,666
Transportation and warehousing.............................	37,684	38,349	38,928	38,772	39,381	40,277	41,993
Information..	44,094	44,847	46,823	45,622	46,161	47,315	48,047
Finance and insurance	56,826	56,432	58,670	61,847	64,086	66,279	68,678
Real estate and rental and leasing...........................	32,873	33,077	33,825	35,659	37,191	37,551	38,987
Professional, scientific, and technical services	55,986	55,621	56,290	58,089	60,311	60,829	63,665
Management of companies and enterprises..................	75,339	65,920	68,478	71,534	75,537	75,206	74,593
Administrative and waste services	31,891	31,622	32,479	32,886	33,337	33,388	34,433
Educational services	32,078	33,148	32,939	34,510	34,576	35,202	36,422
Health care and social assistance............................	39,522	40,296	40,756	41,901	42,663	43,277	44,508
Arts, entertainment, and recreation..........................	24,421	24,304	24,738	25,049	24,819	26,075	26,682
Accommodation and food services............................	17,457	17,310	18,038	18,486	18,931	19,259	20,339
Other services, except public administration..................	24,330	24,498	25,657	26,155	27,057	27,996	29,446
Government and government enterprises.........................	39,766	40,891	41,162	41,194	41,220	41,858	42,857

D = Not shown to avoid disclosure of confidential information, but the estimates for this item are included in the total.

Table ME-10. Employment Characteristics by Family Type

(Number, percent.)

Family type and labor force status	2012		2013		2014	
	Total	Families with own children under 18 years	Total	Families with own children under 18 years	Total	Families with own children under 18 years
All Families...........................	346,950	135,007	338,609	126,751	342,108	128,896
FAMILY TYPE AND LABOR FORCE STATUS						
Married-Couple Families........................	270,568	88,800	263,513	81,309	261,227	81,849
Both husband and wife in labor force................	54.2	72.0	52.0	70.4	53.6	72.7
Husband in labor force, wife not in labor force	16.8	21.6	16.7	20.4	17.3	21.5
Wife in labor force, husband not in labor force	9.0	4.4	10.6	6.8	9.0	4.0
Both husband and wife not in labor force............	19.9	2.0	20.1	2.0	20.1	1.8
Other Families	76,382	46,207	75,096	45,442	80,881	47,047
Female householder, no husband present............	69.6	71.7	68.4	66.9	67.9	68.4
In labor force................	47.2	53.3	47.7	54.1	46.9	54.0
Not in labor force	22.4	18.4	20.8	12.8	21.0	14.4
Male householder, no wife present....................	30.4	28.3	31.6	33.1	32.1	31.6
In labor force...............	22.9	24.1	23.8	27.3	24.7	27.5
Not in labor force	7.5	4.2	7.8	5.8	7.5	4.2

Table ME-11. School Enrollment and Educational Attainment, 2014

(Number, percent.)

Item	State	U.S.
Enrollment		
Total population 3 years and over, enrolled in school....................	296,931	82,063,714
Enrolled in nursery school or preschool (percent)...................	5.1	6.0
Enrolled in kindergarten (percent)...................	4.5	5.1
Enrolled in elementary school, grades 1-8 (percent)................	40.2	40.2
Enrolled in high school, grades 9-12 (percent)	21.7	20.7
Enrolled in college or graduate school (percent).................	28.5	28.0
Attainment		
Total population 25 years and over	959,407	213,725,624
Less than ninth grade (percent)	3.1	5.6
9th to 12th grade, no diploma (percent)	5.2	7.5
High school graduate, including equivalency (percent)............	32.3	27.7
Some college, no degree (percent)	20.3	21.0
Associate's degree (percent)	9.7	8.2
Bachelor's degree (percent)	19.4	18.7
Graduate or professional degree (percent)................	10.0	11.4
High school graduate or higher (percent)	91.7	86.9
Bachelor's degree or higher (percent).................	29.4	30.1

Table ME-12. Public School Characteristics and Educational Indicators

(Number, percent; data derived from National Center of Education Statistics.)

Item	State	U.S.
Public Schools, 2013–2014 (except where noted)		
Number of school districts....................	254	18,194
Number of schools....................	619	98,271
Number of students (in thousands)	184	50,045
Number of teachers (in thousands)	15	3,114
Student-teacher ratio...................	11.9	16.1
Expenditures per student (dollars), FY 2013................	12,655	107,637
Four-year adjusted cohort graduation rate (ACGR)[1][2]	86.5	82.3
Students eligible for free or reduced-price lunch (in thousands)	81	25,596
English language learners (in thousands)	5	4,461
Students age 3 to 21 served under IDEA, part B (in thousands)	32	6,464

Public Schools by Type	Number	Percent of state public schools
Total number of schools....................	619	100.0
Regular...................	589	95.2
Special education....................	3	0.5
Vocational education....................	27	4.4
Alternative education....................	0	-

NOTE: Every school is assigned only one school type based on its instructional emphasis.
[1]ACGR data represents a new method of calculating high-school completion rates and may not be comparable to previous years' data for Averaged Freshmen Graduation Rates (AFGR).
[2]The United States 4-year ACGRs were estimated using both the reported 4-year ACGR data from 49 states and the District of Columbia and using imputed data for Idaho. The estimate for American Indian/Alaska Native students also includes imputed data for Virginia.
- = Zero or rounds to zero.

Table ME-13. Reported Voting and Registration of the Voting-Age Population, November 2014

(Numbers in thousands, percent.)

Item	Total population	Total citizen population	Registered			Voted		
			Total registered	Percent registered (total population)	Percent registered (total citizen population)	Total voted	Percent voted (total population)	Percent voted (total citizen population)
U.S. Total	239,874	219,941	142,166	59.3	64.6	92,251	38.5	41.9
State Total..............................	1,061	1,045	799	75.4	76.5	642	60.5	61.5
Sex								
Male....................................	512	503	373	73.0	74.2	302	59.0	60.0
Female	549	541	426	77.6	78.7	340	61.9	62.8
Race								
White alone............................	1,009	1,002	771	76.4	76.9	616	61.1	61.5
White, non-Hispanic alone...........	999	992	766	76.7	77.3	613	61.4	61.8
Black alone............................	9	7	5	(B)	(B)	3	(B)	(B)
Asian alone	11	3	2	(B)	(B)	2	(B)	(B)
Hispanic (of any race).................	10	10	4	(B)	(B)	3	(B)	(B)
White alone or in combination	1,036	1,029	790	76.2	76.7	635	61.3	61.7
Black alone or in combination.........	19	17	11	(B)	(B)	10	(B)	(B)
Asian alone or in combination..........	13	5	3	(B)	(B)	3	(B)	(B)
Age								
18 to 24 years......................	110	107	54	49.4	50.7	33	30.2	31.0
25 to 34 years......................	154	152	98	63.5	64.4	67	43.4	44.0
35 to 44 years......................	153	149	119	77.8	79.7	90	58.6	60.1
45 to 64 years......................	382	376	310	81.2	82.5	258	67.7	68.7
65 years and over	262	260	218	83.4	83.9	194	74.2	74.7

B = Base is less than 75,000 and therefore too small to show the derived measure.

Table ME-14. Crime

(Number, rate per 100,000. Data are derived from the FBI Uniform Crime Reports.)

Item	State			U.S.[1,2,3,4]		
	2013	2014	Percent change	2013	2014	Percent change
TOTAL POPULATION[5]...........................	1,328,302	1,330,089	0.1	316,128,839	318,857,056	0.9
VIOLENT CRIME						
Number......................................	1,615	1,700	5.3	1,163,146	1,165,383	0.2
Rate	121.6	127.8	5.1	367.9	365.5	-0.7
Murder and Nonnegligent Manslaughter						
Number......................................	24	21	-12.5	14,196	14,249	0.4
Rate	1.8	1.6	-11.1	4.5	4.5	-
Rape[6]						
Number......................................	447	485	X	108,612	116,645	X
Rate	33.7	36.5	X	34.4	36.6	X
Robbery						
Number......................................	335	304	-9.3	345,031	325,802	-5.6
Rate	25.2	22.9	-9.1	109.1	102.2	-6.3
Aggravated Assault						
Number......................................	912	890	-2.4	724,149	741,291	2.4
Rate	68.7	66.9	-2.6	229.1	232.5	1.5
PROPERTY CRIME						
Number......................................	30,447	26,421	-13.2	8,632,512	8,277,829	-4.1
Rate	2,292.2	1,986.4	-13.3	2,730.7	2,596.1	-4.9
Burglary						
Number......................................	6,483	5,030	-22.4	1,928,465	1,729,806	-10.3
Rate	488.1	378.2	-22.5	610.0	542.5	-11.1
Larceny-Theft						
Number......................................	23,050	20,592	-10.7	6,004,453	5,858,496	-2.4
Rate	1,735.3	1,548.2	-10.8	1,899.4	1,837.3	-3.3
Motor Vehicle Theft						
Number......................................	914	799	-12.6	699,594	689,527	-1.4
Rate	68.8	60.1	-12.6	221.3	216.2	-2.3

NOTE: Although arson data are included in the trend and clearance tables, sufficient data are not available to estimate totals for this offense. Therefore, no arson data are published in this table.
X = Not applicable.
- = Zero or rounds to zero.
[1]The crime figures have been adjusted.
[2]The data collection methodology for the offense of forcible rape used by the Minnesota state Uniform Crime Reporting (UCR) Program (with the exception of Minneapolis and St. Paul, Minnesota) does not comply with national UCR Program guidelines. Consequently, its figures for forcible rape and violent crime (of which forcible rape is a part) are not published in this table.
[3]Includes offenses reported by the Zoological Police and the Metro Transit Police.
[4]Because of changes in the state's reporting practices, figures are not comparable to previous years' data.
[5]Populations are U.S. Census Bureau provisional estimates as of July 1 of each year.
[6]The figures shown for the offense of rape were estimated using the revised Uniform Crime Reporting (UCR) definition of rape.

Table ME-15. State Government Finances, 2014

(Dollar amounts in thousands, percent distribution.)

Item	Dollars	Percent distribution
Total Revenue	10,528,889	100.0
General revenue	8,192,598	77.8
Intergovernmental revenue	3,028,373	28.8
Taxes	3,847,181	36.5
General sales	1,191,685	11.3
Selective sales	719,713	6.8
License taxes	254,251	2.4
Individual income tax	1,414,110	13.4
Corporate income tax	182,928	1.7
Other taxes	84,494	0.8
Current charges	766,281	7.3
Miscellaneous general revenue	550,763	5.2
Utility revenue	9,743	0.1
Liquor stores revenue	33	-
Insurance trust revenue[1]	2,326,515	22.1
Total Expenditure	9,258,232	100.0
Intergovernmental expenditure	1,285,064	13.9
Direct expenditure	7,973,168	86.1
Current operation	6,272,326	67.7
Capital outlay	341,814	3.7
Insurance benefits and repayments	1,004,891	10.9
Assistance and subsidies	136,545	1.5
Interest on debt	217,592	2.4
Exhibit: Salaries and wages	757,774	8.2
Total Expenditure	9,258,232	100.0
General expenditure	8,233,355	88.9
Intergovernmental expenditure	1,285,064	13.9
Direct expenditure	6,948,291	75.0
General expenditure, by function:		
Education	2,086,599	22.5
Public welfare	3,361,727	36.3
Hospitals	113,791	1.2
Health	459,578	5.0
Highways	582,645	6.3
Police protection	76,457	0.8
Correction	141,375	1.5
Natural resources	161,656	1.7
Parks and recreation	7,385	0.1
Governmental administration	285,847	3.1
Interest on general debt	217,592	2.4
Other and unallocable	738,703	8.0
Utility expenditure	19,986	0.2
Liquor stores expenditure	0	-
Insurance trust expenditure	1,004,891	10.9
Debt at End of Fiscal Year	5,473,870	X
Cash and Security Holdings	19,037,456	X

X = Not applicable.
- = Zero or rounds to zero.
[1]Within insurance trust revenue, net earnings of state retirement systems is a calculated statistic (the item code in the data file is X08), and thus can be positive or negative. Net earnings is the sum of earnings on investments plus gains on investments minus losses on investments. The change made in 2002 for asset valuation from book to market value in accordance with Statement 34 of the Governmental Accounting Standards Board is reflected in the calculated statistics.

Table ME-16. State Government Tax Collections, 2014

(Dollars in thousands, percent.)

Item	Dollars	Percent distribution
Total Taxes	3,847,181	100.0
Property taxes	35,755	0.9
Sales and gross receipts	1,911,398	49.7
General sales and gross receipts	1,191,685	31.0
Selective sales and gross receipts	719,713	18.7
Alcoholic beverages	17,923	0.5
Amusements	50,854	1.3
Insurance premiums	106,372	2.8
Motor fuels	240,901	6.3
Pari-mutuels	1,816	-
Public utilities	32,432	0.8
Tobacco products	136,160	3.5
Other selective sales	133,255	3.5
Licenses	254,251	6.6
Alcoholic beverages	5,393	0.1
Amusements	654	-
Corporations in general	9,343	0.2
Hunting and fishing	16,282	0.4
Motor vehicle	102,306	2.7
Motor vehicle operators	10,064	0.3
Public utilities	0	-
Occupation and business, NEC	101,562	2.6
Other licenses	8,647	0.2
Income taxes	1,597,038	41.5
Individual income	1,414,110	36.8
Corporation net income	182,928	4.8
Other taxes	48,739	1.3
Death and gift	23,962	0.6
Documentary and stock transfer	24,777	0.6
Severance	X	X
Taxes, NEC	0	-

X = Not applicable.
- = Zero or rounds to zero.

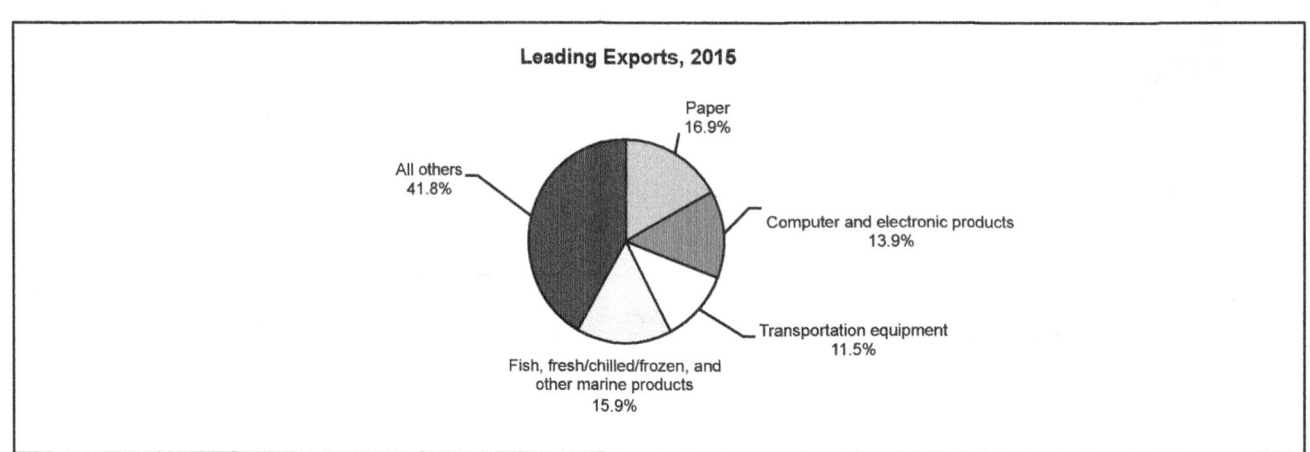

Leading Exports, 2015

Paper 16.9%

Computer and electronic products 13.9%

Transportation equipment 11.5%

Fish, fresh/chilled/frozen, and other marine products 15.9%

All others 41.8%

Facts and Figures

Location: Eastern United States; bordered on the N by Pennsylvania, on the E by Delaware and the Atlantic Ocean, and on the S and W by Virginia and West Virginia

Area: 12,407 sq. mi. (32,133 sq. km.); rank—42nd

Population: 6,006,401 (2015 est.); rank—19th

Principal Cities: capital—Annapolis; largest—Baltimore

Statehood: April 28, 1788; 7th state

U.S. Congress: 2 senators, 8 representatives

State Motto: *Fatti maschii parole femine* ("Manly deeds, womanly words")

State Song: "Maryland, My Maryland"

State Nicknames: The Old Line State; The Free State

Abbreviations: MD; Md.

State Symbols: flower—black-eyed susan; tree—white oak; bird—Baltimore oriole

At a Glance

- With an increase in population of 3.8 percent, Maryland ranked 22nd among the states in growth from 2010 to 2015.

- Maryland's median household income in 2014 was $73,971, the highest in the country, and 10.1 percent of the population lived below the poverty level.

- Maryland's violent crime rate in 2014 was 446.1 per 100,000 population, compared to 365.5 for the entire nation.

- In 2014, 7.9 percent of all Marylanders and 3.2 percent of children under age 18 in Maryland were uninsured, compared to the national averages of 11.7 percent and 6.0 percent respectively.

- Approximately 30.5 percent of Marylanders self-identified their race as "Black or African American alone" in 2015, the 5th highest percentage in the country.

Table MD-1. Population by Age, Sex, Race, and Hispanic Origin

(Number, percent, except where noted.)

Sex, age, race, and Hispanic origin	2000	2010	2015[1]	Average annual percent change, 2010–2015
Total Population..	5,296,486	5,773,552	6,006,401	0.3
Percent of total U.S. population	1.9	1.9	1.9	X
Sex				
Male..	2,557,794	2,791,762	2,911,085	0.3
Female	2,738,692	2,981,790	3,095,316	0.3
Age				
Under 5 years...	353,393	364,488	369,035	0.1
5 to 19 years..	1,139,572	1,152,138	1,134,444	-0.1
20 to 64 years..	3,204,214	3,549,284	3,653,351	0.2
65 years and over...	599,307	707,642	849,571	1.3
Median age (years)	36.0	38.0	38.4	0.1
Race and Hispanic Origin				
One race				
White...	3,391,308	3,542,379	3,581,757	0.1
Black..	1,477,411	1,731,513	1,829,583	0.4
American Indian and Alaska Native	15,423	30,885	33,792	0.6
Asian..	210,929	326,655	391,985	1.3
Native Hawaiian or Other Pacific Islander	2,303	5,391	6,479	1.3
Two or more races	103,587	137,729	162,805	1.2
Hispanic (of any race)...	227,916	493,811	572,373	1.1

X = Not applicable.
[1]Population figures for 2015 are July 1 estimates. The 2010 estimates are taken from the 2010 Census.

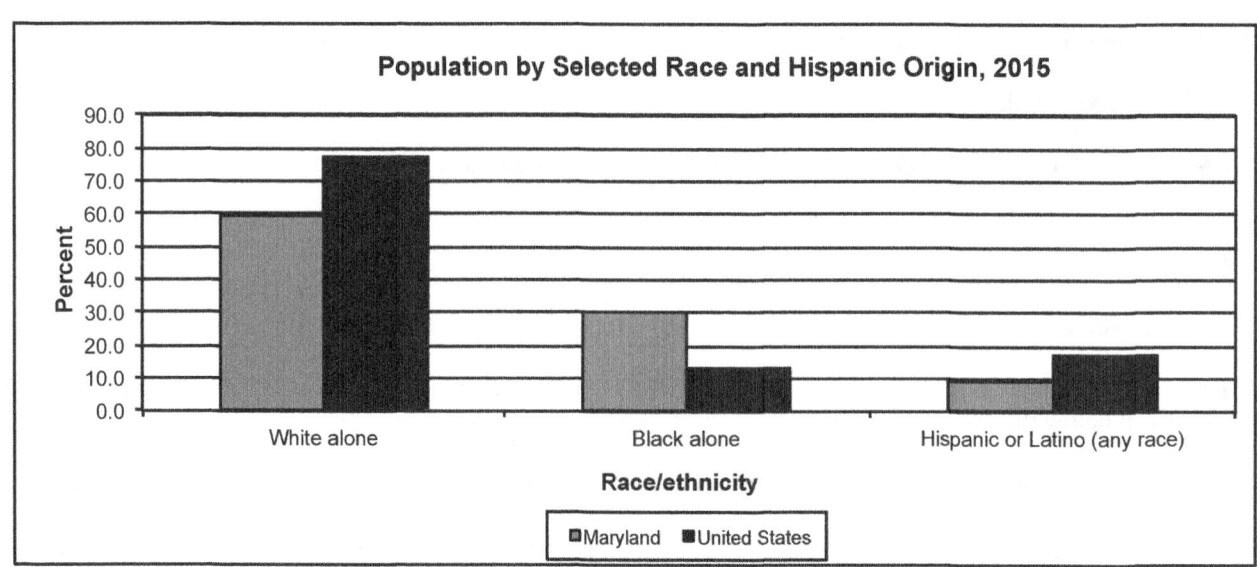

Population by Selected Race and Hispanic Origin, 2015

Maryland / United States

Table MD-2. Marital Status

(Number, percent distribution.)

Sex, age, race, and Hispanic origin	2000	2010	2014
Males, 15 Years and Over	1,972,921	2,232,162	2,282,784
Never married	31.0	36.8	37.2
Now married, except separated...	56.3	50.2	49.8
Separated..	2.8	2.3	2.2
Widowed..	2.5	2.7	2.5
Divorced..	7.4	8.0	8.3
Females, 15 Years and Over	2,186,715	2,442,021	2,489,684
Never married	26.8	32.2	32.7
Now married, except separated...	49.7	45.3	44.6
Separated..	3.4	2.9	2.8
Widowed..	10.1	9.0	8.7
Divorced..	10.1	10.7	11.2

Table MD-3. Households and Housing Characteristics

(Number, percent, dollars.)

Item	2000	2010	2014	Average annual percent change, 2000–2014
Total Households..	1,980,859	2,127,439	2,165,438	0.7
Family households...	1,359,318	1,431,958	1,445,972	0.5
Married-couple family.......................................	994,549	1,022,613	1,022,058	0.2
Other family..	364,789	409,345	423,914	1.2
Male householder, no wife present....................	84,893	104,112	106,105	1.8
Female householder, no husband present...........	279,876	305,233	317,809	1.0
Nonfamily households	621,541	695,481	719,466	1.1
Householder living alone..................................	495,459	570,388	582,835	1.3
Householder not living alone............................	126,082	125,093	136,631	0.6
Housing Characteristics				
Total housing units..	2,145,283	2,380,605	2,422,317	0.9
Occupied housing units	1,980,859	2,127,439	2,165,438	0.7
Owner occupied...	1,341,751	1,426,267	1,426,748	0.5
Renter occupied...	639,108	701,172	738,690	1.1
Average household size.....................................	2.61	2.65	2.7	0.2
Financial Characteristics				
Median gross rent of renter-occupied housing	689	1,131	1,242	5.7
Median monthly owner costs for housing units with a mortgage	1,296	2,016	1,903	3.3
Median value of owner-occupied housing units...........	146,000	301,400	288,500	7.0

Table MD-4. Migration, Origin, and Language

(Number, percent.)

Characteristic	State			U.S.		
	2013	2014	Percent change	2013	2014	Percent change
Residence 1 Year Ago						
Population 1 year and over	5,857,213	5,911,235	0.9	312,432,820	315,095,393	0.9
Same house	86.7	86.1	X	85.0	85.1	X
Different house in the U.S.	12.5	13.1	X	14.4	14.3	X
Same county	7.2	7.6	X	8.9	8.7	X
Different county	5.4	5.5	X	5.5	5.6	X
Same state	2.6	2.8	X	3.2	3.3	X
Different state	2.8	2.7	X	2.3	2.3	X
Abroad	0.8	0.8	X	0.6	0.6	X
Place of Birth						
Native born	5,086,564	5,085,968	-	274,780,773	276,465,262	0.6
Male	48.6	48.5	X	49.3	49.3	X
Female	51.4	51.5	X	50.7	50.7	X
Foreign born	842,250	890,439	5.7	41,348,066	42,391,794	2.5
Male	48.1	48.4	X	48.8	48.7	X
Female	51.9	51.6	X	51.2	51.3	X
Foreign born; naturalized U.S. citizen.................	420,344	434,791	3.4	19,294,710	19,984,738	3.6
Male	45.3	46.1	X	45.9	45.9	X
Female	54.7	53.9	X	54.1	54.1	X
Foreign born; not a U.S. citizen.........................	421,906	455,648	8.0	22,053,356	22,407,056	1.6
Male	50.9	50.6	X	51.3	51.2	X
Female	49.1	49.4	X	48.7	48.8	X
Entered 2010 or later	10.8	14.4	X	9.7	12.3	X
Entered 2000 to 2009	35.2	33.5	X	29.4	28.6	X
Entered before 2000...	54.0	52.1	X	61.0	59.1	X
World Region of Birth, Foreign						
Foreign-born population, excluding population born at sea	842,250	890,439	5.7	41,347,945	42,390,705	2.5
Europe	10.1	10.5	X	11.6	11.2	X
Asia	33.3	33.1	X	29.5	30.1	X
Africa	16.4	16.1	X	4.4	4.6	X
Oceania	0.3	0.3	X	0.5	0.6	X
Latin America	39.0	39.0	X	51.9	51.6	X
North America	1.0	1.0	X	2.0	1.9	X
Language Spoken at Home and Ability to Speak English						
Population 5 years and over...............................	5,562,102	5,609,124	0.8	296,358,760	299,084,046	0.9
English only	83.0	82.9	X	79.2	78.9	X
Language other than English.............................	17.0	17.1	X	20.8	21.1	X
Speaks English less than "very well"..................	6.3	6.4	X	8.5	8.6	X

X = Not applicable.
- = Zero or rounds to zero.

Table MD-5. Median Income and Poverty Status, 2014

(Number, percent, except as noted.)

Characteristic	State		U.S.	
	Number	Percent	Number	Percent
Median Income				
Households (dollars)...	73,971	X	53,657	X
Families (dollars)	89,678	X	65,910	X
Below Poverty Level (All People)	589,818	10.1	48,208,387	15.5
Sex				
Male..	255,434	9.1	21,590,918	14.2
Female	334,384	11.1	26,617,469	16.8
Age				
Under 18 years...	173,305	13.0	15,686,012	21.7
Related children under 18 years........................	168,388	12.7	15,372,705	21.3
18 to 64 years..	357,390	9.6	28,267,482	14.6
65 years and over	59,123	7.4	4,254,893	9.5

X = Not applicable.

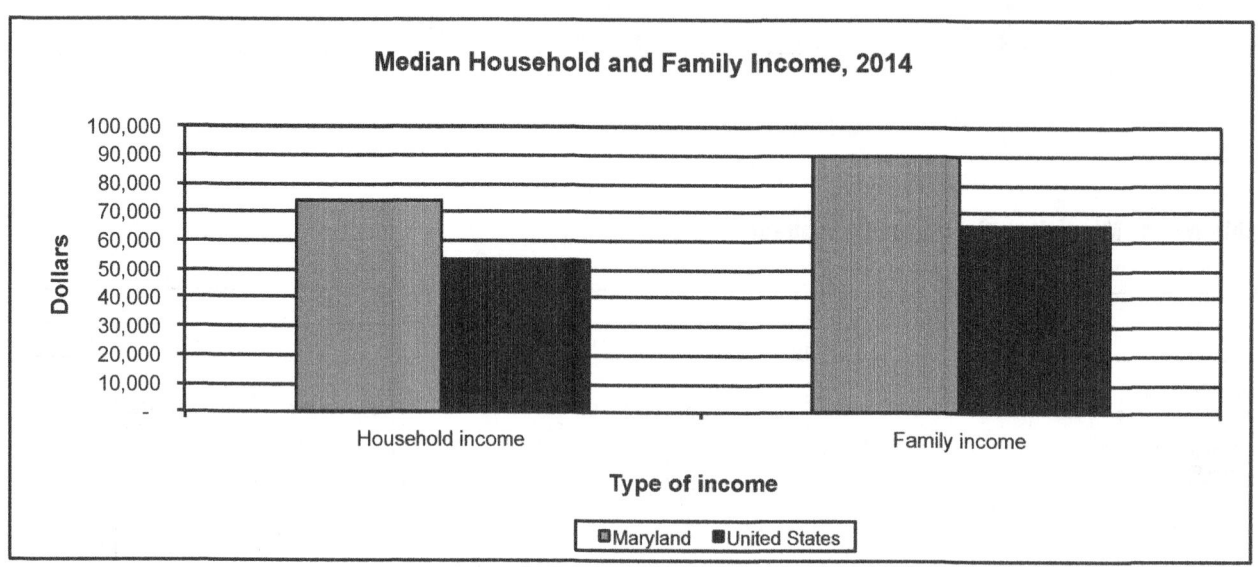

Table MD-6. Health Insurance Coverage Status for the Civilian Noninstitutionalized Population and Children Under 18 Years of Age

(Numbers in thousands, percent.)

Item	2006	2007	2008	2009	2010	2011	2012	2013	2014
Civilian Noninstitutionalized Population	5,613	5,565	5,530	5,590	5,688	5,737	5,788	5,834	5,886
Covered by Private or Public Insurance									
Number...	4,836	4,804	4,919	4,969	5,047	5,138	5,191	5,241	5,423
Percent...	86.2	86.3	89.0	88.9	88.7	89.6	89.7	89.8	92.1
Not Covered									
Number...	776	762	611	621	641	598	597	593	463
Percent...	13.8	13.7	11.0	11.1	11.3	10.4	10.3	10.2	7.9
Percent in the U.S. not covered..............................	15.8	15.3	15.1	15.1	15.5	15.1	14.8	14.5	11.7
Children Under 18 Years of Age	1,384	1,382	1,339	1,348	1,350	1,344	1,341	1,343	1,350
Covered by Private or Public Insurance									
Number...	1,247	1,237	1,269	1,283	1,286	1,283	1,290	1,284	1,307
Percent...	90.1	89.5	94.8	95.2	95.2	95.4	96.2	95.6	96.8
Not Covered									
Number...	137	146	70	65	64	61	51	59	43
Percent...	9.9	10.5	5.2	4.8	4.8	4.6	3.8	4.4	3.2
Percent in the U.S. not covered..............................	11.7	11.0	9.7	8.6	8.0	7.5	7.2	7.1	6.0

Table MD-7. Employment Status by Demographic Group, 2015

(Numbers in thousands, percent.)

Characteristic	Civilian noninstitutional population	Civilian labor force		Employed		Unemployed	
		Number	Percent of population	Number	Percent of population	Number	Percent of population
Total..	4,717	3,180	67.4	3,014	63.9	165	5.2
Sex							
Male..	2,237	1,636	73.2	1,553	69.4	83	5.1
Female..	2,480	1,543	62.2	1,461	58.9	82	5.3
Race, Sex, and Hispanic Origin							
White...	2,898	1,965	67.8	1,894	65.4	71	3.6
Male..	1,428	1,071	75.0	1,034	72.4	37	3.5
Female..	1,470	894	60.8	860	58.5	34	3.8
Black or African American.......................	1,390	906	65.2	831	59.8	75	8.3
Male..	621	418	67.4	380	61.2	38	9.2
Female..	770	488	63.4	452	58.7	37	7.5
Hispanic or Latino ethnicity[1]..................	341	262	76.9	248	72.7	14	5.4
Male..	173	154	88.7	147	84.6	7	4.6
Female..	168	109	64.7	102	60.5	7	6.5
Age							
16 to 19 years.....................................	302	108	35.9	90	29.8	18	16.9
20 to 24 years.....................................	395	297	75.2	266	67.2	31	10.6
25 to 34 years.....................................	819	688	84.1	644	78.7	44	6.4
35 to 44 years.....................................	743	641	86.2	612	82.3	29	4.5
45 to 54 years.....................................	861	721	83.8	701	81.4	21	2.8
55 to 64 years.....................................	796	545	68.4	530	66.6	15	2.7
65 years and over.................................	801	179	22.4	172	21.5	7	4.1

NOTE: Data in Table 7 are from the Current Population Survey (CPS) and do not match the estimates in Table 8. See notes and definitions for further information.
[1]May be of any race.

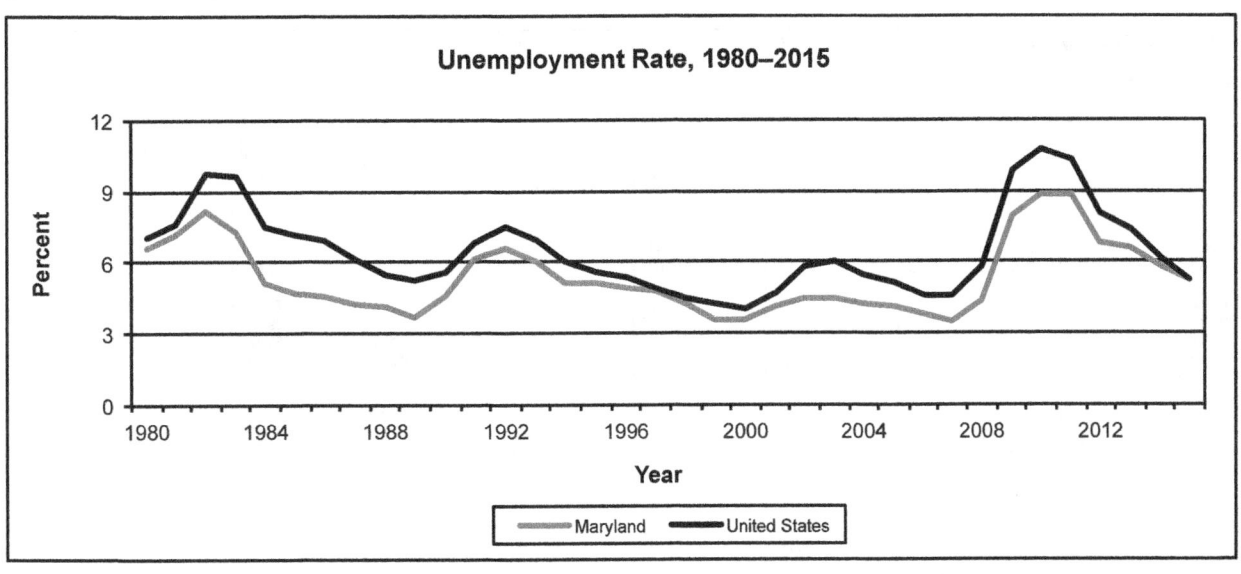

Table MD-8. Employment Status of the Civilian Noninstitutional Population Age 16 Years and Over

(Number, percent.)

Year	Civilian labor force	Civilian participation rate	Employed	Unemployed	Unemployment rate
2007..	2,970,094	68.7	2,867,348	102,746	3.5
2008..	3,001,953	68.9	2,874,987	126,966	4.2
2009..	3,032,700	69.0	2,820,245	212,455	7.0
2010..	3,073,826	68.5	2,838,492	235,334	7.7
2011..	3,096,561	68.0	2,872,084	224,477	7.2
2012..	3,120,678	67.8	2,903,673	217,005	7.0
2013..	3,127,825	67.3	2,921,375	206,450	6.6
2014..	3,128,296	66.8	2,946,520	181,776	5.8
2015..	3,151,929	66.8	2,988,101	163,828	5.2

Table MD-9. Employment and Average Wages by Industry

(Estimates through 2010 are based on the 2007 North American Industry Classification System [NAICS]. Estimates from 2011 onward are based on the 2012 NAICS.)

Industry	2008	2009	2010	2011	2012	2013	2014
	\multicolumn{7}{c}{Number of jobs}						
Wage and Salary Employment by Industry................	2,721,297	2,643,648	2,636,857	2,664,514	2,691,293	2,709,290	2,729,502
Farm Wage and Salary Employment........................	4,436	4,298	4,816	4,670	6,052	5,790	6,408
Nonfarm Wage and Salary Employment....................	2,716,861	2,639,350	2,632,041	2,659,844	2,685,241	2,703,500	2,723,094
Private wage and salary employment.......................	2,165,616	2,081,971	2,066,491	2,089,409	2,115,694	2,135,042	2,156,379
Forestry, fishing, and related activities..................	2,166	2,109	2,186	2,094	1,977	1,980	2,067
Mining...	1,616	1,492	1,468	1,431	1,523	1,333	1,260
Utilities..	10,274	10,104	9,719	10,071	10,103	9,776	9,739
Construction..	185,201	160,300	149,522	150,948	148,037	151,472	154,194
Manufacturing...	128,368	118,788	115,083	112,946	108,879	106,357	103,353
Durable goods manufacturing........................	69,424	63,902	61,503	60,185	57,882	56,329	53,747
Nondurable goods manufacturing....................	58,944	54,886	53,580	52,761	50,997	50,028	49,606
Wholesale trade	93,753	88,238	86,123	86,777	86,591	86,222	85,338
Retail trade...	296,824	281,097	281,817	284,893	286,844	287,209	289,428
Transportation and warehousing.......................	68,277	65,511	66,017	66,581	67,771	68,717	71,177
Information..	49,955	46,319	43,949	41,019	39,950	39,578	38,927
Finance and insurance	105,486	101,598	99,412	98,965	99,367	99,412	98,484
Real estate and rental and leasing....................	48,013	44,864	44,307	43,659	43,708	44,421	44,660
Professional, scientific, and technical services	229,406	227,426	227,311	232,290	235,950	237,689	241,227
Management of companies and enterprises..............	20,997	19,877	19,532	22,148	24,685	25,873	25,588
Administrative and waste services	153,452	141,599	145,057	147,597	152,755	156,885	160,049
Educational services	68,717	69,358	70,351	73,095	73,114	71,788	73,215
Health care and social assistance.......................	315,336	324,909	329,891	335,766	342,993	345,907	350,538
Arts, entertainment, and recreation....................	37,072	35,893	36,289	37,094	38,283	42,506	44,607
Accommodation and food services......................	201,902	197,244	196,821	199,636	207,455	213,744	217,501
Other services, except public administration.............	148,801	145,245	141,636	142,399	145,709	144,173	145,027
Government and government enterprises	551,245	557,379	565,550	570,435	569,547	568,458	566,715
	\multicolumn{7}{c}{Dollars}						
Average Wages and Salaries by Industry	50,629	51,705	52,945	54,281	55,493	55,446	56,830
Average Farm Wages and Salaries	32,039	31,414	26,481	24,431	21,131	30,094	27,086
Average Nonfarm Wages and Salaries	50,660	51,738	52,993	54,333	55,571	55,500	56,900
Average private wages and salaries...........................	48,463	49,201	50,463	51,659	53,160	53,082	54,322
Forestry, fishing, and related activities.................	25,850	25,811	26,607	27,450	27,796	28,870	29,203
Mining...	54,404	53,982	55,858	61,188	61,664	60,410	62,716
Utilities..	101,535	96,608	107,058	109,583	119,093	115,148	114,292
Construction	53,314	54,431	54,972	55,910	57,143	57,191	59,147
Manufacturing...	63,443	64,848	67,792	68,579	70,623	70,921	72,182
Durable goods manufacturing........................	69,976	72,442	75,905	75,857	77,664	78,255	77,916
Nondurable goods manufacturing....................	55,748	56,006	58,479	60,276	62,632	62,663	65,971
Wholesale trade	67,812	68,505	70,546	72,673	74,502	75,054	77,348
Retail trade...	28,262	28,394	28,841	28,948	29,560	29,467	30,058
Transportation and warehousing.......................	45,986	46,262	47,989	50,118	50,475	50,460	52,664
Information..	68,618	70,584	74,037	78,331	80,562	82,945	84,934
Finance and insurance	79,960	78,522	82,242	85,075	93,791	93,408	96,484
Real estate and rental and leasing....................	52,211	51,876	55,258	56,471	58,194	57,983	60,584
Professional, scientific, and technical services	80,094	82,925	85,262	88,177	91,557	90,239	92,493
Management of companies and enterprises..................	94,427	97,673	107,580	106,464	105,754	107,573	111,081
Administrative and waste services	36,580	37,256	38,149	38,668	39,583	39,484	40,159
Educational services	41,290	42,967	43,527	45,390	46,788	47,063	48,405
Health care and social assistance.......................	46,612	47,362	47,646	48,623	49,607	50,001	50,924
Arts, entertainment, and recreation....................	29,359	29,861	31,151	31,522	32,493	32,456	33,114
Accommodation and food services......................	19,610	19,498	20,084	20,594	20,881	20,841	21,603
Other services, except public administration..................	33,191	33,741	34,951	35,414	36,132	37,330	38,557
Government and government enterprises	59,290	61,217	62,239	64,128	64,527	64,582	66,707

Table MD-10. Employment Characteristics by Family Type

(Number, percent.)

Family type and labor force status	2012		2013		2014	
	Total	Families with own children under 18 years	Total	Families with own children under 18 years	Total	Families with own children under 18 years
All Families.................................	1,437,113	633,449	1,443,796	632,608	1,437,457	625,063
FAMILY TYPE AND LABOR FORCE STATUS						
Married-Couple Families............................	1,018,129	420,489	1,022,394	423,061	1,013,543	415,627
Both husband and wife in labor force........................	60.1	73.5	58.8	72.6	58.4	72.9
Husband in labor force, wife not in labor force	19.3	22.4	19.3	22.6	19.9	22.6
Wife in labor force, husband not in labor force	7.3	3.1	7.7	3.3	7.4	3.3
Both husband and wife not in labor force.....................	13.3	1.0	13.4	1.0	14.4	1.1
Other Families	418,984	212,960	421,402	209,547	423,914	209,436
Female householder, no husband present.....................	74.6	76.2	75.8	78.4	75.0	76.2
In labor force................................	57.0	66.3	57.8	67.0	56.6	66.0
Not in labor force	17.6	10.0	17.9	11.4	18.4	10.2
Male householder, no wife present..........................	25.4	23.8	24.2	21.6	25.0	23.8
In labor force................................	21.1	22.2	20.1	20.5	20.1	22.5
Not in labor force	4.4	1.6	4.1	1.1	4.9	1.3

Table MD-11. School Enrollment and Educational Attainment, 2014

(Number, percent.)

Item	State	U.S.
Enrollment		
Total population 3 years and over, enrolled in school............................	1,563,158	82,063,714
Enrolled in nursery school or preschool (percent)	6.3	6.0
Enrolled in kindergarten (percent)............................	5.1	5.1
Enrolled in elementary school, grades 1-8 (percent)............................	37.9	40.2
Enrolled in high school, grades 9-12 (percent)............................	19.7	20.7
Enrolled in college or graduate school (percent)............................	31.0	28.0
Attainment		
Total population 25 years and over	4,062,813	213,725,624
Less than ninth grade (percent)............................	4.1	5.6
9th to 12th grade, no diploma (percent)	6.3	7.5
High school graduate, including equivalency (percent)............................	25.7	27.7
Some college, no degree (percent)	19.1	21.0
Associate's degree (percent)............................	6.5	8.2
Bachelor's degree (percent)............................	20.7	18.7
Graduate or professional degree (percent)............................	17.5	11.4
High school graduate or higher (percent)	89.6	86.9
Bachelor's degree or higher (percent)............................	38.2	30.1

Table MD-12. Public School Characteristics and Educational Indicators

(Number, percent; data derived from National Center of Education Statistics.)

Item	State	U.S.
Public Schools, 2013–2014 (except where noted)		
Number of school districts............................	25	18,194
Number of schools............................	1,442	98,271
Number of students (in thousands)	866	50,045
Number of teachers (in thousands)	59	3,114
Student-teacher ratio............................	14.8	16.1
Expenditures per student (dollars), FY 2013............................	140,867	107,637
Four-year adjusted cohort graduation rate (ACGR)[1,2]	86.4	82.3
Students eligible for free or reduced-price lunch (in thousands)	382	25,596
English language learners (in thousands)	56	4,461
Students age 3 to 21 served under IDEA, part B (in thousands)	104	6,464

Public Schools by Type	Number	Percent of state public schools
Total number of schools............................	1,442	100.0
Regular	1,324	91.8
Special education............................	38	2.6
Vocational education............................	26	1.8
Alternative education............................	54	3.7

NOTE: Every school is assigned only one school type based on its instructional emphasis.
[1]ACGR data represents a new method of calculating high-school completion rates and may not be comparable to previous years' data for Averaged Freshmen Graduation Rates (AFGR).
[2]The United States 4-year ACGRs were estimated using both the reported 4-year ACGR data from 49 states and the District of Columbia and using imputed data for Idaho. The estimate for American Indian/Alaska Native students also includes imputed data for Virginia.

Table MD-13. Reported Voting and Registration of the Voting-Age Population, November 2014

(Numbers in thousands, percent.)

Item	Total population	Total citizen population	Registered			Voted		
			Total registered	Percent registered (total population)	Percent registered (total citizen population)	Total voted	Percent voted (total population)	Percent voted (total citizen population)
U.S. Total	239,874	219,941	142,166	59.3	64.6	92,251	38.5	41.9
State Total............................	4,542	4,148	2,995	65.9	72.2	2,028	44.7	48.9
Sex								
Male................................	2,135	1,947	1,378	64.6	70.8	938	43.9	48.2
Female	2,407	2,201	1,617	67.2	73.5	1,090	45.3	49.6
Race								
White alone.....................	2,752	2,613	1,941	70.5	74.3	1,345	48.9	51.5
White, non-Hispanic alone	2,508	2,480	1,857	74.1	74.9	1,300	51.8	52.4
Black alone......................	1,325	1,208	856	64.6	70.8	581	43.8	48.1
Asian alone	343	231	135	39.4	58.4	69	20.2	30.0
Hispanic (of any race)	332	189	120	36.1	63.6	58	17.5	30.8
White alone or in combination	2,824	2,659	1,983	70.2	74.6	1,363	48.2	51.2
Black alone or in combination	1,353	1,236	875	64.7	70.8	589	43.5	47.6
Asian alone or in combination..........	365	253	152	41.7	60.2	79	21.6	31.2
Age								
18 to 24 years.....................	490	434	210	42.9	48.4	106	21.7	24.5
25 to 34 years.....................	964	822	544	56.4	66.1	265	27.5	32.3
35 to 44 years.....................	649	571	432	66.6	75.8	285	44.0	50.0
45 to 64 years.....................	1,682	1,583	1,229	73.0	77.6	912	54.2	57.6
65 years and over	757	738	580	76.6	78.5	460	60.8	62.3

Table MD-14. Crime

(Number, rate per 100,000. Data are derived from the FBI Uniform Crime Reports.)

Item	State			U.S.[1,2,3,4]		
	2013	2013	Percent change	2013	2014	Percent change
TOTAL POPULATION[5].............................	5,928,814	5,976,407	0.8	316,128,839	318,857,056	0.9
VIOLENT CRIME						
Number.............................	27,734	26,661	-3.9	1,163,146	1,165,383	0.2
Rate	467.8	446.1	-4.6	367.9	365.5	-0.7
Murder and Nonnegligent Manslaughter						
Number.............................	381	365	-4.2	14,196	14,249	0.4
Rate	6.4	6.1	-4.7	4.5	4.5	-
Rape[6]						
Number.............................	1,532	1,619	X	108,612	116,645	X
Rate	25.8	27.1	X	34.4	36.6	X
Robbery						
Number.............................	10,048	9,544	-5.0	345,031	325,802	-5.6
Rate	169.5	159.7	-5.8	109.1	102.2	-6.3
Aggravated Assault						
Number.............................	16,128	15,133	-6.2	724,149	741,291	2.4
Rate	272.0	253.2	-6.9	229.1	232.5	1.5
PROPERTY CRIME						
Number.............................	157,913	149,859	-5.1	8,632,512	8,277,829	-4.1
Rate	2,663.5	2,507.5	-5.9	2,730.7	2,596.1	-4.9
Burglary						
Number.............................	31,949	28,012	-12.3	1,928,465	1,729,806	-10.3
Rate	538.9	468.7	-13.0	610.0	542.5	-11.1
Larceny-Theft						
Number.............................	112,546	108,745	-3.4	6,004,453	5,858,496	-2.4
Rate	1,898.3	1,819.6	-4.1	1,899.4	1,837.3	-3.3
Motor Vehicle Theft						
Number.............................	13,418	13,102	-2.4	699,594	689,527	-1.4
Rate	226.3	219.2	-3.1	221.3	216.2	-2.3

NOTE: Although arson data are included in the trend and clearance tables, sufficient data are not available to estimate totals for this offense. Therefore, no arson data are published in this table.
X = Not applicable.
- = Zero or rounds to zero.
[1]The crime figures have been adjusted.
[2]The data collection methodology for the offense of forcible rape used by the Minnesota state Uniform Crime Reporting (UCR) Program (with the exception of Minneapolis and St. Paul, Minnesota) does not comply with national UCR Program guidelines. Consequently, its figures for forcible rape and violent crime (of which forcible rape is a part) are not published in this table.
[3]Includes offenses reported by the Zoological Police and the Metro Transit Police.
[4]Because of changes in the state's reporting practices, figures are not comparable to previous years' data.
[5]Populations are U.S. Census Bureau provisional estimates as of July 1 of each year.
[6]The figures shown for the offense of rape were estimated using the revised Uniform Crime Reporting (UCR) definition of rape.

Table MD-15. State Government Finances, 2014

(Dollar amounts in thousands, percent distribution.)

Item	Dollars	Percent distribution
Total Revenue	44,699,507	100.0
General revenue	36,280,744	81.2
Intergovernmental revenue	11,038,357	24.7
Taxes	18,929,069	42.3
General sales	4,195,996	9.4
Selective sales	3,826,541	8.6
License taxes	853,851	1.9
Individual income tax	7,773,773	17.4
Corporate income tax	982,784	2.2
Other taxes	1,296,124	2.9
Current charges	3,578,323	8.0
Miscellaneous general revenue	2,734,995	6.1
Utility revenue	139,038	0.3
Liquor stores revenue	0	-
Insurance trust revenue[1]	8,279,725	18.5
Total Expenditure	41,308,885	100.0
Intergovernmental expenditure	8,733,983	21.1
Direct expenditure	32,574,902	78.9
Current operation	22,620,810	54.8
Capital outlay	2,700,117	6.5
Insurance benefits and repayments	4,200,588	10.2
Assistance and subsidies	1,911,815	4.6
Interest on debt	1,141,572	2.8
Exhibit: Salaries and wages	5,049,188	12.2
Total Expenditure	41,308,885	100.0
General expenditure	36,037,087	87.2
Intergovernmental expenditure	8,733,983	21.1
Direct expenditure	27,303,104	66.1
General expenditure, by function:		
Education	11,984,843	29.0
Public welfare	10,833,807	26.2
Hospitals	522,942	1.3
Health	2,174,952	5.3
Highways	2,185,900	5.3
Police protection	577,061	1.4
Correction	1,397,131	3.4
Natural resources	469,547	1.1
Parks and recreation	166,138	0.4
Governmental administration	1,874,178	4.5
Interest on general debt	1,141,572	2.8
Other and unallocable	2,709,016	6.6
Utility expenditure	1,071,210	2.6
Liquor stores expenditure	0	-
Insurance trust expenditure	4,200,588	10.2
Debt at End of Fiscal Year	26,378,595	X
Cash and Security Holdings	66,549,295	X

X = Not applicable.
- = Zero or rounds to zero.
[1]Within insurance trust revenue, net earnings of state retirement systems is a calculated statistic (the item code in the data file is X08), and thus can be positive or negative. Net earnings is the sum of earnings on investments plus gains on investments minus losses on investments. The change made in 2002 for asset valuation from book to market value in accordance with Statement 34 of the Governmental Accounting Standards Board is reflected in the calculated statistics.

Table MD-16. State Government Tax Collections, 2014

(Dollars in thousands, percent.)

Item	Dollars	Percent distribution
Total Taxes	18,929,069	100.0
Property taxes	725,694	3.8
Sales and gross receipts	8,022,537	42.4
General sales and gross receipts	4,195,996	22.2
Selective sales and gross receipts	3,826,541	20.2
Alcoholic beverages	30,808	0.2
Amusements	431,851	2.3
Insurance premiums	475,294	2.5
Motor fuels	812,739	4.3
Pari-mutuels	3,071	-
Public utilities	139,346	0.7
Tobacco products	402,403	2.1
Other selective sales	1,531,029	8.1
Licenses	853,851	4.5
Alcoholic beverages	1,358	-
Amusements	1,158	-
Corporations in general	106,658	0.6
Hunting and fishing	18,149	0.1
Motor vehicle	474,475	2.5
Motor vehicle operators	36,859	0.2
Public utilities	0	-
Occupation and business, NEC	213,324	1.1
Other licenses	1,870	-
Income taxes	8,756,557	46.3
Individual income	7,773,773	41.1
Corporation net income	982,784	5.2
Other taxes	570,430	3.0
Death and gift	213,780	1.1
Documentary and stock transfer	158,844	0.8
Severance	X	X
Taxes, NEC	197,806	1.0

X = Not applicable.
- = Zero or rounds to zero.

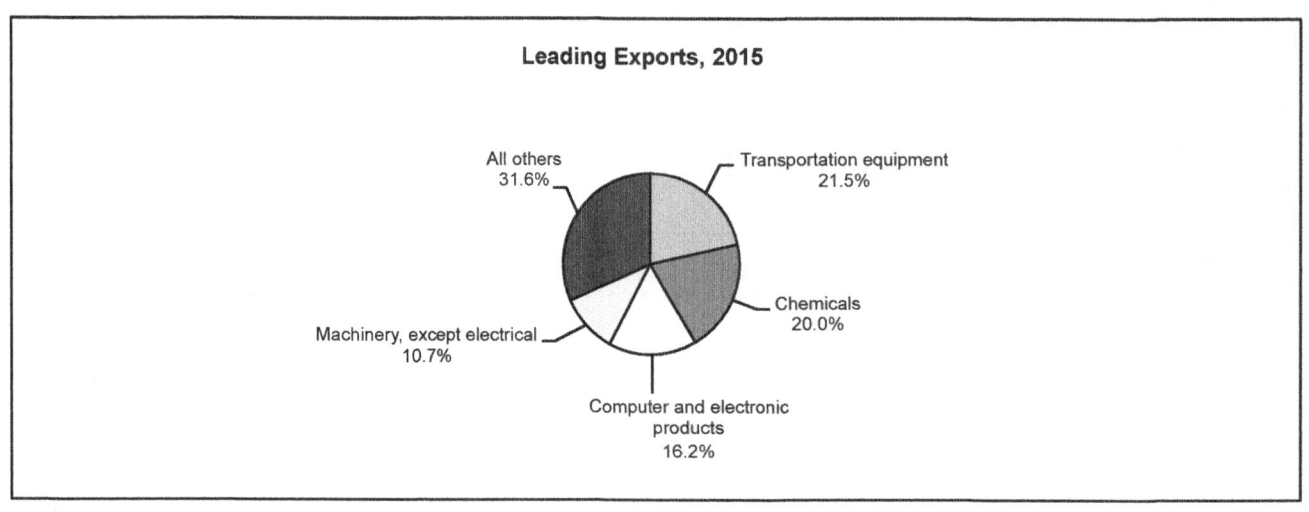

Leading Exports, 2015

All others 31.6%

Transportation equipment 21.5%

Chemicals 20.0%

Computer and electronic products 16.2%

Machinery, except electrical 10.7%

MASSACHUSETTS

Facts and Figures

Location: Northeastern United States; bordered on the N by Vermont and New Hampshire, on the E by the Atlantic Ocean, on the S by Connecticut and Rhode Island, and on the W by New York

Area: 10,555 sq. mi. (27,336 sq. km.); rank—44th

Population: 6,794,422 (2015 est.); rank—15th

Principal Cities: capital—Boston; largest—Boston

Statehood: February 6, 1788; 6th state

U.S. Congress: 2 senators, 9 representatives

State Motto: *Ense petit placidam sub libertate quietem* ("By the sword we seek peace, but peace only under liberty")

State Song: "All Hail to Massachusetts"

State Nickname: The Bay State

Abbreviations: MA; Mass.

State Symbols: flower—mayflower; tree—American elm; bird—chickadee

At a Glance

- With an increase in population of 3.5 percent, Massachusetts ranked 26th among the states in growth from 2010 to 2015.

- Massachusetts's median household income in 2014 was $69,160, the 7th highest in the country.

- Approximately 11.6 percent of the state's population lived below the poverty level in 2014, compared to 15.5 percent of the entire U.S. population.

- Massachusetts's violent crime rate in 2014 was 391.4 per 100,000 population, compared to 365.5 for the entire nation.

- Massachusetts's infant mortality rate of 4.38 per 1,000 live births was the third lowest in the country in 2014.

Table MA-1. Population by Age, Sex, Race, and Hispanic Origin

(Number, percent, except where noted.)

Sex, age, race, and Hispanic origin	2000	2010	2015[1]	Average annual percent change, 2010–2015
Total Population..	6,349,097	6,547,629	6,794,422	0.3
Percent of total U.S. population	2.3	2.1	2.1	X
Sex				
Male..	3,058,816	3,166,628	3,296,118	0.3
Female	3,290,281	3,381,001	3,498,304	0.2
Age				
Under 5 years..	397,268	367,087	366,562	-
5 to 19 years...	1,277,845	1,254,056	1,226,408	-0.2
20 to 64 years...	3,813,822	4,023,762	4,156,230	0.2
65 years and over	860,162	902,724	1,045,222	1.1
Median age (years)	36.5	39.1	39.4	0.1
Race and Hispanic Origin				
One race				
White...	5,367,286	5,524,937	5,580,385	0.1
Black..	343,454	504,365	574,106	0.9
American Indian and Alaska Native	15,015	29,944	32,751	0.6
Asian...	238,124	359,673	445,927	1.5
Native Hawaiian or Other Pacific Islander	2,489	5,971	6,863	1.0
Two or more races..	146,005	122,739	154,390	1.7
Hispanic (of any race)...	428,729	656,888	759,194	1.0

X = Not applicable.
- = Zero or rounds to zero.
[1]Population figures for 2015 are July 1 estimates. The 2010 estimates are taken from the 2010 Census.

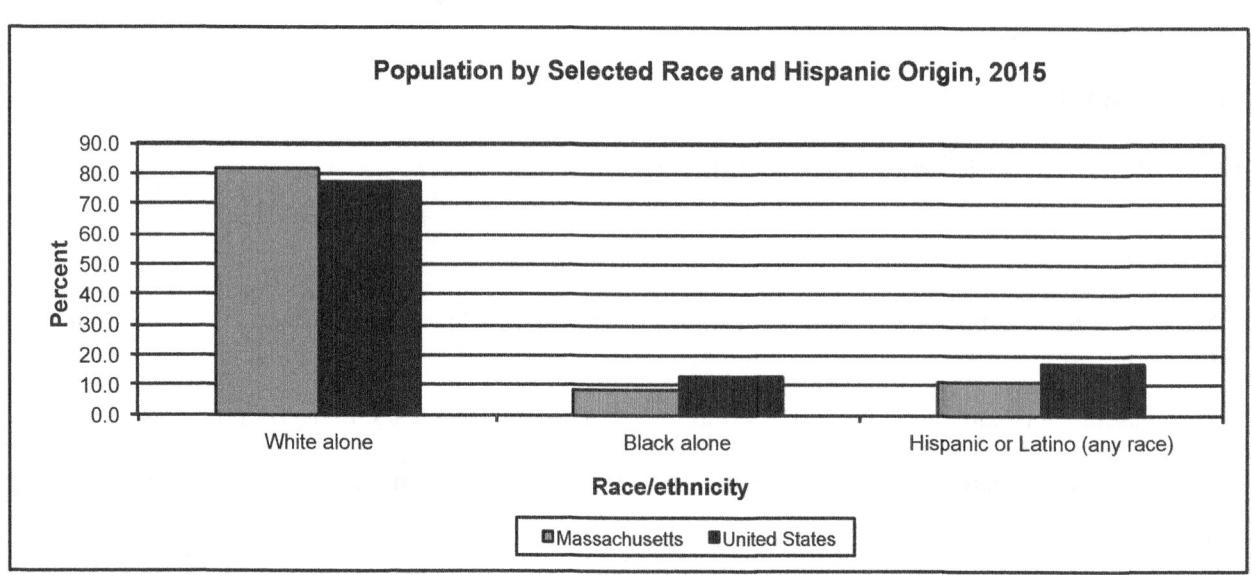

Table MA-2. Marital Status

(Number, percent distribution.)

Sex, age, race, and Hispanic origin	2000	2010	2014
Males, 15 Years and Over	2,412,349	2,579,221	2,637,974
Never married	33.9	38.7	38.7
Now married, except separated..	54.7	49.1	49.2
Separated..	1.6	1.6	1.6
Widowed..	2.7	2.7	2.6
Divorced..	7.0	8.0	7.9
Females, 15 Years and Over	2,679,020	2,819,768	2,871,070
Never married	28.5	33.2	33.5
Now married, except separated..	48.9	44.1	44.5
Separated..	2.3	2.4	2.2
Widowed..	10.8	9.1	8.9
Divorced..	9.5	11.1	11.0

Table MA-3. Households and Housing Characteristics

(Number, percent, dollars.)

Item	2000	2010	2014	Average annual percent change, 2000–2014
Total Households..	2,443,580	2,520,419	2,549,336	0.3
Family households..	1,576,696	1,590,257	1,610,581	0.2
Married-couple family................................	1,197,917	1,166,204	1,183,524	-0.1
Other family................................	378,779	424,053	427,057	0.9
Male householder, no wife present................	88,835	100,400	107,701	1.5
Female householder, no husband present........	289,944	323,653	319,356	0.7
Nonfamily households................................	866,884	930,162	938,755	0.6
Householder living alone................................	684,345	736,320	739,844	0.6
Householder not living alone........................	182,539	193,842	198,911	0.6
Housing Characteristics				
Total housing units................................	2,621,989	2,808,727	2,828,592	0.6
Occupied housing units	2,443,580	2,520,419	2,549,336	0.3
Owner occupied................................	1,508,052	1,568,382	1,570,332	0.3
Renter occupied................................	935,528	952,037	979,004	0.3
Average household size................................	2.51	2.51	2.55	0.1
Financial Characteristics				
Median gross rent of renter-occupied housing	684	1,009	1,107	4.4
Median monthly owner costs for housing units with a mortgage	1,353	2,036	2,014	3.5
Median value of owner-occupied housing units...............	185,700	334,100	338,900	5.9

Table MA-4. Migration, Origin, and Language

(Number, percent.)

Characteristic	State			U.S.		
	2013	2014	Percent change	2013	2014	Percent change
Residence 1 Year Ago						
Population 1 year and over	6,619,999	6,674,907	0.8	312,432,820	315,095,393	0.9
Same house	86.5	86.7	X	85.0	85.1	X
Different house in the U.S.	12.6	12.3	X	14.4	14.3	X
Same county	7.7	7.4	X	8.9	8.7	X
Different county	4.9	4.9	X	5.5	5.6	X
Same state	2.9	2.7	X	3.2	3.3	X
Different state	2.0	2.2	X	2.3	2.3	X
Abroad	0.9	1.1	X	0.6	0.6	X
Place of Birth						
Native born	5,646,669	5,685,127	0.7	274,780,773	276,465,262	0.6
Male	48.6	48.4	X	49.3	49.3	X
Female	51.4	51.6	X	50.7	50.7	X
Foreign born	1,046,155	1,060,281	1.4	41,348,066	42,391,794	2.5
Male	48.1	48.7	X	48.8	48.7	X
Female	51.9	51.3	X	51.2	51.3	X
Foreign born; naturalized U.S. citizen................	549,009	554,211	0.9	19,294,710	19,984,738	3.6
Male	45.7	46.9	X	45.9	45.9	X
Female	54.3	53.1	X	54.1	54.1	X
Foreign born; not a U.S. citizen................	497,146	506,070	1.8	22,053,356	22,407,056	1.6
Male	50.7	50.7	X	51.3	51.2	X
Female	49.3	49.3	X	48.7	48.8	X
Entered 2010 or later	13.2	16.6	X	9.7	12.3	X
Entered 2000 to 2009	30.1	28.9	X	29.4	28.6	X
Entered before 2000................................	56.7	54.4	X	61.0	59.1	X
World Region of Birth, Foreign						
Foreign-born population, excluding population born at sea	1,046,155	1,060,281	1.4	41,347,945	42,390,705	2.5
Europe	22.9	21.7	X	11.6	11.2	X
Asia	29.2	30.5	X	29.5	30.1	X
Africa	8.7	9.7	X	4.4	4.6	X
Oceania	0.3	0.4	X	0.5	0.6	X
Latin America................................	35.8	34.9	X	51.9	51.6	X
North America................................	3.2	2.8	X	2.0	1.9	X
Language Spoken at Home and Ability to Speak English						
Population 5 years and over................................	6,328,899	6,379,441	0.8	296,358,760	299,084,046	0.9
English only	77.6	77.4	X	79.2	78.9	X
Language other than English................................	22.4	22.6	X	20.8	21.1	X
Speaks English less than "very well"................	8.9	8.9	X	8.5	8.6	X

X = Not applicable.
- = Zero or rounds to zero.

Table MA-5. Median Income and Poverty Status, 2014

(Number, percent, except as noted.)

Characteristic	State Number	State Percent	U.S. Number	U.S. Percent
Median Income				
Households (dollars)...	69,160	X	53,657	X
Families (dollars)	87,951	X	65,910	X
Below Poverty Level (All People)	757,235	11.6	48,208,387	15.5
Sex				
Male...	327,326	10.4	21,590,918	14.2
Female	429,909	12.8	26,617,469	16.8
Age				
Under 18 years...	207,673	15.2	15,686,012	21.7
Related children under 18 years...............	202,976	14.9	15,372,705	21.3
18 to 64 years..	459,130	11.0	28,267,482	14.6
65 years and over	90,432	9.3	4,254,893	9.5

X = Not applicable.

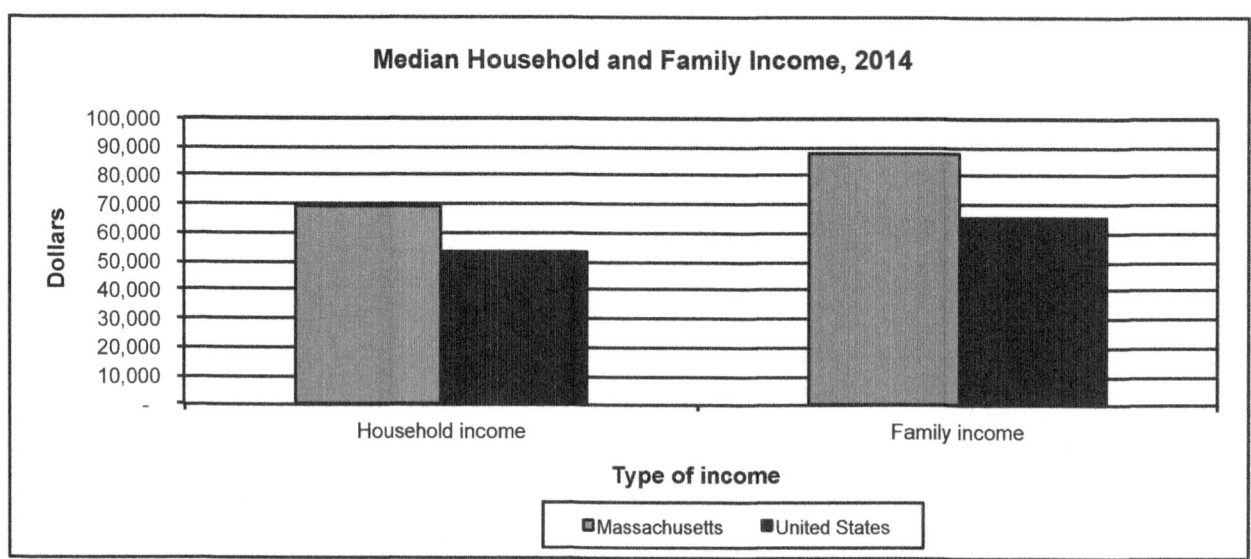

Table MA-6. Health Insurance Coverage Status for the Civilian Noninstitutionalized Population and Children Under 18 Years of Age

(Numbers in thousands, percent.)

Item	2006	2007	2008	2009	2010	2011	2012	2013	2014
Civilian Noninstitutionalized Population	6,335	6,340	6,399	6,496	6,478	6,508	6,567	6,614	6,668
Covered by Private or Public Insurance									
Number...	5,678	6,000	6,135	6,225	6,192	6,231	6,313	6,367	6,450
Percent...	89.6	94.6	95.9	95.8	95.6	95.7	96.1	96.3	96.7
Not Covered									
Number...	657	340	264	271	286	277	254	247	219
Percent...	10.4	5.4	4.1	4.2	4.4	4.3	3.9	3.7	3.3
Percent in the U.S. not covered.................................	15.8	15.3	15.1	15.1	15.5	15.1	14.8	14.5	11.7
Children Under 18 Years of Age	1,470	1,435	1,427	1,431	1,415	1,402	1,398	1,389	1,387
Covered by Private or Public Insurance									
Number...	1,367	1,392	1,397	1,411	1,393	1,378	1,378	1,368	1,366
Percent...	93.0	97.0	97.9	98.6	98.5	98.3	98.6	98.5	98.5
Not Covered									
Number...	103	43	30	20	22	24	20	21	21
Percent...	7.0	3.0	2.1	1.4	1.5	1.7	1.4	1.5	1.5
Percent in the U.S. not covered.................................	11.7	11.0	9.7	8.6	8.0	7.5	7.2	7.1	6.0

Table MA-7. Employment Status by Demographic Group, 2015

(Numbers in thousands, percent.)

Characteristic	Civilian noninstitutional population	Civilian labor force		Employed		Unemployed	
		Number	Percent of population	Number	Percent of population	Number	Percent of population
Total...	5,493	3,586	65.3	3,410	62.1	176	4.9
Sex							
Male................................	2,629	1,841	70.0	1,740	66.2	101	5.5
Female..............................	2,863	1,746	61.0	1,670	58.3	75	4.3
Race, Sex, and Hispanic Origin							
White................................	4,588	3,008	65.6	2,877	62.7	132	4.4
Male..............................	2,188	1,534	70.1	1,456	66.5	78	5.1
Female...........................	2,400	1,474	61.4	1,421	59.2	54	3.7
Black or African American................	429	287	67.1	257	60.0	30	10.6
Male..............................	201	141	70.0	125	62.2	16	11.2
Female...........................	228	147	64.4	132	58.0	15	9.9
Hispanic or Latino ethnicity[1]............	504	314	62.2	279	55.4	34	11.0
Male..............................	227	153	67.3	133	58.6	20	13.0
Female...........................	277	161	58.1	147	52.8	15	9.1
Age							
16 to 19 years...........................	329	118	35.9	96	29.3	22	18.5
20 to 24 years...........................	526	364	69.2	338	64.2	26	7.3
25 to 34 years...........................	980	835	85.2	790	80.6	45	5.4
35 to 44 years...........................	779	654	83.9	632	81.1	22	3.3
45 to 54 years...........................	910	740	81.3	708	77.8	32	4.3
55 to 64 years...........................	922	645	69.9	621	67.4	23	3.6
65 years and over.......................	1,047	232	22.1	226	21.6	6	2.6

NOTE: Data in Table 7 are from the Current Population Survey (CPS) and do not match the estimates in Table 8. See notes and definitions for further information.
[1] May be of any race.

Unemployment Rate, 1980–2015

Table MA-8. Employment Status of the Civilian Noninstitutional Population Age 16 Years and Over

(Number, percent.)

Year	Civilian labor force	Civilian participation rate	Employed	Unemployed	Unemployment rate
2007............................	3,426,009	66.7	3,268,096	157,913	4.6
2008............................	3,452,468	66.6	3,261,408	191,060	5.5
2009............................	3,470,382	66.3	3,189,010	281,372	8.1
2010............................	3,480,083	66.3	3,190,818	289,265	8.3
2011............................	3,469,308	65.5	3,217,754	251,554	7.3
2012............................	3,486,326	65.2	3,254,060	232,266	6.7
2013............................	3,513,565	65.0	3,277,801	235,764	6.7
2014............................	3,557,362	65.2	3,353,138	204,224	5.7
2015............................	3,569,956	64.9	3,392,107	177,849	5.0

Table MA-9. Employment and Average Wages by Industry

(Estimates through 2010 are based on the 2007 North American Industry Classification System [NAICS]. Estimates from 2011 onward are based on the 2012 NAICS.)

Industry	2008	2009	2010	2011	2012	2013	2014
	Number of jobs						
Wage and Salary Employment by Industry..................	3,410,858	3,300,521	3,311,859	3,350,292	3,396,978	3,480,691	3,543,360
Farm Wage and Salary Employment.........................	3,858	3,721	3,730	3,956	4,005	4,746	5,079
Nonfarm Wage and Salary Employment....................	3,407,000	3,296,800	3,308,129	3,346,336	3,392,973	3,475,945	3,538,281
Private wage and salary employment............................	2,953,629	2,844,590	2,853,964	2,896,415	2,938,862	3,017,111	3,075,244
Forestry, fishing, and related activities..........................	4,578	4,879	4,971	4,058	4,053	3,894	3,993
Mining..	1,273	1,220	1,048	1,002	866	886	930
Utilities...	10,026	10,209	10,432	10,453	10,250	10,052	10,680
Construction..	137,785	116,521	112,186	116,555	119,310	126,675	132,765
Manufacturing..	287,097	259,629	254,857	254,195	252,185	250,777	250,442
Durable goods manufacturing.............................	190,450	170,461	166,166	167,191	165,397	163,595	162,328
Nondurable goods manufacturing.........................	96,647	89,168	88,691	87,004	86,788	87,182	88,114
Wholesale trade	137,445	128,466	123,891	124,165	122,136	123,858	124,569
Retail trade...	352,469	339,954	345,194	348,742	349,005	350,581	352,975
Transportation and warehousing..............................	76,041	72,101	73,879	74,670	75,673	77,351	80,323
Information..	89,450	84,864	85,363	84,355	87,170	86,274	86,213
Finance and insurance...	182,975	176,477	173,524	173,682	171,932	170,560	171,415
Real estate and rental and leasing...........................	43,947	42,062	41,765	41,714	42,051	43,288	44,108
Professional, scientific, and technical services.................	261,255	254,688	251,989	259,996	268,005	276,169	285,585
Management of companies and enterprises.................	61,351	59,060	57,436	58,604	63,326	64,260	63,552
Administrative and waste services............................	169,591	151,742	158,625	163,472	165,163	169,534	173,250
Educational services	180,664	183,512	182,461	186,329	190,356	192,938	195,151
Health care and social assistance............................	488,580	498,869	510,601	518,706	527,909	570,257	586,965
Arts, entertainment, and recreation..........................	49,935	48,383	49,611	50,570	51,352	52,993	55,100
Accommodation and food services............................	259,566	255,091	261,794	268,399	276,792	283,713	289,886
Other services, except public administration.................	159,601	156,863	154,337	156,748	161,328	163,051	167,342
Government and government enterprises..........................	453,371	452,210	454,165	449,921	454,111	458,834	463,037
	Dollars						
Average Wages and Salaries by Industry	55,737	55,235	56,808	58,620	59,859	60,307	62,608
Average Farm Wages and Salaries	28,799	28,366	26,728	22,546	24,963	28,701	31,259
Average Nonfarm Wages and Salaries	55,767	55,265	56,842	58,662	59,900	60,350	62,653
Average private wages and salaries............................	56,563	55,879	57,689	59,541	60,792	61,140	63,509
Forestry, fishing, and related activities	51,525	51,403	54,008	57,093	54,715	52,872	49,468
Mining..	51,901	53,072	56,133	57,184	57,645	58,316	62,105
Utilities...	99,517	102,825	104,102	109,970	107,949	107,780	110,025
Construction..	62,174	61,845	62,162	63,266	65,123	66,463	68,670
Manufacturing..	68,978	69,237	75,206	77,553	79,513	79,820	83,359
Durable goods manufacturing.............................	75,487	75,716	83,905	86,712	89,034	88,657	91,972
Nondurable goods manufacturing.........................	56,151	56,850	58,908	59,953	61,369	63,237	67,490
Wholesale trade	76,919	76,456	79,192	82,166	82,376	84,386	88,330
Retail trade...	27,741	27,777	27,823	27,919	28,325	28,938	30,080
Transportation and warehousing..............................	43,716	43,730	44,150	45,425	46,127	46,499	47,974
Information..	86,277	84,680	91,985	95,875	97,033	97,270	103,326
Finance and insurance...	118,230	110,406	114,391	119,299	124,439	126,337	136,185
Real estate and rental and leasing...........................	56,632	55,582	60,295	63,205	66,408	69,763	72,818
Professional, scientific, and technical services	96,720	95,743	100,957	103,816	108,219	110,221	113,947
Management of companies and enterprises.................	100,424	101,498	104,263	123,065	115,671	118,633	126,711
Administrative and waste services............................	38,683	38,397	38,535	39,779	40,987	41,079	42,277
Educational services	41,583	42,058	44,404	45,969	46,037	47,200	48,209
Health care and social assistance............................	49,150	50,269	51,327	52,111	53,259	51,672	52,612
Arts, entertainment, and recreation..........................	37,412	36,356	37,237	37,556	38,240	38,377	38,653
Accommodation and food services............................	21,316	21,000	21,409	21,976	22,340	22,653	23,752
Other services, except public administration.................	31,103	30,998	31,666	32,245	32,550	33,579	34,180
Government and government enterprises..........................	50,586	51,400	51,519	53,008	54,130	55,158	56,969

Table MA-10. Employment Characteristics by Family Type

(Number, percent.)

Family type and labor force status	2012		2013		2014	
	Total	Families with own children under 18 years	Total	Families with own children under 18 years	Total	Families with own children under 18 years
All Families........................	1,598,867	698,945	1,620,802	701,258	1,596,764	693,261
FAMILY TYPE AND LABOR FORCE STATUS						
Married-Couple Families.............................	1,173,287	479,890	1,190,249	482,070	1,169,707	475,565
Both husband and wife in labor force...............	60.1	73.5	58.5	72.1	59.2	73.1
Husband in labor force, wife not in labor force	17.7	21.7	18.4	22.1	18.4	22.5
Wife in labor force, husband not in labor force	7.7	3.5	7.7	3.7	7.5	3.3
Both husband and wife not in labor force...............	14.6	1.3	14.3	1.3	15.0	1.1
Other Families	425,580	219,055	430,553	219,188	427,057	217,696
Female householder, no husband present............	75.6	80.4	74.9	79.3	74.8	80.3
In labor force........................	53.3	63.2	53.2	62.7	54.1	66.5
Not in labor force........................	22.3	17.1	21.7	16.6	20.7	13.8
Male householder, no wife present...............	24.4	19.6	25.1	20.7	25.2	19.7
In labor force........................	18.9	17.3	19.2	18.1	20.3	18.0
Not in labor force........................	5.5	2.4	5.9	2.6	4.9	1.7

Table MA-11. School Enrollment and Educational Attainment, 2014

(Number, percent.)

Item	State	U.S.
Enrollment		
Total population 3 years and over, enrolled in school...................	1,737,678	82,063,714
Enrolled in nursery school or preschool (percent)	6.4	6.0
Enrolled in kindergarten (percent)...................	4.5	5.1
Enrolled in elementary school, grades 1-8 (percent)...................	35.6	40.2
Enrolled in high school, grades 9-12 (percent)...................	19.5	20.7
Enrolled in college or graduate school (percent)...................	33.9	28.0
Attainment		
Total population 25 years and over	4,654,351	213,725,624
Less than ninth grade (percent)...................	5.0	5.6
9th to 12th grade, no diploma (percent)...................	5.4	7.5
High school graduate, including equivalency (percent)...................	24.9	27.7
Some college, no degree (percent)	15.7	21.0
Associate's degree (percent)	7.9	8.2
Bachelor's degree (percent)...................	23.2	18.7
Graduate or professional degree (percent)...................	18.0	11.4
High school graduate or higher (percent)	89.7	86.9
Bachelor's degree or higher (percent)	41.2	30.1

Table MA-12. Public School Characteristics and Educational Indicators

(Number, percent; data derived from National Center of Education Statistics.)

Item	State	U.S.
Public Schools, 2013–2014 (except where noted)		
Number of school districts...................	409	
Number of schools...................	1,865	
Number of students (in thousands)	956	
Number of teachers (in thousands)	70	
Student-teacher ratio...................	13.6	
Expenditures per student (dollars), FY 2013...................	15,321	
Four-year adjusted cohort graduation rate (ACGR)[1,2]	86.1	
Students eligible for free or reduced-price lunch (in thousands)	365	
English language learners (in thousands)	67	
Students age 3 to 21 served under IDEA, part B (in thousands)	167	

Public Schools by Type	Number	Percent of state public schools
Total number of schools...................	1,865	100.0
Regular...................	1,782	95.5
Special education...................	22	1.2
Vocational education...................	39	2.1
Alternative education...................	22	1.2

NOTE: Every school is assigned only one school type based on its instructional emphasis.
[1]ACGR data represents a new method of calculating high-school completion rates and may not be comparable to previous years' data for Averaged Freshmen Graduation Rates (AFGR).
[2]The United States 4-year ACGRs were estimated using both the reported 4-year ACGR data from 49 states and the District of Columbia and using imputed data for Idaho. The estimate for American Indian/Alaska Native students also includes imputed data for Virginia.

Table MA-13. Reported Voting and Registration of the Voting-Age Population, November 2014

(Numbers in thousands, percent.)

Item	Total population	Total citizen population	Registered			Voted		
			Total registered	Percent registered (total population)	Percent registered (total citizen population)	Total voted	Percent voted (total population)	Percent voted (total citizen population)
U.S. Total	239,874	219,941	142,166	59.3	64.6	92,251	38.5	41.9
State Total..............................	5,279	4,815	3,250	61.6	67.5	2,259	42.8	46.9
Sex								
Male..	2,504	2,241	1,485	59.3	66.3	1,036	41.4	46.2
Female	2,775	2,574	1,765	63.6	68.6	1,223	44.1	47.5
Race								
White alone...............................	4,441	4,205	2,980	67.1	70.9	2,117	47.7	50.4
White, non-Hispanic alone	4,113	3,969	2,860	69.5	72.1	2,073	50.4	52.2
Black alone................................	408	310	141	34.6	45.4	80	19.6	25.7
Asian alone	325	214	85	26.2	39.8	37	11.5	17.4
Hispanic (of any race)	462	312	155	33.6	49.7	53	11.5	17.0
White alone or in combination	4,513	4,268	3,013	66.8	70.6	2,137	47.3	50.1
Black alone or in combination.........	454	348	160	35.3	46.0	87	19.2	25.0
Asian alone or in combination..........	345	234	94	27.2	40.1	46	13.3	19.7
Age								
18 to 24 years............................	590	536	238	40.4	44.4	109	18.5	20.3
25 to 34 years............................	983	845	427	43.4	50.5	233	23.7	27.5
35 to 44 years............................	844	718	504	59.8	70.3	298	35.3	41.5
45 to 64 years............................	1,813	1,696	1,271	70.1	74.9	974	53.7	57.4
65 years and over	1,049	1,021	810	77.3	79.4	646	61.6	63.3

Table MA-14. Crime

(Number, rate per 100,000. Data are derived from the FBI Uniform Crime Reports.)

Item	State			U.S.[1,2,3,4]		
	2013	2014	Percent change	2013	2014	Percent change
TOTAL POPULATION[5]...	6,692,824	6,745,408	0.8	316,128,839	318,857,056	0.9
VIOLENT CRIME						
Number..	27,038	26,399	-2.4	1,163,146	1,165,383	0.2
Rate	404.0	391.4	-3.1	367.9	365.5	-0.7
Murder and Nonnegligent Manslaughter						
Number..	137	132	-3.6	14,196	14,249	0.4
Rate	2.0	2.0	0.0	4.5	4.5	-
Rape[6]						
Number..	2,718	2,180	X	108,612	116,645	X
Rate	40.6	32.3	X	34.4	36.6	X
Robbery						
Number..	6,706	6,036	-10.0	345,031	325,802	-5.6
Rate	100.2	89.5	-10.7	109.1	102.2	-6.3
Aggravated Assault						
Number..	18,106	18,051	-0.3	724,149	741,291	2.4
Rate	270.5	267.6	-1.1	229.1	232.5	1.5
PROPERTY CRIME						
Number..	137,285	125,267	-8.8	8,632,512	8,277,829	-4.1
Rate	2,051.2	1,857.1	-9.5	2,730.7	2,596.1	-4.9
Burglary						
Number..	30,735	24,964	-18.8	1,928,465	1,729,806	-10.3
Rate	459.2	370.1	-19.4	610.0	542.5	-11.1
Larceny-Theft						
Number..	97,428	92,043	-5.5	6,004,453	5,858,496	-2.4
Rate	1,455.7	1,364.5	-6.3	1,899.4	1,837.3	-3.3
Motor Vehicle Theft						
Number..	9,122	8,260	-9.4	699,594	689,527	-1.4
Rate	136.3	122.5	-10.1	221.3	216.2	-2.3

NOTE: Although arson data are included in the trend and clearance tables, sufficient data are not available to estimate totals for this offense. Therefore, no arson data are published in this table.
X = Not applicable.
- = Zero or rounds to zero.
[1]The crime figures have been adjusted.
[2]The data collection methodology for the offense of forcible rape used by the Minnesota state Uniform Crime Reporting (UCR) Program (with the exception of Minneapolis and St. Paul, Minnesota) does not comply with national UCR Program guidelines. Consequently, its figures for forcible rape and violent crime (of which forcible rape is a part) are not published in this table.
[3]Includes offenses reported by the Zoological Police and the Metro Transit Police.
[4]Because of changes in the state's reporting practices, figures are not comparable to previous years' data.
[5]Populations are U.S. Census Bureau provisional estimates as of July 1 of each year.
[6]The figures shown for the offense of rape were estimated using the revised Uniform Crime Reporting (UCR) definition of rape.

Table MA-15. State Government Finances, 2014

(Dollar amounts in thousands, percent distribution.)

Item	Dollars	Percent distribution
Total Revenue	61,746,528	100.0
General revenue	49,046,286	79.4
Intergovernmental revenue	14,165,615	22.9
Taxes	25,235,726	40.9
General sales	5,518,580	8.9
Selective sales	2,414,450	3.9
License taxes	1,012,557	1.6
Individual income tax	13,246,221	21.5
Corporate income tax	2,194,620	3.6
Other taxes	849,298	1.4
Current charges	4,862,786	7.9
Miscellaneous general revenue	4,782,159	7.7
Utility revenue	807,618	1.3
Liquor stores revenue	0	-
Insurance trust revenue[1]	11,892,624	19.3
Total Expenditure	58,304,754	100.0
Intergovernmental expenditure	9,811,813	16.8
Direct expenditure	48,492,941	83.2
Current operation	33,756,215	57.9
Capital outlay	3,274,466	5.6
Insurance benefits and repayments	7,596,912	13.0
Assistance and subsidies	824,465	1.4
Interest on debt	3,040,883	5.2
Exhibit: Salaries and wages	6,546,198	11.2
Total Expenditure	58,304,754	100.0
General expenditure	48,306,414	82.9
Intergovernmental expenditure	9,811,813	16.8
Direct expenditure	38,494,601	66.0
General expenditure, by function:		
Education	13,476,969	23.1
Public welfare	16,656,061	28.6
Hospitals	516,179	0.9
Health	1,120,235	1.9
Highways	2,231,116	3.8
Police protection	845,126	1.4
Correction	1,196,619	2.1
Natural resources	415,175	0.7
Parks and recreation	207,548	0.4
Governmental administration	1,845,743	3.2
Interest on general debt	2,683,075	4.6
Other and unallocable	7,112,568	12.2
Utility expenditure	2,401,428	4.1
Liquor stores expenditure	0	-
Insurance trust expenditure	7,596,912	13.0
Debt at End of Fiscal Year	74,234,582	X
Cash and Security Holdings	96,031,087	X

X = Not applicable.
- = Zero or rounds to zero.
[1]Within insurance trust revenue, net earnings of state retirement systems is a calculated statistic (the item code in the data file is X08), and thus can be positive or negative. Net earnings is the sum of earnings on investments plus gains on investments minus losses on investments. The change made in 2002 for asset valuation from book to market value in accordance with Statement 34 of the Governmental Accounting Standards Board is reflected in the calculated statistics.

Table MA-16. State Government Tax Collections, 2014

(Dollars in thousands, percent.)

Item	Dollars	Percent distribution
Total Taxes	25,235,726	100.0
Property taxes	3,433	-
Sales and gross receipts	7,933,030	31.4
General sales and gross receipts	5,518,580	21.9
Selective sales and gross receipts	2,414,450	9.6
Alcoholic beverages	78,817	0.3
Amusements	3,758	-
Insurance premiums	346,828	1.4
Motor fuels	732,207	2.9
Pari-mutuels	337	-
Public utilities	23,736	0.1
Tobacco products	660,029	2.6
Other selective sales	568,738	2.3
Licenses	1,012,557	4.0
Alcoholic beverages	3,056	-
Amusements	762	-
Corporations in general	25,972	0.1
Hunting and fishing	5,456	-
Motor vehicle	390,879	1.5
Motor vehicle operators	105,322	0.4
Public utilities	0	-
Occupation and business, NEC	317,250	1.3
Other licenses	163,860	0.6
Income taxes	15,440,841	61.2
Individual income	13,246,221	52.5
Corporation net income	2,194,620	8.7
Other taxes	845,865	3.4
Death and gift	401,512	1.6
Documentary and stock transfer	246,850	1.0
Severance	X	X
Taxes, NEC	197,503	0.8

X = Not applicable.
- = Zero or rounds to zero.

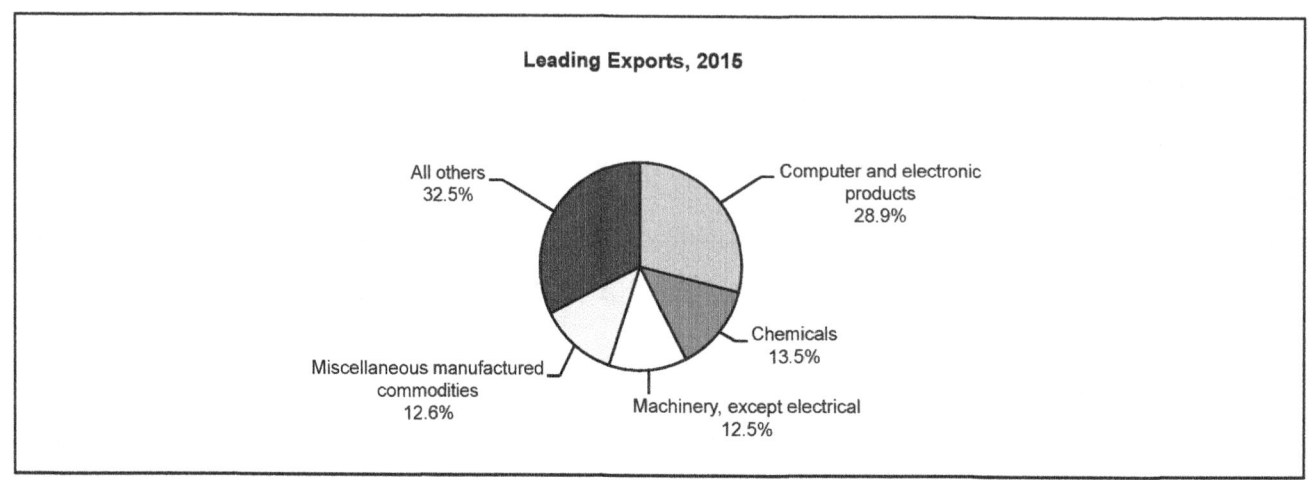

Leading Exports, 2015

- All others 32.5%
- Computer and electronic products 28.9%
- Chemicals 13.5%
- Machinery, except electrical 12.5%
- Miscellaneous manufactured commodities 12.6%

Facts and Figures

Location: East north central United States; bordered on the N by Lake Superior, on the E by Ontario, Canada, and Lakes Huron and Erie, on the S by Indiana and Ohio, and on the W by Wisconsin and Lake Michigan

Area: 96,716 sq. mi. (250,494 sq. km.); rank—11th

Population: 9,922,576 (2015 est.); rank—10th

Principal Cities: capital—Lansing; largest—Detroit

Statehood: January 26, 1837; 26th state

U.S. Congress: 2 senators, 14 representatives

State Motto: *Si quaeris peninsulam amoenam, circumspice* ("If you seek a pleasant peninsula, look about you")

State Song: "Michigan, My Michigan"

State Nicknames: The Wolverine State; The Great Lakes State

Abbreviations: MI; Mich.

State Symbols: flower—apple blossom; tree—Eastern white pine; bird—robin

At a Glance

- With an increase in population of 0.5 percent, Michigan ranked 45th among the states in growth from 2010 to 2015.

- In 2014, 8.5 percent of Michiganders did not have health insurance, compared to 11.7 percent of the total U.S. population.

- Michigan's violent crime rate in 2014 was 427.3 per 100,000 population, compared to the U.S. rate of 365.5 per 100,000 population.

- Approximately 16.2 percent of Michiganders lived below the poverty level in 2014.

- Michigan's unemployment rate of 5.4 ranked 21st in the nation in 2015.

Table MI-1. Population by Age, Sex, Race, and Hispanic Origin

(Number, percent, except where noted.)

Sex, age, race, and Hispanic origin	2000	2010	2015[1]	Average annual percent change, 2010–2015
Total Population................................	9,938,444	9,883,640	9,922,576	-
Percent of total U.S. population	3.5	3.2	3.1	X
Sex				
Male................................	4,873,095	4,848,114	4,878,148	-
Female	5,065,349	5,035,526	5,044,428	-
Age				
Under 5 years................................	672,005	596,286	571,776	-0.3
5 to 19 years................................	2,212,060	2,052,599	1,903,407	-0.5
20 to 64 years................................	5,835,361	5,873,225	5,876,722	-
65 years and over................................	1,219,018	1,361,530	1,570,671	1.0
Median age (years)................................	35.5	38.9	39.7	0.1
Race and Hispanic Origin				
One race				
White	7,966,053	7,949,497	7,909,096	-
Black................................	1,412,742	1,416,067	1,410,066	-
American Indian and Alaska Native	58,479	68,396	71,545	0.3
Asian................................	176,510	243,062	297,650	1.5
Native Hawaiian or Other Pacific Islander	2,692	3,442	3,998	1.1
Two or more races	192,416	203,176	230,221	0.9
Hispanic (of any race)................................	323,877	459,751	485,974	0.4

X = Not applicable.
- = Zero or rounds to zero.
[1]Population figures for 2015 are July 1 estimates. The 2010 estimates are taken from the 2010 Census.

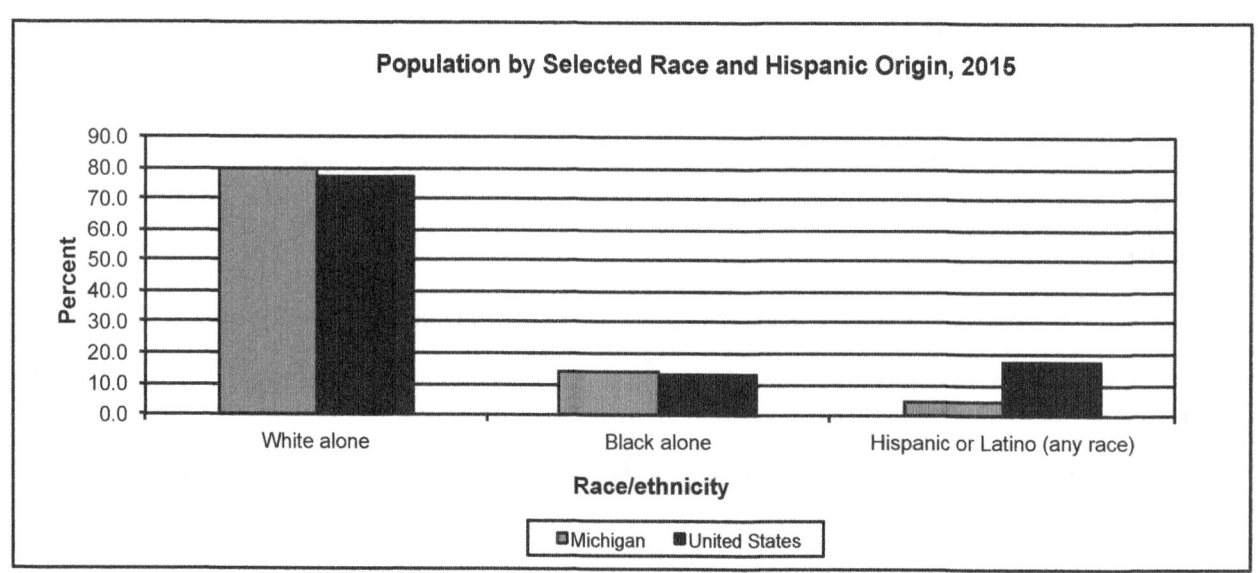

Table MI-2. Marital Status

(Number, percent distribution.)

Sex, age, race, and Hispanic origin	2000	2010	2014
Males, 15 Years and Over	3,761,881	3,875,107	3,903,030
Never married	30.8	34.9	35.5
Now married, except separated................................	56.1	50.5	50.0
Separated................................	1.3	1.3	1.2
Widowed................................	2.5	2.7	2.7
Divorced................................	9.3	10.6	10.6
Females, 15 Years and Over	4,013,722	4,099,384	4,127,252
Never married	25.0	29.0	29.4
Now married, except separated................................	51.8	47.2	46.9
Separated................................	1.6	1.6	1.6
Widowed................................	10.4	9.7	9.5
Divorced................................	11.2	12.5	12.5

Table MI-3. Households and Housing Characteristics

(Number, percent, dollars.)

Item	2000	2010	2014	Average annual percent change, 2000–2014
Total Households...	3,785,661	3,806,621	3,834,574	0.1
Family households...	2,575,699	2,508,780	2,485,159	-0.3
Married-couple family....................................	1,947,610	1,845,094	1,814,961	-0.5
Other family...	627,989	663,686	670,198	0.5
Male householder, no wife present..............	154,187	168,337	182,312	1.3
Female householder, no husband present....	473,802	495,349	487,886	0.2
Nonfamily households.......................................	1,209,962	1,297,841	1,349,415	0.8
Householder living alone...............................	993,607	1,090,126	1,115,614	0.9
Householder not living alone..........................	216,335	207,715	233,801	0.6
Housing Characteristics				
Total housing units..	4,234,279	4,531,231	4,540,088	0.5
Occupied housing units....................................	3,785,661	3,806,621	3,834,574	0.1
Owner occupied...	2,793,124	2,769,474	2,693,284	-0.3
Renter occupied..	992,537	1,037,147	1,141,290	1.1
Average household size..................................	2.56	2.53	2.53	-0.1
Financial Characteristics				
Median gross rent of renter-occupied housing	546	730	788	3.2
Median monthly owner costs for housing units with a mortgage	972	1,288	1,217	1.8
Median value of owner-occupied housing units...........................	115,600	123,300	125,700	0.6

- = Zero or rounds to zero.

Table MI-4. Migration, Origin, and Language

(Number, percent.)

Characteristic	State 2013	State 2014	State Percent change	U.S. 2013	U.S. 2014	U.S. Percent change
Residence 1 Year Ago						
Population 1 year and over	9,784,094	9,795,659	0.1	312,432,820	315,095,393	0.9
Same house...	84.8	85.1	X	85.0	85.1	X
Different house in the U.S............................	14.7	14.4	X	14.4	14.3	X
Same county.......................................	9.2	9	X	8.9	8.7	X
Different county.................................	5.5	5.4	X	5.5	5.6	X
Same state......................................	4.0	3.9	X	3.2	3.3	X
Different state................................	1.5	1.5	X	2.3	2.3	X
Abroad...	0.5	0.5	X	0.6	0.6	X
Place of Birth						
Native born	9,278,836	9,273,308	-0.1	274,780,773	276,465,262	0.6
Male..	49.1	49.1	X	49.3	49.3	X
Female..	50.9	50.9	X	50.7	50.7	X
Foreign born	616,786	636,569	3.2	41,348,066	42,391,794	2.5
Male..	48.8	48.7	X	48.8	48.7	X
Female..	51.2	51.3	X	51.2	51.3	X
Foreign born; naturalized U.S. citizen...............	315,064	328,337	4.2	19,294,710	19,984,738	3.6
Male..	47.5	47.4	X	45.9	45.9	X
Female..	52.5	52.6	X	54.1	54.1	X
Foreign born; not a U.S. citizen.......................	301,722	308,232	2.2	22,053,356	22,407,056	1.6
Male..	50.2	50.1	X	51.3	51.2	X
Female..	49.8	49.9	X	48.7	48.8	X
Entered 2010 or later	15.2	17.5	X	9.7	12.3	X
Entered 2000 to 2009	28.0	27	X	29.4	28.6	X
Entered before 2000....................................	56.8	55.5	X	61.0	59.1	X
World Region of Birth, Foreign						
Foreign-born population, excluding population born at sea	616,786	636,569	3.2	41,347,945	42,390,705	2.5
Europe	20.9	19.8	X	11.6	11.2	X
Asia	49.1	50.1	X	29.5	30.1	X
Africa	4.1	4.5	X	4.4	4.6	X
Oceania	0.4	0.4	X	0.5	0.6	X
Latin America......................................	18.4	19.3	X	51.9	51.6	X
North America	7.1	5.9	X	2.0	1.9	X
Language Spoken at Home and Ability to Speak English						
Population 5 years and over...........................	9,325,319	9,340,973	0.2	296,358,760	299,084,046	0.9
English only	91.0	90.8	X	79.2	78.9	X
Language other than English........................	9.0	9.2	X	20.8	21.1	X
Speaks English less than "very well"..........	3.3	3.4	X	8.5	8.6	X

X = Not applicable.
- = Zero or rounds to zero.

Table MI-5. Median Income and Poverty Status, 2014

(Number, percent, except as noted.)

Characteristic	State		U.S.	
	Number	Percent	Number	Percent
Median Income				
Households (dollars)...	49,847	X	53,657	X
Families (dollars)	62,143	X	65,910	X
Below Poverty Level (All People)	1,568,844	16.2	48,208,387	15.5
Sex				
Male...	714,862	15.1	21,590,918	14.2
Female	853,982	17.2	26,617,469	16.8
Age				
Under 18 years..	492,853	22.6	15,686,012	21.7
Related children under 18 years...........................	481,270	22.2	15,372,705	21.3
18 to 64 years	954,488	15.9	28,267,482	14.6
65 years and over	121,503	8.1	4,254,893	9.5

X = Not applicable.

Median Household and Family Income, 2014

Table MI-6. Health Insurance Coverage Status for the Civilian Noninstitutionalized Population and Children Under 18 Years of Age

(Numbers in thousands, percent.)

Item	2006	2007	2008	2009	2010	2011	2012	2013	2014
Civilian Noninstitutionalized Population	9,970	9,927	9,866	9,835	9,764	9,762	9,773	9,784	9,799
Covered by Private or Public Insurance									
Number..	8,928	8,776	8,734	8,632	8,556	8,612	8,658	8,713	8,962
Percent..	89.5	88.4	88.5	87.8	87.6	88.2	88.6	89.0	91.5
Not Covered									
Number..	1,043	1,151	1,132	1,203	1,207	1,150	1,115	1,072	837
Percent..	10.5	11.6	11.5	12.2	12.4	11.8	11.4	11.0	8.5
Percent in the U.S. not covered...............................	15.8	15.3	15.1	15.1	15.5	15.1	14.8	14.5	11.7
Children Under 18 Years of Age	2,446	2,419	2,389	2,343	2,331	2,290	2,264	2,240	2,220
Covered by Private or Public Insurance									
Number..	2,330	2,270	2,265	2,236	2,236	2,196	2,174	2,150	2,137
Percent..	95.3	93.8	94.8	95.4	95.9	95.9	96.0	96.0	96.2
Not Covered									
Number..	116	149	124	107	95	94	90	90	83
Percent..	4.7	6.2	5.2	4.6	4.1	4.1	4.0	4.0	3.8
Percent in the U.S. not covered...............................	11.7	11.0	9.7	8.6	8.0	7.5	7.2	7.1	6.0

Table MI-7. Employment Status by Demographic Group, 2015

(Numbers in thousands, percent.)

Characteristic	Civilian noninstitutional population	Civilian labor force		Employed		Unemployed	
		Number	Percent of population	Number	Percent of population	Number	Percent of population
Total.............................	7,882	4,763	60.4	4,505	57.2	258	5.4
Sex							
Male........................	3,811	2,511	65.9	2,365	62.1	146	5.8
Female.....................	4,072	2,252	55.3	2,139	52.5	112	5.0
Race, Sex, and Hispanic Origin							
White........................	6,436	3,948	61.3	3,772	58.6	176	4.5
Male.....................	3,152	2,128	67.5	2,023	64.2	105	4.9
Female..................	3,284	1,819	55.4	1,748	53.2	71	3.9
Black or African American..................	1,056	557	52.8	493	46.6	65	11.6
Male.....................	477	248	52.0	212	44.4	36	14.6
Female..................	579	310	53.4	281	48.5	29	9.2
Hispanic or Latino ethnicity[1]	368	258	70.1	236	64.1	22	8.6
Male.....................	184	146	79.2	139	75.5	7	4.8
Female..................	184	112	61.0	97	52.7	15	13.5
Age							
16 to 19 years............	494	206	41.8	172	34.8	35	16.7
20 to 24 years............	686	498	72.6	449	65.4	49	9.9
25 to 34 years............	1,203	957	79.6	903	75.1	54	5.6
35 to 44 years............	1,213	972	80.2	930	76.7	42	4.3
45 to 54 years............	1,375	1,097	79.8	1,057	76.9	39	3.6
55 to 64 years............	1,340	769	57.4	741	55.3	28	3.6
65 years and over............	1,572	264	16.8	252	16.0	11	4.3

NOTE: Data in Table 7 are from the Current Population Survey (CPS) and do not match the estimates in Table 8. See notes and definitions for further information.
[1]May be of any race.

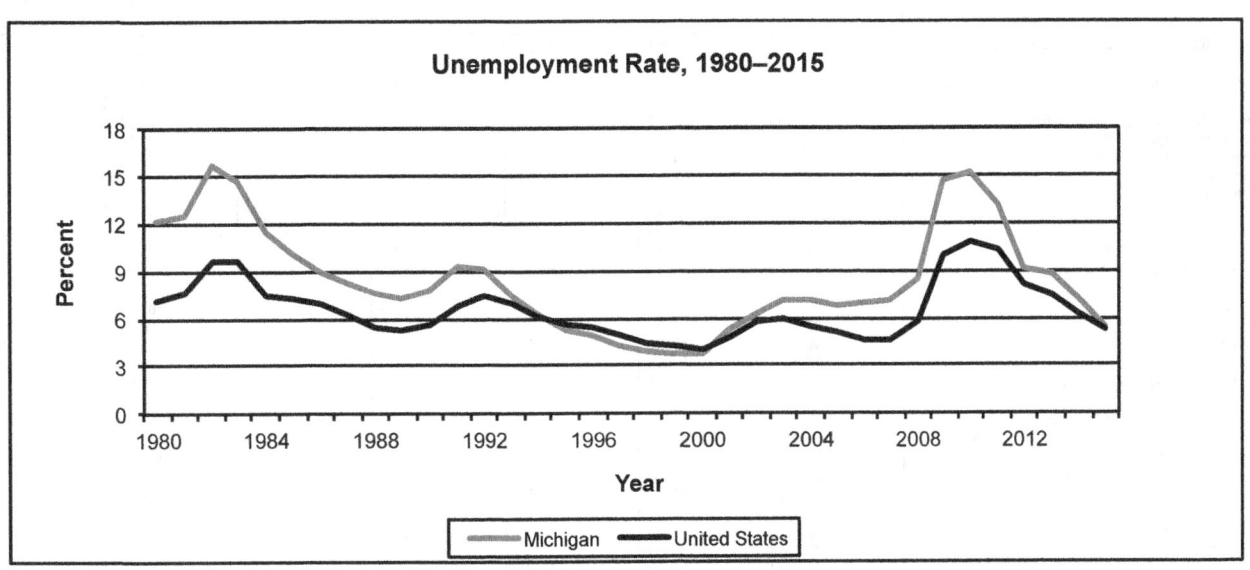

Table MI-8. Employment Status of the Civilian Noninstitutional Population Age 16 Years and Over

(Number, percent.)

Year	Civilian labor force	Civilian participation rate	Employed	Unemployed	Unemployment rate
2007........................	5,011,120	64.4	4,658,939	352,181	7.0
2008........................	4,921,466	63.3	4,529,289	392,177	8.0
2009........................	4,903,544	63.1	4,233,803	669,741	13.7
2010........................	4,798,954	62.0	4,194,041	604,913	12.6
2011........................	4,685,164	60.5	4,198,349	486,815	10.4
2012........................	4,672,484	60.0	4,246,233	426,251	9.1
2013........................	4,729,625	60.5	4,311,262	418,363	8.8
2014........................	4,754,282	60.6	4,408,144	346,138	7.3
2015........................	4,750,627	60.3	4,492,989	257,638	5.4

Table MI-9. Employment and Average Wages by Industry

(Estimates through 2010 are based on the 2007 North American Industry Classification System [NAICS]. Estimates from 2011 onward are based on the 2012 NAICS.)

Industry	2008	2009	2010	2011	2012	2013	2014
	Number of jobs						
Wage and Salary Employment by Industry..................	4,257,567	3,960,939	3,955,898	4,049,195	4,108,945	4,186,832	4,265,676
Farm Wage and Salary Employment.........................	17,600	18,072	16,719	22,521	19,054	22,198	22,952
Nonfarm Wage and Salary Employment....................	4,239,967	3,942,867	3,939,179	4,026,674	4,089,891	4,164,634	4,242,724
Private wage and salary employment............................	3,576,307	3,283,032	3,288,111	3,394,605	3,467,631	3,554,581	3,636,124
Forestry, fishing, and related activities	6,518	6,529	6,914	7,197	7,113	7,804	8,905
Mining..	6,372	5,561	5,616	5,913	6,300	6,484	6,646
Utilities...	20,784	20,269	19,480	19,337	19,210	19,359	19,774
Construction	156,768	131,059	126,044	131,659	132,531	138,379	145,999
Manufacturing...	580,835	469,570	478,601	513,416	538,329	556,930	578,671
Durable goods manufacturing............................	441,778	345,961	352,953	383,282	405,915	421,523	439,273
Nondurable goods manufacturing......................	139,057	123,609	125,648	130,134	132,414	135,407	139,398
Wholesale trade	167,482	153,228	151,528	156,142	159,961	164,610	168,525
Retail trade..	484,299	458,394	452,882	454,646	453,517	459,788	464,827
Transportation and warehousing..........................	105,892	94,526	95,225	100,170	103,890	107,008	111,807
Information	62,210	58,739	57,287	55,819	56,222	58,003	60,496
Finance and insurance	150,208	139,717	137,114	139,336	143,824	147,468	148,138
Real estate and rental and leasing.........................	55,028	52,015	51,539	51,930	49,396	50,966	51,863
Professional, scientific, and technical services	243,722	223,044	226,352	238,825	250,004	262,213	269,746
Management of companies and enterprises.................	54,259	48,686	48,132	50,858	52,119	54,679	55,246
Administrative and waste services	267,688	233,079	247,251	270,635	280,910	289,652	294,563
Educational services	74,388	74,690	76,157	77,917	77,407	78,952	80,747
Health care and social assistance........................	537,862	538,699	540,771	548,958	557,854	561,779	565,656
Arts, entertainment, and recreation......................	56,812	53,730	51,868	49,049	47,638	48,954	49,806
Accommodation and food services........................	344,926	330,301	328,629	334,721	344,073	352,455	359,367
Other services, except public administration..............	200,254	191,196	186,721	188,077	187,333	189,098	195,342
Government and government enterprises	663,660	659,835	651,068	632,069	622,260	610,053	606,600
	Dollars						
Average Wages and Salaries by Industry	43,674	43,076	43,865	45,194	46,153	46,623	47,935
Average Farm Wages and Salaries	34,099	33,837	28,444	25,937	31,325	35,726	38,031
Average Nonfarm Wages and Salaries	43,713	43,118	43,930	45,302	46,222	46,681	47,989
Average private wages and salaries...........................	43,665	42,693	43,557	45,219	46,182	46,648	48,002
Forestry, fishing, and related activities	23,844	24,077	25,024	25,591	26,360	27,547	27,663
Mining..	64,932	62,502	73,681	74,926	73,530	73,358	77,186
Utilities...	84,167	89,233	93,787	98,236	102,234	104,152	109,026
Construction	50,543	49,648	50,564	52,013	53,231	53,631	55,604
Manufacturing...	59,557	58,613	59,744	62,235	62,823	63,406	64,432
Durable goods manufacturing............................	62,368	61,167	62,268	65,352	65,346	66,018	66,979
Nondurable goods manufacturing......................	50,628	51,464	52,655	53,054	55,088	55,273	56,403
Wholesale trade	63,504	61,587	64,279	67,009	67,790	67,437	69,913
Retail trade..	25,035	25,250	25,648	26,037	26,408	26,519	27,353
Transportation and warehousing..........................	46,459	45,789	47,516	49,077	50,150	50,860	51,795
Information	57,452	57,371	58,548	62,044	62,067	64,237	65,451
Finance and insurance	60,081	60,305	62,076	63,967	66,392	68,195	70,854
Real estate and rental and leasing.........................	32,892	33,255	34,119	36,048	37,625	38,226	39,732
Professional, scientific, and technical services	74,099	70,491	70,668	73,096	74,423	74,459	76,438
Management of companies and enterprises.................	104,241	99,959	103,246	113,268	116,195	110,606	119,913
Administrative and waste services	30,908	30,661	30,907	31,068	31,727	31,704	32,041
Educational services	28,132	28,107	28,602	28,637	29,414	29,855	30,614
Health care and social assistance........................	42,059	42,996	43,341	44,373	44,902	45,545	46,447
Arts, entertainment, and recreation......................	30,364	30,594	30,778	30,484	31,960	32,454	33,072
Accommodation and food services........................	15,136	15,186	15,790	16,551	16,770	16,717	17,410
Other services, except public administration.................	27,906	27,711	28,533	29,016	29,541	30,289	31,167
Government and government enterprises	43,972	45,232	45,813	45,748	46,446	46,874	47,911

Table MI-10. Employment Characteristics by Family Type

(Number, percent.)

Family type and labor force status	2012 Total	2012 Families with own children under 18 years	2013 Total	2013 Families with own children under 18 years	2014 Total	2014 Families with own children under 18 years
All Families................................	2,482,612	1,041,802	2,484,558	1,041,331	2,478,645	1,026,180
FAMILY TYPE AND LABOR FORCE STATUS						
Married-Couple Families...........................	1,821,915	682,944	1,809,823	675,621	1,808,447	670,411
Both husband and wife in labor force.................	50.1	67.1	49.5	66.7	48.9	67.2
Husband in labor force, wife not in labor force	19.9	26.3	20.0	26.0	20.2	26.2
Wife in labor force, husband not in labor force	8.8	4.4	8.8	5.0	8.8	4.3
Both husband and wife not in labor force................	21.2	2.2	21.4	2.1	22.1	2.3
Other Families	660,697	358,858	674,735	365,710	670,198	355,769
Female householder, no husband present.............	74.7	77.3	73.4	76.2	72.8	74.0
In labor force	50.7	62.4	49.9	61.7	49.5	60.6
Not in labor force	24.0	14.9	23.5	14.5	23.3	13.4
Male householder, no wife present...................	25.3	22.7	26.6	23.8	27.2	26.0
In labor force....................................	19.0	19.9	19.9	21.0	20.0	22.7
Not in labor force	6.3	2.8	6.7	2.8	7.2	3.3

Table MI-11. School Enrollment and Educational Attainment, 2014

(Number, percent.)

Item	State	U.S.
Enrollment		
Total population 3 years and over, enrolled in school...............................	2,555,615	82,063,714
Enrolled in nursery school or preschool (percent)	5.4	6.0
Enrolled in kindergarten (percent)...	4.8	5.1
Enrolled in elementary school, grades 1-8 (percent)...............................	39.0	40.2
Enrolled in high school, grades 9-12 (percent)....................................	21.3	20.7
Enrolled in college or graduate school (percent)..................................	29.5	28.0
Attainment		
Total population 25 years and over	6,680,525	213,725,624
Less than ninth grade (percent)	3.2	5.6
9th to 12th grade, no diploma (percent)...	6.9	7.5
High school graduate, including equivalency (percent).............................	29.7	27.7
Some college, no degree (percent)..	23.6	21.0
Associate's degree (percent)	9.3	8.2
Bachelor's degree (percent)	16.5	18.7
Graduate or professional degree (percent)...	10.8	11.4
High school graduate or higher (percent)	89.9	86.9
Bachelor's degree or higher (percent)...	27.4	30.1

Table MI-12. Public School Characteristics and Educational Indicators

(Number, percent; data derived from National Center of Education Statistics.)

Item	State	U.S.
Public Schools, 2013–2014 (except where noted)		
Number of school districts...	907	18,194
Number of schools..	3,538	98,271
Number of students (in thousands)	1,549	50,045
Number of teachers (in thousands)	86	3,114
Student-teacher ratio...	18.1	16.1
Expenditures per student (dollars), FY 2013	10,515	107,637
Four-year adjusted cohort graduation rate (ACGR)[1,2]	78.6	82.3
Students eligible for free or reduced-price lunch (in thousands)	727	25,596
English language learners (in thousands)	63	4,461
Students age 3 to 21 served under IDEA, part B (in thousands)	200	6,464

Public Schools by Type	Number	Percent of state public schools
Total number of schools...	3,538	100.0
Regular	3,039	85.9
Special education	183	5.2
Vocational education	6	0.2
Alternative education...	310	8.8

NOTE: Every school is assigned only one school type based on its instructional emphasis.

[1]ACGR data represents a new method of calculating high-school completion rates and may not be comparable to previous years' data for Averaged Freshmen Graduation Rates (AFGR).

[2]The United States 4-year ACGRs were estimated using both the reported 4-year ACGR data from 49 states and the District of Columbia and using imputed data for Idaho. The estimate for American Indian/Alaska Native students also includes imputed data for Virginia.

Table MI-13. Reported Voting and Registration of the Voting-Age Population, November 2014

(Numbers in thousands, percent.)

Item	Total population	Total citizen population	Registered			Voted		
			Total registered	Percent registered (total population)	Percent registered (total citizen population)	Total voted	Percent voted (total population)	Percent voted (total citizen population)
U.S. Total	239,874	219,941	142,166	59.3	64.6	92,251	38.5	41.9
State Total..............................	7,576	7,246	5,159	68.1	71.2	3,416	45.1	47.1
Sex								
Male..	3,615	3,456	2,397	66.3	69.4	1,551	42.9	44.9
Female	3,961	3,791	2,762	69.7	72.9	1,864	47.1	49.2
Race								
White alone................................	6,164	5,965	4,280	69.4	71.7	2,875	46.6	48.2
White, non-Hispanic alone	5,836	5,720	4,128	70.7	72.2	2,808	48.1	49.1
Black alone................................	979	965	685	70.0	71.0	438	44.8	45.4
Asian alone	277	177	86	31.2	48.9	51	18.4	28.8
Hispanic (of any race)	395	295	179	45.3	60.6	82	20.8	27.8
White alone or in combination	6,243	6,045	4,344	69.6	71.9	2,905	46.5	48.1
Black alone or in combination..........	1,026	1,012	714	69.6	70.6	455	44.4	45.0
Asian alone or in combination..........	291	191	93	32.1	49.0	58	19.9	30.4
Age								
18 to 24 years.............................	915	899	448	48.9	49.8	167	18.3	18.6
25 to 34 years.............................	1,127	1,039	674	59.8	64.9	340	30.1	32.7
35 to 44 years.............................	1,271	1,193	863	67.9	72.3	546	43.0	45.8
45 to 64 years.............................	2,660	2,553	1,888	71.0	74.0	1,312	49.3	51.4
65 years and over	1,602	1,562	1,285	80.2	82.3	1,051	65.6	67.3

Table MI-14. Crime

(Number, rate per 100,000. Data are derived from the FBI Uniform Crime Reports.)

Item	State			U.S.[1,2,3,4]		
	2013	2014	Percent change	2013	2014	Percent change
TOTAL POPULATION[5]..	9,895,622	9,909,877	0.1	316,128,839	318,857,056	0.9
VIOLENT CRIME						
Number..	42,536	42,348	-0.4	1,163,146	1,165,383	0.2
Rate	429.8	427.3	-0.6	367.9	365.5	-0.7
Murder and Nonnegligent Manslaughter						
Number..	631	535	-15.2	14,196	14,249	0.4
Rate	6.4	5.4	-15.6	4.5	4.5	-
Rape[6]						
Number..	6,593	6,273	X	108,612	116,645	X
Rate	66.6	63.3	X	34.4	36.6	X
Robbery						
Number..	10,105	8,021	-20.6	345,031	325,802	-5.6
Rate	102.1	80.9	-20.8	109.1	102.2	-6.3
Aggravated Assault						
Number..	27,194	27,519	1.2	724,149	741,291	2.4
Rate	274.8	277.7	1.1	229.1	232.5	1.5
PROPERTY CRIME						
Number..	230,334	202,547	-12.1	8,632,512	8,277,829	-4.1
Rate	2,327.6	2,043.9	-12.2	2,730.7	2,596.1	-4.9
Burglary						
Number..	56,344	44,184	-21.6	1,928,465	1,729,806	-10.3
Rate	569.4	445.9	-21.7	610.0	542.5	-11.1
Larceny-Theft						
Number..	149,423	137,206	-8.2	6,004,453	5,858,496	-2.4
Rate	1,510.0	1,384.5	-8.3	1,899.4	1,837.3	-3.3
Motor Vehicle Theft						
Number..	24,567	21,157	-13.9	699,594	689,527	-1.4
Rate	248.3	213.5	-14.0	221.3	216.2	-2.3

NOTE: Although arson data are included in the trend and clearance tables, sufficient data are not available to estimate totals for this offense. Therefore, no arson data are published in this table.
X = Not applicable.
- = Zero or rounds to zero.
[1]The crime figures have been adjusted.
[2]The data collection methodology for the offense of forcible rape used by the Minnesota state Uniform Crime Reporting (UCR) Program (with the exception of Minneapolis and St. Paul, Minnesota) does not comply with national UCR Program guidelines. Consequently, its figures for forcible rape and violent crime (of which forcible rape is a part) are not published in this table.
[3]Includes offenses reported by the Zoological Police and the Metro Transit Police.
[4]Because of changes in the state's reporting practices, figures are not comparable to previous years' data.
[5]Populations are U.S. Census Bureau provisional estimates as of July 1 of each year.
[6]The figures shown for the offense of rape were estimated using the revised Uniform Crime Reporting (UCR) definition of rape.

Table MI-15. State Government Finances, 2014

(Dollar amounts in thousands, percent distribution.)

Item	Dollars	Percent distribution
Total Revenue	68,884,416	100.0
General revenue	54,834,376	79.6
Intergovernmental revenue	17,929,672	26.0
Taxes	24,803,973	36.0
General sales	8,419,195	12.2
Selective sales	3,890,369	5.6
License taxes	1,511,695	2.2
Individual income tax	7,874,712	11.4
Corporate income tax	881,011	1.3
Other taxes	2,226,991	3.2
Current charges	7,752,191	11.3
Miscellaneous general revenue	4,348,540	6.3
Utility revenue	0	-
Liquor stores revenue	957,064	1.4
Insurance trust revenue[1]	13,092,976	19.0
Total Expenditure	63,861,993	100.0
Intergovernmental expenditure	19,779,302	31.0
Direct expenditure	44,082,691	69.0
Current operation	31,467,830	49.3
Capital outlay	2,022,385	3.2
Insurance benefits and repayments	7,794,453	12.2
Assistance and subsidies	1,288,655	2.0
Interest on debt	1,509,368	2.4
Exhibit: Salaries and wages	7,937,015	12.4
Total Expenditure	63,861,993	100.0
General expenditure	55,288,264	86.6
Intergovernmental expenditure	19,779,302	31.0
Direct expenditure	35,508,962	55.6
General expenditure, by function:		
Education	23,548,582	36.9
Public welfare	15,679,564	24.6
Hospitals	3,221,713	5.0
Health	1,304,723	2.0
Highways	2,628,372	4.1
Police protection	427,914	0.7
Correction	1,876,087	2.9
Natural resources	302,488	0.5
Parks and recreation	137,879	0.2
Governmental administration	999,521	1.6
Interest on general debt	1,509,368	2.4
Other and unallocable	3,652,053	5.7
Utility expenditure	0	-
Liquor stores expenditure	779,276	1.2
Insurance trust expenditure	7,794,453	12.2
Debt at End of Fiscal Year	31,528,074	X
Cash and Security Holdings	94,660,666	X

X = Not applicable.
- = Zero or rounds to zero.
[1]Within insurance trust revenue, net earnings of state retirement systems is a calculated statistic (the item code in the data file is X08), and thus can be positive or negative. Net earnings is the sum of earnings on investments plus gains on investments minus losses on investments. The change made in 2002 for asset valuation from book to market value in accordance with Statement 34 of the Governmental Accounting Standards Board is reflected in the calculated statistics.

Table MI-16. State Government Tax Collections, 2014

(Dollars in thousands, percent.)

Item	Dollars	Percent distribution
Total Taxes	24,803,973	100.0
Property taxes	1,919,910	7.7
Sales and gross receipts	12,309,564	49.6
General sales and gross receipts	8,419,195	33.9
Selective sales and gross receipts	3,890,369	15.7
Alcoholic beverages	143,641	0.6
Amusements	106,903	0.4
Insurance premiums	362,397	1.5
Motor fuels	964,119	3.9
Pari-mutuels	4,252	-
Public utilities	28,412	0.1
Tobacco products	942,148	3.8
Other selective sales	1,338,497	5.4
Licenses	1,511,695	6.1
Alcoholic beverages	16,540	0.1
Amusements	0	-
Corporations in general	22,621	0.1
Hunting and fishing	58,440	0.2
Motor vehicle	979,061	3.9
Motor vehicle operators	54,695	0.2
Public utilities	27,357	0.1
Occupation and business, NEC	164,127	0.7
Other licenses	188,854	0.8
Income taxes	8,755,723	35.3
Individual income	7,874,712	31.7
Corporation net income	881,011	3.6
Other taxes	307,081	1.2
Death and gift	177	-
Documentary and stock transfer	233,416	0.9
Severance	73,488	0.3
Taxes, NEC	0	-

- = Zero or rounds to zero.

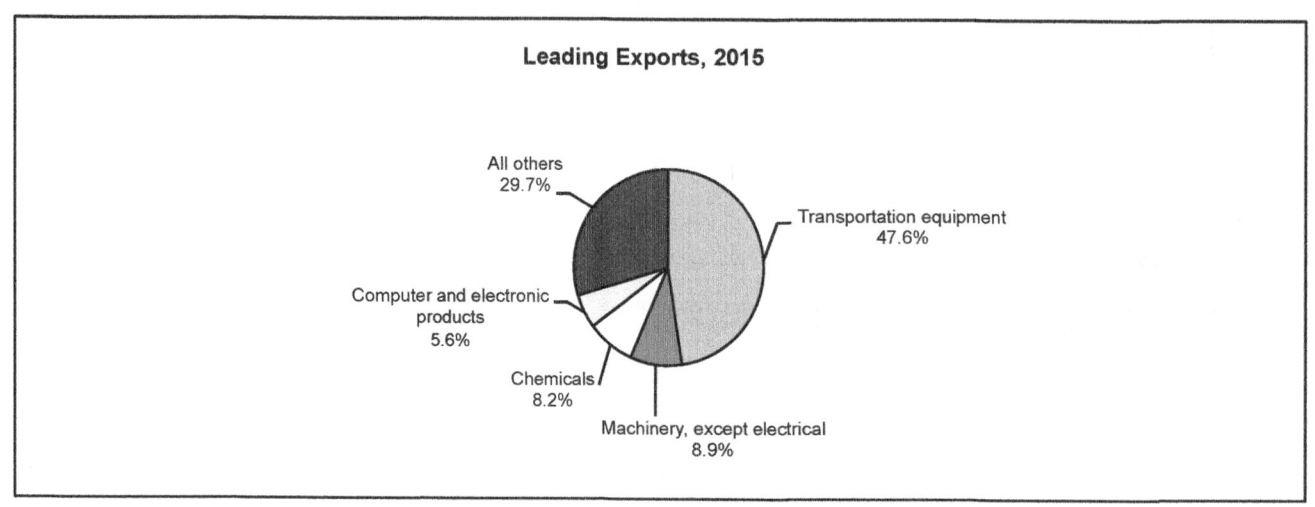

Leading Exports, 2015

All others 29.7%
Transportation equipment 47.6%
Computer and electronic products 5.6%
Chemicals 8.2%
Machinery, except electrical 8.9%

MINNESOTA

Facts and Figures

Location: North central United States; bordered on the N by Canada (Manitoba and Ontario), on the E by Lake Superior and Wisconsin, on the S by Iowa, and on the W by North Dakota and South Dakota

Area: 86,939 sq. mi. (225,171 sq. km.); rank—12th

Population: 5,489,594 (2015 est.); rank—21st

Principal Cities: capital—St. Paul; largest—Minneapolis

Statehood: May 11, 1858; 32nd state

U.S. Congress: 2 senators, 8 representatives

State Motto: *L'Etoile du Nord* ("The Star of the North")

State Song: "Hail! Minnesota"

State Nicknames: The North Star State; The Land of 10,000 Lakes; The Gopher State

Abbreviations: MN; Minn.

State Symbols: flower—showy (pink and white) lady's slipper; tree—red (Norway) pine; bird—loon

At a Glance

- With an increase in population of 3.4 percent, Minnesota ranked 27th among the states in growth from 2010 to 2015.

- Minnesota's violent crime rate in 2014 was 229.1 per 100,000 population, compared to 365.5 for the entire nation.

- With a property crime rate of 2,297.5 per 100,000 population in 2014, Minnesota ranked 31st in the nation.

- Minnesota's median household income was $61,481 in 2014, the 11th highest in the country.

- In 2014, 11.5 percent of all Minnesotans and 14.9 percent of children in Minnesota lived below the poverty level, compared to 15.5 percent of the entire U.S. population and 21.7 percent of all U.S. children.

Table MN-1. Population by Age, Sex, Race, and Hispanic Origin

(Number, percent, except where noted.)

Sex, age, race, and Hispanic origin	2000	2010	2015[1]	Average annual percent change, 2010–2015
Total Population..	4,919,479	5,303,925	5,489,594	0.2
Percent of total U.S. population	1.7	1.7	1.7	X
Sex				
Male...	2,435,631	2,632,132	2,729,864	0.3
Female...	2,483,848	2,671,793	2,759,730	0.2
Age				
Under 5 years..	329,594	355,504	350,534	-0.1
5 to 19 years..	1,105,251	1,075,707	1,075,263	-
20 to 64 years...	2,890,368	3,189,593	3,258,154	0.2
65 years and over..	594,266	683,121	805,643	1.2
Median age (years)...	35.4	37.4	37.9	0.1
Race and Hispanic Origin				
One race				
White	4,400,282	4,623,461	4,685,506	0.1
Black...	171,731	280,949	328,815	1.1
American Indian and Alaska Native	54,967	67,325	73,101	0.6
Asian...	141,968	217,792	268,042	1.5
Native Hawaiian or Other Pacific Islander	1,979	2,958	3,567	1.3
Two or more races	82,742	111,440	130,563	1.1
Hispanic (of any race)..	143,382	264,432	284,214	0.5

X = Not applicable.
- = Zero or rounds to zero.
[1]Population figures for 2015 are July 1 estimates. The 2010 estimates are taken from the 2010 Census.

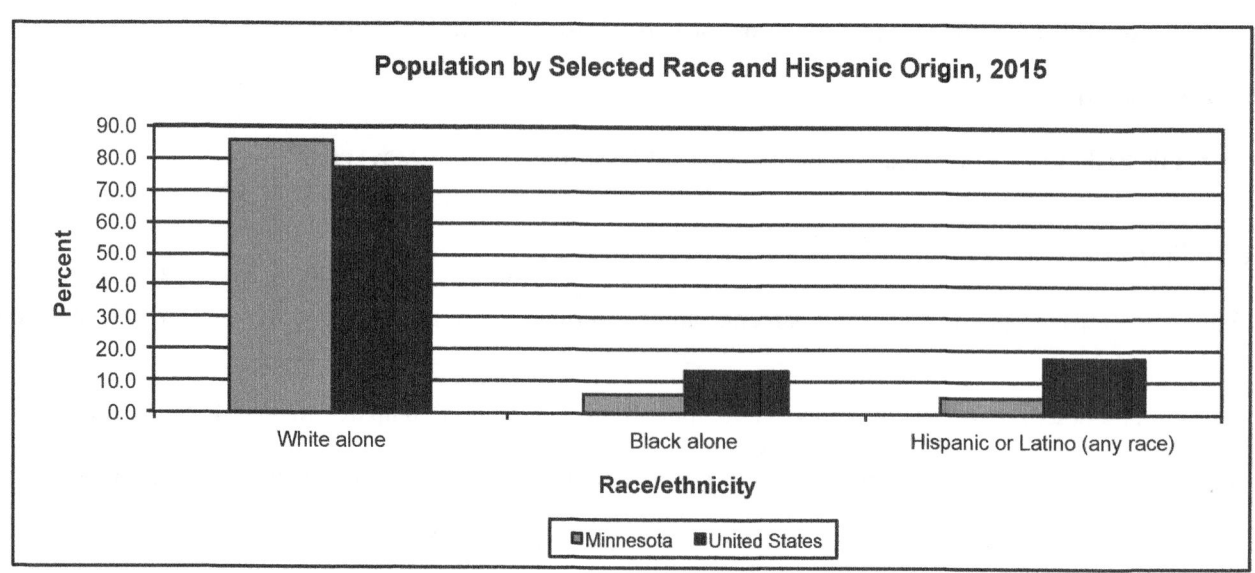

Table MN-2. Marital Status

(Number, percent distribution.)

Sex, age, race, and Hispanic origin	2000	2010	2014
Males, 15 Years and Over	1,889,936	2,090,940	2,130,079
Never married	31.3	34.6	34.7
Now married, except separated..	57.7	53.5	53.3
Separated...	0.9	0.9	1.0
Widowed...	2.1	2.2	2.2
Divorced..	8.0	8.7	8.9
Females, 15 Years and Over	1,967,819	2,155,042	2,189,134
Never married	25.0	28.2	28.2
Now married, except separated..	55.0	51.5	51.5
Separated...	1.2	1.2	1.3
Widowed...	9.4	8.4	8.2
Divorced..	9.5	10.7	10.9

Table MN-3. Households and Housing Characteristics

(Number, percent, dollars.)

Item	2000	2010	2014	Average annual percent change, 2000–2014
Total Households...	1,895,127	2,091,548	2,129,195	0.9
Family households	1,255,141	1,353,758	1,369,594	0.7
Married-couple family	1,018,245	1,069,000	1,075,956	0.4
Other family	236,986	284,758	293,638	1.7
Male householder, no wife present............	68,114	87,757	89,801	2.3
Female householder, no husband present....	168,782	197,001	203,837	1.5
Nonfamily households	639,986	737,790	759,601	1.3
Householder living alone..........................	509,468	591,124	611,108	1.4
Householder not living alone.....................	130,518	146,666	148,493	1.0
Housing Characteristics				
Total housing units....................................	2,065,946	2,348,242	2,385,261	1.1
Occupied housing units	1,895,127	2,091,548	2,129,195	0.9
Owner occupied.......................................	1,412,865	1,527,328	1,526,406	0.6
Renter occupied.......................................	482,262	564,220	602,789	1.8
Average household size................................	2.52	2.47	2.5	-0.1
Financial Characteristics				
Median gross rent of renter-occupied housing	566	764	859	3.7
Median monthly owner costs for housing units with a mortgage	1,044	1,503	1,454	2.8
Median value of owner-occupied housing units........................	122,400	194,300	188,300	3.8

Table MN-4. Migration, Origin, and Language

(Number, percent.)

Characteristic	State 2013	State 2014	State Percent change	U.S. 2013	U.S. 2014	U.S. Percent change
Residence 1 Year Ago						
Population 1 year and over	5,353,441	5,385,219	0.6	312,432,820	315,095,393	0.9
Same house	85.6	85.7	X	85.0	85.1	X
Different house in the U.S.	13.8	13.8	X	14.4	14.3	X
Same county	7.3	7.2	X	8.9	8.7	X
Different county	6.5	6.6	X	5.5	5.6	X
Same state	4.6	4.7	X	3.2	3.3	X
Different state	2.0	2	X	2.3	2.3	X
Abroad	0.5	0.6	X	0.6	0.6	X
Place of Birth						
Native born	5,016,866	5,029,116	0.2	274,780,773	276,465,262	0.6
Male	49.8	49.8	X	49.3	49.3	X
Female	50.2	50.2	X	50.7	50.7	X
Foreign born	403,514	428,057	6.1	41,348,066	42,391,794	2.5
Male	48.2	48.6	X	48.8	48.7	X
Female	51.8	51.4	X	51.2	51.3	X
Foreign born; naturalized U.S. citizen................	207,945	215,143	3.5	19,294,710	19,984,738	3.6
Male	44.6	45.5	X	45.9	45.9	X
Female	55.4	54.5	X	54.1	54.1	X
Foreign born; not a U.S. citizen......................	195,569	212,914	8.9	22,053,356	22,407,056	1.6
Male	52.0	51.7	X	51.3	51.2	X
Female	48.0	48.3	X	48.7	48.8	X
Entered 2010 or later	12.2	17.2	X	9.7	12.3	X
Entered 2000 to 2009	37.6	33.6	X	29.4	28.6	X
Entered before 2000......................................	50.1	49.3	X	61.0	59.1	X
World Region of Birth, Foreign						
Foreign-born population, excluding population born at sea	403,514	428,057	6.1	41,347,945	42,390,705	2.5
Europe	10.9	10.8	X	11.6	11.2	X
Asia	38.7	38	X	29.5	30.1	X
Africa	20.2	22	X	4.4	4.6	X
Oceania	0.4	0.5	X	0.5	0.6	X
Latin America..	27.0	25.6	X	51.9	51.6	X
North America	2.7	2.9	X	2.0	1.9	X
Language Spoken at Home and Ability to Speak English						
Population 5 years and over..........................	5,074,032	5,109,770	0.7	296,358,760	299,084,046	0.9
English only	89.4	88.9	X	79.2	78.9	X
Language other than English.........................	10.6	11.1	X	20.8	21.1	X
Speaks English less than "very well".............	4.2	4.5	X	8.5	8.6	X

X = Not applicable.
- = Zero or rounds to zero.

Table MN-5. Median Income and Poverty Status, 2014

(Number, percent, except as noted.)

Characteristic	State		U.S.	
	Number	Percent	Number	Percent
Median Income				
Households (dollars)..	61,481	X	53,657	X
Families (dollars)	77,941	X	65,910	X
Below Poverty Level (All People)	611,354	11.5	48,208,387	15.5
Sex				
Male...	278,568	10.5	21,590,918	14.2
Female	332,786	12.4	26,617,469	16.8
Age				
Under 18 years..	188,717	14.9	15,686,012	21.7
Related children under 18 years......................	183,274	14.6	15,372,705	21.3
18 to 64 years..	366,781	11.0	28,267,482	14.6
65 years and over	55,856	7.5	4,254,893	9.5

X = Not applicable.

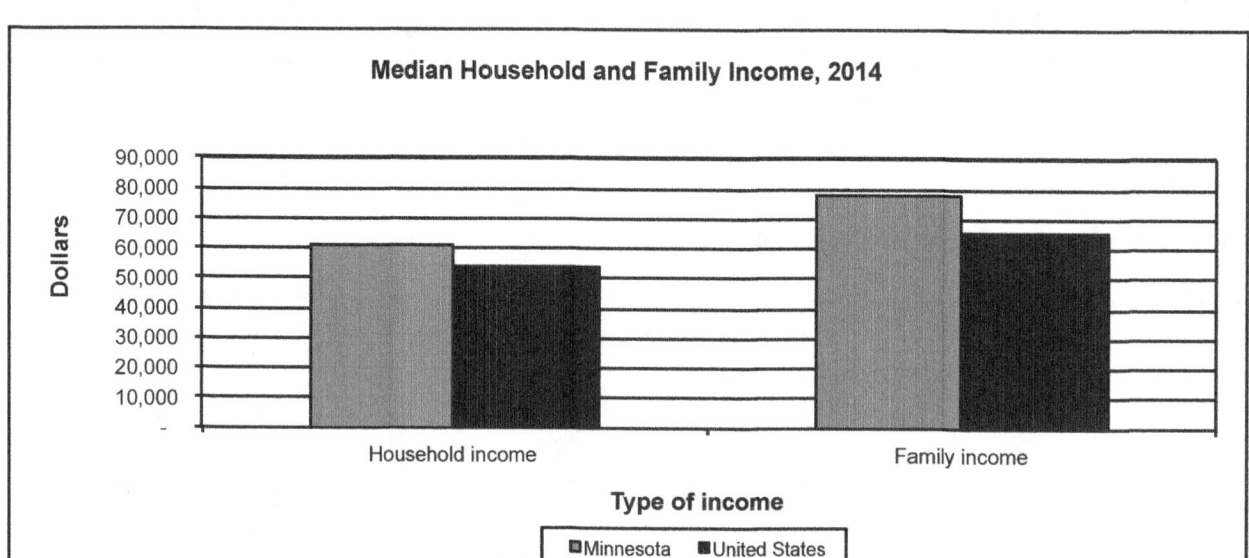

Median Household and Family Income, 2014

Table MN-6. Health Insurance Coverage Status for the Civilian Noninstitutionalized Population and Children Under 18 Years of Age

(Numbers in thousands, percent.)

Item	2006	2007	2008	2009	2010	2011	2012	2013	2014
Civilian Noninstitutionalized Population	5,149	5,190	5,151	5,197	5,252	5,287	5,320	5,363	5,398
Covered by Private or Public Insurance									
Number..	4,675	4,758	4,704	4,724	4,776	4,819	4,895	4,923	5,081
Percent...	90.8	91.7	91.3	90.9	90.9	91.2	92.0	91.8	94.1
Not Covered									
Number..	475	433	447	473	476	467	425	440	317
Percent...	9.2	8.3	8.7	9.1	9.1	8.8	8.0	8.2	5.9
Percent in the U.S. not covered...........................	15.8	15.3	15.1	15.1	15.5	15.1	14.8	14.5	11.7
Children Under 18 Years of Age	1,256	1,246	1,248	1,256	1,281	1,276	1,276	1,280	1,281
Covered by Private or Public Insurance									
Number..	1,153	1,167	1,169	1,173	1,197	1,196	1,208	1,208	1,232
Percent...	91.7	93.6	93.7	93.4	93.4	93.7	94.6	94.4	96.2
Not Covered									
Number..	104	80	79	83	84	80	68	72	49
Percent...	8.3	6.4	6.3	6.6	6.6	6.3	5.4	5.6	3.8
Percent in the U.S. not covered...........................	11.7	11.0	9.7	8.6	8.0	7.5	7.2	7.1	6.0

Table MN-7. Employment Status by Demographic Group, 2015

(Numbers in thousands, percent.)

Characteristic	Civilian noninstitutional population	Civilian labor force		Employed		Unemployed	
		Number	Percent of population	Number	Percent of population	Number	Percent of population
Total..	4,292	3,024	70.5	2,909	67.8	115	3.8
Sex							
Male..	2,115	1,613	76.3	1,543	73.0	69	4.3
Female....................................	2,177	1,411	64.8	1,366	62.8	45	3.2
Race, Sex, and Hispanic Origin							
White......................................	3,740	2,657	71.0	2,579	69.0	78	2.9
Male......................................	1,846	1,414	76.6	1,368	74.1	46	3.3
Female..................................	1,894	1,243	65.6	1,211	63.9	32	2.5
Black or African American................	232	150	64.9	129	55.7	21	14.1
Male......................................	113	82	72.9	71	63.1	11	13.5
Female..................................	119	68	57.3	58	48.7	10	14.8
Hispanic or Latino ethnicity[1]	210	160	76.2	154	73.3	6	3.8
Male......................................	114	98	86.5	93	81.5	6	5.8
Female..................................	96	62	64.0	61	63.5	1	0.8
Age							
16 to 19 years.............................	263	133	50.4	121	45.8	12	9.1
20 to 24 years.............................	325	250	76.8	232	71.5	17	6.9
25 to 34 years.............................	760	669	88.1	643	84.7	26	3.9
35 to 44 years.............................	705	625	88.7	604	85.7	21	3.4
45 to 54 years.............................	734	641	87.4	621	84.6	21	3.2
55 to 64 years.............................	711	524	73.7	512	72.0	12	2.3
65 years and over	795	182	22.9	177	22.3	5	2.8

NOTE: Data in Table 7 are from the Current Population Survey (CPS) and do not match the estimates in Table 8. See notes and definitions for further information.
[1] May be of any race.

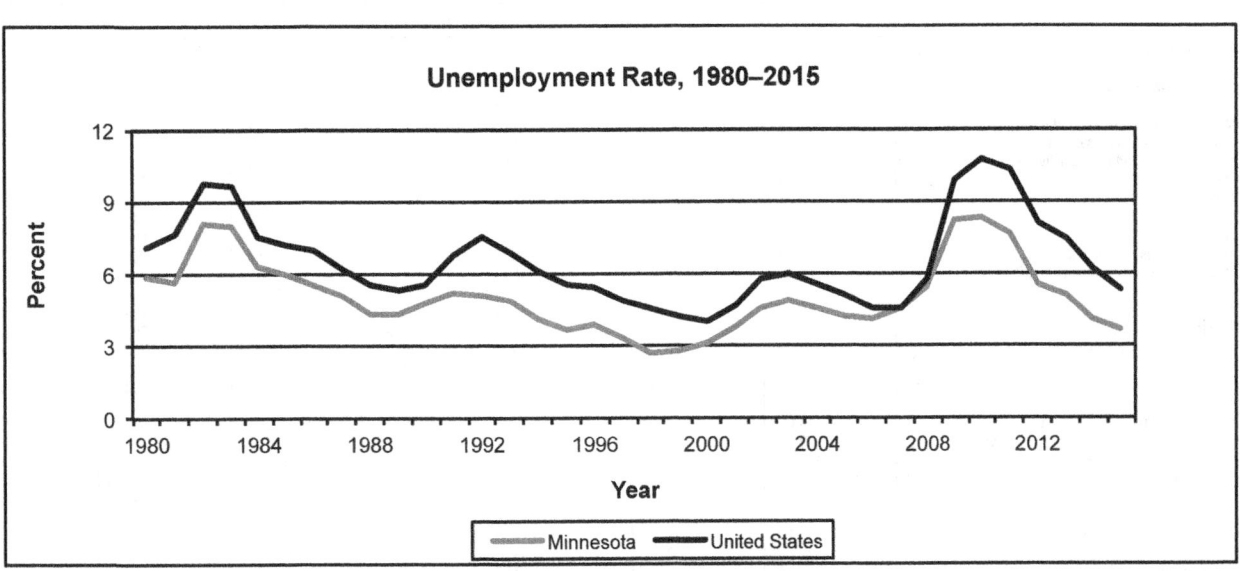

Unemployment Rate, 1980–2015

Table MN-8. Employment Status of the Civilian Noninstitutional Population Age 16 Years and Over

(Number, percent.)

Year	Civilian labor force	Civilian participation rate	Employed	Unemployed	Unemployment rate
2007..	2,906,390	72.4	2,773,704	132,686	4.6
2008..	2,925,088	72.2	2,766,342	158,746	5.4
2009..	2,941,976	72.0	2,713,426	228,550	7.8
2010..	2,938,795	71.4	2,721,194	217,601	7.4
2011..	2,946,279	71.0	2,755,264	191,015	6.5
2012..	2,958,273	70.6	2,793,143	165,130	5.6
2013..	2,971,523	70.3	2,824,970	146,553	4.9
2014..	2,982,750	70.1	2,858,592	124,158	4.2
2015..	3,010,367	70.2	2,898,864	111,503	3.7

Table MN-9. Employment and Average Wages by Industry

(Estimates through 2010 are based on the 2007 North American Industry Classification System [NAICS]. Estimates from 2011 onward are based on the 2012 NAICS.)

Industry	2008	2009	2010	2011	2012	2013	2014
	Number of jobs						
Wage and Salary Employment by Industry	2,828,921	2,725,314	2,718,113	2,759,615	2,797,535	2,838,575	2,877,568
Farm Wage and Salary Employment	13,424	18,409	19,372	16,349	18,940	15,758	14,232
Nonfarm Wage and Salary Employment	2,815,497	2,706,905	2,698,741	2,743,266	2,778,595	2,822,817	2,863,336
Private wage and salary employment	2,395,555	2,288,567	2,278,070	2,329,716	2,361,625	2,405,022	2,443,263
Forestry, fishing, and related activities	5,343	5,305	5,560	5,857	5,799	5,786	6,069
Mining	5,549	4,423	5,220	5,812	6,250	6,220	6,369
Utilities	12,515	12,726	12,691	12,807	12,716	13,007	12,864
Construction	114,760	97,786	91,776	96,726	98,137	104,390	111,024
Manufacturing	335,168	300,075	292,717	301,429	305,952	307,587	312,364
Durable goods manufacturing	215,463	188,537	183,413	190,285	194,517	195,392	198,757
Nondurable goods manufacturing	119,705	111,538	109,304	111,144	111,435	112,195	113,607
Wholesale trade	133,858	126,920	124,523	126,851	129,100	131,139	132,575
Retail trade	298,169	284,478	282,103	284,601	285,461	289,207	291,149
Transportation and warehousing	83,086	78,347	77,968	80,081	80,101	81,195	84,128
Information	58,384	55,751	54,322	53,743	53,838	53,360	52,653
Finance and insurance	140,441	137,888	138,560	141,436	141,797	144,335	142,220
Real estate and rental and leasing	39,018	37,533	37,602	37,220	39,964	40,860	40,245
Professional, scientific, and technical services	134,271	127,256	125,404	130,053	131,666	137,153	142,317
Management of companies and enterprises	71,126	69,812	70,657	72,693	74,843	77,002	78,718
Administrative and waste services	127,456	114,424	122,830	130,706	133,185	134,210	134,895
Educational services	64,442	66,222	68,249	70,521	70,617	70,742	71,397
Health care and social assistance	382,788	392,413	395,097	400,501	409,196	420,943	429,678
Arts, entertainment, and recreation	39,253	38,709	37,762	38,719	39,327	40,091	40,777
Accommodation and food services	209,464	202,402	200,927	204,507	208,027	211,984	215,420
Other services, except public administration	140,464	136,097	134,102	135,453	135,649	135,811	138,401
Government and government enterprises	419,942	418,338	420,671	413,550	416,970	417,795	420,073
	Dollars						
Average Wages and Salaries by Industry	45,091	44,585	45,910	46,990	48,412	49,222	50,711
Average Farm Wages and Salaries	36,202	35,677	29,421	27,805	33,022	37,300	38,849
Average Nonfarm Wages and Salaries	45,133	44,646	46,029	47,105	48,517	49,289	50,770
Average private wages and salaries	45,592	44,814	46,510	47,659	49,281	50,026	51,533
Forestry, fishing, and related activities	24,652	25,112	25,894	27,025	28,649	29,395	29,367
Mining	71,798	63,524	73,484	81,167	82,175	84,081	85,550
Utilities	82,755	81,799	86,375	90,413	92,783	97,296	99,317
Construction	52,759	52,270	51,887	53,447	55,572	57,321	58,942
Manufacturing	53,154	53,552	56,320	57,531	58,722	59,544	61,092
Durable goods manufacturing	56,620	57,398	60,764	61,822	63,087	64,204	65,818
Nondurable goods manufacturing	46,914	47,052	48,863	50,184	51,104	51,428	52,825
Wholesale trade	68,081	66,800	69,494	71,753	74,420	75,975	76,990
Retail trade	23,973	24,118	24,477	24,886	25,382	25,983	27,221
Transportation and warehousing	47,436	44,281	44,607	46,035	47,829	48,365	49,668
Information	60,148	60,124	62,098	66,119	65,000	66,675	69,447
Finance and insurance	76,451	74,681	77,746	82,075	89,515	88,627	92,741
Real estate and rental and leasing	44,610	43,831	44,962	46,859	51,826	53,617	55,082
Professional, scientific, and technical services	72,001	72,030	74,432	76,038	79,032	80,956	83,807
Management of companies and enterprises	114,802	94,856	110,451	109,296	112,103	112,757	115,370
Administrative and waste services	30,678	31,042	31,377	31,635	32,370	32,249	33,879
Educational services	28,353	29,225	29,137	29,660	29,926	29,910	30,256
Health care and social assistance	41,160	42,135	43,231	43,429	44,637	44,953	45,801
Arts, entertainment, and recreation	29,938	28,869	31,935	31,887	31,447	32,150	32,541
Accommodation and food services	15,545	15,533	16,044	16,682	17,016	17,131	18,062
Other services, except public administration	27,296	27,546	27,716	28,474	28,711	29,728	30,853
Government and government enterprises	42,513	43,726	43,424	43,980	44,189	45,046	46,335

Table MN-10. Employment Characteristics by Family Type

(Number, percent.)

Family type and labor force status	2012 Total	2012 Families with own children under 18 years	2013 Total	2013 Families with own children under 18 years	2014 Total	2014 Families with own children under 18 years
All Families...........................	1,374,436	619,780	1,372,189	617,391	1,362,032	603,414
FAMILY TYPE AND LABOR FORCE STATUS						
Married-Couple Families............................	1,079,809	437,066	1,077,897	436,434	1,068,394	428,952
Both husband and wife in labor force.........	62.0	78.1	61.0	75.7	60.6	77.1
Husband in labor force, wife not in labor force.........	15.5	18.4	15.7	19.4	15.7	18.5
Wife in labor force, husband not in labor force.........	6.8	2.5	7.3	3.7	7.5	3.6
Both husband and wife not in labor force...........	15.7	1.0	15.6	1.0	16.3	0.8
Other Families	294,627	182,714	294,292	180,957	293,638	174,462
Female householder, no husband present........	69.5	73.4	70.8	74.0	69.4	71.5
In labor force................	53.6	61.4	55.8	64.0	52.5	60.0
Not in labor force	15.9	12.0	15.0	10.0	16.9	11.5
Male householder, no wife present...........	30.5	26.6	29.2	26.0	30.6	28.5
In labor force...........	26.2	24.8	24.6	24.7	25.4	26.3
Not in labor force	4.3	1.8	4.6	1.3	5.2	2.2

Table MN-11. School Enrollment and Educational Attainment, 2014

(Number, percent.)

Item	State	U.S.
Enrollment		
Total population 3 years and over, enrolled in school...........	1,398,073	82,063,714
Enrolled in nursery school or preschool (percent)	6.4	6.0
Enrolled in kindergarten (percent)...........	5.3	5.1
Enrolled in elementary school, grades 1-8 (percent)...........	40.8	40.2
Enrolled in high school, grades 9-12 (percent)...........	20.8	20.7
Enrolled in college or graduate school (percent)	26.7	28.0
Attainment		
Total population 25 years and over	3,672,583	213,725,624
Less than ninth grade (percent)	3.0	5.6
9th to 12th grade, no diploma (percent)	4.5	7.5
High school graduate, including equivalency (percent)	25.7	27.7
Some college, no degree (percent)	21.6	21.0
Associate's degree (percent)	11.0	8.2
Bachelor's degree (percent)	22.7	18.7
Graduate or professional degree (percent)...........	11.6	11.4
High school graduate or higher (percent)	92.6	86.9
Bachelor's degree or higher (percent)	34.3	30.1

Table MN-12. Public School Characteristics and Educational Indicators

(Number, percent; data derived from National Center of Education Statistics.)

Item	State	U.S.
Public Schools, 2013–2014 (except where noted)		
Number of school districts...........	548	18,194
Number of schools...........	2,414	98,271
Number of students (in thousands)	851	50,045
Number of teachers (in thousands)	54	3,114
Student-teacher ratio...........	15.6	16.1
Expenditures per student (dollars), FY 2013...........	110,657	107,637
Four-year adjusted cohort graduation rate (ACGR)[1,2]	81.2	82.3
Students eligible for free or reduced-price lunch (in thousands)	327	25,596
English language learners (in thousands)	56	4,461
Students age 3 to 21 served under IDEA, part B (in thousands)	125	6,464

Public Schools by Type	Number	Percent of state public schools
Total number of schools...........	2,414	100.0
Regular	1,645	68.1
Special education	279	11.6
Vocational education...........	11	0.5
Alternative education...........	479	19.8

NOTE: Every school is assigned only one school type based on its instructional emphasis.
[1]ACGR data represents a new method of calculating high-school completion rates and may not be comparable to previous years' data for Averaged Freshmen Graduation Rates (AFGR).
[2]The United States 4-year ACGRs were estimated using both the reported 4-year ACGR data from 49 states and the District of Columbia and using imputed data for Idaho. The estimate for American Indian/Alaska Native students also includes imputed data for Virginia.

Table MN-13. Reported Voting and Registration of the Voting-Age Population, November 2014

(Numbers in thousands, percent.)

Item	Total population	Total citizen population	Registered			Voted		
			Total registered	Percent registered (total population)	Percent registered (total citizen population)	Total voted	Percent voted (total population)	Percent voted (total citizen population)
U.S. Total	239,874	219,941	142,166	59.3	64.6	92,251	38.5	41.9
State Total..............................	4,104	3,933	2,822	68.8	71.8	2,047	49.9	52.0
Sex								
Male..	2,007	1,924	1,346	67.1	70.0	974	48.5	50.6
Female......................................	2,097	2,009	1,476	70.4	73.5	1,073	51.2	53.4
Race								
White alone...............................	3,670	3,579	2,667	72.7	74.5	1,958	53.4	54.7
White, non-Hispanic alone...........	3,538	3,517	2,623	74.1	74.6	1,925	54.4	54.7
Black alone................................	196	155	83	42.5	53.6	34	17.2	21.7
Asian alone...............................	112	78	34	30.5	43.7	29	25.9	37.1
Hispanic (of any race).................	183	100	48	26.2	47.8	34	18.4	33.5
White alone or in combination........	3,715	3,624	2,688	72.4	74.2	1,969	53.0	54.3
Black alone or in combination.........	220	179	99	45.3	55.5	40	18.0	22.0
Asian alone or in combination..........	119	85	36	30.3	42.4	31	26.0	36.3
Age								
18 to 24 years.........................	537	520	206	38.4	39.6	112	20.9	21.6
25 to 34 years.........................	710	660	416	58.6	63.1	252	35.4	38.1
35 to 44 years.........................	628	598	465	74.0	77.7	292	46.5	48.9
45 to 64 years.........................	1,409	1,343	1,080	76.7	80.5	802	56.9	59.7
65 years and over.....................	819	812	654	79.9	80.6	588	71.8	72.5

Table MN-14. Crime

(Number, rate per 100,000. Data are derived from the FBI Uniform Crime Reports.)

Item	State[1]			U.S.[1,2,3,4]		
	2013	2014	Percent change	2013	2014	Percent change
TOTAL POPULATION[5]................................	5,420,380	5,457,173	0.7	316,128,839	318,857,056	0.9
VIOLENT CRIME						
Number..	12,100	12,505	3.3	1,163,146	1,165,383	0.2
Rate	223.2	229.1	2.6	367.9	365.5	-0.7
Murder and Nonnegligent Manslaughter						
Number..	114	88	-22.8	14,196	14,249	0.4
Rate	2.1	1.6	-23.8	4.5	4.5	-
Rape[6]						
Number..	2,008	2,001	X	108,612	116,645	X
Rate	37.0	36.7	X	34.4	36.6	X
Robbery						
Number..	3,674	3,687	0.4	345,031	325,802	-5.6
Rate	67.8	67.6	-0.3	109.1	102.2	-6.3
Aggravated Assault						
Number..	6,909	6,729	-2.6	724,149	741,291	2.4
Rate	127.5	123.3	-3.3	229.1	232.5	1.5
PROPERTY CRIME						
Number..	131,195	125,377	-4.4	8,632,512	8,277,829	-4.1
Rate	2,420.4	2,297.5	-5.1	2,730.7	2,596.1	-4.9
Burglary						
Number..	22,713	20,773	-8.5	1,928,465	1,729,806	-10.3
Rate	419.0	380.7	-9.1	610.0	542.5	-11.1
Larceny-Theft						
Number..	100,516	96,237	-4.3	6,004,453	5,858,496	-2.4
Rate	1,854.4	1,763.5	-4.9	1,899.4	1,837.3	-3.3
Motor Vehicle Theft						
Number..	7,966	8,367	5.0	699,594	689,527	-1.4
Rate	147.0	153.3	4.3	221.3	216.2	-2.3

NOTE: Although arson data are included in the trend and clearance tables, sufficient data are not available to estimate totals for this offense. Therefore, no arson data are published in this table.

X = Not applicable.

- = Zero or rounds to zero.

[1]The data collection methodology for the offense of forcible rape used by the Minnesota state Uniform Crime Reporting (UCR) Program (with the exception of Minneapolis and St. Paul, Minnesota) does not comply with national UCR Program guidelines. Consequently, its figures for forcible rape and violent crime (of which forcible rape is a part) are not published in this table.

[2]The crime figures have been adjusted.

[3]Includes offenses reported by the Zoological Police and the Metro Transit Police.

[4]Because of changes in the state's reporting practices, figures are not comparable to previous years' data.

[5]Populations are U.S. Census Bureau provisional estimates as of July 1 of each year.

[6]The figures shown for the offense of rape were estimated using the revised Uniform Crime Reporting (UCR) definition of rape.

Table MN-15. State Government Finances, 2014

(Dollar amounts in thousands, percent distribution.)

Item	Dollars	Percent distribution
Total Revenue	50,419,432	100.0
General revenue	37,645,695	74.7
Intergovernmental revenue	9,838,098	19.5
Taxes	23,128,901	45.9
General sales	5,441,934	10.8
Selective sales	4,317,412	8.6
License taxes	1,314,463	2.6
Individual income tax	9,528,454	18.9
Corporate income tax	1,315,762	2.6
Other taxes	1,210,876	2.4
Current charges	2,513,445	5.0
Miscellaneous general revenue	2,165,251	4.3
Utility revenue	98644	0.2
Liquor stores revenue	0	-
Insurance trust revenue[1]	12,675,093	25.1
Total Expenditure	41,845,094	100.0
Intergovernmental expenditure	12,620,852	30.2
Direct expenditure	29,224,242	69.8
Current operation	21,056,988	50.3
Capital outlay	1,558,704	3.7
Insurance benefits and repayments	5,029,774	12.0
Assistance and subsidies	1,099,384	2.6
Interest on debt	479,392	1.1
Exhibit: Salaries and wages	5,838,309	14.0
Total Expenditure	41,845,094	100.0
General expenditure	36,498,533	87.2
Intergovernmental expenditure	12,620,852	30.2
Direct expenditure	23,877,681	57.1
General expenditure, by function:		
Education	14,695,831	35.1
Public welfare	12,442,106	29.7
Hospitals	303,833	0.7
Health	480,262	1.1
Highways	2,763,034	6.6
Police protection	418,581	1.0
Correction	544,697	1.3
Natural resources	702,009	1.7
Parks and recreation	286,079	0.7
Governmental administration	989,949	2.4
Interest on general debt	477,944	1.1
Other and unallocable	2,394,208	5.7
Utility expenditure	316,787	0.8
Liquor stores expenditure	0	-
Insurance trust expenditure	5,029,774	12.0
Debt at End of Fiscal Year	15,818,353	X
Cash and Security Holdings	77,009,863	X

X = Not applicable.
- = Zero or rounds to zero.
[1]Within insurance trust revenue, net earnings of state retirement systems is a calculated statistic (the item code in the data file is X08), and thus can be positive or negative. Net earnings is the sum of earnings on investments plus gains on investments minus losses on investments. The change made in 2002 for asset valuation from book to market value in accordance with Statement 34 of the Governmental Accounting Standards Board is reflected in the calculated statistics.

Table MN-16. State Government Tax Collections, 2014

(Dollars in thousands, percent.)

Item	Dollars	Percent distribution
Total Taxes	23,128,901	100.0
Property taxes	836,743	3.6
Sales and gross receipts	9,759,346	42.2
General sales and gross receipts	5,441,934	23.5
Selective sales and gross receipts	4,317,412	18.7
Alcoholic beverages	81,328	0.4
Amusements	44,705	0.2
Insurance premiums	403,280	1.7
Motor fuels	893,351	3.9
Pari-mutuels	492	-
Public utilities	51	-
Tobacco products	581,872	2.5
Other selective sales	2,312,333	10.0
Licenses	1,314,463	5.7
Alcoholic beverages	2,211	-
Amusements	1,211	-
Corporations in general	7,382	-
Hunting and fishing	59,156	0.3
Motor vehicle	695,796	3.0
Motor vehicle operators	43,544	0.2
Public utilities	284	-
Occupation and business, NEC	440,372	1.9
Other licenses	64,507	0.3
Income taxes	10,844,216	46.9
Individual income	9,528,454	41.2
Corporation net income	1,315,762	5.7
Other taxes	374,133	1.6
Death and gift	165,159	0.7
Documentary and stock transfer	166,912	0.7
Severance	42,062	0.2
Taxes, NEC	0	-

- = Zero or rounds to zero.

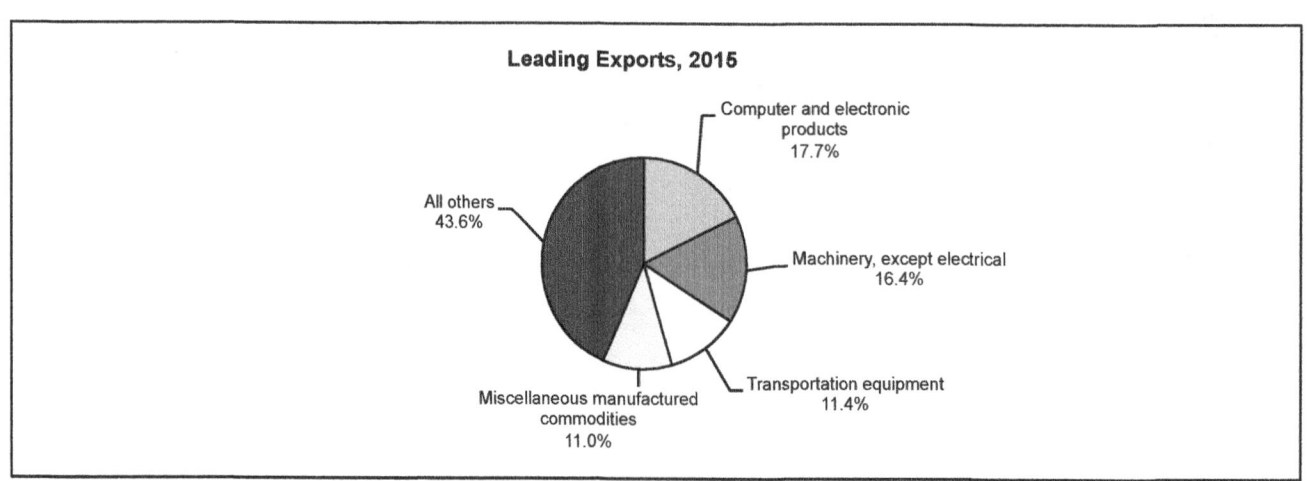

Leading Exports, 2015

Computer and electronic products 17.7%

Machinery, except electrical 16.4%

Transportation equipment 11.4%

Miscellaneous manufactured commodities 11.0%

All others 43.6%

Facts and Figures

Location: South central United States; bordered on the N by Tennessee, on the E by Alabama, on the S by Louisiana and the Gulf of Mexico, and on the W by Arkansas and Louisiana

Area: 48,430 sq. mi. (125,434 sq. km.); rank—32nd

Population: 2,992,333 (2015 est.); rank—32nd

Principal Cities: capital—Jackson; largest—Jackson

Statehood: December 10, 1817; 20th state

U.S. Congress: 2 senators, 4 representatives

State Motto: *Virtute et armis* ("By valor and arms")

State Song: "Go, Mississippi"

State Nicknames: The Magnolia State; The Hospitality State

Abbreviations: MS; Miss.

State Symbols: flower—magnolia blossom; tree—Southern magnolia; bird—mockingbird

At a Glance

- With an increase in population of 0.7 percent, Mississippi ranked 42nd among the states in growth from 2010 to 2015.

- In 2014, Mississippi had the lowest median household income in the country ($39,680) and the highest percent of population living the below the poverty level (21.5 percent).

- In 2014, 14.5 percent of Mississippians did not have health insurance, compared to 11.7 percent of the total U.S. population.

- Mississippi's infant mortality rate in 2014 was 8.24 deaths per 1,000 live births, the second highest in the country.

- Mississippi's birth rate of 12.9 per 1,000 population was slightly higher than the national average of 12.5 births per 1,000 population in 2014.

Table MS-1. Population by Age, Sex, Race, and Hispanic Origin

(Number, percent, except where noted.)

Sex, age, race, and Hispanic origin	2000	2010	2015[1]	Average annual percent change, 2010–2015
Total Population.....................	2,844,658	2,967,297	2,992,333	0.1
Percent of total U.S. population	1.0	1.0	0.9	X
Sex				
Male.............................	1,373,554	1,441,240	1,451,850	0.1
Female	1,471,104	1,526,057	1,540,483	0.1
Age				
Under 5 years.................	204,364	210,956	192,782	-0.6
5 to 19 years..................	668,850	638,539	616,775	-0.2
20 to 64 years................	1,627,921	1,737,395	1,743,075	-
65 years and over	343,523	380,407	439,701	1.0
Median age (years)...........	33.8	36.0	36.9	0.2
Race and Hispanic Origin				
One race				
White...........................	1,746,099	1,789,391	1,779,783	-
Black...........................	1,033,809	1,103,101	1,124,875	0.1
American Indian and Alaska Native	11,652	16,837	17,810	0.4
Asian...........................	18,626	26,477	31,774	1.3
Native Hawaiian or Other Pacific Islander	667	1,700	1,826	0.5
Two or more races	20,021	29,791	36,265	1.4
Hispanic (of any race)........	39,569	85,107	91,564	0.5

X = Not applicable.
- = Zero or rounds to zero.
[1]Population figures for 2015 are July 1 estimates. The 2010 estimates are taken from the 2010 Census.

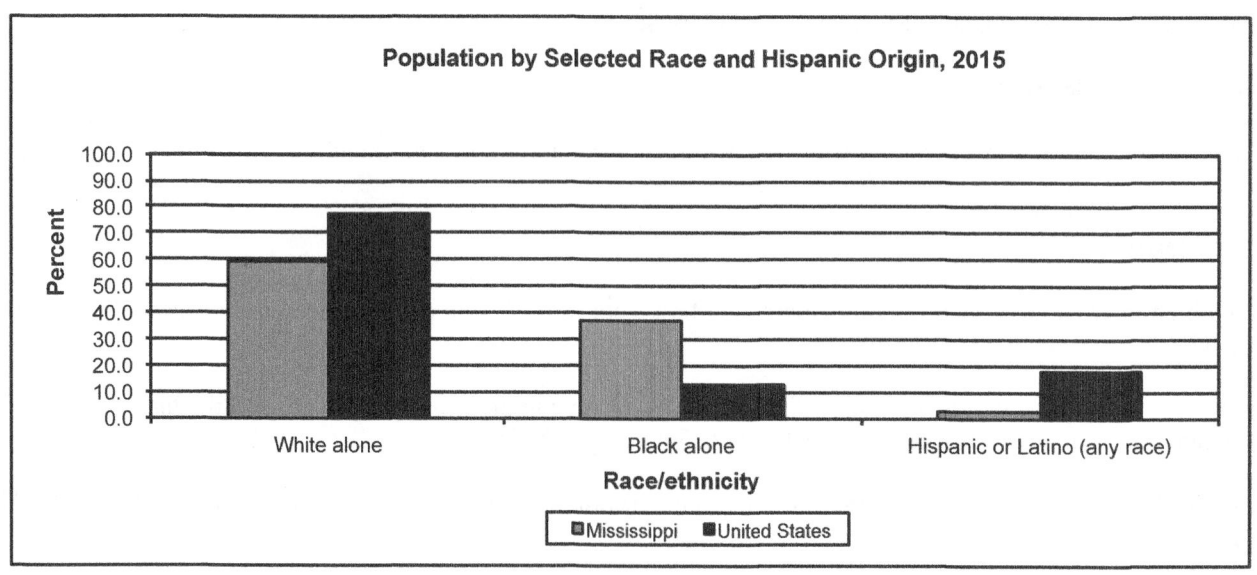

Population by Selected Race and Hispanic Origin, 2015

Table MS-2. Marital Status

(Number, percent distribution.)

Sex, age, race, and Hispanic origin	2000	2010	2014
Males, 15 Years and Over	1,046,252	1,121,265	1,133,229
Never married	30.6	34.9	35.5
Now married, except separated..........................	54.6	48.3	47.9
Separated..................................	2.4	2.5	2.7
Widowed...................................	2.9	2.7	2.9
Divorced...................................	9.5	11.7	11.0
Females, 15 Years and Over	1,157,363	1,224,423	1,232,668
Never married	25.1	29.8	30.4
Now married, except separated..........................	48.6	43.8	42.7
Separated..................................	3.2	3.4	3.5
Widowed...................................	12.5	10.8	10.9
Divorced...................................	10.6	12.3	12.5

Table MS-3. Households and Housing Characteristics

(Number, percent, dollars.)

Item	2000	2010	2014	Average annual percent change, 2000–2014
Total Households..	1,046,434	1,079,999	1,095,823	0.3
Family households	747,159	746,115	738,463	-0.1
Married-couple family	520,884	501,571	482,221	-0.5
Other family	226,315	244,544	256,242	0.9
Male householder, no wife present..................	45,610	51,400	55,629	1.6
Female householder, no husband present........	180,705	193,144	200,613	0.8
Nonfamily households	299,275	333,884	357,360	1.4
Householder living alone	257,708	293,185	313,403	1.5
Householder not living alone..........................	41,567	40,699	43,957	0.4
Housing Characteristics				
Total housing units..	1,161,953	1,276,441	1,294,738	0.8
Occupied housing units	1,046,434	1,079,999	1,095,823	0.3
Owner occupied	756,967	753,374	741,504	-0.1
Renter occupied	289,467	326,625	354,319	1.6
Average household size......................................	2.63	2.66	2.64	-
Financial Characteristics				
Median gross rent of renter-occupied housing	439	672	711	4.4
Median monthly owner costs for housing units with a mortgage ...	762	1,043	1,079	3.0
Median value of owner-occupied housing units........	71,400	100,100	104,000	3.3

- = Zero or rounds to zero.

Table MS-4. Migration, Origin, and Language

(Number, percent.)

Characteristic	State 2013	State 2014	State Percent change	U.S. 2013	U.S. 2014	U.S. Percent change
Residence 1 Year Ago						
Population 1 year and over	2,957,797	2,957,658	-	312,432,820	315,095,393	0.9
Same house	85.6	86.4	X	85.0	85.1	X
Different house in the U.S.	14.2	13.4	X	14.4	14.3	X
Same county	8.1	7.0	X	8.9	8.7	X
Different county	6.1	6.3	X	5.5	5.6	X
Same state	3.7	3.8	X	3.2	3.3	X
Different state	2.3	2.5	X	2.3	2.3	X
Abroad	0.2	0.3	X	0.6	0.6	X
Place of Birth						
Native born	2,928,308	2,928,929	-	274,780,773	276,465,262	0.6
Male	48.5	48.6	X	49.3	49.3	X
Female	51.5	51.4	X	50.7	50.7	X
Foreign born	62,899	65,150	3.6	41,348,066	42,391,794	2.5
Male	51.6	52.7	X	48.8	48.7	X
Female	48.4	47.3	X	51.2	51.3	X
Foreign born; naturalized U.S. citizen................	24,044	23,340	-2.9	19,294,710	19,984,738	3.6
Male	42.2	41.7	X	45.9	45.9	X
Female	57.8	58.3	X	54.1	54.1	X
Foreign born; not a U.S. citizen	38,855	41,810	7.6	22,053,356	22,407,056	1.6
Male	57.4	58.8	X	51.3	51.2	X
Female	42.6	41.2	X	48.7	48.8	X
Entered 2010 or later	15.9	16.5	X	9.7	12.3	X
Entered 2000 to 2009	34.6	35.2	X	29.4	28.6	X
Entered before 2000..	49.5	48.4	X	61.0	59.1	X
World Region of Birth, Foreign						
Foreign-born population, excluding population born at sea	62,899	65,150	3.6	41,347,945	42,390,705	2.5
Europe	10.9	11.1	X	11.6	11.2	X
Asia	35.6	31.6	X	29.5	30.1	X
Africa	3.4	2.9	X	4.4	4.6	X
Oceania	0.2	0.3	X	0.5	0.6	X
Latin America	47.5	52.1	X	51.9	51.6	X
North America	2.4	2.0	X	2.0	1.9	X
Language Spoken at Home and Ability to Speak English						
Population 5 years and over..................................	2,793,325	2,802,072	0.3	296,358,760	299,084,046	0.9
English only	96.3	96.3	X	79.2	78.9	X
Language other than English............................	3.7	3.7	X	20.8	21.1	X
Speaks English less than "very well".............	1.3	1.5	X	8.5	8.6	X

X = Not applicable.
- = Zero or rounds to zero.

Table MS-5. Median Income and Poverty Status, 2014

(Number, percent, except as noted.)

Characteristic	State		U.S.	
	Number	Percent	Number	Percent
Median Income				
Households (dollars)..	39,680	X	53,657	X
Families (dollars)	50,178	X	65,910	X
Below Poverty Level (All People)	623,113	21.5	48,208,387	15.5
Sex				
Male..	270,536	19.4	21,590,918	14.2
Female	352,577	23.5	26,617,469	16.8
Age				
Under 18 years...	211,726	29.4	15,686,012	21.7
Related children under 18 years..............................	208,199	29.0	15,372,705	21.3
18 to 64 years..	356,623	20.3	28,267,482	14.6
65 years and over	54,764	13.2	4,254,893	9.5

X = Not applicable.

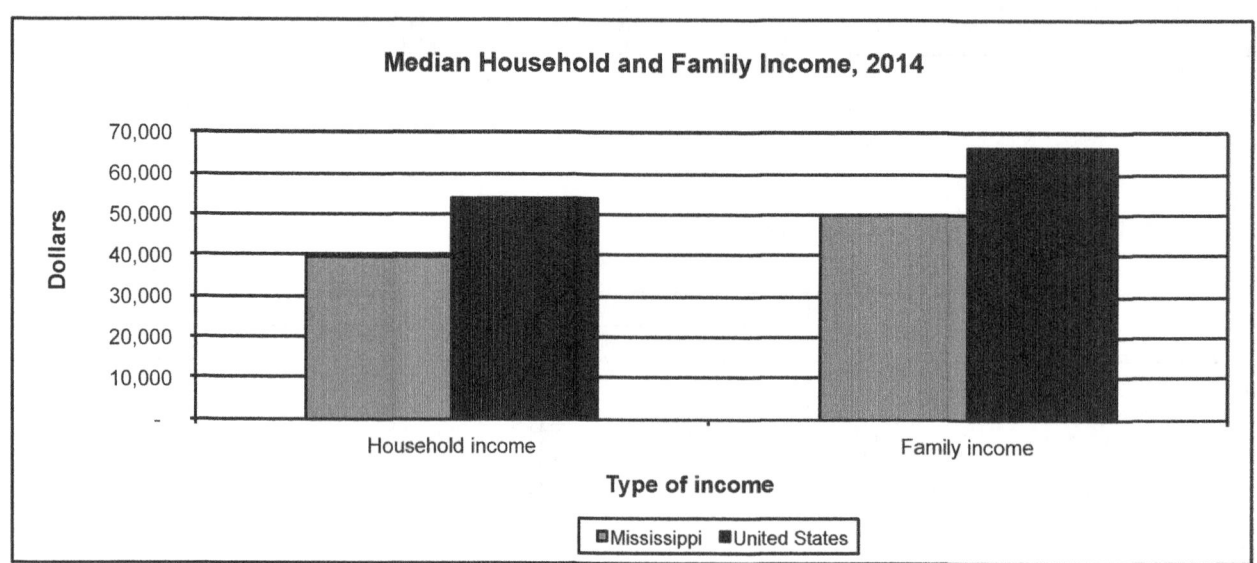

Table MS-6. Health Insurance Coverage Status for the Civilian Noninstitutionalized Population and Children Under 18 Years of Age

(Numbers in thousands, percent.)

Item	2006	2007	2008	2009	2010	2011	2012	2013	2014
Civilian Noninstitutionalized Population	2,892	2,903	2,868	2,880	2,903	2,912	2,918	2,925	2,927
Covered by Private or Public Insurance									
Number...	2,292	2,358	2,355	2,366	2,375	2,395	2,421	2,425	2,503
Percent..	79.2	81.2	82.1	82.1	81.8	82.3	83.0	82.9	85.5
Not Covered									
Number...	600	545	513	514	528	516	497	500	424
Percent..	20.8	18.8	17.9	17.9	18.2	17.7	17.0	17.1	14.5
Percent in the U.S. not covered...	15.8	15.3	15.1	15.1	15.5	15.1	14.8	14.5	11.7
Children Under 18 Years of Age	774	778	763	764	752	750	746	734	730
Covered by Private or Public Insurance									
Number...	628	684	666	685	688	689	691	678	691
Percent..	81.1	87.9	87.3	89.7	91.6	91.9	92.7	92.4	94.7
Not Covered									
Number...	146	94	97	79	64	61	55	56	39
Percent..	18.9	12.1	12.7	10.3	8.4	8.1	7.3	7.6	5.3
Percent in the U.S. not covered...	11.7	11.0	9.7	8.6	8.0	7.5	7.2	7.1	6.0

Table MS-7. Employment Status by Demographic Group, 2015

(Numbers in thousands, percent.)

Characteristic	Civilian noninstitutional population	Civilian labor force		Employed		Unemployed	
		Number	Percent of population	Number	Percent of population	Number	Percent of population
Total...	2,283	1,281	56.1	1,199	52.5	83	6.5
Sex							
Male..	1,072	661	61.6	621	57.9	40	6.0
Female..	1,211	621	51.3	578	47.7	43	6.9
Race, Sex, and Hispanic Origin							
White..	1,412	791	56.0	754	53.4	37	4.7
Male..	682	436	63.9	417	61.2	19	4.3
Female...	730	355	48.7	337	46.1	19	5.2
Black or African American.....................	819	462	56.4	419	51.1	43	9.4
Male..	364	209	57.3	189	51.8	20	9.6
Female...	455	253	55.7	230	50.5	23	9.2
Hispanic or Latino ethnicity[1]	53	34	63.6	32	60.1	2	5.4
Male..	29	23	80.7	22	78.2	1	3.2
Female...	NA	NA	NA	NA	NA	NA	NA
Age							
16 to 19 years......................................	160	42	26.1	33	20.9	8	20.1
20 to 24 years......................................	225	147	65.4	128	57.0	19	12.9
25 to 34 years......................................	332	259	77.9	240	72.2	19	7.2
35 to 44 years......................................	386	310	80.3	295	76.3	15	4.9
45 to 54 years......................................	381	272	71.3	261	68.4	11	4.1
55 to 64 years......................................	381	195	51.1	186	48.9	9	4.4
65 years and over	417	57	13.7	55	13.2	2	3.5

NOTE: Data in Table 7 are from the Current Population Survey (CPS) and do not match the estimates in Table 8. See notes and definitions for further information.
NA = Not available.
[1]May be of any race.

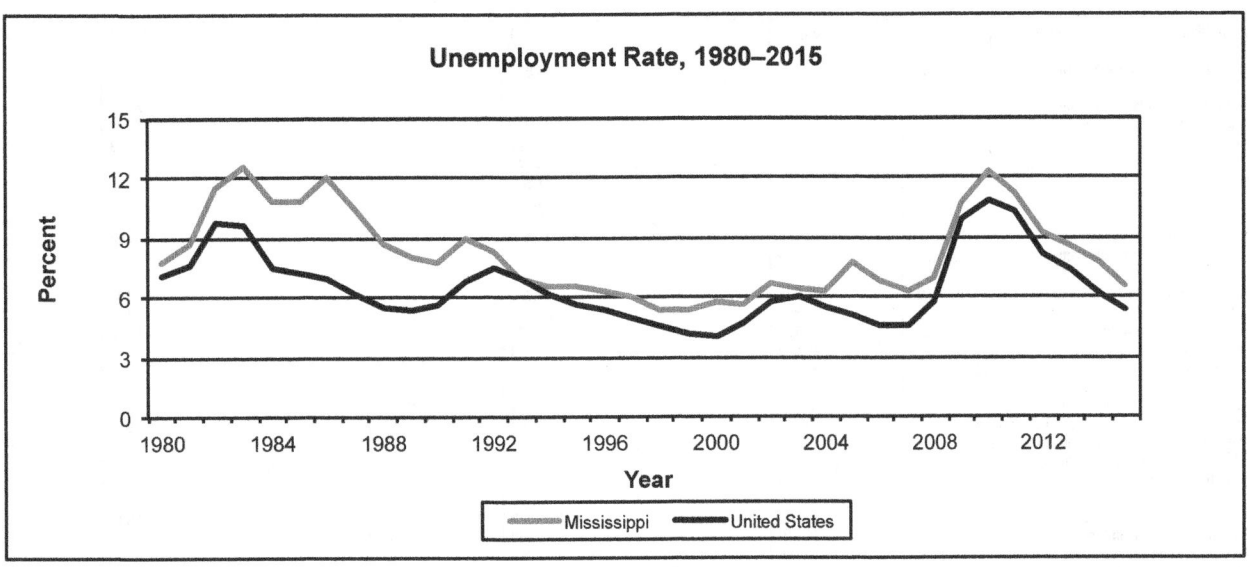

Table MS-8. Employment Status of the Civilian Noninstitutional Population Age 16 Years and Over

(Number, percent.)

Year	Civilian labor force	Civilian participation rate	Employed	Unemployed	Unemployment rate
2007..	1,303,514	60.0	1,224,059	79,455	6.1
2008..	1,306,772	59.8	1,220,991	85,781	6.6
2009..	1,269,219	57.7	1,148,930	120,289	9.5
2010..	1,306,608	58.6	1,170,879	135,729	10.4
2011..	1,342,808	59.8	1,208,747	134,061	10.0
2012..	1,317,447	58.4	1,198,914	118,533	9.0
2013..	1,271,436	56.1	1,161,814	109,622	8.6
2014..	1,249,288	54.9	1,154,812	94,476	7.6
2015..	1,272,657	55.8	1,189,646	83,011	6.5

Table MS-9. Employment and Average Wages by Industry

(Estimates through 2010 are based on the 2007 North American Industry Classification System [NAICS]. Estimates from 2011 onward are based on the 2012 NAICS.)

Industry	2008	2009	2010	2011	2012	2013	2014
	Number of jobs						
Wage and Salary Employment by Industry..................	1,230,068	1,179,833	1,172,459	1,173,633	1,177,334	1,182,655	1,194,871
Farm Wage and Salary Employment..........................	8,617	9,824	9,993	9,012	7,752	7,003	12,104
Nonfarm Wage and Salary Employment.....................	1,221,451	1,170,009	1,162,466	1,164,621	1,169,582	1,175,652	1,182,767
Private wage and salary employment........................	937,690	885,322	880,596	885,304	890,508	898,417	908,195
Forestry, fishing, and related activities........................	8,183	7,591	7,994	8,230	7,903	7,726	7,926
Mining...	6,513	5,667	5,700	6,126	6,311	6,175	6,251
Utilities...	7,626	7,714	7,733	7,733	7,723	7,871	7,826
Construction	63,234	53,950	52,070	51,468	50,029	53,114	50,671
Manufacturing...	159,641	141,508	136,188	135,493	137,267	136,976	139,734
Durable goods manufacturing................................	105,221	90,678	87,373	88,112	90,931	90,681	93,632
Nondurable goods manufacturing..........................	54,420	50,830	48,815	47,381	46,336	46,295	46,102
Wholesale trade	36,773	35,103	34,521	34,561	34,380	34,294	34,247
Retail trade...	141,108	135,253	134,361	134,996	134,785	134,794	136,875
Transportation and warehousing................................	41,408	39,490	39,545	40,037	40,299	41,033	42,675
Information	13,482	12,815	12,315	11,886	12,597	12,811	13,206
Finance and insurance	34,983	34,143	33,974	34,093	34,181	33,523	33,177
Real estate and rental and leasing...........................	12,733	12,382	11,911	11,801	11,726	11,819	11,775
Professional, scientific, and technical services	33,876	32,219	32,138	32,161	31,539	30,948	31,301
Management of companies and enterprises..................	9,890	9,816	9,749	10,139	10,153	10,773	10,630
Administrative and waste services............................	52,431	46,671	51,490	52,749	55,697	58,113	60,567
Educational services	18,841	18,642	19,134	19,720	20,074	20,022	20,039
Health care and social assistance.............................	116,457	118,460	120,870	122,437	122,973	123,667	124,915
Arts, entertainment, and recreation...........................	12,895	12,260	12,074	11,021	11,290	11,639	11,349
Accommodation and food services............................	113,635	108,839	107,503	109,490	111,085	113,210	115,296
Other services, except public administration...............	53,981	52,799	51,326	51,163	50,086	49,909	49,735
Government and government enterprises..........................	283,761	284,687	281,870	279,317	279,484	277,235	274,572
	Dollars						
Average Wages and Salaries by Industry	34,240	34,559	35,274	35,951	36,990	37,571	38,032
Average Farm Wages and Salaries	21,338	18,757	18,556	18,447	23,865	27,285	22,596
Average Nonfarm Wages and Salaries	34,331	34,692	35,418	36,086	37,077	37,633	38,190
Average private wages and salaries...........................	33,839	34,004	34,699	35,486	36,719	37,433	37,925
Forestry, fishing, and related activities........................	28,441	28,466	29,121	29,948	30,896	33,133	33,914
Mining...	67,919	64,256	65,743	70,024	75,344	76,009	78,736
Utilities...	66,823	66,225	67,384	68,006	71,420	72,381	74,029
Construction	42,339	41,392	41,424	42,437	44,885	46,901	47,275
Manufacturing...	40,150	41,196	42,220	43,610	45,233	46,085	47,620
Durable goods manufacturing................................	41,460	42,837	43,813	45,175	46,585	47,494	49,084
Nondurable goods manufacturing..........................	37,618	38,267	39,368	40,699	42,580	43,325	44,646
Wholesale trade	48,838	48,284	48,893	50,327	52,124	53,192	54,656
Retail trade...	22,854	23,062	23,691	24,012	24,809	25,166	25,389
Transportation and warehousing................................	40,173	39,800	40,843	41,834	43,302	44,287	44,468
Information	40,676	40,359	42,190	44,033	45,106	46,571	47,828
Finance and insurance	47,229	47,250	48,978	50,007	52,639	55,269	56,027
Real estate and rental and leasing...........................	29,801	29,536	30,689	31,823	33,698	33,686	34,846
Professional, scientific, and technical services	50,764	52,024	52,203	53,074	55,122	55,991	56,309
Management of companies and enterprises..................	70,716	70,928	73,586	77,992	82,498	80,868	82,431
Administrative and waste services............................	24,452	25,108	25,816	25,596	26,701	27,805	27,808
Educational services	23,653	24,664	25,469	26,816	27,450	28,440	28,061
Health care and social assistance.............................	37,562	38,602	38,853	39,568	40,680	40,904	41,085
Arts, entertainment, and recreation...........................	24,819	24,332	24,800	24,240	23,827	23,774	23,528
Accommodation and food services............................	17,785	17,340	18,057	18,495	18,590	18,557	18,761
Other services, except public administration...............	24,684	24,744	26,043	26,362	27,528	28,554	29,367
Government and government enterprises..........................	35,957	36,831	37,662	37,988	38,162	38,281	39,065

Table MS-10. Employment Characteristics by Family Type

(Number, percent.)

Family type and labor force status	2012 Total	2012 Families with own children under 18 years	2013 Total	2013 Families with own children under 18 years	2014 Total	2014 Families with own children under 18 years
All Families......................................	747,620	322,759	745,079	310,168	736,864	305,343
FAMILY TYPE AND LABOR FORCE STATUS						
Married-Couple Families..........................	481,032	180,872	487,648	176,292	480,622	173,656
Both husband and wife in labor force.................	49.1	65.7	47.4	67.9	48.6	67.6
Husband in labor force, wife not in labor force......	22.6	26.0	21.1	23.4	21.8	24.9
Wife in labor force, husband not in labor force......	8.8	5.6	10.7	6.0	9.1	4.4
Both husband and wife not in labor force.............	19.6	2.7	20.5	2.5	20.5	3.1
Other Families	266,588	141,887	257,431	133,876	256,242	131,687
Female householder, no husband present..............	78.6	81.6	79.2	84.2	78.3	79.4
In labor force..................................	50.9	63.6	51.9	67.5	49.7	63.7
Not in labor force..............................	27.7	18.0	27.3	16.7	28.6	15.7
Male householder, no wife present...................	21.4	18.4	20.8	15.8	21.7	20.6
In labor force..................................	15.1	16.7	13.5	13.7	16.0	18.3
Not in labor force..............................	6.3	1.7	7.3	2.1	5.7	2.3

Table MS-11. School Enrollment and Educational Attainment, 2014

(Number, percent.)

Item	State	U.S.
Enrollment		
Total population 3 years and over, enrolled in school...............	806,652	82,063,714
Enrolled in nursery school or preschool (percent)...................	5.8	6.0
Enrolled in kindergarten (percent).................................	5.9	5.1
Enrolled in elementary school, grades 1-8 (percent)................	41.7	40.2
Enrolled in high school, grades 9-12 (percent).....................	20.4	20.7
Enrolled in college or graduate school (percent)...................	26.3	28.0
Attainment		
Total population 25 years and over	1,950,710	213,725,624
Less than ninth grade (percent)...................................	5.8	5.6
9th to 12th grade, no diploma (percent)...........................	11.4	7.5
High school graduate, including equivalency (percent)..............	30.0	27.7
Some college, no degree (percent).................................	23.1	21.0
Associate's degree (percent)......................................	8.6	8.2
Bachelor's degree (percent).......................................	13.0	18.7
Graduate or professional degree (percent).........................	8.0	11.4
High school graduate or higher (percent)	82.8	86.9
Bachelor's degree or higher (percent).............................	21.1	30.1

Table MS-12. Public School Characteristics and Educational Indicators

(Number, percent; data derived from National Center of Education Statistics.)

Item	State	U.S.
Public Schools, 2013–2014 (except where noted)		
Number of school districts..	162	18,194
Number of schools...	1,066	98,271
Number of students (in thousands).................................	493	50,045
Number of teachers (in thousands)	32	3,114
Student-teacher ratio	15	16.1
Expenditures per student (dollars), FY 2013.......................	8,117	107,637
Four-year adjusted cohort graduation rate (ACGR)[1,2]	77.6	82.3
Students eligible for free or reduced-price lunch (in thousands) ..	355.5	25,596
English language learners (in thousands)	7	4,461
Students age 3 to 21 served under IDEA, part B (in thousands)	66	6,464

Public Schools by Type	Number	Percent of state public schools
Total number of schools...	1,066	100.0
Regular	910	85.4
Special education...	4	0.4
Vocational education..	90	8.4
Alternative education...	62	5.8

NOTE: Every school is assigned only one school type based on its instructional emphasis.

[1]ACGR data represents a new method of calculating high-school completion rates and may not be comparable to previous years' data for Averaged Freshmen Graduation Rates (AFGR).

[2]The United States 4-year ACGRs were estimated using both the reported 4-year ACGR data from 49 states and the District of Columbia and using imputed data for Idaho. The estimate for American Indian/Alaska Native students also includes imputed data for Virginia.

Table MS-13. Reported Voting and Registration of the Voting-Age Population, November 2014

(Numbers in thousands, percent.)

Item	Total population	Total citizen population	Registered			Voted		
			Total registered	Percent registered (total population)	Percent registered (total citizen population)	Total voted	Percent voted (total population)	Percent voted (total citizen population)
U.S. Total	239,874	219,941	142,166	59.3	64.6	92,251	38.5	41.9
State Total.............................	2,182	2,142	1,628	74.6	76.0	907	41.6	42.3
Sex								
Male..	1,028	1,008	740	72.0	73.4	413	40.2	41.0
Female....................................	1,154	1,135	888	77.0	78.3	493	42.8	43.5
Race								
White alone.............................	1,352	1,326	964	71.3	72.6	536	39.7	40.4
White, non-Hispanic alone...........	1,308	1,303	948	72.5	72.8	525	40.2	40.3
Black alone..............................	769	768	639	83.2	83.3	357	46.4	46.5
Asian alone..............................	27	21	5	(B)	(B)	1	(B)	(B)
Hispanic (of any race).................	60	32	17	(B)	(B)	13	(B)	(B)
White alone or in combination.........	1,377	1,344	975	70.8	72.5	540	39.2	40.2
Black alone or in combination.........	779	773	644	82.6	83.2	361	46.3	46.6
Asian alone or in combination.........	33	28	11	(B)	(B)	3	(B)	(B)
Age								
18 to 24 years...........................	327	322	218	66.6	67.8	85	26.1	26.5
25 to 34 years...........................	371	360	234	63.1	64.9	88	23.8	24.5
35 to 44 years...........................	311	302	210	67.7	69.7	111	35.8	36.8
45 to 64 years...........................	739	730	591	80.0	81.0	374	50.6	51.2
65 years and over.......................	434	429	375	86.4	87.5	248	57.2	57.9

B = Base is less than 75,000 and therefore too small to show the derived measure.

Table MS-14. Crime

(Number, rate per 100,000. Data are derived from the FBI Uniform Crime Reports.)

Item	State			U.S.[1,2,3,4]		
	2013	2014	Percent change	2013	2014	Percent change
TOTAL POPULATION[5].............................	2,991,207	2,994,079	0.1	316,128,839	318,857,056	0.9
VIOLENT CRIME						
Number..................................	7,999	8,338	4.2	1,163,146	1,165,383	0.2
Rate	267.4	278.5	4.2	367.9	365.5	-0.7
Murder and Nonnegligent Manslaughter						
Number..................................	195	258	32.3	14,196	14,249	0.4
Rate	6.5	8.6	32.3	4.5	4.5	-
Rape[6]						
Number..................................	930	1,058	X	108,612	116,645	X
Rate	31.1	35.3	X	34.4	36.6	X
Robbery						
Number..................................	2,409	2,430	0.9	345,031	325,802	-5.6
Rate	80.5	81.2	0.9	109.1	102.2	-6.3
Aggravated Assault						
Number..................................	4,680	4,592	-1.9	724,149	741,291	2.4
Rate	156.5	153.4	-2.0	229.1	232.5	1.5
PROPERTY CRIME						
Number..................................	81,500	87,462	7.3	8,632,512	8,277,829	-4.1
Rate	2,724.7	2,921.2	7.2	2,730.7	2,596.1	-4.9
Burglary						
Number..................................	24,995	24,352	-2.6	1,928,465	1,729,806	-10.3
Rate	835.6	813.3	-2.7	610.0	542.5	-11.1
Larceny-Theft						
Number..................................	52,117	58,591	12.4	6,004,453	5,858,496	-2.4
Rate	1,742.3	1,956.9	12.3	1,899.4	1,837.3	-3.3
Motor Vehicle Theft						
Number..................................	4,388	4,519	3.0	699,594	689,527	-1.4
Rate	146.7	150.9	2.9	221.3	216.2	-2.3

NOTE: Although arson data are included in the trend and clearance tables, sufficient data are not available to estimate totals for this offense. Therefore, no arson data are published in this table.
X = Not applicable.
- = Zero or rounds to zero.
[1]The crime figures have been adjusted.
[2]The data collection methodology for the offense of forcible rape used by the Minnesota state Uniform Crime Reporting (UCR) Program (with the exception of Minneapolis and St. Paul, Minnesota) does not comply with national UCR Program guidelines. Consequently, its figures for forcible rape and violent crime (of which forcible rape is a part) are not published in this table.
[3]Includes offenses reported by the Zoological Police and the Metro Transit Police.
[4]Because of changes in the state's reporting practices, figures are not comparable to previous years' data.
[5]Populations are U.S. Census Bureau provisional estimates as of July 1 of each year.
[6]The figures shown for the offense of rape were estimated using the revised Uniform Crime Reporting (UCR) definition of rape.

Table MS-15. State Government Finances, 2014

(Dollar amounts in thousands, percent distribution.)

Item	Dollars	Percent distribution
Total Revenue	23,346,924	100.0
General revenue	17,576,209	75.3
Intergovernmental revenue	7,377,669	31.6
Taxes	7,574,515	32.4
General sales	3,304,632	14.2
Selective sales	1,400,323	6.0
License taxes	559,218	2.4
Individual income tax	1,667,344	7.1
Corporate income tax	526,302	2.3
Other taxes	116,696	0.5
Current charges	1,983,695	8.5
Miscellaneous general revenue	640,330	2.7
Utility revenue	0	-
Liquor stores revenue	292,878	1.3
Insurance trust revenue[1]	5,477,837	23.5
Total Expenditure	20,013,073	100.0
Intergovernmental expenditure	4,919,968	24.6
Direct expenditure	15,093,105	75.4
Current operation	10,888,369	54.4
Capital outlay	1,110,581	5.5
Insurance benefits and repayments	2,507,777	12.5
Assistance and subsidies	308,343	1.5
Interest on debt	278,035	1.4
Exhibit: Salaries and wages	2,550,047	12.7
Total Expenditure	20,013,073	100.0
General expenditure	17,272,737	86.3
Intergovernmental expenditure	4,919,968	24.6
Direct expenditure	12,352,769	61.7
General expenditure, by function:		
Education	5,506,928	27.5
Public welfare	5,808,953	29.0
Hospitals	1,164,932	5.8
Health	368,897	1.8
Highways	1,363,706	6.8
Police protection	113,475	0.6
Correction	379,382	1.9
Natural resources	263,772	1.3
Parks and recreation	55,945	0.3
Governmental administration	434,792	2.2
Interest on general debt	278,035	1.4
Other and unallocable	1,533,920	7.7
Utility expenditure	0	-
Liquor stores expenditure	232,559	1.2
Insurance trust expenditure	2,507,777	12.5
Debt at End of Fiscal Year	7,104,085	X
Cash and Security Holdings	32,920,518	X

X = Not applicable.
= Zero or rounds to zero.
[1]Within insurance trust revenue, net earnings of state retirement systems is a calculated statistic (the item code in the data file is X08), and thus can be positive or negative. Net earnings is the sum of earnings on investments plus gains on investments minus losses on investments. The change made in 2002 for asset valuation from book to market value in accordance with Statement 34 of the Governmental Accounting Standards Board is reflected in the calculated statistics.

Table MS-16. State Government Tax Collections, 2014

(Dollars in thousands, percent.)

Item	Dollars	Percent distribution
Total Taxes	7,574,515	100.0
Property taxes	25,103	0.3
Sales and gross receipts	4,704,955	62.1
General sales and gross receipts	3,304,632	43.6
Selective sales and gross receipts	1,400,323	18.5
Alcoholic beverages	42,402	0.6
Amusements	127,777	1.7
Insurance premiums	263,809	3.5
Motor fuels	409,836	5.4
Pari-mutuels	0	-
Public utilities	4,384	0.1
Tobacco products	146,050	1.9
Other selective sales	406,065	5.4
Licenses	559,218	7.4
Alcoholic beverages	2,945	-
Amusements	18,619	0.2
Corporations in general	182,624	2.4
Hunting and fishing	17,862	0.2
Motor vehicle	154,677	2.0
Motor vehicle operators	40,086	0.5
Public utilities	3,212	0.0
Occupation and business, NEC	100,025	1.3
Other licenses	39,168	0.5
Income taxes	2,193,646	29.0
Individual income	1,667,344	22.0
Corporation net income	526,302	6.9
Other taxes	91,593	1.2
Death and gift	9	-
Documentary and stock transfer	0	-
Severance	91,059	1.2
Taxes, NEC	525	-

- = Zero or rounds to zero.

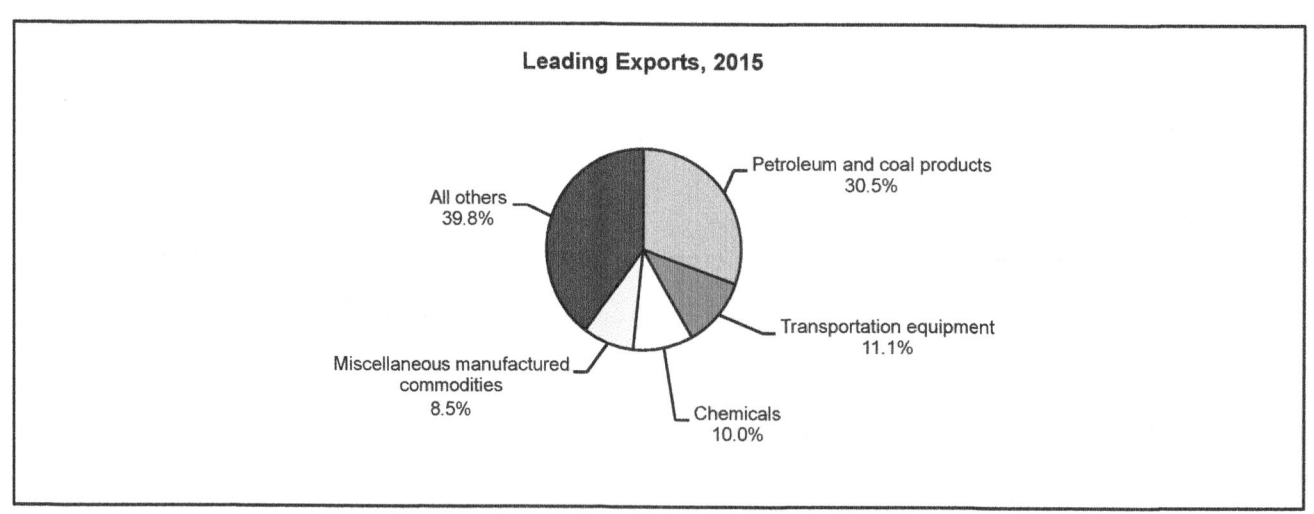

Leading Exports, 2015

Petroleum and coal products 30.5%

Transportation equipment 11.1%

Chemicals 10.0%

Miscellaneous manufactured commodities 8.5%

All others 39.8%

Facts and Figures

Location: Central United States; bordered on the N by Iowa, on the E by Illinois, Kentucky, and Tennessee, on the S by Arkansas, and on the W by Oklahoma, Kansas, and Nebraska

Area: 69,704 sq. mi. (180,533 sq. km.); rank—21st

Population: 6,083,672 (2015 est.); rank—18th

Principal Cities: capital—Jefferson City; largest—Kansas City

Statehood: August 10, 1821; 24th state

U.S. Congress: 2 senators, 8 representatives

State Motto: *Salus populi suprema lex esto* ("The welfare of the people shall be the supreme law")

State Song: "Missouri Waltz"

State Nickname: The Show Me State

Abbreviations: MO; Mo.

State Symbols: flower—hawthorn; tree—flowering dogwood; bird—Eastern bluebird

At a Glance

- With an increase in population of 1.5 percent, Missouri ranked 37th among the states in growth from 2010 to 2015.

- In 2014, 11.7 percent of Missourians did not have health insurance, which was the same as the national average.

- Missouri's violent crime rate was 442.9 per 100,000 population in 2014, compared to the U.S. rate of 365.5 per 100,000 population.

- Missouri's median household income of $48,363 ranked 37th in the country in 2014.

- In Missouri in 2014, 15.5 percent of residents lived below the poverty level, which was the same as the national average; 22.1 percent of Missouri children lived in poverty, which was slightly higher than the national average of 21.7 percent.

Table MO-1. Population by Age, Sex, Race, and Hispanic Origin

(Number, percent, except where noted.)

Sex, age, race, and Hispanic origin	2000	2010	2015[1]	Average annual percent change, 2010–2015
Total Population	5,595,211	5,988,927	6,083,672	0.1
Percent of total U.S. population	2.0	1.9	1.9	X
Sex				
Male	2,720,177	2,933,477	2,985,045	0.1
Female	2,875,034	3,055,450	3,098,627	0.1
Age				
Under 5 years	269,898	390,237	374,360	-0.3
5 to 19 years	1,224,274	1,211,174	1,174,346	-0.2
20 to 64 years	3,245,660	3,549,222	3,580,044	0.1
65 years and over	755,379	838,294	954,922	0.9
Median age (years)	36.1	37.9	38.4	0.1
Race and Hispanic Origin				
One race				
White	4,748,083	5,038,407	5,069,110	-
Black	629,391	700,178	718,518	0.2
American Indian and Alaska Native	25,076	30,595	33,499	0.6
Asian	61,595	100,213	121,406	1.4
Native Hawaiian or Other Pacific Islander	3,178	7,178	8,857	1.5
Two or more races	82,061	112,356	132,282	1.2
Hispanic (of any race)	118,592	223,421	247,567	0.7

X = Not applicable.
- = Zero or rounds to zero.
[1]Population figures for 2015 are July 1 estimates. The 2010 estimates are taken from the 2010 Census.

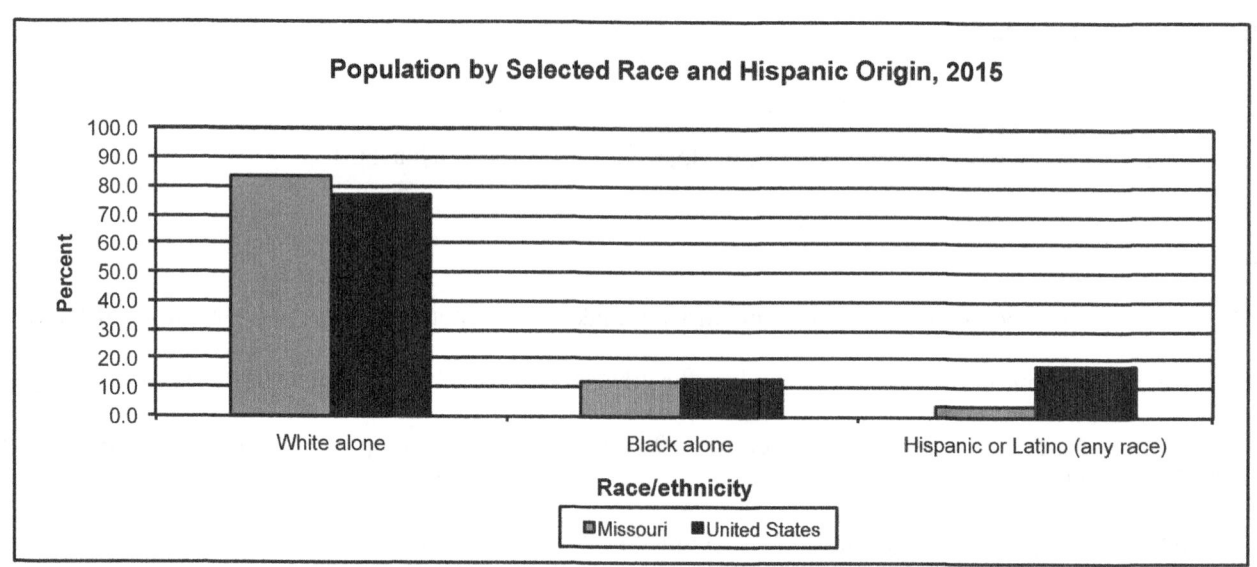

Table MO-2. Marital Status

(Number, percent distribution.)

Sex, age, race, and Hispanic origin	2000	2010	2014
Males, 15 Years and Over	2,114,280	2,332,888	2,356,977
Never married	27.8	32.1	32.6
Now married, except separated	58.0	52.5	51.8
Separated	1.6	1.7	1.7
Widowed	2.6	2.6	2.8
Divorced	10.0	11.0	11.1
Females, 15 Years and Over	2,300,111	2,492,198	2,505,060
Never married	22.1	26.8	26.9
Now married, except separated	53.1	48.2	48.2
Separated	2.0	2.2	2.1
Widowed	11.3	10.0	9.8
Divorced	11.5	12.8	13.0

Table MO-3. Households and Housing Characteristics

(Number, percent, dollars.)

Item	2000	2010	2014	Average annual percent change, 2000–2014
Total Households..	2,194,594	2,350,628	2,354,809	0.5
Family households	1,476,516	1,524,078	1,508,816	0.2
Married-couple family	1,140,866	1,146,501	1,124,715	-0.1
Other family	335,650	377,577	384,101	1.0
Male householder, no wife present..	81,890	99,807	103,300	1.9
Female householder, no husband present	253,760	277,770	280,801	0.8
Nonfamily households	718,078	826,550	845,993	1.3
Householder living alone	599,808	689,361	702,018	1.2
Householder not living alone	118,270	137,189	143,975	1.6
Housing Characteristics				
Total housing units..	2,442,017	2,714,017	2,735,803	0.9
Occupied housing units	2,194,594	2,350,628	2,354,809	0.5
Owner occupied	1,542,149	1,621,371	1,575,626	0.2
Renter occupied	652,445	729,257	779,183	1.4
Average household size..	2.48	2.48	2.5	0.1
Financial Characteristics				
Median gross rent of renter-occupied housing	484	682	754	4.0
Median monthly owner costs for housing units with a mortgage	861	1,182	1,187	2.7
Median value of owner-occupied housing units..	89,900	139,000	138,500	3.9

Table MO-4. Migration, Origin, and Language

(Number, percent.)

Characteristic	State			U.S.		
	2013	2014	Percent change	2013	2014	Percent change
Residence 1 Year Ago						
Population 1 year and over	5,973,448	5,992,195	0.3	312,432,820	315,095,393	0.9
Same house	84.0	84.1	X	85.0	85.1	X
Different house in the U.S.	15.7	15.5	X	14.4	14.3	X
Same county	8.7	8.9	X	8.9	8.7	X
Different county	7.0	6.7	X	5.5	5.6	X
Same state	4.4	4.1	X	3.2	3.3	X
Different state	2.7	2.6	X	2.3	2.3	X
Abroad	0.3	0.3	X	0.6	0.6	X
Place of Birth						
Native born	5,810,910	5,838,467	0.5	274,780,773	276,465,262	0.6
Male	49.0	49	X	49.3	49.3	X
Female	51.0	51	X	50.7	50.7	X
Foreign born	233,261	225,122	-3.5	41,348,066	42,391,794	2.5
Male	48.6	48.4	X	48.8	48.7	X
Female	51.4	51.6	X	51.2	51.3	X
Foreign born; naturalized U.S. citizen..	105,387	102,996	-2.3	19,294,710	19,984,738	3.6
Male	44.2	46	X	45.9	45.9	X
Female	55.8	54	X	54.1	54.1	X
Foreign born; not a U.S. citizen..	127,874	122,126	-4.5	22,053,356	22,407,056	1.6
Male	52.1	50.4	X	51.3	51.2	X
Female	47.9	49.6	X	48.7	48.8	X
Entered 2010 or later	15.1	17.5	X	9.7	12.3	X
Entered 2000 to 2009	33.0	32	X	29.4	28.6	X
Entered before 2000..	51.8	50.5	X	61.0	59.1	X
World Region of Birth, Foreign						
Foreign-born population, excluding population born at sea	233,261	225,122	-3.5	41,347,945	42,390,705	2.5
Europe	21.3	18.7	X	11.6	11.2	X
Asia	37.6	39	X	29.5	30.1	X
Africa	7.3	8.8	X	4.4	4.6	X
Oceania	1.2	0.8	X	0.5	0.6	X
Latin America..	30.0	29.9	X	51.9	51.6	X
North America	2.6	2.8	X	2.0	1.9	X
Language Spoken at Home and Ability to Speak English						
Population 5 years and over..	5,669,938	5,691,365	0.4	296,358,760	299,084,046	0.9
English only	94.2	94.4	X	79.2	78.9	X
Language other than English..	5.8	5.6	X	20.8	21.1	X
Speaks English less than "very well"..	2.1	1.9	X	8.5	8.6	X

X = Not applicable.
- = Zero or rounds to zero.

Table MO-5. Median Income and Poverty Status, 2014

(Number, percent, except as noted.)

Characteristic	State		U.S.	
	Number	Percent	Number	Percent
Median Income				
Households (dollars)...	48,363	X	53,657	X
Families (dollars)	61,299	X	65,910	X
Below Poverty Level (All People)	908,628	15.5	48,208,387	15.5
Sex				
Male..	401,848	14	21,590,918	14.2
Female	506,780	16.8	26,617,469	16.8
Age				
Under 18 years..	287,081	21.1	15,686,012	21.7
Related children under 18 years.................	279,206	20.7	15,372,705	21.3
18 to 64 years..	540,714	14.9	28,267,482	14.6
65 years and over	80,833	9	4,254,893	9.5

X = Not applicable.

Median Household and Family Income, 2014

Table MO-6. Health Insurance Coverage Status for the Civilian Noninstitutionalized Population and Children Under 18 Years of Age

(Numbers in thousands, percent.)

Item	2006	2007	2008	2009	2010	2011	2012	2013	2014
Civilian Noninstitutionalized Population	5,800	5,791	5,795	5,871	5,880	5,899	5,909	5,931	5,951
Covered by Private or Public Insurance									
Number...	5,028	5,062	5,040	5,098	5,106	5,092	5,108	5,158	5,257
Percent...	86.7	87.4	87.0	86.8	86.8	86.3	86.4	87.0	88.3
Not Covered									
Number...	772	729	755	773	774	807	801	773	694
Percent...	13.3	12.6	13.0	13.2	13.2	13.7	13.6	13.0	11.7
Percent in the U.S. not covered.........................	15.8	15.3	15.1	15.1	15.5	15.1	14.8	14.5	11.7
Children Under 18 Years of Age	1,398	1,442	1,418	1,427	1,414	1,409	1,400	1,395	1,388
Covered by Private or Public Insurance									
Number...	1,271	1,291	1,317	1,329	1,326	1,314	1,302	1,297	1,288
Percent...	90.9	89.6	92.9	93.1	93.8	93.3	93.0	93.0	92.8
Not Covered									
Number...	127	150	101	98	88	95	98	98	100
Percent...	9.1	10.4	7.1	6.9	6.2	6.7	7.0	7.0	7.2
Percent in the U.S. not covered.........................	11.7	11.0	9.7	8.6	8.0	7.5	7.2	7.1	6.0

Table MO-7. Employment Status by Demographic Group, 2015

(Numbers in thousands, percent.)

Characteristic	Civilian noninstitutional population	Civilian labor force		Employed		Unemployed	
		Number	Percent of population	Number	Percent of population	Number	Percent of population
Total...	4,748	3,107	65.4	2,951	62.2	156	5.0
Sex							
Male..	2,286	1,614	70.6	1,531	67.0	83	5.1
Female.......................................	2,462	1,493	60.6	1,420	57.7	73	4.9
Race, Sex, and Hispanic Origin							
White..	4,027	2,626	65.2	2,510	62.3	116	4.4
Male...	1,958	1,382	70.6	1,320	67.4	62	4.5
Female......................................	2,069	1,244	60.1	1,190	57.5	54	4.3
Black or African American.................	518	340	65.6	306	59.1	34	10.0
Male...	233	162	69.4	143	61.4	19	11.7
Female......................................	285	178	62.5	163	57.2	15	8.5
Hispanic or Latino ethnicity[1]...........	152	109	71.9	103	68.0	6	5.5
Male...	75	60	80.0	57	76.1	3	4.9
Female......................................	77	49	64.1	46	60.1	3	6.2
Age							
16 to 19 years.............................	320	152	47.3	128	40.0	23	15.4
20 to 24 years.............................	375	302	80.4	277	73.8	25	8.3
25 to 34 years.............................	772	671	86.9	637	82.5	34	5.1
35 to 44 years.............................	761	660	86.8	638	83.8	23	3.4
45 to 54 years.............................	812	657	80.9	629	77.5	28	4.2
55 to 64 years.............................	752	497	66.1	481	64.0	16	3.2
65 years and over..........................	956	169	17.6	161	16.9	7	4.2

NOTE: Data in Table 7 are from the Current Population Survey (CPS) and do not match the estimates in Table 8. See notes and definitions for further information.
[1]May be of any race.

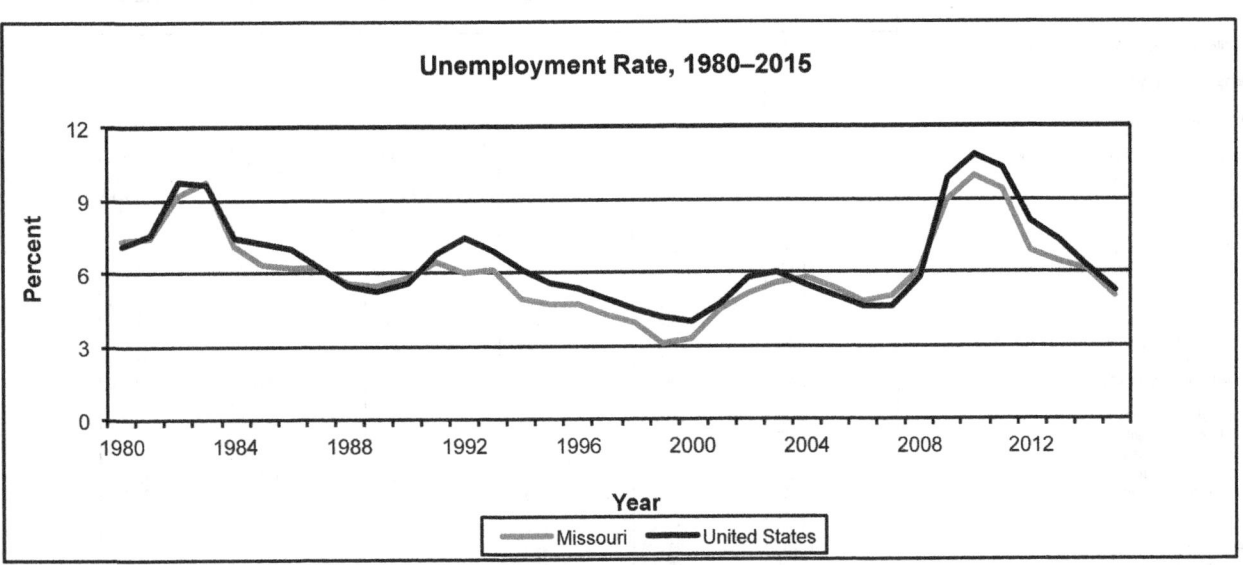

Table MO-8. Employment Status of the Civilian Noninstitutional Population Age 16 Years and Over

(Number, percent.)

Year	Civilian labor force	Civilian participation rate	Employed	Unemployed	Unemployment rate
2007..........................	3,034,579	66.9	2,879,647	154,932	5.1
2008..........................	3,028,857	66.2	2,842,845	186,012	6.1
2009..........................	3,049,563	66.1	2,766,711	282,852	9.3
2010..........................	3,056,484	66.0	2,763,535	292,949	9.6
2011..........................	3,047,786	65.6	2,789,224	258,562	8.5
2012..........................	3,016,161	64.6	2,806,121	210,040	7.0
2013..........................	3,011,601	64.2	2,809,402	202,199	6.7
2014..........................	3,051,812	64.7	2,863,982	187,830	6.2
2015..........................	3,113,760	65.6	2,958,176	155,584	5.0

Table MO-9. Employment and Average Wages by Industry

(Estimates through 2010 are based on the 2007 North American Industry Classification System [NAICS]. Estimates from 2011 onward are based on the 2012 NAICS.)

Industry	2008	2009	2010	2011	2012	2013	2014
	Number of jobs						
Wage and Salary Employment by Industry..................	2,896,954	2,788,974	2,750,304	2,760,024	2,772,488	2,816,639	2,841,624
Farm Wage and Salary Employment.........................	8,863	8,116	8,921	8,557	8,931	8,669	7,122
Nonfarm Wage and Salary Employment....................	2,888,091	2,780,858	2,741,383	2,751,467	2,763,557	2,807,970	2,834,502
Private wage and salary employment........................	2,394,176	2,281,338	2,250,632	2,268,829	2,286,856	2,332,258	2,360,990
Forestry, fishing, and related activities.....................	4,264	4,226	4,495	4,814	4,631	5,254	5,549
Mining..	4,941	4,134	4,092	4,018	3,977	3,947	3,895
Utilities..	12,331	12,658	12,601	12,345	12,177	12,115	11,961
Construction	145,995	124,519	111,287	108,890	107,958	111,594	113,593
Manufacturing..	289,656	255,609	243,699	246,939	248,935	252,934	256,210
Durable goods manufacturing...........................	173,322	146,730	140,234	143,541	144,143	147,842	152,338
Nondurable goods manufacturing......................	116,334	108,879	103,465	103,398	104,792	105,092	103,872
Wholesale trade	126,199	119,174	117,277	117,049	117,921	119,171	121,493
Retail trade..	315,917	305,987	303,854	306,198	305,245	304,891	308,045
Transportation and warehousing..........................	97,805	91,795	87,770	88,187	90,187	92,208	94,344
Information	64,172	62,346	58,375	55,695	52,833	52,591	52,301
Finance and insurance	122,837	122,059	124,107	124,873	129,249	128,006	128,033
Real estate and rental and leasing.......................	40,926	38,664	37,860	36,335	35,649	35,354	35,771
Professional, scientific, and technical services	132,081	126,273	123,375	125,928	131,626	134,023	137,492
Management of companies and enterprises..................	66,282	59,953	59,560	61,213	60,987	63,836	66,112
Administrative and waste services	147,292	134,528	141,668	147,755	147,754	152,249	155,526
Educational services	59,990	61,553	61,765	63,569	66,301	66,084	67,162
Health care and social assistance........................	337,906	344,115	348,782	355,202	360,767	381,230	382,914
Arts, entertainment, and recreation......................	45,422	43,689	43,236	42,394	42,281	43,566	43,942
Accommodation and food services.......................	238,855	233,016	232,403	232,098	234,424	239,449	244,146
Other services, except public administration..............	141,305	137,040	134,426	135,327	133,954	133,756	132,501
Government and government enterprises	493,915	499,520	490,751	482,638	476,701	475,712	473,512
	Dollars						
Average Wages and Salaries by Industry	41,191	40,925	41,677	42,579	43,873	44,094	45,325
Average Farm Wages and Salaries	29,405	33,948	29,826	32,897	38,605	33,341	52,097
Average Nonfarm Wages and Salaries	41,227	40,945	41,716	42,609	43,890	44,128	45,307
Average private wages and salaries.........................	41,772	41,259	42,051	43,052	44,565	44,747	45,989
Forestry, fishing, and related activities.....................	29,364	29,782	27,610	25,881	26,999	27,024	27,281
Mining..	70,036	61,185	59,665	70,043	70,457	68,346	69,773
Utilities..	77,624	77,419	79,424	82,797	83,476	86,206	89,439
Construction..	48,995	50,078	49,247	49,676	51,289	51,609	53,414
Manufacturing..	51,072	50,285	50,976	52,163	54,162	54,785	56,936
Durable goods manufacturing...........................	50,902	52,483	52,524	54,397	55,576	57,416	59,943
Nondurable goods manufacturing........................	51,325	47,324	48,878	49,060	52,217	51,083	52,525
Wholesale trade	57,906	57,634	58,917	60,403	62,279	62,168	64,581
Retail trade..	24,823	25,070	25,389	25,698	26,313	26,482	26,957
Transportation and warehousing..........................	44,092	43,071	44,087	44,978	45,827	47,746	48,288
Information	59,461	62,345	66,726	70,135	72,496	70,489	71,219
Finance and insurance	58,612	59,036	61,974	65,176	69,687	69,718	71,886
Real estate and rental and leasing.......................	34,335	34,683	35,407	36,681	38,934	39,206	40,614
Professional, scientific, and technical services	66,875	67,871	67,950	68,890	71,569	71,165	72,711
Management of companies and enterprises...................	101,489	79,290	88,952	90,430	96,495	98,008	103,266
Administrative and waste services	29,889	30,634	31,365	32,092	32,572	32,995	34,025
Educational services	30,857	31,757	32,327	32,851	33,764	34,907	35,618
Health care and social assistance........................	40,261	41,288	41,649	42,546	43,665	42,878	43,148
Arts, entertainment, and recreation......................	34,415	35,426	35,997	38,107	38,116	39,998	40,087
Accommodation and food services.......................	15,996	16,069	16,686	17,049	17,188	17,226	17,928
Other services, except public administration................	27,957	28,106	28,755	29,192	29,768	30,265	31,510
Government and government enterprises........................	38,583	39,510	40,181	40,528	40,655	41,091	41,910

Table MO-10. Employment Characteristics by Family Type

(Number, percent.)

Family type and labor force status	2012		2013		2014	
	Total	Families with own children under 18 years	Total	Families with own children under 18 years	Total	Families with own children under 18 years
All Families.........	1,517,231	641,438	1,523,085	645,682	1,503,886	629,862
FAMILY TYPE AND LABOR FORCE STATUS						
Married-Couple Families........	1,124,203	417,452	1,133,983	426,596	1,119,785	417,923
Both husband and wife in labor force......	53.7	70.9	52.1	68.6	52.1	70.2
Husband in labor force, wife not in labor force	19.1	23.2	19.9	25.0	19.2	23.5
Wife in labor force, husband not in labor force	8.4	3.9	8.8	3.9	8.9	4.2
Both husband and wife not in labor force.........	18.8	2.0	18.9	2.2	19.8	2.1
Other Families	393,028	223,986	389,102	219,086	384,101	211,939
Female householder, no husband present......	74.4	76.2	74.1	76.4	73.1	72.8
In labor force.........	53.2	62.0	53.9	64.6	50.4	59.4
Not in labor force.........	21.2	14.2	20.2	11.7	22.7	13.4
Male householder, no wife present......	25.6	23.8	25.9	23.6	26.9	27.2
In labor force.........	19.6	21.4	19.7	21.4	21.2	24.2
Not in labor force	6.0	2.3	6.2	2.2	5.7	3.0

Table MO-11. School Enrollment and Educational Attainment, 2014

(Number, percent.)

Item	State	U.S.
Enrollment		
Total population 3 years and over, enrolled in school.........	1,537,651	82,063,714
Enrolled in nursery school or preschool (percent).........	5.8	6.0
Enrolled in kindergarten (percent).........	5.1	5.1
Enrolled in elementary school, grades 1-8 (percent).........	41.2	40.2
Enrolled in high school, grades 9-12 (percent).........	20.0	20.7
Enrolled in college or graduate school (percent).........	28.0	28.0
Attainment		
Total population 25 years and over	4,076,767	213,725,624
Less than ninth grade (percent).........	3.6	5.6
9th to 12th grade, no diploma (percent)	7.6	7.5
High school graduate, including equivalency (percent).........	31.4	27.7
Some college, no degree (percent)	22.5	21.0
Associate's degree (percent).........	7.5	8.2
Bachelor's degree (percent).........	17.1	18.7
Graduate or professional degree (percent).........	10.4	11.4
High school graduate or higher (percent)	88.9	86.9
Bachelor's degree or higher (percent).........	27.5	30.1

Table MO-12. Public School Characteristics and Educational Indicators

(Number, percent; data derived from National Center of Education Statistics.)

Item	State	U.S.
Public Schools, 2013–2014 (except where noted)		
Number of school districts.........	568	18,194
Number of schools.........	2,410	98,271
Number of students (in thousands)	918	50,045
Number of teachers (in thousands)	67	3,114
Student-teacher ratio.........	13.8	16.1
Expenditures per student (dollars), FY 2013.........	97,027	107,637
Four-year adjusted cohort graduation rate (ACGR)[1,2]	87.3	82.3
Students eligible for free or reduced-price lunch (in thousands)	453	25,596
English language learners (in thousands)	25	4,461
Students age 3 to 21 served under IDEA, part B (in thousands)	123	6,464

Public Schools by Type	Number	Percent of state public schools
Total number of schools.........	2,410	100.0
Regular.........	2,179	90.4
Special education.........	63	2.6
Vocational education.........	64	2.7
Alternative education.........	104	4.3

NOTE: Every school is assigned only one school type based on its instructional emphasis.
[1]ACGR data represents a new method of calculating high-school completion rates and may not be comparable to previous years' data for Averaged Freshmen Graduation Rates (AFGR).
[2]The United States 4-year ACGRs were estimated using both the reported 4-year ACGR data from 49 states and the District of Columbia and using imputed data for Idaho. The estimate for American Indian/Alaska Native students also includes imputed data for Virginia.

Table MO-13. Reported Voting and Registration of the Voting-Age Population, November 2014

(Numbers in thousands, percent.)

Item	Total population	Total citizen population	Registered			Voted		
			Total registered	Percent registered (total population)	Percent registered (total citizen population)	Total voted	Percent voted (total population)	Percent voted (total citizen population)
U.S. Total	239,874	219,941	142,166	59.3	64.6	92,251	38.5	41.9
State Total.............................	4,505	4,429	3,194	70.9	72.1	1,713	38.0	38.7
Sex								
Male..	2,172	2,144	1,514	69.7	70.6	863	39.7	40.3
Female.......................................	2,333	2,285	1,680	72.0	73.5	850	36.4	37.2
Race								
White alone..................................	3,861	3,814	2,788	72.2	73.1	1,497	38.8	39.2
White, non-Hispanic alone	3,779	3,773	2,766	73.2	73.3	1,487	39.4	39.4
Black alone..................................	485	479	325	67.1	67.9	177	36.5	37.0
Asian alone	76	53	39	(B)	(B)	13	(B)	(B)
Hispanic (of any race)	88	47	28	(B)	(B)	15	(B)	(B)
White alone or in combination	3,917	3,870	2,817	71.9	72.8	1,510	38.6	39.0
Black alone or in combination..........	508	503	344	67.7	68.5	187	36.7	37.1
Asian alone or in combination..........	93	70	48	(B)	(B)	18	(B)	(B)
Age								
18 to 24 years.............................	442	438	217	49.0	49.4	64	14.5	14.6
25 to 34 years.............................	749	727	477	63.7	65.6	201	26.8	27.6
35 to 44 years.............................	805	776	586	72.8	75.5	305	37.8	39.2
45 to 64 years.............................	1,592	1,580	1,192	74.8	75.4	684	42.9	43.3
65 years and over	916	907	723	78.9	79.7	460	50.2	50.7

B = Base is less than 75,000 and therefore too small to show the derived measure.

Table MO-14. Crime

(Number, rate per 100,000. Data are derived from the FBI Uniform Crime Reports.)

Item	State			U.S.[1,2,3,4]		
	2013	2014	Percent change	2013	2014	Percent change
TOTAL POPULATION[5]............................	6,044,171	6,063,589	0.3	316,128,839	318,857,056	0.9
VIOLENT CRIME						
Number.......................................	25,509	26,856	5.3	1,163,146	1,165,383	0.2
Rate	422.0	442.9	5.0	367.9	365.5	-0.7
Murder and Nonnegligent Manslaughter						
Number.......................................	371	403	8.6	14,196	14,249	0.4
Rate	6.1	6.6	8.2	4.5	4.5	-
Rape[6]						
Number..	2,287	2,379	X	108,612	116,645	X
Rate	37.8	39.2	X	34.4	36.6	X
Robbery						
Number.......................................	5,484	5,592	2.0	345,031	325,802	-5.6
Rate	90.7	92.2	1.7	109.1	102.2	-6.3
Aggravated Assault						
Number.......................................	18,055	18,482	2.4	724,149	741,291	2.4
Rate	298.7	304.8	2.0	229.1	232.5	1.5
PROPERTY CRIME						
Number.......................................	189,606	176,237	-7.1	8,632,512	8,277,829	-4.1
Rate	3,137.0	2,906.5	-7.3	2,730.7	2,596.1	-4.9
Burglary						
Number.......................................	38,865	35,258	-9.3	1,928,465	1,729,806	-10.3
Rate	643.0	581.5	-9.6	610.0	542.5	-11.1
Larceny-Theft						
Number.......................................	134,416	124,622	-7.3	6,004,453	5,858,496	-2.4
Rate	2,223.9	2,055.3	-7.6	1,899.4	1,837.3	-3.3
Motor Vehicle Theft						
Number.......................................	16,325	16,357	0.2	699,594	689,527	-1.4
Rate	270.1	269.8	-0.1	221.3	216.2	-2.3

NOTE: Although arson data are included in the trend and clearance tables, sufficient data are not available to estimate totals for this offense. Therefore, no arson data are published in this table.
X = Not applicable.
- = Zero or rounds to zero.
[1]The crime figures have been adjusted.
[2]The data collection methodology for the offense of forcible rape used by the Minnesota state Uniform Crime Reporting (UCR) Program (with the exception of Minneapolis and St. Paul, Minnesota) does not comply with national UCR Program guidelines. Consequently, its figures for forcible rape and violent crime (of which forcible rape is a part) are not published in this table.
[3]Includes offenses reported by the Zoological Police and the Metro Transit Police.
[4]Because of changes in the state's reporting practices, figures are not comparable to previous years' data.
[5]Populations are U.S. Census Bureau provisional estimates as of July 1 of each year.
[6]The figures shown for the offense of rape were estimated using the revised Uniform Crime Reporting (UCR) definition of rape.

Table MO-15. State Government Finances, 2014

(Dollar amounts in thousands, percent distribution.)

Item	Dollars	Percent distribution
Total Revenue	38,507,812	100.0
General revenue	26,676,937	69.3
Intergovernmental revenue	10,394,689	27.0
Taxes	11,240,657	29.2
General sales	3,285,563	8.5
Selective sales	1,629,647	4.2
License taxes	564,474	1.5
Individual income tax	5,361,976	13.9
Corporate income tax	357,724	0.9
Other taxes	41,273	0.1
Current charges	2,755,336	7.2
Miscellaneous general revenue	2,286,255	5.9
Utility revenue	0	-
Liquor stores revenue	0	-
Insurance trust revenue[1]	11,830,875	30.7
Total Expenditure	30,454,270	100.0
Intergovernmental expenditure	5,785,229	19.0
Direct expenditure	24,669,041	81.0
Current operation	17,897,955	58.8
Capital outlay	1,119,736	3.7
Insurance benefits and repayments	4,304,737	14.1
Assistance and subsidies	593,874	2.0
Interest on debt	752,739	2.5
Exhibit: Salaries and wages	3,853,474	12.7
Total Expenditure	30,454,270	100.0
General expenditure	26,149,533	85.9
Intergovernmental expenditure	5,785,229	19.0
Direct expenditure	20,364,304	66.9
General expenditure, by function:		
Education	9,128,579	30.0
Public welfare	8,069,098	26.5
Hospitals	1,699,793	5.6
Health	1,637,995	5.4
Highways	1,434,567	4.7
Police protection	185,050	0.6
Correction	818,755	2.7
Natural resources	325,393	1.1
Parks and recreation	44,559	0.1
Governmental administration	528,970	1.7
Interest on general debt	752,739	2.5
Other and unallocable	1,524,035	5.0
Utility expenditure	0	-
Liquor stores expenditure	0	-
Insurance trust expenditure	4,304,737	14.1
Debt at End of Fiscal Year	19,041,613	X
Cash and Security Holdings	80,863,913	X

X = Not applicable.
- = Zero or rounds to zero.
[1]Within insurance trust revenue, net earnings of state retirement systems is a calculated statistic (the item code in the data file is X08), and thus can be positive or negative. Net earnings is the sum of earnings on investments plus gains on investments minus losses on investments. The change made in 2002 for asset valuation from book to market value in accordance with Statement 34 of the Governmental Accounting Standards Board is reflected in the calculated statistics.

Table MO-16. State Government Tax Collections, 2014

(Dollars in thousands, percent.)

Item	Dollars	Percent distribution
Total Taxes	11,240,657	100.0
Property taxes	29,725	0.3
Sales and gross receipts	4,915,210	43.7
General sales and gross receipts	3,285,563	29.2
Selective sales and gross receipts	1,629,647	14.5
Alcoholic beverages	35,760	0.3
Amusements	361,046	3.2
Insurance premiums	302,166	2.7
Motor fuels	696,458	6.2
Pari-mutuels	0	-
Public utilities	0	-
Tobacco products	99,527	0.9
Other selective sales	134,690	1.2
Licenses	564,474	5.0
Alcoholic beverages	5,308	-
Amusements	1,980	-
Corporations in general	59,421	0.5
Hunting and fishing	32,740	0.3
Motor vehicle	272,542	2.4
Motor vehicle operators	15,829	0.1
Public utilities	20,118	0.2
Occupation and business, NEC	134,644	1.2
Other licenses	21,892	0.2
Income taxes	5,719,700	50.9
Individual income	5,361,976	47.7
Corporation net income	357,724	3.2
Other taxes	11,548	0.1
Death and gift	129	-
Documentary and stock transfer	11,340	0.1
Severance	5	-
Taxes, NEC	74	-

- = Zero or rounds to zero.

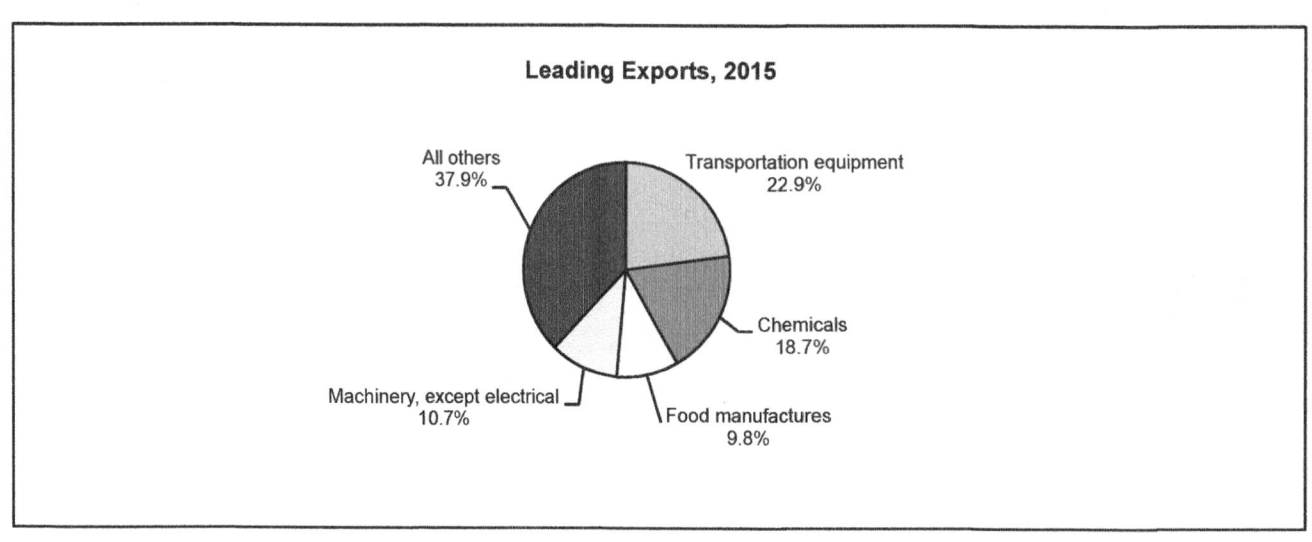

Leading Exports, 2015

All others 37.9%

Transportation equipment 22.9%

Chemicals 18.7%

Food manufactures 9.8%

Machinery, except electrical 10.7%

MONTANA

Facts and Figures

Location: Northwestern United States; bordered on the N by Canada (British Columbia, Alberta, and Saskatchewan), on the E by North Dakota and South Dakota, on the S by Idaho and Wyoming, and on the W by Idaho

Area: 147,042 sq. mi. (380,838 sq. km.); rank—4th

Population: 1,032,949 (2015 est.); rank—44th

Principal Cities: capital—Helena; largest—Billings

Statehood: November 8, 1889; 41st state

U.S. Congress: 2 senators, 1 representative

State Motto: *Oro y plata* ("Gold and silver")

State Song: "Montana"

State Nicknames: The Treasure State; Big Sky Country

Abbreviations: MT; Mont.

State Symbols: flower—bitterroot; tree—ponderosa pine; bird—Western meadowlark

At a Glance

- With an increase in population of 4.3 percent, Montana ranked 20th among the states in growth from 2010 to 2015.

- Montana's violent crime rate in 2014 was 323.7 per 100,000 population, compared to 365.5 for the entire nation.

- In 2015, 17.2 percent of Montana residents were in the 65 and older age group, a percentage that ranked 5th in the country.

- Approximately 0.6 percent of Montana residents self-identified as "Black or African-American alone" in 2015, which was the lowest percentage in the country.

Table MT-1. Population by Age, Sex, Race, and Hispanic Origin

(Number, percent, except where noted.)

Sex, age, race, and Hispanic origin	2000	2010	2015[1]	Average annual percent change, 2010–2015
Total Population.............................	902,195	989,415	1,032,949	0.3
Percent of total U.S. population	0.3	0.3	0.3	X
Sex				
Male..............................	449,480	496,667	519,330	0.3
Female	452,715	492,748	513,619	0.3
Age				
Under 5 years..........................	54,869	62,423	61,886	-0.1
5 to 19 years..........................	202,571	188,613	190,583	0.1
20 to 64 years..........................	523,806	591,637	602,469	0.1
65 years and over.........................	120,949	146,742	178,011	1.4
Median age (years)	37.5	39.8	39.8	-
Race and Hispanic Origin				
One race				
White..............................	817,229	891,529	921,857	0.2
Black..............................	2,692	4,215	6,250	2.9
American Indian and Alaska Native	56,068	63,495	67,916	0.5
Asian..............................	4,691	6,379	8,582	2.1
Native Hawaiian or Other Pacific Islander	470	734	922	1.6
Two or more races.........................	15,730	23,063	27,422	1.2
Hispanic (of any race)..........................	18,081	31,018	37,201	1.3

X = Not applicable.
- = Zero or rounds to zero.
[1]Population figures for 2015 are July 1 estimates. The 2010 estimates are taken from the 2010 Census.

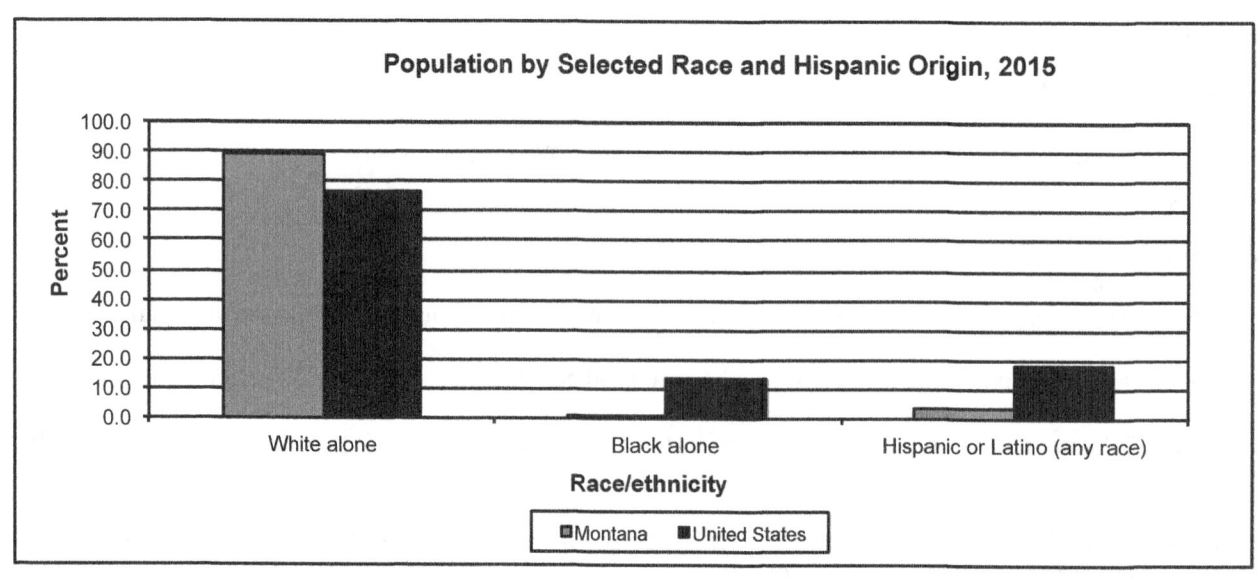

Table MT-2. Marital Status

(Number, percent distribution.)

Sex, age, race, and Hispanic origin	2000	2010	2014
Males, 15 Years and Over	353,801	404,179	410,501
Never married	27.7	30.5	31.5
Now married, except separated.......................	58.3	53.4	52.6
Separated.........................	1.2	1.5	1.3
Widowed.........................	2.6	2.3	2.7
Divorced.........................	10.2	12.4	11.9
Females, 15 Years and Over	362,114	403,766	410,095
Never married	20.4	23.5	24.3
Now married, except separated.......................	56.3	52.9	51.6
Separated.........................	1.3	1.6	1.5
Widowed.........................	10.4	9.7	9.5
Divorced.........................	11.6	12.3	13.1

Table MT-3. Households and Housing Characteristics

(Number, percent, dollars.)

Item	2000	2010	2014	Average annual percent change, 2000–2014
Total Households...	358,667	402,747	410,962	1.0
Family households	237,407	255,199	251,176	0.4
Married-couple family	192,067	203,500	199,495	0.3
Other family	45,340	51,699	51,681	1.0
Male householder, no wife present..................	13,324	16,926	17,819	2.4
Female householder, no husband present.........	32,016	34,773	33,862	0.4
Nonfamily households	121,260	147,548	159,786	2.3
Householder living alone..................................	98,422	119,762	128,311	2.2
Householder not living alone............................	22,838	27,786	31,475	2.7
Housing Characteristics				
Total housing units..	412,633	483,006	491,515	1.4
Occupied housing units	358,667	402,747	410,962	1.0
Owner occupied	247,723	280,633	272,856	0.7
Renter occupied	110,944	122,114	138,106	1.7
Average household size.......................................	2.45	2.39	2.42	-0.1
Financial Characteristics				
Median gross rent of renter-occupied housing	447	642	711	4.2
Median monthly owner costs for housing units with a mortgage	863	1,217	1,251	3.2
Median value of owner-occupied housing units..........................	99,500	181,200	196,800	7.0

Table MT-4. Migration, Origin, and Language

(Number, percent.)

Characteristic	State			U.S.		
	2013	2014	Percent change	2013	2014	Percent change
Residence 1 Year Ago						
Population 1 year and over	1,003,013	1,012,169	0.9	312,432,820	315,095,393	0.9
Same house	82.5	83.5	X	85.0	85.1	X
Different house in the U.S.	17.0	16.2	X	14.4	14.3	X
Same county	9.4	8.9	X	8.9	8.7	X
Different county	7.6	7.3	X	5.5	5.6	X
Same state	3.6	3.6	X	3.2	3.3	X
Different state	4.0	3.7	X	2.3	2.3	X
Abroad	0.5	0.3	X	0.6	0.6	X
Place of Birth						
Native born	995,700	999,697	0.4	274,780,773	276,465,262	0.6
Male..	50.1	50.3	X	49.3	49.3	X
Female..	49.9	49.7	X	50.7	50.7	X
Foreign born	19,465	23,882	22.7	41,348,066	42,391,794	2.5
Male..	43.6	42.4	X	48.8	48.7	X
Female..	56.4	57.6	X	51.2	51.3	X
Foreign born; naturalized U.S. citizen.................	11,127	11,410	2.5	19,294,710	19,984,738	3.6
Male..	37.9	41.7	X	45.9	45.9	X
Female..	62.1	58.3	X	54.1	54.1	X
Foreign born; not a U.S. citizen.........................	8,338	12,472	49.6	22,053,356	22,407,056	1.6
Male..	51.2	43	X	51.3	51.2	X
Female..	48.8	57	X	48.7	48.8	X
Entered 2010 or later	15.7	15.7	X	9.7	12.3	X
Entered 2000 to 2009	19.7	23.6	X	29.4	28.6	X
Entered before 2000...	64.7	60.7	X	61.0	59.1	X
World Region of Birth, Foreign						
Foreign-born population, excluding population born at sea	19,465	23,882	22.7	41,347,945	42,390,705	2.5
Europe	36.1	27.6	X	11.6	11.2	X
Asia	26.5	27.9	X	29.5	30.1	X
Africa	0.4	2.9	X	4.4	4.6	X
Oceania	2.5	1.3	X	0.5	0.6	X
Latin America..	17.1	23.1	X	51.9	51.6	X
North America	17.5	17.1	X	2.0	1.9	X
Language Spoken at Home and Ability to Speak English						
Population 5 years and over................................	954,022	963,804	1.0	296,358,760	299,084,046	0.9
English only	96.3	96.1	X	79.2	78.9	X
Language other than English..............................	3.7	3.9	X	20.8	21.1	X
Speaks English less than "very well"...............	0.7	0.8	X	8.5	8.6	X

X = Not applicable.
- = Zero or rounds to zero.

Table MT-5. Median Income and Poverty Status, 2014

(Number, percent, except as noted.)

Characteristic	State		U.S.	
	Number	Percent	Number	Percent
Median Income				
Households (dollars)...................	46,328	X	53,657	X
Families (dollars)	60,643	X	65,910	X
Below Poverty Level (All People)	153,954	15.4	48,208,387	15.5
Sex				
Male...................	70,703	14.2	21,590,918	14.2
Female	83,251	16.7	26,617,469	16.8
Age				
Under 18 years..................	40,619	18.5	15,686,012	21.7
Related children under 18 years.......	39,377	18.1	15,372,705	21.3
18 to 64 years.................	99,622	16.2	28,267,482	14.6
65 years and over.............	13,713	8.3	4,254,893	9.5

X = Not applicable.

Median Household and Family Income, 2014

Table MT-6. Health Insurance Coverage Status for the Civilian Noninstitutionalized Population and Children Under 18 Years of Age

(Numbers in thousands, percent.)

Item	2006	2007	2008	2009	2010	2011	2012	2013	2014
Civilian Noninstitutionalized Population	931	939	950	958	976	983	990	999	1,008
Covered by Private or Public Insurance									
Number....................	783	772	775	783	807	804	811	835	865
Percent....................	82.9	84.4	81.6	81.8	82.7	81.7	82.0	83.5	85.8
Not Covered									
Number....................	160	146	175	174	169	180	179	165	143
Percent....................	17.1	15.6	18.4	18.2	17.3	18.3	18.0	16.5	14.2
Percent in the U.S. not covered................	15.8	15.3	15.1	15.1	15.5	15.1	14.8	14.5	11.7
Children Under 18 Years of Age	212	219	222	220	221	222	219	223	224
Covered by Private or Public Insurance									
Number....................	181	191	190	192	193	196	195	201	206
Percent....................	85.8	85.5	85.6	87.1	87.6	88.5	88.9	89.9	91.8
Not Covered									
Number....................	31	28	32	28	28	26	24	22	18
Percent....................	14.5	12.6	14.4	12.9	12.4	11.5	11.1	10.1	8.2
Percent in the U.S. not covered................	11.7	11.0	9.7	8.6	8.0	7.5	7.2	7.1	6.0

Table MT-7. Employment Status by Demographic Group, 2015

(Numbers in thousands, percent.)

Characteristic	Civilian noninstitutional population	Civilian labor force		Employed		Unemployed	
		Number	Percent of population	Number	Percent of population	Number	Percent of population
Total...............................	815	523	64.1	501	61.5	21	4.1
Sex							
Male....................	406	276	68.2	263	64.9	13	4.9
Female..................	409	246	60.1	238	58.2	8	3.2
Race, Sex, and Hispanic Origin							
White.....................	764	491	64.2	473	61.9	18	3.7
Male...................	383	261	68.3	251	65.5	11	4.1
Female.................	381	229	60.2	222	58.3	7	3.2
Black or African American.................	NA	NA	NA	NA	NA	NA	NA
Male...................	NA	NA	NA	NA	NA	NA	NA
Female.................	NA	NA	NA	NA	NA	NA	NA
Hispanic or Latino ethnicity[1]	21	15	69.2	14	65.6	1	5.2
Male...................	NA	NA	NA	NA	NA	NA	NA
Female.................	NA	NA	NA	NA	NA	NA	NA
Age							
16 to 19 years.............	51	24	46.2	22	42.1	2	8.8
20 to 24 years.............	72	53	73.5	49	68.8	3	6.4
25 to 34 years.............	130	108	83.5	104	80.1	5	4.2
35 to 44 years.............	113	99	87.3	96	84.9	3	2.7
45 to 54 years.............	123	102	83.5	99	80.4	4	3.7
55 to 64 years.............	160	105	65.5	100	62.9	4	3.9
65 years and over.............	167	32	19.2	31	18.7	1	2.5

NOTE: Data in Table 7 are from the Current Population Survey (CPS) and do not match the estimates in Table 8. See notes and definitions for further information.
NA = Not available.
[1]May be of any race.

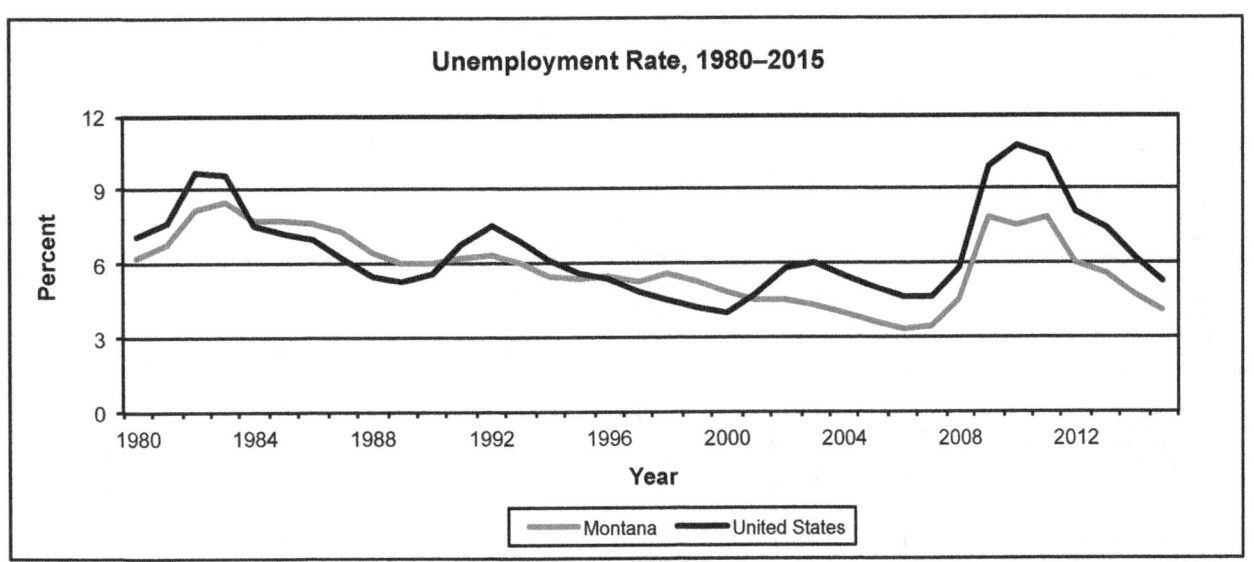

Unemployment Rate, 1980–2015

Table MT-8. Employment Status of the Civilian Noninstitutional Population Age 16 Years and Over

(Number, percent.)

Year	Civilian labor force	Civilian participation rate	Employed	Unemployed	Unemployment rate
2007............	502,070	66.9	484,189	17,881	3.6
2008............	509,163	67.0	483,347	25,816	5.1
2009............	501,014	65.3	466,713	34,301	6.8
2010............	500,525	64.4	463,998	36,527	7.3
2011............	501,225	63.9	466,403	34,822	6.9
2012............	506,446	63.9	476,115	30,331	6.0
2013............	513,255	64.1	485,456	27,799	5.4
2014............	515,947	63.9	491,938	24,009	4.7
2015............	522,727	64.0	501,186	21,541	4.1

Table MT-9. Employment and Average Wages by Industry

(Estimates through 2010 are based on the 2007 North American Industry Classification System [NAICS]. Estimates from 2011 onward are based on the 2012 NAICS.)

Industry	2008	2009	2010	2011	2012	2013	2014
	Number of jobs						
Wage and Salary Employment by Industry..................	468,540	452,213	449,797	454,484	460,085	466,710	470,625
Farm Wage and Salary Employment..........................	5,023	4,705	4,830	5,402	5,593	5,758	6,399
Nonfarm Wage and Salary Employment....................	463,517	447,508	444,967	449,082	454,492	460,952	464,226
Private wage and salary employment.................................	369,354	351,490	347,936	352,843	358,944	366,154	369,063
Forestry, fishing, and related activities.........................	2,771	2,444	2,616	2,742	2,808	3,428	3,679
Mining..	7,541	6,489	6,835	7,561	8,730	8,825	8,528
Utilities...	3,084	3,067	3,047	3,117	3,196	3,178	3,158
Construction...	30,887	25,114	23,796	23,960	23,892	24,983	25,753
Manufacturing..	19,939	17,331	16,352	16,864	17,537	18,365	18,902
Durable goods manufacturing..........................	12,309	10,018	9,405	9,758	10,578	11,127	11,558
Nondurable goods manufacturing.....................	7,630	7,313	6,947	7,106	6,959	7,238	7,344
Wholesale trade	16,887	16,118	15,788	15,770	16,334	17,139	17,024
Retail trade..	59,660	56,579	55,568	55,609	55,826	56,545	57,817
Transportation and warehousing....................	13,803	13,334	13,371	13,848	14,531	15,036	15,363
Information..	7,667	7,475	7,413	7,214	6,949	6,916	6,417
Finance and insurance	16,930	16,571	16,244	16,257	15,707	15,961	16,072
Real estate and rental and leasing....................	6,046	5,619	5,414	5,301	5,262	5,433	5,424
Professional, scientific, and technical services ...	19,607	18,842	18,945	19,341	19,706	20,261	20,308
Management of companies and enterprises..................	1,439	1,570	1,695	2,006	2,057	1,973	1,962
Administrative and waste services...................	19,210	18,019	18,458	19,283	19,727	17,780	17,346
Educational services	5,246	5,310	5,459	5,732	5,672	5,924	6,014
Health care and social assistance...................	57,541	59,202	59,969	60,186	62,185	63,355	64,090
Arts, entertainment, and recreation................	11,759	11,415	10,894	10,965	10,885	11,332	11,321
Accommodation and food services.................	47,908	45,962	45,361	46,157	47,467	49,077	49,377
Other services, except public administration.............	21,429	21,029	20,711	20,930	20,473	20,643	20,508
Government and government enterprises..........................	94,163	96,018	97,031	96,239	95,548	94,798	95,163
	Dollars						
Average Wages and Salaries by Industry	33,379	33,880	34,679	35,814	37,033	37,707	39,024
Average Farm Wages and Salaries	35,694	42,310	35,807	33,217	27,422	39,900	41,987
Average Nonfarm Wages and Salaries	33,354	33,791	34,667	35,846	37,151	37,679	38,983
Average private wages and salaries.............................	32,316	32,605	33,637	34,986	36,469	37,026	38,450
Forestry, fishing, and related activities.....................	28,327	28,029	27,305	28,833	30,654	30,101	31,066
Mining...	72,383	70,377	74,599	80,502	81,885	83,430	88,241
Utilities..	69,686	73,969	74,994	78,167	76,683	78,702	81,097
Construction...	38,937	39,870	40,854	42,713	43,891	44,781	46,116
Manufacturing...	40,594	41,224	42,588	42,588	43,411	43,670	45,754
Durable goods manufacturing..........................	38,533	38,163	39,393	39,934	41,673	42,872	44,095
Nondurable goods manufacturing.....................	43,920	45,417	46,914	46,232	46,053	44,897	48,364
Wholesale trade	45,040	44,642	45,187	47,891	49,846	50,792	53,234
Retail trade..	23,475	23,613	24,217	24,685	25,340	25,856	26,869
Transportation and warehousing....................	42,222	42,125	44,085	47,294	47,750	49,599	50,501
Information..	39,673	40,048	41,624	41,931	43,011	43,991	45,665
Finance and insurance	46,655	47,123	48,886	49,884	53,670	55,558	57,551
Real estate and rental and leasing....................	27,336	25,656	26,554	28,413	30,567	30,432	32,245
Professional, scientific, and technical services	47,435	48,237	49,575	51,672	57,590	54,362	57,884
Management of companies and enterprises..................	63,205	59,889	58,055	59,589	68,618	73,024	71,930
Administrative and waste services...................	24,981	25,690	27,130	27,858	29,301	28,761	30,149
Educational services	20,014	20,566	20,476	21,467	21,358	21,712	22,371
Health care and social assistance...................	35,745	36,876	37,713	39,103	39,929	41,071	42,085
Arts, entertainment, and recreation................	18,767	19,194	19,567	20,341	20,289	20,887	22,619
Accommodation and food services.................	14,475	14,654	15,381	16,149	16,726	16,996	18,027
Other services, except public administration.................	23,544	23,789	24,511	25,008	26,173	26,835	27,747
Government and government enterprises..........................	37,427	38,130	38,360	38,999	39,717	40,201	41,049

Table MT-10. Employment Characteristics by Family Type

(Number, percent.)

Family type and labor force status	2012 Total	2012 Families with own children under 18 years	2013 Total	2013 Families with own children under 18 years	2014 Total	2014 Families with own children under 18 years
All Families..	259,650	105,017	256,091	104,971	250,636	99,341
FAMILY TYPE AND LABOR FORCE STATUS						
Married-Couple Families............................	205,584	73,268	199,251	70,607	198,955	69,152
Both husband and wife in labor force...............	53.7	69.4	51.6	67.2	52.5	69.9
Husband in labor force, wife not in labor force ...	19.1	24.6	20.2	27.1	19.2	24.9
Wife in labor force, husband not in labor force ...	8.2	4.7	8.6	3.5	8.0	3.1
Both husband and wife not in labor force..........	19.0	1.3	19.4	2.0	20.3	2.1
Other Families	54,066	31,749	56,840	34,364	51,681	30,189
Female householder, no husband present..........	64.2	65.5	66.6	69.5	65.5	63.2
In labor force..	48.0	57.6	50.9	56.6	46.0	50.2
Not in labor force	16.2	7.9	15.7	12.9	19.6	13.0
Male householder, no wife present...................	35.8	34.5	33.4	30.5	34.5	36.8
In labor force..	30.4	32.0	26.3	27.3	29.0	34.8
Not in labor force	5.5	2.5	7.0	3.2	5.5	2.0

Table MT-11. School Enrollment and Educational Attainment, 2014

(Number, percent.)

Item	State	U.S.
Enrollment		
Total population 3 years and over, enrolled in school..........................	236,766	82,063,714
Enrolled in nursery school or preschool (percent)	5.9	6.0
Enrolled in kindergarten (percent)	5.7	5.1
Enrolled in elementary school, grades 1-8 (percent)..........................	42.5	40.2
Enrolled in high school, grades 9-12 (percent)	20.5	20.7
Enrolled in college or graduate school (percent)..........................	25.5	28.0
Attainment		
Total population 25 years and over	695,850	213,725,624
Less than ninth grade (percent)	2.2	5.6
9th to 12th grade, no diploma (percent)	5.2	7.5
High school graduate, including equivalency (percent)..........................	30.6	27.7
Some college, no degree (percent)	24.5	21.0
Associate's degree (percent)	8.2	8.2
Bachelor's degree (percent)	19.5	18.7
Graduate or professional degree (percent)..........................	9.8	11.4
High school graduate or higher (percent)	92.6	86.9
Bachelor's degree or higher (percent)	29.3	30.1

Table MT-12. Public School Characteristics and Educational Indicators

(Number, percent; data derived from National Center of Education Statistics.)

Item	State	U.S.
Public Schools, 2013–2014 (except where noted)		
Number of school districts..	493	18,194
Number of schools..	824	98,271
Number of students (in thousands)	144	50,045
Number of teachers (in thousands)	10	3,114
Student-teacher ratio	14.0	16.1
Expenditures per student (dollars), FY 2013..........................	10,662	107,637
Four-year adjusted cohort graduation rate (ACGR)[1,2]	85.4	82.3
Students eligible for free or reduced-price lunch (in thousands)	60	25,596
English language learners (in thousands)	3	4,461
Students age 3 to 21 served under IDEA, part B (in thousands)	16	6,464

Public Schools by Type	Number	Percent of state public schools
Total number of schools..	824	100.0
Regular	818	99.3
Special education..	2	0.2
Vocational education..	0	-
Alternative education..	4	0.5

NOTE: Every school is assigned only one school type based on its instructional emphasis.
- =Zero or rounds to zero.
[1]ACGR data represents a new method of calculating high-school completion rates and may not be comparable to previous years' data for Averaged Freshmen Graduation Rates (AFGR).
[2]The United States 4-year ACGRs were estimated using both the reported 4-year ACGR data from 49 states and the District of Columbia and using imputed data for Idaho. The estimate for American Indian/Alaska Native students also includes imputed data for Virginia.

Table MT-13. Reported Voting and Registration of the Voting-Age Population, November 2014

(Numbers in thousands, percent.)

Item	Total population	Total citizen population	Registered			Voted		
			Total registered	Percent registered (total population)	Percent registered (total citizen population)	Total voted	Percent voted (total population)	Percent voted (total citizen population)
U.S. Total	239,874	219,941	142,166	59.3	64.6	92,251	38.5	41.9
State Total	788	782	506	64.3	64.8	391	49.7	50.1
Sex								
Male	392	389	250	63.7	64.2	191	48.7	49.0
Female	396	393	257	64.8	65.4	201	50.7	51.1
Race								
White alone	728	725	483	66.4	66.6	380	52.2	52.4
White, non-Hispanic alone	714	711	473	66.3	66.5	372	52.2	52.4
Black alone	3	3	3	(B)	(B)	-	(B)	(B)
Asian alone	5	2	2	(B)	(B)	2	(B)	(B)
Hispanic (of any race)	16	16	11	(B)	(B)	8	(B)	(B)
White alone or in combination	742	739	486	65.5	65.8	382	51.5	51.7
Black alone or in combination	3	3	3	(B)	(B)	-	(B)	(B)
Asian alone or in combination	5	2	2	(B)	(B)	2	(B)	(B)
Age								
18 to 24 years	101	99	43	42.8	43.7	21	20.7	21.1
25 to 34 years	136	133	73	53.7	54.8	42	31.0	31.6
35 to 44 years	104	104	73	70.2	70.2	55	52.8	52.8
45 to 64 years	278	277	190	68.2	68.5	159	57.0	57.2
65 years and over	169	169	128	75.6	75.6	115	68.2	68.2

- = Zero or rounds to zero.
B = Base is less than 75,000 and therefore too small to show the derived measure.

Table MT-14. Crime

(Number, rate per 100,000. Data are derived from the FBI Uniform Crime Reports.)

Item	State			U.S.[1,2,3,4]		
	2013	2014	Percent change	2013	2014	Percent change
TOTAL POPULATION[5]	1,015,165	1,023,579	0.8	316,128,839	318,857,056	0.9
VIOLENT CRIME						
Number	2,444	3,313	35.6	1,163,146	1,165,383	0.2
Rate	240.7	323.7	34.5	367.9	365.5	-0.7
Murder and Nonnegligent Manslaughter						
Number	22	37	68.2	14,196	14,249	0.4
Rate	2.2	3.6	63.6	4.5	4.5	-
Rape[6]						
Number	410	541	X	108,612	116,645	X
Rate	40.4	52.9	X	34.4	36.6	X
Robbery						
Number	204	203	-0.5	345,031	325,802	-5.6
Rate	20.1	19.8	-1.5	109.1	102.2	-6.3
Aggravated Assault						
Number	1,931	2,532	31.1	724,149	741,291	2.4
Rate	190.2	247.4	30.1	229.1	232.5	1.5
PROPERTY CRIME						
Number	25,953	25,312	-2.5	8,632,512	8,277,829	-4.1
Rate	2,556.5	2,472.9	-3.3	2,730.7	2,596.1	-4.9
Burglary						
Number	4,064	3,595	-11.5	1,928,465	1,729,806	-10.3
Rate	400.3	351.2	-12.3	610.0	542.5	-11.1
Larceny-Theft						
Number	20,039	19,674	-1.8	6,004,453	5,858,496	-2.4
Rate	1,974.0	1,922.1	-2.6	1,899.4	1,837.3	-3.3
Motor Vehicle Theft						
Number	1,850	2,043	10.4	699,594	689,527	-1.4
Rate	182.2	199.6	9.5	221.3	216.2	-2.3

NOTE: Although arson data are included in the trend and clearance tables, sufficient data are not available to estimate totals for this offense. Therefore, no arson data are published in this table.
X = Not applicable.
- = Zero or rounds to zero.
[1] Because of changes in the state's reporting practices, figures are not comparable to previous years' data.
[2] The crime figures have been adjusted.
[3] The data collection methodology for the offense of forcible rape used by the Minnesota state Uniform Crime Reporting (UCR) Program (with the exception of Minneapolis and St. Paul, Minnesota) does not comply with national UCR Program guidelines. Consequently, its figures for forcible rape and violent crime (of which forcible rape is a part) are not published in this table.
[4] Includes offenses reported by the Zoological Police and the Metro Transit Police.
[5] Populations are U.S. Census Bureau provisional estimates as of July 1 of each year.
[6] The figures shown for the offense of rape were estimated using the revised Uniform Crime Reporting (UCR) definition of rape.

Table MT-15. State Government Finances, 2014

(Dollar amounts in thousands, percent distribution.)

Item	Dollars	Percent distribution
Total Revenue	8,939,148	100.0
General revenue	5,977,163	66.9
Intergovernmental revenue	2,341,686	26.2
Taxes	2,655,553	29.7
General sales	0	-
Selective sales	550,254	6.2
License taxes	314,271	3.5
Individual income tax	1,063,261	11.9
Corporate income tax	150,139	1.7
Other taxes	577,628	6.5
Current charges	549,838	6.2
Miscellaneous general revenue	430,086	4.8
Utility revenue	0	-
Liquor stores revenue	85,346	1.0
Insurance trust revenue[1]	2,876,639	32.2
Total Expenditure	7,218,707	100.0
Intergovernmental expenditure	1,382,045	19.1
Direct expenditure	5,836,662	80.9
Current operation	4,088,225	56.6
Capital outlay	586,918	8.1
Insurance benefits and repayments	918,091	12.7
Assistance and subsidies	118,388	1.6
Interest on debt	125,040	1.7
Exhibit: Salaries and wages	1,057,473	14.6
Total Expenditure	7,218,707	100.0
General expenditure	6,210,681	86.0
Intergovernmental expenditure	1,382,045	19.1
Direct expenditure	4,828,636	66.9
General expenditure, by function:		
Education	1,920,161	26.6
Public welfare	1,501,599	20.8
Hospitals	51,430	0.7
Health	155,415	2.2
Highways	734,448	10.2
Police protection	51,467	0.7
Correction	196,785	2.7
Natural resources	233,466	3.2
Parks and recreation	18,659	0.3
Governmental administration	371,352	5.1
Interest on general debt	125,040	1.7
Other and unallocable	850,859	11.8
Utility expenditure	15,154	0.2
Liquor stores expenditure	74,781	1.0
Insurance trust expenditure	918,091	12.7
Debt at End of Fiscal Year	3,402,199	X
Cash and Security Holdings	18,068,925	X

X = Not applicable.
- = Zero or rounds to zero.
[1]Within insurance trust revenue, net earnings of state retirement systems is a calculated statistic (the item code in the data file is X08), and thus can be positive or negative. Net earnings is the sum of earnings on investments plus gains on investments minus losses on investments. The change made in 2002 for asset valuation from book to market value in accordance with Statement 34 of the Governmental Accounting Standards Board is reflected in the calculated statistics.

Table MT-16. State Government Tax Collections, 2014

(Dollars in thousands, percent.)

Item	Dollars	Percent distribution
Total Taxes	2,655,553	100.0
Property taxes	268,508	10.1
Sales and gross receipts	550,254	20.7
General sales and gross receipts	X	X
Selective sales and gross receipts	550,254	20.7
Alcoholic beverages	30,053	1.1
Amusements	56,900	2.1
Insurance premiums	88,106	3.3
Motor fuels	196,965	7.4
Pari-mutuels	21	-
Public utilities	47,390	1.8
Tobacco products	85,404	3.2
Other selective sales	45,415	1.7
Licenses	314,271	11.8
Alcoholic beverages	3,215	0.1
Amusements	8,512	0.3
Corporations in general	3,311	0.1
Hunting and fishing	45,606	1.7
Motor vehicle	136,787	5.2
Motor vehicle operators	8,042	0.3
Public utilities	12	-
Occupation and business, NEC	98,851	3.7
Other licenses	9,935	0.4
Income taxes	1,213,400	45.7
Individual income	1,063,261	40.0
Corporation net income	150,139	5.7
Other taxes	309,120	11.6
Death and gift	4	-
Documentary and stock transfer	0	-
Severance	305,614	11.5
Taxes, NEC	3,502	0.1

X = Not applicable.
- = Zero or rounds to zero.

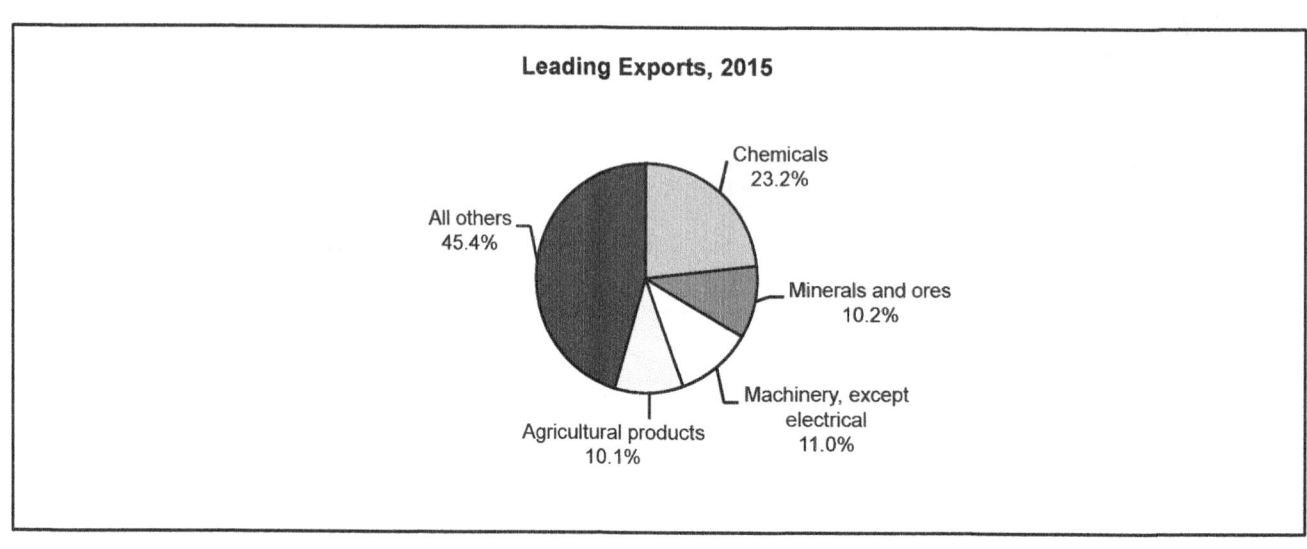

Leading Exports, 2015

Chemicals 23.2%
Minerals and ores 10.2%
Machinery, except electrical 11.0%
Agricultural products 10.1%
All others 45.4%

Facts and Figures

Location: Central United States; bordered on the N by South Dakota, on the E by Iowa and Missouri, on the S by Kansas and Colorado, and on the W by Wyoming

Area: 77,354 sq. mi. (200,345 sq. km.); rank—16th

Population: 1,896,190 (2015 est.); rank—37th

Principal Cities: capital—Lincoln; largest—Omaha

Statehood: March 1, 1867; 37th state

U.S. Congress: 2 senators, 3 representatives

State Motto: Equality Before the Law

State Song: "Beautiful Nebraska"

State Nickname: The Cornhusker State

Abbreviations: NE; Nebr.; Neb.

State Symbols: flower—goldenrod; tree—cottonwood; bird—Western meadowlark

At a Glance

- With an increase in population of 3.6 percent, Nebraska ranked 25th among the states in growth from 2010 to 2015.

- In 2014, 9.7 percent of Nebraskans did not have health insurance, compared to 11.7 percent of the total U.S. population.

- Nebraska's unemployment rate, 3.0 percent, was the second lowest in the country in 2015. The unemployment rate in the entire U.S. was 5.3 percent.

- Nebraska had the 10th highest percentage of residents self-reporting their race as "White alone" in 2015 (89.1 percent).

- The state's violent crime rate in 2014 was 280.4 per 100,000 population, compared to the national rate of 365.5 per 100,000 population.

Table NE-1. Population by Age, Sex, Race, and Hispanic Origin

(Number, percent, except where noted.)

Sex, age, race, and Hispanic origin	2000	2010	2015[1]	Average annual percent change, 2010–2015
Total Population	1,711,263	1,826,341	1,896,190	0.3
Percent of total U.S. population	0.6	0.6	0.6	X
Sex				
Male	843,351	906,296	945,168	0.3
Female	867,912	920,045	951,022	0.2
Age				
Under 5 years	117,048	131,908	130,631	-0.1
5 to 19 years	387,288	380,564	392,651	0.2
20 to 64 years	974,732	1,067,192	1,094,197	0.2
65 years and over	232,195	246,677	278,711	0.9
Median age (years)	35.3	36.2	36.3	-
Race and Hispanic Origin				
One race				
White	1,533,261	1,649,264	1,689,616	0.2
Black	68,541	85,971	93,900	0.6
American Indian and Alaska Native	14,896	23,418	26,492	0.9
Asian	21,931	33,322	44,479	2.1
Native Hawaiian or Other Pacific Islander	836	2,061	2,338	0.9
Two or more races	23,953	32,305	39,365	1.4
Hispanic (of any race)	94,425	173,058	197,416	0.9

X = Not applicable.
- = Zero or rounds to zero.
[1]Population figures for 2015 are July 1 estimates. The 2010 estimates are taken from the 2010 Census.

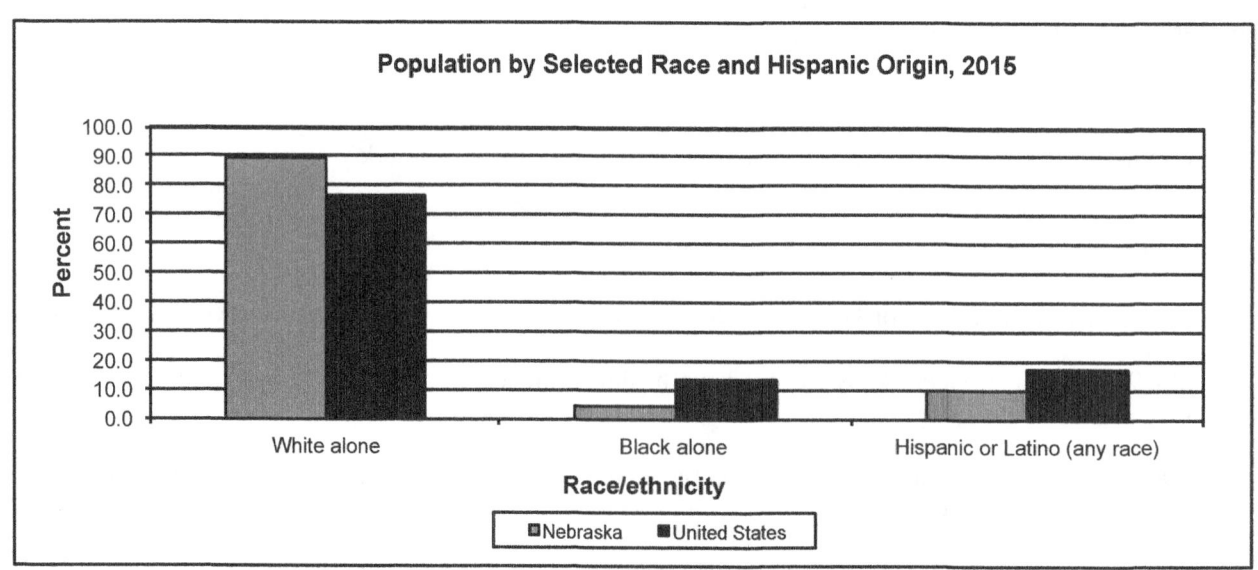

Population by Selected Race and Hispanic Origin, 2015

Table NE-2. Marital Status

(Number, percent distribution.)

Sex, age, race, and Hispanic origin	2000	2010	2014
Males, 15 Years and Over	654,559	708,783	722,917
Never married	29.2	32.4	32.4
Now married, except separated	59.1	54.0	54.4
Separated	1.0	1.4	1.2
Widowed	2.4	2.3	2.5
Divorced	8.3	9.9	9.5
Females, 15 Years and Over	687,863	735,744	744,547
Never married	22.5	25.3	26.0
Now married, except separated	55.7	52.7	52.1
Separated	1.3	1.5	1.4
Widowed	10.8	9.5	9.1
Divorced	9.7	10.9	11.4

Table NE-3. Households and Housing Characteristics

(Number, percent, dollars.)

Item	2000	2010	2014	Average annual percent change, 2000–2014
Total Households..	666,184	719,304	740,765	0.8
Family households	443,411	468,407	480,317	0.6
Married-couple family	360,996	368,023	371,696	0.2
Other family	82,415	100,384	108,621	2.3
Male householder, no wife present..................................	22,072	31,177	30,590	2.8
Female householder, no husband present	60,343	69,207	78,031	2.1
Nonfamily households	222,773	250,897	260,448	1.2
Householder living alone	183,550	205,263	211,536	1.1
Householder not living alone	39,223	45,634	48,912	1.8
Housing Characteristics				
Total housing units..	722,668	797,677	814,957	0.9
Occupied housing units	666,184	719,304	740,765	0.8
Owner occupied	449,317	484,649	488,438	0.6
Renter occupied	216,867	234,655	252,327	1.2
Average household size..	2.49	2.47	2.47	-0.1
Financial Characteristics				
Median gross rent of renter-occupied housing	491	669	742	3.7
Median monthly owner costs for housing units with a mortgage	895	1,218	1,261	2.9
Median value of owner-occupied housing units..................	88,000	127,600	133,800	3.7

Table NE-4. Migration, Origin, and Language

(Number, percent.)

Characteristic	State			U.S.		
	2013	2014	Percent change	2013	2014	Percent change
Residence 1 Year Ago						
Population 1 year and over	1,842,900	1,855,356	0.7	312,432,820	315,095,393	0.9
Same house	83.9	83.1	X	85.0	85.1	X
Different house in the U.S.	15.6	16.4	X	14.4	14.3	X
Same county	9.2	10	X	8.9	8.7	X
Different county	6.4	6.4	X	5.5	5.6	X
Same state	3.9	3.6	X	3.2	3.3	X
Different state	2.5	2.8	X	2.3	2.3	X
Abroad	0.5	0.5	X	0.6	0.6	X
Place of Birth						
Native born	1,745,334	1,756,103	0.6	274,780,773	276,465,262	0.6
Male	49.4	49.6	X	49.3	49.3	X
Female	50.6	50.4	X	50.7	50.7	X
Foreign born	123,182	125,400	1.8	41,348,066	42,391,794	2.5
Male	51.4	51.3	X	48.8	48.7	X
Female	48.6	48.7	X	51.2	51.3	X
Foreign born; naturalized U.S. citizen.............................	41,774	43,971	5.3	19,294,710	19,984,738	3.6
Male	47.7	50.5	X	45.9	45.9	X
Female	52.3	49.5	X	54.1	54.1	X
Foreign born; not a U.S. citizen.......................................	81,408	81,429	-	22,053,356	22,407,056	1.6
Male	53.3	51.8	X	51.3	51.2	X
Female	46.7	48.2	X	48.7	48.8	X
Entered 2010 or later	14.6	18.5	X	9.7	12.3	X
Entered 2000 to 2009	38.5	35.1	X	29.4	28.6	X
Entered before 2000..	46.9	46.4	X	61.0	59.1	X
World Region of Birth, Foreign						
Foreign-born population, excluding population born at sea	123,182	125,400	1.8	41,347,945	42,390,705	2.5
Europe	7.3	7.3	X	11.6	11.2	X
Asia	25.7	27.7	X	29.5	30.1	X
Africa	7.3	7.4	X	4.4	4.6	X
Oceania	0.7	0.4	X	0.5	0.6	X
Latin America..	57.4	56.3	X	51.9	51.6	X
North America	1.5	0.9	X	2.0	1.9	X
Language Spoken at Home and Ability to Speak English						
Population 5 years and over...	1,739,686	1,751,135	0.7	296,358,760	299,084,046	0.9
English only	89.5	89.4	X	79.2	78.9	X
Language other than English...	10.5	10.6	X	20.8	21.1	X
Speaks English less than "very well"...............................	4.7	4.9	X	8.5	8.6	X

X = Not applicable.
- = Zero or rounds to zero.

Table NE-5. Median Income and Poverty Status, 2014

(Number, percent, except as noted.)

Characteristic	State		U.S.	
	Number	Percent	Number	Percent
Median Income				
Households (dollars)..	52,686	X	53,657	X
Families (dollars)	66,120	X	65,910	X
Below Poverty Level (All People)	227,310	12.4	48,208,387	15.5
Sex				
Male..	97,520	10.7	21,590,918	14.2
Female	129,790	14.1	26,617,469	16.8
Age				
Under 18 years..	74,414	16.2	15,686,012	21.7
Related children under 18 years................................	72,556	15.8	15,372,705	21.3
18 to 64 years...	132,413	11.9	28,267,482	14.6
65 years and over	20,483	7.9	4,254,893	9.5

X = Not applicable.

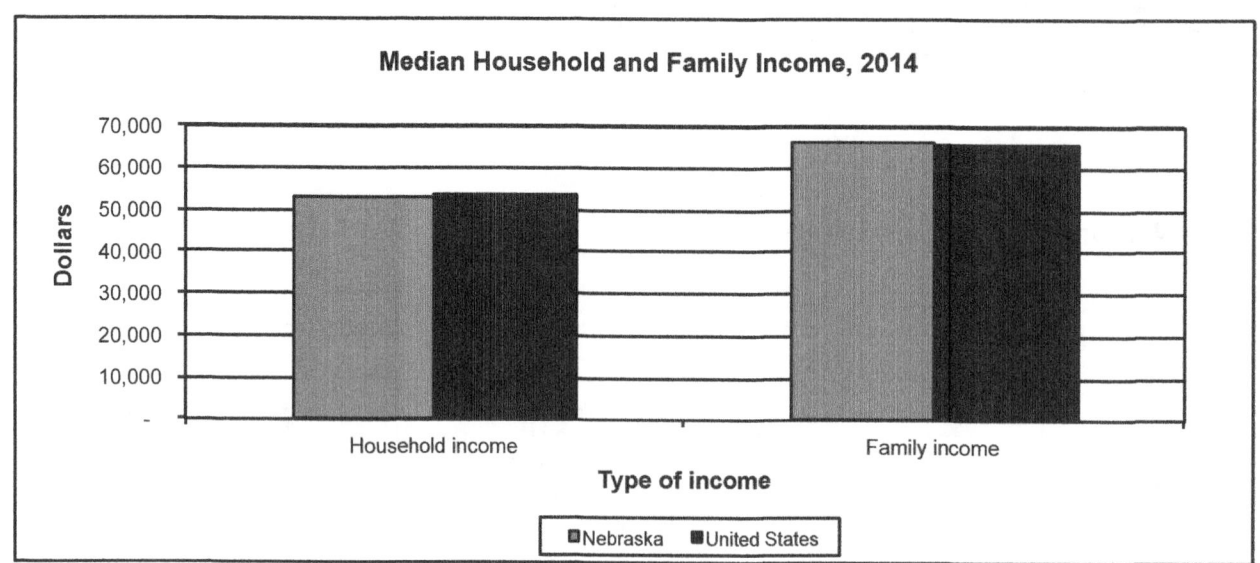

Table NE-6. Health Insurance Coverage Status for the Civilian Noninstitutionalized Population and Children Under 18 Years of Age

(Numbers in thousands, percent.)

Item	2006	2007	2008	2009	2010	2011	2012	2013	2014
Civilian Noninstitutionalized Population	1,767	1,753	1,750	1,763	1,802	1,814	1,827	1,841	1,854
Covered by Private or Public Insurance									
Number..	1,549	1,522	1,555	1,553	1,594	1,607	1,621	1,632	1,674
Percent..	87.7	86.8	88.9	88.1	88.5	88.6	88.7	88.7	90.3
Not Covered									
Number..	217	232	195	210	208	207	206	209	179
Percent..	12.3	13.2	11.1	11.9	11.5	11.4	11.3	11.3	9.7
Percent in the U.S. not covered..................................	15.8	15.3	15.1	15.1	15.5	15.1	14.8	14.5	11.7
Children Under 18 Years of Age	444	452	445	445	459	459	461	463	467
Covered by Private or Public Insurance									
Number..	399	407	414	417	433	432	433	437	442
Percent..	89.9	90.0	93.0	93.7	94.4	94.1	94.0	94.5	94.7
Not Covered									
Number..	45	45	31	28	26	27	28	25	25
Percent..	10.1	10.0	7.0	6.3	5.6	5.9	6.0	5.5	5.3
Percent in the U.S. not covered..................................	11.7	11.0	9.7	8.6	8.0	7.5	7.2	7.1	6.0

Table NE-7. Employment Status by Demographic Group, 2015

(Numbers in thousands, percent.)

Characteristic	Civilian noninstitutional population	Civilian labor force		Employed		Unemployed	
		Number	Percent of population	Number	Percent of population	Number	Percent of population
Total..	1,446	999	69.1	969	67.0	30	3.0
Sex							
Male..	711	528	74.2	510	71.8	17	3.3
Female...	735	471	64.1	458	62.3	13	2.8
Race, Sex, and Hispanic Origin							
White...	1,304	908	69.6	884	67.8	24	2.6
Male..	638	478	74.9	465	72.9	13	2.7
Female...	666	429	64.5	418	62.8	11	2.5
Black or African American...............	60	42	70.0	40	66.3	2	5.3
Male..	NA	NA	NA	NA	NA	NA	NA
Female...	NA	NA	NA	NA	NA	NA	NA
Hispanic or Latino ethnicity[1].........	135	102	75.1	96	71.3	5	5.0
Male..	68	58	84.3	54	79.2	3	5.9
Female...	67	44	65.7	42	63.2	2	3.8
Age							
16 to 19 years.................................	94	45	47.6	40	42.9	4	9.8
20 to 24 years.................................	143	112	78.4	106	74.4	6	5.2
25 to 34 years.................................	247	209	84.7	204	82.6	5	2.5
35 to 44 years.................................	224	190	84.7	184	82.3	5	2.7
45 to 54 years.................................	242	210	86.8	206	85.0	4	2.1
55 to 64 years.................................	230	170	74.0	166	72.4	4	2.2
65 years and over............................	267	63	23.6	62	23.1	1	2.2

NOTE: Data in Table 7 are from the Current Population Survey (CPS) and do not match the estimates in Table 8. See notes and definitions for further information.
NA = Not available.
[1]May be of any race.

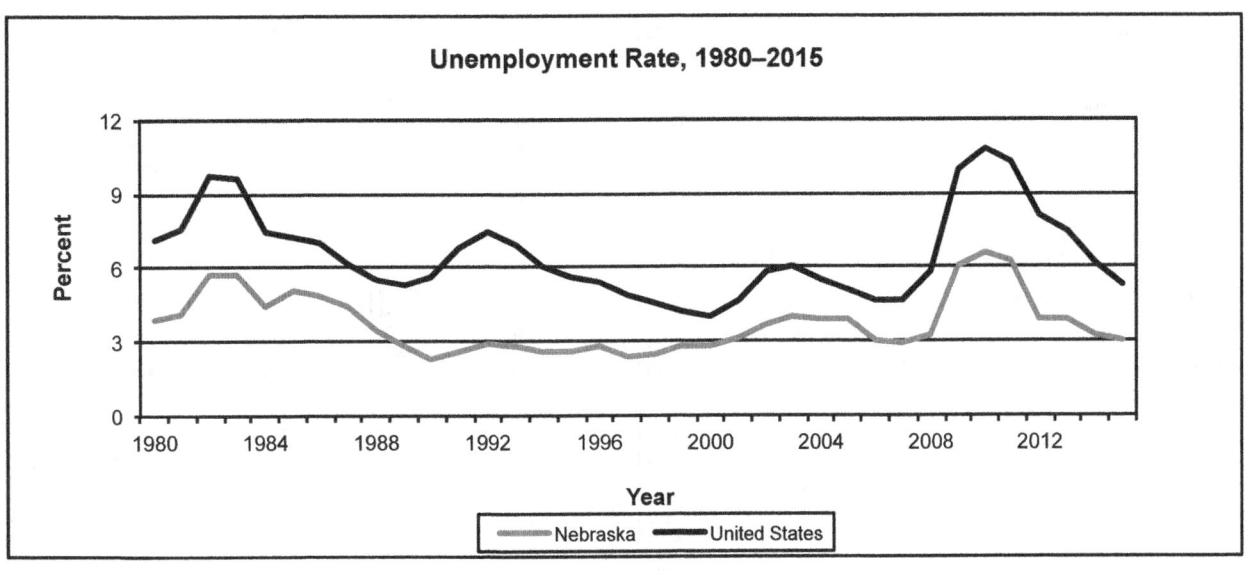

Unemployment Rate, 1980–2015

Table NE-8. Employment Status of the Civilian Noninstitutional Population Age 16 Years and Over

(Number, percent.)

Year	Civilian labor force	Civilian participation rate	Employed	Unemployed	Unemployment rate
2007..	978,763	72.9	949,494	29,269	3.0
2008..	989,757	73.2	956,759	32,998	3.3
2009..	991,583	72.7	945,648	45,935	4.6
2010..	993,398	71.6	947,360	46,038	4.6
2011..	1,003,256	71.6	959,059	44,197	4.4
2012..	1,015,555	71.9	975,032	40,523	4.0
2013..	1,019,345	71.6	980,779	38,566	3.8
2014..	1,013,899	70.7	980,833	33,066	3.3
2015..	1,012,973	70.1	982,707	30,266	3.0

Table NE-9. Employment and Average Wages by Industry

(Estimates through 2010 are based on the 2007 North American Industry Classification System [NAICS]. Estimates from 2011 onward are based on the 2012 NAICS.)

Industry	2008	2009	2010	2011	2012	2013	2014
	Number of jobs						
Wage and Salary Employment by Industry..................	994,614	974,841	972,094	977,551	982,608	1,002,080	1,015,901
Farm Wage and Salary Employment..........................	10,149	11,549	13,017	13,457	10,154	12,271	12,153
Nonfarm Wage and Salary Employment....................	984,465	963,292	959,077	964,094	972,454	989,809	1,003,748
Private wage and salary employment...........................	811,170	787,107	782,045	789,051	798,253	816,370	829,444
Forestry, fishing, and related activities.........................	4,156	4,398	4,634	4,958	5,015	5,896	6,045
Mining...	982	938	940	1,022	1,125	1,043	1,130
Utilities...	1,850	1,918	1,656	1,627	1,605	1,290	1,264
Construction..	51,148	48,453	43,653	42,634	43,637	45,825	47,657
Manufacturing...	101,599	93,466	91,740	93,723	95,232	96,568	97,534
Durable goods manufacturing............................	49,371	42,697	41,435	42,786	44,013	44,994	45,886
Nondurable goods manufacturing.......................	52,228	50,769	50,305	50,937	51,219	51,574	51,648
Wholesale trade	42,354	41,593	40,945	41,178	41,529	42,158	43,165
Retail trade...	109,204	106,159	106,114	106,433	106,547	107,458	109,049
Transportation and warehousing..........................	54,573	51,764	51,086	51,873	52,481	52,627	53,117
Information...	18,847	17,520	16,984	17,190	17,217	17,208	17,056
Finance and insurance.......................................	56,076	55,107	55,283	55,227	55,545	55,754	56,667
Real estate and rental and leasing.......................	9,648	9,434	9,398	9,309	9,067	9,287	9,353
Professional, scientific, and technical services..............	43,687	43,063	43,570	43,950	45,152	44,494	44,433
Management of companies and enterprises................	16,948	17,164	17,150	16,678	16,702	19,335	20,410
Administrative and waste services........................	46,263	41,816	41,965	43,251	45,432	46,813	49,009
Educational services...	17,625	18,087	18,292	18,621	18,636	18,176	18,433
Health care and social assistance...........................	108,710	109,967	111,811	113,518	115,202	122,047	123,241
Arts, entertainment, and recreation........................	12,822	12,906	12,413	12,583	13,017	13,454	13,770
Accommodation and food services.........................	70,762	69,637	69,497	70,316	71,758	73,015	73,865
Other services, except public administration..................	43,916	43,717	44,914	44,960	43,354	43,922	44,246
Government and government enterprises..........................	173,295	176,185	177,032	175,043	174,201	173,439	174,304
	Dollars						
Average Wages and Salaries by Industry	37,942	38,153	38,782	39,869	41,268	41,662	42,747
Average Farm Wages and Salaries	50,981	44,552	35,511	39,151	41,227	44,493	45,009
Average Nonfarm Wages and Salaries	37,808	38,076	38,826	39,879	41,268	41,627	42,720
Average private wages and salaries...........................	37,546	37,643	38,325	39,359	40,901	41,194	42,331
Forestry, fishing, and related activities.........................	21,497	20,949	20,996	23,760	24,749	25,631	26,643
Mining...	44,410	43,762	45,790	48,119	52,144	52,407	53,389
Utilities...	125,026	96,752	88,457	90,972	92,103	86,304	111,399
Construction..	41,048	41,802	41,735	42,097	43,808	44,266	46,640
Manufacturing...	42,117	41,983	43,695	44,641	45,593	45,727	47,348
Durable goods manufacturing............................	44,108	44,151	46,140	48,043	48,525	48,861	50,484
Nondurable goods manufacturing.......................	40,235	40,160	41,681	41,783	43,073	42,993	44,562
Wholesale trade	50,131	49,940	51,243	52,832	55,539	56,209	58,684
Retail trade...	23,069	23,133	23,859	24,064	25,064	25,173	25,653
Transportation and warehousing..........................	48,770	47,360	48,605	51,136	51,825	54,305	53,963
Information...	51,032	50,677	51,205	54,084	55,238	56,400	57,498
Finance and insurance.......................................	52,598	52,848	54,850	57,359	59,873	61,511	62,838
Real estate and rental and leasing.......................	32,267	32,310	32,817	34,225	36,216	37,398	39,118
Professional, scientific, and technical services..............	56,601	57,806	58,533	59,706	62,565	60,892	61,974
Management of companies and enterprises................	79,706	78,977	78,708	80,953	90,716	92,417	95,643
Administrative and waste services........................	28,341	29,233	29,039	30,080	31,654	32,422	34,237
Educational services...	29,585	29,820	30,312	30,479	31,172	30,316	29,457
Health care and social assistance...........................	39,140	39,857	40,084	41,068	42,173	41,060	41,576
Arts, entertainment, and recreation........................	16,663	16,825	17,683	18,106	18,437	18,761	19,205
Accommodation and food services.........................	13,516	13,628	14,152	14,607	15,154	15,181	15,980
Other services, except public administration..................	25,181	25,518	26,120	26,637	28,102	28,476	29,581
Government and government enterprises..........................	39,033	40,012	41,041	42,225	42,952	43,666	44,570

Table NE-10. Employment Characteristics by Family Type

(Number, percent.)

Family type and labor force status	2012 Total	2012 Families with own children under 18 years	2013 Total	2013 Families with own children under 18 years	2014 Total	2014 Families with own children under 18 years
All Families..	474,564	216,935	475,000	212,719	479,357	217,321
FAMILY TYPE AND LABOR FORCE STATUS						
Married-Couple Families...............................	369,338	150,038	372,805	149,660	370,736	150,724
Both husband and wife in labor force..................	61.9	76.2	59.7	73.1	61.9	76.1
Husband in labor force, wife not in labor force........	17.7	20.3	18.6	23.0	16.9	20.4
Wife in labor force, husband not in labor force........	6.6	2.5	6.9	2.6	6.4	2.8
Both husband and wife not in labor force..............	13.8	1.1	14.4	1.1	14.8	0.8
Other Families	105,226	66,897	102,195	63,059	108,621	66,597
Female householder, no husband present..............	69.8	71.3	69.9	72.8	71.8	74.6
In labor force..	55.6	62.5	53.7	63.2	57.3	66.1
Not in labor force.......................................	14.2	8.8	16.2	9.7	14.5	8.6
Male householder, no wife present.....................	30.2	28.7	30.1	27.2	28.2	25.4
In labor force..	26.7	27.7	25.9	25.9	24.4	23.8
Not in labor force.......................................	3.4	1.0	4.2	1.3	3.7	1.5

Table NE-11. School Enrollment and Educational Attainment, 2014

(Number, percent.)

Item	State	U.S.
Enrollment		
Total population 3 years and over, enrolled in school................	501,598	82,063,714
Enrolled in nursery school or preschool (percent)	6.1	6.0
Enrolled in kindergarten (percent)...................................	5.1	5.1
Enrolled in elementary school, grades 1-8 (percent).................	41.4	40.2
Enrolled in high school, grades 9-12 (percent)	20.1	20.7
Enrolled in college or graduate school (percent)....................	27.3	28.0
Attainment		
Total population 25 years and over	1,224,701	213,725,624
Less than ninth grade (percent)......................................	4.3	5.6
9th to 12th grade, no diploma (percent)	5.4	7.5
High school graduate, including equivalency (percent)...............	27.2	27.7
Some college, no degree (percent)	23.1	21.0
Associate's degree (percent)	10.4	8.2
Bachelor's degree (percent)	20.2	18.7
Graduate or professional degree (percent)...........................	9.3	11.4
High school graduate or higher (percent)	90.3	86.9
Bachelor's degree or higher (percent)	29.5	30.1

Table NE-12. Public School Characteristics and Educational Indicators

(Number, percent; data derived from National Center of Education Statistics.)

Item	State	U.S.
Public Schools, 2013–2014 (except where noted)		
Number of school districts...	287	18,194
Number of schools...	1,102	98,271
Number of students (in thousands)	308	50,045
Number of teachers (in thousands)	22	3,114
Student-teacher ratio..	13.7	16.1
Expenditures per student (dollars), FY 2013.........................	11,743	107,637
Four-year adjusted cohort graduation rate (ACGR)[1,2]	89.7	82.3
Students eligible for free or reduced-price lunch (in thousands)	138	25,596
English language learners (in thousands)	15	4,461
Students age 3 to 21 served under IDEA, part B (in thousands)	47	6,464

Public Schools by Type	Number	Percent of state public schools
Total number of schools..	1,102	100.0
Regular...	1,024	92.9
Special education..	26	2.4
Vocational education...	0	-
Alternative education..	52	4.7

NOTE: Every school is assigned only one school type based on its instructional emphasis.
- =Zero or rounds to zero.
[1]ACGR data represents a new method of calculating high-school completion rates and may not be comparable to previous years' data for Averaged Freshmen Graduation Rates (AFGR).
[2]The United States 4-year ACGRs were estimated using both the reported 4-year ACGR data from 49 states and the District of Columbia and using imputed data for Idaho. The estimate for American Indian/Alaska Native students also includes imputed data for Virginia.

Table NE-13. Reported Voting and Registration of the Voting-Age Population, November 2014

(Numbers in thousands, percent.)

Item	Total population	Total citizen population	Registered			Voted		
			Total registered	Percent registered (total population)	Percent registered (total citizen population)	Total voted	Percent voted (total population)	Percent voted (total citizen population)
U.S. Total	239,874	219,941	142,166	59.3	64.6	92,251	38.5	41.9
State Total.............................	1,400	1,306	873	62.4	66.9	579	41.4	44.3
Sex								
Male...	688	635	415	60.3	65.3	286	41.6	45.1
Female	712	671	459	64.4	68.3	293	41.1	43.6
Race								
White alone................................	1,295	1,222	826	63.8	67.6	552	42.6	45.2
White, non-Hispanic alone	1,165	1,160	803	69.0	69.2	541	46.5	46.6
Black alone................................	55	53	36	(B)	(B)	21	(B)	(B)
Asian alone	22	7	3	(B)	(B)	-	(B)	(B)
Hispanic (of any race)......................	135	65	26	(B)	(B)	13	(B)	(B)
White alone or in combination	1,306	1,232	830	63.6	67.4	555	42.5	45.0
Black alone or in combination..........	65	62	36	(B)	(B)	21	(B)	(B)
Asian alone or in combination..........	22	7	3	(B)	(B)	-	(B)	(B)
Age								
18 to 24 years.............................	180	166	76	42.3	45.8	26	14.4	15.5
25 to 34 years.............................	265	237	124	46.7	52.3	68	25.7	28.8
35 to 44 years.............................	219	191	130	59.3	68.1	79	35.9	41.3
45 to 64 years.............................	457	438	322	70.4	73.6	232	50.8	53.1
65 years and over.........................	278	275	221	79.5	80.6	174	62.6	63.4

B = Base is less than 75,000 and therefore too small to show the derived measure.
- = Zero or rounds to zero.

Table NE-14. Crime

(Number, rate per 100,000. Data are derived from the FBI Uniform Crime Reports.)

Item	State			U.S.[1,2,3,4]		
	2013	2014	Percent change	2013	2014	Percent change
TOTAL POPULATION[5]......................	1,868,516	1,881,503	0.7	316,128,839	318,857,056	0.9
VIOLENT CRIME						
Number.....................................	4,712	5,275	11.9	1,163,146	1,165,383	0.2
Rate	252.2	280.4	11.2	367.9	365.5	-0.7
Murder and Nonnegligent Manslaughter						
Number.....................................	57	54	-5.3	14,196	14,249	0.4
Rate	3.1	2.9	-6.5	4.5	4.5	-
Rape[6]						
Number.....................................	801	862	X	108,612	116,645	X
Rate	42.9	45.8	X	34.4	36.6	X
Robbery						
Number.....................................	1,040	1,043	0.3	345,031	325,802	-5.6
Rate	55.7	55.4	-0.5	109.1	102.2	-6.3
Aggravated Assault						
Number.....................................	2,999	3,316	10.6	724,149	741,291	2.4
Rate	160.5	176.2	9.8	229.1	232.5	1.5
PROPERTY CRIME						
Number.....................................	49,018	47,479	-3.1	8,632,512	8,277,829	-4.1
Rate	2,623.4	2,523.5	-3.8	2,730.7	2,596.1	-4.9
Burglary						
Number.....................................	8,900	7,950	-10.7	1,928,465	1,729,806	-10.3
Rate	476.3	422.5	-11.3	610.0	542.5	-11.1
Larceny-Theft						
Number.....................................	35,655	35,074	-1.6	6,004,453	5,858,496	-2.4
Rate	1,908.2	1,864.1	-2.3	1,899.4	1,837.3	-3.3
Motor Vehicle Theft						
Number.....................................	4,463	4,455	-0.2	699,594	689,527	-1.4
Rate	238.9	236.8	-0.9	221.3	216.2	-2.3

NOTE: Although arson data are included in the trend and clearance tables, sufficient data are not available to estimate totals for this offense. Therefore, no arson data are published in this table.
X = Not applicable.
- = Zero or rounds to zero.
[1]The crime figures have been adjusted.
[2]The data collection methodology for the offense of forcible rape used by the Minnesota state Uniform Crime Reporting (UCR) Program (with the exception of Minneapolis and St. Paul, Minnesota) does not comply with national UCR Program guidelines. Consequently, its figures for forcible rape and violent crime (of which forcible rape is a part) are not published in this table.
[3]Includes offenses reported by the Zoological Police and the Metro Transit Police.
[4]Because of changes in the state's reporting practices, figures are not comparable to previous years' data.
[5]Populations are U.S. Census Bureau provisional estimates as of July 1 of each year.
[6]The figures shown for the offense of rape were estimated using the revised Uniform Crime Reporting (UCR) definition of rape.

Table NE-15. State Government Finances, 2014

(Dollar amounts in thousands, percent distribution.)

Item	Dollars	Percent distribution
Total Revenue	12,112,397	100.0
General revenue	9,778,806	80.7
Intergovernmental revenue	3,094,850	25.6
Taxes	4,877,401	40.3
General sales	1,763,695	14.6
Selective sales	540,257	4.5
License taxes	126,745	1.0
Individual income tax	2,124,164	17.5
Corporate income tax	306,591	2.5
Other taxes	15,949	0.1
Current charges	1,069,688	8.8
Miscellaneous general revenue	736,867	6.1
Utility revenue	0	-
Liquor stores revenue	0	-
Insurance trust revenue[1]	2,333,591	19.3
Total Expenditure	10,046,378	100.0
Intergovernmental expenditure	2,202,196	21.9
Direct expenditure	7,844,182	78.1
Current operation	6,134,008	61.1
Capital outlay	775,685	7.7
Insurance benefits and repayments	693,672	6.9
Assistance and subsidies	178,715	1.8
Interest on debt	62,102	0.6
Exhibit: Salaries and wages	2,456,174	24.4
Total Expenditure	10,046,378	100.0
General expenditure	9,352,706	93.1
Intergovernmental expenditure	2,202,196	21.9
Direct expenditure	7,150,510	71.2
General expenditure, by function:		
Education	3,412,086	34.0
Public welfare	2,639,034	26.3
Hospitals	261,995	2.6
Health	473,954	4.7
Highways	742,236	7.4
Police protection	82,128	0.8
Correction	280,999	2.8
Natural resources	277,899	2.8
Parks and recreation	44,585	0.4
Governmental administration	205,585	2.0
Interest on general debt	62,102	0.6
Other and unallocable	870,103	8.7
Utility expenditure	0	-
Liquor stores expenditure	0	-
Insurance trust expenditure	693,672	6.9
Debt at End of Fiscal Year	1,908,707	X
Cash and Security Holdings	19,245,806	X

X = Not applicable.
- = Zero or rounds to zero.

[1]Within insurance trust revenue, net earnings of state retirement systems is a calculated statistic (the item code in the data file is X08), and thus can be positive or negative. Net earnings is the sum of earnings on investments plus gains on investments minus losses on investments. The change made in 2002 for asset valuation from book to market value in accordance with Statement 34 of the Governmental Accounting Standards Board is reflected in the calculated statistics.

Table NE-16. State Government Tax Collections, 2014

(Dollars in thousands, percent.)

Item	Dollars	Percent distribution
Total Taxes	4,877,401	100.0
Property taxes	143	-
Sales and gross receipts	2,303,952	47.2
General sales and gross receipts	1,763,695	36.2
Selective sales and gross receipts	540,257	11.1
Alcoholic beverages	30,258	0.6
Amusements	5,342	0.1
Insurance premiums	42,746	0.9
Motor fuels	335,153	6.9
Pari-mutuels	143	-
Public utilities	53,009	1.1
Tobacco products	63,425	1.3
Other selective sales	10,181	0.2
Licenses	126,745	2.6
Alcoholic beverages	1,475	-
Amusements	1,290	-
Corporations in general	2,123	-
Hunting and fishing	13,576	0.3
Motor vehicle	92,600	1.9
Motor vehicle operators	6,062	0.1
Public utilities	0	-
Occupation and business, NEC	9,619	0.2
Other licenses	0	-
Income taxes	2,430,755	49.8
Individual income	2,124,164	43.6
Corporation net income	306,591	6.3
Other taxes	15,806	0.3
Death and gift	0	-
Documentary and stock transfer	9,044	0.2
Severance	6,762	0.1
Taxes, NEC	0	-

- = Zero or rounds to zero.

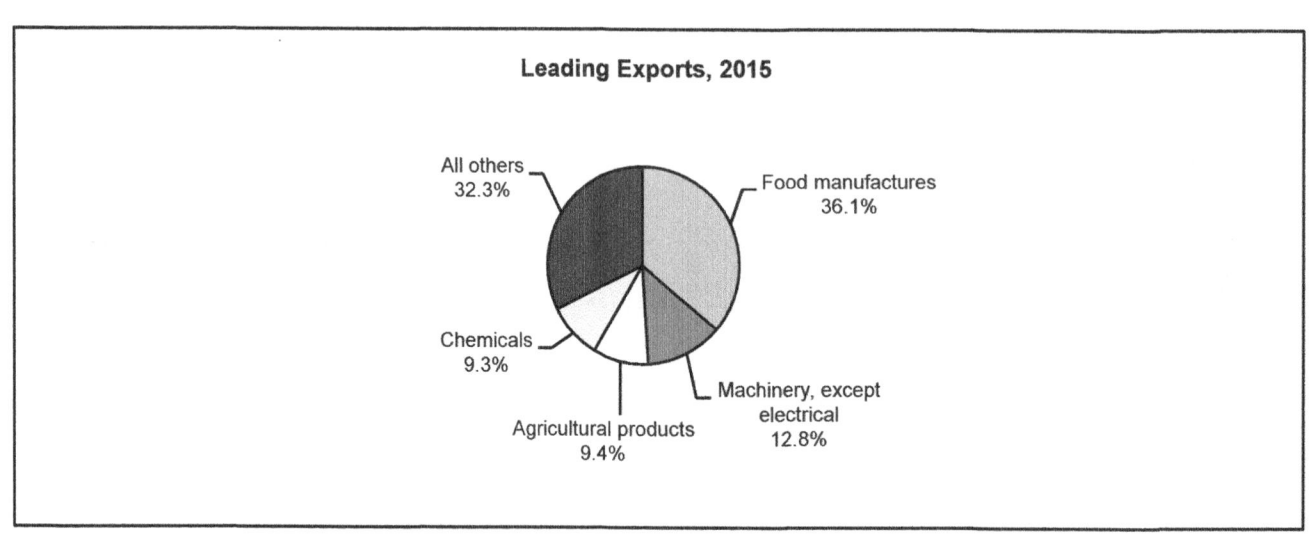

Leading Exports, 2015

All others 32.3%
Food manufactures 36.1%
Machinery, except electrical 12.8%
Agricultural products 9.4%
Chemicals 9.3%

Facts and Figures

Location: Western United States; bordered on the N by Oregon and Idaho, on the E by Utah and Arizona, on the S by Arizona and California, and on the W by California

Area: 110,561 sq. mi. (286,351 sq. km.); rank—7th

Population: 2,890,845 (2015 est.); rank—35th

Principal Cities: capital—Carson City; largest—Las Vegas

Statehood: October 31, 1864; 36th state

U.S. Congress: 2 senators, 4 representatives

State Motto: All for Our Country

State Song: "Home Means Nevada"

State Nicknames: The Silver State; The Sagebrush State

Abbreviations: NV; Nev.

State Symbols: flower—sagebrush; tree—single-leaf piñon and bristlecone pine; bird—mountain bluebird

At a Glance

- With an increase in population of 6.9 percent, Nevada ranked 7th among the states in growth from 2010 to 2015.

- In 2015, 6.7 percent of Nevadans were unemployed, compared to 5.3 percent of the total U.S. population.

- Nevada's violent crime rate in 2014 was 635.6 per 100,000 population, which ranked 3rd among the states. The national violent crime rate was 365.5 per 100,000 population.

- Approximately 28.1 percent of Nevadans self-identified their ethnicity as "Hispanic or Latino" in 2015, the 5th highest percentage in the country.

Table NV-1. Population by Age, Sex, Race, and Hispanic Origin

(Number, percent, except where noted.)

Sex, age, race, and Hispanic origin	2000	2010	2015[1]	Average annual percent change, 2010–2015
Total Population	1,998,257	2,700,551	2,890,845	0.5
Percent of total U.S. population	0.7	0.9	0.9	X
Sex				
Male	1,018,051	1,363,616	1,450,551	0.4
Female	980,206	1,336,935	1,440,294	0.5
Age				
Under 5 years	145,817	187,478	176,617	-0.4
5 to 19 years	415,684	548,850	557,048	0.1
20 to 64 years	1,217,827	1,639,864	1,735,062	0.4
65 years and over	218,929	324,359	422,118	1.9
Median age (years)	35.0	36.3	37.7	0.3
Race and Hispanic Origin				
One race				
White	1,501,886	2,106,494	2,187,769	0.3
Black	135,477	231,224	268,042	1.1
American Indian and Alaska Native	26,420	42,965	47,610	0.7
Asian	90,266	203,478	246,974	1.4
Native Hawaiian or Other Pacific Islander	8,426	19,307	21,876	0.9
Two or more races	76,428	97,083	118,574	1.4
Hispanic (of any race)	393,970	741,200	813,391	0.7

X = Not applicable.
[1]Population figures for 2015 are July 1 estimates. The 2010 estimates are taken from the 2010 Census.

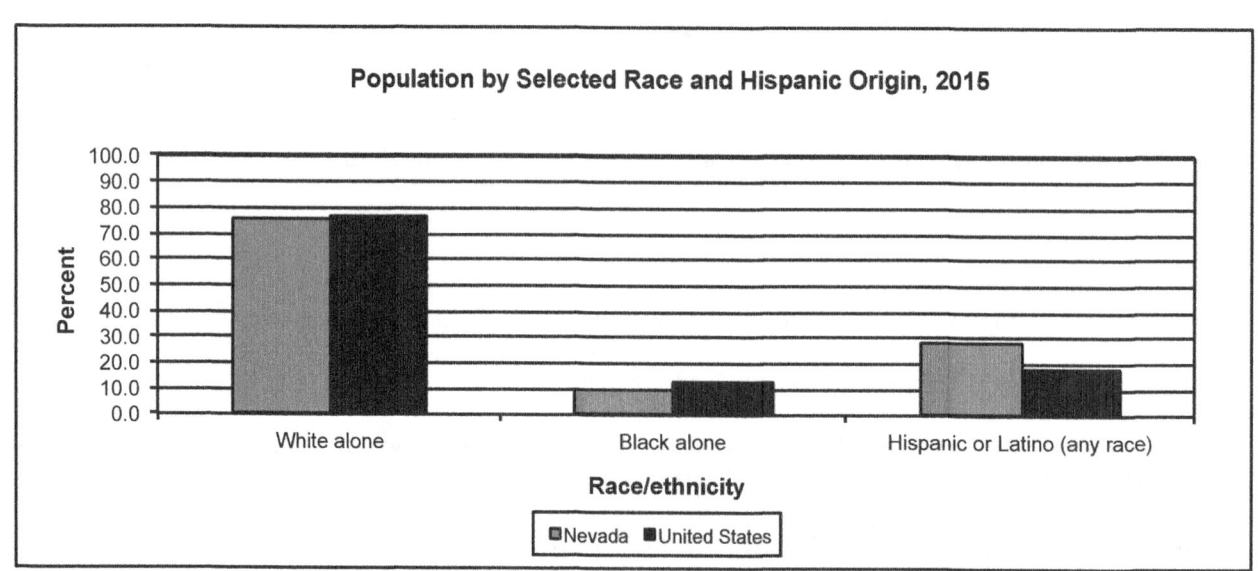

Table NV-2. Marital Status

(Number, percent distribution.)

Sex, age, race, and Hispanic origin	2000	2010	2014
Males, 15 Years and Over	792,317	1,081,514	1,109,661
Never married	28.8	35.0	35.6
Now married, except separated	53.8	47.6	46.9
Separated	2.0	2.0	2.0
Widowed	2.5	2.9	2.5
Divorced	12.9	12.5	13.0
Females, 15 Years and Over	771,263	1,069,123	1,102,036
Never married	20.9	27.2	28.4
Now married, except separated	53.1	47.2	45.9
Separated	2.7	2.8	2.8
Widowed	8.6	8.0	7.9
Divorced	14.7	14.8	14.9

Table NV-3. Households and Housing Characteristics

(Number, percent, dollars.)

Item	2000	2010	2014	Average annual percent change, 2000–2014
Total Households...	751,165	989,811	1,021,519	2.6
Family households	498,333	639,686	642,461	2.1
Married-couple family	373,201	452,361	447,162	1.4
Other family	125,132	187,325	195,299	4.0
Male householder, no wife present............................	41,650	63,327	67,405	4.4
Female householder, no husband present.....................	83,482	123,998	127,894	3.8
Nonfamily households	252,832	350,125	379,058	3.6
Householder living alone	186,745	266,232	298,089	4.3
Householder not living alone	66,087	83,893	80,969	1.6
Housing Characteristics				
Total housing units	827,457	1,175,070	1,198,969	3.2
Occupied housing units	751,165	989,811	1,021,519	2.6
Owner occupied	457,247	565,869	547,905	1.4
Renter occupied	293,918	423,942	473,614	4.4
Average household size..	2.62	2.70	2.74	0.3
Financial Characteristics				
Median gross rent of renter-occupied housing	699	952	955	2.6
Median monthly owner costs for housing units with a mortgage	1,190	1,638	1,331	0.8
Median value of owner-occupied housing units..............	142,000	174,800	192,100	2.5

Table NV-4. Migration, Origin, and Language

(Number, percent.)

Characteristic	State			U.S.		
	2013	2014	Percent change	2013	2014	Percent change
Residence 1 Year Ago						
Population 1 year and over	2,757,365	2,806,170	1.8	312,432,820	315,095,393	0.9
Same house	78.6	79.7	X	85.0	85.1	X
Different house in the U.S.	20.8	19.8	X	14.4	14.3	X
Same county	15.2	14.4	X	8.9	8.7	X
Different county	5.6	5.5	X	5.5	5.6	X
Same state	1.0	0.8	X	3.2	3.3	X
Different state	4.6	4.6	X	2.3	2.3	X
Abroad	0.6	0.5	X	0.6	0.6	X
Place of Birth						
Native born	2,260,972	2,287,377	1.2	274,780,773	276,465,262	0.6
Male	50.8	51.1	X	49.3	49.3	X
Female	49.2	48.9	X	50.7	50.7	X
Foreign born	529,164	551,722	4.3	41,348,066	42,391,794	2.5
Male	47.9	46.9	X	48.8	48.7	X
Female	52.1	53.1	X	51.2	51.3	X
Foreign born; naturalized U.S. citizen	250,949	249,730	-0.5	19,294,710	19,984,738	3.6
Male	46.2	43.1	X	45.9	45.9	X
Female	53.8	56.9	X	54.1	54.1	X
Foreign born; not a U.S. citizen	278,215	301,992	8.5	22,053,356	22,407,056	1.6
Male	49.5	50.1	X	51.3	51.2	X
Female	50.5	49.9	X	48.7	48.8	X
Entered 2010 or later	5.8	8.9	X	9.7	12.3	X
Entered 2000 to 2009	28.8	28.6	X	29.4	28.6	X
Entered before 2000...	65.4	62.5	X	61.0	59.1	X
World Region of Birth, Foreign						
Foreign-born population, excluding population born at sea	529,164	551,722	4.3	41,347,945	42,390,705	2.5
Europe	8.0	7	X	11.6	11.2	X
Asia	30.6	30.5	X	29.5	30.1	X
Africa	3.0	2.7	X	4.4	4.6	X
Oceania	0.4	0.7	X	0.5	0.6	X
Latin America	56.0	57.4	X	51.9	51.6	X
North America	2.0	1.7	X	2.0	1.9	X
Language Spoken at Home and Ability to Speak English						
Population 5 years and over......................................	2,612,849	2,663,364	1.9	296,358,760	299,084,046	0.9
English only	69.7	69.3	X	79.2	78.9	X
Language other than English....................................	30.3	30.7	X	20.8	21.1	X
Speaks English less than "very well"........................	11.6	12.3	X	8.5	8.6	X

X = Not applicable.
- = Zero or rounds to zero.

Table NV-5. Median Income and Poverty Status, 2014

(Number, percent, except as noted.)

Characteristic	State		U.S.	
	Number	Percent	Number	Percent
Median Income				
Households (dollars)...	51,450	X	53,657	X
Families (dollars)	60,824	X	65,910	X
Below Poverty Level (All People)	426,730	15.2	48,208,387	15.5
Sex				
Male......................	200,900	14.4	21,590,918	14.2
Female	225,830	16.1	26,617,469	16.8
Age				
Under 18 years......................	143,621	22.0	15,686,012	21.7
Related children under 18 years......................	141,644	21.7	15,372,705	21.3
18 to 64 years	250,428	14.3	28,267,482	14.6
65 years and over	32,681	8.3	4,254,893	9.5

X = Not applicable.

Median Household and Family Income, 2014

Table NV-6. Health Insurance Coverage Status for the Civilian Noninstitutionalized Population and Children Under 18 Years of Age

(Numbers in thousands, percent.)

Item	2006	2007	2008	2009	2010	2011	2012	2013	2014
Civilian Noninstitutionalized Population	2,535	2,568	2,568	2,610	2,669	2,687	2,724	2,757	2,806
Covered by Private or Public Insurance									
Number...	2,039	2,126	2,020	2,038	2,065	2,098	2,121	2,187	2,379
Percent...	80.4	82.8	78.7	78.1	77.4	78.1	77.8	79.3	84.8
Not Covered									
Number...	496	441	548	572	604	589	603	570	427
Percent...	19.6	17.2	21.3	21.9	22.6	21.9	22.2	20.7	15.2
Percent in the U.S. not covered...	15.8	15.3	15.1	15.1	15.5	15.1	14.8	14.5	11.7
Children Under 18 Years of Age	649	660	667	682	664	662	663	661	662
Covered by Private or Public Insurance									
Number...	527	566	532	561	549	155	553	563	598
Percent...	81.2	85.7	79.8	82.2	82.6	83.8	83.4	85.1	90.4
Not Covered									
Number...	122	94	135	121	115	107	110	99	64
Percent...	18.8	14.3	20.2	17.8	17.4	16.2	16.6	14.9	9.6
Percent in the U.S. not covered...	11.7	11.0	9.7	8.6	8.0	7.5	7.2	7.1	6.0

Table NV-7. Employment Status by Demographic Group, 2015

(Numbers in thousands, percent.)

Characteristic	Civilian noninstitutional population	Civilian labor force		Employed		Unemployed	
		Number	Percent of population	Number	Percent of population	Number	Percent of population
Total..	2,247	1,429	63.6	1,331	59.2	98	6.9
Sex							
Male..........................	1,113	781	70.2	729	65.5	51	6.6
Female........................	1,134	648	57.2	601	53.0	47	7.2
Race, Sex, and Hispanic Origin							
White	1,684	1,063	63.1	998	59.3	65	6.1
Male............................	840	586	69.7	553	65.8	33	5.6
Female.........................	844	477	56.5	445	52.7	32	6.7
Black or African American....................	178	113	63.4	98	54.9	15	13.5
Male............................	86	54	62.6	45	52.8	9	15.7
Female.........................	92	59	64.1	52	56.8	7	11.4
Hispanic or Latino ethnicity[1]	571	417	73.0	384	67.2	33	8.0
Male............................	289	239	82.7	221	76.3	19	7.8
Female.........................	282	178	63.0	163	57.8	15	8.2
Age							
16 to 19 years	145	56	38.5	45	30.7	12	20.5
20 to 24 years	181	141	77.7	126	69.4	15	10.7
25 to 34 years	374	305	81.7	286	76.5	20	6.5
35 to 44 years	401	333	82.9	316	78.8	17	5.0
45 to 54 years	388	309	79.7	289	74.4	20	6.5
55 to 64 years	338	206	61.0	198	58.4	9	4.2
65 years and over	419	79	18.9	73	17.3	7	8.2

NOTE: Data in Table 7 are from the Current Population Survey (CPS) and do not match the estimates in Table 8. See notes and definitions for further information.
[1]May be of any race.

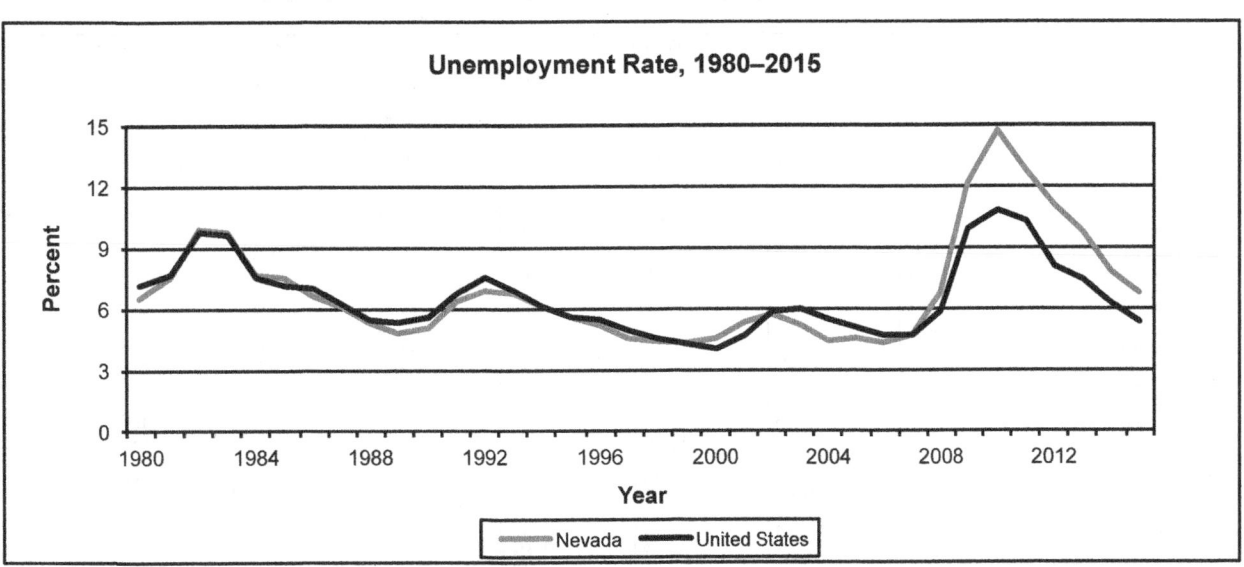

Table NV-8. Employment Status of the Civilian Noninstitutional Population Age 16 Years and Over

(Number, percent.)

Year	Civilian labor force	Civilian participation rate	Employed	Unemployed	Unemployment rate
2007..	1,330,396	68.6	1,270,572	59,824	4.5
2008..	1,363,574	69.0	1,272,187	91,387	6.7
2009..	1,349,299	67.5	1,196,758	152,541	11.3
2010..	1,358,578	65.9	1,174,774	183,804	13.5
2011..	1,373,115	65.5	1,194,264	178,851	13.0
2012..	1,378,094	64.6	1,224,315	153,779	11.2
2013..	1,385,312	63.9	1,252,872	132,440	9.6
2014..	1,401,801	63.4	1,291,040	110,761	7.9
2015..	1,425,711	63.2	1,329,552	96,159	6.7

Table NV-9. Employment and Average Wages by Industry

(Estimates through 2010 are based on the 2007 North American Industry Classification System [NAICS]. Estimates from 2011 onward are based on the 2012 NAICS.)

Industry	2008	2009	2010	2011	2012	2013	2014
				Number of jobs			
Wage and Salary Employment by Industry	1,305,162	1,188,773	1,158,863	1,166,183	1,181,659	1,209,426	1,252,830
Farm Wage and Salary Employment	2,085	2,009	2,130	1,949	1,935	2,140	2,106
Nonfarm Wage and Salary Employment	1,303,077	1,186,764	1,156,733	1,164,234	1,179,724	1,207,286	1,250,724
Private wage and salary employment	1,128,518	1,015,497	987,759	998,170	1,013,156	1,040,308	1,082,544
Forestry, fishing, and related activities	532	524	566	591	595	669	714
Mining	12,292	11,630	12,200	13,884	15,428	15,314	14,384
Utilities	4,585	4,571	4,325	4,188	4,037	3,965	3,884
Construction	121,218	84,657	62,103	54,921	53,620	58,944	65,155
Manufacturing	48,260	40,303	38,004	38,259	39,288	40,634	41,534
Durable goods manufacturing	33,001	26,805	24,810	24,693	25,121	25,683	25,768
Nondurable goods manufacturing	15,259	13,498	13,194	13,566	14,167	14,951	15,766
Wholesale trade	39,389	35,343	33,281	33,009	32,785	33,093	34,146
Retail trade	140,500	130,421	129,415	131,017	133,607	136,628	141,187
Transportation and warehousing	50,686	47,125	46,689	47,965	49,925	50,582	53,758
Information	15,097	13,208	12,549	12,560	12,838	12,859	13,724
Finance and insurance	36,495	33,728	32,258	31,754	32,266	33,073	33,428
Real estate and rental and leasing	27,062	23,748	22,627	22,547	22,359	23,400	24,189
Professional, scientific, and technical services	54,667	49,649	48,141	47,896	48,154	49,567	50,845
Management of companies and enterprises	18,246	17,895	18,267	18,086	19,582	20,216	20,910
Administrative and waste services	81,042	69,953	71,705	75,552	78,437	81,525	85,522
Educational services	8,560	8,950	9,652	9,928	9,856	9,702	10,262
Health care and social assistance	90,841	92,172	94,135	96,043	98,034	100,418	104,518
Arts, entertainment, and recreation	29,294	26,540	25,786	27,388	27,142	27,578	28,435
Accommodation and food services	306,354	283,937	285,722	291,193	291,642	298,154	309,398
Other services, except public administration	43,398	41,143	40,334	41,389	43,561	43,987	46,551
Government and government enterprises	174,559	171,267	168,974	166,064	166,568	166,978	168,180
				Dollars			
Average Wages and Salaries by Industry	44,019	43,596	43,637	44,375	44,915	45,356	46,018
Average Farm Wages and Salaries	34,128	39,325	32,224	36,539	31,457	42,606	44,269
Average Nonfarm Wages and Salaries	44,035	43,603	43,658	44,388	44,937	45,360	46,021
Average private wages and salaries	43,119	42,265	42,328	43,227	43,977	44,450	45,093
Forestry, fishing, and related activities	32,778	34,977	34,133	36,203	36,886	35,876	35,838
Mining	77,126	78,537	82,914	84,536	83,065	87,041	88,642
Utilities	87,670	87,856	89,942	94,683	96,358	107,144	103,153
Construction	57,676	58,683	55,475	53,130	52,114	51,443	52,628
Manufacturing	49,764	49,928	50,384	51,753	53,008	53,721	54,819
Durable goods manufacturing	53,895	54,173	54,952	56,747	58,730	60,372	61,861
Nondurable goods manufacturing	40,829	41,499	41,795	42,663	42,861	42,297	43,309
Wholesale trade	59,277	59,428	60,609	62,925	65,697	65,571	67,763
Retail trade	28,015	27,488	27,711	28,220	28,739	29,172	29,587
Transportation and warehousing	44,431	46,410	48,525	50,346	49,658	49,840	50,962
Information	53,834	55,084	55,526	56,871	58,115	58,421	59,473
Finance and insurance	56,266	55,461	57,152	59,342	62,172	65,327	66,992
Real estate and rental and leasing	39,693	38,795	39,244	40,159	40,823	42,027	43,636
Professional, scientific, and technical services	66,208	65,794	66,306	68,210	69,918	70,248	71,348
Management of companies and enterprises	116,522	99,353	102,450	110,820	116,696	121,122	120,646
Administrative and waste services	29,497	29,904	29,739	30,023	29,832	29,657	30,266
Educational services	34,912	35,875	36,122	35,797	35,398	37,344	37,346
Health care and social assistance	47,976	48,944	48,533	49,399	50,203	50,568	51,224
Arts, entertainment, and recreation	33,225	32,949	32,806	34,671	34,228	34,066	36,016
Accommodation and food services	33,805	32,123	33,345	34,616	35,144	35,206	35,754
Other services, except public administration	30,282	30,384	30,909	31,324	32,325	32,922	32,317
Government and government enterprises	49,959	51,540	51,433	51,365	50,772	51,031	51,994

Table NV-10. Employment Characteristics by Family Type

(Number, percent.)

Family type and labor force status	2012 Total	2012 Families with own children under 18 years	2013 Total	2013 Families with own children under 18 years	2014 Total	2014 Families with own children under 18 years
All Families.............................	650,833	298,464	639,825	286,895	640,193	278,290
FAMILY TYPE AND LABOR FORCE STATUS						
Married-Couple Families...........................	445,312	182,637	456,219	185,645	444,894	175,570
Both husband and wife in labor force............................	50.1	63.1	49.7	63.1	47.7	62.8
Husband in labor force, wife not in labor force	23.3	31.2	23.7	30.6	23.3	30.1
Wife in labor force, husband not in labor force	8.7	4.1	8.3	4.1	8.8	5.5
Both husband and wife not in labor force........................	17.9	1.5	17.8	2.0	20.1	1.7
Other Families	205,521	115,827	183,606	101,250	195,299	102,720
Female householder, no husband present........................	68.1	72.2	69.3	72.9	65.5	67.9
In labor force	51.1	59.6	52.1	61.5	49.8	57.0
Not in labor force	17.0	12.6	17.2	11.4	15.7	11.0
Male householder, no wife present........................	31.9	27.8	30.7	27.1	34.5	32.1
In labor force.......................	26.9	25.6	25.9	25.5	28.9	30.5
Not in labor force	5.0	2.2	4.9	1.6	5.6	1.6

Table NV-11. School Enrollment and Educational Attainment, 2014

(Number, percent.)

Item	State	U.S.
Enrollment		
Total population 3 years and over, enrolled in school.................	699,683	82,063,714
Enrolled in nursery school or preschool (percent)................	4.2	6.0
Enrolled in kindergarten (percent).........................	5.5	5.1
Enrolled in elementary school, grades 1-8 (percent).................	43.4	40.2
Enrolled in high school, grades 9-12 (percent)................	22.1	20.7
Enrolled in college or graduate school (percent)................	24.8	28.0
Attainment		
Total population 25 years and over	1,919,598	213,725,624
Less than ninth grade (percent)	6.1	5.6
9th to 12th grade, no diploma (percent)..................	8.8	7.5
High school graduate, including equivalency (percent)................	28.2	27.7
Some college, no degree (percent)	25.8	21.0
Associate's degree (percent).....................	8.1	8.2
Bachelor's degree (percent)......................	15.2	18.7
Graduate or professional degree (percent)........................	7.9	11.4
High school graduate or higher (percent)	85.1	86.9
Bachelor's degree or higher (percent).........................	23.1	30.1

Table NV-12. Public School Characteristics and Educational Indicators

(Number, percent; data derived from National Center of Education Statistics.)

Item	State	U.S.
Public Schools, 2013–2014 (except where noted)		
Number of school districts........................	19	18,194
Number of schools........................	653	98,271
Number of students (in thousands)	452	50,045
Number of teachers (in thousands)	22	3,114
Student-teacher ratio	20.6	16.1
Expenditures per student (dollars), FY 2013..........................	8,026	107,637
Four-year adjusted cohort graduation rate (ACGR)[1,2]	70.0	82.3
Students eligible for free or reduced-price lunch (in thousands)	239	25,596
English language learners (in thousands)	68	4,461
Students age 3 to 21 served under IDEA, part B (in thousands)	52	6,464

Public Schools by Type	Number	Percent of state public schools
Total number of schools....................	653	100.0
Regular	604	92.5
Special education......................	13	2.0
Vocational education....................	1	0.2
Alternative education......................	35	5.4

NOTE: Every school is assigned only one school type based on its instructional emphasis.
[1]ACGR data represents a new method of calculating high-school completion rates and may not be comparable to previous years' data for Averaged Freshmen Graduation Rates (AFGR).
[2]The United States 4-year ACGRs were estimated using both the reported 4-year ACGR data from 49 states and the District of Columbia and using imputed data for Idaho. The estimate for American Indian/Alaska Native students also includes imputed data for Virginia.

Table NV-13. Reported Voting and Registration of the Voting-Age Population, November 2014

(Numbers in thousands, percent.)

Item	Total population	Total citizen population	Registered			Voted		
			Total registered	Percent registered (total population)	Percent registered (total citizen population)	Total voted	Percent voted (total population)	Percent voted (total citizen population)
U.S. Total	239,874	219,941	142,166	59.3	64.6	92,251	38.5	41.9
State Total.............................	2,128	1,858	1,088	51.1	58.5	693	32.6	37.3
Sex								
Male.................................	1,055	924	524	49.7	56.7	348	33.0	37.6
Female	1,073	934	564	52.5	60.4	345	32.2	37.0
Race								
White alone.......................	1,571	1,388	846	53.8	61.0	573	36.5	41.3
White, non-Hispanic alone	1,143	1,106	690	60.4	62.4	488	42.7	44.1
Black alone........................	193	191	124	64.6	65.2	61	31.6	31.9
Asian alone	181	130	49	27.2	38.0	25	14.0	19.6
Hispanic (of any race)	527	351	189	35.9	53.9	97	18.4	27.6
White alone or in combination	1,626	1,424	862	53.0	60.5	585	36.0	41.1
Black alone or in combination..........	203	201	131	64.7	65.3	62	30.6	30.9
Asian alone or in combination..........	193	142	59	30.6	41.8	30	15.7	21.4
Age								
18 to 24 years.....................	245	233	98	39.9	41.8	42	17.3	18.1
25 to 34 years.....................	388	332	163	42.1	49.1	89	23.0	26.8
35 to 44 years.....................	379	310	176	46.4	56.7	91	23.9	29.3
45 to 64 years.....................	718	606	370	51.5	61.1	248	34.6	41.0
65 years and over	399	377	281	70.5	74.6	223	55.8	59.0

Table NV-14. Crime

(Number, rate per 100,000. Data are derived from the FBI Uniform Crime Reports.)

Item	State			U.S.[1,2,3,4]		
	2013	2014	Percent change	2013	2014	Percent change
TOTAL POPULATION[5]............................	2,790,136	2,839,099	1.8	316,128,839	318,857,056	0.9
VIOLENT CRIME						
Number..............................	16,496	18,045	9.4	1,163,146	1,165,383	0.2
Rate	591.2	635.6	7.5	367.9	365.5	-0.7
Murder and Nonnegligent Manslaughter						
Number..............................	163	170	4.3	14,196	14,249	0.4
Rate	5.8	6.0	3.4	4.5	4.5	-
Rape[6]						
Number..............................	1,418	1,357	X	108,612	116,645	X
Rate	50.8	47.8	X	34.4	36.6	X
Robbery						
Number..............................	5,183	5,954	14.9	345,031	325,802	-5.6
Rate	185.8	209.7	12.9	109.1	102.2	-6.3
Aggravated Assault						
Number..............................	10,060	10,564	5.0	724,149	741,291	2.4
Rate	360.6	372.1	3.2	229.1	232.5	1.5
PROPERTY CRIME						
Number..............................	79,177	74,538	-5.9	8,632,512	8,277,829	-4.1
Rate	2,837.7	2,625.4	-7.5	2,730.7	2,596.1	-4.9
Burglary						
Number..............................	23,047	21,927	-4.9	1,928,465	1,729,806	-10.3
Rate	826.0	772.3	-6.5	610.0	542.5	-11.1
Larceny-Theft						
Number..............................	46,132	42,426	-8.0	6,004,453	5,858,496	-2.4
Rate	1,653.4	1,494.3	-9.6	1,899.4	1,837.3	-3.3
Motor Vehicle Theft						
Number..............................	9,998	10,185	1.9	699,594	689,527	-1.4
Rate	358.3	358.7	0.1	221.3	216.2	-2.3

NOTE: Although arson data are included in the trend and clearance tables, sufficient data are not available to estimate totals for this offense. Therefore, no arson data are published in this table.
X = Not applicable.
- = Zero or rounds to zero.
[1]The crime figures have been adjusted.
[2]The data collection methodology for the offense of forcible rape used by the Minnesota state Uniform Crime Reporting (UCR) Program (with the exception of Minneapolis and St. Paul, Minnesota) does not comply with national UCR Program guidelines. Consequently, its figures for forcible rape and violent crime (of which forcible rape is a part) are not published in this table.
[3]Includes offenses reported by the Zoological Police and the Metro Transit Police.
[4]Because of changes in the state's reporting practices, figures are not comparable to previous years' data.
[5]Populations are U.S. Census Bureau provisional estimates as of July 1 of each year.
[6]The figures shown for the offense of rape were estimated using the revised Uniform Crime Reporting (UCR) definition of rape.

Table NV-15. State Government Finances, 2014

(Dollar amounts in thousands, percent distribution.)

Item	Dollars	Percent distribution
Total Revenue	19,049,438	100.0
General revenue	11,479,806	60.3
Intergovernmental revenue	3,021,228	15.9
Taxes	7,143,169	37.5
General sales	3,828,869	20.1
Selective sales	1,885,328	9.9
License taxes	608,375	3.2
Individual income tax	0	-
Corporate income tax	0	-
Other taxes	820,597	4.3
Current charges	699,421	3.7
Miscellaneous general revenue	615,988	3.2
Utility revenue	62,182	0.3
Liquor stores revenue	0	-
Insurance trust revenue[1]	7,507,450	39.4
Total Expenditure	13,217,485	100.0
Intergovernmental expenditure	4,169,439	31.5
Direct expenditure	9,048,046	68.5
Current operation	5,824,559	44.1
Capital outlay	341,564	2.6
Insurance benefits and repayments	2,370,374	17.9
Assistance and subsidies	344,637	2.6
Interest on debt	166,912	1.3
Exhibit: Salaries and wages	1,556,496	11.8
Total Expenditure	13,217,485	100.0
General expenditure	10,779,735	81.6
Intergovernmental expenditure	4,169,439	31.5
Direct expenditure	6,610,296	50.0
General expenditure, by function:		
Education	4,460,055	33.7
Public welfare	2,719,967	20.6
Hospitals	251,980	1.9
Health	363,059	2.7
Highways	495,263	3.7
Police protection	95,196	0.7
Correction	268,145	2.0
Natural resources	103,302	0.8
Parks and recreation	18,992	0.1
Governmental administration	269,697	2.0
Interest on general debt	164,645	1.2
Other and unallocable	1,569,434	11.9
Utility expenditure	67,376	0.5
Liquor stores expenditure	0	-
Insurance trust expenditure	2,370,374	17.9
Debt at End of Fiscal Year	3,520,774	X
Cash and Security Holdings	38,337,274	X

X = Not applicable.
- = Zero or rounds to zero.
[1]Within insurance trust revenue, net earnings of state retirement systems is a calculated statistic (the item code in the data file is X08), and thus can be positive or negative. Net earnings is the sum of earnings on investments plus gains on investments minus losses on investments. The change made in 2002 for asset valuation from book to market value in accordance with Statement 34 of the Governmental Accounting Standards Board is reflected in the calculated statistics.

Table NV-16. State Government Tax Collections, 2014

(Dollars in thousands, percent.)

Item	Dollars	Percent distribution
Total Taxes	7,143,169	100.0
Property taxes	258,600	3.6
Sales and gross receipts	5,714,197	80.0
General sales and gross receipts	3,828,869	53.6
Selective sales and gross receipts	1,885,328	26.4
Alcoholic beverages	42,917	0.6
Amusements	947,290	13.3
Insurance premiums	264,522	3.7
Motor fuels	296,649	4.2
Pari-mutuels	0	-
Public utilities	22,636	0.3
Tobacco products	102,116	1.4
Other selective sales	209,198	2.9
Licenses	608,375	8.5
Alcoholic beverages	0	-
Amusements	95,717	1.3
Corporations in general	66,665	0.9
Hunting and fishing	10,496	0.1
Motor vehicle	166,067	2.3
Motor vehicle operators	26,517	0.4
Public utilities	0	-
Occupation and business, NEC	239,476	3.4
Other licenses	3,437	-
Income taxes	0	-
Individual income	X	X
Corporation net income	X	X
Other taxes	561,997	7.9
Death and gift	50	-
Documentary and stock transfer	64,712	0.9
Severance	111,395	1.6
Taxes, NEC	385,840	5.4

X = Not applicable.
- = Zero or rounds to zero.

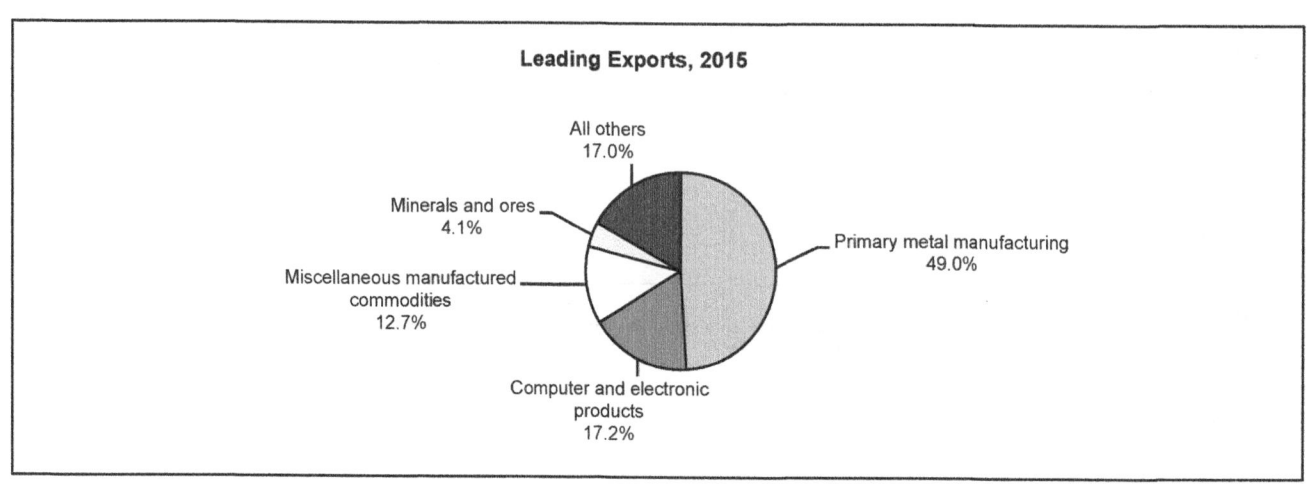

Leading Exports, 2015

- All others 17.0%
- Minerals and ores 4.1%
- Miscellaneous manufactured commodities 12.7%
- Computer and electronic products 17.2%
- Primary metal manufacturing 49.0%

NEW HAMPSHIRE

Facts and Figures

Location: Northeastern United States; bordered on the N by Canada (Quebec), on the E by Maine, on the SE by the Atlantic Ocean, on the S by Massachusetts, and on the W by Vermont

Area: 9,350 sq. mi. (24,216 sq. km.); rank—46th

Population: 1,330,608 (2015 est.); rank—41st

Principal Cities: capital—Concord; largest—Manchester

Statehood: June 21, 1788; 9th state

U.S. Congress: 2 senators, 2 representatives

State Motto: Live Free or Die

State Song: "Old New Hampshire"

State Nickname: The Granite State

Abbreviations: NH; N.H.

State Symbols: flower—purple lilac; tree—white birch; bird—purple finch

At a Glance

- With an increase in population of 1.1 percent, New Hampshire ranked 40th among the states in growth from 2010 to 2015.

- New Hampshire's violent crime rate in 2014 was 196.1 per 100,000 population, the 4th lowest in the country, compared to a rate of 365.5 for the entire nation.

- The state's property crime rate, 1,962.7 per 100,000 population, ranked 42nd in the country in 2014.

- In 2014, 9.2 percent of New Hampshirites did not have health insurance, compared to 11.7 percent of the entire U.S. populace.

- New Hampshire's unemployment rate of 3.4 percent in 2015 ranked 48th nationwide.

- New Hampshire had the lowest birth rate in the country in 2014, with 9.3 births per 1,000 population.

Table NH-1. Population by Age, Sex, Race, and Hispanic Origin

(Number, percent, except where noted.)

Sex, age, race, and Hispanic origin	2000	2010	2015[1]	Average annual percent change, 2010–2015
Total Population...	1,235,786	1,316,470	1,330,608	0.1
Percent of total U.S. population	0.4	0.4	0.4	X
Sex				
Male...	607,687	649,394	657,656	0.1
Female	628,099	667,076	672,952	0.1
Age				
Under 5 years..	75,685	69,806	64,594	-0.6
5 to 19 years...	268,480	255,996	237,160	-0.5
20 to 64 years..	743,651	812,400	809,912	-
65 years and over	147,970	178,268	218,942	1.5
Median age (years)	37.1	41.1	42.8	0.3
Race and Hispanic Origin				
One race				
White	1,186,851	1,248,321	1,249,686	-
Black..	9,035	16,365	19,819	1.4
American Indian and Alaska Native	2,964	3,530	3,885	0.7
Asian..	15,931	28,933	34,843	1.3
Native Hawaiian or Other Pacific Islander	371	532	639	1.3
Two or more races	13,214	18,789	21,736	1.0
Hispanic (of any race)	20,489	38,688	45,619	1.2

X = Not applicable.
- = Zero or rounds to zero.
[1]Population figures for 2015 are July 1 estimates. The 2010 estimates are taken from the 2010 Census.

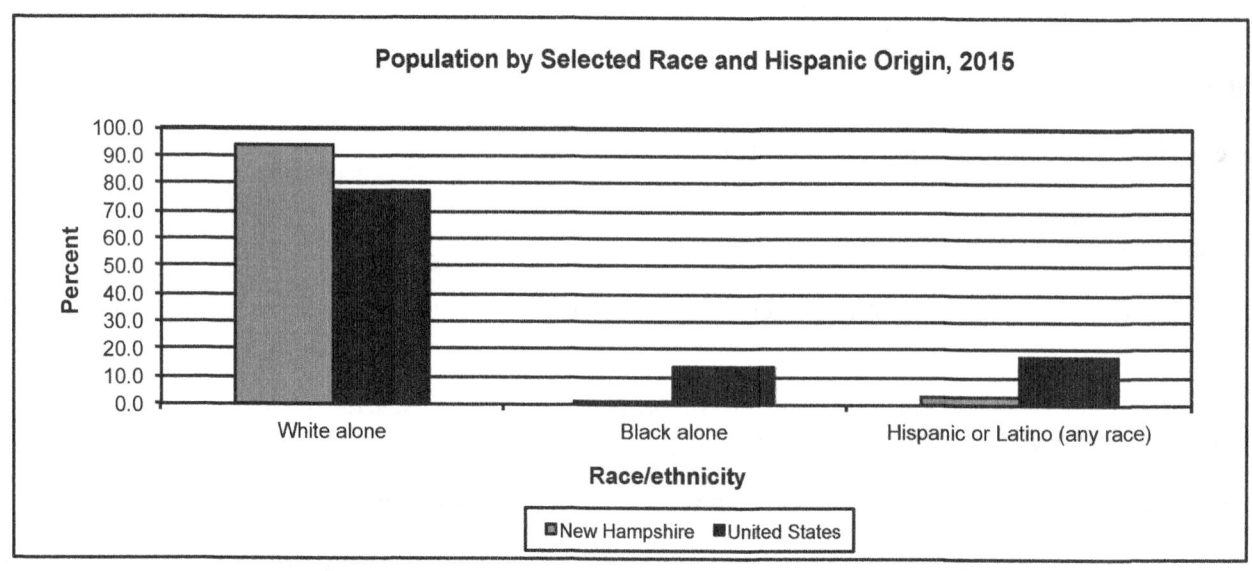

Population by Selected Race and Hispanic Origin, 2015

Table NH-2. Marital Status

(Number, percent distribution.)

Sex, age, race, and Hispanic origin	2000	2010	2014
Males, 15 Years and Over....................................	476,409	529,439	538,166
Never married	27.7	30.5	31.7
Now married, except separated	59.1	54.7	54.2
Separated..	1.2	1.3	1.0
Widowed..	2.4	2.6	2.4
Divorced..	9.6	10.9	10.7
Females, 15 Years and Over..................................	502,232	555,698	560,000
Never married	22.3	25.4	26.0
Now married, except separated	55.7	51.4	51.1
Separated..	1.5	1.3	1.4
Widowed..	9.2	8.6	8.4
Divorced..	11.3	13.4	13.1

Table NH-3. Households and Housing Characteristics

(Number, percent, dollars.)

Item	2000	2010	2014	Average annual percent change, 2000–2014
Total Households	474,606	515,431	519,756	0.7
Family households	323,651	344,057	345,901	0.5
Married-couple family	262,438	274,195	270,978	0.2
Other family	61,213	69,862	74,923	1.6
Male householder, no wife present	18,261	22,205	24,221	2.3
Female householder, no husband present	42,952	47,657	50,702	1.3
Nonfamily households	150,955	171,374	173,855	1.1
Householder living alone	116,014	130,327	132,161	1.0
Householder not living alone	34,941	41,047	41,694	1.4
Housing Characteristics				
Total housing units	547,024	614,996	619,865	1.0
Occupied housing units	474,606	515,431	519,756	0.7
Owner occupied	330,700	369,448	364,996	0.7
Renter occupied	143,906	145,983	154,760	0.5
Average household size	2.53	2.48	2.47	-0.2
Financial Characteristics				
Median gross rent of renter-occupied housing	646	951	994	3.8
Median monthly owner costs for housing units with a mortgage	1,226	1,853	1,828	3.5
Median value of owner-occupied housing units	133,300	243,000	236,400	5.5

Table NH-4. Migration, Origin, and Language

(Number, percent.)

Characteristic	State			U.S.		
	2013	2014	Percent change	2013	2014	Percent change
Residence 1 Year Ago						
Population 1 year and over	1,310,978	1,314,735	0.3	312,432,820	315,095,393	0.9
Same house	86.1	86.3	X	85.0	85.1	X
Different house in the U.S.	13.4	13.3	X	14.4	14.3	X
Same county	7.7	7.6	X	8.9	8.7	X
Different county	5.7	5.7	X	5.5	5.6	X
Same state	2.3	2.6	X	3.2	3.3	X
Different state	3.4	3.1	X	2.3	2.3	X
Abroad	0.5	0.4	X	0.6	0.6	X
Place of Birth						
Native born	1,248,284	1,247,281	-0.1	274,780,773	276,465,262	0.6
Male	49.5	49.6	X	49.3	49.3	X
Female	50.5	50.4	X	50.7	50.7	X
Foreign born	75,175	79,532	5.8	41,348,066	42,391,794	2.5
Male	46.4	45.1	X	48.8	48.7	X
Female	53.6	54.9	X	51.2	51.3	X
Foreign born; naturalized U.S. citizen	40,448	43,744	8.1	19,294,710	19,984,738	3.6
Male	45.6	44	X	45.9	45.9	X
Female	54.4	56	X	54.1	54.1	X
Foreign born; not a U.S. citizen	34,727	35,788	3.1	22,053,356	22,407,056	1.6
Male	47.3	46.3	X	51.3	51.2	X
Female	52.7	53.7	X	48.7	48.8	X
Entered 2010 or later	11.7	14.9	X	9.7	12.3	X
Entered 2000 to 2009	27.2	28.6	X	29.4	28.6	X
Entered before 2000	61.1	56.6	X	61.0	59.1	X
World Region of Birth, Foreign						
Foreign-born population, excluding population born at sea	75,175	79,532	5.8	41,347,945	42,390,705	2.5
Europe	25.6	23.7	X	11.6	11.2	X
Asia	35.3	36.6	X	29.5	30.1	X
Africa	4.3	7.2	X	4.4	4.6	X
Oceania	0.3	0.5	X	0.5	0.6	X
Latin America	21.3	20	X	51.9	51.6	X
North America	13.3	11.9	X	2.0	1.9	X
Language Spoken at Home and Ability to Speak English						
Population 5 years and over	1,257,652	1,261,731	0.3	296,358,760	299,084,046	0.9
English only	91.6	92.5	X	79.2	78.9	X
Language other than English	8.4	7.5	X	20.8	21.1	X
Speaks English less than "very well"	2.5	2.4	X	8.5	8.6	X

X = Not applicable.
- = Zero or rounds to zero.

Table NH-5. Median Income and Poverty Status, 2014

(Number, percent, except as noted.)

Characteristic	State		U.S.	
	Number	Percent	Number	Percent
Median Income				
Households (dollars)...............................	66,532	X	53,657	X
Families (dollars)	80,581	X	65,910	X
Below Poverty Level (All People)............	117,983	9.2	48,208,387	15.5
Sex				
Male..	54,165	8.5	21,590,918	14.2
Female	63,818	9.8	26,617,469	16.8
Age				
Under 18 years....................................	34,463	13.0	15,686,012	21.7
Related children under 18 years............	32,849	12.5	15,372,705	21.3
18 to 64 years.....................................	73,201	8.9	28,267,482	14.6
65 years and over	10,319	5.1	4,254,893	9.5

X = Not applicable.

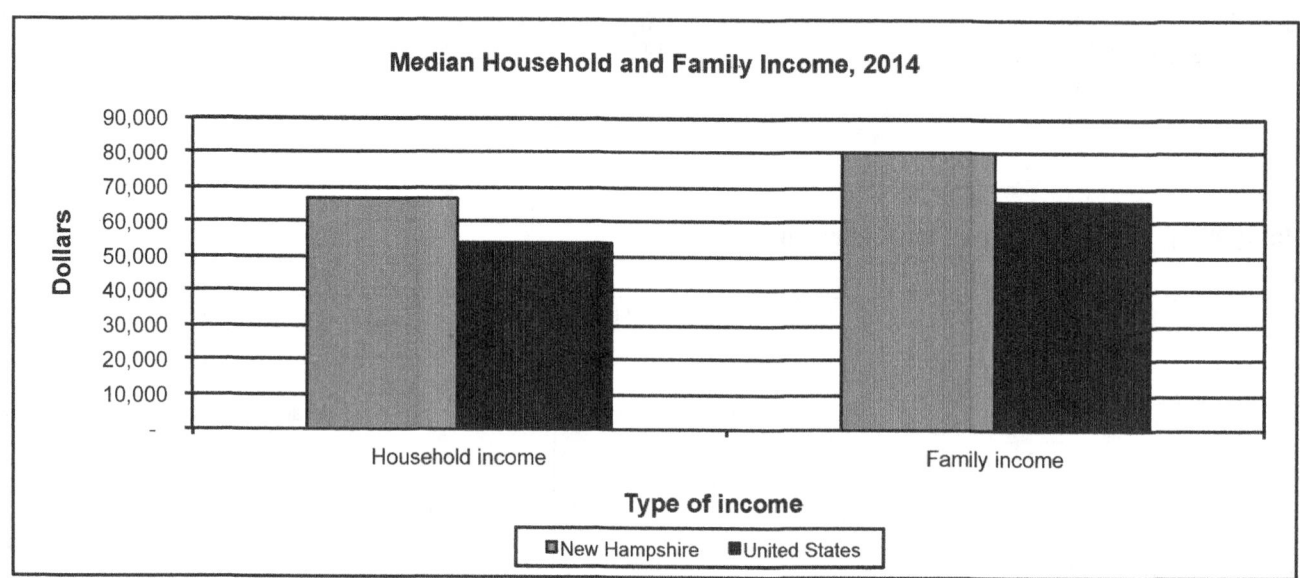

Median Household and Family Income, 2014

Table NH-6. Health Insurance Coverage Status for the Civilian Noninstitutionalized Population and Children Under 18 Years of Age

(Numbers in thousands, percent.)

Item	2006	2007	2008	2009	2010	2011	2012	2013	2014
Civilian Noninstitutionalized Population.................	1,309	1,314	1,299	1,309	1,303	1,304	1,306	1,309	1,312
Covered by Private or Public Insurance									
Number...	119	1,177	1,159	1,175	1,157	1,167	1,167	1,168	1,191
Percent...	88.5	89.5	89.2	89.8	88.9	89.5	89.4	89.3	90.8
Not Covered									
Number...	150	137	140	134	145	137	139	140	120
Percent...	11.5	10.5	10.8	10.2	11.1	10.5	10.6	10.7	9.2
Percent in the U.S. not covered.......................	15.8	15.3	15.1	15.1	15.5	15.1	14.8	14.5	11.7
Children Under 18 Years of Age........................	301	296	293	289	286	279	275	271	267
Covered by Private or Public Insurance									
Number...	278	277	278	276	272	269	264	260	255
Percent...	92.5	93.5	94.9	95.3	95.2	96.3	96.0	96.2	95.6
Not Covered									
Number...	22	19	15	13	14	10	11	10	12
Percent...	7.5	6.5	5.1	4.7	4.8	3.7	4.0	3.8	4.4
Percent in the U.S. not covered.......................	11.7	11.0	9.7	8.6	8.0	7.5	7.2	7.1	6.0

Table NH-7. Employment Status by Demographic Group, 2015

(Numbers in thousands, percent.)

Characteristic	Civilian noninstitutional population	Civilian labor force		Employed		Unemployed	
		Number	Percent of population	Number	Percent of population	Number	Percent of population
Total..........	1,085	743	68.4	717	66.0	26	3.4
Sex							
Male..........	533	391	73.3	377	70.7	14	3.6
Female..........	553	352	63.7	340	61.6	12	3.3
Race, Sex, and Hispanic Origin							
White	1,027	702	68.4	678	66.0	25	3.5
Male..........	505	369	73.2	356	70.5	14	3.7
Female..........	523	333	63.7	322	61.7	11	3.2
Black or African American..........	14	10	70.7	9	64.5	1	8.6
Male..........	NA	NA	NA	NA	NA	NA	NA
Female..........	NA	NA	NA	NA	NA	NA	NA
Hispanic or Latino ethnicity[1]	29	22	76.4	21	72.5	1	5.3
Male..........	14	12	85.2	11	81.8	1	4.2
Female..........	15	10	68.5	10	63.6	1	6.4
Age							
16 to 19 years..........	68	33	49.0	30	44.8	3	8.5
20 to 24 years..........	84	70	83.0	65	77.7	4	6.3
25 to 34 years..........	162	139	86.0	135	83.2	5	3.2
35 to 44 years..........	156	131	83.7	127	81.3	4	2.9
45 to 54 years..........	203	174	85.8	171	84.3	3	1.8
55 to 64 years..........	198	144	72.9	140	70.6	5	3.3
65 years and over	215	51	23.8	49	22.8	2	4.3

NOTE: Data in Table 7 are from the Current Population Survey (CPS) and do not match the estimates in Table 8. See notes and definitions for further information.
[1]May be of any race.
NA = Not available.

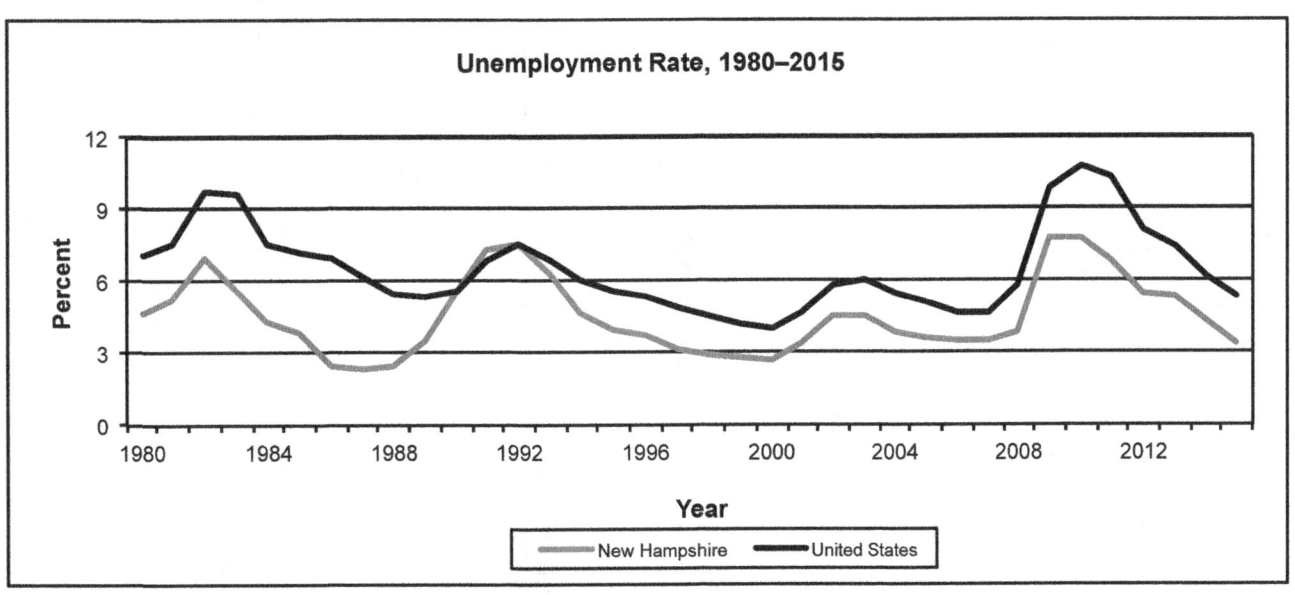

Table NH-8. Employment Status of the Civilian Noninstitutional Population Age 16 Years and Over

(Number, percent.)

Year	Civilian labor force	Civilian participation rate	Employed	Unemployed	Unemployment rate
2007..........	737,942	70.8	712,008	25,934	3.5
2008..........	742,781	70.7	714,104	28,677	3.9
2009..........	744,227	70.4	697,802	46,425	6.2
2010..........	738,257	69.9	695,135	43,122	5.8
2011..........	736,077	69.5	696,326	39,751	5.4
2012..........	740,323	69.4	699,589	40,734	5.5
2013..........	742,017	69.2	704,294	37,723	5.1
2014..........	741,178	68.7	709,219	31,959	4.3
2015..........	741,192	68.4	715,727	25,465	3.4

Table NH-9. Employment and Average Wages by Industry

(Estimates through 2010 are based on the 2007 *North American Industry Classification System* [NAICS]. Estimates from 2011 onward are based on the 2012 NAICS.)

Industry	2008	2009	2010	2011	2012	2013	2014
	Number of jobs						
Wage and Salary Employment by Industry	659,277	636,169	633,655	638,856	642,126	648,182	656,249
Farm Wage and Salary Employment	1,180	1,139	1,141	1,210	1,225	1,452	1,662
Nonfarm Wage and Salary Employment	658,097	635,030	632,514	637,646	640,901	646,730	654,587
Private wage and salary employment	562,461	538,792	534,869	541,705	545,847	552,254	559,640
Forestry, fishing, and related activities	810	785	775	778	764	776	827
Mining	607	510	490	493	501	531	532
Utilities	2,454	2,532	2,513	2,474	2,454	2,480	2,321
Construction	27,161	23,700	22,437	23,338	22,918	23,361	23,939
Manufacturing	76,095	68,115	65,821	66,667	66,075	66,082	66,593
Durable goods manufacturing	58,096	51,982	50,313	51,168	50,230	49,916	49,951
Nondurable goods manufacturing	17,999	16,133	15,508	15,499	15,845	16,166	16,642
Wholesale trade	28,289	26,649	26,093	26,383	26,727	26,882	27,243
Retail trade	98,298	94,565	94,033	94,604	95,347	95,761	95,354
Transportation and warehousing	12,930	12,383	12,346	12,524	12,602	12,614	13,054
Information	12,547	12,181	11,220	11,151	12,103	11,936	12,039
Finance and insurance	29,201	27,870	27,525	28,173	28,889	29,184	29,435
Real estate and rental and leasing	7,850	7,354	7,044	7,051	6,728	6,979	6,994
Professional, scientific, and technical services	31,433	29,948	29,686	30,345	30,696	32,063	32,733
Management of companies and enterprises	8,170	7,968	8,013	8,098	8,155	8,184	8,179
Administrative and waste services	27,753	25,864	27,661	28,856	30,011	30,756	33,262
Educational services	22,160	22,229	22,043	22,280	22,583	22,932	23,279
Health care and social assistance	82,900	84,749	85,391	85,739	86,097	86,737	87,600
Arts, entertainment, and recreation	11,099	11,081	11,199	11,479	11,364	11,447	11,215
Accommodation and food services	53,355	51,513	52,061	52,651	53,654	55,313	56,312
Other services, except public administration	29,349	28,796	28,518	28,621	28,179	28,236	28,729
Government and government enterprises	95,636	96,238	97,645	95,941	95,054	94,476	94,947
	Dollars						
Average Wages and Salaries by Industry	44,249	44,197	45,150	46,380	47,491	48,201	50,360
Average Farm Wages and Salaries	28,812	28,356	26,736	22,556	24,973	28,706	31,259
Average Nonfarm Wages and Salaries	44,277	44,225	45,183	46,425	47,534	48,244	50,408
Average private wages and salaries	44,918	44,684	45,896	47,183	48,441	49,139	51,507
Forestry, fishing, and related activities	34,717	34,851	36,034	37,478	43,800	41,473	45,278
Mining	50,936	52,245	55,849	55,507	56,655	53,305	54,211
Utilities	91,296	87,771	87,860	96,418	94,523	94,702	102,322
Construction	49,942	49,068	49,392	50,144	51,485	52,979	54,179
Manufacturing	58,738	58,299	61,926	63,219	63,337	64,602	66,255
Durable goods manufacturing	62,066	61,533	65,486	66,697	66,557	67,946	69,827
Nondurable goods manufacturing	47,995	47,876	50,376	51,735	53,131	54,276	55,534
Wholesale trade	72,268	70,957	74,646	77,793	80,535	82,132	84,835
Retail trade	26,502	26,350	26,760	27,406	27,935	28,497	29,677
Transportation and warehousing	36,684	36,602	37,434	38,705	39,332	40,299	41,158
Information	71,344	69,375	75,172	74,503	75,499	78,854	91,529
Finance and insurance	73,916	74,362	78,080	81,346	84,450	85,902	94,491
Real estate and rental and leasing	43,846	43,993	40,820	47,017	44,889	46,082	47,691
Professional, scientific, and technical services	73,296	72,500	74,270	76,812	79,566	80,125	84,827
Management of companies and enterprises	77,627	76,944	80,829	82,361	97,872	89,710	106,591
Administrative and waste services	38,712	40,207	40,031	40,296	42,659	42,393	43,546
Educational services	38,585	39,360	40,020	40,638	41,424	42,643	43,745
Health care and social assistance	44,568	45,709	46,500	47,829	48,486	49,120	50,328
Arts, entertainment, and recreation	21,981	21,073	21,263	21,597	22,036	22,969	24,312
Accommodation and food services	18,151	18,462	18,880	19,339	19,612	19,730	20,698
Other services, except public administration	29,282	28,856	29,739	30,126	31,304	32,600	33,256
Government and government enterprises	40,505	41,653	41,277	42,148	42,328	43,016	43,928

Table NH-10. Employment Characteristics by Family Type

(Number, percent.)

Family type and labor force status	2012		2013		2014	
	Total	Families with own children under 18 years	Total	Families with own children under 18 years	Total	Families with own children under 18 years
All Families....................................	341,718	139,546	347,272	145,235	343,363	137,776
FAMILY TYPE AND LABOR FORCE STATUS						
Married-Couple Families..........................	269,048	97,873	272,206	102,397	268,440	94,424
Both husband and wife in labor force.............	59.3	72.1	56.3	71.7	57.3	70.9
Husband in labor force, wife not in labor force.....	17.5	23.3	19.9	23.5	19.4	25.1
Wife in labor force, husband not in labor force.....	7.3	3.1	7.6	3.0	8.0	2.9
Both husband and wife not in labor force..........	15.9	1.5	15.4	1.3	15.3	1.1
Other Families	72,670	41,673	75,066	42,838	74,923	43,352
Female householder, no husband present...........	70.2	71.9	69.8	70.0	67.7	69.3
In labor force..............................	53.8	59.2	53.0	59.7	52.2	60.2
Not in labor force	16.3	12.7	16.8	10.3	15.5	9.1
Male householder, no wife present...............	29.8	28.1	30.2	30.0	32.3	30.7
In labor force..............................	24.6	24.9	24.2	26.5	27.7	29.3
Not in labor force	5.2	3.1	6.0	3.5	4.6	1.4

Table NH-11. School Enrollment and Educational Attainment, 2014

(Number, percent.)

Item	State	U.S.
Enrollment		
Total population 3 years and over, enrolled in school................	314,674	82,063,714
Enrolled in nursery school or preschool (percent)................	5.6	6.0
Enrolled in kindergarten (percent)................	4.8	5.1
Enrolled in elementary school, grades 1-8 (percent)................	38.1	40.2
Enrolled in high school, grades 9-12 (percent)................	22.3	20.7
Enrolled in college or graduate school (percent)................	29.1	28.0
Attainment		
Total population 25 years and over	931,304	213,725,624
Less than ninth grade (percent)................	2.6	5.6
9th to 12th grade, no diploma (percent)................	5.3	7.5
High school graduate, including equivalency (percent)................	28.6	27.7
Some college, no degree (percent)................	18.8	21.0
Associate's degree (percent)................	9.8	8.2
Bachelor's degree (percent)................	21.7	18.7
Graduate or professional degree (percent)................	13.3	11.4
High school graduate or higher (percent)................	92.2	86.9
Bachelor's degree or higher (percent)................	35.0	30.1

Table NH-12. Public School Characteristics and Educational Indicators

(Number, percent; data derived from National Center of Education Statistics.)

Item	State	U.S.
Public Schools, 2013–2014 (except where noted)		
Number of school districts................	292	18,194
Number of schools................	482	98,271
Number of students (in thousands)	186	50,045
Number of teachers (in thousands)	15	3,114
Student-teacher ratio................	12.6	16.1
Expenditures per student (dollars), FY 2013................	14,050	107,637
Four-year adjusted cohort graduation rate (ACGR)[1,2]	88.1	82.3
Students eligible for free or reduced-price lunch (in thousands)	52	25,596
English language learners (in thousands)	4	4,461
Students age 3 to 21 served under IDEA, part B (in thousands)	29	6,464

Public Schools by Type	Number	Percent of state public schools
Total number of schools................	482	100.0
Regular................	482	100.0
Special education................	0	-
Vocational education................	0	-
Alternative education................	0	-

NOTE: Every school is assigned only one school type based on its instructional emphasis.
- = Zero or rounds to zero.
[1]ACGR data represents a new method of calculating high-school completion rates and may not be comparable to previous years' data for Averaged Freshmen Graduation Rates (AFGR).
[2]The United States 4-year ACGRs were estimated using both the reported 4-year ACGR data from 49 states and the District of Columbia and using imputed data for Idaho. The estimate for American Indian/Alaska Native students also includes imputed data for Virginia.

Table NH-13. Reported Voting and Registration of the Voting-Age Population, November 2014

(Numbers in thousands, percent.)

Item	Total population	Total citizen population	Registered			Voted		
			Total registered	Percent registered (total population)	Percent registered (total citizen population)	Total voted	Percent voted (total population)	Percent voted (total citizen population)
U.S. Total	239,874	219,941	142,166	59.3	64.6	92,251	38.5	41.9
State Total..............................	1,047	1,015	694	66.3	68.3	509	48.6	50.2
Sex								
Male..................................	512	498	331	64.6	66.5	246	48.1	49.5
Female	535	517	363	67.8	70.1	263	49.2	50.8
Race								
White alone..........................	996	977	669	67.1	68.5	490	49.2	50.2
White, non-Hispanic alone	974	957	655	67.2	68.4	480	49.3	50.2
Black alone..........................	15	12	7	(B)	(B)	4	(B)	(B)
Asian alone	23	13	7	(B)	(B)	6	(B)	(B)
Hispanic (of any race)	23	21	15	(B)	(B)	10	(B)	(B)
White alone or in combination	1,006	986	676	67.3	68.6	496	49.4	50.3
Black alone or in combination..........	18	15	9	(B)	(B)	6	(B)	(B)
Asian alone or in combination..........	25	15	9	(B)	(B)	7	(B)	(B)
Age								
18 to 24 years........................	113	113	53	46.7	46.7	21	19.0	19.0
25 to 34 years........................	164	151	77	47.0	51.3	40	24.4	26.6
35 to 44 years........................	159	155	106	66.8	68.4	77	48.3	49.5
45 to 64 years........................	398	387	290	72.8	74.9	225	56.5	58.2
65 years and over	213	210	168	78.9	80.1	146	68.7	69.7

B = Base is less than 75,000 and therefore too small to show the derived measure.

Table NH-14. Crime

(Number, rate per 100,000. Data are derived from the FBI Uniform Crime Reports.)

Item	State			U.S.[1,2,3,4]		
	2013	2014	Percent change	2013	2014	Percent change
TOTAL POPULATION[5]..	1,323,459	1,326,813	0.3	316,128,839	318,857,056	0.9
VIOLENT CRIME						
Number..	2,642	2,602	-1.5	1,163,146	1,165,383	0.2
Rate..	199.6	196.1	-1.8	367.9	365.5	-0.7
Murder and Nonnegligent Manslaughter						
Number..	22	12	-45.5	14,196	14,249	0.4
Rate	1.7	0.9	-47.1	4.5	4.5	-
Rape[6]						
Number..	686	594	X	108,612	116,645	X
Rate	51.8	44.8	X	34.4	36.6	X
Robbery						
Number..	649	537	-17.3	345,031	325,802	-5.6
Rate	49.0	40.5	-17.3	109.1	102.2	-6.3
Aggravated Assault						
Number..	1,492	1,459	-2.2	724,149	741,291	2.4
Rate	112.7	110.0	-2.4	229.1	232.5	1.5
PROPERTY CRIME						
Number..	29,040	26,041	-10.3	8,632,512	8,277,829	-4.1
Rate	2,194.3	1,962.7	-10.6	2,730.7	2,596.1	-4.9
Burglary						
Number..	4,936	4,162	-15.7	1,928,465	1,729,806	-10.3
Rate	373.0	313.7	-15.9	610.0	542.5	-11.1
Larceny-Theft						
Number..	23,164	21,022	-9.2	6,004,453	5,858,496	-2.4
Rate	1,750.3	1,584.4	-9.5	1,899.4	1,837.3	-3.3
Motor Vehicle Theft						
Number..	940	857	-8.8	699,594	689,527	-1.4
Rate	71.0	64.6	-9.0	221.3	216.2	-2.3

NOTE: Although arson data are included in the trend and clearance tables, sufficient data are not available to estimate totals for this offense. Therefore, no arson data are published in this table.
X = Not applicable.
- = Zero or rounds to zero.
[1]The crime figures have been adjusted.
[2]The data collection methodology for the offense of forcible rape used by the Minnesota state Uniform Crime Reporting (UCR) Program (with the exception of Minneapolis and St. Paul, Minnesota) does not comply with national UCR Program guidelines. Consequently, its figures for forcible rape and violent crime (of which forcible rape is a part) are not published in this table.
[3]Includes offenses reported by the Zoological Police and the Metro Transit Police.
[4]Because of changes in the state's reporting practices, figures are not comparable to previous years' data.
[5]Populations are U.S. Census Bureau provisional estimates as of July 1 of each year.
[6]The figures shown for the offense of rape were estimated using the revised Uniform Crime Reporting (UCR) definition of rape.

Table NH-15. State Government Finances, 2014

(Dollar amounts in thousands, percent distribution.)

Item	Dollars	Percent distribution
Total Revenue	8,261,811	100.0
General revenue	5,912,732	71.6
Intergovernmental revenue	1,853,129	22.4
Taxes	2,282,507	27.6
General sales	0	-
Selective sales	877,035	10.6
License taxes	280,011	3.4
Individual income tax	92,743	1.1
Corporate income tax	542,847	6.6
Other taxes	489,871	5.9
Current charges	882,524	10.7
Miscellaneous general revenue	894,572	10.8
Utility revenue	0	-
Liquor stores revenue	611,157	7.4
Insurance trust revenue[1]	1,737,922	21.0
Total Expenditure	7,344,811	100.0
Intergovernmental expenditure	1,268,583	17.3
Direct expenditure	6,076,228	82.7
Current operation	4,504,053	61.3
Capital outlay	344,400	4.7
Insurance benefits and repayments	731,299	10.0
Assistance and subsidies	153,352	2.1
Interest on debt	343,124	4.7
Exhibit: Salaries and wages	903,848	12.3
Total Expenditure	7,344,811	100.0
General expenditure	6,124,043	83.4
Intergovernmental expenditure	1,268,583	17.3
Direct expenditure	4,855,460	66.1
General expenditure, by function:		
Education	2,038,385	27.8
Public welfare	1,759,697	24.0
Hospitals	53,597	0.7
Health	104,918	1.4
Highways	512,418	7.0
Police protection	56,332	0.8
Correction	98,358	1.3
Natural resources	72,645	1.0
Parks and recreation	23,417	0.3
Governmental administration	242,260	3.3
Interest on general debt	343,124	4.7
Other and unallocable	818,892	11.1
Utility expenditure	8,820	0.1
Liquor stores expenditure	480,649	6.5
Insurance trust expenditure	731,299	10.0
Debt at End of Fiscal Year	8,098,921	X
Cash and Security Holdings	14,345,224	X

X = Not applicable.
- = Zero or rounds to zero.
[1]Within insurance trust revenue, net earnings of state retirement systems is a calculated statistic (the item code in the data file is X08), and thus can be positive or negative. Net earnings is the sum of earnings on investments plus gains on investments minus losses on investments. The change made in 2002 for asset valuation from book to market value in accordance with Statement 34 of the Governmental Accounting Standards Board is reflected in the calculated statistics.

Table NH-16. State Government Tax Collections, 2014

(Dollars in thousands, percent.)

Item	Dollars	Percent distribution
Total Taxes	2,282,507	100.0
Property taxes	383,126	16.8
Sales and gross receipts	877,035	38.4
General sales and gross receipts	X	
Selective sales and gross receipts	877,035	38.4
Alcoholic beverages	9,545	0.4
Amusements	444	-
Insurance premiums	84,518	3.7
Motor fuels	146,101	6.4
Pari-mutuels	827	-
Public utilities	69,877	3.1
Tobacco products	215,012	9.4
Other selective sales	350,711	15.4
Licenses	280,011	12.3
Alcoholic beverages	4,306	0.2
Amusements	244	-
Corporations in general	50,783	2.2
Hunting and fishing	9,804	0.4
Motor vehicle	94,395	4.1
Motor vehicle operators	12,125	0.5
Public utilities	9,081	0.4
Occupation and business, NEC	91,654	4.0
Other licenses	7,619	0.3
Income taxes	635,590	27.8
Individual income	92,743	4.1
Corporation net income	542,847	23.8
Other taxes	106,745	4.7
Death and gift	0	-
Documentary and stock transfer	106,745	4.7
Severance	X	X
Taxes, NEC	0	-

X = Not applicable.
- = Zero or rounds to zero.

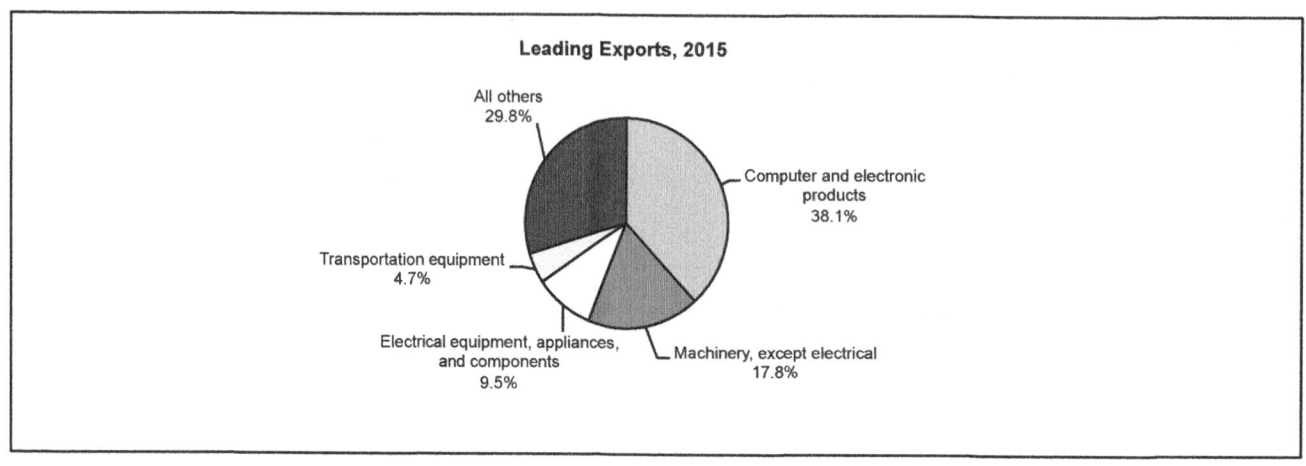

Leading Exports, 2015

- All others 29.8%
- Computer and electronic products 38.1%
- Transportation equipment 4.7%
- Electrical equipment, appliances, and components 9.5%
- Machinery, except electrical 17.8%

Facts and Figures

Location: Middle Atlantic region of the United States; bordered on the N and NE by New York, on the E by the Atlantic Ocean, on the S by Delaware Bay, and on the W by Delaware and Pennsylvania

Area: 8,721 sq. mi. (22,588 sq. km.); rank—47th

Population: 8,958,013 (2015 est.); rank—11th

Principal Cities: capital—Trenton; largest—Newark

Statehood: December 18, 1787; 3rd state

U.S. Congress: 2 senators, 12 representatives

State Motto: Liberty and Prosperity

State Song: None

State Nickname: The Garden State

Abbreviations: NJ; N.J.

State Symbols: flower—common meadow violet; tree—red oak; bird—Eastern goldfinch

At a Glance

- With an increase in population of 1.8 percent, New Jersey ranked 34th among the states in growth from 2010 to 2015.

- New Jersey's median household income was $71,919 in 2014, the second highest in the country.

- In 2014, 11.1 percent of the New Jersey's population lived below the poverty level, compared to 15.5 percent of the entire U.S. population.

- New Jersey's property crime rate of 1,734.1 incidents per 100,000 population, was the third lowest rate in the country in 2014.

- Approximately 37.4 percent of New Jersey residents had a bachelor's degree or more in 2014, the 6th highest percentage in the country.

Table NJ-1. Population by Age, Sex, Race, and Hispanic Origin

(Number, percent, except where noted.)

Sex, age, race, and Hispanic origin	2000	2010	2015[1]	Average annual percent change, 2010–2015
Total Population	8,414,350	8,791,894	8,958,013	0.1
Percent of total U.S. population	3.0	2.8	2.8	X
Sex				
Male	4,082,813	4,279,600	4,372,116	0.2
Female	4,331,357	4,512,294	4,585,897	0.1
Age				
Under 5 years	563,785	541,020	530,134	-0.1
5 to 19 years	1,720,332	1,750,184	1,687,398	-0.3
20 to 64 years	5,017,107	5,314,697	5,396,855	0.1
65 years and over	1,113,136	1,185,993	1,343,626	0.9
Median age (years)	36.7	39.0	39.6	0.1
Race and Hispanic Origin				
One race				
White	6,104,705	6,546,498	6,506,870	-
Black	1,141,821	1,282,005	1,329,948	0.3
American Indian and Alaska Native	19,492	49,907	53,775	0.5
Asian	480,276	746,212	868,800	1.1
Native Hawaiian or Other Pacific Islander	3,329	7,731	9,202	1.3
Two or more races	13,755	159,541	189,418	1.2
Hispanic (of any race)	1,117,191	1,606,006	1,762,181	0.7

X = Not applicable.
[1]Population figures for 2015 are July 1 estimates. The 2010 estimates are taken from the 2010 Census.
- = Zero or rounds to zero.

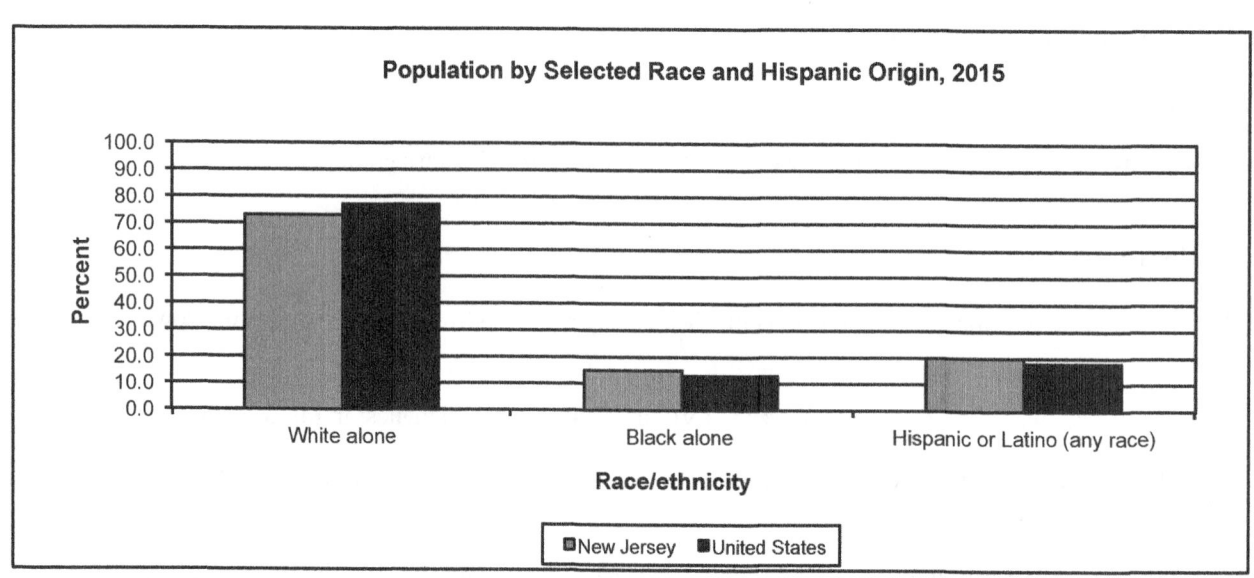

Population by Selected Race and Hispanic Origin, 2015

Table NJ-2. Marital Status

(Number, percent distribution.)

Sex, age, race, and Hispanic origin	2000	2010	2014
Males, 15 Years and Over	3,176,413	3,419,050	3,471,402
Never married	31.1	36.4	37.0
Now married, except separated	57.7	52.1	51.9
Separated	2.0	1.8	1.6
Widowed	2.9	2.6	2.6
Divorced	6.2	7.1	6.9
Females, 15 Years and Over	3,478,920	3,690,673	3,728,556
Never married	25.3	30.2	31.0
Now married, except separated	51.8	47.6	46.9
Separated	2.7	2.2	2.3
Widowed	11.5	10.2	9.8
Divorced	8.7	9.8	10.0

Table NJ-3. Households and Housing Characteristics

(Number, percent, dollars.)

Item	2000	2010	2014	Average annual percent change, 2000–2014
Total Households...	3,064,645	3,172,421	3,194,844	0.3
Family households	2,154,539	2,185,732	2,203,675	0.2
Married-couple family	1,638,322	1,614,230	1,607,880	-0.1
Other family	516,217	571,502	595,795	1.1
Male householder, no wife present.......................	129,205	154,036	154,428	1.4
Female householder, no husband present.............	387,012	417,466	441,367	1.0
Nonfamily households	910,106	986,689	991,169	0.6
Householder living alone	751,287	827,294	826,340	0.7
Householder not living alone...............................	158,819	159,395	164,829	0.3
Housing Characteristics				
Total housing units..	3,310,275	3,554,909	3,591,847	0.6
Occupied housing units	3,064,645	3,172,421	3,194,844	0.3
Owner occupied	2,012,473	2,106,728	2,021,062	-
Renter occupied	1,053,172	1,065,693	1,173,782	0.8
Average household size..	2.68	2.72	2.74	0.2
Financial Characteristics				
Median gross rent of renter-occupied housing	751	1,114	1,202	4.3
Median monthly owner costs for housing units with a mortgage	1,560	2,370	2,313	3.4
Median value of owner-occupied housing units...........	170,800	339,200	313,200	6.0

- = Zero or rounds to zero

Table NJ-4. Migration, Origin, and Language

(Number, percent.)

Characteristic	State			U.S.		
	2013	2014	Percent change	2013	2014	Percent change
Residence 1 Year Ago						
Population 1 year and over	8,803,679	8,840,346	0.4	312,432,820	315,095,393	0.9
Same house	90.2	90.1	X	85.0	85.1	X
Different house in the U.S.	9.1	9.2	X	14.4	14.3	X
Same county	5.3	5.5	X	8.9	8.7	X
Different county	3.8	3.7	X	5.5	5.6	X
Same state	2.3	2.2	X	3.2	3.3	X
Different state	1.6	1.5	X	2.3	2.3	X
Abroad	0.7	0.7	X	0.6	0.6	X
Place of Birth						
Native born	6,973,566	6,977,441	0.1	274,780,773	276,465,262	0.6
Male	48.8	48.8	X	49.3	49.3	X
Female	51.2	51.2	X	50.7	50.7	X
Foreign born	1,925,773	1,960,734	1.8	41,348,066	42,391,794	2.5
Male	48.8	48.8	X	48.8	48.7	X
Female	51.2	51.2	X	51.2	51.3	X
Foreign born; naturalized U.S. citizen.....................	1,021,084	1,066,460	4.4	19,294,710	19,984,738	3.6
Male	46.9	46.8	X	45.9	45.9	X
Female	53.1	53.2	X	54.1	54.1	X
Foreign born; not a U.S. citizen	904,689	894,274	-1.2	22,053,356	22,407,056	1.6
Male	51.0	51.2	X	51.3	51.2	X
Female	49.0	48.8	X	48.7	48.8	X
Entered 2010 or later	9.3	12.1	X	9.7	12.3	X
Entered 2000 to 2009	30.5	29.6	X	29.4	28.6	X
Entered before 2000..	60.2	58.3	X	61.0	59.1	X
World Region of Birth, Foreign						
Foreign-born population, excluding population born at sea	1,925,773	1,960,734	1.8	41,347,945	42,390,705	2.5
Europe	16.3	15.6	X	11.6	11.2	X
Asia	32.2	32.5	X	29.5	30.1	X
Africa	5.2	5.2	X	4.4	4.6	X
Oceania	0.2	0.2	X	0.5	0.6	X
Latin America..	45.3	45.7	X	51.9	51.6	X
North America	0.8	0.8	X	2.0	1.9	X
Language Spoken at Home and Ability to Speak English						
Population 5 years and over.....................................	8,368,158	8,406,007	0.5	296,358,760	299,084,046	0.9
English only	69.6	69.4	X	79.2	78.9	X
Language other than English.................................	30.4	30.6	X	20.8	21.1	X
Speaks English less than "very well"...................	12.0	12.2	X	8.5	8.6	X

X = Not applicable.
- = Zero or rounds to zero.

Table NJ-5. Median Income and Poverty Status, 2014

(Number, percent, except as noted.)

Characteristic	State Number	State Percent	U.S. Number	U.S. Percent
Median Income				
Households (dollars)........................	71,919	X	53,657	X
Families (dollars)	88,419	X	65,910	X
Below Poverty Level (All People)	972,903	11.1	48,208,387	15.5
Sex				
Male...........................	424,554	10.0	21,590,918	14.2
Female	548,349	12.2	26,617,469	16.8
Age				
Under 18 years...........................	315,563	15.9	15,686,012	21.7
Related children under 18 years........................	310,524	15.7	15,372,705	21.3
18 to 64 years...........................	548,101	10.0	28,267,482	14.6
65 years and over...........................	109,239	8.6	4,254,893	9.5

X = Not applicable.

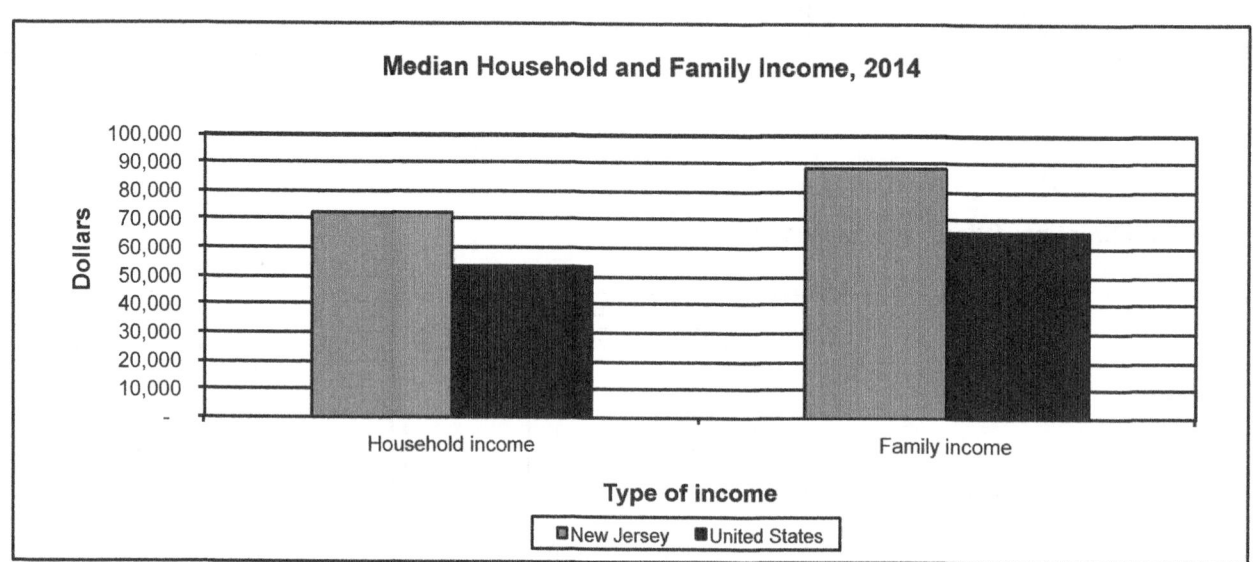

Median Household and Family Income, 2014

Table NJ-6. Health Insurance Coverage Status for the Civilian Noninstitutionalized Population and Children Under 18 Years of Age

(Numbers in thousands, percent.)

Item	2006	2007	2008	2009	2010	2011	2012	2013	2014
Civilian Noninstitutionalized Population	8,660	8,556	8,557	8,583	8,694	8,713	8,757	8,792	8,831
Covered by Private or Public Insurance									
Number...........................	7,319	7,208	7,499	7,499	7,542	7,574	7,644	7,631	7,866
Percent...........................	84.5	84.2	87.6	87.4	86.8	86.9	87.3	86.8	89.1
Not Covered									
Number...........................	1,341	1,348	1,058	1,084	1,151	1,139	1,113	1,160	965
Percent...........................	15.5	15.8	12.4	12.6	13.2	13.1	12.7	13.2	10.9
Percent in the U.S. not covered...........................	15.8	15.3	15.1	15.1	15.5	15.1	14.8	14.5	11.7
Children Under 18 Years of Age	2,088	2,091	2,045	2,044	2,057	2,038	2,024	2,017	2,007
Covered by Private or Public Insurance									
Number...........................	1,810	1,821	1,897	1,914	1,934	1,933	1,921	1,906	1,916
Percent...........................	86.7	87.1	92.8	93.6	94.0	94.8	94.9	94.4	95.4
Not Covered									
Number...........................	277	270	148	130	123	105	103	112	92
Percent...........................	13.3	12.9	7.2	6.4	6.0	5.2	5.1	5.6	4.6
Percent in the U.S. not covered...........................	11.7	11.0	9.7	8.6	8.0	7.5	7.2	7.1	6.0

Table NJ-7. Employment Status by Demographic Group, 2015

(Numbers in thousands, percent.)

Characteristic	Civilian noninstitutional population	Civilian labor force		Employed		Unemployed	
		Number	Percent of population	Number	Percent of population	Number	Percent of population
Total.............................	7,105	4,545	64.0	4,281	60.2	264	5.8
Sex							
Male..............................	3,408	2,442	71.7	2,305	67.6	137	5.6
Female	3,698	2,103	56.9	1,976	53.4	127	6.0
Race, Sex, and Hispanic Origin							
White	5,334	3,418	64.1	3,242	60.8	176	5.2
Male..........................	2,582	1,847	71.5	1,750	67.8	97	5.2
Female	2,752	1,571	57.1	1,492	54.2	80	5.1
Black or African American....................	1,007	631	62.6	568	56.4	63	10.0
Male..........................	452	310	68.6	281	62.2	29	9.3
Female	556	321	57.8	287	51.6	34	10.6
Hispanic or Latino ethnicity[1]	1,208	822	68.0	759	62.8	63	7.6
Male..........................	616	478	77.7	446	72.5	32	6.7
Female	592	344	58.0	313	52.8	31	8.9
Age							
16 to 19 years..................	486	130	26.7	107	21.9	23	18.0
20 to 24 years..................	585	375	64.1	338	57.8	37	9.8
25 to 34 years..................	1,153	938	81.3	885	76.8	53	5.6
35 to 44 years..................	1,075	890	82.8	849	79.0	41	4.6
45 to 54 years..................	1,336	1,081	80.9	1,032	77.2	49	4.5
55 to 64 years..................	1,112	800	71.9	757	68.1	43	5.4
65 years and over	1,358	332	24.4	313	23.1	19	5.7

NOTE: Data in Table 7 are from the Current Population Survey (CPS) and do not match the estimates in Table 8. See notes and definitions for further information.
[1]May be of any race.

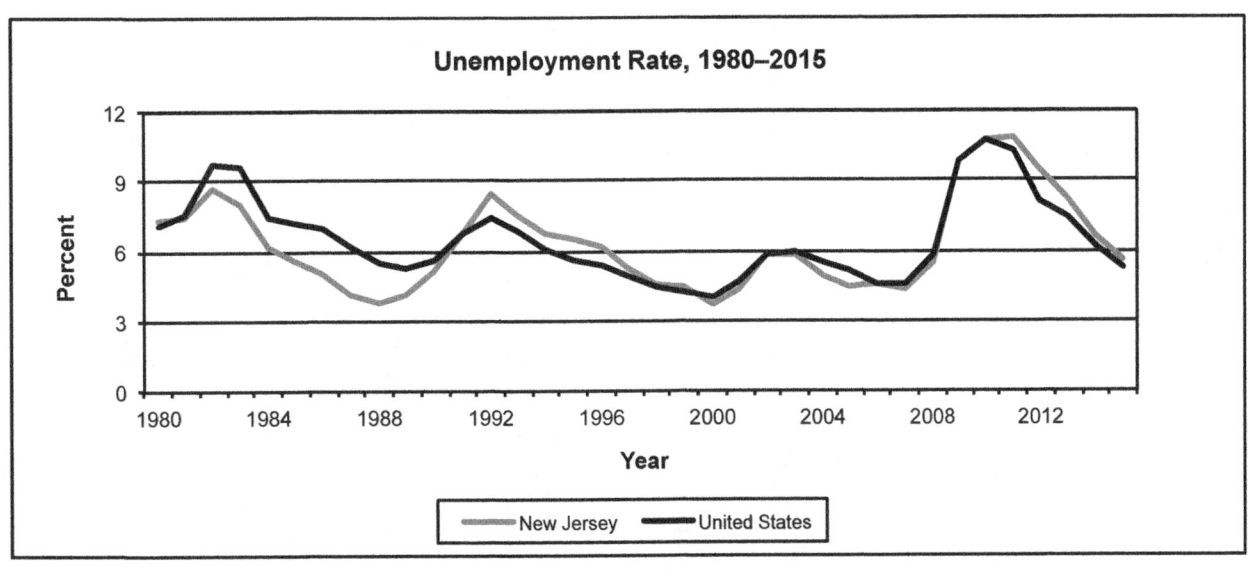

Table NJ-8. Employment Status of the Civilian Noninstitutional Population Age 16 Years and Over

(Number, percent.)

Year	Civilian labor force	Civilian participation rate	Employed	Unemployed	Unemployment rate
2007...	4,441,797	66.4	4,251,815	189,982	4.3
2008...	4,504,432	67.0	4,263,965	240,467	5.3
2009...	4,550,645	67.3	4,138,570	412,075	9.1
2010...	4,555,330	66.4	4,121,455	433,875	9.5
2011...	4,565,272	65.9	4,138,464	426,808	9.3
2012...	4,585,318	65.8	4,158,553	426,765	9.3
2013...	4,528,492	64.6	4,157,649	370,843	8.2
2014...	4,513,600	64.0	4,209,699	303,901	6.7
2015...	4,543,777	64.1	4,288,825	254,952	5.6

Table NJ-9. Employment and Average Wages by Industry

(Estimates through 2010 are based on the 2007 North American Industry Classification System [NAICS]. Estimates from 2011 onward are based on the 2012 NAICS.)

Industry	2008	2009	2010	2011	2012	2013	2014
				Number of jobs			
Wage and Salary Employment by Industry..................	4,118,820	3,960,283	3,922,946	3,923,939	3,951,205	3,989,089	4,022,164
Farm Wage and Salary Employment.........................	6,971	6,755	7,570	7,339	9,511	9,099	9,540
Nonfarm Wage and Salary Employment....................	4,111,849	3,953,528	3,915,376	3,916,600	3,941,694	3,979,990	4,012,624
Private wage and salary employment........................	3,452,565	3,293,683	3,267,478	3,290,968	3,320,739	3,359,773	3,393,143
Forestry, fishing, and related activities........................	2,945	3,078	3,677	3,811	3,890	2,870	3,570
Mining..	1,605	1,492	1,371	1,305	1,251	1,317	1,412
Utilities...	11,939	11,776	14,345	13,596	13,805	13,668	13,663
Construction.....................................	170,499	145,200	136,019	136,803	134,904	142,821	146,199
Manufacturing...................................	298,064	266,926	257,696	253,333	245,520	243,022	242,406
Durable goods manufacturing........................	135,115	118,946	114,308	114,628	112,106	110,998	108,889
Nondurable goods manufacturing....................	162,949	147,980	143,388	138,705	133,414	132,024	133,517
Wholesale trade	234,458	218,250	212,135	211,455	213,869	214,116	215,518
Retail trade......................................	464,036	443,251	444,675	448,211	448,461	453,082	458,977
Transportation and warehousing...................	163,582	153,789	151,198	152,332	151,671	150,777	153,534
Information..	92,278	84,171	79,458	75,774	77,882	75,339	75,613
Finance and insurance...........................	205,875	195,473	193,181	192,542	191,736	191,347	184,886
Real estate and rental and leasing....................	61,663	57,963	56,975	55,182	54,272	56,048	56,037
Professional, scientific, and technical services	293,729	281,110	276,511	281,203	281,409	286,136	290,413
Management of companies and enterprises..................	74,702	75,743	72,785	77,400	79,573	83,312	79,022
Administrative and waste services...................	252,539	235,034	241,793	250,969	261,602	267,697	274,892
Educational services	91,383	92,550	93,419	96,108	94,821	95,353	97,721
Health care and social assistance...................	490,545	497,698	505,292	509,745	519,172	527,688	536,650
Arts, entertainment, and recreation...................	54,877	53,763	53,664	54,897	56,869	58,238	60,504
Accommodation and food services...................	290,812	283,892	285,282	285,593	291,880	297,865	299,927
Other services, except public administration...................	197,034	192,524	188,002	190,709	198,152	199,077	202,199
Government and government enterprises..........................	659,284	659,845	647,898	625,632	620,955	620,217	619,481
				Dollars			
Average Wages and Salaries by Industry	54,523	54,370	55,587	56,722	57,784	58,712	59,825
Average Farm Wages and Salaries	32,043	31,414	26,478	24,434	21,133	30,097	27,089
Average Nonfarm Wages and Salaries	54,561	54,409	55,643	56,783	57,873	58,778	59,903
Average private wages and salaries...........................	54,412	53,986	55,228	56,377	57,556	58,548	59,687
Forestry, fishing, and related activities.....................	23,952	24,754	23,878	24,140	24,155	27,852	27,417
Mining..	62,782	64,157	67,177	66,959	70,261	72,102	71,375
Utilities...	96,909	95,359	99,507	106,182	108,470	107,170	112,824
Construction.....................................	60,266	60,519	60,678	61,676	62,269	63,766	64,896
Manufacturing...................................	70,564	71,230	74,016	74,981	75,929	77,224	79,935
Durable goods manufacturing........................	63,105	63,700	65,867	68,023	68,931	69,603	72,138
Nondurable goods manufacturing....................	76,748	77,283	80,512	80,732	81,809	83,630	86,294
Wholesale trade	73,633	74,077	76,696	79,469	81,011	82,326	85,149
Retail trade......................................	29,742	29,686	30,003	30,392	30,578	30,969	31,704
Transportation and warehousing...................	47,455	47,215	48,360	49,321	50,206	51,643	52,411
Information..	82,775	83,274	86,114	89,636	92,730	96,140	98,801
Finance and insurance...........................	101,375	97,256	104,128	106,852	108,681	110,930	115,832
Real estate and rental and leasing....................	52,884	51,637	54,032	54,103	58,945	58,512	60,364
Professional, scientific, and technical services	85,411	85,976	88,091	90,889	95,576	97,568	100,084
Management of companies and enterprises..................	124,500	124,666	132,582	136,761	146,350	150,391	151,769
Administrative and waste services...................	37,284	36,723	37,264	38,182	38,560	39,149	39,647
Educational services	35,196	36,281	37,226	37,976	38,313	39,670	40,370
Health care and social assistance...................	46,364	46,792	46,802	47,448	48,267	48,632	49,506
Arts, entertainment, and recreation...................	35,863	35,868	36,633	35,269	36,753	36,910	36,267
Accommodation and food services...................	22,987	22,057	22,536	22,779	22,985	23,287	24,257
Other services, except public administration.................	31,519	31,359	32,027	32,429	32,161	32,866	33,449
Government and government enterprises..........................	55,343	56,525	57,740	58,919	59,570	60,021	61,089

Table NJ-10. Employment Characteristics by Family Type

(Number, percent.)

Family type and labor force status	2012 Total	2012 Families with own children under 18 years	2013 Total	2013 Families with own children under 18 years	2014 Total	2014 Families with own children under 18 years
All Families	2,211,642	1,009,713	2,207,108	985,032	2,194,075	971,317
FAMILY TYPE AND LABOR FORCE STATUS						
Married-Couple Families	1,626,018	720,912	1,609,473	703,827	1,598,280	689,184
Both husband and wife in labor force	56.4	67.9	55.1	67.4	55.7	67.6
Husband in labor force, wife not in labor force	22.3	27.6	22.9	27.8	22.5	27.9
Wife in labor force, husband not in labor force	7.4	3.4	7.4	3.6	7.5	3.4
Both husband and wife not in labor force	13.9	1.1	14.2	0.9	14.3	1.0
Other Families	585,624	288,801	597,635	281,205	595,795	282,133
Female householder, no husband present	73.7	78.2	73.2	76.2	74.1	77.7
In labor force	53.4	64.8	52.7	63.2	54.2	65.8
Not in labor force	20.3	13.4	20.5	13.0	19.9	11.9
Male householder, no wife present	26.3	21.8	26.8	23.8	25.9	22.3
In labor force	21.2	20.4	21.0	21.4	20.9	21.0
Not in labor force	5.1	1.4	5.8	2.4	5.0	1.3

Table NJ-11. School Enrollment and Educational Attainment, 2014

(Number, percent.)

Item	State	U.S.
Enrollment		
Total population 3 years and over, enrolled in school	2,272,659	82,063,714
Enrolled in nursery school or preschool (percent)	7.7	6.0
Enrolled in kindergarten (percent)	4.9	5.1
Enrolled in elementary school, grades 1-8 (percent)	39.7	40.2
Enrolled in high school, grades 9-12 (percent)	21.3	20.7
Enrolled in college or graduate school (percent)	26.5	28.0
Attainment		
Total population 25 years and over	6,127,931	213,725,624
Less than ninth grade (percent)	5.2	5.6
9th to 12th grade, no diploma (percent)	5.8	7.5
High school graduate, including equivalency (percent)	28.2	27.7
Some college, no degree (percent)	17.1	21.0
Associate's degree (percent)	6.4	8.2
Bachelor's degree (percent)	23.1	18.7
Graduate or professional degree (percent)	14.3	11.4
High school graduate or higher (percent)	89.1	86.9
Bachelor's degree or higher (percent)	37.4	30.1

Table NJ-12. Public School Characteristics and Educational Indicators

(Number, percent; data derived from National Center of Education Statistics.)

Item	State	U.S.
Public Schools, 2013–2014 (except where noted)		
Number of school districts	680	18,194
Number of schools	2,508	98,271
Number of students (in thousands)	1,370	50,045
Number of teachers (in thousands)	115	3,114
Student-teacher ratio	12.0	16.1
Expenditures per student (dollars), FY 2013	18,523	107,637
Four-year adjusted cohort graduation rate (ACGR)[1,2]	88.6	82.3
Students eligible for free or reduced-price lunch (in thousands)	519	25,596
English language learners (in thousands)	61	4,461
Students age 3 to 21 served under IDEA, part B (in thousands)	229	6,464

Public Schools by Type	Number	Percent of state public schools
Total number of schools	2,508	100.0
Regular	2,370	94.5
Special education	58	2.3
Vocational education	57	2.3
Alternative education	23	0.9

NOTE: Every school is assigned only one school type based on its instructional emphasis.
[1]ACGR data represents a new method of calculating high-school completion rates and may not be comparable to previous years' data for Averaged Freshmen Graduation Rates (AFGR).
[2]The United States 4-year ACGRs were estimated using both the reported 4-year ACGR data from 49 states and the District of Columbia and using imputed data for Idaho. The estimate for American Indian/Alaska Native students also includes imputed data for Virginia.

Table NJ-13. Reported Voting and Registration of the Voting-Age Population, November 2014

(Numbers in thousands, percent.)

Item	Total population	Total citizen population	Registered			Voted		
			Total registered	Percent registered (total population)	Percent registered (total citizen population)	Total voted	Percent voted (total population)	Percent voted (total citizen population)
U.S. Total	239,874	219,941	142,166	59.3	64.6	92,251	38.5	41.9
State Total............................	6,820	5,909	3,919	57.5	66.3	2,151	31.5	36.4
Sex								
Male....................................	3,277	2,825	1,808	55.2	64.0	969	29.6	34.3
Female	3,543	3,084	2,112	59.6	68.5	1,182	33.4	38.3
Race								
White alone..........................	5,146	4,645	3,161	61.4	68.0	1,771	34.4	38.1
White, non-Hispanic alone..........	4,036	3,912	2,705	67.0	69.1	1,527	37.8	39.0
Black alone...........................	953	779	496	52.0	63.6	276	29.0	35.4
Asian alone	641	425	226	35.3	53.2	82	12.9	19.4
Hispanic (of any race)................	1,229	805	497	40.4	61.7	274	22.3	34.1
White alone or in combination	5,194	4,682	3,183	61.3	68.0	1,782	34.3	38.1
Black alone or in combination..........	972	798	511	52.5	64.0	276	28.4	34.6
Asian alone or in combination..........	655	438	237	36.2	54.1	93	14.3	21.3
Age								
18 to 24 years......................	772	698	328	42.5	47.0	100	12.9	14.3
25 to 34 years......................	1,139	877	485	42.6	55.3	160	14.0	18.3
35 to 44 years......................	1,124	860	591	52.5	68.7	263	23.4	30.5
45 to 64 years......................	2,427	2,181	1,576	65.0	72.3	963	39.7	44.2
65 years and over	1,358	1,292	940	69.2	72.7	666	49.0	51.5

Table NJ-14. Crime

(Number, rate per 100,000. Data are derived from the FBI Uniform Crime Reports.)

Item	State			U.S.[1,2,3,4]		
	2013	2014	Percent change	2013	2014	Percent change
TOTAL POPULATION[5].............................	8,899,339	8,938,175	0.4	316,128,839	318,857,056	0.9
VIOLENT CRIME						
Number..............................	25,415	23,346	-8.1	1,163,146	1,165,383	0.2
Rate	285.6	261.2	-8.5	367.9	365.5	-0.7
Murder and Nonnegligent Manslaughter						
Number..............................	401	349	-13.0	14,196	14,249	0.4
Rate	4.5	3.9	-13.3	4.5	4.5	-
Rape[6]						
Number..............................	1,120	1,274	X	108,612	116,645	X
Rate	12.6	14.3	X	34.4	36.6	X
Robbery						
Number..............................	12,082	10,498	-13.1	345,031	325,802	-5.6
Rate	135.8	117.5	-13.5	109.1	102.2	-6.3
Aggravated Assault						
Number..............................	12,071	11,225	-7.0	724,149	741,291	2.4
Rate	135.6	125.6	-7.4	229.1	232.5	1.5
PROPERTY CRIME						
Number..............................	167,556	154,993	-7.5	8,632,512	8,277,829	-4.1
Rate	1,882.8	1,734.1	-7.9	2,730.7	2,596.1	-4.9
Burglary						
Number..............................	35,873	31,710	-11.6	1,928,465	1,729,806	-10.3
Rate	403.1	354.8	-12.0	610.0	542.5	-11.1
Larceny-Theft						
Number..............................	117,936	111,578	-5.4	6,004,453	5,858,496	-2.4
Rate	1,325.2	1,248.3	-5.8	1,899.4	1,837.3	-3.3
Motor Vehicle Theft						
Number..............................	13,747	11,705	-14.9	699,594	689,527	-1.4
Rate	154.5	131.0	-15.2	221.3	216.2	-2.3

NOTE: Although arson data are included in the trend and clearance tables, sufficient data are not available to estimate totals for this offense. Therefore, no arson data are published in this table.
X = Not applicable.
- = Zero or rounds to zero.
[1]The crime figures have been adjusted.
[2]The data collection methodology for the offense of forcible rape used by the Minnesota state Uniform Crime Reporting (UCR) Program (with the exception of Minneapolis and St. Paul, Minnesota) does not comply with national UCR Program guidelines. Consequently, its figures for forcible rape and violent crime (of which forcible rape is a part) are not published in this table.
[3]Includes offenses reported by the Zoological Police and the Metro Transit Police.
[4]Because of changes in the state's reporting practices, figures are not comparable to previous years' data.
[5]Populations are U.S. Census Bureau provisional estimates as of July 1 of each year.
[6]The figures shown for the offense of rape were estimated using the revised Uniform Crime Reporting (UCR) definition of rape.

Table NJ-15. State Government Finances, 2014

(Dollar amounts in thousands, percent distribution.)

Item	Dollars	Percent distribution
Total Revenue	65,657,635	100.0
General revenue	56,558,996	86.1
Intergovernmental revenue	16,049,091	24.4
Taxes	29,679,226	45.2
General sales	8,885,847	13.5
Selective sales	3,866,004	5.9
License taxes	1,516,698	2.3
Individual income tax	11,973,673	18.2
Corporate income tax	2,368,068	3.6
Other taxes	1,068,936	1.6
Current charges	6,270,757	9.6
Miscellaneous general revenue	4,559,922	6.9
Utility revenue	1,029,118	1.6
Liquor stores revenue	0	-
Insurance trust revenue[1]	8,069,521	12.3
Total Expenditure	69,081,342	100.0
Intergovernmental expenditure	12,104,168	17.5
Direct expenditure	56,977,174	82.5
Current operation	36,511,499	52.9
Capital outlay	3,635,710	5.3
Insurance benefits and repayments	13,367,146	19.3
Assistance and subsidies	1,358,014	2.0
Interest on debt	2,104,805	3.0
Exhibit: Salaries and wages	10,247,660	14.8
Total Expenditure	69,081,342	100.0
General expenditure	53,517,630	77.5
Intergovernmental expenditure	12,104,168	17.5
Direct expenditure	41,413,462	59.9
General expenditure, by function:		
Education	17,087,383	24.7
Public welfare	15,922,690	23.0
Hospitals	2,267,061	3.3
Health	1,464,909	2.1
Highways	3,607,065	5.2
Police protection	871,267	1.3
Correction	1,409,867	2.0
Natural resources	441,991	0.6
Parks and recreation	210,407	0.3
Governmental administration	1,693,019	2.5
Interest on general debt	2,102,526	3.0
Other and unallocable	6,439,445	9.3
Utility expenditure	2,196,566	3.2
Liquor stores expenditure	0	-
Insurance trust expenditure	13,367,146	19.3
Debt at End of Fiscal Year	66,089,959	X
Cash and Security Holdings	122,220,439	X

X = Not applicable.
- = Zero or rounds to zero.
[1]Within insurance trust revenue, net earnings of state retirement systems is a calculated statistic (the item code in the data file is X08), and thus can be positive or negative. Net earnings is the sum of earnings on investments plus gains on investments minus losses on investments. The change made in 2002 for asset valuation from book to market value in accordance with Statement 34 of the Governmental Accounting Standards Board is reflected in the calculated statistics.

Table NJ-16. State Government Tax Collections, 2014

(Dollars in thousands, percent.)

Item	Dollars	Percent distribution
Total Taxes	29,679,226	100.0
Property taxes	6,705	-
Sales and gross receipts	12,751,851	43.0
General sales and gross receipts	8,885,847	29.9
Selective sales and gross receipts	3,866,004	13.0
Alcoholic beverages	139,438	0.5
Amusements	219,000	0.7
Insurance premiums	599,169	2.0
Motor fuels	539,155	1.8
Pari-mutuels	0	-
Public utilities	1,012,028	3.4
Tobacco products	740,605	2.5
Other selective sales	616,609	2.1
Licenses	1,516,698	5.1
Alcoholic beverages	3,965	-
Amusements	49,618	0.2
Corporations in general	275,705	0.9
Hunting and fishing	13,206	-
Motor vehicle	617,428	2.1
Motor vehicle operators	53,016	0.2
Public utilities	6,765	-
Occupation and business, NEC	495,599	1.7
Other licenses	1,396	-
Income taxes	14,341,741	48.3
Individual income	11,973,673	40.3
Corporation net income	2,368,068	8.0
Other taxes	1,062,231	3.6
Death and gift	685,459	2.3
Documentary and stock transfer	376,772	1.3
Severance	X	X
Taxes, NEC	0	-

X = Not applicable.
- = Zero or rounds to zero.

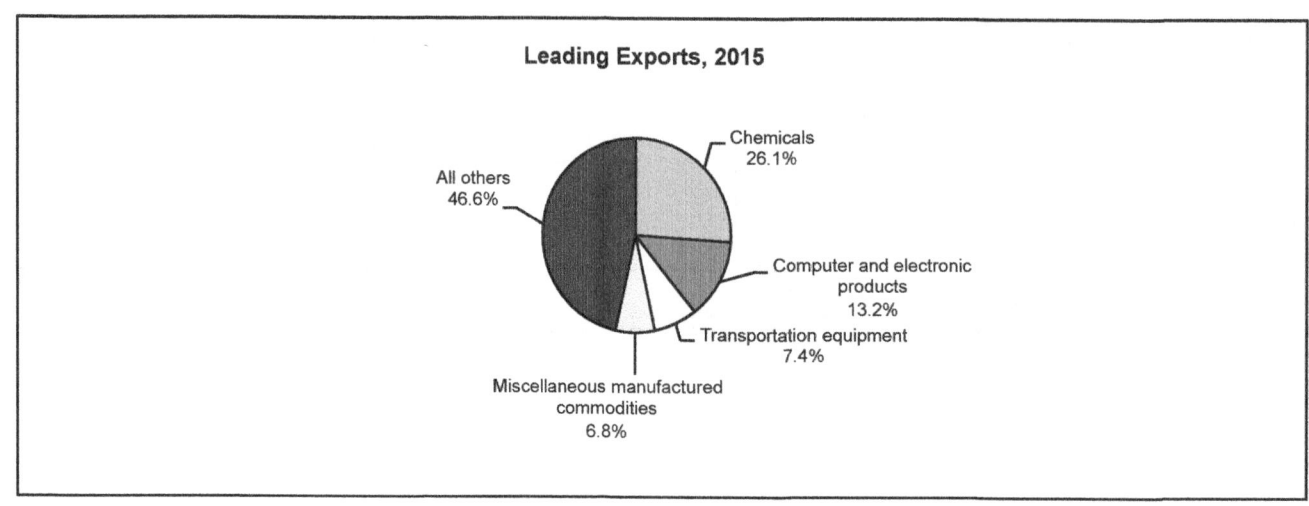

Leading Exports, 2015

Chemicals 26.1%

All others 46.6%

Computer and electronic products 13.2%

Transportation equipment 7.4%

Miscellaneous manufactured commodities 6.8%

NEW MEXICO

Facts and Figures

Location: Southwestern United States; bordered on the N by Colorado, on the E by Oklahoma and Texas, on the S by Texas and Mexico, and on the W by Arizona; New Mexico is one of the Four Corner states—at its NW corner it touches Arizona, Colorado, and Utah

Area: 121,590 sq. mi. (314,915 sq. km.); rank—5th

Population: 2,085,109 (2015 est.); rank—36th

Principal Cities: capital—Santa Fe; largest—Albuquerque

Statehood: January 6, 1912; 47th state

U.S. Congress: 2 senators, 3 representatives

State Motto: *Crescit eundo* ("It grows as it goes")

State Song: "O, Fair New Mexico"

State Nickname: The Land of Enchantment

Abbreviations: NM; N. Mex.

State Symbols: flower—yucca; tree—piñon; bird—roadrunner

At a Glance

- With an increase in population of 1.0 percent, New Mexico ranked 41st among the states in growth from 2010 to 2015.

- In 2014, New Mexico's violent crime rate of 597.4 per 100,000 population was the 5th highest rate in the country, and its property crime rate of 3,542.3 per 100,000 population, was the 3rd highest in the country.

- With approximately 48.0 percent of its residents self-identifying as "Hispanic or Latino," New Mexico was the state with the highest percentage of this population in 2015.

- New Mexico had the 2nd highest percentage of residents living below the poverty line in 2014 (21.3 percent).

- In 2015, 6.6 percent of New Mexico residents were unemployed, compared to 5.3 percent of the entire U.S. population.

Table NM-1. Population by Age, Sex, Race, and Hispanic Origin

(Number, percent, except where noted.)

Sex, age, race, and Hispanic origin	2000	2010	2015[1]	Average annual percent change,2010–2015
Total Population.............................	1,819,046	2,059,179	2,085,109	0.1
Percent of total U.S. population	0.6	0.7	0.6	X
Sex				
Male.............................	894,317	1,017,421	1,033,421	0.1
Female	924,729	1,041,758	1,051,688	0.1
Age				
Under 5 years.............................	130,628	144,981	135,024	-0.5
5 to 19 years.............................	434,231	434,860	416,561	-0.3
20 to 64 years.............................	1,041,962	1,207,083	1,203,119	-
65 years and over	212,225	272,255	330,405	1.4
Median age (years)	34.6	36.7	37.3	0.1
Race and Hispanic origin.............................				
One race				
White	1,214,253	1,720,992	1,721,137	-
Black.............................	34,343	49,006	53,429	0.6
American Indian and Alaska Native	173,483	208,890	219,237	0.3
Asian.............................	19,255	31,253	35,933	1.0
Native Hawaiian or Other Pacific Islander	1,503	3,132	3,485	0.8
Two or more races	66,327	45,906	51,888	0.9
Hispanic (of any race)	765,386	973,088	1,001,258	0.2

X = Not applicable.
- = Zero or rounds to zero.
[1]Population figures for 2015 are July 1 estimates. The 2010 estimates are taken from the 2010 Census.

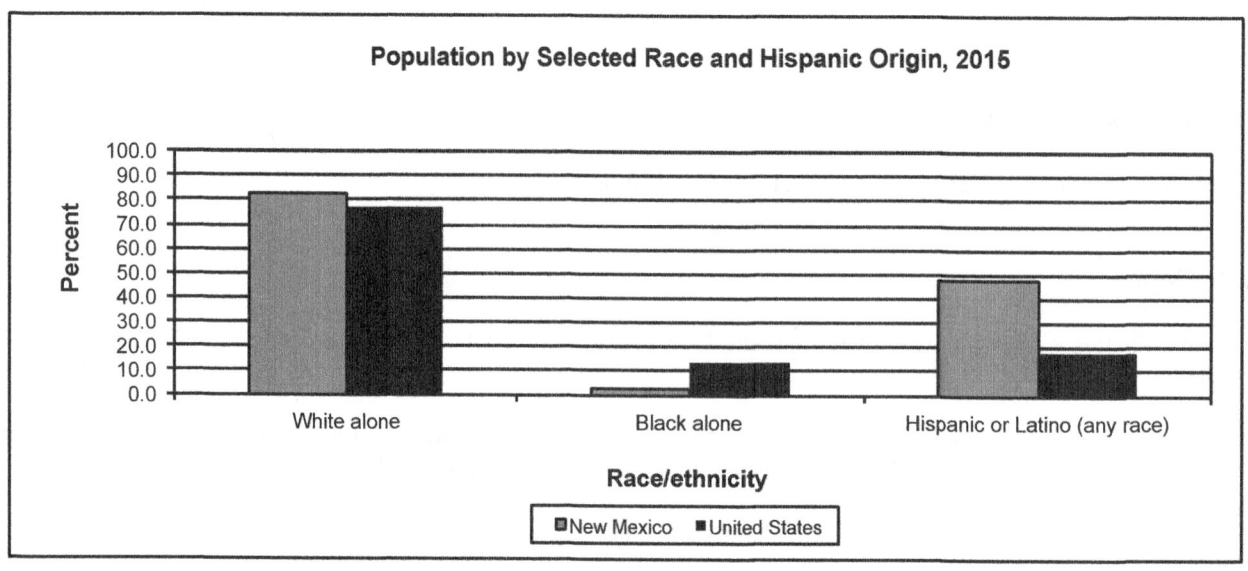

Population by Selected Race and Hispanic Origin, 2015

Table NM-2. Marital Status

(Number, percent distribution.)

Sex, age, race, and Hispanic origin	2000	2010	2014
Males, 15 Years and Over	677,967	801,901	812,255
Never married	30.5	35.4	36.4
Now married, except separated.............................	55.0	48.4	47.7
Separated.............................	1.6	1.6	1.5
Widowed.............................	2.6	2.6	2.8
Divorced.............................	10.4	11.9	11.6
Females, 15 Years and Over	720,529	833,357	841,695
Never married	24.7	29.9	30.3
Now married, except separated.............................	51.2	45.0	44.3
Separated.............................	2.0	2.6	2.3
Widowed.............................	9.4	8.5	8.9
Divorced.............................	12.8	14.1	14.2

Table NM-3. Households and Housing Characteristics

(Number, percent, dollars.)

Item	2000	2010	2014	Average annual percent change, 2000–2014
Total Households...	677,971	765,183	760,916	0.9
Family households....................................	466,515	501,092	489,532	0.4
Married-couple family.............................	341,818	349,344	340,733	-0.0
Other family...	124,697	151,748	148,799	1.4
Male householder, no wife present.........	35,075	49,041	42,076	1.4
Female householder, no husband present........	89,622	102,707	106,723	1.4
Nonfamily households..............................	211,456	264,091	271,384	2.0
Householder living alone..........................	172,181	216,704	227,301	2.3
Householder not living alone.....................	39,275	47,387	44,083	0.9
Housing Characteristics				
Total housing units..................................	780,579	902,242	912,910	1.2
Occupied housing units	677,971	765,183	760,916	0.9
Owner occupied......................................	474,445	519,864	509,151	0.5
Renter occupied......................................	203,526	245,319	251,765	1.7
Average household size............................	2.63	2.64	2.68	0.1
Financial Characteristics				
Median gross rent of renter-occupied housing	503	699	777	3.9
Median monthly owner costs for housing units with a mortgage	929	1,202	1,195	2.0
Median value of owner-occupied housing units....................	108,100	161,200	158,400	3.3

Table NM-4. Migration, Origin, and Language

(Number, percent.)

Characteristic	State			U.S.		
	2013	2014	Percent change	2013	2014	Percent change
Residence 1 Year Ago						
Population 1 year and over	2,059,689	2,060,189	-	312,432,820	315,095,393	0.9
Same house..	85.7	85.9	X	85.0	85.1	X
Different house in the U.S.	13.7	13.7	X	14.4	14.3	X
Same county...	8.6	7.8	X	8.9	8.7	X
Different county.......................................	5.1	5.9	X	5.5	5.6	X
Same state..	2.3	2.5	X	3.2	3.3	X
Different state......................................	2.8	3.3	X	2.3	2.3	X
Abroad	0.7	0.4	X	0.6	0.6	X
Place of Birth						
Native born...	1,874,038	1,879,919	0.3	274,780,773	276,465,262	0.6
Male..	49.6	49.8	X	49.3	49.3	X
Female...	50.4	50.2	X	50.7	50.7	X
Foreign born	211,249	205,653	-2.6	41,348,066	42,391,794	2.5
Male..	49.1	47.3	X	48.8	48.7	X
Female...	50.9	52.7	X	51.2	51.3	X
Foreign born; naturalized U.S. citizen...........	72,651	75,607	4.1	19,294,710	19,984,738	3.6
Male..	43.4	43.7	X	45.9	45.9	X
Female...	56.6	56.3	X	54.1	54.1	X
Foreign born; not a U.S. citizen..................	138,598	130,046	-6.2	22,053,356	22,407,056	1.6
Male..	52.1	49.3	X	51.3	51.2	X
Female...	47.9	50.7	X	48.7	48.8	X
Entered 2010 or later	8.1	8.4	X	9.7	12.3	X
Entered 2000 to 2009	28.5	29.9	X	29.4	28.6	X
Entered before 2000.................................	63.4	61.7	X	61.0	59.1	X
World Region of Birth, Foreign						
Foreign-born population, excluding population born at sea	211,249	205,653	-2.6	41,347,945	42,390,705	2.5
Europe...	8.3	6.6	X	11.6	11.2	X
Asia...	10.6	11.9	X	29.5	30.1	X
Africa	1.0	1.7	X	4.4	4.6	X
Oceania..	0.3	0.3	X	0.5	0.6	X
Latin America..	78.6	77.9	X	51.9	51.6	X
North America...	1.2	1.7	X	2.0	1.9	X
Language Spoken at Home and Ability to Speak English						
Population 5 years and over.......................	1,946,891	1,950,156	0.2	296,358,760	299,084,046	0.9
English only	64.0	63.2	X	79.2	78.9	X
Language other than English.......................	36.0	36.8	X	20.8	21.1	X
Speaks English less than "very well"............	9.8	9.1	X	8.5	8.6	X

X = Not applicable.
- = Zero or rounds to zero.

Table NM-5. Median Income and Poverty Status, 2014

(Number, percent, except as noted.)

Characteristic	State		U.S.	
	Number	Percent	Number	Percent
Median Income				
Households (dollars)..	44,803	X	53,657	X
Families (dollars)	54,705	X	65,910	X
Below Poverty Level (All People)	436,153	21.3	48,208,387	15.5
Sex				
Male...	196,919	19.6	21,590,918	14.2
Female	239,234	23.0	26,617,469	16.8
Age				
Under 18 years..	145,966	29.5	15,686,012	21.7
Related children under 18 years...........................	142,903	29.1	15,372,705	21.3
18 to 64 years..	248,861	20.1	28,267,482	14.6
65 years and over	41,326	13.2	4,254,893	9.5

X = Not applicable.

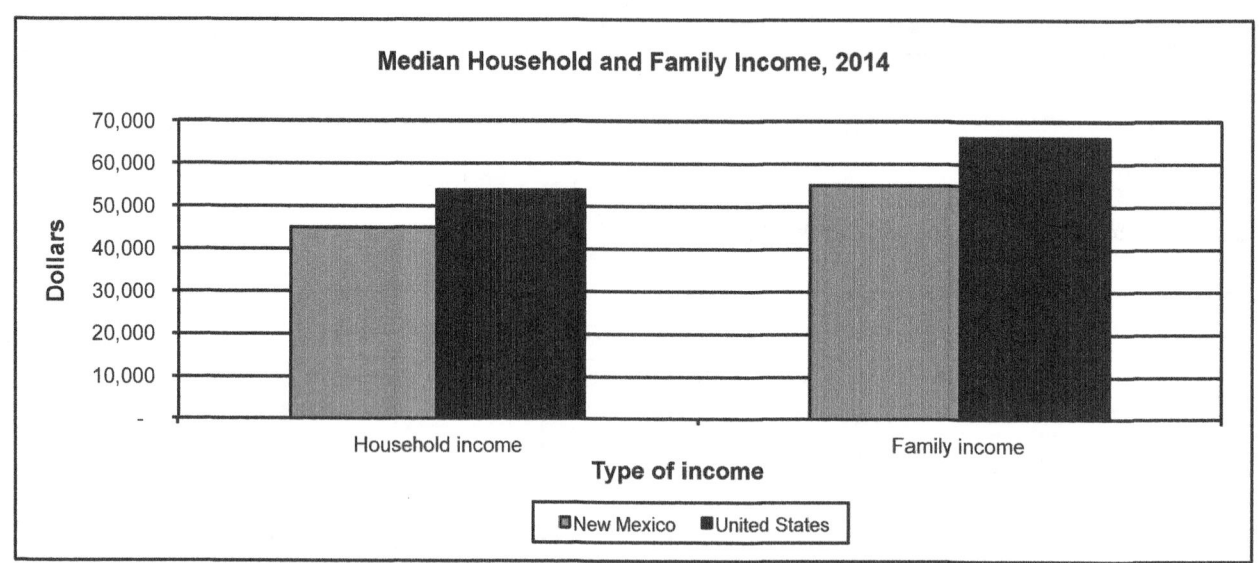

Table NM-6. Health Insurance Coverage Status for the Civilian Noninstitutionalized Population and Children Under 18 Years of Age

(Numbers in thousands, percent.)

Item	2006	2007	2008	2009	2010	2011	2012	2013	2014
Civilian Noninstitutionalized Population	1,943	1,946	1,952	1,976	2,033	2,047	2,052	2,052	2,050
Covered by Private or Public Insurance									
Number..	1,498	1,509	1,533	1,586	1,634	1,641	1,674	1,669	1,753
Percent..	77.1	77.5	78.5	80.3	80.4	80.2	81.6	81.4	85.5
Not Covered									
Number..	445	437	419	390	399	406	378	382	298
Percent..	22.9	22.5	21.5	19.7	19.6	19.8	18.4	18.6	14.5
Percent in the U.S. not covered...............................	15.8	15.3	15.1	15.1	15.5	15.1	14.8	14.5	11.7
Children Under 18 Years of Age	520	495	501	514	518	517	515	507	499
Covered by Private or Public Insurance									
Number..	428	419	432	455	465	470	474	464	462
Percent..	82.1	84.5	86.2	88.6	89.8	90.8	92.0	91.5	92.7
Not Covered									
Number..	93	77	69	59	53	47	41	43	36
Percent..	17.9	15.5	13.8	11.4	10.2	9.2	8.0	8.5	7.3
Percent in the U.S. not covered...............................	11.7	11.0	9.7	8.6	8.0	7.5	7.2	7.1	6.0

Table NM-7. Employment Status by Demographic Group, 2015

(Numbers in thousands, percent.)

Characteristic	Civilian noninstitutional population	Civilian labor force		Employed		Unemployed	
		Number	Percent of population	Number	Percent of population	Number	Percent of population
Total...	1,603	924	57.6	861	53.7	63	6.8
Sex							
Male..	778	491	63.1	454	58.4	37	7.5
Female.......................................	825	433	52.5	407	49.3	26	6.0
Race, Sex, and Hispanic Origin							
White	1,261	740	58.7	698	55.4	42	5.7
Male......................................	616	396	64.2	371	60.2	25	6.3
Female...................................	645	345	53.4	328	50.8	17	4.9
Black or African American..............	42	27	64.5	25	60.3	2	6.5
Male......................................	NA	NA	NA	NA	NA	NA	NA
Female...................................	NA	NA	NA	NA	NA	NA	NA
Hispanic or Latino ethnicity[1]	658	406	61.8	381	57.9	26	6.4
Male......................................	321	214	66.8	200	62.2	15	6.8
Female...................................	337	192	57.0	181	53.7	11	5.8
Age							
16 to 19 years.............................	118	36	30.7	28	23.7	8	23.0
20 to 24 years.............................	149	100	67.5	89	60.2	11	11.0
25 to 34 years.............................	253	192	76.0	178	70.3	15	7.5
35 to 44 years.............................	236	188	79.6	176	74.5	12	6.4
45 to 54 years.............................	262	195	74.7	186	71.3	9	4.6
55 to 64 years.............................	262	158	60.3	152	57.8	7	4.1
65 years and over	324	54	16.8	53	16.3	2	2.9

NOTE: Data in Table 7 are from the Current Population Survey (CPS) and do not match the estimates in Table 8. See notes and definitions for further information.
[1]May be of any race.
NA = Not available.

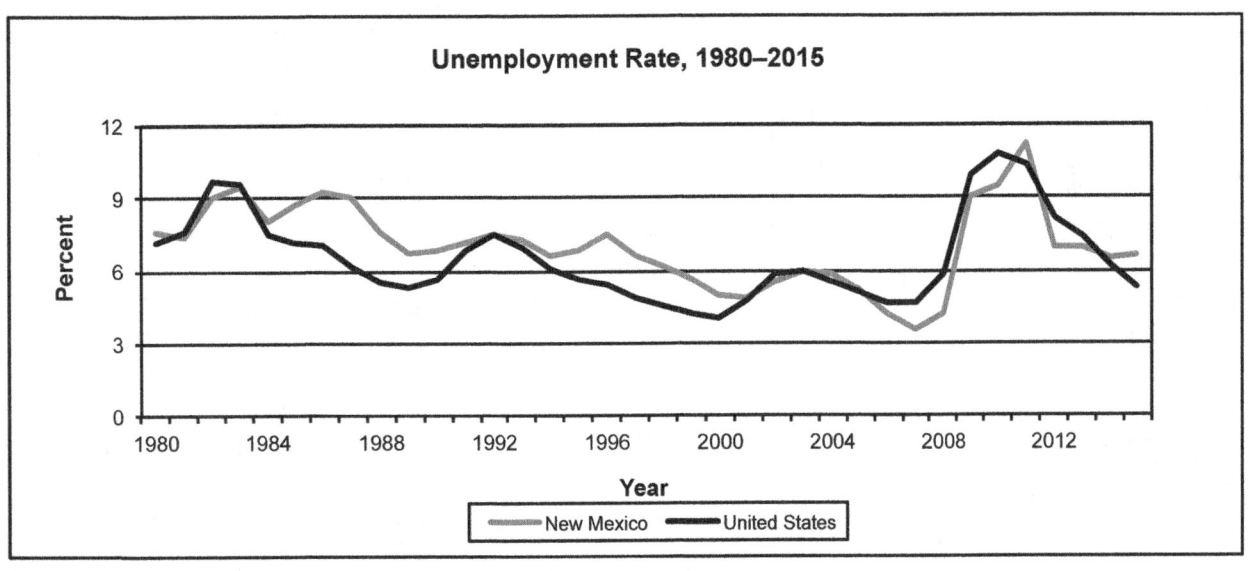

Table NM-8. Employment Status of the Civilian Noninstitutional Population Age 16 Years and Over

(Number, percent.)

Year	Civilian labor force	Civilian participation rate	Employed	Unemployed	Unemployment rate
2007..........................	934,027	63.0	898,998	35,029	3.8
2008..........................	944,548	63.0	902,411	42,137	4.5
2009..........................	940,352	62.0	869,491	70,861	7.5
2010..........................	936,088	60.0	860,154	75,934	8.1
2011..........................	930,356	58.8	860,305	70,051	7.5
2012..........................	928,739	58.4	862,556	66,183	7.1
2013..........................	923,685	57.8	859,428	64,257	7.0
2014..........................	921,380	57.5	859,305	62,075	6.7
2015..........................	919,889	57.2	859,242	60,647	6.6

Table NM-9. Employment and Average Wages by Industry

(Estimates through 2010 are based on the 2007 North American Industry Classification System [NAICS]. Estimates from 2011 onward are based on the 2012 NAICS.)

Industry	2008	2009	2010	2011	2012	2013	2014
	Number of jobs						
Wage and Salary Employment by Industry..................	881,357	848,403	840,219	840,690	842,939	849,701	853,031
Farm Wage and Salary Employment.........................	6,671	6,958	6,643	6,503	6,881	7,886	6,780
Nonfarm Wage and Salary Employment....................	874,686	841,445	833,576	834,187	836,058	841,815	846,251
Private wage and salary employment........................	661,461	625,304	616,320	620,357	623,788	630,455	637,384
Forestry, fishing, and related activities.....................	2,858	2,753	2,923	3,034	3,028	2,899	3,389
Mining........................	21,111	17,511	18,284	21,096	23,795	25,805	27,633
Utilities........................	4,327	4,614	4,374	4,367	4,386	4,445	4,417
Construction	59,690	50,030	45,973	44,534	42,641	43,739	44,050
Manufacturing........................	35,080	30,075	29,064	29,602	29,706	29,111	28,008
Durable goods manufacturing........................	24,052	19,761	19,040	19,346	19,082	18,299	17,284
Nondurable goods manufacturing........................	11,028	10,314	10,024	10,256	10,624	10,812	10,724
Wholesale trade	23,777	21,870	22,074	21,162	21,521	21,684	21,744
Retail trade........................	97,673	93,059	91,272	91,545	91,866	92,853	93,605
Transportation and warehousing........................	20,632	18,301	17,812	18,475	19,264	19,201	19,805
Information	16,000	14,737	14,329	13,470	13,644	13,115	12,563
Finance and insurance	23,069	22,736	22,323	22,167	22,136	22,293	22,865
Real estate and rental and leasing........................	11,376	10,361	10,167	10,012	9,896	10,205	10,241
Professional, scientific, and technical services	56,951	55,923	54,422	54,174	52,831	52,654	53,001
Management of companies and enterprises..................	5,372	5,079	4,954	5,071	4,989	5,072	5,055
Administrative and waste services........................	47,419	42,544	41,722	42,179	40,888	41,895	41,817
Educational services	10,069	10,042	10,319	10,652	10,679	10,351	10,408
Health care and social assistance........................	98,316	101,908	103,733	105,592	107,232	108,183	109,944
Arts, entertainment, and recreation........................	8,763	8,779	8,648	8,668	9,021	9,135	9,019
Accommodation and food services........................	78,725	76,361	76,134	76,763	77,789	79,846	82,438
Other services, except public administration...............	40,253	38,621	37,793	37,794	38,476	37,969	37,382
Government and government enterprises	213,225	216,141	217,256	213,830	212,270	211,360	208,867
	Dollars						
Average Wages and Salaries by Industry	38,686	39,301	40,069	40,905	41,603	41,800	42,959
Average Farm Wages and Salaries	35,732	38,036	34,612	36,685	29,633	38,732	41,810
Average Nonfarm Wages and Salaries	38,709	39,312	40,112	40,938	41,702	41,829	42,968
Average private wages and salaries........................	37,663	37,998	38,919	39,741	40,751	40,855	41,937
Forestry, fishing, and related activities........................	21,006	21,433	21,521	22,348	23,077	23,794	23,505
Mining........................	68,956	66,837	75,764	72,876	74,377	74,348	77,644
Utilities........................	73,015	72,143	72,919	73,908	76,180	77,145	79,274
Construction........................	41,149	41,603	41,389	41,880	42,618	42,373	43,436
Manufacturing........................	48,893	50,838	53,528	55,293	57,181	57,160	58,719
Durable goods manufacturing........................	53,800	55,871	59,412	61,778	64,214	64,152	66,076
Nondurable goods manufacturing........................	38,189	41,197	42,351	43,062	44,549	45,326	46,861
Wholesale trade	49,257	49,111	50,051	50,329	51,553	51,534	53,282
Retail trade........................	25,684	25,631	26,042	26,471	27,101	27,197	27,912
Transportation and warehousing........................	45,026	44,328	45,490	48,050	49,851	50,213	52,020
Information	42,896	43,859	43,071	45,768	47,375	47,465	49,635
Finance and insurance	49,503	50,511	52,482	54,856	57,515	58,911	59,677
Real estate and rental and leasing........................	32,602	32,264	33,893	36,108	36,511	36,846	37,810
Professional, scientific, and technical services	67,105	68,167	70,507	71,223	72,976	72,439	75,193
Management of companies and enterprises..................	56,736	60,495	62,340	63,530	68,018	66,629	69,970
Administrative and waste services........................	31,433	32,809	32,980	34,530	35,245	34,740	34,660
Educational services	30,616	31,175	31,699	32,179	31,535	32,505	32,532
Health care and social assistance........................	37,295	38,311	38,503	39,074	39,863	40,268	40,614
Arts, entertainment, and recreation........................	22,225	21,554	21,532	21,844	22,091	22,580	23,867
Accommodation and food services........................	16,397	16,746	17,224	17,548	17,871	17,980	18,681
Other services, except public administration...............	25,444	25,567	26,325	26,768	27,381	27,615	28,684
Government and government enterprises........................	41,952	43,114	43,497	44,412	44,496	44,735	46,115

Table NM-10. Employment Characteristics by Family Type

(Number, percent.)

Family type and labor force status	2012 Total	2012 Families with own children under 18 years	2013 Total	2013 Families with own children under 18 years	2014 Total	2014 Families with own children under 18 years
All Families.....	501,421	213,058	482,570	210,516	487,117	205,222
FAMILY TYPE AND LABOR FORCE STATUS						
Married-Couple Families.....	347,070	125,725	336,560	125,487	338,318	123,755
Both husband and wife in labor force.....	46.5	62.6	44.1	58.5	44.3	58.8
Husband in labor force, wife not in labor force	22.9	29.4	25.0	34.5	23.7	34.4
Wife in labor force, husband not in labor force	8.9	4.9	9.3	5.0	9.8	4.9
Both husband and wife not in labor force.....	21.7	3.1	21.2	1.8	22.1	1.9
Other Families	154,351	87,333	146,010	85,029	148,799	81,467
Female householder, no husband present.....	71.7	73.2	73.3	73.4	71.7	72.9
In labor force.....	49.2	57.5	50.7	58.3	47.6	56.3
Not in labor force	22.5	15.6	22.6	15.1	24.1	16.6
Male householder, no wife present.....	28.3	26.8	26.7	26.6	28.3	27.1
In labor force.....	22.0	24.1	18.9	22.8	21.8	24.1
Not in labor force	6.3	2.8	7.8	3.8	6.5	3.0

Table NM-11. School Enrollment and Educational Attainment, 2014

(Number, percent.)

Item	State	U.S.
Enrollment		
Total population 3 years and over, enrolled in school.....	560,799	82,063,714
Enrolled in nursery school or preschool (percent).....	4.7	6.0
Enrolled in kindergarten (percent).....	5.7	5.1
Enrolled in elementary school, grades 1-8 (percent).....	40.0	40.2
Enrolled in high school, grades 9-12 (percent)	20.6	20.7
Enrolled in college or graduate school (percent).....	29.0	28.0
Attainment		
Total population 25 years and over	1,373,822	213,725,624
Less than ninth grade (percent)	6.6	5.6
9th to 12th grade, no diploma (percent)	9.2	7.5
High school graduate, including equivalency (percent)	26.4	27.7
Some college, no degree (percent)	23.4	21.0
Associate's degree (percent)	8.0	8.2
Bachelor's degree (percent)	15.1	18.7
Graduate or professional degree (percent).....	11.4	11.4
High school graduate or higher (percent)	84.2	86.9
Bachelor's degree or higher (percent)	26.4	30.1

Table NM-12. Public School Characteristics and Educational Indicators

(Number, percent; data derived from National Center of Education Statistics.)

Item	State	U.S.
Public Schools, 2013–2014 (except where noted)		
Number of school districts.....	150	18,194
Number of schools.....	880	98,271
Number of students (in thousands)	339	50,045
Number of teachers (in thousands)	22	3,114
Student-teacher ratio.....	15.3	16.1
Expenditures per student (dollars), FY 2013.....	9,164	107,637
Four-year adjusted cohort graduation rate (ACGR)[1,2]	68.5	82.3
Students eligible for free or reduced-price lunch (in thousands)	227	25,596
English language learners (in thousands)	50	4,461
Students age 3 to 21 served under IDEA, part B (in thousands)	47	6,464

Public Schools by Type	Number	Percent of state public schools
Total number of schools.....	880	100.0
Regular	831	94.4
Special education	8	0.9
Vocational education.....	1	0.1
Alternative education.....	40	4.5

NOTE: Every school is assigned only one school type based on its instructional emphasis.
[1]ACGR data represents a new method of calculating high-school completion rates and may not be comparable to previous years' data for Averaged Freshmen Graduation Rates (AFGR).
[2]The United States 4-year ACGRs were estimated using both the reported 4-year ACGR data from 49 states and the District of Columbia and using imputed data for Idaho. The estimate for American Indian/Alaska Native students also includes imputed data for Virginia.

Table NM-13. Reported Voting and Registration of the Voting-Age Population, November 2014

(Numbers in thousands, percent.)

Item	Total population	Total citizen population	Registered			Voted		
			Total registered	Percent registered (total population)	Percent registered (total citizen population)	Total voted	Percent voted (total population)	Percent voted (total citizen population)
U.S. Total	239,874	219,941	142,166	59.3	64.6	92,251	38.5	41.9
State Total............................	1,536	1,417	919	59.9	64.9	646	42.1	45.6
Sex								
Male..........	739	676	433	58.7	64.1	304	41.1	44.9
Female	797	740	486	61.0	65.6	342	42.9	46.2
Race								
White alone..........	1,234	1,125	753	61.0	66.9	546	44.2	48.5
White, non-Hispanic alone	674	661	479	71.0	72.4	374	55.5	56.5
Black alone..........	40	39	28	(B)	(B)	8	(B)	(B)
Asian alone	33	26	13	(B)	(B)	11	(B)	(B)
Hispanic (of any race)..........	601	503	302	50.2	60.0	179	29.8	35.6
White alone or in combination	1,254	1,144	761	60.7	66.5	553	44.1	48.3
Black alone or in combination..........	47	46	30	(B)	(B)	10	(B)	(B)
Asian alone or in combination..........	35	28	13	(B)	(B)	11	(B)	(B)
Age								
18 to 24 years..........	196	184	50	25.7	27.3	23	11.6	12.3
25 to 34 years..........	268	243	125	46.9	51.6	63	23.7	26.1
35 to 44 years..........	230	195	136	59.0	69.4	80	34.7	40.8
45 to 64 years..........	504	470	350	69.4	74.4	264	52.4	56.2
65 years and over	338	323	258	76.4	79.8	216	63.8	66.7

B = Base is less than 75,000 and therefore too small to show the derived measure.

Table NM-14. Crime

(Number, rate per 100,000. Data are derived from the FBI Uniform Crime Reports.)

Item	State			U.S.[1,2,3,4]		
	2013	2014	Percent change	2013	2014	Percent change
TOTAL POPULATION[5]..........	2,085,287	2,085,572	-	316,128,839	318,857,056	0.9
VIOLENT CRIME						
Number..........	12,443	12,459	0.1	1,163,146	1,165,383	0.2
Rate	596.7	597.4	0.1	367.9	365.5	-0.7
Murder and Nonnegligent Manslaughter						
Number..........	125	101	-19.2	14,196	14,249	0.4
Rate	6.0	4.8	-20.0	4.5	4.5	-
Rape[6]						
Number..........	1,465	1,475	X	108,612	116,645	X
Rate	70.3	70.7	X	34.4	36.6	X
Robbery						
Number..........	1,810	2,086	15.2	345,031	325,802	-5.6
Rate	86.8	100.0	15.2	109.1	102.2	-6.3
Aggravated Assault						
Number..........	9,382	8,797	-6.2	724,149	741,291	2.4
Rate	449.9	421.8	-6.2	229.1	232.5	1.5
PROPERTY CRIME						
Number..........	77,256	73,877	-4.4	8,632,512	8,277,829	-4.1
Rate	3,704.8	3,542.3	-4.4	2,730.7	2,596.1	-4.9
Burglary						
Number..........	21,476	18,505	-13.8	1,928,465	1,729,806	-10.3
Rate	1,029.9	887.3	-13.8	610.0	542.5	-11.1
Larceny-Theft						
Number..........	49,875	49,082	-1.6	6,004,453	5,858,496	-2.4
Rate	2,391.8	2,353.4	-1.6	1,899.4	1,837.3	-3.3
Motor Vehicle Theft						
Number..........	5,905	6,290	6.5	699,594	689,527	-1.4
Rate	283.2	301.6	6.5	221.3	216.2	-2.3

NOTE: Although arson data are included in the trend and clearance tables, sufficient data are not available to estimate totals for this offense. Therefore, no arson data are published in this table.
X = Not applicable.
- = Zero or rounds to zero.
[1]The crime figures have been adjusted.
[2]The data collection methodology for the offense of forcible rape used by the Minnesota state Uniform Crime Reporting (UCR) Program (with the exception of Minneapolis and St. Paul, Minnesota) does not comply with national UCR Program guidelines. Consequently, its figures for forcible rape and violent crime (of which forcible rape is a part) are not published in this table.
[3]Includes offenses reported by the Zoological Police and the Metro Transit Police.
[4]Because of changes in the state's reporting practices, figures are not comparable to previous years' data.
[5]Populations are U.S. Census Bureau provisional estimates as of July 1 of each year.
[6]The figures shown for the offense of rape were estimated using the revised Uniform Crime Reporting (UCR) definition of rape.

Table NM-15. State Government Finances, 2014

(Dollar amounts in thousands, percent distribution.)

Item	Dollars	Percent distribution
Total Revenue	20,421,122	100.0
General revenue	15,590,791	76.3
Intergovernmental revenue	5,558,490	27.2
Taxes	5,757,432	28.2
General sales	2,098,676	10.3
Selective sales	701,199	3.4
License taxes	282,382	1.4
Individual income tax	1,297,493	6.4
Corporate income tax	205,702	1.0
Other taxes	1,171,980	5.7
Current charges	1,400,320	6.9
Miscellaneous general revenue	2,874,549	14.1
Utility revenue	0	-
Liquor stores revenue	0	-
Insurance trust revenue[1]	4,830,331	23.7
Total Expenditure	17,720,552	100.0
Intergovernmental expenditure	4,604,669	26.0
Direct expenditure	13,115,883	74.0
Current operation	9,624,394	54.3
Capital outlay	738,021	4.2
Insurance benefits and repayments	2,226,310	12.6
Assistance and subsidies	239,847	1.4
Interest on debt	287,311	1.6
Exhibit: Salaries and wages	2,782,904	15.7
Total Expenditure	17,720,552	100.0
General expenditure	15,494,242	87.4
Intergovernmental expenditure	4,604,669	26.0
Direct expenditure	10,889,573	61.5
General expenditure, by function:		
Education	5,501,281	31.0
Public welfare	4,224,310	23.8
Hospitals	1,011,047	5.7
Health	499,939	2.8
Highways	710,283	4.0
Police protection	135,527	0.8
Correction	441,771	2.5
Natural resources	188,758	1.1
Parks and recreation	55,907	0.3
Governmental administration	645,087	3.6
Interest on general debt	287,311	1.6
Other and unallocable	1,793,021	10.1
Utility expenditure	0	-
Liquor stores expenditure	0	-
Insurance trust expenditure	2,226,310	12.6
Debt at End of Fiscal Year	6,887,017	X
Cash and Security Holdings	49,691,660	X

X = Not applicable.
- = Zero or rounds to zero.
[1]Within insurance trust revenue, net earnings of state retirement systems is a calculated statistic (the item code in the data file is X08), and thus can be positive or negative. Net earnings is the sum of earnings on investments plus gains on investments minus losses on investments. The change made in 2002 for asset valuation from book to market value in accordance with Statement 34 of the Governmental Accounting Standards Board is reflected in the calculated statistics.

Table NM-16. State Government Tax Collections, 2014

(Dollars in thousands, percent.)

Item	Dollars	Percent distribution
Total Taxes	5,757,432	100.0
Property taxes	105,637	1.8
Sales and gross receipts	2,799,875	48.6
General sales and gross receipts	2,098,676	36.5
Selective sales and gross receipts	701,199	12.2
Alcoholic beverages	44,968	0.8
Amusements	70,226	1.2
Insurance premiums	99,832	1.7
Motor fuels	234,881	4.1
Pari-mutuels	596	-
Public utilities	29,894	0.5
Tobacco products	81,272	1.4
Other selective sales	139,530	2.4
Licenses	282,382	4.9
Alcoholic beverages	0	-
Amusements	373	-
Corporations in general	24,464	0.4
Hunting and fishing	24,655	0.4
Motor vehicle	188,156	3.3
Motor vehicle operators	3,671	0.1
Public utilities	1,151	-
Occupation and business, NEC	39,912	0.7
Other licenses	0	-
Income taxes	1,503,195	26.1
Individual income	1,297,493	22.5
Corporation net income	205,702	3.6
Other taxes	1,066,343	18.5
Death and gift	0	-
Documentary and stock transfer	0	-
Severance	1,066,343	18.5
Taxes, NEC	0	-

- = Zero or rounds to zero.

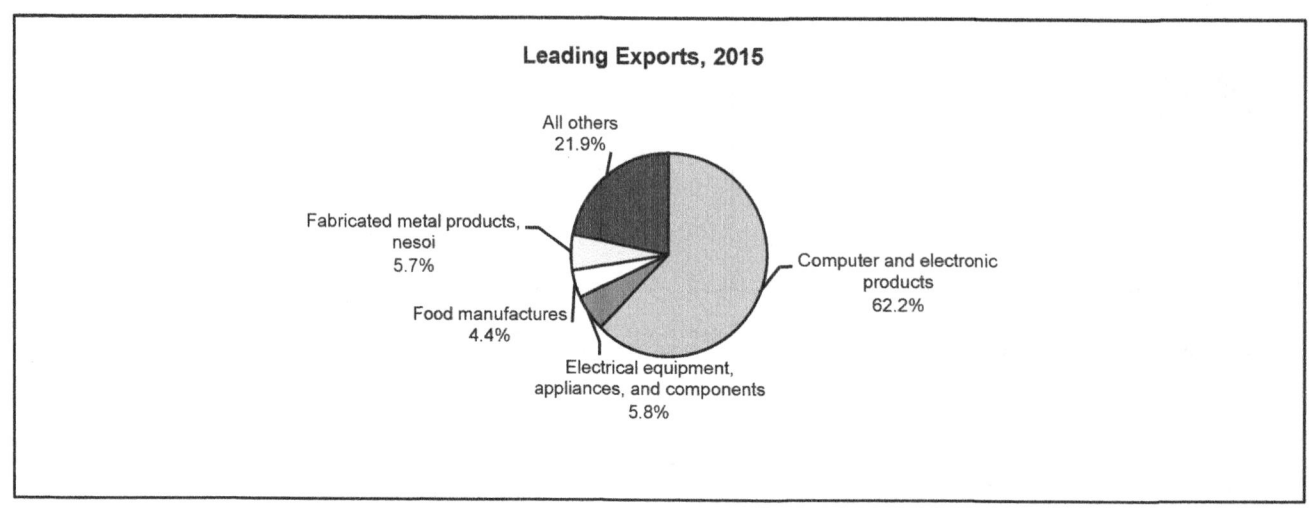

Leading Exports, 2015

All others 21.9%

Fabricated metal products, nesoi 5.7%

Food manufactures 4.4%

Electrical equipment, appliances, and components 5.8%

Computer and electronic products 62.2%

Facts and Figures

Location: Northeastern United States; bordered on the N by Canada (Ontario and Quebec) and Lake Ontario; on the E by Vermont, Massachusetts, and Connecticut; on the S by New Jersey and Pennsylvania; and on the W by Pennsylvania, Lake Erie, Canada (Ontario), and Lake Ontario

Area: 54,556 sq. mi. (141,299 sq. km.); rank—27th

Population: 19,795,791 (2015 est.); rank—4th

Principal Cities: capital—Albany; largest—New York City

Statehood: July 26, 1788; 11th state

U.S. Congress: 2 senators, 27 representatives

State Motto: *Excelsior* ("Ever upward")

State Song: "I Love New York"

State Nickname: The Empire State

Abbreviations: NY; N.Y.

State Symbols: flower—rose; tree—sugar maple; bird—bluebird

At a Glance

- With an increase in population of 2.0 percent, New York ranked 31st among the states in growth from 2010 to 2015.

- In 2014, 8.7 percent of New Yorkers did not have health insurance, compared to 11.7 percent of the total U.S. population.

- New York's infant mortality rate of 4.65 per 1,000 live births ranked 43rd in the nation in 2014.

- New York had the second lowest voter turnout in November 2014, with 30.6 percent of its voting-age population voting in the election.

- New York had the second lowest property crime rate in the country in 2014, at 1,718.2 incidents per 100,000 population.

Table NY-1. Population by Age, Sex, Race, and Hispanic Origin

(Number, percent, except where noted.)

Sex, age, race, and Hispanic origin	2000	2010	2015[1]	Average annual percent change, 2010–2015
Total Population..	18,976,457	19,378,102	19,795,791	0.2
Percent of total U.S. population	6.7	6.3	6.2	X
Sex				
Male..	9,146,748	9,377,147	9,611,513	0.2
Female	9,829,709	10,000,955	10,184,278	0.1
Age				
Under 5 years..	1,239,417	1,155,822	1,184,387	0.2
5 to 19 years..	3,971,834	3,741,689	3,548,028	-0.4
20 to 64 years..	11,316,854	11,862,648	12,099,061	0.1
65 years and over	2,448,352	2,617,943	2,964,315	0.9
Median age (years)..	35.9	38.0	38.3	0.1
Race and Hispanic Origin				
One race				
White	12,893,689	13,901,661	13,874,048	-0.0
Black..	3,014,385	3,378,047	3,491,047	0.2
American Indian and Alaska Native	82,461	183,046	190,539	0.3
Asian..	1,044,976	1,481,555	1,733,570	1.1
Native Hawaiian or Other Pacific Islander	8,818	24,000	26,786	0.8
Two or more races	590,182	409,793	479,801	1.1
Hispanic (of any race)..	2,867,583	3,564,228	3,726,804	0.3

X = Not applicable.
[1]Population figures for 2015 are July 1 estimates. The 2010 estimates are taken from the 2010 Census.
- = Zero or rounds to zero.

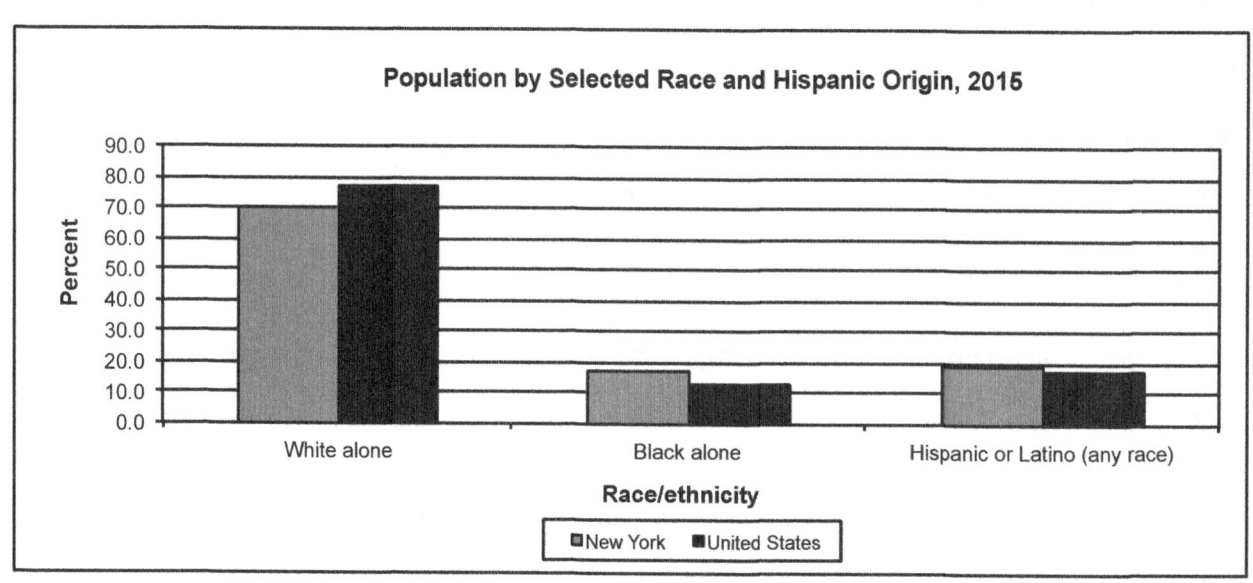

Table NY-2. Marital Status

(Number, percent distribution.)

Sex, age, race, and Hispanic origin	2000	2010	2014
Males, 15 Years and Over	7,125,715	7,586,733	7,699,246
Never married	34.7	40.5	40.7
Now married, except separated..	53.3	47.6	47.3
Separated..	2.7	2.2	2.1
Widowed..	2.8	2.6	2.6
Divorced..	6.5	7.2	7.2
Females, 15 Years and Over	7,932,161	8,283,542	8,380,183
Never married	29.0	34.8	35.2
Now married, except separated..	47.1	42.8	42.3
Separated..	3.7	3.1	3.1
Widowed..	11.2	9.6	9.4
Divorced..	8.9	9.7	9.9

Table NY-3. Households and Housing Characteristics

(Number, percent, dollars.)

Item	2000	2010	2014	Average annual percent change, 2000–2014
Total Households..	7,056,860	7,196,427	7,282,398	0.2
Family households	4,639,387	4,632,676	4,621,954	-
Married-couple family	3,289,514	3,210,895	3,176,379	-0.2
Other family	1,349,873	1,421,781	1,445,575	0.5
Male householder, no wife present....................	311,697	355,236	366,755	1.3
Female householder, no husband present............	1,038,176	1,066,545	1,078,820	0.3
Nonfamily households	2,417,473	2,563,751	2,660,444	0.7
Householder living alone.............................	1,982,742	2,089,816	2,166,287	0.7
Householder not living alone........................	434,731	473,935	494,157	1.0
Housing Characteristics				
Total housing units..	7,679,301	8,108,211	8,191,528	0.5
Occupied housing units	7,056,860	7,196,427	7,282,398	0.2
Owner occupied	3,739,166	3,904,123	3,857,906	0.2
Renter occupied	3,317,694	3,292,304	3,424,492	0.2
Average household size...................................	2.61	2.61	2.63	0.1
Financial Characteristics				
Median gross rent of renter-occupied housing	627	1,020	1,148	5.9
Median monthly owner costs for housing units with a mortgage	1,357	1,963	1,982	3.3
Median value of owner-occupied housing units...........................	148,700	296,500	279,100	6.3

- = Zero or rounds to zero.

Table NY-4. Migration, Origin, and Language

(Number, percent.)

Characteristic	State			U.S.		
	2013	2014	Percent change	2013	2014	Percent change
Residence 1 Year Ago						
Population 1 year and over	19,431,954	19,528,220	0.5	312,432,820	315,095,393	0.9
Same house	89.0	89.2	X	85.0	85.1	X
Different house in the U.S.	10.2	10.0	X	14.4	14.3	X
Same county	6.3	6.3	X	8.9	8.7	X
Different county	3.9	3.7	X	5.5	5.6	X
Same state	2.5	2.4	X	3.2	3.3	X
Different state	1.4	1.3	X	2.3	2.3	X
Abroad	0.8	0.8	X	0.6	0.6	X
Place of Birth						
Native born	15,267,816	15,280,758	0.1	274,780,773	276,465,262	0.6
Male	48.9	48.9	X	49.3	49.3	X
Female	51.1	51.1	X	50.7	50.7	X
Foreign born	4,383,311	4,465,469	1.9	41,348,066	42,391,794	2.5
Male	47.2	47.1	X	48.8	48.7	X
Female	52.8	52.9	X	51.2	51.3	X
Foreign born; naturalized U.S. citizen................	2,359,247	2,416,184	2.4	19,294,710	19,984,738	3.6
Male	44.7	44.5	X	45.9	45.9	X
Female	55.3	55.5	X	54.1	54.1	X
Foreign born; not a U.S. citizen.......................	2,024,064	2,049,285	1.2	22,053,356	22,407,056	1.6
Male	50.1	50.1	X	51.3	51.2	X
Female	49.9	49.9	X	48.7	48.8	X
Entered 2010 or later	9.5	12.0	X	9.7	12.3	X
Entered 2000 to 2009	26.8	26.6	X	29.4	28.6	X
Entered before 2000.......................................	63.7	61.4	X	61.0	59.1	X
World Region of Birth, Foreign						
Foreign-born population, excluding population born at sea	4,383,311	4,465,415	1.9	41,347,945	42,390,705	2.5
Europe	17.1	16.5	X	11.6	11.2	X
Asia	27.6	28.3	X	29.5	30.1	X
Africa	4.2	4.3	X	4.4	4.6	X
Oceania	0.3	0.3	X	0.5	0.6	X
Latin America..	49.4	49.4	X	51.9	51.6	X
North America	1.4	1.2	X	2.0	1.9	X
Language Spoken at Home and Ability to Speak English						
Population 5 years and over.............................	18,480,702	18,563,935	0.5	296,358,760	299,084,046	0.9
English only	69.9	69.6	X	79.2	78.9	X
Language other than English...........................	30.1	30.4	X	20.8	21.1	X
Speaks English less than "very well"..............	13.4	13.8	X	8.5	8.6	X

X = Not applicable.
- = Zero or rounds to zero.

Table NY-5. Median Income and Poverty Status, 2014

(Number, percent, except as noted.)

Characteristic	State		U.S.	
	Number	Percent	Number	Percent
Median Income				
Households (dollars)..	58,878	X	53,657	X
Families (dollars)	71,115	X	65,910	X
Below Poverty Level (All People)	3,062,938	15.9	48,208,387	15.5
Sex				
Male...	1,360,616	14.6	21,590,918	14.2
Female..	1,702,322	17.1	26,617,469	16.8
Age				
Under 18 years..	936,938	22.6	15,686,012	21.7
Related children under 18 years............................	918,641	22.2	15,372,705	21.3
18 to 64 years...	1,798,638	14.6	28,267,482	14.6
65 years and over	327,362	11.7	4,254,893	9.5

X = Not applicable.

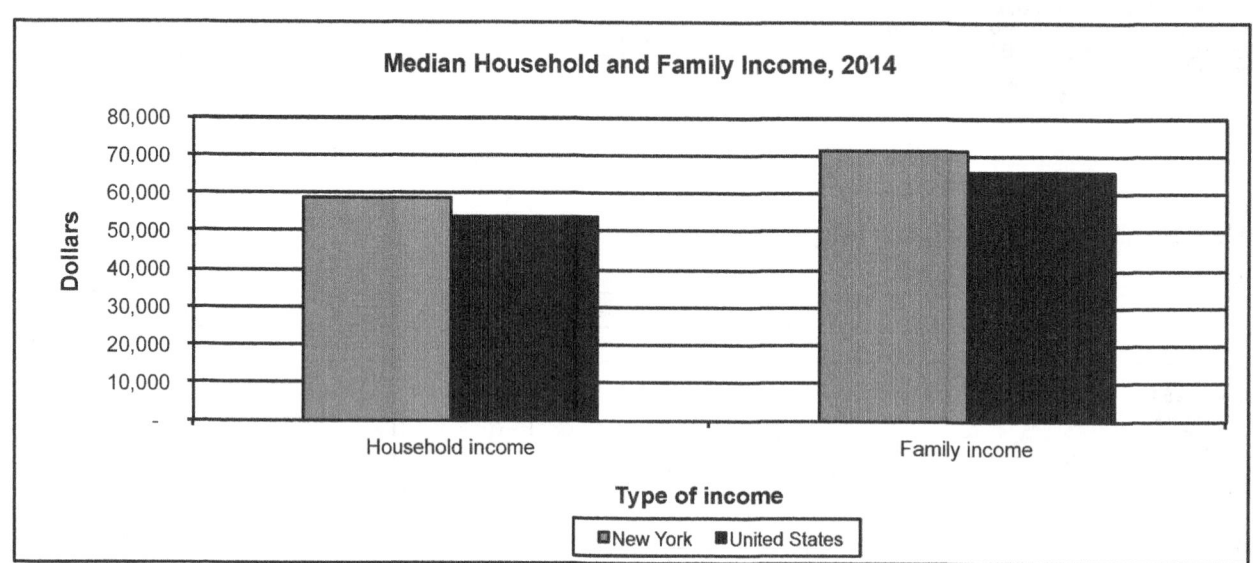

Table NY-6. Health Insurance Coverage Status for the Civilian Noninstitutionalized Population and Children Under 18 Years of Age

(Numbers in thousands, percent.)

Item	2006	2007	2008	2009	2010	2011	2012	2013	2014
Civilian Noninstitutionalized Population	19,040	19,062	19,207	19,264	19,134	19,208	19,317	19,400	19,500
Covered by Private or Public Insurance									
Number...	16,378	16,543	16,949	17,070	16,857	17,013	17,214	17,331	17,803
Percent..	86.0	86.8	88.2	88.6	88.1	88.6	89.1	89.3	91.3
Not Covered									
Number...	2,662	2,519	2,258	2,195	2,277	2,195	2,103	2,070	1,697
Percent..	14.0	13.2	11.8	11.4	11.9	11.4	10.9	10.7	8.7
Percent in the U.S. not covered..............................	15.8	15.3	15.1	15.1	15.5	15.1	14.8	14.5	11.7
Children Under 18 Years of Age	4,547	4,437	4,402	4,414	4,302	4,270	4,253	4,231	4,217
Covered by Private or Public Insurance									
Number...	4,167	4,042	4,147	4,209	4,094	4,089	4,085	4,060	4,080
Percent..	91.6	91.1	94.2	95.4	95.2	95.8	96.1	96.0	96.7
Not Covered									
Number...	380	395	255	205	208	181	168	171	138
Percent..	8.4	8.9	5.8	4.6	4.8	4.2	3.9	4.0	3.3
Percent in the U.S. not covered..............................	11.7	11.0	9.7	8.6	8.0	7.5	7.2	7.1	6.0

Table NY-7. Employment Status by Demographic Group, 2015

(Numbers in thousands, percent.)

Characteristic	Civilian noninstitutional population	Civilian labor force		Employed		Unemployed	
		Number	Percent of population	Number	Percent of population	Number	Percent of population
Total..	15,853	9,672	61.0	9,160	57.8	512	5.3
Sex							
Male..........................	7,559	5,102	67.5	4,830	63.9	272	5.3
Female........................	8,294	4,570	55.1	4,330	52.2	239	5.2
Race, Sex, and Hispanic Origin							
White	11,310	6,951	61.5	6,636	58.7	315	4.5
Male..........................	5,477	3,730	68.1	3,561	65.0	169	4.5
Female........................	5,833	3,221	55.2	3,075	52.7	146	4.5
Black or African American....................	2,675	1,601	59.9	1,471	55.0	131	8.2
Male..........................	1,188	756	63.6	687	57.8	69	9.1
Female........................	1,486	846	56.9	784	52.7	62	7.3
Hispanic or Latino ethnicity[1]	2,609	1,603	61.4	1,496	57.3	107	6.7
Male..........................	1,279	919	71.8	858	67.1	61	6.6
Female........................	1,330	684	51.4	638	47.9	47	6.8
Age							
16 to 19 years................	1,022	284	27.8	223	21.8	61	21.5
20 to 24 years................	1,438	905	62.9	797	55.4	108	11.9
25 to 34 years................	2,826	2,243	79.3	2,131	75.4	112	5.0
35 to 44 years................	2,408	1,920	79.7	1,856	77.1	64	3.3
45 to 54 years................	2,695	2,140	79.4	2,063	76.5	77	3.6
55 to 64 years................	2,515	1,617	64.3	1,551	61.7	66	4.1
65 years and over	2,948	565	19.2	540	18.3	24	4.3

NOTE: Data in Table 7 are from the Current Population Survey (CPS) and do not match the estimates in Table 8. See notes and definitions for further information.
[1]May be of any race.

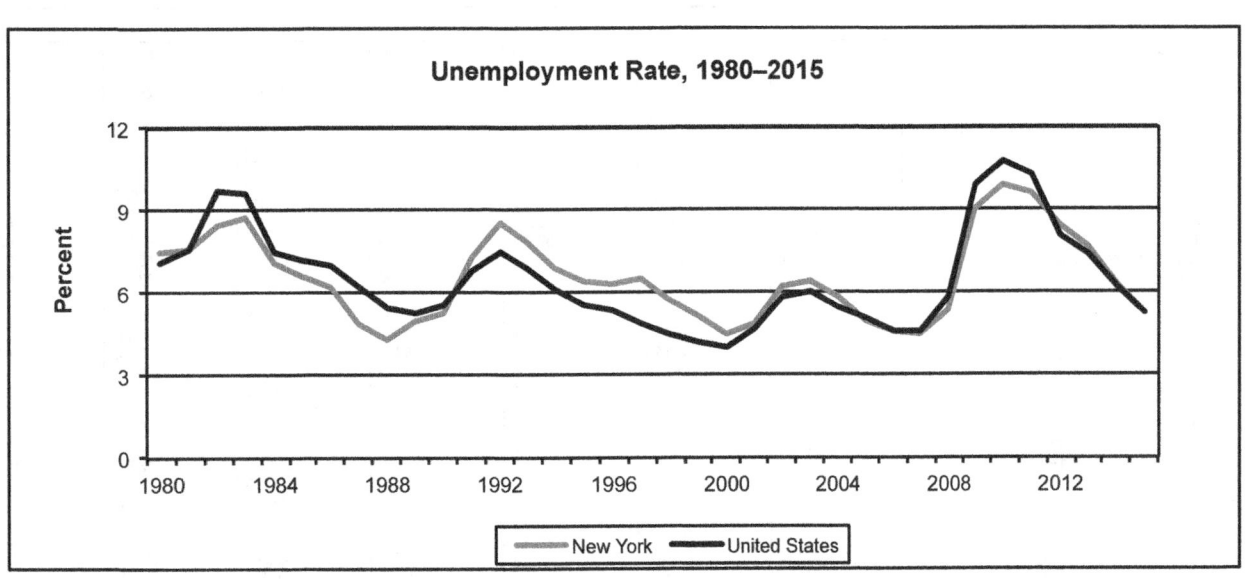

Table NY-8. Employment Status of the Civilian Noninstitutional Population Age 16 Years and Over

(Number, percent.)

Year	Civilian labor force	Civilian participation rate	Employed	Unemployed	Unemployment rate
2007................................	9,522,056	62.7	9,088,207	433,849	4.6
2008................................	9,664,773	63.3	9,139,080	525,693	5.4
2009................................	9,647,485	62.8	8,844,486	802,999	8.3
2010................................	9,595,362	62.4	8,769,723	825,639	8.6
2011................................	9,517,361	61.4	8,728,057	789,304	8.3
2012................................	9,617,611	61.7	8,797,832	819,779	8.5
2013................................	9,636,411	61.4	8,893,628	742,783	7.7
2014................................	9,595,304	60.8	8,989,429	605,875	6.3
2015................................	9,679,321	61.1	9,166,246	513,075	5.3

Table NY-9. Employment and Average Wages by Industry

(Estimates through 2010 are based on the 2007 North American Industry Classification System [NAICS]. Estimates from 2011 onward are based on the 2012 NAICS.)

Industry	2008	2009	2010	2011	2012	2013	2014
				Number of jobs			
Wage and Salary Employment by Industry..................	9,003,322	8,735,423	8,732,197	8,837,168	8,935,624	9,066,866	9,232,209
Farm Wage and Salary Employment.........................	19,023	18,351	18,392	19,509	19,751	23,408	22,579
Nonfarm Wage and Salary Employment....................	8,984,299	8,717,072	8,713,805	8,817,659	8,915,873	9,043,458	9,209,630
Private wage and salary employment........................	7,455,737	7,191,241	7,195,895	7,339,851	7,458,722	7,584,862	7,754,448
Forestry, fishing, and related activities..........................	5,029	5,045	5,158	5,446	4,988	5,194	5,592
Mining..	5,635	4,777	4,634	4,681	4,678	4,405	4,620
Utilities...	38,886	39,359	38,327	37,278	36,043	36,355	37,701
Construction...	375,382	340,039	321,327	324,855	325,097	338,963	353,652
Manufacturing...	534,317	477,631	458,109	459,252	459,568	456,471	453,281
Durable goods manufacturing..............................	317,602	281,194	268,367	271,254	269,657	266,892	265,158
Nondurable goods manufacturing.........................	216,715	196,437	189,742	187,998	189,911	189,579	188,123
Wholesale trade	354,528	332,696	328,545	334,142	336,350	337,993	340,172
Retail trade..	910,003	878,238	891,411	907,655	922,498	936,377	952,000
Transportation and warehousing.............................	242,217	230,532	226,846	230,202	231,718	231,997	240,806
Information...	265,147	253,295	253,220	256,473	261,625	262,108	265,687
Finance and insurance	547,195	509,996	503,703	517,938	517,035	511,941	520,957
Real estate and rental and leasing..........................	194,552	188,380	187,147	185,901	184,649	188,926	191,312
Professional, scientific, and technical services	597,315	571,505	564,281	584,824	604,447	620,320	635,781
Management of companies and enterprises..................	131,576	130,725	132,092	133,230	134,734	138,666	142,245
Administrative and waste services...........................	443,118	410,762	420,108	432,763	443,111	455,797	462,105
Educational services	353,266	353,666	359,334	366,831	374,891	378,982	385,402
Health care and social assistance...........................	1,271,880	1,293,921	1,318,983	1,331,403	1,344,308	1,365,381	1,399,317
Arts, entertainment, and recreation.........................	146,531	143,117	143,118	145,968	150,564	158,222	163,037
Accommodation and food services..........................	580,974	579,229	603,010	632,911	659,140	688,203	715,404
Other services, except public administration................	458,186	448,328	436,542	448,098	463,278	468,561	485,377
Government and government enterprises........................	1,528,562	1,525,831	1,517,910	1,477,808	1,457,151	1,458,596	1,455,182
				Dollars			
Average Wages and Salaries by Industry	59,418	57,004	59,511	61,042	61,863	62,327	65,069
Average Farm Wages and Salaries	28,804	27,627	26,371	22,547	24,963	28,400	31,259
Average Nonfarm Wages and Salaries	59,483	57,066	59,581	61,127	61,945	62,415	65,152
Average private wages and salaries..........................	61,252	58,106	60,831	62,437	63,333	63,655	66,604
Forestry, fishing, and related activities........................	27,844	28,753	28,865	29,137	29,420	30,011	30,326
Mining..	60,086	55,486	58,210	67,444	63,460	60,295	65,260
Utilities...	93,933	92,583	97,932	103,008	108,849	106,014	107,794
Construction...	58,868	59,674	60,281	61,489	62,343	63,448	65,252
Manufacturing...	57,040	57,052	59,391	59,979	60,917	61,160	62,061
Durable goods manufacturing..............................	60,327	60,591	62,768	64,386	65,990	66,322	66,896
Nondurable goods manufacturing.........................	52,223	51,987	54,614	53,620	53,713	53,893	55,245
Wholesale trade	68,900	68,769	71,633	73,738	77,718	76,862	79,611
Retail trade..	29,469	29,215	29,626	30,299	30,725	31,485	32,478
Transportation and warehousing.............................	44,356	44,025	45,460	46,132	47,038	48,197	48,948
Information...	89,110	89,193	90,840	95,814	100,128	102,414	110,387
Finance and insurance	204,962	171,837	191,436	198,094	197,340	197,220	216,864
Real estate and rental and leasing..........................	54,783	52,242	54,584	56,582	59,437	60,014	63,881
Professional, scientific, and technical services	87,363	86,296	90,752	93,826	96,078	97,881	103,105
Management of companies and enterprises..................	133,419	119,634	140,138	142,451	144,017	142,725	143,779
Administrative and waste services...........................	40,668	40,503	42,540	41,922	43,713	43,900	44,960
Educational services	39,096	40,537	41,077	42,297	43,178	44,548	45,585
Health care and social assistance...........................	42,536	43,733	44,359	45,135	45,775	46,602	47,432
Arts, entertainment, and recreation.........................	47,315	46,484	47,111	48,224	48,865	48,565	51,428
Accommodation and food services..........................	24,269	23,693	24,573	25,483	26,121	26,116	27,472
Other services, except public administration................	32,397	32,576	33,582	33,971	34,578	35,503	36,377
Government and government enterprises........................	50,850	52,168	53,654	54,618	54,841	55,969	57,418

Table NY-10. Employment Characteristics by Family Type

(Number, percent.)

Family type and labor force status	2012		2013		2014	
	Total	Families with own children under 18 years	Total	Families with own children under 18 years	Total	Families with own children under 18 years
All Families...	4,587,857	2,015,419	4,584,095	1,980,127	4,592,706	1,938,644
FAMILY TYPE AND LABOR FORCE STATUS						
Married-Couple Families...............................	3,147,912	1,307,147	3,158,468	1,303,725	3,147,131	1,269,381
Both husband and wife in labor force........................	53.5	65.4	52.6	64.6	53.0	65.5
Husband in labor force, wife not in labor force............	21.6	28.2	21.7	28.3	21.5	28.1
Wife in labor force, husband not in labor force...........	8.5	4.6	8.7	4.8	8.6	4.6
Both husband and wife not in labor force.....................	16.4	1.8	16.2	1.7	16.8	1.8
Other Families	1,439,945	708,272	1,425,627	676,402	1,445,575	669,263
Female householder, no husband present....................	74.3	78.1	74.5	78.9	74.6	77.9
In labor force...	51.8	63.0	51.0	62.2	49.9	61.6
Not in labor force	22.5	15.1	23.5	16.7	24.7	16.3
Male householder, no wife present.........................	25.7	21.9	25.5	21.1	25.4	22.1
In labor force..	19.9	19.6	19.7	18.7	19.3	19.6
Not in labor force	5.8	2.3	5.9	2.4	6.1	2.5

Table NY-11. School Enrollment and Educational Attainment, 2014

(Number, percent.)

Item	State	U.S.
Enrollment		
Total population 3 years and over, enrolled in school...........	4,874,923	82,063,714
Enrolled in nursery school or preschool (percent).............	6.2	6.0
Enrolled in kindergarten (percent)...........................	5.0	5.1
Enrolled in elementary school, grades 1-8 (percent)...........	37.9	40.2
Enrolled in high school, grades 9-12 (percent)...............	20.5	20.7
Enrolled in college or graduate school (percent).............	30.4	28.0
Attainment		
Total population 25 years and over	13,539,612	213,725,624
Less than ninth grade (percent)..............................	6.7	5.6
9th to 12th grade, no diploma (percent)......................	7.6	7.5
High school graduate, including equivalency (percent).........	26.6	27.7
Some college, no degree (percent)	16.1	21.0
Associate's degree (percent)	8.6	8.2
Bachelor's degree (percent)	19.6	18.7
Graduate or professional degree (percent)....................	14.9	11.4
High school graduate or higher (percent)	85.7	86.9
Bachelor's degree or higher (percent)........................	34.5	30.1

Table NY-12. Public School Characteristics and Educational Indicators

(Number, percent; data derived from National Center of Education Statistics.)

Item	State	U.S.
Public Schools, 2013–2014 (except where noted)		
Number of school districts....................................	970	18,194
Number of schools..	4,801	98,271
Number of students (in thousands)	2,733	50,045
Number of teachers (in thousands)	207	3,114
Student-teacher ratio..	13.2	16.1
Expenditures per student (dollars), FY 2013..................	195,297	107,637
Four-year adjusted cohort graduation rate (ACGR)[1,2].........	77.8	82.3
Students eligible for free or reduced-price lunch (in thousands) ...	1292	25,596
English language learners (in thousands)	185	4,461
Students age 3 to 21 served under IDEA, part B (in thousands) ...	455	6,464

Public Schools by Type	Number	Percent of state public schools
Total number of schools......................................	4,801	100.0
Regular..	4,618	96.2
Special education..	128	2.7
Vocational education...	25	0.5
Alternative education..	30	0.6

NOTE: Every school is assigned only one school type based on its instructional emphasis.
[1]ACGR data represents a new method of calculating high-school completion rates and may not be comparable to previous years' data for Averaged Freshmen Graduation Rates (AFGR).
[2]The United States 4-year ACGRs were estimated using both the reported 4-year ACGR data from 49 states and the District of Columbia and using imputed data for Idaho. The estimate for American Indian/Alaska Native students also includes imputed data for Virginia.

Table NY-13. Reported Voting and Registration of the Voting-Age Population, November 2014

(Numbers in thousands, percent.)

Item	Total population	Total citizen population	Registered			Voted		
			Total registered	Percent registered (total population)	Percent registered (total citizen population)	Total voted	Percent voted (total population)	Percent voted (total citizen population)
U.S. Total	239,874	219,941	142,166	59.3	64.6	92,251	38.5	41.9
State Total...............................	15,274	13,611	8,078	52.9	59.4	4,680	30.6	34.4
Sex								
Male..	7,294	6,460	3,679	50.4	56.9	2,131	29.2	33.0
Female	7,980	7,150	4,399	55.1	61.5	2,548	31.9	35.6
Race								
White alone	11,147	10,287	6,185	55.5	60.1	3,683	33.0	35.8
White, non-Hispanic alone	9,385	8,994	5,471	58.3	60.8	3,321	35.4	36.9
Black alone...............................	2,581	2,211	1,385	53.7	62.6	762	29.5	34.5
Asian alone	1,206	807	366	30.4	45.4	156	13.0	19.3
Hispanic (of any race)....................	2,394	1,784	995	41.6	55.8	502	21.0	28.1
White alone or in combination	11,351	10,476	6,262	55.2	59.8	3,730	32.9	35.6
Black alone or in combination.........	2,734	2,342	1,454	53.2	62.1	799	29.2	34.1
Asian alone or in combination..........	1,269	867	392	30.9	45.2	175	13.8	20.2
Age								
18 to 24 years..............................	1,959	1,738	733	37.4	42.2	258	13.2	14.9
25 to 34 years..............................	2,882	2,444	1,213	42.1	49.6	509	17.7	20.8
35 to 44 years..............................	2,310	1,946	1,195	51.7	61.4	602	26.1	30.9
45 to 64 years..............................	5,153	4,653	2,948	57.2	63.3	1,899	36.9	40.8
65 years and over	2,971	2,830	1,989	66.9	70.3	1,411	47.5	49.9

Table NY-14. Crime

(Number, rate per 100,000. Data are derived from the FBI Uniform Crime Reports.)

Item	State			U.S.[1,2,3,4]		
	2013	2014	Percent change	2013	2014	Percent change
TOTAL POPULATION[5]..	19,651,127	19,746,227	0.5	316,128,839	318,857,056	0.9
VIOLENT CRIME						
Number......................................	76,596	75,398	-1.6	1,163,146	1,165,383	0.2
Rate	389.8	381.8	-2.1	367.9	365.5	-0.7
Murder and Nonnegligent Manslaughter						
Number......................................	648	617	-4.8	14,196	14,249	0.4
Rate	3.3	3.1	-6.1	4.5	4.5	-
Rape[6]						
Number......................................	3,353	5,433	X	108,612	116,645	X
Rate	17.1	27.5	X	34.4	36.6	X
Robbery						
Number......................................	27,241	24,045	-11.7	345,031	325,802	-5.6
Rate	138.6	121.8	-12.1	109.1	102.2	-6.3
Aggravated Assault						
Number......................................	46,130	45,303	-1.8	724,149	741,291	2.4
Rate	234.7	229.4	-2.3	229.1	232.5	1.5
PROPERTY CRIME						
Number......................................	358,598	339,282	-5.4	8,632,512	8,277,829	-4.1
Rate	1,824.8	1,718.2	-5.8	2,730.7	2,596.1	-4.9
Burglary						
Number......................................	56,442	50,781	-10.0	1,928,465	1,729,806	-10.3
Rate	287.2	257.2	-10.4	610.0	542.5	-11.1
Larceny-Theft						
Number......................................	286,674	272,765	-4.9	6,004,453	5,858,496	-2.4
Rate	1,458.8	1,381.4	-5.3	1,899.4	1,837.3	-3.3
Motor Vehicle Theft						
Number......................................	15,482	15,736	1.6	699,594	689,527	-1.4
Rate	78.8	79.7	1.1	221.3	216.2	-2.3

NOTE: Although arson data are included in the trend and clearance tables, sufficient data are not available to estimate totals for this offense. Therefore, no arson data are published in this table.
X = Not applicable.
- = Zero or rounds to zero.
[1]The crime figures have been adjusted.
[2]The data collection methodology for the offense of forcible rape used by the Minnesota state Uniform Crime Reporting (UCR) Program (with the exception of Minneapolis and St. Paul, Minnesota) does not comply with national UCR Program guidelines. Consequently, its figures for forcible rape and violent crime (of which forcible rape is a part) are not published in this table.
[3]Includes offenses reported by the Zoological Police and the Metro Transit Police.
[4]Because of changes in the state's reporting practices, figures are not comparable to previous years' data.
[5]Populations are U.S. Census Bureau provisional estimates as of July 1 of each year.
[6]The figures shown for the offense of rape were estimated using the revised Uniform Crime Reporting (UCR) definition of rape.

Table NY-15. State Government Finances, 2014

(Dollar amounts in thousands, percent distribution.)

Item	Dollars	Percent distribution
Total Revenue	205,789,823	100.0
General revenue	146,853,198	71.4
Intergovernmental revenue	49,114,188	23.9
Taxes	76,978,982	37.4
General sales	12,668,587	6.2
Selective sales	10,876,202	5.3
License taxes	1,884,841	0.9
Individual income tax	42,964,774	20.9
Corporate income tax	4,861,687	2.4
Other taxes	3,722,891	1.8
Current charges	8,948,398	4.3
Miscellaneous general revenue	11,811,630	5.7
Utility revenue	8,556,719	4.2
Liquor stores revenue	0	-
Insurance trust revenue[1]	50,379,906	24.5
Total Expenditure	178,324,895	100.0
Intergovernmental expenditure	58,134,561	32.6
Direct expenditure	120,190,334	67.4
Current operation	82,652,997	46.3
Capital outlay	8,519,505	4.8
Insurance benefits and repayments	21,438,831	12.0
Assistance and subsidies	1,769,198	1.0
Interest on debt	5,809,803	3.3
Exhibit: Salaries and wages	23,186,104	13.0
Total Expenditure	178,324,895	100.0
General expenditure	144,432,521	81.0
Intergovernmental expenditure	58,134,561	32.6
Direct expenditure	86,297,960	48.4
General expenditure, by function:		
Education	41,599,022	23.3
Public welfare	54,150,085	30.4
Hospitals	4,915,880	2.8
Health	9,108,534	5.1
Highways	4,745,887	2.7
Police protection	881,203	0.5
Correction	3,238,731	1.8
Natural resources	389,639	0.2
Parks and recreation	682,703	0.4
Governmental administration	5,410,454	3.0
Interest on general debt	4,301,618	2.4
Other and unallocable	15,008,765	8.4
Utility expenditure	12,453,543	7.0
Liquor stores expenditure	0	-
Insurance trust expenditure	21,438,831	12.0
Debt at End of Fiscal Year	136,440,657	X
Cash and Security Holdings	350,042,341	X

X = Not applicable.
- = Zero or rounds to zero.
[1]Within insurance trust revenue, net earnings of state retirement systems is a calculated statistic (the item code in the data file is X08), and thus can be positive or negative. Net earnings is the sum of earnings on investments plus gains on investments minus losses on investments. The change made in 2002 for asset valuation from book to market value in accordance with Statement 34 of the Governmental Accounting Standards Board is reflected in the calculated statistics.

Table NY-16. State Government Tax Collections, 2014

(Dollars in thousands, percent.)

Item	Dollars	Percent distribution
Total Taxes	76,978,982	100.0
Property taxes	X	X
Sales and gross receipts	23,544,789	30.6
General sales and gross receipts	12,668,587	16.5
Selective sales and gross receipts	10,876,202	14.1
Alcoholic beverages	250,926	0.3
Amusements	996	-
Insurance premiums	1,345,394	1.7
Motor fuels	1,630,358	2.1
Pari-mutuels	21,420	-
Public utilities	929,929	1.2
Tobacco products	1,446,184	1.9
Other selective sales	5,250,995	6.8
Licenses	1,884,841	2.4
Alcoholic beverages	64,576	0.1
Amusements	50	-
Corporations in general	63,488	0.1
Hunting and fishing	51,775	0.1
Motor vehicle	1,357,553	1.8
Motor vehicle operators	145,500	0.2
Public utilities	24,165	-
Occupation and business, NEC	176,275	0.2
Other licenses	1,459	-
Income taxes	47,826,461	62.1
Individual income	42,964,774	55.8
Corporation net income	4,861,687	6.3
Other taxes	3,722,891	4.8
Death and gift	1,238,320	1.6
Documentary and stock transfer	1,037,341	1.3
Severance	X	X
Taxes, NEC	1,447,230	1.9

X = Not applicable.
- = Zero or rounds to zero.

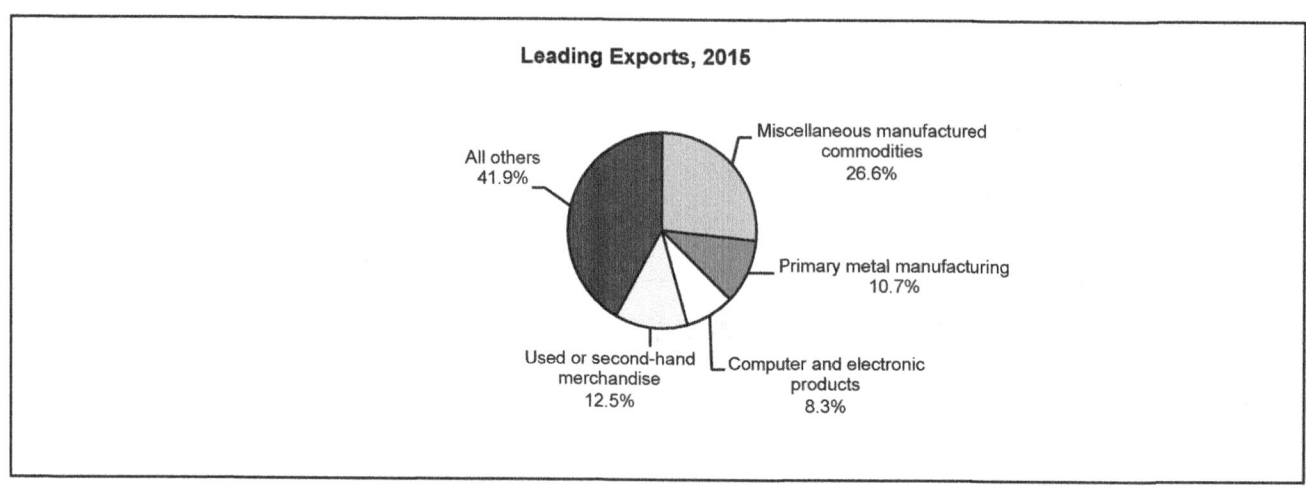

Leading Exports, 2015

Miscellaneous manufactured commodities 26.6%
Primary metal manufacturing 10.7%
Computer and electronic products 8.3%
Used or second-hand merchandise 12.5%
All others 41.9%

Facts and Figures

Location: Southeastern United States; bordered on the N by Virginia, on the E by the Atlantic Ocean, on the S by South Carolina and Georgia, and on the W by Tennessee

Area: 53,819 sq. mi. (139,389 sq. km.); rank—28th

Population: 10,042,802 (2015 est.); rank—9th

Principal Cities: capital—Raleigh; largest—Charlotte

Statehood: November 21, 1789; 12th state

U.S. Congress: 2 senators, 13 representatives

State Motto: *Esse quam videri* ("To be rather than to seem")

State Song: "The Old North State"

State Nicknames: The Tar Heel State; The Old North State

Abbreviations: NC; N.C.

State Symbols: flower—flowering dogwood; tree—pine; bird—cardinal

At a Glance

- With an increase in population of 5.1 percent, North Carolina ranked 14th among the states in growth from 2010 to 2015.

- North Carolina's median household income in 2014 was $46,556, and 17.2 percent of the population lived below the poverty level.

- North Carolina's violent crime rate in 2014 was 329.5 per 100,000 population, compared to 365.5 for the entire nation.

- In 2014, 13.1 percent of North Carolinians did not have health insurance, compared to 11.7 percent of the entire U.S. population.

- North Carolina's unemployment rate of 5.7 percent ranked 16th in the nation in 2015.

Table NC-1. Population by Age, Sex, Race, and Hispanic Origin

(Number, percent, except where noted.)

Sex, age, race, and Hispanic origin	2000	2010	2015[1]	Average annual percent change, 2010–2015
Total Population.....................	8,049,313	9,535,483	10,042,802	0.4
Percent of total U.S. population	2.9	3.1	3.1	X
Sex				
Male.........................	3,942,695	4,645,492	4,892,025	0.4
Female	4,106,618	4,889,991	5,150,777	0.4
Age				
Under 5 years.........................	539,509	632,040	604,711	-0.3
5 to 19 years.........................	1,653,851	1,926,640	1,954,561	0.1
20 to 64 years.........................	4,886,905	5,742,724	5,966,706	0.3
65 years and over	969,048	1,234,079	1,516,824	1.5
Median age (years)	35.3	37.4	38.4	0.2
Race and Hispanic Origin				
One race				
White.........................	5,804,656	6,898,296	7,154,774	0.3
Black.........................	1,737,545	2,088,362	2,223,003	0.4
American Indian and Alaska Native	99,551	147,566	156,173	0.4
Asian.........................	113,689	215,952	284,153	2.0
Native Hawaiian or Other Pacific Islander	3,983	10,309	12,395	1.3
Two or more races.........................	103,260	174,998	212,304	1.4
Hispanic (of any race).........................	378,963	830,172	916,742	0.7

X = Not applicable.
[1]Population figures for 2015 are July 1 estimates. The 2010 estimates are taken from the 2010 Census.

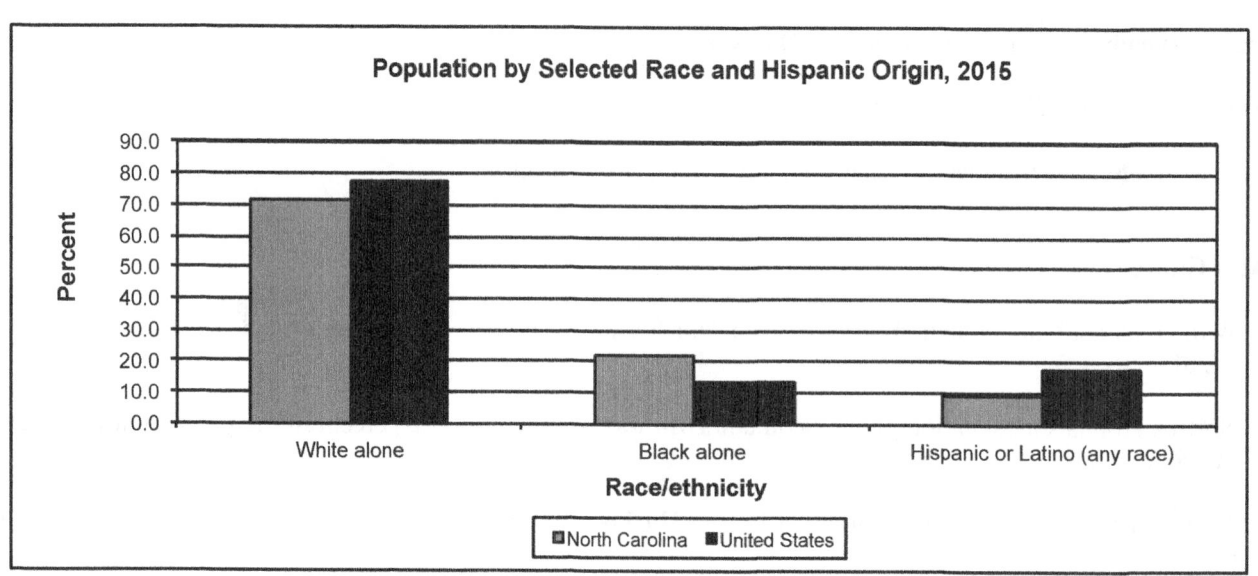

Table NC-2. Marital Status

(Number, percent distribution.)

Sex, age, race, and Hispanic origin	2000	2010	2014
Males, 15 Years and Over	3,092,380	3,678,950	3,778,356
Never married	28.2	33.3	33.7
Now married, except separated.........................	58.7	51.8	51.6
Separated.........................	2.7	2.9	2.7
Widowed.........................	2.4	2.5	2.6
Divorced.........................	8.1	9.6	9.3
Females, 15 Years and Over	3,301,327	3,975,748	4,066,089
Never married	22.0	27.3	27.9
Now married, except separated.........................	53.9	47.3	47.0
Separated.........................	3.3	3.5	3.4
Widowed.........................	10.9	9.8	9.6
Divorced.........................	9.9	12.1	12.0

Table NC-3. Households and Housing Characteristics

(Number, percent, dollars.)

Item	2000	2010	2014	Average annual percent change, 2000–2014
Total Households................................	3,132,012	3,670,859	3,790,620	1.5
Family households	2,158,869	2,441,916	2,492,048	1.1
Married-couple family	1,645,346	1,770,863	1,803,874	0.7
Other family	513,523	671,053	688,174	2.4
Male householder, no wife present................................	123,526	159,752	171,445	2.8
Female householder, no husband present................................	389,997	511,301	516,729	2.3
Nonfamily households	973,144	1,228,943	1,298,572	2.4
Householder living alone	795,271	1,022,017	1,077,581	2.5
Householder not living alone	177,873	206,926	220,991	1.7
Housing Characteristics				
Total housing units	3,523,944	4,333,479	4,452,464	1.9
Occupied housing units	3,132,012	3,670,859	3,790,620	1.5
Owner occupied	2,172,355	2,465,551	2,435,384	0.9
Renter occupied	959,658	1,205,308	1,355,236	2.9
Average household size................................	2.49	2.53	2.56	0.2
Financial Characteristics				
Median gross rent of renter-occupied housing	548	731	803	3.3
Median monthly owner costs for housing units with a mortgage	985	1,250	1,224	1.7
Median value of owner-occupied housing units................................	108,300	154,200	155,000	3.1

Table NC-4. Migration, Origin, and Language

(Number, percent.)

Characteristic	State			U.S.		
	2013	2014	Percent change	2013	2014	Percent change
Residence 1 Year Ago						
Population 1 year and over	9,737,365	9,832,152	1.0	312,432,820	315,095,393	0.9
Same house	84.6	84.7	X	85.0	85.1	X
Different house in the U.S................................	14.9	14.8	X	14.4	14.3	X
Same county	8.4	8.4	X	8.9	8.7	X
Different county	6.5	6.4	X	5.5	5.6	X
Same state	3.7	3.5	X	3.2	3.3	X
Different state	2.8	2.9	X	2.3	2.3	X
Abroad	0.5	0.5	X	0.6	0.6	X
Place of Birth						
Native born	9,098,634	9,180,380	0.9	274,780,773	276,465,262	0.6
Male	48.4	48.5	X	49.3	49.3	X
Female	51.6	51.5	X	50.7	50.7	X
Foreign born	749,426	763,584	1.9	41,348,066	42,391,794	2.5
Male	52.2	50.5	X	48.8	48.7	X
Female	47.8	49.5	X	51.2	51.3	X
Foreign born; naturalized U.S. citizen................................	239,232	269,435	12.6	19,294,710	19,984,738	3.6
Male	47.1	47.3	X	45.9	45.9	X
Female	52.9	52.7	X	54.1	54.1	X
Foreign born; not a U.S. citizen................................	510,194	494,149	-3.1	22,053,356	22,407,056	1.6
Male	54.6	52.2	X	51.3	51.2	X
Female	45.4	47.8	X	48.7	48.8	X
Entered 2010 or later	11.4	13.0	X	9.7	12.3	X
Entered 2000 to 2009	37.5	38.0	X	29.4	28.6	X
Entered before 2000................................	51.1	49.0	X	61.0	59.1	X
World Region of Birth, Foreign						
Foreign-born population, excluding population born at sea	749,426	763,584	1.9	41,347,945	42,390,705	2.5
Europe	10.5	9.9	X	11.6	11.2	X
Asia	24.4	25.8	X	29.5	30.1	X
Africa	5.9	6.4	X	4.4	4.6	X
Oceania	0.5	0.3	X	0.5	0.6	X
Latin America	56.4	55.3	X	51.9	51.6	X
North America	2.3	2.3	X	2.0	1.9	X
Language Spoken at Home and Ability to Speak English						
Population 5 years and over................................	9,240,578	9,342,422	1.1	296,358,760	299,084,046	0.9
English only	89.0	88.8	X	79.2	78.9	X
Language other than English................................	11.0	11.2	X	20.8	21.1	X
Speaks English less than "very well"................................	4.8	4.7	X	8.5	8.6	X

X = Not applicable.
- = Zero or rounds to zero.

Table NC-5. Median Income and Poverty Status, 2014

(Number, percent, except as noted.)

Characteristic	State		U.S.	
	Number	Percent	Number	Percent
Median Income				
Households (dollars)	46,556	X	53,657	X
Families (dollars)	57,380	X	65,910	X
Below Poverty Level (All People)	1,668,686	17.2	48,208,387	15.5
Sex				
Male	736,773	15.7	21,590,918	14.2
Female	931,913	18.6	26,617,469	16.8
Age				
Under 18 years	548,542	24.3	15,686,012	21.7
Related children under 18 years	539,098	24.0	15,372,705	21.3
18 to 64 years	983,033	16.4	28,267,482	14.6
65 years and over	137,111	9.7	4,254,893	9.5

X = Not applicable.

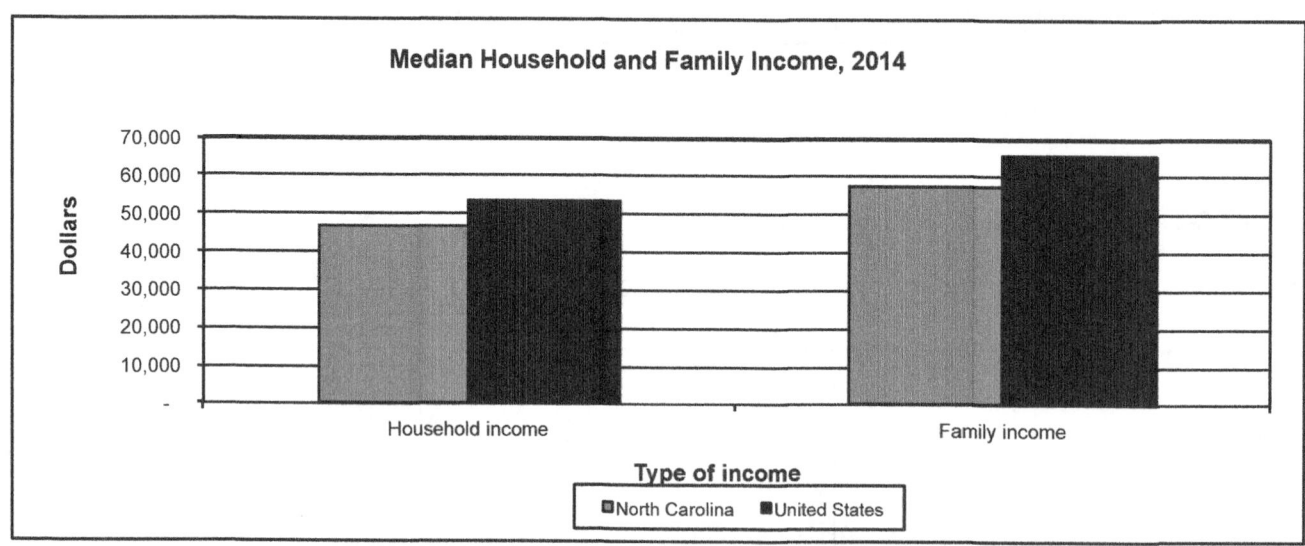

Table NC-6. Health Insurance Coverage Status for the Civilian Noninstitutionalized Population and Children Under 18 Years of Age

(Numbers in thousands, percent.)

Item	2006	2007	2008	2009	2010	2011	2012	2013	2014
Civilian Noninstitutionalized Population	8,851	9,183	9,004	9,149	9,361	9,461	9,553	9,645	9,752
Covered by Private or Public Insurance									
Number	7,266	7,673	7,570	7,679	7,791	7,916	7,970	8,136	8,476
Percent	82.1	83.6	84.1	83.9	83.2	83.7	83.4	84.4	86.9
Not Covered									
Number	1,585	1,510	1,434	1,471	1,570	1,545	1,583	1,509	1,276
Percent	17.9	16.4	15.9	16.1	16.8	16.3	16.6	15.6	13.1
Percent in the U.S. not covered	15.8	15.3	15.1	15.1	15.5	15.1	14.8	14.5	11.7
Children Under 18 Years of Age	2,198	2,247	2,237	2,271	2,281	2,287	2,282	2,281	2,287
Covered by Private or Public Insurance									
Number	1,891	1,975	2,018	2,085	2,104	2,112	2,109	2,136	2,168
Percent	86.0	87.9	90.2	91.8	92.3	92.4	92.4	93.7	94.8
Not Covered									
Number	307	272	219	186	177	175	173	144	119
Percent	14.0	12.1	9.8	8.2	7.7	7.6	7.6	6.3	5.2
Percent in the U.S. not covered	11.7	11.0	9.7	8.6	8.0	7.5	7.2	7.1	6.0

Table NC-7. Employment Status by Demographic Group, 2015

(Numbers in thousands, percent.)

Characteristic	Civilian noninstitutional population	Civilian labor force		Employed		Unemployed	
		Number	Percent of population	Number	Percent of population	Number	Percent of population
Total..	7,780	4,788	61.5	4,508	57.9	281	5.9
Sex							
Male..	3,685	2,495	67.7	2,358	64.0	137	5.5
Female......................................	4,095	2,294	56.0	2,150	52.5	144	6.3
Race, Sex, and Hispanic Origin							
White..	5,616	3,436	61.2	3,272	58.3	164	4.8
Male......................................	2,707	1,871	69.1	1,784	65.9	87	4.6
Female..................................	2,909	1,565	53.8	1,488	51.2	77	4.9
Black or African American...............	1,664	1,040	62.5	933	56.1	107	10.3
Male......................................	743	470	63.3	425	57.3	45	9.6
Female..................................	921	570	61.9	508	55.2	62	10.9
Hispanic or Latino ethnicity[1]	677	486	71.8	450	66.5	36	7.4
Male......................................	351	294	83.9	274	78.0	21	7.0
Female..................................	326	192	58.8	176	54.0	16	8.1
Age							
16 to 19 years............................	516	163	31.7	125	24.2	39	23.7
20 to 24 years............................	698	476	68.2	423	60.6	53	11.1
25 to 34 years............................	1,193	953	79.8	881	73.8	72	7.5
35 to 44 years............................	1,287	1,060	82.4	1,014	78.8	46	4.4
45 to 54 years............................	1,380	1,069	77.4	1,033	74.9	35	3.3
55 to 64 years............................	1,253	783	62.5	756	60.3	28	3.5
65 years and over	1,453	285	19.6	276	19.0	8	2.8

NOTE: Data in Table 7 are from the Current Population Survey (CPS) and do not match the estimates in Table 8. See notes and definitions for further information.
[1]May be of any race.

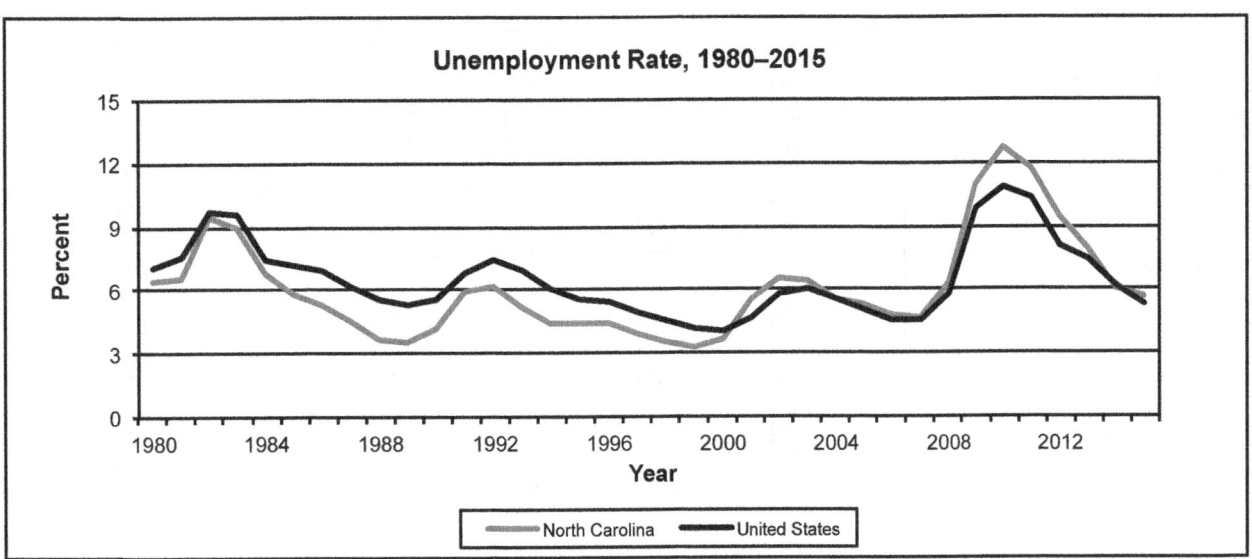

Unemployment Rate, 1980–2015

Table ND-8. Employment Status of the Civilian Noninstitutional Population Age 16 Years and Over

(Number, percent.)

Year	Civilian labor force	Civilian participation rate	Employed	Unemployed	Unemployment rate
2007..	367,234	74.1	355,766	11,468	3.1
2008..	371,025	74.4	359,333	11,692	3.2
2009..	368,665	73.2	353,455	15,210	4.1
2010..	378,342	72.6	364,053	14,289	3.8
2011..	388,634	72.9	375,153	13,481	3.5
2012..	397,812	73.0	385,596	12,216	3.1
2013..	406,602	72.7	394,833	11,769	2.9
2014..	415,286	72.6	404,147	11,139	2.7
2015..	414,344	71.0	403,058	11,286	2.7

Table NC-9. Employment and Average Wages by Industry

(Estimates through 2010 are based on the 2007 North American Industry Classification System [NAICS]. Estimates from 2011 onward are based on the 2012 NAICS.)

Industry	2008	2009	2010	2011	2012	2013	2014
				Number of jobs			
Wage and Salary Employment by Industry..................	4,380,014	4,170,430	4,142,475	4,194,673	4,245,620	4,316,789	4,396,031
Farm Wage and Salary Employment.........................	21,240	19,787	20,537	22,498	18,969	22,756	24,304
Nonfarm Wage and Salary Employment....................	4,358,774	4,150,643	4,121,938	4,172,175	4,226,651	4,294,033	4,371,727
Private wage and salary employment........................	3,509,755	3,291,218	3,255,024	3,311,094	3,366,353	3,432,840	3,518,061
Forestry, fishing, and related activities	13,276	13,184	13,756	14,185	13,932	13,897	14,872
Mining..	3,857	3,421	3,017	3,041	3,004	2,934	2,857
Utilities..	12,696	12,655	12,151	12,142	12,278	12,456	13,640
Construction	246,443	201,912	185,010	183,076	178,009	180,023	184,600
Manufacturing...	520,425	450,378	432,671	435,641	440,116	443,237	449,622
Durable goods manufacturing............................	278,378	233,187	222,044	226,553	234,356	236,402	240,217
Nondurable goods manufacturing.......................	242,047	217,191	210,627	209,088	205,760	206,835	209,405
Wholesale trade	180,249	168,500	166,187	169,313	172,309	174,725	177,680
Retail trade...	470,147	445,199	441,978	447,766	455,304	464,821	475,927
Transportation and warehousing..........................	116,205	106,853	104,879	108,408	110,500	111,506	115,945
Information...	72,418	69,904	68,391	68,765	69,307	69,831	72,539
Finance and insurance	158,175	151,690	152,281	154,409	155,364	157,089	161,163
Real estate and rental and leasing........................	54,845	51,271	49,619	49,191	49,388	51,550	53,551
Professional, scientific, and technical services	190,501	182,479	183,673	191,014	196,984	201,933	209,499
Management of companies and enterprises..............	76,037	73,366	73,211	77,301	80,558	77,921	80,533
Administrative and waste services	243,984	217,521	234,201	251,092	261,258	273,328	284,849
Educational services	82,677	86,226	87,362	89,348	89,503	90,662	93,619
Health care and social assistance.........................	464,786	470,835	465,393	465,269	471,261	480,533	486,015
Arts, entertainment, and recreation.......................	53,965	57,441	56,560	58,051	58,972	61,181	62,303
Accommodation and food services........................	351,085	340,522	340,644	346,828	359,188	372,840	384,457
Other services, except public administration..............	197,984	187,861	184,040	186,254	189,118	192,373	194,390
Government and government enterprises	849,019	859,425	866,914	861,081	860,298	861,193	853,666
				Dollars			
Average Wages and Salaries by Industry	40,708	40,802	42,039	43,107	44,217	44,656	45,849
Average Farm Wages and Salaries	29,361	25,702	18,438	21,834	23,650	28,625	24,684
Average Nonfarm Wages and Salaries	40,763	40,874	42,157	43,221	44,309	44,741	45,966
Average private wages and salaries........................	40,274	40,185	41,689	42,827	44,159	44,696	46,049
Forestry, fishing, and related activities	25,890	26,470	27,046	27,915	28,973	30,810	31,384
Mining..	53,137	51,558	43,772	46,996	47,266	48,091	49,723
Utilities..	78,538	76,185	80,911	82,200	86,571	93,305	90,908
Construction	40,517	40,246	41,015	42,240	44,164	44,779	46,401
Manufacturing...	49,177	50,468	52,809	54,176	54,906	56,201	56,881
Durable goods manufacturing............................	51,999	53,639	56,441	58,112	59,327	61,063	60,931
Nondurable goods manufacturing.......................	45,931	47,064	48,980	49,910	49,870	50,644	52,236
Wholesale trade	58,029	57,951	60,561	62,665	64,539	65,755	68,352
Retail trade...	25,175	24,984	25,594	25,625	26,398	26,788	27,306
Transportation and warehousing..........................	42,174	42,055	42,980	43,845	44,226	45,668	47,205
Information...	60,284	60,354	63,009	65,922	69,672	72,017	75,939
Finance and insurance	72,619	68,467	73,822	76,784	79,594	82,886	86,646
Real estate and rental and leasing........................	37,566	36,701	37,924	39,752	42,764	43,541	45,113
Professional, scientific, and technical services	62,622	63,425	66,463	68,258	71,579	71,219	73,792
Management of companies and enterprises..................	86,643	81,911	88,227	91,823	95,573	97,287	102,876
Administrative and waste services	29,370	30,103	30,982	31,550	33,544	32,656	33,618
Educational services	33,695	33,923	34,997	36,130	36,255	37,172	37,909
Health care and social assistance.........................	38,926	39,811	40,599	41,688	42,909	43,626	44,599
Arts, entertainment, and recreation.......................	32,648	30,330	30,474	31,388	31,749	31,811	33,052
Accommodation and food services........................	15,791	15,875	16,630	16,965	17,379	17,234	17,845
Other services, except public administration..................	26,532	27,128	28,223	28,798	29,314	30,202	31,109
Government and government enterprises	42,784	43,513	43,914	44,736	44,895	44,923	45,626

Table NC-10. Employment Characteristics by Family Type

(Number, percent.)

Family type and labor force status	2012		2013		2014	
	Total	Families with own children under 18 years	Total	Families with own children under 18 years	Total	Families with own children under 18 years
All Families...	2,472,230	1,077,533	2,474,802	1,048,744	2,483,732	1,054,151
FAMILY TYPE AND LABOR FORCE STATUS						
Married-Couple Families...........................	1,795,932	697,959	1,786,356	674,065	1,795,558	683,564
Both husband and wife in labor force................	51.5	65.8	50.7	65.9	49.9	65.1
Husband in labor force, wife not in labor force........	22.0	28.2	21.7	27.4	22.4	28.9
Wife in labor force, husband not in labor force............	8.4	4.3	8.4	4.5	8.5	4.4
Both husband and wife not in labor force............	18.1	1.7	18.9	2.0	19.3	1.6
Other Families	676,298	379,574	688,446	374,679	688,174	370,587
Female householder, no husband present...................	74.7	76.9	75.5	77.6	75.1	76.4
In labor force	52.8	63.2	53.6	64.3	52.5	63.8
Not in labor force	21.9	13.7	21.9	13.3	22.6	12.5
Male householder, no wife present...........................	25.3	23.1	24.5	22.4	24.9	23.6
In labor force..	19.3	20.7	18.7	20.4	18.7	20.9
Not in labor force	6.0	2.4	5.8	2.0	6.2	2.7

Table NC-11. School Enrollment and Educational Attainment, 2014

(Number, percent.)

Item	State	U.S.
Enrollment		
Total population 3 years and over, enrolled in school................	2,556,055	82,063,714
Enrolled in nursery school or preschool (percent).................	5.7	6.0
Enrolled in kindergarten (percent)................................	5.1	5.1
Enrolled in elementary school, grades 1-8 (percent)................	40.6	40.2
Enrolled in high school, grades 9-12 (percent)....................	20.3	20.7
Enrolled in college or graduate school (percent).................	28.2	28.0
Attainment		
Total population 25 years and over	6,661,937	213,725,624
Less than ninth grade (percent)	5.0	5.6
9th to 12th grade, no diploma (percent)	8.5	7.5
High school graduate, including equivalency (percent).............	26.6	27.7
Some college, no degree (percent)	21.9	21.0
Associate's degree (percent).....................................	9.2	8.2
Bachelor's degree (percent)......................................	18.6	18.7
Graduate or professional degree (percent)........................	10.1	11.4
High school graduate or higher (percent)	86.4	86.9
Bachelor's degree or higher (percent)............................	28.7	30.1

Table NC-12. Public School Characteristics and Educational Indicators

(Number, percent; data derived from National Center of Education Statistics.)

Item	State	U.S.
Public Schools, 2013–2014 (except where noted)		
Number of school districts.......................................	265	18,194
Number of schools...	2,588	98,271
Number of students (in thousands)	1,531	50,045
Number of teachers (in thousands)	99	3,114
Student-teacher ratio	15.4	16.1
Expenditures per student (dollars), FY 2013	8,342	107,637
Four-year adjusted cohort graduation rate (ACGR)[1,2]	83.9	82.3
Students eligible for free or reduced-price lunch (in thousands)	801	25,596
English language learners (in thousands)	94	4,461
Students age 3 to 21 served under IDEA, part B (in thousands) ...	193	6,464

Public Schools by Type	Number	Percent of state public schools
Total number of schools...	2,588	100.0
Regular...	2,473	95.6
Special education...	26	1.0
Vocational education..	7	0.3
Alternative education...	82	3.2

NOTE: Every school is assigned only one school type based on its instructional emphasis.

[1]ACGR data represents a new method of calculating high-school completion rates and may not be comparable to previous years' data for Averaged Freshmen Graduation Rates (AFGR).

[2]The United States 4-year ACGRs were estimated using both the reported 4-year ACGR data from 49 states and the District of Columbia and using imputed data for Idaho. The estimate for American Indian/Alaska Native students also includes imputed data for Virginia.

Table NC-13. Reported Voting and Registration of the Voting-Age Population, November 2014

(Numbers in thousands, percent.)

Item	Total population	Total citizen population	Registered			Voted		
			Total registered	Percent registered (total population)	Percent registered (total citizen population)	Total voted	Percent voted (total population)	Percent voted (total citizen population)
U.S. Total	239,874	219,941	142,166	59.3	64.6	92,251	38.5	41.9
State Total...............................	7,412	6,857	4,779	64.5	69.7	3,170	42.8	46.2
Sex								
Male...	3,510	3,204	2,178	62.0	68.0	1,428	40.7	44.6
Female	3,902	3,654	2,601	66.7	71.2	1,742	44.6	47.7
Race								
White alone.................................	5,415	5,004	3,545	65.5	70.9	2,325	42.9	46.5
White, non-Hispanic alone	4,878	4,852	3,461	71.0	71.3	2,290	46.9	47.2
Black alone.................................	1,572	1,527	1,040	66.1	68.1	735	46.7	48.1
Asian alone	190	99	59	30.8	59.1	26	13.5	25.9
Hispanic (of any race)......................	602	204	107	17.7	52.3	53	8.8	26.0
White alone or in combination	5,492	5,081	3,598	65.5	70.8	2,365	43.1	46.5
Black alone or in combination..........	1,628	1,583	1,070	65.7	67.6	761	46.7	48.1
Asian alone or in combination..........	198	107	62	31.6	58.5	29	14.9	27.6
Age								
18 to 24 years.............................	1,092	1,008	451	41.3	44.7	235	21.6	23.4
25 to 34 years.............................	1,199	1,037	669	55.8	64.5	347	28.9	33.5
35 to 44 years.............................	1,091	937	657	60.2	70.2	404	37.1	43.2
45 to 64 years.............................	2,582	2,452	1,869	72.4	76.2	1,262	48.9	51.5
65 years and over	1,448	1,424	1,132	78.2	79.5	921	63.6	64.7

Table NC-14. Crime

(Number, rate per 100,000. Data are derived from the FBI Uniform Crime Reports.)

Item	State			U.S.[1,2,3,4]		
	2013	2014	Percent Change	2013	2014	Percent change
TOTAL POPULATION[5]......................................	9,848,060	9,943,964	1.0	316,128,839	318,857,056	0.9
VIOLENT CRIME						
Number...	33,152	32,767	-1.2	1,163,146	1,165,383	0.2
Rate	336.6	329.5	-2.1	367.9	365.5	-0.7
Murder and Nonnegligent Manslaughter						
Number...	469	510	8.7	14,196	14,249	0.4
Rate	4.8	5.1	6.2	4.5	4.5	-
Rape[6]						
Number...	2,369	2,420	X	108,612	116,645	X
Rate	24.1	24.3	X	34.4	36.6	X
Robbery						
Number...	9,349	8,416	-10.0	345,031	325,802	-5.6
Rate	94.9	84.6	-10.9	109.1	102.2	-6.3
Aggravated Assault						
Number...	21,513	21,421	-0.4	724,149	741,291	2.4
Rate	218.4	215.4	-1.4	229.1	232.5	1.5
PROPERTY CRIME						
Number...	308,049	285,697	-7.3	8,632,512	8,277,829	-4.1
Rate	3,128.0	2,873.1	-8.1	2,730.7	2,596.1	-4.9
Burglary						
Number...	90,702	79,373	-12.5	1,928,465	1,729,806	-10.3
Rate	921.0	798.2	-13.3	610.0	542.5	-11.1
Larceny-Theft						
Number...	202,741	192,694	-5.0	6,004,453	5,858,496	-2.4
Rate	2,058.7	1,937.8	-5.9	1,899.4	1,837.3	-3.3
Motor Vehicle Theft						
Number...	14,606	13,630	-6.7	699,594	689,527	-1.4
Rate	148.3	137.1	-7.6	221.3	216.2	-2.3

NOTE: Although arson data are included in the trend and clearance tables, sufficient data are not available to estimate totals for this offense. Therefore, no arson data are published in this table.
X = Not applicable.
- = Zero or rounds to zero.
[1]The crime figures have been adjusted.
[2]The data collection methodology for the offense of forcible rape used by the Minnesota state Uniform Crime Reporting (UCR) Program (with the exception of Minneapolis and St. Paul, Minnesota) does not comply with national UCR Program guidelines. Consequently, its figures for forcible rape and violent crime (of which forcible rape is a part) are not published in this table.
[3]Includes offenses reported by the Zoological Police and the Metro Transit Police.
[4]Because of changes in the state's reporting practices, figures are not comparable to previous years' data.
[5]Populations are U.S. Census Bureau provisional estimates as of July 1 of each year.
[6]The figures shown for the offense of rape were estimated using the revised Uniform Crime Reporting (UCR) definition of rape.

Table NC-15. State Government Finances, 2014

(Dollar amounts in thousands, percent distribution.)

Item	Dollars	Percent distribution
Total Revenue	61,748,866	100.0
General revenue	46,909,231	76.0
Intergovernmental revenue	15,643,257	25.3
Taxes	23,396,751	37.9
General sales	5,842,182	9.5
Selective sales	4,136,302	6.7
License taxes	1,600,058	2.6
Individual income tax	10,390,520	16.8
Corporate income tax	1,360,628	2.2
Other taxes	67,061	0.1
Current charges	4,869,497	7.9
Miscellaneous general revenue	2,999,726	4.9
Utility revenue	47	-
Liquor stores revenue	0	-
Insurance trust revenue[1]	14,839,588	24.0
Total Expenditure	51,113,382	100.0
Intergovernmental expenditure	13,172,777	25.8
Direct expenditure	37,940,605	74.2
Current operation	27,733,262	54.3
Capital outlay	3,046,212	6.0
Insurance benefits and repayments	5,876,600	11.5
Assistance and subsidies	679,048	1.3
Interest on debt	605,483	1.2
Exhibit: Salaries and wages	9,192,393	18.0
Total Expenditure	51,113,382	100.0
General expenditure	45,116,969	88.3
Intergovernmental expenditure	13,172,777	25.8
Direct expenditure	31,944,192	62.5
General expenditure, by function:		
Education	19,053,531	37.3
Public welfare	12,722,436	24.9
Hospitals	1,729,030	3.4
Health	1,287,441	2.5
Highways	3,752,683	7.3
Police protection	662,476	1.3
Correction	1,178,071	2.3
Natural resources	467,309	0.9
Parks and recreation	159,334	0.3
Governmental administration	1,375,290	2.7
Interest on general debt	605,483	1.2
Other and unallocable	2,123,885	4.2
Utility expenditure	119,813	0.2
Liquor stores expenditure	0	-
Insurance trust expenditure	5,876,600	11.5
Debt at End of Fiscal Year	17,853,232	X
Cash and Security Holdings	100,605,878	X

X = Not applicable.
- = Zero or rounds to zero.
[1]Within insurance trust revenue, net earnings of state retirement systems is a calculated statistic (the item code in the data file is X08), and thus can be positive or negative. Net earnings is the sum of earnings on investments plus gains on investments minus losses on investments. The change made in 2002 for asset valuation from book to market value in accordance with Statement 34 of the Governmental Accounting Standards Board is reflected in the calculated statistics.

Table NC-16. State Government Tax Collections, 2014

(Dollars in thousands, percent.)

Item	Dollars	Percent distribution
Total Taxes	23,396,751	100.0
Property taxes	X	X
Sales and gross receipts	9,978,484	42.6
General sales and gross receipts	5,842,182	25.0
Selective sales and gross receipts	4,136,302	17.7
Alcoholic beverages	343,344	1.5
Amusements	14,157	0.1
Insurance premiums	476,376	2.0
Motor fuels	1,915,670	8.2
Pari-mutuels	X	X
Public utilities	403,194	1.7
Tobacco products	281,773	1.2
Other selective sales	701,788	3.0
Licenses	1,600,058	6.8
Alcoholic beverages	15,916	0.1
Amusements	X	X
Corporations in general	617,408	2.6
Hunting and fishing	17,488	0.1
Motor vehicle	591,457	2.5
Motor vehicle operators	111,132	0.5
Public utilities	X	X
Occupation and business, NEC	233,463	1.0
Other licenses	13,194	0.1
Income taxes	11,751,148	50.2
Individual income	10,390,520	44.4
Corporation net income	1,360,628	5.8
Other taxes	67,061	0.3
Death and gift	19,932	0.1
Documentary and stock transfer	45,353	0.2
Severance	1,776	-
Taxes, NEC	0	-

X = Not applicable.
- = Zero or rounds to zero.

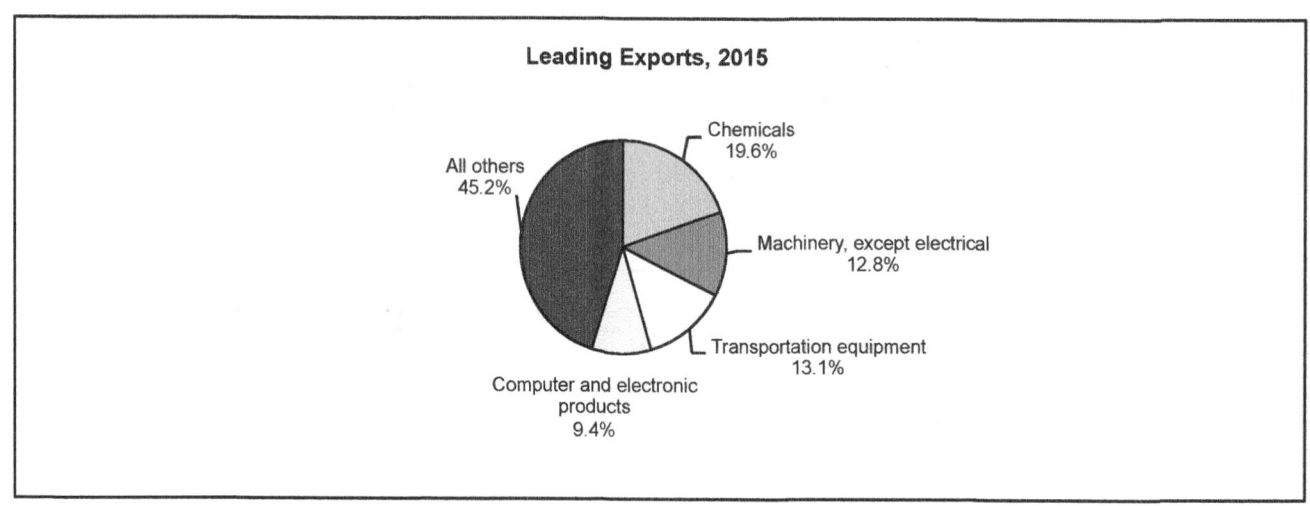

Leading Exports, 2015

Chemicals 19.6%
Machinery, except electrical 12.8%
Transportation equipment 13.1%
Computer and electronic products 9.4%
All others 45.2%

NORTH DAKOTA

Facts and Figures

Location: North central United States; bordered on the N by Canada (Manitoba and Saskatchewan), on the E by Minnesota, on the S by South Dakota, and on the W by Montana

Area: 70,700 sq. mi. (183,112 sq. km.); rank—19th

Population: 756,927 (2015 est.); rank—47th

Principal Cities: capital—Bismarck; largest—Fargo

Statehood: November 2, 1889; 39th state

U.S. Congress: 2 senators, 1 representative

State Motto: Liberty and Union, Now and Forever, One and Inseparable

State Song: "North Dakota Hymn"

State Nicknames: The Peace Garden State; The Flickertail State; The Rough Rider State

Abbreviations: ND; N.D.; N. Dak.

State Symbols: flower—wild prairie rose; tree—American elm; bird—Western meadowlark

At a Glance

- With an increase in population of 12.2 percent, North Dakota ranked 1st for population growth between 2010 and 2015.

- In 2014, 7.9 percent of North Dakotans did not have health insurance, compared to 11.7 percent of the total U.S. population.

- North Dakota had the 3rd highest birth rate in the country in 2014 (15.4 births per 1,000 population).

- In 2015, 2.7 percent of North Dakotans were unemployed, which was the lowest unemployment rate in the country.

- In North Dakota in 2014, 14.8 percent of children under 18 years old lived below the poverty level, compared to the national childhood poverty rate of 21.7 percent.

Table ND-1. Population by Age, Sex, Race, and Hispanic Origin

(Number, percent, except where noted.)

Sex, age, race, and Hispanic origin	2000	2010	2015[1]	Average annual percent change, 2010–2015
Total Population..	642,200	672,591	756,927	0.8
Percent of total U.S. population	0.2	0.2	0.2	X
Sex				
Male...	320,524	339,864	388,853	1.0
Female	321,676	332,727	368,074	0.7
Age				
Under 5 years.................................	39,400	44,595	53,147	1.3
5 to 19 years.................................	144,064	127,340	143,963	0.9
20 to 64 years................................	364,258	403,179	452,536	0.8
65 years and over	94,478	97,477	107,281	0.7
Median age (years)...........................	36.2	37.0	34.6	-0.5
Race and Hispanic Origin				
One race				
White...................................	593,181	609,136	670,430	0.7
Black....................................	3,916	8,248	18,392	5.9
American Indian and Alaska Native	31,329	36,948	41,315	0.8
Asian....................................	3,606	7,032	10,564	2.9
Native Hawaiian or Other Pacific Islander	230	334	623	4.6
Two or more races............................	7,398	10,893	15,603	2.6
Hispanic (of any race)........................	7,786	14,407	26,814	4.5

X = Not applicable.
[1]Population figures for 2015 are July 1 estimates. The 2010 estimates are taken from the 2010 Census.

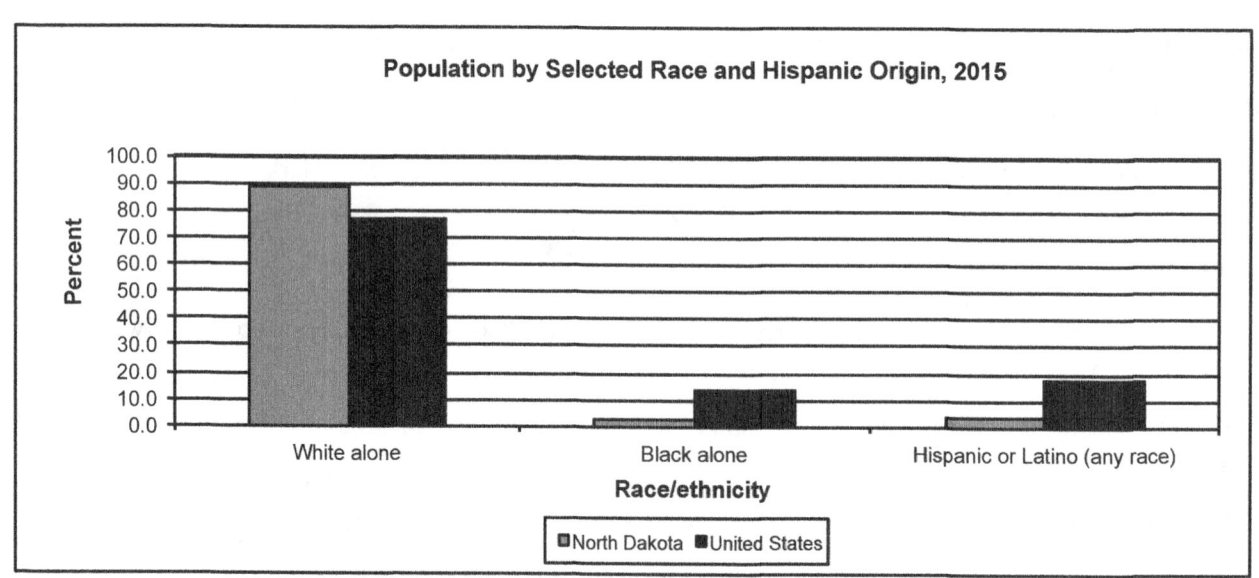

Table ND-2. Marital Status

(Number, percent distribution.)

Sex, age, race, and Hispanic origin	2000	2010	2014
Males, 15 Years and Over	253,900	278,276	290,882
Never married	32.0	35.8	36.0
Now married, except separated.................	57.5	53.1	52.0
Separated...................................	0.6	0.6	0.7
Widowed....................................	2.5	2.1	2.3
Divorced....................................	7.3	8.4	8.9
Females, 15 Years and Over	258,381	271,462	281,379
Never married	23.2	26.6	26.8
Now married, except separated.................	56.0	52.5	52.7
Separated...................................	0.8	0.7	0.9
Widowed....................................	11.7	10.1	9.6
Divorced....................................	8.2	10.2	9.9

Table ND-3. Households and Housing Characteristics

(Number, percent, dollars.)

Item	2000	2010	2014	Average annual percent change, 2000–2014
Total Households...	257,252	280,412	305,431	1.3
Family households	166,150	171,945	187,800	0.9
Married-couple family	137,433	140,277	149,016	0.6
Other family	28,717	31,668	38,784	2.5
Male householder, no wife present.......................	8,569	8,846	14,108	4.6
Female householder, no husband present...............	20,148	22,822	24,676	1.6
Nonfamily households	91,002	108,467	117,631	2.1
Householder living alone.....................................	75,420	87,883	93,963	1.8
Householder not living alone...............................	15,582	20,584	23,668	3.7
Housing Characteristics				
Total housing units..	289,677	318,099	350,534	1.5
Occupied housing units	257,252	280,412	305,431	1.3
Owner occupied	171,299	187,673	195,002	1.0
Renter occupied	85,853	92,739	110,429	2.0
Average household size...	2.41	2.32	2.33	-0.2
Financial Characteristics				
Median gross rent of renter-occupied housing	412	583	728	5.5
Median monthly owner costs for housing units with a mortgage	818	1,133	1,267	3.9
Median value of owner-occupied housing units	74,400	123,000	161,800	8.4

Table ND-4. Migration, Origin, and Language

(Number, percent.)

Characteristic	State 2013	State 2014	State Percent change	U.S. 2013	U.S. 2014	U.S. Percent change
Residence 1 Year Ago						
Population 1 year and over	714,804	729,874	2.1	312,432,820	315,095,393	0.9
Same house	83.1	82.5	X	85.0	85.1	X
Different house in the U.S.	16.5	17.0	X	14.4	14.3	X
Same county	7.7	8.4	X	8.9	8.7	X
Different county	8.8	8.6	X	5.5	5.6	X
Same state..	3.4	3.3	X	3.2	3.3	X
Different state	5.4	5.4	X	2.3	2.3	X
Abroad	0.5	0.4	X	0.6	0.6	X
Place of Birth						
Native born	702,286	715,328	1.9	274,780,773	276,465,262	0.6
Male..	51.1	51.0	X	49.3	49.3	X
Female...	48.9	49.0	X	50.7	50.7	X
Foreign born	21,107	24,154	14.4	41,348,066	42,391,794	2.5
Male..	48.1	48.5	X	48.8	48.7	X
Female...	51.9	51.5	X	51.2	51.3	X
Foreign born; naturalized U.S. citizen.....................	6,548	9,390		19,294,710	19,984,738	3.6
Male..	41.5	43.9	X	45.9	45.9	X
Female...	58.5	56.1	X	54.1	54.1	X
Foreign born; not a U.S. citizen............................	14,559	14,764	1.4	22,053,356	22,407,056	1.6
Male..	51.1	51.4	X	51.3	51.2	X
Female...	48.9	48.6	X	48.7	48.8	X
Entered 2010 or later	35.5	24.6	X	9.7	12.3	X
Entered 2000 to 2009	33.2	38.2	X	29.4	28.6	X
Entered before 2000..	31.3	37.2	X	61.0	59.1	X
World Region of Birth, Foreign						
Foreign-born population, excluding population born at sea	21,107	24,154	14.4	41,347,945	42,390,705	2.5
Europe	13.1	16.5	X	11.6	11.2	X
Asia..	44.3	32.6	X	29.5	30.1	X
Africa	14.8	24.6	X	4.4	4.6	X
Oceania	2.0	0.5	X	0.5	0.6	X
Latin America...	12.0	14.0	X	51.9	51.6	X
North America	13.8	11.9	X	2.0	1.9	X
Language Spoken at Home and Ability to Speak English						
Population 5 years and over..................................	675,918	689,505	2.0	296,358,760	299,084,046	0.9
English only	94.7	94.5	X	79.2	78.9	X
Language other than English.................................	5.3	5.5	X	20.8	21.1	X
Speaks English less than "very well".......................	1.5	1.5	X	8.5	8.6	X

X = Not applicable.
- = Zero or rounds to zero.

Table ND-5. Median Income and Poverty Status, 2014

(Number, percent, except as noted.)

Characteristic	State		U.S.	
	Number	Percent	Number	Percent
Median Income				
Households (dollars)...	59,029	X	53,657	X
Families (dollars)	75,221	X	65,910	X
Below Poverty Level (All People)	82,264	11.5	48,208,387	15.5
Sex				
Male..	35,007	9.7	21,590,918	14.2
Female	47,257	13.5	26,617,469	16.8
Age				
Under 18 years..	24,132	14.8	15,686,012	21.7
Related children under 18 years..	23,260	14.3	15,372,705	21.3
18 to 64 years...	49,539	11.0	28,267,482	14.6
65 years and over	8,593	8.7	4,254,893	9.5

X = Not applicable.

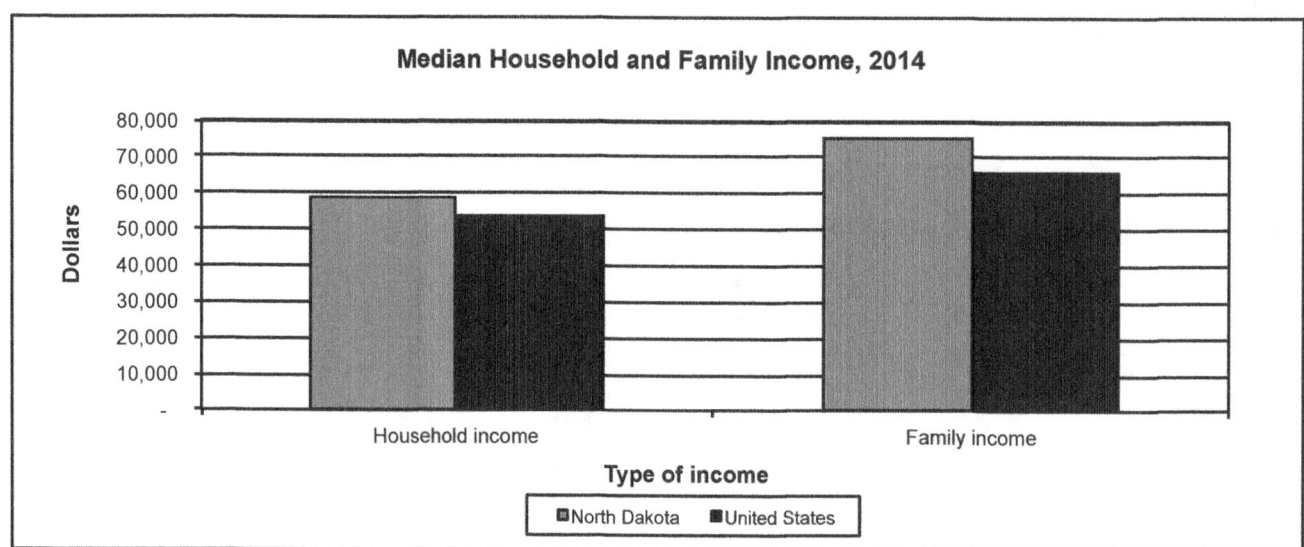

Median Household and Family Income, 2014

Table ND-6. Health Insurance Coverage Status for the Civilian Noninstitutionalized Population and Children Under 18 Years of Age

(Numbers in thousands, percent.)

Item	2006	2007	2008	2009	2010	2011	2012	2013	2014
Civilian Noninstitutionalized Population	617	615	624	630	661	669	685	708	724
Covered by Private or Public Insurance									
Number..	541	553	558	569	596	604	616	635	668
Percent..	87.8	90.0	89.4	90.3	90.2	90.2	90.0	89.6	92.1
Not Covered									
Number..	75	61	66	61	65	65	69	73	57
Percent..	12.2	10.0	10.6	9.7	9.8	9.8	10.0	10.4	7.9
Percent in the U.S. not covered...	15.8	15.3	15.1	15.1	15.5	15.1	14.8	14.5	11.7
Children Under 18 Years of Age	144	146	141	141	150	151	154	160	167
Covered by Private or Public Insurance									
Number..	130	135	130	133	140	141	143	148	156
Percent..	89.7	92.1	92.2	94.4	93.5	93.6	93.1	92.1	93.1
Not Covered									
Number..	15	11	11	8	10	10	11	13	12
Percent..	10.3	7.9	7.8	5.6	6.5	6.4	6.9	7.9	6.9
Percent in the U.S. not covered...	11.7	11.0	9.7	8.6	8.0	7.5	7.2	7.1	6.0

Table ND-7. Employment Status by Demographic Group, 2015

(Numbers in thousands, percent.)

Characteristic	Civilian noninstitutional population	Civilian labor force		Employed		Unemployed	
		Number	Percent of population	Number	Percent of population	Number	Percent of population
Total..	585	414	70.9	403	68.9	11	2.7
Sex							
Male..	298	228	76.6	221	74.3	7	3.0
Female...	287	186	64.9	182	63.4	5	2.4
Race, Sex, and Hispanic Origin							
White..	534	383	71.8	374	70.1	9	2.4
Male...	274	212	77.1	206	75.1	5	2.5
Female..	259	172	66.2	168	64.7	4	2.3
Black or African American.................	NA	NA	NA	NA	NA	NA	NA
Male...	NA	NA	NA	NA	NA	NA	NA
Female..	NA	NA	NA	NA	NA	NA	NA
Hispanic or Latino ethnicity[1]............	NA	NA	NA	NA	NA	NA	NA
Male...	NA	NA	NA	NA	NA	NA	NA
Female..	NA	NA	NA	NA	NA	NA	NA
Age							
16 to 19 years..................................	36	17	47.3	16	44.0	1	6.8
20 to 24 years..................................	58	47	81.3	46	78.6	2	3.6
25 to 34 years..................................	119	102	85.6	99	82.9	3	3.1
35 to 44 years..................................	86	75	86.4	73	84.6	2	2.0
45 to 54 years..................................	90	78	86.9	76	84.8	2	2.4
55 to 64 years..................................	96	74	77.2	73	75.8	1	1.9
65 years and over..............................	99	21	21.4	21	20.9	1.0	2.8

NOTE: Data in Table 7 are from the Current Population Survey (CPS) and do not match the estimates in Table 8. See notes and definitions for further information.
NA = Not available.
[1] May be of any race.

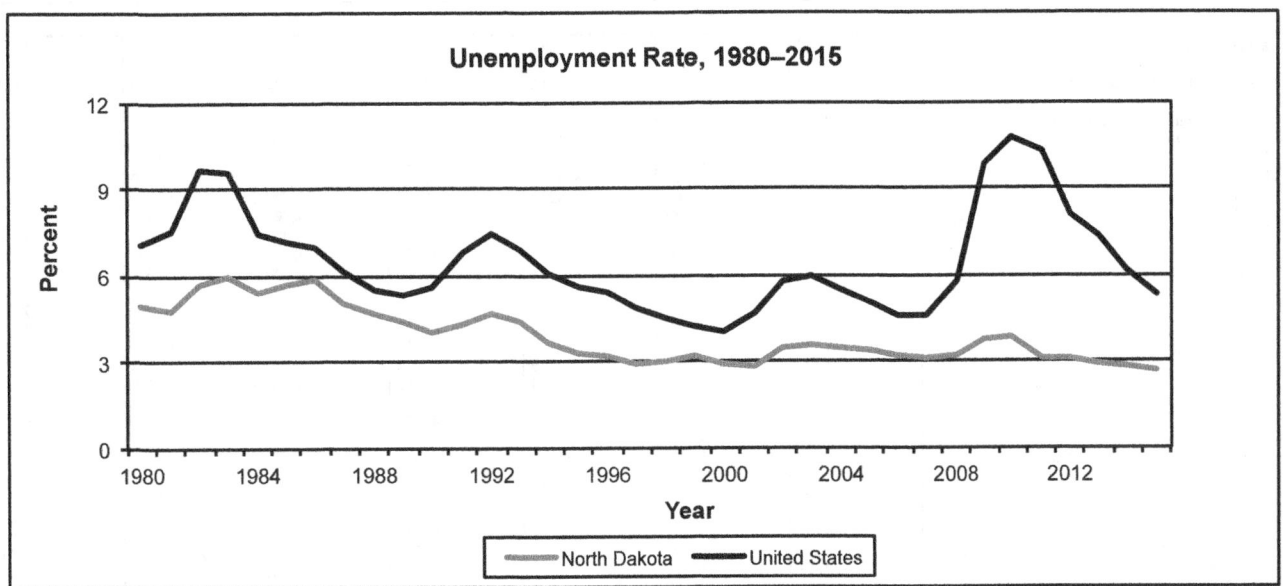

Unemployment Rate, 1980–2015

Table ND-8. Employment Status of the Civilian Noninstitutional Population Age 16 Years and Over

(Number, percent.)

Year	Civilian labor force	Civilian participation rate	Employed	Unemployed	Unemployment rate
2007..	367,234	74.1	355,766	11,468	3.1
2008..	371,025	74.4	359,333	11,692	3.2
2009..	368,665	73.2	353,455	15,210	4.1
2010..	378,342	72.6	364,053	14,289	3.8
2011..	388,634	72.9	375,153	13,481	3.5
2012..	397,812	73.0	385,596	12,216	3.1
2013..	406,602	72.7	394,833	11,769	2.9
2014..	415,286	72.6	404,147	11,139	2.7
2015..	414,344	71.0	403,058	11,286	2.7

Table ND-9. Employment and Average Wages by Industry

(Estimates through 2010 are based on the 2007 North American Industry Classification System [NAICS]. Estimates from 2011 onward are based on the 2012 NAICS.)

Industry	2008	2009	2010	2011	2012	2013	2014
	Number of jobs						
Wage and Salary Employment by Industry..................	384,084	383,488	393,623	415,288	447,570	464,077	482,944
Farm Wage and Salary Employment.........................	5,210	4,395	4,829	5,282	7,088	6,254	7,283
Nonfarm Wage and Salary Employment....................	378,874	379,093	388,794	410,006	440,482	457,823	475,661
Private wage and salary employment...........................	298,381	296,084	304,071	325,678	355,787	371,593	388,090
Forestry, fishing, and related activities.....................	1,630	1,639	1,713	1,790	1,757	2,472	2,625
Mining..	6,791	6,906	10,523	16,580	24,122	25,916	29,607
Utilities...	3,415	3,384	3,418	3,419	3,506	3,592	3,702
Construction	21,428	21,560	22,271	25,607	30,437	33,552	35,857
Manufacturing..	26,362	23,607	22,591	23,792	25,190	25,432	25,956
Durable goods manufacturing...............................	18,002	15,494	14,626	15,850	16,955	17,241	17,640
Nondurable goods manufacturing.........................	8,360	8,113	7,965	7,942	8,235	8,191	8,316
Wholesale trade	20,045	20,377	21,252	22,885	25,223	26,545	27,444
Retail trade...	43,692	43,438	44,221	45,418	47,500	49,488	51,033
Transportation and warehousing...............................	11,854	12,038	12,965	16,287	21,222	22,455	24,495
Information	7,453	7,510	7,325	7,122	6,966	6,827	6,838
Finance and insurance	16,821	16,750	17,061	17,397	17,456	17,940	18,533
Real estate and rental and leasing..........................	3,580	3,563	3,735	4,161	4,735	5,237	5,860
Professional, scientific, and technical services	13,115	12,661	12,657	12,869	14,456	15,717	16,866
Management of companies and enterprises..................	4,288	4,298	4,329	4,470	4,764	5,132	5,291
Administrative and waste services............................	13,216	12,420	11,752	12,852	13,564	13,601	14,343
Educational services	3,734	3,744	3,808	3,862	4,065	4,121	4,258
Health care and social assistance............................	49,289	50,325	52,031	53,345	54,651	55,777	56,224
Arts, entertainment, and recreation..........................	3,765	3,760	3,863	3,829	4,016	4,200	4,326
Accommodation and food services...........................	30,177	30,572	30,865	32,043	34,298	35,272	36,422
Other services, except public administration...............	17,726	17,532	17,691	17,950	17,859	18,317	18,410
Government and government enterprises	80,493	83,009	84,723	84,328	84,695	86,230	87,571
	Dollars						
Average Wages and Salaries by Industry	35,002	35,695	37,653	41,122	45,083	46,775	49,741
Average Farm Wages and Salaries	48,556	43,162	36,388	39,453	40,236	42,118	43,348
Average Nonfarm Wages and Salaries	34,815	35,609	37,668	41,143	45,161	46,838	49,839
Average private wages and salaries...........................	34,861	35,599	37,915	41,952	46,633	48,462	51,856
Forestry, fishing, and related activities......................	23,642	25,836	26,684	27,991	29,367	27,722	28,259
Mining..	74,767	72,801	79,246	89,204	95,806	97,160	103,897
Utilities...	73,221	76,940	78,508	81,965	82,099	86,489	90,563
Construction	44,039	45,341	46,471	51,110	56,396	60,148	64,844
Manufacturing..	41,725	41,559	43,376	44,736	46,673	48,056	49,781
Durable goods manufacturing...............................	43,347	42,539	44,151	45,410	47,348	48,594	49,995
Nondurable goods manufacturing.........................	38,233	39,687	41,953	43,390	45,283	46,924	49,327
Wholesale trade	48,136	48,743	51,324	57,530	51,773	65,249	68,075
Retail trade...	22,883	23,268	24,198	25,689	6,261	28,355	29,714
Transportation and warehousing...............................	46,134	46,621	50,095	56,400	62,114	63,858	67,822
Information	46,629	47,571	49,015	50,884	54,434	55,689	58,382
Finance and insurance	44,360	45,374	46,704	49,865	52,942	54,118	56,329
Real estate and rental and leasing..........................	29,290	30,980	34,482	44,079	50,393	53,306	59,656
Professional, scientific, and technical services	44,349	46,514	51,424	55,841	63,242	67,230	71,676
Management of companies and enterprises..................	58,812	59,976	63,720	65,945	69,354	69,897	76,662
Administrative and waste services............................	22,135	23,060	25,166	27,901	31,639	31,947	34,057
Educational services	20,605	21,310	21,678	22,096	21,756	22,606	22,787
Health care and social assistance............................	36,783	37,922	39,366	41,243	43,406	44,573	46,511
Arts, entertainment, and recreation..........................	14,667	15,121	15,562	16,327	16,809	17,191	17,565
Accommodation and food services...........................	12,907	13,232	14,119	15,422	17,245	18,138	19,391
Other services, except public administration...............	22,051	22,856	23,847	25,122	27,123	28,943	31,832
Government and government enterprises	34,644	35,642	36,785	38,021	38,979	39,841	40,900

Table ND-10. Employment Characteristics by Family Type

(Number, percent.)

Family type and labor force status	2012		2013		2014	
	Total	Families with own children under 18 years	Total	Families with own children under 18 years	Total	Families with own children under 18 years
All Families..	175,380	74,751	180,213	78,738	187,451	84,732
FAMILY TYPE AND LABOR FORCE STATUS						
Married-Couple Families............................	139,907	52,133	145,079	57,092	148,667	59,010
Both husband and wife in labor force..................	61.4	77.3	59.9	72.3	60.8	74.6
Husband in labor force, wife not in labor force	17.5	20.4	18.2	23.4	17.7	21.0
Wife in labor force, husband not in labor force	6.8	1.9	7.0	2.9	6.7	2.9
Both husband and wife not in labor force...............	14.3	0.4	14.5	1.3	14.9	1.5
Other Families	35,473	22,618	35,134	21,646	38,784	25,722
Female householder, no husband present...............	66.1	70.5	63.1	63.8	63.6	68.5
In labor force...	51.6	60.0	47.6	50.8	47.1	55.7
Not in labor force	14.6	10.5	15.4	13.0	16.5	12.8
Male householder, no wife present.....................	33.9	29.5	36.9	36.2	36.4	31.5
In labor force...	30.7	28.6	31.7	34.2	31.1	27.9
Not in labor force	3.2	0.9	5.2	2.0	5.3	3.6

Table ND-11. School Enrollment and Educational Attainment, 2014

(Number, percent.)

Item	State	U.S.
Enrollment		
Total population 3 years and over, enrolled in school................	182,606	82,063,714
Enrolled in nursery school or preschool (percent)	5.7	6.0
Enrolled in kindergarten (percent)...................................	6.0	5.1
Enrolled in elementary school, grades 1-8 (percent).................	38.3	40.2
Enrolled in high school, grades 9-12 (percent)	18.5	20.7
Enrolled in college or graduate school (percent).....................	31.5	28.0
Attainment		
Total population 25 years and over	478,850	213,725,624
Less than ninth grade (percent)	3.3	5.6
9th to 12th grade, no diploma (percent)	4.5	7.5
High school graduate, including equivalency (percent)	27.9	27.7
Some college, no degree (percent)	23.5	21.0
Associate's degree (percent)	13.5	8.2
Bachelor's degree (percent)	19.8	18.7
Graduate or professional degree (percent)............................	7.6	11.4
High school graduate or higher (percent)	92.2	86.9
Bachelor's degree or higher (percent)	27.4	30.1

Table ND-12. Public School Characteristics and Educational Indicators

(Number, percent; data derived from National Center of Education Statistics.)

Item	State	U.S.
Public Schools, 2013–2014 (except where noted)		
Number of school districts..	222	18,194
Number of schools..	512	98,271
Number of students (in thousands)	104	50,045
Number of teachers (in thousands)	9	3,114
Student-teacher ratio	11.8	16.1
Expenditures per student (dollars), FY 2013.........................	11,615	107,637
Four-year adjusted cohort graduation rate (ACGR)[1][2]	87.2	82.3
Students eligible for free or reduced-price lunch (in thousands)	31	25,596
English language learners (in thousands)	3	4,461
Students age 3 to 21 served under IDEA, part B (in thousands)	13	6,464

Public Schools by Type	Number	Percent of state public schools
Total number of schools..	512	100.0
Regular	467	91.2
Special education	33	6.4
Vocational education	12	2.3
Alternative education..	0	-

NOTE: Every school is assigned only one school type based on its instructional emphasis.
[1]ACGR data represents a new method of calculating high-school completion rates and may not be comparable to previous years' data for Averaged Freshmen Graduation Rates (AFGR).
[2]The United States 4-year ACGRs were estimated using both the reported 4-year ACGR data from 49 states and the District of Columbia and using imputed data for Idaho. The estimate for American Indian/Alaska Native students also includes imputed data for Virginia.
- = Zero or rounds to zero.

Table ND-13. Reported Voting and Registration of the Voting-Age Population, November 2014

(Numbers in thousands, percent.)

Item	Total population	Total citizen population	Registered			Voted		
			Total registered	Percent registered (total population)	Percent registered (total citizen population)	Total voted	Percent voted (total population)	Percent voted (total citizen population)
U.S. Total	239,874	219,941	142,166	59.3	64.6	92,251	38.5	41.9
State Total............................	567	547	363	64.1	66.4	279	49.2	51.0
Sex								
Male.................................	290	279	180	61.9	64.4	136	46.7	48.6
Female	276	268	183	66.3	68.5	143	51.8	53.5
Race								
White alone............................	516	508	345	66.8	67.9	266	51.5	52.3
White, non-Hispanic alone	501	497	342	68.2	68.7	264	52.7	53.2
Black alone............................	10	6	2	(B)	(B)	2	(B)	(B)
Asian alone	10	3	1	(B)	(B)	1	(B)	(B)
Hispanic (of any race)	19	14	5	(B)	(B)	2	(B)	(B)
White alone or in combination	526	517	351	66.7	67.8	270	51.4	52.3
Black alone or in combination..........	11	6	3	(B)	(B)	2	(B)	(B)
Asian alone or in combination..........	14	7	4	(B)	(B)	4	(B)	(B)
Age								
18 to 24 years	82	77	36	43.5	46.4	21	25.1	26.7
25 to 34 years.........................	121	114	68	56.2	59.4	45	37.2	39.4
35 to 44 years.........................	78	76	48	60.7	63.0	32	41.2	42.8
45 to 64 years.........................	184	180	128	69.5	71.3	106	57.4	59.0
65 years and over	101	100	84	82.9	83.5	75	74.3	74.8

- = Zero or rounds to zero.
B = Base is less than 75,000 and therefore too small to show the derived measure.

Table ND-14. Crime

(Number, rate per 100,000. Data are derived from the FBI Uniform Crime Reports.)

Item	State			U.S.[1,2,3,4]		
	2013	2014	Percent change	2013	2014	Percent change
TOTAL POPULATION[5]...........................	723,393	739,482	2.2	316,128,839	318,857,056	0.9
VIOLENT CRIME						
Number.................................	1,854	1,960	5.7	1,163,146	1,165,383	0.2
Rate	256.3	265.1	3.4	367.9	365.5	-0.7
Murder and Nonnegligent Manslaughter						
Number.................................	16	22	37.5	14,196	14,249	0.4
Rate	2.2	3.0	36.4	4.5	4.5	-
Rape[6]						
Number.................................	330	358	X	108,612	116,645	X
Rate	45.6	48.4	X	34.4	36.6	X
Robbery						
Number.................................	162	173	6.8	345,031	325,802	-5.6
Rate	22.4	23.4	4.5	109.1	102.2	-6.3
Aggravated Assault						
Number.................................	1,446	1,407	-2.7	724,149	741,291	2.4
Rate	199.9	190.3	-4.8	229.1	232.5	1.5
PROPERTY CRIME						
Number.................................	15,148	15,605	3.0	8,632,512	8,277,829	-4.1
Rate	2,094.0	2,110.3	0.8	2,730.7	2,596.1	-4.9
Burglary						
Number.................................	2,934	2,707	-7.7	1,928,465	1,729,806	-10.3
Rate	405.6	366.1	-9.7	610.0	542.5	-11.1
Larceny-Theft						
Number.................................	10,798	11,384	5.4	6,004,453	5,858,496	-2.4
Rate	1,492.7	1,539.5	3.1	1,899.4	1,837.3	-3.3
Motor Vehicle Theft						
Number.................................	1,416	1,514	6.9	699,594	689,527	-1.4
Rate	195.7	204.7	4.6	221.3	216.2	-2.3

NOTE: Although arson data are included in the trend and clearance tables, sufficient data are not available to estimate totals for this offense. Therefore, no arson data are published in this table.
X = Not applicable.
- = Zero or rounds to zero.
[1] The crime figures have been adjusted.
[2] The data collection methodology for the offense of forcible rape used by the Minnesota state Uniform Crime Reporting (UCR) Program (with the exception of Minneapolis and St. Paul, Minnesota) does not comply with national UCR Program guidelines. Consequently, its figures for forcible rape and violent crime (of which forcible rape is a part) are not published in this table.
[3] Includes offenses reported by the Zoological Police and the Metro Transit Police.
[4] Because of changes in the state's reporting practices, figures are not comparable to previous years' data.
[5] Populations are U.S. Census Bureau provisional estimates as of July 1 of each year.
[6] The figures shown for the offense of rape were estimated using the revised Uniform Crime Reporting (UCR) definition of rape.

Table ND-15. State Government Finances, 2014

(Dollar amounts in thousands, percent distribution.)

Item	Dollars	Percent distribution
Total Revenue	9,966,316	100.0
General revenue	8,849,893	88.8
Intergovernmental revenue	1,534,035	15.4
Taxes	6,120,435	61.4
General sales	1,320,196	13.2
Selective sales	527,934	5.3
License taxes	227,245	2.3
Individual income tax	498,528	5.0
Corporate income tax	250,438	2.5
Other taxes	3,296,094	33.1
Current charges	752,860	7.6
Miscellaneous general revenue	442,563	4.4
Utility revenue	0	-
Liquor stores revenue	0	-
Insurance trust revenue[1]	1,116,423	11.2
Total Expenditure	7,486,329	100.0
Intergovernmental expenditure	2,261,886	30.2
Direct expenditure	5,224,443	69.8
Current operation	3,320,143	44.3
Capital outlay	986,058	13.2
Insurance benefits and repayments	671,734	9.0
Assistance and subsidies	167,513	2.2
Interest on debt	78,995	1.1
Exhibit: Salaries and wages	1,157,901	15.5
Total Expenditure	7,486,329	100.0
General expenditure	6,814,595	91.0
Intergovernmental expenditure	2,261,886	30.2
Direct expenditure	4,552,709	60.8
General expenditure, by function:		
Education	2,124,041	28.4
Public welfare	1,058,618	14.1
Hospitals	57,052	0.8
Health	141,319	1.9
Highways	1,347,130	18.0
Police protection	33,993	0.5
Correction	88,087	1.2
Natural resources	327,196	4.4
Parks and recreation	28,885	0.4
Governmental administration	160,291	2.1
Interest on general debt	78,995	1.1
Other and unallocable	1,368,988	18.3
Utility expenditure	0	-
Liquor stores expenditure	0	-
Insurance trust expenditure	671,734	9.0
Debt at End of Fiscal Year	1,886,865	X
Cash and Security Holdings	23,587,556	X

X = Not applicable.
- = Zero or rounds to zero.
[1]Within insurance trust revenue, net earnings of state retirement systems is a calculated statistic (the item code in the data file is X08), and thus can be positive or negative. Net earnings is the sum of earnings on investments plus gains on investments minus losses on investments. The change made in 2002 for asset valuation from book to market value in accordance with Statement 34 of the Governmental Accounting Standards Board is reflected in the calculated statistics.

Table ND-16. State Government Tax Collections, 2014

(Dollars in thousands, percent.)

Item	Dollars	Percent distribution
Total Taxes	6,120,435	100.0
Property taxes	3,026	-
Sales and gross receipts	1,848,130	30.2
General sales and gross receipts	1,320,196	21.6
Selective sales and gross receipts	527,934	8.6
Alcoholic beverages	9,220	0.2
Amusements	3,620	0.1
Insurance premiums	51,047	0.8
Motor fuels	228,022	3.7
Pari-mutuels	1,159	-
Public utilities	40,411	0.7
Tobacco products	31,262	0.5
Other selective sales	163,193	2.7
Licenses	227,245	3.7
Alcoholic beverages	367	-
Amusements	801	-
Corporations in general	0	-
Hunting and fishing	14,814	0.2
Motor vehicle	119,312	1.9
Motor vehicle operators	5,289	0.1
Public utilities	6	-
Occupation and business, NEC	86,656	1.4
Other licenses	0	-
Income taxes	748,966	12.2
Individual income	498,528	8.1
Corporation net income	250,438	4.1
Other taxes	3,293,068	53.8
Death and gift	15	-
Documentary and stock transfer	0	-
Severance	3,293,053	53.8
Taxes, NEC	0	-

- = Zero or rounds to zero.

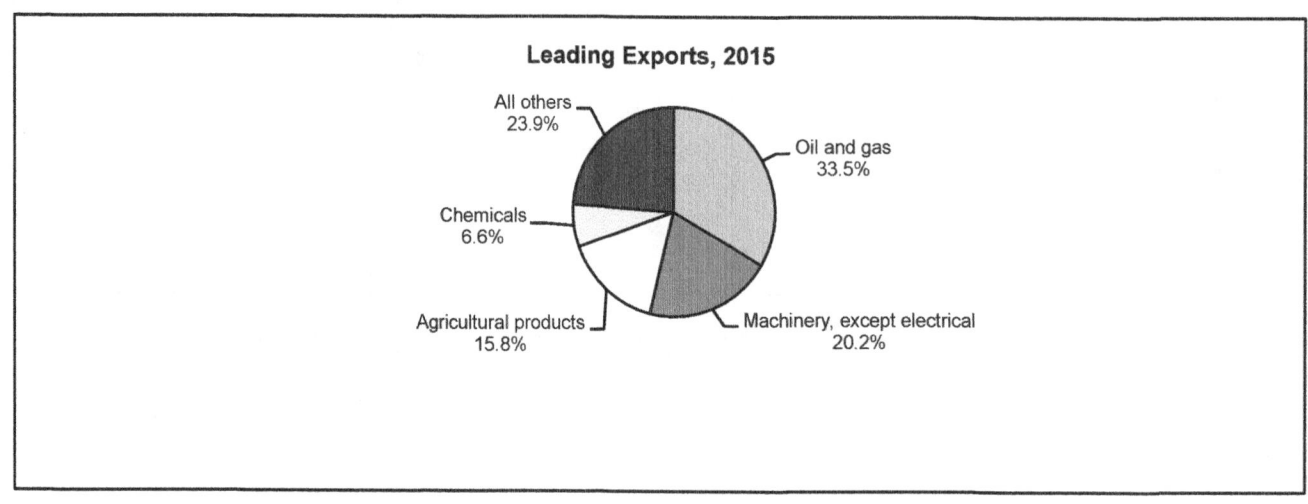

Leading Exports, 2015

All others 23.9%

Oil and gas 33.5%

Chemicals 6.6%

Agricultural products 15.8%

Machinery, except electrical 20.2%

Facts and Figures

Location: East north central United States; bordered on the N by Michigan and Lake Erie, on the E by Pennsylvania and West Virginia, on the S by West Virginia and Kentucky, and on the W by Indiana

Area: 44,825 sq. mi. (116,096 sq. km.); rank—34th

Population: 11,613,423 (2015 est.); rank—7th

Principal Cities: capital—Columbus; largest—Columbus

Statehood: March 1, 1803; 17th state

U.S. Congress: 2 senators, 16 representatives

State Motto: With God, All Things Are Possible

State Song: "Beautiful Ohio"

State Nickname: The Buckeye State

Abbreviations: OH

State Symbols: flower—scarlet carnation; tree—Ohio buckeye; bird—cardinal

At a Glance

- With an increase in population of 0.6 percent, Ohio ranked 44th among the states in growth from 2010 to 2015.

- Ohio's violent crime rate in 2014 was 284.9 per 100,000 population, compared to 365.5 for the entire nation.

- In 2014, 8.4 percent of Ohioans did not have health insurance, compared to 11.7 percent of the entire U.S. population.

- In the November 2014 elections, 38.5 percent of Ohio residents voted, which was the same as the nationwide voter turnout.

- Approximately 26.6 percent of Ohioans had a bachelor's degree or more in 2014, compared to 30.1 percent of residents nationwide.

Table OH-1. Population by Age, Sex, Race, and Hispanic Origin

(Number, percent, except where noted.)

Sex, age, race, and Hispanic origin	2000	2010	2015[1]	Average annual percent change, 2010–2015
Total Population..	11,353,140	11,536,504	11,613,423	-
Percent of total U.S. population	4.0	3.7	3.6	X
Sex				
Male...	5,512,262	5,632,156	5,686,530	0.1
Female	5,840,878	5,904,348	5,926,893	-
Age				
Under 5 years...	754,930	720,856	693,088	-0.3
5 to 19 years..	2,461,025	2,346,270	2,240,765	-0.3
20 to 64 years..	6,629,428	6,847,363	6,836,618	-
65 years and over	1,507,757	1,622,015	1,842,952	0.9
Median age (years)	36.2	38.8	39.3	0.1
Race and Hispanic Origin				
One race				
White	9,645,453	9,664,524	9,604,912	-
Black	1,301,307	1,426,861	1,477,218	0.2
American Indian and Alaska Native	24,486	29,674	31,847	0.5
Asian...	132,633	196,693	244,720	1.6
Native Hawaiian or Other Pacific Islander ...	2,749	5,336	6,155	1.0
Two or more races	157,885	213,416	248,571	1.1
Hispanic (of any race)...................................	217,123	375,004	414,641	0.7

X = Not applicable.
- = Zero or rounds to zero.
[1]Population figures for 2015 are July 1 estimates. The 2010 estimates are taken from the 2010 Census.

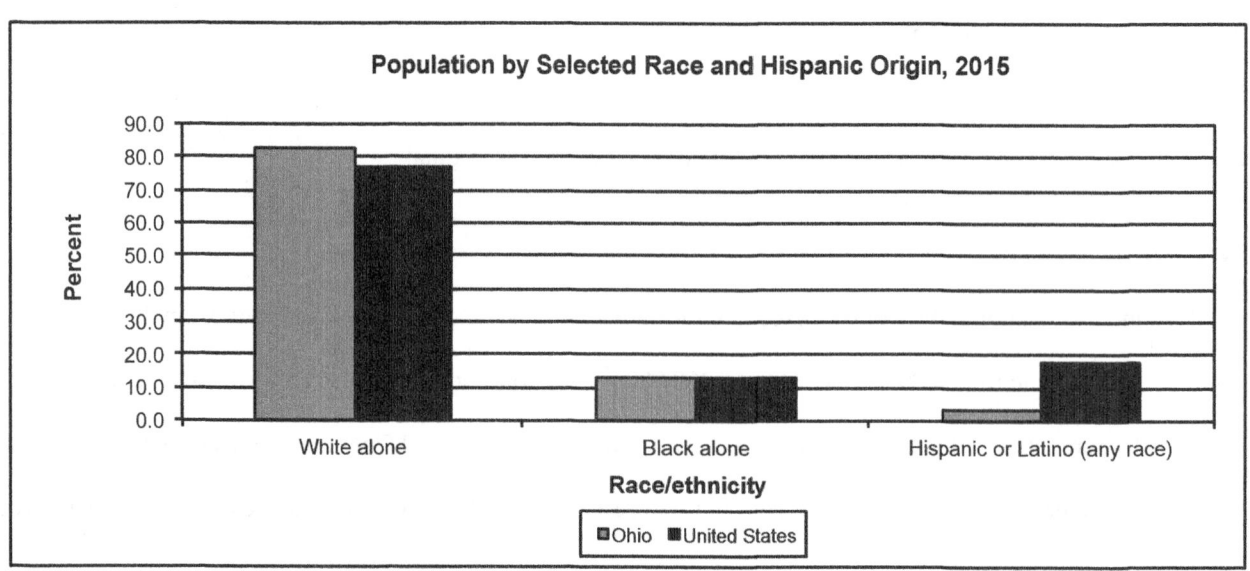

Table OH-2. Marital Status

(Number, percent distribution.)

Sex, age, race, and Hispanic origin	2000	2010	2014
Males, 15 Years and Over	4,281,736	4,487,900	4,524,956
Never married	29.2	33.5	34.2
Now married, except separated..........................	57.0	51.2	50.4
Separated...	1.4	1.7	1.6
Widowed...	2.7	2.9	2.9
Divorced...	9.7	10.8	10.9
Females, 15 Years and Over	4,670,985	4,809,613	4,832,703
Never married	23.5	27.9	28.3
Now married, except separated..........................	52.1	46.9	46.6
Separated...	1.7	2.1	2.0
Widowed...	11.1	10.1	9.9
Divorced...	11.5	12.9	13.1

Table OH-3. Households and Housing Characteristics

(Number, percent, dollars.)

Item	2000	2010	2014	Average annual percent change, 2000–2014
Total Households...	4,445,773	4,525,066	4,593,172	0.2
Family households	2,993,023	2,960,107	2,923,523	-0.2
Married-couple family	2,285,798	2,169,003	2,104,719	-0.6
Other family	707,225	791,104	818,804	1.1
Male householder, no wife present....................	170,347	196,130	214,341	1.8
Female householder, no husband present............	536,878	594,974	604,463	0.9
Nonfamily households	1,452,750	1,564,959	1,669,649	1.1
Householder living alone....................................	1,215,614	1,315,321	1,395,136	1.1
Householder not living alone..............................	237,136	249,638	274,513	1.1
Housing Characteristics				
Total housing units..	4,783,051	5,128,113	5,147,282	0.5
Occupied housing units	4,445,773	4,525,066	4,593,172	0.2
Owner occupied	3,072,522	3,095,197	3,000,748	-0.2
Renter occupied	1,373,251	1,429,869	1,592,424	1.1
Average household size..	2.49	2.48	2.46	-0.1
Financial Characteristics				
Median gross rent of renter-occupied housing	515	685	735	3.1
Median monthly owner costs for housing units with a mortgage	983	1,246	1,211	1.7
Median value of owner-occupied housing units	103,700	134,400	129,100	1.7

Table OH-4. Migration, Origin, and Language

(Number, percent.)

Characteristic	State			U.S.		
	2013	2014	Percent change	2013	2014	Percent change
Residence 1 Year Ago						
Population 1 year and over	11,439,593	11,464,891	0.2	312,432,820	315,095,393	0.9
Same house	85.2	85.0	X	85.0	85.1	X
Different house in the U.S.	14.4	14.7	X	14.4	14.3	X
Same county	9.4	9.5	X	8.9	8.7	X
Different county	4.9	5.1	X	5.5	5.6	X
Same state	3.3	3.4	X	3.2	3.3	X
Different state	1.6	1.7	X	2.3	2.3	X
Abroad	0.4	0.4	X	0.6	0.6	X
Place of Birth						
Native born	11,093,471	11,112,049	0.2	274,780,773	276,465,262	0.6
Male..	48.9	48.9	X	49.3	49.3	X
Female..	51.1	51.1	X	50.7	50.7	X
Foreign born	477,337	482,114	1.0	41,348,066	42,391,794	2.5
Male..	49.7	49.4	X	48.8	48.7	X
Female..	50.3	50.6	X	51.2	51.3	X
Foreign born; naturalized U.S. citizen.................	237,404	240,565	1.3	19,294,710	19,984,738	3.6
Male..	47.6	47.0	X	45.9	45.9	X
Female..	52.4	53.0	X	54.1	54.1	X
Foreign born; not a U.S. citizen	239,933	241,549	0.7	22,053,356	22,407,056	1.6
Male..	51.9	51.7	X	51.3	51.2	X
Female..	48.1	48.3	X	48.7	48.8	X
Entered 2010 or later	15.4	20.0	X	9.7	12.3	X
Entered 2000 to 2009	31.7	31.5	X	29.4	28.6	X
Entered before 2000......................................	53.0	48.4	X	61.0	59.1	X
World Region of Birth, Foreign						
Foreign-born population, excluding population born at sea	477,337	482,114	1.0	41,347,945	42,390,705	2.5
Europe	23.3	21.6	X	11.6	11.2	X
Asia	40.1	43.4	X	29.5	30.1	X
Africa	12.5	12.1	X	4.4	4.6	X
Oceania	0.4	0.5	X	0.5	0.6	X
Latin America..	20.2	19.5	X	51.9	51.6	X
North America...	3.3	3.0	X	2.0	1.9	X
Language Spoken at Home and Ability to Speak English						
Population 5 years and over............................	10,879,145	10,904,728	0.2	296,358,760	299,084,046	0.9
English only	93.4	93.4	X	79.2	78.9	X
Language other than English...........................	6.6	6.6	X	20.8	21.1	X
Speaks English less than "very well"	2.4	2.4	X	8.5	8.6	X

X = Not applicable.
- = Zero or rounds to zero.

Table OH-5. Median Income and Poverty Status, 2014

(Number, percent, except as noted.)

Characteristic	State		U.S.	
	Number	Percent	Number	Percent
Median Income				
Households (dollars)...	49,308	X	53,657	X
Families (dollars)	62,300	X	65,910	X
Below Poverty Level (All People)	1,785,780	15.8	48,208,387	15.5
Sex				
Male..	792,764	14.4	21,590,918	14.2
Female	993,016	17.2	26,617,469	16.8
Age				
Under 18 years..	593,831	22.9	15,686,012	21.7
Related children under 18 years...	580,925	22.5	15,372,705	21.3
18 to 64 years..	1,052,184	15.1	28,267,482	14.6
65 years and over	139,765	8.1	4,254,893	9.5

X = Not applicable.

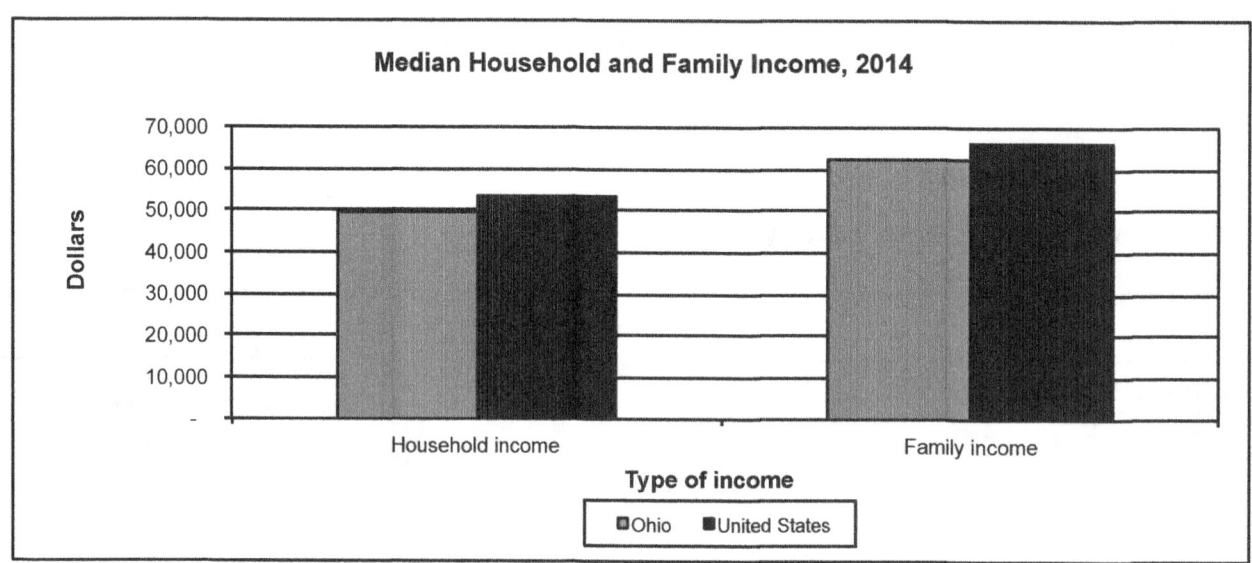

Table OH-6. Health Insurance Coverage Status for the Civilian Noninstitutionalized Population and Children Under 18 Years of Age

(Numbers in thousands, percent.)

Item	2006	2007	2008	2009	2010	2011	2012	2013	2014
Civilian Noninstitutionalized Population	11,319	11,300	11,296	11,352	11,359	11,369	11,372	11,398	11,421
Covered by Private or Public Insurance									
Number...	10,181	9,979	9,966	9,969	9,960	10,015	10,068	10,141	10,466
Percent...	89.9	88.3	88.2	87.8	87.7	88.1	88.5	89.0	91.6
Not Covered									
Number...	1,138	1,322	1,330	1,383	1,399	1,354	1,304	1,258	955
Percent...	10.1	11.7	11.8	12.2	12.3	11.9	11.5	11.0	8.4
Percent in the U.S. not covered...	15.8	15.3	15.1	15.1	15.5	15.1	14.8	14.5	11.7
Children Under 18 Years of Age	2,784	2,790	2,728	2,710	2,715	2,688	2,657	2,645	2,631
Covered by Private or Public Insurance									
Number...	2,626	2,551	2,531	2,538	2,553	2,531	2,516	2,504	2,505
Percent...	94.3	91.4	92.8	93.6	94.0	94.2	94.7	94.7	95.2
Not Covered									
Number...	157	239	197	172	162	157	141	141	126
Percent...	5.7	8.6	7.2	6.4	6.0	5.8	5.3	5.3	4.8
Percent in the U.S. not covered...	11.7	11.0	9.7	8.6	8.0	7.5	7.2	7.1	6.0

Table OH-7. Employment Status by Demographic Group, 2015

(Numbers in thousands, percent.)

Characteristic	Civilian noninstitutional population	Civilian labor force		Employed		Unemployed	
		Number	Percent of population	Number	Percent of population	Number	Percent of population
Total..	9,138	5,692	62.3	5,413	59.2	279	4.9
Sex							
Male..............................	4,403	2,983	67.7	2,834	64.4	148	5.0
Female..........................	4,735	2,709	57.2	2,578	54.4	131	4.8
Race, Sex, and Hispanic Origin							
White.............................	7,709	4,812	62.4	4,618	59.9	194	4.0
Male..........................	3,758	2,581	68.7	2,474	65.8	107	4.1
Female.......................	3,951	2,231	56.5	2,144	54.3	87	3.9
Black or African American..................	1,076	646	60.0	575	53.5	71	10.9
Male..........................	490	289	59.0	255	52.1	34	11.7
Female.......................	587	357	60.8	320	54.6	37	10.3
Hispanic or Latino ethnicity[1].............	252	172	68.2	162	64.2	10	5.8
Male..........................	123	99	80.8	92	75.4	7	6.7
Female.......................	129	73	56.2	69	53.6	3	4.5
Age							
16 to 19 years.....................	637	272	42.7	220	34.5	52	19.2
20 to 24 years.....................	736	550	74.7	500	67.8	51	9.2
25 to 34 years.....................	1,439	1,207	83.9	1,156	80.3	51	4.2
35 to 44 years.....................	1,390	1,150	82.7	1,104	79.4	46	4.0
45 to 54 years.....................	1,509	1,194	79.1	1,158	76.7	36	3.0
55 to 64 years.....................	1,561	989	63.3	957	61.3	32	3.2
65 years and over	1,866	330	17.7	318	17.1	12	3.5

NOTE: Data in Table 7 are from the Current Population Survey (CPS) and do not match the estimates in Table 8. See notes and definitions for further information.
[1]May be of any race.

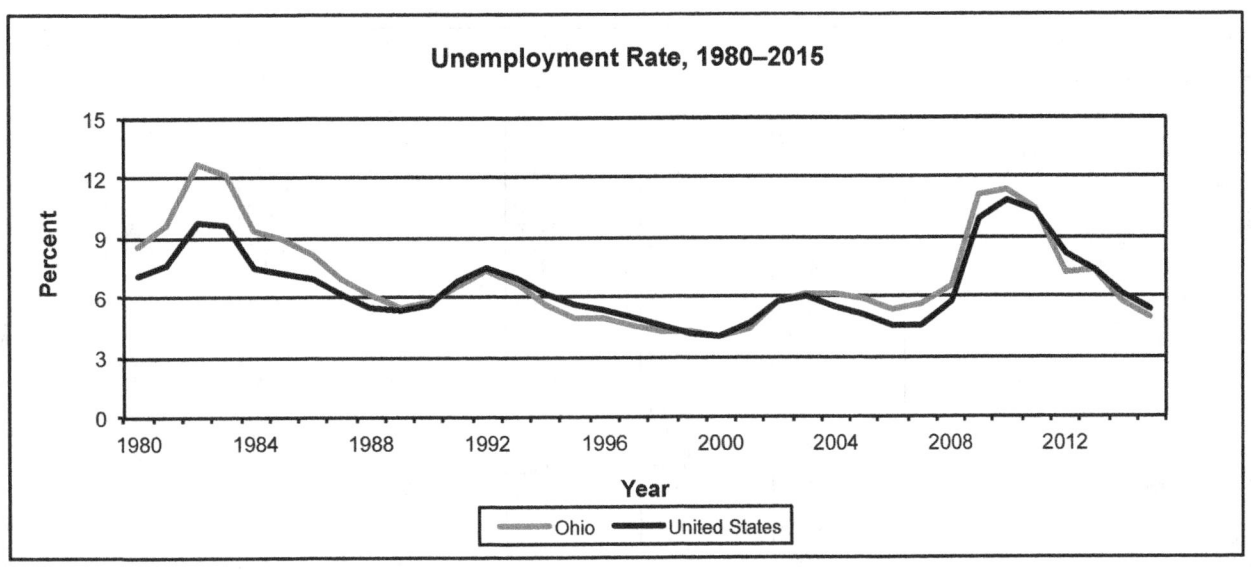

Unemployment Rate, 1980–2015

Table OH-8. Employment Status of the Civilian Noninstitutional Population Age 16 Years and Over

(Number, percent.)

Year	Civilian labor force	Civilian participation rate	Employed	Unemployed	Unemployment rate
2007...	5,990,292	67.3	5,657,718	332,574	5.6
2008...	5,965,166	66.8	5,580,843	384,323	6.4
2009...	5,906,768	66.0	5,297,098	609,670	10.3
2010...	5,846,886	65.2	5,247,050	599,836	10.3
2011...	5,771,469	64.1	5,261,238	510,231	8.8
2012...	5,706,059	63.2	5,284,522	421,537	7.4
2013...	5,717,133	63.1	5,290,147	426,986	7.5
2014...	5,702,698	62.7	5,372,754	329,944	5.8
2015...	5,700,344	62.5	5,423,019	277,325	4.9

Table OH-9. Employment and Average Wages by Industry

(Estimates through 2010 are based on the 2007 North American Industry Classification System [NAICS]. Estimates from 2011 onward are based on the 2012 NAICS.)

Industry	2008	2009	2010	2011	2012	2013	2014
	Number of jobs						
Wage and Salary Employment by Industry..................	5,526,611	5,234,992	5,201,963	5,262,063	5,316,040	5,378,863	5,450,130
Farm Wage and Salary Employment.........................	12,730	13,697	13,802	12,718	17,737	16,197	12,561
Nonfarm Wage and Salary Employment....................	5,513,881	5,221,295	5,188,161	5,249,345	5,298,303	5,362,666	5,437,569
Private wage and salary employment.......................	4,670,242	4,382,490	4,352,940	4,431,887	4,503,667	4,568,746	4,641,626
Forestry, fishing, and related activities..........................	4,247	4,166	4,392	4,529	4,665	4,922	5,269
Mining..	11,681	11,450	10,914	11,393	12,199	12,099	14,386
Utilities...	21,718	21,320	19,957	19,307	19,107	18,792	18,218
Construction	219,940	189,639	177,091	185,850	187,070	192,778	201,644
Manufacturing...	740,114	630,843	621,438	638,984	657,648	663,478	675,122
Durable goods manufacturing............................	506,735	419,584	411,775	429,018	444,988	449,513	459,776
Nondurable goods manufacturing.......................	233,379	211,259	209,663	209,966	212,660	213,965	215,346
Wholesale trade	239,183	223,515	218,849	220,413	225,326	228,855	234,088
Retail trade..	597,304	569,535	561,431	564,106	565,357	568,665	571,386
Transportation and warehousing..........................	191,370	169,014	164,862	168,885	172,871	175,385	181,121
Information	86,190	80,895	77,731	76,034	74,843	75,500	72,725
Finance and insurance	223,876	216,850	215,875	217,771	219,832	220,500	220,411
Real estate and rental and leasing........................	65,570	62,618	60,735	60,051	59,373	61,271	62,522
Professional, scientific, and technical services	254,371	243,084	242,733	249,760	244,314	246,986	250,660
Management of companies and enterprises..................	108,567	107,929	107,288	112,869	127,187	132,331	137,537
Administrative and waste services..........................	310,400	271,613	282,344	295,856	306,404	314,699	325,247
Educational services	111,091	112,079	114,689	116,556	116,759	114,635	115,016
Health care and social assistance..........................	721,396	731,134	741,362	750,158	760,675	769,853	777,270
Arts, entertainment, and recreation........................	65,933	64,222	63,308	64,865	68,823	74,657	76,436
Accommodation and food services..........................	433,322	419,071	418,689	425,014	435,342	447,431	454,038
Other services, except public administration................	263,969	253,513	249,252	249,486	245,872	245,909	248,530
Government and government enterprises	843,639	838,805	835,221	817,458	794,636	793,920	795,943
	Dollars						
Average Wages and Salaries by Industry	41,144	41,283	42,218	43,455	44,988	45,435	46,834
Average Farm Wages and Salaries	31,963	30,403	23,394	31,184	23,067	33,244	37,567
Average Nonfarm Wages and Salaries	41,165	41,312	42,268	43,485	45,062	45,472	46,856
Average private wages and salaries.........................	41,039	40,988	41,986	43,270	44,835	45,298	46,795
Forestry, fishing, and related activities......................	23,940	24,931	25,591	26,626	27,411	28,195	29,086
Mining..	61,679	62,894	66,664	71,352	73,067	65,277	71,289
Utilities...	80,870	82,809	84,143	86,348	88,796	90,502	93,257
Construction...	46,799	47,900	47,887	49,572	51,660	52,958	54,960
Manufacturing...	53,103	52,790	54,852	56,921	57,440	57,525	59,406
Durable goods manufacturing............................	54,876	53,831	56,038	58,076	58,521	58,590	60,486
Nondurable goods manufacturing.......................	49,254	50,723	52,523	54,562	55,179	55,285	57,102
Wholesale trade	58,427	57,871	60,005	62,244	64,097	64,471	66,476
Retail trade..	24,445	24,501	25,095	25,698	26,481	26,593	27,344
Transportation and warehousing..........................	44,342	45,055	45,019	46,216	47,415	47,989	48,977
Information	56,190	56,249	58,293	60,119	62,031	63,392	64,842
Finance and insurance	60,327	60,818	62,884	64,817	66,865	69,420	72,282
Real estate and rental and leasing........................	35,689	35,974	37,253	39,013	40,722	42,323	44,367
Professional, scientific, and technical services	61,854	62,153	63,559	65,853	67,618	68,603	70,590
Management of companies and enterprises..................	91,845	86,569	93,856	96,377	108,260	104,941	109,012
Administrative and waste services..........................	29,099	29,782	29,943	30,547	31,844	32,202	33,149
Educational services	28,585	29,347	29,686	30,562	30,352	30,757	31,092
Health care and social assistance..........................	39,538	40,411	40,701	41,351	42,780	43,607	44,706
Arts, entertainment, and recreation........................	30,293	29,997	31,335	30,675	32,019	31,918	34,152
Accommodation and food services..........................	14,847	14,869	15,343	15,806	16,275	16,336	17,083
Other services, except public administration................	26,024	26,134	26,991	27,575	28,371	29,348	30,179
Government and government enterprises	41,868	43,004	43,734	44,648	46,347	46,472	47,211

Table OH-10. Employment Characteristics by Family Type

(Number, percent.)

Family type and labor force status	2012		2013		2014	
	Total	Families with own children under 18 years	Total	Families with own children under 18 years	Total	Families with own children under 18 years
All Families..	2,913,312	1,230,760	2,923,404	1,232,209	2,914,550	1,218,710
FAMILY TYPE AND LABOR FORCE STATUS						
Married-Couple Families.............................	2,131,425	787,247	2,118,209	781,239	2,095,746	766,196
Both husband and wife in labor force...............	53.0	69.5	52.3	69.7	52.6	69.9
Husband in labor force, wife not in labor force	20.0	24.9	20.3	24.3	20.1	24.5
Wife in labor force, husband not in labor force	8.4	4.0	8.6	3.8	8.3	4.1
Both husband and wife not in labor force..............	18.7	1.7	18.5	2.1	19.0	1.5
Other Families	781,887	443,513	805,195	450,970	818,804	452,514
Female householder, no husband present..............	74.0	76.5	73.6	76.2	73.8	76.6
In labor force	51.8	61.5	51.7	62.9	51.3	63.5
Not in labor force	22.3	14.9	21.9	13.3	22.5	13.1
Male householder, no wife present......................	26.0	23.5	26.4	23.8	26.2	23.4
In labor force...	19.8	21.2	20.0	21.2	20.0	21.0
Not in labor force	6.1	2.4	6.4	2.6	6.2	2.4

Table OH-11. School Enrollment and Educational Attainment, 2014

(Number, percent.)

Item	State	U.S.
Enrollment		
Total population 3 years and over, enrolled in school...............	2,901,361	82,063,714
Enrolled in nursery school or preschool (percent).................	6.0	6.0
Enrolled in kindergarten (percent)................................	5.0	5.1
Enrolled in elementary school, grades 1-8 (percent).............	40.6	40.2
Enrolled in high school, grades 9-12 (percent)...................	21.3	20.7
Enrolled in college or graduate school (percent).................	27.1	28.0
Attainment		
Total population 25 years and over	7,857,460	213,725,624
Less than ninth grade (percent).................................	3.0	5.6
9th to 12th grade, no diploma (percent).........................	7.7	7.5
High school graduate, including equivalency (percent)...........	33.9	27.7
Some college, no degree (percent)	20.4	21.0
Associate's degree (percent)....................................	8.4	8.2
Bachelor's degree (percent).....................................	16.6	18.7
Graduate or professional degree (percent).......................	10.1	11.4
High school graduate or higher (percent)	89.4	86.9
Bachelor's degree or higher (percent)...........................	26.6	30.1

Table OH-12. Public School Characteristics and Educational Indicators

(Number, percent; data derived from National Center of Education Statistics.)

Item	State	U.S.
Public Schools, 2013–2014 (except where noted)		
Number of school districts......................................	1,116	18,194
Number of schools..	3,656	98,271
Number of students (in thousands)	1,724	50,045
Number of teachers (in thousands)	106	3,114
Student-teacher ratio	16.3	16.1
Expenditures per student (dollars), FY 2013.....................	11,276	107,637
Four-year adjusted cohort graduation rate (ACGR)[1,2]	81.8	82.3
Students eligible for free or reduced-price lunch (in thousands)	763	25,596
English language learners (in thousands)	40	4,461
Students age 3 to 21 served under IDEA, part B (in thousands)	255	6,464

Public Schools by Type	Number	Percent of state public schools
Total number of schools..	3,656	100.0
Regular..	3,533	96.6
Special education..	50	1.4
Vocational education	69	1.9
Alternative education..	4	0.1

NOTE: Every school is assigned only one school type based on its instructional emphasis.
[1]ACGR data represents a new method of calculating high-school completion rates and may not be comparable to previous years' data for Averaged Freshmen Graduation Rates (AFGR).
[2]The United States 4-year ACGRs were estimated using both the reported 4-year ACGR data from 49 states and the District of Columbia and using imputed data for Idaho. The estimate for American Indian/Alaska Native students also includes imputed data for Virginia.

Table OH-13. Reported Voting and Registration of the Voting-Age Population, November 2014

(Numbers in thousands, percent.)

Item	Total population	Total citizen population	Registered			Voted		
			Total registered	Percent registered (total population)	Percent registered (total citizen population)	Total voted	Percent voted (total population)	Percent voted (total citizen population)
U.S. Total	239,874	219,941	142,166	59.3	64.6	92,251	38.5	41.9
State Total.............................	8,772	8,509	5,657	64.5	66.5	3,378	38.5	39.7
Sex								
Male....................................	4,197	4,081	2,640	62.9	64.7	1,616	38.5	39.6
Female.................................	4,575	4,428	3,018	66.0	68.2	1,762	38.5	39.8
Race								
White alone...............................	7,404	7,289	4,869	65.8	66.8	2,898	39.1	39.8
White, non-Hispanic alone............	7,235	7,155	4,787	66.2	66.9	2,873	39.7	40.2
Black alone...............................	1,024	991	680	66.4	68.7	403	39.4	40.7
Asian alone..............................	231	116	70	30.2	60.3	44	19.1	38.1
Hispanic (of any race)......................	192	157	93	48.3	58.9	36	19	23.1
White alone or in combination..........	7,501	7,386	4,892	65.2	66.2	2,918	38.9	39.5
Black alone or in combination..........	1,089	1,055	695	63.8	65.8	414	38.0	39.2
Asian alone or in combination..........	259	144	80	30.7	55.3	54	20.8	37.5
Age								
18 to 24 years............................	985	968	421	42.8	43.5	122	12.4	12.6
25 to 34 years............................	1,488	1,408	882	59.2	62.6	404	27.1	28.7
35 to 44 years............................	1,383	1,312	930	67.3	70.9	501	36.2	38.2
45 to 64 years............................	3,033	2,955	2,043	67.4	69.1	1,293	42.6	43.7
65 years and over	1,883	1,867	1,381	73.3	74.0	1,059	56.2	56.7

B = Base is less than 75,000 and therefore too small to show the derived measure.

Table OH-14. Crime

(Number, rate per 100,000. Data are derived from the FBI Uniform Crime Reports.)

Item	State			U.S.[1,2,3,4]		
	2013	2014	Percent change	2013	2014	Percent change
TOTAL POPULATION[5]...	11,570,808	11,594,163	0.2	316,128,839	318,857,056	0.9
VIOLENT CRIME						
Number....................................	31,904	33,030	3.5	1,163,146	1,165,383	0.2
Rate	275.7	284.9	3.3	367.9	365.5	-0.7
Murder and Nonnegligent Manslaughter						
Number....................................	455	464	2.0	14,196	14,249	0.4
Rate	3.9	4.0	2.6	4.5	4.5	-
Rape[6]						
Number....................................	4,041	5,042	X	108,612	116,645	X
Rate	34.9	43.5	X	34.4	36.6	X
Robbery						
Number....................................	14,368	12,753	-11.2	345,031	325,802	-5.6
Rate	124.2	110.0	-11.4	109.1	102.2	-6.3
Aggravated Assault						
Number....................................	14,257	14,771	3.6	724,149	741,291	2.4
Rate	123.2	127.4	3.4	229.1	232.5	1.5
PROPERTY CRIME						
Number....................................	338,731	324,528	-4.2	8,632,512	8,277,829	-4.1
Rate	2,927.5	2,799.1	-4.4	2,730.7	2,596.1	-4.9
Burglary						
Number....................................	91,433	78,845	-13.8	1,928,465	1,729,806	-10.3
Rate	790.2	680.0	-13.9	610.0	542.5	-11.1
Larceny-Theft						
Number....................................	227,766	227,668	-	6,004,453	5,858,496	-2.4
Rate	1,968.5	1,963.6	-0.2	1,899.4	1,837.3	-3.3
Motor Vehicle Theft						
Number....................................	19,532	18,015	-7.8	699,594	689,527	-1.4
Rate	168.8	155.4	-7.9	221.3	216.2	-2.3

NOTE: Although arson data are included in the trend and clearance tables, sufficient data are not available to estimate totals for this offense. Therefore, no arson data are published in this table.
X = Not applicable.
- = Zero or rounds to zero.
[1]The crime figures have been adjusted.
[2]The data collection methodology for the offense of forcible rape used by the Minnesota state Uniform Crime Reporting (UCR) Program (with the exception of Minneapolis and St. Paul, Minnesota) does not comply with national UCR Program guidelines. Consequently, its figures for forcible rape and violent crime (of which forcible rape is a part) are not published in this table.
[3]Includes offenses reported by the Zoological Police and the Metro Transit Police.
[4]Because of changes in the state's reporting practices, figures are not comparable to previous years' data.
[5]Populations are U.S. Census Bureau provisional estimates as of July 1 of each year.
[6]The figures shown for the offense of rape were estimated using the revised Uniform Crime Reporting (UCR) definition of rape.

Table OH-15. State Government Finances, 2014

(Dollar amounts in thousands, percent distribution.)

Item	Dollars	Percent distribution
Total Revenue	96,424,844	100.0
General revenue	62,101,141	64.4
Intergovernmental revenue	22,350,068	23.2
Taxes	27,020,625	28.0
General sales	10,217,826	10.6
Selective sales	5,400,094	5.6
License taxes	2,928,276	3.0
Individual income tax	8,424,843	8.7
Corporate income tax	0	-
Other taxes	49,586	0.1
Current charges	8,181,844	8.5
Miscellaneous general revenue	4,548,604	4.7
Utility revenue	0	-
Liquor stores revenue	1,008,258	1.0
Insurance trust revenue[1]	33,315,445	34.6
Total Expenditure	79,239,198	100.0
Intergovernmental expenditure	16,647,880	21.0
Direct expenditure	62,591,318	79.0
Current operation	38,154,658	48.2
Capital outlay	3,864,670	4.9
Insurance benefits and repayments	16,918,467	21.4
Assistance and subsidies	2,285,823	2.9
Interest on debt	1,367,700	1.7
Exhibit: Salaries and wages	9,597,366	12.1
Total Expenditure	79,239,198	100.0
General expenditure	61,618,069	77.8
Intergovernmental expenditure	16,647,880	21.0
Direct expenditure	44,970,189	56.8
General expenditure, by function:		
Education	21,480,220	27.1
Public welfare	21,476,759	27.1
Hospitals	3,153,148	4.0
Health	2,604,360	3.3
Highways	3,754,744	4.7
Police protection	303,391	0.4
Correction	1,539,877	1.9
Natural resources	371,865	0.5
Parks and recreation	73,637	0.1
Governmental administration	1,773,879	2.2
Interest on general debt	1,367,700	1.7
Other and unallocable	3,718,489	4.7
Utility expenditure	0	-
Liquor stores expenditure	702,662	0.9
Insurance trust expenditure	16,918,467	21.4
Debt at End of Fiscal Year	33,662,042	X
Cash and Security Holdings	250,404,929	X

X = Not applicable.
- = Zero or rounds to zero.
[1]Within insurance trust revenue, net earnings of state retirement systems is a calculated statistic (the item code in the data file is X08), and thus can be positive or negative. Net earnings is the sum of earnings on investments plus gains on investments minus losses on investments. The change made in 2002 for asset valuation from book to market value in accordance with Statement 34 of the Governmental Accounting Standards Board is reflected in the calculated statistics.

Table OH-16. State Government Tax Collections, 2014

(Dollars in thousands, percent.)

Item	Dollars	Percent distribution
Total Taxes	27,020,625	100.0
Property taxes	X	X
Sales and gross receipts	15,617,920	57.8
General sales and gross receipts	10,217,826	37.8
Selective sales and gross receipts	5,400,094	20.0
Alcoholic beverages	98,397	0.4
Amusements	273,393	1.0
Insurance premiums	510,345	1.9
Motor fuels	1,839,594	6.8
Pari-mutuels	5,024	-
Public utilities	1,125,461	4.2
Tobacco products	815,532	3.0
Other selective sales	732,348	2.7
Licensesw	2,928,276	10.8
Alcoholic beverages	41,327	0.2
Amusements	16,209	0.1
Corporations in general	1,026,121	3.8
Hunting and fishing	38,428	0.1
Motor vehicle	725,263	2.7
Motor vehicle operators	82,388	0.3
Public utilities	29,523	0.1
Occupation and business, NEC	940,646	3.5
Other licenses	28,371	0.1
Income taxes	8,424,843	31.2
Individual income	8,424,843	31.2
Corporation net income	0	-
Other taxes	49,586	0.2
Death and gift	39,392	0.1
Documentary and stock transfer	X	X
Severance	10,194	-
Taxes, NEC	0	-

X = Not applicable.
- = Zero or rounds to zero.

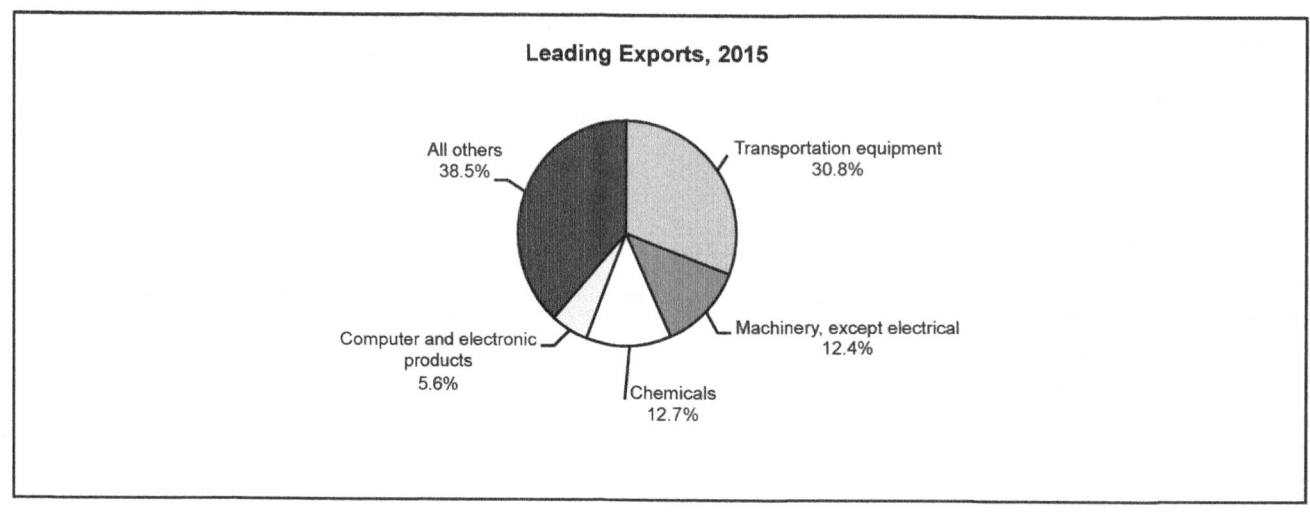

Leading Exports, 2015

All others 38.5%
Transportation equipment 30.8%
Machinery, except electrical 12.4%
Chemicals 12.7%
Computer and electronic products 5.6%

OKLAHOMA

Facts and Figures

Location: West south central United States; bordered on the N by Colorado and Kansas, on the E by Missouri and Arkansas, on the S by Texas, and on the W by Texas and New Mexico

Area: 69,898 sq. mi. (181,036 sq. km.); rank—20th

Population: 3,911,338 (2015 est.); rank—28th

Principal Cities: capital—Oklahoma City; largest—Oklahoma City

Statehood: November 16, 1907; 46th state

U.S. Congress: 2 senators, 5 representatives

State Motto: *Labor omnia vincit* ("Labor conquers all things")

State Song: "Oklahoma!"

State Nickname: The Sooner State

Abbreviations: OK; Okla.

State Symbols: flower—mistletoe; tree—redbud; bird—scissor-tailed flycatcher

At a Glance

- With an increase in population of 4.0 percent, Oklahoma ranked 21st among the states in growth from 2010 to 2015.

- Oklahoma's median household income in 2014 was $47,529, and 16.6 percent of the population lived below the poverty level.

- In 2014, 15.4 percent of Oklahomans did not have health insurance, compared to 11.7 percent of the total U.S. population.

- Oklahoma's violent crime rate in 2014 was 406.0 per 100,000 population, compared to 365.5 for the entire nation.

- The state ranked 14th for property crime rate in 2014, with a rate of 2,990.7 incidents per 100,000 population.

Table OK-1. Population by Age, Sex, Race, and Hispanic Origin

(Number, percent, except where noted.)

Sex, age, race, and Hispanic origin	2000	2010	2015[1]	Average annual percent change, 2010–2015
Total Population	3,450,654	3,751,351	3,911,338	0.3
Percent of total U.S. population	1.2	1.2	1.2	X
Sex				
Male	1,695,895	1,856,977	1,937,124	0.3
Female	1,754,759	1,894,374	1,974,214	0.3
Age				
Under 5 years	236,353	264,126	267,948	0.1
5 to 19 years	765,927	777,484	796,379	0.2
20 to 64 years	1,992,424	2,203,027	2,270,761	0.2
65 years and over	455,950	506,714	576,250	0.9
Median age (years)	35.5	36.2	36.2	-
Race and Hispanic Origin				
One race				
White	2,628,434	2,851,510	2,925,858	0.2
Black	260,968	284,332	303,944	0.5
American Indian and Alaska Native	273,230	335,664	355,795	0.4
Asian	46,767	67,126	85,766	1.8
Native Hawaiian or Other Pacific Islander	2,372	5,354	6,718	1.6
Two or more races	155,985	207,365	233,257	0.8
Hispanic (of any race)	179,304	351,542	396,459	0.9

X = Not applicable.
- = Zero or rounds to zero.
[1]Population figures for 2015 are July 1 estimates. The 2010 estimates are taken from the 2010 Census.

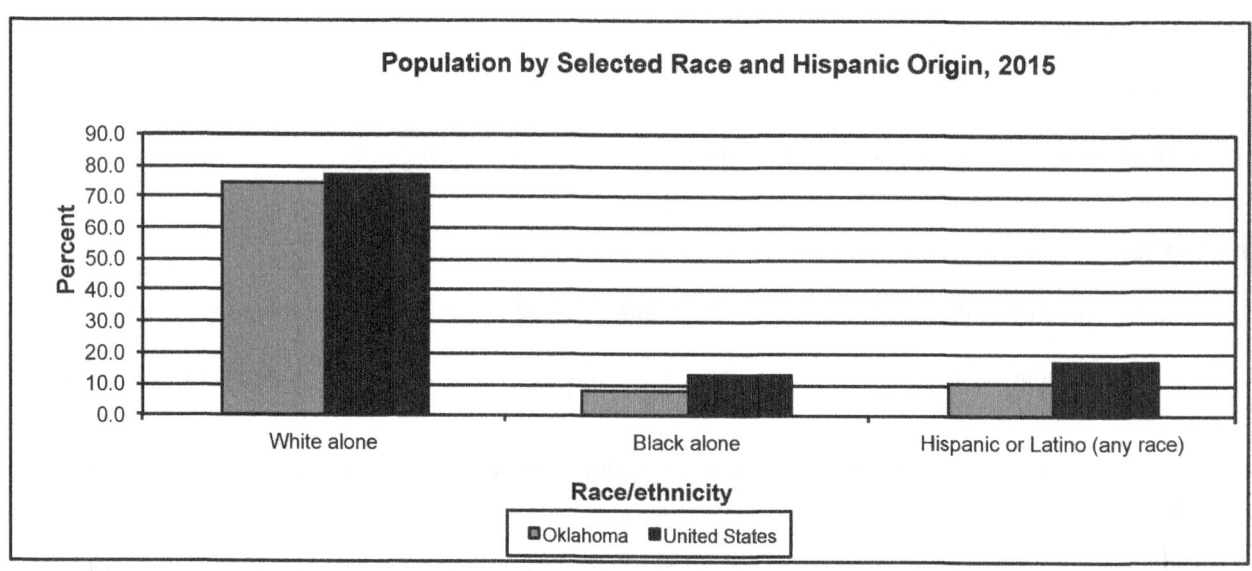

Population by Selected Race and Hispanic Origin, 2015

Table OK-2. Marital Status

(Number, percent distribution.)

Sex, age, race, and Hispanic origin	2000	2010	2014
Males, 15 Years and Over	1,318,729	1,457,860	1,487,422
Never married	25.8	30.7	30.9
Now married, except separated	59.5	52.2	52.1
Separated	1.6	1.8	1.8
Widowed	2.5	3.0	2.9
Divorced	10.6	12.3	12.3
Females, 15 Years and Over	1,398,823	1,521,546	1,541,986
Never married	19.1	23.8	23.9
Now married, except separated	55.3	49.7	49.5
Separated	1.9	2.7	2.5
Widowed	11.1	10.1	9.9
Divorced	12.5	13.7	14.1

Table OK-3. Households and Housing Characteristics

(Number, percent, dollars.)

Item	2000	2010	2014	Average annual percent change, 2000–2014
Total Households..	1,342,293	1,432,959	1,459,759	0.6
Family households	921,750	954,622	966,516	0.3
Married-couple family	717,611	709,256	710,773	-0.1
Other family	204,139	245,366	255,743	1.8
Male householder, no wife present................	51,564	62,855	73,148	3.0
Female householder, no husband present.......	152,575	182,511	182,595	1.4
Nonfamily households	420,543	478,337	493,243	1.2
Householder living alone................................	358,560	400,840	411,134	1.0
Householder not living alone..........................	61,983	77,497	82,109	2.3
Housing Characteristics				
Total housing units..	1,514,400	1,666,205	1,699,556	0.9
Occupied housing units	1,342,293	1,432,959	1,459,759	0.6
Owner occupied	918,259	971,378	950,817	0.3
Renter occupied	424,034	461,581	508,942	1.4
Average household size......................................	2.49	2.55	2.58	0.3
Financial Characteristics				
Median gross rent of renter-occupied housing	456	659	737	4.4
Median monthly owner costs for housing units with a mortgage	764	1,089	1,143	3.5
Median value of owner-occupied housing units..........	70,700	111,400	119,800	5.0

Table OK-4. Migration, Origin, and Language

(Number, percent.)

Characteristic	State			U.S.		
	2013	2014	Percent change	2013	2014	Percent change
Residence 1 Year Ago						
Population 1 year and over	3,801,521	3,827,288	0.7	312,432,820	315,095,393	0.9
Same house	82.4	82.3	X	85.0	85.1	X
Different house in the U.S.	17.2	17.3	X	14.4	14.3	X
Same county	9.9	10	X	8.9	8.7	X
Different county	7.3	7.3	X	5.5	5.6	X
Same state	4.4	4.4	X	3.2	3.3	X
Different state	2.9	2.9	X	2.3	2.3	X
Abroad	0.4	0.4	X	0.6	0.6	X
Place of Birth						
Native born	3,632,136	3,651,386	0.5	274,780,773	276,465,262	0.6
Male..	49.4	49.4	X	49.3	49.3	X
Female...	50.6	50.6	X	50.7	50.7	X
Foreign born	218,432	226,665	3.8	41,348,066	42,391,794	2.5
Male..	52.1	50.9	X	48.8	48.7	X
Female...	47.9	49.1	X	51.2	51.3	X
Foreign born; naturalized U.S. citizen...................	76,353	73,438	-3.8	19,294,710	19,984,738	3.6
Male..	48.2	45.4	X	45.9	45.9	X
Female...	51.8	54.6	X	54.1	54.1	X
Foreign born; not a U.S. citizen..........................	142,079	153,227	7.8	22,053,356	22,407,056	1.6
Male..	54.2	53.6	X	51.3	51.2	X
Female...	45.8	46.4	X	48.7	48.8	X
Entered 2010 or later	14.4	16.7	X	9.7	12.3	X
Entered 2000 to 2009	36.9	35.3	X	29.4	28.6	X
Entered before 2000..	48.7	47.9	X	61.0	59.1	X
World Region of Birth, Foreign						
Foreign-born population, excluding population born at sea	218,432	226,665	3.8	41,347,945	42,390,705	2.5
Europe	6.4	7.7	X	11.6	11.2	X
Asia..	25.3	27.1	X	29.5	30.1	X
Africa	4.6	4.2	X	4.4	4.6	X
Oceania	1.3	0.7	X	0.5	0.6	X
Latin America...	61.0	58.7	X	51.9	51.6	X
North America	1.5	1.7	X	2.0	1.9	X
Language Spoken at Home and Ability to Speak English						
Population 5 years and over................................	3,587,881	3,614,253	0.7	296,358,760	299,084,046	0.9
English only	90.2	90	X	79.2	78.9	X
Language other than English.............................	9.8	10	X	20.8	21.1	X
Speaks English less than "very well".................	4.0	4.2	X	8.5	8.6	X

X = Not applicable.
- = Zero or rounds to zero.

Table OK-5. Median Income and Poverty Status, 2014

(Number, percent, except as noted.)

Characteristic	State		U.S.	
	Number	Percent	Number	Percent
Median Income				
Households (dollars)..	47,529	X	53,657	X
Families (dollars)	58,710	X	65,910	X
Below Poverty Level (All People)	623,840	16.6	48,208,387	15.5
Sex				
Male..	274,577	14.9	21,590,918	14.2
Female	349,263	18.2	26,617,469	16.8
Age				
Under 18 years...	208,310	22.4	15,686,012	21.7
Related children under 18 years...	204,455	22.1	15,372,705	21.3
18 to 64 years..	369,331	16.2	28,267,482	14.6
65 years and over	46,199	8.5	4,254,893	9.5

X = Not applicable.

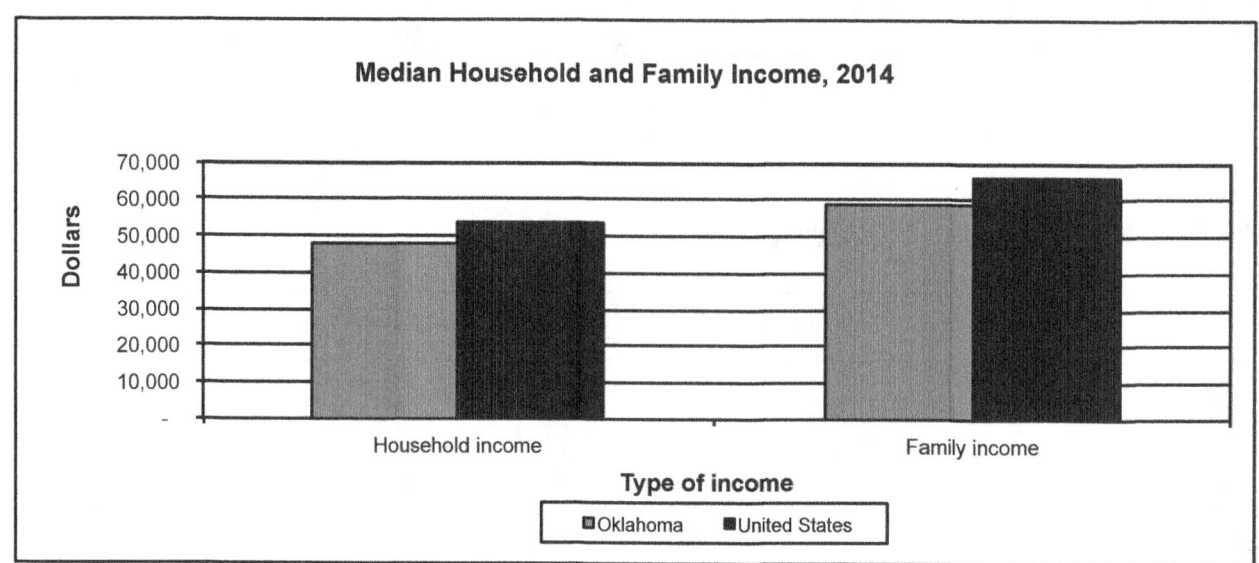

Table OK-6. Health Insurance Coverage Status for the Civilian Noninstitutionalized Population and Children Under 18 Years of Age

(Numbers in thousands, percent.)

Item	2006	2007	2008	2009	2010	2011	2012	2013	2014
Civilian Noninstitutionalized Population	3,492	3,551	3,550	3,590	3,677	3,710	3,733	3,770	3,798
Covered by Private or Public Insurance									
Number..	2,831	2,920	2,858	2,919	2,984	3,017	3,048	3,104	3,214
Percent..	81.1	82.2	80.5	81.3	81.1	81.3	81.6	82.3	84.6
Not Covered									
Number..	661	631	692	672	694	694	685	666	584
Percent..	18.9	17.8	19.5	18.7	18.9	18.7	18.4	17.7	15.4
Percent in the U.S. not covered..	15.8	15.3	15.1	15.1	15.5	15.1	14.8	14.5	11.7
Children Under 18 Years of Age	913	920	903	919	929	934	935	946	950
Covered by Private or Public Insurance									
Number..	799	804	786	816	836	834	841	851	868
Percent..	87.5	87.4	87.0	88.8	90.0	89.4	89.9	90.0	91.3
Not Covered									
Number..	114	116	117	103	93	100	94	95	82
Percent..	12.5	12.6	13.0	11.2	10.0	10.6	10.1	10.0	8.7
Percent in the U.S. not covered..	11.7	11.0	9.7	8.6	8.0	7.5	7.2	7.1	6.0

Table OK-7. Employment Status by Demographic Group, 2015

(Numbers in thousands, percent.)

Characteristic	Civilian noninstitutional population	Civilian labor force		Employed		Unemployed	
		Number	Percent of population	Number	Percent of population	Number	Percent of population
Total...	2,973	1,862	62.6	1,783	60.0	80	4.3
Sex							
Male..........	1,439	1,011	70.3	964	67.0	47	4.6
Female	1,534	851	55.5	818	53.3	33	3.9
Race, Sex, and Hispanic Origin							
White..........	2,364	1,470	62.2	1,415	59.8	55	3.8
Male..........	1,156	818	70.8	785	67.9	33	4.0
Female	1,208	652	54.0	630	52.1	22	3.4
Black or African American..................	198	128	64.3	116	58.7	11	8.8
Male..........	92	62	67.7	56	60.8	6	10.3
Female	107	66	61.4	61	56.9	5	7.4
Hispanic or Latino ethnicity[1]	271	189	69.7	180	66.4	9	4.8
Male..........	134	109	81.3	103	77.2	6	5.1
Female	137	80	58.5	76	55.8	4	4.5
Age							
16 to 19 years..........	197	67	34.0	59	30.1	8	11.5
20 to 24 years..........	263	196	74.4	180	68.4	16	8.1
25 to 34 years..........	557	441	79.1	419	75.2	22	5.0
35 to 44 years..........	439	354	80.7	343	78.2	11	3.1
45 to 54 years..........	484	374	77.3	363	75.0	11	3.0
55 to 64 years..........	473	297	62.8	289	61.0	8	2.8
65 years and over	561	134	23.8	130	23.1	4	2.9

NOTE: Data in Table 7 are from the Current Population Survey (CPS) and do not match the estimates in Table 8. See notes and definitions for further information.
[1]May be of any race.

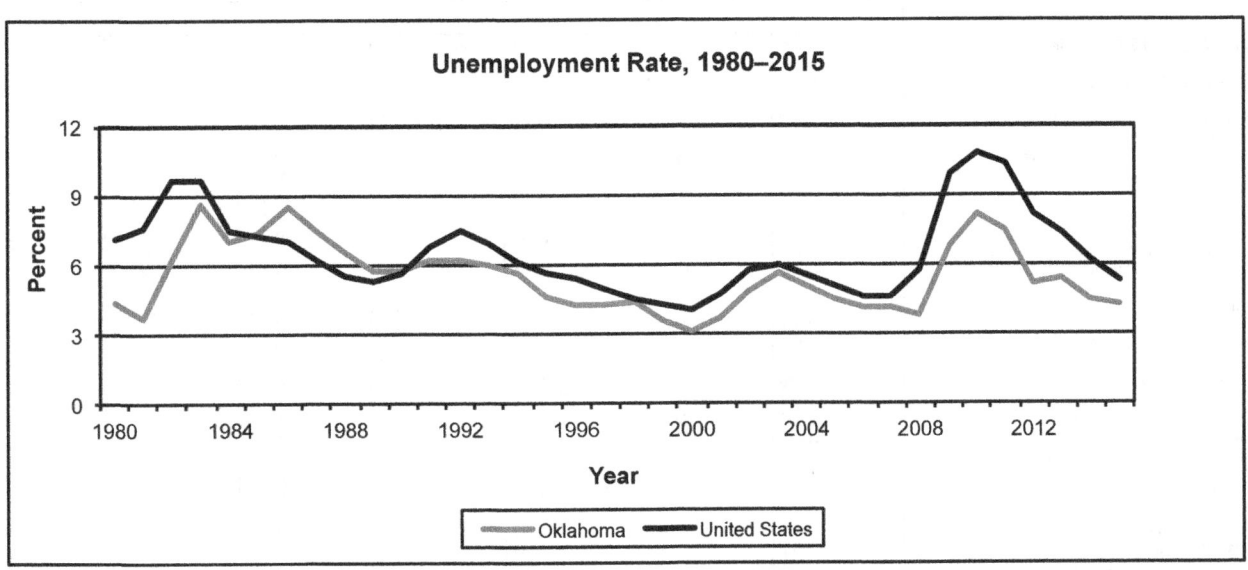

Table OK-8. Employment Status of the Civilian Noninstitutional Population Age 16 Years and Over

(Number, percent.)

Year	Civilian labor force	Civilian participation rate	Employed	Unemployed	Unemployment rate
2007..........	1,726,259	63.5	1,655,490	70,769	4.1
2008..........	1,746,466	63.7	1,681,081	65,385	3.7
2009..........	1,764,432	63.6	1,652,023	112,409	6.4
2010..........	1,768,284	62.4	1,648,138	120,146	6.8
2011..........	1,772,666	61.8	1,668,418	104,248	5.9
2012..........	1,804,071	62.3	1,709,352	94,719	5.3
2013..........	1,806,829	61.8	1,710,781	96,048	5.3
2014..........	1,797,934	61.0	1,717,136	80,798	4.5
2015..........	1,842,049	61.9	1,763,844	78,205	4.2

Table OK-9. Employment and Average Wages by Industry

(Estimates through 2010 are based on the 2007 North American Industry Classification System [NAICS]. Estimates from 2011 onward are based on the 2012 NAICS.)

Industry	2008	2009	2010	2011	2012	2013	2014
				Number of jobs			
Wage and Salary Employment by Industry..................	1,678,945	1,626,342	1,614,647	1,633,708	1,663,796	1,683,711	1,701,311
Farm Wage and Salary Employment.........................	12,605	11,244	9,532	8,599	13,525	13,731	9,760
Nonfarm Wage and Salary Employment....................	1,666,340	1,615,098	1,605,115	1,625,109	1,650,271	1,669,980	1,691,551
Private wage and salary employment........................	1,298,032	1,236,244	1,225,337	1,253,214	1,279,746	1,300,479	1,322,156
Forestry, fishing, and related activities........................	4,189	3,949	4,128	4,111	4,138	4,082	4,471
Mining.........................	50,710	42,591	43,229	50,925	57,564	59,043	60,897
Utilities........................	10,966	11,445	11,234	11,195	11,726	11,712	12,022
Construction	78,639	72,381	70,769	71,827	72,563	77,309	77,684
Manufacturing................	150,338	132,008	125,385	132,255	137,752	138,817	141,835
Durable goods manufacturing................	103,772	87,553	81,836	87,858	94,374	95,750	98,708
Nondurable goods manufacturing................	46,566	44,455	43,549	44,397	43,378	43,067	43,127
Wholesale trade	60,227	56,970	56,037	58,651	60,695	62,417	63,648
Retail trade....................	175,088	172,028	171,161	172,829	174,873	176,510	180,061
Transportation and warehousing................	46,540	44,482	42,453	43,280	45,225	46,520	47,574
Information	28,036	26,504	25,036	24,103	22,696	21,850	21,731
Finance and insurance	59,186	58,452	57,958	57,990	59,226	58,847	59,807
Real estate and rental and leasing................	24,303	22,981	22,460	22,250	21,991	22,730	21,125
Professional, scientific, and technical services	66,899	64,137	63,806	65,688	66,519	67,637	68,311
Management of companies and enterprises................	15,231	14,536	15,159	14,928	15,980	16,564	18,676
Administrative and waste services................	107,178	92,240	93,926	94,967	96,659	97,596	99,916
Educational services	19,188	19,603	19,843	20,339	20,942	21,181	21,906
Health care and social assistance................	178,613	181,094	183,915	185,043	186,423	187,968	188,420
Arts, entertainment, and recreation................	14,905	14,561	14,477	14,976	14,484	14,892	15,089
Accommodation and food services................	126,748	127,327	126,311	129,910	133,457	137,660	141,634
Other services, except public administration................	81,048	78,955	78,050	77,947	76,833	77,144	77,349
Government and government enterprises................	368,308	378,854	379,778	371,895	370,525	369,501	369,395
				Dollars			
Average Wages and Salaries by Industry	37,829	37,764	38,854	40,747	42,110	43,047	44,447
Average Farm Wages and Salaries	30,116	25,316	27,917	35,963	31,642	29,223	34,951
Average Nonfarm Wages and Salaries	37,887	37,851	38,919	40,772	42,196	43,161	44,502
Average private wages and salaries........................	37,860	37,596	38,745	40,918	42,628	43,554	45,047
Forestry, fishing, and related activities........................	22,223	22,178	22,920	23,605	24,361	25,129	26,265
Mining..........................	86,657	81,300	84,802	95,092	92,564	95,308	97,048
Utilities........................	77,270	80,310	79,789	82,744	92,066	96,204	114,306
Construction..................	39,847	40,073	41,572	42,402	44,727	46,927	47,999
Manufacturing................	45,600	45,737	47,704	49,460	51,913	53,128	55,204
Durable goods manufacturing................	47,280	47,470	49,546	51,535	53,845	55,092	57,393
Nondurable goods manufacturing................	41,857	42,325	44,244	45,353	47,708	48,763	50,195
Wholesale trade	52,032	50,717	50,318	52,424	54,855	55,514	58,024
Retail trade....................	24,304	24,436	25,234	25,957	26,986	27,310	27,897
Transportation and warehousing................	47,540	47,528	50,334	53,017	54,181	55,644	57,537
Information	48,045	47,102	47,954	51,776	53,130	54,900	56,447
Finance and insurance	48,050	48,557	50,266	52,328	55,175	56,894	60,066
Real estate and rental and leasing................	36,005	34,460	36,293	39,347	42,519	41,968	42,734
Professional, scientific, and technical services	51,206	52,315	54,200	55,811	59,325	60,907	62,083
Management of companies and enterprises................	71,882	71,789	75,324	96,022	88,331	88,988	82,151
Administrative and waste services................	29,639	30,517	30,975	31,846	33,273	33,487	34,775
Educational services	28,828	29,604	30,274	30,788	30,408	31,055	31,886
Health care and social assistance................	37,031	37,965	38,640	39,954	41,177	42,000	43,434
Arts, entertainment, and recreation................	23,067	27,201	28,064	28,805	31,121	31,143	33,748
Accommodation and food services................	14,711	14,887	15,691	16,127	16,601	16,607	17,328
Other services, except public administration................	25,653	25,637	26,721	27,496	28,466	29,064	30,097
Government and government enterprises................	37,983	38,680	39,480	40,280	40,704	41,777	42,550

Table OK-10. Employment Characteristics by Family Type

(Number, percent.)

Family type and labor force status	2012 Total	2012 Families with own children under 18 years	2013 Total	2013 Families with own children under 18 years	2014 Total	2014 Families with own children under 18 years
All Families....................................	957,067	416,517	956,517	415,825	963,008	418,186
FAMILY TYPE AND LABOR FORCE STATUS						
Married-Couple Families....................	702,265	272,752	702,897	271,793	707,265	274,441
Both husband and wife in labor force...............	49.4	64.2	48.7	62.4	48.7	62.3
Husband in labor force, wife not in labor force	24.4	29.3	24.9	30.9	24.6	30.9
Wife in labor force, husband not in labor force	7.6	4.4	8.0	4.2	8.3	4.5
Both husband and wife not in labor force.............	18.5	2.2	18.2	2.3	18.4	2.3
Other Families	254,802	143,765	253,620	144,032	255,743	143,745
Female householder, no husband present................	71.1	73.7	71.2	73.8	71.4	73.9
In labor force................................	48.3	58.9	48.4	57.5	48.2	58.2
Not in labor force	22.8	14.7	22.8	16.3	23.2	15.7
Male householder, no wife present...................	28.9	26.3	28.8	26.2	28.6	26.1
In labor force................................	22.5	23.9	22.2	23.1	22.3	23.2
Not in labor force	6.3	2.4	6.6	3.1	6.3	2.9

Table OK-11. School Enrollment and Educational Attainment, 2014

(Number, percent.)

Item	State	U.S.
Enrollment		
Total population 3 years and over, enrolled in school............	997,987	82,063,714
Enrolled in nursery school or preschool (percent)	6.7	6.0
Enrolled in kindergarten (percent).........	5.8	5.1
Enrolled in elementary school, grades 1-8 (percent)............	42.9	40.2
Enrolled in high school, grades 9-12 (percent)	20.4	20.7
Enrolled in college or graduate school (percent)...............	24.3	28.0
Attainment		
Total population 25 years and over	2,529,885	213,725,624
Less than ninth grade (percent).........	4.2	5.6
9th to 12th grade, no diploma (percent)	8.5	7.5
High school graduate, including equivalency (percent).........	31.7	27.7
Some college, no degree (percent).........	24.1	21.0
Associate's degree (percent)..................	7.3	8.2
Bachelor's degree (percent)	16.0	18.7
Graduate or professional degree (percent)............	8.1	11.4
High school graduate or higher (percent)	87.3	86.9
Bachelor's degree or higher (percent)...............	24.2	30.1

Table OK-12. Public School Characteristics and Educational Indicators

(Number, percent; data derived from National Center of Education Statistics.)

Item	State	U.S.
Public Schools, 2013–2014 (except where noted)		
Number of school districts.................................	598	18,194
Number of schools..................................	1,789	98,271
Number of students (in thousands)	682	50,045
Number of teachers (in thousands)	42	3,114
Student-teacher ratio	16.2	16.1
Expenditures per student (dollars), FY 2013........	7,914	107,637
Four-year adjusted cohort graduation rate (ACGR)[1,2]	82.7	82.3
Students eligible for free or reduced-price lunch (in thousands)	418	25,596
English language learners (in thousands)	47	4,461
Students age 3 to 21 served under IDEA, part B (in thousands)	103	6,464

Public Schools by Type	Number	Percent of state public schools
Total number of schools.................................	1,789	100.0
Regular	1,781	99.6
Special education	4	0.2
Vocational education	0	-
Alternative education.........................	4	0.2

NOTE. Every school is assigned only one school type based on its instructional emphasis.
[1]ACGR data represents a new method of calculating high-school completion rates and may not be comparable to previous years' data for Averaged Freshmen Graduation Rates (AFGR).
[2]The United States 4-year ACGRs were estimated using both the reported 4-year ACGR data from 49 states and the District of Columbia and using imputed data for Idaho. The estimate for American Indian/Alaska Native students also includes imputed data for Virginia.
- = Zero or rounds to zero.

Table OK-13. Reported Voting and Registration of the Voting-Age Population, November 2014

(Numbers in thousands, percent.)

Item	Total population	Total citizen population	Registered			Voted		
			Total registered	Percent registered (total population)	Percent registered (total citizen population)	Total voted	Percent voted (total population)	Percent voted (total citizen population)
U.S. Total	239,874	219,941	142,166	59.3	64.6	92,251	38.5	41.9
State Total..............................	2,851	2,690	1,644	57.7	61.1	920	32.3	34.2
Sex								
Male..........	1,394	1,296	753	54.1	58.1	418	30.0	32.3
Female	1,457	1,394	890	61.1	63.9	502	34.4	36.0
Race								
White alone...........	2,262	2,149	1,343	59.4	62.5	751	33.2	35.0
White, non-Hispanic alone...........	2,038	2,027	1,286	63.1	63.4	733	35.9	36.1
Black alone...........	192	190	96	49.7	50.3	56	29.2	29.6
Asian alone	65	24	17	(B)	(B)	8	(B)	(B)
Hispanic (of any race)...........	267	156	84	31.3	53.8	28	10.5	18.0
White alone or in combination	2,403	2,290	1,425	59.3	62.2	795	33.1	34.7
Black alone or in combination..........	203	200	100	49.4	50.0	59	29.1	29.5
Asian alone or in combination..........	71	30	21	(B)	(B)	10	(B)	(B)
Age								
18 to 24 years...........	382	352	119	31.1	33.8	42	10.9	11.8
25 to 34 years...........	536	501	286	53.3	57.1	104	19.5	20.9
35 to 44 years...........	419	362	218	52.1	60.3	108	25.7	29.7
45 to 64 years...........	946	917	603	63.8	65.8	366	38.7	39.9
65 years and over	568	558	418	73.5	74.8	300	52.9	53.8

B = Base is less than 75,000 and therefore too small to show the derived measure.

Table OK-14. Crime

(Number, rate per 100,000. Data are derived from the FBI Uniform Crime Reports.)

Item	State			U.S.[1,2,3,4]		
	2013	2014	Percent change	2013	2014	Percent change
TOTAL POPULATION[5]..	3,850,568	3,878,051	0.7	316,128,839	318,857,056	0.9
VIOLENT CRIME						
Number...........	16,484	15,744	-4.5	1,163,146	1,165,383	0.2
Rate	428.1	406.0	-5.2	367.9	365.5	-0.7
Murder and Nonnegligent Manslaughter						
Number...........	195	175	-10.3	14,196	14,249	0.4
Rate	5.1	4.5	-11.8	4.5	4.5	-
Rape[6]						
Number...........	2,180	1,777	X	108,612	116,645	X
Rate	56.6	45.8	X	34.4	36.6	X
Robbery						
Number...........	3,031	3,048	0.6	345,031	325,802	-5.6
Rate	78.7	78.6	-0.1	109.1	102.2	-6.3
Aggravated Assault						
Number...........	11,583	10,744	-7.2	724,149	741,291	2.4
Rate	300.8	277.0	-7.9	229.1	232.5	1.5
PROPERTY CRIME						
Number...........	126,057	115,982	-8.0	8,632,512	8,277,829	-4.1
Rate	3,273.7	2,990.7	-8.6	2,730.7	2,596.1	-4.9
Burglary						
Number...........	33,348	29,508	-11.5	1,928,465	1,729,806	-10.3
Rate	866.1	760.9	-12.1	610.0	542.5	-11.1
Larceny-Theft						
Number...........	81,495	75,891	-6.9	6,004,453	5,858,496	-2.4
Rate	2,116.4	1,956.9	-7.5	1,899.4	1,837.3	-3.3
Motor Vehicle Theft						
Number...........	11,214	10,583	-5.6	699,594	689,527	-1.4
Rate	291.2	272.9	-6.3	221.3	216.2	-2.3

NOTE: Although arson data are included in the trend and clearance tables, sufficient data are not available to estimate totals for this offense. Therefore, no arson data are published in this table.
X = Not applicable.
- = Zero or rounds to zero.
[1]The crime figures have been adjusted.
[2]The data collection methodology for the offense of forcible rape used by the Minnesota state Uniform Crime Reporting (UCR) Program (with the exception of Minneapolis and St. Paul, Minnesota) does not comply with national UCR Program guidelines. Consequently, its figures for forcible rape and violent crime (of which forcible rape is a part) are not published in this table.
[3]Includes offenses reported by the Zoological Police and the Metro Transit Police.
[4]Because of changes in the state's reporting practices, figures are not comparable to previous years' data.
[5]Populations are U.S. Census Bureau provisional estimates as of July 1 of each year.
[6]The figures shown for the offense of rape were estimated using the revised Uniform Crime Reporting (UCR) definition of rape.

Table OK-15. State Government Finances, 2014

(Dollar amounts in thousands, percent distribution.)

Item	Dollars	Percent distribution
Total Revenue	28,534,050	100.0
General revenue	21,441,335	75.1
Intergovernmental revenue	7,409,652	26.0
Taxes	9,103,302	31.9
General sales	2,599,203	9.1
Selective sales	1,390,155	4.9
License taxes	1,057,768	3.7
Individual income tax	2,962,128	10.4
Corporate income tax	397,290	1.4
Other taxes	696,758	2.4
Current charges	2,574,897	9.0
Miscellaneous general revenue	2,353,484	8.2
Utility revenue	634,446	2.2
Liquor stores revenue	0	-
Insurance trust revenue[1]	6,458,269	22.6
Total Expenditure	23,377,996	100.0
Intergovernmental expenditure	4,278,505	18.3
Direct expenditure	19,099,491	81.7
Current operation	13,861,017	59.3
Capital outlay	1,756,699	7.5
Insurance benefits and repayments	2,535,530	10.8
Assistance and subsidies	470,398	2.0
Interest on debt	475,847	2.0
Exhibit: Salaries and wages	3,288,701	14.1
Total Expenditure	23,377,996	100.0
General expenditure	20,126,703	86.1
Intergovernmental expenditure	4,278,505	18.3
Direct expenditure	15,848,198	67.8
General expenditure, by function:		
Education	7,552,546	32.3
Public welfare	6,523,375	27.9
Hospitals	239,214	1.0
Health	961,802	4.1
Highways	1,887,893	8.1
Police protection	198,656	0.8
Correction	585,519	2.5
Natural resources	224,968	1.0
Parks and recreation	84,720	0.4
Governmental administration	747,880	3.2
Interest on general debt	403,849	1.7
Other and unallocable	716,281	3.1
Utility expenditure	715,763	3.1
Liquor stores expenditure	0	-
Insurance trust expenditure	2,535,530	10.8
Debt at End of Fiscal Year	9,047,456	X
Cash and Security Holdings	45,383,325	X

X = Not applicable.
- = Zero or rounds to zero.
[1]Within insurance trust revenue, net earnings of state retirement systems is a calculated statistic (the item code in the data file is X08), and thus can be positive or negative. Net earnings is the sum of earnings on investments plus gains on investments minus losses on investments. The change made in 2002 for asset valuation from book to market value in accordance with Statement 34 of the Governmental Accounting Standards Board is reflected in the calculated statistics.

Table OK-16. State Government Tax Collections, 2014

(Dollars in thousands, percent.)

Item	Dollars	Percent distribution
Total Taxes	9,103,302	100.0
Property taxes	X	X
Sales and gross receipts	3,989,358	43.8
General sales and gross receipts	2,599,203	28.6
Selective sales and gross receipts	1,390,155	15.3
Alcoholic beverages	110,941	1.2
Amusements	20,823	0.2
Insurance premiums	294,762	3.2
Motor fuels	450,807	5.0
Pari-mutuels	1,113	-
Public utilities	46,306	0.5
Tobacco products	292,752	3.2
Other selective sales	172,651	1.9
Licenses	1,057,768	11.6
Alcoholic beverages	1,326	-
Amusements	146,857	1.6
Corporations in general	35,351	0.4
Hunting and fishing	19,910	0.2
Motor vehicle	754,435	8.3
Motor vehicle operators	20,109	0.2
Public utilities	947	-
Occupation and business, NEC	78,572	0.9
Other licenses	261	-
Income taxes	3,359,418	36.9
Individual income	2,962,128	32.5
Corporation net income	397,290	4.4
Other taxes	696,758	7.7
Death and gift	1,056	-
Documentary and stock transfer	16,296	0.2
Severance	679,406	7.5
Taxes, NEC	0	-

X = Not applicable.
- = Zero or rounds to zero.

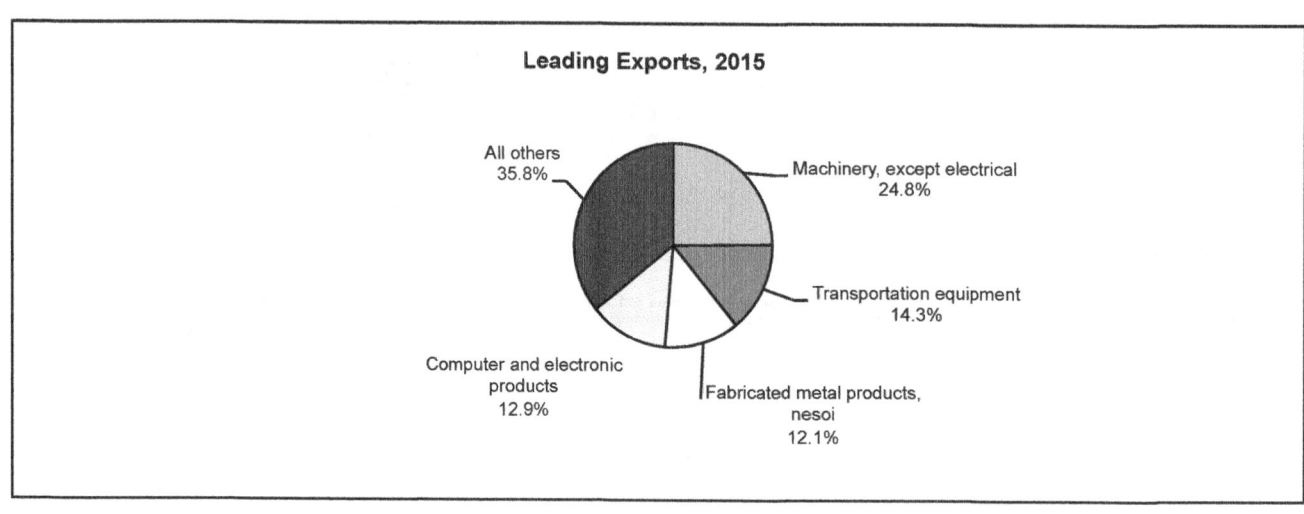

Leading Exports, 2015

All others 35.8%
Machinery, except electrical 24.8%
Transportation equipment 14.3%
Fabricated metal products, nesoi 12.1%
Computer and electronic products 12.9%

OREGON

Facts and Figures

Location: Northwestern United States; bordered on the N by Washington, on the E by Idaho, on the S by Nevada and California, and on the W by the Pacific Ocean

Area: 98,381 sq. mi. (254,805 sq. km.); rank—9th

Population: 4,028,977 (2015 est.); rank—27th

Principal Cities: capital—Salem; largest—Portland

Statehood: February 14, 1859; 33rd state

U.S. Congress: 2 senators, 5 representatives

State Motto: She Flies With Her Own Wings

State Song: "Oregon, My Oregon"

State Nickname: The Beaver State

Abbreviations: OR; Oreg.

State Symbols: flower—Oregon grape; tree—Douglas fir; bird—Western meadowlark

At a Glance

- With an increase in population of 5.0 percent, Oregon ranked 16th among the states in growth from 2010 to 2015.

- In 2014, 9.7 percent of Oregonians did not have health insurance, compared to 11.7 percent of the total U.S. population.

- Oregon's violent crime rate in 2014 was 232.3 per 100,000 population, compared to 365.5 for the entire nation.

- Oregon's median income in 2014 was $51,075, and 16.6 percent of its residents lived below the poverty level.

- Oregon had the third highest increase in employees on nonfarm payrolls between 2014 and 2015 (3.3 percent).

Table OR-1. Population by Age, Sex, Race, and Hispanic Origin

(Number, percent, except where noted.)

Sex, age, race, and Hispanic origin	2000	2010	2015[1]	Average annual percent change, 2010–2015
Total Population...	3,421,399	3,831,074	4,028,977	0.4
Percent of total U.S. population	1.2	1.2	1.3	X
Sex				
Male...	1,696,550	1,896,002	1,993,170	0.4
Female...	1,724,849	1,935,072	2,035,807	0.4
Age				
Under 5 years..	223,005	237,556	230,790	-0.2
5 to 19 years..	720,999	734,627	729,011	-0.1
20 to 64 years...	2,039,218	2,325,358	2,408,300	0.3
65 years and over..	438,177	533,533	660,876	1.5
Median age (years)..	36.3	38.4	39.3	0.2
Race and Hispanic Origin				
One race				
White..	2,961,623	3,403,252	3,529,686	0.3
Black..	55,662	74,414	83,636	0.8
American Indian and Alaska Native	45,211	66,784	72,327	0.6
Asian..	101,350	145,009	177,473	1.5
Native Hawaiian or Other Pacific Islander	7,976	14,649	17,674	1.3
Two or more races..	104,745	126,966	148,181	1.1
Hispanic (of any race).......................................	275,314	467,030	511,901	0.7

X = Not applicable.

[1]Population figures for 2015 are July 1 estimates. The 2010 estimates are taken from the 2010 Census.

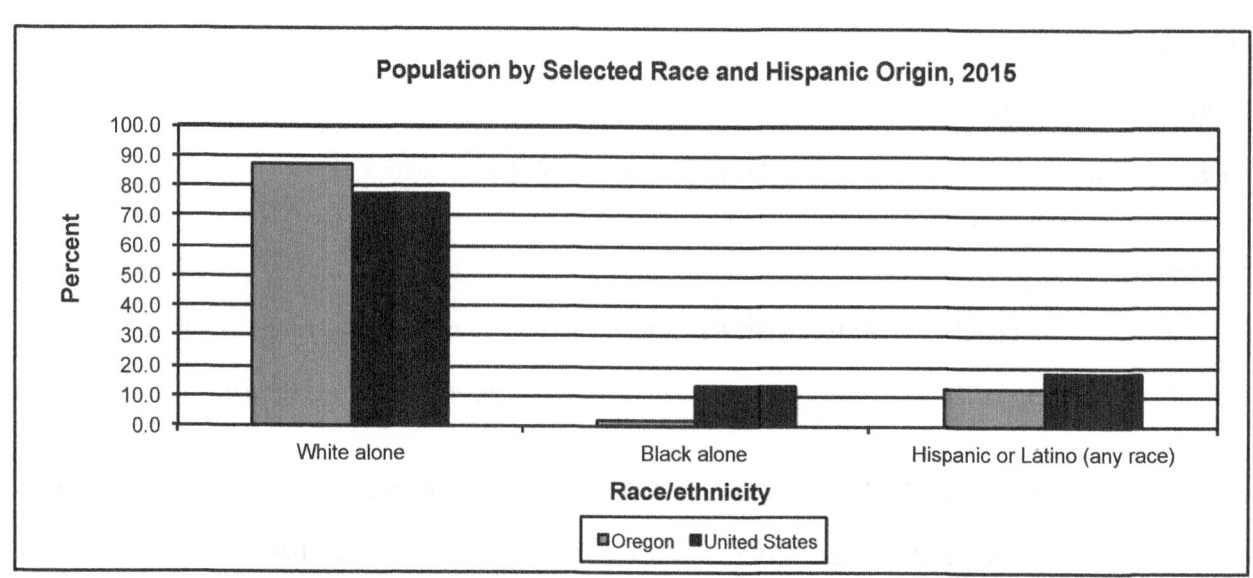

Table OR-2. Marital Status

(Number, percent distribution.)

Sex, age, race, and Hispanic origin	2000	2010	2014
Males, 15 Years and Over	1,336,805	1,533,177	1,564,715
Never married	28.5	32.6	33.2
Now married, except separated..............................	57.1	51.4	50.9
Separated...	1.5	1.6	1.6
Widowed...	2.4	2.7	2.6
Divorced..	10.6	11.8	11.8
Females, 15 Years and Over	1,385,329	1,588,428	1,623,076
Never married	21.9	25.8	26.6
Now married, except separated..............................	53.9	48.9	48.4
Separated...	1.9	1.9	2.0
Widowed...	9.6	8.5	8.3
Divorced..	12.7	14.9	14.6

Table OR-3. Households and Housing Characteristics

(Number, percent, dollars.)

Item	2000	2010	2014	Average annual percent change, 2000–2014
Total Households...	1,333,723	1,507,137	1,535,511	1.1
Family households	877,671	963,362	966,250	0.7
Married-couple family	692,532	733,095	730,615	0.4
Other family	185,139	230,267	235,635	1.9
Male householder, no wife present.......................	54,357	65,972	71,466	2.2
Female householder, no husband present	130,782	164,295	164,169	1.8
Nonfamily households	456,032	543,775	569,261	1.8
Householder living alone..	347,624	416,500	431,526	1.7
Householder not living alone..	108,428	127,275	137,735	1.9
Housing Characteristics				
Total housing units..	1,452,709	1,676,476	1,700,611	1.2
Occupied housing units	1,333,723	1,507,137	1,535,511	1.1
Owner occupied	856,951	942,674	932,392	0.6
Renter occupied	476,772	564,463	603,119	1.9
Average household size..	2.51	2.49	2.53	0.1
Financial Characteristics				
Median gross rent of renter-occupied housing	620	816	924	3.5
Median monthly owner costs for housing units with a mortgage	1,125	1,577	1,500	2.4
Median value of owner-occupied housing units	152,100	244,500	239,800	4.1

- = Zero or rounds to zero.

Table OR-4. Migration, Origin, and Language

(Number, percent.)

Characteristic	State			U.S.		
	2013	2014	Percent change	2013	2014	Percent change
Residence 1 Year Ago						
Population 1 year and over	3,888,216	3,927,857	1.0	312,432,820	315,095,393	0.9
Same house	81.1	81.4	X	85.0	85.1	X
Different house in the U.S.	18.4	18	X	14.4	14.3	X
Same county	10.7	10.5	X	8.9	8.7	X
Different county	7.7	7.5	X	5.5	5.6	X
Same state	4.0	4	X	3.2	3.3	X
Different state	3.7	3.5	X	2.3	2.3	X
Abroad	0.5	0.6	X	0.6	0.6	X
Place of Birth						
Native born	3,538,859	3,576,587	1.1	274,780,773	276,465,262	0.6
Male	49.5	49.4	X	49.3	49.3	X
Female	50.5	50.6	X	50.7	50.7	X
Foreign born	391,206	393,652	0.6	41,348,066	42,391,794	2.5
Male	49.4	49.9	X	48.8	48.7	X
Female	50.6	50.1	X	51.2	51.3	X
Foreign born; naturalized U.S. citizen............................	155,415	159,830	2.8	19,294,710	19,984,738	3.6
Male	45.9	45.9	X	45.9	45.9	X
Female	54.1	54.1	X	54.1	54.1	X
Foreign born; not a U.S. citizen	235,791	233,822	-0.8	22,053,356	22,407,056	1.6
Male	51.7	52.7	X	51.3	51.2	X
Female	48.3	47.3	X	48.7	48.8	X
Entered 2010 or later	9.3	13.3	X	9.7	12.3	X
Entered 2000 to 2009	28.3	27.3	X	29.4	28.6	X
Entered before 2000..	62.4	59.4	X	61.0	59.1	X
World Region of Birth, Foreign						
Foreign-born population, excluding population born at sea	391,206	393,652	0.6	41,347,945	42,390,705	2.5
Europe	16.7	14.6	X	11.6	11.2	X
Asia	28.5	30	X	29.5	30.1	X
Africa	3.1	4.1	X	4.4	4.6	X
Oceania	1.7	1.7	X	0.5	0.6	X
Latin America..	46.4	45.7	X	51.9	51.6	X
North America...	3.6	3.8	X	2.0	1.9	X
Language Spoken at Home and Ability to Speak English						
Population 5 years and over..	3,701,662	3,743,771	1.1	296,358,760	299,084,046	0.9
English only	85.1	84.5	X	79.2	78.9	X
Language other than English...	14.9	15.5	X	20.8	21.1	X
Speaks English less than "very well"............................	5.9	6.1	X	8.5	8.6	X

X = Not applicable.
- = Zero or rounds to zero.

Table OR-5. Median Income and Poverty Status, 2014

(Number, percent, except as noted.)

Characteristic	State		U.S.	
	Number	Percent	Number	Percent
Median Income				
Households (dollars)...	51,075	X	53,657	X
Families (dollars)	62,670	X	65,910	X
Below Poverty Level (All People)	644,450	16.6	48,208,387	15.5
Sex				
Male...	301,552	15.7	21,590,918	14.2
Female	342,898	17.4	26,617,469	16.8
Age				
Under 18 years..	181,714	21.6	15,686,012	21.7
Related children under 18 years...............................	175,974	21.1	15,372,705	21.3
18 to 64 years..	407,565	16.8	28,267,482	14.6
65 years and over	55,171	8.8	4,254,893	9.5

X = Not applicable.

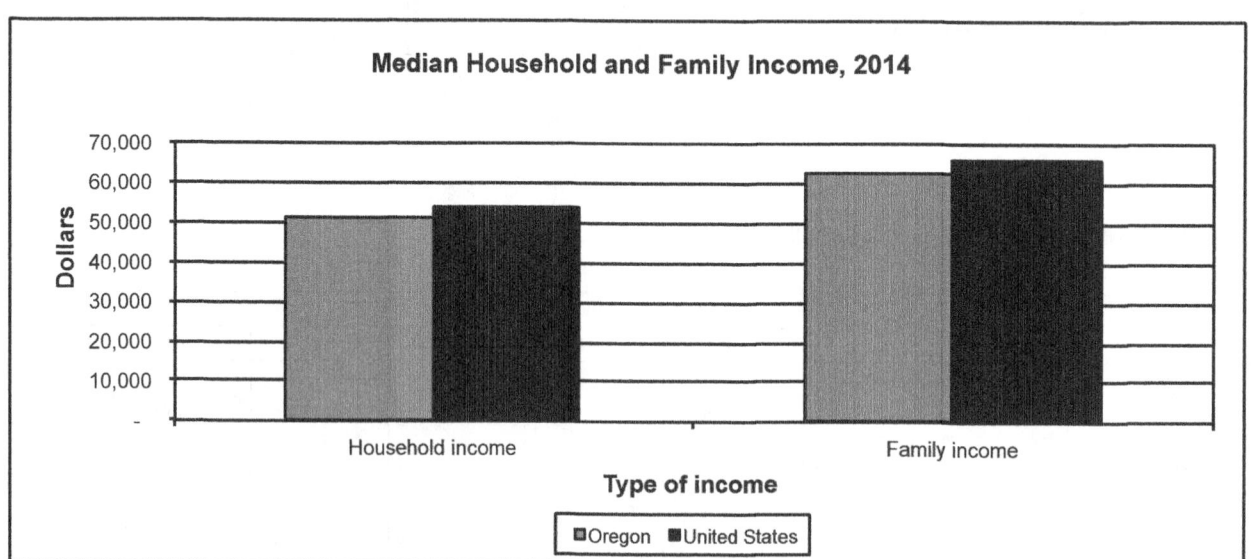

Table OR-6. Health Insurance Coverage Status for the Civilian Noninstitutionalized Population and Children Under 18 Years of Age

(Numbers in thousands, percent.)

Item	2006	2007	2008	2009	2010	2011	2012	2013	2014
Civilian Noninstitutionalized Population	3,715	3,762	3,746	3,780	3,799	3,833	3,860	3,893	3,931
Covered by Private or Public Insurance									
Number...	3,051	3,130	3,132	3,137	3,148	3,230	3,284	3,322	3,549
Percent...	82.1	83.2	83.6	83.0	82.9	84.3	85.1	85.3	90.3
Not Covered									
Number...	665	632	614	643	652	602	576	571	383
Percent...	17.9	16.8	16.4	17.0	17.1	15.7	14.9	14.7	9.7
Percent in the U.S. not covered..	15.8	15.3	15.1	15.1	15.5	15.1	14.8	14.5	11.7
Children Under 18 Years of Age	870	864	865	871	865	861	860	858	857
Covered by Private or Public Insurance									
Number...	755	772	755	781	789	798	805	808	818
Percent...	86.9	89.4	87.3	89.6	91.2	92.7	93.6	94.2	95.4
Not Covered									
Number...	114	92	110	90	76	63	55	50	39
Percent...	13.1	10.6	12.7	10.4	8.8	7.3	6.4	5.8	4.6
Percent in the U.S. not covered..	11.7	11.0	9.7	8.6	8.0	7.5	7.2	7.1	6.0

Table OR-7. Employment Status by Demographic Group, 2015

(Numbers in thousands, percent.)

Characteristic	Civilian noninstitutional population	Civilian labor force		Employed		Unemployed	
		Number	Percent of population	Number	Percent of population	Number	Percent of population
Total..	3,206	1,955	61.0	1,844	57.5	111	5.7
Sex							
Male	1,563	1,034	66.1	973	62.2	61	5.9
Female	1,643	921	56.0	871	53.0	50	5.4
Race, Sex, and Hispanic Origin							
White	2,860	1,730	60.5	1,631	57.0	99	5.7
Male	1,385	900	65.0	846	61.1	53	5.9
Female	1,475	830	56.3	785	53.2	45	5.5
Black or African American....................	59	40	67.3	37	62.4	3	7.4
Male	36	29	79	27	74	2	6
Female	NA	NA	NA	NA	NA	NA	NA
Hispanic or Latino ethnicity[1]	336	236	70.3	221	65.8	15	6.5
Male	180	143	79.6	135	74.7	9	6.1
Female	155	93	59.5	86	55.4	7	7.0
Age							
16 to 19 years	206	69	33.5	54	26.1	15	22.2
20 to 24 years	238	172	72.2	157	65.9	15	8.8
25 to 34 years	551	450	81.7	430	78.1	20	4.4
35 to 44 years	512	418	81.6	401	78.4	17	3.9
45 to 54 years	497	385	77.5	371	74.6	15	3.8
55 to 64 years	517	325	62.8	305	58.9	20	6.2
65 years and over	685	136	19.8	127	18.5	9	6.5

NOTE: Data in Table 7 are from the Current Population Survey (CPS) and do not match the estimates in Table 8. See notes and definitions for further information.

[1] May be of any race.

NA = Not available.

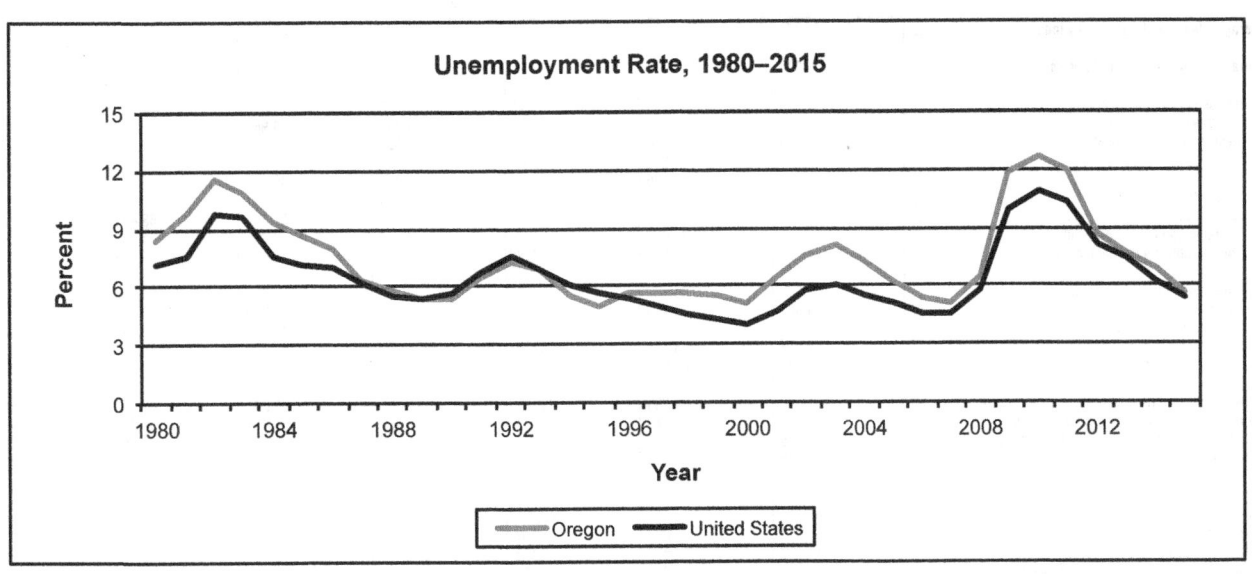

Unemployment Rate, 1980–2015

Table OR-8. Employment Status of the Civilian Noninstitutional Population Age 16 Years and Over

(Number, percent.)

Year	Civilian labor force	Civilian participation rate	Employed	Unemployed	Unemployment rate
2007..	1,921,766	65.7	1,822,772	98,994	5.2
2008..	1,955,121	65.8	1,827,352	127,769	6.5
2009..	1,976,638	65.7	1,753,682	222,956	11.3
2010..	1,984,039	65.4	1,773,076	210,963	10.6
2011..	1,993,889	65.1	1,804,320	189,569	9.5
2012..	1,954,098	63.1	1,781,428	172,670	8.8
2013..	1,909,842	61.0	1,759,197	150,645	7.9
2014..	1,939,396	61.1	1,807,328	132,068	6.8
2015..	1,969,466	61.1	1,857,114	112,352	5.7

Table OR-9. Employment and Average Wages by Industry

(Estimates through 2010 are based on the 2007 North American Industry Classification System [NAICS]. Estimates from 2011 onward are based on the 2012 NAICS.)

Industry	2008	2009	2010	2011	2012	2013	2014
	Number of jobs						
Wage and Salary Employment by Industry..................	1,810,443	1,707,674	1,701,494	1,720,379	1,719,728	1,756,815	1,801,023
Farm Wage and Salary Employment.........................	30,351	30,942	33,578	33,358	30,302	32,834	29,578
Nonfarm Wage and Salary Employment....................	1,780,092	1,676,732	1,667,916	1,687,021	1,689,426	1,723,981	1,771,445
Private wage and salary employment........................	1,484,093	1,378,007	1,367,286	1,392,299	1,409,680	1,447,306	1,493,846
Forestry, fishing, and related activities	20,701	18,818	19,157	19,894	19,685	21,908	22,570
Mining...	1,989	1,676	1,575	1,600	1,592	1,527	1,543
Utilities...	4,757	4,713	4,548	4,493	4,561	4,497	4,512
Construction	96,526	75,992	69,366	70,932	71,394	76,074	81,787
Manufacturing...	195,054	166,964	163,545	167,984	171,712	174,944	179,261
Durable goods manufacturing............................	142,762	117,683	114,793	118,572	121,582	123,272	125,995
Nondurable goods manufacturing.......................	52,292	49,281	48,752	49,412	50,130	51,672	53,266
Wholesale trade	80,878	75,856	73,576	74,573	75,492	71,731	72,708
Retail trade..	199,067	185,856	185,643	187,109	188,621	193,095	197,653
Transportation and warehousing...........................	54,585	49,670	48,640	49,738	50,303	50,864	53,125
Information..	35,546	33,114	32,262	32,081	32,697	32,451	32,164
Finance and insurance	61,199	58,711	57,793	58,489	58,552	58,972	59,217
Real estate and rental and leasing.........................	27,617	26,058	25,241	24,317	23,950	24,478	24,853
Professional, scientific, and technical services	73,537	70,752	71,233	74,713	77,324	80,723	84,778
Management of companies and enterprises..............	32,306	30,737	30,529	30,417	30,490	37,908	40,165
Administrative and waste services........................	92,256	80,225	81,936	84,103	88,476	91,418	95,519
Educational services	40,274	41,272	42,398	43,746	43,805	44,607	45,524
Health care and social assistance.........................	203,894	207,421	212,172	215,966	218,727	222,947	230,396
Arts, entertainment, and recreation.......................	23,489	22,212	21,827	22,402	21,978	22,734	23,583
Accommodation and food services........................	150,923	142,293	142,362	145,034	149,010	154,779	160,186
Other services, except public administration..............	89,495	85,667	83,483	84,708	81,311	81,649	84,302
Government and government enterprises..................	295,999	298,725	300,630	294,722	279,746	276,675	277,599
	Dollars						
Average Wages and Salaries by Industry	40,993	41,087	42,014	43,464	45,021	45,783	47,233
Average Farm Wages and Salaries	30,087	29,122	25,649	26,787	25,205	34,844	31,736
Average Nonfarm Wages and Salaries	41,179	41,308	42,343	43,794	45,377	45,991	47,492
Average private wages and salaries........................	40,930	40,842	41,985	43,486	44,981	45,513	46,993
Forestry, fishing, and related activities....................	32,026	30,616	30,165	32,435	34,131	34,901	36,265
Mining..	47,813	45,646	45,480	48,768	48,648	50,654	51,351
Utilities...	81,550	84,565	84,415	87,030	89,150	89,681	93,593
Construction	46,849	47,701	48,104	50,135	51,755	52,513	54,130
Manufacturing...	54,743	55,243	59,172	62,062	64,224	63,496	65,611
Durable goods manufacturing............................	59,582	60,969	66,380	70,223	72,736	71,763	74,670
Nondurable goods manufacturing.......................	41,532	41,567	42,200	42,479	43,582	43,772	44,183
Wholesale trade	63,628	63,188	66,367	69,594	71,719	63,023	65,022
Retail trade..	26,521	26,556	26,970	27,377	28,050	28,262	29,023
Transportation and warehousing...........................	42,335	42,123	43,417	44,345	44,945	45,462	46,842
Information..	64,256	63,423	64,691	67,921	68,035	68,882	72,333
Finance and insurance	61,237	60,791	62,564	64,080	67,832	69,827	71,349
Real estate and rental and leasing.........................	32,757	32,283	33,180	34,391	35,830	36,249	38,182
Professional, scientific, and technical services	59,581	59,170	61,348	63,638	66,854	67,672	70,468
Management of companies and enterprises..............	77,415	75,014	76,861	81,449	85,024	107,240	112,454
Administrative and waste services........................	29,578	30,308	30,294	30,931	32,037	32,073	33,336
Educational services	22,868	23,281	23,864	24,737	25,048	25,677	25,813
Health care and social assistance.........................	41,870	42,419	42,924	44,224	45,295	46,001	46,980
Arts, entertainment, and recreation.......................	24,917	24,686	26,357	25,509	28,090	27,112	27,510
Accommodation and food services........................	17,498	17,598	18,175	18,737	19,290	19,419	20,315
Other services, except public administration..............	27,148	27,009	27,986	28,489	29,736	30,726	31,565
Government and government enterprises..................	42,429	43,459	43,970	45,247	47,368	48,494	50,178

Table OR-10. Employment Characteristics by Family Type

(Number, percent.)

Family type and labor force status	2012 Total	2012 Families with own children under 18 years	2013 Total	2013 Families with own children under 18 years	2014 Total	2014 Families with own children under 18 years
All Families..	964,892	406,243	961,197	405,368	960,100	398,763
FAMILY TYPE AND LABOR FORCE STATUS						
Married-Couple Families............................	729,381	270,464	731,763	276,074	724,465	267,628
Both husband and wife in labor force..................	50.1	64.2	49.2	65.1	49.1	66.0
Husband in labor force, wife not in labor force.........	21.4	29.8	20.7	28.3	21.0	27.9
Wife in labor force, husband not in labor force.........	8.2	4.0	8.6	4.3	8.5	4.3
Both husband and wife not in labor force...............	20.4	2.0	21.1	2.0	21.4	1.8
Other Families	235,511	135,779	229,434	129,294	235,635	131,135
Female householder, no husband present...............	70.7	72.1	71.1	73.7	69.7	72.0
In labor force	49.3	57.1	48.9	59.7	48.5	57.8
Not in labor force	21.4	15.0	22.1	14.0	21.2	14.2
Male householder, no wife present....................	29.3	27.9	28.9	26.3	30.3	28.0
In labor force.......................................	23.2	25.2	22.5	23.5	24.1	25.1
Not in labor force	6.1	2.8	6.5	2.8	6.3	2.9

Table OR-11. School Enrollment and Educational Attainment, 2014

(Number, percent.)

Item	State	U.S.
Enrollment		
Total population 3 years and over, enrolled in school........	956,494	82,063,714
Enrolled in nursery school or preschool (percent)	5.4	6.0
Enrolled in kindergarten (percent)	4.9	5.1
Enrolled in elementary school, grades 1-8 (percent)..........	40.2	40.2
Enrolled in high school, grades 9-12 (percent)	20.3	20.7
Enrolled in college or graduate school (percent).............	29.1	28.0
Attainment		
Total population 25 years and over	2,746,957	213,725,624
Less than ninth grade (percent)	4.2	5.6
9th to 12th grade, no diploma (percent)	6.1	7.5
High school graduate, including equivalency (percent)........	24.3	27.7
Some college, no degree (percent)	26.2	21.0
Associate's degree (percent)...............................	8.4	8.2
Bachelor's degree (percent)	19.2	18.7
Graduate or professional degree (percent)...................	11.6	11.4
High school graduate or higher (percent)	89.7	86.9
Bachelor's degree or higher (percent)	30.8	30.1

Table OR-12. Public School Characteristics and Educational Indicators

(Number, percent; data derived from National Center of Education Statistics.)

Item	State	U.S.
Public Schools, 2013–2014 (except where noted)		
Number of school districts.................................	220	18,194
Number of schools..	1,246	98,271
Number of students (in thousands)	593	50,045
Number of teachers (in thousands)	27	3,114
Student-teacher ratio	22.2	16.1
Expenditures per student (dollars), FY 2013.................	9,183	107,637
Four-year adjusted cohort graduation rate (ACGR)[1,2]	72.0	82.3
Students eligible for free or reduced-price lunch (in thousands) ...	282	25,596
English language learners (in thousands)	50	4,461
Students age 3 to 21 served under IDEA, part B (in thousands) ...	83	6,464

Public Schools by Type	Number	Percent of state public schools
Total number of schools....................................	1,246	100.0
Regular..	1,206	96.8
Special education	1	0.1
Vocational education	0	-
Alternative education......................................	39	3.1

NOTE: Every school is assigned only one school type based on its instructional emphasis.
[1] ACGR data represents a new method of calculating high-school completion rates and may not be comparable to previous years' data for Averaged Freshmen Graduation Rates (AFGR).
[2] The United States 4-year ACGRs were estimated using both the reported 4-year ACGR data from 49 states and the District of Columbia and using imputed data for Idaho. The estimate for American Indian/Alaska Native students also includes imputed data for Virginia.
- = Zero or rounds to zero.

Table OR-13. Reported Voting and Registration of the Voting-Age Population, November 2014

(Numbers in thousands, percent.)

Item	Total population	Total citizen population	Registered			Voted		
			Total registered	Percent registered (total population)	Percent registered (total citizen population)	Total voted	Percent voted (total population)	Percent voted (total citizen population)
U.S. Total	239,874	219,941	142,166	59.3	64.6	92,251	38.5	41.9
State Total.............................	3,078	2,870	2,008	65.2	70.0	1,594	51.8	55.5
Sex								
Male...	1,512	1,394	950	62.8	68.1	741	49.0	53.2
Female	1,566	1,475	1,058	67.6	71.7	852	54.4	57.8
Race								
White alone................................	2,768	2,608	1,861	67.2	71.4	1,510	54.5	57.9
White, non-Hispanic alone	2,475	2,448	1,770	71.5	72.3	1,458	58.9	59.5
Black alone................................	56	50	29	(B)	(B)	14	(B)	(B)
Asian alone	123	99	47	38.7	48.0	24	19.7	24.4
Hispanic (of any race).....................	322	184	106	33.1	57.7	62	19.2	33.6
White alone or in combination	2,839	2,675	1,900	66.9	71.0	1,537	54.1	57.5
Black alone or in combination	63	53	29	(B)	(B)	14	(B)	(B)
Asian alone or in combination..........	125	102	50	40.0	49.3	27	21.4	26.4
Age								
18 to 24 years.............................	380	358	149	39.1	41.6	89	23.4	24.9
25 to 34 years.............................	531	483	333	62.7	69.0	242	45.6	50.2
35 to 44 years.............................	497	436	311	62.6	71.4	237	47.8	54.4
45 to 64 years.............................	1,066	994	757	71.0	76.2	615	57.6	61.8
65 years and over	604	599	457	75.8	76.3	410	68.0	68.5

B = Base is less than 75,000 and therefore too small to show the derived measure.

Table OR-14. Crime

(Number, rate per 100,000. Data are derived from the FBI Uniform Crime Reports.)

Item	State			U.S.[1,2,3,4]		
	2013	2014	Percent change	2013	2014	Percent change
TOTAL POPULATION[5].....................................	3,930,065	3,970,239	1.0	316,128,839	318,857,056	0.9
VIOLENT CRIME						
Number...	9,546	9,224	-3.4	1,163,146	1,165,383	0.2
Rate	242.9	232.3	-4.4	367.9	365.5	-0.7
Murder and Nonnegligent Manslaughter						
Number..	80	81	1.3	14,196	14,249	0.4
Rate	2.0	2.0	-	4.5	4.5	-
Rape[6]						
Number..	1,897	1,458	X	108,612	116,645	X
Rate	48.3	36.7	X	34.4	36.6	X
Robbery						
Number..	2,397	2,093	-12.7	345,031	325,802	-5.6
Rate	61.0	52.7	-13.6	109.1	102.2	-6.3
Aggravated Assault						
Number..	5,610	5,592	-0.3	724,149	741,291	2.4
Rate	142.7	140.8	-1.3	229.1	232.5	1.5
PROPERTY CRIME						
Number..	124,737	114,305	-8.4	8,632,512	8,277,829	-4.1
Rate	3,173.9	2,879.0	-9.3	2,730.7	2,596.1	-4.9
Burglary						
Number..	20,769	17,230	-17.0	1,928,465	1,729,806	-10.3
Rate	528.5	434.0	-17.9	610.0	542.5	-11.1
Larceny-Theft						
Number..	94,106	87,526	-7.0	6,004,453	5,858,496	-2.4
Rate	2,394.5	2,204.6	-7.9	1,899.4	1,837.3	-3.3
Motor Vehicle Theft						
Number..	9,862	9,549	-3.2	699,594	689,527	-1.4
Rate	250.9	240.5	-4.1	221.3	216.2	-2.3

NOTE: Although arson data are included in the trend and clearance tables, sufficient data are not available to estimate totals for this offense. Therefore, no arson data are published in this table.
X = Not applicable.
- = Zero or rounds to zero.
[1]The crime figures have been adjusted.
[2]The data collection methodology for the offense of forcible rape used by the Minnesota state Uniform Crime Reporting (UCR) Program (with the exception of Minneapolis and St. Paul, Minnesota) does not comply with national UCR Program guidelines. Consequently, its figures for forcible rape and violent crime (of which forcible rape is a part) are not published in this table.
[3]Includes offenses reported by the Zoological Police and the Metro Transit Police.
[4]Because of changes in the state's reporting practices, figures are not comparable to previous years' data.
[5]Populations are U.S. Census Bureau provisional estimates as of July 1 of each year.
[6]The figures shown for the offense of rape were estimated using the revised Uniform Crime Reporting (UCR) definition of rape.

Table OR-15. State Government Finances, 2014

(Dollar amounts in thousands, percent distribution.)

Item	Dollars	Percent distribution
Total Revenue	37,665,178	100.0
General revenue	24,355,892	64.7
Intergovernmental revenue	8,791,134	23.3
Taxes	9,683,640	25.7
General sales	0	-
Selective sales	1,444,542	3.8
License taxes	960,777	2.6
Individual income tax	6,649,418	17.7
Corporate income tax	495,134	1.3
Other taxes	133,769	0.4
Current charges	3,972,594	10.5
Miscellaneous general revenue	1,908,524	5.1
Utility revenue	0	-
Liquor stores revenue	518,659	1.4
Insurance trust revenue[1]	12,790,627	34.0
Total Expenditure	29,413,524	100.0
Intergovernmental expenditure	6,007,393	20.4
Direct expenditure	23,406,131	79.6
Current operation	16,336,067	55.5
Capital outlay	1,115,204	3.8
Insurance benefits and repayments	4,994,133	17.0
Assistance and subsidies	563,677	1.9
Interest on debt	397,050	1.3
Exhibit: Salaries and wages	5,277,593	17.9
Total Expenditure	29,413,524	100.0
General expenditure	24,146,193	82.1
Intergovernmental expenditure	6,007,393	20.4
Direct expenditure	18,138,800	61.7
General expenditure, by function:		
Education	7,894,773	26.8
Public welfare	8,024,261	27.3
Hospitals	2,082,330	7.1
Health	626,178	2.1
Highways	1,313,047	4.5
Police protection	181,241	0.6
Correction	785,514	2.7
Natural resources	516,795	1.8
Parks and recreation	80,870	0.3
Governmental administration	1,187,088	4.0
Interest on general debt	397,050	1.3
Other and unallocable	1,057,046	3.6
Utility expenditure	18,594	0.1
Liquor stores expenditure	254,604	0.9
Insurance trust expenditure	4,994,133	17.0
Debt at End of Fiscal Year	14,583,105	X
Cash and Security Holdings	83,639,767	X

X = Not applicable.
- = Zero or rounds to zero.
[1]Within insurance trust revenue, net earnings of state retirement systems is a calculated statistic (the item code in the data file is X08), and thus can be positive or negative. Net earnings is the sum of earnings on investments plus gains on investments minus losses on investments. The change made in 2002 for asset valuation from book to market value in accordance with Statement 34 of the Governmental Accounting Standards Board is reflected in the calculated statistics.

Table OR-16. State Government Tax Collections, 2014

(Dollars in thousands, percent.)

Item	Dollars	Percent distribution
Total Taxes	9,683,640	100.0
Property taxes	21,740	0.2
Sales and gross receipts	1,444,542	14.9
General sales and gross receipts	X	X
Selective sales and gross receipts	1,444,542	14.9
Alcoholic beverages	17,627	0.2
Amusements	0	-
Insurance premiums	85,196	0.9
Motor fuels	512,342	5.3
Pari-mutuels	2,253	-
Public utilities	85,401	0.9
Tobacco products	257,583	2.7
Other selective sales	484,140	5.0
Licenses	960,777	9.9
Alcoholic beverages	4,609	-
Amusements	812	-
Corporations in general	29,471	0.3
Hunting and fishing	54,100	0.6
Motor vehicle	514,003	5.3
Motor vehicle operators	41,484	0.4
Public utilities	14,061	0.1
Occupation and business, NEC	295,379	3.1
Other licenses	6,858	0.1
Income taxes	7,144,552	73.8
Individual income	6,649,418	68.7
Corporation net income	495,134	5.1
Other taxes	112,029	1.2
Death and gift	85,491	0.9
Documentary and stock transfer	3,114	-
Severance	23,424	0.2
Taxes, NEC	0	-

X = Not applicable.
- = Zero or rounds to zero.

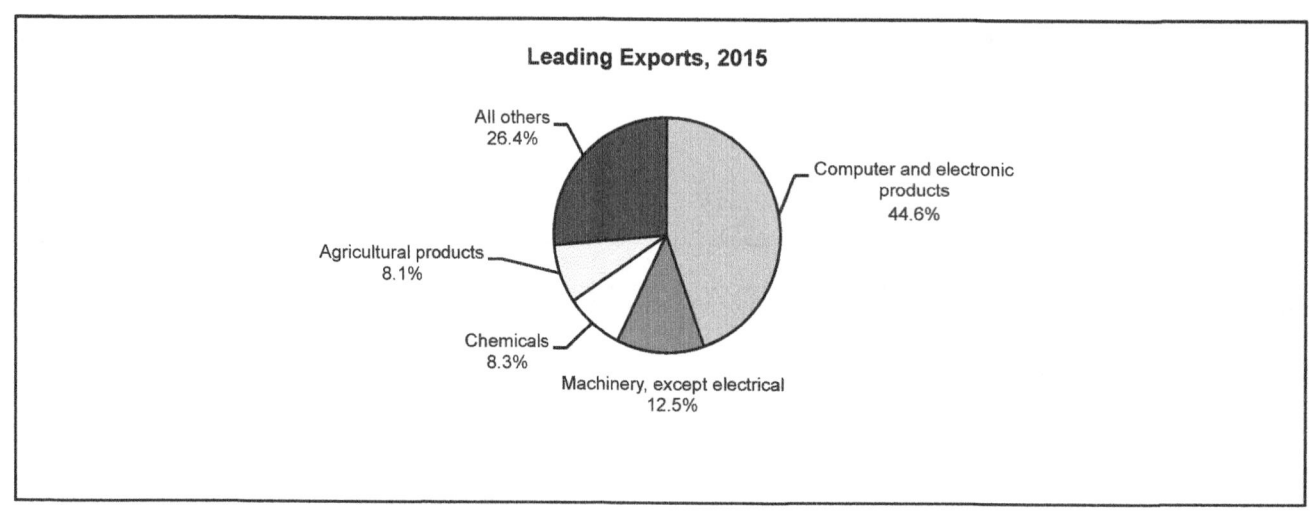

Leading Exports, 2015

All others 26.4%
Computer and electronic products 44.6%
Agricultural products 8.1%
Chemicals 8.3%
Machinery, except electrical 12.5%

PENNSYLVANIA

Facts and Figures

Location: Northeastern United States; bordered on the N by Lake Erie and New York, on the E by New York and New Jersey, on the S by Delaware, Maryland, and West Virginia, and on the W by West Virginia and Ohio

Area: 46,055 sq. mi. (119,283 sq. km.); rank—33rd

Population: 12,802,503 (2015 est.); rank—6th

Principal Cities: capital—Harrisburg; largest—Philadelphia

Statehood: December 12, 1787; 2nd state

U.S. Congress: 2 senators, 18 representatives

State Motto: Virtue, Liberty, and Independence

State Song: "Pennsylvania"

State Nicknames: The Keystone State; The Quaker State

Abbreviations: PA; Penn.

State Symbols: flower—mountain laurel; tree—Eastern hemlock; bird—ruffed grouse

At a Glance

- With an increase in population of 0.7 percent, Pennsylvania ranked 42nd among the states in growth from 2010 to 2015.

- Pennsylvania's median household income in 2014 was $53,234, and 13.6 percent of the population lived below the poverty level.

- Approximately 8.5 percent of Pennsylvanians did not have health insurance in 2014, compared to the national rate of 11.7 percent.

- Pennsylvania's violent crime rate in 2014 was 314.1 per 100,000 population, compared to 365.5 for the entire nation.

- The unemployment rate in Pennsylvania was 5.1 percent in 2015, compared to the national unemployment rate of 5.3 percent.

Table PA-1. Population by Age, Sex, Race, and Hispanic Origin

(Number, percent, except where noted.)

Sex, age, race, and Hispanic origin	2000	2010	2015[1]	Average annual percent change, 2010–2015
Total Population.....................	12,281,054	12,702,379	12,802,503	0.1
Percent of total U.S. population	4.4	4.1	4.0	X
Sex				
Male......................	5,929,663	6,190,363	6,264,374	0.1
Female......................	6,351,391	6,512,016	6,538,129	-
Age				
Under 5 years......................	727,804	729,538	714,919	-0.1
5 to 19 years......................	2,542,780	2,449,852	2,326,413	-0.4
20 to 64 years......................	7,091,305	7,563,682	7,581,383	-
65 years and over	1,919,165	1,959,307	2,179,788	0.8
Median age (years)	38.0	40.1	40.7	0.1
Race and Hispanic Origin				
One race				
White	10,484,203	10,663,774	10,573,536	-0.1
Black......................	1,224,612	1,431,826	1,497,476	0.3
American Indian and Alaska Native	18,348	39,735	45,343	0.9
Asian......................	219,813	358,195	435,121	1.4
Native Hawaiian or Other Pacific Islander	3,417	7,115	8,799	1.5
Two or more races	142,224	201,734	242,228	1.3
Hispanic (of any race)......................	394,088	758,058	872,386	1.0

X = Not applicable.
[1]Population figures for 2015 are July 1 estimates. The 2010 estimates are taken from the 2010 Census.
- = Zero or rounds to zero.

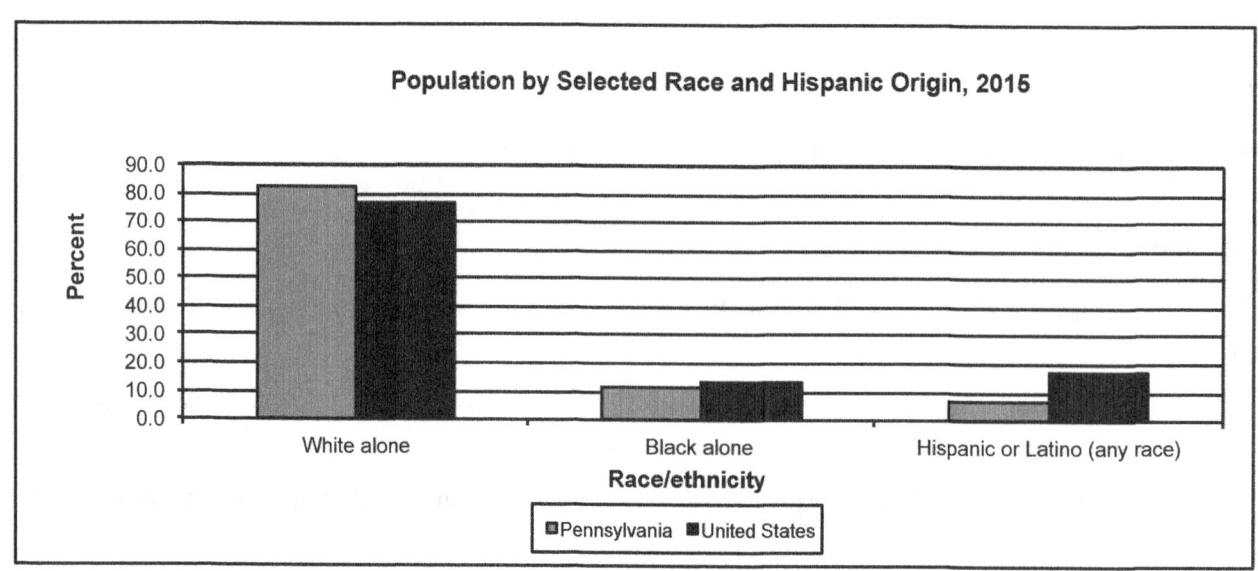

Population by Selected Race and Hispanic Origin, 2015

Table PA-2. Marital Status

(Number, percent distribution.)

Sex, age, race, and Hispanic origin	2000	2010	2014
Males, 15 Years and Over	4,686,277	5,031,761	5,082,468
Never married	30.1	35.9	36.1
Now married, except separated......................	57.4	50.6	50.4
Separated......................	1.9	2.0	2.0
Widowed......................	3.3	3.1	3.1
Divorced......................	7.3	8.5	8.4
Females, 15 Years and Over	5,175,436	5,406,494	5,430,136
Never married	24.6	29.8	30.2
Now married, except separated......................	51.5	46.2	46.3
Separated......................	2.4	2.7	2.4
Widowed......................	12.7	11.2	10.8
Divorced......................	8.8	10.2	10.4

Table PA-3. Households and Housing Characteristics

(Number, percent, dollars.)

Item	2000	2010	2014	Average annual percent change, 2000–2014
Total Households...	4,777,003	4,936,030	4,945,972	0.3
Family households	3,208,388	3,197,710	3,185,054	-0.1
Married-couple family	2,467,673	2,381,094	2,364,442	-0.3
Other family	740,715	816,616	820,612	0.8
Male householder, no wife present.......................	186,022	215,082	224,880	1.5
Female householder, no husband present	554,693	601,534	595,732	0.5
Nonfamily households	1,568,615	1,738,320	1,760,918	0.9
Householder living alone.....................................	1,320,941	1,458,055	1,463,776	0.8
Householder not living alone...............................	247,674	280,265	297,142	1.4
Housing Characteristics				
Total housing units...	5,249,750	5,568,820	5,590,712	0.5
Occupied housing units	4,777,003	4,936,030	4,945,972	0.3
Owner occupied	3,406,337	3,461,678	3,404,164	-
Renter occupied	1,370,666	1,474,352	1,541,808	0.9
Average household size..	2.48	2.49	2.50	0.1
Financial Characteristics				
Median gross rent of renter-occupied housing	531	763	848	4.3
Median monthly owner costs for housing units with a mortgage	1,010	1,390	1,400	2.8
Median value of owner-occupied housing units	97,000	165,500	165,400	5.0

- = Zero or rounds to zero.

Table PA-4. Migration, Origin, and Language

(Number, percent.)

Characteristic	State			U.S.		
	2013	2014	Percent change	2013	2014	Percent change
Residence 1 Year Ago						
Population 1 year and over	12,639,493	12,645,888	0.1	312,432,820	315,095,393	0.9
Same house	87.9	87.8	X	85.0	85.1	X
Different house in the U.S.	11.6	11.7	X	14.4	14.3	X
Same county	7.2	7.2	X	8.9	8.7	X
Different county	4.3	4.5	X	5.5	5.6	X
Same state	2.6	2.6	X	3.2	3.3	X
Different state	1.8	1.8	X	2.3	2.3	X
Abroad	0.5	0.5	X	0.6	0.6	X
Place of Birth						
Native born	11,977,642	11,965,509	-0.1	274,780,773	276,465,262	0.6
Male...	48.9	48.9	X	49.3	49.3	X
Female..	51.1	51.1	X	50.7	50.7	X
Foreign born	796,159	821,700	3.2	41,348,066	42,391,794	2.5
Male...	48.8	48.9	X	48.8	48.7	X
Female..	51.2	51.1	X	51.2	51.3	X
Foreign born; naturalized U.S. citizen....................	410,524	419,991	2.3	19,294,710	19,984,738	3.6
Male...	46.9	45.4	X	45.9	45.9	X
Female..	53.1	54.6	X	54.1	54.1	X
Foreign born; not a U.S. citizen	385,635	401,709	4.2	22,053,356	22,407,056	1.6
Male...	50.7	52.5	X	51.3	51.2	X
Female..	49.3	47.5	X	48.7	48.8	X
Entered 2010 or later	14.1	17.5	X	9.7	12.3	X
Entered 2000 to 2009	31.4	31.5	X	29.4	28.6	X
Entered before 2000...	54.5	51.0	X	61.0	59.1	X
World Region of Birth, Foreign						
Foreign-born population, excluding population born at sea	796,159	821,700	3.2	41,347,945	42,390,705	2.5
Europe	21.2	20.0	X	11.6	11.2	X
Asia..	39.1	39.2	X	29.5	30.1	X
Africa	8.2	7.2	X	4.4	4.6	X
Oceania..	0.4	0.5	X	0.5	0.6	X
Latin America	29.2	31.3	X	51.9	51.6	X
North America	1.9	1.8	X	2.0	1.9	X
Language Spoken at Home and Ability to Speak English						
Population 5 years and over..................................	12,059,233	12,075,749	0.1	296,358,760	299,084,046	0.9
English only	89.4	89.2	X	79.2	78.9	X
Language other than English................................	10.6	10.8	X	20.8	21.1	X
Speaks English less than "very well"...................	4.1	4.2	X	8.5	8.6	X

X = Not applicable.
- = Zero or rounds to zero.

Table PA-5. Median Income and Poverty Status, 2014

(Number, percent, except as noted.)

Characteristic	State		U.S.	
	Number	Percent	Number	Percent
Median Income				
Households (dollars)	53,234	X	53,657	X
Families (dollars)	67,876	X	65,910	X
Below Poverty Level (All People)	1,682,212	13.6	48,208,387	15.5
Sex				
Male	746,833	12.4	21,590,918	14.2
Female	935,379	14.7	26,617,469	16.8
Age				
Under 18 years	514,292	19.4	15,686,012	21.7
Related children under 18 years	501,858	19.0	15,372,705	21.3
18 to 64 years	1,002,146	13.1	28,267,482	14.6
65 years and over	165,774	8.1	4,254,893	9.5

X = Not applicable.

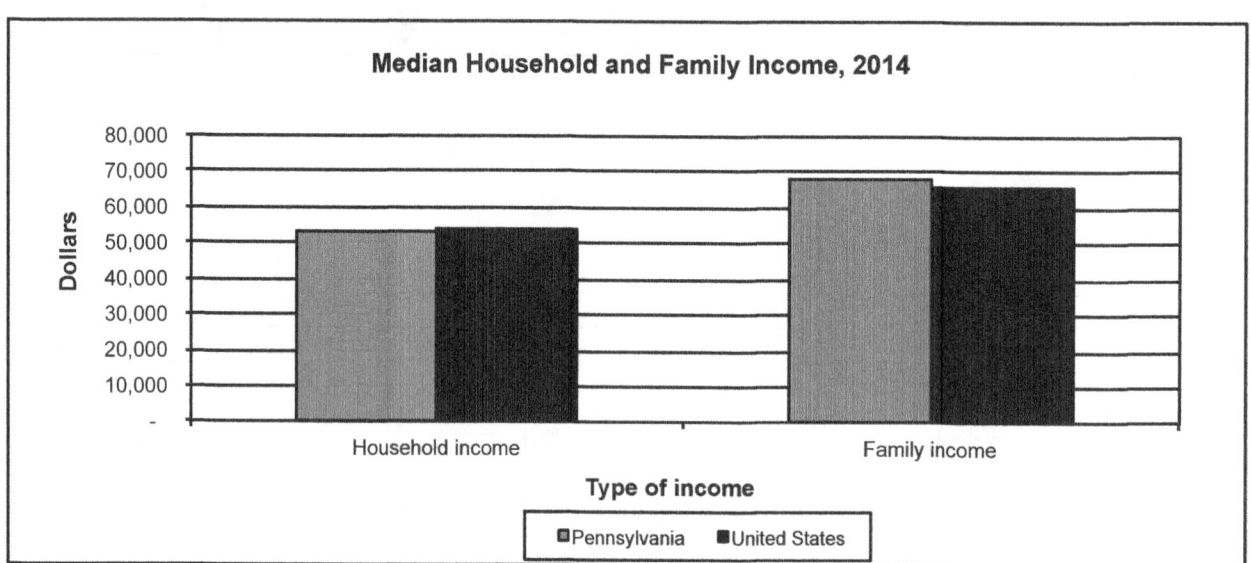

Table PA-6. Health Insurance Coverage Status for the Civilian Noninstitutionalized Population and Children Under 18 Years of Age

(Numbers in thousands, percent.)

Item	2006	2007	2008	2009	2010	2011	2012	2013	2014
Civilian Noninstitutionalized Population	12,345	12,313	12,209	12,366	12,506	12,540	12,559	12,569	12,583
Covered by Private or Public Insurance									
Number	11,108	11,138	11,058	11,146	11,235	11,275	11,335	11,347	11,518
Percent	90.0	90.5	90.6	90.1	89.8	89.9	90.2	90.3	91.5
Not Covered									
Number	1,237	1,176	1,151	1,220	1,271	1,265	1,224	1,222	1,065
Percent	10.0	9.5	9.4	9.9	10.2	10.1	9.8	9.7	8.5
Percent in the U.S. not covered	15.8	15.3	15.1	15.1	15.5	15.1	14.8	14.5	11.7
Children Under 18 Years of Age	2,778	2,775	2,757	2,766	2,778	2,755	2,731	2,709	2,693
Covered by Private or Public Insurance									
Number	2,575	2,568	2,588	2,619	2,634	2,606	2,592	2,562	2,554
Percent	92.7	92.6	93.9	94.7	94.8	94.6	94.9	94.6	94.8
Not Covered									
Number	203	207	169	147	144	149	139	147	139
Percent	7.3	7.4	6.1	5.3	5.2	5.4	5.1	5.4	5.2
Percent in the U.S. not covered	11.7	11.0	9.7	8.6	8.0	7.5	7.2	7.1	6.0

Table PA-7. Employment Status by Demographic Group, 2015

(Numbers in thousands, percent.)

Characteristic	Civilian noninstitutional population	Civilian labor force		Employed		Unemployed	
		Number	Percent of population	Number	Percent of population	Number	Percent of population
Total..	10,248	6,436	62.8	6,101	59.5	334	5.2
Sex							
Male..........................	4,931	3,370	68.4	3,187	64.6	184	5.4
Female........................	5,317	3,066	57.7	2,915	54.8	151	4.9
Race, Sex, and Hispanic Origin							
White........................	8,583	5,434	63.3	5,192	60.5	243	4.5
Male........................	4,169	2,887	69.2	2,749	65.9	138	4.8
Female......................	4,413	2,548	57.7	2,442	55.3	105	4.1
Black or African American............	1,087	654	60.2	585	53.9	69	10.5
Male........................	490	301	61.4	266	54.2	36	11.8
Female......................	597	353	59.1	320	53.6	33	9.4
Hispanic or Latino ethnicity[1]	636	419	65.9	387	60.8	32	7.7
Male........................	290	215	74.2	200	69.2	15	6.7
Female......................	346	204	59.0	186	53.8	18	8.8
Age							
16 to 19 years...............	650	256	39.4	230	35.3	27	10.4
20 to 24 years...............	917	679	74.1	611	66.6	68	10.0
25 to 34 years...............	1,583	1,295	81.8	1,217	76.9	78	6.0
35 to 44 years...............	1,437	1,216	84.6	1,157	80.5	59	4.9
45 to 54 years...............	1,723	1,402	81.4	1,359	78.9	43	3.0
55 to 64 years...............	1,807	1,188	65.7	1,146	63.4	42	3.5
65 years and over............	2,132	399	18.7	381	17.9	18	4.5

NOTE: Data in Table 7 are from the Current Population Survey (CPS) and do not match the estimates in Table 8. See notes and definitions for further information.
[1]May be of any race.

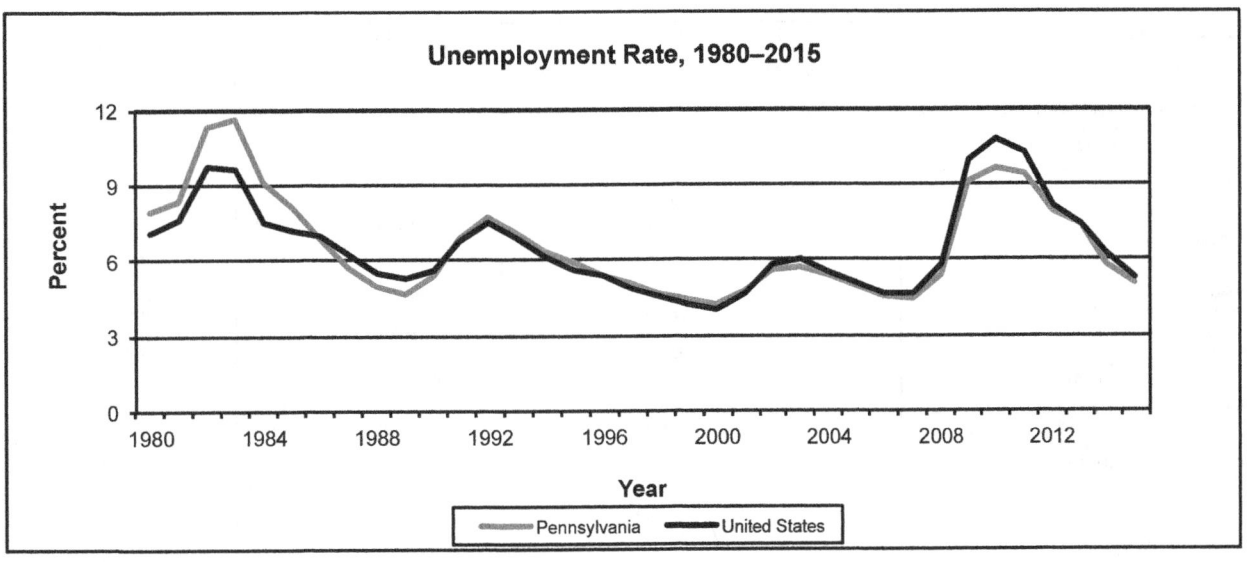

Table PA-8. Employment Status of the Civilian Noninstitutional Population Age 16 Years and Over

(Number, percent.)

Year	Civilian labor force	Civilian participation rate	Employed	Unemployed	Unemployment rate
2007....................	6,342,997	64.5	6,064,063	278,934	4.4
2008....................	6,451,535	65.2	6,109,645	341,890	5.3
2009....................	6,400,263	64.4	5,885,351	514,912	8.0
2010....................	6,380,949	63.5	5,840,887	540,062	8.5
2011....................	6,395,506	63.2	5,888,745	506,761	7.9
2012....................	6,463,922	63.6	5,957,326	506,596	7.8
2013....................	6,440,444	63.2	5,964,726	475,718	7.4
2014....................	6,391,421	62.6	6,015,668	375,753	5.9
2015....................	6,423,903	62.8	6,093,858	330,045	5.1

Table PA-9. Employment and Average Wages by Industry

(Estimates through 2010 are based on the 2007 North American Industry Classification System [NAICS]. Estimates from 2011 onward are based on the 2012 NAICS.)

Industry	2008	2009	2010	2011	2012	2013	2014
	Number of jobs						
Wage and Salary Employment by Industry..................	5,999,422	5,812,006	5,821,316	5,882,592	5,920,251	5,945,600	5,992,480
Farm Wage and Salary Employment.........................	17,328	16,794	18,821	18,245	23,646	22,621	21,070
Nonfarm Wage and Salary Employment.....................	5,982,094	5,795,212	5,802,495	5,864,347	5,896,605	5,922,979	5,971,410
Private wage and salary employment.........................	5,165,218	4,972,955	4,978,951	5,061,393	5,108,422	5,135,279	5,190,704
Forestry, fishing, and related activities.....................	7,711	7,699	8,047	8,442	8,452	7,816	8,078
Mining...	21,573	21,563	25,871	32,359	35,913	34,982	36,790
Utilities...	21,711	21,757	21,789	22,307	22,310	22,001	21,479
Construction	264,504	235,072	226,635	234,753	233,627	234,094	238,344
Manufacturing...	643,396	576,265	561,421	565,523	567,871	564,472	568,016
Durable goods manufacturing...........................	398,373	346,316	334,818	342,113	347,985	346,811	346,625
Nondurable goods manufacturing.......................	245,023	229,949	226,603	223,410	219,886	217,661	221,391
Wholesale trade	241,597	227,853	225,618	229,466	228,893	226,626	227,205
Retail trade..	657,690	635,555	636,332	639,415	640,009	639,012	639,016
Transportation and warehousing...........................	220,879	212,539	212,878	219,226	221,640	224,279	231,620
Information	106,479	99,971	93,374	91,157	90,700	88,662	85,282
Finance and insurance..	269,922	263,622	261,039	261,035	262,634	263,606	266,937
Real estate and rental and leasing.........................	67,550	63,329	61,569	60,481	59,956	60,706	62,309
Professional, scientific, and technical services	321,572	310,690	307,556	312,866	319,652	327,656	331,753
Management of companies and enterprises.................	113,669	113,124	117,387	123,164	129,633	133,428	132,865
Administrative and waste services..........................	282,632	256,985	272,269	286,829	288,284	294,869	300,786
Educational services	231,463	236,232	238,936	242,115	244,154	244,396	246,790
Health care and social assistance..........................	882,144	895,324	907,540	919,745	933,110	936,747	954,142
Arts, entertainment, and recreation.........................	88,252	88,277	90,597	94,463	94,667	93,933	92,923
Accommodation and food services.........................	421,383	411,940	416,964	422,777	432,461	442,794	448,778
Other services, except public administration...............	301,091	295,158	293,129	295,270	294,456	295,200	297,591
Government and government enterprises	816,876	822,257	823,544	802,954	788,183	787,700	780,706
	Dollars						
Average Wages and Salaries by Industry	43,502	43,920	44,805	46,100	47,334	48,035	49,477
Average Farm Wages and Salaries	32,047	30,538	26,133	24,434	21,132	29,743	29,001
Average Nonfarm Wages and Salaries	43,535	43,959	44,865	46,168	47,439	48,105	49,549
Average private wages and salaries........................	43,592	43,851	44,795	46,160	47,596	48,239	49,758
Forestry, fishing, and related activities.....................	23,902	24,674	25,283	25,795	26,597	28,500	29,193
Mining...	59,901	61,585	67,930	72,635	75,604	77,752	82,916
Utilities...	96,558	92,745	94,549	100,402	101,798	103,374	109,220
Construction	51,852	52,439	53,080	54,636	56,024	56,801	58,763
Manufacturing...	51,203	51,527	53,646	55,211	56,367	56,701	58,548
Durable goods manufacturing...........................	51,584	51,590	54,131	56,158	56,867	57,288	59,333
Nondurable goods manufacturing.......................	50,583	51,432	52,928	53,761	55,575	55,765	57,318
Wholesale trade	63,407	63,607	65,473	68,682	70,827	72,399	76,350
Retail trade..	24,438	24,676	25,028	25,347	25,693	25,806	26,258
Transportation and warehousing...........................	39,813	39,795	40,556	41,626	42,230	43,154	44,275
Information	59,566	60,666	63,432	65,779	67,445	68,999	70,651
Finance and insurance..	71,680	69,934	71,965	74,930	78,947	80,529	84,371
Real estate and rental and leasing.........................	44,949	44,338	46,437	48,655	51,160	51,170	54,120
Professional, scientific, and technical services	73,643	75,651	77,352	78,901	82,312	82,720	84,852
Management of companies and enterprises.................	98,287	98,095	101,145	106,922	114,405	114,849	120,750
Administrative and waste services.........................	30,914	31,024	31,168	31,316	31,981	32,316	32,932
Educational services	37,330	38,527	39,373	40,340	40,946	42,185	42,810
Health care and social assistance..........................	40,937	41,838	42,260	43,178	44,151	44,916	45,808
Arts, entertainment, and recreation.........................	28,790	29,414	30,550	32,233	32,254	32,416	33,359
Accommodation and food services.........................	16,388	16,260	16,773	17,292	17,646	17,891	18,601
Other services, except public administration...............	27,319	27,588	28,299	28,828	29,391	30,022	31,132
Government and government enterprises	43,178	44,610	45,288	46,218	46,423	47,233	48,159

Table PA-10. Employment Characteristics by Family Type

(Number, percent.)

Family type and labor force status	2012 Total	2012 Families with own children under 18 years	2013 Total	2013 Families with own children under 18 years	2014 Total	2014 Families with own children under 18 years
All Families....................	3,202,089	1,285,713	3,152,234	1,253,201	3,173,379	1,256,610
FAMILY TYPE AND LABOR FORCE STATUS						
Married-Couple Families.....................	2,386,165	864,021	2,354,778	845,149	2,352,767	841,562
Both husband and wife in labor force..........	54.1	70.2	53.1	69.3	53.0	70.0
Husband in labor force, wife not in labor force.........	20.1	24.7	20.0	24.9	19.8	24.7
Wife in labor force, husband not in labor force..........	7.8	3.5	8.3	3.7	8.4	3.8
Both husband and wife not in labor force........	18.0	1.6	18.3	1.8	18.9	1.5
Other Families	815,924	421,692	797,456	408,052	820,612	415,048
Female householder, no husband present...........	73.6	75.7	73.8	76.0	72.6	75.1
In labor force	49.8	59.9	51.2	62.6	49.2	59.6
Not in labor force	23.8	15.8	22.6	13.4	23.4	15.5
Male householder, no wife present...........	26.4	24.3	26.2	24.0	27.4	24.9
In labor force...........	19.7	21.3	19.6	21.3	20.5	22.2
Not in labor force	6.7	3.0	6.6	2.8	6.9	2.7

Table PA-11. School Enrollment and Educational Attainment, 2014

(Number, percent.)

Item	State	U.S.
Enrollment		
Total population 3 years and over, enrolled in school............	3,011,245	82,063,714
Enrolled in nursery school or preschool (percent)...........	5.8	6.0
Enrolled in kindergarten (percent)..........	4.7	5.1
Enrolled in elementary school, grades 1-8 (percent)...........	40.3	40.2
Enrolled in high school, grades 9-12 (percent)...........	20.9	20.7
Enrolled in college or graduate school (percent)...........	28.3	28.0
Attainment		
Total population 25 years and over	8,858,865	213,725,624
Less than ninth grade (percent)	3.5	5.6
9th to 12th grade, no diploma (percent)	7.1	7.5
High school graduate, including equivalency (percent)...........	36.4	27.7
Some college, no degree (percent)	16.2	21.0
Associate's degree (percent)...........	7.9	8.2
Bachelor's degree (percent)...........	17.5	18.7
Graduate or professional degree (percent)...........	11.4	11.4
High school graduate or higher (percent)	89.4	86.9
Bachelor's degree or higher (percent)	29.0	30.1

Table PA-12. Public School Characteristics and Educational Indicators

(Number, percent; data derived from National Center of Education Statistics.)

Item	State	U.S.
Public Schools, 2013–2014 (except where noted)		
Number of school districts...........	789	18,194
Number of schools...........	3,068	98,271
Number of students (in thousands)	1,755	50,045
Number of teachers (in thousands)	121	3,114
Student-teacher ratio	14.5	16.1
Expenditures per student (dollars), FY 2013	13,445	107,637
Four-year adjusted cohort graduation rate (ACGR)[1,2]...........	85.3	82.3
Students eligible for free or reduced-price lunch (in thousands)	753	25,596
English language learners (in thousands)	45	4,461
Students age 3 to 21 served under IDEA, part B (in thousands)	296	6,464

Public Schools by Type	Number	Percent of state public schools
Total number of schools...........	3,068	100.0
Regular...........	2,968	96.7
Special education...........	5	0.2
Vocational education...........	85	2.8
Alternative education...........	10	0.3

NOTE: Every school is assigned only one school type based on its instructional emphasis.

[1] ACGR data represents a new method of calculating high-school completion rates and may not be comparable to previous years' data for Averaged Freshmen Graduation Rates (AFGR).

[2] The United States 4-year ACGRs were estimated using both the reported 4-year ACGR data from 49 states and the District of Columbia and using imputed data for Idaho. The estimate for American Indian/Alaska Native students also includes imputed data for Virginia.

Table PA-13. Reported Voting and Registration of the Voting-Age Population, November 2014

(Numbers in thousands, percent.)

Item	Total population	Total citizen population	Registered			Voted		
			Total registered	Percent registered (total population)	Percent registered (total citizen population)	Total voted	Percent voted (total population)	Percent voted (total citizen population)
U.S. Total	239,874	219,941	142,166	59.3	64.6	92,251	38.5	41.9
State Total.............................	9,924	9,511	6,121	61.7	64.4	3,803	38.3	40.0
Sex								
Male...	4,779	4,571	2,845	59.5	62.2	1,768	37.0	38.7
Female.....................................	5,145	4,940	3,276	63.7	66.3	2,035	39.6	41.2
Race								
White alone.................................	8,451	8,291	5,452	64.5	65.8	3,375	39.9	40.7
White, non-Hispanic alone	8,015	7,934	5,252	65.5	66.2	3,272	40.8	41.2
Black alone.................................	1,001	920	492	49.2	53.5	341	34.1	37.1
Asian alone	295	165	93	31.7	56.6	46	15.6	27.9
Hispanic (of any race).....................	689	540	260	37.7	48.1	119	17.3	22.1
White alone or in combination	8,600	8,398	5,519	64.2	65.7	3,416	39.7	40.7
Black alone or in combination..........	1,076	984	513	47.6	52.1	341	31.7	34.7
Asian alone or in combination..........	322	192	121	37.4	62.8	73	22.7	38.1
Age								
18 to 24 years.............................	1,119	1,062	404	36.1	38.0	116	10.4	10.9
25 to 34 years.............................	1,667	1,511	852	51.1	56.4	424	25.4	28.0
35 to 44 years.............................	1,484	1,385	972	65.5	70.1	509	34.3	36.8
45 to 64 years.............................	3,607	3,525	2,398	66.5	68.0	1,633	45.3	46.3
65 years and over	2,047	2,027	1,496	73.1	73.8	1,121	54.8	55.3

Table PA-14. Crime

(Number, rate per 100,000. Data are derived from the FBI Uniform Crime Reports.)

Item	State			U.S.[1,2,3,4]		
	2013	2014	Percent change	2013	2014	Percent change
TOTAL POPULATION[5]	12,773,801	12,787,209	0.1	316,128,839	318,857,056	0.9
VIOLENT CRIME						
Number...	41,713	40,164	-3.7	1,163,146	1,165,383	0.2
Rate	326.6	314.1	-3.8	367.9	365.5	-0.7
Murder and Nonnegligent Manslaughter						
Number...	594	614	3.4	14,196	14,249	0.4
Rate	4.7	4.8	2.1	4.5	4.5	-
Rape[6]						
Number...	3,774	3,827	X	108,612	116,645	X
Rate	29.5	29.9	X	34.4	36.6	X
Robbery						
Number...	14,762	13,534	-8.3	345,031	325,802	-5.6
Rate	115.6	105.8	-8.5	109.1	102.2	-6.3
Aggravated Assault						
Number...	23,719	22,189	-6.5	724,149	741,291	2.4
Rate	185.7	173.5	-6.6	229.1	232.5	1.5
PROPERTY CRIME						
Number...	263,240	247,016	-6.2	8,632,512	8,277,829	-4.1
Rate	2,060.8	1,931.7	-6.3	2,730.7	2,596.1	-4.9
Burglary						
Number...	52,034	45,720	-12.1	1,928,465	1,729,806	-10.3
Rate	407.3	357.5	-12.2	610.0	542.5	-11.1
Larceny-Theft						
Number...	197,436	188,256	-4.6	6,004,453	5,858,496	-2.4
Rate	1,545.6	1,472.2	-4.7	1,899.4	1,837.3	-3.3
Motor Vehicle Theft						
Number...	13,770	13,040	-5.3	699,594	689,527	-1.4
Rate	107.8	102.0	-5.4	221.3	216.2	-2.3

NOTE: Although arson data are included in the trend and clearance tables, sufficient data are not available to estimate totals for this offense. Therefore, no arson data are published in this table.
X = Not applicable.
- = Zero or rounds to zero.
[1]The crime figures have been adjusted.
[2]The data collection methodology for the offense of forcible rape used by the Minnesota state Uniform Crime Reporting (UCR) Program (with the exception of Minneapolis and St. Paul, Minnesota) does not comply with national UCR Program guidelines. Consequently, its figures for forcible rape and violent crime (of which forcible rape is a part) are not published in this table.
[3]Includes offenses reported by the Zoological Police and the Metro Transit Police.
[4]Because of changes in the state's reporting practices, figures are not comparable to previous years' data.
[5]Populations are U.S. Census Bureau provisional estimates as of July 1 of each year.
[6]The figures shown for the offense of rape were estimated using the revised Uniform Crime Reporting (UCR) definition of rape.

Table PA-15. State Government Finances, 2014

(Dollar amounts in thousands, percent distribution.)

Item	Dollars	Percent distribution
Total Revenue	89,537,550	100.0
General revenue	70,354,934	78.6
Intergovernmental revenue	21,868,995	24.4
Taxes	34,192,869	38.2
General sales	9,497,906	10.6
Selective sales	7,921,523	8.8
License taxes	2,302,934	2.6
Individual income tax	10,809,736	12.1
Corporate income tax	2,301,589	2.6
Other taxes	1,359,181	1.5
Current charges	9,891,633	11.0
Miscellaneous general revenue	4,401,437	4.9
Utility revenue	0	-
Liquor stores revenue	1,786,501	2.0
Insurance trust revenue[1]	17,396,115	19.4
Total Expenditure	86,985,760	100.0
Intergovernmental expenditure	18,835,531	21.7
Direct expenditure	68,150,229	78.3
Current operation	46,464,080	53.4
Capital outlay	5,639,107	6.5
Insurance benefits and repayments	12,463,559	14.3
Assistance and subsidies	2,123,046	2.4
Interest on debt	1,460,437	1.7
Exhibit: Salaries and wages	8,402,893	9.7
Total Expenditure	86,985,760	100.0
General expenditure	72,881,492	83.8
Intergovernmental expenditure	18,835,531	21.7
Direct expenditure	54,045,961	62.1
General expenditure, by function:		
Education	22,857,967	26.3
Public welfare	24,369,130	28.0
Hospitals	4,040,856	4.6
Health	2,951,617	3.4
Highways	6,866,562	7.9
Police protection	934,579	1.1
Correction	1,956,876	2.2
Natural resources	633,077	0.7
Parks and recreation	257,919	0.3
Governmental administration	2,954,271	3.4
Interest on general debt	1,460,437	1.7
Other and unallocable	3,598,201	4.1
Utility expenditure	2168	-
Liquor stores expenditure	1,638,541	1.9
Insurance trust expenditure	12,463,559	14.3
Debt at End of Fiscal Year	47,572,612	X
Cash and Security Holdings	133,011,194	X

X = Not applicable.
- = Zero or rounds to zero.
[1]Within insurance trust revenue, net earnings of state retirement systems is a calculated statistic (the item code in the data file is X08), and thus can be positive or negative. Net earnings is the sum of earnings on investments plus gains on investments minus losses on investments. The change made in 2002 for asset valuation from book to market value in accordance with Statement 34 of the Governmental Accounting Standards Board is reflected in the calculated statistics.

Table PA-16. State Government Tax Collections, 2014

(Dollars in thousands, percent.)

Item	Dollars	Percent distribution
Total Taxes	34,192,869	100.0
Property taxes..	45,017	0.1
Sales and gross receipts	17,419,429	50.9
General sales and gross receipts	9,497,906	27.8
Selective sales and gross receipts	7,921,523	23.2
Alcoholic beverages	346,008	1.0
Amusements...	1,400,232	4.1
Insurance premiums......................................	773,462	2.3
Motor fuels	2,231,348	6.5
Pari-mutuels	11,758	-
Public utilities	1,284,892	3.8
Tobacco products..	1,028,006	3.0
Other selective sales	845,817	2.5
Licenses..	2,302,934	6.7
Alcoholic beverages	16,952	-
Amusements...	12,157	-
Corporations in general................................	229,686	0.7
Hunting and fishing......................................	74,679	0.2
Motor vehicle	837,823	2.5
Motor vehicle operators	54,847	0.2
Public utilities	75,269	0.2
Occupation and business, NEC	981,965	2.9
Other licenses	19,556	0.1
Income taxes...	13,111,325	38.3
Individual income...	10,809,736	31.6
Corporation net income	2,301,589	6.7
Other taxes...	1,314,164	3.8
Death and gift...	849,194	2.5
Documentary and stock transfer	438,984	1.3
Severance	X	X
Taxes, NEC	25,986	0.1

X = Not applicable.
- = Zero or rounds to zero.

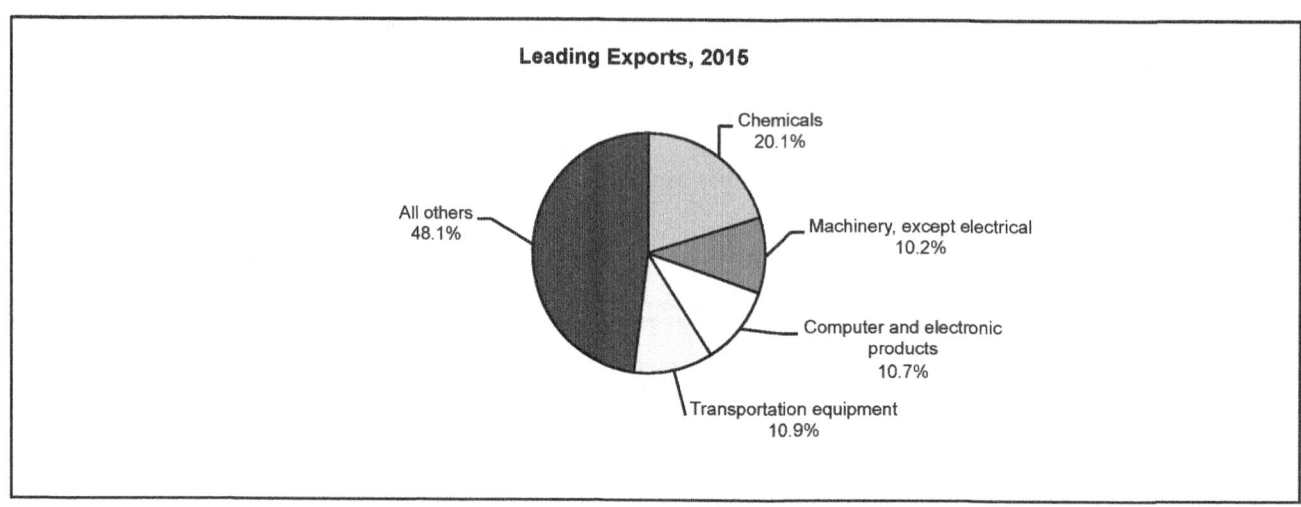

Leading Exports, 2015

Chemicals 20.1%
Machinery, except electrical 10.2%
Computer and electronic products 10.7%
Transportation equipment 10.9%
All others 48.1%

RHODE ISLAND

Facts and Figures

Location: Eastern United States; bordered on the N by Massachusetts, on the E by Massachusetts and the Atlantic Ocean, on the S by Block Island Sound and the Atlantic Ocean, and on the W by Connecticut

Area: 1,545 sq. mi. (4,002 sq. km.); rank—50th

Population: 1,056,298 (2015 est.); rank—43rd

Principal Cities: capital—Providence; largest—Providence

Statehood: May 29, 1790; 13th state

U.S. Congress: 2 senators, 2 representatives

State Motto: Hope

State Song: "Rhode Island"

State Nickname: The Ocean State

Abbreviations: RI; R.I.

State Symbols: flower—violet; tree—red maple; bird—Rhode Island red

At a Glance

- With an increase in population of 0.3 percent, Rhode Island ranked 46th among the states in growth from 2010 to 2015.

- In 2014, 7.4 percent of Rhode Islanders did not have health insurance, compared to 11.7 percent of the total U.S. population.

- Rhode Island's violent crime rate in 2014 was 219.2 per 100,000 population, compared to 365.5 for the entire nation.

- The state's median income in 2014 was $54,891, and 14.3 percent of its residents lived below the poverty level.

- In 2015, 20.0 percent of Rhode Island's population was under 18 years old, and 16.1 percent of its population was 65 years or older, compared to the national averages of 22.9 percent and 14.9 percent respectively.

Table RI-1. Population by Age, Sex, Race, and Hispanic Origin

(Number, percent, except where noted.)

Sex, age, race, and Hispanic origin	2000	2010	2015[1]	Average annual percent change, 2010–2015
Total Population	1,048,319	1,052,567	1,056,298	-
Percent of total U.S. population	0.4	0.3	0.3	X
Sex				
Male	503,635	508,400	511,949	-
Female	544,684	544,167	544,349	-
Age				
Under 5 years	63,896	57,448	55,128	-0.3
5 to 19 years	218,720	204,310	191,061	-0.5
20 to 64 years	613,301	638,928	640,133	-
65 years and over	152,402	151,881	169,976	0.8
Median age (years)	36.7	39.4	39.9	0.1
Race and Hispanic Origin				
One race				
White	891,191	910,253	895,343	-0.1
Black	46,908	75,073	83,101	0.7
American Indian and Alaska Native	5,121	9,173	10,192	0.8
Asian	23,665	31,768	37,871	1.3
Native Hawaiian or Other Pacific Islander	567	1,602	1,882	1.2
Two or more races	28,251	24,698	27,909	0.9
Hispanic (of any race)	90,820	137,169	152,084	0.7

X = Not applicable.
- = Zero or rounds to zero.
[1]Population figures for 2015 are July 1 estimates. The 2010 estimates are taken from the 2010 Census.

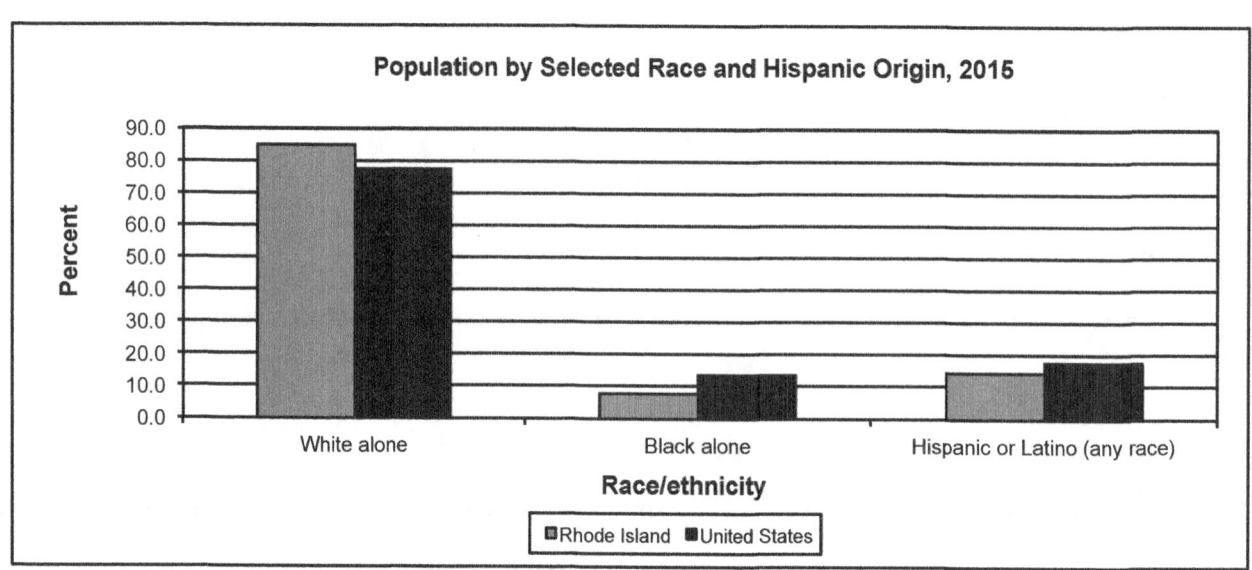

Table RI-2. Marital Status

(Number, percent distribution.)

Sex, age, race, and Hispanic origin	2000	2010	2014
Males, 15 Years and Over	396,396	414,628	418,818
Never married	32.5	39.8	39.2
Now married, except separated	54.9	45.2	47.1
Separated	1.5	1.6	1.5
Widowed	3.0	3.1	2.7
Divorced	8.0	10.3	9.5
Females, 15 Years and Over	445,107	456,425	457,008
Never married	27.1	32.4	32.7
Now married, except separated	48.5	41.8	42.2
Separated	2.3	2.4	2.2
Widowed	11.5	10.4	10.1
Divorced	10.7	13.0	12.8

Table RI-3. Households and Housing Characteristics

(Number, percent, dollars.)

Item	2000	2010	2014	Average annual percent change, 2000–2014
Total Households..	408,424	402,295	409,654	-
Family households	265,398	246,028	257,165	-0.2
Married-couple family	196,757	173,848	179,215	-0.6
Other family	68,641	72,180	77,950	1.0
Male householder, no wife present........................	16,032	17,525	20,253	1.9
Female householder, no husband present..............	52,609	54,655	57,697	0.7
Nonfamily households	143,026	156,267	152,489	0.5
Householder living alone.......................................	116,678	125,371	121,626	0.3
Householder not living alone.................................	26,348	30,896	30,863	1.2
Housing Characteristics				
Total housing units..	439,837	463,416	462,630	0.4
Occupied housing units	408,424	402,295	409,654	-
Owner occupied	245,156	244,516	240,878	-0.1
Renter occupied	163,268	157,779	168,776	0.2
Average household size...	2.47	2.51	2.47	-
Financial Characteristics				
Median gross rent of renter-occupied housing	553	868	934	4.9
Median monthly owner costs for housing units with a mortgage	1,205	1,837	1,745	3.2
Median value of owner-occupied housing units..........	133,000	254,500	236,000	5.5

- = Zero or rounds to zero.

Table RI-4. Migration, Origin, and Language

(Number, percent.)

Characteristic	State			U.S.		
	2013	2014	Percent change	2013	2014	Percent change
Residence 1 Year Ago						
Population 1 year and over	1,040,986	1,045,791	0.5	312,432,820	315,095,393	0.9
Same house	86.9	86.7	X	85.0	85.1	X
Different house in the U.S.	12.3	12.6	X	14.4	14.3	X
Same county	7.3	8.0	X	8.9	8.7	X
Different county	5.0	4.6	X	5.5	5.6	X
Same state	1.7	1.5	X	3.2	3.3	X
Different state	3.3	3.1	X	2.3	2.3	X
Abroad	0.7	0.7	X	0.6	0.6	X
Place of Birth						
Native born	915,539	913,940	-0.2	274,780,773	276,465,262	0.6
Male...	48.9	48.4	X	49.3	49.3	X
Female...	51.1	51.6	X	50.7	50.7	X
Foreign born..	135,972	141,233	3.9	41,348,066	42,391,794	2.5
Male...	48.0	48.8	X	48.8	48.7	X
Female...	52.0	51.2	X	51.2	51.3	X
Foreign born; naturalized U.S. citizen.......................	69,709	72,884	4.6	19,294,710	19,984,738	3.6
Male...	45.6	46.8	X	45.9	45.9	X
Female...	54.4	53.2	X	54.1	54.1	X
Foreign born; not a U.S. citizen	66,263	68,349	3.1	22,053,356	22,407,056	1.6
Male...	50.5	51.0	X	51.3	51.2	X
Female...	49.5	49.0	X	48.7	48.8	X
Entered 2010 or later	10.2	14.1	X	9.7	12.3	X
Entered 2000 to 2009	26.3	24.3	X	29.4	28.6	X
Entered before 2000...	63.5	61.6	X	61.0	59.1	X
World Region of Birth, Foreign						
Foreign-born population, excluding population born at sea	135,972	141,233	3.9	41,347,945	42,390,705	2.5
Europe	21.3	21.9	X	11.6	11.2	X
Asia...	18.6	20.4	X	29.5	30.1	X
Africa...	12.5	11.7	X	4.4	4.6	X
Oceania...	0.3	0.1	X	0.5	0.6	X
Latin America..	45.6	44.5	X	51.9	51.6	X
North America..	1.6	1.2	X	2.0	1.9	X
Language Spoken at Home and Ability to Speak English						
Population 5 years and over.......................................	997,310	1,000,317	0.3	296,358,760	299,084,046	0.9
English only	78.7	79.0	X	79.2	78.9	X
Language other than English..................................	21.3	21.0	X	20.8	21.1	X
Speaks English less than "very well"...................	7.7	8.4	X	8.5	8.6	X

X = Not applicable.
- = Zero or rounds to zero.

Table RI-5. Median Income and Poverty Status, 2014

(Number, percent, except as noted.)

Characteristic	State		U.S.	
	Number	Percent	Number	Percent
Median Income				
Households (dollars)........................	54,891	X	53,657	X
Families (dollars)	71,212	X	65,910	X
Below Poverty Level (All People)	145,596	14.3	48,208,387	15.5
Sex				
Male..	61,980	12.6	21,590,918	14.2
Female	83,616	16.0	26,617,469	16.8
Age				
Under 18 years..............................	41,629	19.8	15,686,012	21.7
Related children under 18 years.............	40,822	19.5	15,372,705	21.3
18 to 64 years..............................	88,457	13.7	28,267,482	14.6
65 years and over...........................	15,510	9.7	4,254,893	9.5

X = Not applicable.

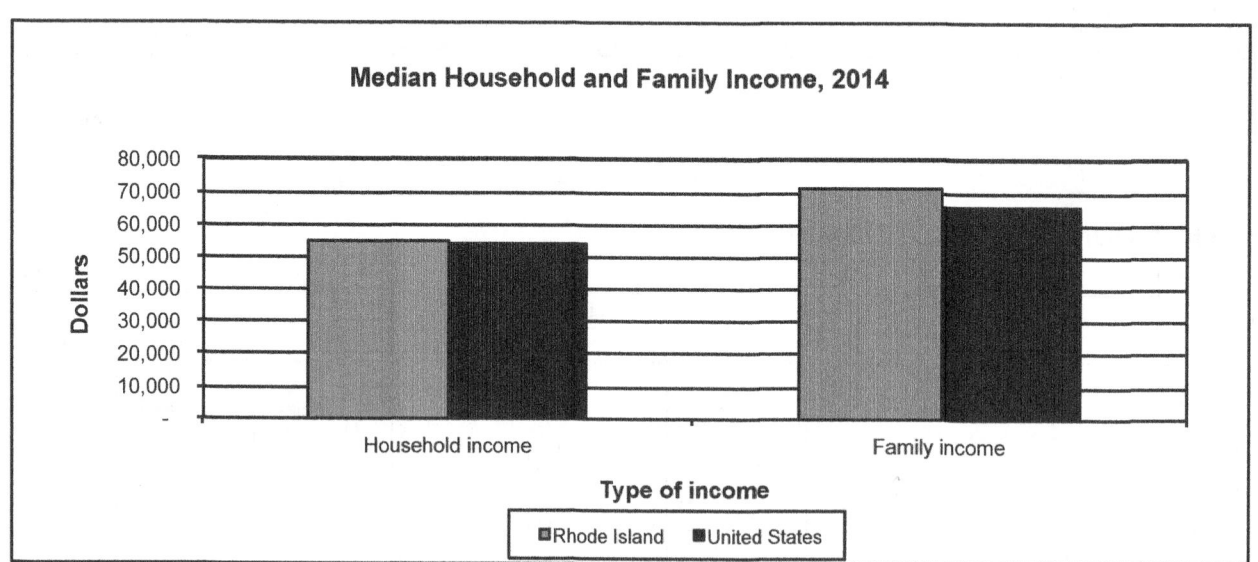

Table RI-6. Health Insurance Coverage Status for the Civilian Noninstitutionalized Population and Children Under 18 Years of Age

(Numbers in thousands, percent.)

Item	2006	2007	2008	2009	2010	2011	2012	2013	2014
Civilian Noninstitutionalized Population	1,054	1,044	1,030	1,035	1,037	1,035	1,035	1,036	1,040
Covered by Private or Public Insurance									
Number..........................	963	931	922	919	911	923	920	916	963
Percent..........................	91.4	89.2	89.5	88.7	87.8	89.2	88.9	88.4	92.6
Not Covered									
Number..........................	91	113	108	117	126	112	115	120	77
Percent..........................	8.6	10.8	10.5	11.3	12.2	10.8	11.1	11.6	7.4
Percent in the U.S. not covered..........................	15.8	15.3	15.1	15.1	15.5	15.1	14.8	14.5	11.7
Children Under 18 Years of Age	237	238	228	227	224	219	217	212	212
Covered by Private or Public Insurance									
Number..........................	227	217	215	215	212	211	207	201	205
Percent..........................	95.8	91.2	94.3	94.6	94.4	96.0	95.5	94.6	96.7
Not Covered									
Number..........................	10	21	13	12	12	8	10	12	7
Percent..........................	4.1	8.8	5.7	5.4	5.6	4.0	4.5	5.4	3.3
Percent in the U.S. not covered..........................	11.7	11.0	9.7	8.6	8.0	7.5	7.2	7.1	6.0

Table RI-7. Employment Status by Demographic Group, 2015

(Numbers in thousands, percent.)

Characteristic	Civilian noninstitutional population	Civilian labor force		Employed		Unemployed	
		Number	Percent of population	Number	Percent of population	Number	Percent of population
Total..	857	559	65.3	526	61.4	33	5.9
Sex							
Male..	409	285	69.7	265	64.9	20	6.9
Female.....................................	448	274	61.2	261	58.2	13	4.9
Race, Sex, and Hispanic Origin							
White.......................................	744	486	65.3	461	61.9	25	5.2
Male.....................................	357	250	70.0	235	65.8	15	6.0
Female..................................	386	236	61.1	226	58.4	10	4.3
Black or African American................	61	41	66.2	36	58.2	5	12.2
Male.....................................	30	19	65.2	16	55.6	3	14.6
Female..................................	32	21	67.1	19	60.5	2	9.9
Hispanic or Latino ethnicity[1]...........	104	74	71.0	67	64.5	7	9.1
Male.....................................	49	37	74.8	33	66.7	4	10.7
Female..................................	54	37	67.7	34	62.5	3	7.5
Age							
16 to 19 years............................	54	22	41.1	19	34.6	4	16.1
20 to 24 years............................	78	60	76.7	55	70.2	5	8.7
25 to 34 years............................	135	114	85.0	108	79.9	7	6.0
35 to 44 years............................	133	112	84.5	107	80.1	6	5.2
45 to 54 years............................	146	117	80.2	112	76.5	5	4.5
55 to 64 years............................	152	103	67.7	98	64.4	5	5.0
65 years and over.........................	160	31	19.4	30	18.7	1	3.9

NOTE: Data in Table 7 are from the Current Population Survey (CPS) and do not match the estimates in Table 8. See notes and definitions for further information.
[1]May be of any race.

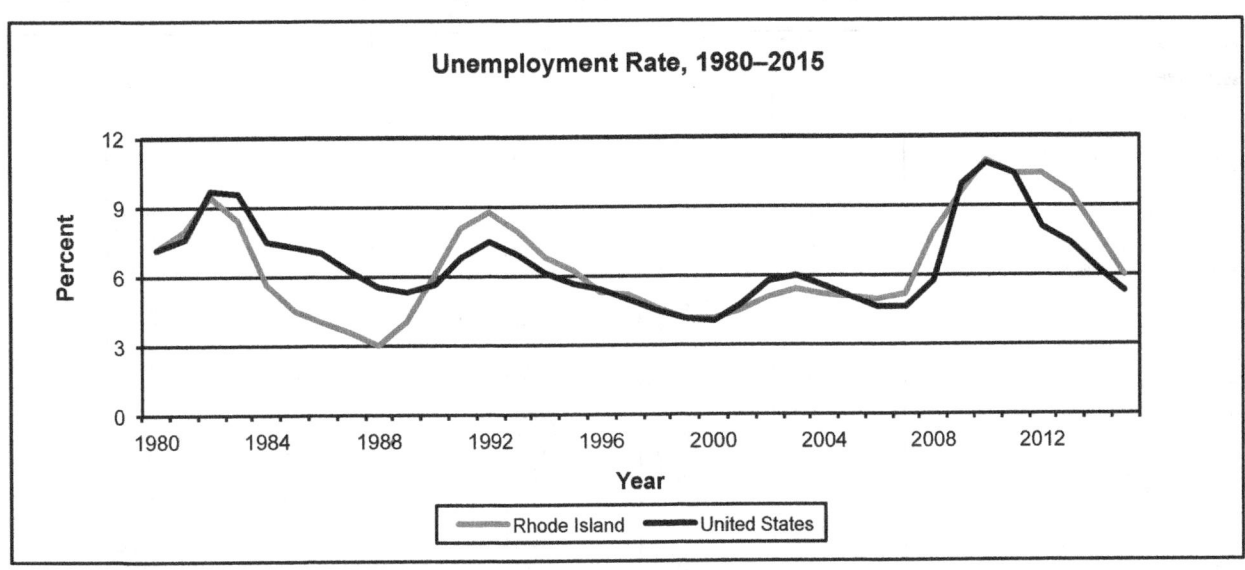

Unemployment Rate, 1980–2015

Table RI-8. Employment Status of the Civilian Noninstitutional Population Age 16 Years and Over

(Number, percent.)

Year	Civilian labor force	Civilian participation rate	Employed	Unemployed	Unemployment rate
2007..	573,173	68.4	543,401	29,772	5.2
2008..	570,328	68.0	525,941	44,387	7.8
2009..	567,280	67.4	504,951	62,329	11.0
2010..	566,704	67.3	503,216	63,488	11.2
2011..	560,056	66.4	498,248	61,808	11.0
2012..	558,392	66.0	500,316	58,076	10.4
2013..	557,256	65.7	505,686	51,570	9.3
2014..	555,955	65.3	513,217	42,738	7.7
2015..	554,558	64.9	521,434	33,124	6.0

Table RI-9. Employment and Average Wages by Industry

(Estimates through 2010 are based on the 2007 North American Industry Classification System [NAICS]. Estimates from 2011 onward are based on the 2012 NAICS.)

Industry	2008	2009	2010	2011	2012	2013	2014
	Number of jobs						
Wage and Salary Employment by Industry.................	499,308	477,886	476,805	478,046	478,698	485,026	491,884
Farm Wage and Salary Employment..........................	527	509	510	541	548	649	615
Nonfarm Wage and Salary Employment....................	498,781	477,377	476,295	477,505	478,150	484,377	491,269
Private wage and salary employment........................	424,126	403,989	403,247	405,394	406,575	412,600	419,466
Forestry, fishing, and related activities............	514	558	D	D	600	D	D
Mining..	246	194	D	D	188	D	D
Utilities..	1,111	1,119	1,130	1,077	1,056	1,059	1,057
Construction	21,182	17,990	16,719	16,523	16,548	16,705	17,010
Manufacturing...	48,034	41,841	40,431	40,416	39,701	40,121	40,925
Durable goods manufacturing....................	31,219	26,904	25,828	25,863	25,352	25,619	26,133
Nondurable goods manufacturing...............	16,815	14,937	14,603	14,553	14,349	14,502	14,792
Wholesale trade	16,957	16,226	15,935	16,278	16,896	16,767	16,918
Retail trade...	50,320	47,840	47,701	47,640	47,373	47,030	47,626
Transportation and warehousing.....................	9,883	9,186	9,247	9,693	9,815	9,761	9,983
Information	10,757	10,158	10,033	10,172	9,600	9,088	8,864
Finance and insurance	25,603	24,136	24,148	23,919	24,226	24,735	25,079
Real estate and rental and leasing.................	6,699	6,229	5,931	5,887	5,934	6,091	6,082
Professional, scientific, and technical services	21,967	21,470	21,248	21,287	21,677	22,213	23,044
Management of companies and enterprises..................	9,302	9,207	9,326	9,856	10,524	11,342	12,016
Administrative and waste services.................	24,211	22,483	23,554	23,702	24,351	25,608	26,321
Educational services	24,403	24,847	25,068	25,340	24,329	24,121	24,782
Health care and social assistance....................	78,004	78,388	79,691	79,534	79,742	81,394	81,434
Arts, entertainment, and recreation.................	8,166	7,768	7,679	7,703	7,739	8,525	8,943
Accommodation and food services..................	43,387	41,803	42,533	43,064	44,403	45,494	46,660
Other services, except public administration..............	23,380	22,546	22,127	22,554	21,873	21,801	21,923
Government and government enterprises.........................	74,655	73,388	73,048	72,111	71,575	71,777	71,803
	Dollars						
Average Wages and Salaries by Industry	43,525	43,930	45,275	46,375	47,510	48,305	49,866
Average Farm Wages and Salaries	28,825	28,354	26,727	22,543	24,943	28,696	31,237
Average Nonfarm Wages and Salaries	43,541	43,947	45,295	46,402	47,536	48,332	49,889
Average private wages and salaries...........................	42,069	42,271	43,650	44,760	46,018	46,946	48,618
Forestry, fishing, and related activities.........................	39,484	37,618	D	D	38,045	D	D
Mining..	48,297	48,582	D	D	51,580	D	D
Utilities..	81,681	85,218	86,633	93,909	86,992	96,837	97,592
Construction	51,431	53,037	52,520	53,841	54,691	55,247	56,021
Manufacturing...	47,975	48,872	50,989	52,722	53,956	55,263	56,544
Durable goods manufacturing....................	48,842	49,863	52,470	54,322	55,482	56,865	57,890
Nondurable goods manufacturing...............	46,365	47,087	48,371	49,877	51,261	52,434	54,165
Wholesale trade	61,469	61,378	64,751	65,451	67,262	69,237	70,265
Retail trade...	27,456	27,294	28,154	27,821	28,412	28,603	29,737
Transportation and warehousing.....................	37,934	38,992	39,861	40,949	41,488	41,893	42,925
Information	59,222	61,392	62,900	65,816	69,087	67,584	70,217
Finance and insurance	69,842	69,956	75,543	80,261	84,493	86,698	93,511
Real estate and rental and leasing.................	37,713	37,323	38,914	40,170	41,909	42,592	44,153
Professional, scientific, and technical services	63,007	63,211	65,446	66,555	67,827	69,273	72,166
Management of companies and enterprises..................	107,131	95,224	104,620	106,642	115,243	116,768	122,399
Administrative and waste services.................	30,903	31,200	31,606	32,403	33,564	34,493	35,300
Educational services	38,160	38,554	39,520	40,155	40,132	42,158	42,743
Health care and social assistance....................	40,384	41,708	42,311	43,169	43,679	44,120	45,042
Arts, entertainment, and recreation.................	26,444	26,487	27,149	28,115	28,769	29,196	31,111
Accommodation and food services..................	17,756	17,832	18,360	18,946	19,309	19,547	20,397
Other services, except public administration..................	27,915	28,124	28,941	29,190	29,713	30,680	31,907
Government and government enterprises.........................	51,902	53,171	54,370	55,634	56,158	56,294	57,314

D = Not shown to avoid disclosure of confidential information, but the estimates for this item are included in the total.

Table RI-10. Employment Characteristics by Family Type

(Number, percent.)

Family type and labor force status	2012		2013		2014	
	Total	Families with own children under 18 years	Total	Families with own children under 18 years	Total	Families with own children under 18 years
All Families...	257,419	106,858	259,863	108,073	256,077	108,359
FAMILY TYPE AND LABOR FORCE STATUS						
Married-Couple Families..............................	180,454	66,254	180,930	66,807	178,127	66,035
Both husband and wife in labor force............	58.5	77.1	56.3	71.6	56.9	74.2
Husband in labor force, wife not in labor force..	17.3	18.3	18.6	22.6	16.5	19.2
Wife in labor force, husband not in labor force..	8.0	3.8	8.8	4.4	9.0	4.7
Both husband and wife not in labor force........	16.2	0.9	15.5	0.9	17.6	1.8
Other Families	76,965	40,604	78,933	41,266	77,950	42,324
Female householder, no husband present..........	75.4	80.0	73.1	78.1	74.0	77.7
In labor force	55.0	65.9	52.7	61.9	52.9	64.8
Not in labor force	20.4	14.1	20.4	16.2	21.1	12.9
Male householder, no wife present..................	24.6	20.0	26.9	21.9	26.0	22.3
In labor force....................................	19.3	18.8	20.1	19.8	20.6	19.8
Not in labor force	5.3	1.3	6.8	2.1	5.3	2.5

Table RI-11. School Enrollment and Educational Attainment, 2014

(Number, percent.)

Item	State	U.S.
Enrollment		
Total population 3 years and over, enrolled in school...............	267,358	82,063,714
Enrolled in nursery school or preschool (percent)...................	5.7	6.0
Enrolled in kindergarten (percent)..................................	4.1	5.1
Enrolled in elementary school, grades 1-8 (percent).................	35.0	40.2
Enrolled in high school, grades 9-12 (percent)......................	20.0	20.7
Enrolled in college or graduate school (percent)....................	35.2	28.0
Attainment		
Total population 25 years and over	725,871	213,725,624
Less than ninth grade (percent)....................................	5.7	5.6
9th to 12th grade, no diploma (percent)	8.5	7.5
High school graduate, including equivalency (percent)...............	28.7	27.7
Some college, no degree (percent)	18.4	21.0
Associate's degree (percent)	8.2	8.2
Bachelor's degree (percent)	18.1	18.7
Graduate or professional degree (percent)..........................	12.3	11.4
High school graduate or higher (percent)	85.8	86.9
Bachelor's degree or higher (percent)..............................	30.4	30.1

Table RI-12. Public School Characteristics and Educational Indicators

(Number, percent; data derived from National Center of Education Statistics.)

Item	State	U.S.
Public Schools, 2013–2014 (except where noted)		
Number of school districts...	61	18,194
Number of schools...	304	98,271
Number of students (in thousands)	142	50,045
Number of teachers (in thousands)	10	3,114
Student-teacher ratio	14.5	16.1
Expenditures per student (dollars), FY 2013	14,889	107,637
Four-year adjusted cohort graduation rate (ACGR)[1,2]	80.8	82.3
Students eligible for free or reduced-price lunch (in thousands) ..	66	25,596
English language learners (in thousands)	9	4,461
Students age 3 to 21 served under IDEA, part B (in thousands)	23	6,464

Public Schools by Type	Number	Percent of state public schools
Total number of schools..	304	100.0
Regular..	286	94.1
Special education..	1	0.3
Vocational education...	12	3.9
Alternative education..	5	1.6

NOTE: Every school is assigned only one school type based on its instructional emphasis.

[1]ACGR data represents a new method of calculating high-school completion rates and may not be comparable to previous years' data for Averaged Freshmen Graduation Rates (AFGR).

[2]The United States 4-year ACGRs were estimated using both the reported 4-year ACGR data from 49 states and the District of Columbia and using imputed data for Idaho. The estimate for American Indian/Alaska Native students also includes imputed data for Virginia.

Table RI-13. Reported Voting and Registration of the Voting-Age Population, November 2014

(Numbers in thousands, percent.)

Item	Total population	Total citizen population	Registered			Voted		
			Total registered	Percent registered (total population)	Percent registered (total citizen population)	Total voted	Percent voted (total population)	Percent voted (total citizen population)
U.S. Total	239,874	219,941	142,166	59.3	64.6	92,251	38.5	41.9
State Total............................	819	765	486	59.4	63.6	331	40.4	43.3
Sex								
Male.........................	387	362	231	59.6	63.7	154	39.9	42.6
Female	432	403	255	59.2	63.4	177	41.0	43.9
Race								
White alone..................	717	680	451	62.9	66.3	311	43.4	45.7
White, non-Hispanic alone	659	647	434	65.8	67.0	302	45.8	46.6
Black alone.................	55	47	28	(B)	(B)	16	(B)	(B)
Asian alone	23	15	1	(B)	(B)	-	(B)	(B)
Hispanic (of any race).....................	75	45	22	(B)	(B)	13	(B)	(B)
White alone or in combination	736	697	455	61.9	65.3	313	42.6	44.9
Black alone or in combination..........	69	61	32	(B)	(B)	18	(B)	(B)
Asian alone or in combination..........	24	16	2	(B)	(B)	1	(B)	(B)
Age								
18 to 24 years.....................	108	103	44	41.1	43.3	14	13.0	13.7
25 to 34 years.....................	132	119	61	46.4	51.7	25	18.8	21.0
35 to 44 years.....................	122	109	67	54.9	61.8	45	37.1	41.7
45 to 64 years.....................	289	273	197	68.1	71.9	157	54.4	57.4
65 years and over	167	161	117	69.7	72.2	90	53.7	55.7

B = Base is less than 75,000 and therefore too small to show the derived measure.

Table RI-14. Crime

(Number, rate per 100,000. Data are derived from the FBI Uniform Crime Reports.)

Item	State			U.S.[1,2,3,4]		
	2013	2014	Percent change	2013	2014	Percent change
TOTAL POPULATION[5]........................	1,051,511	1,055,173	0.3	316,128,839	318,857,056	0.9
VIOLENT CRIME						
Number........................	2,572	2,313	-10.1	1,163,146	1,165,383	0.2
Rate	244.6	219.2	-10.4	367.9	365.5	-0.7
Murder and Nonnegligent Manslaughter						
Number........................	31	25	-19.4	14,196	14,249	0.4
Rate	2.9	2.4	-17.2	4.5	4.5	-
Rape[6]						
Number........................	440	361	X	108,612	116,645	X
Rate	41.8	34.2	X	34.4	36.6	X
Robbery						
Number........................	684	529	-22.7	345,031	325,802	-5.6
Rate	65.0	50.1	-22.9	109.1	102.2	-6.3
Aggravated Assault						
Number........................	1,550	1,398	-9.8	724,149	741,291	2.4
Rate	147.4	132.5	-10.1	229.1	232.5	1.5
PROPERTY CRIME						
Number........................	25,678	22,935	-10.7	8,632,512	8,277,829	-4.1
Rate	2,442.0	2,173.6	-11.0	2,730.7	2,596.1	-4.9
Burglary						
Number........................	5,607	4,823	-14.0	1,928,465	1,729,806	-10.3
Rate	533.2	457.1	-14.3	610.0	542.5	-11.1
Larceny-Theft						
Number........................	17,838	16,279	-8.7	6,004,453	5,858,496	-2.4
Rate	1,696.4	1,542.8	-9.1	1,899.4	1,837.3	-3.3
Motor Vehicle Theft						
Number........................	2,233	1,833	-17.9	699,594	689,527	-1.4
Rate	212.4	173.7	-18.2	221.3	216.2	-2.3

NOTE: Although arson data are included in the trend and clearance tables, sufficient data are not available to estimate totals for this offense. Therefore, no arson data are published in this table.
X = Not applicable.
- = Zero or rounds to zero.
[1]The crime figures have been adjusted.
[2]The data collection methodology for the offense of forcible rape used by the Minnesota state Uniform Crime Reporting (UCR) Program (with the exception of Minneapolis and St. Paul, Minnesota) does not comply with national UCR Program guidelines. Consequently, its figures for forcible rape and violent crime (of which forcible rape is a part) are not published in this table.
[3]Includes offenses reported by the Zoological Police and the Metro Transit Police.
[4]Because of changes in the state's reporting practices, figures are not comparable to previous years' data.
[5]Populations are U.S. Census Bureau provisional estimates as of July 1 of each year.
[6]The figures shown for the offense of rape were estimated using the revised Uniform Crime Reporting (UCR) definition of rape.

Table RI-15. State Government Finances, 2014

(Dollar amounts in thousands, percent distribution.)

Item	Dollars	Percent distribution
Total Revenue	8,995,804	100.0
General revenue	7,116,847	79.1
Intergovernmental revenue	2,509,818	27.9
Taxes	2,965,975	33.0
General sales	915,468	10.2
Selective sales	650,723	7.2
License taxes	132,146	1.5
Individual income tax	1,088,405	12.1
Corporate income tax	120,112	1.3
Other taxes	59,121	0.7
Current charges	761,531	8.5
Miscellaneous general revenue	879,523	9.8
Utility revenue	33,031	0.4
Liquor stores revenue	0	-
Insurance trust revenue[1]	1,845,926	20.5
Total Expenditure	8,334,471	100.0
Intergovernmental expenditure	1,198,256	14.4
Direct expenditure	7,136,215	85.6
Current operation	4,735,396	56.8
Capital outlay	419,572	5.0
Insurance benefits and repayments	1,338,318	16.1
Assistance and subsidies	158,901	1.9
Interest on debt	484,028	5.8
Exhibit: Salaries and wages	1,199,140	14.4
Total Expenditure	8,334,471	100.0
General expenditure	6,845,400	82.1
Intergovernmental expenditure	1,198,256	14.4
Direct expenditure	5,647,144	67.8
General expenditure, by function:		
Education	2,026,007	24.3
Public welfare	2,537,727	30.4
Hospitals	67,602	0.8
Health	165,805	2.0
Highways	339,002	4.1
Police protection	73,168	0.9
Correction	186,097	2.2
Natural resources	49,149	0.6
Parks and recreation	31,373	0.4
Governmental administration	363,957	4.4
Interest on general debt	484,028	5.8
Other and unallocable	521,485	6.3
Utility expenditure	150,753	1.8
Liquor stores expenditure	0	-
Insurance trust expenditure	1,338,318	16.1
Debt at End of Fiscal Year	9,388,127	X
Cash and Security Holdings	17,087,879	X

X = Not applicable.
- = Zero or rounds to zero.
[1]Within insurance trust revenue, net earnings of state retirement systems is a calculated statistic (the item code in the data file is X08), and thus can be positive or negative. Net earnings is the sum of earnings on investments plus gains on investments minus losses on investments. The change made in 2002 for asset valuation from book to market value in accordance with Statement 34 of the Governmental Accounting Standards Board is reflected in the calculated statistics.

Table RI-16. State Government Tax Collections, 2014

(Dollars in thousands, percent.)

Item	Dollars	Percent distribution
Total Taxes	2,965,975	100.0
Property taxes	2,591	0.1
Sales and gross receipts	1,566,191	52.8
General sales and gross receipts	915,468	30.9
Selective sales and gross receipts	650,723	21.9
Alcoholic beverages	16,803	0.6
Amusements	0	-
Insurance premiums	85,801	2.9
Motor fuels	95,828	3.2
Pari-mutuels	1,147	-
Public utilities	105,296	3.6
Tobacco products	134,805	4.5
Other selective sales	211,043	7.1
Licenses	132,146	4.5
Alcoholic beverages	174	-
Amusements	223	-
Corporations in general	4,875	0.2
Hunting and fishing	1,748	0.1
Motor vehicle	69,349	2.3
Motor vehicle operat ors	4,988	0.2
Public utilities	0	-
Occupation and business, NEC	46,827	1.6
Other licenses	3,962	0.1
Income taxes	1,208,517	40.7
Individual income	1,088,405	36.7
Corporation net income	120,112	4.0
Other taxes	56,530	1.9
Death and gift	38,899	1.3
Documentary and stock transfer	17,631	0.6
Severance	X	X
Taxes, NEC	0	-

X = Not applicable.
- = Zero or rounds to zero.

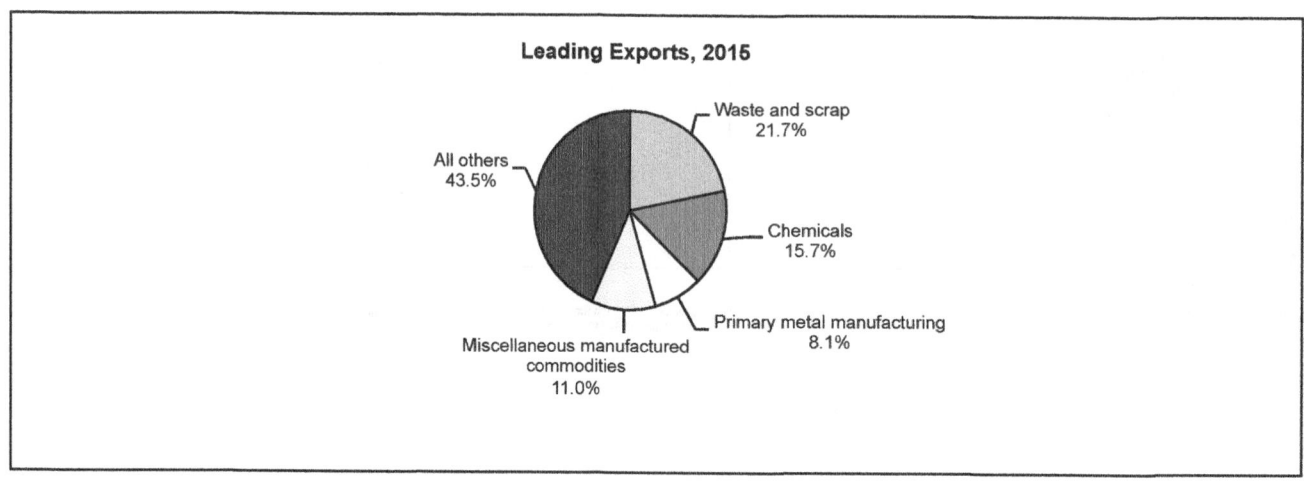

Leading Exports, 2015

- Waste and scrap 21.7%
- Chemicals 15.7%
- Primary metal manufacturing 8.1%
- Miscellaneous manufactured commodities 11.0%
- All others 43.5%

SOUTH CAROLINA

Facts and Figures

Location: Southeastern United States; bordered on the N by North Carolina, on the E by the Atlantic Ocean, on the S by the Atlantic Ocean and Georgia, and on the W by Georgia

Area: 32,020 sq. mi. (82,932 sq. km.); rank—40th

Population: 4,896,146 (2015 est.); rank—23rd

Principal Cities: capital—Columbia; largest—Columbia

Statehood: May 23, 1788; 8th state

U.S. Congress: 2 senators, 7 representatives

State Mottoes: *Animis opibusque parati* ("Prepared in mind and resources"); *Dum spiro, spero* ("While I breathe, I hope")

State Songs: "Carolina"; "South Carolina on My Mind"

State Nickname: The Palmetto State

Abbreviations: SC; S.C.

State Symbols: flower—yellow jessamine; tree—cabbage palmetto; bird—Carolina wren

At a Glance

- With an increase in population of 5.6 percent, South Carolina ranked 10th among the states in growth from 2010 to 2015.

- South Carolina's median household income in 2014 was $45,238, and 18.0 percent of the population lived below the poverty level.

- South Carolina's violent crime rate in 2014 was 497.7 per 100,000 population, compared to 365.5 for the entire nation.

- In 2014, 13.6 percent of South Carolinians did not have health insurance, compared to 11.7 percent of the total U.S. population.

- South Carolina's unemployment rate was 6.0 percent in 2015, compared to the national unemployment rate of 5.3 percent.

Table SC-1. Population by Age, Sex, Race, and Hispanic Origin

(Number, percent, except where noted.)

Sex, age, race, and Hispanic origin	2000	2010	2015[1]	Average annual percent change, 2010–2015
Total Population...	4,012,013	4,625,364	4,896,146	0.4
Percent of total U.S. population	1.4	1.5	1.5	X
Sex				
Male...	1,948,929	2,250,101	2,378,968	0.4
Female...	2,063,083	2,375,263	2,517,178	0.4
Age				
Under 5 years..	264,679	302,297	289,990	-0.3
5 to 19 years..	871,099	922,128	931,392	0.1
20 to 64 years...	2,390,901	2,769,065	2,879,969	0.3
65 years and over	485,333	631,874	794,795	1.7
Median age (years)	35.4	37.9	39	0.2
Race and Hispanic Origin				
One race				
White	2,695,560	3,164,143	3,347,647	0.4
Black..	1,185,216	1,302,865	1,353,056	0.3
American Indian and Alaska Native	13,718	24,665	26,412	0.5
Asian..	36,014	61,247	77,980	1.7
Native Hawaiian or Other Pacific Islander	1,628	3,957	4,580	1.0
Two or more races	39,950	68,487	86,471	1.7
Hispanic (of any race)...	95,076	243,923	268,352	0.7

X = Not applicable.
[1]Population figures for 2015 are July 1 estimates. The 2010 estimates are taken from the 2010 Census.

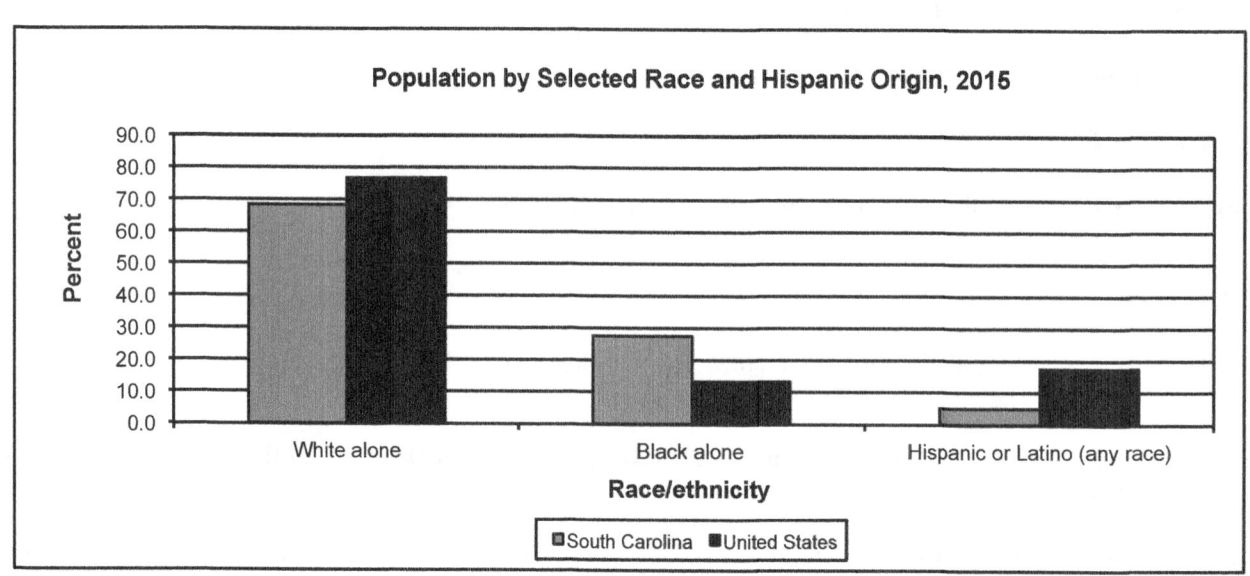

Table SC-2. Marital Status

(Number, percent distribution.)

Sex, age, race, and Hispanic origin	2000	2010	2014
Males, 15 Years and Over	1,516,125	1,797,441	1,841,777
Never married	28.8	35.2	34.6
Now married, except separated......................................	57.3	49.4	49.9
Separated..	2.8	3.0	2.9
Widowed..	2.7	2.8	2.9
Divorced..	8.3	9.5	9.6
Females, 15 Years and Over	1,652,793	1,939,054	1,985,795
Never married	23.4	29.1	28.9
Now married, except separated......................................	51.4	45.2	45.3
Separated..	3.8	3.9	3.8
Widowed..	11.5	10.6	10.4
Divorced..	9.9	11.2	11.5

Table SC-3. Households and Housing Characteristics

(Number, percent, dollars.)

Item	2000	2010	2014	Average annual percent change, 2000–2014
Total Households...	1,533,854	1,761,393	1,826,914	1.4
Family households	1,072,822	1,180,687	1,201,616	0.9
Married-couple family	783,142	827,387	847,329	0.6
Other family	289,680	353,300	354,287	1.6
Male householder, no wife present.............	62,722	77,062	83,380	2.4
Female householder, no husband present.......	226,958	276,238	270,907	1.4
Nonfamily households	461,032	580,706	625,298	2.5
Householder living alone........................	383,142	489,995	526,516	2.7
Householder not living alone...................	77,890	90,711	98,782	1.9
Housing Characteristics				
Total housing units..................................	1,753,670	2,140,337	2,188,258	1.8
Occupied housing units	1,533,854	1,761,393	1,826,914	1.4
Owner occupied	1,107,617	1,210,160	1,243,177	0.9
Renter occupied	426,237	551,233	583,737	2.6
Average household size.............................	2.53	2.55	2.57	0.1
Financial Characteristics				
Median gross rent of renter-occupied housing	510	728	791	3.9
Median monthly owner costs for housing units with a mortgage	894	1,177	1,164	2.2
Median value of owner-occupied housing units.......................	94,900	138,100	140,000	3.4

Table SC-4. Migration, Origin, and Language

(Number, percent.)

Characteristic	State 2013	State 2014	State Percent change	U.S. 2013	U.S. 2014	U.S. Percent change
Residence 1 Year Ago						
Population 1 year and over	4,720,602	4,780,659	1.3	312,432,820	315,095,393	0.9
Same house	84.7	84.6	X	85.0	85.1	X
Different house in the U.S.	14.9	15.0	X	14.4	14.3	X
Same county	8.3	8.2	X	8.9	8.7	X
Different county	6.6	6.8	X	5.5	5.6	X
Same state	3.1	3.2	X	3.2	3.3	X
Different state	3.5	3.6	X	2.3	2.3	X
Abroad	0.4	0.4	X	0.6	0.6	X
Place of Birth						
Native born	4,543,561	4,603,929	1.3	274,780,773	276,465,262	0.6
Male	48.5	48.5	X	49.3	49.3	X
Female	51.5	51.5	X	50.7	50.7	X
Foreign born	231,278	228,553	-1.2	41,348,066	42,391,794	2.5
Male	51.2	51.7	X	48.8	48.7	X
Female	48.8	48.3	X	51.2	51.3	X
Foreign born; naturalized U.S. citizen...........	89,661	86,647	-3.4	19,294,710	19,984,738	3.6
Male	46.9	46.0	X	45.9	45.9	X
Female	53.1	54.0	X	54.1	54.1	X
Foreign born; not a U.S. citizen	141,617	141,906	0.2	22,053,356	22,407,056	1.6
Male	53.9	55.1	X	51.3	51.2	X
Female	46.1	44.9	X	48.7	48.8	X
Entered 2010 or later	8.9	16.5	X	9.7	12.3	X
Entered 2000 to 2009	38.8	33.9	X	29.4	28.6	X
Entered before 2000.............................	52.3	49.6	X	61.0	59.1	X
World Region of Birth, Foreign						
Foreign-born population, excluding population born at sea	231,278	228,553	-1.2	41,347,945	42,390,705	2.5
Europe	15.6	16.2	X	11.6	11.2	X
Asia..	21.3	23.5	X	29.5	30.1	X
Africa	3.8	5.1	X	4.4	4.6	X
Oceania	0.7	1.0	X	0.5	0.6	X
Latin America......................................	54.4	51.4	X	51.9	51.6	X
North America	4.1	2.9	X	2.0	1.9	X
Language Spoken at Home and Ability to Speak English						
Population 5 years and over.........................	4,481,196	4,545,554	1.4	296,358,760	299,084,046	0.9
English only	93.1	93.2	X	79.2	78.9	X
Language other than English......................	6.9	6.8	X	20.8	21.1	X
Speaks English less than "very well"..............	2.8	2.9	X	8.5	8.6	X

X = Not applicable.
- = Zero or rounds to zero.

Table SC-5. Median Income and Poverty Status, 2014

(Number, percent, except as noted.)

Characteristic	State		U.S.	
	Number	Percent	Number	Percent
Median Income				
Households (dollars).............................	45,238	X	53,657	X
Families (dollars)	56,491	X	65,910	X
Below Poverty Level (All People)	843,860	18.0	48,208,387	15.5
Sex				
Male.................................	368,610	16.3	21,590,918	14.2
Female	475,250	19.6	26,617,469	16.8
Age				
Under 18 years.................................	288,564	27.1	15,686,012	21.7
Related children under 18 years.................	283,825	26.7	15,372,705	21.3
18 to 64 years.................................	486,394	16.9	28,267,482	14.6
65 years and over	68,902	9.3	4,254,893	9.5

X = Not applicable.

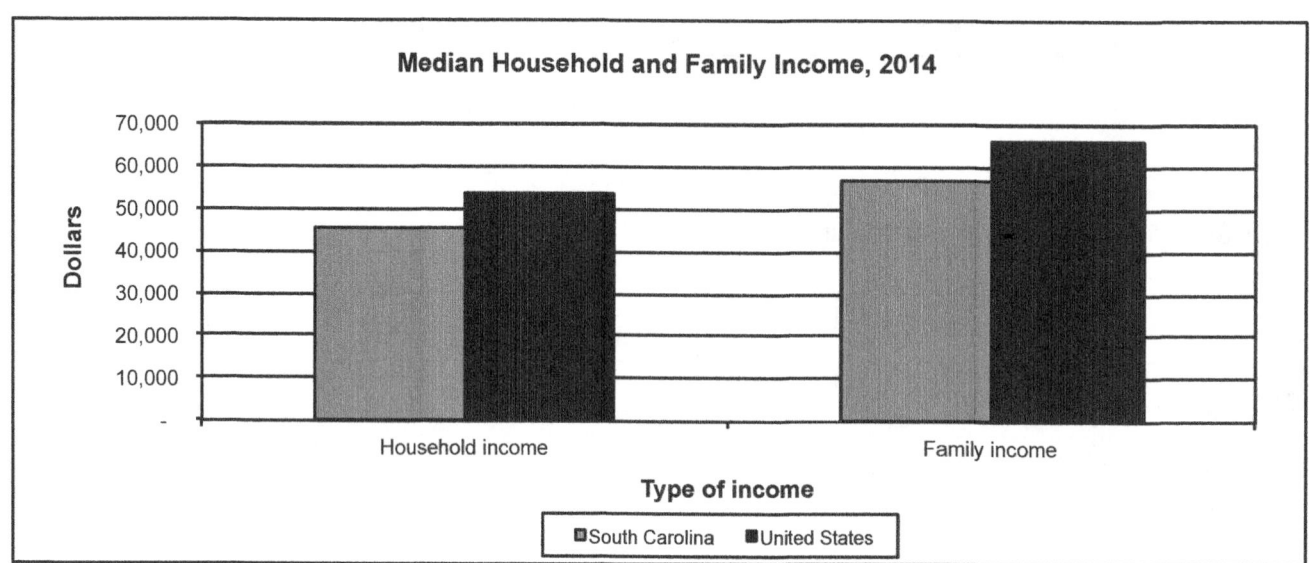

Table SC-6. Health Insurance Coverage Status for the Civilian Noninstitutionalized Population and Children Under 18 Years of Age

(Numbers in thousands, percent.)

Item	2006	2007	2008	2009	2010	2011	2012	2013	2014
Civilian Noninstitutionalized Population	4,226	4,384	4,373	4,454	4,537	4,579	4,623	4,678	4,734
Covered by Private or Public Insurance									
Number.................................	3,553	3,664	3,612	3,705	3,742	3,813	3,845	3,939	4,092
Percent.................................	84.1	83.6	82.6	83.2	82.5	83.3	83.2	84.2	86.4
Not Covered									
Number.................................	672	721	761	750	795	766	778	739	642
Percent.................................	15.9	16.4	17.4	16.8	17.5	16.7	16.8	15.8	13.6
Percent in the U.S. not covered.................................	15.8	15.3	15.1	15.1	15.5	15.1	14.8	14.5	11.7
Children Under 18 Years of Age	1,042	1,070	1,064	1,078	1,078	1,079	1,078	1,077	1,081
Covered by Private or Public Insurance									
Number.................................	930	918	930	971	976	988	989	1,004	1,021
Percent.................................	89.3	85.8	87.4	90.0	90.6	91.6	91.7	93.3	94.5
Not Covered									
Number.................................	112	152	134	107	102	91	89	73	60
Percent.................................	10.7	14.2	12.6	10.0	9.4	8.4	8.3	6.7	5.5
Percent in the U.S. not covered.................................	11.7	11.0	9.7	8.6	8.0	7.5	7.2	7.1	6.0

Table SC-7. Employment Status by Demographic Group, 2015

(Numbers in thousands, percent.)

Characteristic	Civilian noninstitutional population	Civilian labor force		Employed		Unemployed	
		Number	Percent of population	Number	Percent of population	Number	Percent of population
Total..	3,811	2,287	60.0	2,153	56.5	135	5.9
Sex							
Male......................................	1,802	1,183	65.6	1,117	62.0	66	5.6
Female...................................	2,010	1,104	55.0	1,036	51.6	68	6.2
Race, Sex, and Hispanic Origin							
White.....................................	2,700	1,611	59.7	1,545	57.2	65	4.1
Male...................................	1,304	865	66.3	834	64.0	31	3.6
Female................................	1,396	745	53.4	711	50.9	34	4.6
Black or African American...............	1,004	609	60.6	543	54.1	65	10.7
Male...................................	446	281	62.9	246	55.2	34	12.2
Female................................	559	328	58.7	297	53.2	31	9.4
Hispanic or Latino ethnicity[1]............	183	131	71.4	123	67.0	8	6.2
Male...................................	100	86	85.4	80	79.9	6	6.4
Female................................	83	45	54.4	42	51.3	3	5.7
Age							
16 to 19 years............................	244	71	29.0	56	23.1	15	20.5
20 to 24 years............................	302	220	73.0	188	62.2	33	14.8
25 to 34 years............................	637	506	79.4	471	73.8	36	7.0
35 to 44 years............................	578	489	84.7	471	81.5	18	3.7
45 to 54 years............................	646	502	77.6	485	75.1	16	3.3
55 to 64 years............................	648	376	58.0	362	55.9	13	3.6
65 years and over........................	757	124	16.3	120	15.8	4	3.0

NOTE: Data in Table 7 are from the Current Population Survey (CPS) and do not match the estimates in Table 8. See notes and definitions for further information.
[1] May be of any race.

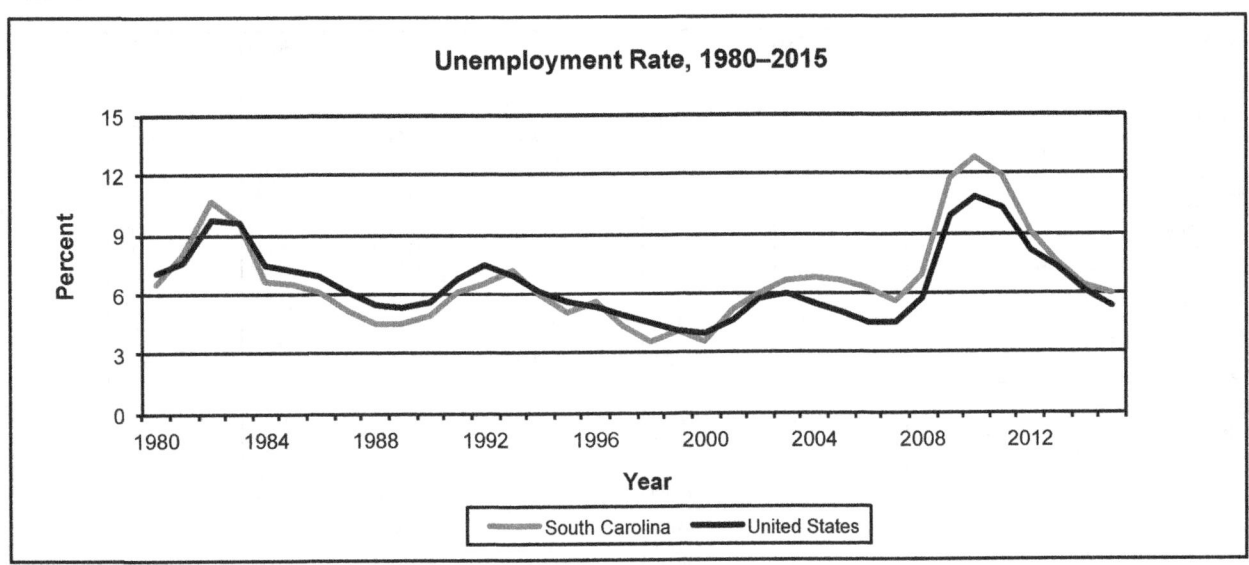

Table SC-8. Employment Status of the Civilian Noninstitutional Population Age 16 Years and Over

(Number, percent.)

Year	Civilian labor force	Civilian participation rate	Employed	Unemployed	Unemployment rate
2007........................	2,125,891	63.0	2,005,686	120,205	5.7
2008........................	2,142,232	62.3	1,996,409	145,823	6.8
2009........................	2,152,745	61.7	1,910,670	242,075	11.2
2010........................	2,155,668	60.5	1,915,045	240,623	11.2
2011........................	2,175,523	60.2	1,945,900	229,623	10.6
2012........................	2,184,113	59.7	1,983,506	200,607	9.2
2013........................	2,189,368	59.1	2,022,444	166,924	7.6
2014........................	2,216,782	58.9	2,074,277	142,505	6.4
2015........................	2,257,077	59.0	2,122,573	134,504	6.0

Table SC-9. Employment and Average Wages by Industry

(Estimates through 2010 are based on the 2007 North American Industry Classification System [NAICS]. Estimates from 2011 onward are based on the 2012 NAICS.)

Industry	2008	2009	2010	2011	2012	2013	2014
	Number of jobs						
Wage and Salary Employment by Industry.................	2,020,732	1,912,435	1,903,467	1,926,026	1,946,432	1,985,162	2,034,900
Farm Wage and Salary Employment.........................	6,453	7,894	6,624	6,722	6,673	7,157	6,077
Nonfarm Wage and Salary Employment....................	2,014,279	1,904,541	1,896,843	1,919,304	1,939,759	1,978,005	2,028,823
Private wage and salary employment...........................	1,613,489	1,502,296	1,498,976	1,526,368	1,544,812	1,578,825	1,627,897
Forestry, fishing, and related activities.....................	6,635	6,468	6,697	6,905	6,305	6,867	7,110
Mining...	1,482	1,340	1,244	1,232	1,195	1,141	1,158
Utilities...	12,363	12,435	12,048	11,922	12,134	12,207	12,349
Construction...	115,006	92,463	83,731	80,892	80,209	82,871	85,208
Manufacturing...	243,301	214,821	208,203	216,381	221,444	225,092	230,602
Durable goods manufacturing..........................	136,638	118,293	114,174	121,111	126,085	129,606	133,647
Nondurable goods manufacturing.....................	106,663	96,528	94,029	95,270	95,359	95,486	96,955
Wholesale trade	71,671	65,668	64,222	65,039	65,974	66,757	68,449
Retail trade..	239,826	227,174	226,866	228,832	228,443	233,103	239,102
Transportation and warehousing...........................	52,830	47,673	47,205	48,312	50,280	52,667	56,505
Information..	28,573	27,229	25,893	25,858	25,801	26,455	26,460
Finance and insurance	72,084	70,386	68,999	68,948	69,762	70,634	70,423
Real estate and rental and leasing.....................	30,955	28,586	27,141	26,660	26,021	26,980	27,881
Professional, scientific, and technical services	77,270	74,138	75,713	80,155	80,284	82,667	85,928
Management of companies and enterprises...................	15,659	14,516	14,290	15,053	16,414	17,238	17,047
Administrative and waste services.......................	131,288	115,370	129,873	136,527	141,475	144,335	153,388
Educational services	28,069	28,271	29,289	29,922	30,679	30,451	31,688
Health care and social assistance.......................	166,737	168,480	172,707	175,238	178,057	180,993	186,239
Arts, entertainment, and recreation.....................	28,779	27,029	26,044	26,805	26,975	27,585	28,225
Accommodation and food services......................	191,371	183,894	183,777	186,392	191,290	196,943	202,242
Other services, except public administration...............	99,590	96,355	95,034	95,295	92,070	93,839	97,893
Government and government enterprises.........................	400,790	402,245	397,867	392,936	394,947	399,180	400,926
	Dollars						
Average Wages and Salaries by Industry	37,330	37,832	38,715	39,627	40,646	41,021	42,054
Average Farm Wages and Salaries	23,101	18,925	22,695	20,051	22,476	21,645	25,422
Average Nonfarm Wages and Salaries	37,375	37,910	38,771	39,696	40,709	41,092	42,104
Average private wages and salaries...........................	36,469	36,798	37,836	38,842	39,967	40,361	41,361
Forestry, fishing, and related activities.....................	29,913	29,906	31,148	31,518	33,322	33,858	35,215
Mining...	46,090	43,035	48,012	50,545	53,413	55,358	57,744
Utilities...	72,803	73,936	78,446	80,316	81,491	85,000	87,572
Construction...	41,013	40,979	41,924	42,903	44,787	45,501	47,238
Manufacturing...	47,851	48,779	51,196	52,793	54,208	54,985	56,985
Durable goods manufacturing..........................	48,930	50,369	53,280	55,232	56,511	57,285	59,856
Nondurable goods manufacturing.....................	46,468	46,832	48,666	49,693	51,164	51,865	53,028
Wholesale trade	55,336	54,676	55,975	58,095	60,513	61,173	63,951
Retail trade..	24,850	24,928	25,432	25,518	26,023	26,245	26,518
Transportation and warehousing...........................	38,908	39,240	40,449	41,243	41,900	42,156	42,454
Information..	50,236	50,835	52,112	52,169	53,915	55,440	57,891
Finance and insurance	52,945	53,973	55,028	57,235	59,551	60,736	62,023
Real estate and rental and leasing.....................	33,909	33,906	34,536	36,297	37,934	39,132	40,804
Professional, scientific, and technical services	57,089	57,937	59,901	61,272	64,002	64,109	65,596
Management of companies and enterprises...................	64,102	65,759	67,177	70,185	72,381	71,074	72,123
Administrative and waste services	30,739	32,200	32,930	33,796	33,615	32,835	33,635
Educational services	26,651	27,675	27,824	28,457	28,983	29,658	30,146
Health care and social assistance.......................	39,183	40,059	41,319	42,089	43,108	43,776	44,854
Arts, entertainment, and recreation.....................	20,390	20,026	20,396	21,023	21,143	20,890	21,306
Accommodation and food services......................	16,294	16,312	17,036	17,494	17,918	17,935	18,389
Other services, except public administration................	26,071	26,257	27,246	27,792	28,898	29,939	30,224
Government and government enterprises.........................	41,025	42,062	42,296	43,015	43,612	43,980	45,121

Table SC-10. Employment Characteristics by Family Type

(Number, percent.)

Family type and labor force status	2012		2013		2014	
	Total	Families with own children under 18 years	Total	Families with own children under 18 years	Total	Families with own children under 18 years
All Families..	1,204,041	491,485	1,195,104	479,885	1,197,456	463,567
FAMILY TYPE AND LABOR FORCE STATUS						
Married-Couple Families..............................	839,168	298,889	840,762	298,898	843,169	284,325
Both husband and wife in labor force..........	48.2	66.7	47.8	66.4	47.5	66.6
Husband in labor force, wife not in labor force	21.2	26.7	21.3	26.1	21.8	27.5
Wife in labor force, husband not in labor force	9.0	4.3	9.4	4.8	8.5	4.4
Both husband and wife not in labor force......	21.6	2.2	21.2	2.5	22.2	1.5
Other Families	364,873	192,596	354,342	180,987	354,287	179,242
Female householder, no husband present.........	76.3	80.6	77.1	80.1	76.5	79.5
In labor force	52.3	66.5	52.2	65.8	50.8	65.6
Not in labor force	24.0	14.1	24.9	14.2	25.7	13.9
Male householder, no wife present..................	23.7	19.4	22.9	19.9	23.5	20.5
In labor force..	17.5	17.8	16.7	17.9	17.5	18.4
Not in labor force	6.2	1.5	6.2	2.0	6.1	2.0

Table SC-11. School Enrollment and Educational Attainment, 2014

(Number, percent.)

Item	State	U.S.
Enrollment		
Total population 3 years and over, enrolled in school................	1,207,095	82,063,714
Enrolled in nursery school or preschool (percent)......................	5.4	6.0
Enrolled in kindergarten (percent)...	6.2	5.1
Enrolled in elementary school, grades 1-8 (percent)...................	40.4	40.2
Enrolled in high school, grades 9-12 (percent)..........................	20.7	20.7
Enrolled in college or graduate school (percent)........................	27.2	28.0
Attainment		
Total population 25 years and over	3,260,929	213,725,624
Less than ninth grade (percent)	4.5	5.6
9th to 12th grade, no diploma (percent)	9.3	7.5
High school graduate, including equivalency (percent).................	30.3	27.7
Some college, no degree (percent)	20.7	21.0
Associate's degree (percent)	8.8	8.2
Bachelor's degree (percent)	16.7	18.7
Graduate or professional degree (percent)................................	9.6	11.4
High school graduate or higher (percent)	86.1	86.9
Bachelor's degree or higher (percent)......................................	26.3	30.1

Table SC-12. Public School Characteristics and Educational Indicators

(Number, percent; data derived from National Center of Education Statistics.)

Item	State	U.S.
Public Schools, 2013–2014 (except where noted)		
Number of school districts...	102	18,194
Number of schools..	1,243	98,271
Number of students (in thousands)	746	50,045
Number of teachers (in thousands)	48	3,114
Student-teacher ratio..	15.5	16.1
Expenditures per student (dollars), FY 2013..................	9,444	107,637
Four-year adjusted cohort graduation rate (ACGR)[1,2]	80.1	82.3
Students eligible for free or reduced-price lunch (in thousands)	426	25,596
English language learners (in thousands)	40	4,461
Students age 3 to 21 served under IDEA, part B (in thousands)	99	6,464

Public Schools by Type	Number	Percent of state public schools
Total number of schools..	1,243	100.0
Regular...	1,172	94.3
Special education	9	0.7
Vocational education	42	3.4
Alternative education..	20	1.6

NOTE: Every school is assigned only one school type based on its instructional emphasis.
[1]ACGR data represents a new method of calculating high-school completion rates and may not be comparable to previous years' data for Averaged Freshmen Graduation Rates (AFGR).
[2]The United States 4-year ACGRs were estimated using both the reported 4-year ACGR data from 49 states and the District of Columbia and using imputed data for Idaho. The estimate for American Indian/Alaska Native students also includes imputed data for Virginia.

Table SC-13. Reported Voting and Registration of the Voting-Age Population, November 2014

(Numbers in thousands, percent.)

Item	Total population	Total citizen population	Registered			Voted		
			Total registered	Percent registered (total population)	Percent registered (total citizen population)	Total voted	Percent voted (total population)	Percent voted (total citizen population)
U.S. Total	239,874	219,941	142,166	59.3	64.6	92,251	38.5	41.9
State Total.............................	3,667	3,569	2,458	67.0	68.9	1,514	41.3	42.4
Sex								
Male..	1,730	1,678	1,132	65.5	67.5	699	40.4	41.6
Female....................................	1,937	1,891	1,325	68.4	70.1	815	42.0	43.1
Race								
White alone.............................	2,622	2,557	1,778	67.8	69.6	1,075	41.0	42.0
White, non-Hispanic alone...........	2,477	2,454	1,730	69.9	70.5	1,061	42.8	43.2
Black alone..............................	965	944	640	66.3	67.9	419	43.4	44.4
Asian alone.............................	50	38	18	(B)	(B)	13	(B)	(B)
Hispanic (of any race)................	171	106	48	28.1	45.1	14	8.1	13.0
White alone or in combination........	2,632	2,568	1,787	67.9	69.6	1,075	40.8	41.9
Black alone or in combination.........	978	956	652	66.7	68.3	426	43.6	44.5
Asian alone or in combination.........	53	42	21	(B)	(B)	16	(B)	(B)
Age								
18 to 24 years........................	462	457	209	45.2	45.7	89	19.3	19.5
25 to 34 years........................	617	590	386	62.5	65.4	156	25.2	26.4
35 to 44 years........................	574	543	379	66.1	69.8	204	35.6	37.6
45 to 64 years........................	1,294	1,267	949	73.3	74.9	688	53.2	54.3
65 years and over....................	720	712	535	74.3	75.1	376	52.2	52.8

B = Base is less than 75,000 and therefore too small to show the derived measure.

Table SC-14. Crime

(Number, rate per 100,000. Data are derived from the FBI Uniform Crime Reports.)

Item	State			U.S.[1,2,3,4]		
	2013	2014	Percent change	2013	2014	Percent change
TOTAL POPULATION[5]...........................	4,774,839	4,832,482	1.2	316,128,839	318,857,056	0.9
VIOLENT CRIME						
Number..	23,625	24,052	1.8	1,163,146	1,165,383	0.2
Rate	494.8	497.7	0.6	367.9	365.5	-0.7
Murder and Nonnegligent Manslaughter						
Number..	297	311	4.7	14,196	14,249	0.4
Rate	6.2	6.4	3.2	4.5	4.5	-
Rape[6]						
Number..	2,171	2,068	X	108,612	116,645	X
Rate	45.5	42.8	X	34.4	36.6	X
Robbery						
Number..	3,972	3,997	0.6	345,031	325,802	-5.6
Rate	83.2	82.7	-0.6	109.1	102.2	-6.3
Aggravated Assault						
Number..	17,838	17,676	-0.9	724,149	741,291	2.4
Rate	373.6	365.8	-2.1	229.1	232.5	1.5
PROPERTY CRIME						
Number..	173,049	167,217	-3.4	8,632,512	8,277,829	-4.1
Rate	3,624.2	3,460.3	-4.5	2,730.7	2,596.1	-4.9
Burglary						
Number..	40,958	36,721	-10.3	1,928,465	1,729,806	-10.3
Rate	857.8	759.9	-11.4	610.0	542.5	-11.1
Larceny-Theft						
Number..	119,511	117,594	-1.6	6,004,453	5,858,496	-2.4
Rate	2,502.9	2,433.4	-2.8	1,899.4	1,837.3	-3.3
Motor Vehicle Theft						
Number..	12,580	12,902	2.6	699,594	689,527	-1.4
Rate	263.5	267.0	1.3	221.3	216.2	-2.3

NOTE: Although arson data are included in the trend and clearance tables, sufficient data are not available to estimate totals for this offense. Therefore, no arson data are published in this table.
X = Not applicable.
- = Zero or rounds to zero.
[1]The crime figures have been adjusted.
[2]The data collection methodology for the offense of forcible rape used by the Minnesota state Uniform Crime Reporting (UCR) Program (with the exception of Minneapolis and St. Paul, Minnesota) does not comply with national UCR Program guidelines. Consequently, its figures for forcible rape and violent crime (of which forcible rape is a part) are not published in this table.
[3]Includes offenses reported by the Zoological Police and the Metro Transit Police.
[4]Because of changes in the state's reporting practices, figures are not comparable to previous years' data.
[5]Populations are U.S. Census Bureau provisional estimates as of July 1 of each year.
[6]The figures shown for the offense of rape were estimated using the revised Uniform Crime Reporting (UCR) definition of rape.

Table SC-15. State Government Finances, 2014

(Dollar amounts in thousands, percent distribution.)

Item	Dollars	Percent distribution
Total Revenue	31,870,556	100.0
General revenue	23,076,006	72.4
Intergovernmental revenue	7,639,636	24.0
Taxes	8,932,564	28.0
General sales	3,370,643	10.6
Selective sales	1,257,720	3.9
License taxes	471,862	1.5
Individual income tax	3,422,532	10.7
Corporate income tax	327,809	1.0
Other taxes	81,998	0.3
Current charges	4,449,801	14.0
Miscellaneous general revenue	2,054,005	6.4
Utility revenue	1,803,512	5.7
Liquor stores revenue	0	-
Insurance trust revenue[1]	6,991,038	21.9
Total Expenditure	28,903,767	100.0
Intergovernmental expenditure	5,581,255	19.3
Direct expenditure	23,322,512	80.7
Current operation	16,966,246	58.7
Capital outlay	1,190,264	4.1
Insurance benefits and repayments	3,522,131	12.2
Assistance and subsidies	1,056,549	3.7
Interest on debt	587,322	2.0
Exhibit: Salaries and wages	3,663,037	12.7
Total Expenditure	28,903,767	100.0
General expenditure	23,683,061	81.9
Intergovernmental expenditure	5,581,255	19.3
Direct expenditure	18,101,806	62.6
General expenditure, by function:		
Education	8,701,760	30.1
Public welfare	6,658,472	23.0
Hospitals	1,520,409	5.3
Health	1,065,220	3.7
Highways	1,101,153	3.8
Police protection	173,571	0.6
Correction	502,417	1.7
Natural resources	214,458	0.7
Parks and recreation	108,372	0.4
Governmental administration	590,524	2.0
Interest on general debt	362,192	1.3
Other and unallocable	2,684,513	9.3
Utility expenditure	1,698,575	5.9
Liquor stores expenditure	0	-
Insurance trust expenditure	3,522,131	12.2
Debt at End of Fiscal Year	15,089,289	X
Cash and Security Holdings	42,817,859	X

X = Not applicable.
- = Zero or rounds to zero.
[1]Within insurance trust revenue, net earnings of state retirement systems is a calculated statistic (the item code in the data file is X08), and thus can be positive or negative. Net earnings is the sum of earnings on investments plus gains on investments minus losses on investments. The change made in 2002 for asset valuation from book to market value in accordance with Statement 34 of the Governmental Accounting Standards Board is reflected in the calculated statistics.

Table SC-16. State Government Tax Collections, 2014

(Dollars in thousands, percent.)

Item	Dollars	Percent distribution
Total Taxes	8,932,564	100.0
Property taxes	21,664	0.2
Sales and gross receipts	4,628,363	51.8
General sales and gross receipts	3,370,643	37.7
Selective sales and gross receipts	1,257,720	14.1
Alcoholic beverages	162,313	1.8
Amusements	38,481	0.4
Insurance premiums	214,600	2.4
Motor fuels	529,655	5.9
Pari-mutuels	0	-
Public utilities	28,450	0.3
Tobacco products	25,632	0.3
Other selective sales	258,589	2.9
Licenses	471,862	5.3
Alcoholic beverages	11,382	0.1
Amusements	1,371	-
Corporations in general	95,139	1.1
Hunting and fishing	17,541	0.2
Motor vehicle	214,192	2.4
Motor vehicle operators	8,813	0.1
Public utilities	10,144	0.1
Occupation and business, NEC	96,472	1.1
Other licenses	16,808	0.2
Income taxes	3,750,341	42.0
Individual income	3,422,532	38.3
Corporation net income	327,809	3.7
Other taxes	60,334	0.7
Death and gift	0	-
Documentary and stock transfer	60,334	0.7
Severance	X	X
Taxes, NEC	0	-

X = Not applicable.
- = Zero or rounds to zero.

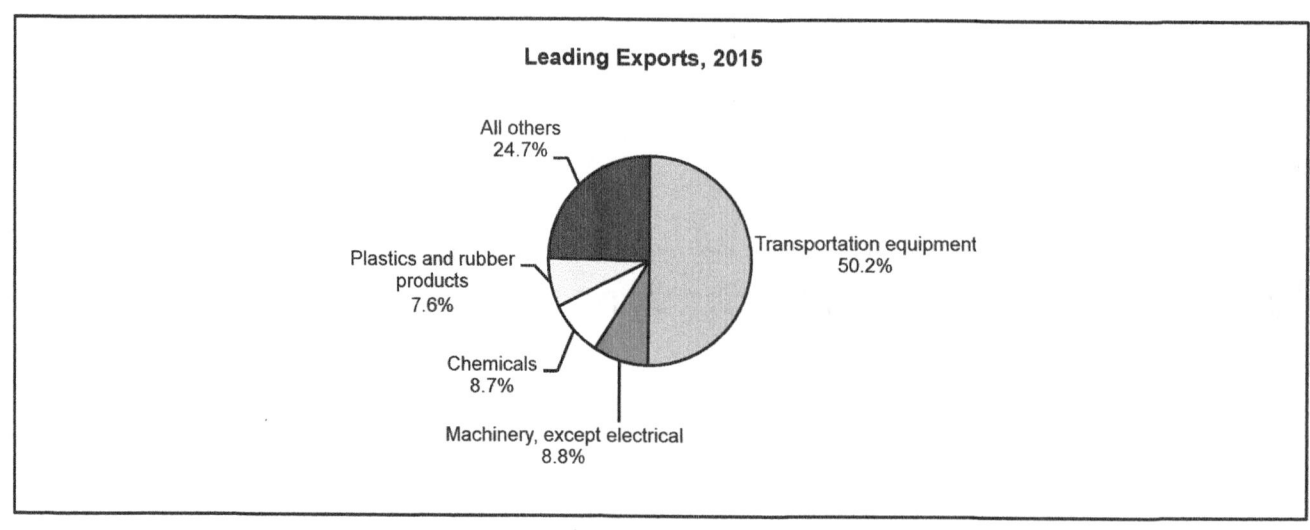

Leading Exports, 2015

- All others 24.7%
- Transportation equipment 50.2%
- Plastics and rubber products 7.6%
- Chemicals 8.7%
- Machinery, except electrical 8.8%

SOUTH DAKOTA

Facts and Figures

Location: North central United States; bordered on the N by North Dakota, on the E by Minnesota and Iowa, on the S by Nebraska, and on the W by Wyoming and Montana

Area: 77,117 sq. mi. (199,731 sq. km.); rank—17th

Population: 858,469 (2015 est.); rank—46th

Principal Cities: capital—Pierre; largest—Sioux Falls

Statehood: November 2, 1889; 40th state

U.S. Congress: 2 senators, 1 representative

State Motto: Under God the People Rule

State Song: "Hail, South Dakota"

State Nickname: The Mount Rushmore State

Abbreviations: SD; S.D.; S. Dak.

State Symbols: flower—pasqueflower; tree—Black Hills spruce; bird—ring-necked pheasant

At a Glance

- With an increase in population of 5.2 percent, South Dakota ranked 12th among the states in growth from 2010 to 2015.

- In 2014, 9.8 percent of South Dakotans did not have health insurance, compared to 11.7 percent of the total U.S. population.

- South Dakota's violent crime rate in 2014 was 326.5 per 100,000 population, compared to 365.5 for the entire nation.

- South Dakota's median income in 2014 was $50,979, and 14.2 percent of its residents lived below the poverty level.

- In 2015, 3.1 percent of South Dakotans were unemployed, compared to 5.3 percent of the entire U.S. population.

Table SD-1. Population by Age, Sex, Race, and Hispanic Origin

(Number, percent, except where noted.)

Sex, age, race, and Hispanic origin	2000	2010	2015[1]	Average annual percent change, 2010–2015
Total Population...	754,844	814,180	858,469	0.4
Percent of total U.S. population	0.4	0.3	0.3	X
Sex				
Male..	374,558	407,381	431,976	0.4
Female	380,286	406,799	426,493	0.3
Age				
Under 5 years..	51,069	59,621	61,244	0.2
5 to 19 years..	176,412	167,119	173,372	0.3
20 to 64 years...	419,232	470,859	489,433	0.3
65 years and over	108,131	116,581	134,420	1.0
Median age (years)..	35.6	36.9	36.9	-
Race and Hispanic Origin				
One race				
White	669,404	706,690	734,385	0.3
Black	4,685	10,533	15,760	2.9
American Indian and Alaska Native	62,283	72,782	76,698	0.4
Asian..	4,378	7,775	11,813	3.0
Native Hawaiian or Other Pacific Islander	261	517	662	1.8
Two or more races	10,156	15,883	19,151	1.3
Hispanic (of any race)..	10,903	23,699	31,214	2.0

X = Not applicable.
[1]Population figures for 2015 are July 1 estimates. The 2010 estimates are taken from the 2010 Census.
- = Zero or rounds to zero.

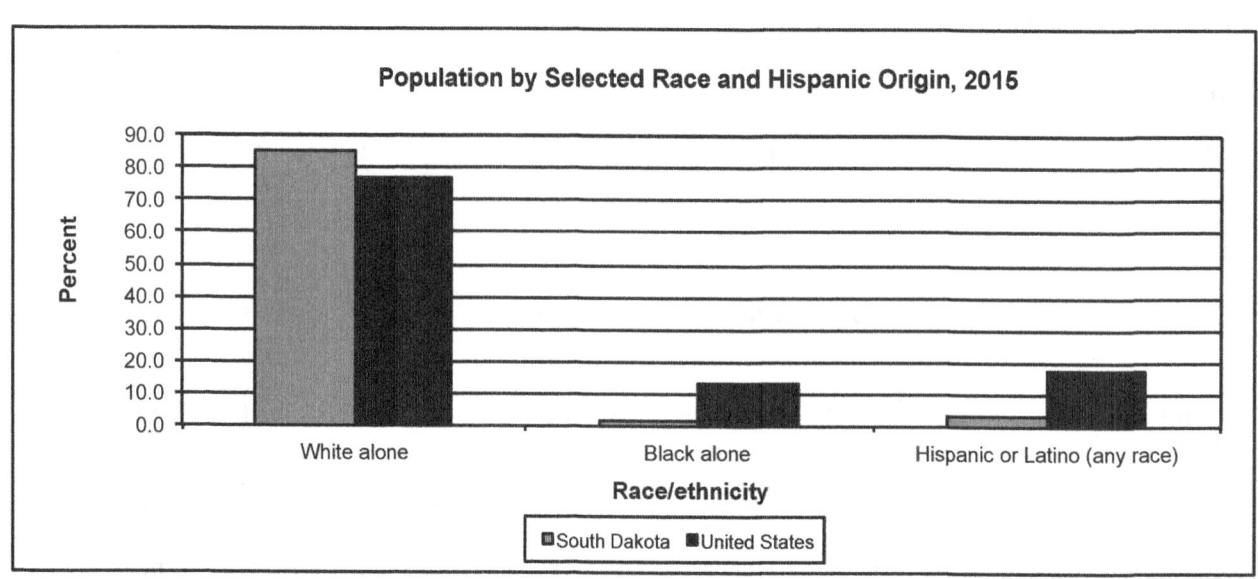

Population by Selected Race and Hispanic Origin, 2015

Legend: ■ South Dakota ■ United States
Y-axis: Percent
X-axis: Race/ethnicity (White alone, Black alone, Hispanic or Latino (any race))

Table SD-2. Marital Status

(Number, percent distribution.)

Sex, age, race, and Hispanic origin	2000	2010	2014
Males, 15 Years and Over	289,858	322,689	330,772
Never married	29.8	33.5	33.6
Now married, except separated...	58.2	52.5	52.5
Separated...	1.0	0.9	1.0
Widowed...	2.4	2.8	2.6
Divorced...	8.5	10.3	10.3
Females, 15 Years and Over	299,754	325,640	331,518
Never married	22.5	26.0	26.4
Now married, except separated...	55.9	52.1	51.8
Separated...	1.1	1.0	1.2
Widowed...	11.4	9.5	9.6
Divorced...	9.0	11.4	11.0

Table SD-3. Households and Housing Characteristics

(Number, percent, dollars.)

Item	2000	2010	2014	Average annual percent change, 2000–2014
Total Households...	290,245	318,955	334,475	1.1
Family households	194,330	204,029	211,235	0.6
Married-couple family	157,391	161,534	165,729	0.4
Other family	36,939	42,495	45,506	1.7
Male householder, no wife present............................	10,734	12,526	14,250	2.3
Female householder, no husband present....................	26,205	29,969	31,256	1.4
Nonfamily households	95,915	114,926	123,240	2.0
Householder living alone...	80,040	95,610	102,607	2.0
Householder not living alone....................................	15,875	19,316	20,633	2.1
Housing Characteristics				
Total housing units...	323,208	364,031	376,347	1.2
Occupied housing units	290,245	318,955	334,475	1.1
Owner occupied	197,940	216,821	228,010	1.1
Renter occupied	92,305	102,134	106,465	1.1
Average household size...	2.50	2.45	2.45	-0.1
Financial Characteristics				
Median gross rent of renter-occupied housing	426	591	647	3.7
Median monthly owner costs for housing units with a mortgage	828	1,151	1,201	3.2
Median value of owner-occupied housing units............	79,600	129,700	142,300	5.6

Table SD-4. Migration, Origin, and Language

(Number, percent.)

Characteristic	State			U.S.		
	2013	2014	Percent change	2013	2014	Percent change
Residence 1 Year Ago						
Population 1 year and over	832,703	842,076	1.1	312,432,820	315,095,393	0.9
Same house	83.1	83.3	X	85.0	85.1	X
Different house in the U.S.	16.7	16.4	X	14.4	14.3	X
Same county	8.7	8.6	X	8.9	8.7	X
Different county	8.0	7.8	X	5.5	5.6	X
Same state	4.4	4.4	X	3.2	3.3	X
Different state	3.6	3.3	X	2.3	2.3	X
Abroad	0.3	0.4	X	0.6	0.6	X
Place of Birth						
Native born	820,418	828,548	1.0	274,780,773	276,465,262	0.6
Male	50.2	50.1	X	49.3	49.3	X
Female	49.8	49.9	X	50.7	50.7	X
Foreign born	24,459	24,627	0.7	41,348,066	42,391,794	2.5
Male	49.0	49.4	X	48.8	48.7	X
Female	51.0	50.6	X	51.2	51.3	X
Foreign born; naturalized U.S. citizen........................	8,035	11,301	40.6	19,294,710	19,984,738	3.6
Male	49.5	49.1	X	45.9	45.9	X
Female	50.5	50.9	X	54.1	54.1	X
Foreign born; not a U.S. citizen................................	16,424	13,326	-18.9	22,053,356	22,407,056	1.6
Male	48.8	49.6	X	51.3	51.2	X
Female	51.2	50.4	X	48.7	48.8	X
Entered 2010 or later	20.6	24.0	X	9.7	12.3	X
Entered 2000 to 2009	39.9	36.0	X	29.4	28.6	X
Entered before 2000..	39.4	40.0	X	61.0	59.1	X
World Region of Birth, Foreign						
Foreign-born population, excluding population born at sea	24,459	24,627	0.7	41,347,945	42,390,705	2.5
Europe	15.6	12.8	X	11.6	11.2	X
Asia	31.8	37.6	X	29.5	30.1	X
Africa	23.9	23.3	X	4.4	4.6	X
Oceania	0.6	0.4	X	0.5	0.6	X
Latin America..	23.9	20.7	X	51.9	51.6	X
North America..	4.2	5.1	X	2.0	1.9	X
Language Spoken at Home and Ability to Speak English						
Population 5 years and over......................................	786,260	792,820	0.8	296,358,760	299,084,046	0.9
English only	93.5	94.3	X	79.2	78.9	X
Language other than English.....................................	6.5	5.7	X	20.8	21.1	X
Speaks English less than "very well".........................	1.9	1.7	X	8.5	8.6	X

X = Not applicable.
- = Zero or rounds to zero.

Table SD-5. Median Income and Poverty Status, 2014

(Number, percent, except as noted.)

Characteristic	State		U.S.	
	Number	Percent	Number	Percent
Median Income				
Households (dollars)...	50,979	X	53,657	X
Families (dollars)	66,936	X	65,910	X
Below Poverty Level (All People)	116,843	14.2	48,208,387	15.5
Sex				
Male...	53,442	13.0	21,590,918	14.2
Female	63,401	15.4	26,617,469	16.8
Age				
Under 18 years..	37,127	18.0	15,686,012	21.7
Related children under 18 years...........................	36,240	17.7	15,372,705	21.3
18 to 64 years...	66,704	13.5	28,267,482	14.6
65 years and over..	13,012	10.6	4,254,893	9.5

X = Not applicable.

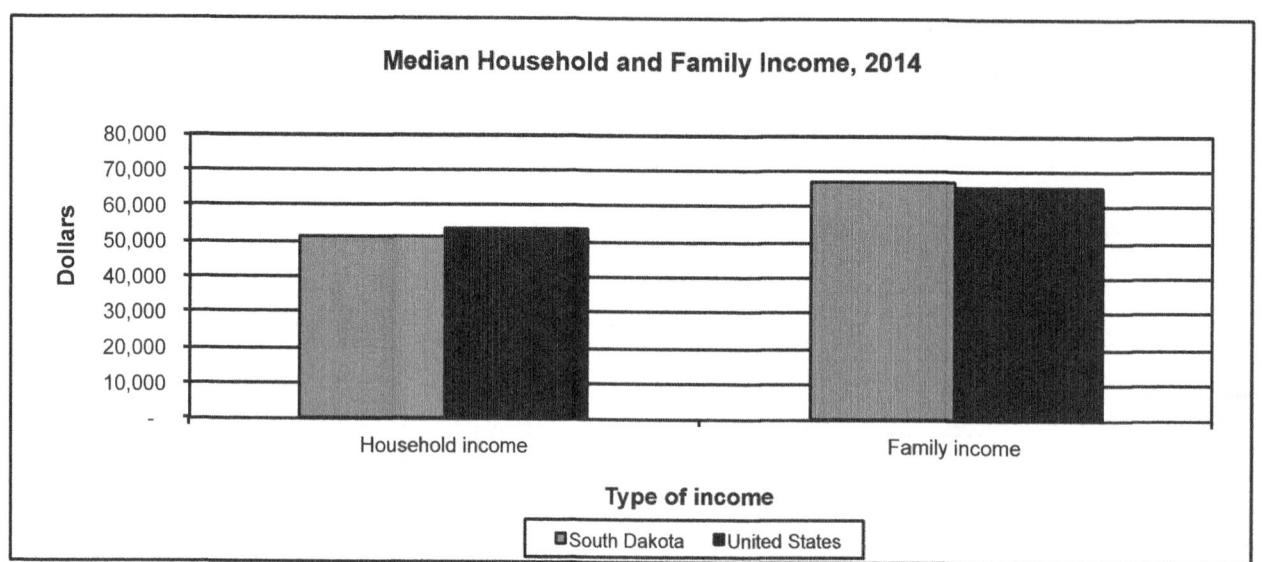

Table SD-6. Health Insurance Coverage Status for the Civilian Noninstitutionalized Population and Children Under 18 Years of Age

(Numbers in thousands, percent.)

Item	2006	2007	2008	2009	2010	2011	2012	2013	2014
Civilian Noninstitutionalized Population	770	788	784	793	798	806	816	827	835
Covered by Private or Public Insurance									
Number..	679	708	692	689	699	710	722	734	753
Percent..	88.2	89.9	88.3	86.9	87.6	88.1	88.5	88.7	90.2
Not Covered									
Number..	91	80	92	104	99	96	94	93	82
Percent..	11.8	10.1	11.7	13.1	12.4	11.9	11.5	11.3	9.8
Percent in the U.S. not covered................................	15.8	15.3	15.1	15.1	15.5	15.1	14.8	14.5	11.7
Children Under 18 Years of Age	193	198	196	195	201	201	203	207	210
Covered by Private or Public Insurance									
Number..	175	183	179	180	184	189	191	194	198
Percent..	90.8	92.0	91.3	92.4	91.7	94.0	94.2	93.7	94.3
Not Covered									
Number..	18	16	17	15	17	12	12	13	12
Percent..	9.2	8.0	8.7	7.6	8.3	6.0	5.8	6.3	5.7
Percent in the U.S. not covered................................	11.7	11.0	9.7	8.6	8.0	7.5	7.2	7.1	6.0

Table SD-7. Employment Status by Demographic Group, 2015

(Numbers in thousands, percent.)

Characteristic	Civilian noninstitutional population	Civilian labor force		Employed		Unemployed	
		Number	Percent of population	Number	Percent of population	Number	Percent of population
Total..	654	456	69.7	440	67.3	16	3.5
Sex							
Male..	325	240	73.9	231	71.2	9	3.7
Female...	329	215	65.5	209	63.5	7	3.2
Race, Sex, and Hispanic Origin							
White...	577	407	70.5	398	69.0	8	2.0
Male..	289	216	74.6	210	72.7	6	2.6
Female...	288	191	66.3	188	65.3	3	1.4
Black or African American..................	NA	NA	NA	NA	NA	NA	NA
Male..	NA	NA	NA	NA	NA	NA	NA
Female...	NA	NA	NA	NA	NA	NA	NA
Hispanic or Latino ethnicity[1]	15	11	72.8	10	69.7	...	3.9
Male..	NA	NA	NA	NA	NA	NA	NA
Female...	NA	NA	NA	NA	NA	NA	NA
Age							
16 to 19 years...............................	40	20	50.2	18	46.0	2	8.4
20 to 24 years...............................	55	45	80.3	40	72.2	5	10.1
25 to 34 years...............................	122	106	87.3	102	84.1	4	3.7
35 to 44 years...............................	92	82	89.6	80	87.2	2	2.8
45 to 54 years...............................	100	86	85.8	84	84.4	1	1.6
55 to 64 years...............................	110	83	75.8	82	74.5	1	1.7
65 years and over...........................	135	34	24.9	33	24.4	1	2.1

NOTE: Data in Table 7 are from the Current Population Survey (CPS) and do not match the estimates in Table 8. See notes and definitions for further information.
[1]May be of any race.
NA = Not available.
... = Fewer than 500 persons

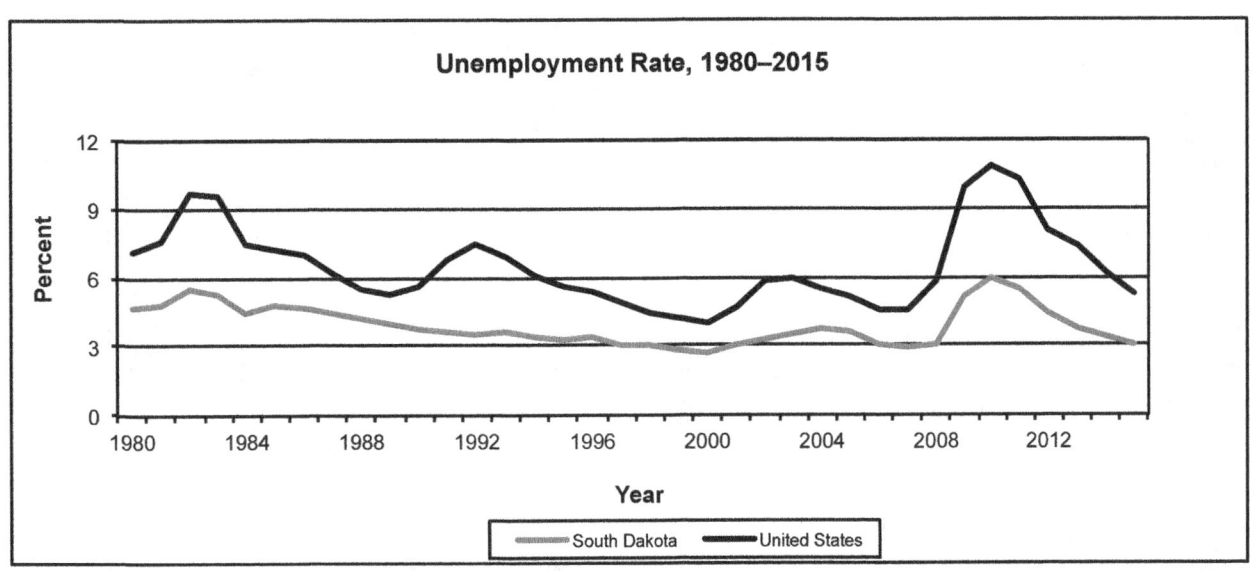

Table SD-8. Employment Status of the Civilian Noninstitutional Population Age 16 Years and Over

(Number, percent.)

Year	Civilian labor force	Civilian participation rate	Employed	Unemployed	Unemployment rate
2007..	442,499	73.2	430,011	12,488	2.8
2008..	446,618	73.0	432,925	13,693	3.1
2009..	446,010	72.2	423,993	22,017	4.9
2010..	441,339	71.3	419,355	21,984	5.0
2011..	440,934	70.6	420,054	20,880	4.7
2012..	442,575	70.0	423,651	18,924	4.3
2013..	444,880	69.4	428,075	16,805	3.8
2014..	448,631	69.3	433,203	15,428	3.4
2015..	452,300	69.4	438,077	14,223	3.1

Table SD-9. Employment and Average Wages by Industry

(Estimates through 2010 are based on the 2007 North American Industry Classification System [NAICS]. Estimates from 2011 onward are based on the 2012 NAICS.)

Industry	2008	2009	2010	2011	2012	2013	2014
	Number of jobs						
Wage and Salary Employment by Industry..................	431,600	423,697	425,114	430,256	436,165	439,202	445,282
Farm Wage and Salary Employment.........................	5,446	4,595	5,049	5,522	7,410	6,538	6,359
Nonfarm Wage and Salary Employment....................	426,154	419,102	420,065	424,734	428,755	432,664	438,923
Private wage and salary employment........................	344,190	334,741	334,353	339,612	344,489	348,757	354,446
Forestry, fishing, and related activities................	1,685	1,659	1,750	1,887	1,888	2,336	2,438
Mining........................	932	836	818	832	849	846	816
Utilities........................	2,073	2,112	2,092	2,071	1,968	1,950	1,967
Construction	23,157	21,842	21,086	21,234	20,833	21,249	21,937
Manufacturing........................	42,789	37,806	37,044	39,291	41,244	41,582	42,453
Durable goods manufacturing........................	29,331	24,780	24,033	25,909	27,225	27,535	28,488
Nondurable goods manufacturing........................	13,458	13,026	13,011	13,382	14,019	14,047	13,965
Wholesale trade	18,854	18,474	18,741	19,138	19,596	19,988	20,908
Retail trade........................	50,829	50,351	50,354	50,958	51,535	51,742	52,306
Transportation and warehousing........................	11,012	10,617	10,484	10,576	10,547	10,563	11,272
Information........................	6,967	6,709	6,556	6,388	6,213	6,034	6,058
Finance and insurance	27,632	27,150	26,098	25,537	26,149	27,155	27,145
Real estate and rental and leasing........................	3,815	3,700	3,540	3,561	3,552	3,649	3,736
Professional, scientific, and technical services	11,167	11,210	11,363	11,353	11,662	12,569	12,500
Management of companies and enterprises.................	3,500	3,474	3,624	3,768	4,145	4,234	4,572
Administrative and waste services........................	13,925	12,568	12,965	13,850	13,645	13,125	13,401
Educational services	7,562	7,547	7,755	7,995	8,257	8,104	8,255
Health care and social assistance........................	55,047	56,043	57,046	57,726	59,188	59,915	60,115
Arts, entertainment, and recreation........................	6,694	6,564	6,492	6,494	6,355	6,218	6,417
Accommodation and food services........................	37,003	36,822	37,067	37,497	38,265	38,738	39,317
Other services, except public administration..............	19,547	19,257	19,478	19,456	18,598	18,760	18,833
Government and government enterprises........................	81,964	84,361	85,712	85,122	84,266	83,907	84,477
	Dollars						
Average Wages and Salaries by Industry	32,681	33,063	33,922	34,997	36,143	36,818	38,246
Average Farm Wages and Salaries	48,558	43,156	36,547	39,449	40,233	42,115	43,377
Average Nonfarm Wages and Salaries	32,478	32,952	33,890	34,939	36,072	36,738	38,172
Average private wages and salaries........................	32,238	32,635	33,664	34,871	36,137	36,880	38,451
Forestry, fishing, and related activities........................	23,228	23,896	25,166	26,424	26,815	27,262	25,842
Mining........................	51,013	46,606	49,559	55,826	57,390	55,916	58,817
Utilities........................	62,172	61,671	64,919	67,087	69,488	73,263	74,712
Construction	36,834	38,064	38,086	38,975	39,916	40,944	42,877
Manufacturing........................	37,766	38,331	39,905	41,470	42,169	42,441	44,512
Durable goods manufacturing........................	38,057	38,738	40,479	42,408	42,827	43,521	45,257
Nondurable goods manufacturing........................	37,130	37,556	38,844	39,653	40,891	40,324	42,991
Wholesale trade	45,108	45,552	46,634	48,900	51,348	52,936	54,996
Retail trade........................	21,951	22,174	23,106	23,737	24,553	25,175	26,199
Transportation and warehousing........................	38,531	38,151	39,442	41,362	42,678	42,658	43,571
Information........................	39,198	39,258	39,883	41,852	42,761	43,315	44,845
Finance and insurance	43,764	44,097	45,798	48,146	49,779	50,341	52,960
Real estate and rental and leasing........................	25,308	25,806	26,736	28,099	29,592	30,629	32,356
Professional, scientific, and technical services	45,148	44,612	46,400	49,024	51,611	49,892	52,661
Management of companies and enterprises.................	78,377	74,858	88,748	88,044	89,097	91,512	92,716
Administrative and waste services........................	23,904	24,478	25,336	25,528	26,948	27,162	29,191
Educational services	22,972	23,579	24,613	24,618	23,821	24,751	24,496
Health care and social assistance........................	38,257	39,496	40,093	41,580	43,084	44,302	45,795
Arts, entertainment, and recreation........................	17,459	17,863	17,795	18,001	17,939	18,142	18,781
Accommodation and food services........................	13,271	13,390	14,050	14,494	14,922	15,243	15,939
Other services, except public administration..............	22,661	23,171	23,623	24,220	25,654	26,270	27,787
Government and government enterprises........................	33,486	34,210	34,770	35,210	35,806	36,147	37,001

Table SD-10. Employment Characteristics by Family Type

(Number, percent.)

Family type and labor force status	2012		2013		2014	
	Total	Families with own children under 18 years	Total	Families with own children under 18 years	Total	Families with own children under 18 years
All Families....................................	206,668	88,894	213,838	94,183	210,903	88,396
FAMILY TYPE AND LABOR FORCE STATUS						
Married-Couple Families......................	159,567	58,663	166,793	62,905	165,397	59,765
Both husband and wife in labor force............	61.6	79.2	62.3	79.6	61.7	78.8
Husband in labor force, wife not in labor force......	16.0	17.0	15.5	15.6	16.2	17.2
Wife in labor force, husband not in labor force.........	7.3	3.0	6.9	3.1	7.0	2.7
Both husband and wife not in labor force.........	15.1	0.8	14.9	1.4	15.1	1.3
Other Families	47,101	30,231	47,045	31,278	45,506	28,631
Female householder, no husband present..................	70.4	73.9	67.4	69.9	68.7	73.3
In labor force............................	54.9	65.9	51.0	58.5	51.7	61.6
Not in labor force	15.5	8.0	16.4	11.4	17.0	11.7
Male householder, no wife present..................	29.6	26.1	32.6	30.1	31.3	26.7
In labor force..................................	23.9	23.4	25.6	26.9	26.8	26.0
Not in labor force	5.6	2.7	7.0	3.2	4.5	0.7

Table SD-11. School Enrollment and Educational Attainment, 2014

(Number, percent.)

Item	State	U.S.
Enrollment		
Total population 3 years and over, enrolled in school..............	223,281	82,063,714
Enrolled in nursery school or preschool (percent)	7.5	6.0
Enrolled in kindergarten (percent)............................	4.8	5.1
Enrolled in elementary school, grades 1-8 (percent)............	41.3	40.2
Enrolled in high school, grades 9-12 (percent)................	20.7	20.7
Enrolled in college or graduate school (percent)................	25.8	28.0
Attainment		
Total population 25 years and over	555,488	213,725,624
Less than ninth grade (percent)..............................	3.4	5.6
9th to 12th grade, no diploma (percent)	4.9	7.5
High school graduate, including equivalency (percent)...........	30.6	27.7
Some college, no degree (percent)	22.0	21.0
Associate's degree (percent)	11.3	8.2
Bachelor's degree (percent)	20.0	18.7
Graduate or professional degree (percent).....................	7.8	11.4
High school graduate or higher (percent)	91.7	86.9
Bachelor's degree or higher (percent)	27.8	30.1

Table SD-12. Public School Characteristics and Educational Indicators

(Number, percent; data derived from National Center of Education Statistics.)

Item	State	U.S.
Public Schools, 2013–2014 (except where noted)		
Number of school districts............................	170	18,194
Number of schools..	699	98,271
Number of students (in thousands)	131	50,045
Number of teachers (in thousands)	10	3,114
Student-teacher ratio	13.8	16.1
Expenditures per student (dollars), FY 2013..............	8,630	107,637
Four-year adjusted cohort graduation rate (ACGR)[1,2]	82.7	82.3
Students eligible for free or reduced-price lunch (in thousands)	52	25,596
English language learners (in thousands)	4	4,461
Students age 3 to 21 served under IDEA, part B (in thousands)	19	6,464

Public Schools by Type	Number	Percent of state public schools
Total number of schools...................................	699	100.0
Regular..	656	93.8
Special education..	9	1.3
Vocational education.....................................	3	0.4
Alternative education....................................	31	4.4

NOTE: Every school is assigned only one school type based on its instructional emphasis.
[1]ACGR data represents a new method of calculating high-school completion rates and may not be comparable to previous years' data for Averaged Freshmen Graduation Rates (AFGR).
[2]The United States 4-year ACGRs were estimated using both the reported 4-year ACGR data from 49 states and the District of Columbia and using imputed data for Idaho. The estimate for American Indian/Alaska Native students also includes imputed data for Virginia.

Table SD-13. Reported Voting and Registration of the Voting-Age Population, November 2014

(Numbers in thousands, percent.)

Item	Total population	Total citizen population	Registered			Voted		
			Total registered	Percent registered (total population)	Percent registered (total citizen population)	Total voted	Percent voted (total population)	Percent voted (total citizen population)
U.S. Total	239,874	219,941	142,166	59.3	64.6	92,251	38.5	41.9
State Total..............................	625	618	401	64.2	64.9	273	43.7	44.1
Sex								
Male..	308	304	189	61.4	62.1	132	42.8	43.3
Female....................................	317	314	212	67.0	67.7	141	44.5	45.0
Race								
White alone.............................	562	558	369	65.7	66.1	259	46.2	46.5
White, non-Hispanic alone...........	551	549	367	66.6	66.8	259	46.9	47.0
Black alone..............................	12	11	5	(B)	(B)	3	(B)	(B)
Asian alone.............................	4	1	-	(B)	(B)	-	(B)	(B)
Hispanic (of any race)......................	12	10	3	(B)	(B)	-	(B)	(B)
White alone or in combination.........	565	562	372	65.9	66.3	262	46.3	46.6
Black alone or in combination..........	14	13	7	(B)	(B)	5	(B)	(B)
Asian alone or in combination..........	4	1	-	(B)	(B)	-	(B)	(B)
Age								
18 to 24 years.........................	69	67	24	(B)	(B)	8	(B)	(B)
25 to 34 years.........................	125	122	67	53.7	55.3	32	25.2	26.0
35 to 44 years.........................	86	85	62	71.7	72.6	42	48.1	48.7
45 to 64 years.........................	233	233	161	68.8	68.9	124	52.9	53.0
65 years and over	111	111	87	78.8	78.8	68	61.4	61.4

- = Zero or rounds to zero.
B = Base is less than 75,000 and therefore too small to show the derived measure.

Table SD-14. Crime

(Number, rate per 100,000. Data are derived from the FBI Uniform Crime Reports.)

Item	State			U.S.[1,2,3,4]		
	2013	2014	Percent change	2013	2014	Percent change
TOTAL POPULATION[5].............................	844,877	853,175	1.0	316,128,839	318,857,056	0.9
VIOLENT CRIME						
Number.............................	2,524	2,786	10.4	1,163,146	1,165,383	0.2
Rate	298.7	326.5	9.3	367.9	365.5	-0.7
Murder and Nonnegligent Manslaughter						
Number.............................	20	20	0.0	14,196	14,249	0.4
Rate	2.4	2.3	-4.2	4.5	4.5	-
Rape[6]						
Number.............................	499	470	X	108,612	116,645	X
Rate	59.1	55.1	X	34.4	36.6	X
Robbery						
Number.............................	159	200	25.8	345,031	325,802	-5.6
Rate	18.8	23.4	24.5	109.1	102.2	-6.3
Aggravated Assault						
Number.............................	1,996	2,096	5.0	724,149	741,291	2.4
Rate	236.2	245.7	4.0	229.1	232.5	1.5
PROPERTY CRIME						
Number.............................	16,177	15,902	-1.7	8,632,512	8,277,829	-4.1
Rate	1,914.7	1,863.9	-2.7	2,730.7	2,596.1	-4.9
Burglary						
Number.............................	3,372	2,818	-16.4	1,928,465	1,729,806	-10.3
Rate	399.1	330.3	-17.2	610.0	542.5	-11.1
Larceny-Theft						
Number.............................	11,867	12,077	1.8	6,004,453	5,858,496	-2.4
Rate	1,404.6	1,415.5	0.8	1,899.4	1,837.3	-3.3
Motor Vehicle Theft						
Number.............................	938	1,007	7.4	699,594	689,527	-1.4
Rate	111.0	118.0	6.3	221.3	216.2	-2.3

NOTE: Although arson data are included in the trend and clearance tables, sufficient data are not available to estimate totals for this offense. Therefore, no arson data are published in this table.
X = Not applicable.
- = Zero or rounds to zero.
[1]The crime figures have been adjusted.
[2]The data collection methodology for the offense of forcible rape used by the Minnesota state Uniform Crime Reporting (UCR) Program (with the exception of Minneapolis and St. Paul, Minnesota) does not comply with national UCR Program guidelines. Consequently, its figures for forcible rape and violent crime (of which forcible rape is a part) are not published in this table.
[3]Includes offenses reported by the Zoological Police and the Metro Transit Police.
[4]Because of changes in the state's reporting practices, figures are not comparable to previous years' data.
[5]Populations are U.S. Census Bureau provisional estimates as of July 1 of each year.
[6]The figures shown for the offense of rape were estimated using the revised Uniform Crime Reporting (UCR) definition of rape.

Table SD-15. State Government Finances, 2014

(Dollar amounts in thousands, percent distribution.)

Item	Dollars	Percent distribution
Total Revenue	6,124,116	100.0
General revenue	4,161,877	68.0
Intergovernmental revenue	1,573,610	25.7
Taxes	1,608,496	26.3
General sales	914,979	14.9
Selective sales	381,769	6.2
License taxes	277,787	4.5
Individual income tax	0	0.0
Corporate income tax	24,819	0.4
Other taxes	9,142	0.1
Current charges	353,860	5.8
Miscellaneous general revenue	625,911	10.2
Utility revenue	0	-
Liquor stores revenue	0	-
Insurance trust revenue[1]	1,962,239	32.0
Total Expenditure	4,520,937	100.0
Intergovernmental expenditure	745,993	16.5
Direct expenditure	3,774,944	83.5
Current operation	2,542,615	56.2
Capital outlay	556,804	12.3
Insurance benefits and repayments	481,797	10.7
Assistance and subsidies	86,008	1.9
Interest on debt	107,720	2.4
Exhibit: Salaries and wages	976,144	21.6
Total Expenditure	4,520,937	100.0
General expenditure	4,039,140	89.3
Intergovernmental expenditure	745,993	16.5
Direct expenditure	3,293,147	72.8
General expenditure, by function:		
Education	1,277,578	28.3
Public welfare	986,197	21.8
Hospitals	22,598	0.5
Health	188,174	4.2
Highways	615,254	13.6
Police protection	38,553	0.9
Correction	123,618	2.7
Natural resources	179,499	4.0
Parks and recreation	48,256	1.1
Governmental administration	179,037	4.0
Interest on general debt	107,720	2.4
Other and unallocable	272,656	6.0
Utility expenditure	0	-
Liquor stores expenditure	0	-
Insurance trust expenditure	481,797	10.7
Debt at End of Fiscal Year	3,239,167	X
Cash and Security Holdings	15,655,347	X

X = Not applicable.
- = Zero or rounds to zero.
[1]Within insurance trust revenue, net earnings of state retirement systems is a calculated statistic (the item code in the data file is X08), and thus can be positive or negative. Net earnings is the sum of earnings on investments plus gains on investments minus losses on investments. The change made in 2002 for asset valuation from book to market value in accordance with Statement 34 of the Governmental Accounting Standards Board is reflected in the calculated statistics.

Table SD-16. State Government Tax Collections, 2014

(Dollars in thousands, percent.)

Item	Dollars	Percent distribution
Total Taxes	1,608,496	100.0
Property taxes	X	X
Sales and gross receipts	1,296,748	80.6
General sales and gross receipts	914,979	56.9
Selective sales and gross receipts	381,769	~
Alcoholic beverages	16,205	1.0
Amusements	8,885	0.6
Insurance premiums	77,374	4.8
Motor fuels	138,087	8.6
Pari-mutuels	461	-
Public utilities	3,709	0.2
Tobacco products	61,811	3.8
Other selective sales	75,237	4.7
Licenses	277,787	17.3
Alcoholic beverages	840	0.1
Amusements	6,980	0.4
Corporations in general	4,688	0.3
Hunting and fishing	27,781	1.7
Motor vehicle	76,143	4.7
Motor vehicle operators	3,773	0.2
Public utilities	0	-
Occupation and business, NEC	135,841	8.4
Other licenses	21,741	1.4
Income taxes	24,819	1.5
Individual income	X	X
Corporation net income	24,819	1.5
Other taxes	9,142	0.6
Death and gift	0	-
Documentary and stock transfer	192	-
Severance	8,950	0.6
Taxes, NEC	0	-

X = Not applicable.
- = Zero or rounds to zero.

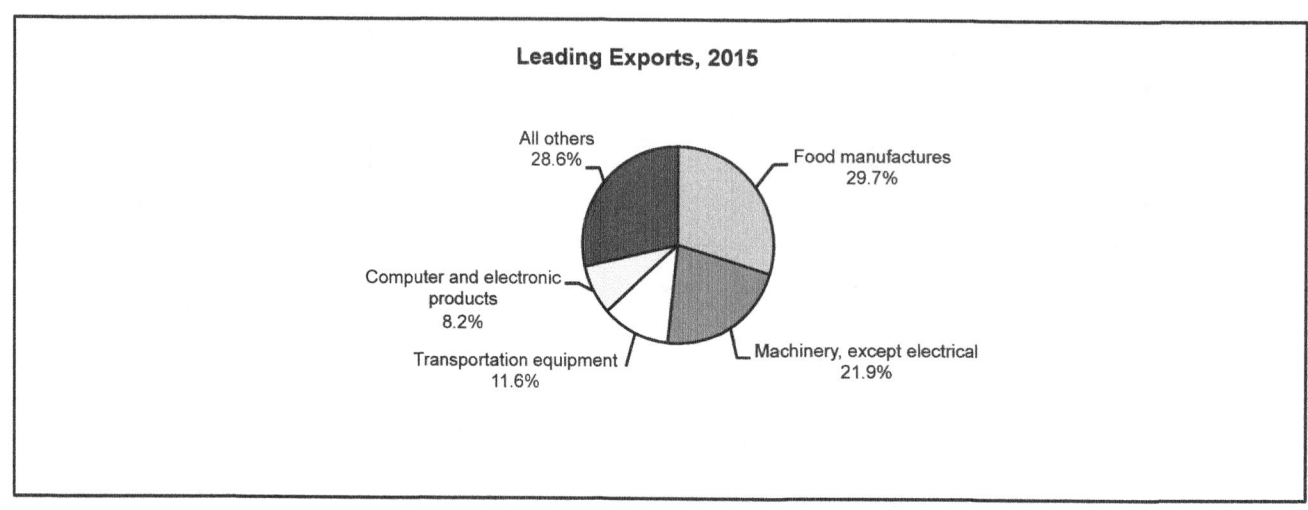

Leading Exports, 2015

All others 28.6%
Food manufactures 29.7%
Computer and electronic products 8.2%
Transportation equipment 11.6%
Machinery, except electrical 21.9%

TENNESSEE

Facts and Figures

Location: South central United States; bordered on the N by Kentucky and Virginia, on the E by North Carolina, on the S by Georgia, Alabama, and Mississippi, and on the W by Arkansas and Missouri

Area: 42,143 sq. mi. (109,151 sq. km.); rank—36th

Population: 6,600,299 (2015 est.); rank—17th

Principal Cities: capital—Nashville; largest—Memphis

Statehood: June 1, 1796; 16th state

U.S. Congress: 2 senators, 9 representatives

State Motto: Agriculture and Commerce

State Song: "The Tennessee Waltz"

State Nickname: The Volunteer State

Abbreviations: TN; Tenn.

State Symbols: flower—iris; tree—yellow poplar (tulip poplar); bird—mockingbird

At a Glance

- With an increase in population of 3.8 percent, Tennessee ranked 22nd among the states in growth from 2010 to 2015.

- Tennessee's median household income in 2014 was $44,361, and 18.3 percent of the population lived below the poverty level.

- In 2014, 12.0 percent of Tennesseans did not have health insurance, compared to 11.7 percent of the total U.S. population.

- Tennessee's violent crime rate in 2014 was 608.4 per 100,000 population, compared to 365.5 for the entire nation; this was the 4th highest rate in the country.

- Tennessee's unemployment rate of 5.8 percent ranked 15th among the states in 2015 and was slightly higher than the national rate of 5.3 percent.

Table TN-1. Population by Age, Sex, Race, and Hispanic Origin

(Number, percent, except where noted.)

Sex, age, race, and Hispanic origin	2000	2010	2015[1]	Average annual percent change, 2010–2015
Total Population..	5,689,283	6,346,105	6,600,299	0.3
Percent of total U.S. population	2.0	2.1	2.1	X
Sex				
Male..	2,770,275	3,093,504	3,217,461	0.3
Female...	2,919,008	3,252,601	3,382,838	0.3
Age				
Under 5 years...	374,880	407,813	402,183	-0.1
5 to 19 years..	1,186,152	1,268,308	1,258,718	-0.1
20 to 64 years...	3,424,940	3,816,522	3,922,846	0.2
65 years and over	703,311	853,462	1,016,552	1.3
Median age (years)	35.9	38.0	38.6	0.1
Race and Hispanic Origin				
One race				
White	4,563,310	5,056,311	5,199,238	0.2
Black	932,809	1,068,010	1,129,765	0.4
American Indian and Alaska Native	15,152	26,256	29,480	0.8
Asian..	56,662	93,897	117,196	1.6
Native Hawaiian or Other Pacific Islander	2,205	5,426	6,419	1.2
Two or more races	63,109	96,205	118,201	1.5
Hispanic (of any race)	123,838	301,090	340,508	0.9

X = Not applicable.
[1]Population figures for 2015 are July 1 estimates. The 2010 estimates are taken from the 2010 Census.

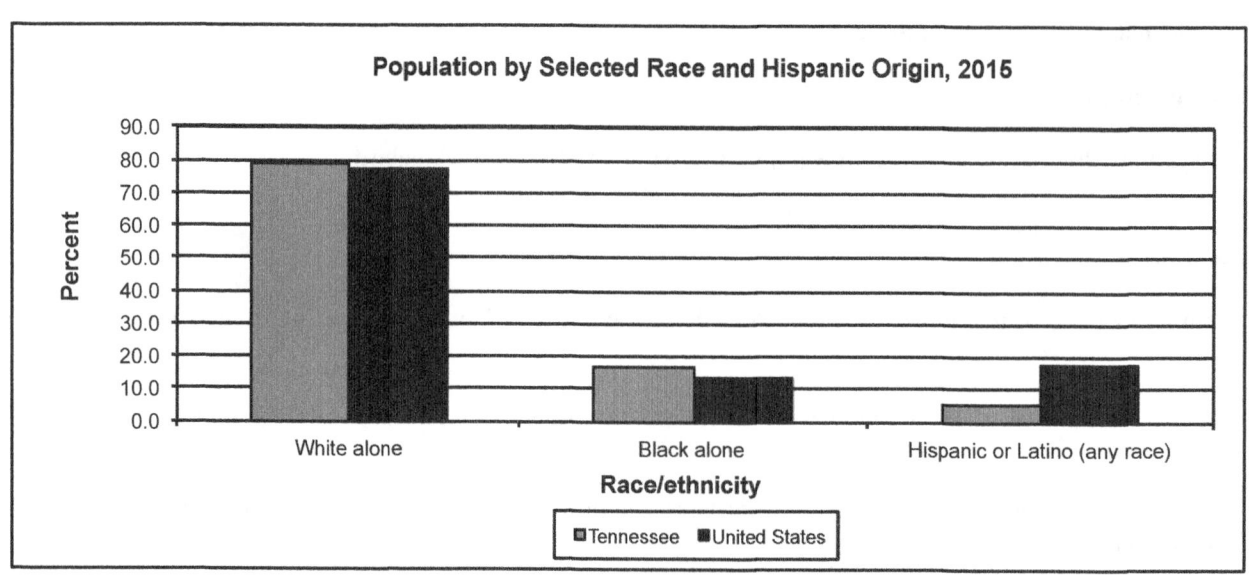

Table TN-2. Marital Status

(Number, percent distribution.)

Sex, age, race, and Hispanic origin	2000	2010	2014
Males, 15 Years and Over	2,169,327	2,461,573	2,510,764
Never married	26.6	31.4	31.7
Now married, except separated.....................................	58.9	52.2	51.9
Separated..	1.7	2.1	2.0
Widowed..	2.5	2.7	2.8
Divorced..	10.4	11.7	11.6
Females, 15 Years and Over	2,353,303	2,652,823	2,701,222
Never married	20.7	25.3	26.0
Now married, except separated.....................................	53.6	47.9	47.7
Separated..	2.3	2.7	2.6
Widowed..	11.2	10.3	10.0
Divorced..	12.2	13.7	13.7

Table TN-3. Households and Housing Characteristics

(Number, percent, dollars.)

Item	2000	2010	2014	Average annual percent change, 2000–2014
Total Households	2,232,905	2,440,663	2,509,665	0.9
Family households	1,547,835	1,644,896	1,660,344	0.5
Married-couple family	1,173,960	1,195,406	1,203,038	0.2
Other family	373,875	449,490	457,306	1.6
Male householder, no wife present	85,976	106,616	114,935	2.4
Female householder, no husband present	287,899	342,874	342,371	1.4
Nonfamily households	685,070	795,767	849,321	1.7
Householder living alone	576,401	675,565	709,149	1.6
Householder not living alone	108,669	120,202	140,172	2.1
Housing Characteristics				
Total housing units	2,439,443	2,815,087	2,869,419	1.3
Occupied housing units	2,232,905	2,440,663	2,509,665	0.9
Owner occupied	1,561,363	1,662,768	1,659,797	0.5
Renter occupied	671,542	777,895	849,868	1.9
Average household size	2.48	2.54	2.55	0.2
Financial Characteristics				
Median gross rent of renter-occupied housing	505	697	770	3.7
Median monthly owner costs for housing units with a mortgage	882	1,161	1,167	2.3
Median value of owner-occupied housing units	93,000	139,000	142,900	3.8

Table TN-4. Migration, Origin, and Language

(Number, percent.)

Characteristic	State 2013	State 2014	State Percent change	U.S. 2013	U.S. 2014	U.S. Percent change
Residence 1 Year Ago						
Population 1 year and over	6,419,226	6,471,445	0.8	312,432,820	315,095,393	0.9
Same house	84.6	84.4	X	85.0	85.1	X
Different house in the U.S.	15.0	15.1	X	14.4	14.3	X
Same county	9.2	9.1	X	8.9	8.7	X
Different county	5.9	6.1	X	5.5	5.6	X
Same state	3.0	3.3	X	3.2	3.3	X
Different state	2.9	2.8	X	2.3	2.3	X
Abroad	0.4	0.4	X	0.6	0.6	X
Place of Birth						
Native born	6,191,177	6,228,094	0.6	274,780,773	276,465,262	0.6
Male	48.7	48.6	X	49.3	49.3	X
Female	51.3	51.4	X	50.7	50.7	X
Foreign born	304,801	321,258	5.4	41,348,066	42,391,794	2.5
Male	53.2	51.7	X	48.8	48.7	X
Female	46.8	48.3	X	51.2	51.3	X
Foreign born; naturalized U.S. citizen	114,362	115,725	1.2	19,294,710	19,984,738	3.6
Male	48.8	47.1	X	45.9	45.9	X
Female	51.2	52.9	X	54.1	54.1	X
Foreign born; not a U.S. citizen	190,439	205,533	7.9	22,053,356	22,407,056	1.6
Male	55.8	54.3	X	51.3	51.2	X
Female	44.2	45.7	X	48.7	48.8	X
Entered 2010 or later	12.8	16.5	X	9.7	12.3	X
Entered 2000 to 2009	41.8	39.5	X	29.4	28.6	X
Entered before 2000	45.4	44.0	X	61.0	59.1	X
World Region of Birth, Foreign						
Foreign-born population, excluding population born at sea	304,801	321,258	5.4	41,347,945	42,390,705	2.5
Europe	9.6	10.5	X	11.6	11.2	X
Asia	29.9	30.1	X	29.5	30.1	X
Africa	10.7	9.8	X	4.4	4.6	X
Oceania	0.4	0.5	X	0.5	0.6	X
Latin America	46.8	46.5	X	51.9	51.6	X
North America	2.6	2.5	X	2.0	1.9	X
Language Spoken at Home and Ability to Speak English						
Population 5 years and over	6,098,770	6,150,997	0.9	296,358,760	299,084,046	0.9
English only	93.5	93.0	X	79.2	78.9	X
Language other than English	6.5	7.0	X	20.8	21.1	X
Speaks English less than "very well"	2.7	2.9	X	8.5	8.6	X

X = Not applicable.
- = Zero or rounds to zero.

Table TN-5. Median Income and Poverty Status, 2014

(Number, percent, except as noted.)

Characteristic	State		U.S.	
	Number	Percent	Number	Percent
Median Income				
Households (dollars)..	44,361	X	53,657	X
Families (dollars)	55,557	X	65,910	X
Below Poverty Level (All People)	1,171,307	18.3	48,208,387	15.5
Sex				
Male..	521,616	16.8	21,590,918	14.2
Female	649,691	19.8	26,617,469	16.8
Age				
Under 18 years..	384,065	26.2	15,686,012	21.7
Related children under 18 years............................	378,596	25.9	15,372,705	21.3
18 to 64 years	690,357	17.4	28,267,482	14.6
65 years and over	96,885	10.1	4,254,893	9.5

X = Not applicable.

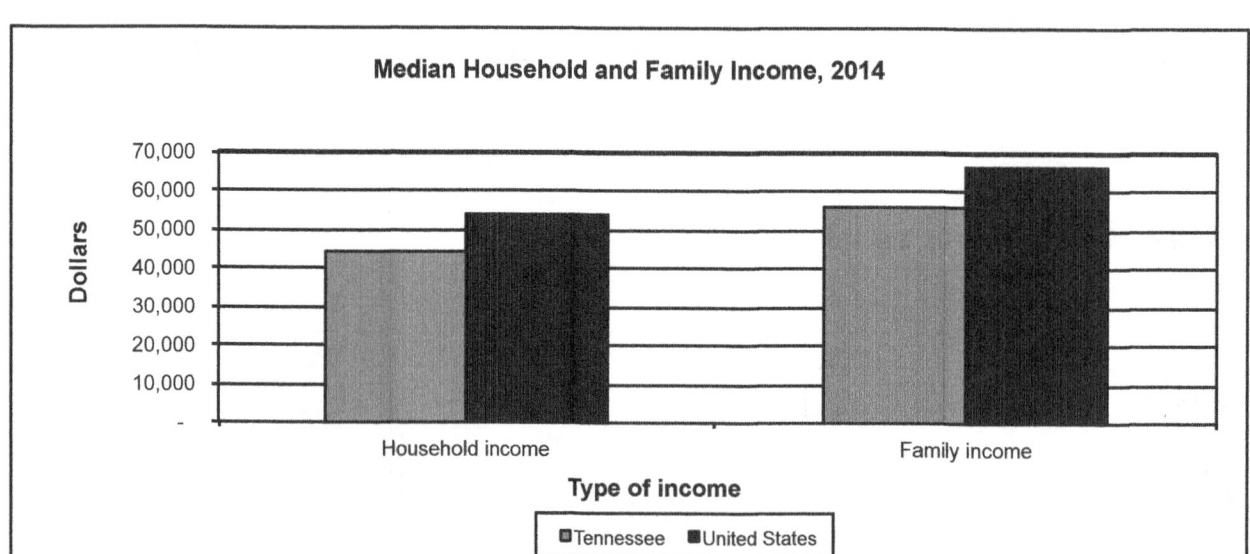

Table TN-6. Health Insurance Coverage Status for the Civilian Noninstitutionalized Population and Children Under 18 Years of Age

(Numbers in thousands, percent.)

Item	2006	2007	2008	2009	2010	2011	2012	2013	2014
Civilian Noninstitutionalized Population	5,920	6,150	6,113	6,188	6,260	6,302	6,355	6,395	6,449
Covered by Private or Public Insurance									
Number...	5,111	5,268	5,279	5,305	5,361	5,380	5,473	5,508	5,672
Percent..	86.3	85.6	86.4	85.7	85.6	85.4	86.1	86.1	88.0
Not Covered									
Number...	809	883	834	883	899	923	882	887	776
Percent..	13.7	14.4	13.6	14.3	14.4	14.6	13.9	13.9	12.0
Percent in the U.S. not covered.............................	15.8	15.3	15.1	15.1	15.5	15.1	14.8	14.5	11.7
Children Under 18 Years of Age	1,468	1,479	1,476	1,488	1,493	1,488	1,490	1,490	1,490
Covered by Private or Public Insurance									
Number...	1,376	1,344	1,370	1,401	1,414	1,403	1,405	1,404	1,412
Percent..	93.6	90.9	92.8	94.1	94.7	94.3	94.3	94.3	94.8
Not Covered									
Number...	94	135	106	87	79	85	85	85	78
Percent..	6.4	9.1	7.2	5.9	5.3	5.7	5.7	5.7	5.2
Percent in the U.S. not covered.............................	11.7	11.0	9.7	8.6	8.0	7.5	7.2	7.1	6.0

Table TN-7. Employment Status by Demographic Group, 2015

(Numbers in thousands, percent.)

Characteristic	Civilian noninstitutional population	Civilian labor force		Employed		Unemployed	
		Number	Percent of population	Number	Percent of population	Number	Percent of population
Total...	5,169	3,088	59.7	2,913	56.4	175	5.7
Sex							
Male.............................	2,472	1,660	67.2	1,569	63.5	91	5.5
Female	2,697	1,428	52.9	1,344	49.8	84	5.9
Race, Sex, and Hispanic Origin							
White	4,149	2,439	58.8	2,315	55.8	124	5.1
Male.............................	2,012	1,351	67.1	1,284	63.8	67	5.0
Female	2,137	1,088	50.9	1,031	48.3	57	5.2
Black or African American....................	834	531	63.7	491	58.9	40	7.5
Male.............................	375	247	66.0	230	61.4	18	7.1
Female	459	284	61.8	261	56.9	23	8.0
Hispanic or Latino ethnicity[1]	244	169	69.3	162	66.5	7	4.0
Male.............................	134	112	83.4	108	80.3	4	3.7
Female	110	57	52.1	55	49.7	3	4.5
Age							
16 to 19 years	315	121	38.4	97	30.8	24	19.9
20 to 24 years	440	332	75.4	299	67.9	33	10.0
25 to 34 years	919	723	78.8	686	74.7	37	5.1
35 to 44 years	778	611	78.5	578	74.2	33	5.4
45 to 54 years	851	636	74.7	611	71.8	25	3.9
55 to 64 years	836	497	59.4	480	57.4	17	3.4
65 years and over	1,030	168	16.3	162	15.8	6	3.6

NOTE: Data in Table 7 are from the Current Population Survey (CPS) and do not match the estimates in Table 8. See notes and definitions for further information.
[1]May be of any race.

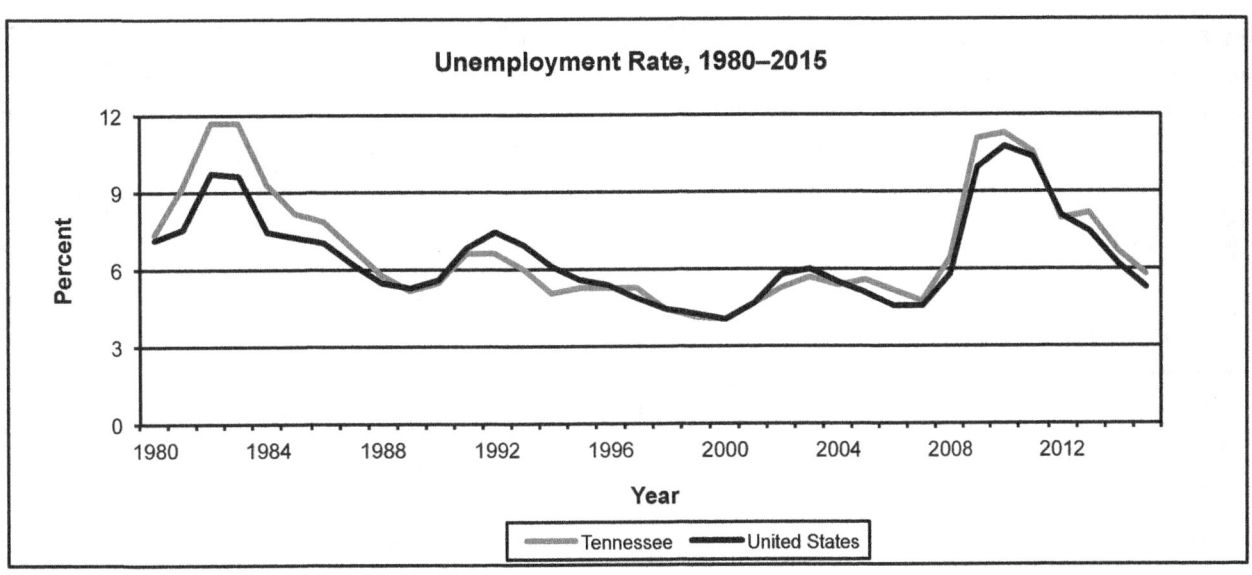

Table TN-8. Employment Status of the Civilian Noninstitutional Population Age 16 Years and Over

(Number, percent.)

Year	Civilian labor force	Civilian participation rate	Employed	Unemployed	Unemployment rate
2007..........................	3,063,669	64.4	2,920,352	143,317	4.7
2008..........................	3,054,785	63.4	2,853,746	201,039	6.6
2009..........................	3,052,678	62.7	2,733,113	319,565	10.5
2010..........................	3,090,795	62.7	2,792,063	298,732	9.7
2011..........................	3,125,307	62.8	2,844,662	280,645	9.0
2012..........................	3,103,047	61.8	2,860,355	242,692	7.8
2013..........................	3,077,048	60.7	2,837,898	239,150	7.8
2014..........................	3,046,632	59.6	2,847,777	198,855	6.5
2015..........................	3,062,775	59.3	2,886,024	176,751	5.8

Table TN-9. Employment and Average Wages by Industry

(Estimates through 2010 are based on the 2007 North American Industry Classification System [NAICS]. Estimates from 2011 onward are based on the 2012 NAICS.)

Industry	2008	2009	2010	2011	2012	2013	2014
	Number of jobs						
Wage and Salary Employment by Industry	2,888,909	2,728,711	2,724,777	2,769,845	2,812,441	2,849,940	2,909,569
Farm Wage and Salary Employment	9,417	8,408	8,553	9,176	9,592	9,183	9,914
Nonfarm Wage and Salary Employment	2,879,492	2,720,303	2,716,224	2,760,669	2,802,849	2,840,757	2,899,655
Private wage and salary employment	2,425,718	2,267,069	2,258,202	2,306,093	2,353,034	2,394,111	2,454,139
Forestry, fishing, and related activities	4,435	4,364	4,640	4,946	5,061	4,672	5,057
Mining	3,921	3,228	3,549	3,595	3,429	3,424	3,426
Utilities	3,502	3,557	3,358	3,318	3,375	3,341	3,383
Construction	133,007	110,843	105,805	110,330	108,364	107,599	109,921
Manufacturing	361,391	310,581	300,054	304,462	314,069	319,023	325,261
Durable goods manufacturing	220,844	183,414	177,658	183,824	194,495	199,166	205,388
Nondurable goods manufacturing	140,547	127,167	122,396	120,638	119,574	119,857	119,873
Wholesale trade	133,097	121,872	117,878	118,463	121,131	122,885	123,833
Retail trade	330,882	311,720	312,020	314,622	315,881	318,240	323,798
Transportation and warehousing	142,618	132,539	131,704	135,709	141,067	144,189	147,726
Information	49,457	46,328	44,465	43,166	42,858	43,563	43,346
Finance and insurance	110,908	108,330	108,748	107,450	108,597	106,915	109,260
Real estate and rental and leasing	37,054	34,418	33,566	32,197	32,483	33,816	35,266
Professional, scientific, and technical services	113,057	109,270	108,798	111,188	112,012	115,315	121,101
Management of companies and enterprises	25,011	25,384	26,049	28,981	31,555	35,187	37,311
Administrative and waste services	186,666	162,171	172,034	186,512	195,911	205,247	217,706
Educational services	50,179	51,646	52,859	54,018	55,506	55,925	57,114
Health care and social assistance	319,706	324,095	329,625	337,410	344,253	347,840	350,819
Arts, entertainment, and recreation	31,678	30,643	30,098	30,688	30,776	31,888	32,973
Accommodation and food services	245,713	236,137	235,798	240,228	248,324	256,544	265,547
Other services, except public administration	143,436	139,943	137,154	138,810	138,382	138,498	141,291
Government and government enterprises	453,774	453,234	458,022	454,576	449,815	446,646	445,516
	Dollars						
Average Wages and Salaries by Industry	39,445	39,703	41,014	41,876	43,328	43,516	44,632
Average Farm Wages and Salaries	21,405	22,775	21,148	17,635	18,909	26,911	24,615
Average Nonfarm Wages and Salaries	39,504	39,755	41,076	41,957	43,411	43,570	44,700
Average private wages and salaries	39,735	39,966	41,469	42,371	43,971	44,032	45,141
Forestry, fishing, and related activities	21,564	21,791	22,823	23,723	24,422	25,446	25,854
Mining	58,717	56,977	63,525	61,540	64,397	63,443	67,968
Utilities	58,384	60,849	61,574	63,018	63,663	65,546	67,942
Construction	43,717	43,063	44,294	45,565	47,108	47,568	49,874
Manufacturing	48,142	48,676	51,869	52,883	54,726	54,654	56,303
Durable goods manufacturing	47,416	47,799	50,763	51,775	54,256	53,186	55,140
Nondurable goods manufacturing	49,282	49,942	53,474	54,572	55,490	57,093	58,297
Wholesale trade	55,927	55,571	57,503	59,658	62,080	61,569	64,269
Retail trade	26,000	26,140	27,034	27,726	28,105	27,871	28,633
Transportation and warehousing	46,866	46,212	48,116	49,590	50,007	50,847	51,144
Information	52,288	52,156	54,018	57,046	59,006	58,898	61,783
Finance and insurance	62,796	62,915	66,006	68,066	72,406	72,240	74,916
Real estate and rental and leasing	37,351	37,077	38,103	39,862	42,098	42,620	44,689
Professional, scientific, and technical services	60,904	61,699	64,532	65,860	70,896	70,483	71,997
Management of companies and enterprises	77,906	73,568	82,160	83,175	99,429	98,288	97,018
Administrative and waste services	29,674	30,985	31,425	31,174	32,651	33,174	32,254
Educational services	32,786	33,462	33,653	34,218	34,605	35,561	35,913
Health care and social assistance	42,791	44,015	44,835	45,500	46,352	46,680	47,757
Arts, entertainment, and recreation	38,710	37,798	40,385	41,880	44,209	44,020	47,130
Accommodation and food services	16,981	17,059	17,829	18,186	18,365	17,957	18,681
Other services, except public administration	27,052	27,517	28,455	29,204	29,825	30,171	31,760
Government and government enterprises	38,271	38,701	39,142	39,856	40,485	41,093	42,274

Table TN-10. Employment Characteristics by Family Type

(Number, percent.)

Family type and labor force status	2012		2013		2014	
	Total	Families with own children under 18 years	Total	Families with own children under 18 years	Total	Families with own children under 18 years
All Families................................	1,641,665	681,582	1,658,071	677,544	1,655,480	684,060
FAMILY TYPE AND LABOR FORCE STATUS						
Married-Couple Families.....................	1,200,647	446,140	1,208,430	439,638	1,198,174	447,165
Both husband and wife in labor force............	48.4	63.5	48.6	64.3	48.0	64.3
Husband in labor force, wife not in labor force.........	23.3	30.0	22.4	28.6	23.2	29.2
Wife in labor force, husband not in labor force.........	8.8	4.2	9.1	4.7	9.1	4.2
Both husband and wife not in labor force.........	19.5	2.3	19.8	2.2	19.8	2.3
Other Families	441,018	235,442	449,641	237,906	457,306	236,895
Female householder, no husband present............	74.9	76.0	74.1	75.6	74.9	77.9
In labor force	50.8	60.8	50.5	60.9	49.8	61.8
Not in labor force	24.1	15.2	23.6	14.7	25.1	16.2
Male householder, no wife present............	25.1	24.0	25.9	24.4	25.1	22.1
In labor force............................	19.1	21.3	19.8	21.9	18.2	19.5
Not in labor force	6.0	2.7	6.1	2.6	7.0	2.6

Table TN-11. School Enrollment and Educational Attainment, 2014

(Number, percent.)

Item	State	U.S.
Enrollment		
Total population 3 years and over, enrolled in school..............	1,589,191	82,063,714
Enrolled in nursery school or preschool (percent)...............	5.5	6.0
Enrolled in kindergarten (percent)...............	5.0	5.1
Enrolled in elementary school, grades 1-8 (percent)...............	42.2	40.2
Enrolled in high school, grades 9-12 (percent)...............	21.5	20.7
Enrolled in college or graduate school (percent)...............	25.8	28.0
Attainment		
Total population 25 years and over	4,425,073	213,725,624
Less than ninth grade (percent)	5.4	5.6
9th to 12th grade, no diploma (percent)	8.8	7.5
High school graduate, including equivalency (percent)...............	33.3	27.7
Some college, no degree (percent)	20.5	21.0
Associate's degree (percent)	6.7	8.2
Bachelor's degree (percent)	16.2	18.7
Graduate or professional degree (percent)...............	9.1	11.4
High school graduate or higher (percent)	85.8	86.9
Bachelor's degree or higher (percent)	25.3	30.1

Table TN-12. Public School Characteristics and Educational Indicators

(Number, percent; data derived from National Center of Education Statistics.)

Item	State	U.S.
Public Schools, 2013–2014 (except where noted)		
Number of school districts..............	140	18,194
Number of schools..............	1,855	98,271
Number of students (in thousands)	994	50,045
Number of teachers (in thousands)	66	3,114
Student-teacher ratio	15.1	16.1
Expenditures per student (dollars), FY 2013	8,588	107,637
Four-year adjusted cohort graduation rate (ACGR)[1,2]	87.2	82.3
Students eligible for free or reduced-price lunch (in thousands)	578	25,596
English language learners (in thousands)	34	4,461
Students age 3 to 21 served under IDEA, part B (in thousands)	130	6,464

Public Schools by Type	Number	Percent of state public schools
Total number of schools..............	1,855	100.0
Regular..............	1,797	96.9
Special education..............	16	0.9
Vocational education..............	19	1.0
Alternative education..............	23	1.2

NOTE: Every school is assigned only one school type based on its instructional emphasis.
[1]ACGR data represents a new method of calculating high-school completion rates and may not be comparable to previous years' data for Averaged Freshmen Graduation Rates (AFGR).
[2]The United States 4-year ACGRs were estimated using both the reported 4-year ACGR data from 49 states and the District of Columbia and using imputed data for Idaho. The estimate for American Indian/Alaska Native students also includes imputed data for Virginia.

Table TN-13. Reported Voting and Registration of the Voting-Age Population, November 2014

(Numbers in thousands, percent.)

Item	Total population	Total citizen population	Registered			Voted		
			Total registered	Percent registered (total population)	Percent registered (total citizen population)	Total voted	Percent voted (total population)	Percent voted (total citizen population)
U.S. Total	239,874	219,941	142,166	59.3	64.6	92,251	38.5	41.9
State Total.............................	4,975	4,815	3,088	62.1	64.1	1,763	35.4	36.6
Sex								
Male....................................	2,366	2,275	1,376	58.2	60.5	793	33.5	34.8
Female	2,609	2,539	1,712	65.6	67.4	970	37.2	38.2
Race								
White alone...........................	4,014	3,895	2,545	63.4	65.3	1,481	36.9	38.0
White, non-Hispanic alone	3,821	3,799	2,503	65.5	65.9	1,467	38.4	38.6
Black alone............................	793	782	473	59.7	60.5	244	30.7	31.2
Asian alone	84	54	21	(B)	(B)	12	(B)	(B)
Hispanic (of any race).................	202	105	42	20.6	39.8	13	6.6	12.7
White alone or in combination	4,079	3,960	2,588	63.5	65.4	1,504	36.9	38.0
Black alone or in combination.........	803	792	480	59.8	60.6	247	30.7	31.2
Asian alone or in combination.........	91	61	24	(B)	(B)	12	(B)	(B)
Age								
18 to 24 years.........................	661	652	272	41.1	41.7	78	11.8	11.9
25 to 34 years.........................	803	741	387	48.2	52.2	137	17.1	18.5
35 to 44 years.........................	817	772	515	63.1	66.7	300	36.7	38.8
45 to 64 years.........................	1,750	1,714	1,184	67.7	69.1	747	42.7	43.6
65 years and over	945	935	730	77.3	78.1	502	53.1	53.7

B = Base is less than 75,000 and therefore too small to show the derived measure.

Table TN-14. Crime

(Number, rate per 100,000. Data are derived from the FBI Uniform Crime Reports.)

Item	State			U.S.[1,2,3,4]		
	2013	2014	Percent change	2013	2014	Percent change
TOTAL POPULATION[5]...........................	6,495,978	6,549,352	0.8	316,128,839	318,857,056	0.9
VIOLENT CRIME						
Number...............................	37,655	39,848	5.8	1,163,146	1,165,383	0.2
Rate	579.7	608.4	5.0	367.9	365.5	-0.7
Murder and Nonnegligent Manslaughter						
Number...............................	328	371	13.1	14,196	14,249	0.4
Rate	5.0	5.7	14.0	4.5	4.5	-
Rape[6]						
Number...............................	2,351	2,531	X	108,612	116,645	X
Rate	36.2	38.6	X	34.4	36.6	X
Robbery						
Number...............................	7,307	7,265	-0.6	345,031	325,802	-5.6
Rate	112.5	110.9	-1.4	109.1	102.2	-6.3
Aggravated Assault						
Number...............................	28,378	29,681	4.6	724,149	741,291	2.4
Rate	436.9	453.2	3.7	229.1	232.5	1.5
PROPERTY CRIME						
Number...............................	206,629	200,447	-3.0	8,632,512	8,277,829	-4.1
Rate	3,180.9	3,060.6	-3.8	2,730.7	2,596.1	-4.9
Burglary						
Number...............................	50,999	46,642	-8.5	1,928,465	1,729,806	-10.3
Rate	785.1	712.2	-9.3	610.0	542.5	-11.1
Larceny-Theft						
Number...............................	143,802	141,206	-1.8	6,004,453	5,858,496	-2.4
Rate	2,213.7	2,156.0	-2.6	1,899.4	1,837.3	-3.3
Motor Vehicle Theft						
Number...............................	11,828	12,599	6.5	699,594	689,527	-1.4
Rate	182.1	192.4	5.7	221.3	216.2	-2.3

NOTE: Although arson data are included in the trend and clearance tables, sufficient data are not available to estimate totals for this offense. Therefore, no arson data are published in this table.
X = Not applicable.
- = Zero or rounds to zero.
[1]The crime figures have been adjusted.
[2]The data collection methodology for the offense of forcible rape used by the Minnesota state Uniform Crime Reporting (UCR) Program (with the exception of Minneapolis and St. Paul, Minnesota) does not comply with national UCR Program guidelines. Consequently, its figures for forcible rape and violent crime (of which forcible rape is a part) are not published in this table.
[3]Includes offenses reported by the Zoological Police and the Metro Transit Police.
[4]Because of changes in the state's reporting practices, figures are not comparable to previous years' data.
[5]Populations are U.S. Census Bureau provisional estimates as of July 1 of each year.
[6]The figures shown for the offense of rape were estimated using the revised Uniform Crime Reporting (UCR) definition of rape.

Table TN-15. State Government Finances, 2014

(Dollar amounts in thousands, percent distribution.)

Item	Dollars	Percent distribution
Total Revenue	31,290,576	100.0
General revenue	26,493,021	84.7
Intergovernmental revenue	10,645,251	34.0
Taxes	11,806,329	37.7
General sales	6,192,281	19.8
Selective sales	2,565,804	8.2
License taxes	1,335,392	4.3
Individual income tax	239,219	0.8
Corporate income tax	1,176,971	3.8
Other taxes	296,662	0.9
Current charges	2,113,069	6.8
Miscellaneous general revenue	1,928,372	6.2
Utility revenue	0	-
Liquor stores revenue	0	-
Insurance trust revenue[1]	4,797,555	15.3
Total Expenditure	30,518,934	100.0
Intergovernmental expenditure	7,221,663	23.7
Direct expenditure	23,297,271	76.3
Current operation	18,065,274	59.2
Capital outlay	1,364,863	4.5
Insurance benefits and repayments	2,436,140	8.0
Assistance and subsidies	1,175,812	3.9
Interest on debt	255,182	0.8
Exhibit: Salaries and wages	3,915,962	12.8
Total Expenditure	30,518,934	100.0
General expenditure	28,082,794	92.0
Intergovernmental expenditure	7,221,663	23.7
Direct expenditure	20,861,131	68.4
General expenditure, by function:		
Education	10,115,387	33.1
Public welfare	10,922,445	35.8
Hospitals	413,232	1.4
Health	664,920	2.2
Highways	1,640,075	5.4
Police protection	241,188	0.8
Correction	934,521	3.1
Natural resources	294,152	1.0
Parks and recreation	88,262	0.3
Governmental administration	884,716	2.9
Interest on general debt	255,182	0.8
Other and unallocable	1,628,714	5.3
Utility expenditure	0	-
Liquor stores expenditure	0	-
Insurance trust expenditure	2,436,140	8.0
Debt at End of Fiscal Year	6,049,178	X
Cash and Security Holdings	46,888,874	X

X = Not applicable.
- = Zero or rounds to zero.
[1]Within insurance trust revenue, net earnings of state retirement systems is a calculated statistic (the item code in the data file is X08), and thus can be positive or negative. Net earnings is the sum of earnings on investments plus gains on investments minus losses on investments. The change made in 2002 for asset valuation from book to market value in accordance with Statement 34 of the Governmental Accounting Standards Board is reflected in the calculated statistics.

Table TN-16. State Government Tax Collections, 2014

(Dollars in thousands, percent.)

Item	Dollars	Percent distribution
Total Taxes	11,806,329	100.0
Property taxes	X	X
Sales and gross receipts	8,758,085	74.2
General sales and gross receipts	6,192,281	52.4
Selective sales and gross receipts	2,565,804	21.7
Alcoholic beverages	147,812	1.3
Amusements	0	-
Insurance premiums	749,470	6.3
Motor fuels	845,395	7.2
Pari-mutuels	0	-
Public utilities	6,840	0.1
Tobacco products	261,101	2.2
Other selective sales	555,186	4.7
Licenses	1,335,392	11.3
Alcoholic beverages	1,317	-
Amusements	376	-
Corporations in general	676,478	5.7
Hunting and fishing	32,959	0.3
Motor vehicle	269,317	2.3
Motor vehicle operators	47,194	0.4
Public utilities	5,840	-
Occupation and business, NEC	293,122	2.5
Other licenses	8,789	0.1
Income taxes	1,416,190	12.0
Individual income	239,219	2.0
Corporation net income	1,176,971	10.0
Other taxes	296,662	2.5
Death and gift	107,341	0.9
Documentary and stock transfer	167,055	1.4
Severance	2,487	-
Taxes, NEC	19,779	0.2

X = Not applicable.
- = Zero or rounds to zero.

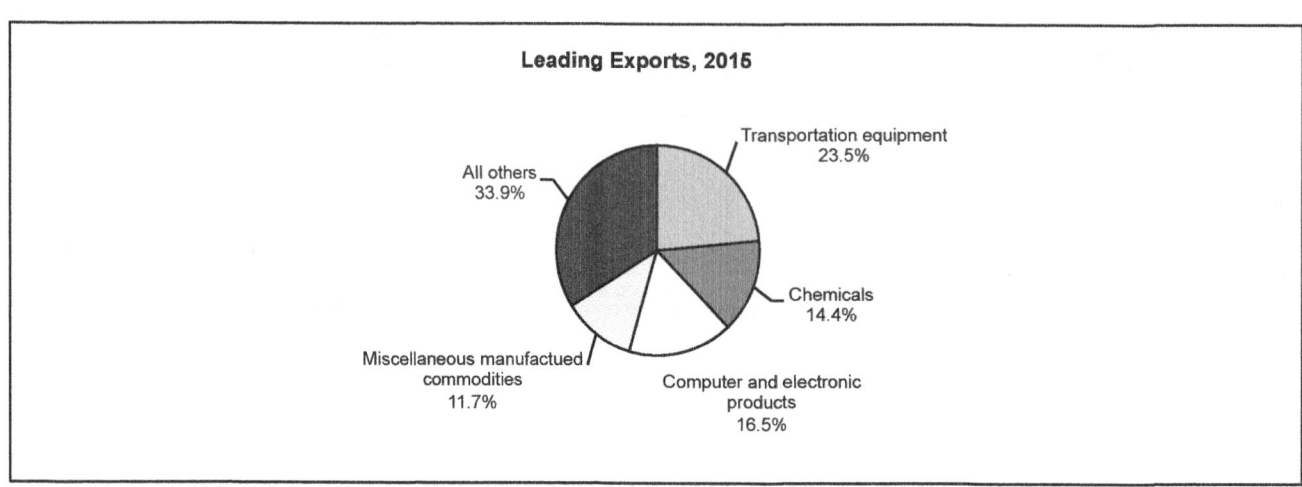

Leading Exports, 2015

Transportation equipment 23.5%
Chemicals 14.4%
Computer and electronic products 16.5%
Miscellaneous manufactued commodities 11.7%
All others 33.9%

Facts and Figures

Location: West South Central United States; bordered on the N by Oklahoma, on the E by Arkansas and Louisiana, on the S by Mexico and the Gulf of Mexico, and on the W by Mexico and New Mexico

Area: 268,581 sq. mi. (695,621 sq. km.); rank—2nd

Population: 27,469,114 (2015 est.); rank—2nd

Principal Cities: capital—Austin; largest—Houston

Statehood: December 29, 1845; 28th state

U.S. Congress: 2 senators, 36 representatives

State Motto: Friendship

State Song: "Texas, Our Texas"

State Nickname: The Lone Star State

Abbreviations: TX; Tex.

State Symbols: flower—bluebonnet; tree—pecan; bird—mockingbird

At a Glance

- With an increase in population of 8.8 percent, Texas ranked 3rd among the states in growth from 2010 to 2015.

- Texas's median household income in 2014 was $53,035, and 17.2 percent of the population lived below the poverty level.

- In 2014, 19.1 percent of Texans did not have health insurance, compared to 11.7 percent of the total U.S. population.

- Texas's violent crime rate in 2014 was 405.9 per 100,000 population, compared to 365.5 for the entire nation.

- The property crime rate in Texas in 2014, 3,019.4 per 100,000 population, ranked 13th in the United States.

Table TX-1. Population by Age, Sex, Race, and Hispanic Origin

(Number, percent, except where noted.)

Sex, age, race, and Hispanic origin	2000	2010	2015[1]	Average annual percent change, 2010–2015
Total Population..	20,851,820	25,145,561	27,469,114	0.6
Percent of total U.S. population	7.4	8.1	8.5	X
Sex				
Male...	10,352,910	12,472,280	13,637,790	0.6
Female..	10,498,910	12,673,281	13,831,324	0.6
Age				
Under 5 years...	1,625,628	1,928,473	1,983,640	0.2
5 to 19 years...	4,291,608	5,693,241	5,982,490	0.4
20 to 64 years...	12,233,052	14,921,961	16,277,816	0.6
65 years and over...	2,072,532	2,601,886	3,225,168	1.5
Median age (years)...	32.3	33.6	34.3	0.1
Race and Hispanic Origin				
One race				
White...	14,799,505	20,389,793	21,889,275	0.5
Black...	2,404,566	3,070,440	3,444,190	0.8
American Indian and Alaska Native	118,362	251,209	280,463	0.8
Asian...	562,319	1,000,473	1,299,874	1.9
Native Hawaiian or Other Pacific Islander	14,434	31,242	38,217	1.4
Two or more races..	514,633	402,404	517,095	1.8
Hispanic (of any race)...	6,699,666	9,578,505	10,670,101	0.8

X = Not applicable.
[1]Population figures for 2015 are July 1 estimates. The 2010 estimates are taken from the 2010 Census.

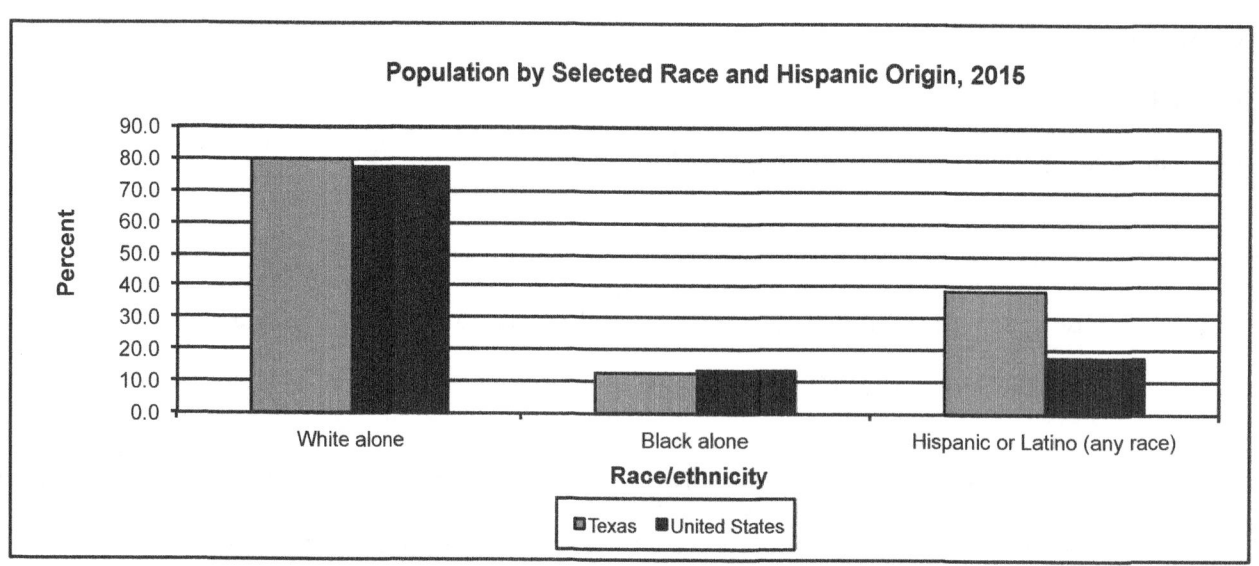

Table TX-2. Marital Status

(Number, percent distribution.)

Sex, age, race, and Hispanic origin	2000	2010	2014
Males, 15 Years and Over	7,820,248	9,587,343	9,961,996
Never married	28.6	34.6	34.8
Now married, except separated....................................	58.8	51.6	51.3
Separated..	2.0	2.3	2.2
Widowed..	2.1	2.2	2.2
Divorced..	8.5	9.4	9.4
Females, 15 Years and Over	8,117,395	9,903,147	10,276,164
Never married	22.6	27.6	28.4
Now married, except separated....................................	54.3	48.5	48.0
Separated..	2.9	3.3	3.2
Widowed..	9.1	8.1	8.1
Divorced..	11.0	12.5	12.3

Table TX-3. Households and Housing Characteristics

(Number, percent, dollars.)

Item	2000	2010	2014	Average annual percent change, 2000–2014
Total Households...	7,393,354	8,738,664	9,277,197	1.8
Family households	5,247,794	6,091,590	6,407,165	1.6
Married-couple family	3,989,741	4,386,996	4,603,234	1.1
Other family	1,258,053	1,704,594	1,803,931	3.1
Male householder, no wife present...........................	320,464	436,727	477,204	3.5
Female householder, no husband present...................	937,489	1,267,867	1,326,727	3.0
Nonfamily households	2,145,560	2,647,074	2,870,032	2.4
Householder living alone.....................................	1,752,141	2,166,469	2,346,941	2.4
Householder not living alone................................	393,419	480,605	523,091	2.4
Housing Characteristics				
Total housing units...	8,157,575	9,996,209	10,426,760	2.0
Occupied housing units	7,393,354	8,738,664	9,277,197	1.8
Owner occupied	4,716,959	5,555,903	5,674,241	1.4
Renter occupied	2,676,395	3,182,761	3,602,956	2.5
Average household size..	2.74	2.82	2.84	0.3
Financial Characteristics				
Median gross rent of renter-occupied housing	574	801	896	4.0
Median monthly owner costs for housing units with a mortgage	986	1,402	1,419	3.1
Median value of owner-occupied housing units	82,500	128,100	139,600	4.9

Table TX-4. Migration, Origin, and Language

(Number, percent.)

Characteristic	State			U.S.		
	2013	2014	Percent change	2013	2014	Percent change
Residence 1 Year Ago						
Population 1 year and over	26,087,349	26,588,600	1.9	312,432,820	315,095,393	0.9
Same house	83.0	83.3	X	85.0	85.1	X
Different house in the U.S.	16.3	15.9	X	14.4	14.3	X
Same county	10.0	9.8	X	8.9	8.7	X
Different county	6.2	6.1	X	5.5	5.6	X
Same state	4.1	4.1	X	3.2	3.3	X
Different state	2.1	2.0	X	2.3	2.3	X
Abroad	0.7	0.8	X	0.6	0.6	X
Place of Birth						
Native born	22,078,922	22,434,530	1.6	274,780,773	276,465,262	0.6
Male	49.5	49.5	X	49.3	49.3	X
Female	50.5	50.5	X	50.7	50.7	X
Foreign born	4,369,271	4,522,428	3.5	41,348,066	42,391,794	2.5
Male	50.6	50.3	X	48.8	48.7	X
Female	49.4	49.7	X	51.2	51.3	X
Foreign born; naturalized U.S. citizen	1,491,058	1,579,958	6.0	19,294,710	19,984,738	3.6
Male	47.4	47.6	X	45.9	45.9	X
Female	52.6	52.4	X	54.1	54.1	X
Foreign born; not a U.S. citizen	2,878,213	2,942,470	2.2	22,053,356	22,407,056	1.6
Male	52.3	51.7	X	51.3	51.2	X
Female	47.7	48.3	X	48.7	48.8	X
Entered 2010 or later	9.6	12.8	X	9.7	12.3	X
Entered 2000 to 2009	31.2	30.6	X	29.4	28.6	X
Entered before 2000..	59.2	56.6	X	61.0	59.1	X
World Region of Birth, Foreign						
Foreign-born population, excluding population born at sea	4,369,271	4,522,428	3.5	41,347,945	42,390,705	2.5
Europe	4.3	4.4	X	11.6	11.2	X
Asia	19.5	20.3	X	29.5	30.1	X
Africa	3.8	4.2	X	4.4	4.6	X
Oceania	0.2	0.3	X	0.5	0.6	X
Latin America	71.1	69.9	X	51.9	51.6	X
North America	1.2	1.0	X	2.0	1.9	X
Language Spoken at Home and Ability to Speak English						
Population 5 years and over..	24,521,695	25,010,570	2.0	296,358,760	299,084,046	0.9
English only	65.3	64.5	X	79.2	78.9	X
Language other than English...	34.7	35.5	X	20.8	21.1	X
Speaks English less than "very well"	14.0	14.4	X	8.5	8.6	X

X = Not applicable.
- = Zero or rounds to zero.

Table TX-5. Median Income and Poverty Status, 2014

(Number, percent, except as noted.)

Characteristic	State		U.S.	
	Number	Percent	Number	Percent
Median Income				
Households (dollars)..	53,035	X	53,657	X
Families (dollars)	62,830	X	65,910	X
Below Poverty Level (All People)	4,523,708	17.2	48,208,387	15.5
Sex				
Male...	2,020,844	15.6	21,590,918	14.2
Female..	2,502,864	18.7	26,617,469	16.8
Age				
Under 18 years..	1,728,982	24.6	15,686,012	21.7
Related children under 18 years..	1,702,958	24.3	15,372,705	21.3
18 to 64 years...	2,465,330	15.1	28,267,482	14.6
65 years and over	329,396	10.9	4,254,893	9.5

X = Not applicable.

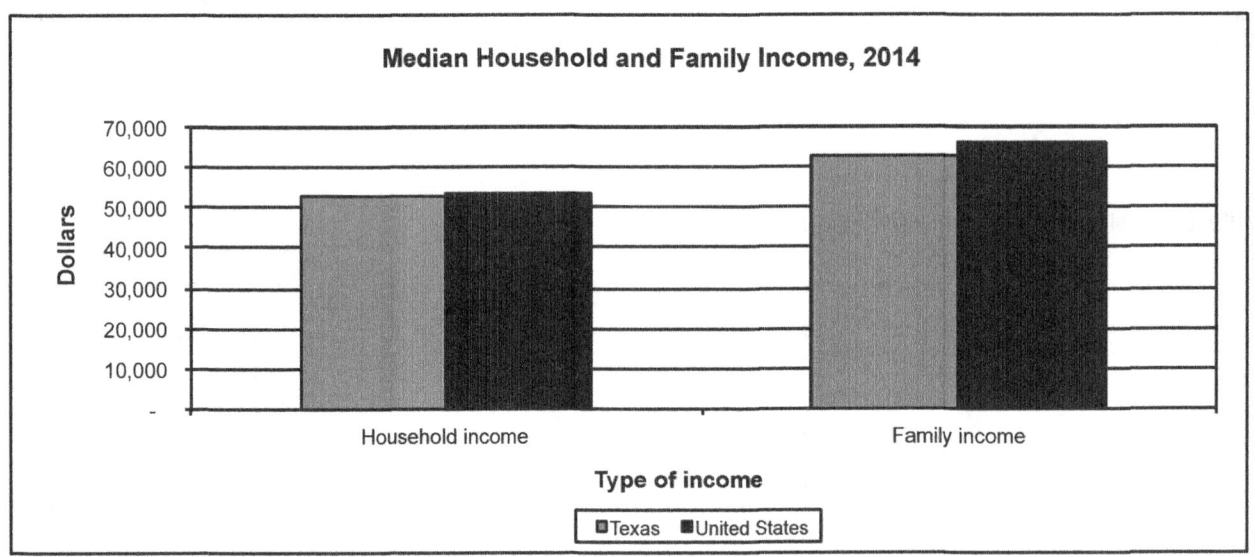

Table TX-6. Health Insurance Coverage Status for the Civilian Noninstitutionalized Population and Children Under 18 Years of Age

(Numbers in thousands, percent.)

Item	2006	2007	2008	2009	2010	2011	2012	2013	2014
Civilian Noninstitutionalized Population	23,236	23,704	23,827	24,292	24,779	25,197	25,584	25,977	26,486
Covered by Private or Public Insurance									
Number..	17,533	17,742	18,082	18,508	18,904	19,408	19,822	20,228	21,438
Percent..	75.5	74.8	75.9	76.2	76.3	77.0	77.5	77.9	80.9
Not Covered									
Number..	5,704	5,962	5,745	5,783	5,875	5,790	5,762	5,748	5,047
Percent..	24.5	25.2	24.1	23.8	23.7	23.0	22.5	22.1	19.1
Percent in the U.S. not covered...	15.8	15.3	15.1	15.1	15.5	15.1	14.8	14.5	11.7
Children Under 18 Years of Age	6,556	6,720	6,714	6,878	6,876	6,947	6,972	7,029	7,107
Covered by Private or Public Insurance									
Number..	5,164	5,285	5,518	5,758	5,880	6,030	6,109	6,140	6,323
Percent..	78.8	78.6	82.2	83.7	85.5	86.8	87.6	87.4	89.0
Not Covered									
Number..	1,392	1,435	1,196	1,120	996	917	863	888	784
Percent..	21.2	21.4	17.8	16.3	14.5	13.2	12.4	12.6	11.0
Percent in the U.S. not covered...	11.7	11.0	9.7	8.6	8.0	7.5	7.2	7.1	6.0

Table TX-7. Employment Status by Demographic Group, 2015

(Numbers in thousands, percent.)

Characteristic	Civilian noninstitutional population	Civilian labor force		Employed		Unemployed	
		Number	Percent of population	Number	Percent of population	Number	Percent of population
Total..	20,470	13,010	63.6	12,434	60.7	576	4.4
Sex							
Male..................	9,942	7,174	72.2	6,846	68.9	328	4.6
Female	10,529	5,836	55.4	5,587	53.1	249	4.3
Race, Sex, and Hispanic Origin							
White.....................	16,405	10,354	63.1	9,934	60.6	420	4.1
Male...........	8,020	5,822	72.6	5,586	69.6	236	4.1
Female	8,385	4,532	54.0	4,349	51.9	183	4.0
Black or African American.................................	2,487	1,605	64.5	1,485	59.7	120	7.5
Male...........	1,142	762	66.7	691	60.5	71	9.3
Female	1,345	842	62.6	793	59.0	49	5.8
Hispanic or Latino ethnicity[1]	7,195	4,652	64.6	4,426	61.5	226	4.9
Male...........	3,550	2,724	76.7	2,600	73.2	124	4.6
Female	3,646	1,928	52.9	1,826	50.1	102	5.3
Age							
16 to 19 years..................	1,478	447	30.2	388	26.2	59	13.1
20 to 24 years..................	2,007	1,415	70.5	1,300	64.8	114	8.1
25 to 34 years..................	3,827	3,015	78.8	2,874	75.1	141	4.7
35 to 44 years..................	3,580	2,920	81.6	2,821	78.8	99	3.4
45 to 54 years..................	3,380	2,689	79.6	2,607	77.1	82	3.1
55 to 64 years..................	3,056	1,928	63.1	1,869	61.2	59	3.0
65 years and over	3,142	597	19.0	575	18.3	22	3.7

NOTE: Data in Table 7 are from the Current Population Survey (CPS) and do not match the estimates in Table 8. See notes and definitions for further information.
[1]May be of any race.

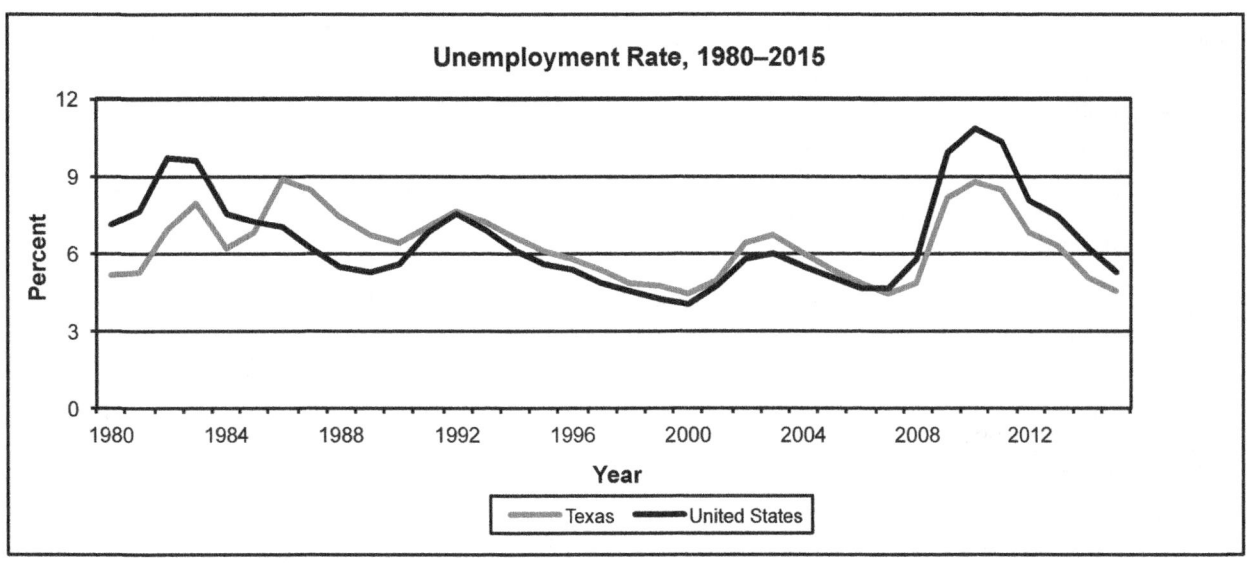

Table TX-8. Employment Status of the Civilian Noninstitutional Population Age 16 Years and Over

(Number, percent.)

Year	Civilian labor force	Civilian participation rate	Employed	Unemployed	Unemployment rate
2007..................	11,431,631	65.7	10,941,413	490,218	4.3
2008..................	11,664,390	65.8	11,104,115	560,275	4.8
2009..................	11,910,799	65.8	11,008,903	901,896	7.6
2010..................	12,241,970	65.9	11,244,632	997,338	8.1
2011..................	12,504,498	65.9	11,535,095	969,403	7.8
2012..................	12,682,204	65.6	11,830,356	851,848	6.7
2013..................	12,891,255	65.4	12,090,501	800,754	6.2
2014..................	13,022,851	64.7	12,358,703	664,148	5.1
2015..................	13,078,304	63.7	12,494,350	583,954	4.5

Table TX-9. Employment and Average Wages by Industry

(Estimates through 2010 are based on the 2007 North American Industry Classification System [NAICS]. Estimates from 2011 onward are based on the 2012 NAICS.)

Industry	2008	2009	2010	2011	2012	2013	2014
	Number of jobs						
Wage and Salary Employment by Industry..................	11,096,319	10,808,235	10,828,653	11,072,783	11,354,264	11,679,288	12,034,808
Farm Wage and Salary Employment..........................	42,703	48,479	44,051	41,328	38,762	45,186	47,052
Nonfarm Wage and Salary Employment....................	11,053,616	10,759,756	10,784,602	11,031,455	11,315,502	11,634,102	11,987,756
Private wage and salary employment............................	9,116,924	8,776,668	8,771,530	9,046,768	9,347,629	9,660,191	10,003,808
Forestry, fishing, and related activities........................	28,127	27,127	28,302	28,775	27,464	31,184	33,209
Mining..	230,088	203,229	203,461	234,092	267,802	287,554	304,261
Utilities...	47,516	48,042	48,316	49,026	48,682	48,928	49,003
Construction	700,532	626,586	592,472	595,688	605,212	636,359	672,200
Manufacturing..	924,271	838,653	811,550	837,471	864,944	874,683	887,940
Durable goods manufacturing................................	608,562	537,342	515,868	543,706	569,709	579,102	590,128
Nondurable goods manufacturing............................	315,709	301,311	295,682	293,765	295,235	295,581	297,812
Wholesale trade	533,936	502,987	501,522	519,424	543,048	563,205	580,402
Retail trade..	1,190,978	1,159,288	1,155,041	1,178,723	1,199,113	1,232,635	1,267,536
Transportation and warehousing...............................	398,766	376,704	377,833	391,232	408,016	416,353	432,883
Information	217,408	205,464	196,069	195,523	197,153	201,393	203,118
Finance and insurance	467,810	458,773	464,849	477,157	493,384	507,422	517,505
Real estate and rental and leasing............................	192,012	182,340	179,127	180,900	184,237	193,518	201,168
Professional, scientific, and technical services	595,415	570,446	577,632	596,946	627,178	653,131	684,600
Management of companies and enterprises...................	74,981	77,042	79,307	83,489	87,586	90,106	110,357
Administrative and waste services	683,145	622,713	637,018	676,759	708,116	731,265	763,295
Educational services	143,269	148,431	153,919	158,713	165,372	166,484	169,054
Health care and social assistance.............................	1,108,291	1,155,375	1,196,470	1,228,565	1,257,684	1,296,295	1,326,634
Arts, entertainment, and recreation...........................	110,219	111,675	111,881	112,998	113,287	119,044	125,914
Accommodation and food services............................	908,255	905,928	909,188	942,578	979,898	1,028,949	1,070,515
Other services, except public administration................	561,905	555,865	547,573	558,709	569,453	581,683	604,214
Government and government enterprises.........................	1,936,692	1,983,088	2,013,072	1,984,687	1,967,873	1,973,911	1,983,948
	Dollars						
Average Wages and Salaries by Industry	45,526	45,255	46,542	48,351	50,087	50,643	52,626
Average Farm Wages and Salaries	31,452	25,333	27,486	35,284	30,938	29,150	33,572
Average Nonfarm Wages and Salaries	45,580	45,345	46,619	48,400	50,153	50,726	52,701
Average private wages and salaries...................................	46,247	45,703	47,146	49,079	51,111	51,652	53,714
Forestry, fishing, and related activities........................	24,408	24,805	25,451	25,907	27,055	26,577	27,453
Mining..	113,073	111,559	117,244	122,085	120,842	119,782	123,759
Utilities...	88,718	88,531	90,004	90,239	98,792	97,694	100,461
Construction...	48,950	48,943	49,195	50,908	54,188	55,707	58,604
Manufacturing...	60,462	60,239	63,181	65,897	68,333	68,729	71,184
Durable goods manufacturing................................	61,921	62,256	65,452	68,327	70,252	70,533	73,154
Nondurable goods manufacturing............................	57,648	56,641	59,220	61,401	64,630	65,196	67,282
Wholesale trade	65,786	65,020	67,874	71,415	74,561	74,164	77,208
Retail trade..	26,668	26,511	27,165	27,902	28,838	29,124	30,043
Transportation and warehousing...............................	51,143	50,639	53,376	55,373	58,444	58,845	60,180
Information	67,122	66,835	67,330	70,722	73,374	75,405	76,682
Finance and insurance	67,795	65,364	68,514	71,569	74,610	75,777	79,575
Real estate and rental and leasing............................	45,620	44,045	45,764	49,099	52,594	53,918	57,353
Professional, scientific, and technical services	73,749	73,877	76,448	79,425	81,796	83,760	86,479
Management of companies and enterprises...................	96,622	94,096	100,017	106,866	113,626	114,060	124,598
Administrative and waste services	34,895	35,198	36,084	36,965	38,382	38,891	40,608
Educational services	34,008	35,127	35,508	36,131	36,912	38,350	38,578
Health care and social assistance.............................	39,377	40,482	40,945	41,719	42,649	42,708	43,895
Arts, entertainment, and recreation...........................	31,476	31,916	31,827	32,702	33,899	32,824	33,600
Accommodation and food services............................	17,625	17,679	18,429	18,982	19,424	19,480	20,343
Other services, except public administration................	27,049	27,341	28,346	29,197	29,883	30,922	31,957
Government and government enterprises.........................	42,445	43,757	44,323	45,306	45,603	46,195	47,590

Table TX-10. Employment Characteristics by Family Type

(Number, percent.)

	2012		2013		2014	
Family type and labor force status	Total	Families with own children under 18 years	Total	Families with own children under 18 years	Total	Families with own children under 18 years
All Families...	6,239,195	3,027,703	6,322,542	3,033,950	6,386,885	3,036,494
FAMILY TYPE AND LABOR FORCE STATUS						
Married-Couple Families..............................	4,492,603	2,051,269	4,552,753	2,049,461	4,582,954	2,049,534
Both husband and wife in labor force..............	51.2	60.3	50.4	59.2	49.9	59.2
Husband in labor force, wife not in labor force	28.1	34.8	28.4	35.6	28.7	36.0
Wife in labor force, husband not in labor force	6.5	3.3	6.9	3.4	6.7	3.2
Both husband and wife not in labor force...............	14.1	1.6	14.0	1.6	14.7	1.6
Other Families	1,746,592	976,434	1,769,789	984,489	1,803,931	986,960
Female householder, no husband present...................	73.3	77.4	74.0	77.9	73.5	77.4
In labor force	52.9	63.3	54.2	64.9	53.1	63.6
Not in labor force	20.5	14.1	19.7	13.0	20.4	13.8
Male householder, no wife present...................	26.7	22.6	26.0	22.1	26.5	22.6
In labor force..	21.8	20.9	21.0	20.1	21.3	20.7
Not in labor force	4.9	1.7	5.1	2.0	5.1	1.8

Table TX-11. School Enrollment and Educational Attainment, 2014

(Number, percent.)

Item	State	U.S.
Enrollment		
Total population 3 years and over, enrolled in school...........	7,467,266	82,063,714
Enrolled in nursery school or preschool (percent)	6.0	6.0
Enrolled in kindergarten (percent)...............	5.6	5.1
Enrolled in elementary school, grades 1-8 (percent)...............	43.2	40.2
Enrolled in high school, grades 9-12 (percent)	20.6	20.7
Enrolled in college or graduate school (percent)...............	24.5	28.0
Attainment		
Total population 25 years and over	17,087,888	213,725,624
Less than ninth grade (percent)	9.0	5.6
9th to 12th grade, no diploma (percent)	8.8	7.5
High school graduate, including equivalency (percent)...............	25.2	27.7
Some college, no degree (percent)	22.5	21.0
Associate's degree (percent)	6.7	8.2
Bachelor's degree (percent)	18.2	18.7
Graduate or professional degree (percent)...............	9.6	11.4
High school graduate or higher (percent)	82.2	86.9
Bachelor's degree or higher (percent)...............	27.8	30.1

Table TX-12. Public School Characteristics and Educational Indicators

(Number, percent; data derived from National Center of Education Statistics.)

Item	State	U.S.
Public Schools, 2013–2014 (except where noted)		
Number of school districts...........	1,252	18,194
Number of schools...........	8,748	98,271
Number of students (in thousands)	5,154	50,045
Number of teachers (in thousands)	335	3,114
Student-teacher ratio	15.4	16.1
Expenditures per student (dollars), FY 2013	8,261	107,637
Four-year adjusted cohort graduation rate (ACGR)[1,2]	88.3	82.3
Students eligible for free or reduced-price lunch (in thousands)	3092	25,596
English language learners (in thousands)	766	4,461
Students age 3 to 21 served under IDEA, part B (in thousands)	444	6,464

Public Schools by Type	Number	Percent of state public schools
Total number of schools...........	8,748	100.0
Regular	7,750	88.6
Special education...........	21	0.2
Vocational education...........	0	0.0
Alternative education...........	977	11.2

NOTE: Every school is assigned only one school type based on its instructional emphasis.
[1]ACGR data represents a new method of calculating high-school completion rates and may not be comparable to previous years' data for Averaged Freshmen Graduation Rates (AFGR).
[2]The United States 4-year ACGRs were estimated using both the reported 4-year ACGR data from 49 states and the District of Columbia and using imputed data for Idaho. The estimate for American Indian/Alaska Native students also includes imputed data for Virginia.

Table TX-13. Reported Voting and Registration of the Voting-Age Population, November 2014

(Numbers in thousands, percent.)

Item	Total population	Total citizen population	Registered			Voted		
			Total registered	Percent registered (total population)	Percent registered (total citizen population)	Total voted	Percent voted (total population)	Percent voted (total citizen population)
U.S. Total	239,874	219,941	142,166	59.3	64.6	92,251	38.5	41.9
State Total.............................	19,354	16,844	9,946	51.4	59.1	5,836	30.2	34.6
Sex								
Male..................................	9,412	8,076	4,606	48.9	57.0	2,600	27.6	32.2
Female	9,941	8,767	5,340	53.7	60.9	3,236	32.5	36.9
Race								
White alone..........................	15,676	13,693	8,124	51.8	59.3	4,820	30.7	35.2
White, non-Hispanic alone	9,238	9,033	5,982	64.8	66.2	3,776	40.9	41.8
Black alone..........................	2,327	2,198	1,334	57.3	60.7	777	33.4	35.3
Asian alone..........................	853	565	259	30.3	45.8	102	11.9	18.0
Hispanic (of any race)	6,762	4,878	2,255	33.4	46.2	1,092	16.2	22.4
White alone or in combination	15,905	13,899	8,255	51.9	59.4	4,906	30.8	35.3
Black alone or in combination..........	2,402	2,264	1,380	57.4	60.9	809	33.7	35.7
Asian alone or in combination..........	877	589	271	30.9	46.0	105	12.0	17.9
Age								
18 to 24 years......................	2,611	2,371	864	33.1	36.4	287	11.0	12.1
25 to 34 years......................	3,815	3,137	1,551	40.6	49.4	687	18.0	21.9
35 to 44 years......................	3,558	2,816	1,646	46.3	58.4	835	23.5	29.7
45 to 64 years......................	6,416	5,681	3,801	59.2	66.9	2,478	38.6	43.6
65 years and over	2,954	2,839	2,085	70.6	73.4	1,548	52.4	54.5

Table TX-14. Crime

(Number, rate per 100,000. Data are derived from the FBI Uniform Crime Reports.)

Item	State			U.S.[1,2,3,4]		
	2013	2014	Percent change	2013	2014	Percent change
TOTAL POPULATION[5]...........................	26,448,193	26,956,958	1.9	313,873,685	316,128,839	0.7
VIOLENT CRIME						
Number..................................	105,736	109,414	3.5	1,217,067	1,163,146	-4.4
Rate	399.8	405.9	1.5	387.8	367.9	-5.1
Murder and Nonnegligent Manslaughter						
Number..................................	1,139	1,184	4.0	14,866	14,196	-4.5
Rate	4.3	4.4	2.3	4.7	4.5	-5.2
Rape[6]						
Number..................................	9,766	11,393	X	X	108,612	X
Rate	36.9	42.3	X	X	34.4	X
Robbery						
Number..................................	31,801	31,181	-1.9	355,051	345,031	-2.8
Rate	120.2	115.7	-3.7	113.1	109.1	-3.5
Aggravated Assault						
Number..................................	65,292	65,656	0.6	762,009	724,149	-5.0
Rate	246.9	243.6	-1.3	242.8	229.1	-5.6
PROPERTY CRIME						
Number..................................	861,734	813,934	-5.5	9,001,992	8,632,512	-4.1
Rate	3,258.2	3,019.4	-7.3	2,868.0	2,730.7	-4.8
Burglary						
Number..................................	190,898	169,234	-11.3	2,109,932	1,928,465	-8.6
Rate	721.8	627.8	-13.0	672.2	610.0	-9.3
Larceny-Theft						
Number..................................	605,091	576,154	-4.8	6,168,874	6,004,453	-2.7
Rate	2,287.8	2,137.3	-6.6	1,965.4	1,899.4	-3.4
Motor Vehicle Theft						
Number..................................	65,745	68,546	4.3	723,186	699,594	-3.3
Rate	248.6	254.3	2.3	230.4	221.3	-4.0

NOTE: Although arson data are included in the trend and clearance tables, sufficient data are not available to estimate totals for this offense. Therefore, no arson data are published in this table.
X = Not applicable.
- = Zero or rounds to zero.
[1]The crime figures have been adjusted.
[2]The data collection methodology for the offense of forcible rape used by the Minnesota state Uniform Crime Reporting (UCR) Program (with the exception of Minneapolis and St. Paul, Minnesota) does not comply with national UCR Program guidelines. Consequently, its figures for forcible rape and violent crime (of which forcible rape is a part) are not published in this table.
[3]Includes offenses reported by the Zoological Police and the Metro Transit Police.
[4]Because of changes in the state's reporting practices, figures are not comparable to previous years' data.
[5]Populations are U.S. Census Bureau provisional estimates as of July 1 of each year.
[6]The figures shown for the offense of rape were estimated using the revised Uniform Crime Reporting (UCR) definition of rape.

Table TX-15. State Government Finances, 2014

(Dollar amounts in thousands, percent distribution.)

Item	Dollars	Percent distribution
Total Revenue	160,134,265	100.0
General revenue	121,679,260	76.0
Intergovernmental revenue	40,561,370	25.3
Taxes	55,260,850	34.5
General sales	32,336,032	20.2
Selective sales	13,410,566	8.4
License taxes	3,499,902	2.2
Individual income tax	0	-
Corporate income tax	0	-
Other taxes	6,014,350	3.8
Current charges	13,297,878	8.3
Miscellaneous general revenue	12,559,162	7.8
Utility revenue	0	-
Liquor stores revenue	0	-
Insurance trust revenue[1]	38,455,005	24.0
Total Expenditure	130,573,820	100.0
Intergovernmental expenditure	29,191,904	22.4
Direct expenditure	101,381,916	77.6
Current operation	72,474,094	55.5
Capital outlay	8,688,183	6.7
Insurance benefits and repayments	15,929,854	12.2
Assistance and subsidies	2,661,749	2.0
Interest on debt	1,628,036	1.2
Exhibit: Salaries and wages	17,088,610	13.1
Total Expenditure	130,573,820	100.0
General expenditure	114,643,966	87.8
Intergovernmental expenditure	29,191,904	22.4
Direct expenditure	85,452,062	65.4
General expenditure, by function:		
Education	50,419,906	38.6
Public welfare	32,833,975	25.1
Hospitals	5,468,585	4.2
Health	2,881,374	2.2
Highways	8,711,014	6.7
Police protection	848,949	0.7
Correction	3,740,764	2.9
Natural resources	1,072,559	0.8
Parks and recreation	164,372	0.1
Governmental administration	1,875,560	1.4
Interest on general debt	1,628,036	1.2
Other and unallocable	4,998,872	3.8
Utility expenditure	0	-
Liquor stores expenditure	0	-
Insurance trust expenditure	15,929,854	12.2
Debt at End of Fiscal Year	41,855,106	X
Cash and Security Holdings	331,456,378	X

X = Not applicable.
- = Zero or rounds to zero.
[1]Within insurance trust revenue, net earnings of state retirement systems is a calculated statistic (the item code in the data file is X08), and thus can be positive or negative. Net earnings is the sum of earnings on investments plus gains on investments minus losses on investments. The change made in 2002 for asset valuation from book to market value in accordance with Statement 34 of the Governmental Accounting Standards Board is reflected in the calculated statistics.

Table TX-16. State Government Tax Collections, 2014

(Dollars in thousands, percent.)

Item	Dollars	Percent distribution
Total Taxes	55,260,850	100.0
Property taxes	X	X
Sales and gross receipts	45,746,598	82.8
General sales and gross receipts	32,336,032	58.5
Selective sales and gross receipts	13,410,566	24.3
Alcoholic beverages	1,066,512	1.9
Amusements	29,659	0.1
Insurance premiums	1,886,289	3.4
Motor fuels	3,325,916	6.0
Pari-mutuels	7,356	-
Public utilities	768,000	1.4
Tobacco products	1,446,144	2.6
Other selective sales	4,880,690	8.8
Licenses	3,499,902	6.3
Alcoholic beverages	71,661	0.1
Amusements	20,664	0.0
Corporations in general	124,996	0.2
Hunting and fishing	104,390	0.2
Motor vehicle	2,177,571	3.9
Motor vehicle operators	139,337	0.3
Public utilities	28,080	0.1
Occupation and business, NEC	668,807	1.2
Other licenses	164,396	0.3
Income taxes	0	-
Individual income	X	X
Corporation net income	X	X
Other taxes	6,014,350	10.9
Death and gift	X	X
Documentary and stock transfer	0	-
Severance	6,014,350	10.9
Taxes, NEC	0	-

X = Not applicable.
- = Zero or rounds to zero.

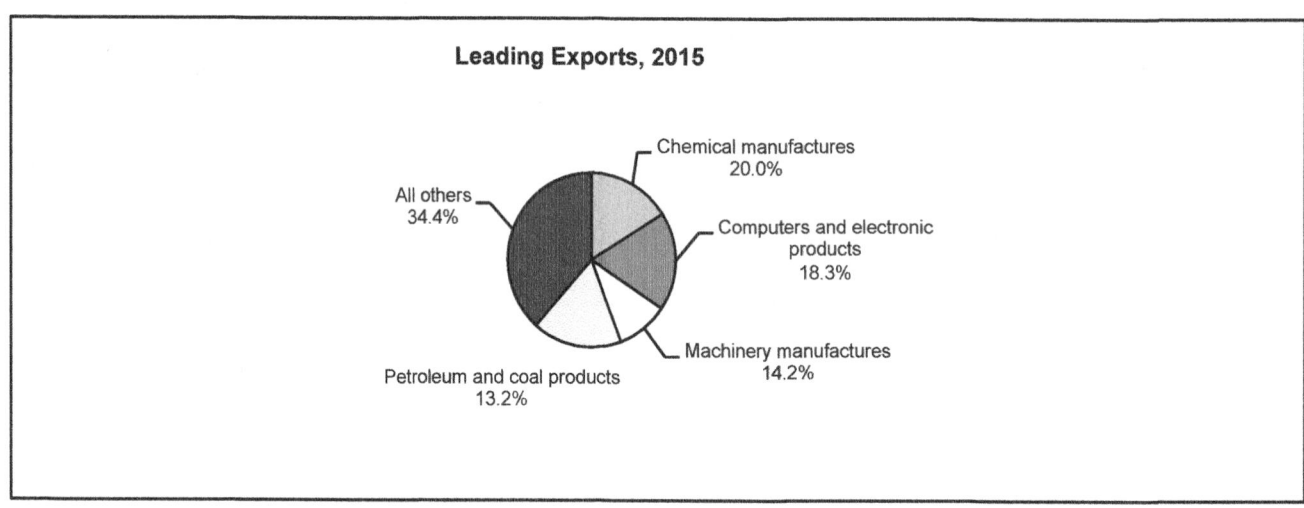

Leading Exports, 2015

Chemical manufactures 20.0%

Computers and electronic products 18.3%

Machinery manufactures 14.2%

Petroleum and coal products 13.2%

All others 34.4%

Facts and Figures

Location: Western United States; bordered on the N by Idaho and Wyoming, on the E by Colorado, on the S by Arizona, and on the W by Nevada; Utah is one of the Four Corner states—at its SE corner it touches Arizona, Colorado, and New Mexico

Area: 84,899 sq. mi. (219,887 sq. km.); rank—13th

Population: 2,995,919 (2015 est.); rank—31st

Principal Cities: capital—Salt Lake City; largest—Salt Lake City

Statehood: January 4, 1896; 45th state

U.S. Congress: 2 senators, 4 representatives

State Motto: Industry

State Song: "Utah, We Love Thee"

State Nickname: The Beehive State

Abbreviations: UT

State Symbols: flower—sego lily; tree—blue spruce; bird—California seagull

At a Glance

- With an increase in population of 7.9 percent, Utah ranked 5th among the states in growth from 2010 to 2015.

- Utah's violent crime rate in 2014 was 215.6 per 100,000 population, compared to 365.5 for the entire nation.

- Of all the states, Utah had the highest percent children in 2015, with 30.5 percent of its population under age 18.

- Utah's median household income in 2014 was $60,922, and 11.7 percent of the population lived below the poverty level.

- In 2014, 12.5 percent of Utahns did not have health insurance, compared to 11.7 percent of the total U.S. population.

Table UT-1. Population by Age, Sex, Race, and Hispanic Origin

(Number, percent, except where noted.)

Sex, age, race, and Hispanic origin	2000	2010	2015[1]	Average annual percent change, 2010–2015
Total Population..	2,233,169	2,763,885	2,995,919	0.6
Percent of total U.S. population	0.8	0.9	0.9	X
Sex				
Male..	1,119,031	1,388,317	1,507,100	0.6
Female	1,114,138	1,375,568	1,488,819	0.6
Age				
Under 5 years..	209,378	263,924	250,703	-0.4
5 to 19 years...	601,599	698,613	750,629	0.5
20 to 64 years..	1,231,970	1,551,886	1,686,720	0.6
65 years and over	190,222	249,462	307,867	1.5
Median age (years)..	27.1	29.2	30.7	0.4
Race and Hispanic Origin				
One race				
White	1,992,975	2,547,328	2,732,481	0.5
Black..	17,657	33,864	40,163	1.2
American Indian and Alaska Native	29,684	40,729	46,023	0.9
Asian..	37,108	57,800	74,734	1.9
Native Hawaiian or Other Pacific Islander	15,145	26,049	30,195	1.1
Two or more races	47,185	58,114	72,323	1.6
Hispanic (of any race)..	201,559	370,870	411,143	0.7

X = Not applicable.
[1]Population figures for 2015 are July 1 estimates. The 2010 estimates are taken from the 2010 Census.

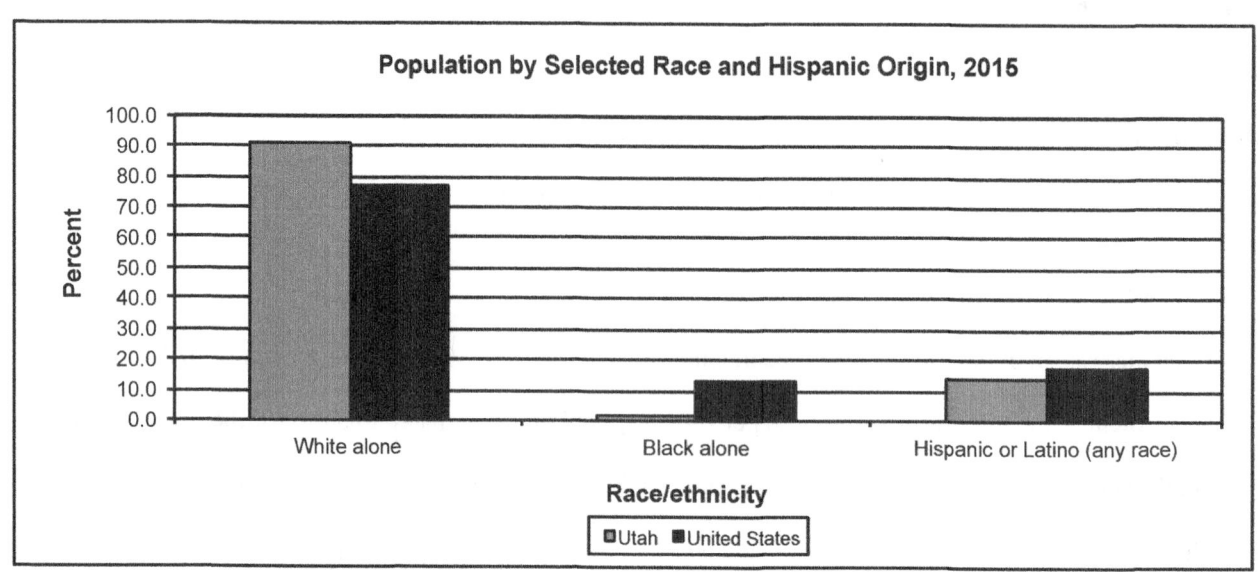

Population by Selected Race and Hispanic Origin, 2015

Table UT-2. Marital Status

(Number, percent distribution.)

Sex, age, race, and Hispanic origin	2000	2010	2014
Males, 15 Years and Over	813,693	1,014,706	1,049,058
Never married	30.6	31.3	32.1
Now married, except separated.................................	59.5	58.0	56.8
Separated..	1.1	1.3	1.3
Widowed..	1.6	1.8	1.7
Divorced..	7.3	7.6	8.1
Females, 15 Years and Over	852,995	1,019,010	1,054,539
Never married	25.2	25.8	26.1
Now married, except separated.................................	58.0	56.6	56.1
Separated..	1.4	1.6	1.8
Widowed..	6.6	5.8	5.8
Divorced..	8.8	10.1	10.2

Table UT-3. Households and Housing Characteristics

(Number, percent, dollars.)

Item	2000	2010	2014	Average annual percent change, 2000–2014
Total Households...	701,281	880,025	918,370	2.2
Family households	535,294	665,964	691,495	2.1
Married-couple family	442,931	543,212	566,881	2.0
Other family	92,363	122,752	124,614	2.5
Male householder, no wife present............................	26,422	37,258	37,803	3.1
Female householder, no husband present...................	65,941	85,494	86,811	2.3
Nonfamily households	165,987	214,061	226,875	2.6
Householder living alone	124,756	164,863	177,104	3.0
Householder not living alone	41,231	49,198	49,771	1.5
Housing Characteristics				
Total housing units..	768,594	981,821	1,022,593	2.4
Occupied housing units	701,281	880,025	918,370	2.2
Owner occupied	501,547	615,142	635,163	1.9
Renter occupied	188,734	264,883	283,207	3.6
Average household size...	3.13	3.10	3.16	0.1
Financial Characteristics				
Median gross rent of renter-occupied housing	597	796	886	3.5
Median monthly owner costs for housing units with a mortgage	1,102	1,433	1,393	1.9
Median value of owner-occupied housing units...........................	146,100	217,200	223,200	3.8

Table UT-4. Migration, Origin, and Language

(Number, percent.)

Characteristic	State			U.S.		
	2013	2014	Percent change	2013	2014	Percent change
Residence 1 Year Ago						
Population 1 year and over	2,854,667	2,894,001	1.4	312,432,820	315,095,393	0.9
Same house	82.7	83.2	X	85.0	85.1	X
Different house in the U.S.	16.7	16.1	X	14.4	14.3	X
Same county	10.2	9.7	X	8.9	8.7	X
Different county	6.5	6.4	X	5.5	5.6	X
Same state	3.0	3.3	X	3.2	3.3	X
Different state	3.4	3.1	X	2.3	2.3	X
Abroad	0.6	0.7	X	0.6	0.6	X
Place of Birth						
Native born	2,663,918	2,692,985	1.1	274,780,773	276,465,262	0.6
Male	50.4	50.4	X	49.3	49.3	X
Female	49.6	49.6	X	50.7	50.7	X
Foreign born	236,954	249,917	5.5	41,348,066	42,391,794	2.5
Male	48.9	49.1	X	48.8	48.7	X
Female	51.1	50.9	X	51.2	51.3	X
Foreign born; naturalized U.S. citizen...	88,045	95,039	7.9	19,294,710	19,984,738	3.6
Male	45.6	45.3	X	45.9	45.9	X
Female	54.4	54.7	X	54.1	54.1	X
Foreign born; not a U.S. citizen...	148,909	154,878	4.0	22,053,356	22,407,056	1.6
Male	50.9	51.5	X	51.3	51.2	X
Female	49.1	48.5	X	48.7	48.8	X
Entered 2010 or later	11.3	13.4	X	9.7	12.3	X
Entered 2000 to 2009	33.9	32.7	X	29.4	28.6	X
Entered before 2000..	54.8	53.9	X	61.0	59.1	X
World Region of Birth, Foreign						
Foreign-born population, excluding population born at sea	236,954	249,831	5.4	41,347,945	42,390,705	2.5
Europe	12.1	9.5	X	11.6	11.2	X
Asia	19.5	21.7	X	29.5	30.1	X
Africa	3.0	3.2	X	4.4	4.6	X
Oceania	3.3	3.5	X	0.5	0.6	X
Latin America	57.9	59.0	X	51.9	51.6	X
North America	4.1	3.1	X	2.0	1.9	X
Language Spoken at Home and Ability to Speak English						
Population 5 years and over..	2,647,463	2,693,093	1.7	296,358,760	299,084,046	0.9
English only	85.9	85.3	X	79.2	78.9	X
Language other than English...	14.1	14.7	X	20.8	21.1	X
Speaks English less than "very well"...................................	4.8	5.1	X	8.5	8.6	X

X = Not applicable.
- = Zero or rounds to zero.

Table UT-5. Median Income and Poverty Status, 2014

(Number, percent, except as noted.)

Characteristic	State		U.S.	
	Number	Percent	Number	Percent
Median Income				
Households (dollars)...	60,922	X	53,657	X
Families (dollars)	69,535	X	65,910	X
Below Poverty Level (All People)	339,900	11.7	48,208,387	15.5
Sex				
Male...	156,974	10.8	21,590,918	14.2
Female	182,926	12.6	26,617,469	16.8
Age				
Under 18 years...	118,789	13.3	15,686,012	21.7
Related children under 18 years........................	115,973	13.0	15,372,705	21.3
18 to 64 years..	201,724	11.8	28,267,482	14.6
65 years and over	19,387	6.7	4,254,893	9.5

X = Not applicable.

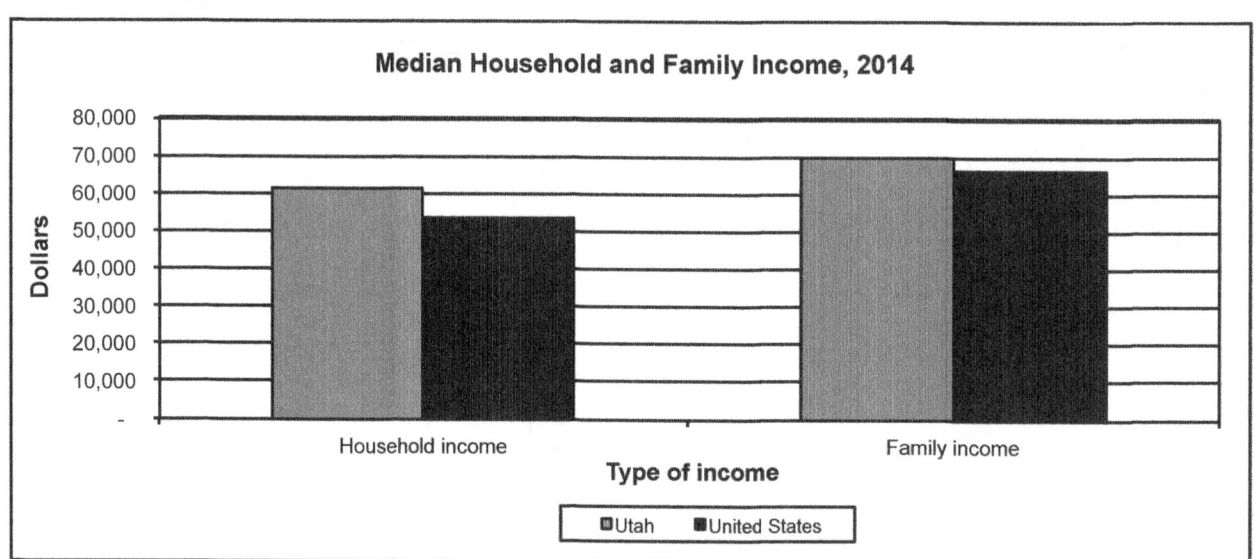

Table UT-6. Health Insurance Coverage Status for the Civilian Noninstitutionalized Population and Children Under 18 Years of Age

(Numbers in thousands, percent.)

Item	2006	2007	2008	2009	2010	2011	2012	2013	2014
Civilian Noninstitutionalized Population	2,537	2,657	2,705	2,755	2,750	2,790	2,829	2,874	2,916
Covered by Private or Public Insurance									
Number..	2,094	2,317	2,286	2,354	2,328	2,364	2,420	2,472	2,551
Percent..	82.6	87.2	84.5	85.4	84.7	84.7	85.5	86.0	87.5
Not Covered									
Number..	442	340	419	401	422	426	409	402	366
Percent..	17.4	12.8	15.5	14.6	15.3	15.3	14.5	14.0	12.5
Percent in the U.S. not covered..........................	15.8	15.3	15.1	15.1	15.5	15.1	14.8	14.5	11.7
Children Under 18 Years of Age	801	832	849	869	870	878	884	894	902
Covered by Private or Public Insurance									
Number..	681	746	738	780	775	781	794	809	818
Percent..	85.0	89.6	86.9	89.7	89.1	88.9	89.9	90.5	90.6
Not Covered									
Number..	120	87	111	89	95	97	90	85	85
Percent..	15.0	10.4	13.1	10.3	10.9	11.1	10.1	9.5	9.4
Percent in the U.S. not covered..........................	11.7	11.0	9.7	8.6	8.0	7.5	7.2	7.1	6.0

Table UT-7. Employment Status by Demographic Group, 2015

(Numbers in thousands, percent.)

Characteristic	Civilian noninstitutional population	Civilian labor force		Employed		Unemployed	
		Number	Percent of population	Number	Percent of population	Number	Percent of population
Total..............................	2,140	1,456	68.0	1,405	65.6	52	3.6
Sex							
Male........................	1,064	834	78.4	807	75.9	26	3.1
Female	1,077	623	57.8	597	55.5	26	4.1
Race, Sex, and Hispanic Origin							
White	2,012	1,369	68.1	1,320	65.6	49	3.6
Male....................	994	781	78.6	756	76.1	25	3.2
Female	1,018	588	57.8	564	55.4	24	4.0
Black or African American............	NA	NA	NA	NA	NA	NA	NA
Male....................	NA	NA	NA	NA	NA	NA	NA
Female	NA	NA	NA	NA	NA	NA	NA
Hispanic or Latino ethnicity[1]	253	181	71.6	170	67.3	11	6.0
Male....................	130	108	83.0	102	78.6	6	5.3
Female	123	73	59.5	68	55.3	5	6.9
Age							
16 to 19 years	172	87	50.4	77	44.7	10	11.3
20 to 24 years	245	196	80.2	186	76.0	10	5.1
25 to 34 years	426	335	78.7	325	76.4	10	3.0
35 to 44 years	410	330	80.5	322	78.5	8	2.5
45 to 54 years	308	254	82.3	247	79.9	7	2.8
55 to 64 years	282	198	70.2	193	68.5	5	2.5
65 years and over	298	57	19.1	55	18.6	2	3.0

NOTE: Data in Table 7 are from the Current Population Survey (CPS) and do not match the estimates in Table 8. See notes and definitions for further information.
[1]May be of any race.
NA = Not available.

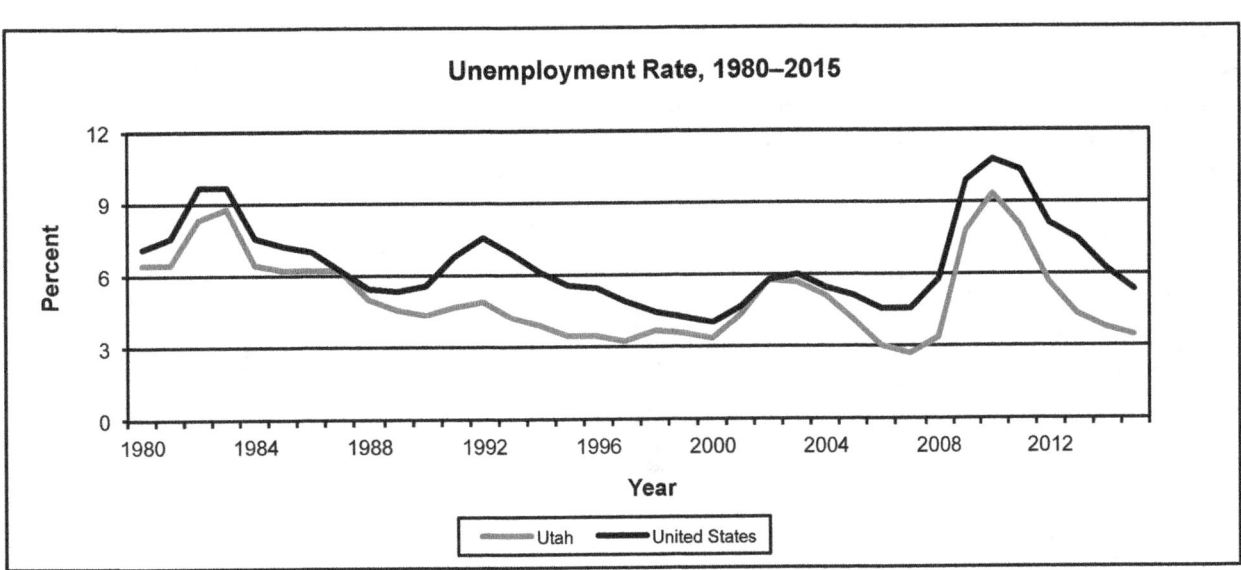

Unemployment Rate, 1980–2015

Table UT-8. Employment Status of the Civilian Noninstitutional Population Age 16 Years and Over

(Number, percent.)

Year	Civilian labor force	Civilian participation rate	Employed	Unemployed	Unemployment rate
2007..	1,359,129	71.9	1,324,060	35,069	2.6
2008..	1,371,201	70.9	1,322,089	49,112	3.6
2009..	1,365,850	69.2	1,266,009	99,841	7.3
2010..	1,356,097	68.8	1,249,814	106,283	7.8
2011..	1,350,444	67.8	1,259,337	91,107	6.7
2012..	1,373,479	67.7	1,299,289	74,190	5.4
2013..	1,409,366	68.2	1,344,637	64,729	4.6
2014..	1,431,553	68.0	1,377,013	54,540	3.8
2015..	1,464,404	68.1	1,412,473	51,931	3.5

Table UT-9. Employment and Average Wages by Industry

(Estimates through 2010 are based on the 2007 North American Industry Classification System [NAICS]. Estimates from 2011 onward are based on the 2012 NAICS.)

Industry	2008	2009	2010	2011	2012	2013	2014
	Number of jobs						
Wage and Salary Employment by Industry..................	1,311,608	1,247,606	1,241,818	1,268,399	1,305,665	1,346,365	1,382,435
Farm Wage and Salary Employment..........................	4,713	4,542	4,814	4,406	4,373	4,836	4,496
Nonfarm Wage and Salary Employment....................	1,306,895	1,243,064	1,237,004	1,263,993	1,301,292	1,341,529	1,377,939
Private wage and salary employment......................	1,078,399	1,011,524	1,002,726	1,026,412	1,060,080	1,098,297	1,133,114
Forestry, fishing, and related activities..........................	1,382	1,345	1,416	1,520	1,516	1,419	1,537
Mining..	12,538	10,661	10,377	11,594	12,493	12,043	12,096
Utilities..	4,152	4,138	4,063	4,020	4,019	3,905	3,888
Construction	94,065	73,808	68,344	68,728	71,628	76,148	81,122
Manufacturing...	125,310	112,322	110,493	113,063	116,022	118,140	119,987
Durable goods manufacturing..........................	84,643	73,484	71,763	74,057	76,652	77,925	79,050
Nondurable goods manufacturing.....................	40,667	38,838	38,730	39,006	39,370	40,215	40,937
Wholesale trade	48,489	45,518	44,329	46,413	48,009	48,520	48,882
Retail trade..	150,693	143,176	140,395	140,822	145,085	149,257	152,989
Transportation and warehousing..........................	47,263	44,387	43,566	45,111	46,662	47,139	48,747
Information..	29,633	28,441	28,184	28,366	30,274	31,344	32,178
Finance and insurance	57,218	55,562	53,534	54,128	55,260	57,687	59,466
Real estate and rental and leasing..........................	18,706	17,314	17,051	17,247	17,196	18,170	18,670
Professional, scientific, and technical services	69,048	66,306	66,276	69,200	73,072	79,214	83,702
Management of companies and enterprises.................	18,575	17,631	16,747	16,759	17,363	17,410	18,148
Administrative and waste services	74,471	65,477	69,473	73,645	76,581	80,522	82,732
Educational services	36,706	37,869	39,440	40,781	42,207	42,909	44,117
Health care and social assistance........................	113,600	116,693	119,358	121,951	124,463	130,117	132,846
Arts, entertainment, and recreation.....................	17,880	17,726	17,724	18,363	19,377	19,785	20,286
Accommodation and food services......................	98,236	94,413	94,375	96,696	100,053	104,719	108,673
Other services, except public administration..................	60,434	58,737	57,581	58,005	58,800	59,849	63,048
Government and government enterprises...........................	228,496	231,540	234,278	237,581	241,212	243,232	244,825
	Dollars						
Average Wages and Salaries by Industry	38,692	39,319	40,174	41,105	42,220	42,693	43,856
Average Farm Wages and Salaries	34,123	39,314	32,225	36,531	31,459	42,613	44,260
Average Nonfarm Wages and Salaries	38,708	39,319	40,205	41,121	42,256	42,693	43,855
Average private wages and salaries........................	38,652	39,162	40,273	41,292	42,729	43,188	44,432
Forestry, fishing, and related activities.........................	25,229	25,462	26,348	26,901	27,600	30,378	31,614
Mining..	70,405	66,927	70,788	74,076	77,188	77,857	79,140
Utilities..	81,494	83,143	87,092	87,564	86,843	89,133	90,952
Construction	39,977	41,563	42,876	43,528	45,044	44,350	45,697
Manufacturing...	47,864	49,081	50,872	51,558	52,795	53,191	54,499
Durable goods manufacturing..........................	50,955	52,739	54,604	55,385	56,122	56,264	57,742
Nondurable goods manufacturing.....................	41,429	42,159	43,958	44,293	46,319	47,235	48,236
Wholesale trade	54,896	54,677	55,743	58,575	60,147	62,269	62,819
Retail trade..	26,213	26,129	26,850	27,280	28,480	28,771	29,779
Transportation and warehousing..........................	42,733	42,455	43,839	44,729	45,091	46,736	47,429
Information..	49,037	50,251	53,670	57,933	60,721	61,302	64,992
Finance and insurance	52,538	53,399	55,963	58,425	63,047	63,627	66,168
Real estate and rental and leasing..........................	35,780	35,628	36,662	38,749	40,374	40,684	42,813
Professional, scientific, and technical services	59,646	60,220	60,855	62,758	63,937	63,434	66,875
Management of companies and enterprises.................	68,704	70,365	80,746	78,792	86,277	85,448	85,115
Administrative and waste services	27,890	28,582	28,863	29,656	30,629	31,372	32,203
Educational services	26,326	26,558	27,559	28,441	28,510	29,067	29,978
Health care and social assistance........................	37,112	38,548	38,536	39,100	40,067	40,593	41,407
Arts, entertainment, and recreation.....................	24,260	24,477	25,277	25,180	24,973	26,383	26,758
Accommodation and food services......................	16,298	15,971	16,567	17,056	17,529	17,420	18,205
Other services, except public administration..................	36,713	38,518	40,508	40,876	42,603	44,771	44,831
Government and government enterprises...........................	38,977	40,005	39,914	40,384	40,181	40,459	41,181

Table UT-10. Employment Characteristics by Family Type

(Number, percent.)

Family type and labor force status	2012 Total	2012 Families with own children under 18 years	2013 Total	2013 Families with own children under 18 years	2014 Total	2014 Families with own children under 18 years
All Families..	666,661	345,172	677,332	352,191	688,140	351,950
FAMILY TYPE AND LABOR FORCE STATUS						
Married-Couple Families................................	542,587	274,021	551,975	283,134	563,526	281,444
Both husband and wife in labor force........................	52.4	57.7	49.9	54.1	51.8	57.5
Husband in labor force, wife not in labor force	29.2	39.0	31.2	41.1	29.7	39.5
Wife in labor force, husband not in labor force	5.4	2.2	5.9	3.5	5.3	2.3
Both husband and wife not in labor force..................	13.0	1.1	12.6	1.1	13.2	0.8
Other Families	124,074	71,151	125,357	69,057	124,614	70,506
Female householder, no husband present.....................	69.4	71.4	69.0	70.6	69.7	72.9
In labor force...	50.4	60.0	51.1	58.7	50.2	61.8
Not in labor force	18.9	11.4	17.9	11.9	19.5	11.1
Male householder, no wife present...........................	30.6	28.6	31.0	29.4	30.3	27.1
In labor force...	25.3	26.2	25.0	28.3	24.7	25.1
Not in labor force.......................................	5.3	2.3	5.9	1.2	5.6	2.0

Table UT-11. School Enrollment and Educational Attainment, 2014

(Number, percent.)

Item	State	U.S.
Enrollment		
Total population 3 years and over, enrolled in school...........	953,887	82,063,714
Enrolled in nursery school or preschool (percent)...............	6.3	6.0
Enrolled in kindergarten (percent).............................	5.5	5.1
Enrolled in elementary school, grades 1-8 (percent)............	42.3	40.2
Enrolled in high school, grades 9-12 (percent).................	20.3	20.7
Enrolled in college or graduate school (percent)...............	25.6	28.0
Attainment		
Total population 25 years and over	1,704,734	213,725,624
Less than ninth grade (percent)	3.0	5.6
9th to 12th grade, no diploma (percent).......................	5.6	7.5
High school graduate, including equivalency (percent).........	23.0	27.7
Some college, no degree (percent)	27.4	21.0
Associate's degree (percent)...................................	9.9	8.2
Bachelor's degree (percent)...................................	20.8	18.7
Graduate or professional degree (percent).....................	10.3	11.4
High school graduate or higher (percent)	91.4	86.9
Bachelor's degree or higher (percent).........................	31.1	30.1

Table UT-12. Public School Characteristics and Educational Indicators

(Number, percent; data derived from National Center of Education Statistics.)

Item	State	U.S.
Public Schools, 2013–2014 (except where noted)		
Number of school districts....................................	138	18,194
Number of schools..	1,006	98,271
Number of students (in thousands)	625	50,045
Number of teachers (in thousands)	27	3,114
Student-teacher ratio	23.0	16.1
Expenditures per student (dollars), FY 2013	6,432	107,637
Four-year adjusted cohort graduation rate (ACGR)[1,2]	83.9	82.3
Students eligible for free or reduced-price lunch (in thousands)	231	25,596
English language learners (in thousands)	33	4,461
Students age 3 to 21 served under IDEA, part B (in thousands).	75	6,464

Public Schools by Type	Number	Percent of state public schools
Total number of schools......................................	1,006	100.0
Regular..	907	90.2
Special education..	69	6.9
Vocational education...	4	0.4
Alternative education..	26	2.6

NOTE: Every school is assigned only one school type based on its instructional emphasis.
[1]ACGR data represents a new method of calculating high-school completion rates and may not be comparable to previous years' data for Averaged Freshmen Graduation Rates (AFGR).
[2]The United States 4-year ACGRs were estimated using both the reported 4-year ACGR data from 49 states and the District of Columbia and using imputed data for Idaho. The estimate for American Indian/Alaska Native students also includes imputed data for Virginia.

Table UT-13. Reported Voting and Registration of the Voting-Age Population, November 2014

(Numbers in thousands, percent.)

Item	Total population	Total citizen population	Registered			Voted		
			Total registered	Percent registered (total population)	Percent registered (total citizen population)	Total voted	Percent voted (total population)	Percent voted (total citizen population)
U.S. Total	239,874	219,941	142,166	59.3	64.6	92,251	38.5	41.9
State Total.............................	2,026	1,924	1,101	54.3	57.2	703	34.7	36.5
Sex								
Male..........	1,011	955	539	53.3	56.4	339	33.5	35.5
Female	1,016	969	562	55.4	58.0	364	35.8	37.6
Race								
White alone....................	1,919	1,840	1,064	55.5	57.8	678	35.3	36.8
White, non-Hispanic alone	1,704	1,684	1,009	59.2	59.9	650	38.2	38.6
Black alone...................	26	16	6	(B)	(B)	6	(B)	(B)
Asian alone	37	24	13	(B)	(B)	10	(B)	(B)
Hispanic (of any race)	222	156	56	25.0	35.6	28	12.7	18.1
White alone or in combination	1,939	1,860	1,070	55.2	57.5	681	35.1	36.6
Black alone or in combination..........	34	24	11	(B)	(B)	8	(B)	(B)
Asian alone or in combination..........	43	30	14	(B)	(B)	10	(B)	(B)
Age								
18 to 24 years.....................	259	250	74	28.7	29.8	35	13.4	13.9
25 to 34 years.....................	457	428	195	42.7	45.6	99	21.8	23.3
35 to 44 years.....................	436	410	242	55.6	59.2	121	27.7	29.5
45 to 64 years.....................	589	558	374	63.5	67.0	258	43.9	46.3
65 years and over	286	279	215	75.3	77.3	189	66.1	67.9

B = Base is less than 75,000 and therefore too small to show the derived measure.

Table UT-14. Crime

(Number, rate per 100,000. Data are derived from the FBI Uniform Crime Reports.)

Item	State			U.S.[1,2,3,4]		
	2013	2014	Percent change	2013	2014	Percent change
TOTAL POPULATION[5]...........................	2,900,872	2,942,902	1.4	316,128,839	318,857,056	0.9
VIOLENT CRIME						
Number................	6,070	6,346	4.5	1,163,146	1,165,383	0.2
Rate	209.2	215.6	3.1	367.9	365.5	-0.7
Murder and Nonnegligent Manslaughter						
Number................	49	67	36.7	14,196	14,249	0.4
Rate	1.7	2.3	35.3	4.5	4.5	-
Rape[6]						
Number................	1,422	1,454	X	108,612	116,645	X
Rate	49.0	49.4	X	34.4	36.6	X
Robbery						
Number................	1,243	1,312	5.6	345,031	325,802	-5.6
Rate	42.8	44.6	4.2	109.1	102.2	-6.3
Aggravated Assault						
Number................	3,784	3,513	-7.2	724,149	741,291	2.4
Rate	130.4	119.4	-8.4	229.1	232.5	1.5
PROPERTY CRIME						
Number................	85,586	84,711	-1.0	8,632,512	8,277,829	-4.1
Rate	2,950.4	2,878.5	-2.4	2,730.7	2,596.1	-4.9
Burglary						
Number................	13,333	11,518	-13.6	1,928,465	1,729,806	-10.3
Rate	459.6	391.4	-14.8	610.0	542.5	-11.1
Larceny-Theft						
Number................	64,788	65,895	1.7	6,004,453	5,858,496	-2.4
Rate	2,233.4	2,239.1	0.3	1,899.4	1,837.3	-3.3
Motor Vehicle Theft						
Number................	7,465	7,298	-2.2	699,594	689,527	-1.4
Rate	257.3	248.0	-3.6	221.3	216.2	-2.3

NOTE: Although arson data are included in the trend and clearance tables, sufficient data are not available to estimate totals for this offense. Therefore, no arson data are published in this table.
X = Not applicable.
- = Zero or rounds to zero.
[1]The crime figures have been adjusted.
[2]The data collection methodology for the offense of forcible rape used by the Minnesota state Uniform Crime Reporting (UCR) Program (with the exception of Minneapolis and St. Paul, Minnesota) does not comply with national UCR Program guidelines. Consequently, its figures for forcible rape and violent crime (of which forcible rape is a part) are not published in this table.
[3]Includes offenses reported by the Zoological Police and the Metro Transit Police.
[4]Because of changes in the state's reporting practices, figures are not comparable to previous years' data.
[5]Populations are U.S. Census Bureau provisional estimates as of July 1 of each year.
[6]The figures shown for the offense of rape were estimated using the revised Uniform Crime Reporting (UCR) definition of rape.

Table UT-15. State Government Finances, 2014

(Dollar amounts in thousands, percent distribution.)

Item	Dollars	Percent distribution
Total Revenue	19,413,736	100.0
General revenue	14,974,256	77.1
Intergovernmental revenue	4,211,310	21.7
Taxes	6,312,489	32.5
General sales	1,823,355	9.4
Selective sales	858,745	4.4
License taxes	276,824	1.4
Individual income tax	2,889,912	14.9
Corporate income tax	307,910	1.6
Other taxes	155,743	0.8
Current charges	3,367,177	17.3
Miscellaneous general revenue	1,083,280	5.6
Utility revenue	0	-
Liquor stores revenue	310,228	1.6
Insurance trust revenue[1]	4,129,252	21.3
Total Expenditure	17,039,808	100.0
Intergovernmental expenditure	3,266,053	19.2
Direct expenditure	13,773,755	80.8
Current operation	10,270,811	60.3
Capital outlay	882,781	5.2
Insurance benefits and repayments	1,673,285	9.8
Assistance and subsidies	683,852	4.0
Interest on debt	263,026	1.5
Exhibit: Salaries and wages	3,006,183	17.6
Total Expenditure	17,039,808	100.0
General expenditure	15,147,203	88.9
Intergovernmental expenditure	3,266,053	19.2
Direct expenditure	11,881,150	69.7
General expenditure, by function:		
Education	7,025,833	41.2
Public welfare	3,147,342	18.5
Hospitals	1,292,253	7.6
Health	370,615	2.2
Highways	827,568	4.9
Police protection	142,226	0.8
Correction	317,480	1.9
Natural resources	176,731	1.0
Parks and recreation	41,664	0.2
Governmental administration	598,903	3.5
Interest on general debt	263,026	1.5
Other and unallocable	943,562	5.5
Utility expenditure	0	-
Liquor stores expenditure	219,320	1.3
Insurance trust expenditure	1,673,285	9.8
Debt at End of Fiscal Year	7,327,147	X
Cash and Security Holdings	33,019,290	X

X = Not applicable.
- = Zero or rounds to zero.
[1]Within insurance trust revenue, net earnings of state retirement systems is a calculated statistic (the item code in the data file is X08), and thus can be positive or negative. Net earnings is the sum of earnings on investments plus gains on investments minus losses on investments. The change made in 2002 for asset valuation from book to market value in accordance with Statement 34 of the Governmental Accounting Standards Board is reflected in the calculated statistics.

Table UT-16. State Government Tax Collections, 2014

(Dollars in thousands, percent.)

Item	Dollars	Percent distribution
Total Taxes	6,312,489	100.0
Property taxes	X	X
Sales and gross receipts	2,682,100	42.5
General sales and gross receipts	1,823,355	28.9
Selective sales and gross receipts	858,745	13.6
Alcoholic beverages	48,413	0.8
Amusements	0	-
Insurance premiums	113,316	1.8
Motor fuels	372,935	5.9
Pari-mutuels	0	-
Public utilities	24,319	0.4
Tobacco products	113,184	1.8
Other selective sales	186,578	3.0
Licenses	276,824	4.4
Alcoholic beverages	1,936	0.0
Amusements	0	-
Corporations in general	484	0.0
Hunting and fishing	28,720	0.5
Motor vehicle	175,679	2.8
Motor vehicle operators	15,733	0.2
Public utilities	0	-
Occupation and business, NEC	53,264	0.8
Other licenses	1,008	-
Income taxes	3,197,822	50.7
Individual income	2,889,912	45.8
Corporation net income	307,910	4.9
Other taxes	155,743	2.5
Death and gift	0	-
Documentary and stock transfer	0	-
Severance	155,743	2.5
Taxes, NEC	0	-

X = Not applicable.
- = Zero or rounds to zero.

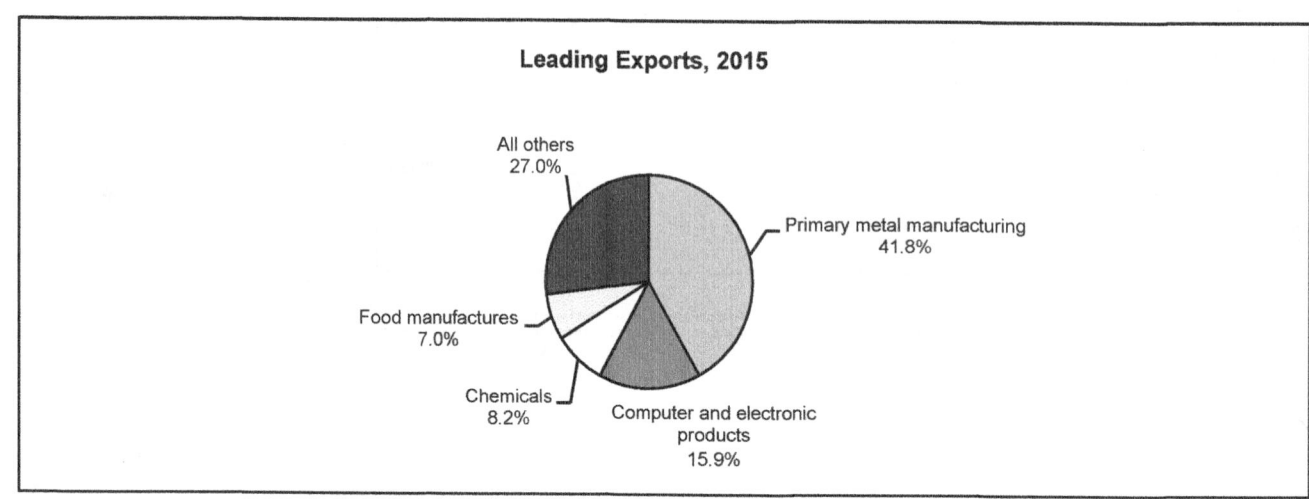

Leading Exports, 2015

All others 27.0%
Primary metal manufacturing 41.8%
Food manufactures 7.0%
Chemicals 8.2%
Computer and electronic products 15.9%

Facts and Figures

Location: Northeastern United States; bordered on the N by Canada (Quebec), on the E by New Hampshire, on the S by Massachusetts, and on the W by New York

Area: 9,614 sq. mi. (24,901 sq. km.); rank—45th

Population: 626,042 (2015 est.); rank—50th

Principal Cities: capital—Montpelier; largest—Burlington

Statehood: March 4, 1791; the 14th state

U.S. Congress: 2 senators, 1 representative

State Motto: Freedom and Unity

State Song: "These Green Mountains"

State Nickname: The Green Mountain State

Abbreviations: VT; Vt.

State Symbols: flower—red clover; tree—sugar maple; bird—hermit thrush

At a Glance

- Vermont's population did not change much between 2010 and 2015, with the percent change rounding to zero. This placed Vermont 50th among the states for population growth.

- Vermont's median household income in 2014 was $54,166, and 12.2 percent of the population lived below the poverty level.

- Vermont's violent crime rate in 2014 was the lowest in the nation at 99.3 incidents per 100,000 population.

- In 2014, 5.0 percent of Vermonters did not have health insurance, compared to 11.7 percent of the total U.S. population.

- Vermont had the second lowest percent of its population under age 18 in 2015, with 19.2 percent of its residents in this age group.

Table VT-1. Population by Age, Sex, Race, and Hispanic Origin

(Number, percent, except where noted.)

Sex, age, race, and Hispanic origin	2000	2010	2015[1]	Average annual percent change, 2010–2015
Total Population	608,827	625,741	626,042	-
Percent of total U.S. population	0.2	0.2	0.2	X
Sex				
Male	298,337	308,206	308,526	-
Female	310,490	317,535	317,516	-
Age				
Under 5 years	33,989	31,952	30,408	-0.4
5 to 19 years	132,268	118,323	110,275	-0.5
20 to 64 years	365,060	384,388	375,466	-0.2
65 years and over	77,510	91,078	109,893	1.4
Median age (years)	37.7	41.5	42.8	0.2
Race and Hispanic Origin				
One race				
White	589,208	598,592	593,361	-0.1
Black	3,063	6,456	8,140	1.7
American Indian and Alaska Native	2,420	2,308	2,381	0.2
Asian	5,217	8,069	10,277	1.7
Native Hawaiian or Other Pacific Islander	141	175	241	2.3
Two or more races	7,335	10,141	11,642	1.0
Hispanic (of any race)	5,504	9,962	11,525	1.0

X = Not applicable.
- = Zero or rounds to zero.
[1]Population figures for 2015 are July 1 estimates. The 2010 estimates are taken from the 2010 Census.

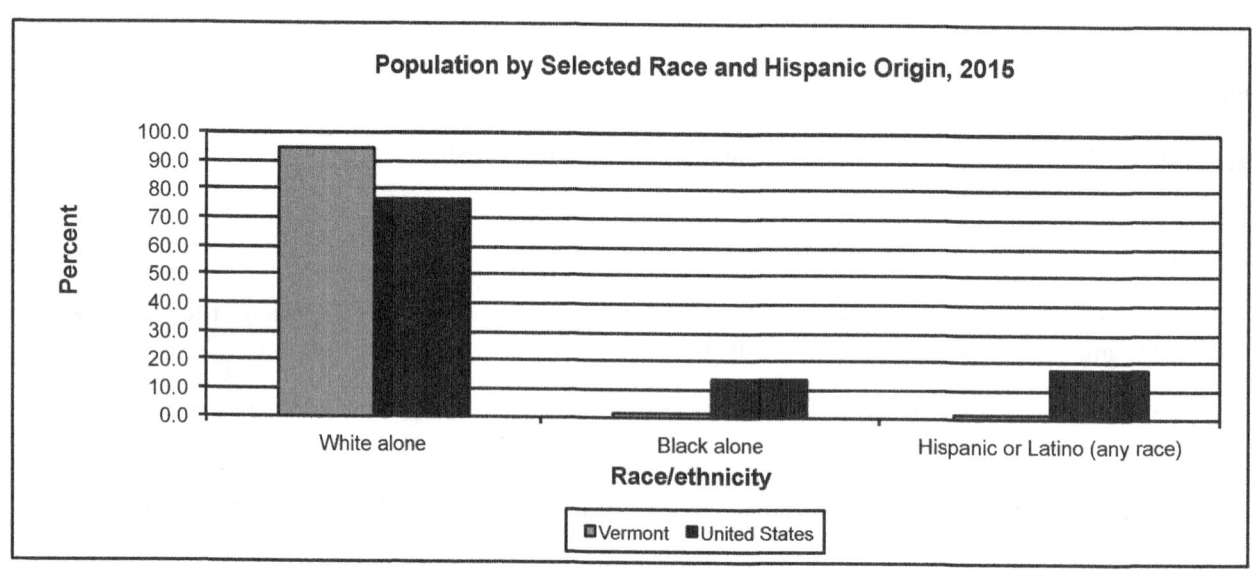

Population by Selected Race and Hispanic Origin, 2015

Table VT-2. Marital Status

(Number, percent distribution.)

Sex, age, race, and Hispanic origin	2000	2010	2014
Males, 15 Years and Over	236,517	254,288	256,277
Never married	29.7	34.2	34.1
Now married, except separated	57.1	51.3	51.3
Separated	1.2	1.3	1.2
Widowed	2.4	2.5	2.4
Divorced	9.6	10.7	11.1
Females, 15 Years and Over	251,764	266,860	268,759
Never married	23.9	27.7	27.9
Now married, except separated	53.3	49.7	49.2
Separated	1.4	1.4	1.4
Widowed	10.0	8.2	8.5
Divorced	11.5	13.0	13.0

Table VT-3. Households and Housing Characteristics

(Number, percent, dollars.)

Item	2000	2010	2014	Average annual percent change, 2000–2014
Total Households..	240,634	256,922	257,229	0.5
Family households	157,763	159,846	162,017	0.2
Married-couple family	126,413	125,678	125,741	-
Other family	31,350	34,168	36,276	1.1
Male householder, no wife present..........	9,078	10,887	11,469	1.9
Female householder, no husband present............	22,272	23,281	24,807	0.8
Nonfamily households	82,871	97,076	95,212	1.1
Householder living alone	63,112	75,243	73,617	1.2
Householder not living alone	19,759	21,833	21,595	0.7
Housing Characteristics				
Total housing units....................................	294,382	322,698	325,774	0.8
Occupied housing units	240,634	256,922	257,229	0.5
Owner occupied	169,784	180,847	180,184	0.4
Renter occupied	70,850	76,075	77,045	0.6
Average household size................................	2.44	2.34	2.34	-0.3
Financial Characteristics				
Median gross rent of renter-occupied housing	553	823	917	4.7
Median monthly owner costs for housing units with a mortgage	1,021	1,445	1,504	3.4
Median value of owner-occupied housing units....................	111,500	216,800	214,600	6.6

- = Zero or rounds to zero

Table VT-4. Migration, Origin, and Language

(Number, percent.)

Characteristic	State			U.S.		
	2013	2014	Percent change	2013	2014	Percent change
Residence 1 Year Ago						
Population 1 year and over	621,256	620,898	-0.1	312,432,820	315,095,393	0.9
Same house	87.2	86.5	X	85.0	85.1	X
Different house in the U.S.	12.4	13.3	X	14.4	14.3	X
Same county	6.7	7.1	X	8.9	8.7	X
Different county	5.7	6.2	X	5.5	5.6	X
Same state	2.0	2.5	X	3.2	3.3	X
Different state	3.7	3.6	X	2.3	2.3	X
Abroad	0.4	0.2	X	0.6	0.6	X
Place of Birth						
Native born	599,618	600,984	0.2	274,780,773	276,465,262	0.6
Male..	49.4	49.4	X	49.3	49.3	X
Female...	50.6	50.6	X	50.7	50.7	X
Foreign born	27,012	25,578	-5.3	41,348,066	42,391,794	2.5
Male..	46.9	44.8	X	48.8	48.7	X
Female...	53.1	55.2	X	51.2	51.3	X
Foreign born; naturalized U.S. citizen................	15,904	13,360	-16.0	19,294,710	19,984,738	3.6
Male..	41.4	41.7	X	45.9	45.9	X
Female...	58.6	58.3	X	54.1	54.1	X
Foreign born; not a U.S. citizen....................	11,108	12,218	10.0	22,053,356	22,407,056	1.6
Male..	54.7	48.1	X	51.3	51.2	X
Female...	45.3	51.9	X	48.7	48.8	X
Entered 2010 or later	11.3	18.5	X	9.7	12.3	X
Entered 2000 to 2009	28.1	26.8	X	29.4	28.6	X
Entered before 2000..................................	60.6	54.7	X	61.0	59.1	X
World Region of Birth, Foreign						
Foreign-born population, excluding population born at sea	27,012	25,578	-5.3	41,347,945	42,390,705	2.5
Europe	29.7	31.5	X	11.6	11.2	X
Asia..	28.5	34.7	X	29.5	30.1	X
Africa	8.7	6.0	X	4.4	4.6	X
Oceania	0.5	0.4	X	0.5	0.6	X
Latin America..	11.0	10.5	X	51.9	51.6	X
North America.......................................	21.6	16.9	X	2.0	1.9	X
Language Spoken at Home and Ability to Speak English						
Population 5 years and over...........................	596,324	595,681	-0.1	296,358,760	299,084,046	0.9
English only	95.0	95.0	X	79.2	78.9	X
Language other than English.........................	5.0	5.0	X	20.8	21.1	X
Speaks English less than "very well"............	1.3	1.3	X	8.5	8.6	X

X = Not applicable.
- = Zero or rounds to zero.

Table VT-5. Median Income and Poverty Status, 2014

(Number, percent, except as noted.)

Characteristic	State		U.S.	
	Number	Percent	Number	Percent
Median Income				
Households (dollars)	54,166	X	53,657	X
Families (dollars)	67,154	X	65,910	X
Below Poverty Level (All People)	73,149	12.2	48,208,387	15.5
Sex				
Male	31,891	10.8	21,590,918	14.2
Female	41,258	13.4	26,617,469	16.8
Age				
Under 18 years	18,819	15.8	15,686,012	21.7
Related children under 18 years	18,090	15.3	15,372,705	21.3
18 to 64 years	47,028	12.4	28,267,482	14.6
65 years and over	7,302	7.1	4,254,893	9.5

X = Not applicable.

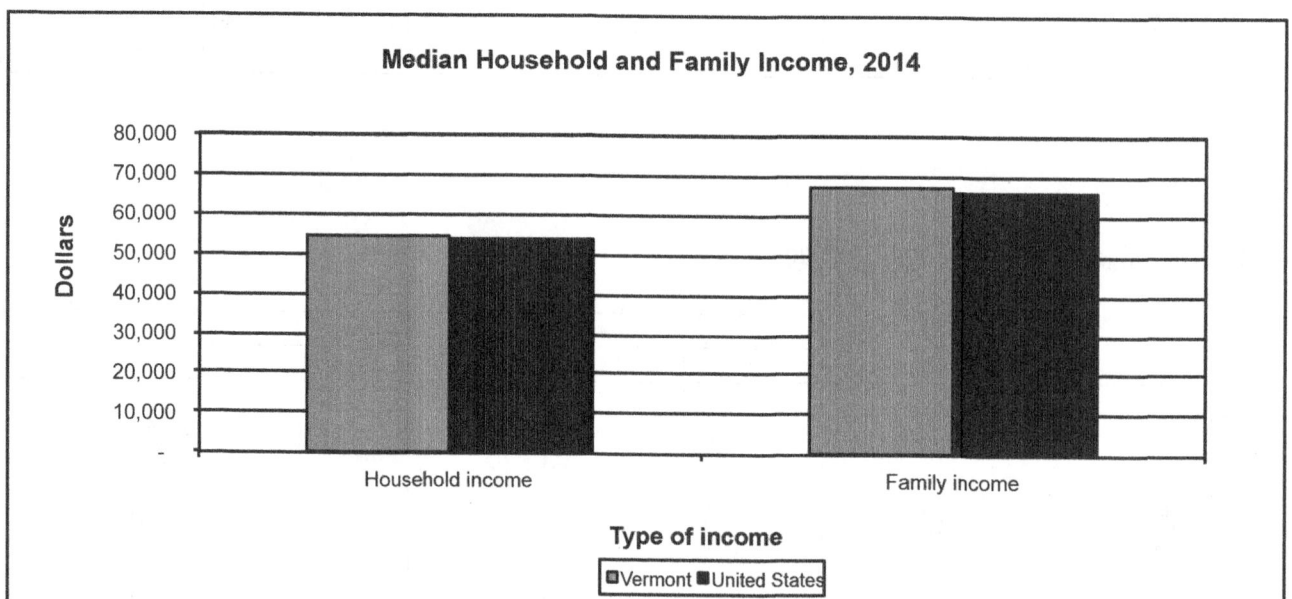

Table VT-6. Health Insurance Coverage Status for the Civilian Noninstitutionalized Population and Children Under 18 Years of Age

(Numbers in thousands, percent.)

Item	2006	2007	2008	2009	2010	2011	2012	2013	2014
Civilian Noninstitutionalized Population	620	614	615	615	620	620	620	621	620
Covered by Private or Public Insurance									
Number	557	545	559	562	570	579	580	576	590
Percent	89.8	88.8	90.9	91.4	92.0	93.4	93.5	92.8	95.0
Not Covered									
Number	63	69	56	53	50	41	40	45	31
Percent	10.2	11.2	9.1	8.6	8.0	6.6	6.5	7.2	5.0
Percent in the U.S. not covered	15.8	15.3	15.1	15.1	15.5	15.1	14.8	14.5	11.7
Children Under 18 Years of Age	133	129	129	126	130	126	124	124	121
Covered by Private or Public Insurance									
Number	122	117	124	122	127	123	121	120	119
Percent	92.0	90.6	96.1	96.8	98.0	97.6	97.2	96.9	97.8
Not Covered									
Number	11	12	5	4	3	3	3	4	3
Percent	8.0	9.4	3.9	3.2	2.0	2.4	2.8	3.1	2.2
Percent in the U.S. not covered	11.7	11.0	9.7	8.6	8.0	7.5	7.2	7.1	6.0

Table VT-7. Employment Status by Demographic Group, 2015

(Numbers in thousands, percent.)

Characteristic	Civilian noninstitutional population	Civilian labor force		Employed		Unemployed	
		Number	Percent of population	Number	Percent of population	Number	Percent of population
Total...	515	344	66.8	332	64.4	12	3.6
Sex							
Male	252	176	69.9	169	67.1	7	4.0
Female	264	168	63.8	163	61.8	5	3.1
Race, Sex, and Hispanic Origin							
White	494	331	67.1	320	64.7	12	3.6
Male	242	170	70.3	163	67.4	7	4.0
Female	252	162	64.1	157	62.1	5	3.1
Black or African American....................	NA	NA	NA	NA	NA	NA	NA
Male	NA	NA	NA	NA	NA	NA	NA
Female	NA	NA	NA	NA	NA	NA	NA
Hispanic or Latino ethnicity[1]	8	6	78	6	76	...	4
Male	NA	NA	NA	NA	NA	NA	NA
Female	NA	NA	NA	NA	NA	NA	NA
Age							
16 to 19 years	31	14	46.5	13	40.8	2	12.2
20 to 24 years	36	27	73.9	25	67.9	2	7.8
25 to 34 years	81	66	82.3	64	79.4	2	3.5
35 to 44 years	75	64	85.5	63	83.2	2	2.5
45 to 54 years	87	73	84.1	71	81.7	2	2.6
55 to 64 years	101	74	72.7	72	70.8	2	2.4
65 years and over	104	26	24.7	25	24.0	1	3.1

NOTE: Data in Table 7 are from the Current Population Survey (CPS) and do not match the estimates in Table 8. See notes and definitions for further information.
[1]May be of any race.
NA = Not available.
... = Fewer than 500 persons.

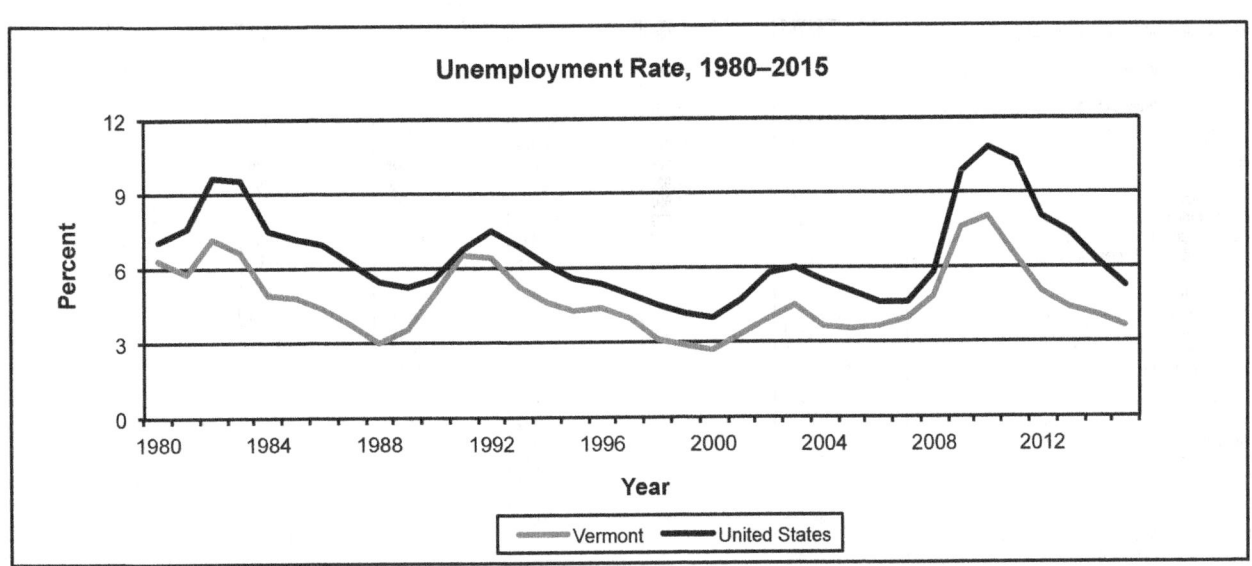

Table VT-8. Employment Status of the Civilian Noninstitutional Population Age 16 Years and Over

(Number, percent.)

Year	Civilian labor force	Civilian participation rate	Employed	Unemployed	Unemployment rate
2007................................	353,739	70.4	339,547	14,192	4.0
2008................................	354,899	70.3	338,273	16,626	4.7
2009................................	359,836	71.0	336,104	23,732	6.6
2010................................	359,402	70.8	337,488	21,914	6.1
2011................................	358,108	70.2	338,463	19,645	5.5
2012................................	354,849	69.4	337,247	17,602	5.0
2013................................	351,342	68.5	335,856	15,486	4.4
2014................................	347,898	67.6	334,044	13,854	4.0
2015................................	344,414	66.8	331,824	12,590	3.7

Table VT-9. Employment and Average Wages by Industry

(Estimates through 2010 are based on the 2007 North American Industry Classification System [NAICS]. Estimates from 2011 onward are based on the 2012 NAICS.)

Industry	2008	2009	2010	2011	2012	2013	2014
	Number of jobs						
Wage and Salary Employment by Industry..................	321,435	311,317	312,230	314,778	317,523	321,355	323,871
Farm Wage and Salary Employment..........................	2,359	2,276	2,282	2,420	2,450	2,903	2,957
Nonfarm Wage and Salary Employment.....................	319,076	309,041	309,948	312,358	315,073	318,452	320,914
Private wage and salary employment............................	262,280	251,913	252,545	255,425	257,885	259,611	262,555
Forestry, fishing, and related activities.....................	801	886	903	950	843	858	926
Mining..	740	650	594	611	649	621	600
Utilities..	1,699	1,756	1,801	1,801	1,828	1,790	1,727
Construction	16,221	14,400	14,201	14,835	14,677	14,599	15,243
Manufacturing..	34,790	31,153	30,853	30,948	31,908	31,739	31,235
Durable goods manufacturing..............................	25,179	22,088	21,787	21,628	21,695	21,228	20,384
Nondurable goods manufacturing........................	9,611	9,065	9,066	9,320	10,213	10,511	10,851
Wholesale trade	10,347	9,675	9,634	9,687	9,237	9,258	9,291
Retail trade...	40,675	38,854	38,709	38,661	38,017	38,130	38,306
Transportation and warehousing............................	7,101	6,763	6,896	7,191	7,098	6,997	7,038
Information..	5,777	5,510	5,369	4,945	4,675	4,683	4,761
Finance and insurance	9,618	9,373	9,348	9,370	9,299	9,199	9,251
Real estate and rental and leasing.........................	3,388	3,157	3,093	3,066	3,069	3,155	3,158
Professional, scientific, and technical services	13,728	13,450	13,795	13,881	14,189	14,213	13,986
Management of companies and enterprises..................	735	778	893	1,417	1,962	1,950	2,081
Administrative and waste services...........................	8,995	8,424	8,867	9,705	10,259	10,498	10,762
Educational services	13,785	13,641	13,683	13,916	14,238	14,438	14,548
Health care and social assistance..........................	46,670	47,664	47,699	47,799	48,977	49,542	50,096
Arts, entertainment, and recreation.........................	3,994	3,866	3,880	3,981	4,050	4,101	4,271
Accommodation and food services...........................	29,080	28,145	28,853	29,023	29,588	30,466	31,098
Other services, except public administration..............	14,136	13,768	13,474	13,638	13,322	13,374	14,177
Government and government enterprises........................	56,796	57,128	57,403	56,933	57,188	58,841	58,359
	Dollars						
Average Wages and Salaries by Industry	37,682	38,085	38,735	39,541	39,706	41,099	42,155
Average Farm Wages and Salaries	28,809	28,367	26,723	22,544	21,065	28,702	31,262
Average Nonfarm Wages and Salaries	37,748	38,157	38,823	39,672	39,875	41,212	42,256
Average private wages and salaries............................	37,110	37,411	38,141	39,048	39,449	40,765	41,703
Forestry, fishing, and related activities.........................	28,313	27,828	28,373	29,278	28,803	30,249	31,225
Mining..	53,784	55,386	55,665	54,286	54,940	54,383	55,895
Utilities..	88,943	87,929	92,295	92,736	97,755	98,080	104,389
Construction	41,293	41,697	42,705	43,287	43,894	45,447	46,196
Manufacturing..	50,530	51,677	53,103	53,784	54,583	54,662	55,282
Durable goods manufacturing..............................	54,343	56,034	57,401	58,356	60,167	59,083	59,218
Nondurable goods manufacturing........................	40,541	41,061	42,774	43,174	43,305	45,732	47,889
Wholesale trade	50,397	51,531	52,483	54,634	56,206	56,594	56,437
Retail trade...	25,291	25,572	25,990	26,772	26,530	27,469	28,388
Transportation and warehousing............................	36,821	36,804	37,304	37,830	38,492	38,798	40,331
Information..	44,230	45,173	45,091	49,309	48,797	51,341	53,819
Finance and insurance	64,673	61,497	62,219	64,123	66,751	67,653	69,790
Real estate and rental and leasing.........................	32,135	32,853	33,356	34,472	35,121	37,800	38,466
Professional, scientific, and technical services	59,530	60,257	63,808	64,562	65,847	68,728	70,840
Management of companies and enterprises..................	79,751	77,545	78,471	78,258	78,404	81,783	87,202
Administrative and waste services...........................	29,521	30,555	28,779	29,257	30,950	34,511	36,634
Educational services	30,689	31,420	30,674	31,054	30,266	31,759	32,807
Health care and social assistance..........................	36,793	37,601	38,420	39,255	39,474	41,204	42,008
Arts, entertainment, and recreation.........................	22,383	22,841	23,529	23,643	23,561	25,090	25,633
Accommodation and food services...........................	19,587	19,387	19,802	20,710	20,435	21,506	22,478
Other services, except public administration..............	24,985	25,123	25,701	26,235	26,495	27,512	28,216
Government and government enterprises........................	40,695	41,444	41,826	42,474	41,755	43,184	44,741

Table VT-10. Employment Characteristics by Family Type

(Number, percent.)

Family type and labor force status	2012		2013		2014	
	Total	Families with own children under 18 years	Total	Families with own children under 18 years	Total	Families with own children under 18 years
All Families............................	160,878	64,915	155,933	60,395	160,392	65,545
FAMILY TYPE AND LABOR FORCE STATUS						
Married-Couple Families........................	126,519	44,208	123,176	40,361	124,116	42,593
Both husband and wife in labor force...............	59.2	75.9	57.7	75.4	59.5	76.6
Husband in labor force, wife not in labor force	16.1	18.7	15.6	18.1	15.3	17.7
Wife in labor force, husband not in labor force	9.7	4.5	8.3	4.1	8.5	3.6
Both husband and wife not in labor force............	15.0	1.0	17.2	1.5	16.8	2.1
Other Families	34,359	20,707	32,757	20,034	36,276	22,952
Female householder, no husband present........................	70.5	72.8	70.4	71.0	68.4	70.6
In labor force	53.4	61.7	50.1	55.0	49.1	58.0
Not in labor force	17.1	11.1	20.3	16.0	19.3	12.6
Male householder, no wife present........................	29.5	27.2	29.6	29.0	31.6	29.4
In labor force........................	22.1	22.9	22.5	24.5	25.4	26.4
Not in labor force	7.4	4.4	7.1	4.5	6.2	2.9

Table VT-11. School Enrollment and Educational Attainment, 2014

(Number, percent.)

Item	State	U.S.
Enrollment		
Total population 3 years and over, enrolled in school........................	146,261	82,063,714
Enrolled in nursery school or preschool (percent)........................	5.8	6.0
Enrolled in kindergarten (percent)........................	5.3	5.1
Enrolled in elementary school, grades 1-8 (percent)........................	36.3	40.2
Enrolled in high school, grades 9-12 (percent)........................	21.6	20.7
Enrolled in college or graduate school (percent)........................	31.0	28.0
Attainment		
Total population 25 years and over	438,279	213,725,624
Less than ninth grade (percent)........................	2.8	5.6
9th to 12th grade, no diploma (percent)........................	5.2	7.5
High school graduate, including equivalency (percent)........................	30.7	27.7
Some college, no degree (percent)........................	18.7	21.0
Associate's degree (percent)........................	7.8	8.2
Bachelor's degree (percent)........................	20.9	18.7
Graduate or professional degree (percent)........................	14.0	11.4
High school graduate or higher (percent)........................	92.0	86.9
Bachelor's degree or higher (percent)........................	34.9	30.1

Table VT-12. Public School Characteristics and Educational Indicators

(Number, percent; data derived from National Center of Education Statistics.)

Item	State	U.S.
Public Schools, 2013–2014 (except where noted)		
Number of school districts........................	360	18,194
Number of schools........................	316	98,271
Number of students (in thousands)	89	50,045
Number of teachers (in thousands)	8	3,114
Student-teacher ratio........................	10.6	16.1
Expenditures per student (dollars), FY 2013........................	17,286	107,637
Four-year adjusted cohort graduation rate (ACGR)[1,2]	87.8	82.3
Students eligible for free or reduced-price lunch (in thousands)	34	25,596
English language learners (in thousands)	1	4,461
Students age 3 to 21 served under IDEA, part B (in thousands)	14	6,464

Public Schools by Type	Number	Percent of state public schools
Total number of schools........................	316	100.0
Regular	300	94.9
Special education........................	0	-
Vocational education........................	15	4.7
Alternative education........................	1	0.3

NOTE: Every school is assigned only one school type based on its instructional emphasis.
[1]ACGR data represents a new method of calculating high-school completion rates and may not be comparable to previous years' data for Averaged Freshmen Graduation Rates (AFGR).
[2]The United States 4-year ACGRs were estimated using both the reported 4-year ACGR data from 49 states and the District of Columbia and using imputed data for Idaho. The estimate for American Indian/Alaska Native students also includes imputed data for Virginia.
- = Zero or rounds to zero.

Table VT-13. Reported Voting and Registration of the Voting-Age Population, November 2014

(Numbers in thousands, percent.)

Item	Total population	Total citizen population	Registered			Voted		
			Total registered	Percent registered (total population)	Percent registered (total citizen population)	Total voted	Percent voted (total population)	Percent voted (total citizen population)
U.S. Total	239,874	219,941	142,166	59.3	64.6	92,251	38.5	41.9
State Total.............................	493	482	324	65.7	67.2	205	41.6	42.5
Sex								
Male..	240	233	152	63.3	65.0	93	38.7	39.7
Female....................................	253	248	172	67.9	69.2	112	44.3	45.1
Race								
White alone.............................	475	466	318	67.0	68.3	202	42.6	43.5
White, non-Hispanic alone	471	463	316	67.0	68.2	201	42.6	43.3
Black alone.............................	4	4	2	(B)	(B)	-	(B)	(B)
Asian alone	7	5	-	(B)	(B)	-	(B)	(B)
Hispanic (of any race)	4	3	2	(B)	(B)	2	(B)	(B)
White alone or in combination	480	471	321	66.8	68.1	204	42.4	43.2
Black alone or in combination..........	6	6	3	(B)	(B)	-	(B)	(B)
Asian alone or in combination..........	8	6	1	(B)	(B)	1	(B)	(B)
Age								
18 to 24 years.........................	55	55	19	(B)	(B)	6	(B)	(B)
25 to 34 years.........................	74	72	30	(B)	(B)	12	(B)	(B)
35 to 44 years.........................	74	72	49	(B)	(B)	28	(B)	(B)
45 to 64 years.........................	184	179	140	75.7	78.1	93	50.7	52.3
65 years and over	106	105	86	81.0	82.0	65	61.5	62.2

B = Base is less than 75,000 and therefore too small to show the derived measure.
- = Zero or rounds to zero.

Table VT-14. Crime

(Number, rate per 100,000. Data are derived from the FBI Uniform Crime Reports.)

Item	State			U.S.[1,2,3,4]		
	2013	2014	Percent change	2013	2014	Percent change
TOTAL POPULATION[5]............................	626,630	626,562	-	316,128,839	318,857,056	0.9
VIOLENT CRIME						
Number..	720	622	-13.6	1,163,146	1,165,383	0.2
Rate	114.9	99.3	-13.6	367.9	365.5	-0.7
Murder and Nonnegligent Manslaughter						
Number..	10	10	-	14,196	14,249	0.4
Rate	1.6	1.6	-	4.5	4.5	-
Rape[6]						
Number..	130	110	X	108,612	116,645	X
Rate	20.7	17.6	X	34.4	36.6	X
Robbery						
Number..	73	70	-4.1	345,031	325,802	-5.6
Rate	11.6	11.2	-3.4	109.1	102.2	-6.3
Aggravated Assault						
Number..	546	432	-20.9	724,149	741,291	2.4
Rate	87.1	68.9	-20.9	229.1	232.5	1.5
PROPERTY CRIME						
Number..	13,875	9,551	-31.2	8,632,512	8,277,829	-4.1
Rate	2,214.2	1,524.4	-31.2	2,730.7	2,596.1	-4.9
Burglary						
Number..	3,313	2,034	-38.6	1,928,465	1,729,806	-10.3
Rate	528.7	324.6	-38.6	610.0	542.5	-11.1
Larceny-Theft						
Number..	10,228	7,273	-28.9	6,004,453	5,858,496	-2.4
Rate	1,632.2	1,160.8	-28.9	1,899.4	1,837.3	-3.3
Motor Vehicle Theft						
Number..	334	244	-26.9	699,594	689,527	-1.4
Rate	53.3	38.9	-27.0	221.3	216.2	-2.3

NOTE: Although arson data are included in the trend and clearance tables, sufficient data are not available to estimate totals for this offense. Therefore, no arson data are published in this table.
X = Not applicable.
- = Zero or rounds to zero.
[1] The crime figures have been adjusted.
[2] The data collection methodology for the offense of forcible rape used by the Minnesota state Uniform Crime Reporting (UCR) Program (with the exception of Minneapolis and St. Paul, Minnesota) does not comply with national UCR Program guidelines. Consequently, its figures for forcible rape and violent crime (of which forcible rape is a part) are not published in this table.
[3] Includes offenses reported by the Zoological Police and the Metro Transit Police.
[4] Because of changes in the state's reporting practices, figures are not comparable to previous years' data.
[5] Populations are U.S. Census Bureau provisional estimates as of July 1 of each year.
[6] The figures shown for the offense of rape were estimated using the revised Uniform Crime Reporting (UCR) definition of rape.

Table VT-15. State Government Finances, 2014

(Dollar amounts in thousands, percent distribution.)

Item	Dollars	Percent distribution
Total Revenue	6,545,351	100.0
General revenue	5,771,744	88.2
Intergovernmental revenue	1,943,173	29.7
Taxes	2,962,531	45.3
General sales	354,541	5.4
Selective sales	660,419	10.1
License taxes	109,996	1.7
Individual income tax	675,240	10.3
Corporate income tax	105,817	1.6
Other taxes	1,056,518	16.1
Current charges	531,903	8.1
Miscellaneous general revenue	334,137	5.1
Utility revenue	0	-
Liquor stores revenue	53,009	0.8
Insurance trust revenue[1]	720,598	11.0
Total Expenditure	6,302,744	100.0
Intergovernmental expenditure	1,570,909	24.9
Direct expenditure	4,731,835	75.1
Current operation	3,902,750	61.9
Capital outlay	201,350	3.2
Insurance benefits and repayments	382,782	6.1
Assistance and subsidies	155,385	2.5
Interest on debt	89,568	1.4
Exhibit: Salaries and wages	819,518	13.0
Total Expenditure	6,302,744	100.0
General expenditure	5,864,932	93.1
Intergovernmental expenditure	1,570,909	24.9
Direct expenditure	4,294,023	68.1
General expenditure, by function:		
Education	2,482,331	39.4
Public welfare	1,671,302	26.5
Hospitals	2732	0.0
Health	332,224	5.3
Highways	473,963	7.5
Police protection	92,234	1.5
Correction	139,146	2.2
Natural resources	101,284	1.6
Parks and recreation	13,209	0.2
Governmental administration	188,918	3.0
Interest on general debt	89,568	1.4
Other and unallocable	278,021	4.4
Utility expenditure	0	-
Liquor stores expenditure	55,030	0.9
Insurance trust expenditure	382,782	6.1
Debt at End of Fiscal Year	3,291,205	X
Cash and Security Holdings	7,894,308	X

X = Not applicable.
- = Zero or rounds to zero.
[1]Within insurance trust revenue, net earnings of state retirement systems is a calculated statistic (the item code in the data file is X08), and thus can be positive or negative. Net earnings is the sum of earnings on investments plus gains on investments minus losses on investments. The change made in 2002 for asset valuation from book to market value in accordance with Statement 34 of the Governmental Accounting Standards Board is reflected in the calculated statistics.

Table VT-16. State Government Tax Collections, 2014

(Dollars in thousands, percent.)

Item	Dollars	Percent distribution
Total Taxes	2,962,531	100.0
Property taxes	985,478	33.3
Sales and gross receipts	1,014,960	34.3
General sales and gross receipts	354,541	12.0
Selective sales and gross receipts	660,419	22.3
Alcoholic beverages	24,065	0.8
Amusements	0	-
Insurance premiums	60,020	2.0
Motor fuels	103,551	3.5
Pari-mutuels	0	-
Public utilities	21,791	0.7
Tobacco products	71,854	2.4
Other selective sales	379,138	12.8
Licenses	109,996	3.7
Alcoholic beverages	430	-
Amusements	36	-
Corporations in general	3,276	0.1
Hunting and fishing	7,319	0.2
Motor vehicle	70,398	2.4
Motor vehicle operators	7,795	0.3
Public utilities	0	-
Occupation and business, NEC	18,869	0.6
Other licenses	1,873	0.1
Income taxes	781,057	26.4
Individual income	675,240	22.8
Corporation net income	105,817	3.6
Other taxes	71,040	2.4
Death and gift	35,542	1.2
Documentary and stock transfer	30,931	1.0
Severance	X	X
Taxes, NEC	4,567	0.2

X = Not applicable.
- = Zero or rounds to zero.

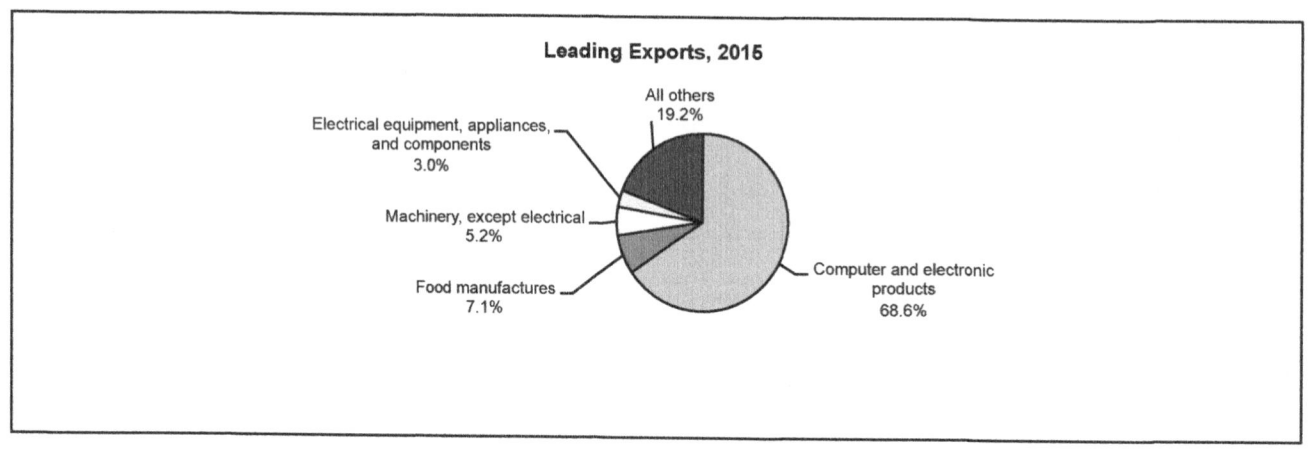

Leading Exports, 2015

- All others 19.2%
- Electrical equipment, appliances, and components 3.0%
- Machinery, except electrical 5.2%
- Food manufactures 7.1%
- Computer and electronic products 68.6%

VIRGINIA

Facts and Figures

Location: Eastern United States; bordered on the N and NE by Maryland and the District of Columbia, on the E by the Atlantic Ocean, on the S by North Carolina and Tennessee, and on the W by Kentucky and West Virginia

Area: 42,774 sq. mi. (110,785 sq. km.); rank—35th

Population: 8,382,993 (2015 est.); rank—12th

Principal Cities: capital—Richmond; largest—Virginia Beach

Statehood: June 25, 1788; 10th state

U.S. Congress: 2 senators, 11 representatives

State Motto: *Sic semper tyrannis* ("Thus always to tyrants")

State Song: "Our Great Virginia" and "Sweet Virginia Breeze"

State Nickname: The Old Dominion State

Abbreviations: VA; Va.

State Symbols: flower—flowering dogwood; tree—flowering dogwood; bird—cardinal

At a Glance

- With an increase in population of 4.5 percent, Virginia ranked 19th among the states in growth from 2010 to 2015.

- Virginia's violent crime rate (196.2 incidents per 100,000 population) was the 5th lowest in the country in 2014.

- In 2015, 4.4 percent of Virginians were unemployed, compared to 5.3 percent of the total U.S. population.

- Virginia's median household income in 2014 was $64,902, and 11.8 percent of the population lived below the poverty level.

- In 2014, 10.9 percent of Virginians did not have health insurance, compared to 11.7 percent of the total U.S. population.

Table VA-1. Population by Age, Sex, Race, and Hispanic Origin

(Number, percent, except where noted.)

Sex, age, race, and Hispanic origin	2000	2010	2015[1]	Average annual percent change, 2010–2015
Total Population...	7,078,515	8,001,024	8,382,993	0.3
Percent of total U.S. population	2.5	2.6	2.6	X
Sex				
Male...	3,471,895	3,925,983	4,124,765	0.4
Female	3,606,620	4,075,041	4,258,228	0.3
Age				
Under 5 years...	461,982	509,625	515,157	0.1
5 to 19 years...	1,475,104	1,574,060	1,578,186	-
20 to 64 years...	4,349,096	4,940,402	5,101,257	0.2
65 years and over...	79,233	976,937	1,188,393	1.4
Median age (years)...	35.7	37.5	37.8	0.1
Race and Hispanic Origin				
One race				
White...	5,120,110	5,725,432	5,886,416	0.2
Black...	1,390,293	1,579,414	1,654,264	0.3
American Indian and Alaska Native	21,172	41,525	45,483	0.7
Asian...	261,025	449,149	545,973	1.4
Native Hawaiian or Other Pacific Islander	3,946	8,201	9,777	1.3
Two or more races...	143,069	197,303	241,080	1.4
Hispanic (of any race)...	329,540	660,501	754,737	1.0

X = Not applicable.
[1]Population figures for 2015 are July 1 estimates. The 2010 estimates are taken from the 2010 Census.
- = Zero or rounds to zero.

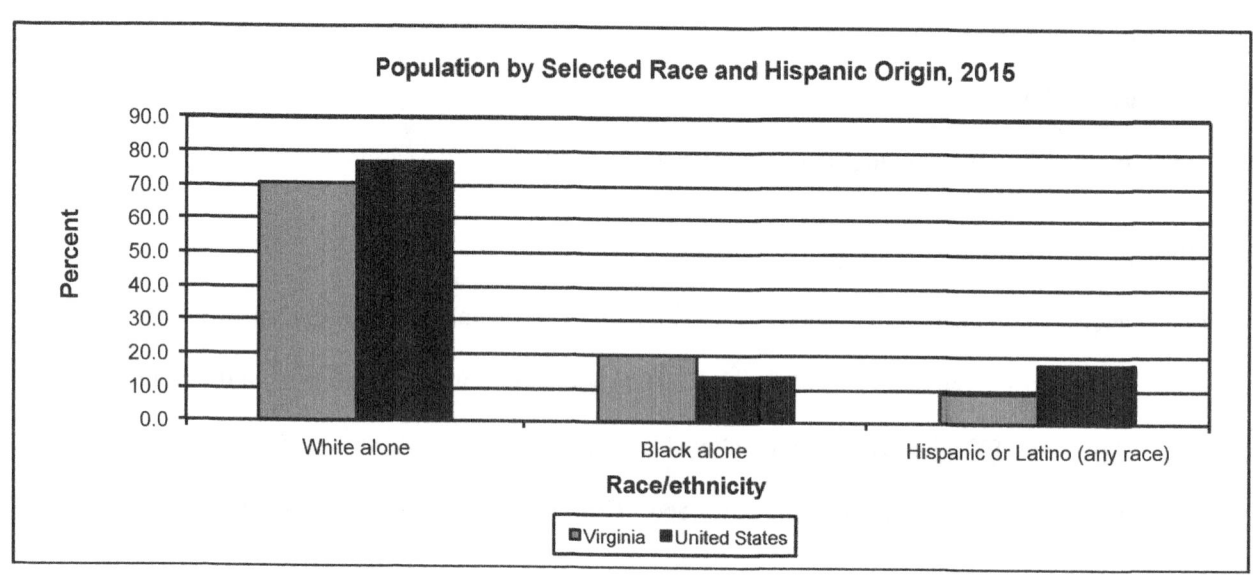

Table VA-2. Marital Status

(Number, percent distribution.)

Sex, age, race, and Hispanic origin	2000	2010	2014
Males, 15 Years and Over	2,724,334	3,156,115	3,232,491
Never married	29.1	34.2	34.6
Now married, except separated...	58.2	52.6	52.3
Separated...	2.6	2.3	2.2
Widowed...	2.3	2.3	2.4
Divorced...	7.9	8.5	8.6
Females, 15 Years and Over	2,899,294	3,331,264	3,404,862
Never married	23.5	28.0	28.5
Now married, except separated...	53.4	49.0	48.6
Separated...	3.2	2.9	2.8
Widowed...	9.9	8.7	8.7
Divorced...	10.0	11.4	11.4

Table VA-3. Households and Housing Characteristics

(Number, percent, dollars.)

Item	2000	2010	2014	Average annual percent change, 2000–2014
Total Households...	2,699,173	2,992,732	3,083,820	1.0
Family households	1,847,796	2,013,520	2,058,820	0.8
Married-couple family	1,426,044	1,517,627	1,544,439	0.6
Other family	421,752	495,893	514,381	1.6
Male householder, no wife present.......................	101,462	124,273	133,347	2.2
Female householder, no husband present.................	320,290	371,620	381,034	1.4
Nonfamily households	851,377	979,212	1,025,000	1.5
Householder living alone	676,907	794,535	833,523	1.7
Householder not living alone...............................	174,470	184,677	191,477	0.7
Housing Characteristics				
Total housing units...	2,904,192	3,368,674	3,446,585	1.3
Occupied housing units	2,699,173	2,992,732	3,083,820	1.0
Owner occupied	1,837,939	2,025,240	2,014,812	0.7
Renter occupied	861,234	967,492	1,069,008	1.7
Average household size..	2.54	2.60	2.62	0.2
Financial Characteristics				
Median gross rent of renter-occupied housing	650	1,019	1,116	5.1
Median monthly owner costs for housing units with a mortgage	1,144	1,728	1,664	3.2
Median value of owner-occupied housing units............	125,400	249,100	247,800	7.0

Table VA-4. Migration, Origin, and Language

(Number, percent.)

Characteristic	State			U.S.		
	2013	2014	Percent change	2013	2014	Percent change
Residence 1 Year Ago						
Population 1 year and over	8,163,664	8,224,054	0.7	312,432,820	315,095,393	0.9
Same house	84.2	83.8	X	85.0	85.1	X
Different house in the U.S.	15.1	15.3	X	14.4	14.3	X
Same county	6.7	6.9	X	8.9	8.7	X
Different county	8.3	8.4	X	5.5	5.6	X
Same state	5.1	5.2	X	3.2	3.3	X
Different state	3.3	3.2	X	2.3	2.3	X
Abroad	0.7	0.9	X	0.6	0.6	X
Place of Birth						
Native born	7,311,442	7,320,669	0.1	274,780,773	276,465,262	0.6
Male	49.3	49.3	X	49.3	49.3	X
Female	50.7	50.7	X	50.7	50.7	X
Foreign born	948,963	1,005,620	6.0	41,348,066	42,391,794	2.5
Male	48.1	48.0	X	48.8	48.7	X
Female	51.9	52.0	X	51.2	51.3	X
Foreign born; naturalized U.S. citizen.........................	477,236	496,809	4.1	19,294,710	19,984,738	3.6
Male	46.3	46.3	X	45.9	45.9	X
Female	53.7	53.7	X	54.1	54.1	X
Foreign born; not a U.S. citizen	471,727	508,811	7.9	22,053,356	22,407,056	1.6
Male	49.9	49.7	X	51.3	51.2	X
Female	50.1	50.3	X	48.7	48.8	X
Entered 2010 or later	11.3	14.7	X	9.7	12.3	X
Entered 2000 to 2009	34.0	33.5	X	29.4	28.6	X
Entered before 2000...	54.7	51.8	X	61.0	59.1	X
World Region of Birth, Foreign						
Foreign-born population, excluding population born at sea	948,963	1,005,620	6.0	41,347,945	42,390,705	2.5
Europe	10.4	10.0	X	11.6	11.2	X
Asia..	41.6	41.9	X	29.5	30.1	X
Africa	9.9	10.4	X	4.4	4.6	X
Oceania	0.5	0.3	X	0.5	0.6	X
Latin America	36.1	35.9	X	51.9	51.6	X
North America..	1.6	1.4	X	2.0	1.9	X
Language Spoken at Home and Ability to Speak English						
Population 5 years and over..	7,750,801	7,818,739	0.9	296,358,760	299,084,046	0.9
English only	85.1	84.4	X	79.2	78.9	X
Language other than English....................................	14.9	15.6	X	20.8	21.1	X
Speaks English less than "very well"........................	5.3	5.6	X	8.5	8.6	X

X = Not applicable.
- = Zero or rounds to zero.

Table VA-5. Median Income and Poverty Status, 2014

(Number, percent, except as noted.)

Characteristic	State		U.S.	
	Number	Percent	Number	Percent
Median Income				
Households (dollars)............	64,902	X	53,657	X
Families (dollars)	78,290	X	65,910	X
Below Poverty Level (All People)	953,395	11.8	48,208,387	15.5
Sex				
Male............	411,485	10.4	21,590,918	14.2
Female	541,910	13.1	26,617,469	16.8
Age				
Under 18 years............	291,260	15.8	15,686,012	21.7
Related children under 18 years............	283,702	15.5	15,372,705	21.3
18 to 64 years............	574,323	11.2	28,267,482	14.6
65 years and over............	87,812	7.8	4,254,893	9.5

X = Not applicable.

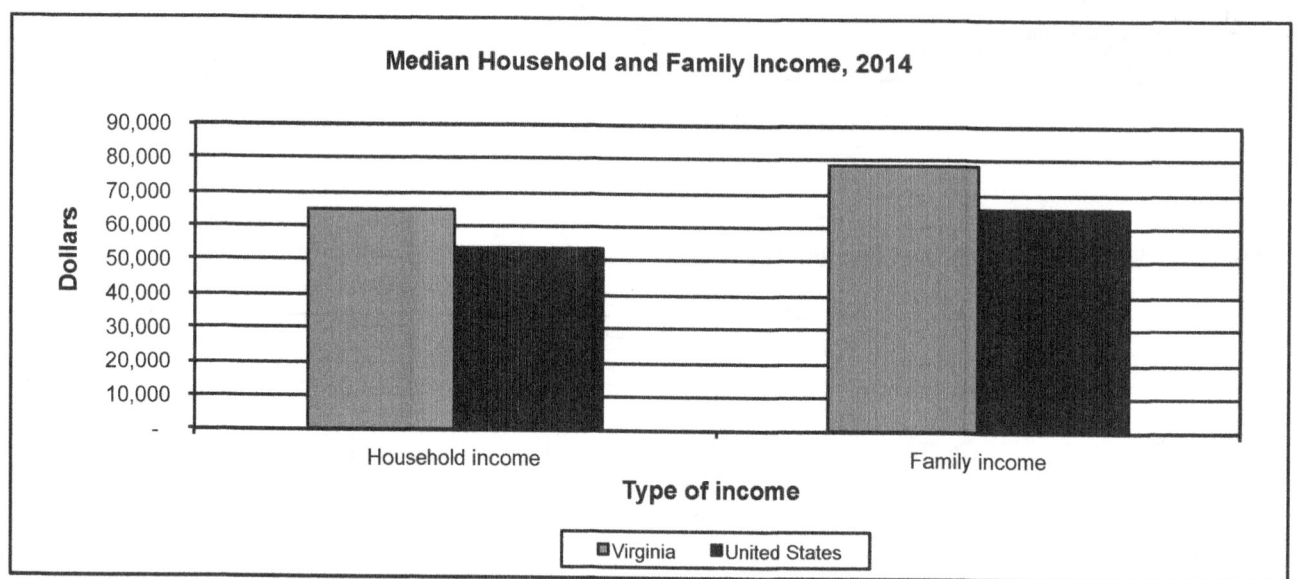

Table VA-6. Health Insurance Coverage Status for the Civilian Noninstitutionalized Population and Children Under 18 Years of Age

(Numbers in thousands, percent.)

Item	2006	2007	2008	2009	2010	2011	2012	2013	2014
Civilian Noninstitutionalized Population	7,538	7,684	7,520	7,644	7,807	7,887	7,973	8,054	8,115
Covered by Private or Public Insurance									
Number............	6,532	6,548	6,621	6,736	6,787	6,904	6,974	7,064	7,231
Percent............	86.7	85.2	88.0	88.1	86.9	87.5	87.5	87.7	89.1
Not Covered									
Number............	1,006	1,135	899	908	1,020	983	999	991	884
Percent............	13.3	14.8	12.0	11.9	13.1	12.5	12.5	12.3	10.9
Percent in the U.S. not covered............	15.8	15.3	15.1	15.1	15.5	15.1	14.8	14.5	11.7
Children Under 18 Years of Age	1,827	1,833	1,815	1,843	1,850	1,849	1,852	1,862	1,865
Covered by Private or Public Insurance									
Number............	1,643	1,646	1,677	1,721	1,729	1,741	1,748	1,760	1,758
Percent............	89.9	89.8	92.4	93.4	93.4	94.1	94.4	94.6	94.3
Not Covered									
Number............	185	187	138	122	121	108	104	101	107
Percent............	10.1	10.2	7.6	6.6	6.6	5.9	5.6	5.4	5.7
Percent in the U.S. not covered............	11.7	11.0	9.7	8.6	8.0	7.5	7.2	7.1	6.0

Table VA-7. Employment Status by Demographic Group, 2015

(Numbers in thousands, percent.)

Characteristic	Civilian noninstitutional population	Civilian labor force		Employed		Unemployed	
		Number	Percent of population	Number	Percent of population	Number	Percent of population
Total..............................	6,503	4,218	64.9	4,029	62.0	189	4.5
Sex							
Male	3,117	2,233	71.6	2,130	68.3	103	4.6
Female	3,386	1,986	58.7	1,899	56.1	87	4.4
Race, Sex, and Hispanic Origin							
White	4,725	3,063	64.8	2,952	62.5	111	3.6
Male	2,319	1,664	71.7	1,597	68.9	67	4.0
Female	2,406	1,399	58.2	1,355	56.3	44	3.2
Black or African American....	1,227	780	63.5	718	58.5	62	7.9
Male	558	378	67.7	349	62.5	29	7.6
Female	669	402	60.1	369	55.1	33	8.2
Hispanic or Latino ethnicity[1]	500	373	74.5	350	70.1	22	6.0
Male	246	204	83.0	190	77.3	14	6.8
Female	255	169	66.3	160	63.0	8	4.9
Age							
16 to 19 years...................	426	143	33.7	118	27.8	25	17.5
20 to 24 years...................	536	381	70.9	353	65.9	27	7.1
25 to 34 years...................	1,095	902	82.3	852	77.8	50	5.5
35 to 44 years...................	1,099	938	85.3	903	82.2	35	3.7
45 to 54 years...................	1,127	914	81.1	888	78.7	26	2.9
55 to 64 years...................	1,041	689	66.2	668	64.1	21	3.1
65 years and over..............	1,179	252	21.4	247	21.0	5	2.0

NOTE: Data in Table 7 are from the Current Population Survey (CPS) and do not match the estimates in Table 8. See notes and definitions for further information.
[1]May be of any race.

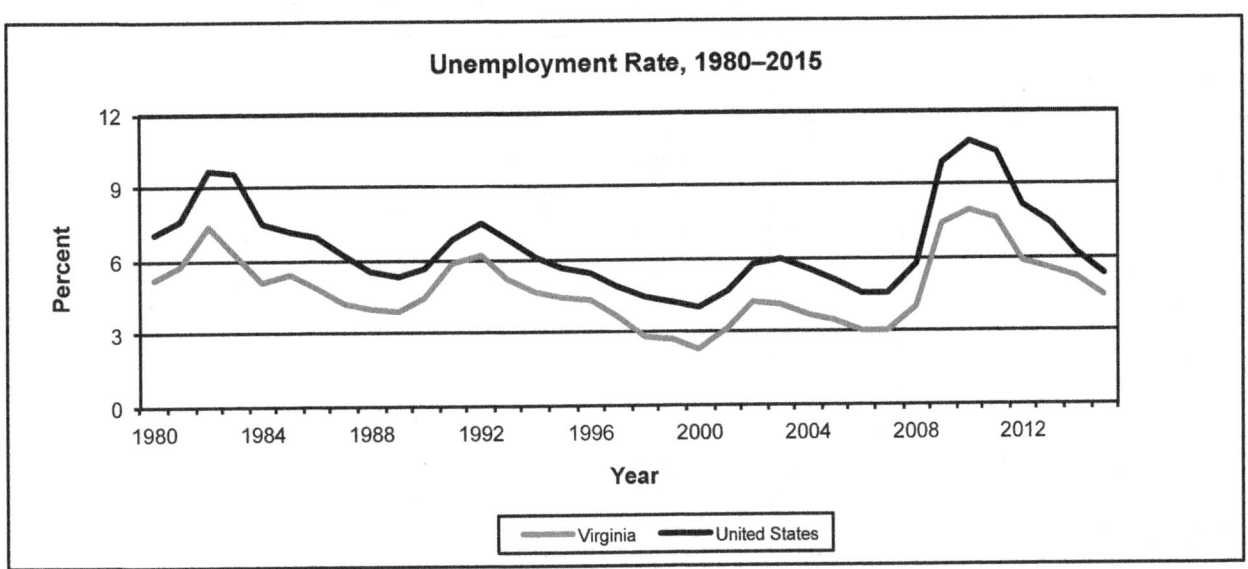

Unemployment Rate, 1980–2015

Legend: Virginia — United States

Table VA-8. Employment Status of the Civilian Noninstitutional Population Age 16 Years and Over

(Number, percent.)

Year	Civilian labor force	Civilian participation rate	Employed	Unemployed	Unemployment rate
2007..............................	4,036,835	68.9	3,914,087	122,748	3.0
2008..............................	4,133,443	69.7	3,970,428	163,015	3.9
2009..............................	4,118,171	68.6	3,842,516	275,655	6.7
2010..............................	4,157,658	67.7	3,860,386	297,272	7.1
2011..............................	4,211,802	67.4	3,934,326	277,476	6.6
2012..............................	4,225,252	66.8	3,969,890	255,362	6.0
2013..............................	4,239,491	66.3	3,998,244	241,247	5.7
2014..............................	4,257,986	66.0	4,036,280	221,706	5.2
2015..............................	4,240,470	65.2	4,051,908	188,562	4.4

Table VA-9. Employment and Average Wages by Industry

(Estimates through 2010 are based on the 2007 North American Industry Classification System [NAICS]. Estimates from 2011 onward are based on the 2012 NAICS.)

Industry	2008	2009	2010	2011	2012	2013	2014
	Number of jobs						
Wage and Salary Employment by Industry..................	4,006,870	3,882,095	3,874,473	3,909,375	3,930,655	3,952,806	3,973,687
Farm Wage and Salary Employment.........................	9,264	9,879	13,127	10,085	10,564	11,579	14,283
Nonfarm Wage and Salary Employment....................	3,997,606	3,872,216	3,861,346	3,899,290	3,920,091	3,941,227	3,959,404
Private wage and salary employment........................	3,125,203	2,998,974	2,987,308	3,027,512	3,047,898	3,072,442	3,095,066
Forestry, fishing, and related activities................	5,452	5,348	5,498	5,694	5,639	5,839	6,110
Mining..	9,288	8,489	8,593	9,040	9,019	8,074	7,462
Utilities...	11,479	11,448	10,917	10,892	10,640	10,534	10,645
Construction	232,599	199,691	192,176	188,046	182,833	183,581	184,104
Manufacturing..	264,666	239,445	230,767	230,872	231,745	231,327	232,080
Durable goods manufacturing..........................	153,764	137,113	132,380	134,413	136,528	136,624	137,526
Nondurable goods manufacturing.....................	110,902	102,332	98,387	96,459	95,217	94,703	94,554
Wholesale trade	121,211	114,278	111,017	113,126	111,914	111,874	111,481
Retail trade..	425,957	404,814	404,937	408,642	409,926	414,940	417,712
Transportation and warehousing..........................	109,508	103,624	103,663	104,960	105,996	106,141	108,945
Information	87,883	81,318	76,442	74,404	71,786	71,254	71,648
Finance and insurance	130,268	124,833	124,539	128,440	131,586	134,152	135,852
Real estate and rental and leasing........................	58,634	56,098	54,237	52,920	52,891	53,451	52,905
Professional, scientific, and technical services	378,425	381,689	387,686	396,367	399,046	397,704	392,442
Management of companies and enterprises................	77,465	74,741	73,963	73,355	76,391	76,061	74,474
Administrative and waste services.........................	211,823	193,815	197,862	204,193	207,857	210,765	216,994
Educational services	68,208	68,662	70,827	73,178	73,304	72,864	72,853
Health care and social assistance.........................	364,700	374,283	381,407	389,687	398,241	406,107	411,256
Arts, entertainment, and recreation.......................	48,248	47,108	47,434	48,582	49,245	50,643	50,165
Accommodation and food services........................	305,294	298,526	298,471	305,160	312,287	318,506	323,494
Other services, except public administration..............	214,095	210,764	206,872	209,954	207,552	208,625	214,444
Government and government enterprises	872,403	873,242	874,038	871,778	872,193	868,785	864,338
	Dollars						
Average Wages and Salaries by Industry	48,470	49,461	50,948	52,072	53,104	53,267	54,250
Average Farm Wages and Salaries	29,824	25,703	18,648	21,993	23,534	28,909	24,008
Average Nonfarm Wages and Salaries	48,513	49,521	51,057	52,150	53,184	53,338	54,359
Average private wages and salaries.........................	47,667	48,533	50,122	51,372	52,536	52,772	53,661
Forestry, fishing, and related activities.....................	26,746	26,474	27,556	28,453	29,105	30,284	31,526
Mining..	60,398	61,570	67,349	70,807	68,916	69,203	71,084
Utilities...	91,812	93,856	100,019	100,599	101,588	101,264	105,726
Construction	45,565	46,052	47,559	48,597	49,195	49,701	50,933
Manufacturing..	50,193	51,111	53,412	54,527	55,655	56,229	58,359
Durable goods manufacturing..........................	51,970	52,904	55,166	57,091	58,134	58,977	61,796
Nondurable goods manufacturing.....................	47,729	48,710	51,051	50,954	52,100	52,265	53,361
Wholesale trade	66,487	67,121	69,087	72,211	72,613	73,468	75,407
Retail trade..	25,823	25,992	26,482	26,853	27,477	27,646	28,173
Transportation and warehousing..........................	45,326	45,935	47,102	48,214	49,578	51,594	51,903
Information	77,818	78,360	80,670	81,724	84,425	87,837	92,538
Finance and insurance	72,672	72,433	75,333	78,514	83,444	83,723	86,013
Real estate and rental and leasing........................	44,021	43,876	45,192	46,823	48,868	49,558	51,347
Professional, scientific, and technical services	87,808	90,030	93,372	96,059	97,996	97,879	99,025
Management of companies and enterprises................	98,278	98,693	103,532	107,867	112,565	113,665	114,626
Administrative and waste services.........................	33,861	35,412	36,980	37,923	38,927	38,529	39,211
Educational services	37,631	39,014	39,727	40,256	38,081	38,747	38,654
Health care and social assistance.........................	43,340	44,110	44,676	45,691	46,533	47,043	47,947
Arts, entertainment, and recreation.......................	26,107	26,084	27,443	26,558	27,184	27,030	28,154
Accommodation and food services........................	18,100	17,906	18,614	19,030	19,362	19,349	20,054
Other services, except public administration..............	33,828	34,073	35,211	35,625	36,573	37,139	37,828
Government and government enterprises.........................	51,547	52,916	54,253	54,851	55,448	55,338	56,859

Table VA-10. Employment Characteristics by Family Type

(Number, percent.)

Family type and labor force status	2012		2013		2014	
	Total	Families with own children under 18 years	Total	Families with own children under 18 years	Total	Families with own children under 18 years
All Families..	2,044,422	895,668	2,049,184	887,364	2,051,042	901,080
FAMILY TYPE AND LABOR FORCE STATUS						
Married-Couple Families..............................	1,541,185	632,612	1,530,934	622,543	1,536,661	635,484
Both husband and wife in labor force......................	55.6	67.9	54.8	67.3	54.8	67.2
Husband in labor force, wife not in labor force	21.8	27.5	21.9	27.9	22.2	27.8
Wife in labor force, husband not in labor force	7.5	3.4	7.3	3.3	7.5	3.5
Both husband and wife not in labor force.................	15.2	1.2	15.6	1.3	15.5	1.5
Other Families	503,237	263,056	518,250	264,821	514,381	265,596
Female householder, no husband present..................	74.8	76.2	74.4	77.9	74.1	76.6
In labor force...	54.7	64.0	54.1	65.1	53.6	64.3
Not in labor force	20.1	12.2	20.3	12.7	20.5	12.3
Male householder, no wife present.........................	25.2	23.8	25.6	22.1	25.9	23.4
In labor force...	20.4	22.1	20.4	20.5	20.7	21.8
Not in labor force	4.8	1.7	5.2	1.7	5.3	1.6

Table VA-11. School Enrollment and Educational Attainment, 2014

(Number, percent.)

Item	State	U.S.
Enrollment		
Total population 3 years and over, enrolled in school...........	2,168,651	82,063,714
Enrolled in nursery school or preschool (percent)	6.0	6.0
Enrolled in kindergarten (percent)...................................	5.0	5.1
Enrolled in elementary school, grades 1-8 (percent)............	38.5	40.2
Enrolled in high school, grades 9-12 (percent)	19.9	20.7
Enrolled in college or graduate school (percent).................	30.6	28.0
Attainment		
Total population 25 years and over	5,623,295	213,725,624
Less than ninth grade (percent)......................................	4.8	5.6
9th to 12th grade, no diploma (percent)...........................	6.7	7.5
High school graduate, including equivalency (percent)	24.6	27.7
Some college, no degree (percent)	19.9	21.0
Associate's degree (percent)	7.3	8.2
Bachelor's degree (percent)	20.9	18.7
Graduate or professional degree (percent).........................	15.9	11.4
High school graduate or higher (percent)	88.5	86.9
Bachelor's degree or higher (percent)...............................	36.7	30.1

Table VA-12. Public School Characteristics and Educational Indicators

(Number, percent; data derived from National Center of Education Statistics.)

Item	State	U.S.
Public Schools, 2013–2014 (except where noted)		
Number of school districts...	227	18,194
Number of schools...	2,166	98,271
Number of students (in thousands)	1,274	50,045
Number of teachers (in thousands)	90	3,114
Student-teacher ratio	14.1	16.1
Expenditures per student (dollars), FY 2013......................	10,960	107,637
Four-year adjusted cohort graduation rate (ACGR)[1,2]	85.3	82.3
Students eligible for free or reduced-price lunch (in thousands)	504	25,596
English language learners (in thousands)	94	4,461
Students age 3 to 21 served under IDEA, part B (in thousands)	161	6,464

Public Schools by Type	Number	Percent of state public schools
Total number of schools..	2,166	100.0
Regular..	1,868	86.2
Special education...	53	2.4
Vocational education...	58	2.7
Alternative education..	187	8.6

NOTE: Every school is assigned only one school type based on its instructional emphasis.
[1]ACGR data represents a new method of calculating high-school completion rates and may not be comparable to previous years' data for Averaged Freshmen Graduation Rates (AFGR).
[2]The United States 4-year ACGRs were estimated using both the reported 4-year ACGR data from 49 states and the District of Columbia and using imputed data for Idaho. The estimate for American Indian/Alaska Native students also includes imputed data for Virginia.

Table VA-13. Reported Voting and Registration of the Voting-Age Population, November 2014

(Numbers in thousands, percent.)

Item	Total population	Total citizen population	Registered			Voted		
			Total registered	Percent registered (total population)	Percent registered (total citizen population)	Total voted	Percent voted (total population)	Percent voted (total citizen population)
U.S. Total	239,874	219,941	142,166	59.3	64.6	92,251	38.5	41.9
State Total.............................	6,221	5,888	3,924	63.1	66.6	2,453	39.4	41.7
Sex								
Male	2,975	2,842	1,892	63.6	66.6	1,200	40.3	42.2
Female.....................................	3,246	3,046	2,032	62.6	66.7	1,253	38.6	41.1
Race								
White alone...............................	4,480	4,287	2,939	65.6	68.6	1,924	43.0	44.9
White, non-Hispanic alone	4,145	4,094	2,850	68.8	69.6	1,869	45.1	45.6
Black alone................................	1,188	1,153	712	60.0	61.7	394	33.2	34.2
Asian alone	438	343	209	47.8	61.0	108	24.7	31.6
Hispanic (of any race).....................	389	236	112	28.9	47.4	60	15.4	25.4
White alone or in combination	4,540	4,337	2,973	65.5	68.5	1,934	42.6	44.6
Black alone or in combination..........	1,233	1,199	738	59.8	61.5	401	32.5	33.4
Asian alone or in combination..........	477	372	233	48.9	62.8	116	24.4	31.3
Age								
18 to 24 years.............................	728	681	315	43.2	46.2	112	15.4	16.5
25 to 34 years.............................	1,075	973	606	56.3	62.3	258	24.0	26.6
35 to 44 years.............................	1,094	989	697	63.8	70.5	403	36.9	40.8
45 to 64 years.............................	2,160	2,086	1,449	67.1	69.4	1,017	47.1	48.7
65 years and over	1,165	1,159	858	73.7	74.0	662	56.8	57.1

Table VA-14. Crime

(Number, rate per 100,000. Data are derived from the FBI Uniform Crime Reports.)

Item	State			U.S.[1,2,3,4]		
	2013	2014	Percent change	2013	2014	Percent change
TOTAL POPULATION[5].....................................	8,260,405	8,326,289	0.8	316,128,839	318,857,056	0.9
VIOLENT CRIME						
Number...	15,524	16,340	5.3	1,163,146	1,165,383	0.2
Rate	187.9	196.2	4.4	367.9	365.5	-0.7
Murder and Nonnegligent Manslaughter						
Number...	316	338	7.0	14,196	14,249	0.4
Rate	3.8	4.1	7.9	4.5	4.5	-
Rape[6]						
Number...	2,262	2,310	X	108,612	116,645	X
Rate	27.4	27.7	X	34.4	36.6	X
Robbery						
Number...	4,565	4,292	-6.0	345,031	325,802	-5.6
Rate	55.3	51.5	-6.9	109.1	102.2	-6.3
Aggravated Assault						
Number...	9,062	9,400	3.7	724,149	741,291	2.4
Rate	109.7	112.9	2.9	229.1	232.5	1.5
PROPERTY CRIME						
Number...	170,654	160,720	-5.8	8,632,512	8,277,829	-4.1
Rate	2,065.9	1,930.3	-6.6	2,730.7	2,596.1	-4.9
Burglary						
Number...	26,640	23,122	-13.2	1,928,465	1,729,806	-10.3
Rate	322.5	277.7	-13.9	610.0	542.5	-11.1
Larceny-Theft						
Number...	135,478	129,933	-4.1	6,004,453	5,858,496	-2.4
Rate	1,640.1	1,560.5	-4.9	1,899.4	1,837.3	-3.3
Motor Vehicle Theft						
Number...	8,536	7,665	-10.2	699,594	689,527	-1.4
Rate	103.3	92.1	-10.8	221.3	216.2	-2.3

NOTE: Although arson data are included in the trend and clearance tables, sufficient data are not available to estimate totals for this offense. Therefore, no arson data are published in this table.
X = Not applicable.
- = Zero or rounds to zero.
[1]The crime figures have been adjusted.
[2]The data collection methodology for the offense of forcible rape used by the Minnesota state Uniform Crime Reporting (UCR) Program (with the exception of Minneapolis and St. Paul, Minnesota) does not comply with national UCR Program guidelines. Consequently, its figures for forcible rape and violent crime (of which forcible rape is a part) are not published in this table.
[3]Includes offenses reported by the Zoological Police and the Metro Transit Police.
[4]Because of changes in the state's reporting practices, figures are not comparable to previous years' data.
[5]Populations are U.S. Census Bureau provisional estimates as of July 1 of each year.
[6]The figures shown for the offense of rape were estimated using the revised Uniform Crime Reporting (UCR) definition of rape.

Table VA-15. State Government Finances, 2014

(Dollar amounts in thousands, percent distribution.)

Item	Dollars	Percent distribution
Total Revenue	53,731,192	100.0
General revenue	41,468,565	77.2
Intergovernmental revenue	10,027,820	18.7
Taxes	18,949,272	35.3
General sales	3,555,745	6.6
Selective sales	2,507,437	4.7
License taxes	795,515	1.5
Individual income tax	10,877,689	20.2
Corporate income tax	740,511	1.4
Other taxes	472,375	0.9
Current charges	8,635,737	16.1
Miscellaneous general revenue	3,855,736	7.2
Utility revenue	0	-
Liquor stores revenue	668,660	1.2
Insurance trust revenue[1]	11,593,967	21.6
Total Expenditure	48,187,730	100.0
Intergovernmental expenditure	11,792,595	24.5
Direct expenditure	36,395,135	75.5
Current operation	26,995,082	56.0
Capital outlay	2,159,303	4.5
Insurance benefits and repayments	4,453,815	9.2
Assistance and subsidies	1,664,363	3.5
Interest on debt	1,122,572	2.3
Exhibit: Salaries and wages	6,972,768	14.5
Total Expenditure	48,187,730	100.0
General expenditure	43,198,714	89.6
Intergovernmental expenditure	11,792,595	24.5
Direct expenditure	31,406,119	65.2
General expenditure, by function:		
Education	14,825,305	30.8
Public welfare	10,218,073	21.2
Hospitals	3,797,823	7.9
Health	1,345,494	2.8
Highways	4,284,069	8.9
Police protection	549,728	1.1
Correction	1,724,383	3.6
Natural resources	244,640	0.5
Parks and recreation	119,030	0.2
Governmental administration	1,433,286	3.0
Interest on general debt	1,122,572	2.3
Other and unallocable	3,534,311	7.3
Utility expenditure	0	-
Liquor stores expenditure	535,201	1.1
Insurance trust expenditure	4,453,815	9.2
Debt at End of Fiscal Year	27,739,117	X
Cash and Security Holdings	85,490,610	X

X = Not applicable.
- = Zero or rounds to zero.
[1]Within insurance trust revenue, net earnings of state retirement systems is a calculated statistic (the item code in the data file is X08), and thus can be positive or negative. Net earnings is the sum of earnings on investments plus gains on investments minus losses on investments. The change made in 2002 for asset valuation from book to market value in accordance with Statement 34 of the Governmental Accounting Standards Board is reflected in the calculated statistics.

Table VA-16. State Government Tax Collections, 2014

(Dollars in thousands, percent.)

Item	Dollars	Percent distribution
Total Taxes	18,949,272	100.0
Property taxes	35,561	0.2
Sales and gross receipts	6,063,182	32.0
General sales and gross receipts	3,555,745	18.8
Selective sales and gross receipts	2,507,437	13.2
Alcoholic beverages	207,672	1.1
Amusements	70	-
Insurance premiums	459,993	2.4
Motor fuels	694,833	3.7
Pari-mutuels	0	-
Public utilities	107,394	0.6
Tobacco products	180,733	1.0
Other selective sales	856,742	4.5
Licenses	795,515	4.2
Alcoholic beverages	12,756	0.1
Amusements	101	-
Corporations in general	59,245	0.3
Hunting and fishing	27,983	0.1
Motor vehicle	451,215	2.4
Motor vehicle operators	40,370	0.2
Public utilities	0	-
Occupation and business, NEC	199,707	1.1
Other licenses	4,138	-
Income taxes	11,618,200	61.3
Individual income	10,877,689	57.4
Corporation net income	740,511	3.9
Other taxes	436,814	2.3
Death and gift	196	-
Documentary and stock transfer	310,205	1.6
Severance	2,165	-
Taxes, NEC	124,248	0.7

- = Zero or rounds to zero.

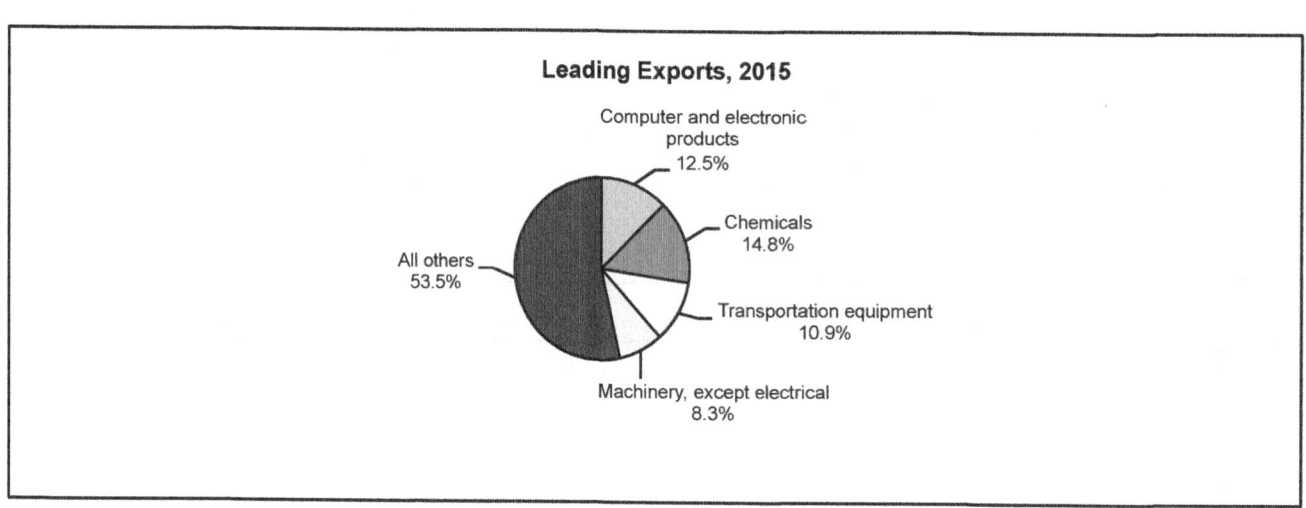

Leading Exports, 2015

Computer and electronic products 12.5%

Chemicals 14.8%

Transportation equipment 10.9%

Machinery, except electrical 8.3%

All others 53.5%

Facts and Figures

Location: Northwestern United States; bordered on the N by Canada (British Columbia), on the E by Idaho, on the S by Oregon, and on the W by the Pacific Ocean

Area: 71,300 sq. mi. (184,665 sq. km.); rank—18th

Population: 7,170,351 (2015 est.); rank—13th

Principal Cities: capital—Olympia; largest—Seattle

Statehood: November 11, 1889; 42nd state

U.S. Congress: 2 senators, 10 representatives

State Motto: *Alki* ("By and by")

State Song: "Washington, My Home"

State Nickname: The Evergreen State

Abbreviations: WA; Wash.

State Symbols: flower—coast rhododendron; tree—Western hemlock; bird—willow goldfinch

At a Glance

- With an increase in population of 6.3 percent, Washington ranked 9th among the states in growth from 2010 to 2015.

- Washington's median household income in 2014 was $61,366, and 13.2 percent of the population lived below the poverty level.

- In 2014, 9.2 percent of Washingtonians did not have health insurance, compared to 11.7 percent of the total U.S. population.

- Washington had the second highest property crime rate in the country (3,706.1 incidents per 100,000 population) in 2014.

- Approximately 33.1 percent of Washingtonians had a bachelor's degree or more in 2014, compared to 30.1 percent of all U.S. residents.

Table WA-1. Population by Age, Sex, Race, and Hispanic Origin

(Number, percent, except where noted.)

Sex, age, race, and Hispanic origin	2000	2010	2015[1]	Average annual percent change, 2010–2015
Total population	5,894,121	6,724,540	7,170,351	0.5
Percent of total U.S. population	2.1	2.2	2.2	X
Sex				
Male	2,934,300	3,349,707	3,584,998	0.5
Female	2,959,821	3,374,833	3,585,353	0.4
Age				
Under 5 years	394,306	439,657	447,922	0.1
5 to 19 years	1,288,713	1,330,238	1,335,385	-
20 to 64 years	3,548,954	4,126,968	4,350,998	0.4
65 years and over	662,148	827,677	1,036,046	1.6
Median age (years)	35.9	37.3	37.6	0.1
Race and Hispanic origin				
One race				
White	4,821,823	5,535,262	5,756,587	0.3
Black	190,267	252,333	294,992	1.1
American Indian and Alaska Native	93,301	122,649	135,957	0.7
Asian	322,335	491,685	603,214	1.5
Native Hawaiian or Other Pacific Islander	23,953	43,505	53,195	1.4
Two or more races	213,519	279,106	326,406	1.1
Hispanic (of any race)	441,509	776,539	886,418	0.9

X = Not applicable.
- = Zero or rounds to zero.
[1]Population figures for 2015 are July 1 estimates. The 2010 estimates are taken from the 2010 Census.

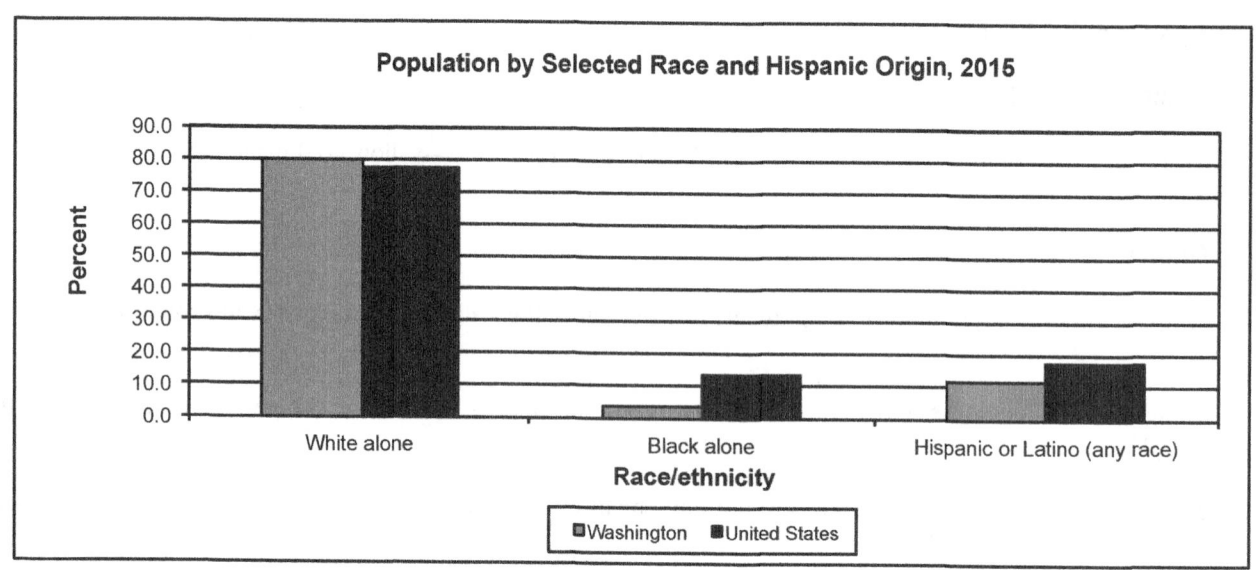

Population by Selected Race and Hispanic Origin, 2015

(Washington / United States)

Table WA-2. Marital Status

(Number, percent distribution.)

Sex, age, race, and Hispanic origin	2000	2010	2014
Males, 15 Years and Over	2,287,431	2,686,801	2,766,340
Never married	29.8	33.8	34.1
Now married, except separated	56.6	52.0	51.7
Separated	1.4	1.6	1.5
Widowed	2.1	2.1	2.2
Divorced	10.1	10.5	10.5
Females, 15 Years and Over	2,352,091	2,746,158	2,810,497
Never married	22.8	26.4	26.9
Now married, except separated	54.1	50.6	49.9
Separated	1.8	2.1	1.9
Widowed	8.6	7.8	7.7
Divorced	12.7	13.2	13.6

Table WA-3. Households and Housing Characteristics

(Number, percent, dollars.)

Item	2000	2010	2014	Average annual percent change, 2000–2014
Total Households...	2,271,398	2,606,863	2,679,601	1.3
Family households	1,499,127	1,681,386	1,725,099	1.1
Married-couple family	1,181,995	1,297,240	1,329,276	0.9
Other family	317,132	384,146	395,823	1.8
Male householder, no wife present..................	92,514	114,187	120,527	2.2
Female householder, no husband present..........	224,618	269,959	275,296	1.6
Nonfamily households	772,271	925,477	954,502	1.7
Householder living alone..................................	594,325	731,452	741,962	1.8
Householder not living alone............................	117,946	194,025	212,540	5.7
Housing Characteristics				
Total housing units..	2,451,075	2,888,594	2,963,293	1.5
Occupied housing units	2,271,398	2,606,863	2,679,601	1.3
Owner occupied	1,467,009	1,644,939	1,654,620	0.9
Renter occupied..	804,389	961,924	1,024,981	2.0
Average household size......................................	2.53	2.53	2.58	0.1
Financial Characteristics				
Median gross rent of renter-occupied housing	663	908	1,032	4.0
Median monthly owner costs for housing units with a mortgage	1,268	1,736	1,673	2.3
Median value of owner-occupied housing units........	168,300	271,800	266,200	4.2

Table WA-4. Migration, Origin, and Language

(Number, percent.)

Characteristic	State			U.S.		
	2013	2014	Percent change	2013	2014	Percent change
Residence 1 Year Ago						
Population 1 year and over	6,888,552	6,979,369	1.3	312,432,820	315,095,393	0.9
Same house	82.8	82.5	X	85.0	85.1	X
Different house in the U.S.	16.5	16.6	X	14.4	14.3	X
Same county	10.6	10.4	X	8.9	8.7	X
Different county	5.8	6.2	X	5.5	5.6	X
Same state	2.8	3.0	X	3.2	3.3	X
Different state	3.0	3.2	X	2.3	2.3	X
Abroad	0.8	1.0	X	0.6	0.6	X
Place of Birth						
Native born	6,027,742	6,116,784	1.5	274,780,773	276,465,262	0.6
Male	50.1	50.2	X	49.3	49.3	X
Female	49.9	49.8	X	50.7	50.7	X
Foreign born	943,664	944,746	0.1	41,348,066	42,391,794	2.5
Male	48.1	48.5	X	48.8	48.7	X
Female	51.9	51.5	X	51.2	51.3	X
Foreign born; naturalized U.S. citizen.................	436,834	437,379	0.1	19,294,710	19,984,738	3.6
Male	44.6	45.1	X	45.9	45.9	X
Female	55.4	54.9	X	54.1	54.1	X
Foreign born; not a U.S. citizen.........................	506,830	507,367	0.1	22,053,356	22,407,056	1.6
Male	51.2	51.4	X	51.3	51.2	X
Female	48.8	48.6	X	48.7	48.8	X
Entered 2010 or later	10.8	14.9	X	9.7	12.3	X
Entered 2000 to 2009	30.8	29.9	X	29.4	28.6	X
Entered before 2000...	58.4	55.2	X	61.0	59.1	X
World Region of Birth, Foreign						
Foreign-born population, excluding population born at sea	943,664	944,746	0.1	41,347,945	42,390,705	2.5
Europe	16.2	16.4	X	11.6	11.2	X
Asia	41.0	41.8	X	29.5	30.1	X
Africa	5.9	5.5	X	4.4	4.6	X
Oceania	1.6	1.6	X	0.5	0.6	X
Latin America..	30.5	29.9	X	51.9	51.6	X
North America...	4.9	4.8	X	2.0	1.9	X
Language Spoken at Home and Ability to Speak English						
Population 5 years and over................................	6,529,296	6,617,324	1.3	296,358,760	299,084,046	0.9
English only	81.1	81.2	X	79.2	78.9	X
Language other than English............................	18.9	18.8	X	20.8	21.1	X
Speaks English less than "very well".................	7.5	7.6	X	8.5	8.6	X

X = Not applicable.
- = Zero or rounds to zero.

Table WA-5. Median Income and Poverty Status, 2014

(Number, percent, except as noted.)

Characteristic	State		U.S.	
	Number	Percent	Number	Percent
Median Income				
Households (dollars)	61,366	X	53,657	X
Families (dollars)	74,193	X	65,910	X
Below Poverty Level (All People)	913,619	13.2	48,208,387	15.5
Sex				
Male	422,812	12.2	21,590,918	14.2
Female	490,807	14.1	26,617,469	16.8
Age				
Under 18 years	276,044	17.5	15,686,012	21.7
Related children under 18 years	265,946	17.0	15,372,705	21.3
18 to 64 years	555,648	12.7	28,267,482	14.6
65 years and over	81,927	8.4	4,254,893	9.5

X = Not applicable.

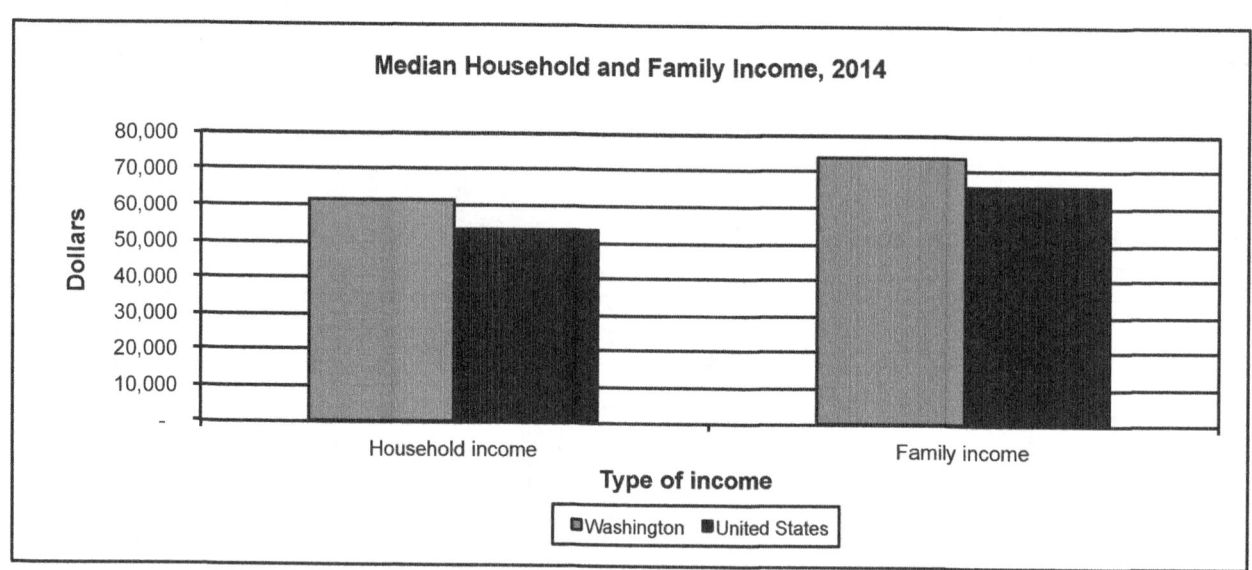

Table WA-6. Health Insurance Coverage Status for the Civilian Noninstitutionalized Population and Children Under 18 Years of Age

(Numbers in thousands, percent.)

Item	2006	2007	2008	2009	2010	2011	2012	2013	2014
Civilian Noninstitutionalized Population	6,318	6,509	6,428	6,546	6,638	6,717	6,793	6,864	6,955
Covered by Private or Public Insurance									
Number	5,572	5,773	5,586	5,669	5,692	5,764	5,848	5,904	6,312
Percent	88.2	88.7	86.9	86.6	85.8	85.8	86.1	86.0	90.8
Not Covered									
Number	746	737	842	878	946	952	945	960	643
Percent	11.8	11.3	13.1	13.4	14.2	14.2	13.9	14.0	9.2
Percent in the U.S. not covered	15.8	15.3	15.1	15.1	15.5	15.1	14.8	14.5	11.7
Children Under 18 Years of Age	1,518	1,558	1,541	1,570	1,583	1,578	1,584	1,595	1,601
Covered by Private or Public Insurance									
Number	1,413	1,452	1,411	1,462	1,481	1,481	1,493	1,500	1,526
Percent	93.1	93.2	91.6	93.1	93.6	93.8	94.2	94.1	95.3
Not Covered									
Number	105	106	130	108	102	97	91	95	75
Percent	6.9	6.8	8.4	6.9	6.4	6.2	5.8	5.9	4.7
Percent in the U.S. not covered	11.7	11.0	9.7	8.6	8.0	7.5	7.2	7.1	6.0

Table WA-7. Employment Status by Demographic Group, 2015

(Numbers in thousands, percent.)

Characteristic	Civilian noninstitutional population	Civilian labor force		Employed		Unemployed	
		Number	Percent of population	Number	Percent of population	Number	Percent of population
Total................................	5,595	3,537	63.2	3,338	59.7	199	5.6
Sex							
Male................................	2,751	1,906	69.3	1,796	65.3	110	5.8
Female............................	2,844	1,632	57.4	1,543	54.2	89	5.5
Race, Sex, and Hispanic Origin							
White..............................	4,543	2,857	62.9	2,705	59.5	152	5.3
Male............................	2,259	1,549	68.6	1,465	64.8	84	5.4
Female........................	2,285	1,308	57.3	1,240	54.3	68	5.2
Black or African American..........	211	138	65.5	126	59.8	12	8.9
Male............................	115	82	70.9	75	65.2	7	8.1
Female........................	96	56	59.0	51	53.2	6	9.9
Hispanic or Latino ethnicity[1].......	650	440	67.8	414	63.7	27	6.1
Male............................	339	264	77.8	251	73.9	13	5.0
Female........................	311	177	56.8	163	52.5	14	7.7
Age							
16 to 19 years....................	378	120	31.8	99	26.2	21	17.6
20 to 24 years....................	430	337	78.3	304	70.8	33	9.6
25 to 34 years....................	1,006	812	80.7	772	76.7	40	4.9
35 to 44 years....................	913	752	82.4	716	78.5	36	4.8
45 to 54 years....................	889	715	80.4	680	76.5	35	4.9
55 to 64 years....................	971	616	63.4	590	60.7	26	4.2
65 years and over.................	1,008	186	18.4	177	17.6	9	4.7

NOTE: Data in Table 7 are from the Current Population Survey (CPS) and do not match the estimates in Table 8. See notes and definitions for further information.
[1]May be of any race.

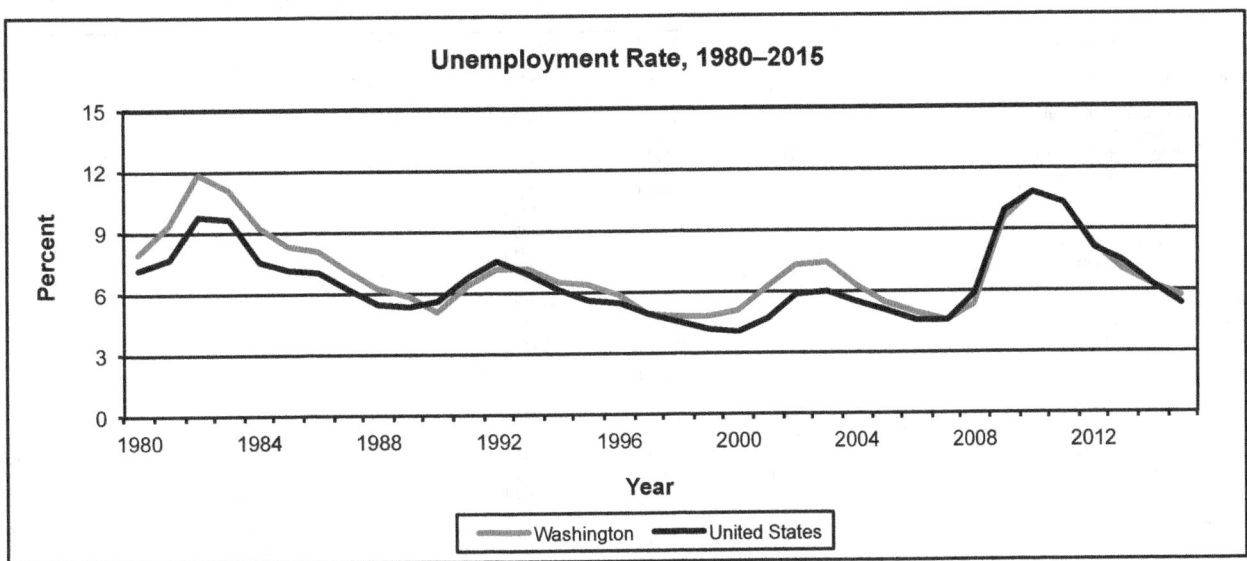

Unemployment Rate, 1980–2015

Washington — United States

Table WA-8. Employment Status of the Civilian Noninstitutional Population Age 16 Years and Over

(Number, percent.)

Year	Civilian labor force	Civilian participation rate	Employed	Unemployed	Unemployment rate
2007................................	3,403,163	68.0	3,243,308	159,855	4.7
2008................................	3,478,577	68.4	3,291,309	187,268	5.4
2009................................	3,535,200	68.3	3,211,649	323,551	9.2
2010................................	3,511,326	66.9	3,160,544	350,782	10.0
2011................................	3,461,428	65.2	3,140,190	321,238	9.3
2012................................	3,472,727	64.5	3,190,421	282,306	8.1
2013................................	3,464,760	63.6	3,220,860	243,900	7.0
2014................................	3,492,866	63.2	3,278,975	213,891	6.1
2015................................	3,544,242	63.0	3,343,992	200,250	5.7

Table WA-9. Employment and Average Wages by Industry

(Estimates through 2010 are based on the 2007 North American Industry Classification System [NAICS]. Estimates from 2011 onward are based on the 2012 NAICS.)

Industry	2008	2009	2010	2011	2012	2013	2014
	Number of jobs						
Wage and Salary Employment by Industry.................	3,190,328	3,055,064	3,017,067	3,050,198	3,089,719	3,202,280	3,283,186
Farm Wage and Salary Employment.........................	47,160	49,636	48,890	46,644	52,776	50,768	53,445
Nonfarm Wage and Salary Employment....................	3,143,168	3,005,428	2,968,177	3,003,554	3,036,943	3,151,512	3,229,741
Private wage and salary employment.......................	2,516,679	2,374,663	2,336,116	2,378,200	2,412,491	2,529,015	2,610,911
Forestry, fishing, and related activities.....................	26,002	27,210	26,656	28,470	27,696	30,856	31,643
Mining.......................................	2,955	2,367	2,202	2,205	2,158	2,165	2,246
Utilities.....................................	4,703	4,767	4,863	4,870	4,913	4,822	4,834
Construction	208,581	166,336	146,762	143,279	143,496	154,574	165,331
Manufacturing..........................	291,067	265,520	257,913	268,681	280,554	286,630	288,656
Durable goods manufacturing............	211,250	190,284	183,718	193,063	204,418	209,283	209,450
Nondurable goods manufacturing.......	79,817	75,236	74,195	75,618	76,136	77,347	79,206
Wholesale trade	130,798	123,355	121,554	123,051	124,363	127,697	130,949
Retail trade.............................	330,081	314,067	313,189	317,476	322,363	332,829	345,811
Transportation and warehousing.........	92,072	87,026	85,243	87,156	89,301	90,079	94,116
Information...............................	105,724	103,817	102,884	104,202	105,535	106,635	109,611
Finance and insurance	104,081	97,037	93,785	93,779	94,517	96,406	98,088
Real estate and rental and leasing........	52,951	49,519	47,356	46,216	45,918	47,623	48,695
Professional, scientific, and technical services	169,754	163,556	164,645	170,210	173,116	177,285	184,354
Management of companies and enterprises....	34,783	32,178	31,796	33,282	36,318	38,869	39,988
Administrative and waste services..........	149,209	132,706	134,751	140,112	143,031	147,868	152,239
Educational services	49,357	49,032	49,908	51,700	52,981	53,463	55,129
Health care and social assistance..........	321,880	331,044	333,660	337,636	340,181	392,861	402,951
Arts, entertainment, and recreation............	48,459	46,577	45,883	46,782	46,452	47,233	48,111
Accommodation and food services............	238,717	225,921	224,183	227,794	232,890	242,575	252,450
Other services, except public administration....	155,505	152,628	148,883	151,299	146,708	148,545	155,709
Government and government enterprises............	626,489	630,765	632,061	625,354	624,452	622,497	618,830
	Dollars						
Average Wages and Salaries by Industry	47,231	48,087	49,282	51,036	52,945	53,334	55,427
Average Farm Wages and Salaries	29,672	27,635	25,520	26,156	24,435	33,317	30,377
Average Nonfarm Wages and Salaries	47,495	48,425	49,673	51,423	53,441	53,656	55,842
Average private wages and salaries.......................	47,552	48,240	49,598	51,602	54,007	54,061	56,253
Forestry, fishing, and related activities.....................	34,826	32,324	33,267	34,648	36,513	35,096	35,274
Mining.......................................	55,819	53,328	56,188	59,809	60,970	63,051	64,086
Utilities.....................................	76,188	83,464	77,235	81,878	83,778	85,809	87,820
Construction	50,782	52,150	51,817	52,859	53,654	54,405	55,900
Manufacturing..........................	61,573	63,039	65,280	68,479	69,786	71,721	75,456
Durable goods manufacturing............	66,644	69,068	72,104	75,748	76,892	79,318	84,335
Nondurable goods manufacturing.......	48,153	47,792	48,381	49,920	50,710	51,167	51,977
Wholesale trade	62,211	62,367	64,253	66,665	69,501	69,087	71,092
Retail trade.............................	30,791	31,024	31,586	32,647	34,587	36,238	38,898
Transportation and warehousing.........	47,439	48,340	49,589	51,898	53,205	54,582	55,061
Information...............................	104,789	106,908	111,436	121,621	135,532	136,788	150,449
Finance and insurance	72,858	71,286	70,283	73,173	77,420	79,407	81,960
Real estate and rental and leasing............	37,586	37,330	38,878	40,332	42,788	44,139	46,216
Professional, scientific, and technical services	71,567	73,019	76,181	77,882	80,678	82,429	85,851
Management of companies and enterprises.........	88,966	89,733	100,110	103,999	107,245	106,911	109,015
Administrative and waste services...........	38,106	39,972	41,923	43,211	43,617	43,529	44,705
Educational services	26,698	27,684	28,562	29,142	29,172	29,883	30,487
Health care and social assistance..........	42,812	44,377	45,386	46,582	47,828	43,919	44,887
Arts, entertainment, and recreation..............	29,727	28,123	27,871	27,657	27,881	30,412	32,574
Accommodation and food services............	18,723	19,121	20,277	21,311	22,617	22,246	22,833
Other services, except public administration....	28,756	28,931	29,844	30,305	33,063	34,255	34,348
Government and government enterprises............	47,268	49,121	49,953	50,741	51,253	52,011	54,109

Table WA-10. Employment Characteristics by Family Type

(Number, percent.)

Family type and labor force status	2012		2013		2014	
	Total	Families with own children under 18 years	Total	Families with own children under 18 years	Total	Families with own children under 18 years
All Families..	1,687,786	752,039	1,705,112	755,115	1,712,570	739,472
FAMILY TYPE AND LABOR FORCE STATUS						
Married-Couple Families.........................	1,301,823	530,116	1,309,075	526,959	1,316,747	521,639
Both husband and wife in labor force................	51.9	62.4	50.8	62.5	50.7	61.5
Husband in labor force, wife not in labor force.........	23.7	32.2	23.5	31.8	23.8	32.7
Wife in labor force, husband not in labor force.........	7.5	3.8	7.7	3.8	7.9	4.2
Both husband and wife not in labor force............	16.9	1.6	17.4	1.5	17.6	1.7
Other Families	385,963	221,923	396,037	228,156	395,823	217,833
Female householder, no husband present.............	70.0	71.5	68.9	70.4	69.6	70.4
In labor force..................................	50.8	57.8	49.2	55.7	50.2	56.9
Not in labor force	19.2	13.7	19.7	14.7	19.4	13.5
Male householder, no wife present..................	30.0	28.5	31.1	29.6	30.4	29.6
In labor force..................................	24.6	25.9	25.0	26.2	24.2	27.0
Not in labor force	5.4	2.6	6.1	3.4	6.2	2.6

Table WA-11. School Enrollment and Educational Attainment, 2014

(Number, percent.)

Item	State	U.S.
Enrollment		
Total population 3 years and over, enrolled in school...........	1,725,154	82,063,714
Enrolled in nursery school or preschool (percent)..............	5.8	6.0
Enrolled in kindergarten (percent)...........................	5.5	5.1
Enrolled in elementary school, grades 1-8 (percent)..........	41.0	40.2
Enrolled in high school, grades 9-12 (percent)...............	20.6	20.7
Enrolled in college or graduate school (percent).............	27.1	28.0
Attainment		
Total population 25 years and over	4,784,484	213,725,624
Less than ninth grade (percent).............................	4.0	5.6
9th to 12th grade, no diploma (percent).....................	5.5	7.5
High school graduate, including equivalency (percent)........	22.8	27.7
Some college, no degree (percent)	24.5	21.0
Associate's degree (percent)	10.0	8.2
Bachelor's degree (percent)	21.0	18.7
Graduate or professional degree (percent)...................	12.1	11.4
High school graduate or higher (percent)	90.4	86.9
Bachelor's degree or higher (percent).......................	33.1	30.1

Table WA-12. Public School Characteristics and Educational Indicators

(Number, percent; data derived from National Center of Education Statistics.)

Item	State	U.S.
Public Schools, 2013–2014 (except where noted)		
Number of school districts..................................	318	18,194
Number of schools..	2,381	98,271
Number of students (in thousands)	1,059	50,045
Number of teachers (in thousands)	55	3,114
Student-teacher ratio	19.3	16.1
Expenditures per student (dollars), FY 2013.................	9,714	107,637
Four-year adjusted cohort graduation rate (ACGR)[1,2]	78.2	82.3
Students eligible for free or reduced-price lunch (in thousands) ...	490	25,596
English language learners (in thousands)	100	4,461
Students age 3 to 21 served under IDEA, part B (in thousands)	132	6,464

Public Schools by Type	Number	Percent of state public schools
Total number of schools.....................................	2,381	100.0
Regular	1,940	81.5
Special education	96	4.0
Vocational education	20	0.8
Alternative education.......................................	325	13.6

NOTE: Every school is assigned only one school type based on its instructional emphasis.
[1]ACGR data represents a new method of calculating high-school completion rates and may not be comparable to previous years' data for Averaged Freshmen Graduation Rates (AFGR).
[2]The United States 4-year ACGRs were estimated using both the reported 4-year ACGR data from 49 states and the District of Columbia and using imputed data for Idaho. The estimate for American Indian/Alaska Native students also includes imputed data for Virginia.

Table WA-13. Reported Voting and Registration of the Voting-Age Population, November 2014

(Numbers in thousands, percent.)

Item	Total population	Total citizen population	Registered			Voted		
			Total registered	Percent registered (total population)	Percent registered (total citizen population)	Total voted	Percent voted (total population)	Percent voted (total citizen population)
U.S. Total	239,874	219,941	142,166	59.3	64.6	92,251	38.5	41.9
State Total............................	5,333	4,776	3,281	61.5	68.7	2,390	44.8	50.0
Sex								
Male...	2,616	2,331	1,543	59.0	66.2	1,125	43.0	48.3
Female.....................................	2,717	2,445	1,739	64.0	71.1	1,265	46.5	51.7
Race								
White alone............................	4,238	3,939	2,819	66.5	71.6	2,088	49.3	53.0
White, non-Hispanic alone..........	3,716	3,644	2,683	72.2	73.6	2,022	54.4	55.5
Black alone..............................	195	159	74	37.9	46.6	53	27.4	33.7
Asian alone	451	268	161	35.6	59.9	110	24.4	41.2
Hispanic (of any race)......................	635	378	169	26.7	44.8	95	15.0	25.1
White alone or in combination	4,407	4,099	2,927	66.4	71.4	2,143	48.6	52.3
Black alone or in combination..........	236	196	88	37.5	45.2	60	25.3	30.5
Asian alone or in combination..........	483	300	180	37.2	59.9	127	26.3	42.4
Age								
18 to 24 years.............................	592	522	237	40.0	45.4	127	21.4	24.3
25 to 34 years.............................	1,008	840	458	45.4	54.5	247	24.5	29.4
35 to 44 years.............................	908	773	565	62.3	73.2	345	38.0	44.6
45 to 64 years.............................	1,796	1,655	1,242	69.1	75.0	981	54.6	59.3
65 years and over	1,029	986	779	75.7	79.0	690	67.1	70.0

Table WA-14. Crime

(Number, rate per 100,000. Data are derived from the FBI Uniform Crime Reports.)

Item	State			U.S.[1,2,3,4]		
	2013	2014	Percent change	2013	2014	Percent change
TOTAL POPULATION[5].........................	6,971,406	7,061,530	1.3	316,128,839	318,857,056	0.9
VIOLENT CRIME						
Number..	19,377	20,136	3.9	1,163,146	1,165,383	0.2
Rate	277.9	285.2	2.6	367.9	365.5	-0.7
Murder and Nonnegligent Manslaughter						
Number..	160	174	8.8	14,196	14,249	0.4
Rate	2.3	2.5	8.7	4.5	4.5	-
Rape[6]						
Number..	2,573	2,695	X	108,612	116,645	X
Rate	36.9	38.2	X	34.4	36.6	X
Robbery						
Number..	5,819	5,640	-3.1	345,031	325,802	-5.6
Rate	83.5	79.9	-4.3	109.1	102.2	-6.3
Aggravated Assault						
Number..	11,601	11,627	0.2	724,149	741,291	2.4
Rate	166.4	164.7	-1.0	229.1	232.5	1.5
PROPERTY CRIME						
Number..	258,662	261,706	1.2	8,632,512	8,277,829	-4.1
Rate	3,710.3	3,706.1	-0.1	2,730.7	2,596.1	-4.9
Burglary						
Number..	58,353	55,290	-5.2	1,928,465	1,729,806	-10.3
Rate	837.0	783.0	-6.5	610.0	542.5	-11.1
Larceny-Theft						
Number..	171,910	175,769	2.2	6,004,453	5,858,496	-2.4
Rate	2,465.9	2,489.1	0.9	1,899.4	1,837.3	-3.3
Motor Vehicle Theft						
Number..	28,399	30,647	7.9	699,594	689,527	-1.4
Rate	407.4	434.0	6.5	221.3	216.2	-2.3

NOTE: Although arson data are included in the trend and clearance tables, sufficient data are not available to estimate totals for this offense. Therefore, no arson data are published in this table.
X = Not applicable.
- = Zero or rounds to zero.
[1]The crime figures have been adjusted.
[2]The data collection methodology for the offense of forcible rape used by the Minnesota state Uniform Crime Reporting (UCR) Program (with the exception of Minneapolis and St. Paul, Minnesota) does not comply with national UCR Program guidelines. Consequently, its figures for forcible rape and violent crime (of which forcible rape is a part) are not published in this table.
[3]Includes offenses reported by the Zoological Police and the Metro Transit Police.
[4]Because of changes in the state's reporting practices, figures are not comparable to previous years' data.
[5]Populations are U.S. Census Bureau provisional estimates as of July 1 of each year.
[6]The figures shown for the offense of rape were estimated using the revised Uniform Crime Reporting (UCR) definition of rape.

Table WA-15. State Government Finances, 2014

(Dollar amounts in thousands, percent distribution.)

Item	Dollars	Percent distribution
Total Revenue	55,071,735	100.0
General revenue	38,295,614	69.5
Intergovernmental revenue	11,474,963	20.8
Taxes	19,447,899	35.3
General sales	11,767,488	21.4
Selective sales	3,442,776	6.3
License taxes	1,414,960	2.6
Individual income tax	0	-
Corporate income tax	0	-
Other taxes	2,822,675	5.1
Current charges	4,925,015	8.9
Miscellaneous general revenue	2,447,737	4.4
Utility revenue	0	-
Liquor stores revenue	0	-
Insurance trust revenue[1]	16,776,121	30.5
Total Expenditure	47,971,432	100.0
Intergovernmental expenditure	10,439,034	21.8
Direct expenditure	37,532,398	78.2
Current operation	24,772,727	51.6
Capital outlay	2,881,528	6.0
Insurance benefits and repayments	6,898,620	14.4
Assistance and subsidies	1,615,893	3.4
Interest on debt	1,363,630	2.8
Exhibit: Salaries and wages	10,661,561	22.2
Total Expenditure	47,971,432	100.0
General expenditure	40,464,592	84.4
Intergovernmental expenditure	10,439,034	21.8
Direct expenditure	30,025,558	62.6
General expenditure, by function:		
Education	16,189,021	33.7
Public welfare	9,771,308	20.4
Hospitals	2,229,129	4.6
Health	2,489,729	5.2
Highways	3,022,871	6.3
Police protection	337,484	0.7
Correction	959,264	2.0
Natural resources	954,773	2.0
Parks and recreation	112,504	0.2
Governmental administration	996,524	2.1
Interest on general debt	1,363,630	2.8
Other and unallocable	2,038,355	4.2
Utility expenditure	145,220	0.3
Liquor stores expenditure	463,000	1.0
Insurance trust expenditure	6,898,620	14.4
Debt at End of Fiscal Year	31,601,016	X
Cash and Security Holdings	100,562,452	X

X = Not applicable.
- = Zero or rounds to zero.
[1]Within insurance trust revenue, net earnings of state retirement systems is a calculated statistic (the item code in the data file is X08), and thus can be positive or negative. Net earnings is the sum of earnings on investments plus gains on investments minus losses on investments. The change made in 2002 for asset valuation from book to market value in accordance with Statement 34 of the Governmental Accounting Standards Board is reflected in the calculated statistics.

Table WA-16. State Government Tax Collections, 2014

(Dollars in thousands, percent.)

Item	Dollars	Percent distribution
Total Taxes	19,447,899	100.0
Property taxes	1,974,354	10.2
Sales and gross receipts	15,210,264	78.2
General sales and gross receipts	11,767,488	60.5
Selective sales and gross receipts	3,442,776	17.7
Alcoholic beverages	321,412	1.7
Amusements	0	-
Insurance premiums	467,351	2.4
Motor fuels	1,156,242	5.9
Pari-mutuels	1,510	-
Public utilities	497,993	2.6
Tobacco products	443,185	2.3
Other selective sales	555,083	2.9
Licenses	1,414,960	7.3
Alcoholic beverages	153,263	0.8
Amusements	5,699	-
Corporations in general	32,335	0.2
Hunting and fishing	44,906	0.2
Motor vehicle	535,636	2.8
Motor vehicle operators	102,924	0.5
Public utilities	18,689	0.1
Occupation and business, NEC	294,448	1.5
Other licenses	227,060	1.2
Income taxes	0	-
Individual income	X	X
Corporation net income	X	X
Other taxes	848,321	4.4
Death and gift	157,286	0.8
Documentary and stock transfer	649,085	3.3
Severance	41,950	0.2
Taxes, NEC	0	-

X = Not applicable.
- = Zero or rounds to zero.

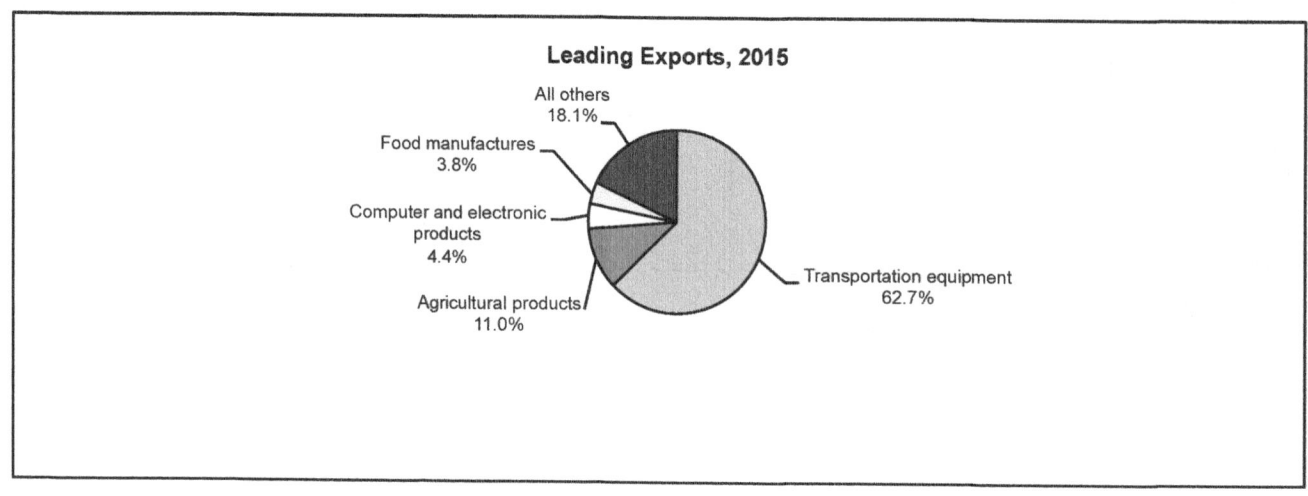

Leading Exports, 2015

All others 18.1%
Food manufactures 3.8%
Computer and electronic products 4.4%
Agricultural products 11.0%
Transportation equipment 62.7%

WEST VIRGINIA

Facts and Figures

Location: East central United States; bordered on the N by Ohio and Pennsylvania, on the E by Pennsylvania, Maryland, and Virginia, on the S by Virginia and Kentucky, and on the W by Kentucky and Ohio

Area: 24,230 sq. mi. (62,755 sq. km.); rank—41st

Population: 1,844,128 (2015 est.); rank—38th

Principal Cities: capital—Charleston; largest—Charleston

Statehood: June 20, 1863; 35th state

U.S. Congress: 2 senators, 3 representatives

State Motto: *Montani semper liberi* ("Mountaineers are always free")

State Songs: "West Virginia Hills"; "This Is My West Virginia"; "West Virginia, My Home Sweet Home"

State Nickname: The Mountain State

Abbreviations: WV; W. Va.

State Symbols: flower—rhododendron (great laurel); tree—sugar maple; bird—cardinal

At a Glance

- West Virginia was the only state to experience a population decline from 2010 to 2015, with its population falling 0.5 percent.

- West Virginia's median household income was $41,059 in 2014, the second lowest among the states, and 18.3 percent of the population lived below the poverty level.

- In 2014, 8.6 percent of West Virginians did not have health insurance, compared to 11.7 percent of the total U.S. population.

- West Virginia had the lowest percent of residents that self-identified as "Hispanic or Latino" in 2015, with 1.5 percent of its population in this category.

- West Virginia ranked in the top 10 states with the highest ratio of state government employees to residents in 2014, with 21.8 employees per 1,000 residents.

Table WV-1. Population by Age, Sex, Race, and Hispanic Origin

(Number, percent, except where noted.)

Sex, age, race, and Hispanic origin	2000	2010	2015[1]	Average annual percent change, 2010–2015
Total Population.....................................	1,808,344	1,852,994	1,844,128	
Percent of total U.S. population	0.6	0.6	0.6	X
Sex				
Male...	879,170	913,586	911,060	-
Female	929,174	939,408	933,068	-
Age				
Under 5 years..	101,805	104,060	103,410	-
5 to 19 years...	352,910	335,153	320,681	-0.3
20 to 64 years...	1,076,734	1,116,377	1,083,749	-0.2
65 years and over..	276,895	297,404	336,288	0.9
Median age (years)......................................	38.9	41.3	42.1	0.1
Race and Hispanic Origin				
One race				
White..	1,718,777	1,746,513	1,726,320	-0.1
Black...	57,232	63,885	67,175	0.4
American Indian and Alaska Native	3,606	3,975	4,459	0.8
Asian..	9,434	12,637	15,538	1.5
Native Hawaiian or Other Pacific Islander	400	485	546	0.8
Two or more races.......................................	15,788	25,499	30,090	1.2
Hispanic (of any race)..................................	12,279	23,679	27,809	1.2

X = Not applicable.
- = Zero or rounds to zero.
[1]Population figures for 2015 are July 1 estimates. The 2010 estimates are taken from the 2010 Census.

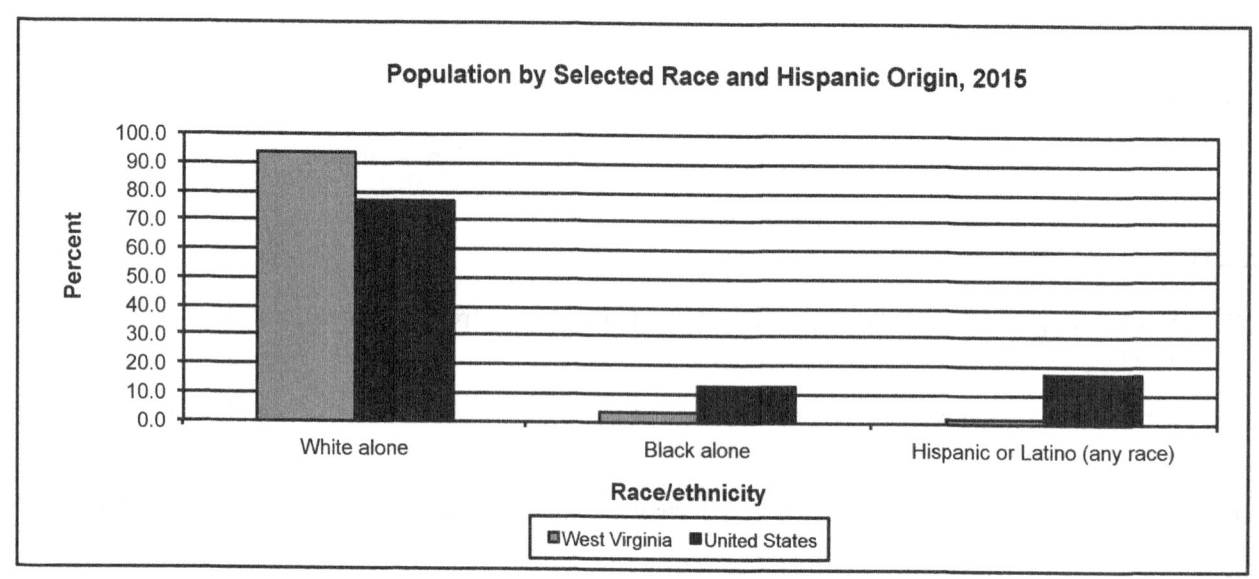

Population by Selected Race and Hispanic Origin, 2015

Table WV-2. Marital Status

(Number, percent distribution.)

Sex, age, race, and Hispanic origin	2000	2010	2014
Males, 15 Years and Over	710,443	750,542	752,192
Never married	25.4	30.3	30.9
Now married, except separated....................................	59.9	52.1	51.9
Separated...	1.3	1.6	1.5
Widowed..	3.2	3.4	3.4
Divorced..	10.1	12.6	12.3
Females, 15 Years and Over	768,858	785,182	784,441
Never married	19.1	22.6	23.3
Now married, except separated....................................	54.7	49.7	49.0
Separated...	1.6	1.7	1.8
Widowed..	13.9	12.8	12.2
Divorced..	10.8	13.2	13.6

Table WV-3. Households and Housing Characteristics

(Number, percent, dollars.)

Item	2000	2010	2014	Average annual percent change, 2000–2014
Total Households..	736,481	741,940	735,375	-
Family households	504,055	485,652	472,869	-0.4
Married-couple family	397,499	372,301	355,690	-0.8
Other family	106,556	113,351	117,179	0.7
Male householder, no wife present........................	27,436	28,515	33,280	1.5
Female householder, no husband present...........	79,120	84,836	83,899	0.4
Nonfamily households	232,426	256,288	262,506	0.9
Householder living alone..................................	199,587	219,848	218,036	0.7
Householder not living alone............................	32,839	36,440	44,470	2.5
Housing Characteristics				
Total housing units...	844,623	882,213	884,574	0.3
Occupied housing units	736,481	741,940	735,375	-
Owner occupied	553,699	553,429	530,755	-0.3
Renter occupied	182,782	188,511	204,620	0.9
Average household size.......................................	2.40	2.43	2.45	0.1
Financial Characteristics				
Median gross rent of renter-occupied housing	401	571	656	4.5
Median monthly owner costs for housing units with a mortgage	713	918	945	2.3
Median value of owner-occupied housing units	72,800	95,100	103,900	3.1

- = Zero or rounds to zero

Table WV-4. Migration, Origin, and Language

(Number, percent.)

Characteristic	State			U.S.		
	2013	2014	Percent change	2013	2014	Percent change
Residence 1 Year Ago						
Population 1 year and over	1,837,863	1,831,414	-0.4	312,432,820	315,095,393	0.9
Same house	88.2	88.3	X	85.0	85.1	X
Different house in the U.S.	11.6	11.5	X	14.4	14.3	X
Same county	6.4	6.4	X	8.9	8.7	X
Different county	5.3	5.1	X	5.5	5.6	X
Same state	2.4	2.5	X	3.2	3.3	X
Different state	2.8	2.6	X	2.3	2.3	X
Abroad	0.2	0.2	X	0.6	0.6	X
Place of Birth						
Native born	1,827,983	1,824,919	-0.2	274,780,773	276,465,262	0.6
Male	49.5	49.4	X	49.3	49.3	X
Female	50.5	50.6	X	50.7	50.7	X
Foreign born	26,321	25,407	-3.5	41,348,066	42,391,794	2.5
Male	47.7	48.9	X	48.8	48.7	X
Female	52.3	51.1	X	51.2	51.3	X
Foreign born; naturalized U.S. citizen...................	13,343	12,651	-5.2	19,294,710	19,984,738	3.6
Male	43.2	37.4	X	45.9	45.9	X
Female	56.8	62.6	X	54.1	54.1	X
Foreign born; not a U.S. citizen..........................	12,978	12,756	-1.7	22,053,356	22,407,056	1.6
Male	52.4	60.3	X	51.3	51.2	X
Female	47.6	39.7	X	48.7	48.8	X
Entered 2010 or later	15.9	23.9	X	9.7	12.3	X
Entered 2000 to 2009	30.4	23.1	X	29.4	28.6	X
Entered before 2000..	53.7	53.0	X	61.0	59.1	X
World Region of Birth, Foreign						
Foreign-born population, excluding population born at sea	26,321	25,407	-3.5	41,347,945	42,390,705	2.5
Europe	17.9	18.1	X	11.6	11.2	X
Asia..	37.7	47.4	X	29.5	30.1	X
Africa	5.1	8.5	X	4.4	4.6	X
Oceania	1.8	0.7	X	0.5	0.6	X
Latin America..	32.5	21.6	X	51.9	51.6	X
North America...	5.0	3.7	X	2.0	1.9	X
Language Spoken at Home and Ability to Speak English						
Population 5 years and over.................................	1,751,468	1,747,774	-0.2	296,358,760	299,084,046	0.9
English only	97.7	98.0	X	79.2	78.9	X
Language other than English..............................	2.3	2.0	X	20.8	21.1	X
Speaks English less than "very well"...................	0.8	0.6	X	8.5	8.6	X

X = Not applicable.
- = Zero or rounds to zero.

Table WV-5. Median Income and Poverty Status, 2014

(Number, percent, except as noted.)

Characteristic	State		U.S.	
	Number	Percent	Number	Percent
Median Income				
Households (dollars)...	41,059	X	53,657	X
Families (dollars)	52,413	X	65,910	X
Below Poverty Level (All People)	327,764	18.3	48,208,387	15.5
Sex				
Male..	148,294	16.8	21,590,918	14.2
Female	179,470	19.7	26,617,469	16.8
Age				
Under 18 years...	91,533	24.7	15,686,012	21.7
Related children under 18 years...............................	89,528	24.3	15,372,705	21.3
18 to 64 years..	206,422	18.7	28,267,482	14.6
65 years and over...	29,809	9.3	4,254,893	9.5

X = Not applicable.

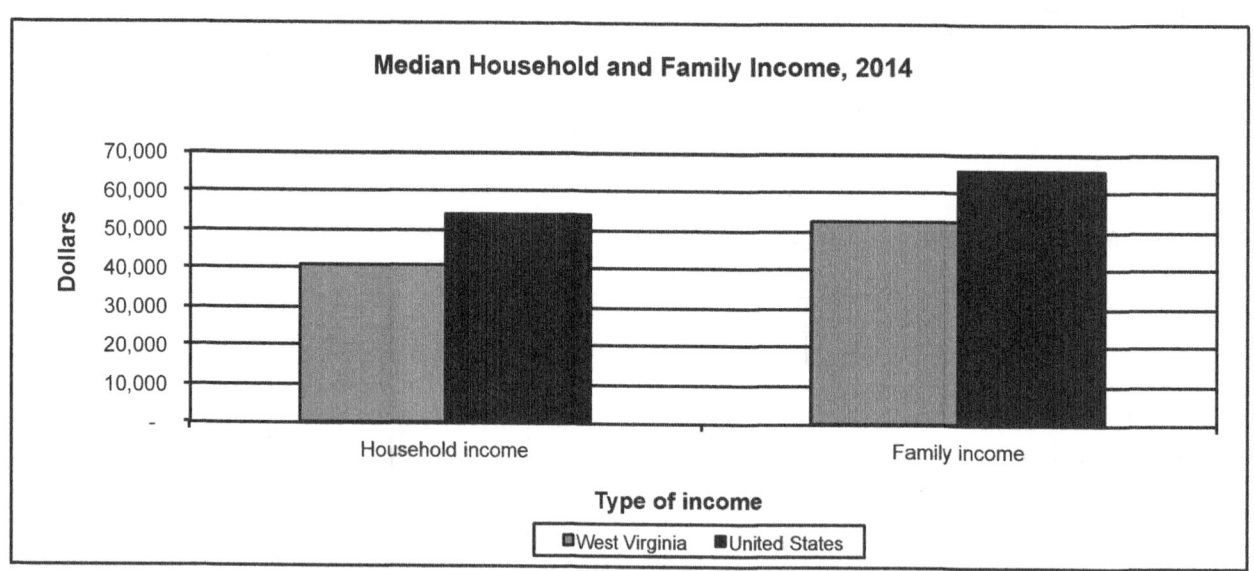

Table WV-6. Health Insurance Coverage Status for the Civilian Noninstitutionalized Population and Children Under 18 Years of Age

(Numbers in thousands, percent.)

Item	2006	2007	2008	2009	2010	2011	2012	2013	2014
Civilian Noninstitutionalized Population	1,814	1,795	1,788	1,793	1,823	1,826	1,827	1,825	1,821
Covered by Private or Public Insurance									
Number...	1,570	1,541	1,505	1,539	1,557	1,554	1,563	1,570	1,665
Percent..	86.5	85.9	84.2	85.8	85.4	85.1	85.6	86.0	91.4
Not Covered									
Number...	245	254	283	254	266	272	264	255	156
Percent..	13.5	14.1	15.8	14.2	14.6	14.9	14.4	14.0	8.6
Percent in the U.S. not covered..............	15.8	15.3	15.1	15.1	15.5	15.1	14.8	14.5	11.7
Children Under 18 Years of Age	395	394	385	383	385	385	383	381	382
Covered by Private or Public Insurance									
Number...	361	376	359	362	367	368	368	361	371
Percent..	91.5	95.4	93.2	94.5	95.5	95.6	96.1	94.7	97.0
Not Covered									
Number...	34	18	26	21	18	17	15	20	11
Percent..	8.5	4.6	6.8	5.5	4.5	4.4	3.9	5.3	3.0
Percent in the U.S. not covered..............	11.7	11.0	9.7	8.6	8.0	7.5	7.2	7.1	6.0

Table WV-7. Employment Status by Demographic Group, 2015

(Numbers in thousands, percent.)

Characteristic	Civilian noninstitutional population	Civilian labor force		Employed		Unemployed	
		Number	Percent of population	Number	Percent of population	Number	Percent of population
Total..	1,486	787	53.0	733	49.3	55	6.9
Sex							
Male...	722	421	58.3	389	53.9	32	7.6
Female	764	367	48.0	344	45.0	23	6.2
Race, Sex, and Hispanic Origin							
White..	1,399	738	52.8	688	49.2	50	6.8
Male.....................................	680	395	58.1	365	53.6	30	7.6
Female..................................	719	343	47.8	323	44.9	20	5.9
Black or African American...................	49	28	57.9	25	51.7	3	10.6
Male.....................................	25	15	58.9	14	54.2	1	8.1
Female..................................	24	14	56.8	12	49.2	2.0	13.3
Hispanic or Latino ethnicity[1]	18	11	65	11	64	...	2
Male.....................................	NA	NA	NA	NA	NA	NA	NA
Female..................................	NA	NA	NA	NA	NA	NA	NA
Age							
16 to 19 years	81	22	27.6	17	20.4	6	26.0
20 to 24 years	126	90	71.7	77	60.8	14	15.3
25 to 34 years	217	161	74.0	149	68.4	12	7.5
35 to 44 years	216	164	75.8	154	71.3	10	5.9
45 to 54 years	233	162	69.4	155	66.4	7	4.3
55 to 64 years	273	139	50.9	135	49.3	4	3.1
65 years and over	339	49	14.4	47	13.9	2	3.7

NOTE: Data in Table 7 are from the Current Population Survey (CPS) and do not match the estimates in Table 8. See notes and definitions for further information.
[1]May be of any race.
NA = Not available.
... = Fewer than 500 persons.

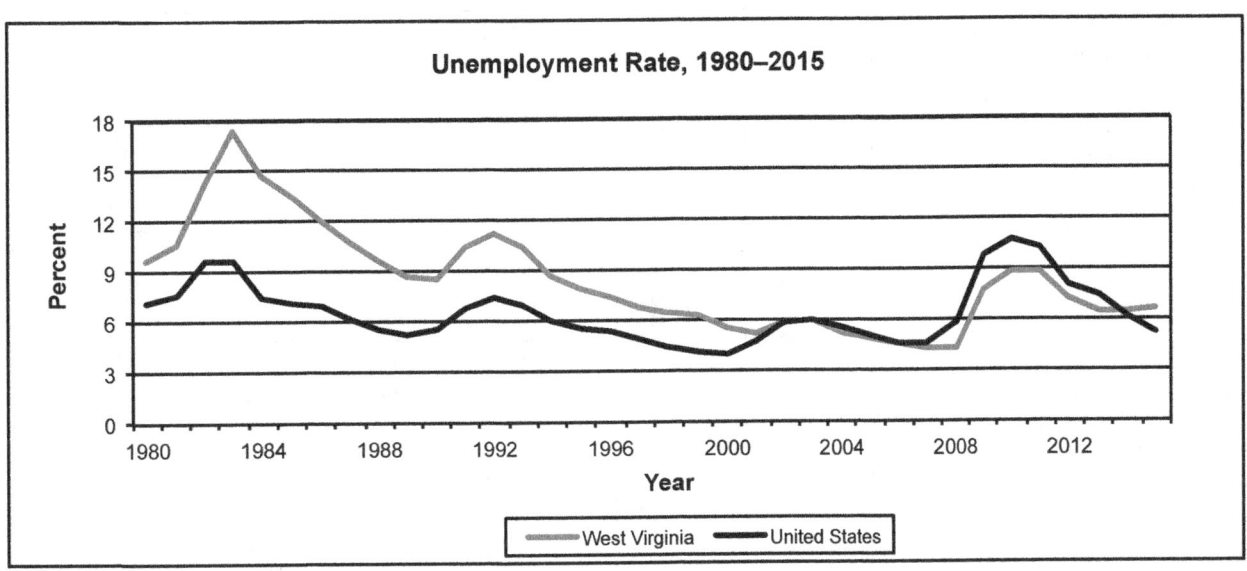

Unemployment Rate, 1980–2015

Table WV-8. Employment Status of the Civilian Noninstitutional Population Age 16 Years and Over

(Number, percent.)

Year	Civilian labor force	Civilian participation rate	Employed	Unemployed	Unemployment rate
2007..........	811,160	56.2	773,990	37,170	4.6
2008..........	812,905	56.1	777,560	35,345	4.3
2009..........	814,027	56.0	751,165	62,862	7.7
2010..........	811,125	54.9	740,910	70,215	8.7
2011..........	807,021	54.3	741,972	65,049	8.1
2012..........	807,595	54.3	747,092	60,503	7.5
2013..........	798,953	53.8	745,081	53,872	6.7
2014..........	789,850	53.2	737,479	52,371	6.6
2015..........	785,049	53.0	732,146	52,903	6.7

Table WV-9. Employment and Average Wages by Industry

(Estimates through 2010 are based on the 2007 North American Industry Classification System [NAICS]. Estimates from 2011 onward are based on the 2012 NAICS.)

Industry	2008	2009	2010	2011	2012	2013	2014
	Number of jobs						
Wage and Salary Employment by Industry......................	755,780	737,945	738,582	747,666	752,413	744,520	741,131
Farm Wage and Salary Employment..............................	1,440	1,286	1,308	1,403	1,467	1,404	1,701
Nonfarm Wage and Salary Employment..........................	754,340	736,659	737,274	746,263	750,946	743,116	739,430
Private wage and salary employment..........................	597,771	577,417	575,076	584,884	588,558	584,953	582,672
Forestry, fishing, and related activities.............................	1,549	1,367	1,320	1,254	1,290	1,337	1,414
Mining..	30,483	28,947	29,251	32,910	32,741	30,878	29,201
Utilities..	6,201	6,194	5,632	5,439	5,307	5,177	5,205
Construction	40,830	35,866	34,324	34,794	36,892	35,621	34,848
Manufacturing...	56,586	50,767	49,180	49,560	49,165	48,467	47,815
Durable goods manufacturing................................	35,426	30,942	29,651	29,944	29,593	29,133	28,866
Nondurable goods manufacturing..........................	21,160	19,825	19,529	19,616	19,572	19,334	18,949
Wholesale trade	24,702	23,555	23,130	23,454	23,605	23,031	22,750
Retail trade...	91,213	88,334	88,004	88,367	88,508	88,511	87,610
Transportation and warehousing.............................	20,763	19,485	19,376	19,847	19,428	20,373	20,994
Information...	11,175	10,468	10,334	10,369	9,638	9,519	9,581
Finance and insurance	21,846	20,932	20,705	20,429	20,250	19,947	19,653
Real estate and rental and leasing..........................	7,645	7,294	7,259	6,966	6,860	6,848	6,984
Professional, scientific, and technical services	25,182	24,467	24,843	25,421	25,753	26,150	26,369
Management of companies and enterprises..................	5,116	5,430	5,469	5,699	6,685	6,501	6,349
Administrative and waste services	31,565	30,410	31,060	32,341	32,777	32,804	34,583
Educational services	8,625	8,477	8,835	9,154	9,131	8,714	8,917
Health care and social assistance...........................	104,748	107,358	109,010	110,883	113,399	114,017	114,185
Arts, entertainment, and recreation.........................	9,147	9,305	9,536	7,366	7,656	7,739	7,776
Accommodation and food services..........................	64,562	63,450	63,555	66,294	67,134	67,304	66,987
Other services, except public administration................	35,833	35,311	34,253	34,337	32,339	32,015	31,451
Government and government enterprises	156,569	159,242	162,198	161,379	162,388	158,163	156,758
	Dollars						
Average Wages and Salaries by Industry	35,468	36,326	37,098	38,477	39,169	39,651	40,589
Average Farm Wages and Salaries	21,402	22,767	21,144	17,636	18,903	26,912	24,613
Average Nonfarm Wages and Salaries	35,495	36,350	37,126	38,516	39,208	39,675	40,625
Average private wages and salaries..........................	35,073	35,863	36,857	38,463	39,262	39,561	40,564
Forestry, fishing, and related activities.............................	24,680	24,825	26,023	27,258	28,415	28,201	29,043
Mining..	69,067	72,252	73,284	78,917	79,266	80,078	80,874
Utilities..	71,679	76,112	77,029	80,512	80,685	81,321	85,135
Construction	43,696	44,623	47,229	46,962	50,782	52,022	53,519
Manufacturing...	47,564	47,934	49,963	51,693	52,787	53,044	55,058
Durable goods manufacturing................................	44,552	45,019	46,548	48,386	50,006	49,654	51,402
Nondurable goods manufacturing..........................	52,607	52,484	55,147	56,741	56,992	58,152	60,629
Wholesale trade	48,153	49,287	49,810	51,245	51,727	52,201	54,992
Retail trade...	21,891	22,608	23,173	23,729	24,147	24,418	24,671
Transportation and warehousing.............................	45,693	46,467	46,947	49,182	50,032	49,750	50,020
Information...	42,125	43,604	46,228	48,520	48,638	47,552	48,758
Finance and insurance	40,220	41,323	42,470	46,743	46,089	47,622	49,380
Real estate and rental and leasing..........................	29,854	31,033	34,849	34,923	20,243	36,490	37,827
Professional, scientific, and technical services	46,393	48,247	50,439	50,623	53,052	53,724	55,202
Management of companies and enterprises..................	66,177	64,248	67,681	81,738	70,891	69,691	72,670
Administrative and waste services	24,682	25,383	26,618	28,502	29,055	29,569	31,279
Educational services	21,205	22,646	23,274	23,980	24,505	24,905	24,587
Health care and social assistance...........................	35,567	36,934	37,129	37,800	38,773	39,641	40,965
Arts, entertainment, and recreation.........................	19,448	20,694	22,315	19,473	19,333	18,929	19,263
Accommodation and food services..........................	15,104	15,231	15,994	17,304	17,588	17,375	17,893
Other services, except public administration................	23,503	24,025	25,163	25,599	26,469	27,351	28,093
Government and government enterprises	37,105	38,118	38,082	38,708	39,013	40,100	40,855

Table WV-10. Employment Characteristics by Family Type

(Number, percent.)

Family type and labor force status	2012		2013		2014	
	Total	Families with own children under 18 years	Total	Families with own children under 18 years	Total	Families with own children under 18 years
All Families.....	471,536	175,829	479,389	177,583	471,865	167,580
FAMILY TYPE AND LABOR FORCE STATUS						
Married-Couple Families.....	358,666	117,691	355,958	113,167	354,686	108,911
Both husband and wife in labor force.....	41.0	58.3	41.3	60.9	41.6	61.6
Husband in labor force, wife not in labor force.....	22.3	30.8	22.5	30.0	22.2	28.2
Wife in labor force, husband not in labor force.....	10.9	7.3	10.3	5.0	9.9	5.5
Both husband and wife not in labor force.....	25.8	3.7	25.7	4.1	26.3	4.6
Other Families.....	112,870	58,138	123,431	64,416	117,179	58,669
Female householder, no husband present.....	71.8	74.9	70.1	70.3	71.6	70.4
In labor force.....	41.6	55.3	40.1	49.8	41.6	51.1
Not in labor force.....	30.2	19.7	30.0	20.5	30.0	19.3
Male householder, no wife present.....	28.2	25.1	29.9	29.7	28.4	29.6
In labor force.....	17.8	19.9	20.3	24.0	17.5	23.7
Not in labor force.....	10.3	5.2	9.6	5.6	10.9	5.9

Table WV-11. School Enrollment and Educational Attainment, 2014

(Number, percent.)

Item	State	U.S.
Enrollment		
Total population 3 years and over, enrolled in school.....	411,243	82,063,714
Enrolled in nursery school or preschool (percent).....	5.8	6.0
Enrolled in kindergarten (percent).....	5.1	5.1
Enrolled in elementary school, grades 1-8 (percent).....	42.2	40.2
Enrolled in high school, grades 9-12 (percent).....	20.8	20.7
Enrolled in college or graduate school (percent).....	26.1	28.0
Attainment		
Total population 25 years and over.....	1,296,350	213,725,624
Less than ninth grade (percent).....	5.0	5.6
9th to 12th grade, no diploma (percent).....	9.9	7.5
High school graduate, including equivalency (percent).....	41.1	27.7
Some college, no degree (percent).....	18.4	21.0
Associate's degree (percent).....	6.5	8.2
Bachelor's degree (percent).....	11.8	18.7
Graduate or professional degree (percent).....	7.4	11.4
High school graduate or higher (percent).....	85.2	86.9
Bachelor's degree or higher (percent).....	19.2	30.1

Table WV-12. Public School Characteristics and Educational Indicators

(Number, percent; data derived from National Center of Education Statistics.)

Item	State	U.S.
Public Schools, 2013–2014 (except where noted)		
Number of school districts.....	57	18,194
Number of schools.....	758	98,271
Number of students (in thousands).....	281	50,045
Number of teachers (in thousands).....	20	3,114
Student-teacher ratio.....	14.1	16.1
Expenditures per student (dollars), FY 2013.....	112,577	107,637
Four-year adjusted cohort graduation rate (ACGR)[1,2].....	84.5	82.3
Students eligible for free or reduced-price lunch (in thousands).....	80	25,596
English language learners (in thousands).....	2	4,461
Students age 3 to 21 served under IDEA, part B (in thousands).....	44	6,464

Public Schools by Type	Number	Percent of state public schools
Total number of schools.....	758	100.0
Regular.....	695	91.7
Special education.....	3	0.4
Vocational education.....	30	4.0
Alternative education.....	30	4.0

NOTE: Every school is assigned only one school type based on its instructional emphasis.
[1]ACGR data represents a new method of calculating high-school completion rates and may not be comparable to previous years' data for Averaged Freshmen Graduation Rates (AFGR).
[2]The United States 4-year ACGRs were estimated using both the reported 4-year ACGR data from 49 states and the District of Columbia and using imputed data for Idaho. The estimate for American Indian/Alaska Native students also includes imputed data for Virginia.

Table WV-13. Reported Voting and Registration of the Voting-Age Population, November 2014

(Numbers in thousands, percent.)

Item	Total population	Total citizen population	Registered			Voted		
			Total registered	Percent registered (total population)	Percent registered (total citizen population)	Total voted	Percent voted (total population)	Percent voted (total citizen population)
U.S. Total	239,874	219,941	142,166	59.3	64.6	92,251	38.5	41.9
State Total.............................	1,449	1,440	896	61.8	62.2	484	33.4	33.6
Sex								
Male..	705	703	431	61.1	61.3	236	33.5	33.6
Female	744	738	465	62.5	63.1	248	33.3	33.6
Race								
White alone.................................	1,376	1,373	863	62.7	62.8	473	34.4	34.5
White, non-Hispanic alone	1,360	1,358	852	62.7	62.8	470	34.6	34.6
Black alone.................................	41	41	17	(B)	(B)	5	(B)	(B)
Asian alone.................................	10	5	4	(B)	(B)	2	(B)	(B)
Hispanic (of any race)	18	16	11	(B)	(B)	3	(B)	(B)
White alone or in combination	1,390	1,387	872	62.7	62.9	475	34.2	34.3
Black alone or in combination..........	49	48	22	(B)	(B)	6	(B)	(B)
Asian alone or in combination..........	10	6	4	(B)	(B)	2	(B)	(B)
Age								
18 to 24 years	185	183	85	46.2	46.6	26	14.3	14.4
25 to 34 years	206	204	120	58.0	58.8	41	19.8	20.0
35 to 44 years	216	212	125	57.8	58.8	63	29.1	29.5
45 to 64 years	505	504	316	62.6	62.7	189	37.4	37.4
65 years and over	338	338	250	74.1	74.1	165	49.0	49.0

B = Base is less than 75,000 and therefore too small to show the derived measure.

Table WV-14. Crime

(Number, rate per 100,000. Data are derived from the FBI Uniform Crime Reports.)

Item	State			U.S.[1,2,3,4]		
	2013	2014	Percent change	2013	2014	Percent change
TOTAL POPULATION[5]......................................	1,854,304	1,850,326	-0.2	316,128,839	318,857,056	0.9
VIOLENT CRIME						
Number...	5,371	5,588	4.0	1,163,146	1,165,383	0.2
Rate	289.7	302.0	4.2	367.9	365.5	-0.7
Murder and Nonnegligent Manslaughter						
Number...	61	74	21.3	14,196	14,249	0.4
Rate	3.3	4.0	21.2	4.5	4.5	-
Rape[6]						
Number...	653	505	X	108,612	116,645	X
Rate	35.2	27.3	X	34.4	36.6	X
Robbery						
Number...	651	651	-	345,031	325,802	-5.6
Rate	35.1	35.2	0.3	109.1	102.2	-6.3
Aggravated Assault						
Number...	4,203	4,358	3.7	724,149	741,291	2.4
Rate	226.7	235.5	3.9	229.1	232.5	1.5
PROPERTY CRIME						
Number...	39,013	37,648	-3.5	8,632,512	8,277,829	-4.1
Rate	2,103.9	2,034.7	-3.3	2,730.7	2,596.1	-4.9
Burglary						
Number...	9,674	8,973	-7.2	1,928,465	1,729,806	-10.3
Rate	521.7	484.9	-7.1	610.0	542.5	-11.1
Larceny-Theft						
Number...	27,423	26,779	-2.3	6,004,453	5,858,496	-2.4
Rate	1,478.9	1,447.3	-2.1	1,899.4	1,837.3	-3.3
Motor Vehicle Theft						
Number...	1,916	1,896	-1.0	699,594	689,527	-1.4
Rate	103.3	102.5	-0.8	221.3	216.2	-2.3

NOTE: Although arson data are included in the trend and clearance tables, sufficient data are not available to estimate totals for this offense. Therefore, no arson data are published in this table.
X = Not applicable.
- = Zero or rounds to zero.
[1]The crime figures have been adjusted.
[2]The data collection methodology for the offense of forcible rape used by the Minnesota state Uniform Crime Reporting (UCR) Program (with the exception of Minneapolis and St. Paul, Minnesota) does not comply with national UCR Program guidelines. Consequently, its figures for forcible rape and violent crime (of which forcible rape is a part) are not published in this table.
[3]Includes offenses reported by the Zoological Police and the Metro Transit Police.
[4]Because of changes in the state's reporting practices, figures are not comparable to previous years' data.
[5]Populations are U.S. Census Bureau provisional estimates as of July 1 of each year.
[6]The figures shown for the offense of rape were estimated using the revised Uniform Crime Reporting (UCR) definition of rape.

Table WV-15. State Government Finances, 2014

(Dollar amounts in thousands, percent distribution.)

Item	Dollars	Percent distribution
Total Revenue	15,381,616	100.0
General revenue	12,246,658	79.6
Intergovernmental revenue	4,350,205	28.3
Taxes	5,379,937	35.0
General sales	1,221,966	7.9
Selective sales	1,339,027	8.7
License taxes	152,754	1.0
Individual income tax	1,770,466	11.5
Corporate income tax	203,508	1.3
Other taxes	692,216	4.5
Current charges	1,393,149	9.1
Miscellaneous general revenue	1,123,367	7.3
Utility revenue	2,084	-
Liquor stores revenue	91,373	0.6
Insurance trust revenue[1]	3,041,501	19.8
Total Expenditure	13,240,704	100.0
Intergovernmental expenditure	2,413,663	18.2
Direct expenditure	10,827,041	81.8
Current operation	7,898,177	59.7
Capital outlay	1,008,311	7.6
Insurance benefits and repayments	1,482,788	11.2
Assistance and subsidies	244,496	1.8
Interest on debt	193,269	1.5
Exhibit: Salaries and wages	1,840,764	13.9
Total Expenditure	13,240,704	100.0
General expenditure	11,678,331	88.2
Intergovernmental expenditure	2,413,663	18.2
Direct expenditure	9,264,668	70.0
General expenditure, by function:		
Education	4,284,504	32.4
Public welfare	3,719,145	28.1
Hospitals	133,665	1.0
Health	330,522	2.5
Highways	1,118,647	8.4
Police protection	76,416	0.6
Correction	300,457	2.3
Natural resources	228,036	1.7
Parks and recreation	49,408	0.4
Governmental administration	434,012	3.3
Interest on general debt	193,269	1.5
Other and unallocable	810,250	6.1
Utility expenditure	4,880	-
Liquor stores expenditure	74,705	0.6
Insurance trust expenditure	1,482,788	11.2
Debt at End of Fiscal Year	7,986,591	X
Cash and Security Holdings	23,644,056	X

X = Not applicable.
- = Zero or rounds to zero.
[1]Within insurance trust revenue, net earnings of state retirement systems is a calculated statistic (the item code in the data file is X08), and thus can be positive or negative. Net earnings is the sum of earnings on investments plus gains on investments minus losses on investments. The change made in 2002 for asset valuation from book to market value in accordance with Statement 34 of the Governmental Accounting Standards Board is reflected in the calculated statistics.

Table WV-16. State Government Tax Collections, 2014

(Dollars in thousands, percent.)

Item	Dollars	Percent distribution
Total Taxes	5,379,937	100.0
Property taxes	0	-
Sales and gross receipts	2,560,993	47.6
General sales and gross receipts	1,221,966	22.7
Selective sales and gross receipts	1,339,027	24.9
Alcoholic beverages	17,295	0.3
Amusements	50,465	0.9
Insurance premiums	155,021	2.9
Motor fuels	441,096	8.2
Pari-mutuels	2,312	-
Public utilities	153,588	2.9
Tobacco products	101,779	1.9
Other selective sales	417,471	7.8
Licenses	152,754	2.8
Alcoholic beverages	1,380	-
Amusements	3,352	0.1
Corporations in general	5,424	0.1
Hunting and fishing	12,599	0.2
Motor vehicle	2,539	-
Motor vehicle operators	108,409	2.0
Public utilities	369	-
Occupation and business, NEC	11,622	0.2
Other licenses	7,060	0.1
Income taxes	1,973,974	36.7
Individual income	1,770,466	32.9
Corporation net income	203,508	3.8
Other taxes	692,216	12.9
Death and gift	0	-
Documentary and stock transfer	10,392	0.2
Severance	681,824	12.7
Taxes, NEC	0	-

- = Zero or rounds to zero.

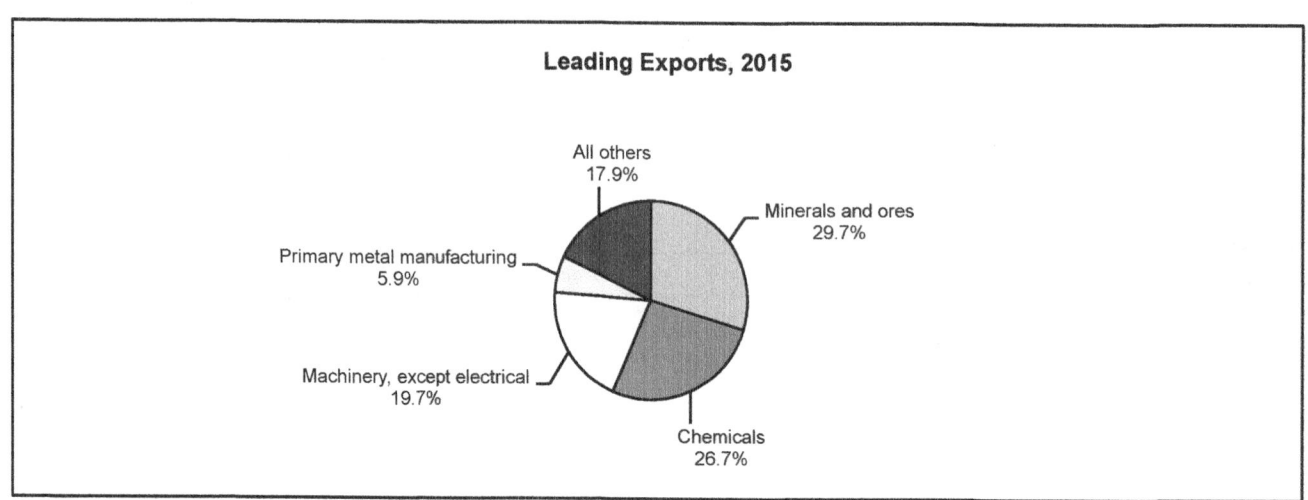

Leading Exports, 2015

All others 17.9%
Minerals and ores 29.7%
Primary metal manufacturing 5.9%
Chemicals 26.7%
Machinery, except electrical 19.7%

WISCONSIN

Facts and Figures

Location: North central United States; bordered on the N by Michigan and Lake Superior, on the E by Lake Michigan, on the S by Illinois, and on the W by Iowa and Minnesota

Area: 65,498 sq. mi. (169,639 sq. km.); rank—23rd

Population: 5,771,337 (2015 est.); rank—20th

Principal Cities: capital—Madison; largest—Milwaukee

Statehood: May 29, 1848; 30th state

U.S. Congress: 2 senators, 8 representatives

State Motto: Forward

State Song: "On, Wisconsin!"

State Nickname: The Badger State

Abbreviations: WI; Wis.; Wisc.

State Symbols: flower—wood violet; tree—sugar maple; bird—robin

At a Glance

- With an increase in population of 1.4 percent, Wisconsin ranked 39th among the states in growth from 2010 to 2015.

- Wisconsin's violent crime rate in 2014 was 290.3 per 100,000 population, compared to 365.5 for the entire nation.

- Wisconsin's median household income in 2014 was $52,622, and 13.2 percent of the population lived below the poverty level.

- In 2014, 7.3 percent of Wisconsin residents did not have health insurance, compared to 11.7 percent of the total U.S. population.

- The unemployment rate in Wisconsin in 2015 was 4.6 percent, compared to the national rate of 5.3 percent.

Table WI-1. Population by Age, Sex, Race, and Hispanic Origin

(Number, percent, except where noted.)

Sex, age, race, and Hispanic origin	2000	2010	2015[1]	Average annual percent change, 2010–2015
Total Population..	5,363,675	5,686,986	5,771,337	0.1
Percent of total U.S. population	1.9	1.8	1.8	X
Sex				
Male..	2,649,041	2,822,400	2,867,600	0.1
Female..	2,714,634	2,864,586	2,903,737	0.1
Age				
Under 5 years..	342,340	358,443	339,726	-0.4
5 to 19 years...	1,189,753	1,143,753	1,110,866	-0.2
20 to 64 years..	3,129,029	3,407,476	3,418,611	-
65 years and over..	702,553	777,314	902,134	1.1
Median age (years)...	36.0	38.5	39.2	0.1
Race and Hispanic Origin				
One race				
White..	4,769,857	5,036,923	5,057,594	-
Black...	304,460	367,021	381,376	0.3
American Indian and Alaska Native	47,228	60,100	65,072	0.6
Asian...	88,763	131,828	159,645	1.4
Native Hawaiian or Other Pacific Islander	1,630	2,505	2,934	1.1
Two or more races...	66,895	88,609	104,716	1.2
Hispanic (of any race)...	192,291	349,366	381,877	0.6

X = Not applicable.
[1]Population figures for 2015 are July 1 estimates. The 2010 estimates are taken from the 2010 Census.

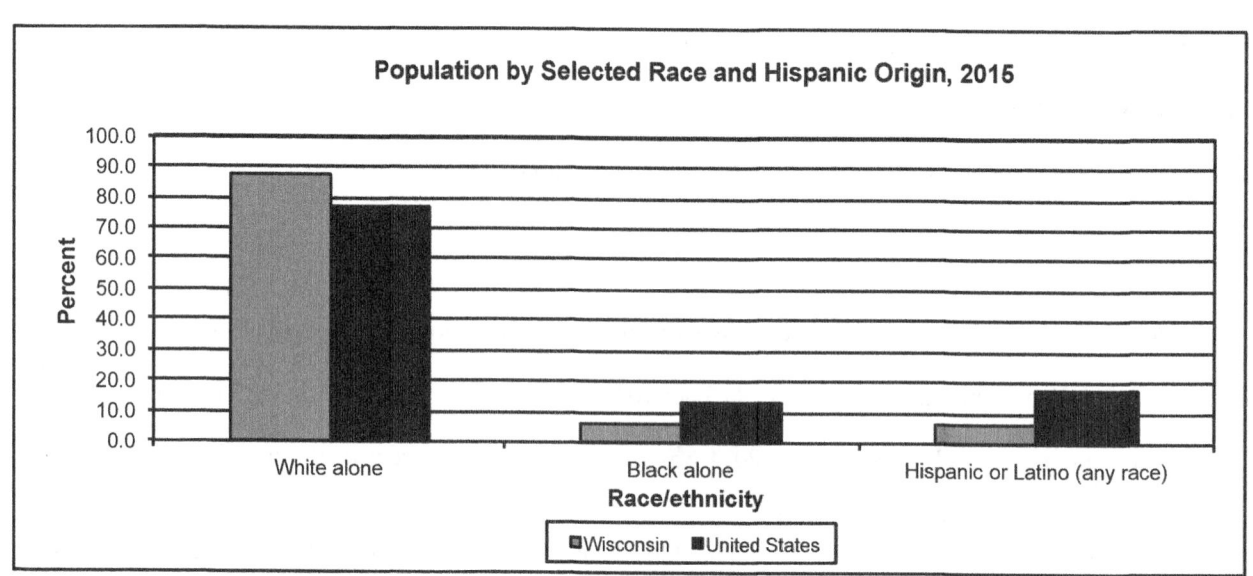

Population by Selected Race and Hispanic Origin, 2015

Table WI-2. Marital Status

(Number, percent distribution.)

Sex, age, race, and Hispanic origin	2000	2010	2014
Males, 15 Years and Over	2,072,397	2,261,022	2,285,427
Never married	30.2	34.1	34.3
Now married, except separated..	57.9	52.1	52.2
Separated..	1.1	1.0	1.0
Widowed...	2.4	2.6	2.5
Divorced...	8.4	10.2	10.0
Females, 15 Years and Over	2,167,164	2,328,733	2,350,966
Never married	24.3	28.1	28.3
Now married, except separated..	54.6	50.1	50.1
Separated..	1.3	1.2	1.2
Widowed...	10.2	9.2	9.0
Divorced...	9.7	11.4	11.4

Table WI-3. Households and Housing Characteristics

(Number, percent, dollars.)

Item	2000	2010	2014	Average annual percent change, 2000–2014
Total Households	2,084,544	2,279,532	2,307,685	0.8
Family households	1,386,815	1,453,332	1,485,877	0.5
Married-couple family	1,108,597	1,125,314	1,133,193	0.2
Other family	278,218	328,018	352,684	1.9
Male householder, no wife present	77,918	96,237	113,960	3.3
Female householder, no husband present	200,300	231,781	238,724	1.4
Nonfamily households	697,729	826,200	821,808	1.3
Householder living alone	557,875	669,106	657,138	1.3
Householder not living alone	139,854	157,094	164,670	1.3
Housing Characteristics				
Total housing units	2,321,144	2,625,477	2,648,342	1.0
Occupied housing units	2,084,544	2,279,532	2,307,685	0.8
Owner occupied	1,426,361	1,566,039	1,536,893	0.6
Renter occupied	658,183	713,493	770,792	1.2
Average household size	2.50	2.43	2.43	-0.2
Financial Characteristics				
Median gross rent of renter-occupied housing	540	715	782	3.2
Median monthly owner costs for housing units with a mortgage	1,024	1,404	1,373	2.4
Median value of owner-occupied housing units	112,200	169,400	164,700	3.3

Table WI-4. Migration, Origin, and Language

(Number, percent.)

Characteristic	State			U.S.		
	2013	2014	Percent change	2013	2014	Percent change
Residence 1 Year Ago						
Population 1 year and over	5,681,024	5,692,727	0.2	312,432,820	315,095,393	0.9
Same house	85.8	85.5	X	85.0	85.1	X
Different house in the U.S.	13.9	14.2	X	14.4	14.3	X
Same county	8.7	8.5	X	8.9	8.7	X
Different county	5.2	5.6	X	5.5	5.6	X
Same state	3.4	3.5	X	3.2	3.3	X
Different state	1.8	2.1	X	2.3	2.3	X
Abroad	0.3	0.3	X	0.6	0.6	X
Place of Birth						
Native born	5,468,026	5,477,407	0.2	274,780,773	276,465,262	0.6
Male	49.6	49.6	X	49.3	49.3	X
Female	50.4	50.4	X	50.7	50.7	X
Foreign born	274,687	280,157	2.0	41,348,066	42,391,794	2.5
Male	51.4	50.9	X	48.8	48.7	X
Female	48.6	49.1	X	51.2	51.3	X
Foreign born; naturalized U.S. citizen	119,720	124,687	4.1	19,294,710	19,984,738	3.6
Male	47.1	47.5	X	45.9	45.9	X
Female	52.9	52.5	X	54.1	54.1	X
Foreign born; not a U.S. citizen	154,967	155,470	0.3	22,053,356	22,407,056	1.6
Male	54.7	53.6	X	51.3	51.2	X
Female	45.3	46.4	X	48.7	48.8	X
Entered 2010 or later	11.8	14.9	X	9.7	12.3	X
Entered 2000 to 2009	33.9	31.7	X	29.4	28.6	X
Entered before 2000	54.4	53.4	X	61.0	59.1	X
World Region of Birth, Foreign						
Foreign-born population, excluding population born at sea	274,687	280,157	2.0	41,347,945	42,390,705	2.5
Europe	17.1	18.2	X	11.6	11.2	X
Asia	34.9	34.6	X	29.5	30.1	X
Africa	3.2	3.5	X	4.4	4.6	X
Oceania	0.5	0.4	X	0.5	0.6	X
Latin America	41.7	40.9	X	51.9	51.6	X
North America	2.6	2.4	X	2.0	1.9	X
Language Spoken at Home and Ability to Speak English						
Population 5 years and over	5,401,273	5,418,476	0.3	296,358,760	299,084,046	0.9
English only	91.3	91.3	X	79.2	78.9	X
Language other than English	8.7	8.7	X	20.8	21.1	X
Speaks English less than "very well"	3.2	3.3	X	8.5	8.6	X

X = Not applicable.
- = Zero or rounds to zero.

Table WI-5. Median Income and Poverty Status, 2014

(Number, percent, except as noted.)

Characteristic	State		U.S.	
	Number	Percent	Number	Percent
Median Income				
Households (dollars)...	52,622	X	53,657	X
Families (dollars)	67,187	X	65,910	X
Below Poverty Level (All People)	738,270	13.2	48,208,387	15.5
Sex				
Male...	330,926	11.9	21,590,918	14.2
Female	407,344	14.4	26,617,469	16.8
Age				
Under 18 years...	234,936	18.4	15,686,012	21.7
Related children under 18 years.........................	228,692	18.1	15,372,705	21.3
18 to 64 years...	442,727	12.7	28,267,482	14.6
65 years and over...	60,607	7.2	4,254,893	9.5

X = Not applicable.

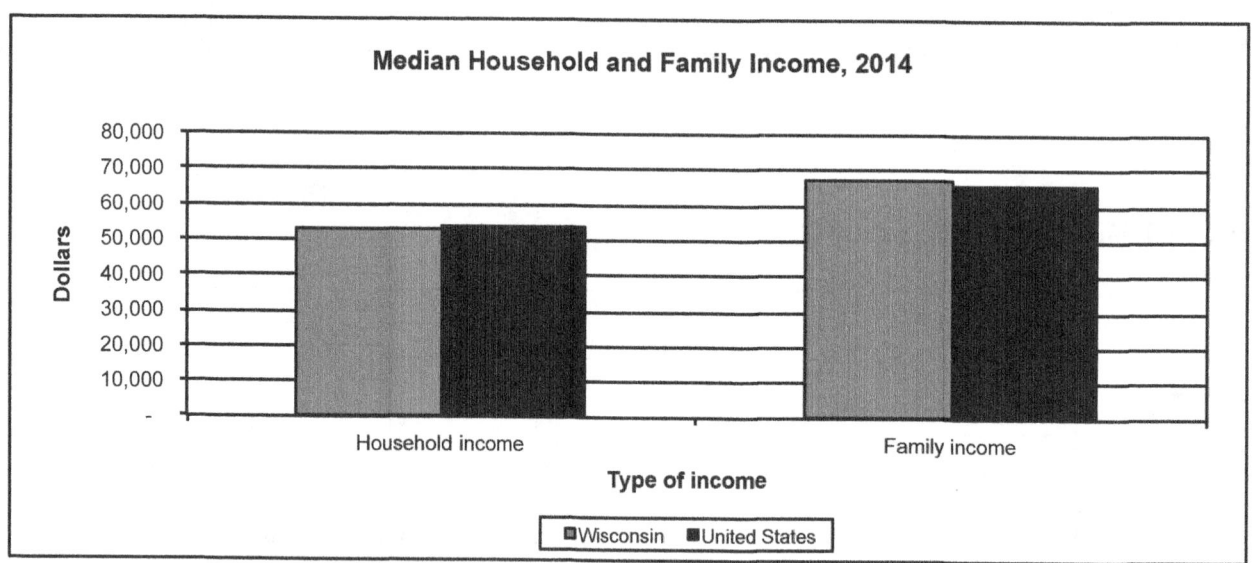

Table WI-6. Health Insurance Coverage Status for the Civilian Noninstitutionalized Population and Children Under 18 Years of Age

(Numbers in thousands, percent.)

Item	2006	2007	2008	2009	2010	2011	2012	2013	2014
Civilian Noninstitutionalized Population	5,476	5,473	5,540	5,566	5,613	5,634	5,652	5,669	5,685
Covered by Private or Public Insurance									
Number...	4,995	5,023	5,034	5,045	5,084	5,127	5,146	5,151	5,267
Percent...	91.2	91.8	90.9	90.6	90.6	91.0	91.0	90.9	92.7
Not Covered									
Number...	481	451	506	521	529	507	506	518	418
Percent...	8.8	8.2	9.1	9.4	9.4	9.0	9.0	9.1	7.3
Percent in the U.S. not covered..................................	15.8	15.3	15.1	15.1	15.5	15.1	14.8	14.5	11.7
Children Under 18 Years of Age	1,290	1,329	1,309	1,303	1,334	1,323	1,315	1,305	1,298
Covered by Private or Public Insurance									
Number...	1,227	1,252	1,241	1,238	1,267	1,265	1,253	1,243	1,240
Percent...	95.1	94.2	94.8	95.0	95.0	95.6	95.3	95.3	95.6
Not Covered									
Number...	63	77	68	65	67	58	62	61	58
Percent...	4.9	5.8	5.2	5.0	5.0	4.4	4.7	4.7	4.4
Percent in the U.S. not covered..................................	11.7	11.0	9.7	8.6	8.0	7.5	7.2	7.1	6.0

Table WI-7. Employment Status by Demographic Group, 2015

(Numbers in thousands, percent.)

Characteristic	Civilian noninstitutional population	Civilian labor force		Employed		Unemployed	
		Number	Percent of population	Number	Percent of population	Number	Percent of population
Total....................................	4,557	3,091	67.8	2,949	64.7	142	4.6
Sex							
Male	2,236	1,611	72.1	1,538	68.8	74	4.6
Female	2,321	1,479	63.7	1,411	60.8	68	4.6
Race, Sex, and Hispanic Origin							
White	4,086	2,767	67.7	2,654	65.0	113	4.1
Male	2,027	1,460	72.0	1,400	69.1	60	4.1
Female	2,059	1,307	63.5	1,254	60.9	53	4.1
Black or African American....................	254	171	67.2	152	59.8	19	11.1
Male	111	80	72.0	70	63.5	9	11.8
Female	143	91	63.6	82	56.9	10	10.5
Hispanic or Latino ethnicity[1]	283	200	70.7	187	66.0	13	6.7
Male	142	114	80.2	104	73.2	10	8.7
Female	140	86	61.1	82	58.7	3	4.0
Age							
16 to 19 years	309	159	51.4	137	44.2	22	14.1
20 to 24 years	420	334	79.6	311	74.0	23	7.0
25 to 34 years	715	623	87.1	587	82.1	36	5.8
35 to 44 years	650	578	88.9	556	85.6	22	3.7
45 to 54 years	819	707	86.3	687	83.9	20	2.8
55 to 64 years	793	550	69.4	536	67.6	14	2.5
65 years and over	852	140	16.4	136	15.9	4	3.0

NOTE: Data in Table 7 are from the Current Population Survey (CPS) and do not match the estimates in Table 8. See notes and definitions for further information.
[1]May be of any race.

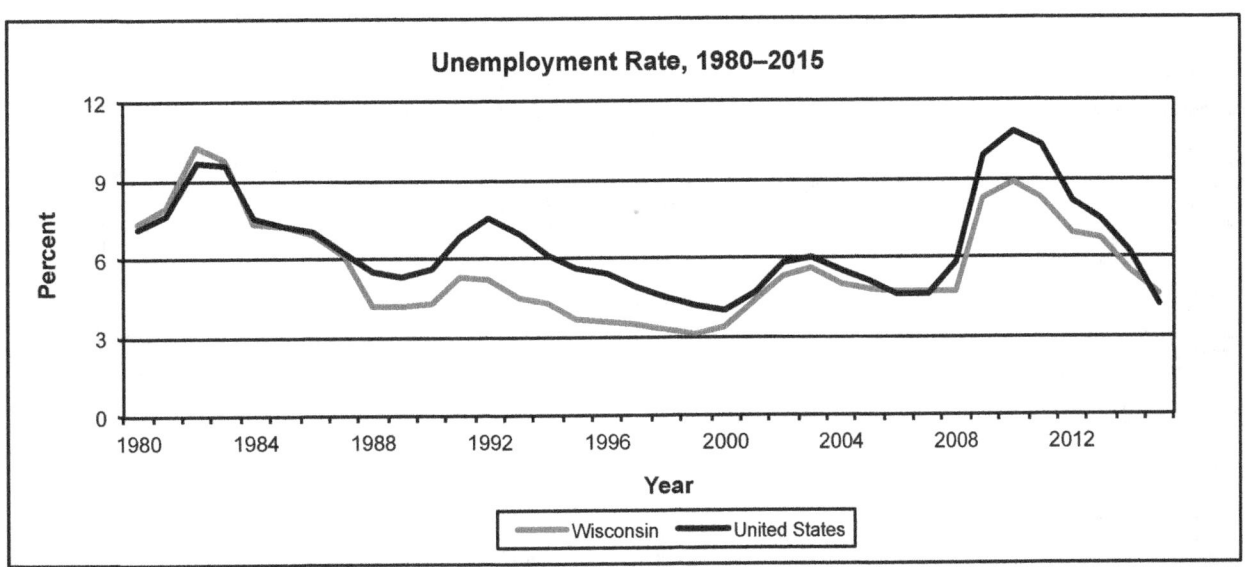

Table WI-8. Employment Status of the Civilian Noninstitutional Population Age 16 Years and Over

(Number, percent.)

Year	Civilian labor force	Civilian participation rate	Employed	Unemployed	Unemployment rate
2007..................	3,087,828	70.9	2,936,452	151,376	4.9
2008..................	3,091,796	70.4	2,940,438	151,358	4.9
2009..................	3,100,348	70.2	2,834,335	266,013	8.6
2010..................	3,081,512	69.5	2,814,393	267,119	8.7
2011..................	3,079,759	69.0	2,840,996	238,763	7.8
2012..................	3,074,339	68.5	2,857,673	216,666	7.0
2013..................	3,083,790	68.4	2,876,037	207,753	6.7
2014..................	3,086,365	68.1	2,918,966	167,399	5.4
2015..................	3,095,376	68.0	2,952,797	142,579	4.6

Table WI-9. Employment and Average Wages by Industry

(Estimates through 2010 are based on the 2007 North American Industry Classification System [NAICS]. Estimates from 2011 onward are based on the 2012 NAICS.)

Industry	2008	2009	2010	2011	2012	2013	2014
	Number of jobs						
Wage and Salary Employment by Industry..................	2,932,840	2,803,520	2,795,211	2,824,652	2,840,951	2,874,843	2,913,690
Farm Wage and Salary Employment..........................	24,483	22,753	23,468	24,791	19,135	25,025	24,465
Nonfarm Wage and Salary Employment....................	2,908,357	2,780,767	2,771,743	2,799,861	2,821,816	2,849,818	2,889,225
Private wage and salary employment.......................	2,476,599	2,344,911	2,334,467	2,368,305	2,389,825	2,418,113	2,454,594
Forestry, fishing, and related activities....................	5,115	5,250	5,412	5,700	5,541	5,738	5,932
Mining...	2,631	2,308	2,227	2,293	2,754	3,009	3,406
Utilities..	11,319	11,271	11,113	10,920	10,896	10,702	10,420
Construction	123,236	106,731	99,226	97,761	96,783	102,124	106,751
Manufacturing..	494,458	437,035	431,729	445,665	456,493	458,139	465,441
Durable goods manufacturing...............................	310,980	264,048	258,729	270,714	279,741	279,901	283,749
Nondurable goods manufacturing..........................	183,478	172,987	173,000	174,951	176,752	178,238	181,692
Wholesale trade	123,652	116,786	113,855	115,475	117,368	119,634	121,052
Retail trade...	314,818	302,760	299,011	299,853	298,278	301,608	305,469
Transportation and warehousing...........................	97,099	91,549	90,637	91,926	91,951	91,687	93,547
Information..	50,426	48,040	46,890	47,056	46,727	47,330	48,035
Finance and insurance	134,603	132,910	130,529	130,186	130,647	129,077	126,745
Real estate and rental and leasing........................	28,348	26,645	26,027	25,295	24,904	25,249	25,078
Professional, scientific, and technical services	102,257	97,654	95,303	97,667	99,466	100,765	102,236
Management of companies and enterprises..............	45,930	46,393	47,130	50,719	53,014	55,750	59,391
Administrative and waste services........................	138,480	119,381	131,733	139,142	140,960	144,783	148,180
Educational services	51,450	52,492	54,321	55,609	55,365	54,930	55,850
Health care and social assistance........................	353,683	358,739	361,818	364,486	369,115	374,304	380,099
Arts, entertainment, and recreation.......................	36,279	35,227	35,238	35,954	36,251	36,648	37,167
Accommodation and food services........................	226,511	220,452	219,644	219,657	222,477	226,574	228,344
Other services, except public administration............	136,304	133,288	132,624	132,941	130,835	130,062	131,451
Government and government enterprises	431,758	435,856	437,276	431,556	431,991	431,705	434,631
	Dollars						
Average Wages and Salaries by Industry	39,678	39,613	40,479	41,558	42,655	43,403	44,471
Average Farm Wages and Salaries	35,038	35,292	29,335	27,175	32,594	35,830	38,338
Average Nonfarm Wages and Salaries	39,717	39,649	40,573	41,686	42,724	43,470	44,523
Average private wages and salaries.......................	39,814	39,642	40,697	41,876	43,105	43,862	44,963
Forestry, fishing, and related activities....................	29,241	28,691	29,757	30,923	32,114	33,510	34,388
Mining...	52,482	53,359	56,996	60,382	61,499	61,633	67,273
Utilities..	91,695	93,364	92,701	95,756	97,979	103,692	101,475
Construction	50,503	49,693	50,070	51,149	52,773	54,296	56,205
Manufacturing..	49,672	49,355	51,943	53,093	54,245	54,780	56,024
Durable goods manufacturing...............................	50,813	50,468	53,717	55,081	55,994	56,430	57,787
Nondurable goods manufacturing..........................	47,739	47,657	49,291	50,016	51,478	52,189	53,270
Wholesale trade	54,176	53,362	55,180	57,311	59,207	60,009	61,751
Retail trade...	23,275	23,343	23,834	24,204	24,608	24,910	25,564
Transportation and warehousing...........................	39,976	39,272	39,724	40,815	42,270	43,040	44,179
Information..	52,156	52,629	54,155	56,149	58,882	61,128	65,530
Finance and insurance	58,325	57,581	59,821	62,356	65,842	67,204	69,364
Real estate and rental and leasing........................	33,097	33,784	33,071	34,171	35,025	35,665	37,115
Professional, scientific, and technical services	58,692	58,569	59,652	61,676	64,218	64,967	67,328
Management of companies and enterprises..............	80,226	78,337	85,041	87,493	89,815	91,926	94,038
Administrative and waste services........................	26,110	26,445	26,507	27,239	27,488	28,113	28,655
Educational services	31,454	32,112	33,076	34,023	34,823	35,580	35,912
Health care and social assistance........................	41,594	42,487	42,855	43,680	44,508	45,356	45,326
Arts, entertainment, and recreation.......................	27,523	27,283	28,299	29,215	28,369	29,786	30,767
Accommodation and food services........................	13,405	13,369	13,956	14,418	14,859	14,888	15,591
Other services, except public administration............	25,680	25,765	26,596	27,231	27,615	28,361	29,362
Government and government enterprises.................	39,160	39,686	39,910	40,638	40,613	41,273	42,037

Table WI-10. Employment Characteristics by Family Type

(Number, percent.)

Family type and labor force status	2012		2013		2014	
	Total	Families with own children under 18 years	Total	Families with own children under 18 years	Total	Families with own children under 18 years
All Families..	1,461,573	629,141	1,458,482	619,727	1,481,237	633,240
FAMILY TYPE AND LABOR FORCE STATUS						
Married-Couple Families..........................	1,126,874	425,308	1,124,707	420,513	1,128,553	416,204
Both husband and wife in labor force..................	58.5	75.2	58.0	75.4	57.3	75.6
Husband in labor force, wife not in labor force.........	16.2	20.3	16.1	19.8	16.5	19.6
Wife in labor force, husband not in labor force........	8.0	3.6	7.9	3.4	8.2	3.7
Both husband and wife not in labor force.............	17.4	0.9	17.6	1.1	18.1	1.2
Other Families...	334,699	203,833	333,775	199,214	352,684	217,036
Female householder, no husband present.............	70.0	72.4	69.9	72.5	67.7	69.4
In labor force...	52.6	60.7	51.8	61.4	50.1	58.1
Not in labor force.......................................	17.3	11.7	18.1	11.1	17.6	11.3
Male householder, no wife present....................	30.0	27.6	30.1	27.5	32.3	30.6
In labor force...	24.1	25.0	24.9	25.0	26.6	27.9
Not in labor force.......................................	5.9	2.6	5.3	2.5	5.7	2.7

Table WI-11. School Enrollment and Educational Attainment, 2014

(Number, percent.)

Item	State	U.S.
Enrollment		
Total population 3 years and over, enrolled in school................	1,451,402	82,063,714
Enrolled in nursery school or preschool (percent).....................	5.3	6.0
Enrolled in kindergarten (percent)......................................	5.7	5.1
Enrolled in elementary school, grades 1-8 (percent)..................	40.3	40.2
Enrolled in high school, grades 9-12 (percent)........................	20.9	20.7
Enrolled in college or graduate school (percent)......................	27.8	28.0
Attainment		
Total population 25 years and over	3,898,162	213,725,624
Less than ninth grade (percent)...	3.0	5.6
9th to 12th grade, no diploma (percent)...............................	5.7	7.5
High school graduate, including equivalency (percent)...............	31.9	27.7
Some college, no degree (percent)	20.7	21.0
Associate's degree (percent)..	10.3	8.2
Bachelor's degree (percent)...	18.9	18.7
Graduate or professional degree (percent)............................	9.5	11.4
High school graduate or higher (percent)	91.4	86.9
Bachelor's degree or higher (percent)..................................	28.4	30.1

Table WI-12. Public School Characteristics and Educational Indicators

(Number, percent; data derived from National Center of Education Statistics.)

Item	State	U.S.
Public Schools, 2013–2014 (except where noted)		
Number of school districts..	466	18,194
Number of schools...	2,249	98,271
Number of students (in thousands).....................................	874	50,045
Number of teachers (in thousands)	58	3,114
Student-teacher ratio	15.1	16.1
Expenditures per student (dollars), FY 2013..........................	111,867	107,637
Four-year adjusted cohort graduation rate (ACGR)[1,2]	88.6	82.3
Students eligible for free or reduced-price lunch (in thousands)	366	25,596
English language learners (in thousands)	43	4,461
Students age 3 to 21 served under IDEA, part B (in thousands)	123	6,464

Public Schools by Type	Number	Percent of state public schools
Total number of schools...	2,249	100.0
Regular	2,139	95.1
Special education..	11	0.5
Vocational education..	4	0.2
Alternative education..	95	4.2

NOTE: Every school is assigned only one school type based on its instructional emphasis.

[1]ACGR data represents a new method of calculating high-school completion rates and may not be comparable to previous years' data for Averaged Freshmen Graduation Rates (AFGR).

[2]The United States 4-year ACGRs were estimated using both the reported 4-year ACGR data from 49 states and the District of Columbia and using imputed data for Idaho. The estimate for American Indian/Alaska Native students also includes imputed data for Virginia.

Table WI-13. Reported Voting and Registration of the Voting-Age Population, November 2014

(Numbers in thousands, percent.)

Item	Total population	Total citizen population	Registered			Voted		
			Total registered	Percent registered (total population)	Percent registered (total citizen population)	Total voted	Percent voted (total population)	Percent voted (total citizen population)
U.S. Total	239,874	219,941	142,166	59.3	64.6	92,251	38.5	41.9
State Total..............................	4,356	4,232	3,005	69.0	71.0	2,343	53.8	55.4
Sex								
Male	2,136	2,059	1,433	67.1	69.6	1,140	53.4	55.4
Female	2,220	2,173	1,572	70.8	72.4	1,203	54.2	55.4
Race								
White alone................................	3,933	3,826	2,791	71.0	72.9	2,213	56.3	57.8
White, non-Hispanic alone	3,715	3,689	2,727	73.4	73.9	2,170	58.4	58.8
Black alone................................	230	227	129	56.1	56.8	93	40.4	40.9
Asian alone	106	91	30	28.8	33.6	9	8.7	10.2
Hispanic (of any race)	248	168	77	31.0	45.8	53	21.4	31.7
White alone or in combination	4,011	3,904	2,846	71.0	72.9	2,241	55.9	57.4
Black alone or in combination..........	270	267	155	57.6	58.2	110	40.9	41.4
Asian alone or in combination...........	116	101	33	28.5	32.8	12	10.2	11.7
Age								
18 to 24 years................................	489	470	223	45.6	47.4	131	26.9	27.9
25 to 34 years................................	756	724	415	54.9	57.3	287	38.0	39.6
35 to 44 years................................	661	639	456	69.0	71.4	336	50.8	52.6
45 to 64 years................................	1,656	1,604	1,282	77.4	79.9	1,041	62.9	64.9
65 years and over	795	794	629	79.1	79.2	548	68.9	68.9

B = Base is less than 75,000 and therefore too small to show the derived measure.

Table WI-14. Crime

(Number, rate per 100,000. Data are derived from the FBI Uniform Crime Reports.)

Item	State			U.S.[1,2,3,4]		
	2013	2014	Percent change	2013	2014	Percent change
TOTAL POPULATION[5]......................................	5,742,713	5,757,564	0.3	316,128,839	318,857,056	0.9
VIOLENT CRIME						
Number................................	15,570	16,714	7.3	1,163,146	1,165,383	0.2
Rate	271.1	290.3	7.1	367.9	365.5	-0.7
Murder and Nonnegligent Manslaughter						
Number................................	162	165	1.9	14,196	14,249	0.4
Rate	2.8	2.9	3.6	4.5	4.5	-
Rape[6]						
Number................................	1,687	1,674	X	108,612	116,645	X
Rate	29.4	29.1	X	34.4	36.6	X
Robbery						
Number................................	4,834	5,066	4.8	345,031	325,802	-5.6
Rate	84.2	88.0	4.5	109.1	102.2	-6.3
Aggravated Assault						
Number................................	9,278	9,809	5.7	724,149	741,291	2.4
Rate	161.6	170.4	5.4	229.1	232.5	1.5
PROPERTY CRIME						
Number................................	125,688	120,238	-4.3	8,632,512	8,277,829	-4.1
Rate	2,188.7	2,088.3	-4.6	2,730.7	2,596.1	-4.9
Burglary						
Number................................	24,347	21,216	-12.9	1,928,465	1,729,806	-10.3
Rate	424.0	368.5	-13.1	610.0	542.5	-11.1
Larceny-Theft						
Number................................	93,953	89,103	-5.2	6,004,453	5,858,496	-2.4
Rate	1,636.0	1,547.6	-5.4	1,899.4	1,837.3	-3.3
Motor Vehicle Theft						
Number................................	7,388	9,919	34.3	699,594	689,527	-1.4
Rate	128.6	172.3	34.0	221.3	216.2	-2.3

NOTE: Although arson data are included in the trend and clearance tables, sufficient data are not available to estimate totals for this offense. Therefore, no arson data are published in this table.
X = Not applicable.
- = Zero or rounds to zero.
[1]The crime figures have been adjusted.
[2]The data collection methodology for the offense of forcible rape used by the Minnesota state Uniform Crime Reporting (UCR) Program (with the exception of Minneapolis and St. Paul, Minnesota) does not comply with national UCR Program guidelines. Consequently, its figures for forcible rape and violent crime (of which forcible rape is a part) are not published in this table.
[3]Includes offenses reported by the Zoological Police and the Metro Transit Police.
[4]Because of changes in the state's reporting practices, figures are not comparable to previous years' data.
[5]Populations are U.S. Census Bureau provisional estimates as of July 1 of each year.
[6]The figures shown for the offense of rape were estimated using the revised Uniform Crime Reporting (UCR) definition of rape.

Table WI-15. State Government Finances, 2014

(Dollar amounts in thousands, percent distribution.)

Item	Dollars	Percent distribution
Total Revenue	47,260,457	100.0
General revenue	32,441,479	68.6
Intergovernmental revenue	9,255,939	19.6
Taxes	16,410,925	34.7
General sales	4,628,338	9.8
Selective sales	2,731,201	5.8
License taxes	1,040,619	2.2
Individual income tax	6,793,269	14.4
Corporate income tax	986,464	2.1
Other taxes	231,034	0.5
Current charges	4,002,858	8.5
Miscellaneous general revenue	2,771,757	5.9
Utility revenue	0	-
Liquor stores revenue	0	-
Insurance trust revenue[1]	14,818,978	31.4
Total Expenditure	38,583,376	100.0
Intergovernmental expenditure	9,890,474	25.6
Direct expenditure	28,692,902	74.4
Current operation	19,801,580	51.3
Capital outlay	1,880,682	4.9
Insurance benefits and repayments	5,305,934	13.8
Assistance and subsidies	739,713	1.9
Interest on debt	964,993	2.5
Exhibit: Salaries and wages	464,527	1.2
Total Expenditure	38,583,376	100.0
General expenditure	33,235,500	86.1
Intergovernmental expenditure	9,890,474	25.6
Direct expenditure	23,345,026	60.5
General expenditure, by function:		
Education	11,195,357	29.0
Public welfare	9,791,106	25.4
Hospitals	1,457,454	3.8
Health	651,238	1.7
Highways	2,487,163	6.4
Police protection	124,027	0.3
Correction	1,118,646	2.9
Natural resources	681,371	1.8
Parks and recreation	26,862	0.1
Governmental administration	725,948	1.9
Interest on general debt	964,993	2.5
Other and unallocable	4,011,335	10.4
Utility expenditure	41,942	0.1
Liquor stores expenditure	0	-
Insurance trust expenditure	5,305,934	13.8
Debt at End of Fiscal Year	22,367,764	X
Cash and Security Holdings	111,263,199	X

X = Not applicable.
- = Zero or rounds to zero.
[1]Within insurance trust revenue, net earnings of state retirement systems is a calculated statistic (the item code in the data file is X08), and thus can be positive or negative. Net earnings is the sum of earnings on investments plus gains on investments minus losses on investments. The change made in 2002 for asset valuation from book to market value in accordance with Statement 34 of the Governmental Accounting Standards Board is reflected in the calculated statistics.

Table WI-16. State Government Tax Collections, 2014

(Dollars in thousands, percent.)

Item	Dollars	Percent distribution
Total Taxes	16,410,925	100.0
Property taxes	159,069	1.0
Sales and gross receipts	7,359,539	44.8
General sales and gross receipts	4,628,338	28.2
Selective sales and gross receipts	2,731,201	16.6
Alcoholic beverages	57,958	0.4
Amusements	222	-
Insurance premiums	185,502	1.1
Motor fuels	1,000,595	6.1
Pari-mutuels	0	
Public utilities	379,549	2.3
Tobacco products	640,728	3.9
Other selective sales	466,647	2.8
Licenses	1,040,619	6.3
Alcoholic beverages	1,785	-
Amusements	666	-
Corporations in general	20,628	0.1
Hunting and fishing	66,962	0.4
Motor vehicle	467,502	2.8
Motor vehicle operators	39,691	0.2
Public utilities	72,199	0.4
Occupation and business, NEC	366,526	2.2
Other licenses	4,660	-
Income taxes	7,779,733	47.4
Individual income	6,793,269	41.4
Corporation net income	986,464	6.0
Other taxes	71,965	0.4
Death and gift	0	-
Documentary and stock transfer	51,179	0.3
Severance	8,984	0.1
Taxes, NEC	11,802	0.1

- = Zero or rounds to zero.

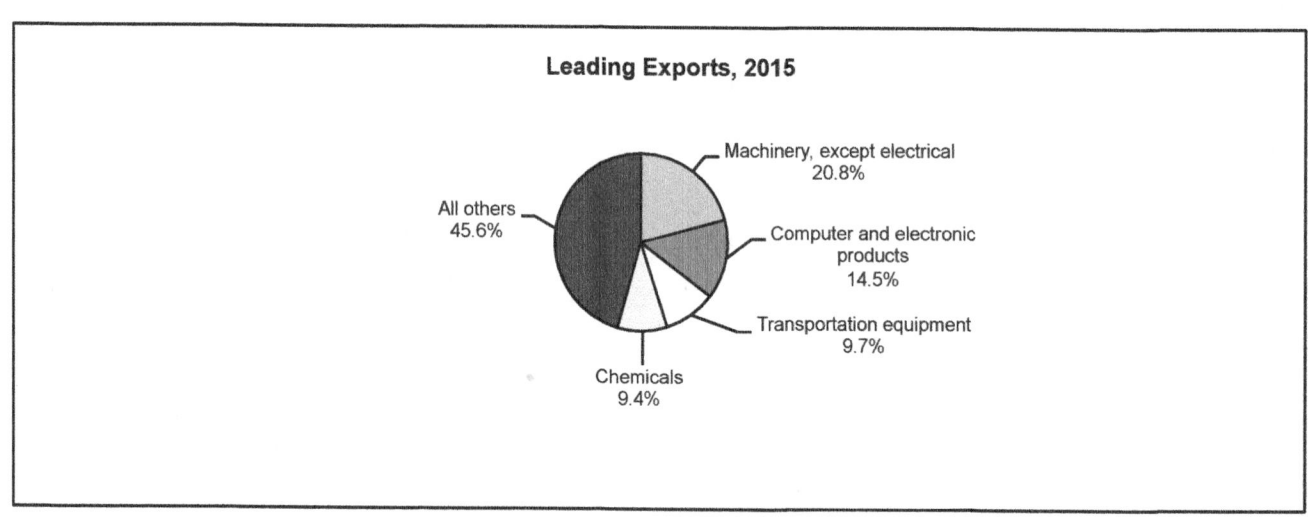

Leading Exports, 2015

- Machinery, except electrical 20.8%
- Computer and electronic products 14.5%
- Transportation equipment 9.7%
- Chemicals 9.4%
- All others 45.6%

WYOMING

Facts and Figures

Location: Western United States; bordered on the N by Montana, on the E by South Dakota and Nebraska, on the S by Colorado and Utah, and on the W by Utah and Idaho

Area: 97,814 sq. mi. (253,336 sq. km.); rank—10th

Population: 586,107 (2015 est.); rank—51st

Principal Cities: capital—Cheyenne; largest—Cheyenne

Statehood: July 10, 1890; 44th state

U.S. Congress: 2 senators, 1 representative

State Motto: Equal Rights

State Song: "Wyoming"

State Nicknames: The Equality State; The Cowboy State

Abbreviations: WY; Wyo.

State Symbols: flower—Indian paintbrush; tree—cottonwood; bird—Western meadowlark

At a Glance

- With an increase in population of 3.8 percent, Wyoming ranked 22nd among the states in growth from 2010 to 2015.

- Wyoming's violent crime rate in 2014 was 195.5 per 100,000 population, the third lowest rate in the country.

- Wyoming's median household income in 2014 was $57,055, and 11.2 percent of the population lived below the poverty level.

- Wyoming had the lowest childhood poverty rate in the country in 2014, with 12.8 percent of children under 18 years of age living in poverty.

- In 2014, 12.0 percent of Wyoming residents did not have health insurance, compared to 11.7 percent of total U.S. residents.

Table WY-1. Population by Age, Sex, Race, and Hispanic Origin

(Number, percent, except where noted.)

Sex, age, race, and Hispanic origin	2000	2010	2015[1]	Average annual percent change, 2010–2015
Total Population	493,782	563,626	586,107	0.3
Percent of total U.S. population	0.2	0.2	0.2	X
Sex				
Male	248,374	287,437	298,901	0.3
Female	245,408	276,189	287,206	0.3
Age				
Under 5 years	30,940	40,203	38,395	-0.3
5 to 19 years	114,406	111,310	114,802	0.2
20 to 64 years	290,743	342,023	348,211	0.1
65 years and over	57,693	70,090	84,699	1.4
Median age (years)	36.2	36.8	36.9	-
Race and Hispanic Origin				
One race				
White	454,670	529,110	543,292	0.2
Black	3,722	5,135	8,286	3.5
American Indian and Alaska Native	11,133	14,457	15,757	0.6
Asian	2,771	4,649	6,072	1.9
Native Hawaiian or Other Pacific Islander	302	521	676	1.9
Two or more races	8,883	9,754	12,024	1.5
Hispanic (of any race)	31,669	52,112	58,207	0.8

X = Not applicable.
- = Zero or rounds to zero.
[1] Population figures for 2015 are July 1 estimates. The 2010 estimates are taken from the 2010 Census.

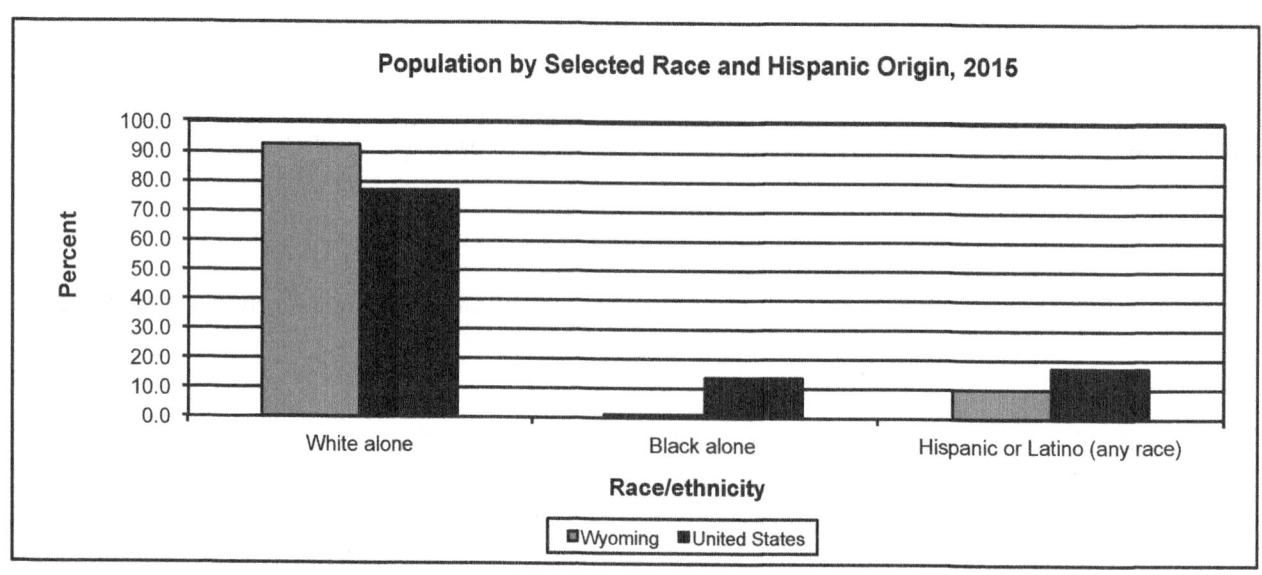

Table WY-2. Marital Status

(Number, percent distribution.)

Sex, age, race, and Hispanic origin	2000	2010	2014
Males, 15 Years and Over	195,412	228,725	234,150
Never married	26.6	29.0	30.3
Now married, except separated	58.8	56.2	53.5
Separated	1.0	1.3	1.6
Widowed	2.3	2.4	2.4
Divorced	11.3	11.2	12.2
Females, 15 Years and Over	195,433	220,169	226,132
Never married	20.0	20.7	22.8
Now married, except separated	57.5	55.1	53.8
Separated	1.3	2.0	1.6
Widowed	9.2	8.6	8.3
Divorced	12.0	13.6	13.4

Table WY-3. Households and Housing Characteristics

(Number, percent, dollars.)

Item	2000	2010	2014	Average annual percent change, 2000–2014
Total Households..	193,608	222,803	232,594	1.4
Family households	130,497	147,394	149,032	1.0
Married-couple family	106,179	119,756	117,040	0.7
Other family	24,318	27,638	31,992	2.3
Male householder, no wife present.............	7,481	7,804	12,147	4.5
Female householder, no husband present.....	16,837	19,834	19,845	1.3
Nonfamily households	63,111	75,409	83,562	2.3
Householder living alone............................	50,980	61,775	67,081	2.3
Householder not living alone......................	12,131	13,634	16,481	2.6
Housing Characteristics				
Total housing units....................................	223,854	262,286	268,205	1.4
Occupied housing units	193,608	222,803	232,594	1.4
Owner occupied	135,514	155,278	155,617	1.1
Renter occupied	58,094	67,525	76,977	2.3
Average household size...............................	2.48	2.47	2.45	-0.1
Financial Characteristics				
Median gross rent of renter-occupied housing	437	693	792	5.8
Median monthly owner costs for housing units with a mortgage	825	1,300	1,311	4.2
Median value of owner-occupied housing units...........................	96,600	180,100	201,000	7.7

Table WY-4. Migration, Origin, and Language

(Number, percent.)

Characteristic	State			U.S.		
	2013	2014	Percent change	2013	2014	Percent change
Residence 1 Year Ago						
Population 1 year and over	575,933	577,782	0.3	312,432,820	315,095,393	0.9
Same house	81.5	82.3	X	85.0	85.1	X
Different house in the U.S.	18.1	17.4	X	14.4	14.3	X
Same county	9.9	10.2	X	8.9	8.7	X
Different county	8.3	7.2	X	5.5	5.6	X
Same state	3.5	2.7	X	3.2	3.3	X
Different state	4.8	4.5	X	2.3	2.3	X
Abroad	0.3	0.3	X	0.6	0.6	X
Place of Birth						
Native born	564,629	561,675	-0.5	274,780,773	276,465,262	0.6
Male...	51.2	51.0	X	49.3	49.3	X
Female..	48.8	49.0	X	50.7	50.7	X
Foreign born	18,029	22,478	24.7	41,348,066	42,391,794	2.5
Male...	45.9	48.9	X	48.8	48.7	X
Female..	54.1	51.1	X	51.2	51.3	X
Foreign born; naturalized U.S. citizen.......................	7,083	7,778	9.8	19,294,710	19,984,738	3.6
Male...	28.1	43.8	X	45.9	45.9	X
Female..	71.9	56.2	X	54.1	54.1	X
Foreign born; not a U.S. citizen	10,946	14,700	34.3	22,053,356	22,407,056	1.6
Male...	57.4	51.6	X	51.3	51.2	X
Female..	42.6	48.4	X	48.7	48.8	X
Entered 2010 or later	13.0	13.5	X	9.7	12.3	X
Entered 2000 to 2009	40.5	36.3	X	29.4	28.6	X
Entered before 2000...	46.5	50.2	X	61.0	59.1	X
World Region of Birth, Foreign						
Foreign-born population, excluding population born at sea	18,029	22,478	24.7	41,347,945	42,390,705	2.5
Europe...	19.6	17.3	X	11.6	11.2	X
Asia...	23.3	17.7	X	29.5	30.1	X
Africa..	7.4	5.4	X	4.4	4.6	X
Oceania...	2.5	3.1	X	0.5	0.6	X
Latin America...	42.8	51.3	X	51.9	51.6	X
North America...	4.5	5.2	X	2.0	1.9	X
Language Spoken at Home and Ability to Speak English						
Population 5 years and over..	544,279	546,224	0.4	296,358,760	299,084,046	0.9
English only	93.7	93.0	X	79.2	78.9	X
Language other than English....................................	6.3	7.0	X	20.8	21.1	X
Speaks English less than "very well"......................	1.8	2.0	X	8.5	8.6	X

X = Not applicable.
- = Zero or rounds to zero.

Table WY-5. Median Income and Poverty Status, 2014

(Number, percent, except as noted.)

Characteristic	State		U.S.	
	Number	Percent	Number	Percent
Median Income				
Households (dollars)...	57,055	X	53,657	X
Families (dollars)	72,460	X	65,910	X
Below Poverty Level (All People)	63,774	11.2	48,208,387	15.5
Sex				
Male...	27,357	9.4	21,590,918	14.2
Female	36,417	13.0	26,617,469	16.8
Age				
Under 18 years..	17,332	12.8	15,686,012	21.7
Related children under 18 years.....................	16,262	12.1	15,372,705	21.3
18 to 64 years...	41,614	11.7	28,267,482	14.6
65 years and over	4,828	6.2	4,254,893	9.5

X = Not applicable.

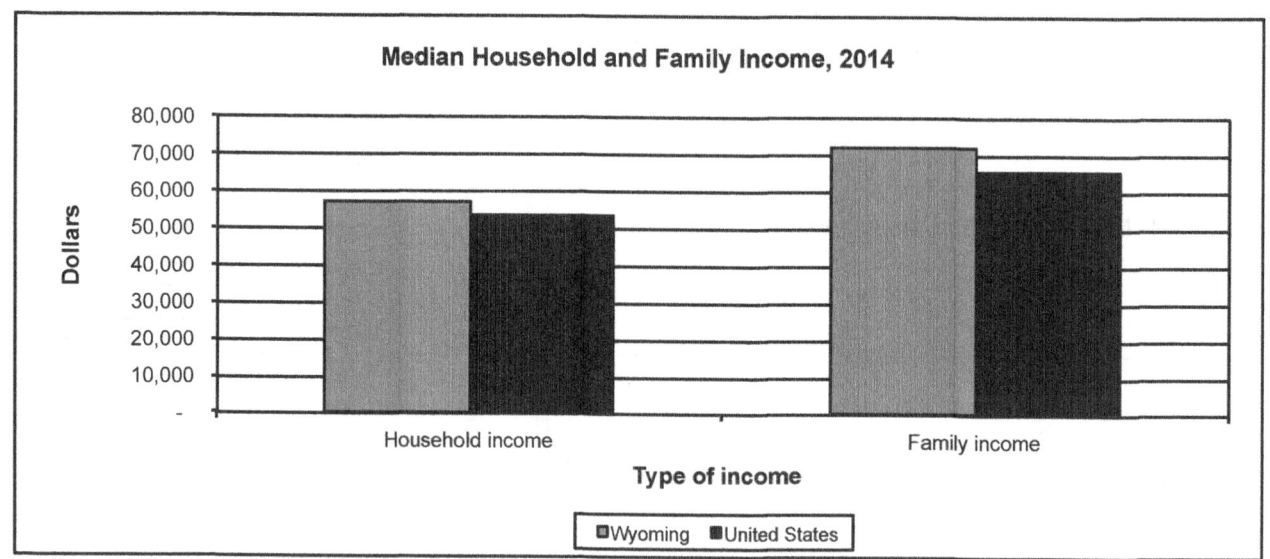

Median Household and Family Income, 2014

Table WY-6. Health Insurance Coverage Status for the Civilian Noninstitutionalized Population and Children Under 18 Years of Age

(Numbers in thousands, percent.)

Item	2006	2007	2008	2009	2010	2011	2012	2013	2014
Civilian Noninstitutionalized Population	516	518	523	534	555	559	567	573	575
Covered by Private or Public Insurance									
Number...	441	447	451	453	472	473	480	496	506
Percent...	85.4	86.4	86.2	84.8	85.1	84.6	84.6	86.6	88.0
Not Covered									
Number...	75	70	72	81	83	86	87	77	69
Percent...	14.6	13.6	13.8	15.2	14.9	15.4	15.4	13.4	12.0
Percent in the U.S. not covered..............................	15.8	15.3	15.1	15.1	15.5	15.1	14.8	14.5	11.7
Children Under 18 Years of Age	123	127	127	128	136	135	136	139	137
Covered by Private or Public Insurance									
Number...	113	115	116	117	125	123	123	131	129
Percent...	91.8	90.4	91.3	91.0	92.1	91.4	90.7	94.3	94.1
Not Covered									
Number...	10	12	11	11	11	12	13	8	8
Percent...	8.2	9.6	8.7	9.0	7.9	8.6	9.3	5.7	5.9
Percent in the U.S. not covered..............................	11.7	11.0	9.7	8.6	8.0	7.5	7.2	7.1	6.0

Table WY-7. Employment Status by Demographic Group, 2015

(Numbers in thousands, percent.)

Characteristic	Civilian noninstitutional population	Civilian labor force		Employed		Unemployed	
		Number	Percent of population	Number	Percent of population	Number	Percent of population
Total.............................	452	306	67.8	294	65.1	13	4.1
Sex							
Male	229	170	74.3	163	71.1	7	4.4
Female	223	136	61.2	131	58.9	5	3.7
Race, Sex, and Hispanic Origin							
White	426	288	67.7	277	65.0	11	3.9
Male	216	160	74.1	153	71.0	7	4.2
Female	210	129	61.1	124	59.0	5	3.6
Black or African American....................	NA	NA	NA	NA	NA	NA	NA
Male	NA	NA	NA	NA	NA	NA	NA
Female	NA	NA	NA	NA	NA	NA	NA
Hispanic or Latino ethnicity[1]	34	25	73.9	24	70.4	1	4.8
Male	18	14	78.9	13	75.0	1	5.2
Female	16	11	68.5	11	65.4	1	4.3
Age							
16 to 19 years....................	27	12	45.0	11	39.1	2	13.0
20 to 24 years....................	40	32	79.1	29	73.4	2	7.3
25 to 34 years....................	82	68	83.1	66	80.2	2	3.4
35 to 44 years....................	70	60	85.4	58	82.1	2	3.7
45 to 54 years....................	74	62	84.5	61	82.4	2	2.6
55 to 64 years....................	81	56	68.6	53	65.9	2	4.0
65 years and over	78	17	21.7	17	21.3	...	1.8

NOTE: Data in Table 7 are from the Current Population Survey (CPS) and do not match the estimates in Table 8. See notes and definitions for further information.
[1] May be of any race.
NA = Not available.
... = Fewer than 500 persons.

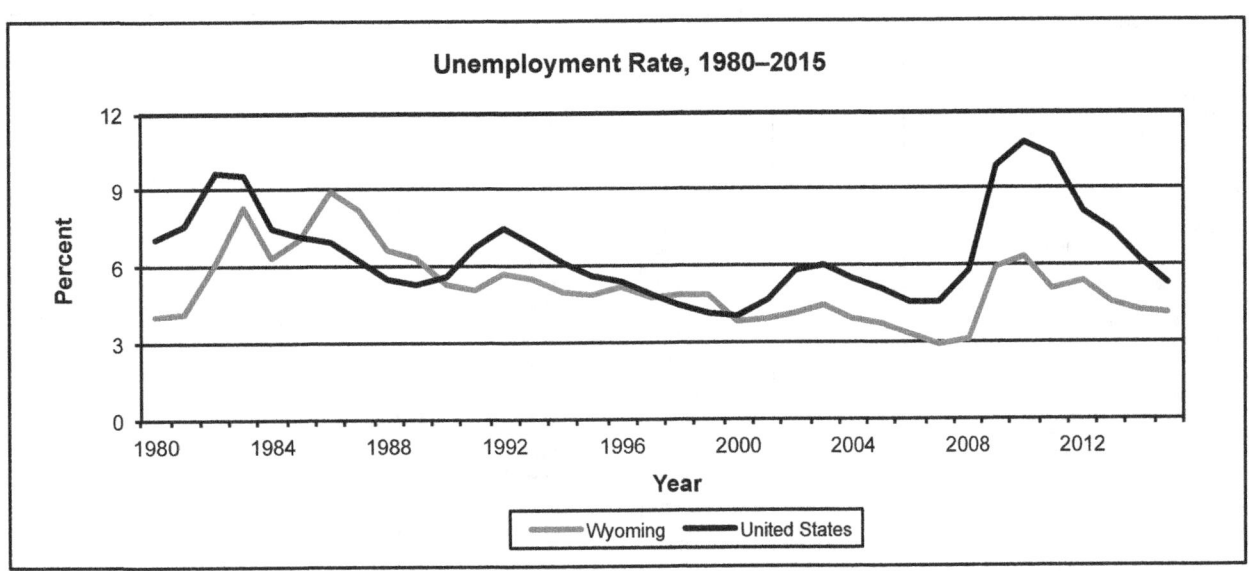

Unemployment Rate, 1980–2015

Table WY-8. Employment Status of the Civilian Noninstitutional Population Age 16 Years and Over

(Number, percent.)

Year	Civilian labor force	Civilian participation rate	Employed	Unemployed	Unemployment rate
2007....................	286,560	71.0	278,486	8,074	2.8
2008....................	293,279	71.4	284,310	8,969	3.1
2009....................	300,120	71.8	281,150	18,970	6.3
2010....................	303,297	70.4	283,744	19,553	6.4
2011....................	306,815	70.2	289,019	17,796	5.8
2012....................	307,425	69.2	291,076	16,349	5.3
2013....................	306,571	68.3	292,157	14,414	4.7
2014....................	306,933	68.1	294,207	12,726	4.1
2015....................	306,012	67.7	293,262	12,750	4.2

Table WY-9. Employment and Average Wages by Industry

(Estimates through 2010 are based on the 2007 North American Industry Classification System [NAICS]. Estimates from 2011 onward are based on the 2012 NAICS.)

Industry	2008	2009	2010	2011	2012	2013	2014
				Number of jobs			
Wage and Salary Employment by Industry..................	307,460	295,383	291,969	295,870	298,049	299,516	304,323
Farm Wage and Salary Employment........................	2,993	2,805	2,878	3,220	3,334	3,432	3,561
Nonfarm Wage and Salary Employment....................	304,467	292,578	289,091	292,650	294,715	296,084	300,762
Private wage and salary employment.......................	232,960	218,671	214,098	217,690	219,151	220,347	225,275
Forestry, fishing, and related activities........................	888	868	902	956	970	1,068	1,173
Mining..	29,320	25,344	24,933	27,215	27,556	26,459	27,121
Utilities..	2,507	2,493	2,483	2,489	2,471	2,482	2,489
Construction	29,299	25,036	23,470	22,221	22,268	22,629	24,514
Manufacturing...	9,964	9,125	8,727	9,185	9,362	9,468	9,822
Durable goods manufacturing...............................	5,209	4,589	4,265	4,617	4,734	4,702	4,876
Nondurable goods manufacturing..........................	4,755	4,536	4,462	4,568	4,628	4,766	4,946
Wholesale trade	9,174	8,809	8,529	8,901	9,196	9,297	9,540
Retail trade..	32,605	31,156	29,989	29,639	29,722	30,079	30,054
Transportation and warehousing................................	12,364	11,668	11,516	12,077	12,307	12,323	13,107
Information	4,011	3,960	3,891	3,850	3,917	3,808	3,776
Finance and insurance	7,441	7,336	7,169	7,108	7,099	7,185	7,189
Real estate and rental and leasing.............................	4,539	4,219	4,101	4,115	4,159	4,445	4,531
Professional, scientific, and technical services	10,064	9,432	9,300	9,236	9,303	9,344	9,606
Management of companies and enterprises..................	801	773	857	865	956	1,032	1,013
Administrative and waste services	8,070	7,380	7,332	7,920	7,916	7,920	7,952
Educational services	1,876	1,984	2,101	2,077	2,032	2,114	2,101
Health care and social assistance...............................	22,663	23,587	23,903	24,147	24,184	24,366	24,494
Arts, entertainment, and recreation.............................	2,896	2,798	2,786	2,835	2,857	2,937	3,041
Accommodation and food services.............................	31,931	30,425	30,194	30,561	31,254	31,877	32,509
Other services, except public administration..................	12,547	12,278	11,915	12,293	11,622	11,514	11,243
Government and government enterprises	71,507	73,907	74,993	74,960	75,564	75,737	75,487
				Dollars			
Average Wages and Salaries by Industry	42,235	41,416	42,587	44,033	45,260	45,751	47,361
Average Farm Wages and Salaries	35,704	42,300	35,817	33,215	27,419	39,899	41,993
Average Nonfarm Wages and Salaries	42,300	41,407	42,655	44,152	45,461	45,818	47,425
Average private wages and salaries..........................	42,439	40,933	42,410	44,204	45,846	46,274	47,902
Forestry, fishing, and related activities........................	21,499	21,665	22,879	24,353	24,779	25,020	25,878
Mining..	76,850	74,342	77,821	80,948	83,511	85,612	88,924
Utilities..	76,946	78,796	81,400	84,114	84,567	85,677	88,761
Construction	48,963	46,153	48,298	48,334	50,202	51,190	52,273
Manufacturing...	50,023	51,068	52,997	56,101	57,356	58,893	62,268
Durable goods manufacturing...............................	44,921	45,518	47,135	48,502	50,248	50,855	53,642
Nondurable goods manufacturing..........................	55,613	56,682	58,601	63,781	64,627	66,823	70,771
Wholesale trade	55,730	53,876	55,449	57,451	59,062	59,328	64,142
Retail trade..	25,637	25,446	25,975	26,736	28,082	27,832	28,561
Transportation and warehousing................................	53,998	51,566	53,696	56,461	56,305	58,138	58,014
Information	38,495	38,927	39,983	41,812	43,207	44,140	45,832
Finance and insurance	50,883	47,880	49,398	50,982	54,158	55,239	57,898
Real estate and rental and leasing.............................	38,304	36,601	38,757	42,987	45,412	46,571	48,832
Professional, scientific, and technical services	51,820	52,648	53,936	55,925	58,844	59,361	62,445
Management of companies and enterprises..................	99,074	95,708	103,743	105,391	114,687	113,459	100,378
Administrative and waste services	30,079	29,254	29,052	32,177	32,015	31,878	32,615
Educational services	26,960	27,387	27,683	28,898	29,673	29,246	29,773
Health care and social assistance...............................	38,401	38,435	39,328	40,364	41,861	41,587	42,552
Arts, entertainment, and recreation.............................	20,696	21,594	21,526	21,483	21,325	21,905	23,727
Accommodation and food services.............................	18,401	17,977	18,517	19,058	19,830	20,421	21,030
Other services, except public administration..................	28,269	28,212	30,297	30,209	32,779	33,344	33,113
Government and government enterprises	41,846	42,811	43,354	44,001	44,345	44,494	46,001

Table WY-10. Employment Characteristics by Family Type

(Number, percent.)

Family type and labor force status	2012		2013		2014	
	Total	Families with own children under 18 years	Total	Families with own children under 18 years	Total	Families with own children under 18 years
All Families..........................	146,745	63,649	148,556	64,587	148,660	63,332
FAMILY TYPE AND LABOR FORCE STATUS						
Married-Couple Families..........................	115,398	43,849	118,017	45,915	116,668	45,397
Both husband and wife in labor force..................	55.7	67.2	57.6	70.9	57.7	68.0
Husband in labor force, wife not in labor force	22.0	30.0	19.8	25.6	19.8	26.8
Wife in labor force, husband not in labor force	6.9	2.1	7.1	1.9	7.2	4.5
Both husband and wife not in labor force..............	15.4	0.8	14.9	1.3	15.3	0.6
Other Families	31,347	19,800	30,539	18,672	31,992	17,935
Female householder, no husband present..............	67.2	66.7	66.3	70.4	62.0	64.0
In labor force..........................	51.7	55.6	49.2	60.8	45.4	51.7
Not in labor force	15.5	11.0	17.1	9.7	16.6	12.3
Male householder, no wife present..............	32.8	33.3	33.7	29.6	38.0	36.0
In labor force..........................	28.3	31.6	28.6	28.0	30.2	32.8
Not in labor force	4.5	1.7	5.1	1.5	7.8	3.2

Table WY-11. School Enrollment and Educational Attainment, 2014

(Number, percent.)

Item	State	U.S.
Enrollment		
Total population 3 years and over, enrolled in school..................	144,582	82,063,714
Enrolled in nursery school or preschool (percent)	5.8	6.0
Enrolled in kindergarten (percent)	5.8	5.1
Enrolled in elementary school, grades 1-8 (percent)..................	42.1	40.2
Enrolled in high school, grades 9-12 (percent)..................	19.8	20.7
Enrolled in college or graduate school (percent)..................	26.5	28.0
Attainment		
Total population 25 years and over	388,962	213,725,624
Less than ninth grade (percent)..................	2.2	5.6
9th to 12th grade, no diploma (percent)..................	5.3	7.5
High school graduate, including equivalency (percent)..................	27.4	27.7
Some college, no degree (percent)	27.9	21.0
Associate's degree (percent)..................	10.7	8.2
Bachelor's degree (percent)..................	17.9	18.7
Graduate or professional degree (percent)..................	8.7	11.4
High school graduate or higher (percent)..................	92.6	86.9
Bachelor's degree or higher (percent)..................	26.6	30.1

Table WY-12. Public School Characteristics and Educational Indicators

(Number, percent; data derived from National Center of Education Statistics.)

Item	State	U.S.
Public Schools, 2013–2014 (except where noted)		
Number of school districts..................	61	18,194
Number of schools..................	366	98,271
Number of students (in thousands)	93	50,045
Number of teachers (in thousands)	8	3,114
Student-teacher ratio	12.3	16.1
Expenditures per student (dollars), FY 2013..................	15,815	107,637
Four-year adjusted cohort graduation rate (ACGR)[1,2]	78.6	82.3
Students eligible for free or reduced-price lunch (in thousands)	35	25,596
English language learners (in thousands)	3	4,461
Students age 3 to 21 served under IDEA, part B (in thousands)	12	6,464

Public Schools by Type	Number	Percent of state public schools
Total number of schools..................	366	100.0
Regular	339	92.6
Special education..................	3	0.8
Vocational education..................	0	-
Alternative education..................	24	6.6

NOTE: Every school is assigned only one school type based on its instructional emphasis.
[1]ACGR data represents a new method of calculating high-school completion rates and may not be comparable to previous years' data for Averaged Freshmen Graduation Rates (AFGR).VC
[2]The United States 4-year ACGRs were estimated using both the reported 4-year ACGR data from 49 states and the District of Columbia and using imputed data for Idaho. The estimate for American Indian/Alaska Native students also includes imputed data for Virginia.
- = Zero or rounds to zero.

Table WY-13. Reported Voting and Registration of the Voting-Age Population, November 2014

(Numbers in thousands, percent.)

Item	Total population	Total citizen population	Registered			Voted		
			Total registered	Percent registered (total population)	Percent registered (total citizen population)	Total voted	Percent voted (total population)	Percent voted (total citizen population)
U.S. Total	239,874	219,941	142,166	59.3	64.6	92,251	38.5	41.9
State Total............................	441	427	241	54.7	56.5	172	39.1	40.3
Sex								
Male...............................	223	215	117	52.6	54.6	85	38.0	39.5
Female............................	217	212	124	56.9	58.4	87	40.2	41.2
Race								
White alone........................	407	399	227	55.8	57.0	164	40.3	41.1
White, non-Hispanic alone...........	384	381	218	56.7	57.2	158	41.0	41.4
Black alone........................	11	9	5	(B)	(B)	3	(B)	(B)
Asian alone........................	3	1	-	(B)	(B)	-	(B)	(B)
Hispanic (of any race).............	29	20	9	(B)	(B)	6	(B)	(B)
White alone or in combination.........	414	406	230	55.5	56.6	166	40.1	41.0
Black alone or in combination.........	11	9	5	(B)	(B)	3	(B)	(B)
Asian alone or in combination.........	4	2	-	(B)	(B)	-	(B)	(B)
Age								
18 to 24 years.....................	52	51	14	(B)	(B)	7	(B)	(B)
25 to 34 years.....................	80	75	39	48.5	51.6	21	26.7	28.4
35 to 44 years.....................	73	70	36	(B)	(B)	21	(B)	(B)
45 to 64 years.....................	153	151	95	62.5	63.1	75	49.0	49.5
65 years and over..................	82	80	57	68.9	71.1	48	58.3	60.1

- = Zero or rounds to zero.
B = Base is less than 75,000 and therefore too small to show the derived measure.

Table WY-14. Crime

(Number, rate per 100,000. Data are derived from the FBI Uniform Crime Reports.)

Item	State			U.S.[1,2,3,4]		
	2013	2014	Percent change	2013	2014	Percent change
TOTAL POPULATION[5].....................	582,658	584,153	0.3	316,128,839	318,857,056	0.9
VIOLENT CRIME						
Number..............................	1,152	1,142	-0.9	1,163,146	1,165,383	0.2
Rate................................	197.7	195.5	-1.1	367.9	365.5	-0.7
Murder and Nonnegligent Manslaughter						
Number..............................	17	16	-5.9	14,196	14,249	0.4
Rate................................	2.9	2.7	-6.9	4.5	4.5	-
Rape[6]						
Number..............................	187	174	X	108,612	116,645	X
Rate................................	32.1	29.8	X	34.4	36.6	X
Robbery						
Number..............................	75	53	-29.3	345,031	325,802	-5.6
Rate................................	12.9	9.1	-29.5	109.1	102.2	-6.3
Aggravated Assault						
Number..............................	916	899	-1.9	724,149	741,291	2.4
Rate................................	157.2	153.9	-2.1	229.1	232.5	1.5
PROPERTY CRIME						
Number..............................	12,809	11,477	-10.4	8,632,512	8,277,829	-4.1
Rate................................	2,198.4	1,964.7	-10.6	2,730.7	2,596.1	-4.9
Burglary						
Number..............................	1,955	1,689	-13.6	1,928,465	1,729,806	-10.3
Rate................................	335.5	289.1	-13.8	610.0	542.5	-11.1
Larceny-Theft						
Number..............................	10,276	9,185	-10.6	6,004,453	5,858,496	-2.4
Rate................................	1,763.6	1,572.4	-10.8	1,899.4	1,837.3	-3.3
Motor Vehicle Theft						
Number..............................	578	603	4.3	699,594	689,527	-1.4
Rate................................	99.2	103.2	4.0	221.3	216.2	-2.3

NOTE: Although arson data are included in the trend and clearance tables, sufficient data are not available to estimate totals for this offense. Therefore, no arson data are published in this table.
X = Not applicable.
- = Zero or rounds to zero.
[1]The crime figures have been adjusted.
[2]The data collection methodology for the offense of forcible rape used by the Minnesota state Uniform Crime Reporting (UCR) Program (with the exception of Minneapolis and St. Paul, Minnesota) does not comply with national UCR Program guidelines. Consequently, its figures for forcible rape and violent crime (of which forcible rape is a part) are not published in this table.
[3]Includes offenses reported by the Zoological Police and the Metro Transit Police.
[4]Because of changes in the state's reporting practices, figures are not comparable to previous years' data.
[5]Populations are U.S. Census Bureau provisional estimates as of July 1 of each year.
[6]The figures shown for the offense of rape were estimated using the revised Uniform Crime Reporting (UCR) definition of rape.

Table WY-15. State Government Finances, 2014

(Dollar amounts in thousands, percent distribution.)

Item	Dollars	Percent distribution
Total Revenue	7,450,967	100.0
General revenue	5,780,141	77.6
Intergovernmental revenue	2,208,034	29.6
Taxes	2,263,387	30.4
General sales	765,543	10.3
Selective sales	160,214	2.2
License taxes	148,092	2.0
Individual income tax	0	-
Corporate income tax	0	-
Other taxes	1,189,538	16.0
Current charges	200,408	2.7
Miscellaneous general revenue	1,108,312	14.9
Utility revenue	0	-
Liquor stores revenue	104674	1.4
Insurance trust revenue[1]	1,566,152	21.0
Total Expenditure	5,894,985	100.0
Intergovernmental expenditure	1,913,090	32.5
Direct expenditure	3,981,895	67.5
Current operation	2,737,907	46.4
Capital outlay	401,742	6.8
Insurance benefits and repayments	737,276	12.5
Assistance and subsidies	69,790	1.2
Interest on debt	35,180	0.6
Exhibit: Salaries and wages	741,567	12.6
Total Expenditure	5,894,985	100.0
General expenditure	5,065,692	85.9
Intergovernmental expenditure	1,913,090	32.5
Direct expenditure	3,152,602	53.5
General expenditure, by function:		
Education	1,762,639	29.9
Public welfare	792,437	13.4
Hospitals	3,708	0.1
Health	271,628	4.6
Highways	521,684	8.8
Police protection	46,366	0.8
Correction	143,777	2.4
Natural resources	359,250	6.1
Parks and recreation	27,726	0.5
Governmental administration	238,174	4.0
Interest on general debt	35,180	0.6
Other and unallocable	863,123	14.6
Utility expenditure	0	-
Liquor stores expenditure	92017	1.6
Insurance trust expenditure	737,276	12.5
Debt at End of Fiscal Year	929,532	X
Cash and Security Holdings	30,215,997	X

X = Not applicable.
- = Zero or rounds to zero.
[1]Within insurance trust revenue, net earnings of state retirement systems is a calculated statistic (the item code in the data file is X08), and thus can be positive or negative. Net earnings is the sum of earnings on investments plus gains on investments minus losses on investments. The change made in 2002 for asset valuation from book to market value in accordance with Statement 34 of the Governmental Accounting Standards Board is reflected in the calculated statistics.

Table WY-16. State Government Tax Collections, 2014

(Dollars in thousands, percent.)

Item	Dollars	Percent distribution
Total Taxes	2,263,387	100.0
Property taxes	300,096	13.3
Sales and gross receipts	925,757	40.9
General sales and gross receipts	765,543	33.8
Selective sales and gross receipts	160,214	7.1
Alcoholic beverages	1,828	0.1
Amusements	0	-
Insurance premiums	25,310	1.1
Motor fuels	100,889	4.5
Pari-mutuels	385	-
Public utilities	4,638	0.2
Tobacco products	24,490	1.1
Other selective sales	2,674	0.1
Licenses	148,092	6.5
Alcoholic beverages	0	-
Amusements	0	-
Corporations in general	13,378	0.6
Hunting and fishing	34,371	1.5
Motor vehicle	71,954	3.2
Motor vehicle operators	2,217	0.1
Public utilities	0	-
Occupation and business, NEC	26,172	1.2
Other licenses	0	-
Income taxes	0	-
Individual income	X	X
Corporation net income	X	X
Other taxes	889,442	39.3
Death and gift	0	-
Documentary and stock transfer	0	-
Severance	883,025	39.0
Taxes, NEC	6,417	0.3

X = Not applicable.
- = Zero or rounds to zero.

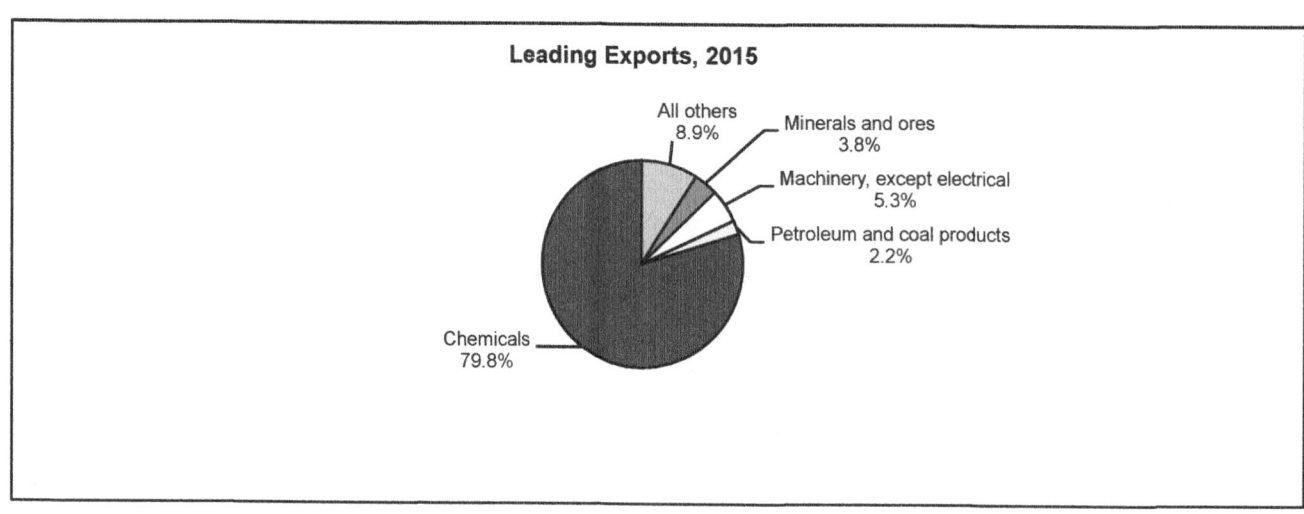

Leading Exports, 2015

All others 8.9%
Minerals and ores 3.8%
Machinery, except electrical 5.3%
Petroleum and coal products 2.2%
Chemicals 79.8%

NOTES AND DEFINITIONS

The state chapters in this book follow a standard plan of organization, and the same data sources are used for the tables and figures found in each chapter. These notes describe the standard data sources, which are presented by topic in the order in which they appear in each chapter. Definitions, brief descriptions of methodology, and sources of additional information are also provided.

Symbols used are included in the footnotes of the tables.

Table 1.
Source: U.S. Department of Commerce. U.S Census Bureau. 2000 and 2010 Decennial Census. Census statistics, 2015.
<http://factfinder.census.gov/>.

Population estimates data are accessed through American FactFinder from the U.S. Census Bureau, as well as from the Census Bureau itself. The data for average annual percent change, 2010–2015, were calculated by the editor.

Population estimates and the decennial census. Population data are estimates produced by the Census Bureau. The Bureau's Population Estimates Program (PEP) produces estimates of the population as of July 1 for each year following the most recently published decennial census (the actual physical count of the population made every ten years, which is described below). Existing data on births, deaths, and domestic and international immigration are used to update the decennial census base. PEP estimates are used to set federal funding allocations, update national surveys, and monitor recent demographic changes.

Noncitizens residing in the United States are included, regardless of their immigration status.

Persons temporarily away from their usual residence on Census Day (April 1), for reasons such as vacation or business trips, were counted as being at their usual residence. People who live at more than one residence during the week, month, or year were counted as being at the place in which they lived most of the year. However, people without a usual residence were counted as being where they were staying on Census Day.

Age, sex, race, and ethnicity. While estimates of the age and sex of the population are straightforward, estimates of race and ethnicity are not. Decennial census data on race and ethnicity are based on self-identification by the respondent, and the same respondent may answer differently on separate occasions. On the 2000 decennial census, respondents could report more than one race; in previous censuses, respondents had to identify themselves as belonging to only one race.

The Census Bureau treats Hispanic or Latino origin as a separate and distinct concept from race. Beginning with the 2000 census, a separate self-identification question was asked regarding Hispanic or Latino origin. Persons of Hispanic or Latino origin are those who classified themselves as belonging to one of the specific categories listed on the questionnaire—Mexican, Puerto Rican, Cuban, or Other Spanish/Hispanic origin (including those whose origins are from Spain, the Spanish-speaking countries of Central and South America, or the Dominican Republic). People who are Hispanic may be of any race, and people in each race group may be Hispanic. The overlap of race and Hispanic origin is a major comparability issue, because Hispanics may be of any race. For a further discussion of this issue, see: U.S. Census Bureau. *U.S. Census Bureau Guidance on the Presentation and Comparison of Race and Hispanic Origin Data.* (June 12, 2003.) <http://www.census.gov/population/www/socdemo/compraceho.html>.

Table 2.
Source: U.S. Department of Commerce. U.S Census Bureau. 2000 Decennial Census. American Community Survey, 2000, 2010, and 2014.
<http://factfinder.census.gov/>.

Data on marital status was tabulated for persons 15 years and over. Marital status was reported for each person as either "now married," "widowed," "divorced," "separated," or "never married." Individuals who were living together (unmarried people, people in commonlaw marriages) reported the marital status they considered most appropriate.

Now Married, Except Separated. Includes people whose current marriage has not ended through widowhood, divorce, or separation (regardless of previous marital history). The category may also include couples who live together or people in common-law marriages if they consider this category the most appropriate. In certain tabulations, currently married people are further classified as "spouse present" or "spouse absent."

Separated. Refers to people who were not living with their spouse due to marital discord.

Divorced. Indicates people who reported being divorced and had not remarried.

Widowed. Refers to people whose last marriage ended with the death of their spouse and who had not remarried.

Never married. The term applies to those who had never been legally married or people whose only marriage ended in an annulment.

Table 3.
Source: U.S. Department of Commerce. U.S Census Bureau. 2000 Decennial Census. American Community Survey, 2000, 2010, and 2014.
<http://factfinder.census.gov/>.

The annual data were obtained from the Census Bureau. The data for average annual percent change, 2000–2014, were calculated by the editor.

Households. A household comprises one or more persons occupying a single housing unit, such as a house, apartment, or a room occupied as separate living quarters. A household may consist of a person living alone, a single family, two or more families living together, or any other group of unrelated individuals sharing a housing unit.

Householder. The person, or one of the people, in whose name the home is owned, being bought, or rented. If there is no such person present, any household member 15 years old and over can serve as the householder for the purposes of the census.

Two types of householders are distinguished: a family householder and a nonfamily householder. A family householder is a householder living with one or more people related to him or her by birth, marriage, or adoption. The householder and all people in the household related to him are family members. A nonfamily householder is a householder living alone or with nonrelatives only.

Housing unit. A house, an apartment, a mobile home or trailer, a group of rooms, or a single room occupied as separate living quarters, or if vacant, intended for occupancy as separate living quarters.

Median gross rent. The monthly amount of contract rent plus the estimated average monthly cost of utilities (electricity, gas, water, and sewer) and fuels (oil, coal, kerosene, wood, etc.).

Median monthly owner costs for housing units with a mortgage. The sum of payments for mortgages, deeds of trust, contracts to purchase, or similar debts on the property (including payments for the first mortgage, second mortgages, home equity loans, and other junior mortgages); real estate taxes; fire, hazard, and flood insurance on the property; utilities (electricity, gas, water, and sewer); and fuels (oil, coal, kerosene, wood, etc.). It also includes, where appropriate, the monthly condominium fee for condominiums and mobile home costs (installment loan payments, personal property taxes, site rent, registration fees, and license fees). Selected monthly owner costs were tabulated for all owner-occupied units, and usually are shown separately for units "with a mortgage" and for units "not mortgaged."

Median value of owner-occupied housing units. Data for the median value of owner-occupied housing units are respondents' estimates of how much their property would sell for if it was currently on the market.

Table 4.
Source: U.S. Department of Commerce. U.S Census Bureau. American Community Survey, 2013 and 2014.
<http://factfinder.census.gov/>.

The annual data derives from Census estimates. The data for percent change were calculated by the editor.

Residence 1 year ago. The data on residence 1 year ago were derived from answers to Question 15, which were asked of the population 1 year and older. For the American Community Survey, people who had moved from another residence in the United States or Puerto Rico 1 year earlier were asked to report the exact address (number and street name); the name of the city, town, or post office; the name of the U.S. county; and the ZIP Code where they lived 1 year ago. People living outside the United States and Puerto Rico were asked to report the name of the foreign country or U.S. Island Area where they were living 1 year ago.

Native born. The native population includes anyone who was a U.S. citizen or a U.S. national at birth. This includes respondents who indicated they were born in the United States, Puerto Rico, a U.S. Island Area (such as Guam), or abroad of an American (U.S. citizen) parent or parents.

Foreign born. The foreign-born population includes anyone who was not a U.S. citizen or a U.S. national at birth. This includes respondents who indicated they were a U.S. citizen by naturalization or not a U.S. citizen.

Respondent's ability to speak English. Respondents who reported speaking a language other than English were asked to indicate their English-speaking ability based on one of the following categories: "Very well," "Well,"

"Not well," or "Not at all." Those who answered "Well," "Not well," or "Not at all" are sometimes referred as "Less than 'very well.'" Respondents were not instructed on how to interpret the response categories in this question. Households in which no one 14 and over speaks English only or speaks a language other than English at home and speaks English "very well" identifies households that may need English language assistance. This arises when no one 14 and over meets either of two conditions: (1) they speak English at home or (2) even though they speak another language, they also report that they speak English "very well."

Table 5.
Source: U.S. Department of Commerce. U.S. Census Bureau. American Community Survey.
<http://factfinder.census.gov/>.

Median household income. Includes the income of the householder and all other individuals 15 years old and over in the household, whether they are related to the householder or not. Because many households consist of only one person, average household income is usually less than average family income. Total income is the sum of the amounts reported separately for wage or salary income; net self-employment income; interest, dividends, or net rental or royalty income or income from estates and trusts; Social Security or railroad retirement income; Supplemental Security Income (SSI); public assistance or welfare payments; retirement, survivor, or disability pensions; and all other income. Receipts from the following sources are not included as income: capital gains, money received from the sale of property (unless the recipient was engaged in the business of selling such property); the value of income "in kind" from food stamps, public housing subsidies, medical care, employer contributions for individuals, etc.; withdrawal of bank deposits; money borrowed; tax refunds; exchange of money between relatives living in the same household; gifts; and lump-sum inheritances, insurance payments, and other types of lump-sum receipts.

Median family income. The incomes of all members 15 years old and over related to the householder are summed and treated as a single amount.

Poverty. Following the Office of Management and Budget standards that have been in use since the late 1960s, the Census Bureau uses a set of money income thresholds that vary by family size and composition to determine the proportion of Americans in poverty. If a household's total income is less than the threshold for the applicable family size, age of householder, and number of children present in the family under 18 years of age, every individual in that household is considered to be living in poverty.

Table 6.
Source: U.S. Department of Commerce. U.S. Census Bureau. American Community Survey.
<http://factfinder.census.gov/>.

The data on health insurance coverage were derived from answers to Question 16 in the American Community Survey (ACS), which was asked of all respondents. Respondents were instructed to report their current coverage and to mark "yes" or "no" for each of the eight types of private and public insurance listed. Health insurance coverage in the ACS and other Census Bureau surveys define coverage to include plans and programs that provide comprehensive health coverage. Plans that provide insurance for specific conditions or situations such as cancer and long-term care policies are not considered coverage. Likewise, other types of insurance like dental, vision, life, and disability insurance are not considered health insurance coverage.

Private health insurance. Coverage through an employer or union, a plan purchased by an individual from a private company, or TRICARE or other military health care.

Public health insurance. Coverage includes the federal programs Medicare, Medicaid, and VA Health Care (provided through the Department of Veterans Affairs); the Children's Health Insurance Program (CHIP); and individual state health plans.

Table 7.
Source: U.S. Department of Labor. Bureau of Labor Statistics. Current Population Survey.
<http://www.bls.gov/cps/>.

Annual data on the labor force, employment, and unemployment for state and local areas are available from two major sources: the Current Population Survey (CPS) and the Local Area Unemployment Statistics (LAUS) program. In Table 7, the data are obtained from the CPS. The CPS is a monthly survey of approximately 60,000 households conducted by the Census Bureau for the Bureau of Labor Statistics. It provides comprehensive data on topics such as the labor force, employment, unemployment, and persons not in the labor force.

Civilian noninstitutional population included are persons 16 years of age and older residing in the 50 States and the District of Columbia who are not inmates of institutions (for example, penal and mental facilities, homes for the aged), and who are not on active duty in the Armed Forces.

Civilian labor force includes all persons classified as employed or unemployed who are not inmates of institutions (for example, penal and mental facilities, homes for the aged), and who are not on active duty in the Armed Forces. Civilians 16 years of age and over in the noninstitutional population who are not classified as employed or unemployed are defined as not in the labor force.

Employment includes persons 16 years and over in the civilian noninstitutional population who, during the reference week, (a) did any work at all (at least 1 hour) as paid employees; worked in their own business, profession, or on their own farm, or worked 15 hours or more as unpaid workers in an enterprise operated by a member of the family; and (b) all those who were not working but who had jobs or businesses from which they were temporarily absent because of vacation, illness, bad weather, childcare problems, maternity or paternity leave, labor-management dispute, job training, or other family or personal reasons, whether or not they were paid for the time off or were seeking other jobs.

Unemployed persons. All civilians who were not employed (according to the above definition) during the reference week, but who were available for work—except for temporary illness—and who had made specific efforts to find employment sometime during the previous four weeks. Persons who did not look for work because they were on layoff are also counted as unemployed.

Unemployment rate. The number of unemployed as a percentage of the civilian labor force.

Table 8.
Source: U.S. Department of Labor. Bureau of Labor Statistics. Local Area Unemployment Statistics.
<http://www.bls.gov/lau/home.htm>.

The Local Area Unemployment Statistics (LAUS) program is a Federal-State cooperative effort in which monthly estimates of total employment and unemployment are prepared for approximately 7,300 areas.

The concepts and definitions underlying LAUS data come from the Current Population Survey (CPS), the household survey that is the official measure of the labor force for the nation. State monthly model estimates are controlled in "real time" to sum to national monthly labor force estimates from the CPS. These models combine current and historical data from the CPS, the Current Employment Statistics (CES) program, and State unemployment insurance (UI) systems. Estimates for seven large areas and their respective balances of State are also model-based. Estimates for the remainder of the substate labor market areas are produced through

a building-block approach known as the "Handbook method." This procedure also uses data from several sources, including the CPS, the CES program, State UI systems, and the decennial census, to create estimates that are adjusted to the statewide measures of employment and unemployment. Below the labor market area level, estimates are prepared using disaggregation techniques based on inputs from the decennial census, annual population estimates, and current UI data.

Table 9.
Source: U.S. Department of Commerce. Bureau of Economic Analysis.
<http://www.bea.gov/regional>.

In this table, the data by industry reflect the North American Industry Classification System (NAICS), a supply- or production-based system that replaced the Standard Industrial Classification (SIC) system in January 2003. Estimates of state employment and earnings by industry use NAICS. NAICS was adopted to more fully reflect the current composition of U.S. businesses and to establish a standard measure of industry classification throughout the United States, Canada, and Mexico, in accordance with the North American Free Trade Agreement, to enhance cross-border comparisons among these trading partners.

Wage and salary employment, also referred to as wage and salary jobs, measures the average annual number of full-time and part-time jobs in each area by place-of-work. All jobs for which wages and salaries are paid are counted. Full-time and part-time jobs are counted with equal weight. Jury and witness service, as well as paid employment of prisoners, are not counted as wage and salary employment; the payments for these activities are classified as "other labor income" in the personal income measure. Corporate directorships are counted as self-employment. This concept of employment differs from that in the Current Population Survey (CPS), which is the source of the employment data in the table on population and labor force. The CPS is a household survey. It counts each individual only once, no matter how many jobs the person holds, and it includes only civilian employment.

Wages and salaries consist of the monetary remuneration of employees, including corporate officer salaries and bonuses, commissions, pay-in-kind, incentive payments, and tips. It reflects the amount of payments disbursed, but not necessarily earned during the year. Wage and salary disbursements are measured before deductions, such as social security contributions and union dues. In recent years, stock options have become a point of discussion. Wage and salary disbursements include stock options of nonqualified plans at the time that they have been exercised by the individual. Stock options are reported in wage and salary disbursements. The value that is included in wages is the difference between the exercise price and the price that the stock options were granted. Average annual wages and salaries were calculated by the editor by dividing total wages and salaries paid during the year in each sector by total wage and salary employment in that sector.

Table 10.
Source: U.S. Department of Commerce. U.S. Census Bureau. American Community Survey, 2012, 2013, 2014. <http://factfinder.census.gov/>.

Civilian labor force. (See definition under Table 7.)

Employment. (See definition under Table 7.)

Family. A family consists of a householder and one or more other people living in the same household who are related to the householder by birth, marriage, or adoption. All people in a household who are related to the householder are regarded as members of his or her family. A family household may contain people not related to the householder, but those people are not included as part of the householder's family in tabulations. Thus, the number of family households is equal to the number of families, but family households may include more members than do families. A household can contain only one family for purposes of tabulations. Not all households contain families since a household may be comprised of a group of unrelated people or of one person living alone – these are called nonfamily households. Families are classified by type as either a "married-couple family" or "other family" according to the sex of the householder and the presence of relatives. The data on family type are based on answers to questions on sex and relationship that were asked of all people.

Married-couple family. A family in which the householder and his or her spouse are listed as members of the same household.

Other family:

Male householder, no wife present. A family with a male householder and no spouse of householder present.

Female householder, no husband present. A family with a female householder and no spouse of householder present.

Table 11.
Source: U.S. Department of Commerce. U.S. Census Bureau. American Community Survey, 2014. <http://www.census.gov/programs-surveys/acs.html>.

Data on school enrollment and educational attainment were derived from a sample of the population. Persons were classified as enrolled in school if they reported attending a "regular" public or private school (or college) during the year. The instructions were to "include only nursery school, kindergarten, elementary school, and schooling which would lead to a high school diploma or a college degree" as regular school. The Census Bureau defines a public school as "any school or college controlled and supported by a local, county, state, or federal government." Schools primarily supported and controlled by religious organizations or other private groups are defined as private schools.

Data on educational attainment are tabulated for the population 25 years old and over. The data were derived from a question that asked respondents for the highest level of school completed or the highest degree received. Persons who had passed a high school equivalency examination were considered high school graduates. Schooling received in foreign schools was to be reported as the equivalent grade or years in the regular American school system.

Vocational and technical training, such as barber school training; business, trade, technical, and vocational schools; or other training for a specific trade are specifically excluded.

High school graduate or more. This category includes persons whose highest degree was a high school diploma or its equivalent, and those who reported any level higher than a high school diploma.

Bachelor's degree or more. This category includes persons who have received bachelor's degrees, master's degrees, professional school degrees (such as law school or medical school degrees), and doctoral degrees.

Graduate degree or more. This category includes persons who have a master's degree, including the traditional MA and MS degrees and field-specific degrees, such as MSW, MEd, MBA, MLS, and MEng., or a professional school degree: medicine, dentistry, chiropractic, optometry, osteopathic medicine, pharmacy, podiatry, veterinary medicine, law, and theology.

Table 12.
Source: U.S. Department of Education, National Center for Education Statistics. *Common Core of Data.* <http://nces.ed.gov/ccd/>.

The data are from the Common Core of Data (CCD), which is made up of a set of five surveys sent to state education departments. Most of the data are obtained from administrative records maintained by the state education agencies (SEAs). Statistical information is collected annually from approximately 100,000 public elementary and secondary schools and approximately 18,000 public school districts (including supervisory unions and regional education service agencies) in the 50 states, the District of Columbia, Department of Defense Schools, and the outlying areas. The SEAs compile CCD requested data into prescribed formats and transmit the information to NCES.

A **school district** or Local Education Agency (LEA) is the agency at the local level whose primary responsibility is to operate public schools or to contract for public school services.

The primary grades include pre-kindergarten through grade 4. Middle school grades included grades 5 through 8. High school grades include grades 9 through 12. Ungraded students are included in the total but are not separately listed. Some states have no ungraded students.

The **student-teacher ratio** is calculated by dividing the number of students in all schools by the number of full-time equivalent teachers employed by all schools and agencies.

Current expenditures per student are derived by dividing total current expenditures by the fall student membership count from the CCD. Current expenditures are comprised of expenditures for the day-to-day operation of schools and school districts for public elementary and secondary education, including expenditures for staff salaries and benefits, supplies, and purchased services. They exclude expenditures for construction, equipment, property, debt services, and programs outside of public elementary and secondary education, such as adult education and community services. Student membership consists of the count of students enrolled on or about October 1 and is comparable across all states. Data are for FY 2013; please see the NCES Web site for the exact beginning and ending dates of fiscal years for each state.

The 4-year adjusted cohort graduation rate (ACGR) is the number of students who graduate in 4 years with a regular high school diploma divided by the number of students who form the adjusted cohort for the graduating class. From the beginning of 9th grade (or the earliest high school grade), students who are entering that grade for the first time form a cohort that is "adjusted" by adding any students who subsequently transfer into the cohort and subtracting any students who subsequently transfer out, emigrate to another country, or die.

Students are eligible for **free and reduced-price lunch** under the National School Lunch Program, which was

established by President Truman in 1946. The program is a federally assisted meal program operated in public and private nonprofit schools and residential child care centers and provides cash subsidies for free or reduced-price meals to students based on family size and income criteria. Participation in the National School Lunch Program depends on income, and eligibility is often used to estimate student needs.

An **English language learner** is an individual who, due to any of the reasons listed below, has enough difficulty speaking, reading, writing, or understanding the English language that it affects their ability to learn in an English-speaking classroom. Such an individual (1) was not born in the United States or has a native language other than English; (2) comes from environments where a language other than English is dominant; or (3) is an American Indian or Alaska Native and comes from environments where a language other than English has had a significant impact on the individual's level of English language proficiency.

Individuals with Disabilities Education Act (IDEA) is a federal law requiring services to children with disabilities throughout the nation. IDEA governs how states and public agencies provide early intervention, special education, and related services to eligible infants, toddlers, children, and youth with disabilities. Infants and toddlers with disabilities (birth–age 2) and their families receive early intervention services under IDEA, Part C. Children and youth (ages 3–21) receive special education and related services under IDEA, Part B.

Public School Types

A **regular school** provides instruction and education services that does not focus primarily on special education, vocational/technical education, or alternative education, or on any of the particular themes associated with magnet/special program emphasis schools.

A **special education school** focuses primarily on special education—including instruction for students with any of the following conditions: autism, deaf-blindness, developmental delay, hearing impairment, mental retardation, multiple disabilities, orthopedic impairment, serious emotional disturbance, specific learning disability, speech or language impairment, traumatic brain injury, visual impairment, and other health impairments—and that adapts curriculum, materials, or instruction for students served.

A **vocational education school** focuses primarily on providing formal preparation for semiskilled, skilled, technical, or professional occupations for high school-age students who have opted to develop or expand their employment opportunities, often in lieu of preparing for college entry.

An **alternative education school** is an elementary/secondary school that (1) addresses needs of students that typically cannot be met in a regular school, (2) provides nontraditional education, (3) serves as an adjunct to a regular school, or (4) falls outside the categories of regular, special education, or vocational education.

Table 13.
Source: U.S. Department of Commerce. U.S. Census Bureau. November Supplement to the Current Population Survey (CPS). *Voting and Registration in the Election of November 2014.*
<http://www.census.gov/hhes/www/socdemo/voting/publications/p20/2014/tables.html>.

Voter participation data are obtained from additional questions regarding voting and voter registration, which are added to the Current Population Survey each November. Because these data are from a sample of the noninstitutional population, they differ from the "official" tally of voter participation reported by the Clerk of the U.S. House of Representatives.

Voting, people eligible to register. The population of voting age includes a considerable number of people who meet the age requirement but cannot register and vote. People who are not citizens are not eligible to vote. Among citizens of voting age, some people are not permitted to vote because they have been committed to penal institutions, mental hospitals, or other institutions, or because they fail to meet state and local resident requirements for various reasons. The eligibility to register is governed by state laws, which differ in many respects.

Registration is the act of qualifying to vote by formally enrolling on a list of voters. People who have moved to another election district must take steps to have their names placed on the voting rolls in their new place of residence.

In a few states or parts of states, no formal registration is required. Voters merely present themselves at the polling place on Election Day with proof that they are of age and have met the appropriate residence requirements. Therefore, in these areas people who are citizens and of voting age, and who meet the residence requirement, would be considered as being registered.

Voter, reported participation. Voter participation data are derived from replies to the following question asked of people (excluding noncitizens) of voting age: "In any election some people are not able to vote because they are sick or busy, or have some other reason, and others do not want to vote. Did (this person) vote in the election held on November (date varies)?"

Those of voting age were classified as "voted" or "did not vote." In most tables, this "did not vote" class includes those reported as "did not vote," "do not know," noncitizens, and nonrespondents. Nonrespondents and people who reported that they did not know if they voted were included in the "did not vote" class because of the general over-reporting by respondents in the sample.

Voter, reported registration. The data on registration were obtained by tabulating replies to the following question for those people included in the category "did not vote." "Was (this person) registered to vote in the November (date varies) election?"

All people reported as having voted were assumed to have been registered. Therefore, the total registered population is obtained by combining the number of people who voted and people included in the category "did not vote," but who had registered.

Table 14.
Source: U.S. Department of Justice. Federal Bureau of Investigation. Uniform Crime Reports. *Crime in the United States, 2014.*
<https://www.fbi.gov/about-us/cjis/ucr/crime-in-the-u.s/2014/crime-in-the-u.s.-2014>.

The Uniform Crime Reports (UCR) Program, administered by the Federal Bureau of Investigation (FBI), was created in 1929 and collects information on the following crimes reported to law enforcement authorities: murder and nonnegligent manslaughter, rape, robbery, aggravated assault, burglary, larceny-theft, motor vehicle theft, and arson. Law enforcement agencies also report arrest data for 21 additional crime categories.

The UCR Program compiles data from monthly law enforcement reports and from individual crime incident records transmitted directly to the FBI or to centralized state agencies that report to the FBI. The program thoroughly examines each report it receives for reasonableness, accuracy, and deviations that may indicate errors. Large variations in crime levels may indicate modified records procedures, incomplete reporting, or changes in a jurisdiction's boundaries. To identify any unusual fluctuations in an agency's crime counts, the program compares monthly reports to previous submissions of the agency and to those for similar agencies.

The FBI annually publishes its findings in a preliminary release in the spring of the following calendar year, followed by a detailed annual report, *Crime in the United States*, issued in the fall. (The printed copy of *Crime in the United States* is published by Bernan Press.) In addition to crime counts and trends, this report includes data on crimes cleared, persons arrested (age, sex, and race), law enforcement personnel (including the number of sworn officers killed or assaulted), and the characteristics of homicides (including age, sex, and race of victims and offenders; victim-offender relationships; weapons used; and circumstances surrounding the homicides). Other periodic reports are also available from the UCR Program. Any deviations from UCR standard data are noted in the table.

Note for Users

Since crime is a sociological phenomenon influenced by a variety of factors, the FBI discourages data users from ranking agencies and using the data as a measurement of the effectiveness of law enforcement. Until data users examine all the variables that affect crime in a town, city, county, state, region, or college or university, they can make no meaningful comparisons.

Violent crime is composed of four offenses: murder and nonnegligent manslaughter, rape, robbery, and aggravated assault. According to the UCR Program's definition, violent crimes involve force or threat of force.

Murder and nonnegligent manslaughter is the willful (nonnegligent) killing of one human being by another. Deaths caused by negligence, attempts to kill, assaults to kill, suicides, and accidental deaths are excluded. The program classifies justifiable homicides separately and limits the definition to (1) the killing of a felon by a law enforcement officer in the line of duty; or (2) the killing of a felon, during the commission of a felony, by a private citizen.

Rape is defined as: penetration, no matter how slight, of the vagina or anus with any body part or object, or oral penetration by a sex organ of another person, without the consent of the victim. The FBI UCR Program's definition of rape, formerly "forcible rape," was revised in 2013. Attempts or assaults to commit rape are also included; however, statutory rape (no force used—victim is under the age of consent) and incest are excluded. Due to the revised definition, figures for rape in 2013 and later are not comparable to data from previous years.

Robbery is the taking or attempted taking of anything of value from the care, custody, or control of a person or persons by force or threat of force or violence and/or by putting the victim in fear.

Aggravated assault is an unlawful attack by one person upon another for the purpose of inflicting severe or aggravated bodily injury. This type of assault usually is accompanied by the use of a weapon or by means likely to produce death or great bodily harm. Attempted aggravated assaults that involve the display of—or threat to use—a gun, knife, or other weapon is included in this crime category because serious personal injury would likely result if the assault were completed. When aggravated assault and larceny-theft occur together, the offense falls under the category of robbery. Simple assaults are excluded.

Property crime includes the offenses of burglary, larceny-theft, motor vehicle theft, and arson. The object of the theft-type offenses is the taking of money or property, but there is no force or threat of force against the victims. The property crime category includes arson because the offense involves the destruction of property; however, arson victims may be subjected to force.

Burglary (breaking or entering) is the unlawful entry of a structure to commit a felony or a theft. The use of force to gain entry need not have occurred. The Program has three subclassifications for burglary: forcible entry, unlawful entry where no force is used, and attempted forcible entry. The UCR definition of "structure" includes, for example, apartment, barn, house trailer or houseboat when used as a permanent dwelling, office, railroad car (but not automobile), stable, and vessel (i.e., ship).

Larceny-theft (except motor vehicle theft) is the unlawful taking, carrying, leading, or riding away of property from the possession or constructive possession of another. Examples are thefts of bicycles or automobile accessories, shoplifting, pocket-picking, or the stealing of any property or article that is not taken by force and violence or by fraud. Attempted larcenies are included. Embezzlement, confidence games, forgery, worthless checks, and the like, are excluded.

Motor vehicle theft is the theft or attempted theft of a motor vehicle. It includes the stealing of automobiles, trucks, buses, motorcycles, snowmobiles, and the like. The taking of a motor vehicle for temporary use by persons having lawful access is excluded from this definition. A motor vehicle is self-propelled and runs on land surface and not on rails. Motorboats, construction equipment, airplanes, and farming equipment are specifically excluded from this category.

Table 15.
Source: U.S. Department of Commerce. U.S Census Bureau.
<http://www.census.gov/govs/index.html>.

The Census Bureau conducts an annual survey covering a range of government finance activities carried out by all state and local governments in the United States, including revenue, expenditures, debt, and assets. The data in this volume relate to state revenues and expenditures only, with the exception of the District of Columbia, for which local government data was used. Data generally reference state government fiscal year 2014, but data for the District of Columbia is for fiscal year 2013. General revenue comprises all revenue except utilities, liquor store, and insurance trust revenue. Intergovernmental revenue is funds from other governments (mainly the federal government), including general support, grants, shared taxes, and loans or advances. Other data on government finance by state, not shown in this volume, include federal government expenditures, obligations, contract awards, and insurance programs.

Table 16.
Source: U.S. Department of Commerce. U.S. Census Bureau.
<http://www.census.gov/govs/statetax/>.

State tax data include all required taxes taken by government for public purposes, except for employer and employee assessments for Social Security and unemployment compensation. The data are shown in this volume are generally for each state's fiscal year 2014. The data for FY2015 were released too late to be included in this edition but can be found at the URL listed above. The Census Bureau does not provide detailed data for the District of Columbia, so there is no Table 16 for D.C.

INDEX

HIGH SCHOOL GRADUATES

HISPANIC OR LATINO ORIGIN, POPULATION BY

HOMEOWNERSHIP RATES

HOUSEHOLDS AND HOUSING CHARACTERISTICS

W
WAGES BY INDUSTRY

WASHINGTON
WEST VIRGINIA